950

실전
모의고사

고경희, 김병기, 박재형 지음

Actual Test 01~06

길벗
이지:톡

시나공 토익
950 실전 모의고사

초판 1쇄 발행 · 2022년 7월 4일
초판 3쇄 발행 · 2024년 2월 21일

지은이 · 고경희, 김병기, 박재형
발행인 · 이종원
발행처 · ㈜도서출판 길벗
브랜드 · 길벗이지톡
출판사 등록일 · 1990년 12월 24일
주소 · 서울시 마포구 월드컵로 10길 56(서교동)
대표전화 · 02) 332–0931 | **팩스** · 02) 322–6766
홈페이지 · www.gilbut.co.kr | **이메일** · eztok@gilbut.co.kr

기획 및 책임편집 · 고경환 (kkh@gilbut.co.kr) | **디자인** · 윤석남 | **제작** · 이준호, 손일순, 이진혁, 김우식
마케팅 · 이수미, 장봉석, 최소영 | **영업관리** · 김명자, 심선숙 | **독자지원** · 윤정아, 최희창

CTP 출력 및 인쇄 · 북솔루션 | **제본** · 북솔루션

ISBN 979-11-407-0042-4 03740
(이지톡 도서번호 301092)

정가 25,000원

· ·

독자의 1초까지 아껴주는 정성 길벗출판사

(주)도서출판 길벗 | IT실용, IT/일반 수험서, 길벗캠퍼스, 경제경영, 취미실용, 인문교양(더퀘스트) www.gilbut.co.kr
길벗스쿨 | 국어학습, 수학학습, 어린이교양, 주니어 어학학습, 교과서 www.gilbutschool.co.kr

950점은 기본, 만점까지 가능한
고득점 완성용 문제집

토익 학습자들의 관심은 '빨리 고득점을 받는 것'입니다. 토익 시행 초기부터 현재까지 학습자들의 이런 욕구는 변하지 않았습니다. 그러면 '어떻게'해야 빨리 고득점을 받을 수 있을까요?

어떤 사람은 학원 강의나 인강이 좋다고 하고, 또 어떤 사람은 책을 여러 권 보라고 합니다. 그러나 그동안 가르치고 직접 코칭해왔던 학생들을 보면 좋은 문제를 많이 풀어보는 것이 제일 도움이 된다고 확신합니다. 여기서 '많이'보다 '좋은 문제'를 강조하고 싶습니다. 고득점에 도움이 되지 않는 문제를 많이 풀어봐야 시간만 낭비하기 때문입니다.

이 책은 실제 토익 경향을 제대로 반영해서 실전 포인트가 살아 있는 문제들만 모았습니다.

이 책에 실린 내용은 실제 시험을 100% 반영했습니다!

토익 시험은 난이도 유지를 위해 매회마다 완전히 새롭게 만들어지는 한 두 문제를 제외하고는 이미 출제되었던 문제와 동일한 문제를 약간 변형시켜 사용합니다. 다시 말하면 유형은 같지만 단어 배열이 다른 문제를 출제합니다. 본 교재는 토익 개정 후 지금까지 시험에 출제된 모든 문제의 유형을 분석한 후, 동일한 유형의 변형 문제를 통해 시험에 나올 만한 문제를 대비할 수 있도록 했습니다. 실전에 출제되지 않았던 내용은 다루지 않았습니다.

고득점을 위한 12세트, 2400문제 훈련!

이 책에는 총 12회분으로 구성된 2400문제가 실려있습니다. 가장 최근 경향까지 반영한 고득점용 2400문제의 힘은《시나공 토익 950 실전 모의고사》이전 시리즈로 학습한 수험생들이 이미 입증한 바 있습니다. 수많은 수험생들이 이 책으로 학습한 후 900점 이상을 얻었고 심지어 만점까지 얻은 학생들도 있었습니다. 이 책에 실린 모든 문제는 억지로 꼬아놓은 문제가 아니라 실제 출제 유형에 기반을 두고 있습니다. 미묘한 함정까지도 알려주기 위해 노력했습니다.

기본 실력을 더 견고하게 해주는 'LC, RC 훈련 노트' 제공!

이 책은 12회분 문제뿐만 아니라 다양한 학습자료를 같이 제공합니다. LC는 기출 표현과 청취력을 모두 잡을 수 있는 '통암기 문장 훈련'을 제공하며, RC는 고득점에 기본인 '핵심 어휘집'을 제공합니다. 이 학습을 하면 단기간 고득점을 얻고 싶은 수험생들이 기본 문제를 틀리는 실수를 절대 하지않게 됩니다. 부록으로 분류되긴 했지만 이 훈련만 꾸준히 해도 기본 200점이 오릅니다.

이 책이 900점 이상을 목표로 하는 독자들에게 큰 도움이 될 책임을 확신합니다. 혼신의 힘을 다해 이 책을 썼습니다. 끝으로 이 책이 나오는데 도움을 준 길벗 편집부와 독자들에게 감사드립니다.

저자 고경희, 김병기, 박재형

이 책의 특징 및 활용 방법

1 'LC+RC' 실전 모의고사 12회분으로 단기간에 950점을 달성하세요!

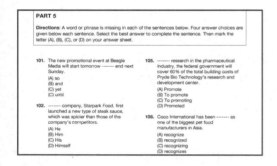

950점은 기본 만점까지 가능한 고득점용 문제집!

이 책은 900점 이상 고득점을 목표로 하는 수험생에게 적합합니다. 난이도가 실제 시험과 비슷하거나 약간 높게 설정되어 실제 토익 시험을 보면 더 수월하게 문제가 풀리는 효과를 얻을 수 있습니다. 이 책에 실린 문제만 충실히 학습해도 950점은 기본이고 990점 만점도 가능합니다.

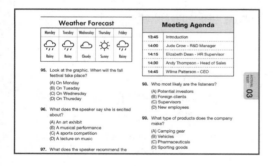

12세트, 2400제의 방대한 분량! 확실한 훈련!

최근 실제 토익 출제 경향을 반영한 12세트 실전 모의고사를 수록했습니다. 12세트, 2400문제를 제공하지만 실전 출제 경향과 난이도를 세심하게 조정했습니다. 이 책에서 벗어난 문제는 출제되지 않습니다.

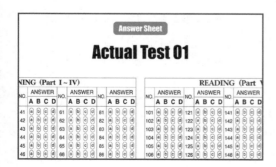

정답표 제공

교재 뒤에 수록된 정답표를 활용해서 실전처럼 답안지 마킹을 연습해 볼 수 있게 했습니다. 실전처럼 정해진 시간에 마킹하는 연습을 하며 실전에 익숙해지세요.

2 상세하고 명쾌한 해석과 해설로 핵심을 파악하세요!

108. With the purchase of any new cosmetic product from CoCo, a stylish gift bag will be ------- for free.

(A) you
(B) your
(C) yours
(D) yourself

해석 CoCo 사의 새로운 화장품을 구입하시면 멋진 선물 가방이 무료로 제공됩니다.

표현 정리 purchase 구매, 구입, 구매하다 cosmetic 화장품 for free 무료로, 공짜로

유형 파악 소유대명사 ★★★

해설 be 동사 뒤에는 위치해야 하는 인칭대명사를 선택하는 문제로 무엇보다 be 동사 뒤에 명사 보어가 위치하려면 앞에 오는 주어와 동일 대상(동격 관계)이 형성되어야 한다는 전제 조건을 충족시켜야 한다. 그러므로 선물 가방이 당신하고 동격일 수 없으니 주격 혹은 목적격 대명사로 쓰이는 you와 재귀대명사 yourself는 동사 뒤에서 목적어로 쓰이거나 혹은 완전한 절의 구조에서 수식어인 부사로 쓰이는 만큼 이들 모두 오답이라고 할 수 있다. 아울러 소유격 대명사 your 역시 단독으로 사용이 불가하니 이 또한 오답이다. 따라서 빈칸에는 선물 가방이 무료로 당신의 것이 될 것이란 문맥을 만들 수 있는 소유대명사 yours가 와야 한다.

정답 (C)

해석
영문의 의미를 명확하게 전달한 해석을 제공하여 해석이 잘 되지 않는 문장의 구조를 파악하는데 도움이 될 수 있게 구성했습니다.

표현 정리-온라인 무료 다운로드
본문에서 나온 어휘중 실제 토익에서 출제율이 높거나 어려운 단어만을 선별해서 정확한 의미와 함께 실었습니다.

유형 파악 및 해설 -온라인 무료 다운로드
정답뿐만 아니라 오답도 정확히 이해되도록 상세한 해설과 용법을 쉽게 풀어냈습니다. 저자가 수업시간에만 알려주는 풀이 노하우도 추가해 읽기만 해도 점수가 오를 수 있게 구성했습니다.

3 다양한 부가 학습자료로 고득점을 완성하세요!

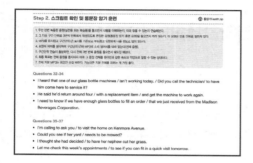

LC 통암기 훈련 노트 제공

저자가 학생들을 직접 가르치며 효과를 본 문장 통암기 훈련을 MP3파일과 PDF 파일로 제공합니다. 저자가 직접 편집하고 만든 이 훈련만 해도 단기에 청취력을 업그레이드 하는 것은 물론 기본적인 영어실력까지 올라갑니다. 문제 12세트에 맞게 12회로 나눠져 있습니다.

RC 핵심 어휘집 제공

저자가 그동안 RC에서 그동안 출제됐던 단어를 추려서 핵심 어휘집으로 제공합니다. 시험에 출제됐던 어휘중에서도 출제 빈도가 높은 어휘만 정리했고 시험에서 같이 붙어서 출제되는 단서까지 정리했습니다. 문제 12세트에 맞게 12회로 나눠져 있습니다.

해설집 & 학습용 MP3 무료 제공

문제의 핵심을 알기 쉽게 이해시켜주고 핵심을 짚어주는 해설집을 홈페이지에서 PDF로 다운로드 할 수 있습니다. 간편하게 태블릿이나 스마트폰에서 확인하며 학습할 수 있습니다. 실전용, 복습용 MP3도 무료로 홈페이지에서 다운로드 하실 수 있습니다. 책에서 QR코드로도 제공합니다.

4 추가 자료 다운로드 방법

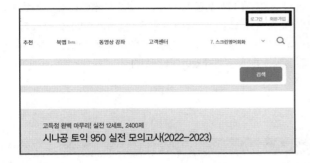

❶
홈페이지(www.gilbut.co.kr)에 접속해 로그인합니다.
(비회원은 회원 가입 권장)

❷
상단 메뉴의 파일 찾기 검색창에
《시나공 토익 950 실전 모의고사》를 입력합니다.

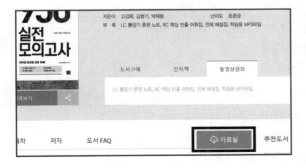

❸
《시나공 토익 950 실전 모의고사》가 검색되면 선택한 후
'자료실'을 클릭하고 자료를 다운로드합니다.

토익 시험 소개

TOEIC이란?

TOEIC은 Test Of English for International Communication의 앞 글자들을 따서 만든 용어로서, 영어가 모국어가 아닌 사람들을 대상으로 하여 언어의 주 기능인 의사소통 능력을 평가하는 시험입니다. 주로 비즈니스와 일상생활 같은 실용적인 주제들을 주로 다루고 있으며, 듣고 이해하는 Listening 분야와 읽고 파악하는 Reading 분야로 나뉩니다. 이 두 부분은 각각 495점의 배점이 주어지며, 총 만점은 990점입니다. 특히 Listening은 미국뿐만 아니라 영국, 호주의 영어발음까지 섞여서 나옵니다.

시험의 구성

구성	Part	내용	문항 수	시간	배점
Listening Comprehension	1	올바른 사진 설명 찾기	6	45분	495점
	2	질문에 알맞은 대답 찾기	25		
	3	짧은 대화 내용 찾기	39		
	4	긴 연설문 내용 찾기	30		
Reading Comprehension	5	문법 / 어휘 빈칸 채우기(문장)	30	75분	495점
	6	문법 / 어휘 빈칸 채우기(지문)	16		
	7	1개 장문의 주제와 세부사항 찾기	29		
		2개 장문의 주제와 세부사항 찾기	10		
		3개 장문의 주제와 세부사항 찾기	15		
Total	7 Part		200	120분	990점

토익 출제분야

토익은 국제적으로 통용되는 비즈니스와 특정 문화에 국한되지 않는 일상생활에 관한 내용을 다룹니다.

비즈니스	일반업무	구매, 영업/판매, 광고, 서비스, 계약, 연구/개발, 인수/합병
	제조	생산 공정, 품질/공장 관리
	인사	채용, 지원, 승진, 퇴직, 급여
	통신	공지, 안내, 회의, 전화, 이메일, 팩스, 회람, 인트라넷, 협조
	재무/회계	투자, 세금 신고, 환급/청구, 은행
	행사	기념일, 행사, 파티, 시상식
일상생활	문화/레저	영화, 공연, 박물관, 여행, 쇼핑, 외식, 캠핑, 스포츠
	구매	주문/예약, 변경/취소, 교환/환불, 배송
	건강	병원 예약, 진료, 의료보험
	생활	고장, 보수, 생활 요금, 일정

토익 접수 및 응시, 성적 확인

토익 접수

접수기간 및 접수처 확인: TOEIC 위원회 홈페이지 / 응시료 : 48,000원

① **방문 접수**
- 해당 회 접수기간에 지정된 접수처에서 응시료를 납부하고, 신청서를 작성한 후 접수합니다.
- 사진(반명함판, 3x4cm) 한 장을 지참합니다.
- 원서 접수시간: 09:00 ~ 18:00(점심시간 12:00 ~ 13:00)

② **인터넷 접수**
해당 회 접수기간에 TOEIC 위원회 홈페이지(www.toeic.co.kr)에서 언제든 등록이 가능합니다. 사진은 jpg 파일로 준비하면 됩니다.

③ **특별 추가 접수**
특별 접수기간 내에 인터넷 접수로만 가능하며 응시료가 52,800원입니다.

토익 응시 준비물

| 규정 신분증 | 연필과 지우개 | 시계 | 수험번호 |

*성적은 정해진 성적 발표일 오전 6시부터 토익위원회 홈페이지와 ARS 060-800-0515를 통해 조회할 수 있습니다. 신분증은 주민등록증, 운전면허증, 공무원증, 기간 만료 전의 여권, 만 17세 미만의 중고생에 한 해 학생증 등도 인정됩니다. 수험번호는 수험장에서도 확인할 수 있습니다. 필기도구는 연필 종류면 다 되지만 사인펜은 사용할 수 없습니다.

시험 시간 안내

시간	내용
AM 09:30 ~ 09:45 (PM 02:30 ~ 02:45)	답안지 배부 및 작성 오리엔테이션
AM 09:45 ~ 09:50 (PM 02:45 ~ 02:50)	휴식 시간
AM 09:50 ~ 10:05 (PM 02:50 ~ 03:05)	1차 신분증 검사
AM 10:05 ~ 10:10 (PM 03:05 ~ 03:10)	문제지 배부 및 파본 확인
AM 10:10 ~ 10:55 (PM 03:10 ~ 03:55)	LC 시험 진행
AM 10:55 ~ 12:10 (PM 03:55 ~ 05:10)	RC 시험 진행(2차 신분 확인)

*아무리 늦어도 9시 50분까지는 입실해야 하며, 고사장의 상황에 따라 위의 시간은 약간 변할 수 있습니다.

성적 확인 및 성적표 수령

성적은 정해진 성적 발표일 오전 6시부터 토익위원회 홈페이지와 ARS 060-800-0515를 통해 조회할 수 있습니다. 성적표는 선택한 방법으로 수령이 가능하며 최초 발급만 무료입니다.

파트별 유형 및 전략

 **Part 1**

사진 묘사 (6문제)
사진을 보고 가장 알맞은 문장을 고르는 유형입니다.

Example

문제지	음성
	**1.** Look at the picture marked number 1 in your test book. (A) She is raking some leaves. (B) She is washing her shorts. (C) She is watering some plants. (D) She is selecting vegetables. 정답 (C)

출제 경향

❶ 파트 1에서 1인/2인 이상 등장하는 사람들의 행동 및 상태를 묘사하는 문제는 평균 3~4문항(전체 60%)이 출제되고 있으며 주로 현재 시제 및 현재 진행형으로 구성된 문장이 정답으로 제시됩니다

❷ 사물/정경을 묘사하는 사진 및 사람과 사물 또는 정경의 복합 사진 문제가 평균 2~3문항(전체 40%)이 출제되고 있으며 이들은 사물의 위치나 배열형태 그리고 정경 묘사에 치중하는 정답이 제시되는 만큼 주로 현재시제, 현재완료 수동태, 현재 수동태 및 There 구문으로 구성된 문장이 정답으로 등장하고 있습니다.

풀이 전략

❶ **사진을 최대한 적절하게 묘사한 사진을 골라야 합니다.**
자주 출제되는 오답유형을 알고 있어야 합니다. 보기를 들으며 o/x를 표시해 가며 확실히 오답을 제거합니다.
- 사진에서 확인이 불가한 행동/대상을 지칭하는 동사/명사가 등장하는 선택지는 오답
- 사진에 인물이 등장하지 않는 상황에서 being이 들리면 선택지는 거의 오답
- 선택지에서 All, Every, Each, Both가 등장하는 경우 거의 대부분 오답

❷ **사진을 보기 전에 나올 단어를 예상 할 수 있어야 합니다.**
보기를 듣기 전에 사진을 보고 나올 동사나 명사를 미리 연상해봅니다. 거의 나오는 어휘가 정해져 있으므로 내용을 파악하는데 큰 도움이 됩니다.

Part 2　질의 응답 (25문제)

질문을 듣고 보기 세 개중 가장 적절한 답을 고르는 유형입니다.

Example

오후	음성
8. Mark your Answer on your answer sheet.	8. Where do you usually go for computer repairs? (A) Last Thursday. (B) I think I can fix it. (C) Do you have a problem? 정답 (C)

출제 경향

❶ 파트 2에서 출제되는 문제 유형의 비중을 살펴보면 '의문사의문문 – 일반/긍정의문문 – 평서문 및 부가의문문 – 일반/부정의문문 – 선택의문문 – 간접의문문' 순이며 이전에 비해 일반의문문과 평서문 및 부가의문문의 출제 비중이 높아졌다고 할 수 있습니다.

❷ 질문에 따른 단서를 우회적으로 제시하는 간접적 답변의 비중이 단서를 직접적으로 제시하는 직접적 답변에 버금갈 정도로 상당히 증가했습니다.

풀이 전략

❶ 의문사의문문에서 자주 출제되는 기본 문형을 바탕으로 초반 의문사를 비롯하여 주어와 동사/형용사로 이어지는 연속적인 3~4단어, 즉 핵심어(키워드)의 의미를 파악하는 것이 관건입니다.
  • 의문사 + 조동사[do/does/did/will/would/can/could/should] + 주어 + 동사원형~?
  • 의문사 + 조동사[be/has/have] + 주어 + 형용사/현재 및 과거분사~?

❷ 질문에 따른 단서를 우회적으로 제시하는 간접적 답변의 비중이 단서를 직접적으로 제시하는 직접적 답변에 버금갈 정도로 상당히 증가했습니다.

❸ 정형화된 오답 유형을 사전에 충실히 익히고 이를 적극적으로 활용하여 정답을 선별하도록 합니다. 대표적으로 의문문에서 등장한 특정 단어를 선택지에서 반복하여 들려주는 동일어휘 오답, 특정 단어와 유사한 발음의 단어를 선택지에서 들려주는 유사발음 어휘 오답, 그리고 특정 단어를 통해 연상할 수 있는 단어를 들려주는 연상어휘 오답은 수시로 접하는 정형화된 오답 유형이므로 이를 적극적으로 활용하면 오답을 수월하게 소거할 수 있습니다.

❹ 절대 정답을 선택함에 시간을 끌지 않도록 합니다. 세 번째 선택지를 다 듣고 난 직후에도 답을 선택하지 못한 상태라면 과감히 찍고 미련을 버린 후 바로 다음 문제를 풀 수 있도록 대비해야 합니다. 파트 2는 문제 사이 간격이 4초 밖에 되지 않으므로 정답 선택을 머뭇거릴수록 이어지는 질문 내용을 파악하는 것에 집중하지 못하여 연이어 문제를 틀리게 되는 도미노 현상이 유독 심하다는 점에 주의하도록 합니다.

Part 3   짧은 대화 [39문제]

2명 또는 3명이 나누는 대화를 듣고 문제지에 있는 질문을 보고 알맞은 보기를 고르는 유형입니다.

Example

문제지	음성
32. Where most likely does the conversation take place? (A) At a restaurant (B) At a hotel (C) At an airport (D) At a food processing company **33.** Why is the man complaining? (A) He did not get a receipt. (B) He was served the dish he didn't order. (C) A bill is higher than he expected. (D) Some food has gone bad. **34.** What does the woman suggest the man do? (A) Speak to a manager (B) Place a new order (C) Check a menu (D) Wait for a replacement <div align="right">정답 32. (B) 33. (D) 34. (D)</div>	**Questions 32 through 34 refer to the following conversation.** W: Reception. How may I help you? M: This is Wesley White in room 101. I ordered some tuna sandwiches from your restaurant and would like to return them. They smell weird. I think the tuna is not fresh. W: Oh, I'm sorry to hear that. I'll call the chef immediately and ask him to bring you a replacement soon. M: Um... Could you please give me a few minutes to have a look at the menu? I don't want to try the same thing again. **32.** Where most likely does the conversation take place? **33.** Why is the man complaining? **33.** What does the woman suggest the man do?

출제 경향

❶ 파트 3 대화들은 주로 회사 업무, 회사 출장 및 여행, 회사 회의, 공사와 같이 회사에서 겪는 다양한 비즈니스 활동 및 일상 생활에 관한 내용이 주류를 이루고 있습니다. 따라서 해당 주제를 다루는 대화 내용을 학습하며 주제별 주요 어휘와 표현을 익히는 것이 매우 중요합니다.

❷ 파트 3 대화의 전반적인 주제 및 대화에서 언급하는 문제점, 대화 장소 및 대화자의 직업, 그리고 세부적인 대화의 내용을 묻는 문제들의 출제 비중이 높습니다. 그러므로 문제 유형별로 대화 내에서 주로 단서가 등장하는 위치를 알아두고 이를 활용하여 효율적으로 단서를 파악하는 문제풀이 방식에 익숙해져야 합니다.

풀이 전략

❶ 대화 지문을 듣기에 앞서 문제와 선택지의 내용을 먼저 파악해야 합니다. 문제와 선택지의 내용을 사전에 알아두는 것만으로도 정답률이 높아집니다. 만약 시간이 없을 경우에는 문제만이라도 읽어봅니다.

❷ 문제 유형에 따른 정답의 위치가 어느 정도 정해져 있으므로 대화 지문을 듣기에 앞서 미리 문제의 유형과 해당 내용을 파악해야 합니다. 각 문제의 유형을 파악한 후에는 이들의 단서가 지문 어디쯤에서 제시될 것이라 예상하며 청해하는, 소위 노려 듣기를 해야 합니다.

❸ 첫 번째 대화 내용과 마지막 대화 내용은 절대 놓치지 말아야 합니다. 첫 번째 대화 내용과 마지막 대화 내용에는 대부분 해당 대화 지문의 첫 번째 문제와 마지막 문제의 단서가 들어가 있습니다.

Part 4

짧은 담화 (30문제)

짧은 담화를 듣고 문제지에 있는 질문을 보고 알맞은 보기를 고르는 유형입니다.

Example

문제지	음성
71. What is the message mainly about? (A) A new library policy (B) An upgraded computer room (C) A special reading program (D) A temporary location **72.** According to the speaker, what can be accessed on a Web site? (A) A new location (B) A moving schedule (C) Specific directions (D) Discount coupons **73.** What should the listeners do to borrow a laptop computer? (A) Complete a form (B) Show a membership card (C) Pay a security deposit (D) Join a free rental service 정답 71. (D) 72. (C) 73. (B)	**Questions 71 through 73 refer to the following recorded message.** Thank you for calling the Warren Public Library. The Warren Public Library will be closed at the end of August for six months for upgrades and remodeling. For your convenience, we are going to open a temporary library facility located at 911 Harder Street next Monday. Please be advised that we will not provide computer rooms at all for library patrons due to limited space. However, you can borrow library laptop computers as usual if you present your library card to any of our librarians. If you need to get step by step directions for your drive or walk to the temporary library, please visit our Web site, www.warrenpl.org. Thank you. **71.** What is the message mainly about? **72.** According to the speaker, what can be accessed on a Web site? **73.** What should the listeners do to borrow a laptop computer?

출제 경향

❶ 파트 4에선 주로 안내(사내, 행사, 관광), 담화/소개, 녹음 메시지, 광고, 일기 예보, 뉴스 등 여러 가지 다양한 소재의 지문이 등장합니다.

❷ 파트 4에서는 전반적인 주제 및 문제점, 장소 및 화자/청자의 정체(직업/직장), 지문 내 세부적인 특정 내용을 묻는 문제, 그리고 화자의 의도/시각 정보 연계 문제들이 비교적 균형있게 출제되고 있습니다.

풀이 전략

❶ 지문을 듣기에 앞서 문제와 선택지의 내용을 먼저 파악해야 한다. 문제와 선택지의 내용을 사전에 알아두는 것만으로도 정답률이 높아집니다. 시간이 없을 경우에는 문제만이라도 먼저 읽어봅니다.

❷ 문제 유형에 따른 정답의 위치가 어느 정도 정해져 있으므로 지문을 듣기에 앞서 미리 문제의 유형과 해당 내용을 파악해야 합니다. 각 문제의 유형을 파악한 후에는 이들의 단서가 지문 어디쯤에서 제시될 것이라 예상하며 청해하는, 소위 노려 듣기를 해야 합니다.

❸ 지문 초반 2문장의 내용과 지문 후반 마지막 2문장의 내용은 절대 놓치지 않도록 합니다. 이 부분에는 해당 지문의 첫 번째 문제와 마지막 문제의 단서가 포함되어 있습니다. 따라서 지문 초반 2문장의 내용과 지문 후반 마지막 2문장의 내용을 놓치지 않는다면 최소한 두 문제는 상대적으로 수월하게 정답을 확보할 수 있습니다.

Part 5 · 단문 빈칸 채우기 (30문제)

문장의 빈칸에 알맞은 보기를 골라 채우는 유형. 늦어도 12~15분 안에 다 풀어야 파트 7에 시간을 더 할애할 수 있습니다. 문법(어형)과 어휘 문제로 구성되어 있습니다.

Example

105. Since the copier we ordered arrived -------, it should be replaced with a new one as soon as possible.

(A) damaged
(B) assembled
(C) discounted
(D) unopened

정답 105. (A)

Part 6 · 장문 빈칸 채우기 (16문제)

파트 6는 지문에 있는 4개의 빈칸에 알맞은 보기를 골라 채우는 유형. 늦어도 8~10분 안에 다 풀어야 파트 7에 시간을 더 할애할 수 있습니다.

Example

Questions 135-138 refer to the following notice.

If your baggage was damaged while being carried or supported by airport employees or by the airport baggage handling system, please ------- it to the airport baggage office on Level
135.
1. According to regulations, domestic travelers must report damage within 48 hours of their actual time of arrival. International travelers must submit a damage report within seven days of a(n) ------- baggage incident. -------. Office personnel will review reports and evaluate all
136. **137.**
damage claims. Please be advised that the airport baggage office is only responsible for damaged baggage ------- by the airport staff and the airport baggage handling system.
138.

135. (A) bring
(B) bringing
(C) brought
(D) brings

136. (A) overweight
(B) unattended
(C) forgotten
(D) mishandled

137. (A) Please fill out a baggage damage claim form as directed.
(B) The new baggage handling system is innovative and efficient
(C) The airport will expand next year to accommodate the increasing demand for air travel.
(D) The airport baggage office will be temporarily closed to travelers while it is renovated.

138. (A) cause
(B) caused
(C) will cause
(D) causing

정답 135. (A) 136. (D) 137. (A) 138. (B)

❶ 파트 5/6은 전체적으로는 문법과 어휘, 그리고 파트 6에서 문장 삽입을 묻는 문제들이 추가되어 있습니다. '문법'과 '어휘'부분은 신토익 실시 이후에도 변화가 거의 없습니다. 간혹 어휘 문제로 새로 등장하는 단어들이 보일 뿐, 특이점들은 많이 발견되지 않습니다. 따라서, 토익이 시작된 시점으로부터 변하지 않고 출제되는 기존의 유형들을 확실하게 다짐과 동시에, 드물지만 새로 추가되는 유형들을 익혀 둔다면 충분한 대비가 될 것입니다.

❷ 전체적인 비율은 바뀐 TOEIC 유형이 나오게 된 2006년 5월이래 사실 크게 달라진 것은 없습니다. 다만, 문법 출제 패턴들 중에 2006년 5월 이전에 강조되었던 명사 부분의 가산/불가산 구분, 수일치, 문제를 읽지 않아도 답이 나오는 숙어 및 관용 표현, 가정법, 생략, 도치 등의 유형들이 많이 사라지고, 질문 내용을 다 읽어야 풀 수 있는 세련된 형태들이 많이 등장하고 있다는 점이 특이점입니다.

꾸준히 출제되는 문법 유형 중에 최근에도 자주 나오는 유형들을 정리하면 다음과 같습니다.
· 관계사나 접속사/부사/전치사 혼합형 문제
· 자동사/타동사를 구분하는 문제
· 문맥을 통해 대명사의 격을 고르는 파트 6문제
· 문맥을 통해 특정 시제를 고르는 파트 6문제
· 부사절접속사들 사이의 차이점 구분 문제
· 사람/사물 또는 수식/보어로 형용사를 구분하는 문제
· 복합어이나 하나인 명사 앞의 형용사나 소유격을 고르는 문제
· 생활영어와 접목된 약간 까다로운 전치사 문제
· 재귀대명사의 강조용법 문제
· 관계사/의문사를 구분하고 들어가야 하는 wh- 문제
· 보기들 중에 동의어가 많이 제시되는 부사 어휘/연결사 문제

❶ 파트 5/6은 항상 보기를 먼저 읽고 문제 유형을 예상 및 파악합니다.

❷ 보기가 같은 어원으로 품사만 달리 나온 어형 문제의 경우, 자리를 묻는 경우가 많으므로 빈칸 주변이나 문장 전체의 [주/목/보어]구조를 따져 봅니다.

❸ 보기가 모두 다른 어휘 문제의 경우 반드시 해석을 해야 합니다.

❹ 보기에 접속사류(wh-로 시작하는 의문사/관계사, 부사절접속사 등)가 보이면 절(주어+동사)의 개수를 파악하고, '하나의 접속사는 두 개의 절을 연결한다'는 내용을 적용하여 접속사의 부족하고 넘침, 빈칸 뒤 문장의 완전/불완전 등을 따져야 합니다.

❺ 보기에 같은 동사가 형태만 달리 나올 때는 (1) 능/수동 (2) 수일치 (3) 시제의 순으로 따져서 풀어야 합니다.

❻ 명사 어휘 문제의 경우, 빈칸 앞의 관사관계를 먼저 살피고, 빈칸 앞이 무관사인 경우는 가산/불가산을 따져 풀어야 하는 문제입니다.

❼ 파트 6에 새로 추가된 유형은 문장 삽입인데, 바로 앞이나 뒤에 제시된 문장과의 연결성을 묻는 것이므로 그 점에 유의해야 합니다.

 **장문 독해 (54문제)**

지문을 읽고 질문에서 가장 적절한 보기를 정답으로 고르는 유형입니다. 4개의 빈칸에 알맞은 보기를 골라 채우는 유형. 단일 지문 29문제, 이중 지문 10문제, 삼중 지문 15문제로 구성되어 있습니다.

Example 단일 지문

Questions 164-167 refer to the following notice.

Kamon Financial Solutions

Yesterday, management and the owners held a meeting to discuss the future of the company. We have seen a great rise in profits during the last two years and also a large increase in our number of clients. So there are many customers that we are unable to serve from our current office. As such, it has been decided that in order to enable the business to grow, we will move to a much larger new office, which will open on October 2. —[1]—.

To make the relocation to the new office as smooth as possible, we have decided to move the majority of our equipment on September 29. —[2]—. On behalf of management, I would like to request that all staff members come to work that Saturday to help us move to the new location. You will be paid for your time at an overtime rate of $50 per/hour. —[3]—. You will be working from 11 A.M. until 3 P.M. In addition, the day before the move, Friday, September 28, management requests that you pack all of your folders and documents into cardboard boxes so that they can be easily loaded into the truck. —[4]—. You will find spare boxes located in the storeroom.

If you have any questions, feel free to contact me directly. My extension is #303. Thank you for your cooperation. Together, we can help Kamon Financial Solutions become a market leader.

164. What is the main purpose of the notice?
(A) To announce a relocation to a new office
(B) To advertise a new product offered by the company
(C) To provide a list of new contact details of clients
(D) To invite employees to attend a conference

165. The word "majority" in paragraph 2, line 2, is closest in meaning to
(A) least
(B) most
(C) absolute
(D) nearly

166. What are employees requested to do on September 29?
(A) Complete some sales reports
(B) Phone some new clients
(C) Come to the office
(D) Park their cars in a different parking lot

167. In which of the positions marked [1], [2], [3], and [4] does the following sentence best belong?

"This day is a Saturday, and our office is usually closed on weekends, so there will be a minimum amount of disruption to our business."

(A) [1]
(B) [2]
(C) [3]
(D) [4]

정답 164. (A) 165. (B) 166. (C) 167. (B)

Questions 181-185 refer to the following announcement and email.

Wallace Zoo Volunteer Program

Requirements:

- 18+ years of age
- High school diploma
- Satisfactory recommendation from previous or current employers
- Ability to commit to one full shift each week
- A clean, professional appearance
- Reliable transportation to the zoo
- The ability to attend employee training

Attendance:

Volunteers will work one full shift each week during the season they are hired. Fall and winter volunteers work shifts from 10 A.M. to 2 P.M. on weekends. Spring and summer volunteers have weekday shifts from 10 A.M. to 4 P.M. However, they might have to work on a weekend shift, which runs from 10 A.M. to 6 P.M. Shifts are assigned by the zoo's assistant manager.

If you are interested in volunteering at the city's best zoo, visit our Web site at wz.org for an application. If you have any questions, contact Kate Kensington at 703-221-8923 or katek@wz.org. Applications for the spring program must be submitted by the end of the business day on March 18. Training for the spring program begins on March 28.

To: katek@wz.org
From: stevel@pgh.com
Date: March 20
Subject: Volunteer work
Attached: Application; Recommendation Letter

Dear Ms. Kensington;

I'm responding to your advertisement for volunteers at the zoo. I saw the advertisement ten days ago; however, I had an illness that put me in the hospital for the past week. So I was unable to respond until now. I understand that the deadline for the spring program has passed. But I hope that you can understand my situation and let me still apply for it. I have attached a completed application and recommendation letter from my current employer.

Only on weekdays am I available for work. I work at a cinema and must work a full shift on both Saturdays and Sundays. I hope this won't be a problem as I would love to work at the zoo. I am a consummate professional, and I am certain I can do great work at the zoo.

Thank you,
Steve Lionsgate

181. What is NOT a requirement of the volunteer position?

(A) Completion of high school
(B) Attendance at staff training
(C) A recommendation letter
(D) Experience at a zoo

182. On what date were applications due for spring positions?

(A) March 10
(B) March 18
(C) March 20
(D) March 28

183. What does Mr. Lionsgate request in his email?

(A) Consideration for her late application
(B) An extra weekend shift at the aquarium
(C) Information about employee training
(D) More time to submit her high school diploma

184. How many hours will Mr. Lionsgate likely volunteer per day at the time he is available?

(A) 4
(B) 6
(C) 8
(D) 16

185. In the email message, the word "consummate" in paragraph 2, line 3, is closest in meaning to

(A) determined
(B) absolute
(C) independent
(D) meticulous

정답 181. (D) 182. (B) 183. (A) 184. (B) 185. (B)

Example 삼중 지문

Questions 196-200 refer to the following Web page, Web search results, and advertisement.

http://www.amityoldtown.com

Old Town in Amity is the perfect place to spend the day with your friends, family, or tour group. You'll love the experience of going on foot through the streets of Amity, which have been preserved to look exactly as they appeared in the 1700s. Go back in time as you tour Old Town.

Discounts are available for groups of 12 or more. In addition, for groups of 15 or more arriving by bus, the driver will get a complimentary ticket. Advance reservations are not required but are recommended for summer weekends. Contact 849-3894 to reserve your tickets today. Group discounts only apply to reservations made at least 24 hours in advance.

Restaurants in Amity

Seascape Features some of the finest dining in the city. Expect to pay high prices, but you'll love the service and the quality of the meals. The specialties are seafood, especially lobster and crab. Located down by the pier.

Hilltop Decorated like an old-style ranch, you'll get some of the finest steaks and ribs in the region. Don't be distracted by the loud music and casual atmosphere. The food here is incredible. About 400 meters from Old Town.

Green Table Enjoy hearty food that takes you back to the 1800s. All the meats and vegetables come from local farmers. Reservations at least a week in advance are a must. Located in the city's center.

Romano's Get a taste of Italian food here. Giuseppe Romano, the owner, has been running this establishment for the past 12 years. It's located just 200 meters from the entrance to Old Town.

Visit Old Town in Amity with the Galway Travel Agency. Enjoy spending a day at Old Town and then dining down by the waterfront. You can do this for the low price of $175.

Your group will depart from the Galway Travel Agency at 9:00 A.M. on August 20. You'll return to the same place sometime around 8:00 P.M. Call 830-1911 for more information. The trip will not be made unless at least 18 people sign up for it.

196. What is indicated about Old Town?

(A) It requires reservations in summer.
(B) It has reduced its admission fees.
(C) It has historical reenactment shows.
(D) It is designed for people to walk through.

197. How can a group get a discount to Old Town?

(A) By purchasing tickets a day in advance
(B) By paying with a credit card
(C) By having 10 or more people
(D) By downloading a coupon from a Web site

198. What is mentioned about Green Table?

(A) It serves vegetarian meals.
(B) Its food is locally produced.
(C) It was established in the 1800s.
(D) It does not require reservations.

199. Where most likely will the excursion organized by the Galway Travel Agency have dinner?

(A) At Seascape
(B) At Hilltop
(C) At Green Table
(D) At Romano's

200. What is suggested about the excursion to Old Town?

(A) It will involve an overnight stay.
(B) It must be paid for in advance.
(C) It may receive a complimentary ticket.
(D) It includes three meals that are paid for.

정답 196. (D) 197. (A) 198. (B) 199. (A) 200. (C)

출제 경향

❶ 파트 7은 신유형이 추가되면서 예전보다 비중이 더 커졌습니다. (1) text–message chain (2) online chat discussion (3) 삼중 지문 (4) 문장 삽입 (5) 특정문구 내용 파악 등이 새로 추가된 유형인데, 삼중지문이 버겁기는 하지만, 이전 토익에 비해 난이도가 전체적으로 높아지지는 않았습니다. 그리고, 유념할 것은 파트 7 전체가 다 어려운 것이 아니라 3–4개의 지문, 그리고 그 지문들 중에서도 특정한 몇 개의 문제들이 어렵다는 것입니다. 주로 (most) likely/probably와 같은 유추/추론의 문제 유형입니다. 논란의 대상이 되는 유형들은 대부분 이 유형으로, 지문에 근거가 100퍼센트 명확히 제시되지 않는 경우가 있어 정답을 골라 내기 쉽지 않습니다. 이외에는 마치 '숨은 그림 찾기'하는 것과 같이 단서를 찾기 어려운 문제들이 대부분인데, 이는 정독을 통해서만 해결할 수 있으므로, 적절한 요령의 숙지와 더불어 정독을 하더라도 시간이 많이 걸리지 않을 정도의 진짜 '독해력'이 필요합니다.

풀이 전략

❶ 해당 문제의 키워드를 찾으며 지문을 정독합니다. 어차피 각 지문당 문제를 다 풀려면, 지문 하나당 3~4번 정도를 읽게 되는데, 읽을 때마다 전에 읽었던 내용들이 머리 속에 남게 되므로 읽는 속도는 빨라지게 되니 읽는 회수가 늘어나는 것에 그리 신경 쓰지 않아도 됩니다. 또한, 가끔 학생들 중에 문제마다 키워드를 미리 다 찾아서 한꺼번에 빈 공간 한 켠에 표시해 두고 풀이하는 사람들이 있는데 이것도 괜찮은 방법입니다.

❷ 독해가 된다는 것은 머리 속에 상황이 그려지는 것이니, 단순히 단어만 읽히고 내용이 머리 속에 들어오지 않는다면, 글 전체의 분위기를 전하는 지문의 제목과 초반부를 다시 한 번 정독합니다.

❸ 이중 지문의 경우, 두 지문 모두에서 부분적인 단서를 찾는 연계문제는 많아야 두 개입니다. 이 말은 다섯 문제 중에 3~4문제는 특정 한 지문만 읽어도 답이 나온다는 것입니다.

❹ 이중/삼중 지문의 경우 꾸준히 출제되는 반복되는 유형들이 있습니다.
• 한 지문에 일정이 나오면, 다른 지문에는 그것이 변경된 내용이 나옵니다.
• 한 지문에 교환/할인/반품에 대한 규정이 나오고, 다른 지문에 특정한 인물이 나오면, 그 인물이 교환/할인/반품의 대상이 되는가와, 또는 되지 않는 이유를 묻는 문제가 나옵니다.
• 특이한 성격의 지문, 예를 들면, draft, invoice, 예약확인 메일 등과 같은 것들은 그 지문의 내용이 아닌 형식이나 성격이 주제로 제시되는 경우가 많습니다.
• 특정 인물에 관한 사실관계, 유추문제가 질문으로 나오면, 그 인물이 발신자인 글을 먼저 읽는 것이 빠릅니다.
• 회사가 여러 개 언급되는 문제의 경우, 지문 맨위 수신자/발신자 이메일 부분의 회사 이름을 반드시 숙지하고 풀어야 합니다.

❺ 평소에 학습할 때 풀고 답을 맞추고 해설 등을 참조한 후에, 반드시 여러 번 정독해야 합니다. 이때, 문제 풀 때는 보이지 않던 많은 단서들이 눈에 들어오게 됩니다.

❻ 파트 7은 오답노트를 만들지 않아도 되지만, 나중에 복습할 때 대략적인 내용을 알 수 있도록 각 문단마다 내용을 한 두 줄로 요약해서 적어 두는 방법도 좋습니다.

목차

＊자세한 해설을 확인하고 싶으시면 홈페이지에서 해설집을 다운로드하세요.(www.gilbut.co.kr)

Actual Test

MP3

해설집

적정 풀이 시간 120분

120 min

시작 시간 ___시 ___분

종료 시간 ___시 ___분

중간에 멈추지 말고 처음부터 끝까지 풀어보세요.
문제를 풀 때에는 실전처럼 답안지에 마킹하세요.

목표 개수 _____ / 200   실제 개수 _____ / 200

예상 점수는 번역 및 정답에 있는 점수 환산표를 참조하세요.

LISTENING TEST

In the Listening test, you will be asked to demonstrate how well you understand spoken English. The entire Listening test will last approximately 45 minutes. There are four parts, and directions are given for each part. You must mark your answers on the separate answer sheet. Do not write your answers in the test book.

PART 1

Directions: For each question in this part, you will hear four statements about a picture in your test book. When you hear the statements, you must select the one statement that best describes what you see in the picture. Then find the number of the question on your answer sheet and mark your answer. The statements will not be printed in your test book and will be spoken only one time.

Statement (B), "They are sitting at a table." is the best description of the picture. So you should select answer (B) and mark it on your answer sheet.

1.

2.

▶ ▶ ▶ GO ON TO THE NEXT PAGE

3.

4.

5.

6.

▶ ▶ ▶ GO ON TO THE NEXT PAGE

PART 2

Directions: You will hear a question or statement and three responses spoken in English. They will not be printed in your test book and will be spoken only one time. Select the best response to the question or statement and mark the letter (A), (B), or (C) on your answer sheet.

7. Mark your answer on your answer sheet.

8. Mark your answer on your answer sheet.

9. Mark your answer on your answer sheet.

10. Mark your answer on your answer sheet.

11. Mark your answer on your answer sheet.

12. Mark your answer on your answer sheet.

13. Mark your answer on your answer sheet.

14. Mark your answer on your answer sheet.

15. Mark your answer on your answer sheet.

16. Mark your answer on your answer sheet.

17. Mark your answer on your answer sheet.

18. Mark your answer on your answer sheet.

19. Mark your answer on your answer sheet.

20. Mark your answer on your answer sheet.

21. Mark your answer on your answer sheet.

22. Mark your answer on your answer sheet.

23. Mark your answer on your answer sheet.

24. Mark your answer on your answer sheet.

25. Mark your answer on your answer sheet.

26. Mark your answer on your answer sheet.

27. Mark your answer on your answer sheet.

28. Mark your answer on your answer sheet.

29. Mark your answer on your answer sheet.

30. Mark your answer on your answer sheet.

31. Mark your answer on your answer sheet.

PART 3

Directions: You will hear some conversations between two or three people. You will be asked to answer three questions about what the speakers say in each conversation. Select the best response to each question and mark the letter (A), (B), (C), or (D) on your answer sheet. The conversations will not be printed in your test book and will be spoken only one time.

32. Where does the woman work?

(A) At an art supply store
(B) At an art gallery
(C) At a publishing company
(D) At a bookstore

33. Why is the woman calling?

(A) To ask about using a picture
(B) To find out about a new display
(D) To inquire about an establishment's hours
(D) To arrange a special tour

34. What does the man ask the woman to provide?

(A) A registration fee
(B) A digital image
(C) A deadline
(D) An identification number

35. What event are the speakers preparing?

(A) A celebratory party
(B) A company retreat
(C) A fundraiser
(D) An anniversary celebration

36. What does the man offer to do?

(A) Send out invitations
(B) Decorate a room
(C) Bake a cake
(D) Ask Mary for assistance

37. What does the woman say she will do?

(A) Ask for a revised budget
(B) Purchase some supplies
(C) Reserve a room
(D) Drop by a bakery

38. What does the man sell at his store?

(A) Electronics
(B) Books
(C) Furniture
(D) Clothing

39. What do the speakers indicate about the convention center?

(A) It is near public transportation.
(B) The tradeshow was held there last year.
(C) Their hotels are located near it.
(D) They had to take a taxi to get there.

40. How are tablet computers used at the man's store?

(A) To sign up new members
(B) To process payments
(C) To collect customer comments
(D) To check inventory

41. What did the man recently learn?

(A) An executive's schedule has changed.
(B) A seminar has just been canceled.
(C) A shipment should be delivered today.
(D) A meeting room has been reserved.

42. What do the speakers need to do?

(A) Review some materials
(B) Schedule a training session
(C) Practice a presentation
(D) Dispose of some documents

43. What does the woman suggest doing?

(A) Ordering in some food
(B) Making a reservation at a restaurant
(C) Arriving early for rehearsal tomorrow
(D) Having lunch after they are done

▶ ▶ ▶GO ON TO THE NEXT PAGE

44. What is Alice's occupation?

(A) Researcher
(B) Lab technician
(C) Office assistant
(D) Office supervisor

45. What will Alice most likely do next?

(A) Take a tour of an office
(B) Complete some paperwork
(C) Conduct a job interview
(D) Speak with the CEO

46. What does Alice suggest about a software?

(A) She hopes it will be replaced.
(B) It is not working properly.
(C) It costs a lot of money.
(D) She knows how to use it.

---

47. Where are the speakers?

(A) At a supermarket
(B) At a health food store
(C) At a restaurant
(D) At a warehouse

48. What does the woman mention about the business?

(A) A sale will start there soon.
(B) It was just renovated.
(C) It opened a second location.
(D) Fewer customers shop there now.

49. What does the woman suggest when she says, "We no longer carry a few brands anymore"?

(A) She no longer works in the that section.
(B) She is expecting a new shipment of the frozen pizza soon.
(C) Some merchandise may not be available.
(D) She thinks the man should buy something else.

50. What type of item are the speakers discussing?

(A) A food product
(B) An electric appliance
(C) A tool
(D) A compact car

51. What still needs to be agreed on?

(A) The name
(B) The price
(C) The release date
(D) The advertising campaign

52. What does the man suggest doing?

(A) Conducting a customer survey
(B) Redesigning the product
(C) Consulting colleagues
(D) Placing an advertisement online

---

53. What will happen in ten days?

(A) A new manager will start working.
(B) The athletic facility will be renovated.
(C) New fitness classes will begin.
(D) Another location will be open.

54. What will be offered to members?

(A) A discount
(B) A T-shirt
(C) A new class
(D) A gift certificate

55. What does the man say he will do?

(A) Interview an applicant
(B) Call all the members
(C) Change a schedule
(D) Send an e-mail

56. What are the speakers mainly discussing?

    (A) Changing hotel rooms
    (B) Relocating an office
    (C) Arranging a presentation for clients
    (D) Organizing a company retreat

57. What information is Mary missing?

    (A) The price estimate for an event
    (B) The confirmed venue
    (C) The complete list of attendees
    (D) A list of potential buyers

58. What does the man recommend doing soon?

    (A) Booking a place for an event
    (B) Reserving airline tickets in advance
    (C) Contacting a local catering service
    (D) Rescheduling a company event

59. Where do the speakers most likely work?

    (A) At a television station
    (B) At a movie studio
    (C) At a radio station
    (D) At a restaurant

60. Why does the man say, "He has won the award three times"?

    (A) To compliment a coworker
    (B) To make a correction
    (C) To express satisfaction
    (D) To reject a suggestion

61. What do the speakers agree to do?

    (A) Ask for employee input
    (B) Extend a deadline
    (C) Postpone an awards ceremony
    (D) Hire a new TV show host

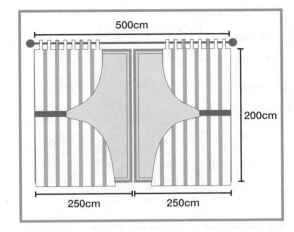

62. Where does the man work?

    (A) At an interior design firm
    (B) At a bookstore
    (C) At a travel agency
    (D) At an architectural firm

63. Look at the graphic. Which measurement will change?

    (A) 200 centimeters
    (B) 250 centimeters
    (C) 300 centimeters
    (D) 500 centimeters

64. What will the woman most likely do next?

    (A) Determine a new price
    (B) Order some extra materials
    (C) Redesign a sketch
    (D) Call another vendor

▶ ▶ ▶GO ON TO THE NEXT PAGE

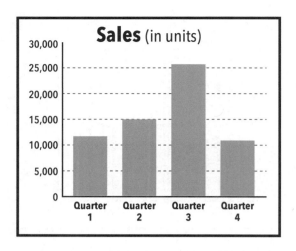

65. Where do the speakers most likely work?

(A) At a mobile phone manufacturer
(B) At a kitchen appliance store
(C) At a computer manufacturer
(D) At a toy maker

66. Look at the graphic. Which sales figure is the man surprised about?

(A) 12,000
(B) 15,000
(C) 26,000
(D) 11,000

67. Who is Jacob Green?

(A) A company president
(B) A marketing expert
(C) A designer
(D) An accountant

Madison Fall Music Festival

October 4

Performance Schedule

YELLOW STAGE		BLUE STAGE	
12:00 P.M.	Country	10:00 A.M.	Jazz
4:00 P.M.	Rock	3:00 P.M.	Pop
		5:00 P.M.	Classical

68. What does the woman offer to do for the man?

(A) Purchase a ticket for him
(B) Look over his report
(C) Give him a ride
(D) Save a seat for him

69. Look at the graphic. What is the man's favorite type of music?

(A) Country
(B) Pop
(C) Jazz
(D) Rock

70. What does the woman remind the man to do?

(A) Purchase a ticket in advance
(B) Wear a jacket
(C) Bring lots of water
(D) Arrive in time for the festival

PART 4

Directions: You will hear some short talks given by a single speaker. You will be asked to answer three questions about what the speaker says in each short talk. Select the best response to each question and mark the letter (A), (B), (C), or (D) on your answer sheet. The talks will not be printed in your test book and will be spoken only one time.

71. What is the topic of the conference?

(A) Vehicle manufacturing
(B) Software development
(C) Engineering
(D) Book publishing

72. According to the speaker, what did Brandon Morris do last month?

(A) He installed solar panels.
(B) He won an award.
(C) He participated in a conference.
(D) He gave a speech.

73. What does the speaker remind the listeners about?

(A) A product demonstration
(B) A reception
(C) A speech
(D) An exhibition

74. Where does the speaker most likely work?

(A) At a government office
(B) At a local weather service
(C) At a construction firm
(D) At a power company

75. What is the cause of the problem?

(A) There was some bad weather.
(B) Some machinery is outdated.
(C) There are not enough work crews.
(D) Electricity rates have risen.

76. What should the listeners do if the problem continues?

(A) Visit a website
(B) Call back later
(C) Visit an office in person
(D) Cancel an electric service

77. What is the museum celebrating?

(A) An anniversary
(B) An executive retirement
(C) A new exhibit
(D) A library opening

78. What will the listeners do first?

(A) Introduce themselves
(B) Go on a tour
(C) Listen to a speech
(D) See a film

79. What will the listeners receive?

(A) Free admission
(B) A gift shop discount
(C) A voucher for a free meal
(D) A complimentary souvenir

80. What is the speaker planning?

(A) A business meeting
(B) A client visit
(C) A corporate fundraiser
(D) A vacation

81. Who most likely is the listener?

(A) A travel agent
(B) A train conductor
(C) A seminar organizer
(D) A hotel clerk

82. What does the speaker mean when she says, "I heard that the scenery in Switzerland is stunning that time of the year"?

(A) She is not happy that her trip was canceled.
(B) She agrees with the listener's recommendation.
(C) She encourages the listener to accompany her.
(D) She thinks a purchase will be worth the money.

▶ ▶ ▶ GO ON TO THE NEXT PAGE

83. What is the speaker's company planning to do next month?

(A) Update its website
(B) Introduce a new product line
(C) Hire more staff for IT team
(D) Attend a trade fair

84. What does the speaker mean when he says, "I must admit that they're quite unique"?

(A) He needs a more detailed explanation.
(B) He just started working at a consulting agency.
(C) He is impressed with some designs.
(D) He is unwilling to follow a recommendation.

85. What does the speaker request?

(A) An estimate
(B) A meeting
(C) A guest list
(D) A shipping address

86. What type of business does the speaker work at?

(A) A department store
(B) A supermarket
(C) An advertisement agency
(D) A marketing firm

87. What will the business start doing?

(A) Offering sale prices to regular customers
(B) Reorganizing the displays of its stores
(C) Adjusting prices throughout the day
(D) Renewing some contracts with its suppliers

88. What does the speaker say that David Lowell will do?

(A) Transfer to headquarters
(B) Ask for volunteers
(C) Hire more employees
(D) Explain a new strategy

89. What will the mobile application allow users to do?

(A) Download maps of banks
(B) Edit photographs and movies
(C) Bank online
(D) Make suggestions

90. What does the speaker suggest when she says, "However, there have already been 15,000 users"?

(A) Another location will be open.
(B) A service is popular.
(C) A system is overwhelmed.
(D) A project needs more employees.

91. What can some users participate in?

(A) A contest
(B) A reception
(C) A training program
(D) A focus group discussion

92. What is the message mainly about?

(A) A temporary location
(B) Library relocation
(C) New programs
(D) A book club

93. According to the speaker, what can be accessed online?

(A) A list of available services
(B) A promotional code
(C) Membership applications
(D) Directions

94. How can listeners borrow a computer?

(A) By sending an e-mail
(B) By calling before they arrive
(C) By filling out a form
(D) By presenting a library card

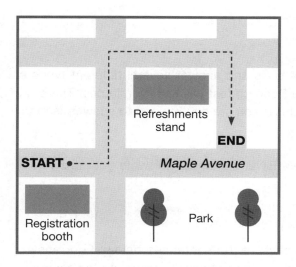

95. What event are the listeners most likely participating in?

(A) An athletic competition
(B) A community cleanup
(C) A charity auction
(D) A city parade

96. According to the speaker, what should the listeners pick up?

(A) A water bottle
(B) A T-shirt
(C) A pair of shoes
(D) A nametag

97. Look at the graphic. Where can the listeners get their pictures taken?

(A) At the park
(B) At the registration booth
(C) At the starting line
(D) At the refreshments stand

98. Who is the announcement intended for?

(A) Airplane passengers
(B) Conference attendees
(C) Hotel guests
(D) Shopping center employees

99. What does the speaker offer to do?

(A) Take drink orders
(B) Provide blankets
(C) Lock up valuable personal belongings
(D) Bring complimentary meals

100. Look at the graphic. Which item is unavailable?

(A) The purse
(B) The necktie
(C) The perfume
(D) The belt

This is the end of the Listening test. Turn to Part 5 in your test book.

▶ ▶ ▶GO ON TO THE NEXT PAGE

READING TEST

In the Reading test, you will read a variety of texts and answer several different types of reading comprehension questions. The entire Reading test will last 75 minutes. There are three parts, and directions are given for each part. You are encouraged to answer as many questions as possible within the time allowed.

You must mark your answer on the separate answer sheet. Do not write your answers in your test book.

PART 5

Directions: A word or phrase is missing in each of the sentences below. Four answer choices are given below each sentence. Select the best answer to complete the sentence. Then mark the letter (A), (B), (C), or (D) on your answer sheet.

101. If you have a question about your bill, your payment options, or applying for or receiving financial assistance, please contact us -------.

(A) recently
(B) really
(C) usually
(D) now

102. Before you leave the office, please turn off the overhead -------, and turn on a soothing, soft nightlight.

(A) lights
(B) lightens
(C) lighted
(D) lightly

103. Our vice president usually attends a marketing conference by -------, but has decided to take Mr. Watson to the one in Los Angeles.

(A) he
(B) him
(C) himself
(D) his

104. It is not fair to judge the candidates on the ability to run a company based on ------- ethnicity.

(A) they
(B) their
(C) them
(D) theirs

105. According to the data, the use of fossil fuels such as coal, natural gas, and oil ------- steadily over the past 150 years.

(A) increase
(B) increases
(C) has increased
(D) will increase

106. Since Joshua Pharmaceuticals moved its manufacturing plant to Spokane, the demand for housing in the city has increased ------- in recent years.

(A) tightly
(B) significantly
(C) distinctly
(D) often

107. ------- of the paintings in our art gallery contains a piece of history that creates a strong impression.

(A) They
(B) All
(C) Each one
(D) Other

108. Teleconferencing technology allows our employees to meet with their clients in other countries without ------- the office.

(A) leave
(B) left
(C) leaving
(D) to leave

109. Bella Corporation currently awards long-serving employees with up to 21 days of vacation ------- three years.

(A) all
(B) much
(C) every
(D) some

110. ------- are the results of the latest residents' survey on the proposed shopping mall construction project.

(A) Enclose
(B) Enclosed
(C) Enclosure
(D) Enclosing

111. After ------- three months of renovations, the manufacturing factory of Ace Technology in Detroit resumed operation yesterday.

(A) mostly
(B) while
(C) approximately
(D) immediately

112. Many companies are currently facing lack of personnel support. -------, there is a shortage of employees who have specialized skills.

(A) Therefore
(B) Otherwise
(C) Moreover
(D) Nevertheless

113. Applicants who passed the final interview for the floor manager position ------- by the human resources director later next week.

(A) have been contacted
(B) was contacted
(C) will be contacted
(D) will contact

114. Some of the directors were very ------- of the new business plan, but the chief executive officer convinced them of its potential.

(A) unanimous
(B) capable
(C) unaware
(D) skeptical

115. ------- new convention centers and hotels being built, London has all the qualifications necessary to become the number one destination for business travelers in Europe.

(A) With
(B) On
(C) To
(D) About

116. Business branding is ------- more important now than ever for local companies because consumer perception and trust are necessary for your business to thrive today.

(A) very
(B) far
(C) extremely
(D) enough

117. Please be ------- that all the flights are currently delayed due to the poor weather conditions and zero visibility.

(A) advise
(B) advising
(C) advised
(D) advisable

118. Construction workers who knowingly fail to comply with safety regulations are ------- to dismissal.

(A) informed
(B) subject
(C) eligible
(D) responsible

▶ ▶ ▶GO ON TO THE NEXT PAGE

119. Dinner will be served at the hotel restaurant ------- after the conclusion of the Annual Conference on New Telecommunication Technology.

(A) shortly
(B) already
(C) frequently
(D) carefully

120. ------- our new car models were released last quarter, they have been astonishingly popular.

(A) During
(B) Since
(C) When
(D) As though

121. In order to ensure the objectivity and the transparency, applicants for business loans must submit several financial documents that have been ------- audited.

(A) primarily
(B) especially
(C) particularly
(D) independently

122. Some customers were ------- with the overall quality of the new products manufactured by the GB Corporation.

(A) disappointing
(B) disappointed
(C) disappoint
(D) disappointment

123. In an effort ------- prices, our company streamlined the production process and minimized package volume and weight.

(A) reduced
(B) reduction
(C) will reduce
(D) to reduce

124. Our warranty does not cover any defects or damage to a product ------- customer's misuse of the product.

(A) in general
(B) alongside
(C) whereabouts
(D) resulting from

125. When you look at stock research websites, they will normally provide you with ratios based on past and ------- earnings.

(A) projecting
(B) projected
(C) projection
(D) projector

126. We usually provide a ------- course schedule for the following academic year so there might be some changes in the future.

(A) pending
(B) sudden
(C) tentative
(D) considerable

127. Unless ------- by one or more parents, minors under the age of 15 are banned from entering movie theaters and amusement parks.

(A) accompany
(B) accompanies
(C) accompanied
(D) accompanying

128. This online presentation will ------- a wide range of marketing techniques and strategies that are effective for your business.

(A) participate
(B) activate
(C) conduct
(D) examine

129. Unfortunately, there are some remote areas in the country ------- our wireless cellular broadband service is unavailable.

(A) which
(B) what
(C) how
(D) where

130. ------- we have suffered more losses this quarter, I see no other way out of this mess than to start making drastic cuts across the board.

(A) If so
(B) Given that
(C) Owing to
(D) Rather than

PART 6

Directions: Read the texts that follow. A word or phrase, or sentence is missing in parts of each text. Four answer choices for each question are given below the text. Select the best answer to complete the text. Then mark the letter (A), (B), (C), or (D) on your answer sheet.

Questions 131-134 refer to the following e-mail.

From: Harry Houston, Plant Manager
To: Plant Employees
Date: March 25
Subject: External Review

I'm writing to inform you that three ------- from Komi Motors will be visiting our plant in
                                       131.
two weeks. Their task is to monitor the ongoing production process and to verify our

automotive parts are being manufactured according to their requirements and standards.

In addition, they will ------- the cleanliness of our manufacturing process.
                        132.

Their review will be released sometime between April 15 and April 17. -------. It is very
                                                                      133.
important that we follow our normal procedures during their visit. If you are planning to

take leave on any day between April 8 and April 10, please inform your supervisor in

advance ------- your replacement can cover your responsibilities.
        134.

Harry Houston
Plant Manager
Houston Precision Machinery

131. (A) investors
(B) inspectors
(C) dealers
(D) trainees

132. (A) assess
(B) mark
(C) award
(D) establish

133. (A) Their arrival date has not been confirmed yet.
(B) Even so, our products are highly commercialized in the industry.
(C) Applications must be submitted by the end of next month.
(D) It will be sent to us and posted on our official website.

134. (A) when
(B) because
(C) so that
(D) admitting that

▶ ▶ ▶GO ON TO THE NEXT PAGE

Questions 135-138 refer to the following advertisement.

Century Home Interior Design

Change Your Home With Perfection!

Do you want to remodel or build an addition to your home and have no idea what to do? -------. Here at Century Home Interior Design, we know exactly what it takes to create a
135.
home that is perfect for you. We ------- a full spectrum of renovation solutions for families
136.
who want to turn their house into a true home.

From picking out new wallpaper to building a new deck for your backyard, our design

consultants can perform ------- any task you require.
137.

We have hired experts in nearly every aspect of home design, whether it is interior design,

home plumbing, structural reconfiguration, and more. This guarantees that each staff

member appointed to ------- your family has the experience to give you exactly what you
138.
need.

You can visit our website at www.chid.com for more details, or stop by our office at 1123

King Street to speak with us personally.

---

135. (A) We have the solutions for your technical problems.
(B) Your interior works have already commenced.
(C) You don't have to look any further.
(D) Our aim is to help you find the best house in the region.

136. (A) provide
(B) were providing
(C) had provided
(D) will be provided

137. (A) recently
(B) almost
(C) enough
(D) carefully

138. (A) assist
(B) treat
(C) affect
(D) introduce

Questions 139-142 refer to the following letter.

Galaxy Technologies
5174 Richmond Avenue
Houston, TX 77056

Dear Mr. Baker,

Thank you for your inquiry of our X63 laptop computer series.

We are very ------- to enclose our latest catalogue. Please note the items in red highlights.
139.
They are special products that we are offering in set with Wave Printers and Velocity video

cards. Our promotion event ------- only for a month. So do not miss this chance, and
140.
please take the advantage of the occasion.

We can assure you that our X63 laptop computer series are the most reliable personal

computer you can buy in the market today. Our ------- in it is supported by our two-year
141.
guarantee and round-the-clock online back-up system that answers any questions of

users 24 hours a day.

-------.
142.

Sincerely,

Donald Harrison
Sales Director
Galaxy Technologies

139. (A) please
(B) pleased
(C) pleasure
(D) pleasing

140. (A) continue
(B) continued
(C) has continued
(D) will continue

141. (A) confide
(B) confident
(C) confidence
(D) confidentiality

142. (A) We look forward to receiving your further inquiry or valued order.
(B) They also need to continually strive to improve their job performance.
(C) Allow three business days for card order processing and delivery.
(D) Our company is proud of the quality products that we manufacture.

▶ ▶ ▶ GO ON TO THE NEXT PAGE

Questions 143-146 refer to the following e-mail.

Dear Ms. Davis,

We are terribly sorry to hear about the problems you encountered during your stay at Bella Resort from June 24 to June 29. Please be assured that the used towels and the unchanged bedding you found in your room are not ------- of the high standards of
143.
service on which our resort has built its reputation. All of our rooms are usually equipped with fresh towels and bedding before guests are allowed to check in. We apologize for the

-------.
144.

We would be happy to ------- you with a complimentary one-night stay at our resort,
145.
including a meal at our Italian restaurant, Luigi's Lasagne. The next time you reserve a room at our resort, simply print out the voucher attached to this e-mail and present it to the front desk staff upon checking in.

-------.
146.

Truly yours,

James Williams
General Manager
Bella Resort

143. (A) represents
(B) represented
(C) representative
(D) representatively

144. (A) factor
(B) attempt
(C) violation
(D) oversight

145. (A) providing
(B) provide
(C) be provided
(D) have provided

146. (A) As always, you will be completely satisfied with our new product.
(B) Please check our website if you need more information about this promotion.
(C) Thank you for your kind words regarding our hotel and its amenities.
(D) Once again, I apologize for the poor standard of service you received.

PART 7

Directions: In this part you will read a selection of texts, such as magazine and newspaper articles, e-mails, and instant messages. Each text or set of texts is followed by several questions. Select the best answer for each question and mark the letter (A), (B), (C), or (D) on your answer sheet.

Questions 147-148 refer to the following advertisement.

BUYNSELL.COM

Rachel Cagle (rcagle@easymail.com)
posted 1 hr ago

Product: *All about Herb Therapy* by Jaquelin Koch

The book is in mint condition and was purchased about 6 months ago for $25.

For those who are interested in herbs or other medicinal plants, you can buy this book from me for $15. The book must be collected by no later than next Wednesday in the Brookside area. The Brookside Community Center would be ideal. I will only accept cash. Please leave me a text message at (647) 555-3921 for further details.

147. What is NOT mentioned about the book?

(A) It is intended for those who want to use plants for medicinal purposes.
(B) It was originally $25.
(C) It is signed by the author.
(D) It has not been damaged.

148. What does the buyer have to do?

(A) Visit the Brookside Community Center
(B) Bring a personal check for $15
(C) Leave a phone number
(D) Pick up the book by next Wednesday

▶ ▶ ▶GO ON TO THE NEXT PAGE

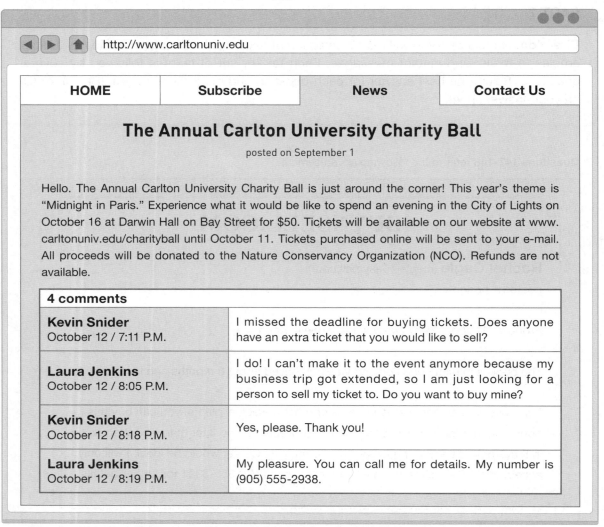

http://www.carltonuniv.edu

| HOME | Subscribe | News | Contact Us |

The Annual Carlton University Charity Ball
posted on September 1

Hello. The Annual Carlton University Charity Ball is just around the corner! This year's theme is "Midnight in Paris." Experience what it would be like to spend an evening in the City of Lights on October 16 at Darwin Hall on Bay Street for $50. Tickets will be available on our website at www.carltonuniv.edu/charityball until October 11. Tickets purchased online will be sent to your e-mail. All proceeds will be donated to the Nature Conservancy Organization (NCO). Refunds are not available.

4 comments

Kevin Snider October 12 / 7:11 P.M.	I missed the deadline for buying tickets. Does anyone have an extra ticket that you would like to sell?
Laura Jenkins October 12 / 8:05 P.M.	I do! I can't make it to the event anymore because my business trip got extended, so I am just looking for a person to sell my ticket to. Do you want to buy mine?
Kevin Snider October 12 / 8:18 P.M.	Yes, please. Thank you!
Laura Jenkins October 12 / 8:19 P.M.	My pleasure. You can call me for details. My number is (905) 555-2938.

149. What is true about the Carlton University Charity Ball?

(A) It will refund tickets for a limited period of time.
(B) It is taking place in Paris.
(C) Tickets for it will go on sale on October 11.
(D) It is supporting an environmental group.

150. At 8:19 P.M., what does Laura Jenkins mean when she writes, "My pleasure"?

(A) She is excited to go on a business trip.
(B) She is happy to help Kevin Snider.
(C) She is interested in attending the next charity ball.
(D) She enjoys talking on the phone.

Questions 151-152 refer to the following itinerary.

Blue Sky Tours

Tasmania Village Tour
August 14, 9:00 A.M. – 6:00 P.M.

*Please arrive at the Hamilton Center 30 minutes prior to the departure time in the morning.

9:00 A.M.	Bus leaves Hamilton Center (please have breakfast before arriving)
10:00 A.M.	Arrival at Tasmania Aboriginal Village
10:15 A.M.	Great Hawk Mountain hiking Hawk Falls sighting
11:00 A.M.	Tour of the Tasmania Aboriginal Museum featuring a special display of Kabu Warseau's pottery
12:30 P.M.	Lunch and free time at Haystack Cafeteria - Free food will be provided.
2:00 P.M.	Tasmania Village onsite tour
4:00 P.M.	Free time in Tasmania Tourists are encouraged to visit the Tasmania Long House, which has traditional sweets and various souvenirs available for purchase.
5:30 P.M.	Departing Tasmania Aboriginal Village
6:30 P.M.	Arrival at Hamilton Center

151. Where most likely can the tourists go shopping?

(A) At the Hamilton Center
(B) At the Tasmania Aboriginal Museum
(C) In the Haystack Cafeteria
(D) At the Tasmania Long House

152. Who most likely is Kabu Warseau?

(A) A tour guide
(B) A curator
(C) An artist
(D) The chief of a tribe

▶ ▶ ▶GO ON TO THE NEXT PAGE

To:	Gayle Leyva <gleyva@enlightfinancials.com>
From:	Scott Adams <sadams@enlightfinacials.com>
Date:	November 2
Subject:	Employee Dinner

Dear Mr. Leyva,

I contacted Gregory Jackson regarding the room setup for the upcoming annual Enlight Financials Employee Dinner, and he told me to contact you as he is currently on a business trip. I need your team to set up a conference room for about 130 guests. In the room, we need 20 round tables with 7 seats each. The tables need to be scattered across the room so that the stage can be viewed from every seat. In addition, please have a podium, two wireless microphones, a projector, and a screen ready.

Here is the schedule for the employee dinner.
3:30 P.M. – Hall setup
5:00 P.M. – Doors open
5:30 P.M. – Opening speech – Rochelle Smith / Employee awards ceremony
7:30 P.M. – Dinner

Scott Adams
Human Resources Assistant Manager

153. By what time should the guests arrive at the Enlight Financials Employee Dinner?

(A) 5:00 P.M.
(B) 5:30 P.M.
(C) 7:00 P.M.
(D) 7:30 P.M.

154. What does Mr. Adams request in the e-mail?

(A) A list of available conference rooms
(B) Information about previous dinner guests
(C) A specific furniture arrangement
(D) A list of presentation equipment

Questions 155-157 refer to the following information.

Lakeview Inn Somerset
Wireless Internet Connection

Please read the following to use the wireless Internet at our hotel.

1. Purchase an Internet connection card at the front desk.

2. Open the network sharing center on your device. Select the network named "Lakeview Inn Somerset" from the list of available networks.

3. Enter the access code, which is printed on the connection card.

4. Read and accept the terms of use of the Internet.

5. Click on "Access the web."

Please note that you can use the Internet for free on desktop computers at the business center. A wireless connection is not available in the parking area and at the outdoor swimming pool. Call the front desk at extension #555 for assistance and inquiries.

155. What is the purpose of the information?

(A) To inform customers of the steps involved in accessing a service
(B) To announce the launching of a new feature
(C) To explain the details of a hotel policy
(D) To outline the advantages of using a program

156. In the information, what is NOT mentioned as something customers should do?

(A) Enable a function on their computers
(B) Enter their personal information
(C) Acquire a code from the reception desk
(D) Agree to comply with some conditions

157. Where is access to wireless Internet limited?

(A) In the hotel rooms
(B) Around the front desk
(C) In the business center
(D) Around the outdoor pool

▶ ▶ ▶GO ON TO THE NEXT PAGE

⊖ ◻ ⊗

To:	All employees
From:	Jose Scott <jscott@beauchamparts.edu>
Date:	February 17
Subject:	Underground parking space

To all employees,

Yesterday, a technician has found a leakage problem in the underground parking area for staff members. Please be advised that the underground parking space will not be available during February due to the pipe reinforcement construction. It is suggested that all employees use local parking spaces around the school. The school will provide reimbursement for parking fees. A list of available parking areas will be posted on www.beauchampartsschool.com/staff. The construction will neither directly affect our upcoming spring concert, nor will it cause problems for the new student orientation program next week. Thank you for your cooperation.

Jose Scott
Secretary, Beauchamp School for the Arts

158. What is the purpose of the e-mail?

(A) To explain about a new program
(B) To announce the construction of a new parking area
(C) To inform the employees of a possible inconvenience
(D) To describe how to get to the parking lot

159. What will happen next week?

(A) A concert will be postponed until the week after.
(B) The underground parking area will be available.
(C) Parking fees will increase.
(D) An instructional session will take place.

160. What are the employees advised to do?

(A) Avoid driving their vehicles to school
(B) Visit a website
(C) Receive reimbursement for damage to their cars
(D) Participate in the construction

Questions 161-163 refer to the following notice.

Attention, Rose Cosmetics Customers!

In response to our customers' repeated requests, we at Rose Cosmetics have decided to extend our hours of operation to welcome more guests. Please refer to the following new schedule:

Location	Opening Hours	
Richmond	Mon – Fri	8:00 A.M. – 6:00 P.M.
	Sun	9:30 A.M. – 4:00 P.M.
Suffolk	Mon – Fri	8:00 A.M. – 6:00 P.M.
	Sat	9:00 A.M. – 5:00 P.M
Portsmouth	Mon – Fri	9:00 A.M. – 7:00 P.M.
	Sat	9:00 A.M. – 6:00 P.M.

To thank our customers for supporting us, we would like to offer all of our customers who visit one of our stores between May 5 and June 4 discounts on selected items and a special gift with every purchase. For a complete list of the discounted items, please visit our website at www.rosecosmetics.com. We at Rose Cosmetics look forward to seeing you soon!

161. Why is Rose Cosmetics changing its hours of operation?

(A) To regain competitiveness in the area
(B) To attract people from other areas
(C) To accommodate increasing clientele
(D) To address customers' complaints

162. How is the Richmond location different from the other locations?

(A) It opens earlier each day.
(B) It operates on Sundays.
(C) It is currently offering a discount.
(D) It will undergo renovations soon.

163. How can customers receive a free item at Rose Cosmetics?

(A) By visiting its website
(B) By purchasing a product
(C) By talking to a representative
(D) By going to a specific store at a designated time

July 8

Matty Romano
3718 Sunrise Road
Las Vegas, NV 89109

Dear Mr. Romano,

Congratulations! Your application for doing volunteer work at the Evergreen Children's Hospital was received, and you are being given a position in our daycare program. However, before you can begin, you have to provide some additional documents for security issues.

You are required to provide a medical record for the last 5 years (this can be retrieved from your personal doctor) and a letter from your school verifying that you are currently attending classes there. This volunteer opportunity is only available to college students, so it is crucial that you send us this document. —[1]—. The required documents are to be mailed directly to the Evergreen social work office. —[2]—. The documents need to be original and hard copies. Please submit them by no later than July 15.

Per your request, I have enclosed this year's volunteer program schedule. —[3]—. Once we have finished reviewing your documents, we will send you a text message with a link to a web page where you should make an account so that you can check your daily volunteering schedule online. —[4]—.

If you have any inquiries regarding these, please do not hesitate to contact me.

Sincerely,

Judy Cruz
Evergreen Children's Hospital Volunteer Program Coordinator

Enclosure

164. Who most likely is Mr. Romano?

    (A) A college student
    (B) A hospital employee
    (C) A recruiting specialist
    (D) A representative of a volunteer group

165. What is Mr. Romano required to do within a week?

    (A) Apply for volunteer work
    (B) Send an e-mail to Ms. Cruz
    (C) Visit Ms. Cruz's office at the Evergreen Children's Hospital
    (D) Receive a document from a doctor

166. What was sent with the letter?

    (A) A certificate for volunteer work
    (B) A letter of attendance
    (C) The address of a web page
    (D) A timetable

167. In which of the positions marked [1], [2], [3], and [4] does the following sentence best belong?

"The address is posted on our website."

    (A) [1]
    (B) [2]
    (C) [3]
    (D) [4]

Questions 168-171 refer to the following online chat discussion.

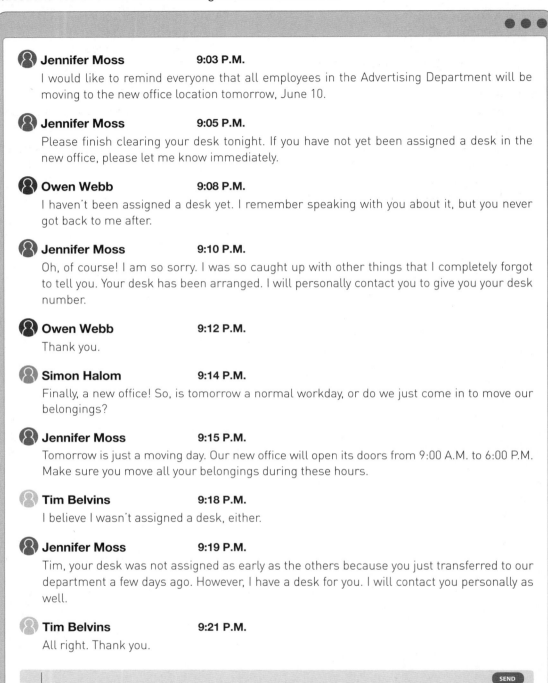

Jennifer Moss　　　9:03 P.M.

I would like to remind everyone that all employees in the Advertising Department will be moving to the new office location tomorrow, June 10.

Jennifer Moss　　　9:05 P.M.

Please finish clearing your desk tonight. If you have not yet been assigned a desk in the new office, please let me know immediately.

Owen Webb　　　9:08 P.M.

I haven't been assigned a desk yet. I remember speaking with you about it, but you never got back to me after.

Jennifer Moss　　　9:10 P.M.

Oh, of course! I am so sorry. I was so caught up with other things that I completely forgot to tell you. Your desk has been arranged. I will personally contact you to give you your desk number.

Owen Webb　　　9:12 P.M.

Thank you.

Simon Halom　　　9:14 P.M.

Finally, a new office! So, is tomorrow a normal workday, or do we just come in to move our belongings?

Jennifer Moss　　　9:15 P.M.

Tomorrow is just a moving day. Our new office will open its doors from 9:00 A.M. to 6:00 P.M. Make sure you move all your belongings during these hours.

Tim Belvins　　　9:18 P.M.

I believe I wasn't assigned a desk, either.

Jennifer Moss　　　9:19 P.M.

Tim, your desk was not assigned as early as the others because you just transferred to our department a few days ago. However, I have a desk for you. I will contact you personally as well.

Tim Belvins　　　9:21 P.M.

All right. Thank you.

SEND

168. What is mentioned about Ms. Moss?

(A) She does not have an assigned desk.
(B) She has been very busy for a while.
(C) She works for a relocation service company.
(D) She is the new advertising manager.

169. Why did Mr. Webb contact Ms. Moss previously?

(A) To get permission to transfer to another department
(B) To mention his promotion
(C) To ask for a designated workstation
(D) To consult about his working hours

170. At 9:14 P.M., what does Mr. Halom most likely mean when he writes, "Finally, a new office!"?

(A) He is indicating that he does not want to work tomorrow.
(B) He plans to visit the new office for the last time.
(C) He is concerned about his new position.
(D) He is excited about working in a new environment.

171. What are the employees instructed to do between 9:00 A.M. and 6:00 P.M. on June 10?

(A) Open a new account online
(B) Move some office furniture
(C) Visit the new office
(D) Contact Ms. Moss

▶ ▶ ▶GO ON TO THE NEXT PAGE

Around Nashville – Business Spotlight

July 19

This week's business spotlight is on Bell Laundro and its owner, Ms. Monica Bell. For those who don't know, Bell Laundro is a one-stop place that is a combination of a launderette, a café, and a bookstore and is based on Jackson Street. This new type of self-service laundry is one of the most successful independent businesses in Nashville today. —[1]—.

At first, Bell Laundro was not as successful as it currently is. —[2]—. However, Ms. Bell was not willing to give up on her business. —[3]—. After months of planning, she renovated a part of her laundry into a café-like lounge. —[4]—. In this waiting area, customers can enjoy a cup of coffee and read books while their clothes are being washed and dried.

The customers at Bell Laundro highly value the convenience and high-quality service Bell Laundro provides. Many residents in the area are students at Welch College, who need to do the laundry and buy books for their classes; they know Bell Laundro is perfect to take care of both tasks at the same time.

Ms. Bell was asked by many local colleges to provide tips and advice for students who plan on opening a new business. As a young entrepreneur herself, she seems very excited to lead her class, entitled "Difficulty into Opportunity."

172. What is indicated about Bell Laundro?

(A) It is located on a college campus.
(B) It has been featured in local magazines.
(C) It sells books via its website.
(D) It is a business with an unusual concept.

173. The word "value" in paragraph 3, line 1, is closest in meaning to

(A) evaluate
(B) appreciate
(C) estimate
(D) support

174. What does Ms. Bell plan to do in the future?

(A) Teach college students
(B) Join an organization
(C) Open another branch
(D) Start a new business

175. In which of the positions marked [1], [2], [3], and [4] does the following sentence best fit?

"Surrounded by large launderettes, it was not able to raise substantial revenue."

(A) [1]
(B) [2]
(C) [3]
(D) [4]

▶ ▶ ▶ GO ON TO THE NEXT PAGE

Questions 176-180 refer to the following notice and e-mail.

Bach's Music Center

Bach's Music Center has expanded to Oakville! We will be having a free open house for our patrons to explore the brand-new center in Oakville, which is equipped with new and improved systems and instruments. Be the first to experience true music at our music center!

Date: July 8
Time: 10:00 A.M. – 5:00 P.M.
What to expect: Taking a tour around the facilities, trying samples of our café items, and meeting our talented instructors.

At Oakville's Bach's Music Center:
- Lyrical Coffee serves delicious and freshly baked goods with a variety of beverage choices to choose from.
- St. Thomas Auditorium, an indoor performance hall with 150 seats.
- Project Eisenach, a junior music class for children under 11 years old.
- Bach Studio – Learn how to sing with a professional vocalist. The first vocal training class ever to be provided at Bach's Music Center.

Oakville's Bach's Music Center will first open our doors to the general public on July 11. We will provide visitors with a free music book and a Bach's Music Center T-shirt. More baked goodies and beverage samples will be waiting for you as well!

To:	Daniel Rupert <drupert@bachmusic.com>
From:	Amy Reyes <areyes@fastmail.com>
Date:	July 12
Subject:	Employment

Dear Mr. Rupert,

Thanks again for your time yesterday. I was very pleased to see the facility with all the newest systems and equipment. Oakville's Bach's Music Center certainly displays an exciting vibe, and that is why I would love to be one of the music instructors at your music center.

I have worked at several music academies as a piano instructor in the past. I have mostly taught young students because I like to work with children to see them grow as musicians as they take their first step in music education by learning the piano. Seeing children develop a passion for music is my main motive and inspiration.

Please e-mail me back or call me at (510) 555-3937 for further inquiries regarding possible positions at your music center. Thank you for your consideration.

Sincerely,
Amy Reyes

176. For whom is the notice most likely intended?

(A) Music instructor applicants
(B) Current students at a music school
(C) Visitors to Oakville
(D) Music contest participants

177. What will be given to visitors for free on July 8?

(A) A T-shirt
(B) A music book
(C) A trial class coupon
(D) Food and beverages

178. What is available exclusively at Oakville's Bach's Music Center?

(A) Instrument rentals
(B) A concert hall
(C) Vocal training
(D) Discounted music lessons

179. When did Mr. Rupert most likely talk to Ms. Reyes?

(A) During the music center's grand opening
(B) During a concert intermission
(C) During his music class
(D) During an open house event

180. Where would Ms. Reyes most likely prefer to work in the music center?

(A) At the St. Thomas Auditorium
(B) At the Project Eisenach
(C) At the Bach Studio
(D) At the Lyrical Coffee

▶ ▶ ▶GO ON TO THE NEXT PAGE

Questions 181-185 refer to the following e-mails.

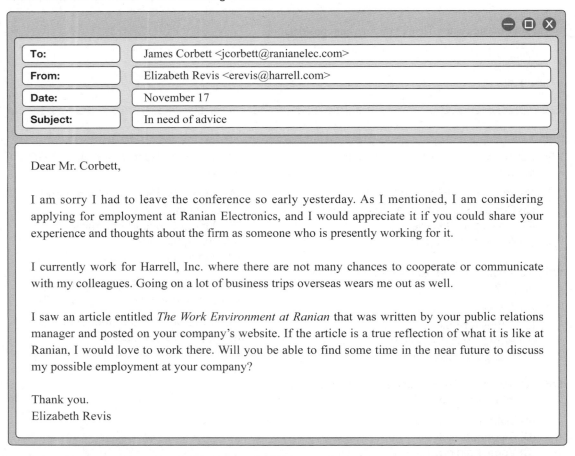

To: James Corbett <jcorbett@ranianelec.com>
From: Elizabeth Revis <erevis@harrell.com>
Date: November 17
Subject: In need of advice

Dear Mr. Corbett,

I am sorry I had to leave the conference so early yesterday. As I mentioned, I am considering applying for employment at Ranian Electronics, and I would appreciate it if you could share your experience and thoughts about the firm as someone who is presently working for it.

I currently work for Harrell, Inc. where there are not many chances to cooperate or communicate with my colleagues. Going on a lot of business trips overseas wears me out as well.

I saw an article entitled *The Work Environment at Ranian* that was written by your public relations manager and posted on your company's website. If the article is a true reflection of what it is like at Ranian, I would love to work there. Will you be able to find some time in the near future to discuss my possible employment at your company?

Thank you.
Elizabeth Revis

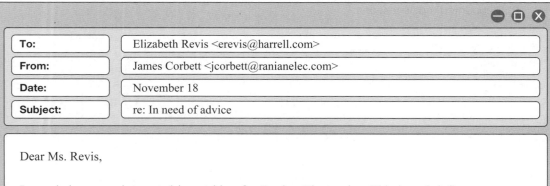

To: Elizabeth Revis <erevis@harrell.com>
From: James Corbett <jcorbett@ranianelec.com>
Date: November 18
Subject: re: In need of advice

Dear Ms. Revis,

I am glad you are interested in working for Ranian Electronics. This is to briefly answer your questions before we meet up to discuss Ranian and your employment here in detail.

The article you mentioned, the one written by Ms. Mary Witt, correctly describes the workplace at Ranian. We have many group assignments that require all members to share their ideas and thoughts with one another. In daily meetings, anyone can suggest a new strategy or insight regardless of rank or title. We rarely go on business trips, which should be a positive factor for you. We are more in-house work oriented.

I am free next Thursday afternoon. How does lunch together that day sound? I look forward to seeing you soon.

Regards,

James Corbett

181. What is the purpose of the first e-mail?

(A) To arrange an appointment
(B) To recommend employment
(C) To accept a job offer
(D) To request compensation

182. What does Ms. Revis mention about Harrell, Inc.?

(A) It does not cover employees' travel expenses.
(B) It has vacant positions to fill.
(C) It posts articles on its website.
(D) It conducts business in more than one country.

183. In the first e-mail, the word "true" in paragraph 3, line 2, is closest in meaning to

(A) certain
(B) natural
(C) direct
(D) accurate

184. What is suggested about Mr. Corbett?

(A) He often works at his home.
(B) He used to be Ms. Revis's coworker.
(C) He has known Ms. Revis for a long time.
(D) He attends meetings frequently.

185. Who is Mary Witt?

(A) A personnel manager
(B) A public relations manager
(C) A journalist
(D) A technician

▶ ▶ ▶GO ON TO THE NEXT PAGE

Questions 186-190 refer to the following instructions, e-mail, and receipt.

Welcome to the Bernardo Mall

To ensure a pleasant and safe experience for all visitors, the Bernardo Mall's parking policy must be strictly abided by and will be enforced at all times. Please read the following rules and instructions carefully:

- All parking is on a first-come, first-served basis. Park in designated spaces only. The Wells Zone, the parking space for large vehicles, such as trucks, buses, or vans, is located next to Carpe Diem, a toy store. All other types of vehicles should be parked in the Pedro Zone, located near the west wing of the mall.

- Parking is complimentary for the first half an hour for all visitors. Afterward, a rate of $2 per hour will apply. Visitors who spend more than $20 at the Bernardo Mall will have their parking fee waived. The receipts must be shown at each gate when leaving. Although we share parking spaces with several restaurants near the Bernardo Mall, restaurant receipts are not accepted.

- Parking is available during the Bernardo Mall's operating hours, 10:00 A.M. to 10:00 P.M., throughout the year.

- Contact the Bernardo Mall at **customerservice@bernardomall.com** for any inquiries, requests, or complaints.

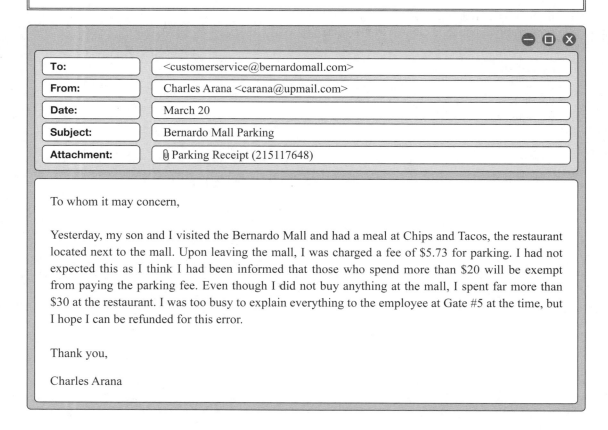

To:	<customerservice@bernardomall.com>
From:	Charles Arana <carana@upmail.com>
Date:	March 20
Subject:	Bernardo Mall Parking
Attachment:	📎 Parking Receipt (215117648)

To whom it may concern,

Yesterday, my son and I visited the Bernardo Mall and had a meal at Chips and Tacos, the restaurant located next to the mall. Upon leaving the mall, I was charged a fee of $5.73 for parking. I had not expected this as I think I had been informed that those who spend more than $20 will be exempt from paying the parking fee. Even though I did not buy anything at the mall, I spent far more than $30 at the restaurant. I was too busy to explain everything to the employee at Gate #5 at the time, but I hope I can be refunded for this error.

Thank you,

Charles Arana

RECEIPT

Bernardo Mall Parking Lot
Receipt Number: 215117648

Parking Location	Wells Zone	Slot Number	B07
Date/Time of Arrival	March 19, 3:19 P.M.	Date/Time of Departure	March 19, 6:41 P.M.

Receipt?	NO	Discount?	NO
Amount Due	$5.73	Hours of Use	3 hrs and 22 min
Amount Paid	$5.73	Payment Type	Cash

Thank you and drive safely!

186. What is implied about the Bernardo Mall?

(A) It has recently amended its parking policy.
(B) It is open every day of the week.
(C) It is currently recruiting customer service representatives.
(D) It may not be available during certain seasons.

187. What is indicated about the parking lot Mr. Arana used on March 19?

(A) It was closed throughout the morning.
(B) It was recently renovated.
(C) It is an underground facility.
(D) It has multiple gates.

188. Why will Mr. Arana be unable to receive a refund?

(A) He did not park his vehicle properly.
(B) He did not spend the required amount of money at the Bernardo Mall.
(C) He did not read the instructions.
(D) He did not contact a customer service representative in time.

189. In the e-mail, the word "far" in paragraph 1, line 4, is closest in meaning to

(A) really
(B) well
(C) beyond
(D) distantly

190. What is NOT true about Mr. Arana?

(A) He drove a large vehicle to the Bernardo Mall.
(B) He dined at Chips and Tacos with his son.
(C) He paid his parking fee in cash on March 19.
(D) He will not visit the Bernardo Mall again.

▶ ▶ ▶GO ON TO THE NEXT PAGE

Sherman Tours

Sherman Tours proudly presents our special one-day trip to the Grand Canyon. You can enjoy a memorable and comfortable trip to the South Rim of the Grand Canyon in a small group of 6. Our expert guide will drive you to the Grand Canyon and other major local tourist attractions in a spacious van and tell you about the history of, as well as tales about, each place. Note that only members of Sherman Tours can take advantage of this very reasonably priced tour. To register and for further information about our trip to the Grand Canyon, please refer to our website at www.shermantours.com.

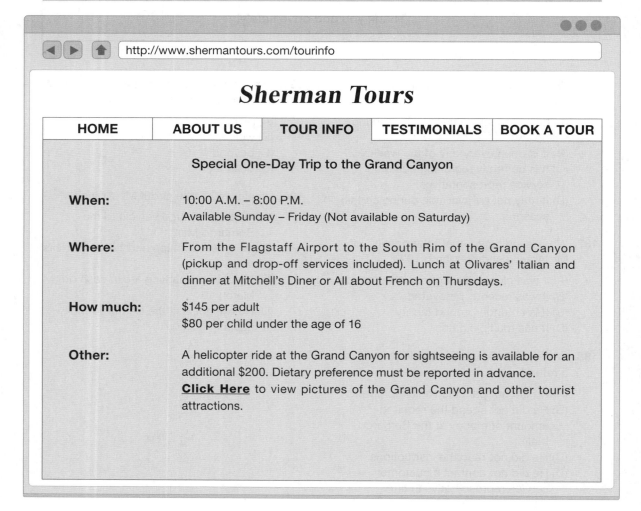

http://www.shermantours.com/tourinfo

Sherman Tours

HOME	ABOUT US	TOUR INFO	TESTIMONIALS	BOOK A TOUR

Special One-Day Trip to the Grand Canyon

When:
10:00 A.M. – 8:00 P.M.
Available Sunday – Friday (Not available on Saturday)

Where:
From the Flagstaff Airport to the South Rim of the Grand Canyon (pickup and drop-off services included). Lunch at Olivares' Italian and dinner at Mitchell's Diner or All about French on Thursdays.

How much:
$145 per adult
$80 per child under the age of 16

Other:
A helicopter ride at the Grand Canyon for sightseeing is available for an additional $200. Dietary preference must be reported in advance.
Click Here to view pictures of the Grand Canyon and other tourist attractions.

Sherman Tours

| HOME | ABOUT US | TOUR INFO | TESTIMONIALS | BOOK A TOUR |

http://www.shermantours.com/testimonials

"Great Trip to the Grand Canyon"

Reviewed by Samantha Watts
Reviewed on October 10

This was such a wonderful and well-organized tour provided by Sherman Tours. I especially liked the fact that I was never rushed, which enabled me to take in the view and appreciate the nature of the beautiful Grand Canyon. Our guide Joshua O'Neil was very informative, knowledgeable, and entertaining. I greatly enjoyed the delicious dinner I had at All about French as well. I would recommend this trip package to all those who want to have an unforgettable experience at the Grand Canyon in a relatively short time.

191. What is true about Sherman Tours?

(A) It is offering its members an exclusive deal.
(B) It consists of six employees.
(C) It issues a newsletter monthly.
(D) It has a long history.

192. What is mentioned about the helicopter ride?

(A) It must be requested in advance.
(B) It will be given to returning guests.
(C) It is offered for an extra fee.
(D) It is currently available for a reduced price.

193. What is included in the one-day trip to the Grand Canyon?

(A) An airline ticket
(B) Meals
(C) A souvenir
(D) Picture-taking service

194. When did Ms. Watts most likely go on a tour to the Grand Canyon?

(A) On a Thursday
(B) On a Friday
(C) On a Saturday
(D) On a Sunday

195. What can be inferred about Mr. O'Neil?

(A) He is a professional entertainer.
(B) He paid $145 for his tour of the Grand Canyon.
(C) He is a new employee at Sherman Tours.
(D) He gave Ms. Watts a ride to the Grand Canyon.

▶ ▶ ▶GO ON TO THE NEXT PAGE

http://www.booksworld.com/category

Books World

HOME	RECENT	CATEGORY	ORDER

Bestselling books by category: culinary arts

1. *Behind the Kitchen* by Anthony Barry
   Dreaming of opening a restaurant? Learn to make good money in the food industry with Mr. Barry's insights and advice.

2. *Happy Table* by Karen Wilson
   The food on your table determines you and your family's health and happiness. Directions on choosing the right ingredients and using the right cooking methods.

3. *Understanding the Food Industry by* Rodney Sanford
   You have to understand the industry in order to become successful in it. See how to avoid mistakes that people new to the food industry often make. If you are interested in owning a restaurant, this is a must-read for you.

4. *Food, Language, and Culture* by Rodney Sanford
   What determines the food, language, and culture of a nation? And how do they, in turn, affect the nation and its people? Find out in Mr. Sanford's book that has been translated into more than 10 languages.

Bloomfield Public Library
Events in the Fourth Week of June

June 20, Monday – Successful author and restaurant owner Rodney Sanford visits our library to discuss methods regarding operating a restaurant that are demonstrated in his latest book. Mr. Sanford will sign his book for participants after the event.

June 22, Wednesday – A fun, interactive event full of music for preschoolers and toddlers with their guardians. Songs about the different seasons and weather will be played along with various instruments. No registration required to join this exciting musical class.

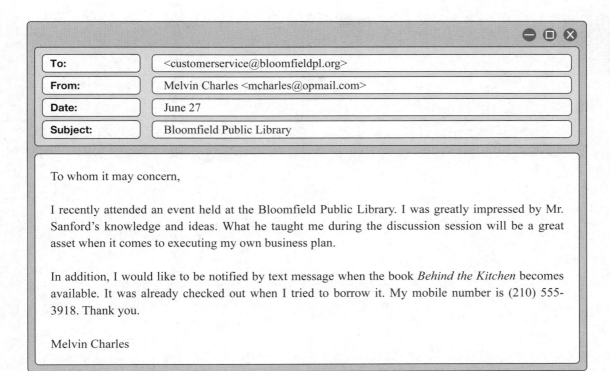

To:	<customerservice@bloomfieldpl.org>
From:	Melvin Charles <mcharles@opmail.com>
Date:	June 27
Subject:	Bloomfield Public Library

To whom it may concern,

I recently attended an event held at the Bloomfield Public Library. I was greatly impressed by Mr. Sanford's knowledge and ideas. What he taught me during the discussion session will be a great asset when it comes to executing my own business plan.

In addition, I would like to be notified by text message when the book *Behind the Kitchen* becomes available. It was already checked out when I tried to borrow it. My mobile number is (210) 555-3918. Thank you.

Melvin Charles

---

196. In the web page, the word "good" in paragraph 1, line 2, is closest in meaning to

(A) pleasant
(B) substantial
(C) generous
(D) real

197. What is indicated about the Bloomfield Public Library?

(A) It hosts events for children.
(B) It requires a membership card for event registration.
(C) It is currently hiring new employees.
(D) Its operating hours vary seasonally.

198. What book was signed at the Bloomfield Public Library by its author recently?

(A) *Behind the Kitchen*
(B) *Happy Table*
(C) *Understanding the Food Industry*
(D) *Food, Language, and Culture*

199. What is probably true about Mr. Charles?

(A) He frequently visits the Bloomfield Public Library.
(B) He works at the Bloomfield Public Library.
(C) He would like to buy one of Mr. Sanford's books.
(D) He is interested in opening a restaurant.

200. What does Mr. Charles request the Bloomfield Public Library do?

(A) Inform him of the release date of a book
(B) Notify him of when there will be another event with Mr. Sanford
(C) Let him know when a book is returned to the library
(D) Send a new book to his address

STOP! This is the end of the test. If you finish before time is called, you may go back to Parts 5, 6, and 7 and check your work.

Actual Test 02

MP3

해설집

적정 풀이 시간 120분

120 min

시작 시간 ___시 ___분

종료 시간 ___시 ___분

중간에 멈추지 말고 처음부터 끝까지 풀어보세요.
문제를 풀 때에는 실전처럼 답안지에 마킹하세요.

목표 개수 _____ / 200 **실제 개수 _____ / 200**

예상 점수는 번역 및 정답에 있는 점수 환산표를 참조하세요.

LISTENING TEST

In the Listening test, you will be asked to demonstrate how well you understand spoken English. The entire Listening test will last approximately 45 minutes. There are four parts, and directions are given for each part. You must mark your answers on the separate answer sheet. Do not write your answers in the test book.

PART 1

Directions: For each question in this part, you will hear four statements about a picture in your test book. When you hear the statements, you must select the one statement that best describes what you see in the picture. Then find the number of the question on your answer sheet and mark your answer. The statements will not be printed in your test book and will be spoken only one time.

Statement (B), "They are sitting at a table." is the best description of the picture. So you should select answer (B) and mark it on your answer sheet.

1.

2.

▶ ▶ ▶ GO ON TO THE NEXT PAGE

3.

4.

5.

6.

▶ ▶ ▶GO ON TO THE NEXT PAGE

PART 2

Directions: You will hear a question or statement and three responses spoken in English. They will not be printed in your test book and will be spoken only one time. Select the best response to the question or statement and mark the letter (A), (B), or (C) on your answer sheet.

7. Mark your answer on your answer sheet.

8. Mark your answer on your answer sheet.

9. Mark your answer on your answer sheet.

10. Mark your answer on your answer sheet.

11. Mark your answer on your answer sheet.

12. Mark your answer on your answer sheet.

13. Mark your answer on your answer sheet.

14. Mark your answer on your answer sheet.

15. Mark your answer on your answer sheet.

16. Mark your answer on your answer sheet.

17. Mark your answer on your answer sheet.

18. Mark your answer on your answer sheet.

19. Mark your answer on your answer sheet.

20. Mark your answer on your answer sheet.

21. Mark your answer on your answer sheet.

22. Mark your answer on your answer sheet.

23. Mark your answer on your answer sheet.

24. Mark your answer on your answer sheet.

25. Mark your answer on your answer sheet.

26. Mark your answer on your answer sheet.

27. Mark your answer on your answer sheet.

28. Mark your answer on your answer sheet.

29. Mark your answer on your answer sheet.

30. Mark your answer on your answer sheet.

31. Mark your answer on your answer sheet.

PART 3

Directions: You will hear some conversations between two or three people. You will be asked to answer three questions about what the speakers say in each conversation. Select the best response to each question and mark the letter (A), (B), (C), or (D) on your answer sheet. The conversations will not be printed in your test book and will be spoken only one time.

32. What product are the speakers discussing?

(A) A motor vehicle
(B) A laptop computer
(C) A cellular phone
(D) A television set

33. What caused a delay?

(A) Unavailable materials
(B) Not enough money in the budget
(C) A problem with an engine
(D) A lack of skilled workers

34. What will happen in two months?

(A) Production will start.
(B) A design will be approved.
(C) Customer surveys will be collected.
(D) A new factory will open.

35. Where do the speakers most likely work?

(A) At a grocery store
(B) At an electronics store
(C) At a bookstore
(D) At a library

36. What did the woman decide to do?

(A) Improve the website
(B) Guarantee a service
(C) Charge customers for membership
(D) Order more products

37. What does the man expect will happen?

(A) Hours will be extended.
(B) Free delivery will be offered.
(C) More staff will be hired.
(D) Sales will improve.

38. Where does the man work?

(A) At a landscaping service
(B) At a real estate agency
(C) At a public library
(D) At a telephone company

39. What is the woman concerned about?

(A) A material
(B) A deadline
(C) A price
(D) A location

40. What do the speakers agree to do in the afternoon?

(A) Check out a manual
(B) Sign a rental contract
(C) Meet with an owner
(D) Visit a property

41. What event are the speakers talking about?

(A) A retirement party
(B) A training seminar
(C) A new cleaning service
(D) An employee appreciation party

42. Why does the man say, "All the recyclables get picked up tomorrow morning"?

(A) To provide a warning
(B) To make a request
(C) To express surprise
(D) To turn down a suggestion

43. What does the man say he will do?

(A) Contact a cleaning service
(B) Go home early
(C) Pick up some trash
(D) Get some cleaning supplies

▶ ▶ ▶ GO ON TO THE NEXT PAGE

44. Where does the man work?

(A) At a train station
(B) At an airport
(C) At a convention center
(D) At a hotel

45. According to the man, what event will take place this week?

(A) A marketing seminar
(B) A trade fair
(C) A music concert
(D) A book release

46. What does the man recommend doing?

(A) Using a shuttle bus
(B) Hiring a local guide
(C) Eating at a restaurant
(D) Taking a taxi

47. What does the business want the woman to do?

(A) Design a new recreation area
(B) Take care of online advertising
(C) Create a new web page
(D) Manage customer account

48. Why is the woman the top job candidate?

(A) She has experience working abroad.
(B) She has good recommendations.
(C) Her work is impressive.
(D) Her schedule is flexible.

49. What do the men point out about their resort?

(A) It was recently renovated.
(B) It has beautiful views.
(C) It is popular with guests.
(D) It is reasonably priced.

50. What does the woman say will happen on the weekend?

(A) Some products will be discounted.
(B) New items will be arriving.
(C) Some lighting fixtures will be installed.
(D) The store's hours will be extended.

51. What does the man mean when he says, "I think we'll be seeing each other a lot"?

(A) He accepted a job at the store.
(B) He is happy about a new business.
(C) He has known a business owner long.
(D) He is a member of a shopping club.

52. Why does the woman apologize?

(A) She misunderstood the man's request.
(B) The store is not currently hiring.
(C) A payment method cannot be used.
(D) An advertised item is out of stock.

53. What type of product are the speakers talking about?

(A) A kitchen appliance
(B) A musical instrument
(C) A light fixture
(D) A smartphone accessory

54. What is the woman's complaint about the item?

(A) It is missing some parts.
(B) It is making strange noises.
(C) It comes with wrong cables.
(D) It is damaged.

55. What does Stuart recommend doing?

(A) Using a manufacturer's warranty
(B) Visiting another repair store
(C) Ordering some replacement parts
(D) Returning later in the day

56. Where do the speakers work?

(A) At a recycling plant
(B) At a technical school
(C) At a manufacturing facility
(D) At a bicycle shop

57. What are the speakers talking about?

(A) An electric motor
(B) Some safety equipment
(C) A bicycle rack
(D) A steering wheel

58. What does the man ask the woman to do?

(A) Call a supplier
(B) Put up a notice
(C) Sign a document
(D) Send an e-mail

59. Where does the woman work?

(A) At a radio station
(B) At a furniture store
(C) At a computer store
(D) At a department store

60. What is mentioned about recent orders?

(A) They are for smaller quantities.
(B) They are mostly from businesses.
(C) They are always placed online.
(D) They must come preassembled.

61. According to the woman, how does her business stay competitive?

(A) By offering a discount on custom-made furniture
(B) By improving customer service
(C) By increasing online marketing
(D) By providing many items for individual customers

Inspection Report	
Item	**Action Taken**
Laptop Computer	Upgraded Operation System
Photocopier	Replaced Toner
Projector	Broken – Repair or Remove
Printer	Connected to New Computer

62. What type of business do the speakers work at?

(A) At a library
(B) At an electronics store
(C) At a university
(D) At a law firm

63. Look at the graphic. Which piece of equipment are the speakers talking about?

(A) The laptop computer
(B) The photocopier
(C) The projector
(D) The printer

64. What does the man say he will do now?

(A) Order some replacement parts
(B) Speak with a coworker
(C) Clean the conference room
(D) Purchase some new equipment

Sam's Schedule

To Do	Time
Meeting with Dean	11:00 A.M.
Conference Call	11:45 A.M.
Client Lunch	12:00 P.M.
Factory Tour	1:30 P.M.
Orientation Speech	4:00 P.M.

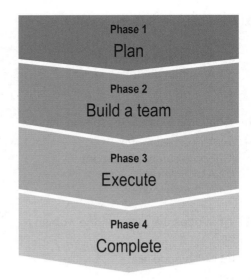

Phase 1
Plan

Phase 2
Build a team

Phase 3
Execute

Phase 4
Complete

65. Where is the conversation taking place?

(A) In Dean's office
(B) At a restaurant
(C) At a factory
(D) In a conference room

66. What are the speakers going to discuss?

(A) The price of a product
(B) The design of a product
(C) The sales of a product
(D) The advertising of a product

67. Look at the graphic. Why does Sam need to leave early?

(A) He has a meeting with Dean.
(B) He has a conference call.
(C) He has a factory tour.
(D) He has an orientation speech.

68. Where does the conversation take place?

(A) At a job fair
(B) At a meeting for managers
(C) At a marketing company
(D) At a trade show

69. Look at the graphic. Which phase does the man think is important to the success of a project?

(A) Plan
(B) Build a team
(C) Execute
(D) Complete

70. What does the woman say she will do when she returns home?

(A) Register for a course
(B) Apply for a position
(C) Talk to the man on the phone
(D) Submit her résumé

PART 4

Directions: You will hear some short talks given by a single speaker. You will be asked to answer three questions about what the speaker says in each short talk. Select the best response to each question and mark the letter (A), (B), (C), or (D) on your answer sheet. The talks will not be printed in your test book and will be spoken only one time.

71. Where does the speaker most likely work?

(A) At a sporting goods store
(B) At a hardware store
(C) At a department store
(D) At a jewelry store

72. According to the speaker, what should the listeners focus on?

(A) Cleaning the store
(B) Handing out promotional flyers
(C) Providing customer service
(D) Rearranging the shelves

73. How can shoppers win a prize?

(A) By sending a text message
(B) By turning in a receipt
(C) By visiting a website
(D) By completing a form

74. What business is being advertised?

(A) An amusement park
(B) A travel agency
(C) A restaurant
(D) A hotel

75. According to the speaker, what is the business recognized for?

(A) Holding swimming competitions
(B) Using environmentally friendly materials
(C) Drawing foreign tourists
(D) Donating to the local charities

76. What job benefit is given to the employees?

(A) Employee discounts
(B) Chances for full-time employment
(C) Flexible work schedules
(D) Training opportunities

77. Why is the speaker calling?

(A) To make a cancelation
(B) To track an order
(C) To talk about an order
(D) To ask for driving directions

78. What does the speaker imply when she says, "We have orders that we need to fill at the end of the month"?

(A) More workers must be hired.
(B) Her request is urgent.
(C) She can pay a higher price.
(D) Items should be sent by special delivery.

79. What is the listener warned about?

(A) The speaker might not be in her office.
(B) There could be a change in working hours.
(C) A reservation cannot be made.
(D) A schedule has been changed.

80. What type of event is being prepared?

(A) A trade show
(B) A local festival
(C) A charity auction
(D) A fundraiser

81. What news does the speaker announce?

(A) An advertisement was successful.
(B) Posters have been put up.
(C) A venue can be rented.
(D) A dinner reservation has been confirmed.

82. According to the speaker, what is the next phase in the planning process?

(A) Placing advertisements
(B) Signing contracts
(C) Creating a web page
(D) Acquiring supplies

▶ ▶ ▶ GO ON TO THE NEXT PAGE

83. What is the topic of the podcast?

(A) Understanding market trends
(B) Expanding a business
(C) Increasing profits
(D) Helping with starting a new business

84. What type of business does Tina Mellon own?

(A) A clothing store
(B) A restaurant
(C) A financial service company
(D) A cosmetics manufacturer

85. What does the speaker say can be found on a website?

(A) An interview
(B) A business tutorial
(C) A list of investors
(D) A job opportunity

---

86. What does the speaker apologize for?

(A) An unexpected fee
(B) A long line
(C) A delayed start
(D) A crowded bus

87. Why does the speaker say, "And that's our next stop"?

(A) To suggest purchasing items later
(B) To complain about a tour schedule
(C) To advise the listeners to hurry up
(D) To answer a listener's question

88. What does the speaker say the listeners will enjoy at the Rudolph Bistro?

(A) The view of the city
(B) The artwork
(C) A musical performance
(D) The fresh food

89. What has the business had difficulty with?

(A) Hiring qualified employees
(B) Promoting its newest products
(C) Expanding into foreign markets
(D) Retaining staff members

90. What did the speaker do last month?

(A) She conducted a survey.
(B) She interviewed some applicants.
(C) She signed a new contract.
(D) She went on a business trip.

91. What does the speaker say the company will do?

(A) Start a mentoring program
(B) Offer an on-the-job training
(C) Create more advertisements
(D) Purchase a new property

---

92. What is Summerville planning to do?

(A) Widen some of the roads in the city
(B) Improve bus services
(C) Encourage residents to use public transportation
(D) Attract more tourists

93. Why does the speaker say, "It has been successful in other cities"?

(A) To hire more bus drivers
(B) To mention a new training program
(C) To develop another mobile app
(D) To praise a job well done

94. What are the listeners asked to do?

(A) E-mail some feedback
(B) Start taking the bus
(C) Visit the mayor's office
(D) Go to other cities

Repairs Plan

Step 1	Inspect a property
Step 2	Make a cost estimate
Step 3	Create a timeline
Step 4	Obtain permits
Step 5	Begin Working

Fayetteville Spring Festival

Saturday, May 2 – Sunday, May 3
Painting and drawing
Local food and performers

◇◇◇◇◇◇◇◇◇◇◇◇◇◇◇◇◇◇◇◇◇◇◇◇◇◇◇◇

Saturday Performances
- Marshall Peters Band
- Fayetteville Orchestra

Sunday Performances
- Dave Sanders Comedy Routine
- Redwood Band

95. Who most likely is the speaker?

(A) A construction manager
(B) An architect
(C) A hardware store owner
(D) An interior decorator

96. Look at the graphic. Which step is the speaker currently working on?

(A) Step 1
(B) Step 2
(C) Step 3
(D) Step 4

97. What will the speaker send the listener?

(A) A contract to sign
(B) Revised blueprints
(C) Some samples of material
(D) A cost estimate

98. Why has an event been postponed?

(A) Some fees have not been paid.
(B) Inclement weather is predicted.
(C) Some performers are not available.
(D) Repair work needs to be done.

99. Look at the graphic. Which performance will the speaker most likely go to?

(A) Redwood Band
(B) Fayetteville Orchestra
(C) Dave Sanders Comedy Routine
(D) Marshall Peters Band

100. What does the speaker offer to do?

(A) Volunteer at the festival
(B) Organize an event
(C) Buy some tickets
(D) Drive to a performance

This is the end of the Listening test. Turn to Part 5 in your test book.

▶ ▶ ▶ GO ON TO THE NEXT PAGE

READING TEST

In the Reading test, you will read a variety of texts and answer several different types of reading comprehension questions. The entire Reading test will last 75 minutes. There are three parts, and directions are given for each part. You are encouraged to answer as many questions as possible within the time allowed.

You must mark your answer on the separate answer sheet. Do not write your answers in your test book.

PART 5

Directions: A word or phrase is missing in each of the sentences below. Four answer choices are given below each sentence. Select the best answer to complete the sentence. Then mark the letter (A), (B), (C), or (D) on your answer sheet.

101. Due to ------- optimistic and cheerful personality, he later became a radio host in New York.

(A) he
(B) him
(C) his
(D) himself

102. Last week, ------- the euro and Swiss franc weakened 3.1 percent against the U.S dollar.

(A) both
(B) either
(C) never
(D) whether

103. Our company decided to hire Mr. Kwon ------- our Head of Marketing because his marketing presentation was impressive.

(A) as
(B) by
(C) so
(D) for

104. Due to the heat wave, BK Construction requested an ------- on the new bridge construction project.

(A) extend
(B) extension
(C) extensive
(D) extended

105. Mandoo Electronics shares rose by about 25 percent almost immediately ------- the release of new memory chips.

(A) when
(B) either
(C) aside from
(D) following

106. With improved search technologies, it is not difficult today to locate ------- to purchase old jazz albums from the 50's and 60's online.

(A) such
(B) and
(C) but
(D) if

107. The landscaper hired by Mr. Jenkins used evergreen bushes to create additional privacy in his garden and to mark a natural ------- for his property.

(A) inventory
(B) building
(C) boundary
(D) source

108. Once the new manufacturing plant in Vietnam has been -------, our productivity is expected to increase by about 30%.

(A) constructed
(B) repaired
(C) incurred
(D) indicated

109. Both the exteriors and interiors of our new car models have been ------- redesigned to appeal to domestic and foreign customers.

(A) complete
(B) completing
(C) completely
(D) completion

110. People usually read newspapers and magazines in order to obtain ------- information about a variety of social phenomena.

(A) accurate
(B) obscure
(C) confidential
(D) sensitive

111. Job applicants should be reminded that false information ------- in the interview may result in automatic dismissal.

(A) give
(B) given
(C) giving
(D) was given

112. The newly-developed battery charger is ------- with almost all types of laptop computers in the domestic market.

(A) popular
(B) innovative
(C) compatible
(D) unavailable

113. Ms. Parker is arguing that the idea for the new inventory system was her own and not ------- of Mr. Evans.

(A) one
(B) this
(C) none
(D) that

114. Drivers must ------- with the rules governing driving time and off-duty time if they drive vehicles transporting dangerous substances.

(A) compete
(B) comply
(C) associate
(D) provide

115. ------- on the recent study, some scientists have concluded that North Pole ice cap is being lost seven times faster than it was in the 1990s.

(A) Based
(B) Basing
(C) Base
(D) Basement

116. ------- who is interested in participating in the technology seminar should contact Mr. McGowan by next Wednesday.

(A) Those
(B) Them
(C) Each other
(D) Anyone

117. The recent survey shows that three out of ten adolescents appeared heavily ------- on their mobile phones.

(A) depend
(B) dependent
(C) dependable
(D) dependence

118. The market analysis report contains some errors that Mr. Hopkins ------- before the board meeting scheduled to take place tomorrow.

(A) to correct
(B) correct
(C) has been corrected
(D) will correct

▶ ▶ ▶ GO ON TO THE NEXT PAGE

119. James Watt, ------- latest album has been the top selling album in the country, has received many prestigious music awards.

(A) whatever
(B) whom
(C) what
(D) whose

120. Please write your recent experience with Global Telecom ------- we can improve our customer services.

(A) now that
(B) while
(C) although
(D) so that

121. The guest speaker should stand ------- the audience to foster their positive engagement and participation.

(A) anywhere
(B) somewhere
(C) in place of
(D) in front of

122. The human resources department will ------- plan many activities that the company offers for newly hired employees.

(A) compatibly
(B) meticulously
(C) considerably
(D) enormously

123. It is recommended that all people ------- a copy of their tax returns and receipts in case they are audited in the future.

(A) retain
(B) imitate
(C) complete
(D) arrange

124. ------- selling fewer trucks and sedans, Autotrade Services reported record profits last year.

(A) Through
(B) Despite
(C) Unless
(D) Upon

125. Ace Computer's manufacturing plant has noticed a sharp increase in productivity ------- the assembly line workers began operating the new machinery.

(A) since
(B) how
(C) even if
(D) as a result of

126. Some of the company's transaction files became damaged ------- being moved to the new data storage system.

(A) in contrast to
(B) in exchange for
(C) in the process of
(D) for the reason that

127. The new office computer course holds thirty employees, all of ------- will learn computer skills, including advanced knowledge of word processing and database management.

(A) who
(B) whom
(C) which
(D) them

128. Although manufacturing jobs have fallen in recent decades, improved productivity has kept manufacturing ------- rising.

(A) amount
(B) quantity
(C) output
(D) consequence

129. Many popular restaurants and hotels are opening their own official websites ------- making reservations and paying with a credit card.

(A) facilitates
(B) facilitation
(C) is facilitating
(D) to facilitate

130. A product that was delivered in packaging will be refunded ------- its original case has not been removed.

(A) therefore
(B) now that
(C) regardless of
(D) provided that

PART 6

Directions: Read the texts that follow. A word or phrase, or sentence is missing in parts of each text. Four answer choices for each question are given below the text. Select the best answer to complete the text. Then mark the letter (A), (B), (C), or (D) on your answer sheet.

Questions 131-134 refer to the following information.

Course Announcement

The Sunhill Community Center is pleased to announce that starting next Wednesday, April

10, Ms. Patricia Hernandez ------- Basic Spanish at the community center. The -------
                      131.   **132.**

meets every Monday from 10:00 A.M. to 11:30 A.M., in room 401.

You can register through our website at www.scc.org, or visit us in person at one of

------- help desks. Tuition is $80 for all four weeks. If you register by this Wednesday, you
133.

will automatically receive a 20 percent discount off of the tuition.

The Sunhill Community Center offers comprehensive foreign language courses starting

next month. -------. More information can be found on the website.
         134.

---

131. (A) to teach
    (B) is taught
    (C) will teach
    (D) has taught

132. (A) faculty
    (B) board
    (C) class
    (D) committee

133. (A) my
    (B) her
    (C) our
    (D) those

134. (A) You need a college degree to satisfy
       licensure requirements for teaching.
    (B) No other prior experience may be
       necessary for our translation jobs.
    (C) All residents of Sunhill age 60 and
       older can attend our courses for free.
    (D) The community center will be
       temporarily closed for extensive
       renovations.

Home > Local News >

Hill Valley Widens The Roads

By Alfred Brantley on December 12, 10:15 A.M.

The city council of Hill Valley is about to commence the road expansion construction on Lombard Street ------- to Hill Valley Convention Center. This construction project consists
135.
of widening the four lanes of Lombard Street so that it can become an eight-lane roadway.

-------.
136.

To enable the construction to be ------- safely, Lombard Street will be closed to vehicular
137.
traffic between Hill Valley Convention Center and the Art Gallery of Hill Valley. The

footbridge next to Hill Valley Convention Center that leads onto Lombard Street will also

be shut to pedestrians.

The pedestrian footway along Lombard Street that provides access to Hill Valley

Convention Center will not be affected by the work. -------, during this period, public
138.
buses that normally use Lombard Street will be diverted via Valencia Lane.

---

135. (A) committed
  (B) pertaining
  (C) related
  (D) adjacent

136. (A) We are concerned about traffic congestion on roads and air pollution.
  (B) It will create many new jobs for local workers and drive our economic growth.
  (C) Workplace safety is all about ensuring people are doing their jobs the right way with zero or very little chance of getting hurt.
  (D) This work is scheduled to begin around March 1, and is expected to take around three months to complete.

137. (A) completed
  (B) intensified
  (C) occurred
  (D) undertaken

138. (A) Similarly
  (B) However
  (C) Additionally
  (D) For example

Dear Mr. Michael Western;

We received your letter of June 1. We regret ------- you any inconvenience.
139.

According to our shipping company, -------, all one hundred cases were delivered in good
140.

frozen condition and no one on the ship observed any cases defrosting before their arrival

in San Diego. Therefore, we assume that the defrosting process started after the cargo

------- to the warehouse in the harbor.
141.

In order to keep pork frozen, the freezer room must be maintained at temperature of

minus 15 degrees centigrade. We believe that the cases began to defrost due to the

insufficient freezing facilities in your warehouse.

Although we are not prepared to offer you a full refund, we would be happy to give you a

30% discount on your next deal. -------.
142.

We look forward to serving you again in the future.

Sincerely yours,

Nina Lee
Product Quality Control Manager
Andrew Farms, Inc.

139. (A) to cause
(B) cause
(C) causing
(D) caused

140. (A) because
(B) however
(C) thereby
(D) at the time

141. (A) move
(B) is moved
(C) will be moving
(D) had been moved

142. (A) We are not responsible for any lost, stolen, or damaged baggage or personal items.
(B) Frozen foods removes any bacteria and allows the foods to be stored for many years.
(C) With speedy delivery and proper packaging, you can send perishable items to your customers.
(D) We hope this arrangement should cover the part of the financial losses you have suffered.

▶ ▶ ▶ GO ON TO THE NEXT PAGE

Walnut Creek Hotel

1411 Tremont Street,
Boston, MA 02120
Tel: (857) 770-7000~3
Fax: (857) 770-7004~5
www.walnutcreekhotel.com

-------. The Walnut Creek Hotel is fully furnished and always prepared with lots of love to
143.

receive you; therefore we would like to ask you to take care of it ------- it were your own
144.

home.

All of the hotel rooms have recently been tastefully redecorated and re-equipped,

combining delicate fabrics and rich marble with the latest technology to ensure the most

------- stay by each and every guest at the hotel.
145.

You can get the necessary information on transportation tips and a variety of services for

your convenience at the front desk located on the ground floor. If you need -------
146.

information, please feel free to call us at ext. 101.

We hope your stay in the Walnut Creek Hotel becomes part of the great memories of your

trip to Boston. Thank you again for choosing the Walnut Creek Hotel for your stay and

enjoy your time with us.

143. (A) On behalf of all the staff, a big thank
you for your kind gifts and your
support this year.
(B) When booking a reservation for a
hotel room, guest may be asked to
make an advance deposit.
(C) No matter what time of year, this
town offers scenic backdrops and
views right on your doorstep.
(D) It is a real pleasure to have you as
our guests and we thank you for
choosing us for your stay.

144. (A) unless
(B) as if
(C) now that
(D) even though

145. (A) satisfy
(B) satisfying
(C) satisfied
(D) satisfaction

146. (A) further
(B) adequate
(C) essential
(D) confidential

PART 7

Directions: In this part you will read a selection of texts, such as magazine and newspaper articles, e-mails, and instant messages. Each text or set of texts is followed by several questions. Select the best answer for each question and mark the letter (A), (B), (C), or (D) on your answer sheet.

Questions 147-148 refer to the following advertisement.

RELAX HERE AT
SERENE SPA

As the premier spa in Southern California, Serene Spa offers services that go far beyond any traditional spa. On July 1, we are opening an additional spa location in San Diego.

Please note that services with asterisk* are available from July 10.

Swedish Massage*	Remedial Massage*	Laser Skincare*
Facials	Waxing	Stone Therapy
Nails	Peels	Aromatherapy

Please print out this page and bring the coupon below.

✂

15% OFF
Any Spa Service

Schedule Your Appointment Today!
- Offer is valid through July 31.
- Only one coupon may be used per visit.

---

147. Which service is NOT available on July 9?

(A) Facials
(B) Stone therapy
(C) Peels
(D) Laser skincare

148. What is indicated about the coupon in the advertisement?

(A) It is available for use in August.
(B) It offers a discount only in the San Diego branch.
(C) It has to be printed out in order to get a discount.
(D) It can be used together with other offers.

▶ ▶ ▶GO ON TO THE NEXT PAGE

Questions 149-150 refer to the following text message chain.

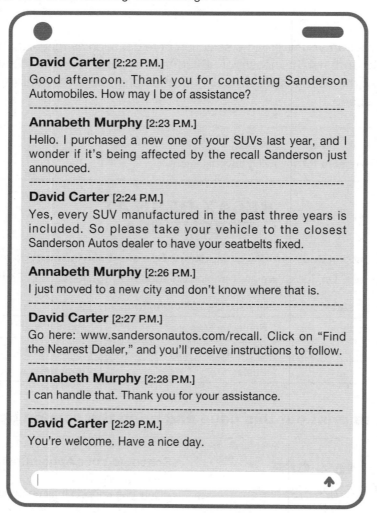

David Carter [2:22 P.M.]

Good afternoon. Thank you for contacting Sanderson Automobiles. How may I be of assistance?

Annabeth Murphy [2:23 P.M.]

Hello. I purchased a new one of your SUVs last year, and I wonder if it's being affected by the recall Sanderson just announced.

David Carter [2:24 P.M.]

Yes, every SUV manufactured in the past three years is included. So please take your vehicle to the closest Sanderson Autos dealer to have your seatbelts fixed.

Annabeth Murphy [2:26 P.M.]

I just moved to a new city and don't know where that is.

David Carter [2:27 P.M.]

Go here: www.sandersonautos.com/recall. Click on "Find the Nearest Dealer," and you'll receive instructions to follow.

Annabeth Murphy [2:28 P.M.]

I can handle that. Thank you for your assistance.

David Carter [2:29 P.M.]

You're welcome. Have a nice day.

149. Why did Ms. Murphy contact Mr. Carter?

(A) To find out how to buy an SUV
(B) To inquire about an engine problem
(C) To ask about a company recall
(D) To request a rebate on a purchase

150. At 2:28 P.M., what does Ms. Murphy most likely mean when she writes, "I can handle that"?

(A) She just followed Mr. Carter's instructions.
(B) She will fix the problem by herself.
(C) She can return to the place she made her purchase.
(D) She understands what she needs to do.

October 14

Alice Watts
Patterson Carpets
557 Longman Street
Portsmouth, OH 45662

Dear Ms. Watts,

It was a pleasure to meet with you at the home furnishings expo in Lexington, Kentucky, last week. —[1]—. You spent a lot of time speaking with me about the carpets your firm manufactures. I enjoyed learning about how your products are different from those of your competitors. I shared the samples you gave me with several employees here, and everyone was impressed with their quality. —[2]—. My colleagues particularly liked the selection of colors available.

We have been searching for a new supplier for our interior design company. —[3]—. We feel that your firm should definitely be able to fulfill all of our needs. I wonder if you are available to meet in person soon so that we can discuss a large order. —[4]—. When do you have time to meet?

Sincerely,

Reginald Wellman
Portsmouth Interior Design

151. What is NOT mentioned about Mr. Wellman?

(A) He is the owner of a company.
(B) He spoke with Ms. Watts in person.
(C) He works at a place that sells carpets.
(D) He traveled to Kentucky a week ago.

152. What does Mr. Wellman indicate about Portsmouth Interior Design?

(A) It recently opened.
(B) It has multiple workers.
(C) It provides free installation.
(D) It is having a sale soon.

153. In which of the positions marked [1], [2], [3], and [4] does the following sentence best belong?

"I'd also like to talk about a possible bulk discount."

(A) [1]
(B) [2]
(C) [3]
(D) [4]

Attention All Customers of Ala Moana

Thanks to all our customers for visiting Ala Moana. We strive to provide you with the finest Hawaiian-style shirts, hats, accessories and a wide variety of fashion items through our website.

Today, we would like to announce a change in our shipping policy. Ala Moana previously offered free shipping on all purchases, but due to the increasing fuel costs, we are no longer able to provide this service. Therefore, we must impose a shipping charge on each purchase less than $50. This was an inevitable decision in order to maintain the area's lowest cost of the products.

We ask for your understanding and Ala Moana promises to remain the most competitive Hawaiian fashion provider.

154. What is the purpose of the information?

(A) To advertise an online business
(B) To post a price list of new products
(C) To confirm a recent order
(D) To announce a change in service

155. What kind of business most likely is Ala Moana?

(A) A resort
(B) A clothing store
(C) A tour operator
(D) A shipping service

156. What is NOT indicated about Ala Moana?

(A) Its items can be purchased online.
(B) It has offered free shipping until recently.
(C) Its products cost less than its competitors'.
(D) It will hold a sale for the first time soon.

PUBLIC ANNOUNCEMENT FOR RESIDENTS OF IRVIING

An area in the City of Irving will be temporarily closed due to the 4th Texas Spring Parade, which will be held near Fritz Park from 3 P.M. to 8 P.M. on May 4.

The road closure will affect:
- The portion of St. Louis Street between Hampton Boulevard and Keys Road

Alternative Routes include:
- Marconi Street
- Bell Boulevard

For additional information, please contact the Traffic Advisory at the City of Irving at 214-885-0830.

157. What is the main purpose of the notice?

(A) To announce the opening of a sports competition
(B) To inform about upcoming traffic interruption
(C) To notify a scheduled road construction
(D) To alert residents to possible dangers on roads

158. Which part of the city will be closed during the event?

(A) The Fritz Park
(B) St. Louis Street
(C) Hampton Boulevard
(D) Marconi Street

▶ ▶ ▶GO ON TO THE NEXT PAGE

Jalalios' Tacos Opens in the Heart of the City of Kearny

by Chritiano Luxemberg

Kearny, August 11 – The residents of Kearny will now be able to enjoy delicious Mexican cuisine in the heart of Kearny. On August 9, the grand opening of Jalalios' Tacos saw local inhabitants flooding into the restaurant.

The owners, Abrahim and Brena Jalalio, are certified chefs who have successfully managed three restaurants in their hometown, Mexico City. Since they moved to the United States last year, they have been planning to open a restaurant in Kearny. When a vacant property, which was once a shoe store, was put on the market on May 22, they did not hesitate to purchase it and then renovate it into a restaurant.

Jalalios' Tacos provides homemade, traditional Mexican fare with a touch of the Jalalios' modern creativity at reasonable prices. Using only the freshest ingredients, Jalalios' Tacos provides not only delicious but healthy food.

Located on the most crowded street of the business district in Kearny, Jalalio's Tacos will now be the favorite restaurant to many businessmen. "I have always been a big fan of Mexican food. I had to eat at the restaurant after trying a free sample at the front door on the opening day. And I was really satisfied with the quality of its food," said Juan Suarez, a customer. On the day before the opening of the restaurant, I interviewed Mr. Jalalio on the outlook of his restaurant. He noted, "I am very pleased to open a new restaurant here on Castanteen Street. I plan to attract university students as well as businessmen. There can be people who have never visited our establishment, but there are none who have just come once."

For detailed information, pricing of the menu and reservation, please call 201-331-9243.

159. What is the purpose of the article?

(A) To advertise a vacant property
(B) To provide information about traditional food
(C) To introduce a new business to the region
(D) To inform residents of an upcoming construction

160. What is indicated about Mr. and Ms. Jalalio?

(A) They have relatives in Kearny.
(B) They previously owned a shoe store.
(C) They use ingredients imported from Mexico.
(D) They have run other restaurants.

161. According to Mr. Suarez, what is true about Jalalio's Tacos?

(A) It is conveniently located near a university.
(B) It gave visitors some food to try.
(C) Its customer service quality is satisfying.
(D) It has been Mr. Suarez's favorite place for a long time.

Questions 162-164 refer to the following review.

A Magical Autumn Night by Blue Souls

Last night, Blue Souls gave a rousing performance to 500 people gathered in the Oklahoma City Plaza. Composed of four musicians from different national backgrounds, Blue Souls is one of the most popular jazz bands in the United States and has been covered in articles numerous times.

Blue Souls was formed four years ago by the world-renowned pianist, David Yakal. Two years after its formation, an old friend of Mr. Yakal joined the Blue Souls. Taylor Clayton, who previously played trumpet in the London City Orchestra, enriched the sound of their performances as a new member of the group. Soon after he joined, Blue Souls was honored with the Best Musician of the Year Award by Oklahoma City for its exceptional quality of brass sound and performance.

The live performance at the outdoor stage of the Oklahoma City Plaza last night showed the audience the unique color of the music Blue Souls play. In addition to their most popular song, *On My Own*, they also performed songs from their upcoming third album, which will be released next month. Their new album contains different styles of music including swing, bossa nova, and modern jazz.

Blue Souls' performance was perfect as usual, but there was a tiny flaw. The concert venue was a little chilly and it would have been better if the organizers had furnished some portable heaters near the seats.

by Lauren Segulla

162. What type of event is being reviewed?

(A) An orchestra concert
(B) A jazz concert
(C) A magic act
(D) A dance performance

163. The word "covered" in paragraph 1, line 4, is closest in meaning to

(A) interviewed
(B) featured
(C) paid for
(D) blocked

164. What is stated about Mr. Clayton?

(A) He plays the piano.
(B) He joined Blue Souls two years ago.
(C) He has been presented an award by the London City Orchestra.
(D) He recently became the leader of Blue Souls.

Mickey Anderson
31 Mountain Road
Cornwall-on-Hudson, NY 12520

April 19

Chelsea Hair Salon
98 Cosmic Drive
Cornwall, NY 12592

To whom it may concern,

I am writing to apply for the advertised position of a fulltime hair stylist at the Chelsea Hair Salon branch in New Hampshire. Although I have enclosed my full résumé with this letter, I would like to briefly summarize my career background.

After receiving the hair stylist certification from the Clark College, I began working at the Berkshire Hair Shop located in Brookline. During the 6 years of employment there, I received professional recognition, including the National Best Hair Perm Styling Award last year. Along with my résumé, I have also added some photos of my awarded hair styles.

Beyond my professional skills, I am an enthusiastic, artistic, and faithful person who is ready to contribute to the national reputation of the Chelsea Hair Salon. I am sure my hair styling will fit the trend-oriented taste of the Chelsea Hair Salon.

Thank you and I look forward to having the opportunity of a personal interview.

Sincerely,

Mickey Anderson
Enclosure

165. Why did Ms. Anderson write the letter?

    (A) To confirm participating in an interview

    (B) To apply to a hair styling competition

    (C) To introduce herself to a potential employer

    (D) To offer a job at a hair salon

166. What is included with the letter?

    (A) Hair stylist certification

    (B) Award prizes

    (C) Sample images

    (D) Reference from another person

167. According to the letter, what is indicated about the Chelsea Hair Salon?

    (A) It is well-known nationally.

    (B) It has been in business for at least 6 years.

    (C) It has many award-winning hair designers in its staff.

    (D) It has a branch located in Brookline.

Questions 168-171 refer to the following online chat discussion.

Russell Thompson   9:55 A.M.

Hi, Steve and Mark. How's work at the Murray residence going?

Steve Gilmore   9:57 A.M.

We are almost finished. The work took a bit longer than expected because Mr. Murray asked us to cut a tree down after we trimmed the hedges. Don't worry. I put it on his bill.

Russell Thompson   9:58 A.M.

Sounds great. We just got an online inquiry from someone new. Anna Granite requested an estimate for her place. She lives at 88 Butler Drive. Do you think you can go there before heading to the Stanton Place?

Mark Stuart   10:00 A.M.

It's only a couple of blocks away.

Steve Gilmore   10:01 A.M.

Our next appointment isn't until 1:00 P.M., so we'll drop by after we finish here. What does she want?

Russell Thompson   10:02 A.M.

Thanks, guys.

Russell Thompson   10:02 A.M.

Ah, she wants the basic service, but she said her yard is larger than most people's. That's why I want you to check it out.

Mark Stuart   10:04 A.M.

I know the place. It covers around three acres.

Russell Thompson   10:05 A.M.

I guess it will be a big job. Give her an estimate based upon how much work you think it will require.

Steve Gilmore   10:06 A.M.

You've got it. I'll call you when we finish to discuss the matter.

SEND

168. Where most likely do the writers work?

(A) At a pool installation company
(B) At a real estate agency
(C) At a construction firm
(D) At a landscaping company

169. What does Mr. Gilmore expect to do in the afternoon?

(A) Provide an estimate
(B) Return to the office
(C) Visit a client
(D) Take part in a conference call

170. What will Mr. Gilmore do after meeting with Ms. Granite?

(A) Contact Mr. Thompson
(B) Submit a bill
(C) Purchase supplies
(D) Send an e-mail

171. At 10:00 A.M., what does Mr. Stuart suggest when he writes, "It's only a couple of blocks away"?

(A) He can comply with Mr. Thompson's request.
(B) He does not have time to make a personal visit.
(C) He does not know an exact location.
(D) He has visited a house in person before.

To:	All Employees of Pizza Stop
From:	Jason Bonanza
Date:	April 5
Subject:	News

Everyone,

Thanks for all of the hard work you have done to make our pizza shop the top one in the city. Unfortunately, our success has led to several imitators, each of whom is attempting to take business from us. —[1]—. As a result, I've decided to implement a few new strategies to attract more customers. Let me fill you in on them.

First, as of tomorrow, April 6, we're going to provide free Wi-Fi to customers in the shop. The password will change daily, so the servers must inform our diners at their tables. We'll also be increasing the number of electrical outlets near tables. —[2]—. That will enable diners to recharge their electric devices. We'll be closed on April 8 in order for electricians to make those changes here.

Next, the recent survey we took indicated that diners would like more options for pizza toppings. So I'll be changing the menu on April 9. —[3]—. We'll have a total of 25 possible pizza toppings, which will be the most in the city.

Finally, we're introducing Pizza Stop membership cards to our customers. —[4]—. Please see the document I've attached to this e-mail for more information.

Regards,

Jason Bonanza
Owner, Pizza Stop

172. Why will Pizza Stop make changes in its policies?

(A) To respond to customer requests
(B) To reduce spending
(C) To make itself more competitive
(D) To improve its advertising

173. What will happen on April 8?

(A) A shop will not open.
(B) A menu will change.
(C) Internet will be installed.
(D) A sale will begin.

174. What is indicated about Pizza Stop?

(A) It currently has a membership program.
(B) It offers discounts to frequent diners.
(C) It will be adding more tables soon.
(D) It is one of the city's leading pizza places.

175. In which of the positions marked [1], [2], [3], and [4] does the following sentence best fit?

"Holders can receive discounts and various free items."

(A) [1]
(B) [2]
(C) [3]
(D) [4]

www.hudsoncollege.edu/notice

HUDSON COLLEGE

| About | Notice | Academics | Community |

Hudson College Lecture Series on Child Education

Department of Child Education and Development proudly presents a series of lectures on early childhood. Lectures will take place at the department every Friday from June 14 through July 5. Renowned professors of Hudson College and professionals from national organizations will provide in-depth presentations about new ideas on analyzing childhood development and appropriate teaching skills.

Seminar Schedule:

Seminar Title and Speaker	Date/Time	Fees
Development of Language in Early Childhood by Mila Trundel, Professor at Hudson College	June 14 2 P.M. – 4 P.M.	$60
Appropriate Curriculum in Childhood Classrooms by Daniel Quinn, Professor at Hudson College	June 21 3 P.M. – 5 P.M.	$70
Managing Childhood and Elementary Classrooms by David Denton, Child education professional at National Institute of Early Childhood Education	June 28 2 P.M. – 4 P.M.	$90
Children's Social Development: Birth through Childhood by Lilith Mills, Child psychiatrist at Cornwall Hospital	July 5 1 P.M. – 3 P.M.	$80
*100 people maximum are permitted to attend each seminar.		

If you would like to register for one of the lectures, CLICK HERE. Please note that all classes are on a first-come, first-served basis and the registration deadline is June 1. Contact Carolina Felton at cfelton@hudsoncollege.edu for any inquiries.

Participants who work in the field of child education and development will receive a $10 discount on the seminar entry fee. An evidentiary document must be presented in the process of registration.

To:	Carolina Felton <cfelton@hudsoncollege.edu>
From:	Olivia Kang <okang@hudsonelementary.com>
Date:	June 3
Subject:	Inquiry

As I frequently heard that the lectures Hudson College offers on these topics are very beneficial, I registered for a lecture, which is to be held on June 21. However, this e-mail is actually to inquire if I may make a change to my reservation.

I am a teacher at a local elementary school. Unfortunately, one of my colleagues has taken an abrupt leave for three weeks due to some family issues. I will have to cover one of his classes on Friday afternoon, June 21. I am still interested in taking one of your lecture series and want to know if I can take the lecture led by David Denton instead. I would also like to know, if the change is possible, when I have to remit the additional fee amount and if I am still eligible for the discount.

Thank you. I look forward to hearing from you soon.

Olivia Kang

176. In the website, what is NOT indicated about the lectures?

(A) They are scheduled in the afternoon.
(B) Their registration deadline is June 1.
(C) Only a limited number of participants can take each lecture.
(D) All lecturers are university professors.

177. How can participants register for the series of lectures?

(A) By sending an e-mail
(B) By visiting a website
(C) By calling a school employee
(D) By coming to the event venue

178. How much did Ms. Kang originally pay?

(A) $60
(B) $70
(C) $80
(D) $90

179. On what date does Ms. Kang wish to take the seminar?

(A) June 14
(B) June 21
(C) June 28
(D) July 5

180. What is suggested about Ms. Kang?

(A) She will be on sick leave for three weeks.
(B) She already paid for the additional charge.
(C) She probably submitted a required document to Hudson college.
(D) She participated in the similar lecture series last quarter.

▶ ▶ ▶ GO ON TO THE NEXT PAGE

7TH ANNUAL ISEE GLOBAL FORUM ON PSYCHOLOGY
CALLS FOR STUDENT VOLUNTEERS!

ISEE Global Forum on Psychology is a renowned conference for psychologists from all over the world to exchange new ideas. Organizing committee of 7th Annual ISEE Global Forum on Psychology (IGFP) is now recruiting student volunteers for various supporting roles during the upcoming conference scheduled from July 5 to July 10 at the Milano Hotel, Chicago, IL.

Volunteer Responsibilities
• **Event Assistant** – The primary role is to set up and clean the area during and after conferences. Also, an event assistant helps with making photocopies, distributing handouts to participants, or preparing water for speakers. This role may involve light furniture moving.

• **AV Operator Assistant** – This job is to check audiovisual equipment in the conference hall. Setting up a projector and microphones, if necessary, will also be one of the roles of an AV operator assistant.

Applicant Requirements
- Official letter from your school indicating your current student status
- Official proof of proficiency for at least one of the following languages: Spanish, Chinese, or German
- Experience in volunteering at a conference
- Knowledge about presentation equipment is strongly preferred

Application Submission
You need to send a copy of your résumé, a cover letter, and official documents by June 1 to the office of IGFP organizing committee stated below:

Claire Stanley, Personnel Manager
IGFP Organizing Committee, 30 Franklin Dr., Chicago, IL 60007

May 10

Ivan Harfield
22 Roosebelt St.
Bridgeport, IL 60608

Claire Stanley
IGFP Organizing Committee
30 Franklin Dr.
Chicago, IL 60007

Dear Ms. Stanley,
I would like to apply for the student volunteer program at ISEE Global Forum on Psychology. I am a junior at the University of Illinois and am highly interested in the field of psychology. I

have participated in numerous conferences on psychology in the past including IWO Psychology and University of Illinois Conference.

Also, I have been involved in many different activities including working at American Student Marketing Association where I interacted with many people from diverse backgrounds. I work very hard to complete tasks given to me. Despite the fact that I do not speak any other language except English, I am sure I can contribute a lot to IGFP.

Please find enclosed the documents you requested. I hope to be contacted for an interview. Thank you for your consideration in advance.

Sincerely,

Ivan Harfield
Enclosure

181. What is suggested about IGFP?

(A) It has been held seven times successfully.
(B) It is sponsored by Milano Hotel.
(C) It will have attendants from different countries.
(D) It provides a certificate to volunteers.

182. What is NOT one of the roles of event assistant?

(A) Handing out documents to participants
(B) Lighting the conference venue
(C) Doing some errands for presenters
(D) Cleaning up when the conference is over

183. When will the organizing committee stop receiving applications?

(A) May 10
(B) June 1
(C) July 5
(D) July 10

184. Why might Mr. Harfield NOT be successful in assuming the volunteer position?

(A) He doesn't speak any languages required.
(B) He didn't submit the documents from his university.
(C) He lacks experience in the field of Psychology.
(D) He doesn't have an academic degree in Psychology.

185. What is indicated about Mr. Harfield?

(A) He may not be available on a certain day during the conference.
(B) He graduated from the University of Illinois.
(C) He is good at handling presentation equipment.
(D) He has attended conferences on psychology before.

http://www.officeshed.com/policies/shippinganddelivery

Office Shed is at your service!

| About Us | Products | Policies | Customer Reviews |

Shipping & Delivery

Office Shed charges a flat rate of $4.50 for domestic standard shipping (5-7 business days) and $6.50 for domestic express shipping (2-3 business days). We currently deliver to the U.S., the U.K., and New Zealand. For detailed rates, refer below:

Destination	Standard Shipping	Express Shipping
United States	$11.00	$15.00
United Kingdom	$13.00	$17.00
New Zealand	$6.00	$8.00

*All prices are in Australian dollars (AUD) unless otherwise indicated.

For registered members of Office Shed, we are now delivering your orders for free for a limited time. This offer only applies to domestic orders.

You will receive a notification e-mail once your order has shipped. After that, you can check the delivery status of your package at no cost by using our program at www.officeshed.com/ordertracker. Please note that you may not be able to track some orders, such as international shipping.

To view our policies on refunds and returns, click **here**, and on membership, click **here**.

OFFICE SHED
Order Confirmation & Receipt

Order Reference: #4865436
Order Placed On: December 12

Shipping Address:
Brooke Binder, 43 Sheldon Rd., Glenhaven, Vic. 4157, Australia

Product Information	Quantity	Price(s)
4-Tier Metal Desk Tray (Color: Black)	1	$10.99
28mm Paper Clips (100/Pack)	3	$6.75
Premium White Envelopes (25/Pack)	1	$8.81
	Subtotal:	$26.55
	Tax:	$2.65
	Shipping Charge:	$0.00
	Total Price:	$29.20
Payment Method: Credit Card (xxxx-xxxx-xxxx-0555)	Amount:	$29.20

In case you need assistance regarding the ordering process, please call the customer service center during our working hours from Monday to Friday between 9:00 A.M. and 5:00 P.M. at 130-111.

To: <cs@officeshed.com>

From: <brookebinder@goldcoastmail.com>

Date: December 17

Subject: Request

To whom it may concern,

I've been very pleased with the service I've received from Office Shed. However, imagine my surprise when I opened the box and couldn't find the envelopes I had ordered. I suppose someone forgot to insert them while packing my items.

I would appreciate having the price of the missing items added to my account as I will be ordering again in the near future. I hope that you can rectify this situation soon.

Regards,

Brooke Binder

---

186. In the website, the word "flat" in paragraph 1, line 1, is closest in meaning to

(A) insufficient
(B) fixed
(C) reduced
(D) vertical

187. Where is Office Shed probably based?

(A) The United States
(B) New Zealand
(C) Australia
(D) The United Kingdom

188. In the receipt, what is mentioned about Office Shed?

(A) It shipped Ms. Binder's order on December 12.
(B) It sells products made by local manufacturers.
(C) It distributes office furniture.
(D) Its customer service center operates only on weekdays.

189. What is suggested about Ms. Binder?

(A) She purchases frequently from Office Shed.
(B) She paid for her order with cash.
(C) She will receive an e-mail from Office Shed.
(D) She is the owner of a small company.

190. How much money does Ms. Binder request she be refunded?

(A) $2.65
(B) $6.75
(C) $8.81
(D) $10.99

▶ ▶ ▶GO ON TO THE NEXT PAGE

Dove Cottage Inspection Notice

Attention, all tenants. Please note that the annual inspection on the building's heating systems will be performed next week. This process is being done in preparation for winter and will help keep the heating system running properly. As always, Four Seasons Maintenance, a local company, will visit and perform the inspections. The checkup will take about 20 minutes for each unit. If any problems are detected, we will schedule further inspections and repair work for the units.

Detailed schedule of the inspection is stated below:
– Units on Building A: November 3, 12:00 P.M. – 6:00 P.M.
– Units on Building B: November 4, 12:00 P.M. – 6:00 P.M.
– Units on Building C: November 5, 10:00 A.M. – 4:00 P.M.

If you are not available on the scheduled date for any reason, please contact Rosa Velasquez, the property manager, at rvelasquez@dovecottage.com immediately to reschedule your inspection.

Check out the website of Four Seasons Maintenance for additional information about the inspections. Thank you in advance for your cooperation.

To: Andrew Rudolph
Telephone Number: 594-9584-1128

Andrew, this is David. I'm supposed to have my apartment inspected this morning, so I wonder if we can reschedule our meeting until the afternoon. Once the inspectors arrive, the process shouldn't take long. How about if we get together in your office at around 3:00? Let me know if that works for you. David.

To:	Rosa Velasquez <rvelasquez@dovecottage.com>
From:	David Yakal <dyakal@smail.com>
Date:	November 6
Subject:	Inquiries

I recently had my apartment inspected and was happy to learn there weren't any problems with my heating system. However, earlier today, I noticed that the inspection crew cracked my balcony window. This same problem also occurred when the crew visited my place last year. I think the large equipment they use caused the damage.

I would like to be compensated for the cost of replacing the window. I will purchase a new window and install it myself. Then, I'll send you the receipt so that I can be repaid. Please be advised that I will be leaving on a business trip this weekend and won't be back for two weeks, so I'd like to receive the payment before I depart.

I look forward to hearing from you soon.

Thanks,

David Yakal

---

191. Why did Dove Cottage undergo inspections?

(A) To prepare the building for the cold season
(B) To fix problems with the central heating system
(C) To follow local regulations for residential buildings
(D) To reduce excessive energy use

192. In the notice, what is stated about the inspection?

(A) It requires registration.
(B) It is performed on a regular basis.
(C) It is done by the property manager.
(D) It takes about a day.

193. When most likely did Mr. Yakal's inspection take place?

(A) On November 3
(B) On November 4
(C) On November 5
(D) On November 6

194. Why did Mr. Yakal send the e-mail?

(A) To reschedule an inspection
(B) To request a problem be addressed
(C) To note where he is going on a trip
(D) To inquire about inspection fees

195. What is indicated about Mr. Yakal?

(A) He went on a business trip on November 3.
(B) He recommended an inspection company to his neighbor.
(C) He intends to complete some repairs by himself.
(D) He has contacted Ms. Velasquez before.

▶ ▶ ▶GO ON TO THE NEXT PAGE

To:	David Linderman <dlinderman@kitavipi.com>
From:	Sam Bankole <sbankole@kitavipi.com>
Date:	July 9
Subject:	Workshop sessions

Dear Mr. Linderman,

I am writing with regard to the schedule for next month's workshop in Istanbul. I reviewed the first draft of the schedule you sent me this morning, and I think I must ask for a change in it. In the morning on the day when the workshop sessions will be held, I have to attend a meeting with an important client in Ankara. The client is coming from Brussels for only two days, and the meeting cannot be rescheduled. My flight back to Istanbul will depart at 11:30 A.M.

I already asked Sayuri Fujita in our department to switch our workshop times, and she agreed to do so. Please reflect these changes in the schedule before it is printed and posted throughout the company to prevent any confusion.

Thank you,

Sam Bankole
Assistant Editor, Editing Department

Kitavi Publishing, Inc.
Istanbul • Ankara • Izmir • Bursa

15th Annual Employee Training Workshop
August 14, Headquarters Building in Istanbul

Time	Workshop Name	Moderator
8:30 A.M. – 10:00 A.M.	Communicating with Both Clients and Colleagues	Sayuri Fujita
10:20 A.M. – 11:30 A.M.	Developing an Idea into a Great Story	Lorenzo Mondi
11:30 A.M. – 1:00 P.M.	Lunch	
1:00 P.M. – 2:30 P.M.	Designing Attractive Book Covers	Katherine Confalonieri
2:50 P.M. – 4:00 P.M.	Editing Your Columns on Your Own	Tyler Butcher
4:20 P.M. – 6:00 P.M.	Time Management – Make It Count	Sam Bankole

*Every attendee will be invited to a luncheon during the lunch break.

All employees are requested to complete this short review of the workshop. You may remain anonymous if you wish. Your feedback will help us improve future sessions.

How was the overall quality of the...

	Excellent	Good	Average	Poor
trainers	X			
presentations		X		
materials	X			

Comments: I really loved the talk by Mr. Mondi. I learned a lot from him. The other instructors were good, too. The microphone kept breaking down during Mr. Butcher's talk, so it was hard to hear him speak.

Name: *Emily Harper*

196. What is indicated about Mr. Bankole?

(A) He contacted Mr. Linderman recently.
(B) He has a business meeting to attend.
(C) He will visit Brussels next month.
(D) He plans to lead a workshop session.

197. Where most likely will Mr. Bankole be at 11:30 A.M. on August 14?

(A) In Brussels
(B) In Istanbul
(C) In Bursa
(D) In Ankara

198. What time was Ms. Fujita originally scheduled to lead a workshop?

(A) At 8:30 A.M.
(B) At 10:20 A.M.
(C) At 1:00 P.M.
(D) At 4:20 P.M.

199. What is indicated in the schedule?

(A) Kitavi Publishing, Inc. has been in business for 15 years.
(B) Mr. Mondi will lead a workshop on article editing.
(C) Mr. Bankole will be present at Ms. Fujita's workshop session.
(D) A meal will be given to the attendees at the workshop.

200. Which presentation did Ms. Harper like the most?

(A) Communicating with Both Clients and Colleagues
(B) Developing an Idea into a Great Story
(C) Designing Attractive Book Covers
(D) Editing Your Columns on Your Own

STOP! This is the end of the test. If you finish before time is called,
you may go back to Parts 5, 6, and 7 and check your work.

Actual Test

MP3

해설집

적정 풀이 시간 120분

120 min

시작 시간 ___시 ___분

종료 시간 ___시 ___분

중간에 멈추지 말고 처음부터 끝까지 풀어보세요.
문제를 풀 때에는 실전처럼 답안지에 마킹하세요.

목표 개수 _____ / 200   실제 개수 _____ / 200

예상 점수는 번역 및 정답에 있는 점수 환산표를 참조하세요.

LISTENING TEST

In the Listening test, you will be asked to demonstrate how well you understand spoken English. The entire Listening test will last approximately 45 minutes. There are four parts, and directions are given for each part. You must mark your answers on the separate answer sheet. Do not write your answers in the test book.

PART 1

Directions: For each question in this part, you will hear four statements about a picture in your test book. When you hear the statements, you must select the one statement that best describes what you see in the picture. Then find the number of the question on your answer sheet and mark your answer. The statements will not be printed in your test book and will be spoken only one time.

Statement (B), "They are sitting at a table." is the best description of the picture. So you should select answer (B) and mark it on your answer sheet.

1.

2.

3.

4.

5.

6.

▶ ▶ ▶GO ON TO THE NEXT PAGE

PART 2

Directions: You will hear a question or statement and three responses spoken in English. They will not be printed in your test book and will be spoken only one time. Select the best response to the question or statement and mark the letter (A), (B), or (C) on your answer sheet.

7. Mark your answer on your answer sheet.

8. Mark your answer on your answer sheet.

9. Mark your answer on your answer sheet.

10. Mark your answer on your answer sheet.

11. Mark your answer on your answer sheet.

12. Mark your answer on your answer sheet.

13. Mark your answer on your answer sheet.

14. Mark your answer on your answer sheet.

15. Mark your answer on your answer sheet.

16. Mark your answer on your answer sheet.

17. Mark your answer on your answer sheet.

18. Mark your answer on your answer sheet.

19. Mark your answer on your answer sheet.

20. Mark your answer on your answer sheet.

21. Mark your answer on your answer sheet.

22. Mark your answer on your answer sheet.

23. Mark your answer on your answer sheet.

24. Mark your answer on your answer sheet.

25. Mark your answer on your answer sheet.

26. Mark your answer on your answer sheet.

27. Mark your answer on your answer sheet.

28. Mark your answer on your answer sheet.

29. Mark your answer on your answer sheet.

30. Mark your answer on your answer sheet.

31. Mark your answer on your answer sheet.

PART 3

Directions: You will hear some conversations between two or three people. You will be asked to answer three questions about what the speakers say in each conversation. Select the best response to each question and mark the letter (A), (B), (C), or (D) on your answer sheet. The conversations will not be printed in your test book and will be spoken only one time.

32. Where is the conversation most likely taking place?

    (A) At a hotel
    (B) In an office
    (C) On an airplane
    (D) At a conference center

33. What did the man bring with him?

    (A) Some pictures
    (B) Some materials
    (C) A hotel confirmation
    (D) Directions to a hotel

34. Why will the woman call a conference center?

    (A) To reserve a conference room
    (B) To change an arrival time
    (C) To ask to see a room
    (D) To get a schedule of events

35. Where do the women most likely work?

    (A) At a radio station
    (B) At an electronics store
    (C) At an auto repair shop
    (D) At a car dealership

36. What did the man recently do?

    (A) He read a car magazine.
    (B) He found a new job.
    (C) He opened a business.
    (D) He completed an automotive repair course.

37. What will the man do next?

    (A) Publish a book
    (B) Call in a radio station
    (C) Buy a vehicle
    (D) Provide some advice

38. What do the speakers say about Jason?

    (A) He is retiring from work.
    (B) He is getting transferred abroad.
    (C) He is being promoted.
    (D) He is moving to another company.

39. What does the man ask about?

    (A) Preparations for a party
    (B) An upcoming meeting
    (C) A business trip
    (D) An urgent call from a client

40. According to the man, what is he planning to do?

    (A) Go to a golf course
    (B) Purchase a present
    (C) Find another caterer
    (D) Donate some money

41. What is the man surprised about?

    (A) The extended hours of operation
    (B) The location of an event
    (C) The number of attendees
    (D) The price of a catering service

42. What does the woman want permission to do?

    (A) Hire a caterer
    (B) Purchase some presents
    (C) Change venues
    (D) Invite more people

43. What is the woman asked to do next?

    (A) Get a price estimate
    (B) Go over a guest list
    (C) Send out some invitations
    (D) Speak with a board member

▶ ▶ ▶GO ON TO THE NEXT PAGE

44. Who most likely is the man?

(A) A sales representative
(B) A human resources employee
(C) A customer service representative
(D) A product designer

45. What does the woman imply when she says, "I only purchased it two weeks ago"?

(A) An item should still function.
(B) An item is damaged in transit.
(C) An order has not been delivered yet.
(D) She wants to purchase another audio device.

46. What will the woman most likely do next?

(A) Get some software updated
(B) Get a refund on an item
(C) Refer to a user's guide
(D) Plug a device in

---

47. Where does the conversation take place?

(A) At a supermarket
(B) At a bakery
(C) At a restaurant
(D) At a cooking school

48. What opportunity does the man offer the woman?

(A) Renewing her contract
(B) Transferring to another location
(C) Managing a bakery
(D) Working extra hours

49. What information does the woman ask about?

(A) Working hours
(B) Company benefits
(C) Hourly wages
(D) Payment options

50. What is the main topic of the conversation?

(A) A relocation
(B) A popular product
(C) A hiring opportunity
(D) A new facility

51. What did the women do today?

(A) They worked on a new design.
(B) They visited a warehouse in person.
(C) They went over a project proposal.
(D) They interviewed job applicants.

52. According to Alice, what information is not correct?

(A) The cost of some items
(B) The address of a building
(C) The size of a warehouse
(D) The number of loading spots

---

53. What does the woman want to discuss?

(A) Improving the safety rules
(B) Hiring other suppliers
(C) Changing a production process
(D) Offering competitive prices

54. What problem does the woman mention about the extra tiles?

(A) They are unable to be sold.
(B) There is no room to put them in storage.
(C) Some of them were damaged in production.
(D) They are not the correct size.

55. Why does the man say the customers were not happy?

(A) Prices were raised recently.
(B) A website had some problems.
(C) Orders were not received on time.
(D) The quality of some work was poor.

56. What did the company recently do?

(A) Rearranged office supplies
(B) Expanded to a foreign country
(C) Offered employees more benefits
(D) Moved to another location

57. What does the woman say she used to do?

(A) Work out every day
(B) Go to work on foot
(C) Bring her lunch to work
(D) Stay at work late

58. What does the man suggest that the woman do?

(A) Move to a different place
(B) Transfer to another department
(C) Become a member at a gym
(D) Drive to work

59. What is the main topic of the conversation?

(A) The design of a product
(B) A change in an advertisement
(C) A product demonstration
(D) The release date of a new car

60. What does the woman imply when she says, "We have until August to finish the project"?

(A) They do not have enough time.
(B) They need to hire more workers.
(C) They have to work faster.
(D) They can still meet their deadline.

61. What does the woman suggest doing?

(A) Hiring a consultant
(B) Speaking with a coworker
(C) Increasing a budget
(D) Reviewing some calculations

Survey

	Satisfactory	Unsatisfactory
1. Performance	☐	☐
2. Story	☐	☐
3. Graphics	☐	☐

4. If you found something unsatisfactory, what is the reason?

_____
_____
_____

62. Who is the survey for?

(A) Designers
(B) Authors
(C) Game players
(D) Computer programmers

63. How did the man choose the items listed in the survey?

(A) He referred to some online reviews.
(B) He read some articles in the online magazines.
(C) He had a meeting with his colleagues.
(D) He looked at a product manual.

64. Look at the graphic. Which item will be taken out from the survey?

(A) Item 1
(B) Item 2
(C) Item 3
(D) Item 4

▶ ▶ ▶GO ON TO THE NEXT PAGE

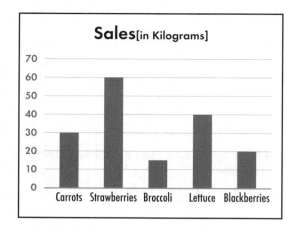

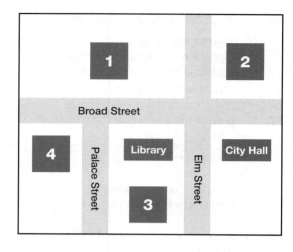

65. What did the speakers do last year?

(A) They bought some fertilizers.
(B) They purchased a new farm vehicle.
(C) They acquired more farmland.
(D) They hired more farmhands.

66. Look at the graphic. Which item will be sold for a lower price this weekend?

(A) Strawberries
(B) Broccoli
(C) Lettuce
(D) Blackberries

67. Why does the woman think more customers will go to the market?

(A) A report aired on a news program.
(B) A newspaper printed an article.
(C) More vendors will be there later.
(D) All prices will be discounted.

68. What kind of business do the speakers most likely work at?

(A) At an advertisement agency
(B) At an accounting firm
(C) At an electronics manufacturer
(D) At an electric company

69. Look at the graphic. Which building will the speakers visit on Friday?

(A) Building 1
(B) Building 2
(C) Building 3
(D) Building 4

70. What does the woman offer to do?

(A) Speak with her supervisor
(B) Change the time of a meeting
(C) Rewrite some presentation material
(D) Change a meeting place

PART 4

Directions: You will hear some short talks given by a single speaker. You will be asked to answer three questions about what the speaker says in each short talk. Select the best response to each question and mark the letter (A), (B), (C), or (D) on your answer sheet. The talks will not be printed in your test book and will be spoken only one time.

71. What product is being promoted?

    (A) A blender
    (B) A coffeemaker
    (C) A toaster
    (D) A scale

72. What does the speaker praise about the product?

    (A) It is environmentally friendly.
    (B) It is inexpensive.
    (C) It is portable.
    (D) It is accurate.

73. What special deal does the speaker offer?

    (A) A discount on cookbooks
    (B) Free installation
    (C) An extended warranty
    (D) Free shipping

74. What will the speaker give a presentation on?

    (A) Retaining more workers
    (B) Providing cost-cutting ideas
    (C) Improving office efficiency
    (D) Getting more cost estimates

75. According to the speaker, what has changed?

    (A) The deadline for a proposal
    (B) A date when the CEO arrives
    (C) A visit by a client
    (D) A meeting location

76. Why does the speaker say, "You do know Peter from Finance, don't you?"

    (A) To express concern about the cost
    (B) To confirm a meeting date
    (C) To suggest a staffing change
    (D) To ask the listener to contact a coworker

77. Who is being introduced?

    (A) A CEO
    (B) A client
    (C) A company director
    (D) A government official

78. What is mentioned about an engine?

    (A) It is currently in use.
    (B) It breaks down at times.
    (C) It needs to be improved.
    (D) It is in the process of being developed.

79. What is suggested about Susan Darcey?

    (A) She was just promoted.
    (B) She frequently travels abroad.
    (C) She intends to retire soon.
    (D) She enjoys assisting others.

80. What is the speaker calling about?

    (A) An advertisement about furniture
    (B) A sofa delivery
    (C) A status on her special order
    (D) Some furniture repairs

81. What problem does the speaker mention?

    (A) Some material is not available.
    (B) An item cannot be repaired.
    (C) A price is higher than the estimate.
    (D) A deadline hasn't been met.

82. What is the listener asked to do?

    (A) Look for another supplier
    (B) Change a release date
    (C) Visit the establishment
    (D) Pick up his equipment

▶ ▶ ▶GO ON TO THE NEXT PAGE

83. According to the speaker, why is the Impressionist Art Collection popular?

(A) Its admission is free.
(B) It was featured in a TV documentary.
(C) It is the museum's largest collection.
(D) It is updated frequently.

84. What does the speaker imply when he says, "I'm an intern here"?

(A) He is not getting paid for leading the tour.
(B) He needs some help from his colleague.
(C) He might not answer some questions.
(D) He is eager to impress the visitors.

85. What does the speaker remind the listeners about?

(A) A gallery policy
(B) A ticket price
(C) A closing time
(D) A new exhibit

86. What is the broadcast mainly about?

(A) Economic conditions
(B) A business acquisition
(C) The results of an election
(D) A completed construction project

87. According to the speaker, what field does Peter Shaw have experience in?

(A) Education
(B) Business
(C) Entertainment
(D) Travel

88. What are the listeners invited to do?

(A) Request some music
(B) Sign up for a membership
(C) Share their thoughts
(D) Enter a raffle

89. What service does the company provide?

(A) Financial consulting
(B) Web security
(C) Online marketing
(D) Property management

90. Why is the speaker unavailable this week?

(A) He is out of the country.
(B) He is at a conference.
(C) He is in a staff meeting.
(D) He is at a training course.

91. What should the listeners do if they need some urgent advice?

(A) Send an e-mail
(B) Visit an office
(C) Call another employee
(D) Call the manager on the cell phone

92. Where do the listeners work?

(A) At a university
(B) At a medical equipment company
(C) At a healthcare facility
(D) At a pharmaceutical company

93. What does the speaker imply when she says, "Lots of people know about Leslie"?

(A) She plans to order more office supplies.
(B) The listeners need to sign up quickly.
(C) A venue for a meeting is too small.
(D) She needs to contact Leslie right away.

94. What does the speaker remind the listeners to do?

(A) Make some proposals
(B) Contact some clients
(C) Improve their efficiency
(D) Prepare some documents

Weather Forecast

Monday	Tuesday	Wednesday	Thursday	Friday
Rainy	Rainy	Cloudy	Sunny	Rainy

95. Look at the graphic. When will the fall festival take place?

(A) On Monday
(B) On Tuesday
(C) On Wednesday
(D) On Thursday

96. What does the speaker say she is excited about?

(A) An art exhibit
(B) A musical performance
(C) A sports competition
(D) A lecture on music

97. What does the speaker recommend the listeners do?

(A) Bring their friends
(B) Buy tickets in advance
(C) Call the station
(D) Enter a contest

Meeting Agenda

13:45	Introduction
14:00	Jude Crow - R&D Manager
14:15	Elizabeth Dean - HR Supervisor
14:30	Andy Thompson - Head of Sales
14:45	Wilma Patterson - CEO

98. Who most likely are the listeners?

(A) Potential investors
(B) Foreign clients
(C) Supervisors
(D) New employees

99. What type of products does the company make?

(A) Camping gear
(B) Vehicles
(C) Pharmaceuticals
(D) Sporting goods

100. Look at the graphic. Who will speak next?

(A) Jude Crow
(B) Elizabeth Dean
(C) Andy Thompson
(D) Wilma Patterson

This is the end of the Listening test. Turn to Part 5 in your test book.

▶ ▶ ▶GO ON TO THE NEXT PAGE

READING TEST

In the Reading test, you will read a variety of texts and answer several different types of reading comprehension questions. The entire Reading test will last 75 minutes. There are three parts, and directions are given for each part. You are encouraged to answer as many questions as possible within the time allowed.

You must mark your answer on the separate answer sheet. Do not write your answers in your test book.

PART 5

Directions: A word or phrase is missing in each of the sentences below. Four answer choices are given below each sentence. Select the best answer to complete the sentence. Then mark the letter (A), (B), (C), or (D) on your answer sheet.

101. James Watson, one of the popular singers in the country, has agreed to allow Coco Jewelry to use ------- name in an upcoming advertising campaign.

(A) he
(B) his
(C) him
(D) himself

102. Bella Communications provides ------- Internet and mobile phone services to local residents.

(A) only if
(B) either
(C) both
(D) but also

103. The firm has been a leading company in educating people to design advertising campaigns more ------- for years.

(A) efficiency
(B) efficiencies
(C) efficient
(D) efficiently

104. Some of the office desks in the personnel department are too heavy for Brian and Harry to carry by -------.

(A) them
(B) their
(C) theirs
(D) themselves

105. Our firm decided to push ahead our original plan for the ------- of the two banks in China.

(A) merge
(B) merger
(C) merged
(D) merging

106. The new desktop computer is equipped ------- the latest word processor softwares and high-resolution screen.

(A) for
(B) by
(C) with
(D) through

107. With two weeks of added musical shows, *Romance With Cats* will ------- run through November 14 at our theater.

(A) now
(B) mostly
(C) nearly
(D) immediately

108. Many companies have been ------- awaiting the new free trade agreement with European countries in the hope of raising their market shares there.

(A) eagerness
(B) eager
(C) more eager
(D) eagerly

109. Mr. Jenkins said yesterday that the exported frozen food products ------- with the food safety regulations of 20 countries.

(A) comply
(B) complying
(C) compliance
(D) compliant

110. According to the data, the number of earthquakes caused by volcanic activity ------- significantly over the last ten years.

(A) increase
(B) has increased
(C) had increased
(D) will increase

111. A work environment that is clean and visually appealing can have a great ------- in your workforce's performance and mood.

(A) impact
(B) comfort
(C) enthusiasm
(D) responsibility

112. Some passengers on the flight were ill ------- arrival at the international airport and were immediately hospitalized.

(A) with
(B) along
(C) upon
(D) towards

113. Please be aware that our data must be ------- transmitted to the central data repository for analysis and feedback.

(A) securely
(B) systematically
(C) precisely
(D) potentially

114. If you are ------- to keep your scheduled medical appointment, please notify us at least two days in advance.

(A) impossible
(B) absent
(C) unable
(D) ready

115. Please fill out the form to see if your office building is ------- from requirements for fire drills and safety inspections.

(A) reliant
(B) exempt
(C) intact
(D) absolute

116. When ------- one of our customer service representatives to ask questions, it would be better to have a list of questions ready.

(A) call
(B) calling
(C) called
(D) to call

117. The investment by One International is the ------- largest foreign direct investment in the nation's financial industry.

(A) every
(B) quite
(C) much
(D) single

118. With ------- facts and evidence, the presentation was conducted in a logical and analytical manner.

(A) attentive
(B) verifiable
(C) incredible
(D) renewable

119. Mr. McDonald was hired only two months ago, but has ------- devised some effective sales strategies for the company.

(A) namely
(B) simultaneously
(C) nevertheless
(D) notwithstanding

▶ ▶ ▶ GO ON TO THE NEXT PAGE

120. According to our office policy, ------- leaves last is responsible for turning off all the lights and locking the door in the office.

(A) several
(B) this
(C) which
(D) whoever

121. It appears that many office workers overuse energy drinks ------- they get tired or stressed from work and their daily routines.

(A) even if
(B) whenever
(C) whichever
(D) so that

122. The magazine was ------- successful, selling many more issues than anyone had thought likely, but its circulation dropped rapidly in several years.

(A) tightly
(B) phenomenally
(C) abundantly
(D) profitably

123. Orders placed to commercial websites in Asia are usually ------- with merchandise from their warehouses in Vietnam.

(A) filled
(B) positioned
(C) occurred
(D) committed

124. Our employees will receive a significant bonus at the end of this year ------- the company's net profits exceed the expectations of the board.

(A) provided that
(B) while
(C) in that
(D) unless

125. Starpark Sports is committed to designing and producing different running shoes that ------- wants to wear.

(A) everyone
(B) anywhere
(C) whoever
(D) one another

126. ------- for our brand to remain popular as it is today, high quality contents need to be provided in convenient forms on the Internet.

(A) Not only
(B) As a result
(C) In case
(D) In order

127. ------- the high waves and bad weather, all the passengers onboard the flight were successfully rescued.

(A) In spite of
(B) On account of
(C) As a result of
(D) With regard to

128. City residents rarely think about growing their own gardens ------- building a small garden is not that difficult.

(A) for one thing
(B) therefore
(C) similarly
(D) even though

129. -------, most of our employees are permitted to leave the office earlier than usual before a national holiday.

(A) At that time
(B) By the time
(C) Once in a while
(D) In a moment

130. In recent years, consumption of electronic products has increased so much ------- today this represents one of the most environmentally problematic product groups.

(A) because
(B) that
(C) when
(D) although

PART 6

Directions: Read the texts that follow. A word or phrase, or sentence is missing in parts of each text. Four answer choices for each question are given below the text. Select the best answer to complete the text. Then mark the letter (A), (B), (C), or (D) on your answer sheet.

Questions 131-134 refer to the following information.

Bella Airlines Frequently Asked Questions

What if I did not receive an e-mail confirmation of my Bella Airlines flight?

-------. Bella Airlines ------- takes up to three hours to send the e-mail confirmation to a
  131.   **132.**

passenger after booking. In case you don't receive your e-mail confirmation even after

booking, make sure that your payment was successful. If the payment doesn't show up

on your credit card, it is ------- that your flight reservation did not go through.
                    133.

-------, please call us at 692-9815 so that we can look into the matter. Calls to this number
  134.

are paid for by Bella Airlines, making them free for our customers.

131. (A) Mobile phones cannot be used during flight at any time.
    (B) We will correct your account if the transaction was posted in error.
    (C) Your flight details will be sent to the e-mail address you provided.
    (D) Please keep hard copies of your purchase order and confirmation number.

132. (A) potentially
    (B) normally
    (C) accordingly
    (D) temporarily

133. (A) right
    (B) likely
    (C) proper
    (D) correct

134. (A) Finally
    (B) Moreover
    (C) In contrast
    (D) In this case

▶ ▶ ▶GO ON TO THE NEXT PAGE

Lucky 7 Mart

"Only the fresh!"

5801 Sundale Ave.

Bakersfield, CA 93307

The Lucky 7 Mart is full of the ------- fruits and vegetables available during all seasons!
135.

From California, Arizona, Florida, and beyond, our ------- is SUPER FRESH! When
136.

available, the Lucky 7 Mart offers fresh local food, which is grown by nearby farmers, to

your family.

The Lucky 7 Mart has products at prices you'll love! We have a fabulous selection of lunch

meats and cheeses freshly sliced to your order! We ------- only the finest beef, grade-A
137.

poultry, grade-A fresh pork, homemade smoked hams, and ground meats. -------.
138.

If you need help while shopping, ask a store clerk. He or she will gladly take you to the

items.

135. (A) fresh
(B) fresher
(C) freshest
(D) freshly

136. (A) produce
(B) producer
(C) production
(D) productivity

137. (A) carry
(B) access
(C) transport
(D) promote

138. (A) Learn about our upcoming special promotions.
(B) Customer reviews have been consistently positive.
(C) Business competition can be very fierce, especially in fast-moving markets.
(D) You'll love our everyday low prices, on-sale items, and new items.

Questions 139-142 refer to the following e-mail.

To: Charlotte Parker <cp@hdmail.com>
From: Lisa Preston <lpreston@nybc.com>
Subject: Your application
Date: February 14

Dear Ms. Parker,

Thank you for your application for the administrative assistant position. We very much

appreciate your interest in ------- our firm. -------. However, our human resources team
           139.   **140.**

read your résumé with great interest. Your professional experience and educational

background are very -------, which will make you an excellent addition to the firm.
                    141.

If you have no -------, we will keep your résumé on file and get in touch with you as soon
              142.

as a suitable position becomes available.

In the meantime, we wish you all the best with your job hunt.

Kind regards,

Lisa Preston
Head of Personnel
New York Business Consulting

---

139. (A) purchasing
(B) visiting
(C) joining
(D) contracting

140. (A) We are concerned about the result of your job interview.
(B) The position you applied for is no longer available.
(C) You are highly qualified to be an administrative assistant.
(D) Our recruiters must go through many applications to fill a position.

141. (A) impress
(B) impressed
(C) impressing
(D) impressive

142. (A) option
(B) objection
(C) intention
(D) confidentiality

▶ ▶ ▶ GO ON TO THE NEXT PAGE

June 20
Classic Shades, Inc.
401 Scott Street
Atlanta, GA 30303

Miramax Home Improvement
265 Peachtree Street
Atlanta, GA 30303

Dear whom it may concern,

We received 40 one-gallon cans of Floral White house paint yesterday, but they are not what we ordered from your company. -------.
143.

Please refer to our purchase order BK365020 of June 12, in which we asked ------- 50
144.
one-pint cans of Snowflake house paint, your product catalog No. SF-909. Please confirm the receipt of this letter and ------- of the request with a fax to 1-800-521-6313 as soon as
145.
possible.

-------, please rush this order so that we may meet our customers' demands promptly.
146.
Sincerely yours,

Aurora Lane
Head of Purchasing
Miramax Home Improvement

143. (A) We are happy to supply you with the estimate you requested.
(B) Unfortunately, the client expressed disappointment at the deadline being missed.
(C) We, therefore, are returning them to your Rocksville plant in Maryland.
(D) Your paint products are most commonly used to protect or provide texture to objects.

144. (A) after
(B) for
(C) into
(D) around

145. (A) routine
(B) execution
(C) termination
(D) collection

146. (A) In summary
(B) In fact
(C) Conversely
(D) Furthermore

PART 7

Directions: In this part you will read a selection of texts, such as magazine and newspaper articles, e-mails, and instant messages. Each text or set of texts is followed by several questions. Select the best answer for each question and mark the letter (A), (B), (C), or (D) on your answer sheet.

Questions 147-148 refer to the following form.

East Village, Inc.

109 Pitts Street
Dover, Delaware 19028

Date of Order: June 5

Order Number: 0194570
Customer Name: Angela Rose
Delivery Address: 42 Charity Dr., Highland Acres, Delaware, 19010
Delivery Date & Time: June 9, 12:00 P.M.
Return Date & Time: June 10, 10:00 A.M.

Items	Qty	Price
Color Reception Tableware Set (Rental)	2	$ 24.00
Flower Decorations – White and Yellow (Rental)	5	$ 20.00
Folding Banquet Table & Chair Set (Rental)	2	$ 40.00
Party Tent (Rental)	2	$ 50.00
Shipping & Setting		$ 50.00
Total		$ 184.00

* We provide corporate customers with a 10% discount.

* Pick-up charge is included in the shipping & set-up fee.

* All items must be ready for pick-up by the return time stated above.

147. What is suggested about Ms. Rose?

(A) She resides on Pitts Street.
(B) She is a corporate customer.
(C) She is preparing an event.
(D) She will use the delivered items in the morning.

148. What is NOT indicated about East Village, Inc.?

(A) It charges additional 10% of the service fee for late returns.
(B) It provides a discount to certain customers.
(C) It charges customers a shipping cost.
(D) It will pick up the rental items on June 10.

▶ ▶ ▶GO ON TO THE NEXT PAGE

Questions 149-150 refer to the following text message chain.

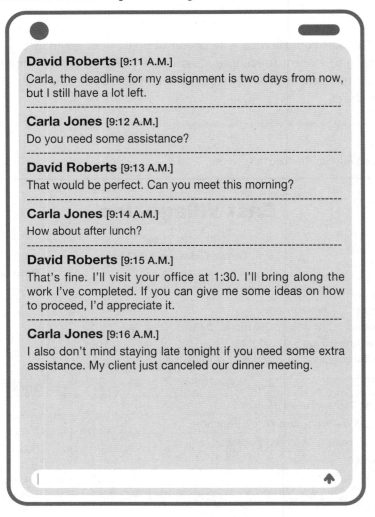

David Roberts [9:11 A.M.]

Carla, the deadline for my assignment is two days from now, but I still have a lot left.

Carla Jones [9:12 A.M.]

Do you need some assistance?

David Roberts [9:13 A.M.]

That would be perfect. Can you meet this morning?

Carla Jones [9:14 A.M.]

How about after lunch?

David Roberts [9:15 A.M.]

That's fine. I'll visit your office at 1:30. I'll bring along the work I've completed. If you can give me some ideas on how to proceed, I'd appreciate it.

Carla Jones [9:16 A.M.]

I also don't mind staying late tonight if you need some extra assistance. My client just canceled our dinner meeting.

149. What is Mr. Roberts' problem?

(A) He needs more ideas for a new project.

(B) He has to complete a project by this evening.

(C) His client just canceled a meeting.

(D) He has not finished some work yet.

150. At 9:14 A.M., why does Ms. Jones write, "How about after lunch?"

(A) To change a reservation

(B) To reject a suggestion

(C) To make an apology

(D) To propose a location

The 2nd Brown Design Competition

Brown, Inc., the leading manufacturer of household goods, is excited to present the 2nd Brown Design Competition. This year's design entry will be of a food storage container, which we intend to develop for the first time in our history.

Various forms of entries including drafts and sketches using different art materials are welcome. Please refer to the previous product designs of Brown, Inc. at www.browninc.com. The portable teapot designed by Walter Cho is an excellent example, as it was the winning design of the Brown Design Competition last year that broke all previous sales records of Brown, Inc.

This year's winning entry will be selected and launched as an official product of Brown, Inc. in the next market year. Also, the first-prize winner will be offered a fulltime employment position with the company. All winners will be invited to the awards ceremony scheduled on August 20 at the headquarters in Dover. The awards will be presented by design executives of Brown, Inc.

In addition, the winners will be given monetary awards worth a total of $6,000.

1st Prize: $3,000
2nd Prize: $2,000
3rd Prize: $1,000

If you are interested in participating, please visit our website at www.browninc.com/application to download detailed guidelines for submission and e-mail us your entry. The entries begin on July 1, and the deadline for submission is July 31.

151. What is suggested about Brown, Inc.?

(A) It only sells food containers.
(B) It has been in business for two years.
(C) Its portable teapot has been popular with customers.
(D) It will hold the awards ceremony of the competition next year.

152. What will NOT be offered to the first place prize winner?

(A) $3,000 in cash
(B) Invitation to a formal event
(C) An airfare to Dover
(D) A full-time position at Brown, Inc.

153. What is indicated about the application?

(A) It requires a processing fee.
(B) It is due on July 31.
(C) It will be judged by a group of executives.
(D) It has to be submitted by mail.

▶ ▶ ▶ GO ON TO THE NEXT PAGE

Questions 154-156 refer to the following e-mail.

To: John Baker <jbaker@easymail.com>

From: Amber Lee <alee@hotelconcord.com>

Date: September 20

Subject: RE: About my last visit

Dear Mr. Baker,

First of all, I would like to thank you for your recent visit to Hotel Concord New Orleans. It was truly an honor for us to serve you.

We have received your inquiry. Please kindly accept my sincere apologies on behalf of Hotel Concord for your unpleasant stay at our hotel last week. An unknown error occurred in our reservation system and we apologize for not being able to provide you with the room that you had originally reserved.

To compensate for this inconvenience, we would like to provide you a $200 certificate, which you may use at any branch of Hotel Concord in the United States. You can download the certificate through our official website at www.hotelconcord.com.

Thank you, and I hope to see you again.

Sincerely,

Amber Lee
Manager, Hotel Concord New Orleans

154. What is the main purpose of the e-mail?

(A) To thank a customer for visiting the hotel
(B) To give an excuse about overbooking
(C) To confirm the reservation
(D) To make up for a recent mistake

155. What is implied about Mr. Baker?

(A) He visited Hotel Concord with his family.
(B) He recently wrote an e-mail to Hotel Concord.
(C) He lives in New Orleans.
(D) He paid $200 for his room.

156. According to the e-mail, what is indicated about Hotel Concord?

(A) It will open its website.
(B) Its rooms are currently fully booked.
(C) It has more than one location.
(D) It gives coupons to all first-time visitors.

SAM'S PIZZA

Celebrating the 5th anniversary of Sam's Pizza, we are offering our customers special weekday deals throughout July. Please bring a coupon from below to enjoy delicious pizzas at special prices.

Coupons

$3.00 OFF On Any Specialty Pizza	**<FREE>** **2 Pepperoni Rolls** **Or** **2 Toppings of Your Choice** *With Purchase of a Large Pizza*
Wednesday & Thursday BIG DEAL **Large Cheese Pizza** **$7.99** **2 For $15.00**	**BUY 1 GET 1 FREE** Any Large Pizza

- All coupons are for "Take Out" only.
- Only one coupon may be used per order.

157. What can be inferred about Sam's Pizza?

(A) It has been in business for five years.
(B) It closes on weekends.
(C) Its customers don't have topping choices.
(D) It doesn't offer a delivery service.

158. What should a customer do to buy two large cheese pizzas for $15.00?

(A) Pay in cash
(B) Dine in the restaurant on a Thursday in July
(C) Use a coupon on a specific date
(D) Buy another regularly-priced pizza

Questions 159-161 refer to the following advertisement.

Tree House Solutions

Are you bothered by household pests such as termites and bedbugs? Tree House Solutions can solve your insect problems with our individualized three-step extermination solution for your home.

1. Detection

Our highly qualified inspectors, who undergo 10 hours of annual training, will start by carefully examining your house after a consultation with you. Then, we will prescribe an optimal treatment for maximum protection based on your unique situation.

2. Treatment

After detection, we effectively and quickly eradicate pests by applying our pest control treatments three times. We have two types of treatments, both of which are non-toxic and environmentally safe: liquid and foam. Liquid treatment is applied to the foundation of house whereas foam treatment is applied to surfaces such as exterior walls and pipes.

3. Monitoring

Our monitoring service ensures the ongoing effectiveness of the protection. We visit your house quarterly for two years and apply additional treatment as needed.

159. What most likely is being advertised?

(A) A house cleaning service
(B) A bug extermination service
(C) Environment-friendly interior design
(D) A gardening service

160. How often do staff of Tree House Solutions visit for monitoring?

(A) Once a year
(B) Twice a year
(C) Three times a year
(D) Four times a year

161. What is NOT indicated about the staff of Tree House Solutions?

(A) They must take annual training.
(B) They discuss symptoms with clients before the detection of the cause.
(C) They give a treatment kit to customers who renew the contract.
(D) They use treatments, which do little harm on the environment.

Questions 162-164 refer to the following e-mail.

To:	Jessica Cisneros <jcisneros@sevelia.com>
From:	Mark Demont <mdemont@sku.edu>
Date:	April 15
Subject:	Last Night

Dear Ms. Cisneros,

Since my first visit to Sevelia on its opening night, I have been a big fan. I couldn't believe that a small local restaurant could provide such delicious Thai food with excellent service. —[1]—. Since then, I have frequently visited Sevelia, and I have been delighted every single time until last night.

—[2]—.We ordered two main dishes, but we were served only one. Though we were quite upset about this mistake, we did not have time to wait, so we decided to share the dish and leave. After finishing the meal, I paid with my credit card but did not check the bill or the receipt. —[3]—. However, when I checked the receipt later, I discovered that you charged me for two main dishes instead of one.

It was the most disappointing service I have received in the two years that I have dined at your establishment. —[4]—. Because of this experience, I have to consider whether or not to visit your restaurant again in the future. I demand your prompt attention to this matter.

Thank you,

Mark Demont

162. What is the purpose of the e-mail?

(A) To recommend a local restaurant
(B) To ask for monetary compensation
(C) To complain about increased meal prices
(D) To report some poor service

163. What is indicated about Sevelia?

(A) It is a big chain store.
(B) It does not have many customers.
(C) It has been in business for about 2 years.
(D) It recently hired a new employee.

164. In which of the positions marked [1], [2], [3], and [4] does the following sentence best fit?

"Last night, my wife and I went to your restaurant for dinner."

(A) [1]
(B) [2]
(C) [3]
(D) [4]

Old Dusty City Hall Reborn

June 17

The old City Hall located on Vie Street has been subject to much curiosity and anticipation over the past 8 months. Finally, the building will be presented to the public on the night of July 1 under a new name, Indianapolis City Museum for Art.

Ian Kensington, the architect who created the city's icon, Spiral Tower, assumed the responsibility of designing the museum. He worked closely with Dorian Webster, the engineer of the city electricity system, to make the space eco-friendly. Two wings have been added, connecting the museum to a sculpture garden. Windmills and solar panels disguised as sculptures will generate enough power to run the entire museum.

The renovation project was actually initiated by the architect himself. After he submitted the proposal to the city council, he also donated a significant sum of funds to the project. "It is not an exaggeration when I say that Mr. Kensington made the project possible," commented Caitlin Tristan, the mayor of Indianapolis. "He raised the majority of the renovation costs required by hosting fund-raising dinners. All I did was merely approve his proposal."

The museum will open with an exhibition of the renowned photographer, Amy Nijinsky. She will deliver an appreciation speech to Mr. Kensington that night on behalf of the city council.

The museum will be open Monday through Friday from 9 A.M. to 7 P.M. For more information about the city museum, visit its website at www.icma.org.

165. How has Mr. Kensington contributed to the museum?

    (A) By allowing his private properties to be used as the construction site

    (B) By planning out how the budget should be used

    (C) By coming up with the idea of renovating the City Hall building

    (D) By organizing the opening ceremony

166. Who most likely is Ms. Tristan?

    (A) A famous photographer

    (B) A museum curator

    (C) A city official

    (D) A professional engineer

167. What is stated about the opening ceremony?

    (A) It will be followed by a fund-raising dinner.

    (B) It will be held on a Monday.

    (C) It is an invitation-only event.

    (D) It will include a formal talk.

▶ ▶ ▶ GO ON TO THE NEXT PAGE

Teresa Harper   10:48 A.M.

Don't forget about the brainstorming session scheduled for today. The location has changed to room 453, but it's still going to take place at 3:00.

Kate Martin   10:50 A.M.

I'm not going to make it there on time. My meeting at Duncan, Inc. isn't supposed to finish until 2:30. Shall I bring some refreshments for everyone?

Teresa Harper   10:51 A.M.

Why not? Oh, everyone, please remember to print the information I e-mailed you this morning and bring it with you.

Darryl Waltrip   10:52 A.M.

I'm looking at my inbox, and I don't see anything from you.

Eric Reed   10:53 A.M.

Me, neither.

Teresa Harper   10:55 A.M.

Really? I must have forgotten to send it. I'll e-mail it to everyone right now.

Eric Reed   10:56 A.M.

Got it. Thanks.

Darryl Waltrip   10:57 A.M.

I'll read it during lunch so that I'm fully prepared for the meeting.

Teresa Harper   10:59 A.M.

Thanks, everyone. We really need to land this contract, so I hope you have some creative ideas for our proposal. It's due at the end of the week.

SEND

168. Why does Ms. Harper invite the writers to the meeting?

(A) To go over the results of a survey
(B) To consider a recent proposal
(C) To examine the terms of a contract
(D) To come up with some new ideas

169. Why will Ms. Martin be late for the meeting?

(A) She has not prepared for it yet.
(B) She needs to complete a work proposal.
(C) She has to attend a business meeting.
(D) She will be meeting with her supervisor.

170. What does Mr. Waltrip indicate he will do?

(A) Read some information
(B) Print a document for everyone
(C) Set up the meeting room
(D) Let his colleagues know about a meeting

171. At 10:51 A.M. why does Ms. Harper write, "Why not?"

(A) To question the suggestion made by Ms. Martin
(B) To refuse to allow anyone to attend the meeting late
(C) To agree to have food and drinks at the meeting
(D) To approve a request to change the time of the meeting

▶ ▶ ▶GO ON TO THE NEXT PAGE

Tokyo Daily

"I still cannot believe this is really happening to me," said Sakutaro Kimoto. Mr. Kimoto moved to the United States with his parents from Tokyo, Japan, when he was only 16. "When I first came to New York, I was very lonely. Everything was new and confusing, so I spent most of my time by myself after school. The only way to ease my boredom was to spend time cooking at home." —[1]—.

When he turned 20, Mr. Kimoto started working as a kitchen staff member at a Boston-based Italian restaurant, Charley's, instead of going to college. Recognized for his outstanding ability and effort, he was promoted to head chef in just 2 years. There, he learned to manage a kitchen staff and to cook various Italian dishes. As he built a reputation as a chef, Mr. Kimoto began to consider opening his own restaurant. —[2]—. After working there for 3 more years as the head chef, he left Charley's, moved back to his hometown, and opened a small restaurant, named Iratshai Italy, that specializes in Japanese-Italian fusion cuisine. The restaurant soon acquired considerable local interest and became one of the most popular dining places in the region only a year after its opening.

—[3]—. The establishment has undergone renovations and been enlarged two times already, but it still needs more space to meet the needs of its customers. In fact, the second Iratshai Italy will be opening in Yokohama, Japan, next weekend. "I am so excited to open another restaurant. I am grateful for the opportunities given to me, and I will continue to put all my efforts into serving quality Japanese-Italian foods to local residents," Mr. Kimoto said. —[4]—.

172. What is mainly being discussed in the article?

(A) The achievements of an individual
(B) The requirements for the success of a local business
(C) Dining trends in a local area
(D) Successful ways to open a restaurant

173. What did Mr. Kimoto do for a living right before opening his own restaurant?

(A) A kitchen staff at a restaurant
(B) The owner of Charley's
(C) A student at a college
(D) A manager of a local business

174. According to the article, what will Mr. Kimoto do soon?

(A) Hire more employees
(B) Relocate his original restaurant
(C) Launch another restaurant
(D) Invest in another field of business

175. In which of the positions marked [1], [2], [3], and [4] does the following sentence best fit?

"Mr. Kimoto's restaurant has been expanding in size."

(A) [1]
(B) [2]
(C) [3]
(D) [4]

Magical Intelligence

There is nothing we are unable to fix, so count on us!

Branch Location:

■ Manchester ☐ London ☐ Bradford

Date of Visit and Pick Up: July 6
Work Completion Date: July 22 **Service Number**: CR7902

Customer Information	Service Information
Name: Steve Jackson	Item: Washing machine
Address: 134 Ridge Ave., Manchester	Brand: Shalatt
Telephone: 161-555-2267	Model: S3

Service Description	Rate
• Leaking Washing Machine: Door Seal and Pump Replacement	£65.00
• Visit and Pick Up Service	£15.00
• Delivery and Installation Fee	£12.00
Subtotal	£92.00
Tax	£9.20
Total	£101.20

Payment Received on:	July 22
Form of Payment:	Cash

We especially regard the speed of our service highly, thus, we will refund 30% of all services that take longer than the originally estimated time to be repaired and returned to your home. Indicate the total duration of the process in the survey form that the technician gave you when picking up your appliance.

Magical Intelligence

Thank you for choosing Magical Intelligence! Please take some time to complete the survey below so that we may improve our service and serve you better next time.

Customer Name	Steve Jackson
Date of Receipt	July 22
Service Number	CR 7902
Technician	William Luke

Please indicate the level of satisfaction with...

	Excellent	Good	Fair	Poor
Promptness				V
Quality	V			
Cost		V		

Was the technician...?

	Excellent	Good	Fair	Poor
Professional	V			
Polite	V			
Informative	V			

Please note any comments you might have:

I must say that I am quite disappointed by the service I received this time. The quality of service was fair and satisfying as always, but how long it took was really frustrating. When I called Magical Intelligence on July 2, I was informed that the repair would be completed by July 10. However, I have been forced to go to a local laundry for over 2 weeks now, and my washing machine arrived just yesterday. I think I will have to reconsider coming back for your service in the future.

---

176. What kind of business most likely is Magical Intelligence?

(A) A local laundry
(B) A shipping company
(C) A repair service provider
(D) An electronics store

177. What is implied about Magical Intelligence?

(A) It requires customers to pick up their appliances.
(B) It offers discounts to all customers.
(C) It has more than one location.
(D) It provides free shipping and handling.

178. What most likely is true about Mr. Luke?

(A) He filled out a survey.
(B) He owns a washing machine made by Shalatt.
(C) He visited Mr. Jackson on July 6.
(D) He is a new employee at Magical Intelligence.

179. What will probably happen in the future?

(A) Mr. Jackson will receive a certain amount of money back.
(B) The fixed washing machine will arrive.
(C) Magical Intelligence will send a technician to Mr. Jackson again.
(D) A discount coupon will expire.

180. What is indicated in the survey?

(A) Mr. Jackson is upset with the quality of the new washing machine.
(B) The cost of Magical Intelligence is the least expensive in the region.
(C) Mr. Jackson has done business with Magical Intelligence before.
(D) Magical Intelligence has been featured in a publication.

▶ ▶ ▶GO ON TO THE NEXT PAGE

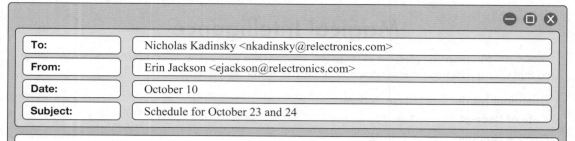

To:	Nicholas Kadinsky <nkadinsky@relectronics.com>
From:	Erin Jackson <ejackson@relectronics.com>
Date:	October 10
Subject:	Schedule for October 23 and 24

Dear Mr. Kadinsky,

I am sure you are well aware of your upcoming business trip to Tokyo from October 23 to October 24, but I just wanted to remind you about it.

Your flight will depart from Los Angeles Airport at 7:15 A.M. on October 23 and arrive at Tokyo Airport at 12:50 P.M. (local time). A representative from our Tokyo branch, Takuya Akira, will greet you at the airport to pick you up. Then, you will arrive at Sakura Hotel to have lunch with Tsubasa Honda, the branch manager.

The Futures Conference, where you will deliver your keynote speech, will commence at 4:00 P.M. at the Grande Conference Hall of Sakura Hotel. Afterwards, you are scheduled to attend the banquet to which all chief executives and presidents of companies, who participate in the conference, are invited.

On the following day, you will be attending the board of directors meeting at our Tokyo branch conference hall in the morning to discuss the company's direction in the next financial year. Your return flight departs at 4:25 P.M., and I will pick you up from the airport upon your arrival.

Regards,

Erin Jackson
Chief Secretary
Rami Electronics

To:	Tsubasa Honda <thonda@relectronics.com>
From:	Erin Jackson <ejackson@relectronics.com>
Date:	October 23
Subject:	Lunch Appointment Cancellation

Dear Ms. Honda,

I regret to inform you that Mr. Kadinsky's flight has been delayed due to mechanical problems and therefore, he is unable to have lunch with you today. I have scheduled an alternate flight that departs 2 hours later than originally planned. Please rearrange the schedule accordingly so that Mr. Kadinsky can be picked up from the airport promptly.

Mr. Kadinsky apologizes for not being able to meet with you personally and hopes for another opportunity in the future. Despite the delay, he will be able to deliver his keynote speech at the conference, and the rest of the schedule is to remain unchanged.

Regards,

Erin Jackson
Chief Secretary
Rami Electronics

181. Why did Ms. Jackson e-mail Mr. Kadinsky?

(A) To provide details about an event
(B) To ask for a conference agenda
(C) To outline the plans for a trip
(D) To remind of a department meeting

182. Who most likely is Mr. Kadinsky?

(A) A corporate executive
(B) A branch manager
(C) A regional representative
(D) A chief secretary

183. What will Mr. Akira probably do on October 23?

(A) Deliver a keynote speech at 4:00 P.M.
(B) Have lunch with Ms. Honda
(C) Pick up Mr. Kadinsky from Sakura Hotel
(D) Be present at an airport by 2:50 P.M.

184. What is suggested about the Futures Conference?

(A) It is exclusively for employees of Rami Electronics.
(B) It will be followed by a formal dinner.
(C) It will be held in Los Angeles.
(D) It is organized by Ms. Jackson.

185. In the second e-mail, the word "rest" in paragraph 2, line 3 is closest in meaning to

(A) break
(B) detail
(C) remainder
(D) addition

Make Your Own Magazine

Nielsen Publishing is pleased to announce another addition to our variety of magazines. Over the past ten years, we have expanded our focus from women's interests to other fields. This year's addition will be launched in May.

Make Your Own is the very first magazine of its kind. With *Make Your Own*, you can select topics you are interested in and have them compiled into a personalized monthly magazine. Nielsen Publishing provides twelve different categories from which you may choose. The subscription rate varies depending on the number of categories you want.

Membership	Number of Topics	Subscription Rate
Platinum	6	$200/yr
Gold	4	$170/yr
Silver	2	$145/yr

Platinum members will receive an extra three months of the magazine as well as a free bestselling novel. When you subscribe to *Make Your Own*, enter the book code of the novel you want. The list of books and codes can be found on Nielsen Publishing's website. Gold members will receive an extra month of the magazine.

Check out our exclusive promotion for those who already subscribe to any of Nielsen Publishing's magazines. They will receive a 50% discount for the first year's subscription to *Make Your Own*. This offer will last from May to August.

Subscribe to *Make Your Own* today and have it delivered to you within 30 days!

---

 www.nielsenpublishing.com/subscribe/payment/confirmation

Nielsen Publishing Co.
120 Chambers St., New York, NY 10007

HOME	SUBSCRIBE	DONATION	CONTACT US

Subscription confirmed.
Thank you for your subscription to *Make Your Own*!

Date	June 19
Name	Kelsey Perry
Telephone	917-659-7834
Address	98 Mountain Rd., Cornwall-on-Hudson, NY 12520

Payment Received: $200
Subscription Details:

	Business & Economics	V	Science & Nature		Sports & Recreation	V	Fashion & Style
	Parenting		Health & Fitness	V	Literature	V	Music
V	Lifestyle	V	Medicine		News & Politics		Children

Your Complimentary Book Code: _____

* For Platinum-level members who leave the book code column blank, a book will be selected randomly.

To:	<customerservice@nielsonpublishing.com>
From:	<kperry@personalmail.com>
Date:	June 20
Subject:	My Subscription

To whom it may concern,

I just realized that I omitted the special code that I was supposed to send you along with my subscription. The code that I want is 5954-93A. Please make sure that it is added to my subscription record. Thank you very much.

I am looking forward to receiving the first issue of my magazine soon.

Sincerely,

Kelsey Perry

186. What is mentioned about *Make Your Own*?

(A) It is popular with its readers.
(B) It will be published monthly.
(C) It will be available in bookstores in May.
(D) It has been published for ten years.

187. What is indicated about Nielsen Publishing?

(A) It specializes in magazines for women only.
(B) It publishes magazines in multiple countries.
(C) Its headquarters is located on Chambers Street.
(D) It has published many bestselling novels.

188. When will Ms. Perry receive her first issue of *Make Your Own*?

(A) In May
(B) In June
(C) In July
(D) In August

189. In which topic is Ms. Perry NOT interested?

(A) Literature
(B) Medicine
(C) Fashion & Style
(D) Health & Fitness

190. Why did Ms. Perry send the e-mail?

(A) To select a free novel
(B) To name the bonus magazine she wants
(C) To praise the quality of the magazine
(D) To ask for an extension on her subscription

International Paliburg Award to Be Given

by Frank Jameson

North Arlington (September 19) – On September 28, the ceremony for the International Paliburg Award (IPA), an award given to authors for exceptional achievements in literature, will take place at the Paliburg Center as it always has for the last 8 decades. The winner will receive $8,000 in cash and a medal. This year, 4 nominees have been selected: Rosa Perry, Justin Otter, Genevieve Swift, and Bruce Moore.

Ms. Perry and Mr. Moore are both award-winning authors. Ms. Perry's nominated work, *Fireworks*, is of the biography genre, like many of her other novels. Mr. Moore's *The Way* is a tragic love story of a young boy named Luke West.

Among the nominations is Justin Otter's *Never Say Never*. During his interview with us at the Paris Book Festival last month, Mr. Otter said that his adventure-themed work is somewhat based on his own experiences as a young student in his hometown of Melbourne.

What is most notable about one of the selected books, *Belonging*, is that it is Genevieve Swift's first novel. "Last year, I finally quit my teaching job to concentrate on writing. When I saw a copy of my novel at a bookstore, I thought that I had finally realized my dream," noted Ms. Swift.

For more information and a list of past award winners, please visit IPA's website, www. ipalibergaward.org.

To:	Justin Otter <jotter@ccpmail.com>
From:	Selena Jetson <sjetson@kearnyhs.edu>
Date:	September 30
Subject:	Congratulations!

Hello, Justin,

Congratulations on winning the International Paliburg Award. When I saw your novel on the nomination list, I had no doubt that you would win.

I noticed that the apple farm in the book is the one my father used to own. I remember we would help my father during summer breaks. After you moved to New York a couple of years ago, it was quite difficult for us to keep in touch. Reading your book made me think of the time we spent together in our hometown.

Congratulations again! I look forward to hearing from you soon.

Sincerely,

Selena

For Immediate Release

Primrose Publishing has just signed Genevieve Swift to an exclusive writing contract. Ms. Swift will produce 5 books in the next 6 years. The first book, tentatively entitled *Swan Lake*, is a sequel to *Belonging*, which Ms. Swift published several months ago. More information regarding this new deal can be found at www.primrosepublishing.com.

191. What is suggested about the International Paliburg Award?

(A) It was established about 80 years ago.
(B) It has been given only two fiction writers.
(C) It is sponsored by a local business.
(D) It accepts personal submissions from authors.

192. Who is a former educator?

(A) Frank Jameson
(B) Rosa Perry
(C) Genevieve Swift
(D) Luke West

193. In the article, the word "realized" in paragraph 4, line 3, is closest in meaning to

(A) possessed
(B) fulfilled
(C) recognized
(D) understood

194. What is true about Mr. Otter?

(A) He was hired by the Paliburg Center.
(B) He received a monetary prize.
(C) He won other awards for his work in the past.
(D) He majored in literature.

195. What is suggested about Ms. Swift?

(A) The title of her second novel will be *Swan Lake*.
(B) It was not possible for her to attend the awards ceremony.
(C) She will collaborate with Mr. Otter on a new work.
(D) She works during the day and writes at night.

Questions 196-200 refer to the following memo, e-mail, and comment form.

To: All Employees
From: Erin Lindsey, HR Director
Subject: Employee Training
Date: September 21

We will be installing new machinery this weekend. We are acquiring computers from Synth, Inc., printers from CompuBest, copy machines from Powderhouse, and scanners from Tyndale. Because we are replacing so much equipment, it is imperative that all employees be trained on how to use everything properly as soon as possible. The following is the schedule for the training courses that will be given on Monday, September 28, and Tuesday, September 29:

Dates/Times	Departments
September 28, 9:00 A.M – 12:00 P.M.	Sales
September 28, 1:00 P.M. – 4:00 P.M.	Accounting, HR
September 29, 10:00 A.M. – 1:00 P.M.	R&D
September 29, 2:00 P.M. – 5:00 P.M.	Marketing

Please be sure to attend the proper training session with your colleagues. Speak with me at extension 89 if you are unable to attend your assigned session. I will do my best to assign you to another one.

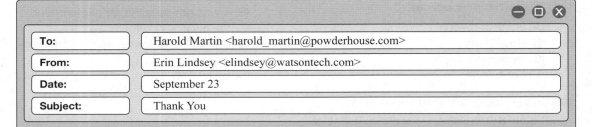

To:	Harold Martin <harold_martin@powderhouse.com>
From:	Erin Lindsey <elindsey@watsontech.com>
Date:	September 23
Subject:	Thank You

Mr. Martin,

Thank you for informing me about the recent sale that Powderhouse is offering its long-term customers. In light of that information, I would like to purchase six units of the XJ45 instead of only five. I hope you can accommodate this request. I would still like all of the machines to be delivered and installed at the company this coming weekend. Please let me know if there are any problems with my request.

Regards,

Erin Lindsey
HR Director, Watson Tech

Employee Training Comment Form

Training Date/Time: September 29, 2:00 P.M.

Employee Name: Regina Stewart

Comments:

I found the training session to be quite beneficial overall. The trainers were knowledgeable about the equipment they were teaching us to use. They were also willing to answer all of our questions. However, I wish that the representative from Tyndale had provided us with handouts. I had to write down everything she told us instead, and I'm afraid that I was unable to record all of the necessary information.

196. What is one purpose of the memo?

(A) To request work schedules from employees
(B) To confirm an upcoming office move
(C) To assign training slots to workers
(D) To request volunteers to work on the weekend

197. What is suggested about Watson Tech?

(A) It is moving its office to a new location on the weekend.
(B) It is providing its own trainers for the upcoming sessions.
(C) It has purchased equipment from Powderhouse in the past.
(D) It needs new equipment because it recently hired more employees.

198. What equipment was Ms. Lindsey able to purchase for a discount?

(A) Computers
(B) Printers
(C) Copy machines
(D) Scanners

199. What department does Ms. Stewart most likely work in?

(A) Sales
(B) Accounting
(C) R&D
(D) Marketing

200. What problem does Ms. Stewart mention?

(A) The questions that she asked were not answered.
(B) Her training session did not start on time.
(C) She was not provided with written instructions.
(D) Some equipment she trained on did not work properly.

STOP! This is the end of the test. If you finish before time is called, you may go back to Parts 5, 6, and 7 and check your work.

Actual Test 04

MP3 해설집

적정 풀이 시간 120분

120 min

시작 시간 ___시 ___분

종료 시간 ___시 ___분

중간에 멈추지 말고 처음부터 끝까지 풀어보세요.
문제를 풀 때에는 실전처럼 답안지에 마킹하세요.

목표 개수 _____ / 200   실제 개수 _____ / 200

예상 점수는 번역 및 정답에 있는 점수 환산표를 참조하세요.

LISTENING TEST

In the Listening test, you will be asked to demonstrate how well you understand spoken English. The entire Listening test will last approximately 45 minutes. There are four parts, and directions are given for each part. You must mark your answers on the separate answer sheet. Do not write your answers in the test book.

PART 1

Directions: For each question in this part, you will hear four statements about a picture in your test book. When you hear the statements, you must select the one statement that best describes what you see in the picture. Then find the number of the question on your answer sheet and mark your answer. The statements will not be printed in your test book and will be spoken only one time.

Statement (B), "They are sitting at a table." is the best description of the picture. So you should select answer (B) and mark it on your answer sheet.

1.

2.

▶ ▶ ▶ GO ON TO THE NEXT PAGE

3.

4.

5.

6.

▶ ▶ ▶GO ON TO THE NEXT PAGE

PART 2

Directions: You will hear a question or statement and three responses spoken in English. They will not be printed in your test book and will be spoken only one time. Select the best response to the question or statement and mark the letter (A), (B), or (C) on your answer sheet.

7. Mark your answer on your answer sheet.

8. Mark your answer on your answer sheet.

9. Mark your answer on your answer sheet.

10. Mark your answer on your answer sheet.

11. Mark your answer on your answer sheet.

12. Mark your answer on your answer sheet.

13. Mark your answer on your answer sheet.

14. Mark your answer on your answer sheet.

15. Mark your answer on your answer sheet.

16. Mark your answer on your answer sheet.

17. Mark your answer on your answer sheet.

18. Mark your answer on your answer sheet.

19. Mark your answer on your answer sheet.

20. Mark your answer on your answer sheet.

21. Mark your answer on your answer sheet.

22. Mark your answer on your answer sheet.

23. Mark your answer on your answer sheet.

24. Mark your answer on your answer sheet.

25. Mark your answer on your answer sheet.

26. Mark your answer on your answer sheet.

27. Mark your answer on your answer sheet.

28. Mark your answer on your answer sheet.

29. Mark your answer on your answer sheet.

30. Mark your answer on your answer sheet.

31. Mark your answer on your answer sheet.

PART 3

Directions: You will hear some conversations between two or three people. You will be asked to answer three questions about what the speakers say in each conversation. Select the best response to each question and mark the letter (A), (B), (C), or (D) on your answer sheet. The conversations will not be printed in your test book and will be spoken only one time.

32. Who most likely is the woman?

    (A) A yoga coach
    (B) A culinary teacher
    (C) A lab technician
    (D) A computer programmer

33. What does the woman say she recently did?

    (A) Joined a fitness center
    (B) Changed departments
    (C) Bought some supplies
    (D) Reviewed a budget

34. What does the man suggest?

    (A) Reusing some items
    (B) Buying some more equipment
    (C) Meeting with their supervisor
    (D) Holding a fundraiser

35. What event are the speakers discussing?

    (A) A training program
    (B) An orientation session
    (C) A charity luncheon
    (D) A product demonstration

36. What does the woman imply when she says, "I requested 25 laptops"?

    (A) She plans to conduct an online meeting.
    (B) A request was not fulfilled properly.
    (C) Not everyone will attend an event.
    (D) Some machines are not working.

37. What does the man ask the woman to do?

    (A) Make a payment
    (B) Pick up some food coupons
    (C) Reserve an event venue
    (D) Clean up a room

38. What problem does the woman mention?

    (A) A truck's engine will not start.
    (B) An oven is broken.
    (C) A bathroom window is jammed.
    (D) A sink is leaking.

39. What does the man ask about?

    (A) Where some tools are
    (B) How much he needs to pay
    (C) When a repair can be done
    (D) How to complete a form

40. What does the woman say she will do next?

    (A) Check her toolbox
    (B) Inspect the rest of the house
    (C) Look for some parts
    (D) Call her supervisor

41. What is the purpose of the man's business trip?

    (A) To present some results
    (B) To meet with a new supplier
    (C) To sign a contract
    (D) To demonstrate a product

42. What does the woman suggest the man visit?

    (A) A museum
    (B) A theater district
    (C) A restaurant
    (D) A monument

43. What does the man say he will do during his break?

    (A) Conduct some research
    (B) Reserve a plane ticket
    (C) Look for some tickets
    (D) Contact his client

► ► ►GO ON TO THE NEXT PAGE

44. Who most likely is the woman?

(A) A newspaper reporter
(B) A company owner
(C) A talk show host
(D) An advertising executive

45. According to the woman, why was the man busy recently?

(A) He took part in convention.
(B) He was training some new workers.
(C) He wrote some news reports.
(D) He conducted some interviews.

46. Why does the man say, "My employees are incredibly dedicated and reliable"?

(A) To recommend his workers for new jobs
(B) To help secure a new contract with a client
(C) To address a complaint by a customer
(D) To recognize the contribution of some others

47. What has the man been doing?

(A) Interviewing job applicants
(B) Writing an article on international travel
(C) Going over some survey results
(D) Updating some rules

48. What problem does the woman mention?

(A) Some costs have gone up.
(B) A company's branches are closing down.
(C) Some equipment is malfunctioning.
(D) Writers are reluctant to go abroad.

49. What does the man suggest doing?

(A) Transferring some workers to a new branch
(B) Allowing electronic payment
(C) Producing an online version of the magazine
(D) Hiring more staff members

50. What are the speakers mainly discussing?

(A) An available position
(B) A proposed budget
(C) An advertisement campaign
(D) A business trip

51. What did the man say he received?

(A) A job offer
(B) A meal voucher
(C) Some new information
(D) Sales numbers

52. What will the woman most likely do next?

(A) Meet with a client
(B) Make a presentation
(C) Reschedule a meeting
(D) Attend a luncheon

53. Where does the conversation most likely take place?

(A) At a construction site
(B) At a duty-free store
(C) At a hardware store
(D) At a rental car agency

54. What does the woman say she is looking for in a product?

(A) An extended warranty
(B) Durable material
(C) Ease of transport
(D) Something that is waterproof

55. What will Todd probably do next?

(A) Show a user's guide
(B) Arrange a delivery
(C) Provide a demonstration
(D) Offer a discount

56. Where does the conversation take place?

(A) At an airport
(B) At an office building
(C) At a hotel
(D) At a supermarket

57. Why has the man visited the business?

(A) To install a lighting fixture
(B) To repair some lights
(C) To redecorate a room
(D) To paint some walls

58. What does the woman say happened last week?

(A) Some equipment was purchased.
(B) A new tenant arrived.
(C) Renovations were made.
(D) Operating hours were extended.

59. Why does Sarah Doyle want a loan?

(A) To purchase some equipment
(B) To pay her monthly rent
(C) To run some advertisements
(D) To hire additional staffers

60. Why does the man ask for assistance?

(A) He does not do a certain task.
(B) He is helping another customer.
(C) He is currently on his break.
(D) He does not understand a question.

61. What requirement for a loan is mentioned?

(A) A letter of recommendation
(B) Legal documentation for property
(C) Some financial records
(D) A bank account

Restaurant Reviews	
Susan's Corner	★ ★ ☆ ☆ ☆
Westside Café	★ ★ ★ ☆ ☆
Steak 45	★ ★ ★ ★ ☆
Thompson Place	★ ★ ★ ★ ★

62. What did the man look over for the woman?

(A) A product review
(B) A meeting schedule
(C) A presentation
(D) A company catalog

63. What is the woman worried about?

(A) An upcoming training course
(B) Her presentation at a seminar
(C) Her performance review
(D) A meeting with a client

64. Look at the graphic. Which restaurant does the man recommend?

(A) Susan's Corner
(B) Westside Café
(C) Steak 45
(D) Thompson Place

▶ ▶ ▶GO ON TO THE NEXT PAGE

	Ground (price per package)	Air (price per package)
1-20 packages	$3.00	$6.00
21-50 packages	$2.50	$5.00
51-100 packages	$2.00	$4.00

Project-Related Agenda Items

1. Timeline
2. Project Managing
3. Budget
4. Vendors for supplies

65. What recently happened to Harrison Manufacturing?

(A) It hired more workers.
(B) It obtained some new customers.
(C) It opened a factory in Europe.
(D) It signed a contract with a supplier.

66. Look at the graphic. How much will it most likely cost to send each package?

(A) $2.00
(B) $2.50
(C) $4.00
(D) $5.00

67. What will the man most likely do next?

(A) Send packaging boxes
(B) Provide his contact information
(C) Sign a contract
(D) Ship some packages

68. Where do the speakers most likely work?

(A) At a library
(B) At a museum
(C) At an art supply store
(D) At an architect office

69. Look at the graphic. Which agenda item are the speakers discussing?

(A) Item 1
(B) Item 2
(C) Item 3
(D) Item 4

70. What does the woman say she will do later?

(A) Contact a colleague
(B) Review a proposal
(C) Post an advertisement
(D) Call in a meeting

PART 4

Directions: You will hear some short talks given by a single speaker. You will be asked to answer three questions about what the speaker says in each short talk. Select the best response to each question and mark the letter (A), (B), (C), or (D) on your answer sheet. The talks will not be printed in your test book and will be spoken only one time.

71. Who most likely is the listener?

(A) An editor-in-chief
(B) A writer
(C) A photographer
(D) A teacher

72. According to the speaker, what is he impressed with?

(A) A budget proposal
(B) A job description
(C) Some photographs
(D) Some samples of work

73. What does the speaker say he wants to do?

(A) Confirm an e-mail address
(B) Arrange an interview
(C) Provide a price estimate
(D) Schedule a release date

74. What will take place on Sunday?

(A) A product demonstration
(B) An information session
(C) A sales conference
(D) A job interview

75. What does the Jospin Institute offer?

(A) Business audits
(B) Computer classes
(C) Online market research
(D) Security consulting

76. Why should the listeners text a number?

(A) To respond to a survey
(B) To receive a newsletter
(C) To request an application
(D) To provide comments

77. What is the speaker mainly discussing?

(A) A departmental budget
(B) A speech at a conference
(C) A new phone system
(D) A new conference room

78. According to the speaker, what should the listeners do if they have any further issues?

(A) Notify an expert
(B) Write an online review
(C) Use some different equipment
(D) Restart their computer

79. Why does the speaker ask the listeners to call him?

(A) To reserve a meeting room
(B) To request new machinery
(C) To ask for a transfer
(D) To order some supplies

80. Who most likely is the speaker?

(A) A restaurant owner
(B) A government inspector
(C) A kitchen staff member
(D) A financial advisor

81. Why does the speaker say, "Our kitchen is always busy"?

(A) To tell the listeners that a wait time could be longer
(B) To explain a reason for a change
(C) To show that a business is successful
(D) To prove that the work will be difficult

82. What does the speaker ask the listeners to do?

(A) Confirm their work schedules
(B) Work overtime
(C) Wear hard hats at all times
(D) Have their name tags on

▶ ▶ ▶ GO ON TO THE NEXT PAGE

83. What kind of product is the speaker discussing?

(A) An exercise machine
(B) A software program
(C) A skincare item
(D) A running shoe

84. What will the listeners start working on?

(A) Working with a focus group
(B) Creating some marketing materials
(C) Making a TV commercial
(D) Training some new workers

85. What does the speaker say she will do this week?

(A) Meet with each employee
(B) Arrange a conference call with staff
(C) Travel abroad on business
(D) Visit the company's factory

86. What type of business is the news report mainly about?

(A) An airplane manufacturer
(B) A car rental service
(C) An automobile maker
(D) A photography studio

87. According to the speaker, what is the goal of the company's action?

(A) To expand into overseas markets
(B) To help protect the environment
(C) To cut its production costs
(D) To use fewer raw materials

88. What does the speaker imply when he says, "I've already ordered a new one"?

(A) He thinks the vehicles are high in demand.
(B) Some models will not be available soon.
(C) The vehicles' prices are not too high.
(D) He likes the looks of the new models.

89. What problem does the speaker mention?

(A) A shipper is sending items late.
(B) A building needs renovations.
(C) Some products are getting damaged.
(D) Wrong items have been shipped out.

90. What does the company intend to do?

(A) Change its packaging options
(B) Hire another shipping service
(C) Provide more employee benefits
(D) Introduce new policy guidelines

91. What has been prepared for some employees?

(A) Food and drinks
(B) A tutorial for packaging
(C) An employee handbook
(D) Some samples of packaging

92. Where does the speaker work?

(A) At a government office
(B) At an elementary school
(C) At an art supply store
(D) At a community center

93. According to the speaker, what is different about this summer's program?

(A) It will include additional activities.
(B) It will be at a different venue.
(C) It will cost money to participate.
(D) It will start later in the summer.

94. Why does the speaker say, "We hope you feel the same way"?

(A) To apologize to the listeners for changing a date
(B) To encourage the listeners to make a donation
(C) To thank the listeners for volunteering
(D) To ask for feedback from the listeners

Catalog

Ivory #R4852	Light Blue #R4853
Green #R4854	Cream #R4855

95. Look at the graphic. Which color is the speaker interested in?

(A) Ivory
(B) Light blue
(C) Green
(D) Cream

96. What does the speaker want to know?

(A) If refunds are allowed
(B) If a special price is available
(C) If an item is out of stock
(D) If delivery can be made for free

97. When does the speaker want to be contacted?

(A) In the morning
(B) At lunchtime
(C) At night
(D) On the weekend

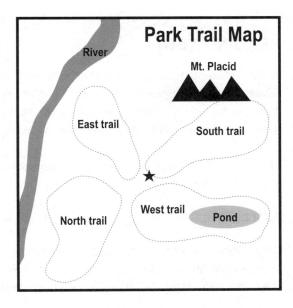

Park Trail Map

98. Look at the graphic. Which trail does the speaker say is the easiest?

(A) North trail
(B) South trail
(C) East trail
(D) West trail

99. According to the speaker, what should the listeners take with them?

(A) Sunblock lotion
(B) Raingear
(C) Plenty of water
(D) A tent

100. What are the listeners asked to do next?

(A) Complete a survey for hikers
(B) Watch a short video
(C) Look at some photos
(D) Get a permit for hiking

This is the end of the Listening test. Turn to Part 5 in your test book.

▶ ▶ ▶GO ON TO THE NEXT PAGE

READING TEST

In the Reading test, you will read a variety of texts and answer several different types of reading comprehension questions. The entire Reading test will last 75 minutes. There are three parts, and directions are given for each part. You are encouraged to answer as many questions as possible within the time allowed.

You must mark your answer on the separate answer sheet. Do not write your answers in your test book.

PART 5

Directions: A word or phrase is missing in each of the sentences below. Four answer choices are given below each sentence. Select the best answer to complete the sentence. Then mark the letter (A), (B), (C), or (D) on your answer sheet.

101. Regular customers of Coffee House have been surprised at the sharp price increases which were ------- imposed last week.

(A) unexpected
(B) more unexpected
(C) unexpectedly
(D) unexpectedness

102. The weather satellite project began ten years ago, but suffered from several -------.

(A) delay
(B) delayed
(C) delaying
(D) delays

103. The speech of the chief executive officer focused on our Mr. Jenkins and ------- successes in India.

(A) he
(B) his
(C) him
(D) himself

104. Economic uncertainty is one of the biggest challenges we face while doing business in this city, ------- comparatively little effort is devoted to fixing it.

(A) so
(B) yet
(C) nor
(D) although

105. Our town is a ------- community made up of different nationalities, cultural backgrounds, and religious groups.

(A) successful
(B) profitable
(C) diverse
(D) external

106. The president of Speed Freight Services has been considering ------- another warehouse in Toronto in two years.

(A) build
(B) building
(C) to build
(D) built

107. Most employees are ------- to vacation time and vacation pay after being employed for one year.

(A) entitled
(B) eliminated
(C) limited
(D) trained

108. Customers who wish to be ------- should return defective products within three days of purchase and bring an original receipt as well.

(A) fulfilled
(B) reimbursed
(C) exchanged
(D) collaborated

109. ------- the high volume of applications that we receive, only qualified applicants will be contacted next week.

(A) Due to
(B) Aside from
(C) Regardless of
(D) On behalf of

110. It is quite ------- that Bella Motors has become the leader in the hybrid car industry in just six years.

(A) amaze
(B) amazing
(C) amazed
(D) amazes

111. All of the researchers at BK Pharmaceutical's Lab are required to wear safety equipment on the -------.

(A) phases
(B) premises
(C) technologies
(D) remarks

112. The government ------- announced that it would grant generous tax breaks for foreign companies doing business in the country.

(A) immediately
(B) soon
(C) recently
(D) exclusively

113. The environmental project was designed to raise ------- of the serious garbage problem in the oceans.

(A) approach
(B) maintenance
(C) awareness
(D) influence

114. It is ------- necessary to turn off the computer data servers to upgrade their operating system.

(A) lately
(B) occasionally
(C) helpfully
(D) carefully

115. Some employees ------- usually work late are likely to think that the best way to refresh themselves is to get some energy drinks.

(A) who
(B) which
(C) where
(D) what

116. Don't put off making necessary repairs or performing ------- maintenance to make your car last as long as possible in top condition.

(A) routine
(B) beneficial
(C) upcoming
(D) cautious

117. Sign up for the BK Cable Television membership to get hundreds of channels ------- your choice of three sports channels for absolutely no charge.

(A) whichever
(B) plus
(C) additionally
(D) that

118. According to our personnel records, Mr. Jones works the ------- of all of the employees working at Cheese Bread Factory.

(A) hardly
(B) harder
(C) hardest
(D) hard

▶ ▶ ▶ **GO ON TO THE NEXT PAGE**

119. The health care system is basically a service-based industry and is at ------- just as in other service-oriented sectors.

(A) utmost
(B) farthest
(C) relative
(D) apparent

120. Most people rarely think about sharing their cars ------- crude oil prices are currently rising sharply.

(A) if so
(B) therefore
(C) even though
(D) since

121. Mr. Parker ------- a managerial position last year, but declined since he was looking for a high-paying job.

(A) offers
(B) offered
(C) was offered
(D) will be offered

122. Tourism International will award 'Agency of the Year' to ------- travel agency gets the most votes from the board members.

(A) whoever
(B) whichever
(C) wherever
(D) however

123. The human resources department will come up with several ways to ------- the sales staff to improve their competitiveness in the overseas market.

(A) consolidate
(B) contact
(C) raise
(D) motivate

124. The company cafeteria opens from 8 A.M. to 8 P.M. during the weekdays, so you can plan your lunch and dinner hour -------.

(A) subsequently
(B) seasonally
(C) primarily
(D) accordingly

125. ------- Mr. Brown, actual profit and loss should be precisely reflected in the next accounting report.

(A) With respect to
(B) In addition to
(C) The fact that
(D) As stated by

126. According to our policy, ------- who violates the "no mobile phone" rule can be asked to leave the theater.

(A) those
(B) both
(C) several
(D) anyone

127. The individual ------- responsibility is to trace all business transactions that result in changes in the property and finance of our company is Mr. Brian Walker, the head accountant.

(A) whose
(B) what
(C) whether
(D) this

128. Even though most customers find the new product easy to use, ------- less familiar with it should refer to the user's guide before use.

(A) those
(B) who
(C) these
(D) none

129. Ms. Rodriguez will participate in a training course for her new position, in ------- she will be in charge of statistical analysis.

(A) whom
(B) which
(C) that
(D) where

130. The launch of the new mobile device ------- at least a week after a problem was detected.

(A) were postponed
(B) will postpone
(C) has been postponed
(D) had been postponed

PART 6

Directions: Read the texts that follow. A word or phrase, or sentence is missing in parts of each text. Four answer choices for each question are given below the text. Select the best answer to complete the text. Then mark the letter (A), (B), (C), or (D) on your answer sheet.

Questions 131-134 refer to the following letter.

Dear Ms. Schickler;

In connection with our annual symposium on the electronics industry, we invite an expert in the field to address us. ------- our emphasis this year is on the future of the electronics,
131.
we would be honored if you could speak to us on your experience of business.

Future Electronics Symposium will be ------- at Los Angeles Metropolitan Hotel on
132.
October 1, from 10:00 A.M. to 3:00 P.M. We ------- your speech from 1:00 P.M. to 2:00
133.
P.M., and would like you to speak for an hour including questions and answer period.

-------.
134.
Very truly yours,

Siobhan Kelly
Vice President
Andromeda Electronics

131. (A) Since
(B) Although
(C) Even if
(D) While

132. (A) hold
(B) holding
(C) held
(D) to hold

133. (A) is scheduling
(B) have scheduled
(C) had been scheduled
(D) will be scheduled

134. (A) We very much appreciated your attendance at our presentation on October 1.
(B) As agreed, your payment for our transaction will be made in Canadian dollars.
(C) It is our pleasure to host a number of seminars and presentations related to the international community.
(D) We are pleased to be able to pay your traveling costs and to offer you a modest honorarium.

Dear all staff,

I'm writing to inform you that we have recently revised our business travel reimbursement policy. This policy defines the conditions, rules, and procedures that apply to staff members who undertake business travel ------- the company and where the company
135.
may reimburse the expenses associated with business travel.

From now on, after approval for your business travel, flight tickets and hotels must be booked through the personnel department. -------. If there is any reason you need to book
136.
your business travel, you must ------- the reason in your business travel expense report
137.
and submit all receipts to the personnel department. Additionally, employees ------- up to
138.
$100 per day to pay for your incidentals, including food and ground transportation.

Please be aware that reimbursement will not be made if you do not follow this new policy when booking your business travel.

Do not hesitate to contact me with any questions or concerns.

Truly yours,

Jennifer Grant
Head of Accounting

---

135. (A) in charge of
(B) in compliance with
(C) with regard to
(D) on behalf of

136. (A) You will be satisfied with the quality of our service here.
(B) We should discuss the amount permitted for incidentals next week.
(C) It will help to remove the confusion we had in the past.
(D) To take advantage of this opportunity, you must respond by May 15.

137. (A) document
(B) consider
(C) perform
(D) persuade

138. (A) allows
(B) allowed
(C) will allow
(D) will be allowed

Uptown Furniture

Event Notice

Many thanks for purchasing our couch set. Seats should be comfortable for all members

of family. We greatly appreciate your -------, and we trust that you are getting lots of
139.

enjoyment from your new furniture.

-------. We would therefore be grateful if you could take a moment to complete the
140.

enclosed customer satisfaction survey. Your answers will help us ensure that we always

------- our future customers' needs.
141.

Furthermore, your completed survey will be entered into a special prize draw. The winning

customer will get a $500 gift certificate to use in-store. Please return your survey by July

15 to be included in the draw. The winner ------- on August 1.
142.

---

139. (A) requirement
(B) supervision
(C) custom
(D) prediction

140. (A) Prior experience is preferred for this
position.
(B) We always strive to improve our
customer care.
(C) All of your complaints are to be
treated equally.
(D) It's often used for heavy items like
dressers and dining tables.

141. (A) satisfy
(B) desire
(C) research
(D) replace

142. (A) announces
(B) should announce
(C) was announced
(D) will be announced

▶ ▶ ▶GO ON TO THE NEXT PAGE

Questions 143-146 refer to the following article.

Syracuse Chronicle
Culture Section

A New Photo Exhibit Is Coming to Town
Brandon Lee

November 1) Starting next Wednesday, the National Art Gallery will be holding an exhibit on the works of photographer Ms. Cecil Beaton. Ms. Beaton's photos ------- many awards

143.

internationally. The rising artist is renowned for her black and white photos that feature the socially oppressed. She was the sole apprentice of the late Peter Jackson, a prominent photographer who focused on capturing the lives of indigenous peoples. Based on -------

144.

she learned from Mr. Jackson, Ms. Beaton went on to take photos of homeless people, beggars, child workers, and other socially ignored citizens. "Like the indigenous people that are not being fully recognized globally, there are people within our own cities that are being ignored," stated Ms. Beaton. "I wanted to capture their lives through photography

------- my audience can see and reconnect to their forgotten neighbors." The

145.

photographer hopes to contribute to society through her works. -------. The exhibit will

146.

last for four months.

143. (A) receives
(B) were received
(C) have received
(D) will receive

144. (A) that
(B) which
(C) what
(D) how

145. (A) however
(B) although
(C) so
(D) therefore

146. (A) The exhibition will be based on Mr. Jackson's photos on indigenous people.
(B) Several magazine companies will contact her to use her pictures soon.
(C) She plans to donate all of the exhibition's profits to charity organizations.
(D) The photographer mentioned future plans of taking photos of homeless people.

PART 7

Directions: In this part you will read a selection of texts, such as magazine and newspaper articles, e-mails, and instant messages. Each text or set of texts is followed by several questions. Select the best answer for each question and mark the letter (A), (B), (C), or (D) on your answer sheet.

Questions 147-148 refer to the following e-mail.

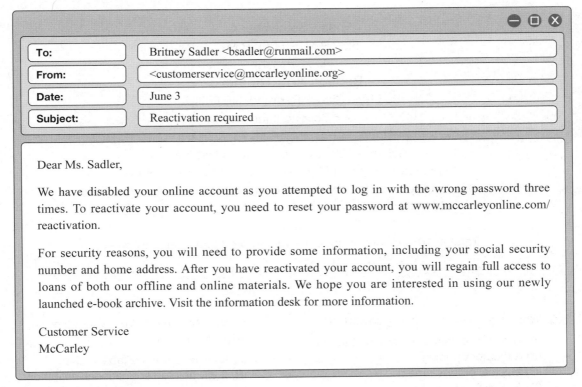

To: Britney Sadler <bsadler@runmail.com>

From: <customerservice@mccarleyonline.org>

Date: June 3

Subject: Reactivation required

Dear Ms. Sadler,

We have disabled your online account as you attempted to log in with the wrong password three times. To reactivate your account, you need to reset your password at www.mccarleyonline.com/reactivation.

For security reasons, you will need to provide some information, including your social security number and home address. After you have reactivated your account, you will regain full access to loans of both our offline and online materials. We hope you are interested in using our newly launched e-book archive. Visit the information desk for more information.

Customer Service
McCarley

147. Why was the e-mail probably sent to Ms. Sadler?

(A) She was unable to purchase a book online.
(B) She canceled a transaction with McCarley.
(C) She needs to renew her account.
(D) She forgot her password.

148. What most likely is McCarley?

(A) A bank
(B) A online bookstore
(C) A library
(D) A security agency

5th Annual Hot Potato Market

A Rock & Roll Night

presented by Iratshai – a local Japanese restaurant

Come and enjoy a night full of energy!
Guest Performer: Green Tomatoes Band

Friday, September 4
5:30 P.M. – 11:00 P.M.

Benson Arts Theater
958 Kyle Street, Bertrand, NE 68927
Second floor

Tickets - $20 (Sales start on August 30)
All proceeds to benefit the Jacksonville Music Academy.
Visit www.hotpotatomarket.org for more information or to reserve a ticket.
You'd better hurry! Tickets are expected to sell out quickly.

* Iratshai 10% discount coupons will be provided to all attendees.

149. What type of event is being advertised?

(A) The anniversary party of a restaurant
(B) A theater opening
(C) Musical entertainment
(D) A local food festival

150. What is NOT mentioned about the advertised event?

(A) Its tickets are available online.
(B) It will help an educational institution.
(C) It will conclude at 11:00 P.M.
(D) Its tickets will be available on September 4.

Questions 151-152 refer to the following text message chain.

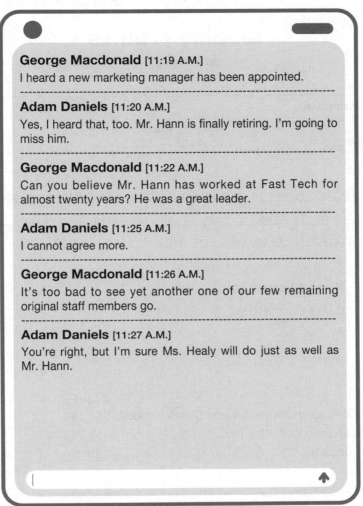

George Macdonald [11:19 A.M.]

I heard a new marketing manager has been appointed.

Adam Daniels [11:20 A.M.]

Yes, I heard that, too. Mr. Hann is finally retiring. I'm going to miss him.

George Macdonald [11:22 A.M.]

Can you believe Mr. Hann has worked at Fast Tech for almost twenty years? He was a great leader.

Adam Daniels [11:25 A.M.]

I cannot agree more.

George Macdonald [11:26 A.M.]

It's too bad to see yet another one of our few remaining original staff members go.

Adam Daniels [11:27 A.M.]

You're right, but I'm sure Ms. Healy will do just as well as Mr. Hann.

---

151. What is indicated about Fast Tech?

(A) It has been in business for fewer than two decades.
(B) It has recently hired a new employee.
(C) It will post a job advertisement soon.
(D) It is expanding its Marketing Department.

152. At 11:25 A.M., what does Mr. Daniels mean when he writes, "I cannot agree more"?

(A) He is indicating that Mr. Macdonald is giving incorrect information.
(B) He thinks greatly of Mr. Hann as well.
(C) He does not have any close colleagues now.
(D) He refuses to work with Mr. Healy.

▶ ▶ ▶GO ON TO THE NEXT PAGE

Quality Frames

1086 College Avenue
Dayton, OH 45434

Customer Information	
Name:	Victor Clark
Phone Number:	(513)555-2903

Special Memo:

I would like to frame a painting. This painting was painted by my grandfather, and it has a very high sentimental value. As you will see, the painting is timeworn, so please take special care of it.

Frame Type: Michelangelo

Color: Classic Gold & Silver

Pickup Date: July 10

Cost Summary:

- Service: $35.00
- Material Cost: Michelangelo frame (2 5/8 inches): $95.00
- Membership Discount (10%): -$9.50
- Prepaid Deposit: -$30.00

Balance Due at Pickup: $90.50

153. What can be inferred about the painting?

(A) It was created by a famous artist.
(B) Its original frame broke.
(C) It is fragile.
(D) It is expensive.

154. How much money does Mr. Clark need to pay on July 10?

(A) $30.00
(B) $35.00
(C) $90.50
(D) $95.00

Jazzy Numbers

Jazzy Numbers is a 3-year-old jazz instrumental band that has members who play the piano, saxophone, clarinet, double bass, and drums. We have turned out many famous musicians, including Aaron Mills, who is one of our original members. He recently joined the prestigious Ersel Orchestra as the lead clarinetist.

Do you have a passion for jazz music?

Then do not hesitate to apply to be a member! As a freelance jazz band, we play anytime, anywhere for various events such as parties, weddings, and other ceremonies. We are currently looking for new members. All we need is a recording of you playing as well as a brief personal statement by November 3. Once we have evaluated your submission, we will call you for an audition. E-mail Jeffry Henderson at jhenderson@boostmail.com for audition file submissions or questions.

155. What is the purpose of the advertisement?

(A) To announce a retirement
(B) To recruit additional artists
(C) To publicize an upcoming performance
(D) To ask for donations

156. What is NOT true about Aaron Mills?

(A) He will be judging the audition.
(B) He played in Jazzy Numbers about 3 years ago.
(C) He is a well-known clarinetist.
(D) He is currently a member of the Ersel Orchestra.

157. What is suggested about the musicians in Jazzy Numbers?

(A) They record their performances on electronic files.
(B) They are amateurs.
(C) They travel to different places.
(D) They work for Mr. Henderson.

Barney's Hill
Barney's Signature Cereal Bars

Barney's Hill Cereal Bars are made from the traditional homemade family recipe created by Canadian farmer Barney Pierres. For 50 years, Mr. Pierres had run the business, but now his son, Romeo Pierres, has taken over the business. Using no artificial flavors, each bar is filled with toasted oats, cashews, and almonds and dipped in real maple syrup to produce a sweet, great-tasting, wholesome snack that you can take anywhere. Our cereal bars are full of classic crunch and whole grain goodness making them a nutritious snack that will keep you full without guilty pleasures.

- High in fiber and low in sugar
- Zero trans-fats and gluten-free
- Quick and easy to consume
- Provides a boost of energy
- Approved by the Organic Farm Association (OFA)

Visit our website at www.barneyshill.com/naturebars to download a printable coupon. When purchasing a package of Barney's Hill Cereal Bars containing a dozen bars, present the coupon to the cashier and receive a second pack for free!

158. What is the purpose of the information?

(A) To describe the history of a business
(B) To introduce a traditional food
(C) To advertise a product made with natural ingredients.
(D) To show how to cook a homemade dish

159. What is indicated about Barney's Hill?

(A) It prints Mr. Pierres' signature on its products.
(B) Its products are manufactured on a farm.
(C) It is a family-owned business.
(D) It will merge with the OFA.

160. What is available on the website?

(A) Ordering a pack of cereal bars
(B) Downloading an application
(C) Requesting some free product samples
(D) Receiving a buy-one-get-one-free voucher

Questions 161-163 refer to the following e-mail.

To:	Sofia Elliot <selliot@neymail.com>
From:	Oskar Viren <oviren@valverdeshoes.com>
Date:	August 13, Monday
Subject:	re: Request

Dear Ms. Elliot,

Thank you for contacting us on August 9 to report that you have not yet received a response regarding the online message you sent to us on August 4. Your message, which mentions that you received shoes in the wrong size on August 2, was processed today after a delay caused by a technical issue with our online server.

You may already know that return requests made due to problems caused by Valverde Shoes are processed free of charge. In addition, we will provide you with a $20 discount coupon to apologize for the inconvenience we have caused you. Please log in to our website to claim it. —[1]—.

To return your shoes, please download a return request form from our website, print it, and fill it out. —[2]—. In the original package, you will see a prepaid shipping label. —[3]—. You must include the shoes, the original receipt, and a completed return request form in your shipment.

—[4]—. Make sure to have the package delivered to us by August 20.

Truly yours,

Oskar Viren
Customer Service, Valverde Shoes

161. What is implied about Valverde Shoes?

(A) It normally charges a fee for return requests.
(B) It will include a discount coupon in a shipment.
(C) It is currently experiencing technical problems.
(D) It offers discount coupons to return customers.

162. When did Ms. Elliot first report a problem with her order to Valverde Shoes?

(A) On August 2
(B) On August 4
(C) On August 9
(D) On August 13

163. In which of the positions marked [1], [2], [3], and [4] does the following sentence best belong?

"It should be glued on top of your shipment when being sent as our office address is printed on it."

(A) [1]
(B) [2]
(C) [3]
(D) [4]

Questions 164-167 refer to the following online chat discussion.

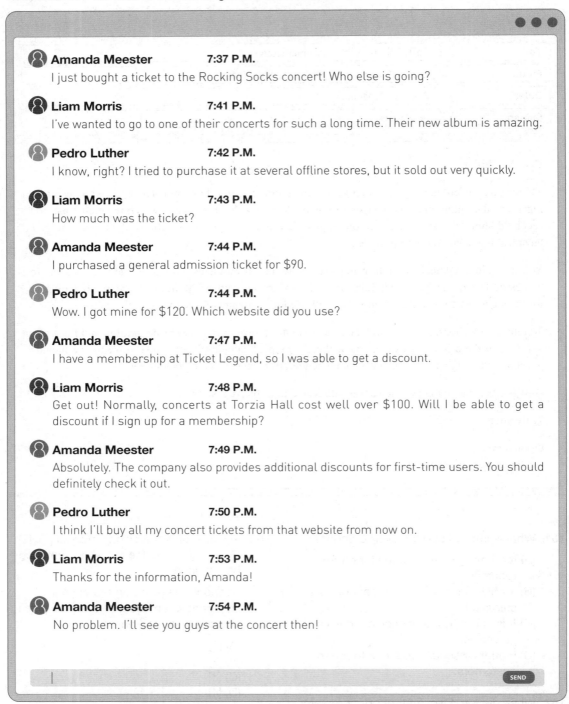

Amanda Meester   7:37 P.M.
I just bought a ticket to the Rocking Socks concert! Who else is going?

Liam Morris   7:41 P.M.
I've wanted to go to one of their concerts for such a long time. Their new album is amazing.

Pedro Luther   7:42 P.M.
I know, right? I tried to purchase it at several offline stores, but it sold out very quickly.

Liam Morris   7:43 P.M.
How much was the ticket?

Amanda Meester   7:44 P.M.
I purchased a general admission ticket for $90.

Pedro Luther   7:44 P.M.
Wow. I got mine for $120. Which website did you use?

Amanda Meester   7:47 P.M.
I have a membership at Ticket Legend, so I was able to get a discount.

Liam Morris   7:48 P.M.
Get out! Normally, concerts at Torzia Hall cost well over $100. Will I be able to get a discount if I sign up for a membership?

Amanda Meester   7:49 P.M.
Absolutely. The company also provides additional discounts for first-time users. You should definitely check it out.

Pedro Luther   7:50 P.M.
I think I'll buy all my concert tickets from that website from now on.

Liam Morris   7:53 P.M.
Thanks for the information, Amanda!

Amanda Meester   7:54 P.M.
No problem. I'll see you guys at the concert then!

SEND

164. Why is Mr. Luther's ticket more expensive than Ms. Meester's?

(A) His ticket is exclusive to fan club members.
(B) He did not purchase his ticket at a discounted price.
(C) He purchased a front-row seat.
(D) He paid more than he should have by mistake.

165. What is indicated about Rocking Socks?

(A) Tickets to their upcoming concert are sold out.
(B) They recently debuted.
(C) They are currently on tour.
(D) Their new album is a big hit.

166. At 7:48 P.M., what does Mr. Morris mean when he writes, "Get out"?

(A) He thinks the website is offering a great deal.
(B) He is suggesting that Ms. Meester leave early on the day of the concert.
(C) He will receive the ticket from Ms. Meester once she buys it for him.
(D) He is surprised to learn how easy it is to purchase a ticket online.

167. What can be inferred from the online chat discussion?

(A) Mr. Morris will get a refund for his ticket.
(B) There will be a long line at the Rocking Socks concert.
(C) Ms. Meester will go to Mr. Luther's concert with Mr. Morris.
(D) The upcoming Rocking Socks concert will be held at Torzia Hall.

December 18

Lillie Martinez
Associate Editor
Dysart Publishing
551 Eagles Road
San Diego, CA 92155

Dear Ms. Martinez,

I am a professor of journalism at Cupouse University. I was very impressed with your innovative ideas on creating and using e-publications that you explained in your online column on your company's website. Your knowledge and expertise in the field of editing and publishing are admirable.

In an effort to provide my students with current information on the professional writing field, I have been organizing a program with special guest lecturers. Would you be interested in coming to one of my classes to meet with my students and to deliver a lecture on the same topic as your online column? Last semester, the manager of your department, Mr. Phillips, came to deliver a lecture to the students, and they benefited from it very much.

If you are interested, please contact Brenda Smith at bsmith@cupouse.edu to discuss the date and time of your visit. I look forward to seeing you.

Sincerely,

Joseph Cleveland
Professor of Journalism, Cupouse University

168. What is the purpose of the letter?

(A) To give information about an upcoming event

(B) To compliment a student

(C) To request a web design

(D) To recruit a lecturer

169. How did Mr. Cleveland find out about Ms. Martinez's ideas?

(A) He read an online article that she wrote.

(B) He attended a seminar that she led.

(C) He delivered a speech at her company.

(D) He interviewed her for a report.

170. According to the letter, who previously visited Cupouse University?

(A) A group of web designers

(B) An employee at a publishing company

(C) The head of a company

(D) The organizer of a seminar series

171. Why should Ms. Martinez contact Ms. Smith?

(A) To reserve a seat for a seminar

(B) To submit some documents

(C) To discuss compensation

(D) To arrange an appointment

August 9 – The Moon Circus is making its first appearance in New York to present *Zora*, a show based on an astounding story of the nature. This latest extravaganza is finally ready for the stage after 2 years of production.

At a press conference held in Philadelphia last week, Mr. Gregory Karminski, the director of *Zora*, described in detail how the show came to be. —[1]—. The show is inspired by Julia Simms' famous work of fiction, *Jungle Tales*, taking on the majestic and wild characteristics of the jungle and its inhabitants.

—[2]—. Mr. Karminski emphasized portraying the colors of nature on the stage that *Jungle Tales* illustrates in words. He paid close attention to the details of the stage designs, costumes, and props to make them look as realistic as possible. He collaborated with Aria Fernandez, a choreographer who created routines for *the Seattle Horizon*, in creating of the choreography that makes the audience feel as if they are in the actual jungle. —[3]—. These efforts contributed to the creation of a masterpiece, a circus that is beyond imaginable.

—[4]—.

Zora's premiere at Loren's Theater will be shown on September 3. The *Zora* National Tour will be visiting Boston and Las Vegas in the future. Do not miss the chance to see the most stunning show of all time, *Zora*, by the Moon Circus.

172. What is the main purpose of the article?

(A) To advertise a movie based on a novel
(B) To introduce a debuting director
(C) To share information about a show
(D) To describe an event featuring animals from the jungle

173. What is NOT indicated about Mr. Karminski?

(A) He talked to a group of reporters last week.
(B) He visited the jungle to prepare for his show.
(C) He worked with Aria Fernandez.
(D) He worked on *Zora* for two years.

174. Where is Loren's Theater located?

(A) In New York
(B) In Philadelphia
(C) In Las Vegas
(D) In Boston

175. In which of the positions marked [1], [2], [3], and [4] does the following sentence best fit?

"The director also worked closely with an award-winning scriptwriter Louis Bell in the making of *Zora*'s script."

(A) [1]
(B) [2]
(C) [3]
(D) [4]

▶ ▶ ▶GO ON TO THE NEXT PAGE

Valley Fitness Center

~ Celebrating our first anniversary ~

"We needed just a year to become
the top personal training provider in the region."

Personal Training Room 201 Availability for December 12 – 16

	MONDAY	TUESDAY	WEDNESDAY	THURSDAY	FRIDAY
9 A.M. – 12 P.M.	Daniel Andrews	Robert Stone	Robert Stone	Alexander Nielson	Allan Grayson
1 P.M. – 4 P.M.	Sylvia Pereira	Allan Grayson	Robert Stone	Alexander Nielson	Sylvia Pereira
4 P.M. – 6 P.M.	Daniel Andrews	Allan Grayson	Daniel Andrews	Victoria Burke	Victoria Burke

This week, Mr. Robert Stone will fill in for Ms. Ashley Snider, who is recovering from a minor injury, and provide personal training for her clients. On Saturdays, all the personal training rooms are reserved for clients to make up for their missed sessions.

To:	Linda Cronin <lcronin@cuzmail.com>
From:	Carl Johnson <cjohnson@valleyfitness.com>
Date:	December 10
Subject:	Your personal training

Dear Ms. Cronin,

We are sorry to inform you that Valley Fitness Center will be closed on Monday and Tuesday of this week due to the unexpected heavy snowfall Sacramento experienced. As a result, your Monday morning personal training originally scheduled to be held in Room 201 had to be canceled. Please call the center at your earliest convenience to discuss a convenient day for you to come to our center for training.

Our records also indicate that your annual membership will expire on December 20. Renew your membership before December 15 to receive a 15% discount on the membership and a special gift. Go to our website to see more than 20 gifts that you can choose from.

Carl Johnson
Valley Fitness Center

176. What is indicated about Valley Fitness Center?

(A) It is a fast-growing business.
(B) It invites makeup artists on Saturdays.
(C) It hired Mr. Stone recently.
(D) It plans to open another location.

177. What is a purpose of the e-mail?

(A) To warn about the harsh weather
(B) To respond to a request
(C) To confirm the shutdown of a business
(D) To announce a schedule change

178. Who did Ms. Cronin intend to receive personal training from?

(A) Alexander Neilson
(B) Allan Grayson
(C) Daniel Andrews
(D) Sylvia Pereira

179. What is indicated about Ms. Cronin?

(A) She lives in Sacramento.
(B) She will renew her membership on Saturday.
(C) She has been a member of Valley Fitness Center for about a year.
(D) She is a personal trainer at Valley Fitness Center.

180. Why should Ms. Cronin visit the website?

(A) To reschedule an appointment
(B) To check out a list
(C) To renew a membership
(D) To receive a discount

Auckara

Auckara is a Pottsville-based convention center that provides venues for both businesses in and residents of Pottsville and Kirington. Our venue experts will not stop until you are completely satisfied.

Featured Venues

Barbara Hall

This main hall in the Burton Building is the perfect venue for both business and personal events. Snack bar included. Can accommodate up to 200 people.

Catalina Garden

A beautiful garden for outside events such as weddings and receptions. Venue availability dependent on weather conditions. Catering service available at an extra charge.

Disquito Hall

This conference hall is equipped with a projector, round tables for groups of 6, and comfortable chairs. Suitable for presentations and seminars with about 40 people.

Professionals Room

A classroom-type room ideal for seminars, presentations, and lectures. A whiteboard, a microphone, a laser pointer, a projector, and other necessary items are included. Accommodates about 50 people.

All venues featured on this page are equipped with free wireless Internet. For specific details, the price of each venue, and more information about Auckara, please visit our website at www.auckara.com. Please send an e-mail to our venue manager, Katherine Washington, at k.washington@auckara.com to make a reservation.

To:	Katherine Washington <k.washington@auckara.com>
From:	Rose Guarin <rguarin@voepublishing.com>
Date:	June 10
Subject:	Venue

Dear Ms. Washington,

I am planning to hold a seminar on public relations in July. A colleague of mine, Michael Greenmier, from the Event Planning Department referred me to Auckara after holding a banquet in the Barbara Hall in April. He said the place was very well prepared and its price is reasonable. I am looking for a venue for about 35 people. As the seminar will include discussion sessions, a place where participants can break into smaller groups is needed.

If there is a suitable venue for my needs, please reply to this e-mail with your recommendation. I would like to talk to you over the phone to discuss further details and prices. In addition, as our department will be holding the seminar biannually, I want to know whether I can receive a discount. Thank you in advance for your assistance.

Sincerely,

Rose Guarin

181. What is mentioned about Auckara?

(A) It requires a deposit when reserving a venue.
(B) It may be closed depending on the weather conditions.
(C) It sells equipment for business meetings.
(D) It has venues for various events.

182. According to the advertisement, what is available at all featured venues?

(A) Refreshments
(B) A projector
(C) Tables and chairs
(D) Internet access

183. What is mentioned about Mr. Greenmier?

(A) He works for Auckara.
(B) He will send an e-mail to Ms. Guarin.
(C) He visited the Burton Building in April.
(D) He is knowledgeable about public relations.

184. Which venue would Ms. Washington most likely recommend to Ms. Guarin?

(A) Barbara Hall
(B) Disquito Hall
(C) Catalina Garden
(D) Professionals Room

185. What does Ms. Guarin ask about in the e-mail?

(A) Her eligibility for a discount
(B) The catering service fee
(C) The dates of a seminar series
(D) The size of a venue

▶ ▶ ▶ GO ON TO THE NEXT PAGE

3rd Homemade Cuisine Contest

Food Empire Magazine is inviting amateur cooks to participate in our 3rd annual Homemade Cuisine Contest. We are looking for dishes in the following four categories:

Categories	Judges
Chinese	Donald Liu, owner of the restaurant Red Dragon and author of *Finest Ingredients, Finest Dishes*
French	Corinne Desilets, head chef at the Grand Palace Hotel and author of *The Most Important Factor in Life: Food*
Italian	Mario Panicucci, TV show *Gourmet Spot*'s food critic and author of *The Secret Recipes*
Mexican	Alicia Rodriguez, award-winning food stylist and author of *How to Take the Best Snapshot of Dishes*

The first round of selections will be based on photographs and recipes submitted by the participants. Submit your entries on our website by July 5. On July 20, 15 candidates in each category will be announced. They will be invited to Food Empire's convention center to show off their cooking skills and cuisines in front of the judges on July 30. Two winners in each category will be announced on August 10. All winners will be featured in our September issue with pictures of their kitchens and dishes taken by our professional photographers. First-place winners will be given $2,500 as a prize, and second-place winners will receive a free subscription to our magazine for a whole year.

---

http://www.foodempire.com/contest_submission

Homemade Cuisine Contest
Online Submission Form

Name:  Helen McDaniels
E-mail Address: hmcdaniels@riomail.com
Phone Number: 843-555-5265
Address: 35 Khale Street, Roswell, SC 29455

Brief Description of Your Dish:

Classic cream pasta with mushrooms and bacon and home-baked cheese pizza. Affogato with vanilla ice cream as a dessert included as well.

 If I am chosen as a winner of the contest, I approve of *Food Empire Magazine* publishing photographs of my dishes and kitchen.

Please Attach Photos and Recipe of Your Dishes:

🖼 Pasta_McDaniels.jpg	🖼 Affogato_McDaniels.jpg
🖼 Pizza_McDaniels.jpg	📄 Recipes_McDaniels.doc

Homemade Cuisine Contest
Winners Announcement

It is finally time for us to announce the winners of the 3rd Homemade Cuisine Contest!

Chinese	1st Place: Justin Harnois	2nd Place: Robert Wilson
Italian	1st Place: Kimberly Smith	2nd Place: Helen McDaniels
French	1st Place: Brian Lopez	2nd Place: Tyson Sullivan
Mexican	1st Place: Michelle Mason	2nd Place: Joseph Tang

Congratulations to the winners! To see the pictures and recipes of the dishes of the winners, **Click Here.**

186. What do the judges have in common?

(A) They have all won awards for cooking.
(B) They went to the same cooking school.
(C) They have each judged the contest three times.
(D) They each wrote a book about food.

187. When is the due date for the first round of selections?

(A) July 5
(B) July 20
(C) July 30
(D) August 10

188. Who most likely evaluated Ms. McDaniels' entry?

(A) Mr. Liu
(B) Ms. Desilets
(C) Mr. Panicucci
(D) Ms. Rodriguez

189. What does Ms. McDaniels agree to do?

(A) Appear on a TV show
(B) Allow Food Empire to check if she is an amateur cook
(C) Photograph the kitchens of the contest winners
(D) Let Food Empire's employees visit her kitchen

190. What is indicated about Ms. Mason?

(A) She will receive a free magazine subscription.
(B) She will be given a monetary award.
(C) She works for *Food Empire Magazine*.
(D) She is a professional Mexican food chef.

Questions 191-195 refer to the following e-mails.

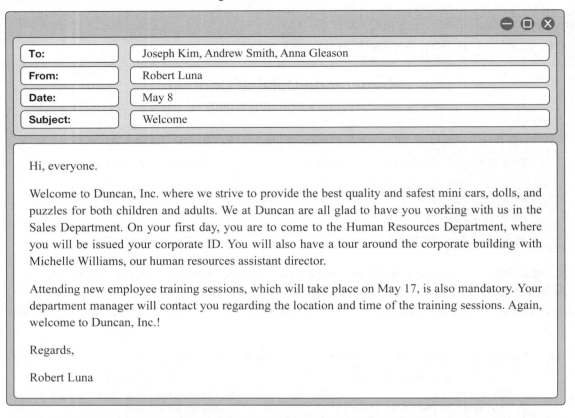

To: Joseph Kim, Andrew Smith, Anna Gleason
From: Robert Luna
Date: May 8
Subject: Welcome

Hi, everyone.

Welcome to Duncan, Inc. where we strive to provide the best quality and safest mini cars, dolls, and puzzles for both children and adults. We at Duncan are all glad to have you working with us in the Sales Department. On your first day, you are to come to the Human Resources Department, where you will be issued your corporate ID. You will also have a tour around the corporate building with Michelle Williams, our human resources assistant director.

Attending new employee training sessions, which will take place on May 17, is also mandatory. Your department manager will contact you regarding the location and time of the training sessions. Again, welcome to Duncan, Inc.!

Regards,

Robert Luna

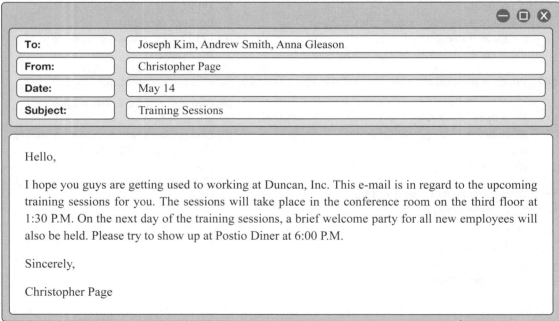

To: Joseph Kim, Andrew Smith, Anna Gleason
From: Christopher Page
Date: May 14
Subject: Training Sessions

Hello,

I hope you guys are getting used to working at Duncan, Inc. This e-mail is in regard to the upcoming training sessions for you. The sessions will take place in the conference room on the third floor at 1:30 P.M. On the next day of the training sessions, a brief welcome party for all new employees will also be held. Please try to show up at Postio Diner at 6:00 P.M.

Sincerely,

Christopher Page

To:	Christopher Page
From:	Laura Morgan
Date:	May 21
Subject:	Your business proposal

Dear Mr. Page,

Thank you for choosing Postio Diner for your company's recent party for your new employees. I hope everyone had a good time at my establishment. As we discussed at the party, we at Postio will be happy to provide food at your annual celebration to take place in June at your company's conference room. Please pay a visit again to talk about the terms and conditions of the contract.

Thank you,

Laura Morgan

191. What is NOT suggested about Duncan, Inc.?

(A) It provides educational courses for its employees.
(B) It recently hired a group of employees.
(C) It sells playthings for children.
(D) It covers employees' tour expenses.

192. In the first e-mail, the word "issued" in paragraph 1, line 4, is closest in meaning to

(A) printed
(B) charged
(C) given
(D) published

193. Who most likely is Mr. Page?

(A) A Sales Department manager
(B) An instructor at a training session
(C) A business owner
(D) A human resources director

194. When did Ms. Morgan and Mr. Page probably meet?

(A) On May 14
(B) On May 17
(C) On May 18
(D) On May 21

195. What does Ms. Morgan ask Mr. Page to do?

(A) Provide catering service
(B) Send an e-mail
(C) Pay for a recent event
(D) Come to her business

Booktree.com is an online bookstore where you can find both new and second-hand books at the most reasonable prices. In business for more than 20 years, Booktree.com is becoming increasingly popular with booklovers and was selected as the Bookstore of the Year by *Trend Today Magazine* last year.

As a summer special promotional event, we are currently giving back 20% of what you spent on your book purchase in Booktree points. This is 15% more than the 5% you usually get. Booktree points are our rewards points that you can use in the future for more books. This offer applies only to your first purchase and is valid until August 30.

Request expedited shipping for only $3.00 and receive your shipment within just 2 days of order. This service is available for domestic customers only.

Booktree.com
Always the best books at the best prices

Order Number:	FS094810	Order Date:	August 28
Booktree Account:	jbrown09	Shipping Date:	September 2
Customer Name:	Joseph Brown		
Address:	425 Cambridge Drive Phoenix, AZ 85040		

Order Details

Book Title	Author	Item Number	Price
The Art of Designing Software	Leonard Castro	D148501	$27.50
Computer Programming Patterns	Frank Mosley	R720958	$16.75
Programming Fundamentals	Howard Jackson	R012290	$31.10
Productive Computing	Lucy Rodriguez	C890271	$28.80
		Subtotal:	$104.15
		Shipping and Handling:	-
		Tax (8%):	$8.33
		Total:	$112.48

Booktree Points Provided on this Transaction:
22.50 Points (Promotional – 20%)

*Return or refund request must be made within 10 days of purchase. Submit an online request or send an e-mail to returnrequest@booktree.com. Refer to our website for detailed return and refund policy.

To:	Joseph Brown <jbrown@bkmail.com>
From:	Customer Service <customerservice@booktree.com>
Date:	September 5
Subject:	re: My Recent Order

Dear Mr. Brown,

We are sorry to hear that you received a wrong book, *Elements of Computer Programming*, written by Dr. Mosley, this morning. I believe there happened to be a mistake in packing your shipment as the author and the price of the book are the same as the one you actually ordered. We will expedite the correct book to your address. Please send the title you received to 55 Ilford Avenue, Houston, TX 73550 at your earliest convenience. In addition, to apologize for our mistake, we have provided you with a $10 discount coupon; log into your account on our website to claim it.

Sincerely,

Booktree.com Customer Service

196. What is suggested about Booktree.com?

(A) It sells used books online.
(B) It has received several awards.
(C) It ships books to domestic customers only.
(D) It launched a magazine last year.

197. What is probably true about Mr. Brown?

(A) He manufactures computers.
(B) He subscribes to *Trend Today Magazine*.
(C) He requested expedited shipping.
(D) He placed an order at Booktree.com for the first time.

198. When was the order sent to Mr. Brown?

(A) On August 28
(B) On August 30
(C) On September 2
(D) On September 5

199. In the e-mail, the word "claim" in paragraph 1, line 7, is closest in meaning to

(A) insist
(B) complain
(C) spend
(D) take

200. How much is *Elements of Computer Programming*?

(A) $16.75
(B) $27.50
(C) $28.80
(D) $31.10

STOP! This is the end of the test. If you finish before time is called,
you may go back to Parts 5, 6, and 7 and check your work.

Actual Test

MP3

해설집

적정 풀이 시간 120분

120 min

시작 시간 ___시 ___분

종료 시간 ___시 ___분

중간에 멈추지 말고 처음부터 끝까지 풀어보세요.
문제를 풀 때에는 실전처럼 답안지에 마킹하세요.

목표 개수 _____ / 200   실제 개수 _____ / 200

예상 점수는 번역 및 정답에 있는 점수 환산표를 참조하세요.

LISTENING TEST

In the Listening test, you will be asked to demonstrate how well you understand spoken English. The entire Listening test will last approximately 45 minutes. There are four parts, and directions are given for each part. You must mark your answers on the separate answer sheet. Do not write your answers in the test book.

PART 1

Directions: For each question in this part, you will hear four statements about a picture in your test book. When you hear the statements, you must select the one statement that best describes what you see in the picture. Then find the number of the question on your answer sheet and mark your answer. The statements will not be printed in your test book and will be spoken only one time.

Statement (B), "They are sitting at a table." is the best description of the picture. So you should select answer (B) and mark it on your answer sheet.

1.

2.

▶ ▶ ▶GO ON TO THE NEXT PAGE

3.

4.

5.

6.

▶ ▶ ▶GO ON TO THE NEXT PAGE

ACTUAL
TEST ••• **05**

PART 2

Directions: You will hear a question or statement and three responses spoken in English. They will not be printed in your test book and will be spoken only one time. Select the best response to the question or statement and mark the letter (A), (B), or (C) on your answer sheet.

7. Mark your answer on your answer sheet.

8. Mark your answer on your answer sheet.

9. Mark your answer on your answer sheet.

10. Mark your answer on your answer sheet.

11. Mark your answer on your answer sheet.

12. Mark your answer on your answer sheet.

13. Mark your answer on your answer sheet.

14. Mark your answer on your answer sheet.

15. Mark your answer on your answer sheet.

16. Mark your answer on your answer sheet.

17. Mark your answer on your answer sheet.

18. Mark your answer on your answer sheet.

19. Mark your answer on your answer sheet.

20. Mark your answer on your answer sheet.

21. Mark your answer on your answer sheet.

22. Mark your answer on your answer sheet.

23. Mark your answer on your answer sheet.

24. Mark your answer on your answer sheet.

25. Mark your answer on your answer sheet.

26. Mark your answer on your answer sheet.

27. Mark your answer on your answer sheet.

28. Mark your answer on your answer sheet.

29. Mark your answer on your answer sheet.

30. Mark your answer on your answer sheet.

31. Mark your answer on your answer sheet.

PART 3

Directions: You will hear some conversations between two or three people. You will be asked to answer three questions about what the speakers say in each conversation. Select the best response to each question and mark the letter (A), (B), (C), or (D) on your answer sheet. The conversations will not be printed in your test book and will be spoken only one time.

32. Where do the speakers work?

(A) At a retail shop
(B) At a textile manufacturer
(C) At a drugstore
(D) At a supermarket

33. What will happen this weekend?

(A) A sale will be held.
(B) Employees will work overtime.
(C) New equipment will be installed.
(D) A training program will take place.

34. What does the woman say she has been preparing?

(A) A work schedule
(B) A store directory
(C) An inventory
(D) An advertisement

35. Who most likely is the man?

(A) A customer service representative
(B) An electric engineer
(C) A sales consultant
(D) A marketing expert

36. Why is the woman frustrated?

(A) She does not have her receipt.
(B) She didn't get the computer fixed.
(C) She cannot get her money back.
(D) She had to wait a long time.

37. What is the woman asked to provide?

(A) An account number
(B) An item number
(C) A coupon code
(D) A street address

38. Who most likely is the woman?

(A) A bus driver
(B) A railroad engineer
(C) A rental car agent
(D) A bus station employee

39. What problem does the woman mention?

(A) A phone number is incorrect.
(B) A meeting was canceled.
(C) A bus is delayed.
(D) An Internet connection is not available.

40. What will Steve do next?

(A) Contact a customer
(B) Cancel a meeting
(C) Pay for some tickets
(D) Ask for a refund on tickets

41. What does the woman ask the man about?

(A) An auto repair shop
(B) An upcoming seminar
(C) Bike parking
(D) A rental car reservation

42. What problem does the woman have?

(A) She misplaced her car keys.
(B) Her car is in the shop.
(C) Her computer is not working.
(D) She is late for work again.

43. What does the man suggest the woman do?

(A) Take some time off work
(B) Move closer to work
(C) Speak with a coworker
(D) Print some files

▶ ▶ ▶GO ON TO THE NEXT PAGE

44. What does the woman congratulate the man for?

(A) Being promoted
(B) Getting a transfer
(C) Receiving a bonus
(D) Winning an award

45. What is the man looking forward to doing?

(A) Moving to his hometown
(B) Signing a new contract
(C) Working as a manager
(D) Greeting employees from abroad

46. Why does the man say, "I heard about a new Indian restaurant downtown"?

(A) To accept an invitation
(B) To indicate that there is heavy traffic downtown
(C) To request a change of menu
(D) To express concern about the cost

47. Why are the speakers meeting?

(A) To have a job interview
(B) To view a demonstration
(C) To conduct an experiment
(D) To discuss a new software program

48. What most likely is the man's profession?

(A) Chemical engineer
(B) Software developer
(C) Automobile designer
(D) Sales representative

49. What does the man say he likes about the company?

(A) It pays high salaries to its workers.
(B) It offers opportunities for personal growth.
(C) It has offices in many foreign countries.
(D) It provides gym memberships to its employees.

50. Where does the woman most likely work?

(A) At a university
(B) At a medical clinic
(C) At a shopping center
(D) At a drugstore

51. What new policy does the woman tell the man about?

(A) He needs to have a referral.
(B) He must pay for a cancelation.
(C) He needs to register in advance.
(D) He does not need an appointment.

52. What does the man say he will do?

(A) Fill out a medical form
(B) Reschedule an appointment for tomorrow
(C) Arrive after work
(D) Visit in the morning

53. What are the speakers mainly discussing?

(A) A rescheduled event
(B) A proposal for expansion
(C) The impact of a construction project
(D) Employment opportunities

54. What does the woman mean when she says, "We just got four new interns"?

(A) There is not enough space.
(B) She needs additional office equipment.
(C) They need an orientation session.
(D) Her department is over its budget.

55. What does the woman offer to do?

(A) Call Facilities
(B) Look at the budget report
(C) Speak with a client
(D) Address a customer complaint

56. What does the man want to do?

(A) Install an updated version of software
(B) Hire some more employees
(C) Arrange a training session
(D) Schedule a departmental meeting

57. What does the woman suggest doing?

(A) Taking a look at online reviews
(B) Upgrading computers
(C) Taking a client out to lunch
(D) Providing food

58. What will the man most likely do next?

(A) Find some missing supplies
(B) Hire a catering service
(C) Look at a budget
(D) Make a telephone call

59. What are the speakers mainly discussing?

(A) A hiring process
(B) A durable device
(C) A timesheet system
(D) A digital door lock

60. What will be provided to employees this afternoon?

(A) A revised work schedule
(B) A new security code
(C) An electronic badge
(D) A laptop computer

61. What does the woman indicate about the XLS 500?

(A) It is easy for employees to use.
(B) It is costly to be installed companywide.
(C) It comes with a two-year warranty.
(D) Its installation work takes long.

Team Safety Helmet Color	
Welders	Yellow
Plumbers	Blue
Bricklayers	Orange
Roofers	White

62. What type of building are the speakers discussing?

(A) A sports stadium
(B) A factory
(C) A parking garage
(D) A shopping center

63. Look at the graphic. Which team of workers will begin in one week?

(A) Welders
(B) Plumbers
(C) Roofers
(D) Bricklayers

64. What will the woman do next?

(A) Put an advertisement online
(B) Visit a project site
(C) Check a construction timeline
(D) Put in an order

Jackson's Ice Cream Shop

Today's Special Prices

Scoop	$2.00
Pint	$3.50
Quart	$5.00
Gallon	$9.00

Credit Card Statement

Date	Description	Amount
February 5	Sylvan Clothes	$73.45
February 9	Bus Terminal	$15.00
February 11	Jerry's Grill	$42.00
February 12	Westside Groceries	$89.98

65. Who is the woman?

(A) A restaurant owner
(B) A delivery person
(C) A school teacher
(D) A company manager

66. Look at the graphic. How much will the woman pay for her order?

(A) $2.00
(B) $3.50
(C) $5.00
(D) $9.00

67. What will the woman do next?

(A) Pay a bill for ice scream
(B) Sample some of strawberry ice cream
(C) Retrieve her purse from her car
(D) Get her car to the mechanic

68. What information is the woman asked to provide?

(A) Her name
(B) Her e-mail address
(C) Her phone number
(D) Her home address

69. Look at the graphic. Which amount does the woman say is not incorrect?

(A) $73.45
(B) $15.00
(C) $42.00
(D) $89.98

70. What does the man tell the woman to do?

(A) Visit the office in person
(B) Provide her account number
(C) Complete paperwork
(D) Speak with his manager

PART 4

Directions: You will hear some short talks given by a single speaker. You will be asked to answer three questions about what the speaker says in each short talk. Select the best response to each question and mark the letter (A), (B), (C), or (D) on your answer sheet. The talks will not be printed in your test book and will be spoken only one time.

71. Where does the announcement take place?

(A) At a movie theater
(B) At a museum
(C) At a television station
(D) At a library

72. What new service does the speaker say is provided?

(A) Online customer support
(B) Complimentary online tutorials
(C) E-book downloading service
(D) Movie streaming

73. How can the listeners get further information?

(A) By reading a brochure
(B) By subscribing to a newsletter
(C) By consulting a librarian
(D) By visiting a web page

74. What is the topic of the workshop?

(A) Hiring new employees
(B) Writing résumés
(C) Marketing goods
(D) Managing workers

75. How will the workshop help the listeners?

(A) It will attract more customers.
(B) It will let them retain clients.
(C) It will let them save money.
(D) It will improve performance.

76. What does the speaker ask the listeners to do?

(A) Sign a form
(B) Watch an informational video
(C) Set up a slide projector
(D) Introduce themselves

77. Where do the listeners work?

(A) At a hotel
(B) At a supermarket
(C) At a restaurant
(D) At a department store

78. What does the speaker imply when she says, "The tourists are flocking to this area"?

(A) More employees will be hired.
(B) Parking will be hard to find.
(C) A deadline is not likely to be met.
(D) A business will become busier.

79. What does the speaker remind the listeners to do?

(A) Pick up their new uniforms
(B) Arrive at work on time
(C) Update a calendar
(D) Wear their nametags

80. What is the speaker calling about?

(A) An equipment order
(B) A mobile application
(C) A job opening
(D) A release of a new mobile phone

81. Why is the listener suitable for a new project?

(A) He is familiar with a city.
(B) He has good leadership skills.
(C) He is a computer programmer.
(D) He is well organized.

82. What does the speaker want to do?

(A) Place an advertisement
(B) Talk about employment opportunities
(C) Consult with an expert
(D) Arrange a meeting

▶ ▶ ▶GO ON TO THE NEXT PAGE

83. What did the speaker recently do?

(A) She started a company.
(B) She requested a job interview.
(C) She wrote a book.
(D) She gave a presentation.

84. What does the speaker imply when she says, "I've worked as a recruiting manager at a few large companies for more than two decades"?

(A) People can trust her advice.
(B) She has an excellent job.
(C) She withdrew her résumé.
(D) She does not work with small companies.

85. What can the listeners receive by checking out a website?

(A) A discount on some course material
(B) A trial version of software
(C) An autographed book
(D) A free consultation

86. Who is the speaker?

(A) A singer
(B) An actress
(C) A radio host
(D) A sports reporter

87. What does the speaker say inspired her to choose her career?

(A) Talking with a famous singer
(B) Winning a prize
(C) Listening to an interview
(D) Traveling around the country

88. What will the speaker do next?

(A) Announce some news
(B) Interview some famous people
(C) Answer a question
(D) Play a song

89. What event is being planned?

(A) A charity auction
(B) A sporting event
(C) A fundraiser
(D) A musical concert

90. According to the speaker, what will volunteers be doing for the event?

(A) Serving food to the guests
(B) Putting flower arrangements on each table
(C) Greeting guests at the entrance
(D) Setting up a room

91. What does the speaker ask the listeners for?

(A) A signed contract
(B) A suggestion for a band
(C) A credit card number
(D) A recommendation for a caterer

92. Where does the talk take place?

(A) At a conference
(B) At a training session
(C) At an orientation event
(D) At a job fair

93. Why does the speaker say, "Your employees could turn out to be effective product testers"?

(A) To advise selling more products
(B) To suggest an alternative approach
(C) To praise some employees
(D) To recommend hiring more workers

94. What does the speaker give the listeners?

(A) A business card
(B) A website address
(C) A brochure
(D) A picture

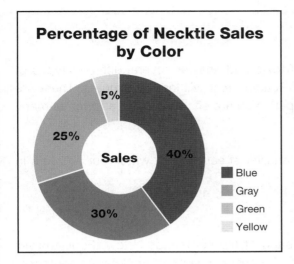

Percentage of Necktie Sales by Color

Sales

- Blue 40%
- Gray 30%
- Green 25%
- Yellow 5%

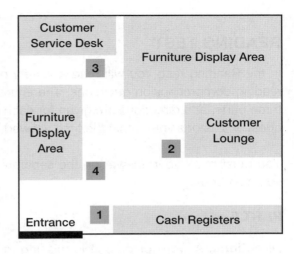

Customer Service Desk

Furniture Display Area

3

Furniture Display Area

Customer Lounge

2

4

Entrance

1

Cash Registers

95. Who most likely are the listeners?

(A) Marketers
(B) Designers
(C) Salespeople
(D) Programmers

96. Which aspect of a new product will the team discuss in small groups?

(A) Its size
(B) Its color
(C) Its style
(D) Its price

97. Look at the graphic. What will the color of the new product be?

(A) Gray
(B) Green
(C) Yellow
(D) Blue

98. What is the speaker mainly discussing?

(A) A training session
(B) A yearly clearance sale
(C) A sales conference
(D) A customer appreciation day

99. What are the listeners advised to do when people arrive?

(A) Give them shopping carts
(B) Assist them in finding items
(C) Distribute promotional flyers
(D) Inform them about refreshments

100. Look at the graphic. Where will the additional signs be located?

(A) Location 1
(B) Location 2
(C) Location 3
(D) Location 4

This is the end of the Listening test. Turn to Part 5 in your test book.

READING TEST

In the Reading test, you will read a variety of texts and answer several different types of reading comprehension questions. The entire Reading test will last 75 minutes. There are three parts, and directions are given for each part. You are encouraged to answer as many questions as possible within the time allowed.

You must mark your answer on the separate answer sheet. Do not write your answers in your test book.

PART 5

Directions: A word or phrase is missing in each of the sentences below. Four answer choices are given below each sentence. Select the best answer to complete the sentence. Then mark the letter (A), (B), (C), or (D) on your answer sheet.

101. The catering service company offers various Italian dishes ------- desserts for special occasions such as anniversary celebrations and business banquets.

(A) and
(B) so
(C) for
(D) nor

102. Consumers need to check whether a product ------- purchase through foreign direct shopping has been recalled.

(A) they
(B) them
(C) their
(D) themselves

103. If you have difficulty ------- a particular book, please come to the circulation desk and ask one of our librarians for assistance.

(A) location
(B) to locate
(C) locating
(D) located

104. Our restaurant ------- the right to refuse service to any patrons if they disturb the enjoyment of other patrons.

(A) guarantees
(B) violates
(C) reserves
(D) grants

105. The personnel manager mentioned to me that the board was ------- somebody to take charge of the new manufacturing plant.

(A) looking
(B) seeking
(C) searching
(D) consulting

106. ------- the lack of research and development for new products, Coco Sports couldn't remain the leading company in the sports equipment market.

(A) Neither
(B) Despite
(C) Due to
(D) Along with

107. Any errors in the articles should be reported to the editing department ------- so corrections can be made before the newspaper is published.

(A) prompt
(B) promptly
(C) prompted
(D) prompting

108. Some local businesspeople were ------- in getting a law passed that promoted fair competition for the protection of consumers.

(A) instruct
(B) instructor
(C) instrument
(D) instrumental

109. The city will provide a variety of complimentary drinks to ------- who participates in the film festival from May 14-19.

(A) anyone
(B) some
(C) those
(D) many

110. Applicants who passed the final interview for the floor manager position ------- by the human resources director later next week.

(A) have been contacted
(B) was contacted
(C) will contact
(D) will be contacted

111. BK Electronics announced its new plan yesterday to ------- their semiconductor manufacturing facilities in Alabama.

(A) extend
(B) accomplish
(C) enlarge
(D) anticipate

112. It is essential that we try harder to improve customer satisfaction levels and keep our company more -------.

(A) competitive
(B) competitively
(C) compete
(D) competition

113. Several investment companies saw the ------- for return at a time of slowing economic growth, and so they launched financial products tailored to the emerging markets.

(A) mark
(B) potential
(C) proposal
(D) allowance

114. Please note that payment for this shipment is due within 21 days of ------- of this invoice.

(A) receiving
(B) receive
(C) receipt
(D) receiver

115. ------- arrival at the airport, every passenger should go through customs, and it'll take about twenty five minutes or so.

(A) For
(B) Upon
(C) Owing to
(D) Despite

116. All the participants in the upcoming forum may stay at the Bella Hotel or the Grand Hotel, ------- they find more pleasant and convenient.

(A) that
(B) whoever
(C) whichever
(D) everyone

117. In order to ------- expenses incurred, it is necessary that original receipts or invoices be submitted with expense claims.

(A) schedule
(B) verify
(C) discount
(D) complicate

118. Hit by the surging costs of raw materials, food -------, steel, and textile industries are pinpointed to have a pretty gloomy economic outlook.

(A) proceed
(B) process
(C) processing
(D) procedure

▶ ▶ ▶GO ON TO THE NEXT PAGE

119. Mr. Stanford ------- the reins of his father's company by stepping down as CEO two years ago.

(A) reported
(B) inaugurated
(C) assumed
(D) relinquished

120. Prices are ------- to change based upon your choice of travel dates, number of travelers, departure city, and your choice of flight, hotels or other items.

(A) public
(B) subject
(C) imperative
(D) willing

121. Anything done to change some major rivers will only destroy the environment and ecosystem ------- repair.

(A) in
(B) toward
(C) beyond
(D) since

122. The assessment report states ------- that improvement to our distribution system has resulted in savings of more than millions of dollars for the past two years.

(A) explicitly
(B) randomly
(C) intangibly
(D) cooperatively

123. Success in this consumer-electronics industry depends on technological capability to introduce new products to the market in a ------- manner.

(A) time
(B) timer
(C) timely
(D) timing

124. ------- the current state of the economy, most customers cannot afford to buy our expensive new products.

(A) Provided
(B) Given
(C) Regarding
(D) Now that

125. Ace Medical has developed several low-cost imaging devices, two of ------- are considered for this year's Brandon Prize for Technology.

(A) them
(B) that
(C) whose
(D) which

126. If Jet Red Airlines ------- outsourcing some reservations jobs overseas, about 1,000 new jobs will be created in California this year.

(A) had started
(B) starting
(C) will start
(D) starts

127. ------- one of us must assume personal responsibility, not only for ourselves and our families, but for our neighbors and our society.

(A) Entire
(B) Every
(C) Total
(D) Complete

128. The company's personnel director will stop accepting applications ------- the administrative position has been filled.

(A) while
(B) once
(C) despite
(D) whereas

129. The new governor ------- to widen the four main highways to accommodate increasing freight shipments and reduce travel delays.

(A) insisted
(B) suggested
(C) supported
(D) proposed

130. ------- you need any help with the presentation or further assistance, please do not hesitate to contact us.

(A) In order
(B) Although
(C) Should
(D) So that

PART 6

Directions: Read the texts that follow. A word or phrase, or sentence is missing in parts of each text. Four answer choices for each question are given below the text. Select the best answer to complete the text. Then mark the letter (A), (B), (C), or (D) on your answer sheet.

Questions 131-134 refer to the following article.

SAN FRANCISCO DAILY

Ace Supermarket Is Expanding Into South America

Peter Smith

San Francisco - March 3) Ace Supermarket, the world's largest supermarket chain based in the U.S., is planning to get a ------- in the markets in South America. The headquarters
131.
of Ace Supermarket announced yesterday that five branch locations will come to Chile and Brazil, with the first two supermarkets scheduled to open on March 30 in Chile. -------.
132.
Basically, Ace Supermarket implements a unique ------- of management to open small
133.
supermarkets and provide its house brand products and local agriculture produces with affordable prices. "We are ------- to open our supermarkets in South America and
134.
introduce customers to our high quality products at lower costs," said the spokesperson of Ace Supermarket Benjamin Wilson.

131. (A) share
(B) foothold
(C) permission
(D) settlement

132. (A) The other three ones will open in Brazil by the end of next month.
(B) About one-fifth of our supermarkets will have energy efficient lighting this year.
(C) They have competed against traditional grocery chains throughout South America.
(D) Many of the stores are being built in overcrowded cities where land is scarce.

133. (A) event
(B) strategy
(C) regulation
(D) control

134. (A) eligible
(B) necessary
(C) capable
(D) eager

▶ ▶ ▶GO ON TO THE NEXT PAGE

May 30   Edinburgh College of Art & Design
Mr. Lewis Burton   74 Lauriston Place
184 Cheetham Hill Road   Edinburgh, EH3 9DF
Manchester, UK   eca@ed.ac.uk
M4 1PW   +44 (0)131 651 5800

Dear Mr. Burton,

Thank you for your inquiry regarding evening classes at the Edinburgh College of Art &

Design. I am contacting you with details of our classes, ------- the classes that we run
                                                        135.

every week on Tuesdays or Thursdays, as you requested.

First, there is our Beginner Oil Painting class, which provides instruction on basic

techniques and emphasizes the importance of color. Second, there is our Technical

Drawing class, which is designed for those interested in engineering and architecture.

Unfortunately, these are the only ------- classes that we currently run in the evenings.
                                   136.
-------, we do also offer various online classes for individuals who have particularly
   137.
busy schedules. Those who enroll in such courses are supplied with a list of necessary

materials that they should purchase in advance. -------.
                                             138.

Best regards,

Annabel Taylor
Manager of Student Services
Edinburgh College of Art & Design

---

135. (A) specify
(B) specific
(C) specified
(D) specifically

136. (A) midweek
(B) weekend
(C) monthly
(D) annual

137. (A) Indeed
(B) Nevertheless
(C) In spite of
(D) For example

138. (A) We appreciate your interest in employment opportunities at our institution.
(B) Further details for all the above listed options are available on our website.
(C) Your application for enrollment in the class is currently being processed.
(D) Please contact me should you wish to withdraw from any of these classes.

To: Scarlett Welsh <sw@cocomail.com>
From: Eleanor Fletcher <ef@sjfc.com>
Subject: Record Store Shows
Date: April 21

Dear Ms. Welsh,

It is my distinct pleasure to inform you about the upcoming shows that Stanley Jordan's

management is organizing for ------- fan club members.
139.

Mr. Jordan will play twenty-five concerts in Sound Factory Hall, and these shows will

provide an amazing opportunity for fans to joyfully ------- a Stanley Jordan performance in
140.

a small, intimate setting. -------, they will be able to meet with their favorite pop singer
141.

during an autograph session, which will immediately follow his performance. Copies of

Stanley Jordan's new record will be available for purchase, and fans can also have these

signed during the autograph session.

Tickets will be affordably priced and may be purchased online. The record store concerts

will take place between May 10 and May 15, and the exact tour schedule will be posted

on www.sjfc.com within the next few days. -------.
142.

Best wishes,

Eleanor Fletcher
Manager of Stanley Jordan Fan Club

139. (A) value
(B) valuing
(C) valuation
(D) valued

140. (A) interest
(B) present
(C) benefit
(D) experience

141. (A) Even though
(B) Afterward
(C) Instead
(D) In advance

142. (A) Thank you for your recent inquiry
about Stanley Jordan.
(B) You will receive your free tickets
within seven days.
(C) Don't miss this chance to see your
beloved artist up close.
(D) The first show will be held at the end
of the month.

▶ ▶ ▶GO ON TO THE NEXT PAGE

Cork is essentially a piece of bark from a cork oak known as Quercus suber. The cork tree grows naturally in a region ------- the western Mediterranean Sea. -------. But, so far, the
143. **144.**
results have not been encouraging. Although there is some historical evidence suggesting that cork was used as a stopper about 2,000 years ago, its use became more ------- with
145.
the introduction of glass bottles in the 17th century. In recent years, other alternatives such as plastic stoppers ------- as closures for wine bottles. However, cork still remains
146.
the principal closure of choice for premium wines.

144. (A) locating
(B) exploring
(C) bordering
(D) corresponding

145. (A) competitive
(B) authentic
(C) prevalent
(D) familiar

143. (A) Several efforts have been made to grow this species in other parts of the world.
(B) That means there are some trees that are adapted to the Mediterranean climate.
(C) The corking machine should be cleaned and maintained according to the manufacturer's directions.
(D) The region is producing some of the most remarkable grapes and wines in the world.

146. (A) introduce
(B) are introducing
(C) will be introduced
(D) have been introduced

PART 7

Directions: In this part you will read a selection of texts, such as magazine and newspaper articles, e-mails, and instant messages. Each text or set of texts is followed by several questions. Select the best answer for each question and mark the letter (A), (B), (C), or (D) on your answer sheet.

Questions 147-148 refer to the following information.

East Seattle Laundry
Nicest, Cleanest Launderette in Town!
Open 24 Hours

1. Place your laundry into one of the washing machines.

2. Put laundry detergent into the washing machine. Detergent is available from the vending machine by the front door.

3. Set the washing machine's controls. Generally, hot water is suitable for whites, and cold water for colors.

4. Insert the exact amount of coins required for each machine into the coin slot. Do not open the machine until the washing process is finished.

Call (206) 408-3180 with any problems.

---

147. What is the purpose of the information?

(A) To inform ways to purchase a washing machine
(B) To explain the procedure of using a facility
(C) To instruct how to request a repair service for equipment
(D) To advertise a laundry service

148. What would a customer have to do if hot water does not come out?

(A) Go to the front desk
(B) Add laundry to the washing machine
(C) Report to an employee on the phone
(D) Insert additional coins

Questions 149-150 refer to the following text message chain.

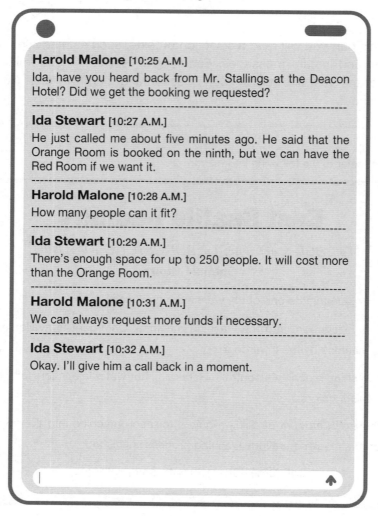

Harold Malone [10:25 A.M.]

Ida, have you heard back from Mr. Stallings at the Deacon Hotel? Did we get the booking we requested?

Ida Stewart [10:27 A.M.]

He just called me about five minutes ago. He said that the Orange Room is booked on the ninth, but we can have the Red Room if we want it.

Harold Malone [10:28 A.M.]

How many people can it fit?

Ida Stewart [10:29 A.M.]

There's enough space for up to 250 people. It will cost more than the Orange Room.

Harold Malone [10:31 A.M.]

We can always request more funds if necessary.

Ida Stewart [10:32 A.M.]

Okay. I'll give him a call back in a moment.

149. What is the text message chain mainly about?

(A) Preparations for an upcoming event
(B) The price to rent a room
(C) The need to book a hotel room
(D) Some changes in the date of an event

150. At 10:31 A.M., what does Mr. Malone most likely mean when he writes, "We can always request more funds if necessary"?

(A) He needs to submit a budget report.
(B) He should talk to his supervisor soon.
(C) He just requested more money for the budget.
(D) He is willing to reserve the Red Room.

THEATRICAL PIZZA

Business hours: 10:00 A.M. – 11:00 P.M.
Open 7 days a week

Small	Medium	Large	Giant
$12.95	$14.95	$18.95	$20.95

All prices are subject to change without notice.
Free delivery on orders of $20 or more.

Pizzas of the Month (Buy One & Get One Free!)

Vegetarian	Tomatoes, Mushrooms, Red Onions, Green Bell Peppers, Cilantro, Olives
Supreme	Pepperoni, Tomatoes, Mushrooms, Red Onions, Red & Green Bell Peppers, Olives
BBQ Chicken	Special BBQ Sauce, Chicken, Tomatoes, Mushrooms, Onions, Bell Peppers

Visit our website at www.theatricalpizza.com for a complete list of items on the menu.

ADDITIONAL TOPPINGS

Small	Medium	Large	Giant
$1.65	$2.25	$2.85	$3.55

Mushroom, Tomato, Bell Peppers, Cheddar Cheese, Shrimp, Ham, Pepperoni,
Chicken, Roasted Garlic, Onions, Olives, and Many More!

We offer catering services for all types of occasions.
Please call 555-329-0504 for pricing.

151. What ingredient is included in all pizzas of the month?

(A) Cilantro
(B) Tomatoes
(C) Chicken
(D) Olives

152. What information is provided in the advertisement?

(A) The prices of beverages
(B) Rates for catering services
(C) Topping choices
(D) The address of the shop

153. What is NOT indicated about Theatrical Pizza?

(A) It is open on Sundays.
(B) It delivers orders free of charge to some customers.
(C) It has a website.
(D) It recently opened a new branch.

▶ ▶ ▶ GO ON TO THE NEXT PAGE

Nathaniel Cooper Bed

Thank you for purchasing a Nathaniel Cooper bed from Nathaniel Furniture Ltd., the city's best furniture provider. We believe that this bed, which has won awards for its durability, will perfectly satisfy you. Please read the instructions below carefully before you start assembling the bed. —[1]—.

Assembly Instructions

Step 1. Install the headboard at its desired location.

Step 2. Attach a side rail to the headboard by matching the red dot on the side rail with the dot on the headboard. —[2]—.

Step 3. Attach the footboard to the side rails.

Step 4. Tighten the roll bolts securely to the headboard and the footboard. —[3]—.

Step 5. Drop in the slats and screw them in by using a screwdriver.

Step 6. Place the mattress on the frame. —[4]—.

Visit our website to see photographs depicting these steps. If you have any questions regarding our product, please call us at 1-555-932-3333, or send an e-mail to staff@ nathanielbed.com.

154. For whom is this information intended?

(A) Employees at a furniture delivery company
(B) Customer service representatives
(C) Furniture manufacturers
(D) Customers

155. What is indicated about the product?

(A) The bedrails can be used as handles.
(B) Extra items can be used to assemble the bed.
(C) It is designed for young children.
(D) The bed is recognized for its sturdy construction.

156. In which of the positions marked [1], [2], [3], and [4] does the following sentence best fit?

"Repeat the above procedure with the other side rail."

(A) [1]
(B) [2]
(C) [3]
(D) [4]

Caring Hands

24 Franklin Drive
Seaside, OR 97160
(503) 762-0847

April 10, 9:35 A.M.

Item	Qty.	Price	Amount
Pocketbook, *All About First Aid*	1	$2.80	$2.80
Bandage (2ea)	1	$2.00	$2.00
Antiseptic Ointment (25mg)	1	$4.70	$4.70
Painkiller Pills (10 tablets)	1	$4.00	$4.00
Total Item(s)	4		
Subtotal			$13.50
Frequent-Buyer Discount			- $2.00
Balance Due			$11.50
Credit Card			$11.50
*********5621			
Change			$0.00

Thank You!

157. What type of business most likely is Caring Hands?

(A) A hospital
(B) A pharmacy
(C) A bookstore
(D) A beauty salon

158. What is indicated about the customer?

(A) The customer works at a clinic.
(B) The customer purchased the items in the afternoon.
(C) The customer paid in cash.
(D) The customer often shops at Caring Hands.

ACTUAL TEST 05

To:	Jake Herald <jherald@chelsea.com>
From:	Lilian Mulvey <lmulvey@chelsea.com>
Date:	January 23
Subject:	Inquiry

Dear Mr. Herald,

On January 2, the copy machine in the Marketing Department broke down. So I submitted a request for a new copy machine to the Purchasing Department on January 8. You told me that it would be handled within a week, but it has now been two weeks since I submitted the proposal, and nothing has been done yet.

Our department is currently using the copy machine in the Human Resources Department. This has caused a serious delay in the preparations for a conference we are holding on January 30.

I hope this problem can be solved shortly. Please let me know if there is anything I can do.

Thanks,

Lilian Mulvey

159. What is the problem?

(A) An item has not been replaced.
(B) A conference has been delayed.
(C) Funds have not been provided.
(D) A replacement has not been hired.

160. Where does Mr. Herald work?

(A) In the Marketing Department
(B) In the Human Resources Department
(C) In the Purchasing Department
(D) In the Maintenance Department

161. When was the proposal for a new copy machine submitted?

(A) On January 2
(B) On January 8
(C) On January 23
(D) On January 30

Questions 162-164 refer to the following e-mail.

To: <jhbuskers@chmail.com>
From: <tmyers@ggmail.com>
Date: December 15
Subject: Congratulations!

Dear members of the Buskers,

I would like to congratulate you on your recent success with the concert at the Cruz Arena. I read on *St. Cruz City Herald* that you are the first musicians to hold a concert there within just three years of your first debut. I was especially impressed when I learned that you have donated a part of the proceeds to the children's hospital.

Both as an owner of a bar and a big fan of yours, I would like to invite you to perform at my bar. The majority of our customers are university students and in their mid-twenties, so I think you will be a good fit for my customers. My bar, Sailboat, is located at 46 Reindeer Dr., St. Cruz City and is open from 8 P.M. to 4 A.M. every day. The time of your performance and your payment are negotiable. Please get back to me if you are interested.

Thanks,

Tessa Myers

162. What is the main purpose of the e-mail?

(A) To address the achievements of a band
(B) To offer a job at a bar
(C) To inform about details of a concert
(D) To confirm a performance schedule

163. Who is Tessa Myers?

(A) A customer at a bar
(B) A band member
(C) A patient
(D) A music fan

164. What is indicated about the Buskers?

(A) It was formed 4 years ago.
(B) It recently recruited a new member.
(C) It was featured in a local publication.
(D) It held a concert at a hospital.

MC Steps Forward

By Samantha Provoost, Staff Writer

August 7 — The Brussels-based carmaker, Aqua Motors Corp. (AMC), will begin producing vehicles in China this week as the construction of its manufacturing factory in Beijing is finally completed.

"This is the first step of AMC's strategy to dominate the automotive industry and hold an edge over other competitors in China," explained CEO of AMC, Jean Bergmann. "We had decided to build the new facility to maintain stable sales of our vehicles in the Chinese market and promote future models."

AMC has been gaining popularity in China since the critically acclaimed compact car model, the Jaws, was put out on the market last year. "Demand for AMC cars, especially for the Jaws series, has risen sharply. I believe local customers are interested in the Jaws model because they are affordable, fuel efficient, and creatively designed," commented a local car dealer in Shanghai, Joe Wang.

The company is planning to release an upgraded version of the Jaws, the Jaws-2, in October. The new line of Jaws will feature a built-in navigation system, improved safety technology, and even better fuel efficiency. The newly built plant will be focusing mainly on manufacturing this model to meet the demand in China's major cities such as Chongqing and Tianjin. AMC is currently preparing to aggressively promote the model in China through TV commercials, starring popular Belgian celebrity, Mr. Filip Gilliams. The commercials will be broadcast once the Jaws-2 is released.

165. The word "edge" in paragraph 2, line 1, is closest in meaning to

(A) blade
(B) revenue
(C) advantage
(D) trend

166. According to Mr. Wang, what is NOT suggested about the Jaws model?

(A) It is reasonably priced.
(B) It consumes relatively less energy.
(C) Its sales are quite robust in China.
(D) It is currently being manufactured in China.

167. Where will the Jaws-2 be primarily produced?

(A) In Brussels
(B) In Shanghai
(C) In Tianjin
(D) In Beijing

Rosemary Waters   **2:42 P.M.**

Hello, Sylvia. How is your training program going?

Sylvia Smith   **2:43 P.M.**

It's really educational. I'm learning a lot here, and the information should be a big help when I start my official duties next week.

Rosemary Waters   **2:44 P.M.**

I'm glad to hear that. I'm sure that you'll fit in really well here.

Sylvia Smith   **2:45 P.M.**

I'm pleased that you're confident in me.

Trent Sutter   **2:47 P.M.**

Sylvia, when you get here next Monday, please drop by my office at 10:00 in the morning. I have an assignment for you.

Sylvia Smith   **2:48 P.M.**

I'd love to, but I'm supposed to meet Patsy Roth in HR from 9:00 to noon. Can we meet after lunch?

Trent Sutter   **2:49 P.M.**

I'm going to be out of the office starting at noon, and I won't be back until Friday. How do you feel about me e-mailing you an assignment?

Sylvia Smith   **2:51 P.M.**

That works for me. But I don't have a work e-mail account yet.

Rosemary Waters   **2:53 P.M.**

I'll get someone in IT to set that up for you right now. I'll text you the login and the password within an hour.

Sylvia Smith   **2:54 P.M.**

Thank you so much. I'll let you know my new e-mail address as soon as I get it, Trent. And then we can get to work.

SEND

168. Who most likely is Ms. Smith?

    (A) A manager
    (B) A trainee
    (C) A customer
    (D) An executive

169. What problem does Ms. Smith have?

    (A) She cannot meet at a proposed time.
    (B) She does not have enough experience.
    (C) She is unable to go on a business trip.
    (D) She has not completed some forms.

170. What does Ms. Waters offer to do for Ms. Smith?

    (A) Arrange for a new computer
    (B) Order her a new desk
    (C) Set up an online account
    (D) Assist her with a project

171. At 2:51 P.M., why does Ms. Smith write, "That works for me"?

    (A) To complain about a new assignment
    (B) To offer to work overtime
    (C) To indicate how busy she is
    (D) To agree with Mr. Sutter's idea

Come Feel the African Soul!

Brookline, April 22— The sound of Africa comes to Brookline, where many music festivals have been held in previous years. A marvelous outdoor African music festival, the African Soul Festival, will be held at Brookline Square on May 30 and 31. —[1]—. Hundreds of African music fans as well as local residents are expected to attend it.

Hosted by the Recreation Department of Brookline, the African Soul Festival has many notable features. One is the diversity of the music. —[2]—. There will be many different kinds of African music performed, including tunes from Eastern, Central, and Southern Africa.

Many renowned African musicians will fly to Brookline to perform in the African Soul Festival. Papa Kelle, the winner of the 4th African Musicians Contest, will perform on the opening day. —[3]—. Popular in their countries but not yet world renowned artists, such as Alan GaM'olla, Daddy Solomon, and Simba Omonga, will also perform in the festival.

On the first day of the event, samples of traditional African foods and drinks will be served for free near the entrance in the evening.

Tickets can be purchased at the box office near the entrance to Brookline Square on the days of the festival. —[4]—. Tickets are also available at reduced prices until May 20 at www.brooklinetickets.com.

172. What is the topic of the article?

(A) Free performances for residents
(B) A trip to Africa
(C) The history of African music
(D) An outdoor event

173. What is mentioned about tickets?

(A) They will be discounted for a limited time.
(B) They are not available onsite.
(C) They will be given to local residents for free.
(D) They can be reserved by calling the Recreation Department.

174. When will free food be served?

(A) On April 22
(B) On May 20
(C) On May 30
(D) On May 31

175. In which of the positions marked [1], [2], [3], and [4] does the following sentence best fit?

"On the second day, Moulin Noir, a Ska music band now famous after appearing on TV, will participate."

(A) [1]
(B) [2]
(C) [3]
(D) [4]

Questions 176-180 refer to the following flyer and website.

CALL THE CUE

Seymour Park, London
October 1-5

The International Theatre Society (ITS) once again returns with its 5th Call the Cue! Join our annual week-long festival filled with vibrant performances from both major and independent productions, including the Claymore College of Performing Arts (CCPA).

Main Stage Showcases include:

Day 1 James Garza & Roxanne Swanson performing *Man with the Tiger*

Day 2 Anne-Sophie Wynter performing a series of monologues; Royal Theatre Company performing *Merchant's City*

Day 3 Curtain Call Company performing *Fountain of Color*; Elaine Edina's one-man show

Day 4 Prize-winning scripts from this year's ITS Short Play Competition including Russell Chan's *Yellow Umbrella*

Day 5 JMS Production & the Rhodes Actors Association performing *Dragonia*; Roderick Doherty performing *The Solitary Tree*

And many more! For the complete list of performances on each day, visit our website at www.its.org/callthecue.

A special discount offer is extended to those attending the CCPA. Enter the promotion code CCASTD upon checkout. Proof of enrollment will be requested upon entry.

International Theatre Society
1 Pattison Street, London
0844 555 0787

TICKET BOOK

www.ticketbook.com/theatre/its-call-the-cue/payment

Welcome! Chris Fyfe | My Account

HOME	CONCERTS	THEATRE	EXHIBITS	SPORTS

QUICK SEARCH

TODAY'S DEALS
THIS WEEK
THIS MONTH

MY PAGE
RESERVATIONS
BOOKMARKS
MY POINTS

Ticket Type	Single Day Admission
Select Date	October 3
Delivery Method	On-site collection
Promotion Code	CCASTD

Ticket	$30
Delivery Fee	$0
Discount	-$5
Total	$25

Payment Method	Credit Card
	XXXX-XXXX-XXXX-0333

---

176. What type of event most likely is Call the Cue?

(A) Art exhibitions
(B) A sequence of animal shows
(C) A series of plays
(D) School festivals

177. Who will perform *The Solitary Tree*?

(A) Ms. Swanson
(B) Mr. Garza
(C) Ms. Wynter
(D) Mr. Doherty

178. In the flyer, the word "extended" in paragraph 4, line 1 is closest in meaning to

(A) postponed
(B) created
(C) offered
(D) enlarged

179. What is NOT indicated about the International Theatre Society?

(A) It has arranged festivals before.
(B) It is based in London.
(C) It was established about 5 years ago.
(D) It hosts a short play competition.

180. What is suggested about Mr. Fyfe?

(A) He purchased a ticket for someone else.
(B) He has a membership at ITS.
(C) He is a student at an art school.
(D) He will perform a short play.

Valpoa Cave Tours

Welcome to Valpoa Cave, the amazing masterpiece created by nature. Located in a national park in the province of Laguna, the Philippines, this cave, thousands of years old, is one of the largest tourist attractions in the nation. Choose one of the following tours and witness the magnificence of nature that will take your breath away! In each tour, you can learn about the history, geography, and culture of the region with the help of our guides, who are certified by the National Tourist Association (NTA).

Regular Tour
Includes comfortable rides to the cave in an SUV. 450 pesos per adult and 300 pesos per child (ages 4-11), and children under the age of 4 are admitted for free.

Prime Time Tour
Departs at the time of the day when the most sunlight enters the cave. Adults 550 pesos and children (ages 4-11) 380 pesos, and children under the age of 4 are admitted for free.

Photography Tour
Take your own pictures of beautiful Valpoa Cave. For both amateur and professional photographers alike. Experts are there to help you with camera settings and angles. You can bring a tripod with you. Adults 650 pesos and children (ages 4-11) 470 pesos, and children under the age of 4 are admitted for free.

Open 365 days a year. For reservations and detailed information, visit www.valpoacave.com. For any questions, please send an e-mail to customerservice@valpoa.com or call 632-555-9270.

To:	Valpoa Cave Tours <customerservice@valpoa.com>
From:	Kurt Toka <ktoka@polemail.com>
Date:	July 5
Subject:	About my last tour

To whom it may concern,

Last month, I visited Valpoa Cave with my wife. We enjoyed the beauty of the cave very much. However, the place was too crowded, and I had difficulty taking pictures of the cave, as there was not enough space to set up my tripod. I told David Neeson, our tour guide, about this inconvenience, and he acknowledged the problem. He promised to arrange a partial refund and a set of Valpoa Cave postcards to be delivered to my house within a week as compensation. I have received the partial payment, 200 pesos, which is reasonable because I did enjoy the cave. However, it has been more than 2 weeks, and I have not received the postcards yet.

If you have not yet mailed the postcards to me, could you please include a brochure in the parcel? I noticed a discount coupon on your advertisement and would like to visit Valpoa Cave again in the near future.

Thank you,

Kurt Toka

181. What is indicated about the tours at Valpoa Cave?

(A) They require visitors to drive their own SUVs.
(B) They depart every hour.
(C) They are available year round.
(D) They charge the same fee regardless of age.

182. How can a customer book a tour?

(A) By talking to a guide
(B) By writing an e-mail
(C) By visiting a website
(D) By calling a phone number

183. What is the purpose of the e-mail?

(A) To complain about a tour guide
(B) To inform a person of an item that has not been delivered
(C) To request a complete schedule of tours
(D) To ask about the location of a cave

184. How much did Mr. Toka originally pay for his visit in June?

(A) 200 pesos
(B) 450 pesos
(C) 470 pesos
(D) 650 pesos

185. What is suggested about Mr. Neeson?

(A) He will lead another tour for Mr. Toka.
(B) He will send postcards to Mr. Toka.
(C) He is licensed by an organization.
(D) He brought his own tripod to Valpoa Cave.

Rudolf Toys

Rudolf Toys is pleased to announce that the annual employee training courses will take place next week. These are held to improve the efficiency and knowledge of the staff. The following is the course schedule:

Project Planning

Setsuko Asada, Marketing Department Director		
Tuesday, June 10	9:00 A.M. – 10:30 A.M.	Room 501

Engineering   *All Engineering Department members must attend.

Orlando Ibrahimovic, Senior Engineering Manager		
Tuesday, June 10	1:00 P.M. – 3:00 P.M.	Room 502

Communication Skills

Anna Dvorkin, Accounting Department Assistant Manager		
Thursday, June 12	1:00 P.M. – 2:30 P.M.	Room 401

Safety Regulations and Equipment Use

Kimberley Jade, Plant Manager		
Thursday, June 12	3:00 P.M. – 6:00 P.M.	Room 603

Following the latter session on June 12, dinner will be served to the attendees. Please arrive 5 minutes prior to the beginning of each session to be seated. No food or drinks are allowed. Any comments, suggestions, or questions should be submitted to the Human Resources Department.

To:	Remy Yves <ryves@rudolftoys.com>
From:	Setsuko Asada <sasada@rudolftoys.com>
Date:	June 3
Subject:	Training Courses

Dear Mr. Yves,

I am writing with regard to the upcoming training courses. I was supposed to lead a session, but I will be unable to do so due to an urgent business trip I must go on. Fortunately, the assistant director in my department, Linda Sommers, is available on the day of my session. She will handle the training course in my place.

Please correct the posts with the schedule at your earliest convenience to prevent any confusion. I am sorry for the inconvenience this may cause. While on my trip, I will be available by e-mail or phone at (135)-555-6432.

Sincerely,

Setsuko Asada
Director, Marketing Department

To:	Remy Yves <ryves@rudolftoys.com>
From:	Anna Dvorkin <annad@rudolftoys.com>
Date:	June 13
Subject:	Thank You

Mr. Yves,

Thank you so much for allowing me to switch course times with Kimberley. I regret only giving you one day's notice, so I am truly appreciative that you were able to make the change.

In addition, this was my first time to lead a training course here. I thoroughly enjoyed the process and hope to have the opportunity to do it again in the future. If you need more assistance from me at a later time, please feel free to ask.

Thank you.

Anna Dvorkin

186. What is indicated about Rudolf Toys in the schedule?

(A) It requires training course attendees to sign up in advance.
(B) It is currently recruiting new employees.
(C) It plans to hold a regular event soon.
(D) It evaluates the performances of its employees annually.

187. What is mentioned about the training course led by Mr. Ibrahimovic?

(A) It requires certain people to participate.
(B) It will last for 3 hours.
(C) It will have refreshments for attendees.
(D) It is intended for new staff members.

188. After which session will a complimentary meal be given?

(A) Project Planning
(B) Engineering
(C) Communication Skills
(D) Safety Regulations and Equipment Use

189. What can be inferred about Mr. Yves?

(A) He will lead a training session.
(B) He is planning to go on a business trip.
(C) He will contact Ms. Asada soon.
(D) He works in the Human Resources Department.

190. When did Ms. Dvorkin lead a training course?

(A) On Tuesday at 9:00 A.M.
(B) On Tuesday at 1:00 P.M.
(C) On Thursday at 1:00 P.M.
(D) On Thursday at 3:00 P.M.

Scarlatium
Make Your Special Day Extraordinary

Choose the city's favorite place, Scarlatium, to hold special occasions. We have been nominated as the finest service provider in Washington, D.C. in the event management field for the past five consecutive years.

•Banquet Hall

This option includes a ballroom lit by chandeliers, which creates an elegant look. It seats 200 guests comfortably at tables of 10 and includes a stage for speeches.

•Rose Garden

Hold your event under the sun in the elegant gazebo. The bench setting with no meals accommodates 300 guests and the banquet arrangement 150 guests. Please note that events may be relocated to vacant ballrooms depending on weather conditions.

•Chapel

High arches and large stained-glass windows provide a divine space for your day. This room is only available for ceremonies as food is not served there. Guests can be served meals in another hall upon request.

•Photography

Hamilton's, a local photography studio, will capture the days' special moments. This service is provided free of charge except during the peak season from March to May.

---

www.scarlatium.com/testimonials

Scarlatium *Make Your Special Day Extraordinary*

HOME	CONSULTING	RESERVATION	TESTIMONIALS

Perfection

- by Nathalie White, posted June 13

Holding my wedding at Scarlatium was a decision I do not regret. The day was flawless, and I have my event coordinator, Evelyn George, to thank for it. Evelyn was invaluable in organizing every detail of the event. I was very stressed out in the morning because I was informed that the audio system was malfunctioning in the room I had booked. I became even more nervous upon hearing that every other ballroom was booked. Then, Evelyn arranged for the event to be held in the garden. She also refunded the money I paid for photographs as an apology. The food served by Scarlatium was beyond my expectations, too. I could not have asked for more.

To:	Jacob Thomas <jthomas@hamiltons.com>
From:	Evelyn George <egeorge@scarlatium.com>
Date:	June 14
Subject:	Re: Payment

Mr. Thomas,

I just read the e-mail you sent me. Please do not be worried as you will receive the payment for the services you rendered for Ms. White at her wedding. While we refunded her money, we still intend to pay you. Once we receive an invoice from you, the payment will be deposited into your account within three business days. Please let me know if you have any other concerns.

Regards,

Evelyn George
Scarlatium

191. In the advertisement, the word "occasions" in paragraph 1, line 1, is closest in meaning to

(A) cases
(B) events
(C) breaks
(D) dates

192. What is mentioned about Scarlatium?

(A) It was founded five years ago.
(B) It only accommodates wedding ceremonies.
(C) It has a space with ornate windows.
(D) It can host a maximum of 300 guests at a time.

193. Why did Ms. White make a post on the web page?

(A) To request a refund
(B) To make a suggestion
(C) To file a complaint
(D) To praise a service

194. What can be inferred about Ms. White?

(A) She requested a refund from Scarlatium.
(B) She initially planned to hold her event outside.
(C) She held her event during Scarlatium's peak season.
(D) She used an external catering service.

195. Who most likely is Mr. Thomas?

(A) A photographer
(B) An employee at Scarlatium
(C) A wedding guest
(D) A Scarlatium customer

▶▶▶GO ON TO THE NEXT PAGE

ORIENTAL STAR HOTEL

Located in the heart of Bangkok, the Oriental Star Hotel has been hosting guests for the last sixty years. The hotel was recently renovated. Free wireless Internet is now available in the entire hotel. Here are the features of the newly refurbished rooms:

Standard	twin bed, hair dryer, and air conditioning
Deluxe	2 twin beds, hair dryer, refrigerator, and air conditioning
Suite	2 twin beds, living room, 2 bathrooms with bathtubs, hair dryer, refrigerator, state-of-the-art audio system, high-definition television, and air conditioning
Executive Suite	2 bedrooms, living room, 2 bathrooms with bathtubs, hair dryer, 2 refrigerators, audio system, 2 high-definition televisions, air conditioning, and complimentary breakfast

The Oriental Star Hotel's restaurant, Blue Plates, serves food prepared by internationally renowned award-winning master chef Isra Ta. Ms. Ta has 15 years of experience in cooking the traditional foods of Thailand, Korea, Japan, and Italy.

To learn more about the Oriental Star Hotel, please visit us at www.orientalstarhotel.com. Given the large number of visitors during the peak season, we recommend booking a room two months in advance.

To:	Customer Service <customerservice@orientalstarhotel.com>
From:	Anurak Horvejkul <ahorvejkul@pmtextiles.com>
Date:	November 20
Subject:	Wonderful experience

To whom it may concern,

I am writing to thank you for a wonderful experience at your establishment. I arranged for my client, Tahan Santisakul, to stay at your hotel last week when he visited Bangkok for business. Mr. Santisakul said he was satisfied with the overall service you provided for him. He especially appreciated the free breakfast he enjoyed each morning.

In addition, both Mr. Santisakul and I enjoyed the cuisine at Blue Plates. On November 16, we both ordered the grilled salmon. The head chef herself served us. It was a pleasant experience to speak with someone whom I had seen on TV before. I look forward to doing business with you again in the future.

Sincerely,

Anurak Horvejkul
Account Manager
PM Textiles, Inc.

To: <reservations@orientalstarhotel.com>

From: <tahans@promenadecarpets.com>

Date: December 1

Subject: Booking

Dear Sir/Madam,

My name is Tahan Santisakul, and I would like to make a reservation at your hotel. I stayed there last month and thoroughly enjoyed it. I will be in Bangkok from December 6 to 12. I hope to have the same type of room that I stayed in the last time.

I realize that I should have made this reservation a couple of months ago, but I still hope that you can accommodate my request. Please let me know if you have any available rooms.

Regards,

Tahan Santisakul

196. What is indicated about the Oriental Star Hotel in the advertisement?

(A) It was closed for a certain period of time.
(B) It is the biggest hotel in Bangkok.
(C) It is located near several tourist attractions.
(D) It has been in business for decades.

197. What is available in a deluxe room?

(A) A high-quality TV
(B) A refrigerator
(C) A living room
(D) A bathtub

198. What is NOT suggested about Ms. Ta?

(A) She has worked at the Oriental Star Hotel for 15 years.
(B) She has won awards for her cooking.
(C) She cooks various styles of dishes.
(D) She is known to people in other countries.

199. What can be inferred about Mr. Santisakul?

(A) He is Mr. Horvejkul's coworker.
(B) He has visited Bangkok many times.
(C) He stayed in an executive suite.
(D) He recently read a magazine about culinary arts.

200. What is indicated about Mr. Santisakul?

(A) He will stay in Bangkok the entire month of December.
(B) He will meet with Mr. Horvejkul daily.
(C) He wants to stay in a different room on his next trip.
(D) He plans to visit Bangkok during the peak season.

STOP! This is the end of the test. If you finish before time is called, you may go back to Parts 5, 6, and 7 and check your work.

Actual Test 06

MP3   해설집

적정 풀이 시간 120분

120 min

시작 시간 ___시 ___분

종료 시간 ___시 ___분

중간에 멈추지 말고 처음부터 끝까지 풀어보세요.
문제를 풀 때에는 실전처럼 답안지에 마킹하세요.

목표 개수 _____ / 200   실제 개수 _____ / 200

예상 점수는 번역 및 정답에 있는 점수 환산표를 참조하세요.

LISTENING TEST

In the Listening test, you will be asked to demonstrate how well you understand spoken English. The entire Listening test will last approximately 45 minutes. There are four parts, and directions are given for each part. You must mark your answers on the separate answer sheet. Do not write your answers in the test book.

PART 1

Directions: For each question in this part, you will hear four statements about a picture in your test book. When you hear the statements, you must select the one statement that best describes what you see in the picture. Then find the number of the question on your answer sheet and mark your answer. The statements will not be printed in your test book and will be spoken only one time.

Statement (B), "They are sitting at a table." is the best description of the picture. So you should select answer (B) and mark it on your answer sheet.

1.

2.

▶ ▶ ▶ **GO ON TO THE NEXT PAGE**

3.

4.

5.

6.

▶ ▶ ▶GO ON TO THE NEXT PAGE

7. Mark your answer on your answer sheet.

8. Mark your answer on your answer sheet.

9. Mark your answer on your answer sheet.

10. Mark your answer on your answer sheet.

11. Mark your answer on your answer sheet.

12. Mark your answer on your answer sheet.

13. Mark your answer on your answer sheet.

14. Mark your answer on your answer sheet.

15. Mark your answer on your answer sheet.

16. Mark your answer on your answer sheet.

17. Mark your answer on your answer sheet.

18. Mark your answer on your answer sheet.

19. Mark your answer on your answer sheet.

20. Mark your answer on your answer sheet.

21. Mark your answer on your answer sheet.

22. Mark your answer on your answer sheet.

23. Mark your answer on your answer sheet.

24. Mark your answer on your answer sheet.

25. Mark your answer on your answer sheet.

26. Mark your answer on your answer sheet.

27. Mark your answer on your answer sheet.

28. Mark your answer on your answer sheet.

29. Mark your answer on your answer sheet.

30. Mark your answer on your answer sheet.

31. Mark your answer on your answer sheet.

PART 3

Directions: You will hear some conversations between two or three people. You will be asked to answer three questions about what the speakers say in each conversation. Select the best response to each question and mark the letter (A), (B), (C), or (D) on your answer sheet. The conversations will not be printed in your test book and will be spoken only one time.

32. What did the woman do yesterday?

(A) She conducted an interview.
(B) She gave a presentation.
(C) She recruited a new employee.
(D) She updated a website.

33. What industry do the speakers work in?

(A) Clothing
(B) Electronics
(C) Engineering
(D) Catering service

34. What will the company do next Monday?

(A) Have a meeting with clients
(B) Replace some devices
(C) Negotiate a takeover
(D) Test a new product

35. What does the man ask the woman to do at an event?

(A) Introduce some speakers
(B) Make a list of attendees
(C) Arrange a venue
(D) Sell tickets

36. What kind of event is being planned?

(A) A charity auction
(B) A training session
(C) A fundraiser
(D) A product demonstration

37. What does the man say he needs to do?

(A) Create some invitations
(B) Contact the guest speakers
(C) Hire a caterer
(D) Pay a deposit

38. Where do the speakers work?

(A) At an amusement park
(B) At a bank
(C) At a zoo
(D) At a museum

39. According to the man, what will happen on Tuesday?

(A) A person will start working.
(B) A group will visit a building.
(C) A new program will begin.
(D) An exhibit will be launched.

40. What does the man say the woman should do?

(A) Provide some badges
(B) Collect some tickets
(C) Restock some more brochures
(D) Print some tour schedules

41. What product are the speakers talking about?

(A) A running shoe
(B) A sports beverage
(C) A skateboard
(D) A bicycle

42. Why is the man concerned?

(A) A flight has been cancelled.
(B) A factory is located far away.
(C) A workload is too great.
(D) A project is not on schedule.

43. What does the woman suggest doing?

(A) Purchasing a fuel-efficient vehicle
(B) Relocating a factory
(C) Changing a production timeline
(D) Finding a local inspector

▶ ▶ ▶GO ON TO THE NEXT PAGE

44. Who is the man?

(A) A recruiter
(B) A trainer
(C) An interviewer
(D) A car dealer

45. Why did the woman take a new job?

(A) To be closer to her family
(B) To make a bigger salary
(C) To take a course at a local university
(D) To acquire some new skills

46. What will the woman most likely do next?

(A) Get hands-on experience
(B) Review a manual
(C) Fill out the paperwork
(D) Give a demonstration

47. What is the problem with the elevator?

(A) It is down for maintenance.
(B) It is being cleaned up.
(C) It is not big enough.
(D) It is being repaired.

48. What does Emily offer to do?

(A) Carry some bags
(B) Park a vehicle
(C) Drive the man to the airport
(D) Provide a discount to the man

49. What does the man hope to do tomorrow?

(A) Rent a vehicle
(B) Sell some books
(C) Shop at a bookstore
(D) Reserve a booth for a book fair

50. Who most likely is the woman?

(A) A government inspector
(B) A bus driver
(C) A tour guide
(D) A travel agent

51. What does the man want the woman to do?

(A) Look over some documents
(B) Take a park tour
(C) Give out some surveys
(D) Send him an e-mail

52. What does the woman say she has?

(A) A map of the park
(B) Some nametags
(C) Some visitor passes
(D) A e-mail list

53. What is the conversation mainly about?

(A) A leaking pipe
(B) A broken lock
(C) A missing item
(D) An electrical problem

54. What does the woman mean when she says, "The maintenance team is working on some pipes this morning"?

(A) The man needs to call somebody else.
(B) Some repair work will be expensive.
(C) Some work cannot be done immediately.
(D) The team members are busy all day long.

55. What does the man say he will do in the afternoon?

(A) Visit a warehouse
(B) Meet with a client
(C) Attend a company outing
(D) Prepare some documents

56. What does the woman suggest the company do?

(A) Change the hours of operation
(B) Provide gym memberships
(C) Offer better benefits
(D) Open an in-house health center

57. What does the man imply when he says, "We have lots of employees here"?

(A) The company will add more offices soon.
(B) A suggestion will be too costly.
(C) Some employees will be transferred.
(D) Many of the employees should work from home.

58. What does the man say he will do?

(A) Put off a staff meeting
(B) Review a budget report
(C) Do some research on his own
(D) Add a topic to an agenda

---

59. What does the woman want to purchase?

(A) Postcards
(B) Photo frames
(C) Hanging flowers
(D) Key rings

60. What does Peter say about the engraving service?

(A) It would require additional time.
(B) It isn't currently in stock.
(C) It was featured in a magazine this year.
(D) It is an award-winning service.

61. What does Jason say is available for free?

(A) Engraving service
(B) Delivery
(C) Maintenance
(D) An extended warranty

Jeff's Schedule
Thursday, Nov. 5

9:00 A.M. – 10:00 A.M.	Conference Call with Tudor Pharmaceuticals
10:30 A.M. – 12:00 P.M.	Product Demonstration with Edward Wright
1:00 P.M. – 2:30 P.M.	Contract Negotiation with Stuart Duncan
5:00 P.M. – 6:00 P.M.	Presentation at the Harper Convention Center

62. What is the woman organizing?

(A) A product demonstration
(B) A conference
(C) A charity auction
(D) An orientation event

63. What does the woman ask the man to do?

(A) Fill in for a colleague
(B) Organize a reception
(C) Go on a business trip
(D) Meet with a customer

64. Look at the graphic. Which activity will the man reschedule?

(A) The conference call
(B) The product demonstration
(C) The contract negotiation
(D) The presentation

Last Week's Sales by Team Three

| 30% Eric |
| 25% Tom |
| 20% Steve |
| 15% Peter |
| 10% Robert |

File name	Size
Kingswood.mov	15MB
Bernstein.mov	30MB
Perez.mov	40MB
LIttlebrook.mov	25MB

65. According to the woman, what will happen next week?

(A) A work schedule will change.
(B) A new worker will be transferred.
(C) A sales promotion will take place.
(D) An employee will stop working.

66. Where do the speakers most likely work?

(A) At an appliance store
(B) At a clothing shop
(C) At an outdoor market
(D) At a tool manufacturer

67. Look at the graphic. What is the man's name?

(A) Eric
(B) Tom
(C) Steve
(D) Peter

68. What kind of business do the speakers work in?

(A) Marketing
(B) Advertising
(C) Manufacturing
(D) Software

69. Look at the graphic. Which file did the man try to e-mail?

(A) Kingswood.mov
(B) Bernstein.mov
(C) Perez.mov
(D) LIttlebrook.mov

70. What does the woman suggest the man do?

(A) Attempt to e-mail a file again
(B) Wait for a manager to come back
(C) Speak with an IT specialist
(D) Have his computer repaired

PART 4

Directions: You will hear some short talks given by a single speaker. You will be asked to answer three questions about what the speaker says in each short talk. Select the best response to each question and mark the letter (A), (B), (C), or (D) on your answer sheet. The talks will not be printed in your test book and will be spoken only one time.

71. Who most likely is the listener?

(A) A government official
(B) A shopkeeper
(C) An apartment supervisor
(D) A delivery person

72. What information does the speaker inquire about?

(A) An apartment address
(B) A place for recycling items
(C) A pickup day
(D) A service fee amount

73. What does the speaker ask the listener to do?

(A) E-mail some information
(B) Return a telephone call
(C) Check some policies for tenants
(D) Call Maintenance

74. What does the speaker discuss?

(A) Changing rules
(B) Ordering supplies
(C) Cleaning the office
(D) Getting another supplier

75. What does the speaker request that the listeners do?

(A) Submit their timesheets
(B) Stay late at work this evening
(C) Complete a form accurately
(D) Share ideas for workplace efficiency

76. What does the speaker say is in Sharon's office?

(A) An employee directory
(B) A product catalog
(C) A user's manual
(D) A visitor's pass

77. What product is being discussed?

(A) Pizza
(B) Bread
(C) Coffee
(D) Cake

78. What did Justin Groceries recently do?

(A) It canceled an order.
(B) It changed its operating hours.
(C) It released a new line of pizza.
(D) It increased an order.

79. What does the speaker mean when she says, "I need to hear your thoughts"?

(A) More funding will be needed to meet the demand.
(B) Meetings will be held biweekly.
(C) Some production lines are not working properly.
(D) Some information is needed to make a decision.

80. Where does the speaker work?

(A) At a restaurant
(B) At a hospital
(C) At an airport
(D) At a theater

81. What does the speaker imply when he says, "We have a good team working on it now"?

(A) A replacement part will arrive shortly.
(B) A problem will be solved soon.
(C) All of the workers are too busy.
(D) More training is not necessary.

82. What does the speaker say he will do next?

(A) Offer everyone a refund
(B) Change the gate number
(C) Answer anyone's questions
(D) Provide an update soon

▶ ▶ ▶ GO ON TO THE NEXT PAGE

83. What are the listeners most likely experts in?

(A) Design
(B) Tourism
(C) Marketing
(D) Computers

84. What does the speaker suggest doing?

(A) Focusing on specific individuals
(B) Releasing a new line of running shoes
(C) Improving the quality of an item
(D) Hiring more marketing consultants

85. What will happen on Friday?

(A) An advertisement will be recorded.
(B) A specific group will be surveyed.
(C) A career fair will be held.
(D) A strategy will be discussed.

---

86. According to the broadcast, what is the sponsor looking for?

(A) Cooking contestants
(B) Celebrity chefs
(C) Product testers
(D) TV announcers

87. What kind of products does the sponsor manufacture?

(A) Computer games
(B) Kitchen appliances
(C) Gardening supplies
(D) Sporting goods

88. What should the listeners interested in participating do?

(A) Visit a store
(B) Mail in a survey
(C) Send a recipe
(D) Make a phone call

89. Who most likely are the listeners?

(A) College students
(B) Writers
(C) Publishers
(D) Business owners

90. Why does the speaker say, "He owns a chain of stores all across the country"?

(A) To put an emphasis on a speaker's qualification
(B) To thank a colleague for his dedication
(C) To encourage the listeners to do their best
(D) To suggest a topic for an agenda

91. What will the listeners get at the end of the day?

(A) A book of coupons
(B) An autographed poster
(C) A signed book
(D) A free subscription

---

92. What will happen next week?

(A) A grand opening
(B) A going-away party
(C) A sale
(D) A road closure

93. What does the speaker want the listeners to do?

(A) Arrive at work on time
(B) Park in a pay lot
(C) Use public transportation
(D) Check a store directory

94. What does the speaker tell the listeners to do by the end of the week?

(A) Put up sale posters
(B) Complete a training course
(C) Confirm their working hours
(D) Read a document

Weather Forecast

Sunday	Monday	Tuesday	Wednesday	Thursday
Rain	Cloudy	Rain	Sunny	Sunny

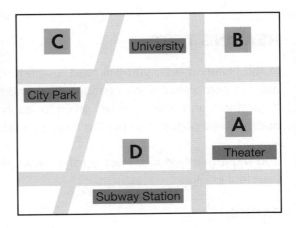

95. What event is the speaker calling about?

(A) A concert
(B) A sporting event
(C) An interview
(D) A conference

96. Look at the graphic. When will the event take place?

(A) On Monday
(B) On Tuesday
(C) On Wednesday
(D) On Thursday

97. What is the listener asked to do?

(A) Send an announcement
(B) Post an advertisement
(C) Sell some tickets
(D) Change a venue for concert

98. What type of business is the speaker discussing?

(A) A retail store
(B) A restaurant
(C) A hardware store
(D) A theater

99. Look at the graphic. Which location does the speaker recommend?

(A) Location A
(B) Location B
(C) Location C
(D) Location D

100. What does the speaker say he will do next?

(A) Show some pictures
(B) Hand out some brochures
(C) Talk about finances
(D) Answer questions

This is the end of the Listening test. Turn to Part 5 in your test book.

▶ ▶ ▶ **GO ON TO THE NEXT PAGE**

READING TEST

In the Reading test, you will read a variety of texts and answer several different types of reading comprehension questions. The entire Reading test will last 75 minutes. There are three parts, and directions are given for each part. You are encouraged to answer as many questions as possible within the time allowed.

You must mark your answer on the separate answer sheet. Do not write your answers in your test book.

PART 5

Directions: A word or phrase is missing in each of the sentences below. Four answer choices are given below each sentence. Select the best answer to complete the sentence. Then mark the letter (A), (B), (C), or (D) on your answer sheet.

101. Sociologists can help ------- to become aware of the barriers that prevent a social problem from being solved.

(A) we
(B) us
(C) our
(D) ourselves

102. During musical shows, there is ------- basic lighting, but also laser beam projectors or fog machines to maximize visual effects.

(A) even
(B) such
(C) just
(D) not only

103. Mr. Harrison pursued the dream ------- owning a business and learned about everything from business insurance to corporate accounting.

(A) on
(B) of
(C) to
(D) with

104. Boutique Coco is one of the popular clothing brands in Europe which creates the ------- trends in women's fashion.

(A) late
(B) latest
(C) lately
(D) lateness

105. The city council has recently made a law ------- all multinational companies to renew their business license every year.

(A) require
(B) requiring
(C) required
(D) requires

106. ------- to the city from all countries remains strictly controlled to help prevent the spread of the harmful virus in the initial stages.

(A) Enter
(B) Entrance
(C) Entry
(D) Entered

107. Some newspapers say that our new chief executive officer is ------- a leader who changes his management style and his business policies.

(A) much
(B) seldom
(C) almost
(D) enough

108. A variety of methods were ------- to get the word out to potential audiences and to increase ticket sales.

(A) use
(B) using
(C) used
(D) usage

109. It is important to distribute a meeting agenda ------- in advance to allow time for the attendees to do necessary thinking of planning.

(A) well
(B) good
(C) best
(D) soon

110. Delta Securities has outlined its management improvement plan to seek a big synergy effect by ------- Sydney Investment with its own banking subsidiary.

(A) consolidation
(B) consolidate
(C) consolidating
(D) console

111. With his extensive hands-on experience, the personnel manager thinks Mr. Collins is a welcome ------- to the sales team.

(A) nominee
(B) article
(C) realty
(D) addition

112. Due to the ------- cost of renting office space in the business district, an increasing number of companies want to move into the outskirts of the city.

(A) rise
(B) rising
(C) rose
(D) risen

113. The installments of new traffic signals on Devonshire Street has been only ------- successful in lowering traffic congestion.

(A) evenly
(B) permanently
(C) specifically
(D) moderately

114. Thanks to careful ------- and consistent advertising on television, Bella & Andrew has finally become the leader in the global toy market.

(A) planner
(B) plan
(C) planning
(D) planned

115. Social media can be described as new kinds of online media with ------- such as participation, openness, and connectedness.

(A) actions
(B) appearance
(C) symptoms
(D) characteristics

116. Candidates ------- have limited experience in sales will be required to attend training session once hired.

(A) who
(B) whom
(C) what
(D) which

117. There are some strict customs formalities to be gone through before the flight passengers are ------- into the country.

(A) needed
(B) appeared
(C) socialized
(D) admitted

▶ ▶ ▶ GO ON TO THE NEXT PAGE

118. In the recent survey of seaport use, many travelers stated that they found the long waiting time at customs -------.

(A) exhausting
(B) exhausted
(C) exhaustingly
(D) exhaustion

119. Customers are invited to tour the manufacturing plant of Winchester Furniture to see ------- their office furniture is made.

(A) whom
(B) during
(C) about
(D) how

120. Our ------- appraisals of the employees are necessary to understand each employee's competency and relative merit and worth for the company.

(A) perform
(B) performer
(C) performance
(D) performing

121. Some advertisers prefer to hand out refrigerator magnets rather than ------- promotional items like pens, towels, or key holders.

(A) other
(B) another
(C) every
(D) others

122. ------- the latest snow storm, our region is currently experiencing a warmer and drier winter.

(A) Since
(B) Despite
(C) Before
(D) During

123. Due to the recent oil price increases, the company ------- its contract to purchase a piece of new heavy machinery until late November or even mid-December.

(A) postponing
(B) has been postponed
(C) are postponing
(D) will postpone

124. Our members can accumulate bonus points ------- they make purchases from any of our affiliated stores across the country.

(A) whoever
(B) whichever
(C) whatever
(D) whenever

125. According to medical experts, ------- who goes outside must wear a mask for protection against viral infections.

(A) anyone
(B) something
(C) everything
(D) themselves

126. Money and trees would be saved if public transportation were free ------- no one would have to print out tickets anymore.

(A) when
(B) because
(C) unless
(D) provided that

127. Many public festivals and events take place throughout the year, but ------- usually do in summer and fall.

(A) most
(B) each
(C) that
(D) another

128. Mr. McGowan will make a presentation about our new mobile phones and there will be a ten-minute question and answer session -------.

(A) before
(B) so as
(C) afterward
(D) subsequent to

129. According to our company policy, ------- is the last to leave the office is responsible for turning on the security alarm system.

(A) that
(B) which
(C) whoever
(D) most

130. In recent years, consumption of electronic products has increased so much ------- this represents one of the most environmentally problematic product groups today.

(A) since
(B) that
(C) which
(D) in addition to

▶ ▶ ▶ GO ON TO THE NEXT PAGE

PART 6

Directions: Read the texts that follow. A word or phrase, or sentence is missing in parts of each text. Four answer choices for each question are given below the text. Select the best answer to complete the text. Then mark the letter (A), (B), (C), or (D) on your answer sheet.

Questions 131-134 refer to the following press release.

New Toll on Highway 585

July 17 - Auckland> Mayor Kenwood has approved a new toll for Highway 585, being built

on the outskirts of the city, ------- completion of construction.
131.

The mayor's new toll fee will take effect ------- after the new highway has been completed
132.

and the toll booth will be constructed at the first mile marker of the highway. The

electronic toll collection system -------, and it will allow motorists the ease of not having to
133.

stop and pay the tolls.

-------. He said he understood that the fee will be unpopular, but ultimately it will help to
134.

decrease traffic while giving the city the ability to pay for the new local roads without

having to raise taxes.

---

131. (A) for
(B) upon
(C) because of
(D) before

132. (A) promptly
(B) accurately
(C) consequently
(D) accordingly

133. (A) were installed
(B) will be installed
(C) have been installed
(D) had installed

134. (A) From August to November, roadway toll fees may be paid in cash.
(B) He joined Tourism Department to promote tourist attractions and arouse tourist visit intention.
(C) The mayor addressed the concern of the new highway and the toll that will be applied.
(D) A highly developed highway system will attract tourists into our city for recreational purposes.

Questions 135-138 refer to the following information.

The Energy Battery you have just purchased was designed to last for over four years or

about 40,000 miles. Nevertheless, when your battery finally dies, you should dispose of it

------. Please do not just throw it in a trash can. Most municipalities currently recommend
135.

users simply not ------- their dead batteries away with trash.
             136.

Most experts say discarded batteries can cause fires and explosions if they ------- loose in
                  137.

boxes or bags with metal items. That's why our company offers a quick and easy disposal

method to our customers. -------. If you turn them over to us, our recycling specialists take
         138.

care of them in the proper fashion at no additional charge.

---

135. (A) immediately
    (B) properly
    (C) confidentially
    (D) respectively

136. (A) throw
    (B) to throw
    (C) throwing
    (D) thrown

137. (A) stores
    (B) are stored
    (C) stored
    (D) will be stored

138. (A) Please do not combine old and new
       batteries or different types or makes
       of batteries.
    (B) Some batteries left in your garage
       can be the cause for several safety
       concerns.
    (C) All you have to do is return your
       dead batteries to one of our recycling
       centers in your area.
    (D) New small-size batteries are used
       in mobile phones and motor-driven
       electric tools.

▶ ▶ ▶GO ON TO THE NEXT PAGE

VIP Membership For Speed Shopping

Tired of waiting for your package to arrive? Desperate for a little bit of shopping therapy?

Hate paying for expedited shipping each time? Become a VIP member today and -------
139.
those problems. Our VIP members ------- free same-day shipping for an unlimited amount
140.
of deliveries every year. -------, they receive a $30 electronic gift certificate once a quarter
141.
which can be used both in-store and online. -------. For an annual fee of just $18, become
142.
our VIP member today. Take an advantage of this golden opportunity! You will never

regret it!

139. (A) embrace
(B) delay
(C) avoid
(D) accept

140. (A) enjoy
(B) enjoyment
(C) will enjoy
(D) have enjoyed

141. (A) Thus
(B) In addition
(C) In other words
(D) Simultaneously

142. (A) We also provide VIP members with special discounts on purchases.
(B) For spending over $100, you will qualify for free same-day shipping.
(C) Thank you for your hard work and commitment that has made the best sales record this year.
(D) We are surprised that you did not receive your shipment and apologize for the delay.

Dear all,

I would like to officially let you know that Mr. Harry McBain will be leaving us on June 30 to start up his own company. Since joining us five years ago, Mr. McBain ------- a key role
143.
in improving the competitiveness of our company. -------.
144.

Under Mr. McBain's leadership, we realigned our planning procedures, introduced rigorous quality standards, and developed a company-wide competitive strategy. While the process of change was not always easy, we can all appreciate the positive results. -------, last quarter we estimate that we overtook all of our rival companies in both
145.
revenue and unit sales, for the first time ever. Mr. McBain deserves a great deal of the ------- for this achievement.
146.

Please join me in wishing Mr. McBain all the best and continued success in his future endeavors.

Best regards,

Sally Murphy
Head of Personnel

143. (A) plays
(B) has played
(C) had been playing
(D) will have played

144. (A) The dedication we have shown to our customers has helped us to expand.
(B) He will continue his role as CEO and will be involved in major decisions.
(C) The prices for our services and products vary widely, which often results in confusion.
(D) As a result, we have dramatically grown sales and become a significantly more profitable company.

145. (A) Even so
(B) In the mean time
(C) For instance
(D) On the other hand

146. (A) aspect
(B) credit
(C) reflection
(D) motivation

▶ ▶ ▶ GO ON TO THE NEXT PAGE

PART 7

Directions: In this part you will read a selection of texts, such as magazine and newspaper articles, e-mails, and instant messages. Each text or set of texts is followed by several questions. Select the best answer for each question and mark the letter (A), (B), (C), or (D) on your answer sheet.

Questions 147-148 refer to the following advertisement.

HOME
SWEET
HOME

Presented by _The Houston Daily_

Looking for brand-new recipes for your family?
Supported by the community's favorite restaurant, Deli Neko, _the Houston Daily_ will provide cooking lessons to local residents starting next week. They will take place at Deli Neko, and the owner of the restaurant, Minoru Toba, will teach the classes.

The lessons offered are:
* Create Your Own Sushi – Monday 2 P.M.
* Japanese Noodles   – Monday 3 P.M.

You can register online at www.thehoustondaily.com. For detailed information including costs, please contact Vanessa Connelly at 917-803-7552.

147. What is being advertised?

(A) A restaurant
(B) A local publication
(C) Culinary classes
(D) Home improvement service

148. What should interested readers do?

(A) Go to a website
(B) Call a restaurant owner
(C) Visit Ms. Connelly
(D) Buy a magazine

Questions 149-150 refer to the following text message chain.

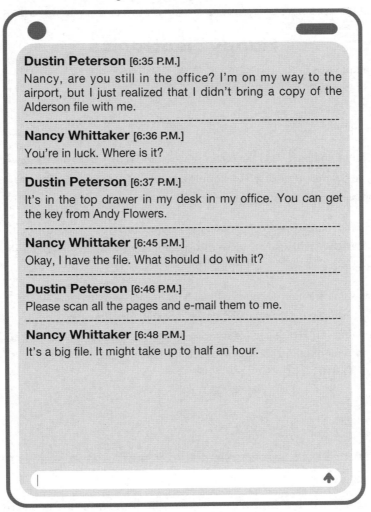

Dustin Peterson [6:35 P.M.]

Nancy, are you still in the office? I'm on my way to the airport, but I just realized that I didn't bring a copy of the Alderson file with me.

Nancy Whittaker [6:36 P.M.]

You're in luck. Where is it?

Dustin Peterson [6:37 P.M.]

It's in the top drawer in my desk in my office. You can get the key from Andy Flowers.

Nancy Whittaker [6:45 P.M.]

Okay, I have the file. What should I do with it?

Dustin Peterson [6:46 P.M.]

Please scan all the pages and e-mail them to me.

Nancy Whittaker [6:48 P.M.]

It's a big file. It might take up to half an hour.

149. What is suggested about Ms. Whittaker?

(A) She shares an office with Mr. Peterson.
(B) She went into Mr. Peterson's office.
(C) She normally stays late at the office.
(D) She could not find Mr. Flowers.

150. At 6:36 P.M., what does Ms. Whittaker most likely mean when she writes, "You're in luck"?

(A) She is working on the Alderson file.
(B) She found the file that Mr. Peterson needs.
(C) She has time to go to the airport.
(D) She has not yet left the office.

▶ ▶ ▶ GO ON TO THE NEXT PAGE

Happy Electronics

To: All employees
From: Marie Davis
Date: Monday, April 1
Subject: New Service Policy

I assume that all of you have read the report released on March 27 about the new customer service policy at ST Electronics. ST Electronics, one of our biggest competitors, announced that it will conduct onsite repairs. —[1]—.

To get ahead in the industry, we will extend our original one-year warranty for all our products by two more years. We will also provide software upgrades without charge for those who visit our centers. —[2]—.

In addition, two-hour training sessions will be held in each store to increase the quality of service and to enhance customer satisfaction. It is mandatory for every sales representative to receive this training. —[3]—. Detailed training schedules for individual stores will be announced at the end of our next monthly meeting. The meeting will be held in Conference Room 302A on April 8. —[4]—.

Marie Davis

Marketing Manager

151. What is the purpose of the e-mail?

(A) To provide the history of a company
(B) To solicit feedback from customers
(C) To ask for the agenda of a meeting
(D) To inform employees of some changes

152. What is NOT indicated about Happy Electronics?

(A) It holds meetings on a regular basis.
(B) It possesses more than one store.
(C) It will soon provide a three-year warranty.
(D) It will start doing onsite repairs.

153. In which of the positions marked [1], [2], [3], and [4] does the following sentence best fit?

"The new policy will go into effect on Tuesday, April 5."

(A) [1]
(B) [2]
(C) [3]
(D) [4]

Come to Charlotte, Enjoy the Performances!

Charlotte City Council presents the following series of marvelous performances!
Visit our city and enjoy our different tourist attractions.

• In case of rain, performances may be canceled •

May 4 / Cyche **Charlotte Adventure World / 7 P.M.**	**May 18 / Kuwaiti Troupe** **Charlotte Theater Hall / 7 P.M.**
Norway's Musician of the Year, Cyche will perform the songs in his 2nd album. Renowned as one of the most enthusiastic singers in the world, he was selected as Musician of the Year by the *Muse* magazine.	Kuwaiti Troupe will perform traditional Kuwait dance using Kuwaiti musical instruments, rubabah and tanbarah.
May 11 / James McLean **Charlotte Amusement Park / 8 P.M.**	**May 25 / Zebras** **Light Factory in Charlotte / 7 P.M.**
Using the traditional Scottish instrument, bagpipes, McLean will sing you amazing songs he himself wrote.	Burundian band, the Zebras, will perform traditional African music with unique instruments and beats.

ACTUAL TEST ···· 06

154. Why will the events be held?

(A) To advertise tour packages
(B) To commemorate a newly constructed amusement park
(C) To promote tourism to Charlotte
(D) To encourage citizens to perform different kinds of music

155. According to the flyer, when will the Zebras perform?

(A) On May 4
(B) On May 11
(C) On May 18
(D) On May 25

156. Where will the dance performance be held?

(A) Charlotte Adventure World
(B) Charlotte Amusement Park
(C) Charlotte City Council
(D) Charlotte Theater Hall

▶ ▶ ▶GO ON TO THE NEXT PAGE

Peter's Gardening

Dear Customer,

Thank you for using our service. We ask you to complete the form below to help us make our service better with your valuable opinions.

Your Name: Scott Hunt

Phone Number: 214-860-2209

Address: 80 Bearpaw Dr., Irving, TX

1. Which service have you received from Peter's Gardening?

☐ Pruning   ☐ Mowing   ☐ Cleanup   ☑ Total Solution

2. How satisfied were you with the costs?

☐ Very Satisfied   ☐ Satisfied   ☑ Dissatisfied   ☐ Very Dissatisfied

3. How satisfied were you with the time the service took?

☑ Very Satisfied   ☐ Satisfied   ☐ Dissatisfied   ☐ Very Dissatisfied

4. How satisfied were you with the outcome?

☐ Very Satisfied   ☑ Satisfied   ☐ Dissatisfied   ☐ Very Dissatisfied

5. Additional comments :

The total solution from Peter's Gardening succeeded in transforming my garden. I liked the fast renovation progress and the results as well. However, the cost of the service seems a bit high compared to your competitors. I recommend adding a discount for frequent customers like myself.

157. Why was the form sent to Mr. Hunt?

(A) To collect the opinions of employees
(B) To get feedback about a finished job
(C) To ask the customer some questions about an upcoming service
(D) To confirm a service order from a customer

158. According to the form, what is indicated about Mr. Hunt?

(A) He recommended Peter's Gardening to his colleagues.
(B) He thinks the prices of the services is reasonable.
(C) He received a discount on his service.
(D) He has received service from Peter's Gardening before.

Questions 159-161 refer to the following information on a website.

www.wholenewworlds.com/register

Welcome to Whole New Worlds

Have you ever wanted to learn a new language, but never had the time or the opportunity? Then Whole New Worlds is just for you. Whole New Worlds is a powerful and respected education provider that offers the following services:

- 1-on-1 pairings with native speakers from over 50 different countries
- Video lectures delivered by certified instructors
- Convenient self-learning tool using flashcards with vocabulary and phrases
- A 3-day free trial period
- A placement test

Become one of the thousands of members of Whole New Worlds and improve your language proficiency starting today!

Tell us about yourself!	
Full Name:	Albert Stahl
E-mail Address:	astahl@quickmail.com
Country You Are From:	Germany
Language You Speak:	German
Language You Want to Learn:	Chinese

Is this your first time using Whole New Worlds? ☐ Yes ☑ No

Registration Type	Available Features
☐ 3-day Trial (FREE)	Placement test and access to self-learning tool and video courses
☐ 1 Month ($30) ☑ 3 Months ($80) ☐ 6 Months ($150)	All features provided by Whole New Worlds including: placement test, 1-on-1 pairing system, self-learning tools, video courses, skill evaluation test and many others

159. What is the purpose of the information?

(A) To recruit new language teachers
(B) To offer a discount for an online publication
(C) To advertise translation services
(D) To promote educational programs

160. What is mentioned about Whole New Worlds?

(A) It offers all of its services for free.
(B) It was recently established.
(C) It has a large number of users.
(D) It is based in Germany.

161. What is suggested about Mr. Stahl?

(A) He plans to register for the 3-day trial.
(B) He speaks Chinese.
(C) He has visited the website before.
(D) He recently took a placement test.

▶ ▶ ▶GO ON TO THE NEXT PAGE

MEMO

To: All Employees of Hotel Mystic Falls
From: Damon Salvatore
Date: February 2
Subject: The result of the nomination

Dear all employees,

I am glad to announce that Elena Gilbert has been selected as the Employee of the Month. The hotel owner, Robert Hood, will present a recognition plaque to her at the next biannual Mystic Falls Night held in June. Additionally, she will receive a two-day paid holiday and a $300 cash prize.

Since she started working at the Hotel Mystic Falls 3 years ago as a housekeeper, Ms. Gilbert has been an exceptional employee who has displayed continuous effort and devotion. Her excellence in service has been recognized several times by customers.

I would like all employees to congratulate her for this remarkable achievement. Since business partners and old friends, Norman Hood and Kevin Costner, first established the hotel, we have continued the tradition of rewarding employees who demonstrate dedication and passion, and I believe any of you could be the next winner of the Best Employee of the Month.

Thanks,

Damon Salvatore
General Manager
Hotel Mystic Falls

162. What is the main topic of the memo?

(A) An award recipient
(B) An upcoming festival
(C) Customer satisfaction survey results
(D) Review of the employees' performance

163. What will most likely happen in June?

(A) Mr. Salvatore will be given a reward.
(B) Submission for a nomination will commence.
(C) A hotel employee will be promoted.
(D) Ms. Gilbert will attend an event.

164. Who is Mr. Costner?

(A) A hotel owner
(B) A friend of Ms. Gilbert's
(C) A co-founder of a business
(D) A housekeeping staff

VEHICLE SALES CONTRACT

J&G Automobile, Ltd.

Contract Number: 121590

This Sales Agreement is made between J&G Automobile, Ltd. (the "Seller") and Michael Bell (the "Buyer").

A. Seller shall transfer the following vehicle to Buyer on February 28.

Maker:	Jensen	Type:	Pickup truck
Model:	J3000i	Color:	Royal Blue
Odometer:	76,291		

B. Buyer agrees to purchase the vehicle from Seller at the price of $19,500 (including tax).

C. Buyer will make a partial installment in the amount of $14,500 on this day and pay the outstanding balance upon the receipt of the vehicle.

D. Seller has presented all inspection records of the vehicle to Buyer and Buyer agrees to purchase the vehicle without warranties.

Signed on February 20 at the J&G Automobile, Ltd. branch in the city of Johnsville.

John Kales	February 20
Seller(Dealership Representative)	Date
Michael Bell	February 20
Buyer	Date
Kyle Wilson	February 20
Witness	Date

165. What will Mr. Bell most likely do on February 28?

(A) Sell a vehicle to J&G Automobile, Ltd.
(B) Submit the balance of five thousand dollars
(C) Purchase a one-year limited warranty
(D) Send Mr. Kales a copy of inspection record

166. According to the contract, what can be inferred about J&G Automobile?

(A) It has more than one location.
(B) It is headquartered in Johnsville.
(C) It has many sales representatives.
(D) It sold a royal blue sedan to Mr. Bell.

167. What is NOT indicated in the contract?

(A) The car was manufactured by Jensen.
(B) Mr. Bell will not receive any warranty.
(C) Kyle Wilson is the previous owner of the vehicle.
(D) John Kales works for J&G Automobiles, Ltd.

▶ ▶ ▶GO ON TO THE NEXT PAGE

Glenn Carter　　　　　2:29 P.M.

Janet Rudolph from the Amber Café e-mailed me. She wants to double her weekly order. Can we handle that?

Marcus Stetson　　　　　2:30 P.M.

I don't see why not. It's not terribly big, so we can do it. What do you think, Greg?

Greg Watkins　　　　　2:31 P.M.

The only problem I can foresee is delivery. She receives six boxes every Monday, and if we double that to twelve, her delivery might be too big to fit in my truck with everything else.

Marcus Stetson　　　　　2:33 P.M.

Oh, I hadn't considered that.

Glenn Carter　　　　　2:34 P.M

Is it possible to rearrange the delivery schedule? After all, her establishment is only a couple of blocks away. How about delivering her items earlier in the day?

Amy Jones　　　　　2:35 P.M.

Let me do it. I drive by her place every morning, so I can drop everything off as I'm going to Harold's Fish and Chips. I can be there by 8:30 A.M.

Glenn Carter　　　　　2:37 P.M.

Sounds good. I'll call Janet and fill her in. Are there any problems I need to know about?

Marcus Stetson　　　　　2:38 P.M.

We're going to be understaffed this weekend. Brad Howard resigned, and we haven't found a replacement yet.

Amy Jones　　　　　2:40 P.M.

I don't have any plans for the weekend.

Glenn Carter　　　　　2:41 P.M.

Thanks, Amy. I'll see you on Saturday then.

SEND

168. What is suggested about Mr. Watkins?

    (A) He drives a delivery truck.
    (B) He works at a café.
    (C) He has met Ms. Rudolph in person.
    (D) He works late at night.

169. What does Ms. Jones offer to do?

    (A) Have a talk with Ms. Rudolph
    (B) Find a potential new employee
    (C) Deliver some items to a store
    (D) Start working earlier each day

170. What will Mr. Carter most likely do next?

    (A) Make a telephone call
    (B) Redo the schedule
    (C) Speak with Mr. Howard
    (D) Visit a customer

171. At 2:40 P.M., what does Ms. Jones suggest when she writes, "I don't have any plans for the weekend"?

    (A) She needs to earn some extra money.
    (B) She has not worked many hours this week.
    (C) She expects to be paid overtime.
    (D) She is willing to work Mr. Howard's shift.

▶ ▶ ▶ GO ON TO THE NEXT PAGE

Pasadena, April 19 — Today, Brilliance Dairy, Inc., a Los Angeles-based international distributor and supplier of dairy products, announced that Jackson Hofstadter, its chief executive officer for the past 10 years, will retire as of April 30. His position will be filled by the company's current vice president, Penelope Garcia. —[1]—.

Spending his whole career at Brilliance Dairy, Mr. Hofstadter has been loyal to the company since its foundation 35 years ago. —[2]—. "It was wonderful to see the company I have put all my passion into rise to become the number-one company in the industry," said Mr. Hofstadter while reminiscing about the past.

Mr. Hofstadter's successor has a history of service to the firm as long as his. Right after earning a degree in business administration from the University of Boston, Ms. Garcia joined the company's subsidiary in New York, CBS Milk, 25 years ago. —[3]—. She worked as the director of marketing at CBS Milk for 11 years before she transferred to Brilliance Dairy.

"Ms. Garcia was a natural choice for the board of directors. I knew Ms. Garcia was going to be selected when I worked as an assistant marketing director with her at CBS Milk. She is the most effective and dedicated leader I have ever seen," said Sean Cooper, the current managing director at CBS Milk.

Brilliance Dairy has arranged an event to say farewell to its old CEO and to welcome its new one at its headquarters. —[4]—. This event will also celebrate the release of Mr. Hofstadter's book, *Everyone Starts at the Bottom*. "I am indebted to numerous people in the industry in many ways. Now it is time for me to help others by passing on my experience and knowledge through books," noted Mr. Hofstadter.

172. What is indicated about Brilliance Dairy Inc.?

(A) It exports its goods abroad.
(B) It is a competitor of CBS Milk.
(C) It has a large dairy farm in Pasadena.
(D) It is currently recruiting new employees.

173. Who is Mr. Cooper?

(A) The new CEO of Brilliance Dairy, Inc.
(B) The former assistant marketing director of CBS Milk
(C) The current vice president of Brilliance Dairy Inc.
(D) The author of *Everyone Starts at the Bottom*

174. What does Mr. Hofstadter plan to do?

(A) Open a new business
(B) Study business management
(C) Train Ms. Garcia
(D) Share his expertise through writing

175. In which of the positions marked [1], [2], [3], and [4] does the following sentence best fit?

"It will be held on April 30."

(A) [1]
(B) [2]
(C) [3]
(D) [4]

▶ ▶ ▶ GO ON TO THE NEXT PAGE

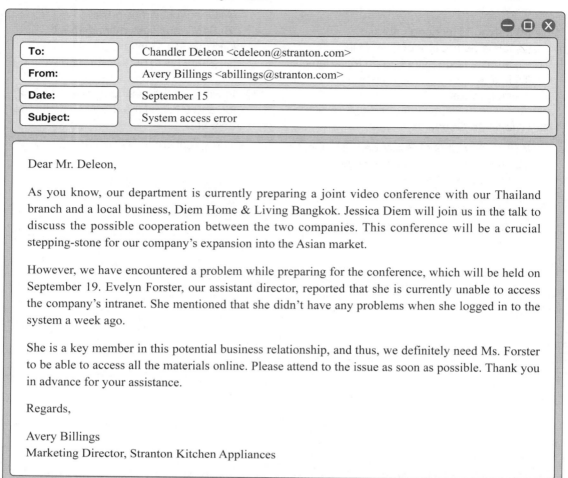

To: Chandler Deleon <cdeleon@stranton.com>

From: Avery Billings <abillings@stranton.com>

Date: September 15

Subject: System access error

Dear Mr. Deleon,

As you know, our department is currently preparing a joint video conference with our Thailand branch and a local business, Diem Home & Living Bangkok. Jessica Diem will join us in the talk to discuss the possible cooperation between the two companies. This conference will be a crucial stepping-stone for our company's expansion into the Asian market.

However, we have encountered a problem while preparing for the conference, which will be held on September 19. Evelyn Forster, our assistant director, reported that she is currently unable to access the company's intranet. She mentioned that she didn't have any problems when she logged in to the system a week ago.

She is a key member in this potential business relationship, and thus, we definitely need Ms. Forster to be able to access all the materials online. Please attend to the issue as soon as possible. Thank you in advance for your assistance.

Regards,

Avery Billings
Marketing Director, Stranton Kitchen Appliances

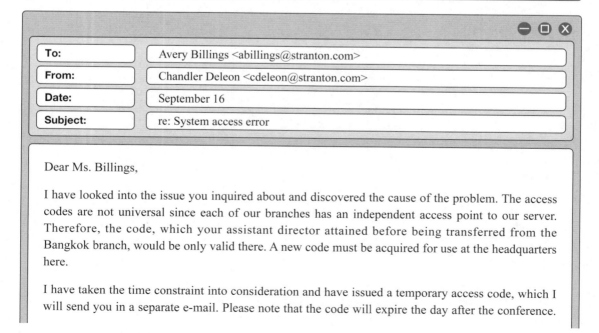

To: Avery Billings <abillings@stranton.com>

From: Chandler Deleon <cdeleon@stranton.com>

Date: September 16

Subject: re: System access error

Dear Ms. Billings,

I have looked into the issue you inquired about and discovered the cause of the problem. The access codes are not universal since each of our branches has an independent access point to our server. Therefore, the code, which your assistant director attained before being transferred from the Bangkok branch, would be only valid there. A new code must be acquired for use at the headquarters here.

I have taken the time constraint into consideration and have issued a temporary access code, which I will send you in a separate e-mail. Please note that the code will expire the day after the conference.

To gain a permanent code, the individual will need to submit a request online. As indicated in the employee manual, fill out the form found at http://intranet.stranton.com/form/100254 and upload the listed materials.

I will be away on a business trip from September 22 and be out of contact. Should there be any issues while I am away, please get in touch with my assistant, Dan Hadley.

Regards,

Chandler Deleon
Technical Support Director, Stranton Kitchen Appliances

176. What is the main purpose of the first e-mail?

(A) To ask for conference attendance
(B) To solicit technological assistance
(C) To inform about business plans
(D) To commend an employee's efforts

177. What is indicated about Stranton Kitchen Appliances?

(A) It is experiencing financial difficulties.
(B) It recruited new employees recently.
(C) It intends to enlarge its business.
(D) It plans to adopt a new system soon.

178. Who has recently joined Ms. Billings' department?

(A) Mr. Deleon
(B) Ms. Diem
(C) Ms. Forster
(D) Mr. Hadley

179. When will the temporary code expire?

(A) On September 16
(B) On September 19
(C) On September 20
(D) On September 22

180. What will Ms. Forster most likely do next?

(A) Submit a report to her manager
(B) Read an instruction manual
(C) Request a new authorization code
(D) Schedule a conference

4th Sand & Music Festival
July 13-14, Salisbury Beach

Visit Salisbury, the hometown of many world-famous musicians, to enjoy your summer days and nights with the 4th Sand & Music Festival. The weekend-long festival at the Salisbury Beach will provide all visitors with great food, excitement, and unforgettable memories! Below is the list of activities you can participate in:

Sand Sculpture Exhibition

Walk along the magnificent sand sculptures displayed on the wonderful shore of Salisbury Beach. The theme of this year's exhibition is 'Under the Ocean.'

Beach Volleyball Competition (July 14 Only)

Join us at the coed beach volleyball competition. Quick and easy registration is available online until July 8.

Summer Night Concerts

Enjoy the sound of music calling in the sunsets. A stage will be set up on the shore of Salisbury Beach. The concerts will be held in a local bar if it rains.

Fireworks Display

Experience amazingly beautiful fireworks each night at 9 P.M.

- For further inquiries about the 4th Sand & Music Festival, please give us a call at 555-0095.
- Press must receive official permission to cover the festival. Prior registration by July 10 with Jake Seiz at jseiz@salisbury.com is required.

Salisbury Times

By Helena Maliosa

July 15, Salisbury — Last weekend, over ten thousand people attended the 4th Sand & Music Festival at Salisbury Beach to enjoy some exciting activities.

My sons and I personally enjoyed this year's sand sculpture exhibition the most. When I visited the festival with my sons last year, the sand sculpture exhibition only had about 10 sculptures. This year's village of giant sea creatures definitely provided a splendid view. Ten world-class sand sculptors from across the nation built 30 pieces of art.

The first day's jazz concert was a huge success. The large stage set up on the shore actually seemed small among the large crowd. Unlike the jazz concert, the pop concert on the second day was disappointing. It was held in a local pub, and because of the size of the pub, a lot of people could not even enter. Also, the sound equipment in the pub was so dated that the crowd could not hear the music clearly. It seems like the organizers of the festival next year should come up with another indoor venue for concerts.

Without a doubt, the highlight of the festival was the fireworks rounding off each day of the event. The best local pyrotechnic company designed the fireworks this year, and all visitors were invited to watch the fabulous show free of charge.

181. In the announcement, what is mentioned about Salisbury?

(A) It is famous for its weekly fireworks.
(B) It is open to public only in summer.
(C) It is overly crowded with visitors.
(D) It produced some well-known musicians.

182. By when does the registration for beach volleyball competition have to be completed?

(A) July 8
(B) July 10
(C) July 14
(D) July 15

183. What had Ms. Maliosa probably done before the festival?

(A) Registered for a membership
(B) Contacted Mr. Seiz
(C) Paid for admission
(D) Called the organizers

184. What is NOT suggested about the festival this year?

(A) It was held near a body of water.
(B) It hosted the sand sculpture exhibition for the first time.
(C) It was open to children.
(D) It rained on the second day.

185. What does Ms. Maliosa indicate about the festival in the review?

(A) The festival lacks events for children.
(B) The firework display needs more safety staff.
(C) The alternative location for a concert was inadequate.
(D) There were not enough places for visitors to eat.

INCREDIBLE LODGE

Alice Springs, Northern Territory, Australia

+61 230777199

In search of a unique getaway? Then come to the Incredible Lodge for an extraordinary encounter in the heart of the Australian continent. Get in touch with an ancient land and dig up stories buried in the sand.

- Tour Uluru with a guide from an Aboriginal tribe, one of the indigenous people of Australia
- Take part in a festival of the Anangu people, a local tribe
- Take a sunrise camel tour exploring central Australia
- Dine under the beautiful starry sky in the desert

As the biggest hotel in the area, we cater to your every need, including providing an airport shuttle, laundry service, and cleaning at no cost. In celebration of our tenth anniversary, all guests can enjoy a complimentary buffet breakfast.

Visit www.incrediblelodge.com to discover more. Visit before the end of January and receive a 10% discount at our souvenir shop.

INCREDIBLE LODGE

Customer Feedback

Please complete this short survey so that we can better serve our guests.

Name: Kieran Achino   **E-mail:** kachino@mail.com

Date of Stay: January 20-25

Please indicate your level of satisfaction (1 = highest / 4 = lowest)

	1	2	3	4
Politeness of staff	○	●	○	○
Responsiveness of staff	●	○	○	○
Cleanliness of the facilities	○	●	○	○
Quality of your room	○	●	○	○

Most Memorable Experience: The Uluru tour. When I visited Uluru, I was guided by Bakana, who was a wonderful storyteller. She told a traditional dreamtime story of her tribe, adding depth to my experience. It was nice to see her again at her people's festival that night, where she told more stories.

Issues You Had: On the second day of my stay, the air conditioner stopped working. However, the problem was fixed within half an hour of my reporting it. I was impressed with the level of service.

To: All Staff, Maintenance Department
From: Jason Wheelock
Subject: Room Problem
Date: January 30

The air conditioner in room 34 on the third floor has broken down for the second time in the past week. I looked into the matter and discovered that we purchased it more than ten years ago. As such, I've ordered a new unit. It's scheduled to arrive in two days. Once it arrives, please install it immediately. That room will remain empty until the new unit is running properly.

186. For whom is the advertisement intended?

(A) Historians
(B) Business owners
(C) Tourists
(D) Traditional artists

187. What is NOT suggested about the Incredible Lodge?

(A) It only accepts online bookings.
(B) It does its guests' laundry for free.
(C) It can hold more guests than all other nearby hotels.
(D) It opened a decade ago.

188. According to the advertisement, what is being offered for a limited period of time?

(A) Room upgrades
(B) A free camel hire
(C) Complimentary dinners
(D) A discount at a gift store

189. What is indicated about Bakana?

(A) She is a famous author.
(B) She is from the Anangu tribe.
(C) She was recently hired by the Incredible Lodge.
(D) She was satisfied with her recent tour.

190. What is suggested about Mr. Achino?

(A) He felt that the Incredible Lodge was too expensive.
(B) He was somewhat displeased with his tour.
(C) He stayed on the third floor of the Incredible Lodge.
(D) He intends to return to Uluru later in the year.

July 25

Barbados Grill
97A Plate Avenue
Toronto M4C 5B5

Dear Store Manager,

This is to inquire about the billing process during my last visit to your establishment. At 6:30 P.M. on July 20, my wife and I visited your restaurant for dinner before attending a concert. My wife ordered the lamb chops with Italian herbs while I ordered the stuffed pork belly. Each dish was priced at $60. However, I was served the chef's special, which was pork chops with artichokes.

When I spoke to you, you asked me whether I would like to wait for the correct dish or have the served dish. You also said that since it was your mistake, you would offer the $90 dish at the same price as my original order. Since we were pressed for time, I ate the pork chops.

When we were leaving, we were in a hurry so we didn't examine the bill carefully. However, when I received my monthly credit card statement, I noticed that I had been charged $150 for the meal. I hereby request a refund of $30.

We have been customers at your restaurant for almost two years, and this incident has been disappointing. I hope something similar does not happen again.

Regards,

Bruce McGee

July 31

Bruce McGee
555 Victoria Street
Toronto, M3M 5G9

Dear Mr. McGee,

Please accept my sincere apology for the mistake. I spoke with Mark Harrington about your visit, and he confirmed that you were accidentally served the wrong meal and that he offered it to you at a reduced price. $30 has therefore been refunded to your credit card.

I feel bad that something like this has happened to valued customers such as you and your wife. Please accept this coupon that you can use on your next visit. If there is anything else I can do for you, please let me know.

Yours respectfully,

Lorraine Bracco
Owner, Barbados Grill

COUPON
Barbados Grill

This coupon is good for one free chef's special meal.
Please show this coupon to your server when placing your order.
Limit one coupon per customer.

Expiration Date: December 31

---

191. Why was the first letter written?

(A) To describe a pleasant experience
(B) To report a payment error
(C) To make a reservation for a meal
(D) To inquire about the menu

192. What is indicated about Mr. McGee?

(A) He was late for a concert.
(B) He dined with his spouse on July 20.
(C) He likes to try new menu items.
(D) He will not return to the restaurant again.

193. What is suggested about Mr. Harrington?

(A) He was working at Barbados Grill on July 31.
(B) His credit card was wrongly charged.
(C) He is the manager of Barbados Grill.
(D) He usually recommends lamb chops to customers.

194. What can be inferred about Barbados Grill?

(A) It closes at 7:30 P.M.
(B) It offers gift cards to all customers.
(C) It has been in business for about two years.
(D) Its owner cares about its customers.

195. What is the value of the coupon?

(A) $30
(B) $60
(C) $90
(D) $150

ACTUAL TEST ... 06

▶ ▶ ▶GO ON TO THE NEXT PAGE

Victoria (October 10) – The Flourishing Trees Organization (FTO) will host a fundraising event, the One Earth Festival, at Gilmour Park on Friday, October 13, from 8:30 A.M. to 6:00 P.M. FTO is a nonprofit organization focusing on reminding people of the importance of the environment and nature. This festival is intended to promote the environment to residents of Victoria.

The festival will feature speeches by invited speakers, including Willow Lawrence. "I'm pleased this event will be finally held in my hometown. It's a good cause and will definitely help increase environmental awareness in the region," remarked Ms. Lawrence.

"I want everybody from Victoria to enjoy the festival like people did at previous festivals in other cities. There will be food vendors, short performances, and music concerts by locals," said FTO spokesman Dexter Voorhees. "What is special about this year's festival is that it will be held outdoors for the first time."

Everyone is welcome at the festival. All donations are appreciated. Businesses donating more than $3,000 will be given an advertisement slot on the front page of the organization's website and in its brochure. For more information, please call the planning director, Declan Jackman, at 852-555-0958 or send an e-mail to djackman@ ftomail.com.

To: Declan Jackman, Felicia Stewart, Rodney West
From: Jason Greene, CEO
Date: October 11
Subject: Slight Changes

We have had to make a few changes regarding the festival in Victoria. Please note the new duties of the following individuals:

Aaron Hampton: entertainment coordinator
Patricia Ermine: catering coordinator
Rodney West: public speaking facilitator
Nancy Marsh: public relations advisor

If you have any questions, get in touch with me at once. Let's make this year's festival the best one ever.

To:	Declan Jackman <djackman@ftomail.com>
From:	Arnold Xavier <axavier@lesfeuilles.com>
Date:	October 17
Subject:	Thank you!

Dear Mr. Jackman,

Thank you for putting my restaurant's logo on your website and in the brochure. I'm pleased the festival went so well. The entire event seemed to run smoothly. My restaurant has seen an increasing number of diners lately as well as increased sales thanks to the ads.

I was happy to be involved with the event and hope to do so in the future. Please keep me advised of any opportunities that may arise later.

Thank you,

Arnold Xavier
Owner
Les Feuilles

196. In the article, the word "cause" in paragraph 2, line 4, is closest in meaning to

(A) promotion
(B) goal
(C) fund
(D) result

197. What is indicated about Ms. Lawrence?

(A) She will lead a team of volunteers.
(B) She founded the FTO.
(C) She is from Victoria.
(D) She is world famous.

198. According to Mr. Voorhees, what is true about the One Earth Festival?

(A) It is expecting the most attendees in its history.
(B) It has been held in Victoria several times.
(C) It will only admit residents of Victoria.
(D) It took place indoors last year.

199. Who most likely worked with Ms. Lawrence?

(A) Mr. Hampton
(B) Ms. Ermine
(C) Mr. West
(D) Ms. Marsh

200. What can be inferred about Mr. Xavier?

(A) He contributed over $3,000 to the festival.
(B) He sold food from his restaurant at the festival.
(C) He founded Les Feuilles a few years ago.
(D) His restaurant's logo was redesigned recently.

STOP! This is the end of the test. If you finish before time is called,
you may go back to Parts 5, 6, and 7 and check your work.

Actual Test 정답표

01

1. (D)	2. (D)	3. (C)	4. (A)	5. (A)	101. (D)	102. (A)	103. (C)	104. (B)	105. (C)
6. (D)	7. (A)	8. (B)	9. (B)	10. (A)	106. (B)	107. (C)	108. (C)	109. (C)	110. (B)
11. (B)	12. (A)	13. (A)	14. (B)	15. (A)	111. (C)	112. (C)	113. (C)	114. (D)	115. (A)
16. (C)	17. (C)	18. (C)	19. (B)	20. (C)	116. (B)	117. (C)	118. (B)	119. (A)	120. (B)
21. (C)	22. (A)	23. (A)	24. (B)	25. (A)	121. (D)	122. (B)	123. (D)	124. (D)	125. (B)
26. (B)	27. (C)	28. (A)	29. (B)	30. (B)	126. (C)	127. (C)	128. (D)	129. (D)	130. (B)
31. (A)	32. (C)	33. (A)	34. (D)	35. (A)	131. (B)	132. (A)	133. (D)	134. (C)	135. (C)
36. (C)	37. (B)	38. (B)	39. (C)	40. (D)	136. (A)	137. (B)	138. (A)	139. (B)	140. (D)
41. (A)	42. (C)	43. (A)	44. (C)	45. (B)	141. (C)	142. (A)	143. (C)	144. (B)	145. (B)
46. (D)	47. (A)	48. (B)	49. (C)	50. (C)	146. (D)	147. (C)	148. (D)	149. (D)	150. (B)
51. (A)	52. (C)	53. (B)	54. (A)	55. (D)	151. (D)	152. (C)	153. (B)	154. (C)	155. (A)
56. (D)	57. (C)	58. (A)	59. (A)	60. (D)	156. (B)	157. (D)	158. (C)	159. (D)	160. (B)
61. (A)	62. (C)	63. (A)	64. (A)	65. (C)	161. (C)	162. (B)	163. (B)	164. (A)	165. (D)
66. (D)	67. (B)	68. (C)	69. (B)	70. (B)	166. (D)	167. (B)	168. (B)	169. (C)	170. (D)
71. (C)	72. (B)	73. (B)	74. (D)	75. (A)	171. (C)	172. (D)	173. (B)	174. (A)	175. (B)
76. (B)	77. (C)	78. (D)	79. (B)	80. (D)	176. (B)	177. (D)	178. (C)	179. (A)	180. (B)
81. (A)	82. (D)	83. (D)	84. (C)	85. (B)	181. (A)	182. (D)	183. (D)	184. (D)	185. (B)
86. (A)	87. (C)	88. (D)	89. (C)	90. (B)	186. (B)	187. (D)	188. (B)	189. (B)	190. (D)
91. (A)	92. (A)	93. (D)	94. (D)	95. (A)	191. (A)	192. (C)	193. (B)	194. (A)	195. (D)
96. (B)	97. (A)	98. (A)	99. (B)	100. (D)	196. (B)	197. (A)	198. (C)	199. (D)	200. (C)

02

1. (C)	2. (C)	3. (C)	4. (A)	5. (C)	101. (C)	102. (A)	103. (A)	104. (B)	105. (D)
6. (B)	7. (B)	8. (C)	9. (C)	10. (B)	106. (B)	107. (C)	108. (A)	109. (C)	110. (A)
11. (A)	12. (B)	13. (B)	14. (B)	15. (A)	111. (B)	112. (C)	113. (D)	114. (B)	115. (A)
16. (A)	17. (C)	18. (B)	19. (B)	20. (C)	116. (D)	117. (B)	118. (D)	119. (D)	120. (D)
21. (B)	22. (B)	23. (C)	24. (A)	25. (C)	121. (D)	122. (B)	123. (A)	124. (B)	125. (A)
26. (C)	27. (B)	28. (B)	29. (A)	30. (A)	126. (C)	127. (B)	128. (C)	129. (D)	130. (D)
31. (B)	32. (A)	33. (C)	34. (A)	35. (C)	131. (C)	132. (C)	133. (C)	134. (C)	135. (D)
36. (B)	37. (D)	38. (B)	39. (C)	40. (D)	136. (D)	137. (D)	138. (B)	139. (C)	140. (B)
41. (A)	42. (D)	43. (D)	44. (D)	45. (B)	141. (D)	142. (D)	143. (D)	144. (B)	145. (B)
46. (A)	47. (B)	48. (C)	49. (B)	50. (D)	146. (A)	147. (D)	148. (C)	149. (C)	150. (D)
51. (B)	52. (C)	53. (B)	54. (D)	55. (A)	151. (A)	152. (B)	153. (D)	154. (D)	155. (B)
56. (D)	57. (A)	58. (B)	59. (B)	60. (A)	156. (D)	157. (B)	158. (B)	159. (C)	160. (D)
61. (D)	62. (D)	63. (C)	64. (B)	65. (B)	161. (B)	162. (B)	163. (B)	164. (B)	165. (C)
66. (B)	67. (C)	68. (D)	69. (B)	70. (A)	166. (C)	167. (A)	168. (D)	169. (C)	170. (A)
71. (A)	72. (C)	73. (D)	74. (D)	75. (C)	171. (A)	172. (C)	173. (A)	174. (D)	175. (D)
76. (C)	77. (C)	78. (B)	79. (A)	80. (D)	176. (D)	177. (B)	178. (A)	179. (C)	180. (C)
81. (C)	82. (C)	83. (B)	84. (D)	85. (A)	181. (C)	182. (B)	183. (B)	184. (A)	185. (D)
86. (C)	87. (A)	88. (C)	89. (D)	90. (A)	186. (B)	187. (C)	188. (D)	189. (C)	190. (C)
91. (A)	92. (B)	93. (D)	94. (A)	95. (A)	191. (A)	192. (B)	193. (C)	194. (B)	195. (C)
96. (B)	97. (C)	98. (B)	99. (D)	100. (C)	196. (B)	197. (D)	198. (D)	199. (D)	200. (B)

Actual Test 정답표

Listening Comprehension   **Reading Comprehension**

03

1. (C)	2. (C)	3. (A)	4. (C)	5. (C)	101. (B)	102. (C)	103. (D)	104. (D)	105. (B)
6. (C)	7. (C)	8. (A)	9. (C)	10. (A)	106. (C)	107. (A)	108. (D)	109. (A)	110. (B)
11. (A)	12. (A)	13. (C)	14. (C)	15. (A)	111. (A)	112. (C)	113. (A)	114. (C)	115. (B)
16. (A)	17. (B)	18. (B)	19. (B)	20. (A)	116. (B)	117. (D)	118. (B)	119. (C)	120. (D)
21. (C)	22. (C)	23. (A)	24. (B)	25. (B)	121. (B)	122. (B)	123. (A)	124. (A)	125. (A)
26. (C)	27. (C)	28. (B)	29. (B)	30. (B)	126. (D)	127. (A)	128. (D)	129. (C)	130. (B)
31. (A)	32. (C)	33. (B)	34. (C)	35. (A)	131. (C)	132. (B)	133. (D)	134. (D)	135. (C)
36. (C)	37. (D)	38. (D)	39. (A)	40. (B)	136. (A)	137. (A)	138. (D)	139. (C)	140. (B)
41. (D)	42. (B)	43. (B)	44. (C)	45. (A)	141. (D)	142. (B)	143. (C)	144. (B)	145. (B)
46. (A)	47. (B)	48. (D)	49. (C)	50. (D)	146. (D)	147. (C)	148. (A)	149. (D)	150. (B)
51. (C)	52. (D)	53. (C)	54. (A)	55. (C)	151. (C)	152. (C)	153. (B)	154. (D)	155. (B)
56. (D)	57. (B)	58. (C)	59. (A)	60. (D)	156. (C)	157. (A)	158. (C)	159. (D)	160. (D)
61. (B)	62. (C)	63. (A)	64. (D)	65. (A)	161. (C)	162. (D)	163. (C)	164. (D)	165. (C)
66. (B)	67. (A)	68. (A)	69. (B)	70. (B)	166. (C)	167. (D)	168. (D)	169. (C)	170. (A)
71. (D)	72. (D)	73. (A)	74. (B)	75. (A)	171. (C)	172. (A)	173. (A)	174. (C)	175. (C)
76. (D)	77. (C)	78. (A)	79. (D)	80. (D)	176. (C)	177. (C)	178. (C)	179. (A)	180. (C)
81. (A)	82. (D)	83. (D)	84. (C)	85. (A)	181. (C)	182. (A)	183. (D)	184. (B)	185. (C)
86. (C)	87. (B)	88. (C)	89. (A)	90. (D)	186. (B)	187. (C)	188. (D)	189. (D)	190. (A)
91. (C)	92. (C)	93. (B)	94. (D)	95. (C)	191. (A)	192. (C)	193. (B)	194. (B)	195. (A)
96. (B)	97. (D)	98. (D)	99. (A)	100. (C)	196. (C)	197. (C)	198. (C)	199. (D)	200. (C)

04

1. (B)	2. (C)	3. (B)	4. (C)	5. (A)	101. (C)	102. (D)	103. (B)	104. (B)	105. (C)
6. (D)	7. (C)	8. (C)	9. (B)	10. (C)	106. (B)	107. (A)	108. (B)	109. (A)	110. (B)
11. (B)	12. (A)	13. (A)	14. (B)	15. (B)	111. (B)	112. (C)	113. (C)	114. (B)	115. (A)
16. (B)	17. (B)	18. (B)	19. (B)	20. (C)	116. (A)	117. (B)	118. (C)	119. (A)	120. (C)
21. (A)	22. (A)	23. (A)	24. (A)	25. (B)	121. (C)	122. (B)	123. (D)	124. (D)	125. (D)
26. (B)	27. (C)	28. (C)	29. (A)	30. (B)	126. (D)	127. (A)	128. (A)	129. (B)	130. (C)
31. (C)	32. (A)	33. (C)	34. (D)	35. (A)	131. (A)	132. (C)	133. (B)	134. (D)	135. (D)
36. (B)	37. (B)	38. (D)	39. (C)	40. (C)	136. (C)	137. (A)	138. (D)	139. (C)	140. (B)
41. (A)	42. (C)	43. (A)	44. (C)	45. (A)	141. (A)	142. (D)	143. (C)	144. (C)	145. (C)
46. (D)	47. (C)	48. (A)	49. (D)	50. (B)	146. (C)	147. (D)	148. (C)	149. (C)	150. (D)
51. (C)	52. (A)	53. (C)	54. (C)	55. (C)	151. (A)	152. (B)	153. (C)	154. (C)	155. (B)
56. (C)	57. (B)	58. (C)	59. (C)	60. (A)	156. (A)	157. (C)	158. (C)	159. (C)	160. (D)
61. (D)	62. (C)	63. (D)	64. (C)	65. (B)	161. (A)	162. (B)	163. (D)	164. (B)	165. (D)
66. (C)	67. (B)	68. (B)	69. (B)	70. (A)	166. (A)	167. (B)	168. (D)	169. (A)	170. (B)
71. (B)	72. (D)	73. (B)	74. (B)	75. (B)	171. (D)	172. (C)	173. (B)	174. (A)	175. (C)
76. (B)	77. (C)	78. (A)	79. (A)	80. (A)	176. (A)	177. (D)	178. (C)	179. (C)	180. (B)
81. (C)	82. (D)	83. (D)	84. (B)	85. (A)	181. (D)	182. (D)	183. (C)	184. (B)	185. (A)
86. (C)	87. (B)	88. (D)	89. (C)	90. (A)	186. (D)	187. (A)	188. (C)	189. (D)	190. (B)
91. (D)	92. (D)	93. (A)	94. (B)	95. (C)	191. (D)	192. (C)	193. (A)	194. (C)	195. (D)
96. (B)	97. (C)	98. (D)	99. (B)	100. (C)	196. (A)	197. (D)	198. (C)	199. (D)	200. (A)

Actual Test 정답표

05

1. (C)	2. (B)	3. (D)	4. (C)	5. (C)	101. (A)	102. (A)	103. (C)	104. (C)	105. (B)
6. (D)	7. (B)	8. (A)	9. (A)	10. (C)	106. (C)	107. (B)	108. (D)	109. (A)	110. (D)
11. (B)	12. (B)	13. (A)	14. (B)	15. (A)	111. (C)	112. (A)	113. (B)	114. (C)	115. (B)
16. (C)	17. (A)	18. (C)	19. (C)	20. (C)	116. (C)	117. (B)	118. (D)	119. (D)	120. (B)
21. (C)	22. (A)	23. (B)	24. (B)	25. (A)	121. (C)	122. (A)	123. (C)	124. (B)	125. (D)
26. (A)	27. (A)	28. (C)	29. (B)	30. (C)	126. (D)	127. (B)	128. (B)	129. (D)	130. (C)
31. (B)	32. (A)	33. (C)	34. (A)	35. (A)	131. (B)	132. (A)	133. (B)	134. (D)	135. (D)
36. (D)	37. (B)	38. (D)	39. (C)	40. (A)	136. (A)	137. (B)	138. (B)	139. (D)	140. (D)
41. (C)	42. (B)	43. (C)	44. (B)	45. (C)	141. (B)	142. (C)	143. (C)	144. (A)	145. (C)
46. (A)	47. (A)	48. (B)	49. (B)	50. (B)	146. (D)	147. (B)	148. (C)	149. (A)	150. (D)
51. (D)	52. (D)	53. (C)	54. (A)	55. (A)	151. (B)	152. (C)	153. (D)	154. (D)	155. (D)
56. (C)	57. (D)	58. (C)	59. (C)	60. (C)	156. (B)	157. (D)	158. (D)	159. (A)	160. (C)
61. (A)	62. (C)	63. (B)	64. (D)	65. (C)	161. (B)	162. (B)	163. (D)	164. (C)	165. (C)
66. (D)	67. (C)	68. (A)	69. (C)	70. (C)	166. (D)	167. (B)	168. (B)	169. (A)	170. (C)
71. (D)	72. (D)	73. (D)	74. (C)	75. (C)	171. (D)	172. (D)	173. (A)	174. (C)	175. (C)
76. (D)	77. (D)	78. (D)	79. (C)	80. (B)	176. (C)	177. (D)	178. (C)	179. (C)	180. (C)
81. (A)	82. (D)	83. (C)	84. (A)	85. (D)	181. (A)	182. (C)	183. (B)	184. (D)	185. (C)
86. (C)	87. (C)	88. (D)	89. (C)	90. (D)	186. (C)	187. (A)	188. (C)	189. (D)	190. (D)
91. (D)	92. (A)	93. (B)	94. (C)	95. (B)	191. (B)	192. (C)	193. (D)	194. (C)	195. (A)
96. (C)	97. (D)	98. (B)	99. (D)	100. (C)	196. (D)	197. (B)	198. (A)	199. (C)	200. (D)

06

1. (C)	2. (B)	3. (A)	4. (D)	5. (C)	101. (B)	102. (D)	103. (B)	104. (B)	105. (B)
6. (A)	7. (B)	8. (B)	9. (B)	10. (C)	106. (C)	107. (B)	108. (C)	109. (A)	110. (C)
11. (A)	12. (C)	13. (C)	14. (C)	15. (A)	111. (D)	112. (B)	113. (D)	114. (C)	115. (D)
16. (C)	17. (B)	18. (C)	19. (A)	20. (C)	116. (A)	117. (D)	118. (A)	119. (D)	120. (C)
21. (B)	22. (C)	23. (B)	24. (A)	25. (B)	121. (A)	122. (B)	123. (D)	124. (D)	125. (A)
26. (B)	27. (B)	28. (A)	29. (C)	30. (B)	126. (B)	127. (A)	128. (C)	129. (C)	130. (B)
31. (C)	32. (B)	33. (B)	34. (D)	35. (A)	131. (B)	132. (A)	133. (B)	134. (C)	135. (B)
36. (C)	37. (A)	38. (D)	39. (B)	40. (A)	136. (B)	137. (B)	138. (C)	139. (C)	140. (A)
41. (C)	42. (B)	43. (D)	44. (B)	45. (A)	141. (B)	142. (C)	143. (B)	144. (D)	145. (C)
46. (B)	47. (D)	48. (A)	49. (B)	50. (C)	146. (B)	147. (C)	148. (A)	149. (B)	150. (D)
51. (C)	52. (D)	53. (D)	54. (C)	55. (A)	151. (D)	152. (D)	153. (B)	154. (C)	155. (D)
56. (B)	57. (B)	58. (D)	59. (B)	60. (D)	156. (D)	157. (B)	158. (D)	159. (D)	160. (C)
61. (B)	62. (B)	63. (A)	64. (C)	65. (D)	161. (C)	162. (A)	163. (D)	164. (C)	165. (C)
66. (A)	67. (C)	68. (A)	69. (C)	70. (B)	166. (C)	167. (C)	168. (A)	169. (C)	170. (A)
71. (C)	72. (C)	73. (B)	74. (B)	75. (C)	171. (D)	172. (A)	173. (B)	174. (D)	175. (D)
76. (B)	77. (A)	78. (D)	79. (D)	80. (C)	176. (B)	177. (C)	178. (C)	179. (C)	180. (C)
81. (B)	82. (D)	83. (C)	84. (A)	85. (D)	181. (D)	182. (A)	183. (B)	184. (B)	185. (C)
86. (C)	87. (B)	88. (C)	89. (D)	90. (A)	186. (C)	187. (A)	188. (D)	189. (B)	190. (C)
91. (C)	92. (C)	93. (B)	94. (D)	95. (A)	191. (B)	192. (B)	193. (C)	194. (D)	195. (C)
96. (C)	97. (A)	98. (B)	99. (D)	100. (A)	196. (B)	197. (C)	198. (D)	199. (C)	200. (A)

Actual Test

01
02
03
04
05
06

번역 및 정답

1. 미M
(A) She is paying for purchases.
(B) She is weighing some vegetables.
(C) She is exiting a store.
(D) She is placing food in a basket.

(A) 그녀는 구매한 물건에 대해 값을 치르고 있다.
(B) 그녀는 채소 무게를 달고 있다.
(C) 그녀는 가게에서 나오고 있다.
(D) 그녀는 바구니에 식품을 담고 있다. 　　　　정답 (D)

2. 영M
(A) The man has his hands on the steering wheel.
(B) A vehicle is being repaired.
(C) A package is being delivered to a man.
(D) The man is writing on a clipboard.

(A) 남자가 차의 핸들에 손을 대고 있다.
(B) 차량이 수리되고 있다.
(C) 소포가 남자에게 배달되고 있다.
(D) 남자가 클립보드에 적고 있다. 　　　　정답 (D)

3. 호W
(A) She is pouring coffee into a cup.
(B) She is holding onto a handrail.
(C) She is descending a staircase.
(D) She is taking a wallet from her backpack.

(A) 그녀는 컵에 커피를 따르고 있다.
(B) 그녀는 난간을 꽉 잡고 있다.
(C) 그녀는 계단을 내려가고 있다.
(D) 그녀는 배낭에서 지갑을 꺼내고 있다. 　　　　정답 (C)

4. 미M
(A) Some tables have been arranged in the middle of a room.
(B) Some objects are scattered around on the table.
(C) Some potted plants have been arranged in rows.
(D) Folded chairs are leaning against the wall.

(A) 테이블 몇 개가 방 한가운데에 정돈 배치되어 있다.
(B) 몇 개의 물건들이 테이블 위에 흩어져 있다.
(C) 화초가 있는 화분이 줄지어 정돈되어 있다.
(D) 접혀진 의자들이 벽에 기대어져 있다. 　　　　정답 (A)

5. 미W
(A) Some people are assembled on the patio.
(B) Some people are adjusting an umbrella.
(C) A chair has been set on the lawn.
(D) They are arranging chairs on the patio.

(A) 몇 명의 사람들이 옥외 테라스에 모여 있다.
(B) 몇 명의 사람들이 파라솔을 조정하고 있다.
(C) 의자가 잔디밭 위에 놓여 있다.
(D) 그들은 옥외 테라스에 있는 의자를 정리하고 있다. 　　　　정답 (A)

6. 영M
(A) One of the women is reaching into an oven.
(B) Some containers are being emptied.
(C) One of the women is leaning against the counter.

(D) Some candy is being displayed in a glass case.

(A) 여자 중 한 명이 오븐 안으로 손을 뻗고 있다.
(B) 용기 몇 개가 비워지고 있다.
(C) 여자 중 한 명이 카운터에 기대고 있다.
(D) 사탕이 유리 케이스에 진열되어 있다. 　　　　정답 (D)

Part 2

7. 미M 미W
Who is supposed to work at the loading dock this morning?
(A) Karl and Jeff.
(B) I know the name of that road.
(C) More than 10 crates of bananas.

오늘 오전에 누가 하역장에서 일하기로 되어 있어요?
(A) 칼과 제프예요.
(B) 제가 그 도로 이름을 알아요.
(C) 열 상자 이상의 바나나요. 　　　　정답 (A)

8. 미W 호W
When is Margo coming to the product demonstration?
(A) There's more in the supply cabinet.
(B) She said she'd be five minutes late.
(C) Yes, she arrived last Monday.

마고는 언제 제품 시연회에 오죠?
(A) 비품함에 좀 더 있어요.
(B) 그녀는 5분 늦는다고 했어요.
(C) 예, 그녀는 지난주 월요일에 도착했어요. 　　　　정답 (B)

9. 호W 미M
Do you work out every day?
(A) A nearby fitness facility.
(B) I jog each morning.
(C) That's not the right size.

매일 운동하세요?
(A) 근처 헬스 시설이요.
(B) 저는 매일 아침 조깅해요.
(C) 그건 사이즈가 맞지 않아요. 　　　　정답 (B)

10. 미W 미M
Where is our team taking the clients out to dinner?
(A) Somewhere in the commercial district.
(B) No, put it here on the dinner table.
(C) They have great vegetarian dishes.

우리 팀은 고객들을 어디로 모시고 나가서 저녁을 먹을 거예요?
(A) 상업 지구 어딘가에서요.
(B) 아뇨, 그것을 여기 디너 테이블에 놓으세요.
(C) 거기에 괜찮은 채식 요리가 있어요. 　　　　정답 (A)

11. 미W 영M
Could you call the Royal Restaurant to make dinner reservations?
(A) Today's chef's specialty.
(B) They don't accept reservations.
(C) Yes, the security code has changed.

로열 식당에 전화해서 저녁 식사를 예약해 주실래요?
(A) 오늘의 주방장 특선요리예요.

(B) 거기는 예약을 받지 않아요.
(C) 예, 보안 코드가 변경되었어요.　　　　　　　정답 (B)

12. 미M 미W
How did your presentation go yesterday?
(A) It went very well, thanks.
(B) Sorry, I can't go by bus.
(C) It was a present from my colleagues.

어제 당신 발표는 어떻게 되었어요?
(A) 아주 잘되었어요, 감사해요.
(B) 죄송해요, 저는 버스로 갈 수 없어요.
(C) 그건 제 동료들이 준 선물이었어요.　　　정답 (A)

13. 미W 미M
This laptop model here is new, isn't it?
(A) Yes, but it isn't selling well.
(B) We need new cables.
(C) Thanks for leaving it turned on.

여기 이 노트북 모델은 새로 나온 거죠, 그렇죠?
(A) 예, 그런데 그게 잘 팔리지는 않아요.
(B) 우리는 새 케이블이 필요해요.
(C) 그것을 켜두어 주셔서 감사해요.　　　　정답 (A)

14. 미W 호W
Would you like to see the promotional flyer I designed?
(A) He got a promotion last week.
(B) I'll go to a meeting in just ten minutes.
(C) I resigned last year.

제가 디자인한 홍보 전단지를 보실래요?
(A) 그는 지난주에 승진했어요.
(B) 제가 10분 후에 회의에 갈 거예요.
(C) 저는 작년에 사임했어요.　　　　　　　정답 (B)

15. 미M 영M
Didn't you have a doctor's appointment yesterday afternoon?
(A) Yeah, that's why I left work early.
(B) Here is your prescription.
(C) He is not available today.

어제 오후에 의사와의 진료 예약이 있지 않았어요?
(A) 예, 그래서 제가 일찍 퇴근했잖아요.
(B) 여기 처방전 있어요.
(C) 그는 오늘 자리에 없어요.　　　　　　　정답 (A)

16. 영M 미W
How is our manager getting to the Seattle Convention?
(A) It was a great trip.
(B) Sure, I'd like to go there, too.
(C) I'm going to give him a ride.

우리 매니저는 시애틀 컨벤션에 어떻게 가시죠?
(A) 그건 아주 괜찮은 여행이었어요.
(B) 좋아요. 저도 거기에 가고 싶어요.
(C) 제가 그 분을 태워다 드릴 거예요.　　　정답 (C)

17. 호W 미M
You're attending the safety training on Thursday, aren't you?
(A) The desk for registration over there.
(B) The safety inspector is arriving in any minute.

(C) I'm leaving for the marketing conference.

목요일에 안전 교육에 참석하실 거죠, 그렇죠?
(A) 저쪽에 있는 등록 데스크요.
(B) 안전 검사원이 곧 도착해요.
(C) 저는 마케팅 회의에 참석하기 위해 나갈 거예요.　정답 (C)

18. 미W 영M
Why has the storage closet been locked all day?
(A) Did you buy some more office supplies?
(B) It is close to our office.
(C) Because I misplaced the key.

보관실이 왜 하루 종일 잠겨 있는 거죠?
(A) 사무용품을 좀 더 구매했어요?
(B) 그곳은 우리 사무실과 가까워요.
(C) 왜냐하면 제가 열쇠를 잃어버렸기 때문이에요.　정답 (C)

19. 미M 호W
The company is going to cover the damages for the shipment, isn't it?
(A) It was shipped out yesterday.
(B) I'm sure they will.
(C) The model has many advantages.

회사가 운송에 대한 피해를 보상해 주는 거죠, 그렇죠?
(A) 그것은 어제 발송되었어요.
(B) 분명히 그럴 거예요.
(C) 그 모델은 장점이 많아요.　　　　　　　정답 (B)

20. 미W 미M
Should we have the meeting this week or next week?
(A) We've met before, haven't we?
(B) It lasted for more than half an hour.
(C) Next Monday would be better.

회의를 이번 주에 할까요, 아니면 다음 주에 할까요?
(A) 우리는 전에 만난 적이 있죠, 그렇죠?
(B) 그건 30분 이상 지속되었어요.
(C) 다음 주 월요일이 더 좋겠어요.　　　　정답 (C)

21. 영M 미W
When will the company outing be held?
(A) No, it hasn't been taken care of yet.
(B) I set it on the lawn yesterday.
(C) Management is still deciding.

회사 야유회가 언제 열리나요?
(A) 아뇨, 그건 아직 처리되지 않았어요.
(B) 제가 그것을 어제 잔디 위에 두었어요.
(C) 경영진이 아직 결정 중이에요.　　　　정답 (C)

22. 미M 호W
Who's helping you work on the quarterly sales report?
(A) It's already finished.
(B) Turn to the page 52 of the report.
(C) No, it comes out annually.

당신이 분기별 판매 보고서 작업하는 것을 누가 도와주고 있어요?
(A) 그건 이미 끝났어요.
(B) 보고서 52쪽으로 넘기세요.
(C) 아뇨, 그건 일년에 한 번 나와요.　　　정답 (A)

23. 미W 미M

Doesn't the ticket office open at 7 P.M.?

(A) Aren't they closed on Mondays?

(B) Yes, the office is close to the bookstore.

(C) No, the performer will arrive at 6 P.M.

매표소는 저녁 7시에 열지 않나요?

(A) 월요일에는 문을 닫지 않나요?

(B) 예, 사무실은 서점과 가까워요.

(C) 아뇨, 공연자는 오후 6시에 도착할 거예요.　　　정답 (A)

24. 호W 미M

Do you have the flight and accommodations details for our business trip?

(A) I flew to New York.

(B) Ms. Wilson is making arrangements for our travel.

(C) They had a paid vacation.

우리 출장 관련 항공편 및 숙소 세부 내용을 갖고 있으세요?

(A) 저는 뉴욕에 비행기 타고 갔어요.

(B) 윌슨 씨가 우리 출장 관련 준비를 하고 있어요.

(C) 그들은 유급 휴가를 받았어요.　　　정답 (B)

25. 미W 영M

Which one are we serving at the welcome reception, beef or chicken?

(A) The guests will have several options.

(B) The servers look busy.

(C) I didn't go to the party, either.

환영회에서 어느 것을 제공할까요, 소고기요 아니면 닭고기요?

(A) 손님들에게 몇 가지 옵션이 있을 거예요.

(B) 서빙하는 사람들이 바빠 보여요.

(C) 저도 파티에 가지 않았어요.　　　정답 (A)

26. 미M 영M

How many attendees are we expecting for the product demonstration?

(A) Right after 10.

(B) The number keeps changing.

(C) The upgraded version of the software.

제품 시연회에 참석자가 몇 명 올 거라고 예상하고 있나요?

(A) 10시 직후에요.

(B) 숫자가 계속 바뀌어요.

(C) 소프트웨어 업그레이드 버전이요.　　　정답 (B)

27. 미W 호W

I'm wondering if you could e-mail me next quarter's sales projections.

(A) Yes, all items are on sale.

(B) I'd really appreciate it.

(C) Chris faxed it to you this morning.

다음 분기 예상 판매량을 이메일로 제게 보내주실 수 있을까 모르겠네요.

(A) 예, 모든 품목이 세일 중이에요.

(B) 그렇게 해주시면 정말 감사할게요.

(C) 크리스가 오늘 아침에 당신에게 그것을 팩스로 보냈어요.　　　정답 (C)

28. 영M 미M

There isn't Internet access available on this shuttle bus, is there?

(A) This is one of the older buses our company has.

(B) About 30 minutes at rush hour.

(C) The tickets are available on the Internet.

이 셔틀 버스에서는 인터넷 접속이 안 되는 거죠, 그렇죠?

(A) 이 버스는 우리 회사가 보유하고 있는 오래된 버스 중 하나예요.

(B) 러시 아워 시간에는 약 30분이요.

(C) 표는 인터넷에서 구입 가능해요.　　　정답 (A)

29. 미W 호W

Why don't we publish this article in the May issue of our magazine?

(A) In the publisher conference.

(B) Yes, I think it's very timely.

(C) I don't subscribe to the magazine.

이 기사를 우리 잡지 5월호에 싣는 게 어때요?

(A) 출판업체 총회에서요

(B) 예, 아주 시의적절한 것 같아요.

(C) 저는 그 잡지를 구독하지 않아요.　　　정답 (B)

30. 미M 호W

Is the art gallery under renovation this month?

(A) I forgot to close the drawer.

(B) I don't work there anymore.

(C) Oh, I was there last month.

미술관은 이달에 보수공사 중인가요?

(A) 제가 서랍을 닫는 것을 깜빡 잊었어요.

(B) 저는 더 이상 그곳에서 근무하지 않아요.

(C) 아, 저는 지난달에 거기 있었어요.　　　정답 (B)

31. 미M 미W

This article looks at ways to improve energy efficiency.

(A) Can I read it when you are done?

(B) The magazine editor-in-chief.

(C) The new vehicle is fuel-efficient.

이 기사는 에너지 효율을 개선하기 위한 방법을 살펴보는 거예요.

(A) 다 끝내시면 제가 읽어봐도 될까요?

(B) 잡지 편집장이요.

(C) 그 새 차량은 연비가 좋아요.　　　정답 (A)

Part 3

문제 32-34번은 다음 대화를 참조하시오. 미M 미W

M: Hello. You've reached the Perkins Art Gallery. How can I help you?

W: Good morning. **(32)I'm calling from Russell Publishing. (33) I saw a work of art in your digital collection last weekend, and I'd love to use it on the front cover of a book I'm working on. Can I do that?**

M: Of course. **(34)Could you let me know the image ID number of the work?** Each and every document here in our museum collection has one. If you do that, I can provide you with a digital image.

M: 안녕하세요. 퍼킨스 미술관입니다. 무엇을 도와드릴까요?

W: 안녕하세요. 러셀 출판사에서 전화드립니다. 지난 주말에 거기 디지털 소장품에서 작품 하나를 봤는데, 그 작품을 제가 작업하고 있는 책의 앞 표

지로 사용하고 싶습니다. 그렇게 해도 될까요?

M: 물론입니다. 그 작품의 이미지 식별 번호를 알려 주시겠어요? 여기 저희 미술관에 있는 모든 작품에 각각 번호가 있어요. 그 번호를 알려 주시면, 디지털 이미지를 제공해 드릴 수 있습니다.

32. 여자는 어디에서 근무하는가?
    (A) 화방
    (B) 미술관
    (C) 출판사
    (D) 서점   정답 (C)

33. 여자가 전화를 거는 이유는?
    (A) 사진 사용에 대해 문의하기 위해
    (B) 새 전시품에 대해 알아보기 위해
    (C) 한 업체의 영업 시간을 물어보기 위해
    (D) 특별 투어를 준비하기 위해   정답 (A)

34. 남자는 여자에게 무엇을 달라고 요청하는가?
    (A) 등록비
    (B) 디지털 이미지
    (C) 마감시한
    (D) 식별 번호   정답 (D)

문제 35-37번은 다음 대화를 참조하시오. 호W 미M

W: All right, (35)**the party to celebrate Mary's promotion is soon,** so we need to figure out what we need to buy for it. We definitely need a cake as well as some drinks, cups, and plates.
M: Don't worry about the cake. There's no need to buy one. (36)**Remember how Mary loved that chocolate cake I made at the party last spring? I can make another one.**
W: That sounds perfect, Dave. So let's just get the other things I mentioned. (37)**I'll visit the store tomorrow after work to purchase the cups and the plates.**

W: 자, 메리의 승진을 축하하기 위한 파티가 곧 있어서, 파티를 위해 우리가 뭘 사야 하는지 생각해 봐야 해요. 음료, 컵, 접시뿐 아니라 케이크도 꼭 필요해요.
M: 케이크에 대해서는 걱정하지 마세요. 살 필요 없어요. 지난 봄 파티에서 내가 만든 초콜릿 케이크를 메리가 얼마나 좋아했는지 기억나요? 내가 또 하나 만들 수 있어요.
W: 딱이네요, 데이브. 그러면 내가 말한 나머지 것들만 삽시다. 내일 퇴근 후에 내가 가게에 들러 컵과 접시를 살게요.

35. 화자들은 어떤 행사를 준비하고 있는가?
    (A) 축하 파티
    (B) 회사 연수회
    (C) 기금 모금 행사
    (D) 기념일 축하 행사   정답 (A)

36. 남자는 무엇을 하겠다고 제의하는가?
    (A) 초대장 보내기
    (B) 방 장식하기
    (C) 케이크 굽기
    (D) 메리에게 도움 청하기   정답 (C)

37. 여자는 무엇을 하겠다고 말하는가?
    (A) 개정된 예산안 요청하기

    (B) 물품 구매하기
    (C) 방 예약하기
    (D) 제과점 들르기   정답 (B)

문제 38-40번은 다음 대화를 참조하시오. 미W 영M

W: Hello, Kevin. Are you having a good time at this year's book tradeshow?
M: It's really great. (38)**I've discovered several new authors whose works I can sell at my bookstore.** I'm also pleased about the new venue this year. (39)**This convention center is much closer to my hotel.**
W: I know what you mean. (39)**I only had to walk for three minutes and didn't need to take a taxi like I did last year.** Oh, by the way, you told me that you purchased some tablet computers for the sales staff at your store to use. How well are they working out?
M: Quite well. (40)**My employees find them convenient, especially when it comes to checking on item availability.**

W: 안녕하세요, 케빈. 올해 도서 박람회에서 좋은 시간 보내고 있어요?
M: 정말 좋아요. 작품을 우리 서점에서 판매할 수 있는 신규 작가 몇 분을 발견했어요. 또한 올해 박람회 장소가 바뀐 것도 좋았어요. 이 컨벤션 센터는 제 호텔에서 훨씬 더 가까워요.
W: 무슨 말인지 알겠어요. 저는 3분만 걸어가면 되어서, 작년처럼 택시를 탈 필요가 없었죠. 아, 그런데, 당신 서점의 영업 담당 직원들이 쓸 태블릿 컴퓨터를 샀다고 얘기하셨죠. 그건 잘 쓰고 있나요?
M: 아주 잘 써요. 직원들이 태블릿 컴퓨터가 아주 편하다고 생각해요. 특히 재고 확인에 관해서는요.

38. 남자는 자신의 매장에서 무엇을 판매하는가?
    (A) 전자제품
    (B) 도서
    (C) 가구
    (D) 의류   정답 (B)

39. 화자들은 컨벤션 센터에 대해 무엇을 암시하는가?
    (A) 컨벤션 센터는 대중교통 근처에 있다.
    (B) 무역 박람회가 작년에 그곳에서 개최되었다.
    (C) 그들의 호텔들이 컨벤션 센터 근처에 있다.
    (D) 그들은 그곳에 가기 위해 택시를 타야 했다.   정답 (C)

40. 태블릿 컴퓨터는 남자의 매장에서 어떻게 사용되는가?
    (A) 신규 회원을 등록시키기 위해
    (B) 지불을 처리하기 위해
    (C) 고객들의 의견을 수집하기 위해
    (D) 재고를 확인하기 위해   정답 (D)

문제 41-43번은 다음 대화를 참조하시오. 미M 호W

M: Samantha, (41)**I just learned that the vice president changed his schedule.** He's going to arrive tomorrow instead of on Friday.
W: In that case, we'd better complete our presentation file by this afternoon. (42)**We only have a couple of slides left and still need to rehearse it a couple of times, too.**
M: You're right, but I think we'll be ready by the time he arrives.

Let's not stop working today.

W: Okay. You know, it's nearly lunch time. (43)**How about having some food delivered from the Marcos Deli?** That way, we won't need to waste time going out to a restaurant.

M: Sure, good idea. Let's do it.

M: 사만다, 부사장님이 일정을 바꾸셨다고 막 들었어요. 금요일 대신 내일 도착하실 거예요.

W: 그렇다면, 오늘 오후까지 프레젠테이션 자료를 끝내는 게 낫겠어요. 슬라이드 자료 두 개밖에 안 남았는데, 그래도 프레젠테이션 리허설도 두 번은 해야 해요.

M: 맞아요, 그런데 내 생각에는 부사장님이 도착할 때쯤이면 우리 준비는 다 될 것 같아요. 오늘은 쉬지 말고 일합시다.

W: 좋아요, 그런데 거의 점심 시간이에요. 마르코 델리에서 음식을 배달시키는 게 어때요? 그렇게 해야, 식당으로 나가느라 시간을 낭비할 필요가 없을 테니까요.

M: 물론이에요, 좋은 생각이에요. 그렇게 합시다.

41. 남자는 최근에 무엇을 알게 되었는가?
(A) 한 경영진의 일정이 변경되었다.
(B) 세미나가 막 취소되었다.
(C) 배송품이 오늘 배달된다.
(D) 회의실이 예약되었다.   정답 (A)

42. 화자들은 무엇을 할 필요가 있는가?
(A) 자료 검토하기
(B) 교육 일정 잡기
(C) 프레젠테이션 연습하기
(D) 일부 서류 치우기   정답 (C)

43. 여자는 무엇을 할 것을 제안하는가?
(A) 음식을 배달 주문하기
(B) 식당 예약하기
(C) 내일 리허설을 위해 일찍 오기
(D) 다 끝낸 후 점심 먹기   정답 (A)

문제 44-46번은 다음 3자 대화를 참조하시오. 영M 호W 미W

M: Hello, Alice. I'm Robert. It's great that you're joining us on the staff here at Watson Medical Center. I'm your supervisor, and (44)**I'll be teaching you how to handle office assistant duties.**

W1: Hi, Robert. It's a pleasure to meet you.

M: This is Karen. Karen, this is Alice, our newest office assistant.

W2: Hi, Alice. I'm glad to meet you. I guess we'll be working together.

M: Here's Alice's new employee binder. (45)**Could you help her fill out some of these orientation forms, please, Karen?**

W2: (45)**Sure. I've got some time now.**

M: Thanks. Once you are done, I'll show Alice how to use the patient tag software program.

W1: (46)**Actually, I used one at my previous job.**

M: 안녕하세요, 앨리스. 로버트예요. 당신이 여기 왓슨 메디컬 센터 직원으로 함께하게 되어 기쁘군요. 나는 당신의 상사고요. 사무 보조직원 업무들을 어떻게 처리할지 가르쳐 드릴게요.

W1: 안녕하세요, 로버트. 만나뵙게 되어 반갑습니다.

M: 여기는 카렌이에요. 카렌, 여기는 가장 최근에 들어온 사무 보조직원, 앨리스예요.

W2: 안녕하세요, 앨리스. 만나게 되어 반가워요. 우리 같이 근무하게 될 것 같네요.

M: 여기 앨리스의 신입 사원 바인더가 있어요. 앨리스가 이 오리엔테이션 서식 일부를 작성하는 것을 도와주실래요, 카렌?

W2: 물론이죠. 저는 지금 시간이 좀 있어요.

M: 고마워요. 일단 당신이 끝나면, 나는 앨리스에게 환자 신원 확인 밴드 소프트웨어 프로그램을 사용하는 방법을 보여줄 거예요.

W1: 사실 전 이전 직장에서도 환자 신원 확인 밴드 소프트웨어를 사용했어요.

44. 앨리스의 직업은 무엇인가?
(A) 연구원
(B) 실험실 기사
(C) 사무 보조직원
(D) 사무장   정답 (C)

45. 앨리스는 이후에 무엇을 할 것 같은가?
(A) 사무실 둘러보기
(B) 서식 작성
(C) 취업 면접 실시
(D) CEO와 대화   정답 (B)

46. 앨리스는 소프트웨어에 대해 무엇을 시사하는가?
(A) 그녀는 그게 교체되기를 바란다.
(B) 그것이 제대로 작동하지 않는다.
(C) 그것이 비용이 많이 든다.
(D) 그녀는 그것의 사용법을 안다.   정답 (D)

문제 47-49번은 다음 대화를 참조하시오. 미M 미W

M: Pardon me, but where is the honey? (47)**I thought I knew where it was, but I can't seem to find it anywhere in this supermarket store.**

W: Ah, (48)**the building was recently remodeled, so we changed the locations of some merchandise.** You can find the honey in aisle number three. Do you need anything else?

M: Yes, please. (49)**Do you still sell Denton's frozen pizzas?**

W: (49)**Let me ask my manager. We no longer carry a few brands anymore.**

M: 실례합니다만, 꿀이 어디에 있나요? 있는 장소를 안다고 생각했는데, 이 슈퍼마켓 매장 어디에서도 찾을 수가 없는 것 같군요.

W: 아, 이 건물이 최근에 리모델링을 해서, 상품 위치를 좀 바꿨어요. 3번 통로에 가면 꿀이 있을 거예요. 뭐 다른 거 또 필요한 거 있으세요?

M: 네, 있어요. 덴턴 사의 냉동 피자를 계속 판매하나요?

W: 매니저님께 여쭤볼게요. 우리는 몇몇 브랜드는 더 이상 취급하지 않고 있어요.

47. 화자들은 어디에 있는가?
(A) 슈퍼마켓
(B) 건강식품점
(C) 식당
(D) 창고   정답 (A)

48. 여자는 업체에 대해 무엇을 언급하는가?
(A) 곧 거기에서 세일을 시작할 것이다.
(B) 막 보수공사를 했다.
(C) 두 번째 매장을 개설했다.

(D) 이제 더 적은 사람들이 거기서 쇼핑한다.   정답 (B)

49. 여자가 "우리는 몇몇 브랜드는 더 이상 취급하지 않고 있어요"라고 말할 때 무엇을 시사하는가?
(A) 그녀는 그 코너에서 더 이상 근무하지 않는다.
(B) 그녀는 곧 새로 배송될 냉동 피자를 기다리고 있다.
(C) 일부 상품은 구입할 수 없을 것이다.
(D) 그녀는 남자가 다른 것을 구매해야 한다고 생각한다.   정답 (C)

문제 50~52번은 다음 대화를 참조하시오. 영M 미W

M: Hello, Janet. **(50)Stefan told me your design for the new multi-purpose tool is almost finished.**
W: That's right. I'm really pleased with it. The lightweight and compact tool has seven separate units that fit into one holdable hardwood handle.
M: Wonderful. How far along are we on the ad campaign for the multi-use tool?
W: I'm not sure yet. **(51)We're still in the process of deciding what to call it. We have come up with some interesting ideas, but we have yet to agree on the best one.**
M: **(52)Why don't you ask everyone to give some comments at the staff meeting tomorrow?** Maybe you'll get an idea or two of what name might appeal to most customers.

M: 안녕하세요, 자넷. 스테판이 말하는데 새 다목적 연장의 디자인이 거의 끝났다면서요.
W: 맞아요. 그래서 저도 기뻐요. 가볍고 작은 이 연장은 7개의 각기 다른 도구가 들어가 있는데, 손에 쥘 수 있는 한 개의 단단한 나무 손잡이에 다 들어가요.
M: 훌륭하군요. 얼마나 있어야 그 다목적 연장에 대한 광고 캠페인에 들어가요?
W: 아직 잘 몰라요. 우리는 아직 그것의 이름을 뭘로 할지 결정하는 중이에요. 몇 가지 흥미로운 아이디어를 내긴 했는데, 가장 좋은 이름에 대해서는 아직 합의를 못 했어요.
M: 내일 직원 회의에서 모두에게 의견 좀 달라고 요청하지 그러세요? 어쩌면 어떤 이름이 대부분의 고객에게 매력적일 수 있는지 아이디어 한두 개쯤 얻을지도 몰라요.

50. 화자들은 어떤 종류의 제품에 대해 논의하고 있는가?
(A) 식품
(B) 전기 제품
(C) 연장
(D) 초소형 차   정답 (C)

51. 아직 무엇에 대해 합의해야 하는가?
(A) 이름
(B) 가격
(C) 출시일
(D) 광고 캠페인   정답 (A)

52. 남자는 무엇을 할 것을 제안하는가?
(A) 고객 설문조사 실시하기
(B) 제품 재디자인하기
(C) 동료들과 상의하기
(D) 온라인에 광고 내기   정답 (C)

문제 53~55번은 다음 대화를 참조하시오. 호W 미M

W: Ted, I just got off the phone with the manager of all the Dynamo Fitness Center locations in the city. **(53)He confirmed that our location will be closing ten days from now to undergo renovations that will last for two months.**
M: Okay, we'd better put some signs up to inform our members of what's going to happen. We can provide directions to other Dynamo Fitness Centers nearby.
W: Oh, one more thing. Mr. Sullivan informed me that **(54)any members who travel to alternate locations should receive half off their monthly fee.**
M: Sounds good. **(55)I'll send a mass e-mail to our members at once.**

W: 테드, 이 도시의 모든 다이나모 피트니스 센터 지점의 총괄 매니저와 지금 막 통화를 끝냈어요. 매니저가 우리 지점이 앞으로 10일 후에 문을 닫고 2개월간 보수공사를 진행한다고 확인해 주었어요.
M: 좋아요. 우리 회원들에게 무슨 일이 있을지 알리는 표지판 몇 개를 붙여야겠어요. 근처 다른 다이나모 피트니스 센터로 가는 길 안내를 제공하면 돼요.
W: 아, 한 가지 더 있어요. 설리반 씨가 저에게 다른 지점으로 가는 회원은 월 회비에서 50% 할인 받을 거라고 알려 주었어요.
M: 좋아요. 제가 당장 우리 회원들에게 단체 이메일을 보낼게요.

53. 10일 후에 무슨 일이 있겠는가?
(A) 새 매니저가 근무를 시작할 것이다.
(B) 운동 시설이 보수공사를 하게 될 것이다.
(C) 새 운동 강좌가 시작될 것이다.
(D) 다른 지점이 문을 열 것이다.   정답 (B)

54. 회원들에게 무엇이 제공될 것인가?
(A) 할인
(B) 티셔츠
(C) 새 강좌
(D) 상품권   정답 (A)

55. 남자는 무엇을 하겠다고 말하는가?
(A) 지원자 면접 보기
(B) 모든 회원에게 전화하기
(C) 일정 변경하기
(D) 이메일 보내기   정답 (D)

문제 56~58번은 다음 3자 대화를 참조하시오. 미M 미W 호W

M: **(56)Susan, are you having any problems planning this year's company retreat? I know it's your first time working on this.**
W1: No worries. I've already got all the activities planned.
M: I'm glad to hear that. How about reserving the venue? Did you reserve the hotel rooms?
W1: Mary is handling that. She's right over there. Mary, have you booked the hotel reservations for our company retreat yet?
W2: No, I haven't. I haven't been told how many will participate in it. **(57)I need a final list of attendees.**
M: Okay, but we're running out of time. **(58)Just make sure the hotel rooms are available at that time. I recommend that you make a reservation as soon as possible even without**

that information.

M: 수잔, 올해 회사 연수회 기획하는 데 문제 있어요? 이런 행사를 준비하는 게 처음인 것으로 아는데요.
W1: 괜찮아요. 이미 모든 행사를 기획했어요.
M: 그 말을 들으니 기쁘네요. 장소 예약은 어때요? 호텔 객실을 예약했어요?
W1: 메리가 그것을 담당하고 있어요. 메리가 바로 저쪽에 있네요. 메리, 우리 회사 수련회를 위한 호텔을 예약했어요?
W2: 아뇨, 안 했어요. 몇 명이 참석할지 아직 못 들었거든요. 최종 참석자 명단이 필요해요.
M: 알았어요. 그런데 시간이 별로 안 남았어요. 그 때 꼭 호텔 객실을 구할 수 있게 해두세요. 그 정보 없이도 가능한 한 빨리 예약을 하시는 게 좋겠어요.

56. 화자들은 주로 무엇을 논의하고 있는가?
(A) 호텔 객실 변경하기
(B) 사무실 이전하기
(C) 고객을 위한 프레젠테이션 준비하기
(D) 회사 연수회 준비하기 　　　　　정답 (D)

57. 메리에게 어떤 정보가 없는가?
(A) 행사에 대한 견적
(B) 확정된 장소
(C) 참석자 전체 명단
(D) 잠재 구매자 명단 　　　　　정답 (C)

58. 남자는 빨리 무엇을 할 것을 권하는가?
(A) 행사 장소 예약
(B) 항공권 사전 예약
(C) 지역 출장 요리 업체에 연락
(D) 회사 행사 일정 변경 　　　　　정답 (A)

문제 59-61번은 다음 대화를 참조하시오. 영M 미W

M: Hello, Ms. Sanders. I want to talk about the employee appreciation dinner with you. We're having it next month, but (59)we still haven't selected the winner of the TV host of the year award.
W: How about Peter? His morning show has been very popular with our viewers and gets great ratings.
M: (60)He has won the award three times. And a lot of other hosts have also made a remarkable contribution to our program.
W: You're right. (61)Why don't we nominate three people and send the list to our employees? We can let them choose.
M: (61)That's a good idea. It will be a first for us to have our staff members vote for the winner.

M: 안녕하세요, 샌더스 씨. 직원 감사 만찬에 대해 얘기 나누고 싶어요. 다음 달에 만찬을 여는데, 우리는 아직도 올해의 TV 진행자상 수상자를 선정하지 못했어요.
W: 피터가 어때요? 그의 모닝쇼가 시청자들에게 계속 인기 있고, 시청률도 좋잖아요.
M: 그는 그 상을 세 번이나 탔어요. 그리고 다른 많은 진행자들도 우리 프로그램에 괄목할 만한 기여를 했어요.
W: 그 말이 맞긴 해요. 세 명을 추천해서 그 명단을 직원들에게 보내는 것은 어떨까요? 직원들이 뽑을 수 있게요.
M: 좋은 생각이네요. 이번이 처음으로 직원들로 하여금 투표로 수상자를

뽑게 하는 것이겠군요.

59. 화자들은 어디에서 근무하는 것 같은가?
(A) TV 방송국
(B) 영화사
(C) 라디오 방송국
(D) 식당 　　　　　정답 (A)

60. 남자가 "그는 그 상을 세 번이나 탔어요"라고 말하는 이유는?
(A) 동료를 칭찬하기 위해
(B) 정정하기 위해
(C) 만족을 표하기 위해
(D) 제안을 거절하기 위해 　　　　　정답 (D)

61. 화자들은 무엇을 하기로 동의하는가?
(A) 직원의 의견 요청하기
(B) 마감시한 연장하기
(C) 시상식 연기하기
(D) 새 TV쇼 진행자 고용하기 　　　　　정답 (A)

문제 62-64번은 다음 대화와 스케치를 참조하시오. 호W 미M

W: Welcome to Delvin Interior. How may I help you?
M: Hello. (62)I spoke on the phone with you about placing an order for some curtains for the travel agency I work at.
W: Oh, hello, Mr. Carter. How did you like the samples I sent?
M: They were great.
W: Did you get the sketch of the design I e-mailed you?
M: I did. It looks nice, and I want to get some curtains made for the office. However, the windows in the office go from the floor to the ceiling, (63)so I'd like them to hang down longer than what you have recommended so that they can reach all the way to the floor. I want them to be 280 centimeters long instead.
W: No problem at all. But I think this will affect the cost slightly. (64)Could you please hold on while I calculate the new price?

W: 델빈 인테리어에 오신 것을 환영합니다. 무엇을 도와드릴까요?
M: 안녕하세요. 제가 일하는 여행사의 커튼 주문 건 때문에 전화 통화를 했었어요.
W: 아, 안녕하세요, 카터 씨. 제가 보낸 견본은 마음에 드셨나요?
M: 좋았어요.
W: 제가 이메일로 보내 드린 디자인 스케치는 받으셨어요?
M: 받았어요. 좋아 보여요. 그리고 사무실을 위한 커튼을 제작하고 싶어요. 그런데, 사무실 창문이 바닥부터 천장까지 있어서, 커튼이 바닥까지 닿을 수 있도록 여기에서 추천해 주신 것보다 좀 더 길게 늘어뜨리면 좋겠어요. 커튼은 280센티미터 정도 길이가 되었으면 해요.
W: 전혀 문제가 없어요. 그런데 이게 비용에 약간 영향이 있을 것 같아요. 제가 새 가격을 계산하는 동안 잠시 기다려 주실래요?

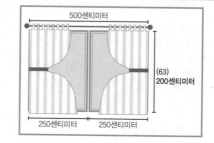

62. 남자는 어디서 근무하는가?
(A) 인테리어 디자인 회사
(B) 서점
(C) 여행사
(D) 건축 회사　　　　　　　　　　정답 (C)

63. 그래픽을 보시오. 어느 수치가 변경되겠는가?
(A) 200센티미터
(B) 250센티미터
(C) 300센티미터
(D) 500센티미터　　　　　　　　　정답 (A)

64. 여자가 이후에 무엇을 할 것 같은가?
(A) 새 가격 결정
(B) 추가 재료 주문
(C) 스케치 재디자인
(D) 다른 납품업체에 전화　　　　　정답 (A)

문제 65-67번은 다음 대화와 그래프를 참조하시오. 호W 미M

W: (65)**Here are last year's sales figures for our high-end laptops.** What do you think?
M: Hmm… I had expected sales for the third quarter to rise, (66) **but I'm shocked by how much they declined the following quarter.**
W: Well, we did have a few special sales during the third quarter, but we didn't do anything at the end of the year.
M: (67)**We'd better talk to Jacob Green, the new director of marketing. He should be able to arrange a promotional campaign or two for us.**

W: 여기 작년 우리 최고 사양의 노트북 컴퓨터 판매 수치가 있습니다. 어떻게 생각하세요?
M: 음… 3분기 매출은 오를 거라고 기대했었어요. 그런데 그 다음 분기에 매출이 얼마나 하락했는지 정말 충격 받았어요.
W: 저기, 3분기에는 우리가 몇 번의 특별 할인을 했지만, 연말에는 아무것도 하지 않았어요.
M: 신임 마케팅 국장이신 제이콥 그린과 얘기해 보는 게 낫겠어요. 우리를 위해 홍보 캠페인 한두 개쯤 준비하실 수 있을 거예요.

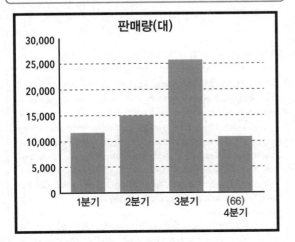

판매량(대)

65. 화자들은 어디에서 근무하는 것 같은가?
(A) 휴대 전화 제조업체

(B) 주방 가전제품 매장
(C) 컴퓨터 제조업체
(D) 장난감 제조업체　　　　　　　정답 (C)

66. 그래픽을 보시오. 남자가 어느 판매 수치에 놀라는가?
(A) 12,000
(B) 15,000
(C) 26,000
(D) 11,000　　　　　　　　　　　정답 (D)

67. 제이콥 그린은 누구인가?
(A) 회사 사장
(B) 마케팅 전문가
(C) 디자이너
(D) 회계사　　　　　　　　　　　정답 (B)

문제 68-70번은 다음 대화와 포스터를 참조하시오. 호W 영M

W: Dave, I can't wait to go to the music festival tomorrow.
M: I agree. There's such a big variety of musical acts that will be performing this year.
W: (68)**I am wondering if you need a ride to the festival.** I'm going to drive with some other colleagues in the sales department.
M: Actually, I have a dental appointment tomorrow morning, (69) **but I'll be sure to arrive there in time for the performance by my favorite act at 3:00.** Shall we meet near the blue stage?
W: No problem. (70)**Be sure to wear a jacket. I hear it's going to be a bit windy tomorrow.**

W: 데이브, 내일 음악 축제에 가는 게 너무 기다려져요.
M: 동감이에요. 올해 공연할 음악 공연자들이 아주 다양해요.
W: 축제까지 차편이 필요하신지 모르겠네요. 저는 영업부 동료들 몇 명과 같이 차로 갈 거예요.
M: 사실 저는 내일 아침에 치과 진료 약속이 있어요. 그렇지만 3시에 있는 제가 가장 좋아하는 그룹의 공연을 위해 거기에 제 시간에 꼭 도착할 거예요. 블루 스테이지 근처에서 만날까요?
W: 좋아요. 꼭 재킷을 입고 오세요. 내일 약간 바람이 분다고 들었어요.

매디슨 가을 음악 축제
10월 4일

공연 일정			
옐로 스테이지		블루 스테이지	
오후 12:00	컨트리	오전 10:00	재즈
오후 4:00	록	(69) 오후 3:00	팝
		오후 5:00	클래식

68. 여자는 남자를 위해 무엇을 하겠다고 제의하는가?
- (A) 그를 위해 표 구매하기
- (B) 그의 보고서 검토하기
- (C) 그를 차에 태워 주기
- (D) 그를 위해 좌석 맡아 두기
  정답 (C)

69. 그래픽을 보시오. 남자가 가장 좋아하는 음악 종류는 무엇인가?
- (A) 컨트리
- (B) 팝
- (C) 재즈
- (D) 록
  정답 (B)

70. 여자가 남자에게 상기시켜 주는 것은 무엇인가?
- (A) 표를 미리 구매할 것
- (B) 재킷을 입을 것
- (C) 물을 많이 가져올 것
- (D) 축제 시간에 맞춰 도착할 것
  정답 (B)

Part 4

문제 71-73번은 다음 소개를 참조하시오. 미W

W: Hello, everyone. **(71)I hope you've been having a great time at this year's engineering conference.** We're about to hear from the final speaker of the day, Brandon Morris. Anyone who has kept up on innovations in engineering would be familiar with his name since he's been recognized for a variety of innovative ideas. **(72)In fact, just one month ago, Mr. Morris won the prestigious Lorentz prize for designing a solar-powered portable water pump.** Mr. Morris is going to tell us more about his latest work momentarily. **(73)But first I'd like to remind you all about the reception we'll be having as soon as his talk ends.**

안녕하세요, 여러분. 올해 공학 기술 총회에서 좋은 시간을 보내고 계시기를 바랍니다. 오늘의 마지막 강연자, 브랜든 모리스의 연설을 곧 들으실 것입니다. 공학 기술의 혁신에 대한 소식을 계속 파악해 왔던 분이라면 누구든지 모리스 씨가 다양한 혁신적인 아이디어로 인정을 받아 왔기 때문에 이분의 이름이 익숙하실 겁니다. 사실 바로 한 달 전에, 모리스 씨는 태양열이 동력인 휴대용 양수기를 설계하여 명망 있는 로렌츠 상을 수상하셨습니다. 모리스 씨는 잠시 후에 저희에게 그의 가장 최근 업적에 대해 좀 더 많은 얘기를 해주실 것입니다. 그런데 먼저, 여러분 모두에게 모리스 씨의 연설이 끝나자마자 저희가 개최하는 환영회에 대해 잊지 마실 것을 말씀드리고자 합니다.

71. 총회의 주제는 무엇인가?
- (A) 차량 제조
- (B) 소프트웨어 개발
- (C) 공학 기술
- (D) 도서 출판
  정답 (C)

72. 화자에 따르면, 브랜든 모리스는 지난달에 무엇을 했는가?
- (A) 그는 태양 열판을 설치했다.
- (B) 그는 상을 수상했다.
- (C) 그는 총회에 참석했다.
- (D) 그는 연설을 했다.
  정답 (B)

73. 화자는 청자들에게 무엇에 대해 상기시켜 주는가?
- (A) 제품 시연회

- (B) 환영회
- (C) 연설
- (D) 전시회
  정답 (B)

문제 74-76번은 다음 녹음 메시지를 참조하시오. 영M

M: **(74)Thank you for choosing Lincoln Electricity as your energy provider.** We are well aware that **(75)the severe thunderstorms caused numerous power outages throughout the city during the night.** Work crews are busy attempting to restore power. We anticipate that all homes and businesses in the city will have full power no later than 10 a.m. this morning. **(76)If electricity has not been restored to your location by that time, please call us again** and press the number five to speak with one of our representatives.

여러분의 전력 공급업체로 링컨 전력 회사를 선택해 주셔서 감사합니다. 맹렬한 뇌우로 지난밤 도시 전역에서 수많은 정전이 발생했음을 잘 알고 있습니다. 작업반원들이 전력을 복구하느라 바쁩니다. 우리는 이 도시의 모든 가정과 사업체에 늦어도 오늘 오전 10시까지는 전력이 완전히 돌아올 것으로 예상하고 있습니다. 만약 그 시각까지 여러분이 있는 곳에 전력이 복구되지 않는다면, 저희에게 다시 전화하여 5번을 누르시면 저희 직원 중 한 명과 통화하실 수 있습니다.

74. 화자는 어디에서 근무하는 것 같은가?
- (A) 관공서
- (B) 지역 기상청
- (C) 건설 회사
- (D) 전력 회사
  정답 (D)

75. 문제의 원인이 무엇인가?
- (A) 악천후가 있었다.
- (B) 기계 일부가 구식이다.
- (C) 작업반원이 충분히 있지 않다.
- (D) 전기 요금이 올랐다.
  정답 (A)

76. 문제가 계속된다면, 청자들은 무엇을 해야 하는가?
- (A) 웹사이트 방문
- (B) 나중에 다시 전화
- (C) 사무실을 직접 방문
- (D) 전력 서비스 취소
  정답 (B)

문제 77-79번은 다음 안내를 참조하시오. 미M

M: **(77)Thank you for attending the opening celebration of our museum's Native American art exhibit.** It's wonderful to see so many people from the local area here today. This exhibit features all kinds of artwork made by Native Americans in this region. **(78)Now, before the tour begins, let's head to the auditorium to watch a short video about Native American art.** And please be aware that as a way of expressing gratitude for your support, **(79)we're offering a 30% discount for purchases made at our gift shop today only.**

우리 미술관의 미국 원주민 미술 전시회의 개막식에 참석해 주셔서 감사합니다. 오늘 이 자리에서 이 지역의 많은 분들을 보게 되어 정말 좋습니다. 이 전시회는 주로 이 지역의 미국 원주민들이 만든 모든 종류의 예술품을 전시

하고 있습니다. 이제 전시회 관람을 시작하기 전에, 미국 원주민 예술에 대한 짧은 비디오를 시청하러 대강당으로 갑시다. 그리고 여러분의 지지에 대한 감사를 표시하는 방법으로, 오늘 하루만 저희 선물 가게에서 이루어지는 구매품에 대해 30% 할인을 제공해 드린다는 것도 알아 두세요.

77. 미술관이 무엇을 축하하고 있는가?
(A) 기념일
(B) 임원 은퇴
(C) 새 전시회
(D) 도서관 개관   정답 (C)

78. 청자들은 맨 먼저 무엇을 할 것인가?
(A) 자기 소개
(B) 관람
(C) 연설 청취
(D) 영상 시청   정답 (D)

79. 청자들은 무엇을 받을 것인가?
(A) 무료 입장
(B) 선물 가게 할인
(C) 무료 식사 쿠폰
(D) 무료 기념품   정답 (B)

문제 80-82번은 다음 전화 메시지를 참조하시오. 호W

W: Hello. (81)**One of my colleagues that just got back from a vacation highly recommended your agency.** (80) (81)**So I'm calling because I'd love for you to assist me with my own trip for this winter.** I noticed on the Swiss Railways website that an unlimited travel pass is being offered in January for the equivalent of $400. (82)**I know it's the peak season for travel, which is why the fare is rather expensive. However, I heard that the scenery in Switzerland is stunning that time of the year.** So I thought I'd check with you before I reserve anything. Please call me back at 867-3339.

안녕하세요. 휴가에서 막 돌아온 제 동료 중 한 명이 귀 대리점을 강력 추천했어요. 그래서 귀사에서 올 겨울 저만의 여행을 좀 도와주셨으면 해서 전화드렸습니다. 스위스 철도 웹사이트에서 1월에 400달러에 상당하는 가격으로 무제한 여행권이 제공되고 있다는 것을 알게 되었어요. 1월이 여행 성수기이고, 그래서 요금이 다소 비싸다는 것을 알고 있어요. 그렇지만, 스위스 경치는 해마다 그때쯤이 굉장히 멋있다고 들었어요. 그래서 뭐든 예약하기 전에 귀사에 확인해 봐야겠다고 생각했습니다. 867-3339로 제게 연락 주세요.

80. 화자는 무엇을 계획하고 있는가?
(A) 업무 회의
(B) 고객 방문
(C) 회사의 기금 모금 행사
(D) 휴가   정답 (D)

81. 청자는 누구일 것 같은가?
(A) 여행사 직원
(B) 기차의 차장
(C) 세미나 조직인
(D) 호텔 직원   정답 (A)

82. 화자가 "스위스의 경치는 해마다 그때쯤이 굉장히 멋있다고 들었어요"라고 말할 때 무엇을 의미하는가?
(A) 그녀는 여행이 취소되어서 기분이 좋지 않다.
(B) 그녀는 청자의 추천에 동의한다.
(C) 그녀는 청자가 자신과 동행할 것을 권하고 있다.
(D) 그녀는 구매가 돈 값어치를 할 것이라고 생각한다.   정답 (D)

문제 83-85번은 다음 전화 메시지를 참조하시오. 미M

M: Hello. I'm calling from Sanderson Consulting. (83)**We'll be attending the Northeastern IT Trade Show next month**, and we need a display designed for us. I've gone over some of the designs you did for prior exhibitions on your website, and (84) **I must admit that they're quite unique. I'd love for you to work for us.** We didn't rent a big space, but I hope that your team can work with it and make something nice. Will you be available this Friday? (85)**If you are free, how about getting together to discuss what I'd like to have done?**

안녕하세요. 샌더슨 컨설팅에서 전화드렸어요. 저희가 다음달 북동부 IT 박람회에 참가하는데, 저희 회사를 위해 진열대를 디자인해 주셨으면 해서요. 이전 전시회들에서 당신이 작업한 여러 디자인 중 일부를 귀사의 웹사이트에서 훑어봤는데, 그것들이 아주 독특하다는 것을 인정하지 않을 수 없군요. 저희를 위해서 작업을 해주셨으면 합니다. 저희 회사는 큰 공간을 임대하지는 않았지만, 당신 팀이 그곳에 작업을 하여 뭔가 멋지게 만들어 주시기를 희망합니다. 이번 주 금요일에 시간이 되시나요? 시간이 되신다면, 만나서 제가 작업이 되길 원하는 것에 대해 논의하는 게 어떨까요?

83. 화자의 회사는 다음 달에 무엇을 할 계획인가?
(A) 자사 웹사이트 업데이트
(B) 신제품 소개
(C) IT 팀의 추가 직원 채용
(D) 무역 박람회 참석   정답 (D)

84. 화자가 "그것들이 아주 독특하다는 것을 인정하지 않을 수 없군요"라고 말할 때 무엇을 의미하는가?
(A) 그는 좀 더 자세한 설명이 필요하다.
(B) 그는 컨설팅 회사에서 일을 막 시작했다.
(C) 그는 일부 디자인에 대해 좋은 인상을 받았다.
(D) 그는 추천을 따르는 것이 꺼려진다.   정답 (C)

85. 화자는 무엇을 요청하는가?
(A) 견적서
(B) 회의
(C) 고객 명단
(D) 배송 주소   정답 (B)

문제 86-88번은 다음 회의 발췌 내용을 참조하시오. 호W

W: (86)**I wanted to have this meeting to discuss a new strategy for our department stores. (87)We're going to experiment with a strategy where the prices of items change all throughout the day.** We'd like to encourage customers to make more purchases at off-peak times. For example, young adult clothing sells quite well in the evenings. So if we lower the prices in the morning, we can sell more clothing items throughout the day. That should also encourage young adults to make other purchases. (88)David Lowell, the vice president of Marketing, came up with this idea, and he's going to tell us exactly how we're going to implement the strategy in our departments.

우리 백화점을 위한 새로운 전략에 대해 논의하기 위해서 이 회의를 열고 싶었습니다. 우리는 하루 종일 물건의 가격이 변동되는 전략을 실험할 것입니다. 손님들이 한산한 시간에 구입을 더 하도록 장려하고자 합니다. 예를 들어, 청소년층 의류는 저녁에 아주 잘 판매됩니다. 그래서 오전에는 가격을 낮춘다면, 하루 종일 더 많은 의류를 판매할 수 있을 것입니다. 그렇게 되면 또한 젊은이들이 다른 구매도 하게끔 촉진하게 될 것입니다. 마케팅 부사장님이신 데이비드 로웰 씨가 이 아이디어를 제안하셨는데, 부사장님이 우리 백화점에서 이 전략을 어떻게 실행에 옮길 것인지 말씀해 주실 겁니다.

86. 화자는 어떤 업종에 근무하는가?
(A) 백화점
(B) 슈퍼마켓
(C) 광고 대행사
(D) 마케팅 회사 　　　　　　　　　　　정답 (A)

87. 업체에서는 무엇을 하기 시작할 것인가?
(A) 단골 고객에게 할인가 제공하기
(B) 매장의 진열대 다시 정리하기
(C) 하루 종일 가격 조정하기
(D) 납품업체들과 계약 갱신하기 　　　　정답 (C)

88. 화자는 데이비드 로웰이 무엇을 할 것이라고 말하는가?
(A) 본사로 전근
(B) 자원봉사자 요청
(C) 추가 직원 고용
(D) 새로운 전략 설명 　　　　　　　　정답 (D)

문제 89~91번은 다음 뉴스 보도를 참조하시오. 미W

W: This is Helen Watson with Channel 3 News. In tonight's financial news, banking combines technology with Cisco Bank's new mobile banking app. (89)With this new app, you can access the details of your account and complete transactions on your own electronic devices within minutes. Some industry experts have doubted whether Cisco could be successful in the competitive banking technology field. (90) However, there have already been 15,000 users since the application was released two days ago. To promote the app, (91)any users who complete two transactions within five days of downloading the app will automatically be entered into a raffle to win a new laptop.

채널 3 뉴스의 헬렌 왓슨입니다. 오늘 밤 금융 뉴스에서는, 금융업이 시스코 은행의 새 모바일 금융 앱에 기술을 결합합니다. 이 새 앱으로, 여러분은 자기 계좌의 세부정보에 접근할 수 있고, 몇 분에 자신의 전자기기에서 거래를 끝낼 수 있습니다. 일부 업계 전문가들은 시스코가 경쟁이 치열한 금융 기술 분야에서 성공할 수 있을지 의문을 품어왔습니다. 그런데 이 앱이 2일 전에 공개된 이후로 벌써 이용자가 15,000명이나 되었습니다. 이 앱을 홍보하기 위해서, 앱을 내려받고 5일 이내로 2회 거래를 완료한 이용자는 누구든 새 노트북을 받는 경품 추첨 행사에 자동으로 참가하게 됩니다.

89. 모바일 앱으로 이용자들은 무엇을 할 수 있게 되는가?
(A) 은행 지도 내려받기

(B) 사진과 영화 편집하기
(C) 온라인으로 은행 거래 하기
(D) 제안하기 　　　　　　　　　　　정답 (C)

90. 화자가 "그런데, 벌써 이용자가 15,000명이나 되었습니다"라고 말할 때 무엇을 시사하는가?
(A) 또 다른 지점이 개점할 것이다.
(B) 서비스가 인기 있다.
(C) 시스템이 너무 많은 이용자들로 인해 감당을 못한다.
(D) 프로젝트에 더 많은 직원이 필요하다. 　정답 (B)

91. 일부 이용자들은 무엇에 참가할 수 있는가?
(A) 콘테스트
(B) 환영회
(C) 교육 프로그램
(D) 관심 집단 토론 　　　　　　　　　정답 (A)

문제 92~94번은 다음 녹음 메시지를 참조하시오. 영M

M: You've reached the Burton Public Library. This month, our library building is closed for some remodeling. (92)During the period of renovation, library patrons can visit our temporary location at 58 Creek Avenue. (93)Detailed directions can be found on our website. Since the space in the temporary library facility is small, it does not have a multi-media room for patrons to use. However, this facility can provide laptop computers upon request. (94)To borrow one, what you have to do is show your library card at the front desk.

버튼 공립 도서관에 연결되셨습니다. 이번 달에 우리 도서관 건물이 리모델링 작업 때문에 문을 닫습니다. 보수공사 기간 동안, 도서관 이용객들은 크릭 애비뉴 58번지에 있는 우리 임시 도서관을 방문하시면 됩니다. 자세한 길 안내는 우리 웹사이트에서 보실 수 있습니다. 임시 도서관의 공간이 작기 때문에, 이용객들이 이용할 수 있는 멀티미디어실은 없습니다. 그렇지만, 요청하시면 이 시설에서 노트북 컴퓨터를 제공해드릴 수 있습니다. 노트북 컴퓨터를 빌리시려면, 여러분은 안내 데스크에서 도서관증을 제시하시기만 하면 됩니다.

92. 메시지는 주로 무엇에 관한 것인가?
(A) 임시 장소
(B) 도서관 이전
(C) 새 프로그램
(D) 독서 동아리 　　　　　　　　　　정답 (A)

93. 화자에 따르면, 온라인으로 무엇을 볼 수 있는가?
(A) 이용 가능한 서비스 목록
(B) 할인 쿠폰 번호
(C) 회원 신청서
(D) 길 안내 　　　　　　　　　　　　정답 (D)

94. 청자들은 어떻게 컴퓨터를 빌릴 수 있는가?
(A) 이메일을 보냄으로써
(B) 도착하기 전에 전화를 함으로써
(C) 양식을 작성함으로써
(D) 도서관증을 제시함으로써 　　　　　정답 (D)

M: (95)**Thank you all for participating in this year's three-mile race for charity fundraising.** We hope everyone enjoys themselves today. Now, let me review the event instructions with you today. First, all participants need to report to the registration booth by 9:30 A.M. (96)**Here at the registration booth, you can not only check in but also pick up a free T-shirt.** Go ahead and wear it during the race. While you run, you should keep to the designated course. (97)**Remember that once you make it to the end of the course, cross Maple Avenue to have your picture taken.** Several photographers we hired will be waiting for you there.

여러분 모두 자선 기금 모금을 위한 올해의 3마일 경주에 참가해 주셔서 감사합니다. 우리는 오늘 모든 분들이 좋은 시간이 되시길 바랍니다. 이제, 오늘 행사 안내사항에 대해 여러분과 같이 확인해 보겠습니다. 먼저, 모든 참가자들은 아침 9시 30분까지 등록대로 가서 참석했음을 알리셔야 합니다. 여기 등록대에서, 참가 수속을 밟을 뿐만 아니라 무료 티셔츠도 받으실 수 있습니다. 망설이지 말고 경주 중에 그 티셔츠를 착용하세요. 달리는 동안 지정된 코스를 지키셔야 합니다. 그리고 잊지 마셔야 할 것은, 일단 코스 끝까지 완주하고 나면, 메이플 애비뉴를 건너가서 사진을 찍으십시오. 우리가 고용한 사진사 여러 명이 그곳에서 여러분들을 기다리고 있을 겁니다.

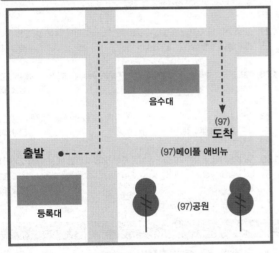

95. 청자들은 어떤 행사에 참석하고 있는 것 같은가?
(A) 운동 대회
(B) 지역사회 대청소
(C) 자선 경매
(D) 도시 퍼레이드   정답 (A)

96. 화자에 따르면, 청자들은 무엇을 받아야 하는가?
(A) 물병
(B) 티셔츠
(C) 신발
(D) 이름표   정답 (B)

97. 그래픽을 보시오. 청자들은 어디서 자기 사진을 찍을 수 있는가?
(A) 공원
(B) 등록대
(C) 출발선
(D) 음수대   정답 (A)

W: Your attention, please. (98)**Before we get the lights dimmed down for today's three-hour flight to Houston, I have a couple of announcements to make.** First, for the sake of passengers' convenience, (99)**complimentary blankets are available for use during your flight.** If you are feeling cold and need a blanket, please let me or any of the other flight attendants know and (99)**we'll provide you with one.** We'll also be opening the duty-free shop in around an hour. Feel free to check out the catalog listing a great selection of items that you can purchase on the flight. (100)**Unfortunately, Item number 183 is not in stock at the moment,** but we have all other items in the catalog available for purchase today.

안내 말씀 드립니다. 오늘 휴스턴 행 세 시간 비행을 위해서 조명을 어둡게 하기 전에, 몇 가지 알려 드릴 것이 있습니다. 먼저, 승객들의 편의를 위해서 비행하는 동안, 무료 담요가 준비되어 있습니다. 추위를 느껴서 담요가 필요하시면, 저나 다른 승무원 누구에게든 알려 주세요, 그러면 하나 갖다 드리겠습니다. 또한 약 한 시간 후에 면세점을 시작합니다. 여러분이 비행 중에 구매할 수 있는 아주 다양한 종류의 물건들이 나열되어 있는 카탈로그를 편안하게 확인해 보세요. 유감스럽게도, 품목 번호 183은 현재 재고가 없습니다만, 카탈로그에 있는 그 밖에 다른 모든 물건들은 오늘 구매하실 수 있도록 준비되어 있습니다.

98. 안내 방송은 누구를 대상으로 하는 것인가?
(A) 비행기 승객
(B) 총회 참석자
(C) 호텔 손님
(D) 쇼핑 센터 직원   정답 (A)

99. 화자는 무엇을 해주겠다고 제안하는가?
(A) 음료 주문 받기
(B) 담요 제공하기
(C) 개인의 귀중품 보관하기
(D) 무료 식사 갖다 주기   정답 (B)

100. 그래픽을 보시오. 어떤 품목을 구할 수 없는가?
(A) 지갑
(B) 넥타이
(C) 향수
(D) 벨트   정답 (D)

Part 5

101. 만약 귀하의 고지서, 납부 수단, 또는 재정 지원의 신청이나 수령에 관해 궁금한 점이 있으시면 지금 저희에게 연락하세요. 정답 (D)

102. 퇴근하기 전에, 천장에 있는 등은 소등하시고 차분하고 부드러운 야간등을 켜주세요. 정답 (A)

103. 부사장은 평소에 마케팅 회의에 혼자 참석하지만, 로스앤젤레스에서 열리는 회의에는 왓슨 씨를 데려가기로 결정했다. 정답 (C)

104. 기업을 경영하는 능력에 대해 그의 인종을 토대로 후보자를 평가하는 것은 불공정하다. 정답 (B)

105. 자료에 따르면, 석탄, 천연가스 그리고 석유와 같은 화석 연료의 사용량이 지난 150년간 꾸준하게 증가해 왔다. 정답 (C)

106. 조슈아 제약회사가 제조 공장을 스포케인으로 이전한 이후, 그 도시의 주택 공급에 대한 수요가 최근 몇 년간 크게 증가했다. 정답 (B)

107. 우리 미술관에 있는 각각의 그림은 강한 인상을 주는 역사의 단편을 담고 있다. 정답 (C)

108. 원격 회의 기술은 우리 직원들이 사무실을 나가지 않고 타국에 있는 고객들과의 만남을 가능하게 해준다. 정답 (C)

109. 벨라 법인은 현재 장기 근속 직원들에게 3년마다 최대 21일간의 휴가를 제공한다. 정답 (C)

110. 동봉된 것은 쇼핑몰 건설 프로젝트 제안에 대한 주민들의 최근 설문조사 결과이다. 정답 (B)

111. 약 3개월에 걸친 보수공사 후에, 디트로이트에 있는 에이스 기술 회사의 제조 공장이 어제 가동을 재개했다. 정답 (C)

112. 많은 회사들이 현재 인력 지원 부족에 직면해 있다. 더욱이 전문 기술을 보유한 직원이 부족하다. 정답 (C)

113. 매장 관리자 자리에 대한 최종 면접을 통과한 지원자들은 다음 주 후반 인사 담당자의 연락을 받게 될 것이다. 정답 (C)

114. 일부 이사들은 신사업 계획에 대해 매우 회의적이었으나, 최고 경영자는 그 계획의 잠재성에 대해 그들을 납득시켰다. 정답 (D)

115. 새로운 컨벤션 센터들과 호텔들이 건설되면서, 런던은 유럽 지역의 출장자들에게 제 1순위 목적지가 되는 데 필요한 모든 자격을 갖추고 있다. 정답 (A)

116. 오늘날 소비자의 인지도와 신뢰가 사업이 번창하는 데 있어 필수이므로 지역 기업들에게 사업 브랜딩의 중요성은 그 어느 때보다 훨씬 더 중요하다. 정답 (B)

117. 현재 악천후와 그에 따른 시계 불량으로 인해 모든 항공편이 지연되고 있음을 알려 드립니다. 정답 (C)

118. 안전 규정을 알고서도 이를 준수하지 않는 건설 작업자들은 해고될 것이다. 정답 (B)

119. 새로운 이동통신 기술에 관한 연차 총회가 끝난 직후 호텔 식당에서 만찬이 제공될 것이다. 정답 (A)

120. 지난 분기에 우리의 새로운 자동차 모델들이 출시된 이후로, 그것들은 놀라울 정도로 인기가 있다. 정답 (B)

121. 객관성과 투명성을 보장하기 위해서, 기업 대출 신청자는 필히 독립적으로 감사를 받은 여러 개의 금융 관련 서류를 제출해야 한다. 정답 (D)

122. 일부 고객들은 GB 회사에 의해 제조된 신제품의 전반적인 품질에 실망했다. 정답 (B)

123. 가격을 낮추려는 노력의 일환으로, 우리 회사는 생산 과정을 간소화하고 포장의 부피와 무게를 최소화했다. 정답 (D)

124. 당사의 보증은 고객의 제품 오용으로 인한 결함이나 파손에는 적용되지 않는다. 정답 (D)

125. 주식 연구 웹사이트를 살펴볼 때, 그들은 보통 여러분에게 과거 수익과 미래 예상 수익을 바탕으로 하는 수익률을 제공할 것이다. 정답 (B)

126. 우리는 대개 다음 학년도에 대해 임시의 학사 과정 일정을 제공하므로 향후에 약간의 변경이 발생할 수도 있다. 정답 (C)

127. 한 명 이상의 부모가 동행하지 않는다면, 15세 미만의 미성년자들은 영화관과 놀이 공원 입장이 금지된다. 정답 (C)

128. 이번 온라인 발표는 귀 사업에 효과적인 다양한 마케팅 기법과 전략에 대해 검토해볼 것이다. 정답 (D)

129. 안타깝게도, 국내에 우리 광대역 무선 휴대 전화 서비스를 이용할 수 없는 일부 외딴 지역이 있다. 정답 (D)

130. 우리가 이번 분기에 더 많은 손실을 겪은 점을 고려할 때, 전반에 걸쳐 상당한 비용 절감을 시작하는 것 외에 이 엉망인 상황에서 벗어날 다른 방법은 없어 보인다. 정답 (B)

Part 6

문제 131-134번은 다음 이메일을 참조하시오.

발신: 해리 휴스턴, 공장장
수신: 공장 직원
날짜: 3월 25일
제목: 외부 평가

코미 모터스에서 3명의 조사관들이 2주 후에 우리 공장을 방문할 것임을 알려 드리고자 이메일을 씁니다. 그들의 임무는 진행 중인 생산 공정을 모니터하고 당사의 자동차 부품이 그들의 요구 및 표준에 따라 제조되고 있는지 확인하는 것입니다. 또한, 그들은 우리 제조 공정의 청결도를 평가할 것입니다.

그들의 평가서는 4월 15일에서 4월 17일 사이에 공개될 것입니다. <u>그것은 우리에게 발송되어 우리의 공식 웹사이트에 게시될 것입니다.</u> 이들이 방문하는 동안 정상적인 공정을 따르는 것이 매우 중요합니다. 만약 여러분이 4월 8일에서 4월 10일 사이에 휴가를 가실 계획이라면, 후임자가 자신의 책무를 대신할 수 있도록 사전에 상사에게 알려 주십시오.

해리 휴스턴

공장장
휴스턴 정밀 기계

131. 정답 (B)

132. 정답 (A)

133. (A) 그들의 도착 날짜는 아직 확정되지 않았습니다.
(B) 그렇긴 하지만, 우리 제품은 업계에서 상품성이 높습니다.
(C) 지원서는 다음 달 말까지 제출되어야 합니다.
(D) 그것은 우리에게 발송되어 우리의 공식 웹사이트에 게시될 것입니다.
정답 (D)

134. 정답 (C)

문제 135–138번은 다음 광고를 참조하시오.

센트리 홈 인테리어 디자인

귀하의 주택을 완벽하게 바꾸어 드립니다!

집을 리모델링하거나 부가적인 구조물을 짓고 싶은데 무엇을 해야 할지 모르시나요? 더 이상 알아보실 필요가 없습니다. 저희 센트리 홈 인테리어 디자인은 여러분께 가장 적합한 주택을 만들어 드리는 데 무엇이 필요한지 정확히 알고 있습니다. 저희는 주택을 진짜 집으로 바꾸길 원하는 가정을 위해 모든 범위의 개조 솔루션을 제공해 드립니다.

새로운 벽지를 선택하는 것에서부터 뒤뜰의 새로운 덱을 만드는 것까지 저희 디자인 컨설턴트들이 여러분이 요청하시는 거의 모든 일들을 해 드릴 수 있습니다.

저희는 인테리어 디자인, 주택 배관, 건물 구조 변경 등의 어떤 작업에든 상관없이 주택 디자인의 거의 모든 부문에서 전문가들을 고용하고 있습니다. 이는 여러분의 가족들을 지원하도록 배정된 각 직원들이 여러분께서 필요로 하시는 것을 정확히 제공해 드릴 수 있는 경력이 있음을 보장하는 것입니다.

더 자세한 정보를 원하시면 저희 웹사이트 www.chid.com을 방문하시거나 킹 가 1123번지의 저희 사무실에 들러 직접 상담하실 수 있습니다.

135. (A) 저희에게 여러분의 기술적 문제에 대한 솔루션이 있습니다.
(B) 귀하의 인테리어 공사는 이미 시작되었습니다.
(C) 더 이상 알아보실 필요가 없습니다.
(D) 우리의 목표는 여러분이 이 지역 최고의 주택을 찾는 것을 돕는 것입니다.
정답 (C)

136. 정답 (A)

137. 정답 (B)

138. 정답 (A)

문제 139–142번은 다음 편지를 참조하시오.

갤럭시 테크놀로지
5174 리치몬드 애비뉴
휴스턴, 텍사스 주 77506

베이커 씨께,

저희 X63 노트북 컴퓨터 시리즈에 관해 문의해 주셔서 감사드립니다.

저희는 최신 카탈로그를 첨부해 드리게 되어 기쁩니다. 빨간색으로 강조된 제품들을 주목해 주십시오. 그 제품들은 웨이브 프린터 및 벨로시티 비디오 카드와 함께 저희가 세트로 제공하는 특별 제품들입니다. 저희의 판촉 행사는 한 달간만 지속됩니다. 그러니 이번 기회를 놓치지 마시고, 이번 행사를 이용해 보세요.

저희는 X63 노트북 컴퓨터 시리즈가 요즘 시장에서 구매할 수 있는 가장 신뢰할 만한 개인용 컴퓨터라고 장담할 수 있습니다. 이에 대한 저희의 자신감은 2년간의 보증과 사용자의 어떤 질문에든 답변하는 24시간 온라인 지원 시스템에 의해 뒷받침되고 있습니다.

저희는 고객님으로부터의 추가 문의 혹은 소중한 주문을 받기를 기대하고 있겠습니다.

도널드 해리슨
영업 담당 이사
갤럭시 테크놀로지

139. 정답 (B)

140. 정답 (D)

141. 정답 (C)

142. (A) 저희는 고객님으로부터의 추가 문의 혹은 소중한 주문을 받기를 기대하고 있겠습니다.
(B) 그들은 또한 업무 성과를 향상시키기 위해 지속적으로 노력해야 합니다.
(C) 카드 주문 처리 및 배송에는 영업일 기준 3일이 소요됩니다.
(D) 저희 회사는 우리가 제조하는 고품질의 제품을 자랑스럽게 생각합니다.
정답 (A)

문제 143–146번은 다음 이메일을 참조하시오.

데이비스 씨께,

고객님께서 저희 벨라 리조트에서 6월 24일부터 29일까지 숙박하시는 동안 겪으신 문제점에 관해 듣게 되어 대단히 유감입니다. 고객님의 객실에서 발견하신 사용된 수건 및 교체되지 않은 침구는 저희 리조트가 그 동안 명성을 쌓아 온 높은 수준의 서비스를 대표하는 것이 아님을 알아주셨으면 합니다. 저희 리조트의 모든 객실에는 보통 숙박객들께서 입실 수속을 하실 수 있기 전에 깨끗한 수건과 침구가 구비됩니다. 저희가 실수한 점에 대해 사과드립니다.

고객님께 저희 이탈리아 레스토랑인 루이지스 라자냐에서의 식사를 포함해 리조트에서의 1박 무료 숙박권을 기꺼이 제공해 드리고자 합니다. 다음에 저희 리조트의 객실을 예약하실 때, 이 이메일에 첨부된 쿠폰을 인쇄하여 입실 수속 시 프런트 직원에게 이 쿠폰을 제시하시기만 하면 됩니다.

다시 한 번, 고객님께서 받으신 부적절한 수준의 서비스에 대해 사과드립니다.

안녕히 계십시오.

제임스 윌리엄스
총 지배인
벨라 리조트

143. 정답 (C)

144. 정답 (D)

145. 정답 (B)

146. (A) 늘 그렇듯이, 고객님께서는 저희 신제품에 완전히 만족하실 것입니다.

(B) 만약 이 판촉행사에 관한 더 많은 정보가 필요하시면, 저희 웹사이트에서 확인하십시오.

(C) 저희 호텔과 호텔의 편의시설에 관한 고객님의 따뜻한 칭찬에 감사드립니다.

(D) 다시 한 번, 고객님께서 받으신 부적절한 수준의 서비스에 대해 사과드립니다.

정답 (D)

Part 7

문제 147-148번은 다음 광고를 참조하시오.

> BUYNSELL.COM
>
> 레이첼 케이글(rcagle@easymail.com)
>
> 1시간 전에 게시
>
> 제품: (147A)〈허브 요법에 대한 모든 것〉재클린 코치 지음
>
> (147D)이 책은 거의 새 제품과 다름없는 상태이고, (147B)6개월 전에 25달러에 구매하였습니다.
>
> (147A)허브나 다른 약용 식물에 관심이 있으신 분들은, 이 책을 제게서 15달러에 구매하실 수 있습니다. (148)이 책은 늦어도 다음 주 수요일까지 브룩사이드 지역에서 가져가셔야 합니다. 브룩사이드 커뮤니티 센터가 가장 좋겠습니다. 저는 오직 현금만 받습니다. 더 자세한 내용을 알고 싶으시면 (647) 555-3921로 문자 남겨 주세요.

147. 책에 대해서 언급되지 않은 것은 무엇인가?

(A) 식물을 약용으로 사용하고자 하는 사람들을 대상으로 한 것이다.

(B) 원래 25달러였다.

(C) 저자의 서명이 되어 있다.

(D) 손상되지 않았다.

정답 (C)

148. 구매자는 무엇을 해야 하는가?

(A) 브룩사이드 커뮤니티 센터를 방문해야 한다.

(B) 15달러짜리 개인 수표를 가지고 와야 한다.

(C) 전화 번호를 남겨야 한다.

(D) 다음 주 수요일까지 책을 받아 가야 한다.

정답 (D)

문제 149-150번은 다음 웹 페이지를 참조하시오.

> http://www.carltonuniv.edu
>
> | 홈 | 가입 | 소식 | 연락처 |
> |---|---|---|---|
>
> 연례 칼튼 대학교 자선 무도회
>
> 9월 1일 게시
>
> 안녕하세요. 연례 칼튼 대학교 자선 무도회가 코앞으로 다가왔습니다! 올해의 주제는 "파리의 심야"입니다. 베이 가에 위치한 다윈 홀에서 10월 16일에 50달러로 빛의 도시에서 밤을 보내는 것이 어떨지 경험해 보세요. 표는 10월 11일까지 저희 웹사이트 www.carltonuniv.edu/charityball에서 구매 할 수 있습니다. 온라인으로 구매한 표는 이메일로 발송됩니다. (149)수익금은 전액 자연 보호 기관(NCO)으로 기부됩니다. 환불은 불가합니다.
>
> | 4개의 댓글 | |
> |---|---|
> | 케빈 스나이더
10월 12일
오후 7:11 | 티켓 구매 마감일을 놓쳤어요. (150)누구 남는 티켓을 파실 분 안 계신가요? |
> | 로라 젠킨스
10월 12일
오후 8:05 | 저요! 제 출장 기간이 연장되어 행사에 참여하지 못하게 되어서 마침 티켓을 팔 사람을 찾고 있어요. (150)제 표를 사실래요? |

> | 케빈 스나이더
10월 12일
오후 8:18 | 네 그럴게요. (150)감사합니다! |
> |---|---|
> | (150)로라 젠킨스
10월 12일
오후 8:19 | (150)제가 더 고마워요. 자세한 건 전화로 해주세요. 제 번호는 (905) 555-2938입니다. |

149. 칼튼 대학교 자선 무도회에 대해 사실인 것은?

(A) 정해진 기간 동안 표를 환불해 준다.

(B) 파리에서 열린다.

(C) 10월 11일에 표 판매를 시작한다.

(D) 환경 단체를 후원하고 있다.

정답 (D)

150. 오후 8시 19분에, 로라 젠킨스가 "제가 더 고마워요"라고 쓸 때 무엇을 의미하는가?

(A) 그녀는 출장을 가게 되어 들떠 있다.

(B) 그녀는 케빈 스나이더를 도와 기쁘다.

(C) 그녀는 다음 자선 무도회 참석에 관심이 있다.

(D) 그녀는 전화로 통화하는 것을 즐긴다.

정답 (B)

문제 151-152번은 다음 여행 일정표를 참조하시오.

> **블루 스카이 관광**
>
> 태즈메이니아 마을 관광
>
> 8월 14일, 오전 9시 – 오후 6시
>
> * 아침 출발 시각 30분 전에 해밀턴 센터에 도착해 주십시오.
>
> | 오전 9시 | 해밀턴 센터에서 버스 출발
(도착하기 전에 아침 식사를 하고 오세요) |
> |---|---|
> | 오전 10시 | 태즈메이니아 원주민 마을 도착 |
> | 오전 10시 15분 | 그레이트 호크 산 등산
호크 폭포 관광 |
> | 오전 11시 | (152)카부 워세우의 도자기를 특별 전시하고 있는
태즈메이니아 원주민 박물관 관람 |
> | 오후 12시 30분 | 헤이스택 카페테리아에서 점심과 자유 시간
– 무료 음식이 제공됩니다. |
> | 오후 2시 | 태즈메이니아 마을 현장 관광 |
> | 오후 4시 | 태즈메이니아에서의 자유 시간
(151)관광객 분들은 전통 방식으로 만든 사탕과 다양한 기념품을 살 수 있는 태즈메이니아 롱 하우스에 방문하시길 권합니다. |
> | 오후 5시 30분 | 태즈메이니아 원주민 마을에서 출발 |
> | 오후 6시 30분 | 해밀턴 센터 도착 |

151. 관광객들이 쇼핑할 것 같은 장소는?

(A) 해밀턴 센터

(B) 태즈메이니아 원주민 박물관

(C) 헤이스택 카페테리아

(D) 태즈메이니아 롱 하우스

정답 (D)

152. 카부 워세우는 누구일 것 같은가?

(A) 관광 안내원

(B) 큐레이터

(C) 예술가

(D) 부족장

정답 (C)

문제 153-154번은 다음 이메일을 참조하시오.

수신: 게일 레이바 〈gleyva@enlightfinancials.com〉
발신: 스콧 아담스 〈sadams@enlightfinancials.com〉
날짜: 11월 2일
제목: 직원 만찬

레이바 씨께,

저는 다가오는 연례 인라이트 파이낸셜 직원 만찬회 장소 준비에 관하여 그레고리 잭슨 씨에게 연락했는데, 그는 자신이 현재 출장 중이므로 당신에게 연락하라고 말했습니다. 저는 당신 팀이 130명 정도의 손님을 위한 회의실을 준비해 주셨으면 합니다. (154)회의실에, 각각 7개의 좌석이 있는 20개의 원형 테이블이 필요합니다. 무대가 모든 좌석에서 보이도록 테이블이 회의실 전체에 걸쳐 흩어져 있어야 합니다. 그뿐만 아니라, 연단, 2개의 무선 마이크, 프로젝터 그리고 스크린을 준비해 주세요.

다음은 직원 만찬을 위한 일정입니다.

오후 3시 30분 – 홀 준비
오후 5시 – 문 개방
(153)오후 5시 30분 – 개회사 – 로셀 스미스 / 우수 사원 시상식
오후 7시 30분 – 저녁 식사

스콧 아담스
인사팀 부팀장

153. 손님들은 몇 시까지 인라이트 파이낸셜 직원 만찬회에 도착해야 하는가?

(A) 오후 5시
(B) 오후 5시 30분
(C) 오후 7시
(D) 오후 7시 30분 　　　　　　　정답 (B)

154. 아담스 씨는 이메일에서 무엇을 요청하는가?

(A) 이용 가능한 회의실 목록
(B) 이전 저녁 식사 손님들에 대한 정보
(C) 특정한 가구 배치
(D) 프레젠테이션 장비 목록 　　　　정답 (C)

문제 155-157번은 다음 안내문을 참조하시오.

레이크뷰 인 서머셋
무선 인터넷 접속

(155)저희 호텔에서 무선 인터넷을 이용하시려면 다음 내용을 읽어 주세요.
1. (156C)프런트에서 인터넷 접속 카드를 구매하세요.
2. (156A)귀하의 기기에서 네트워크 공유 센터를 여세요. 이용 가능한 네트워크 목록 중 "Lakeview Inn Somerset"이라는 명칭의 네트워크를 선택하세요.
3. (156C)접속 카드에 인쇄되어 있는 접속 코드를 입력하세요.
4. (156D)인터넷 이용 약관을 읽고 동의하세요.
5. "웹 접속"을 클릭하세요.

비즈니스 센터의 데스크톱 컴퓨터에서 무료로 인터넷을 이용할 수 있습니다. (157)무선 인터넷은 주차장과 야외 수영장에서는 이용할 수 없습니다. 도움이나 질문에 대해서는 내선 번호 #555로 프런트에 전화하세요.

155. 안내문의 목적은 무엇인가?

(A) 어떤 서비스 접속과 관련된 절차를 고객에게 알리기 위한 것
(B) 새로운 서비스의 시작을 알리기 위한 것
(C) 호텔 정책의 세부 사항을 설명하기 위한 것
(D) 어떤 프로그램 이용의 장점을 서술하기 위한 것 　정답 (A)

156. 안내문에서, 고객이 해야 하는 것으로 언급되지 않는 것은 무엇인가?

(A) 자신들의 컴퓨터에 있는 기능 작동시키기
(B) 개인 정보 입력하기
(C) 프런트에서 코드 얻기
(D) 어떤 조건을 준수하기로 동의하기 　정답 (B)

157. 어디에서 무선 인터넷 접속이 제한되는가?

(A) 호텔 방
(B) 프런트 주변
(C) 비즈니스 센터 안
(D) 야외 수영장 주변 　　　　　　정답 (D)

문제 158-160번은 다음 이메일을 참조하시오.

수신: 전 직원
발신: 호세 스콧 〈jscott@beauchamparts.edu〉
날짜: 2월 17일
제목: 지하 주차 공간

모든 직원들에게,

(158)어제, 기술자 한 명이 직원용 지하 주차장에서 누수 문제를 발견했습니다. 파이프 보강 공사 때문에 2월 중에는 지하 주차장을 이용할 수 없다는 사실을 알고 계시기 바랍니다. (160)모든 직원들은 학교 근처의 지역 주차 공간을 이용해 주시기 바랍니다. 학교가 주차 요금을 내드릴 것입니다. (160)이용 가능한 주차장 목록은 www.beauchampartsschool.com/staff에 게시될 겁니다. 공사는 곧 있을 우리의 봄 콘서트에 직접 영향을 주지 않을 뿐만 아니라, (159)다음 주의 신입생 오리엔테이션 프로그램에 대해서도 문제가 되지 않을 것입니다. 협조해 주셔서 감사합니다.

호세 스콧

보상 예술 학교, 총무

158. 이메일의 목적은 무엇인가?

(A) 새로운 프로그램에 관해 설명하기 위한 것
(B) 새로운 주차장 건설을 알리기 위한 것
(C) 직원들에게 있을 수 있는 불편을 알리기 위한 것
(D) 주차장에 가는 방법을 설명하기 위한 것 　정답 (C)

159. 다음 주에 무슨 일이 있을 것인가?

(A) 다음 주까지 콘서트가 연기될 것이다.
(B) 지하 주차장이 이용할 수 있게 될 것이다.
(C) 주차 요금이 인상될 것이다.
(D) 교육 시간이 있을 것이다. 　　　정답 (D)

160. 직원들은 무엇을 하라는 권유를 받는가?

(A) 학교까지 자신의 차량을 운전해서 오는 것 삼가기
(B) 웹사이트 방문하기
(C) 그들의 차량 피해에 대한 변상 받기
(D) 공사에 참여하기 　　　　　　정답 (B)

문제 161-163번은 다음 공고를 참조하시오.

로즈 코스메틱스 고객 여러분, 주목해 주세요!

(161)고객들의 반복되는 요청에 부응하여, 저희 로즈 코스메틱스는 더 많은 고객을 맞아들이기 위해서 영업 시간을 연장하기로 했습니다. 다음의 새로운 영업 시간을 참고해 주십시오.

장소	영업 시간	
리치몬드	월 – 금	오전 8:00 – 오후 6:00
	(162)일	**오전 9:30 – 오후 4:00**
서펔	월 – 금	오전 8:00 – 오후 6:00
	토	오전 9:00 – 오후 5:00
포츠머스	월 – 금	오전 9:00 – 오후 7:00
	토	오전 9:00 – 오후 6:00

고객들께서 저희를 지지해 주신 데 대해 감사하기 위해서 5월 5일과 6월 4일 사이에 저희 매장을 방문해 주시는 모든 고객들에게 선정된 제품에 대해 할인을 제공해 드리고, (163)**모든 구매 건에 대해 특별 선물을 드리고자 합니다.** 할인되는 제품들의 전체 목록을 보시려면 저희의 웹사이트 www. rosecosmetics.com을 방문해 주세요. 저희 로즈 코스메틱스는 고객님을 만나길 고대하고 있습니다.

161. 로즈 코스메틱스가 영업 시간을 변경하는 이유는?
(A) 지역에서 경쟁력을 회복하기 위해
(B) 다른 지역 사람들을 끌어들이기 위해
(C) 증가하는 고객을 수용하기 위해
(D) 고객의 불만을 해결하기 위해 　　　　정답 (C)

162. 리치몬드 지점은 나머지 지점과 어떻게 다른가?
(A) 매일 더 일찍 문을 연다.
(B) 일요일에 영업한다.
(C) 현재 할인을 제공하고 있다.
(D) 곧 수리에 들어갈 것이다. 　　　　정답 (B)

163. 고객들은 어떻게 로즈 코스메틱스에서 무료 제품을 받을 수 있는가?
(A) 로즈 코스메틱스의 웹사이트를 방문함으로써
(B) 제품을 구입함으로써
(C) 직원에게 이야기함으로써
(D) 지정된 시간에 특정 매장을 방문함으로써 　　정답 (B)

문제 164-167번은 다음 편지를 참조하시오.

7월 8일

매티 로마노
3718 선라이즈 로드
라스베이거스, 네바다 주 89109

(164)**로마노 씨께,**

축하합니다! 에버그린 아동 병원 자원봉사 업무에 지원하신 것이 수락되어, 보육 프로그램의 자리가 주어질 것입니다. 그러나 시작하기 전에, 보안상의 이유로 몇 가지 추가 서류를 제출하셔야 합니다.

(164) (165)지난 5년 동안의 의료 기록(주치의로부터 받을 수 있음)과 현재 귀하의 학교에서 재학 중임을 증명할 수 있는 문서를 제출해야 합니다. 이 자원봉사 기회는 오직 대학생들에게만 주어지기 때문에, 이 서류를 제출하는 것은 매우 중요합니다. (167)요청된 서류들은 에버그린 사회복지 사무소로 직접 우편으로 발송되어야 합니다. (165)서류들은 원본으로 인쇄물 형태여야 합니다. 늦어도 7월 15일까지 제출해 주십시오.

(166)귀하의 요청에 따라, 올해의 자원봉사자 프로그램 일정표를 동봉했습니다. 귀하의 서류에 대한 검토가 끝나는 즉시, 귀하가 일일 자원봉사 일정표를 온라인으로 확인할 수 있도록 계정을 만들어야 할 웹사이트의 링크를 문자로 보내 드리겠습니다.

위의 내용에 대한 문의사항이 있으면, 주저하지 마시고 저에게 연락 주세요.

주디 크루즈 드림
에버그린 아동 병원 자원봉사 프로그램 코디네이터
동봉물 재중

164. 로마노 씨는 누구일 것 같은가?
(A) 대학생
(B) 병원 직원
(C) 채용 전문가
(D) 자원봉사 단체의 대표 　　　　정답 (A)

165. 로마노 씨는 일주일 안에 무엇을 해야 하는가?
(A) 자원봉사 업무에 지원하기
(B) 크루즈 씨에게 이메일 보내기
(C) 에버그린 아동 병원의 크루즈 씨 사무실 방문하기
(D) 의사로부터 서류 받기 　　　　정답 (D)

166. 편지와 함께 발송된 것은 무엇인가?
(A) 자원봉사 증명서
(B) 출석 증명서
(C) 한 웹 페이지의 주소
(D) 시간표 　　　　정답 (D)

167. [1], [2], [3] 그리고 [4]로 표시된 곳 중에, 아래 문장이 들어가기에 가장 적절한 곳은?
"주소는 저희 웹사이트에 게시되어 있습니다."
(A) [1]
(B) [2]
(C) [3]
(D) [4] 　　　　정답 (B)

문제 168-171번은 다음 온라인 채팅 토론을 참조하시오.

제니퍼 모스 　　　　　　　　　　　[오후 9:03]
(170) (171)광고부의 모든 직원은 내일 6월 10일 새로운 사무실로 옮겨 가게 됨을 재차 알려 드립니다.

제니퍼 모스 　　　　　　　　　　　[오후 9:05]
오늘 밤에 책상 정리를 마무리해 주세요. 새 사무실에 책상을 아직 배정받지 못했다면, 즉시 저에게 알려 주세요.

(169)**오웬 웹** 　　　　　　　　　　　[오후 9:08]
저는 아직 제 책상을 배정받지 못했습니다. 전에 말씀드렸던 것이 기억나는데, 그 후로 제게 답변을 주지 않으셨어요.

(168)**제니퍼 모스** 　　　　　　　　　　　[오후 9:10]
아, 그럼요! 정말 죄송합니다. 다른 업무들로 정신이 없어서 당신한테 말해주는 걸 까맣게 잊고 있었네요. 당신의 책상은 준비되었습니다. 따로 연락해서 책상 번호를 알려 드릴게요.

오웬 웹 　　　　　　　　　　　[오후 9:12]
감사합니다.

(170)**사이먼 할롬** 　　　　　　　　　　　[오후 9:14]
(170)드디어 새 사무실이네요! 그래서, 내일은 평소처럼 업무를 하면 되나요, 아니면 그냥 짐만 옮기러 오나요?

제니퍼 모스 　　　　　　　　　　　[오후 9:15]
(171)내일은 그냥 이사하는 날이에요. 우리의 새 사무실은 오전 9시에서 오후 6시 사이에 열려 있을 거예요. 꼭 이 시간 동안 개인 소지품을 모두 옮기도록 하세요.

팀 벨빈스 　　　　　　　　　　　[오후 9:18]
저도 책상 배정을 못 받은 것 같은데요.

제니퍼 모스 [오후 9:19]

팀, 당신의 책상은 다른 분들처럼 일찍 배정되지 않았어요. 며칠 전에 저희 부서로 옮기셔서 그렇습니다. 그렇지만 당신 책상도 있어요. 역시 따로 연락 드릴게요.

팀 벨빈스 [오후 9:21]

알겠어요. 감사해요.

168. 모스 씨에 대해 언급된 것은 무엇인가?

(A) 배정된 책상이 없다.
(B) 한동안 매우 바빴다.
(C) 이사 서비스 회사에 근무한다.
(D) 새로운 광고부장이다. 정답 (B)

169. 전에 웹 씨가 모스 씨에게 연락한 이유는?

(A) 다른 부서로의 이동 허가를 받기 위해
(B) 그의 승진을 언급하기 위해
(C) 지정된 사무실 자리를 요청하기 위해
(D) 그의 업무 시간에 대해 상담하기 위해 정답 (C)

170. 오후 9시 14분에, 할룸 씨가 "드디어 새 사무실이네요!"라고 쓸 때 무엇을 의미하는 것 같은가?

(A) 내일 일하고 싶지 않음을 내비치고 있다.
(B) 마지막으로 새 사무실을 방문할 계획이다.
(C) 그의 새 직위에 대해 걱정한다.
(D) 새로운 환경에서 일하는 것에 들떠 있다. 정답 (D)

171. 6월 10일 오전 9시에서 오후 6시 사이에 직원들은 무엇을 하도록 지시 받는가?

(A) 온라인으로 새로운 계정 개설하기
(B) 사무실 가구 옮기기
(C) 새 사무실 방문하기
(D) 모스 씨에게 연락하기 정답 (C)

문제 172 – 175번은 다음 기사를 참조하시오.

내슈빌 소식 – 비즈니스 스포트라이트

7월 19일

이번 주의 비즈니스 스포트라이트는 벨 론드로와 이곳의 소유주인 모니카 벨 씨가 받게 되었습니다. 모르는 사람들을 위해 알려 준다면, (172)벨 론드로는 잭슨 가에 있는 빨래방, 카페, 그리고 서점을 합쳐 놓은 종합 서비스 공간이다. 이 새로운 형태의 셀프 서비스 빨래방은 근래 내슈빌에서 가장 성공적인 자영업소 중 하나이다.

(175)처음에, 벨 론드로는 지금처럼 성공적이지 않았다. 하지만 벨 씨는 그녀의 사업을 포기하지 않았다. 몇 달의 계획을 거쳐, 그녀는 빨래방의 한 부분을 카페 스타일의 휴게실로 개조했다. 이 대기실에서 손님들은 옷이 세탁되고 건조되는 동안 커피 한 잔을 즐기고 책을 읽을 수 있다.

벨 론드로의 고객은 벨 론드로가 제공하는 편리함과 고품질의 서비스를 매우 (173)가치 있게 여긴다. 이 지역의 다수의 주민들은 빨래를 해야 하고 수업을 위한 도서를 구매해야 하는 웰시 대학교 학생들이다. 그래서 그들은 벨 론드로가 두 가지 일을 한 번에 처리하기에 완벽한 곳이라는 것을 알고 있다.

(174)벨 씨는 지역의 많은 대학교로부터 창업을 계획하고 있는 학생들에게 정보와 조언을 제공해 달라고 요청받았다. 젊은 사업가로서, 그녀는 "어려움을 기회로"라는 제목이 붙여진 자신의 강의를 진행하게 되어 매우 들떠 있는 것 같다.

172. 벨 론드로에 대해 나타나 있는 것은 무엇인가?

(A) 대학교 캠퍼스에 위치해 있다.
(B) 지역 잡지들에 실린 적이 있다.
(C) 자사 웹사이트를 통해 도서를 판매한다.
(D) 평범하지 않은 콘셉트의 업체이다. 정답 (D)

173. 세 번째 단락의 1행에 있는 단어 "value"와 의미상 가장 가까운 것은?

(A) 평가하다
(B) 진가를 알아보다
(C) 추정하다
(D) 지지하다 정답 (B)

174. 벨 씨는 앞으로 무엇을 할 계획인가?

(A) 대학생 가르치기
(B) 단체에 가입하기
(C) 또 다른 지점 개설하기
(D) 새로운 사업 시작하기 정답 (A)

175. [1], [2], [3] 그리고 [4]로 표시된 곳 중에, 아래 문장이 들어가기에 가장 적절한 곳은?

"이곳은 대형 빨래방에 둘러싸여, 큰 수익을 올릴 수가 없었다."

(A) [1]
(B) [2]
(C) [3]
(D) [4] 정답 (B)

문제 176–180번은 다음 공지문과 이메일을 참조하시오.

바흐 음악 센터

(176)바흐 음악 센터가 오크빌로 확장했습니다! 우리 고객님들이 오크빌의 새로운 센터를 둘러보실 수 있도록 무료 공개 체험 행사를 열 것이며, 이곳은 향상된 새 시스템과 악기를 갖추고 있습니다. 저희 음악 센터에서 진정한 음악을 경험하는 첫 번째 고객이 되십시오!

(177)날짜: 7월 8일
시간: 오전 10:00 – 오후 5:00
예정 활동: 시설 둘러보기, 카페 메뉴 시식해 보기, 그리고 센터의 재능 있는 강사 만나기

(177)오크빌의 바흐 음악 센터에서:

– 리리컬 커피가 선택할 수 있는 다양한 종류의 음료와 함께 갓 구운 맛있는 빵을 제공합니다.

– 세인트 토마스 강당, 150개 좌석의 실내 공연장

– (180)프로젝트 아이제나흐, 11세 이하의 어린이들을 위한 주니어 음악 교실

– (178)바흐 스튜디오 – 프로 가수에게 노래하는 법을 배우세요. 바흐 음악 센터가 제공하는 최초의 보컬 트레이닝 수업입니다.

(176) (179)오크빌의 바흐 음악 센터는 7월 11일 일반인에게 처음으로 개방됩니다. 방문객에게는 무료 음악책과 바흐 음악 센터의 티셔츠를 드립니다. 또한 모두를 위해 더 많은 빵과 시식용 음료도 준비되어 있습니다!

수신: 다니엘 루퍼트 〈drupert@bachmusic.com〉
발신: 에이미 레이에스 〈areyes@fastmail.com〉
날짜: (179)7월 12일
제목: 일자리

루퍼트 씨에게,

(179)어제 저에게 내주신 시간에 재차 감사드립니다. 최신 시스템과 장비를 갖춘 시설을 보게 되어 정말 즐거웠습니다. 오크빌의 바흐 음악 센터는 정말 신나는 분위기를 드러내고 있어서 저는 귀 음악 센터에서 음악 강사가 되고 싶습니다.

저는 과거에 여러 음악 학원에서 피아노 강사로 일을 한 적이 있습니다. (180)저는 대부분 어린 학생들을 가르쳤는데, 그것은 제가 아이들이 피아노를 배우는 것으로 음악 교육에 첫발을 내디디고 음악인으로 성장하는 것을 보며 아이들과 일하는 것을 좋아하기 때문입니다. 어린이들이 음악에 대한 열정을 키워가는 것을 보는 것이 제게 주된 동기와 영감을 줍니다.

귀 음악 센터에서 가능한 자리에 대한 추가 질문이 있으시면 저에게 다시 이메일을 주시거나 (510) 555-3937로 전화 주십시오. 고려해 주셔서 감사합니다.

에이미 레이에스 드림

176. 공지문은 누구를 대상으로 한 것 같은가?
(A) 음악 강사 지원자
(B) 음악 센터에 재학 중인 학생
(C) 오크빌의 방문자
(D) 음악 경연 대회 참가자 　　　　　　　　정답 (B)

177. 7월 8일 방문객들에게 무료로 제공될 것은 무엇인가?
(A) 티셔츠
(B) 음악책
(C) 수업 체험 쿠폰
(D) 음식과 음료 　　　　　　　　정답 (D)

178. 오직 오크빌의 바흐 음악 센터에서만 이용 가능한 것은 무엇인가?
(A) 악기 대여
(B) 콘서트장
(C) 보컬 트레이닝
(D) 할인된 음악 수업 　　　　　　　　정답 (C)

179. 루퍼트 씨는 레이에스 씨와 언제 이야기를 나누었을 것 같은가?
(A) 음악 센터의 개원일에
(B) 콘서트의 중간 휴식 시간 동안
(C) 그의 음악 수업 시간 동안
(D) 공개 체험 행사 동안 　　　　　　　　정답 (A)

180. 레이에스 씨는 음악 센터의 어디에서 일하는 것을 선호할 것 같은가?
(A) 세인트 토마스 강당
(B) 프로젝트 아이제나흐
(C) 바흐 스튜디오
(D) 리리컬 커피 　　　　　　　　정답 (B)

문제 181-185번은 다음 이메일들을 참조하시오.

수신: 제임스 코빗 〈jcorbett@ranianelec.com〉
발신: 엘리자베스 레비스 〈 erevis@harrell.com〉
날짜: 11월 17일
제목: 조언을 구하며

코빗 씨에게,

어제 회의에서 먼저 자리를 떠서 죄송합니다. 제가 말했듯이, 저는 라니안 일렉트로닉스의 채용에 지원할 것을 고려하고 있습니다. 그래서, 당신이 현재 그 회사에서 일하고 있는 사람으로서 그 회사에 대한 당신의 경험과 생각을 저에게 공유해 주실 수 있다면 정말 감사하겠습니다.

(182)저는 현재 해럴 주식회사에서 일하고 있는데, 이곳은 동료들과 협력해

일하거나 의사소통할 기회가 많지 않습니다. (182)많은 해외 출장을 가는 것이 저를 많이 지치게 하기도 합니다.

(185)당신 회사의 웹사이트에 올라온 홍보 부장이 쓴 〈라니안의 작업 환경〉이라는 제목의 기사를 읽었습니다. 만약 그 기사가 라니안이 어떤 회사인지에 대한 (183)정확한 묘사라면, 그 곳에서 일하고 싶습니다. (181)당신 회사에 제가 고용될 수 있는지에 대해 이야기를 나눌 수 있게 조만간 시간을 내어 주실 수 있을까요?

감사합니다.

엘리자베스 레비스

수신: 엘리자베스 레비스 〈 erevis@harrell.com〉
발신: 제임스 코빗 〈jcorbett@ranianelec.com〉
날짜: 11월 18일
제목: 답장: 조언을 구하며

레비스 씨에게,

라니안 일렉트로닉스에서 근무하는 것에 관심이 있으시다니 기쁩니다. 우리가 만나서 라니안과 당신의 고용 건에 대해 자세히 얘기 나누기 전에 간단히 당신의 질문에 답변을 드리고자 합니다.

(185)당신이 언급한 메리 위트 씨가 작성한 기사는 라니안의 업무 현장을 정확하게 묘사하고 있습니다. 우리는 모든 조원이 서로서로 아이디어와 생각을 공유해야 하는 조별 임무가 많습니다. (184)매일 있는 회의에서는, 누구나 직급과 직책에 상관없이 새로운 방안이나 견해를 말할 수 있습니다. 우리는 출장을 거의 가지 않는데, 이것이 당신에게 긍정적인 요인이 될 것입니다. 우리는 좀 더 내부 업무를 중시합니다.

저는 다음 주 목요일 오후에 시간이 됩니다. 그날 점심을 같이하는 것이 어떨까요? 곧 뵙기를 바랍니다.

제임스 코빗 드림

181. 첫 번째 이메일의 목적은 무엇인가?
(A) 약속을 잡기 위한 것
(B) 일자리를 추천하기 위한 것
(C) 일자리 제안을 받아들이기 위한 것
(D) 보상을 요구하기 위한 것 　　　　　　　　정답 (A)

182. 레비스 씨가 해럴 주식회사에 대해 언급하는 것은 무엇인가?
(A) 직원의 출장비를 대주지 않는다.
(B) 충원이 필요한 공석이 있다.
(C) 회사 웹사이트에 기사를 올린다.
(D) 여러 국가에서 사업을 한다. 　　　　　　　　정답 (D)

183. 첫 번째 이메일의 세 번째 단락 2행에 있는 단어 "true"와 의미상 가장 가까운 것은?
(A) 확실한
(B) 자연스러운
(C) 직접적인
(D) 정확한 　　　　　　　　정답 (D)

184. 코빗 씨에 대해 시사된 것은 무엇인가?
(A) 그는 자주 재택근무를 한다.
(B) 레비스 씨의 직장 동료였다.
(C) 그는 오랫동안 레비스 씨와 알고 지내고 있다.
(D) 그는 자주 회의에 참석한다. 　　　　　　　　정답 (D)

185. 메리 위트는 누구인가?

(A) 인사 부장
(B) 홍보 부장
(C) 기자
(D) 기술자

정답 (B)

문제 186-190번은 다음 설명서와 이메일 그리고 영수증을 참조하시오.

베르나르도 몰에 오신 것을 환영합니다

모든 방문객의 쾌적하고 안전한 방문을 보장하기 위해, 베르나르도 몰의 주차 규정은 엄격히 준수되어야 하며 항시 시행될 것입니다. 다음 규칙과 안내 사항들을 주의 깊게 읽어 보십시오:

- 모든 주차는 선착순 기준입니다. 지정된 공간에만 주차하십시오. (190A)웰스 존은 트럭, 버스, 또는 밴 같은 대형차를 위한 주차 공간으로 장난감 가게인 카르페 디엠 옆에 위치해 있습니다. 다른 차종은 모두 쇼핑 센터의 서쪽 동 가까이에 있는 페드로 존에 주차되어야 합니다.

- 주차는 모든 고객에게 첫 30분 동안은 무료입니다. 그 후 시간 당 2달러의 요금이 적용됩니다. (188)베르나르도 몰에서 20달러 이상을 쓰시는 방문 객은 주차 요금이 면제됩니다. (187)나가실 때 각 출구에서 영수증이 제시되어야 합니다. 베르나르도 몰 주변의 몇몇 식당들과 주차장을 공동으로 사용하지만, 식당의 영수증은 받지 않습니다.

- (186)주차는 연중 내내 베르나르도 몰의 영업 시간인 오전 10시부터 오후 10시까지 이용 가능합니다.

- 문의, 요청, 또는 불만사항에 대해서는 customerservice@bernardomall. com에서 베르나르도 몰로 연락 주십시오.

수신: 〈customerservice@bernardomall.com〉
발신: 찰스 아라나 〈carana@upmail.com〉
날짜: 3월 20일
제목: 베르나르도 몰 주차
첨부: (190A)주차 영수증 (215117648)

관계자 분께,

(188) (190B)어제, 제 아들과 저는 베르나르도 몰을 방문해서 쇼핑 센터 옆에 있는 식당인 칩스앤타코스에서 식사했어요. 쇼핑 센터를 떠날 때, 주차 요금으로 5.73달러를 청구받았습니다. 20달러 이상을 사용한 사람들에게는 주차 요금 지불이 면제되는 것으로 알고 있었던 것 같아 이를 전혀 예상치 못했습니다. (188)쇼핑 센터에서 아무것도 사지는 않았지만, 음식점에서 30 달러 (189)훨씬 넘게 지출했습니다. (187)그 당시에는 너무 바빠서 5번 출구의 직원에게 모든 것을 설명할 수 없었지만, 잘못 지불된 이 주차 요금을 환불받고 싶습니다.

감사합니다.

찰스 아라나

영수증

베르나르도 몰 주차장
(190A)영수증 번호: 215117648

(190A)주차 구역	웰스 존	주차 위치 번호	B07
입차 날짜/시간	(190C)3월 19일, 오후 3:19	출차 날짜/시간	(190C)3월 19일, 오후 6:41

영수증?	없음	할인?	없음

지불할 금액	5.73달러	이용 시간	3시간 22분
지불된 금액	5.73달러	(190C)지불 방식	현금

감사드리며, 안전 운전 하세요!

186. 베르나르도 몰에 대해 암시된 것은 무엇인가?

(A) 최근에 주차 규정을 개정했다.
(B) 모든 요일에 영업한다.
(C) 현재 고객 서비스 상담원을 모집하고 있다.
(D) 특정 시기에는 운영되지 않을 수 있다.

정답 (B)

187. 아라나 씨가 3월 19일에 이용한 주차장에 대해 나타나 있는 것은 무엇인가?

(A) 오전 내내 운영을 안 했다.
(B) 최근에 개보수되었다.
(C) 지하 시설이다.
(D) 여러 개의 출구가 있다.

정답 (D)

188. 아라나 씨가 환불을 받을 수 없게 되는 이유는?

(A) 그의 차를 제대로 주차하지 않았다.
(B) 베르나르도 몰에서 필요 금액을 지출하지 않았다.
(C) 안내사항을 읽지 않았다.
(D) 시간 내에 고객 서비스 상담원에게 연락하지 않았다.

정답 (B)

189. 이메일의 첫 번째 단락 4행에 있는 단어 "far"와 의미상 가장 가까운 것은?

(A) 정말로
(B) 훨씬
(C) 넘어서
(D) 멀리

정답 (B)

190. 아라나 씨에 대해 사실이 아닌 것은?

(A) 그는 베르나르도 몰로 대형차를 운전해 갔다.
(B) 그는 자기 아들과 칩스앤타코스에서 식사했다.
(C) 그는 3월 19일에 주차비를 현금으로 냈다.
(D) 그는 베르나르도 몰을 다시 방문하지 않을 것이다.

정답 (D)

문제 191-195번은 다음 광고와 웹 페이지들을 참조하시오.

셔먼 투어

셔먼 투어는 그랜드 캐년으로 가는 특별 당일 여행을 자신 있게 선보입니다. 6명의 소그룹으로 그랜드 캐년의 사우스 림으로 가는 기억에 남을 만한 편안한 여행을 즐기실 수 있습니다. (195)저희 전문 가이드가 여러분을 널찍한 밴으로 그랜드 캐년과 다른 주요 지역 관광 명소로 모셔다 드리고 각 명소의 역사와 전해지는 이야기도 들려 드립니다. (191)셔먼 투어의 회원만이 이 합리적인 가격의 여행 상품을 이용하실 수 있는 점에 주목해 주십시오. 이 상품을 신청하시거나 그랜드 캐년 여행 상품에 대한 추가적인 정보를 원하시면 저희 웹사이트 www.shermantours.com을 참조해 주십시오.

---

http://www.shermantours.com/tourinfo

셔먼 투어

메인 페이지	회사 소개	여행 상품 정보	고객 평가	예약하기

(193)그랜드 캐년으로 떠나는 특별한 당일 여행

일시: 오전 10:00 - 오후 8:00
일요일 - 금요일 출발 (토요일 일정 없음)

장소: 플래그스태프 공항에서 그랜드 캐년의 사우스 림까지 (공항에서 사우스 림까지 차편 제공 서비스 포함). **(193)올리바레 이탈리안에서 점심 식사와 미첼스 다이너에서 저녁 식사 또는 (194)목요일에는 올어바웃 프렌치에서 저녁 식사**

비용: 성인 한 명당 145달러
16세 이하의 아동 한 명당 80달러

기타: **(192)추가 200달러로 그랜드 캐년 헬기 탑승 관광을 할 수 있습니다.** 원하시는 식사 종류는 사전에 알려 주셔야 합니다. 그랜드 캐년과 다른 관광 명소들의 사진을 보시려면, 여기를 누르세요.

---

http://www.shermantours.com/testimonials

셔먼 투어

메인 페이지	회사 소개	여행 상품 정보	고객 평가	예약하기

"그랜드 캐년으로의 멋진 여행"
사만다 와츠 평가
10월 10일 작성

이것은 셔먼 투어가 제공해준 정말 멋지고 잘 짜인 여행이었어요. 저는 특히 결코 서두를 필요 없이 아름다운 그랜드 캐년의 경관을 보러 가고 자연을 감상할 수 있었던 점이 좋았어요. **(195)가이드 조슈아 오닐 씨는 정말 유익한 정보를 알려 주었고, 박식하고 재미있었어요. (194)올어바웃 프렌치에서 먹었던 저녁도 정말 맛있었어요.** 비교적 짧은 시간에 그랜드 캐년에서 잊지 못할 경험을 하고 싶은 사람들에게 이 여행 상품을 추천합니다.

191. 셔먼 투어에 대해 사실인 것은?
(A) 회원들에게만 특정 상품을 제공하고 있다.
(B) 6명의 직원이 있다.
(C) 매달 사보를 낸다.
(D) 긴 역사가 있다. 정답 (A)

192. 헬기 탑승에 대해 언급되는 것은 무엇인가?
(A) 사전에 신청되어야 한다.
(B) 재구매 고객에게 주어진다.
(C) 추가 요금으로 제공된다.
(D) 현재 할인된 금액에 이용할 수 있다. 정답 (C)

193. 그랜드 캐년 당일 여행에 포함된 것은 무엇인가?
(A) 비행기 표
(B) 식사
(C) 기념품
(D) 사진 촬영 서비스 정답 (B)

194. 와츠 씨는 언제 그랜드 캐년으로 여행을 갔을 것 같은가?
(A) 목요일
(B) 금요일
(C) 토요일
(D) 일요일 정답 (A)

195. 오닐 씨에 대해 추론될 수 있는 것은 무엇인가?
(A) 그는 직업 연예인이다.
(B) 그는 그랜드 캐년 관광에 145달러를 냈다.
(C) 그는 셔먼 투어의 신입 사원이다.
(D) 그는 와츠 씨를 그랜드 캐년으로 태워다 주었다. 정답 (D)

문제 196-200번은 다음 웹 페이지와 공지 그리고 이메일을 참조하시오.

http://www.booksworld.com/category

북스 월드

메인 페이지	최신	카테고리	주문

요리법 분야 베스트셀러 도서

1. 〈부엌 뒤에서〉 앤서니 베리
식당 여는 것을 꿈꾸고 있나요? 베리 씨의 남다른 통찰력과 조언으로 요식업에서 **(196)큰 돈을 버는 법을 배우세요.**

2. 〈행복한 식탁〉 카렌 윌슨
당신의 식탁 위 음식이 당신과 당신 가족의 건강과 행복을 결정합니다. 올바른 재료들을 선택하고 올바르게 요리하는 방법을 알려 드립니다.

3. **(198)〈요식업계 이해하기〉 로드니 샌포드**
요식업계에서 성공하기 위해서는 업계를 이해해야 합니다. 요식업에 막 뛰어든 사람들이 자주 범하는 실수를 피하는 법을 확인하세요. 음식점 운영에 관심이 있다면, 이것은 꼭 읽어야 할 책입니다.

4. 〈음식, 언어, 그리고 문화〉 로드니 샌포드
무엇이 한 국가의 음식, 언어, 그리고 문화를 결정하는 걸까요? 그리고 결과적으로 그것들이 어떻게 그 국가와 국민에게 영향을 미칠까요? 10개 이상의 언어로 번역된 샌포드 씨의 책에서 알아보세요.

블룸필드 공공 도서관
6월 넷째 주의 행사

(199)6월 20일, 월요일 - (198)성공한 작가이자 레스토랑 소유주 로드니 샌포드 씨가 그의 최신 저서에 설명된 음식점 운영에 관한 방법에 대해 얘기하기 위해 우리 도서관을 방문합니다. 샌포드 씨는 행사 후에 참가자들을 위해 그의 책에 사인해줄 것입니다.

6월 22일, 수요일 - **(197)보호자 동반 유치원생들과 유아들을 위한 재미있고 함께 즐길 수 있는 음악으로 가득한 행사가 준비되어 있습니다.** 여러 계절과 날씨에 관한 곡들이 다양한 악기로 연주됩니다. 이 신나는 음악 수업 참여를 위해 따로 신청하실 필요는 없습니다.

수신: 〈customerservice@bloomfieldpl.org〉
발신: 멜빈 찰스 〈mcharles@opmail.com〉
날짜: 6월 27일
제목: 블룸필드 공공 도서관

관계자 분께,

(199)저는 최근 블룸필드 공공 도서관에서 진행된 행사에 참석했습니다. 저는 샌포드 씨의 지식과 생각에 깊은 인상을 받았습니다. 그가 토론 시간에 가르쳐준 것들은 저의 사업 계획을 실행하는 것과 관련하여 정말 큰 자산이 될 것입니다.

(200)또한, 도서, 〈부엌 뒤에서〉가 대여 가능할 때 문자로 알림을 받고 싶습니다. 제가 빌리려 했을 때 이미 대출된 상태였습니다. 제 휴대 전화 번호는 (210) 555-3918입니다. 감사합니다.

(199)멜빈 찰스

196. 웹 페이지의 첫 번째 단락의 2행에 있는 단어 "good"과 의미상 가장 가까운 것은?
(A) 쾌적한
(B) 상당한
(C) 후한
(D) 진짜의 정답 (B)

197. 블룸필드 공공 도서관에 대해 나타나 있는 것은 무엇인가?

(A) 어린이들을 위한 행사를 연다.

(B) 행사 등록을 위하여 회원 카드가 있어야 한다.

(C) 현재 신입 직원을 채용하고 있다.

(D) 시기에 따라 운영 시간이 바뀐다. 　　　　　　　정답 (A)

198. 어떤 책이 최근에 블룸필드 공공 도서관에서 저자에 의해 서명되었는가?

(A) 부엌 뒤에서

(B) 행복한 식탁

(C) 요식업계 이해하기

(D) 음식, 언어, 그리고 문화 　　　　　　　정답 (C)

199. 찰스 씨에 대해 사실인 것은?

(A) 자주 블룸필드 공공 도서관을 방문한다.

(B) 블룸필드 공공 도서관에서 일한다.

(C) 샌포드 씨의 도서 중 하나를 구매하기 원한다.

(D) 음식점 개업에 관심이 있다. 　　　　　　　정답 (D)

200. 찰스 씨는 블룸필드 공공 도서관에 무엇을 해달라고 요청하는가?

(A) 도서의 출간일 알려 주기

(B) 샌포드 씨의 행사가 또 언제 있을지 알려 주기

(C) 책이 언제 도서관으로 반납되는지 알려 주기

(D) 그의 주소지로 새 책 보내 주기 　　　　　　　정답 (C)

---

1. [미M]

(A) He is leaving the window open.

(B) He is taking off his hat.

(C) He is wearing a coat.

(D) He is exiting an aircraft.

(A) 그는 창문을 열어 두고 있다.

(B) 그는 모자를 벗고 있다.

(C) 그는 코트를 입고 있다.

(D) 그는 비행기에서 내리고 있다. 　　　　　　　정답 (C)

2. [미W]

(A) A hammer is placed in the tool box.

(B) New equipment is being installed in a work station.

(C) The man is leaning over his work.

(D) The man is measuring some building materials.

(A) 망치가 연장함에 놓여 있다.

(B) 새 장비가 작업장에 설치되고 있다.

(C) 남자가 작업하는 것 위로 몸을 구부리고 있다.

(D) 남자가 건축 자재의 치수를 재고 있다. 　　　　　　　정답 (C)

3. [영M]

(A) One of the men is handing a pen to a presenter.

(B) Some folders have been left open on the table.

(C) A clock has been mounted on a wall.

(D) One of the women is reaching for a cup.

(A) 남자 중 한 명이 발표자에게 펜을 건네고 있다.

(B) 폴더 몇 개가 테이블 위에 펼쳐진 채로 있다.

(C) 시계가 벽에 걸려 있다.

(D) 여자 중 한 명이 컵을 잡으려고 손을 뻗고 있다. 　　　　　　　정답 (C)

4. [미M]

(A) They are approaching a doorway.

(B) Some recycling bins have been left on the street.

(C) One of the men is parking a truck beside a store.

(D) Both of the men are hanging a sign on the wall.

(A) 그들은 출입구로 다가가고 있다.

(B) 재활용 수거함 몇 개가 길거리에 놓여 있다.

(C) 남자 중 한 명이 가게 옆에 트럭을 주차하고 있다.

(D) 남자 둘 다 간판을 벽에 걸고 있다. 　　　　　　　정답 (A)

5. [호W]

(A) Some branches of a tree are being trimmed.

(B) Some flowers are being planted in a parking lot.

(C) Some traffic cones have been put near a truck.

(D) A vehicle is being towed by a truck.

(A) 나뭇가지들이 가지치기 되고 있다.

(B) 꽃들이 주차장에 심어지고 있다.

(C) 원뿔형 도로 표지들이 트럭 근처에 놓여 있다.

(D) 차량 한 대가 트럭에 의해 견인되고 있다. 　　　　　　　정답 (C)

6. [미W]

(A) The audience is applauding the presenter.

(B) The audience is facing the front of the room.

(C) The presenter is walking toward a podium.

(D) The presenter is connecting a projector to a computer.

(A) 청중이 발표자에게 박수 갈채를 보내고 있다.
(B) 청중이 방 앞쪽을 향하고 있다.
(C) 발표자가 연단을 향해서 걸어가고 있다.
(D) 발표자가 프로젝터를 컴퓨터에 연결하고 있다. 정답 (B)

Part 2

7. 〔미M〕〔미W〕
Who's introducing the new marketing expert tomorrow?
(A) It will be on the market next week.
(B) The manager's going to.
(C) Nice talking to you, too.

내일 새로 오는 마케팅 전문가를 누가 소개하나요?
(A) 그것은 다음 주에 시판될 거예요.
(B) 매니저가 하실 거예요.
(C) 저도 얘기 나누게 되어 반가웠어요. 정답 (B)

8. 〔호W〕〔미M〕
What ingredients are in this wedding cake?
(A) Not that I know of.
(B) Cookbooks will be on display today.
(C) Some blueberries and powdered nuts.

이 웨딩 케이크에 어떤 재료들이 들어가 있어요?
(A) 제가 알기로는 아니에요.
(B) 요리책이 오늘 진열될 거예요.
(C) 블루베리와 분말 견과류요. 정답 (C)

9. 〔미W〕〔영M〕
Why did the management decide to hold the company picnic at the City Park?
(A) It was crowded.
(B) You should bring some paper plates and cups.
(C) They think it has lots of space.

경영진은 왜 시티 파크에서 회사 야유회를 열기로 결정한 건가요?
(A) 거기는 사람들이 붐볐어요.
(B) 종이접시와 종이컵을 좀 가져오셔야 해요.
(C) 경영진은 거기가 공간이 넓다고 생각해요. 정답 (C)

10. 〔미M〕〔호W〕
Could you water my potted plants while I'm away on business?
(A) Take a tour of the new plant.
(B) Sure. I'd be glad to.
(C) At the botanical garden.

제가 출장 가 있는 동안 제 화분에 물 좀 주실래요?
(A) 새 공장을 둘러보세요.
(B) 알았어요. 기꺼이 해 드릴게요.
(C) 식물원에서요. 정답 (B)

11. 〔미W〕〔호W〕
When did you last replace the water purifying filter?
(A) A few days ago.
(B) It should take about an hour to fix it.
(C) Because I was so thirsty.

정수기 필터를 언제 마지막으로 교체하셨어요?
(A) 며칠 전이요.

(B) 그것을 수리하는 데 한 시간 정도 걸릴 거예요.
(C) 제가 너무 목이 말랐거든요. 정답 (A)

12. 〔미M〕〔미W〕
Should we drive or take the bus to the conference?
(A) Half an hour if there's no traffic.
(B) I'd prefer to drive myself.
(C) On the conference table.

총회까지 운전해서 갈까요, 아니면 버스를 탈까요?
(A) 차들이 없으면 30분이요.
(B) 제가 직접 운전해서 가고 싶어요.
(C) 회의 테이블 위에요. 정답 (B)

13. 〔영M〕〔미W〕
What is supposed to happen at his job interview?
(A) At the office on the second floor.
(B) He'll meet with the marketing director.
(C) It starts Tuesday morning at 9 o'clock.

그의 취업 면접에서 어떤 일이 있게 되나요?
(A) 2층 사무실에서요.
(B) 그는 마케팅 이사를 만나게 될 거예요.
(C) 그것은 화요일 아침 9시에 시작해요. 정답 (B)

14. 〔호W〕〔미M〕
How long do you think it will take to fix the air purifier?
(A) No. I didn't repair it.
(B) It should be ready in about an hour.
(C) It will fit in the corner.

공기 청정기를 수리하는 데 얼마나 걸릴 것 같아요?
(A) 아뇨. 제가 그것을 수리하지 않았어요.
(B) 대략 한 시간 후면 될 거예요.
(C) 그건 구석에 딱 맞게 들어갈 거예요. 정답 (B)

15. 〔미W〕〔영M〕
Who's giving a speech first at the sales conference?
(A) Carrie is, I think.
(B) Not all of the attendees did.
(C) A very informative presentation.

영업 총회에서 누가 처음으로 연설하나요?
(A) 캐리가 하는 것 같아요.
(B) 모든 참석자들이 한 것은 아니었어요.
(C) 매우 유익한 프레젠테이션이에요. 정답 (A)

16. 〔영M〕〔호W〕
Would you like to reschedule an appointment for next Monday?
(A) How about Tuesday at 2 P.M.?
(B) I scheduled a meeting.
(C) A new security policy.

약속을 다음 주 월요일로 일정을 조정하시겠어요?
(A) 화요일 오후 2시가 어때요?
(B) 저는 회의 일정을 잡았어요.
(C) 새로운 보안 정책이요. 정답 (A)

17. 〔호W〕〔미M〕
Why didn't Elaine attend the rock festival last night?
(A) I won't be able to be there until 7:00.
(B) I want to play some music.

(C) Because she had to work late.

일레인은 어젯밤 왜 록 페스티벌에 안 갔어요?
(A) 저는 7시나 되어야 거기에 갈 수 있을 거예요.
(B) 저는 음악을 좀 틀고 싶어요.
(C) 그녀는 늦게까지 근무해야 했기 때문이에요.   정답 (C)

18. 미W 영M
Laura commutes an hour and a half to work every day.
(A) There was heavy traffic.
(B) That sure is a very long ride.
(C) Yes, my lunch break is in thirty minutes.

로라는 매일 1시간 30분씩 출퇴근해요.
(A) 교통체증이 있었어요.
(B) 그거 정말 차 타고 다니는 시간이 기네요.
(C) 예, 제 점심 시간은 30분 후예요.   정답 (B)

19. 미M 미W
You're from Oxford, right?
(A) Wednesday afternoons will be fine.
(B) Yes, I lived there for 30 years or so.
(C) It was good to meet our overseas employees.

당신은 옥스포드 출신이죠, 그렇죠?
(A) 수요일 오후는 괜찮을 거예요.
(B) 예, 거기서 30년 정도 살았어요.
(C) 해외 직원들을 만나게 되어 좋았어요.   정답 (B)

20. 영M 호W
Does your company use any recycled materials in the factory?
(A) The recycling bin is over there.
(B) Please put on this safety gear.
(C) Not yet, but we are planning to.

당신 회사는 공장에서 재활용 물질을 사용하나요?
(A) 재활용 통은 저쪽에 있어요.
(B) 이 안전 장비를 착용하세요.
(C) 아직 아니지만, 그럴 계획이에요.   정답 (C)

21. 미M 호W
Do you want to post the study results on the website or publish them in our magazine?
(A) The post office stays open until 4 o'clock.
(B) I think online would be much better.
(C) I subscribe to the magazine, too.

연구 결과를 웹사이트에 올리고 싶으세요, 아니면 우리 잡지에 발표하고 싶으세요?
(A) 우체국은 4시까지 문을 열어요.
(B) 온라인이 훨씬 더 나을 것 같아요.
(C) 저도 그 잡지를 구독해요.   정답 (B)

22. 영M 미W
The weather forecast said it is supposed to rain all day tomorrow.
(A) Joshua was supposed to handle that.
(B) Then we'd better cancel the outdoor event.
(C) Where did you buy that raincoat?

일기예보에 따르면 내일 하루 종일 비가 올 거라고 했어요.
(A) 조슈아가 그것을 담당하게 되어 있었어요.

(B) 그렇다면 우리는 야외 행사를 취소하는 게 낫겠어요.
(C) 그 우비는 어디서 샀어요?   정답 (B)

23. 미M 호W
Why can't I get this accounting program to work?
(A) He is a new accountant.
(B) I didn't watch that television program, either.
(C) You haven't installed the software update, have you?

이 회계 프로그램이 왜 작동하지 않는 거죠?
(A) 그는 새로 들어온 회계사예요.
(B) 저 역시 그 텔레비전 프로를 시청하지 않았어요.
(C) 소프트웨어 업데이트를 설치하지 않으셨죠, 그렇죠?   정답 (C)

24. 미W 영M
You approved the remodeling of the employee breakroom, didn't you?
(A) Yes, construction will begin next Monday.
(B) His room has a nice mountain view.
(C) Let's take a coffee break.

직원 휴게실의 리모델링을 승인하셨죠, 그렇죠?
(A) 예, 공사는 다음 주 월요일에 시작할 거예요.
(B) 그의 방은 산 전망이 좋아요.
(C) 커피 타임을 가집시다.   정답 (A)

25. 미W 미M
We need to formally announce when we are relocating.
(A) They require formal attire.
(B) Movers arrived late.
(C) Didn't Sue send an e-mail?

우리가 언제 이전하는지 공식적으로 발표할 필요가 있어요.
(A) 그들은 정장을 입을 것을 요구해요.
(B) 이삿짐 직원들이 늦게 도착했어요.
(C) 수가 이메일을 보내지 않았어요?   정답 (C)

26. 호W 영M
When will you be available to start working as a tour guide?
(A) Of course, I'm ready to work on it.
(B) He's been with us for 20 years.
(C) I still have three weeks left of school.

관광 가이드로서 언제 근무 시작이 가능하신가요?
(A) 물론이죠, 저는 그것을 작업할 준비가 되어 있어요.
(B) 그는 20년 동안 우리와 함께 해왔어요.
(C) 저는 아직도 학교 수업이 3주가 남았어요.   정답 (C)

27. 미W 영M
Will the farewell party for Jessy be held at the office or at a restaurant?
(A) Yes, it sure is more spacious.
(B) Our conference room is not large enough.
(C) Yes. We'll need more workers.

제시를 위한 송별 파티가 사무실에서 열리나요, 아니면 식당에서 열리나요?
(A) 예, 거긴 분명히 더 넓어요.
(B) 우리 회의실은 충분히 크지 않아요.
(C) 예, 우리는 직원이 더 필요할 거예요.   정답 (B)

28. 미M 호W

Where's the main entrance to the amusement park?
(A) He is the park ranger.
(B) You see a long line of people over there, don't you?
(C) There are many rides you can enjoy.

놀이 공원의 주 입구가 어디예요?
(A) 그는 공원 관리인이에요.
(B) 저기 길게 줄 서 있는 사람들이 보이죠, 그렇죠?
(C) 당신이 즐길 수 있는 놀이 기구가 많이 있어요.　　　정답 (B)

29. 미W 영M

Will we discuss the expansion project at the manager meeting?
(A) Haven't you seen the agenda?
(B) Yes, it was well responded.
(C) Yes, that conference room will do.

관리자 회의에서 확장 프로젝트에 대해 논의를 할 건가요?
(A) 의제를 보지 못하셨어요?
(B) 예, 그건 반응이 좋았어요.
(C) 예, 그 회의실이면 될 거예요.　　　정답 (A)

30. 미W 미M

Haven't you ordered more of the rosemary shampoo yet?
(A) It's not that popular with shoppers.
(B) Actually, I'd like to rinse it.
(C) Put them back on the shelf.

로즈마리 샴푸를 아직도 더 주문하지 않았어요?
(A) 그게 쇼핑객들에게 그렇게 인기 있지 않아요.
(B) 사실, 저는 그것을 헹구고 싶어요.
(C) 그것들을 다시 선반에 갖다 놓으세요.　　　정답 (A)

31. 미W 영M

When can we reopen the factory we are expanding?
(A) Does the rent include utilities?
(B) The renovation project was delayed again.
(C) That tool belongs to Jenny.

우리가 확장하는 공장을 언제 다시 열 수 있죠?
(A) 임대료에 공과금이 포함되어 있나요?
(B) 보수공사 프로젝트가 다시 지연되었어요.
(C) 그 연장은 제니 거예요.　　　정답 (B)

Part 3

문제 32-34번은 다음 대화를 참조하시오. 영M 미W

M: (32)How is everything going with the development of the Dynasty sport utility vehicle?
W: (33)We're running a bit behind schedule with this vehicle. The engine is being overhauled. The one we had planned to use simply wasn't powerful enough.
M: Good. When do you think we can start manufacturing it?
W: We'll need to let some potential customers test drive it first, but (34)we are planning to begin production in two months.

M: 다이내스티 스포츠 유틸리티 차량 개발은 어떻게 다 잘되어가고 있어요?
W: 이 차량은 약간 일정이 뒤쳐지고 있어요. 엔진을 철저히 점검하고 있는 중이에요. 우리가 사용하려고 계획했던 엔진이 강력한 힘을 충분히 내지 못

했어요.
M: 좋아요. 언제부터 우리가 차량 생산을 시작할 수 있을 것 같아요?
W: 먼저 잠재 고객 몇 사람에게 시운전하게 할 필요가 있긴 하지만, 두 달 후에는 생산을 시작할 계획이에요.

32. 화자들은 어떤 제품에 관해 논의하고 있는가?
(A) 자동차
(B) 노트북 컴퓨터
(C) 휴대폰
(D) 텔레비전 수상기　　　정답 (A)

33. 무엇 때문에 지연이 발생했는가?
(A) 구할 수 없는 재료
(B) 충분하지 않은 예산 자금
(C) 엔진의 문제
(D) 숙련 노동자의 부족　　　정답 (C)

34. 2개월 후에 무슨 일이 있겠는가?
(A) 생산이 시작될 것이다.
(B) 디자인이 승인될 것이다.
(C) 고객 설문지가 수거될 것이다.
(D) 새 공장이 문을 열 것이다.　　　정답 (A)

문제 35-37번은 다음 대화를 참조하시오. 호W 영M

W: Hello, Jeff. It's great to see you. Did you have a good vacation?
M: Yes, I did. Thanks for asking. You know, I noticed a sign on the front window when I came in. (35)What's this about guaranteeing same-day delivery on all book purchases?
W: (36)I made the decision to do that while you were away. We have an arrangement with a local delivery service that will let us get books to customers within a couple of hours.
M: (37)That should help sales. I imagine that our website will attract more customers if we keep ensuring that kind of reliability for swift delivery.

W: 안녕하세요, 제프. 얼굴 보니 반갑네요. 휴가는 잘 보냈어요?
M: 예, 좋았어요. 물어봐 줘서 고마워요. 있잖아요, 들어오다가, 앞 유리창에 붙어 있는 공지를 봤는데요. 모든 도서 구입에 대해 당일 배송 서비스를 보장한다고 한 이게 뭐예요?
W: 당신이 없는 동안에 그렇게 하기로 결정했어요. 우리는 지역 택배 서비스와 계약을 맺어서 시간 내로 고객들에게 책을 배달하게 될 거예요.
M: 그러면 매출에 도움되겠군요. 우리가 신속 배송이라는 그런 신뢰도를 계속 유지하면, 우리 웹사이트가 더 많은 고객을 유치할 거라고 생각해요.

35. 화자들은 어디에서 근무하는 것 같은가?
(A) 식료품점
(B) 전자제품 대리점
(C) 서점
(D) 도서관　　　정답 (C)

36. 여자는 무엇을 하기로 결정했는가?
(A) 웹사이트 개선
(B) 서비스 보장
(C) 회원 자격에 대해 고객에게 비용 청구
(D) 추가 제품 주문　　　정답 (B)

37. 남자는 무슨 일이 있을 것으로 예상하는가?
(A) 영업 시간이 연장될 것이다.
(B) 무료 배송이 제공될 것이다.
(C) 추가 직원이 고용될 것이다.
(D) 매출이 향상될 것이다.　　　　　　　정답 (D)

문제 38-40번은 다음 대화를 참조하시오. ⓜM ⓦW

M: Hello, Ms. Buford. (38)**This is Samuel, the realtor with Kline Realty.** I've got some great news for you. There's a new home up for sale in the Golden Forest neighborhood. Are you interested?
W: I know that's a good neighborhood. Can you tell me about what the house is like?
M: Sure. It has four bedrooms and three bathrooms. It's selling for $250,000.
W: (39)**Well, the location and the house sound perfect, but it's a bit beyond my budget.** Would the owners consider negotiating a lower price?
M: They would. (40)**How about checking out the property first? Do you have time today at 1:00 P.M.?**
W: (40)**Yes, I do. If you tell me the address, I'll meet you there.**

M: 안녕하세요, 뷰퍼드 씨. 저는 클라인 부동산의 중개사 사무엘이에요. 좋은 소식이 있어요. 골든 포레스트 동네에 새 집이 매물로 나왔어요. 관심 있으세요?
W: 거기는 좋은 동네라는 것을 알고 있어요. 그 집이 어떤 집인지 얘기 좀 해 주실래요?
M: 물론이죠. 방이 4개에 욕실이 3개예요. 250,000달러에 팔아요.
W: 음, 위치와 집은 완벽한 것 같은데, 제 예산을 약간 초과하는군요. 집주인이 좀 더 낮은 가격 협상을 고려할까요?
M: 그럴 겁니다. 먼저 집부터 보시는 게 어떠세요? 오늘 오후 1시에 시간 있으세요?
W: 예, 시간 됩니다. 주소를 말씀해 주시면, 거기서 뵐게요.

38. 남자는 어디에서 근무하는가?
(A) 조경업체
(B) 부동산 중개소
(C) 공립 도서관
(D) 전화 회사　　　　　　　정답 (B)

39. 여자는 무엇에 대해 걱정하는가?
(A) 자재
(B) 마감일
(C) 가격
(D) 위치　　　　　　　정답 (C)

40. 화자들은 오후에 무엇을 하기로 동의하는가?
(A) 사용 설명서 확인하기
(B) 임대 계약서에 서명하기
(C) 주인 만나기
(D) 부동산 방문하기　　　　　　　정답 (D)

문제 41-43번은 다음 대화를 참조하시오. ⓦW ⓜM

W: Well, that was a great party. (41)**It was wonderful to be all together and celebrate John's retirement.**

M: You can say that again. Now for the hard part, we have to clean up this mess.
W: (42)**I'm tired, so how about leaving that for tomorrow?**
M: (42)**All the recyclables get picked up tomorrow morning.**
W: I totally forgot about that. Okay, let's take care of it now.
M: Don't worry. We'll be finished in no time. (43)**I'll get the broom and dustpan, and you get some garbage bags from the back closet.**

W: 정말 대단한 파티였어요. 전부 다 모여서 존의 은퇴를 축하한 것은 멋졌어요.
M: 당신 말이 백 번 옳아요. 이제 힘든 부분은, 우리가 이 난장판을 깨끗이 치워야 한다는 거예요.
W: 난 좀 피곤한데, 그 상태로 그냥 두었다가 내일 하는 게 어때요?
M: 모든 재활용품은 내일 아침에 수거돼요.
W: 그거는 까마득히 잊고 있었어요. 좋아요, 청소를 지금 합시다.
M: 걱정 마세요. 금방 끝날 거예요. 내가 빗자루와 쓰레받기를 가져올 테니, 당신은 뒤쪽 비품실에서 쓰레기 봉투를 가지고 오세요.

41. 화자들은 무엇에 관해 얘기하고 있는가?
(A) 은퇴 파티
(B) 교육 세미나
(C) 새로운 청소업체
(D) 직원 감사 파티　　　　　　　정답 (A)

42. 남자가 "모든 재활용품은 내일 아침에 수거돼요"라고 말하는 이유는?
(A) 경고하기 위해
(B) 요청하기 위해
(C) 놀라움을 표현하기 위해
(D) 제안을 거절하기 위해　　　　　　　정답 (D)

43. 남자는 자신이 무엇을 할 것이라고 말하는가?
(A) 청소업체에 연락하기
(B) 일찍 집에 가기
(C) 쓰레기 줍기
(D) 청소용품 가져오기　　　　　　　정답 (D)

문제 44-46번은 다음 대화를 참조하시오. ⓜM ⓦW

M: Hello. (44)**You have reached the Everest Hotel.** How may I be of assistance?
W: Good morning. I need to reserve a room for this Thursday and Friday nights. Are there any rooms still available?
M: It's your lucky day. (45)**There's a trade show going on this weekend,** but we still have a couple of rooms available. Are you planning to attend the event?
W: Actually, I'll be hosting a booth there.
M: Just so you know, (46)**we will be providing shuttle buses to and from the convention center every thirty minutes. That should be convenient since you won't need to take a taxi or a bus.**

M: 여보세요. 에베레스트 호텔입니다. 무엇을 도와드릴까요?
W: 안녕하세요. 이번 주 목요일과 금요일 밤에 방 하나를 예약해야 해요. 아직 빈방이 남아 있는 게 있나요?
M: 오늘 운이 좋으시네요. 이번 주말에 무역 박람회가 있는데, 그래도 아직 방 몇 개가 남아 있어요. 그 행사에 참석하실 계획인가요?
W: 사실, 그곳에서 부스 하나를 운영할 거예요.

M: 참고하시라고 드리는 말씀인데요. 우리는 30분마다 컨벤션 센터를 왕복하는 셔틀 버스를 제공할 거예요. 그러면 택시나 버스를 탈 필요가 없으니까 편리할 거예요.

44. 남자는 어디에서 근무하는가?
(A) 기차 역
(B) 공항
(C) 컨벤션 센터
(D) 호텔   정답 (D)

45. 남자에 따르면, 이번 주에 어떤 행사가 열리는가?
(A) 마케팅 세미나
(B) 무역 박람회
(C) 음악 콘서트
(D) 도서 출간   정답 (B)

46. 남자는 무엇을 할 것을 권하는가?
(A) 셔틀 버스 이용
(B) 현지 가이드 고용
(C) 식당에서 식사
(D) 택시 타기   정답 (A)

문제 47-49번은 다음 3자 대화를 참조하시오. 미M 미W 영M

M1: We appreciate your coming to this job interview, Anna. As you're aware, (47)**we need someone to handle our online advertisements as well as manage our social media accounts.**
W: Yes. I've been in charge of my company's social media campaigns for the past three years.
M2: We noticed that on your résumé. (48)**We checked out those online campaigns and were impressed. That's why you're the leading candidate for the job now.**
M1: (49)**Well, now that you're here at our resort, you can see its beautiful scenery and views for yourself.** Do you think you'd be able to incorporate images from here into our accounts?
W: Definitely. I can't believe how beautiful it is.
M1: We'll take you on a tour of the grounds soon so that you can see the natural beauty in person.

M1: 안나, 이번 취업 면접에 와주셔서 감사합니다. 아시다시피, 우리는 우리 소셜 미디어 계정을 관리하는 것뿐만 아니라 온라인 광고를 담당할 사람이 필요합니다.
W: 그렇군요. 저는 지난 3년 동안 우리 회사의 소셜 미디어 광고를 담당해 왔습니다.
M2: 당신의 이력서를 보고 그건 알았어요. 그 온라인 광고들을 확인했는데, 깊은 인상을 받았어요. 그래서 지금 이 자리에 당신이 최우선적인 후보자입니다.
M1: 자, 이제 이곳 우리 휴양지에 오셨으니, 우리 휴양지의 아름다운 풍경과 전망을 직접 보실 수 있습니다. 이곳의 모습을 우리 계정에 넣을 수 있을 것 같으세요?
W: 물론이죠. 얼마나 아름다운지 믿을 수가 없네요.
M1: 직접 자연적인 아름다움을 보실 수 있도록 곧 이곳 부지를 구경시켜 드릴게요.

47. 업체는 여자가 무엇을 해주기를 원하는가?
(A) 새 레크리에이션 구역 설계
(B) 온라인 광고 담당
(C) 새로운 웹 페이지 제작
(D) 고객 계정 관리   정답 (B)

48. 여자가 최우선적인 후보자인 이유는?
(A) 그녀는 해외에서 근무한 경험이 있다.
(B) 그녀의 추천서가 괜찮다.
(C) 그녀의 작업이 인상적이다.
(D) 그녀의 일정이 융통성이 있다.   정답 (C)

49. 남자들은 그들의 휴양지에 대해 무엇을 언급하는가?
(A) 최근에 보수공사를 했다.
(B) 아름다운 전망이 있다.
(C) 투숙객들에게 인기가 있다.
(D) 가격이 합리적이다.   정답 (B)

문제 50-52번은 다음 대화를 참조하시오. 미W 영M

W: Were you able to find everything you wanted?
M: I was. This grocery store just opened, right? It's my first time to see it.
W: We opened two days ago. We're still organizing everything. (50)**We'll be having a grand opening sale this weekend, and most items will be offered at a reduced price.** Please drop by.
M: I'm really pleased there's a supermarket so close to my home. (51)**Given that you have a good selection here, I think we'll be seeing each other a lot.**
W: If our sales so far are any criterion, it would seem that we can expect to see a lot of people here.
M: I'm happy to hear that. Anyway, I'd like to check out now. (52)**Do you take credit cards?**
W: (52)**I'm really sorry, but the card readers haven't been connected yet.**

W: 원하시는 모든 것을 찾으실 수 있었어요?
M: 예, 다 찾았어요. 이 식료품점은 지금 막 개업했군요, 맞죠? 이 가게를 처음 봐서요.
W: 이틀 전에 개업했어요. 아직 모든 물건들을 정리 중이에요. 이번 주말에 대개장 세일을 하는데, 대부분의 품목들이 할인 가격에 제공될 거예요. 그 때 오세요.
M: 집과 이렇게 가까운 곳에 슈퍼마켓이 있어서 정말 기쁘네요. 여기에 물건들을 다양하게 갖추고 있는 것을 감안하면, 서로 자주 뵙게 될 것 같아요.
W: 지금까지의 매출이 기준이 된다면, 이곳에 많은 사람들이 올 것으로 예상되긴 해요.
M: 그 얘기 들으니 기쁘네요. 어쨌든 지금 계산하려고요. 신용 카드를 받나요?
W: 정말 죄송하지만, 카드 리더기가 아직 연결되어 있지 않아요.

50. 여자는 주말에 무슨 일이 있을 것이라고 말하는가?
(A) 일부 제품이 할인될 것이다.
(B) 새로운 품목들이 도착할 것이다.
(C) 몇 개의 조명 장치가 설치될 것이다.
(D) 매장 영업 시간이 연장될 것이다.   정답 (A)

51. 남자가 "우리 서로 자주 뵙게 될 것 같아요"라고 말할 때 무엇을 의미하는가?

(A) 그는 그 가게의 일자리를 수락했다.

(B) 그는 새로운 업체에 대해 만족스럽다.

(C) 그는 가게 주인을 안 지 오래되었다.

(D) 그는 쇼핑 클럽의 회원이다. 　　　　정답 (B)

52. 여자가 사과하는 이유는?

(A) 그녀는 남자의 요청을 오해했다.

(B) 가게에서 현재 채용하지 않고 있다.

(C) 어떤 지불 방법을 이용할 수가 없다.

(D) 광고된 제품이 품절되었다. 　　　　정답 (C)

문제 53-55번은 다음 3자 대화를 참조하시오. 미W 미M 영M

W: Hello. (53) (54)I purchased this violin here two months ago, but yesterday I found a crack in it. I wonder if I can get a refund.

M1: I'm not sure. Let me ask the manager. Oh, here he comes. Stuart, this customer has a question.

M2: Hello. I'm Stuart. What can I help you with?

W: Um, I bought this violin here two months ago, but it's already broken. Is it possible to return it for a refund?

M2: Sorry, but the store policy is that items must be returned within four weeks of purchase to get a refund. (55)However, that particular item comes with a company warranty that's valid for one year.

W: 안녕하세요. 두 달 전에 여기서 이 바이올린을 구매했는데, 어제 안에 금이 가 있는 것을 발견했어요. 환불을 받을 수 있을지 궁금해요.

M1: 잘 모르겠어요. 매니저에게 물어볼게요. 아, 여기 오시네요. 스튜어트, 이 손님이 질문이 있어요.

M2: 안녕하세요. 스튜어트입니다. 뭐를 도와드릴까요?

W: 음, 여기서 두 달 전에 이 바이올린을 샀는데, 벌써 망가졌어요. 반품하고 환불받을 수 있을까요?

M2: 죄송합니다만, 저희 가게 방침으로는 환불을 받으려면 물품을 구매한 지 4주 이내로만 반품할 수 있습니다. 그런데, 이 특정 제품은 1년간 유효한 회사 품질 보증서가 같이 나옵니다.

53. 어떤 종류의 제품에 대해 얘기하고 있는가?

(A) 부엌 가전제품

(B) 악기

(C) 조명 기구

(D) 스마트폰 액세서리 　　　　정답 (B)

54. 제품에 대한 여자의 불만사항은 무엇인가?

(A) 그것에 일부 부속이 빠져 있다.

(B) 그것이 이상한 소음을 내고 있다.

(C) 그것에 맞지 않는 케이블이 같이 왔다.

(D) 그것이 파손되어 있다. 　　　　정답 (D)

55. 스튜어트는 무엇을 할 것을 권하는가?

(A) 제조업체의 품질 보증 이용

(B) 다른 수리점 방문

(C) 교체 부속 주문

(D) 오늘 나중에 다시 오기 　　　　정답 (A)

문제 56-58번은 다음 대화를 참조하시오. 호W 영M

W: Hello, Tim. Are you available now?

M: (56)I'm just about to finish repairing this bicycle. What's going on?

W: (57)We finally received that shipment of electric motors. I'm sure our customers will be pleased.

M: Great. There have been a lot of people asking if they could convert their bikes to electric ones. They're not hard to install, are they?

W: Not at all. You simply attach the motor. It's great for people who want to travel long distances on their bikes.

M: Wonderful. (58)Could you please hang up a sign saying that the motors are currently in stock? We need to inform our customers of their arrival as soon as possible.

W: 안녕하세요, 팀. 지금 시간 있어요?

M: 이 자전거 고치는 거 막 끝내던 참이에요. 무슨 일이에요?

W: 드디어 전기 모터 배송품을 받았어요. 우리 고객들이 분명 기뻐할 거예요.

M: 잘됐군요. 자신들의 자전거를 전기 자전거로 바꿀 수 있는지 묻는 사람들이 많았어요. 그 모터는 설치가 어렵지 않죠, 그렇죠?

W: 전혀요. 그냥 모터를 달기만 하면 돼요. 자전거로 장거리를 다니고 싶어하는 사람들에게 잘됐네요.

M: 아주 잘됐어요. 현재 모터가 재고가 있다고 알리는 표지판을 붙여 주시겠어요? 가능하면 빨리 고객들에게 모터가 도착한 것을 알릴 필요가 있어요.

56. 화자들은 어디에서 근무하는가?

(A) 재활용 공장

(B) 기술 학교

(C) 제조 시설

(D) 자전거 가게 　　　　정답 (D)

57. 화자들은 무엇에 대해 얘기하고 있는가?

(A) 전기 모터

(B) 안전 장비

(C) 자전거 보관대

(D) 자동차 핸들 　　　　정답 (A)

58. 남자는 여자에게 무엇을 해달라고 부탁하는가?

(A) 납품업체에 전화

(B) 안내문 게시

(C) 서류 서명

(D) 이메일 발송 　　　　정답 (B)

문제 59-61번은 다음 대화를 참조하시오. 미M 호W

M: Welcome back to my talk show on radio 103.4. (59)My guest today is Susan Briggs, the owner of Briggs Furniture. She'll be talking about how her industry has changed. Welcome, Susan.

W: Thanks for having me on the show.

M: I know that custom-made furniture isn't as popular as it once was. How has your store managed to remain profitable considering this changing trend?

W: (60)Recently, we haven't gotten as many orders as we used to. (61)However, the orders we do get tend to be extensive.

M: And is it profitable to fill those orders?

W: **(61)Many homeowners request custom-made furniture for every room in their home,** and those orders provide us with plenty of work, which helps us still stay competitive.

M: 라디오 103.4의 토크쇼에 다시 오신 것을 환영합니다. 오늘 초대 손님은 브릭스 가구 소유주이신 수잔 브릭스입니다. 수잔은 자신의 업계가 어떻게 변화해 왔는지에 대해 얘기해 주실 것입니다. 어서 오세요, 수잔.

W: 이 프로에 초대해 주셔서 감사합니다.

M: 맞춤 가구가 한때는 인기 있었지만 이제는 그만큼 인기가 없는 것으로 알고 있어요. 귀사는 이런 변화하는 동향을 고려하면서 어떻게 운영하여 수익을 유지하시나요?

W: 최근에는, 예전만큼 많은 주문이 들어오지는 않아요. 그런데, 우리가 받는 주문이 광범위해지는 경향이 있어요.

M: 그런 주문에 응해서 수익이 나고 있나요?

W: 많은 주택 소유자들이 자신의 집의 각 방에 맞춤형 가구를 요청하고 있어요. 그리고 그런 주문들로 우리에게 많은 일거리가 생기기 때문에, 그런 상황이 아직 계속해서 경쟁력을 유지하는 데 도움이 되고 있어요.

59. 여자는 어디에서 근무하는가?
(A) 라디오 방송국
(B) 가구점
(C) 컴퓨터 가게
(D) 백화점 　　　　　　　　　　　　　　정답 (B)

60. 최근의 주문에 대하여 무엇이 언급되는가?
(A) 물량이 더 적어졌다
(B) 주로 기업체에서 온다.
(C) 항상 온라인에서 이루어진다.
(D) 미리 조립되어서 나와야 한다. 　　　　정답 (A)

61. 여자에 따르면, 그녀의 업체는 어떻게 경쟁력을 유지하는가?
(A) 맞춤 가구에 대해 할인을 제공함으로써
(B) 고객 서비스를 개선함으로써
(C) 온라인 마케팅을 늘림으로써
(D) 개별 고객들에게 많은 품목들을 제공함으로써 　정답 (D)

문제 62–64번은 다음 대화와 보고서를 참조하시오. 영M 미W

M: Hello, Alice. **(62)I just inspected the office equipment here at the law firm.** But I need your advice about something before I turn in my report.

W: Sure. What's your question?

M: Almost everything is working properly, **(63)but there's one piece of equipment in the main conference room which hasn't worked in a while, and I don't know if I should repair it or throw it away.** What should I do?

W: Talk to Joseph. The main conference room is his responsibility. See what he wants to do.

M: **(64)He was in a meeting just a while ago, but I'll go there to see if it's over now.**

M: 안녕하세요, 앨리스. 지금 막 여기 법률 사무소의 사무 장비를 점검했어요. 그런데 내가 보고서를 제출하기 전에 당신의 조언이 필요한 일이 있어요.

W: 좋아요, 질문이 무엇인가요?

M: 거의 모든 게 제대로 작동되고 있는데, 주 회의실에 있는 장비 하나만

꽤나 오래 작동이 안 되고 있어요. 그걸 수리해야 할지 그냥 버려야 할지 잘 모르겠어요. 어떻게 하면 좋을까요?

W: 조셉과 얘기해 보세요. 주 회의실은 그 사람 책임이에요. 그가 어떻게 하고 싶은지 알아보세요.

M: 조셉은 좀 전에 회의 들어갔는데, 거기 가서 지금쯤 회의가 끝났는지 알아봐야겠네요.

점검 보고서	
품목	**조치**
노트북 컴퓨터	운영 시스템 업그레이드
복사기	토너 교체
(63)영사기	고장 – 수리 또는 폐기
프린터	새 컴퓨터에 연결

62. 화자들은 어떤 종류의 업종에서 근무하는가?
(A) 도서관
(B) 전자제품 대리점
(C) 대학교
(D) 법률 사무소 　　　　　　　　　　　정답 (D)

63. 그래픽을 보시오. 화자들은 어떤 장비에 대해 얘기하고 있는가?
(A) 노트북 컴퓨터
(B) 복사기
(C) 영사기
(D) 프린터 　　　　　　　　　　　　　　정답 (C)

64. 남자는 지금 무엇을 하겠다고 말하는가?
(A) 교체 부속 주문
(B) 동료와 대화
(C) 회의실 청소
(D) 새 장비 구매 　　　　　　　　　　　정답 (B)

문제 65–67번은 다음 대화와 일정표를 참조하시오. 호W 미M

W: Sam, I thought you said you'd have to skip lunch with our clients.

M: **(65)My conference call with Fred got canceled, so I had time to make it to the restaurant.** I'm glad the clients aren't already here.

W: So am I. I'm pleased you're here. **(66)You worked on the design of the appliance a lot, so I hope you can help me describe it.**

M: Okay. However, **(67)I can't stay for too long because I have to be somewhere at 1:30.**

W: I understand. In that case, why don't you start by talking about the new appliance when the clients arrive? Then, when you need to go, I'll take over and respond to all of their questions.

M: That sounds perfect to me.

W: 샘, 우리 고객과의 점심식사에 빠져야 한다고 말씀하신 것으로 알았는데요.

M: 프레드와의 전화 회의가 취소되어서 식당으로 올 시간이 생겼어요. 고객 분들이 아직 여기 오지 않으셔서 다행이네요.

W: 저도 그래요. 당신이 오니 좋네요. 당신이 가전제품 디자인 작업을 많이

하셨으니, 그것을 설명하는 것을 도와주실 수 있으면 좋겠네요.

M: 좋아요. 그런데, 1시 30분에 다른 데 가야 해서 오래 있을 수는 없어요.

W: 알았어요. 그렇다면, 고객 분들이 도착하면 당신이 새 가전제품에 대해 먼저 얘기를 시작하시는 게 어때요? 그 다음, 당신이 가야 할 때가 되면, 제가 인계 받아서 그들의 모든 질문에 답변할게요.

M: 그게 저한테 딱 맞는 것 같아요.

샘의 일정

할 일	시간
딘과 회의	오전 11:00
전화 회의	오전 11:45
고객과 점심	오후 12:00
(67)공장 견학	오후 1:30
오리엔테이션 연설	오후 4:00

65. 대화는 어디에서 이루어지고 있는가?
(A) 딘의 사무실
(B) 식당
(C) 공장
(D) 회의실 　　　　　　　　　　　　　정답 (B)

66. 화자들은 무엇에 대해 논의할 것인가?
(A) 제품의 가격
(B) 제품의 디자인
(C) 제품의 매출
(D) 제품의 광고 　　　　　　　　　　　정답 (B)

67. 그래픽을 보시오. 샘이 일찍 가야 하는 이유는?
(A) 딘과 회의가 있다.
(B) 전화 회의가 있다.
(C) 공장 견학이 있다
(D) 오리엔테이션 연설이 있다. 　　　　　정답 (C)

문제 68-70번은 다음 대화와 포스터를 참조하시오. 영M 호W

M: Hello. (68)How are you enjoying the trade fair?

W: It's interesting. I'm just checking out booths to see what each company is offering.

M: I can tell you about an online management training program my company offers. It's helpful for those hoping to break into management.

W: It sounds good. I'll be applying for my boss's position when he retires next year.

M: This chart here shows the four phases of managing a project. Most people focus on the first and third phases and (69) don't realize that a project can easily fail if they don't focus enough on the second phase.

W: Interesting. Do you have any brochure about this program or whatever? I'm flying home tonight, (70)but I can sign up for an online training program when I get back home.

- -

M: 안녕하세요. 무역 박람회는 어떻게 재미가 있으신가요?

W: 흥미롭네요. 그냥 저는 각 회사마다 뭐를 내놓고 있나 보려고 부스들을 확인하고 있어요.

M: 우리 회사에서 제공하는 온라인 관리 교육 프로그램에 대해서 말씀드릴게요. 이 프로그램은 관리를 시작하고 싶은 사람들에게 도움이 됩니다.

W: 그거 듣고 보니 좋네요. 내년에 제 상사가 은퇴하면 제가 그 자리에 지원하려고요.

M: 여기 이 차트는 프로젝트를 관리하는 4단계를 보여 줍니다. 대부분의 사람들은 첫 번째와 세 번째 단계에 집중하는데, 두 번째 단계에 충분히 집중하지 못하면 프로젝트는 쉽게 실패할 수 있다는 점을 깨닫지 못하세요.

W: 흥미롭네요. 이 프로그램에 관한 안내책자 같은 거 있나요? 오늘 밤 비행기 타고 집으로 가는데, 집에 도착해서 온라인 교육 프로그램을 신청할 수 있어요.

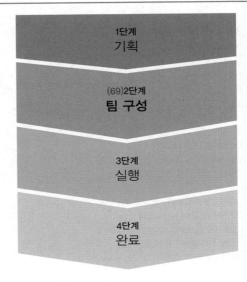

68. 대화가 어디에서 이루어지는가?
(A) 취업 박람회
(B) 관리자를 위한 회의
(C) 마케팅 회사
(D) 무역 박람회 　　　　　　　　　　　정답 (D)

69. 그래픽을 보시오. 남자는 어느 단계가 프로젝트의 성공에 중요하다고 생각하는가?
(A) 기획
(B) 팀 구성
(C) 실행
(D) 완료 　　　　　　　　　　　　　　정답 (B)

70. 여자는 집으로 돌아가면 무엇을 하겠다고 말하는가?
(A) 어떤 과정 등록
(B) 어떤 자리에 지원
(C) 남자와 전화 통화
(D) 자신의 이력서 제출 　　　　　　　　정답 (A)

Part 4

문제 71-73번은 다음 회의 발췌 내용을 참조하시오. 미M

M: Hello, everybody. (71)This is the last day of our special sale, and we expect lots of customers to come to purchase sporting goods. (72)Please be friendly and answer any questions customers have today. I want you to make sure the shelves are fully stocked. (72)But if a customer has trouble finding any item, help that person at once. In addition, because it's the last day of the sale, we're giving away prizes today. (73)All people need to do to win a prize is to make a purchase and then fill out a form you give them.

안녕하세요, 여러분. 오늘은 특별 세일의 마지막 날이어서, 많은 손님들이 스포츠용품을 구입하러 올 것으로 예상합니다. 오늘 친절하게 하시고, 손님들의 질문에 답변을 해주세요. 선반에는 물건들이 가득 채워져 있도록 해주시면 좋겠습니다. 그런데 고객이 어떤 물건이든 찾는 데 애를 먹으면, 즉시 그 사람을 도와주세요. 그 밖에도, 오늘이 세일 마지막 날이기 때문에, 오늘 경품을 나눠줄 것입니다. 경품을 받기 위해서 사람들이 해야 하는 것은 물건을 구매하고 여러분이 고객들에게 주는 양식을 작성하기만 하면 됩니다.

71. 화자는 어디에서 근무하는 것 같은가?
(A) 스포츠용품 회사
(B) 철물점
(C) 백화점
(D) 보석상 　　　　　　　　　　　　　　　정답 (A)

72. 화자에 따르면, 청자들은 무엇에 초점을 맞춰야 하는가?
(A) 매장 청소
(B) 홍보용 전단지 배포
(C) 고객 서비스 제공
(D) 선반 정리 　　　　　　　　　　　　　정답 (C)

73. 쇼핑객들은 어떻게 경품을 받을 수 있는가?
(A) 문자 메시지를 보냄으로써
(B) 영수증을 제출함으로써
(C) 웹사이트를 방문함으로써
(D) 양식을 작성함으로써 　　　　　　　　정답 (D)

문제 74-76번은 다음 광고를 참조하시오. 호W

W: Would you like a fun job during vacation? Then come to the career fair at Stanton Resort this Saturday. We're hiring part-time staff members for all kinds of positions, from lifeguards at our beach to servers at our restaurants. (74)The Stanton Resort is recognized for one of the most popular hotels with tourists (75)as we attract visitors from all around the world. We're also a great place to work. We have the highest hourly wages in the region, (76)and we also offer other benefits, including flexible hours and paid days off.

방학 동안에 재미있는 일자리를 원하세요? 그렇다면 이번 주 토요일 스탠튼 리조트에서 하는 취업 설명회로 오세요. 우리는 해변의 안전요원부터 식당의 서빙 직원까지 온갖 종류의 자리를 위한 시간제 근무 직원들을 채용합니다. 스탠튼 리조트는 전세계 각지에서 방문객들을 유치하고 있어서, 관광객들에게 가장 인기 있는 호텔 중 하나로 인정받고 있습니다. 우리는 또한 근무하기에도 아주 좋은 곳입니다. 이 지역 내에서 가장 높은 시간당 급여를 주고, 또한 탄력 근무 시간과 유급 휴가를 비롯한 기타 복지 혜택도 제공합니다.

74. 어떤 업체가 광고가 되고 있는가?
(A) 놀이 공원
(B) 여행사
(C) 식당
(D) 호텔 　　　　　　　　　　　　　　　정답 (D)

75. 화자에 따르면, 업체는 무엇으로 인정받고 있는가?
(A) 수영 대회 개최
(B) 환경 친화적인 자재 사용
(C) 해외 관광객 유치
(D) 지역 자선기관에 기부 　　　　　　　정답 (C)

76. 직원들에게 어떤 취업 혜택이 주어지는가?
(A) 직원 할인
(B) 상근직 취업 기회
(C) 유연한 근무 일정
(D) 연수 기회 　　　　　　　　　　　　　정답 (C)

문제 77-79번은 다음 전화 메시지를 참조하시오. 미W

W: Hello, Dave. This is Carol at MTR, Inc. (77)We just received a shipment of computer chips from you, but it's much less than we were expecting. (78)Please call me back at once. We have orders that we need to fill at the end of the month. In addition, (79)please be advised that I'll be out of the office most of the day. If I don't answer, dial extension 78, please. Mark will be able to tell you how to get in touch with me.

안녕하세요, 데이브. 저는 MTR 주식회사의 캐롤입니다. 저희가 귀사에서 컴퓨터칩 배송을 막 받았습니다만, 우리가 예상했던 것보다 물량이 훨씬 더 적습니다. 지금 바로 제게 전화 주세요. 이달 말에 우리가 처리해야 할 주문 건들이 있습니다. 또한, 하루 중 대부분 저는 사무실에 없을 것임을 알려 드립니다. 제가 전화를 받지 않으면, 내선번호 78번으로 전화 주세요. 마크가 어떻게 하면 저와 연락이 되는지 알려줄 것입니다.

77. 화자가 전화를 거는 이유는?
(A) 취소를 하기 위해
(B) 주문품을 추적하기 위해
(C) 주문품에 대해 얘기하기 위해
(D) 차로 가는 길 안내를 요청하기 위해 　정답 (C)

78. 화자가 "이달 말에 우리가 처리해야 할 주문 건들이 있습니다"라고 말할 때 무엇을 함축하는가?
(A) 추가 직원이 고용되어야 한다.
(B) 그녀의 요청이 시급하다.
(C) 그녀는 더 높은 가격을 지불할 수 있다.
(D) 물품이 특송으로 발송되어야 한다. 　정답 (B)

79. 청자는 무엇에 대해 주의를 받는가?
(A) 화자는 자신의 사무실에 없을지 모른다.
(B) 근무 시간에 변경이 있을 수 있다.
(C) 예약이 이루어질 수 없다.
(D) 일정이 변경되었다. 　　　　　　　　정답 (A)

문제 80-82번은 다음 회의 발췌 내용을 참조하시오. 영M

M: (80)I need to update you on the fundraiser we're holding for the local hospital next month. (81)It has just been confirmed that we can use the auditorium at city hall. We're really pleased about that since it can hold 1,000 people. Now that we know the location is secured, (82)we can start the next phase of the planning. (82)We need to put together a website for the fundraiser to let people know why we're trying to raise money. I want the site to be up and running no later than next week.

우리가 다음 달에 지역 병원을 위해서 개최하는 기금 모금 행사에 대해 최근 소식을 알려 드리겠습니다. 시청 대강당을 사용할 수 있는 것으로 막 확인되었습니다. 그 곳은 1,000명을 수용할 수 있기 때문에 확정되어 정말 기쁩니다. 이제 장소가 확보가 되었다는 것을 알았으니, 기획 다음 단계를 시작할 수 있습니다. 우리가 왜 기금을 모금하려고 하는지 사람들에게 알리기 위해 기금 모금 행사를 위한 웹사이트를 만들 필요가 있습니다. 늦어도 다음 주까지는 사이트가 정상적으로 운영될 수 있기를 바랍니다.

80. 어떤 종류의 행사가 준비되고 있는가?
(A) 무역 전시회
(B) 지역 축제
(C) 자선 경매
(D) 기금 모금 행사 　　　　　　　　정답 (D)

81. 화자는 어떤 소식을 발표하는가?
(A) 광고가 성공적이었다.
(B) 포스터들이 게시되었다.
(C) 장소를 빌릴 수 있다.
(D) 저녁 예약이 확인되었다. 　　　　정답 (C)

82. 화자에 따르면, 기획 과정에서 다음 단계는 무엇인가?
(A) 광고 내기
(B) 계약서에 서명하기
(C) 웹 페이지 만들기
(D) 물품 구매하기 　　　　　　　　정답 (C)

문제 83-85번은 다음 팟캐스트를 참조하시오. ⓂM

M: It's time to get started with the local news podcast. I'm Tim Davis, the host of the show. (83)**Today, we'll be discussing how to expand your business.** It's important to know when you should open a new store or enlarge your present one. (84)**Today, our special guest is Tina Mellon. Tina started a small cosmetics manufacturer.** Two years later, she decided to hire more workers. At present, she employs more than 1,000 people. (85)**You can read an interview containing her thoughts on doing business by visiting her website.** Go online to check it out.

지역 소식 팟캐스트를 시작할 시간입니다. 저는 이 프로그램의 진행자 팀 데이비스입니다. 오늘, 우리는 여러분의 사업을 어떻게 확장할지에 대해 얘기할 것입니다. 언제 새로운 매장을 열지, 현재의 사업체를 언제 확장할지를 아는 것은 중요합니다. 오늘, 우리 특별 게스트는 티나 멜론입니다. 티나는 작은 화장품 제조업체를 시작했습니다. 2년 후에, 티나는 더 많은 직원을 채용하기로 결정했습니다. 현재, 그녀는 1,000명 이상의 직원을 고용하고 있습니다. 그녀의 웹사이트를 방문하시면 사업을 하는 것에 대한 그녀의 생각이 포함된 인터뷰를 읽을 수 있습니다. 온라인에 접속해서 확인해 보세요.

83. 팟캐스트의 주제는 무엇인가?
(A) 시장 동향 이해하기
(B) 사업체 확장하기
(C) 수익 증대하기
(D) 창업 도와주기 　　　　　　　　정답 (B)

84. 티나 멜론은 어떤 종류의 업체를 소유하고 있는가?
(A) 의류 매장
(B) 식당
(C) 금융 서비스 회사
(D) 화장품 제조업체 　　　　　　　정답 (D)

85. 화자는 웹사이트에서 무엇을 볼 수 있다고 말하는가?
(A) 인터뷰
(B) 사업 교본
(C) 투자자 명단
(D) 취업 기회 　　　　　　　　　　정답 (A)

문제 86-88번은 다음 관광 안내를 참조하시오. ⓂW

W: Thanks for joining us on today's tour. (86)**I'd like to apologize for the late start.** The bus driver encountered some bad traffic on his way here. Fortunately, he took an alternate route, so he wasn't delayed too long. Our first stop will be the commercial district, where we'll stay for about an hour so you can shop. You'll see a variety of ceramic plates and bowls for sale there. (87)**But let me tell you something. Lots of the items for sale there are made in the artisan district. And that's our next stop.** In the afternoon, we'll have lunch at Rudolph Bistro where I think you'll have a good time (88) **because the Jackson Brothers, a popular local guitar duo, will be playing out on the patio there.**

오늘 관광에 저희와 함께해 주셔서 감사합니다. 시작이 늦어진 데 대해 사과를 드리고 싶습니다. 버스 운전사가 여기로 오다가 심한 교통 체증을 만났습니다. 다행스럽게도, 운전사가 다른 길을 택해서, 그렇게 많이 늦지는 않았습니다. 우리가 첫 번째 들를 곳은 상업 지구인데, 여러분이 쇼핑하실 수 있도록 거기서 약 한 시간 정도 있을 것입니다. 그곳에서 판매되는 다양한 도자기 접시와 사발을 보실 겁니다. 그런데 여러분에게 말씀 드릴 게 있습니다. 그곳에서 판매되는 많은 물건들이 장인 구역에서 제작되는 것들입니다. 그리고 그곳은 우리가 뒤이어 들를 곳입니다. 오후에는, 루돌프 비스트로에서 점심을 먹을 것인데, 이 지역의 인기 있는 기타 듀오인 잭슨 브라더스가 그곳 옥외 테라스에서 연주를 할 것이므로 여러분은 좋은 시간을 보내시게 될 것으로 생각합니다.

86. 화자는 무엇에 대해 사과하는가?
(A) 예상치 못한 비용
(B) 긴 줄
(C) 시작 지연
(D) 붐비는 버스 　　　　　　　　　정답 (C)

87. 화자가 "그리고 그곳은 우리가 뒤이어 들를 곳입니다"라고 말하는 이유는?
(A) 물건을 나중에 살 것을 제안하기 위해
(B) 관광 일정에 대해 불평하기 위해
(C) 청자들에게 서두르라고 권하기 위해
(D) 한 청자의 질문에 답하기 위해 　정답 (A)

88. 화자는 청자들이 루돌프 비스트로에서 무엇을 즐길 것이라고 말하는가?
(A) 도시의 전망
(B) 예술 작품
(C) 음악 공연
(D) 신선한 음식 　　　　　　　　　정답 (C)

문제 89–91번은 다음 회의 발췌 내용을 참조하시오. 호W

W: Good morning. Our Human Resources meeting today will be about retaining employees. (89)**For the past several quarters, we've had problems with keeping staff members.** Lots of employees depart after working here a short time. (90)**Last month, I conducted a survey of every employee across the company.** I learned a lot from the results. Several people stated that they would like to have more support and training after being hired. (91)**To address this, we've decided to launch a mentoring program.** We are going to pair all new employees with experienced staff members to help them get settled into their position through informative guidance.

안녕하세요. 오늘 우리 인적자원부 회의는 직원들을 유지하는 것에 관한 것입니다. 지난 몇 분기 동안, 우리는 직원들을 유지하는 데 어려움을 겪었습니다. 많은 직원들이 여기서 짧게 근무하고 떠납니다. 지난달에 저는 전사적으로 모든 직원 대상으로 설문조사를 실시했습니다. 그 결과에서 저는 많은 것을 알게 되었습니다. 여러 사람이 고용된 이후에도 지원과 교육이 있으면 좋겠다고 말했습니다. 이 문제를 해결하기 위해서, 우리는 멘토링 프로그램을 시작하기로 결정했습니다. 우리는 유익한 지도를 통해서 신입 직원들이 자신의 자리에 잘 적응할 수 있도록 신입 사원 전원과 경력 사원을 짝지어줄 예정입니다.

89. 업체가 어려움을 겪어온 것은 무엇인가?
(A) 자격 있는 직원 고용하기
(B) 최신 제품 홍보하기
(C) 해외 시장으로 확장하기
(D) 직원 유지하기 　　　　　　정답 (D)

90. 화자는 지난달에 무엇을 했는가?
(A) 그녀는 설문조사를 실시했다.
(B) 그녀는 지원자 몇 명을 면접 봤다.
(C) 그녀는 새로운 계약에 서명했다.
(D) 그녀는 출장을 갔다. 　　　　정답 (A)

91. 화자는 회사가 무엇을 할 것이라고 말하는가?
(A) 멘토링 프로그램 시작하기
(B) 현장 교육 제공하기
(C) 더 많은 광고 제작하기
(D) 새 부동산 매입하기 　　　　정답 (A)

문제 92–94번은 다음 뉴스 보도를 참조하시오. 미M

M: Hello. This is *News at Ten*. (92)**Summerville has continuously made efforts to improve its bus operations in the city**, and we've been tracking its progress. The mayor just announced that the city is going to launch a mobile app, Bus-tracking Now to help passengers track where the buses are and look up real-time departures and arrivals. (93)**You may be wondering if it's worth downloading another mobile app. Well, we've been told that it has been successful in other cities.** If you download the app and use it, (94)**how about e-mailing your comments to newsatten@Summervillenews.org?** We'd love to know what you think.

안녕하세요. 〈10시 뉴스〉입니다. 서머빌은 도시 버스 운행을 개선하려는 노력을 지속적으로 해왔고, 저희는 그 진행 과정을 계속 파악해 오고 있습니

다. 시장은 승객들이 버스가 어디에 있는지 추적하고 실시간으로 출발 및 도착 정보를 찾아보는 것을 도와줄 버스-트래킹 나우라는 모바일 앱을 시에서 시작할 것이라고 막 발표했습니다. 여러분은 또 다른 모바일 앱을 내려받을 만한 가치가 있을까 궁금하실 수도 있습니다. 자, 우리는 이 앱이 다른 도시에서 성공적이었다고 들었습니다. 여러분이 이 앱을 내려받아 사용하신다면, 이메일로 여러분의 의견을 newsatten@Summervillenews.org에 보내 주시겠습니까? 여러분의 생각이 어떤지 알고 싶습니다.

92. 서머빌은 무엇을 하려고 계획 중인가?
(A) 도시의 도로 일부 확장
(B) 버스 서비스 개선
(C) 주민들에게 대중 교통 이용 권장
(D) 더 많은 관광객 유치 　　　　정답 (B)

93. 화자가 "그것이 다른 도시에서는 성공적이었다"라고 말하는 이유는?
(A) 더 많은 버스 운전사를 고용하기 위해
(B) 새로운 훈련 프로그램을 언급하기 위해
(C) 다른 모바일 앱을 개발하기 위해
(D) 잘 처리된 일을 칭찬하기 위해 　　정답 (D)

94. 청자들은 무엇을 해달라는 요청을 받는가?
(A) 이메일로 의견 보내기
(B) 버스 타기 시작하기
(C) 시장 집무실 방문하기
(D) 다른 도시로 가기 　　　　정답 (A)

문제 95–97번은 다음 전화 메시지와 수리 계획표를 참조하시오. 미W

W: Hello, Carl. This is Amy. (95)**I'm calling regarding the repairs you'd like to have done on your home.** We sent a crew to inspect your property two days ago, and they understand the work that you want done. (96)**Right now, I'm working on an estimate of the price you'll need to pay.** The price mostly depends upon the quality of the paint you want for the interior. (97)**Let me send you a few samples to choose from.** Once you do that, I can give you a final price quote. Please call me back if you have any questions. Thanks.

안녕하세요, 칼. 저는 에이미예요. 고객님 집에 하고자 하시는 수리 건 때문에 전화 드렸습니다. 고객님 집을 점검해 보기 위해 이틀 전에 직원들을 보냈는데, 고객님이 원하시는 작업 내용을 그들이 이해하고 있습니다. 지금은 고객님이 지불하셔야 할 가격의 견적 작업을 하고 있습니다. 가격은 주로 고객님이 실내에 원하시는 페인트 품질에 달려 있습니다. 고르실 수 있게 견본 몇 가지를 보내 드리겠습니다. 일단 페인트를 고르시면, 최종 견적을 드릴 수 있습니다. 질문이 있으시면 다시 연락주세요. 감사합니다.

수리 계획

1단계	건물 조사
(96)2단계	**비용 견적 내기**
3단계	일정표 만들기
4단계	허가 받기
5단계	작업 시작하기

95. 화자는 누구일 것 같은가?
(A) 공사 책임자
(B) 건축가

(C) 철물점 주인

(D) 실내 장식가 정답 (A)

96. 그래픽을 보시오. 화자는 현재 어느 단계 작업을 하고 있는가?

(A) 1단계

(B) 2단계

(C) 3단계

(D) 4단계 정답 (B)

97. 화자는 청자에게 무엇을 보낼 것인가?

(A) 서명할 계약서

(B) 수정된 청사진

(C) 재료 견본

(D) 견적서 정답 (C)

문제 98-100번은 다음 전화 메시지와 포스터를 참조하시오. 호W

W: Hello, Darlene. It's Lisa. I'm calling regarding the spring festival that's taking place in Fayetteville this weekend. (98) **Because of the approaching hurricane, the festival has been pushed back until next weekend.** That's good for me because I really wanted to attend it, but I'll be out of town this weekend. (99)**Anyway, that band we want to see is going to be performing on Saturday**, so how about going to see them together? If you want, (100)**I can pick the tickets up for you after work today.** Just let me know.

안녕하세요, 달린. 리사예요. 이번 주말에 페이엣빌에서 열리는 봄 축제 때문에 전화드렸어요. 허리케인이 다가오고 있기 때문에, 축제가 다음 주말로 미뤄졌어요. 축제에 정말 참가하고 싶었는데 이번 주말에 시외로 나갈 거라서, 그게 저에게는 잘됐어요. 어쨌든, 우리가 보고 싶은 그 밴드가 토요일에 공연을 하니까, 같이 그 밴드를 보러 가는 게 어때요? 원하시면 제가 퇴근 후 당신을 위해서 티켓을 구매할 수 있어요. 어떻게 할 것인지 알려 주세요.

페이엣빌 봄 축제

5월 2일, 토요일 – 5월 3일, 일요일
그림과 스케치
지역 음식과 공연자

◇◇◇◇◇◇◇◇◇◇◇◇◇◇◇◇◇◇◇◇◇

(99)**토요일 공연**	**일요일 공연**
– (99)**마샬 피터스 밴드**	– 데이브 샌더스 코미디 루틴
– 페이엣빌 오케스트라	– 레드우드 밴드

98. 행사가 연기된 이유는?

(A) 일부 비용이 지불되지 않았다.

(B) 악천후가 예상되고 있다.

(C) 일부 공연자들이 시간이 되지 않는다.

(D) 수리 작업이 되어야 한다. 정답 (B)

99. 그래픽을 보시오. 화자는 어떤 공연에 갈 것 같은가?

(A) 레드우드 밴드

(B) 페이엣빌 오케스트라

(C) 데이브 샌더스 코미디 루틴

(D) 마샬 피터스 밴드 정답 (D)

100. 화자는 무엇을 하겠다고 제의하는가?

(A) 축제에서 자원봉사

(B) 행사 준비

(C) 티켓 구매

(D) 공연장까지 운전 정답 (C)

Part 5

101. 그의 낙천적이고 쾌활한 성격 덕분에, 그는 나중에 뉴욕에서 라디오 진행자가 되었다. 정답 (C)

102. 지난주에 유로화와 스위스 프랑 모두 미 달러화에 대한 환율이 3.1퍼센트 하락했다. 정답 (A)

103. 미스터 권의 마케팅 프레젠테이션이 훌륭했기에 우리 회사는 그를 마케팅 책임자로 채용하기로 결정했다. 정답 (A)

104. 폭염으로 인해, BK 건설은 새로운 교량 공사 프로젝트의 연장을 요청했다. 정답 (B)

105. 만두 전자의 주가가 새로운 메모리칩을 출시한 직후 대략 25퍼센트 상승했다. 정답 (D)

106. 여러 검색 기술의 발전으로, 온라인으로 1950–60년대의 오래된 재즈 앨범을 찾아 구매하는 것이 어렵지 않다. 정답 (B)

107. 젠킨스 씨가 채용한 조경업자는 그의 정원에 추가적인 프라이버시를 조성할 뿐만 아니라 그의 소유지에 대한 자연적인 경계를 표시하기 위해 상록수 덤불을 사용했다. 정답 (C)

108. 일단 베트남에 새로운 제조 공장이 건설되면, 우리의 생산성이 약 30퍼센트 증가할 것으로 예상된다. 정답 (A)

109. 새로운 자동차 모델들의 외장과 내장 모두 국내외 고객들의 마음을 끌기 위해 완전히 재설계되었다. 정답 (C)

110. 사람들은 대개 다양한 사회 현상에 대한 정확한 정보를 획득하고자 신문과 잡지를 읽는다. 정답 (A)

111. 취업 지원자들은 면접에서 제공되는 잘못된 정보는 자동적으로 불합격되는 결과에 이를 수 있다는 점을 상기해야 한다. 정답 (B)

112. 새롭게 개발된 배터리 충전기는 국내 시장에 출시된 거의 모든 유형의 노트북 컴퓨터들과 호환이 가능하다. 정답 (C)

113. 파커 씨는 새로운 재고 시스템에 대한 아이디어가 에반스 씨의 것이 아니라 자신의 것이라고 주장하고 있다. 정답 (D)

114. 운전자들은 위험물을 운송하는 차량을 운전할 경우 운전 시간과 비번 시간에 관한 규칙을 준수해야 한다. 정답 (B)

115. 최근 연구에 기초하여, 일부 과학자들은 북극의 만년설이 1990년대에 비해 7배나 더 빨리 없어지고 있다는 결론을 내렸다. 정답 (A)

116. 기술 세미나 참석에 관심이 있는 사람은 다음 주 수요일까지 맥거완 씨에게 연락해야 한다. 정답 (D)

117. 최근 설문조사에서 청소년 10명 중 3명이 과도하게 휴대 전화에 의존하는 것으로 나타났다. 정답 (B)

118. 시장 분석 보고서에는 홉킨스 씨가 내일 열릴 예정인 이사회 전에 수정할 몇몇 오류가 포함되어 있다.   정답 (D)

119. 제임스 와트는 그의 최신 앨범이 국내에서 가장 많이 판매된 앨범이었는데, 많은 권위 있는 음악상을 수상했다.   정답 (D)

120. 글로벌 텔레콤이 고객 서비스를 향상시킬 수 있도록 저희와 관련된 귀하의 최근 경험을 적어 주세요.   정답 (D)

121. 초청 연사는 청중의 긍정적인 연대와 참여를 촉진시키기 위해 청중 앞에 서야 한다.   정답 (D)

122. 인사과는 회사가 신입 사원들에게 제공하는 많은 활동들을 꼼꼼하게 계획할 것이다.   정답 (B)

123. 모든 사람들은 향후 회계 감사를 받을 경우를 대비하여 모든 세금 신고서와 영수증 사본을 보관하도록 권장된다.   정답 (A)

124. 트럭과 승용차를 덜 판매했음에도 불구하고, 오토트레이드 서비스 회사는 작년에 기록적인 이익을 거두었다고 보고했다.   정답 (B)

125. 에이스 컴퓨터 회사의 제조 공장은 조립 라인의 직원들이 새로운 기계를 가동하기 시작한 이후 생산성이 급격하게 증가했다는 사실을 알아챘다.   정답 (A)

126. 회사의 거래 파일 일부가 새로운 데이터 저장 시스템으로 옮겨지는 과정에서 손상되었다.   정답 (C)

127. 새로운 사무용 컴퓨터 강좌는 30명의 직원이 수강하며, 이들 모두는 워드 프로세싱 및 데이터베이스 관리의 고급 지식을 포함한 컴퓨터 기술을 배울 것이다.   정답 (B)

128. 비록 제조업 일자리가 최근 수십 년 동안 감소했지만, 생산성 향상으로 제조업 생산량은 계속 증가하고 있다.   정답 (C)

129. 많은 유명 레스토랑과 호텔들은 예약과 신용 카드 결제를 용이하게 하고자 자체 공식 웹 페이지를 개설하고 있다.   정답 (D)

130. 포장되어 배송된 제품은 정품 케이스가 제거되지 않은 경우에 환불될 것이다.   정답 (D)

Part 6

문제 131-134번은 다음 안내문을 참조하시오.

> **강좌 안내**
>
> 선힐 지역 문화 센터는 패트리샤 헤르난데스 씨가 다음 주 수요일 4월 10일부터 지역 문화 센터에서 기초 스페인어를 가르친다는 것을 발표하게 되어 기쁩니다. 수업은 매주 월요일 오전 10시부터 11시 30분까지 401호에서 모입니다.
>
> 저희 웹사이트 www.scc.org을 통해 등록하시거나 혹은 저희 안내 데스크 중 한 곳을 직접 방문하셔도 됩니다. 4주간의 수강료는 80달러입니다. 이번 주 수요일까지 등록하면 수강료에서 20%를 자동적으로 할인 받게 됩니다.
>
> 선힐 지역 문화 센터에서 다음 달부터 다양한 종합 외국어 과정을 제공합니다. 60세 이상의 모든 선힐 주민들은 저희 강좌를 무료로 수강하실 수 있습니다. 자세한 내용은 저희 웹사이트에서 보실 수 있습니다.

131.   정답 (C)

132.   정답 (C)

133.   정답 (C)

134. (A) 교원 자격증 요건을 충족시키려면 학사 학위가 필요합니다.
(B) 저희의 번역 업무에는 여타 이전 경력이 불필요할 수도 있습니다.
(C) 60세 이상의 모든 선힐 주민들은 저희 강좌를 무료로 수강하실 수 있습니다.
(D) 지역 문화 센터는 종합적인 보수공사를 위해 임시로 폐쇄합니다.   정답 (C)

문제 135-138번은 다음 기사를 참조하시오.

> 홈 〉 지역 뉴스 〉
>
> **힐 밸리 시가 도로를 확장하다**
>
> 알프레드 브랜틀리 작성, 12월 12일 오전 10시 15분
>
> 힐 밸리 시 의회는 힐 밸리 컨벤션 센터에 인접한 롬바르드 가의 도로 확장 공사를 곧 시작할 예정이다. 이 공사 프로젝트는 4차선인 롬바르드 가를 8차선 도로가 될 수 있도록 확장하는 것이다. 이 공사는 3월 1일 즈음에 시작하여 완공까지 대략 3개월이 소요될 것으로 예상된다.
>
> 공사가 안전하게 진행될 수 있도록, 롬바르드 가는 힐 밸리 컨벤션 센터와 힐 밸리 미술관 사이의 차량 통행이 금지될 것이다. 롬바르드 가로 이어지는 힐 밸리 컨벤션 센터 옆의 인도교 또한 보행자들에게는 폐쇄될 것이다.
>
> 힐 밸리 컨벤션 센터로 접근할 수 있는 롬바르드 가를 따라 있는 보도는 공사의 영향을 받지 않을 것이다. 그러나 이 기간 동안 평소 롬바르드 가를 이용하는 대중 버스들은 발렌시아 가로 우회할 것이다.

135.   정답 (D)

136. (A) 우리는 도로의 교통 정체와 공기 오염에 대해 우려하고 있다.
(B) 이는 지역 근로자를 위한 많은 새로운 일자리를 창출하고 우리의 경제 성장을 촉진할 것이다.
(C) 직장의 안전은 직원들이 다칠 가능성이 전혀 혹은 거의 없는 환경에서 올바른 방식으로 그들의 업무를 하도록 보장하는 것이다.
(D) 이 공사는 3월 1일 즈음에 시착하여 완공까지 대략 3개월이 소요될 것으로 예상된다.   정답 (D)

137.   정답 (D)

138.   정답 (B)

문제 139-142번은 다음 편지를 참조하시오.

> 마이클 웨스턴 씨에게;
>
> 6월 1일자 귀하의 편지를 받았습니다. 귀하에게 불편을 끼쳐 드려 유감으로 생각합니다.
>
> 하지만, 저희 배송 회사에 따르면, 총 100상자가 양호한 냉동 상태로 배송되었으며, 운송선에 있는 그 누구도 제품이 샌디에이고에 도착하기 전에 해동되는 것을 보지 못했습니다. 따라서 해동 과정은 제품들이 항구에 있는 창고로 이동되고 난 후 시작한 것으로 저희는 추정하고 있습니다.
>
> 돼지고기가 계속 냉동된 상태를 유지하려면, 냉동실은 섭씨 영하 15도의 온도로 유지되어야 합니다. 저희는 귀사 창고의 부족한 냉동 시설로 인해 상

자들이 해동되기 시작한 것으로 생각합니다.

비록 저희가 귀사에 전액 환불을 해드리고자 하는 것은 아니지만, 저희는 기꺼이 귀사와의 다음 거래에 대해 30% 할인을 해드리고자 합니다. <u>저희는 이러한 조치를 통해 귀사에서 겪은 금전적 손실의 일부를 만회하실 수 있길 바랍니다.</u>

향후에 다시 귀하에게 서비스를 제공할 수 있길 기대합니다.

니나 리 드림
품질 관리 부장
앤드류 팜 주식회사

139. 정답 (C)

140. 정답 (B)

141. 정답 (D)

142. (A) 저희는 분실, 도난 또는 손상된 수하물 또는 개인 물품에 대해 책임을 지지 않습니다.

(B) 냉동 식품은 박테리아를 제거하고 식품을 수년 동안 저장할 수 있습니다.

(C) 빠른 배송과 적절한 포장으로 부패하기 쉬운 품목을 고객에게 보낼 수 있습니다.

(D) 저희는 이러한 조치를 통해 귀사에서 겪은 금전적 손실의 일부를 만회하실 수 있길 바랍니다. 정답 (D)

문제 143-146번은 다음 공지를 참조하시오.

월넛 크릭 호텔

트레몬트 가 1411번지,
보스턴, 매사추세츠 주 02120
전화번호: (857) 770-7000~3
팩스번호: (857) 770-7004~5
www.walnutcreekhotel.com

<u>고객님을 손님으로 모시게 되어 정말 기쁘며 저희 호텔에서의 숙박을 선택해 주신 데 대해 감사드립니다.</u> 월넛 크릭 호텔은 내부 인테리어가 완전하게 구비되어 있으며 항상 귀하를 모시기 위해 많은 사랑으로 준비하고 있습니다; 그러므로 손님께서는 마치 자신의 집인 것처럼 저희 호텔을 잘 이용해주시길 당부드립니다.

이 호텔의 모든 객실은 최근 호텔의 손님 한 분 한 분이 숙박에 최고로 만족하실 수 있도록 최신 기술과 섬세한 직물 및 고급 대리석을 결합하여 세련되게 재단장하고 새로 가구를 갖추었습니다.

교통편 정보, 그리고 손님의 편의를 위한 다양한 서비스에 관한 필요한 정보는 1층에 위치한 프런트에서 얻으실 수 있습니다. 만약 더 필요한 정보가 있으시면, 언제든 내선 번호 101번으로 저희에게 전화 주십시오.

저희는 월넛 크릭 호텔에서의 숙박이 손님의 보스턴 여행에 대한 좋은 기억의 일부가 되길 바랍니다. 다시 한 번 저희 월넛 크릭 호텔을 선택해 주셔서 감사드리며, 이 곳에서 즐거운 시간을 보내시기 바랍니다.

---

143. (A) 올 한 해 동안 모든 직원을 대표하여, 귀하의 친절한 선물과 성원에 대해 정말 감사드립니다.

(B) 호텔 객실 예약 시, 투숙객에게 선입금이 요청될 수도 있습니다.

(C) 일 년 중 언제라도, 귀하는 바로 문 앞에서 이 마을의 아름다운 배경과 풍경을 감상하실 수 있습니다.

(D) 고객님을 손님으로 모시게 되어 정말 기쁘며 저희 호텔에서의 숙박을 선택해 주신 데 대해 감사드립니다. 정답 (D)

---

144. 정답 (B)

145. 정답 (B)

146. 정답 (A)

Part 7

문제 147-148번은 다음 광고를 참조하시오.

세린 스파에서 휴식을 취하세요

캘리포니아 남부에서 최고 스파인 세린 스파가 전통적인 스파를 능가하는 서비스를 제공합니다. 7월 1일에 샌디에이고에 추가 스파 지점을 열 것입니다.

(147)**별표*가 있는 서비스들은 7월 10일부터 이용 가능하다는 것을 알아 두십시오.**

스웨덴식 마사지*	교정 마사지*	(147D)레이저 스킨케어*
(147A)얼굴 마사지	제모	(147B)스톤 테라피
손발톱 관리	(147C)각질 제거	아로마테라피

(148)**이 페이지를 출력해서 아래의 쿠폰을 가져오세요.**

모든 스파 서비스 15% 할인	**오늘 예약하세요!** – 혜택은 7월 31일까지 유효합니다. – 한 번의 방문당 하나의 쿠폰만 사용할 수 있습니다.

147. 7월 9일에 이용 가능하지 않은 서비스는?

(A) 얼굴 마사지

(B) 스톤 테라피

(C) 각질 제거

(D) 레이저 스킨케어 정답 (D)

148. 광고의 쿠폰에 대해 나타나 있는 것은 무엇인가?

(A) 8월에 이용할 수 있다.

(B) 샌디에이고 지점에서만 할인을 제공한다.

(C) 할인을 받기 위해서는 출력되어야 한다.

(D) 다른 혜택들과 함께 사용될 수 있다. 정답 (C)

문제 149-150번은 다음 문자 메시지를 참조하시오.

데이비드 카터 [오후 2시 22분]
안녕하세요. 샌더슨 자동차에 연락 주셔서 감사합니다. 무엇을 도와드릴까요?

애나베스 머피 [오후 2시 23분]
안녕하세요. (149)**작년에 귀사의 SUV를 한 대 새로 구입했는데, 샌더슨이 방금 발표한 리콜에 영향을 받고 있는지 궁금합니다.**

데이비드 카터 [오후 2시 24분]
네, 최근 3년간 생산된 모든 SUV가 포함됩니다. 그러니까 가장 가까운 샌더슨 자동차 대리점에 차를 가지고 가서 안전벨트를 수리 받으세요.

애나베스 머피 [오후 2시 26분]
제가 막 새 도시로 이사 와서, 거기가 어딘지 모르겠어요.

데이비드 카터 [오후 2시 27분]

(150)여기 www.sandersonautos.com/recall로 가보세요. "가장 가까운 대리점 찾기"를 클릭하면 따라야 할 지침이 나타납니다.

애나베스 머피   [오후 2시 28분]
(150)그것은 할 수 있어요. 도와주셔서 감사합니다.

데이비드 카터   [오후 2시 29분]
천만에요. 좋은 하루 되세요.

149. 머피 씨가 카터 씨에게 연락한 이유는?
(A) SUV를 사는 방법을 알아보기 위해
(B) 엔진 문제에 관해 문의하기 위해
(C) 회사 리콜에 대해 문의하기 위해
(D) 구입에 대한 환불을 요청하기 위해   정답 (C)

150. 오후 2시 28분에, 머피 씨가 "제가 그것은 처리할 수 있어요"라고 쓸 때 무엇을 의미하는 것 같은가?
(A) 그녀는 단지 카터 씨의 지시를 따랐다.
(B) 그녀는 문제를 혼자 해결할 것이다.
(C) 그녀는 자신이 구매한 장소로 돌아갈 수 있다.
(D) 그녀는 자신이 무엇을 해야 하는지 이해한다.   정답 (D)

문제 151-153번은 다음 편지를 참조하시오.

10월 14일

앨리스 와츠
(151C)패터슨 카펫
롱맨 가 557번지
포츠머스, 오하이오 주 45662

와츠 씨에게,

(151D)지난주 켄터키 주 렉싱턴에서 열린 가구 박람회에서 뵙게 되어 반가웠습니다. (151B)저와 귀사에서 생산하는 카펫에 대해 얘기하면서 많은 시간을 보내셨죠. 귀사 제품이 경쟁사 제품과 어떻게 다른지 알게 되어 좋았습니다. (152)제게 주신 견본을 여기 직원 여러 명과 공유했는데, 모두들 품질에 깊은 인상을 받았습니다. 제 동료들은 특히 구입 가능한 색상들을 마음에 들어했습니다.

(151C)저희는 저희 인테리어 디자인 회사를 위한 새로운 공급업체를 찾고 있습니다. 저희는 귀사에서 저희 회사의 모든 필요를 분명히 충족시킬 수 있을 것이라고 생각합니다. (153)대량 주문에 대해 논의하기 위해 조만간 직접 만날 수 있는지 궁금합니다. 언제 만날 시간이 있으신가요?

레지널드 웰먼 드림
포츠머스 인테리어 디자인

151. 웰먼 씨에 대해 언급되지 않은 것은 무엇인가?
(A) 그는 회사의 소유주이다.
(B) 그는 와츠 씨와 직접 이야기를 나누었다.
(C) 그는 카펫을 판매하는 곳에서 일한다.
(D) 그는 일주일 전에 켄터키 주로 여행 갔다.   정답 (A)

152. 웰먼 씨가 포츠머스 인테리어 디자인에 대해 나타내는 것은 무엇인가?
(A) 최근에 문을 열었다.
(B) 여러 명의 근로자가 있다.
(C) 무료 설치를 제공한다.
(D) 그것은 곧 세일을 할 예정이다.   정답 (B)

153. [1], [2], [3] 그리고 [4]로 표시된 곳 중에, 아래 문장이 들어가기에 가장 적절한 곳은?
"저는 또한 가능한 대량 할인에 대해 얘기해 보고 싶습니다."

(A) [1]
(B) [2]
(C) [3]
(D) [4]   정답 (D)

문제 154-156번은 다음 안내문을 참조하시오.

알라 모아나의 모든 고객 분들께 알려 드립니다

알라 모아나를 방문해 주신 모든 고객분들께 감사드립니다. (155) (156A)저희는 웹사이트를 통해 가장 좋은 하와이 스타일의 셔츠, 모자, 액세서리와 다양한 패션 물품들을 여러분께 제공하기 위하여 노력합니다.

(154)오늘, 저희는 배송 정책 변경을 알려 드리고자 합니다. (156B)알라 모아나는 이전에는 모든 주문에 대해 무료 배송을 제공해 왔지만, 연료비 인상으로 인해 더 이상 이 서비스를 제공할 수 없게 되었습니다. 그러므로 저희는 50달러 이하의 주문에 대해 배송비를 부과해야 합니다. (156C)이는 지역에서 가장 낮은 상품 가격을 유지하기 위한 불가피한 결정이었습니다.

양해 부탁드리며, 알라 모아나는 가장 경쟁력 있는 하와이 패션 제공업체로 남을 것을 약속드리겠습니다.

154. 안내문의 목적은 무엇인가?
(A) 온라인 사업체를 광고하기 위한 것
(B) 새로운 상품의 가격 목록을 게시하기 위한 것
(C) 최근 주문을 확인하기 위한 것
(D) 서비스 변경을 알리기 위한 것   정답 (D)

155. 알라 모아나는 어떤 유형의 사업체일 것 같은가?
(A) 리조트
(B) 옷 가게
(C) 관광 전문 여행업자
(D) 배송 회사   정답 (B)

156. 알라 모아나에 관해 나타나 있지 않은 것은 무엇인가?
(A) 그곳의 물품들은 온라인으로 구매할 수 있다.
(B) 최근까지 무료 배송을 했다.
(C) 그곳의 상품들은 경쟁 회사에 비해 가격이 저렴하다.
(D) 곧 처음으로 할인 행사를 열 것이다.   정답 (D)

문제 157-158번은 다음 공고를 참조하시오.

어빙 주민들을 위한 공고

(157)프리츠 공원 근처에서 열리는 제 4회 텍사스 봄 퍼레이드 때문에 어빙 시에 있는 한 지역이 5월 4일 오후 3시부터 오후 8시까지 일시적으로 폐쇄될 것입니다.

(158)도로 폐쇄가 영향을 미치는 곳:
– 햄프턴 대로와 키즈 도로 사이의 세인트 루이스 가 부분

우회 도로는 다음과 같습니다:
– 마르코니 가
– 벨 대로

추가적인 정보를 원하시면 어빙 시의 교통 안전부에 214-885-0830으로 연락하십시오.

157. 공고의 주요 목적은 무엇인가?
(A) 한 스포츠 대회의 개막을 알리기 위한 것
(B) 다가오는 교통 통제에 대해 알리기 위한 것
(C) 계획된 도로 공사를 알리기 위한 것

(D) 주민들에게 도로에 있을 수 있는 위험에 대해 알리기 위한 것   정답 (B)

158. 행사 동안 도시의 어떤 곳이 폐쇄될 것인가?
(A) 프리츠 공원
(B) 세인트 루이스 가
(C) 햄프턴 대로
(D) 마르코니 가   정답 (B)

문제 159-161번은 다음 기사를 참조하시오.

잘랄리오스 타코스, 커니 시의 중심지에서 개업하다

크리스티아노 룩셈버그 작성

커니, 8월 11일 – (159)커니의 주민들은 이제 커니의 중심지에서 맛있는 멕시코 요리를 즐길 수 있게 될 것이다. 8월 9일, 잘랄리오스 타코스의 개업날에 지역 주민들이 식당 안으로 물밀듯이 들어왔다.

(160)가게 주인, 아브라힘과 브레나 잘랄리오는 고향인 멕시코 시티에서 3개 식당을 성공적으로 운영한 자격 있는 요리사들이다. 작년 미국으로 옮겨온 후, 그들은 커니에 식당을 열 계획을 하고 있었다. 한때 신발 가게였던 빈 부동산이 5월 22일에 시장에 나왔을 때, 그것을 매수해 식당으로 개조하는 것을 망설이지 않았다.

잘랄리오스 타코스는 잘랄리오 부부의 현대적 창의력이 약간 가미된 직접 만든 전통 멕시코 음식들을 합리적인 가격에 제공한다. 가장 신선한 재료들만 사용하므로, 잘랄리오스 타코스는 맛있을 뿐만 아니라 건강에 좋은 음식을 제공한다.

커니의 상업 지구에서 가장 북적이는 거리에 위치한 잘랄리오스 타코스는 이제 많은 직장인들에게 가장 좋아하는 레스토랑이 될 것이다. "저는 늘 멕시코 음식의 팬이었습니다. (161)개업날 정문에서 무료 시식을 해본 뒤, 저는 이 레스토랑에서 식사할 수밖에 없었습니다. 그리고 음식의 질에 정말 만족했습니다"라고 한 고객인 후안 수아레즈가 말했다. 식당 개업 전날에, 잘랄리오 씨의 레스토랑의 전망에 대해 그를 인터뷰했다. "저는 여기 카스탄틴 가에 새 레스토랑을 열게 되어 무척 기쁩니다. 저는 직장인뿐만 아니라 대학생들도 끌어들일 계획입니다. 저희 식당에 한 번도 오지 않은 사람들은 있을 수 있어도, 한 번만 온 사람은 없습니다"라고 그는 말했다.

더 자세한 정보, 메뉴의 가격과 예약에 대해서는 201-331-9243으로 전화하면 된다.

159. 기사의 목적은 무엇인가?
(A) 빈 부동산을 광고하기 위한 것
(B) 전통 음식에 대한 정보를 제공하기 위한 것
(C) 지역에 새로운 업체를 소개하기 위한 것
(D) 곧 있을 공사에 대해 주민들에게 알려 주기 위한 것   정답 (C)

160. 잘랄리오 씨 부부에 대해 나타나 있는 것은 무엇인가?
(A) 커니에 친척이 있다.
(B) 이전에 신발 가게를 소유했다.
(C) 멕시코에서 수입된 재료를 사용한다.
(D) 다른 식당들을 운영한 적이 있다.   정답 (D)

161. 수아레즈 씨에 따르면, 잘랄리오스 타코스에 대해 사실인 것은?
(A) 대학교 근처에 편리하게 위치해 있다.
(B) 방문객들에게 맛볼 음식을 주었다.
(C) 고객 서비스의 질이 만족스럽다.
(D) 오랫동안 수아레즈 씨가 가장 좋아하는 장소였다.   정답 (B)

문제 162-164번은 다음 비평을 참조하시오.

블루 소울즈에 의한 황홀한 가을 밤

(162)지난밤, 블루 소울즈가 오클라호마 시 광장에 모인 500명의 사람들에게 열렬한 공연을 선보였다. 다양한 국적의 4명의 뮤지션으로 이루어진 블루 소울즈는 미국에서 가장 인기 있는 재즈 밴드 중 하나이며 기사에 여러 번 (163)보도되었다.

블루 소울즈는 세계적으로 유명한 피아니스트인 데이비드 야칼에 의하여 4년 전 결성되었다. (164)결성 2년 후, 야칼 씨의 한 오랜 친구가 블루 소울즈에 합류했다. 런던 시립 오케스트라에서 트럼펫을 연주했던 테일러 클레이턴은 그룹의 새로운 멤버로서 연주의 질을 높였다. 그가 합류하고 나서 머지 않아, 블루 소울즈는 뛰어난 금관 소리와 공연으로 오클라호마 시로부터 올해의 베스트 뮤지션 상을 받으며 인정받았다.

어젯밤 오클라호마 시 광장 야외 무대에서의 라이브 공연은 청중들에게 블루 소울즈가 연주하는 음악의 독특한 색깔을 보여 주었다. 그들의 가장 인기 있는 곡인 〈혼자서〉와 함께, 그들은 다음 달에 발매될 3집 앨범에 있는 곡들도 연주했다. 그들의 새 앨범은 스윙, 보사노바, 그리고 현대 재즈를 포함하는 다양한 스타일의 음악들을 수록하고 있다.

블루 소울즈의 공연은 평소처럼 완벽했지만, 작은 단점이 있었다. 콘서트 장소가 조금 추웠는데, 공연 기획자가 좌석 근처에 휴대용 히터를 비치해 놓았더라면 더 좋았을 것이다.

로렌 세굴라 작성

162. 어떠한 종류의 행사가 리뷰되고 있는가?
(A) 오케스트라 콘서트
(B) 재즈 콘서트
(C) 마술 연기
(D) 댄스 공연   정답 (B)

163. 첫 번째 단락 4행에 있는 단어 "covered"와 의미상 가장 가까운 것은?
(A) 인터뷰된
(B) (특집으로) 다루어진
(C) 지불된
(D) 막아진   정답 (B)

164. 클레이턴 씨에 대해 진술된 것은 무엇인가?
(A) 그는 피아노를 연주한다.
(B) 그는 2년 전 블루 소울즈에 합류했다.
(C) 그는 런던 시립 오케스트라로부터 상을 받았다.
(D) 그는 최근에 블루 소울즈의 리더가 되었다.   정답 (B)

문제 165-167번은 다음 편지를 참조하시오.

미키 앤더슨
31 마운틴 로드
콘월-온-허드슨, 뉴욕 주 12520

4월 19일

첼시 미용실
98 코스믹 드라이브
콘월, 뉴욕 주 12592

관계자 분께,

(165)저는 광고된 뉴 햄프셔에 있는 첼시 미용실 지점의 상근 헤어스타일리스트 자리에 지원하고자 글을 씁니다. 상세한 이력서를 이 편지와 함께 동봉하긴 했지만, 간략하게 저의 경력 배경을 요약해 드리고 싶습니다.

클라크 대학에서 헤어스타일리스트 자격증을 받은 후에, 저는 브루클린에 있는 버크셔 미용실에서 일하기 시작했습니다. 그곳에서 6년간 근무하는 동안, 저는 전국 최고 헤어 파마 스타일링 상을 포함해 전문가로서 인정을 받았습니다. (166)이력서와 함께 상을 받은 헤어스타일의 사진 몇 장도 넣었습니다.

전문 기술 외에도, 저는 (167)첼시 미용실의 전국적인 명성에 기여할 준비가 되어 있는 열정적이고, 예술적이며, 충실한 사람입니다. 저의 헤어스타일링이 첼시 미용실의 유행 추구 성향과 잘 맞을 것임을 확신합니다.

감사드리며 개인 면접의 기회를 가질 수 있기를 고대하겠습니다.

미키 앤더슨 드림

동봉물

165. 앤더슨 씨가 편지를 작성한 이유는?
(A) 면접 참가를 확인하기 위해
(B) 헤어스타일링 대회에 지원하기 위해
(C) 잠재 고용주에게 자신을 소개하기 위해
(D) 헤어 살롱에서의 일자리를 제의하기 위해   정답 (C)

166. 편지에 포함된 것은 무엇인가?
(A) 헤어스타일리스트 자격증
(B) 상
(C) 샘플 사진
(D) 다른 사람으로부터의 추천서   정답 (C)

167. 편지에 따르면, 첼시 미용실에 대해 나타나 있는 것은 무엇인가?
(A) 전국적으로 잘 알려져 있다.
(B) 적어도 6년 동안 영업해 왔다.
(C) 직원 중에 상을 받은 헤어 디자이너들이 많다.
(D) 브루클린에 위치한 지점이 있다.   정답 (A)

문제 168-171번은 다음 온라인 채팅 토론을 참조하시오.

러셀 톰슨 [오전 9시 55분]
안녕하세요. 스티브와 마크. 머레이 씨 집의 작업은 어떻게 되고 있어요?

스티브 길모어 [오전 9시 57분]
거의 다 끝났습니다. (168)우리가 울타리를 손질한 후에 머레이 씨가 나무를 잘라 달라고 요청해서 작업이 예상보다 조금 더 걸렸어요. 걱정하지 마세요. 제가 그것을 그의 계산서에 넣었어요.

러셀 톰슨 [오전 9시 58분]
좋아요. 방금 새로운 사람으로부터 온라인 문의를 받았어요. 안나 그래니트가 자신의 집에 대한 견적을 요청했어요. 그분은 버틀러 드라이브 88번지에 살아요. (169) (171)스탠턴 플레이스에 가기 전에 거기에 갈 수 있을 것 같아요?

마크 스튜어트 [오전 10시]
(171)몇 블록만 가면 돼요.

스티브 길모어 [오전 10시 1분]
(169)우리의 다음 약속은 오후 1시에나 있으니까, 여기를 끝내고 들를게요. 그분은 무엇을 원하는 거예요?

러셀 톰슨 [오전 10시 2분]
고마워요, 여러분.

러셀 톰슨 [오전 10시 2분]
아, 기본 서비스를 원하시는데, 자기 집 마당이 다른 사람들 집보다 더 넓다고 했어요. 그래서 당신이 이걸 확인해 주었으면 하는 거예요.

마크 스튜어트 [오전 10시 4분]

제가 그 곳을 알아요. 마당이 3에이커 정도 돼요.

(170)러셀 톰슨 [오전 10시 5분]
정말 큰 작업이 될 것 같아요. (170)얼마나 되는 작업이 필요할 것 같은지 그분에게 견적을 주세요.

스티브 길모어 [오전 10시 6분]
(170)알겠습니다. 그 문제에 대한 협의가 끝나면 전화드리겠습니다.

168. 작성자들은 어디에서 일할 것 같은가?
(A) 수영장 설치 회사
(B) 부동산 중개소
(C) 건설 회사
(D) 조경 회사   정답 (D)

169. 길모어 씨는 오후에 무엇을 할 예정인가?
(A) 견적 제공
(B) 사무실로 돌아가기
(C) 고객 방문
(D) 전화 회의 참여   정답 (C)

170. 길모어 씨는 그래니트 씨를 만난 후에 무엇을 할 것인가?
(A) 톰슨 씨에게 연락
(B) 계산서 제출
(C) 소모품 구매
(D) 이메일 발송   정답 (A)

171. 오전 10시에 스튜어트 씨가 "몇 블록만 가면 돼요"라고 쓸 때 시사하는 것은 무엇인가?
(A) 그는 톰슨 씨의 요청에 응할 수 있다.
(B) 그는 개인적인 방문을 할 시간이 없다.
(C) 그는 정확한 위치를 모른다.
(D) 그는 전에 어떤 집을 직접 방문한 적이 있다.   정답 (A)

문제 172-175번은 다음 이메일을 참조하시오.

수신: 피자 스탑 전 직원
발신: 제이슨 보난자
날짜: 4월 5일
제목: 소식

여러분,

(174)우리 피자 가게를 시내 최고의 피자 가게로 만들기 위해 여러분이 해주신 많은 노고에 감사드립니다. (172)공교롭게도, 우리의 성공으로 인해 여러 모방업체들이 생겨났고, 그들은 각각 우리로부터 사업을 앗아가려 하고 있습니다. 그 결과, 저는 더 많은 고객을 유치하기 위해 몇 가지 새로운 전략을 실행하기로 결정했습니다. 그에 대해 제가 설명해 드리겠습니다.

우선 4월 6일 내일부터 매장 내 고객에게 무료 와이파이를 제공할 예정입니다. 암호는 매일 바뀌기 때문에, 종업원들은 식탁에 있는 손님들에게 알려 드려야 합니다. 우리는 또한 테이블 가까이에 전기 콘센트의 수도 늘릴 것입니다. 그러면 식사하는 사람들이 그들의 전기 기기를 충전할 수 있게 될 것입니다. (173)4월 8일에 전기 기사가 이곳을 그렇게 바꾸도록 하기 위해 문을 닫을 것입니다.

다음으로, 우리가 실시한 최근 설문조사에서 손님들이 피자 토핑에 대한 옵션이 더 많아지기를 원하는 것으로 나타났습니다. 그래서 4월 9일에 메뉴를 바꿀 예정입니다. 총 25가지 가능한 피자 토핑이 있게 될 것인데, 이는 이 도시에서 가장 많은 토핑이 될 것입니다.

(175)마지막으로, 피자 스탑 회원 카드를 고객에게 소개할 것입니다. 더 자세한 내용은 제가 이 이메일에 첨부한 문서를 보십시오.

제이슨 보낸자 드림
주인, 피자 가게

172. 피자 스탑이 정책을 바꾸려고 하는 이유는?
(A) 고객 요청에 부응하기 위해
(B) 지출을 줄이기 위해
(C) 경쟁력을 더 높이기 위해
(D) 광고를 개선하기 위해   정답 (C)

173. 4월 8일에 무슨 일이 있겠는가?
(A) 가게가 문을 열지 않을 것이다.
(B) 메뉴가 변경될 것이다.
(C) 인터넷이 설치될 것이다.
(D) 세일이 시작될 것이다.   정답 (A)

174. 피자 스탑에 대해 나타나 있는 것은 무엇인가?
(A) 그곳은 현재 회원 프로그램을 운영하고 있다.
(B) 그곳은 자주 식사하는 사람들에게 할인을 제공한다.
(C) 그곳은 곧 더 많은 테이블을 추가할 것이다.
(D) 그곳은 도시 내 대표적인 피자 가게 중 하나이다.   정답 (D)

175. [1], [2], [3] 그리고 [4]로 표시된 곳 중에, 아래 문장이 들어가기에 가장 적
절한 곳은?
"소지자들은 할인과 다양한 무료 물품을 받을 수 있습니다."
(A) [1]
(B) [2]
(C) [3]
(D) [4]   정답 (D)

문제 176-180번은 다음 웹사이트와 이메일을 참조하시오.

www.hudsoncollege.edu/notice

허드슨 대학

소개	공지	학업	커뮤니티

허드슨 대학 아동 교육 강의 시리즈
아동 교육 및 발달학과가 자부심을 갖고 유아기에 대한 일련의 강의를 합니
다. 강의는 6월 14일부터 7월 5일까지 매주 금요일에 학과에서 열릴 것입니
다. (176D)허드슨 대학의 저명한 교수들과 국립 기관의 전문가들이 유아 발
달 분석과 적절한 교육 기술의 새로운 아이디어에 대한 깊이 있는 프레젠테
이션을 제공할 것입니다.

세미나 스케줄:

세미나 제목 및 발표자	날짜/시간	요금
유아기의 언어 발달 밀라 트런들, 허드슨 대학 교수	6월 14일 (176A)오후 2시-4시	60달러
유아 교실(수업)에서의 적절한 커리큘럼 다니엘 킨, 허드슨 대학 교수	(178)6월 21일 (176A)오후 3시-5시	70달러
유아 및 초등 교실(수업) 관리하기 (179)데이비드 덴튼, 국립 유아 교육 협회의 유아 교육 전문가	(179)6월 28일 (176A)오후 2시-4시	90달러
아동의 사회성 발달: 출생부터 유아기까지 릴리스 밀스, 콘월 병원의 아동 정신과 의사	7월 5일 (176A)오후 1시-3시	80달러

(176C)*최대 100명만 각 세미나 참가가 허용됨

(177)강의들 중 하나에 등록하고 싶으시다면, 여기를 클릭해 주세요. (176B)
모든 강의는 선착순이고 등록 마감일이 6월 1일이라는 점에 유의하세요. 문
의사항에 대해서는 cfelton@hudsoncollege.edu로 캐롤라이나 펠턴에
게 연락하세요.

(178) (180)아동 교육 및 발달 분야에 종사하는 참가자들은 세미나 참가 비
용에서 10달러의 할인을 받을 것입니다. 등록 과정에서 입증 자료가 제시되
어야 합니다.

수신: 캐롤라이나 펠턴 〈cfelton@hudsoncollege.edu〉
발신: (180)올리비아 강 〈okang@hudsonelementary.com〉
날짜: 6월 3일
제목: 문의

(178)허드슨 대학이 제공하는 이러한 주제들에 대한 강의가 굉장히 유익하
다고 자주 들어서, 저는 6월 21일에 개최될 강의에 등록했습니다. 하지만
이 이메일은 사실 제 예약을 변경할 수 있는지에 대해 문의하기 위한 것입니
다.

(178) (180)저는 지역 초등학교의 교사입니다. 안타깝게도, 동료 중 한 명이
가족 문제 때문에 갑작스럽게 3주 동안의 휴가를 가게 되었습니다. 저는 6
월 21일 금요일 오후에 그의 수업 중 하나를 대신해야 합니다. 하지만, 강의
중 하나를 듣는 것에 여전히 관심이 있으며, 대신 (179)데이비드 덴튼의 강
의를 들을 수 있는지 알고 싶습니다. 만약 변경이 가능하다면, 제가 언제 추
가 금액을 송금해야 하는지와 (178)여전히 할인을 받을 수 있는지에 대해
알고 싶습니다.

감사합니다. 곧 소식 듣기를 기다리겠습니다.

올리비아 강

176. 웹사이트에서 강의에 대해 나타나 있지 않은 것은 무엇인가?
(A) 오후에 예정되어 있다.
(B) 등록 마감일은 6월 1일이다.
(C) 제한된 수의 참가자들만 각각의 강의를 들을 수 있다.
(D) 모든 강의자들은 대학 교수이다.   정답 (D)

177. 참가자들은 어떻게 강의에 등록할 수 있는가?
(A) 이메일을 보냄으로써
(B) 웹사이트에 방문함으로써
(C) 학교 직원에게 전화함으로써
(D) 행사 장소에 감으로써   정답 (B)

178. 강 씨는 원래 얼마를 지불했는가?
(A) 60달러
(B) 70달러
(C) 80달러
(D) 90달러   정답 (A)

179. 강 씨가 세미나를 듣기를 원하는 날짜는?
(A) 6월 14일
(B) 6월 21일
(C) 6월 28일
(D) 7월 5일   정답 (C)

180. 강 씨에 대해 시사되어 있는 것은 무엇인가?
(A) 3주 동안 병가를 낼 것이다.
(B) 추가 요금을 이미 지불했다.
(C) 아마도 요구되는 서류를 허드슨 대학에 제출했을 것이다.
(D) 지난 분기에 비슷한 강의 시리즈에 참가했다.   정답 (C)

문제 181-185번은 다음 광고와 편지를 참조하시오.

제 7회 연례 ISEE 글로벌 심리학회
학생 자원봉사자 모집!

(181)ISEE 글로벌 심리학회는 전 세계의 심리학자들이 새로운 아이디어를 공유하는 명성 있는 학회입니다. 제 7회 연례 ISEE 글로벌 심리학회(IGFP) 조직 위원회는 현재 7월 5일부터 7월 10일까지 일리노이 주 시카고의 밀라노 호텔에서 열릴 예정인 회의의 다양한 지원 업무를 위한 학생 자원봉사자들을 모집하고 있습니다.

봉사 업무

• 행사 보조 – 주요 업무는 학회 진행 중과 (182D)후에 세팅하고 청소하는 것입니다. 또한, 행사 보조는 복사하는 것, (182A)참가자들에게 유인물을 나누어주는 것, 그리고 (182C)연사들을 위해 물을 준비하는 것을 돕습니다. 이 업무는 가벼운 가구를 옮기는 것도 포함할 수 있습니다.

• 시청각 기사 보조 – 회의장에서 시청각 장비들을 점검하는 일입니다. 필요 시 프로젝터와 마이크를 설치하는 것 또한 시청각 기사 보조의 업무들 중 하나가 될 것입니다.

(184)지원자 자격 요건

– 현재 학생 신분을 나타내는 학교의 공식 문서

– (184)다음 언어들 중 최소 하나에 대한 공식적인 어학 능력 증빙서: 스페인어, 중국어, 혹은 독일어

– 회의장에서의 자원봉사 경험

– 발표 장비 관련 지식 강력 우대

신청서 제출

이력서 1부, 자기소개서 1부와 공식 문서들을 (183)6월 1일까지 아래 표기된 **IGFP 조직 위원회 사무실로 보내셔야 합니다.**

클레어 스탠리, 인사 부장
IGFP 조직 위원회, 30 프랭클린 드라이브, 시카고, 일리노이 주 60007

이반 하필드
22 루즈벨트 가
브리지포트, 일리노이 주 60608

5월 10일

클레어 스탠리
IGFP 조직 위원회
30 프랭클린 드라이브
시카고, 일리노이 주 60007

스탠리 씨께,

저는 ISEE 글로벌 심리학회에서의 학생 자원봉사자 프로그램에 지원하고 싶습니다. 저는 일리노이 대학교 3학년생이며 심리학 분야에 매우 관심이 있습니다. (185)저는 그 동안 IWO 심리학과 일리노이 대학교 학회를 포함하여, 여러 심리학회에 참여한 바 있습니다.

또한, 저는 다양한 배경들을 가진 사람들과 교류했던 미국 학생 마케팅 협회 근무를 포함한 여러 다양한 활동들에 참여해 왔습니다. 저는 주어진 업무들을 끝내기 위해 매우 열심히 일합니다. (184)영어 외에 다른 언어를 구사하지는 못하지만, 저는 IGFP에 많이 기여할 수 있으리라 확신합니다.

요청하신 문서들이 동봉되어 있으니 확인해 주십시오. 면접에 대한 연락을 기다리겠습니다. 숙고해 주셔서 미리 감사드립니다.

이반 하필드 드림
동봉물

---

181. IGFP에 대해 시사되어 있는 것은 무엇인가?
(A) 성공적으로 7회 개최되었다.
(B) 밀라노 호텔로부터 후원을 받는다.
(C) 다양한 나라에서 참가자들이 올 것이다.
(D) 봉사자들에게 확인서를 제공한다. 정답 (C)

182. 행사 보조의 업무가 아닌 것은 무엇인가?
(A) 참가자들에게 서류 나눠주기
(B) 학회 장소에 불 켜기
(C) 발표자들을 위해 심부름하기
(D) 학회가 끝났을 때 청소하기 정답 (B)

183. 조직 위원회는 언제 지원서 받기를 중단할 것인가?
(A) 5월 10일
(B) 6월 1일
(C) 7월 5일
(D) 7월 10일 정답 (B)

184. 하필드 씨가 자원봉사 직책을 맡는 데 성공적이지 않을 수 있는 이유는?
(A) 요구되는 어느 언어도 하지 못한다.
(B) 그의 대학 서류를 제출하지 않았다.
(C) 심리학 분야에서의 경험이 부족하다.
(D) 심리학 학위를 가지고 있지 않다. 정답 (A)

185. 하필드 씨에 대해 나타나 있는 것은 무엇인가?
(A) 학회 기간 중 특정일에는 참석하지 못할 수도 있다.
(B) 일리노이 대학을 졸업했다.
(C) 발표 장비를 잘 다룰 줄 안다.
(D) 이전에 심리학회에 참석한 적이 있다. 정답 (D)

문제 186-190번은 다음 웹사이트와 영수증 그리고 이메일을 참조하시오.

---

http://www.officeshed.com/policies/shippinganddelivery

오피스 셰드는 준비되어 있습니다!

회사 소개	제품	정책	고객 평가

운송 및 배달

오피스 셰드는 (186)국내 표준 배송(5-7영업일)의 경우 4.50달러, 국내 특급 배송(2-3영업일)의 경우 6.50달러의 균일 요금을 부과합니다. 우리는 현재 미국, 영국, 뉴질랜드로 배송하고 있습니다. 자세한 요금은 아래를 참조하십시오:

도착지	표준 배송	특급 배송
미국	$11.00	$15.00
영국	$13.00	$17.00
뉴질랜드	$6.00	$8.00

*모든 가격은 별도의 표시가 없는 한 호주 달러(AUD) 단위입니다.

(187)오피스 셰드에 등록된 회원들을 위해, 우리는 지금 제한된 시간 동안 귀하의 주문을 무료로 배송해 드리고 있습니다. 이번 행사는 국내 주문에만 적용됩니다.

귀하의 주문이 발송되면 알림 이메일을 받게 됩니다. 그 후, www.officeshed.com/ordertracker에서 저희 프로그램을 이용하여 무료로 택배 배송 상태를 확인하실 수 있습니다. 해외 배송과 같은 일부 주문은 추적하지 못할 수 있음에 유의하십시오.

환불 및 반품에 대한 정책을 보시려면 **여기**를 클릭하고, 회원 자격에 대해서는 **여기**를 클릭하십시오.

오피스 셰드
주문 확인 및 영수증

주문 참조: #4865436
주문 날짜: 12월 12일

배송 주소:
브룩 바인더 쉘든 로드 43, 글렌헤이븐, 빅토리아 주 4157, (187)호주

제품 정보	수량	가격
4단 금속 책상용 트레이 (색상: 검정)	1	$10.99
28mm 종이 클립(100/팩)	3	$6.75
(190)프리미엄 흰색 봉투(25/팩)	1	$8.81
소계:		$26.55
세금:		$2.65
(187)배송비:		$0.00
총계:		$29.20
결제 방법: 신용 카드 (xxxx-xxxx-xxxx-0555)	금액:	$29.20

(188)주문 절차에 관하여 도움이 필요하시면, 월요일부터 금요일까지 오전 9시에서 오후 5시 사이 근무 시간 중에 130-111로 고객 서비스 센터에 전화 주십시오.

수신: ⟨cs@officeshed.com⟩
발신: ⟨brookebinder@goldcoastmail.com⟩
날짜: 12월 17일
제목: 요청

관계자 분께,

(189)저는 오피스 셰드에서 받은 서비스에 매우 만족하고 있습니다. 하지만, (190)상자를 열었는데 제가 주문한 봉투를 찾지 못했을 때 제가 놀란 것을 생각해 보십시오. 제 물건을 포장하면서 그것들을 넣는 것을 잊었을 것으로 추정합니다.

(189)조만간에 다시 주문할 예정이니 (190)누락된 물품의 금액을 제 계정에 추가해 주시면 감사하겠습니다. 귀사에서 이 상황을 빨리 바로잡아 주시기를 바랍니다.

브룩 바인더 드림

---

186. 웹사이트에서, 첫 번째 단락의 1행에 있는 단어 "flat"과 의미상 가장 가까운 것은?
(A) 불충분한
(B) 고정된
(C) 할인된
(D) 수직의 　　　　　　　　　　　　　　　정답 (B)

187. 오피스 셰드가 본사를 두고 있는 곳은 어디이겠는가?
(A) 미국
(B) 뉴질랜드
(C) 호주
(D) 영국 　　　　　　　　　　　　　　　　정답 (C)

188. 영수증에서, 오피스 셰드에 대해 언급되는 것은 무엇인가?
(A) 12월 12일에 바인더 씨의 주문을 선적했다.
(B) 지역 제조업체들이 만든 제품을 판매한다.
(C) 사무용 가구를 유통한다.
(D) 고객 서비스 센터가 평일에만 운영된다. 　　정답 (D)

189. 바인더 씨에 대해 시사되어 있는 것은 무엇인가?
(A) 그녀는 오피스 셰드에서 자주 구매한다.
(B) 그녀는 현금으로 주문 금액을 지불했다.
(C) 그녀는 오피스 셰드에서 이메일을 받을 것이다.
(D) 그녀는 작은 회사의 소유주이다. 　　　　정답 (C)

190. 바인더 씨는 얼마를 환불받아야 한다고 요구하는가?
(A) 2달러 65센트
(B) 6달러 75센트
(C) 8달러 81센트
(D) 10달러 99센트 　　　　　　　　　　정답 (C)

문제 191-195번은 다음 안내문과 문자 메시지 그리고 이메일을 참조하시오.

도브 코티지 검사 안내문

모든 세입자 여러분에게 알려 드립니다. (192)건물의 난방 시스템에 대한 연례 점검이 다음 주에 시행될 예정이니 참고 바랍니다. (191)이 절차는 겨울을 대비하여 실시되고 있으며, 난방 시스템이 계속 제대로 가동되도록 하는 데 도움이 될 것입니다. 늘 그렇듯, 지역 기업인 포시즌 유지보수회사가 방문하여 점검을 실시할 것입니다. 점검은 각 호당 20분 정도 소요될 것입니다. 문제가 발견되면, 해당 호의 추가 점검 및 수리 작업 일정을 잡을 것입니다.

점검의 세부 일정은 다음과 같습니다:
– A동 각 호: 11월 3일 오후 12:00 – 오후 6:00
– B동 각 호: 11월 4일 오후 12:00 – 오후 6:00
– (193)C동 각 호: 11월 5일 오전 10:00 – 오후 4:00

어떤 이유로든 예정된 날짜에 시간이 안 되실 경우, 부동산 관리자 로사 벨라스케즈(rvelasquez@dovecottage.com)에게 즉시 연락하여 점검 일정을 조정하십시오.
점검에 대한 추가 정보는 포시즌 유지보수회사 웹사이트를 확인하십시오.
여러분의 협조에 미리 감사드립니다.

받는 사람: 앤드류 루돌프
전화번호: 594-9584-1128

앤드류, 데이비드입니다. (193)오늘 오전에 아파트 점검을 받기로 되어 있어서, 우리 회의 일정을 오후로 바꿀 수 있는지 궁금합니다. 검사원들이 도착하면 절차는 오래 걸리지 않을 거예요. 3시쯤에 당신 사무실에서 만나면 어떨까요? 괜찮으시다면 제게 알려 주세요. 데이비드.

수신: 로사 벨라스케즈 ⟨rvelasquez@dovecottage.com⟩
발신: 데이비드 야칼 ⟨dyakal@smail.com⟩
날짜: 11월 6일
제목: 문의

저는 최근에 아파트 점검을 받았는데 난방 시스템에 문제가 없다는 것을 알고 기뻤습니다. 그러나 오늘 아침, (194)저는 검사원이 제 발코니 창문을 깬 사실을 알았습니다. 지난해 점검원들이 우리 집을 방문했을 때도 같은 문제가 발생했습니다. 그들이 사용하는 큰 장비가 손상을 입힌 것 같습니다.

(194)창문 교체 비용을 보상받고 싶습니다. (195)제가 새 창문을 구매해서 직접 설치할 것입니다. 그 다음, 제가 상환받을 수 있도록 영수증을 보내 드리겠습니다. 이번 주말에 제가 출장을 떠나서 2주 동안 돌아오지 않기 때문에 떠나기 전에 대금을 받고 싶습니다.

빠른 답변 기다리겠습니다.

감사합니다.

데이비드 야칼

191. 도브 코티지가 점검을 받은 이유는?

(A) 건물이 추운 계절에 대비되도록 하기 위해

(B) 중앙 난방 시스템의 문제를 해결하기 위해

(C) 주거용 건물에 대한 지역 규정을 준수하기 위해

(D) 과도한 에너지 사용을 줄이기 위해 　　　　정답 (A)

192. 안내문에서, 점검에 대해 진술된 것은 무엇인가?

(A) 그것은 등록이 요구된다.

(B) 그것은 정기적으로 실시된다.

(C) 그것은 부동산 관리인에 의해 실시된다.

(D) 하루 정도 소요된다. 　　　　정답 (B)

193. 야칼 씨의 점검은 언제 실시되었겠는가?

(A) 11월 3일

(B) 11월 4일

(C) 11월 5일

(D) 11월 6일 　　　　정답 (C)

194. 야칼 씨가 이메일을 보낸 이유는?

(A) 점검 일정을 변경하기 위해

(B) 문제 해결을 요청하기 위해

(C) 그가 어디로 여행을 가는지 언급하기 위해

(D) 점검 수수료에 대해 문의하기 위해 　　　　정답 (B)

195. 야칼 씨에 대해 나타나 있는 것은 무엇인가?

(A) 그는 11월 3일에 출장을 갔다.

(B) 그는 이웃에게 점검 회사를 추천했다.

(C) 그는 혼자서 수리를 마칠 작정이다.

(D) 그는 전에 벨라스케즈 씨에게 연락한 적이 있다. 　　　　정답 (C)

문제 196-200번은 다음 이메일과 공지 그리고 평가서를 참조하시오.

수신: 데이비드 린더만 〈dlinderman@kitavipi.com〉

발신: 샘 뱅콜 〈sbankole@kitavipi.com〉

날짜: 7월 9일

제목: 워크숍 세션

린더만 씨에게,

다음 달 이스탄불 워크숍 일정과 관련하여 글을 씁니다. 오늘 오전에 제게 보내 주신 일정 초안을 검토했는데, 수정을 요청해야 할 것 같습니다. (196) **(197)워크숍이 열리는 날 오전에, 제가 앙카라에서 중요한 거래처와의 회의에 참석해야 합니다.** 거래처가 브뤼셀에서 2일 동안만 오는 것이라서, 회의 일정이 변경될 수 없습니다. **(197)이스탄불로 돌아오는 제 비행기는 오전 11시 30분에 출발합니다.**

(198)저는 이미 우리 부서의 사유리 후지타에게 우리 워크숍 시간을 바꾸어 달라고 요청했고, 그녀는 그렇게 하기로 동의했습니다. 혼동을 방지하기 위해 그것을 인쇄하여 회사 전체에 게시하기 전에 일정에 이러한 변경사항을 반영해 주십시오.

감사합니다.

샘 뱅콜

보조 편집자, 편집부

기타비 출판 주식회사

이스탄불 · 앙카라 · 이즈미르 · 부르사

제 15회 연차 직원 교육 워크숍

(197)8월 14일, 이스탄불 본사 건물

시간	워크숍 명	사회자
오전 8:30 – 오전 10:00	고객 및 동료와 소통하기	사유리 후지타
오전 10:20 – 오전 11:30	**(200)아이디어를 훌륭한 이야기로 발전시키기**	**(200)로렌조 몬디**
오전 11:30 – 오후 1:00	점심	
오후 1:00 – 오후 2:30	매력적인 책 표지 디자인하기	캐서린 콘팔로니에리
오후 2:50 – 오후 4:00	혼자서 자신의 칼럼 편집하기	타일러 부처
(198)오후 4:20 – 오후 6:00	시간 관리 – 그 순간을 가치 있게 만들기	**(198)샘 뱅콜**

(199)*모든 참석자는 점심 시간 동안 오찬에 초대될 것입니다.

전 직원은 워크숍에 대한 이 간단한 평가서를 작성해야 합니다. 원하시면 익명으로 두셔도 됩니다. 귀하의 의견은 향후 세션을 개선하는 데 도움이 될 것입니다.

다음 항목의 전반적인 질은 어땠나요?

	매우 우수	우수	평균	좋지 않음
교육자	X			
발표		X		
자료	X			

의견: **(200)몬디 씨의 강연이 정말 좋았습니다.** 나는 그에게서 많은 것을 배웠습니다. 다른 강사님들도 잘하셨습니다. 부처 씨의 강연 중에 마이크가 계속 고장 나서, 그의 말을 듣기가 힘들었습니다.

이름: 에밀리 하퍼

196. 뱅콜 씨에 대해 나타나 있는 것은 무엇인가?

(A) 그는 최근에 린더만 씨에게 연락했다.

(B) 그는 참석해야 할 업무 회의가 있다.

(C) 그는 다음 달에 브뤼셀을 방문할 것이다.

(D) 그는 워크숍을 이끌 계획이다. 　　　　정답 (B)

197. 뱅콜 씨가 8월 14일 오전 11시 30분에 어디에 있을 것 같은가?

(A) 브뤼셀

(B) 이스탄불

(C) 부르사

(D) 앙카라 　　　　정답 (D)

198. 후지타 씨가 워크숍을 원래 몇 시에 진행하기로 예정되어 있었는가?

(A) 오전 8시 30분

(B) 오전 10시 20분

(C) 오후 1시

(D) 오후 4시 20분 　　　　정답 (D)

199. 일정표에 나타나 있는 것은 무엇인가?

(A) 기타비 출판 주식회사는 15년 동안 사업을 해왔다.

(B) 몬디 씨가 기사 편집에 관한 워크숍을 이끌 것이다.

(C) 뱅콜 씨는 후지타 씨의 워크숍 세션에 참석할 것이다.

(D) 워크숍 참석자들에게 식사가 제공될 것이다. 　　　　정답 (D)

200. 하퍼 씨가 가장 좋아한 발표는 어느 것이었는가?

(A) 고객 및 동료와 소통하기

(B) 아이디어를 훌륭한 이야기로 발전시키기
(C) 매력적인 책 표지 디자인하기
(D) 혼자서 자신의 칼럼 편집하기   정답 (B)

1. 미M
(A) He is moving a rocking chair.
(B) He's sweeping the yard.
(C) He is reading a newspaper.
(D) He is watering the garden.

(A) 그는 흔들의자를 옮기고 있다.
(B) 그는 마당을 쓸고 있다.
(C) 그는 신문을 읽고 있다.
(D) 그는 정원에 물을 주고 있다.   정답 (C)

2. 미W
(A) The woman is standing in the middle of an aisle.
(B) The woman is trying on a blouse in the fitting room.
(C) The woman is hanging up a blouse.
(D) The woman is carrying a clothing rack.

(A) 여자가 통로 한가운데 서 있다.
(B) 여자가 탈의실에서 블라우스를 입어 보고 있다.
(C) 여자가 블라우스를 걸고 있다.
(D) 여자가 옷걸이를 옮기고 있다.   정답 (C)

3. 영M
(A) A man is exiting a vehicle.
(B) A woman is packing her backpack.
(C) Some people are waiting to board a bus.
(D) A man is rolling his suitcase down the aisle.

(A) 남자가 차량에서 내리고 있다.
(B) 여자가 배낭을 싸고 있다.
(C) 몇 사람이 버스에 탑승하려고 기다리고 있다.
(D) 남자가 바퀴 달린 여행가방을 끌고 통로를 내려가고 있다.   정답 (A)

4. 미M
(A) One person is distributing some printouts.
(B) One person is entering some data into a laptop.
(C) Some people are listening to a presentation.
(D) Some people are seated out on the patio.

(A) 한 사람이 인쇄물을 나눠주고 있다.
(B) 한 사람이 노트북에 자료를 입력하고 있다.
(C) 몇 사람이 발표를 듣고 있다.
(D) 몇 사람이 옥외 테라스에 앉아 있다.   정답 (C)

5. 호W
(A) They are emptying their basket.
(B) Shopping baskets are piled in rows.
(C) Items are displayed on shelves.
(D) Some shelves are being measured.

(A) 그들은 그들의 바구니를 비우고 있다.
(B) 쇼핑 바구니가 줄 맞춰 쌓여 있다.
(C) 물건들이 선반 위에 진열되어 있다.
(D) 몇 개의 선반이 측정되고 있다.   정답 (C)

6. 영M
(A) Pots are placed on the stove.
(B) Some chairs are stacked near the entrance.
(C) The refrigerator doors are closed.

(D) Some tables have been pushed against a wall.

(A) 냄비들이 레인지 위에 올려져 있다.
(B) 의자 몇 개가 입구 근처에 쌓여 있다.
(C) 냉장고 문이 닫혀 있다.
(D) 테이블 몇 개가 벽 쪽으로 밀쳐진 상태로 있다.　　　정답 (C)

Part 2

7. 미M 미W
How long will the bike race last?
(A) It's a mountain bike.
(B) It's a 200-meter race track.
(C) It ends at around 5.

자전거 경주는 얼마 동안 하나요?
(A) 그건 산악용 자전거예요.
(B) 그건 200미터 길이의 경주 트랙이에요.
(C) 대략 5시에 끝나요.　　　정답 (C)

8. 영M 호W
Where are you going for your vacation?
(A) To a resort in Hawaii.
(B) An informative presentation.
(C) I'll reserve a ticket.

휴가는 어디로 가실 거예요?
(A) 하와이에 있는 휴양지로요.
(B) 유익한 발표예요.
(C) 제가 표를 예약할게요.　　　정답 (A)

9. 미M 영M
Which manager is on duty after hours?
(A) Yes, I have been.
(B) It's an hourly rate.
(C) I think Paul is.

영업 시간 후에 어느 매니저가 당직인가요?
(A) 예, 제가 한 적이 있어요.
(B) 그건 시간당 요금이에요.
(C) 폴인 것 같아요.　　　정답 (C)

10. 미W 미M
Who do you think I should give this sales report to?
(A) To Ms. Kwon, please.
(B) The sales figures are up.
(C) What time do you report to work?

이 영업 보고서를 누구에게 주어야 할까요?
(A) 권 씨에게요.
(B) 판매 수치가 올라갔어요.
(C) 당신은 몇 시에 출근하세요?　　　정답 (A)

11. 영M 미W
You should buy the sunglasses with the white frames.
(A) I bought a pair like that last year.
(B) Check the filing cabinet.
(C) A regular eye exam.

하얀색 테가 있는 선글라스를 구입하시는 게 좋겠어요.
(A) 작년에 그런 선글라스를 샀어요.
(B) 서류함을 확인해 보세요.

(C) 정기적인 시력 검사요.　　　정답 (A)

12. 미M 호W
Where should we place the new copier?
(A) You'd better ask Jeff.
(B) More than 10 copies might be needed.
(C) It is beyond our budget.

새 복사기를 어디에 둘까요?
(A) 제프에게 물어보는 게 좋아요.
(B) 10부 이상이 필요할지 몰라요.
(C) 그건 우리 예산을 초과해요.　　　정답 (A)

13. 영M 미W
Are you going to participate in the bike race for charity next week?
(A) More than 50 people.
(B) She has a yearly gym membership.
(C) My bike needs to be repaired.

다음 주 자선 자전거 경주에 참가하실 거예요?
(A) 50명 이상이요.
(B) 그녀는 연간 헬스 회원권이 있어요.
(C) 제 자전거는 수리 받아야 해요.　　　정답 (C)

14. 호W 영M
Which team had the best performance results last month?
(A) My train was delayed only 10 minutes.
(B) Some big yellow envelopes.
(C) The director is still reviewing the data.

지난달에 어느 팀이 최고의 실적 결과를 냈나요?
(A) 제 기차는 고작 10분 지연되었어요.
(B) 노란색 큰 봉투 몇 개요.
(C) 이사님이 아직 자료를 검토 중이세요.　　　정답 (C)

15. 미M 호W
Why is it so cold in the conference room?
(A) Because the heater is not working.
(B) Can I have a room with a kitchenette?
(C) Just a brief weather update.

회의실이 왜 이렇게 추워요?
(A) 히터가 작동하지 않고 있기 때문이에요.
(B) 작은 부엌이 딸린 방으로 할 수 있을까요?
(C) 그냥 간략한 날씨 최신 정보예요.　　　정답 (A)

16. 미W 미M
Have you seen the agenda for the board meeting?
(A) I haven't checked my e-mail.
(B) At a reduced rate.
(C) I saw that movie last week.

이사회 회의의 의제를 보셨어요?
(A) 아직 제 이메일을 확인하지 못했어요.
(B) 할인 가격으로요.
(C) 저는 지난주에 그 영화를 봤어요.　　　정답 (A)

17. 호W 영M
When is the new airport location opening?
(A) No, I didn't open it.
(B) In a week or so, I think.

(C) It is a full flight.

신 공항 영업점 개점이 언제예요?
(A) 아뇨, 저는 그것을 열지 않았어요.
(B) 일주일 후쯤일 거예요.
(C) 비행기가 만석이에요. 　　　　　　　정답 (B)

18. 미W 영M
Do you like driving your car or the motorcycle to work?
(A) I thought he had left work early.
(B) I prefer my car.
(C) A car rental agency.

차를 몰고 출근하세요, 아니면 오토바이로 출근하세요?
(A) 저는 그가 일찍 퇴근한 줄 알았어요.
(B) 저는 제 차를 선호해요.
(C) 렌터카 회사요. 　　　　　　　　　정답 (B)

19. 미M 호W
What's the monthly maintenance fee for my savings account?
(A) On a weekly basis.
(B) It's 4 dollars a month.
(C) At the accounting firm.

제 보통 예금 계좌의 월 유지비는 얼마인가요?
(A) 일주일마다요
(B) 한 달에 4달러입니다.
(C) 회계 회사에서요. 　　　　　　　　정답 (B)

20. 영M 미W
None of the clients asked for me this morning, right?
(A) I was out of the office.
(B) It didn't last long.
(C) Sure, you can go ahead and use it.

오늘 아침에 고객 중 아무도 저를 찾은 사람은 없었죠, 그렇죠?
(A) 저는 사무실에 없었어요.
(B) 그것은 오래 가지 않았어요.
(C) 좋아요, 그것을 지체없이 사용해도 됩니다. 　정답 (A)

21. 호W 미M
I just mailed out the survey to our regular customers.
(A) Refunds are possible at the customer service desk.
(B) Check with the director.
(C) I hope all of them complete it.

우리 단골 고객들에게 설문지를 방금 우편으로 발송했어요.
(A) 환불은 고객 서비스 데스크에서 가능합니다.
(B) 이사님에게 확인해 보세요.
(C) 모두가 그것을 작성해 주면 좋겠네요. 　정답 (C)

22. 미W 미M
Jasmine hasn't submitted the reimbursement form yet.
(A) I don't agree with them.
(B) The manager is happy with our budget.
(C) She should do it today.

재스민이 아직도 환급 신청서를 제출하지 않았어요.
(A) 저는 그들의 의견에 동의하지 않아요.
(B) 부장님은 우리 예산에 만족스러워하고 있어요.
(C) 그녀는 그것을 오늘 해야 할 거예요. 　정답 (C)

23. 미W 영M
Why are you late for the morning staff meeting today?
(A) Did you see the traffic?
(B) No. He arrived last night.
(C) Neither am I.

왜 오늘 아침 직원 회의에 늦었어요?
(A) 교통량 보셨어요?
(B) 아뇨. 그는 어제 도착했어요.
(C) 저 역시 아닙니다. 　　　　　　　정답 (A)

24. 미M 호W
How do you like your new job as a salesperson?
(A) Yes, I'd like to.
(B) My first day isn't until next Monday.
(C) Sure, I'll review the sales numbers.

영업 사원으로서의 새 일이 어때요?
(A) 예, 그러고 싶어요.
(B) 제 첫 근무일은 다음 주 월요일이에요.
(C) 좋아요, 제가 판매 수치를 검토할게요. 　정답 (B)

25. 호W 영M
Isn't this back door supposed to stay locked?
(A) I used to live in this neighborhood.
(B) Yes, but it broke this morning.
(C) Put it up on the door.

뒷문은 계속 자물쇠로 잠겨져 있어야 하는 거 아닌가요?
(A) 저는 이 동네에 살았었어요.
(B) 예, 그런데 오늘 아침에 고장 났어요.
(C) 그것을 문에 붙이세요. 　　　　　정답 (B)

26. 호W 미M
Where did you purchase this smartphone?
(A) OK. That day works for me.
(B) Well, I got a great deal.
(C) Actually, it was a present.

이 스마트폰은 어디서 구입했어요?
(A) 좋아요. 그날은 괜찮아요.
(B) 음, 저는 아주 싸게 샀어요.
(C) 사실, 그건 선물이었어요. 　　　　정답 (C)

27. 영M 미W
You're not sold out of this smartphone model, are you?
(A) At an electronic store nearby.
(B) Call me on my cellphone.
(C) Yes, but can I order one for you?

이 스마트폰 모델이 다 팔린 것은 아니죠, 그렇죠?
(A) 근처에 있는 전자 매장에서요.
(B) 제 휴대폰으로 전화 주세요.
(C) 다 팔렸지만, 하나 주문해 드릴까요? 　정답 (C)

28. 미M 호W
Would you like any dessert this evening?
(A) A plastic tablecloth will do.
(B) Do you only serve vanilla ice cream?
(C) It was sold out yesterday afternoon.

오늘 저녁 디저트를 드시겠습니까?

(A) 비닐 식탁보면 괜찮아요.

(B) 바닐라 아이스크림만 제공하시나요?

(C) 그것은 어제 오후에 다 팔렸어요. 정답 (B)

29. 미W 영M

Are you comfortable leading the focus group by yourself or do you need some help?

(A) It's offered at a group rate.

(B) I've done it before.

(C) I came up with those ideas.

혼자서 소비자 제품 평가단 토론을 진행하는 게 편하세요. 아니면 도움이 필요하세요?

(A) 그건 단체 요금으로 제공됩니다.

(B) 전에 그것을 해본 적이 있어요.

(C) 제가 그 아이디어들을 냈어요. 정답 (B)

30. 미M 미W

We should offer employees discounts to the local fitness center.

(A) He is unemployed at the moment.

(B) I think that sounds great.

(C) Two hours every day.

우리는 직원들에게 이 지역 헬스 센터에 대한 할인을 제공하는 게 좋겠어요.

(A) 그는 지금 실업자예요.

(B) 그거 좋은 생각인 것 같아요.

(C) 매일 두 시간씩이요. 정답 (B)

31. 영M 미W

Who do I give my reimbursement form for travel expenses to?

(A) It's an online process now.

(B) The job requires a lot of traveling.

(C) A two-hour flight to Michigan.

출장비에 대한 환급 신청서를 누구에게 주는 건가요?

(A) 그게 이제는 온라인으로 처리해요.

(B) 그 일은 출장을 많이 다녀야 해요.

(C) 미시건으로 가는 2시간 항공편이요. 정답 (A)

Part 3

문제 32–34번은 다음 대화를 참조하시오. 영M 미W

M: Lisa, (32)**don't forget to take your carry-on luggage from under the seat in front of you.**

W: Thanks for the reminder. (32)**This flight has been pretty long.**

M: Well, at least we have landed five minutes ahead of schedule. Once we get to the hotel, we can practice the presentation we're giving at the expo tomorrow.

W: (33)**Did you remember to bring the pamphlets we're going to hand out there?**

M: (33)**Yes, I did.** I've got them in my checked luggage. I have a total of 500, which should be plenty.

W: Now that I think of it, (34)**I'm going to contact the conference center** after we arrive. (34)**I want to ask if we can check out the conference room** that we'll be speaking in to see if it's good enough.

M: 리사, 당신 앞 좌석 밑에서 휴대용 짐 가져가는 것을 잊지 마세요.

W: 잊지 않게 주의를 줘서 고마워요. 이번 비행은 정말 길었어요.

M: 음, 어쨌든 일정보다 5분 일찍 착륙했잖아요. 일단 호텔에 도착하면, 내일 박람회에서 우리가 하게 될 프레젠테이션을 연습할 수 있어요.

W: 거기서 나눠줄 팸플릿을 가져 오는 거 잊지 않으셨죠?

M: 예, 잊지 않았어요. 그것들은 부친 짐에 들어 있어요. 총 500부여서 충분할 거예요.

W: 지금 생각해 보니, 도착한 후에 회의 센터에 연락해야겠어요. 우리가 연설하게 될 회의실이 잘 갖춰진 상태인지 알아보기 위해 그곳을 확인해 볼 수 있는지 물어보고 싶어요.

32. 대화가 어디에서 이루어지고 있는 것 같은가?

(A) 호텔

(B) 사무실

(C) 비행기

(D) 회의 센터 정답 (C)

33. 남자는 무엇을 가지고 왔는가?

(A) 사진

(B) 자료

(C) 호텔 확인서

(D) 호텔 가는 길 안내 정답 (B)

34. 여자가 회의 센터로 전화를 하려는 이유는?

(A) 회의실을 예약하기 위해

(B) 도착 시간을 변경하기 위해

(C) 방을 보자고 요청하기 위해

(D) 행사 일정표를 얻기 위해 정답 (C)

문제 35–37번은 다음 3자 대화를 참조하시오. 미W 호W 미M

W1: (35)**Thank you for listening to *Motor Chat* on Radio 99.8 FM.** I'm Tina.

W2: And I'm Diane, the cohost of the show.

W1: This evening, (36)**we're going to be talking with a man who just launched a new car dealership.** Hello, Tim.

M: Hello. It's a pleasure to be here.

W2: What made you decide to start your own car dealership in the downtown area?

M: To be honest, my family has had a car business for more than 30 years. After working there for quite a long time, I realized I have personality traits suitable for a car salesman and wanted to start my own business.

W2: That is so interesting. (37)**Do you think you could give our listeners some advice on top things to consider when buying a car?**

M: (37)**No problem.**

W1: 라디오 99.8 FM 〈모터 챗〉을 청취해 주셔서 감사합니다. 저는 티나입니다.

W2: 그리고 저는 이 프로그램의 공동 진행자 다이앤입니다.

W1: 오늘 저녁에는 새 자동차 대리점을 막 시작한 남성 분과 얘기를 나눠보겠습니다. 안녕하세요. 팀.

M: 안녕하세요. 출연하게 되어 기쁩니다.

W2: 무엇 때문에 시내 지역에 자동차 대리점을 독자적으로 시작하기로 결정하셨나요?

M: 솔직히 말씀드리면, 저희 가족은 30년 이상 자동차 사업을 해왔습니다. 거기서 꽤 오랫동안 근무하고 나서, 제가 자동차 세일즈맨에 적합한 성격을 갖고 있다는 것을 깨닫고 제 사업을 시작하고 싶었어요.

W2: 참으로 흥미롭네요. 우리 청취자 분들께 차를 살 때 가장 고려해야 할 사항에 대해 조언 좀 해주실 수 있을까요?

M: 그럼요.

35. 여자들은 어디서 근무하는 것 같은가?
(A) 라디오 방송국
(B) 전자제품 대리점
(C) 자동차 정비소
(D) 자동차 대리점 　　　　　　　　　　정답 (A)

36. 남자는 최근에 무엇을 했는가?
(A) 자동차 잡지를 읽었다.
(B) 새로운 일자리를 찾았다.
(C) 사업을 시작했다.
(D) 자동차 정비 과정을 이수했다. 　　정답 (C)

37. 남자는 이후에 무엇을 하겠는가?
(A) 책 출간하기
(B) 라디오 방송국으로 전화하기
(C) 차량 구매하기
(D) 조언해 주기 　　　　　　　　　　정답 (D)

문제 38-40번은 다음 대화를 참조하시오. 영M 미W

M: Have you heard that Jason's last day here is Friday?

W: Yes, I have. **(38)I can't believe he's taking a job at our main rival** after working here for 15 years.

M: It's hard to believe. **(39)By the way, have you made the arrangements for his going-away party yet?**

W: Yes, I have. The caterer will arrive with the food at 3:00. What are you buying for him?

M: **(40)I'm going to get together with a couple of other people in the office to buy him a set of golf clubs.** He'll love them.

W: That sounds good. Maybe I can contribute as well.

M: 여기서 제이슨의 마지막 날이 금요일이라는 거 들었어요?

W: 예, 들었어요. 여기서 15년 근무하고 나서 우리 주요 경쟁업체에 취업을 한다는 게 좀 믿기지가 않아요.

M: 믿기가 어렵죠. 그런데, 송별 파티 준비는 했어요?

W: 예, 했어요. 출장 요리 업체에서 음식을 가지고 3시에 도착할 거예요. 제이슨에게 무엇을 사줄 거예요?

M: 사무실의 다른 두어 명과 함께 골프채 세트를 사주려고요. 제이슨이 무척 좋아할 거예요.

W: 괜찮네요. 어쩌면 저도 거기에 보탤까봐요.

38. 화자들은 제이슨에 대해 무엇을 말하는가?
(A) 그는 회사에서 은퇴할 것이다.
(B) 그는 해외로 전근 갈 것이다.
(C) 그는 승진할 것이다.
(D) 그는 다른 회사로 옮길 것이다. 　　정답 (D)

39. 남자는 무엇에 대해 물어보는가?
(A) 파티 준비
(B) 다가오는 회의
(C) 출장
(D) 고객으로부터 온 급한 전화 　　　정답 (A)

40. 남자에 따르면, 그는 무엇을 할 계획인가?
(A) 골프장 가기
(B) 선물 구입하기
(C) 다른 출장 요리 업체 물색하기
(D) 돈 기부하기 　　　　　　　　　　정답 (B)

문제 41-43번은 다음 대화를 참조하시오. 호W 영M

W: David, I spoke with the manager of the caterer who is going to provide food for our annual end-of-the-year party we are having this weekend. **(41)He told me the food we're planning to order for everyone will cost much less than we budgeted for.**

M: That's very surprising. Fredo's is an expensive place.

W: That's the truth. **(42)So I was thinking that we could use the leftover money to buy some presents for our employees.** Would it be okay? I think that would impress a lot of people here.

M: I agree. Just be sure not to go over the budget. **(43)Oh, would you be sure to check the names on the invitation list?** I want to confirm that we haven't omitted any of the board members.

W: 데이비드, 해마다 하는 이번 주말 연말 송년회에 음식을 제공할 출장 요리 업체 관리자와 통화했는데요. 그가 하는 말을 들어보니, 우리가 모두를 위해 주문하려고 계획한 음식이 우리가 예산으로 책정한 것보다 훨씬 비용이 더 적게 들어요.

M: 그거 매우 놀랍군요. 프레도 식당은 비싼 곳이잖아요.

W: 그건 사실이죠. 그래서 남는 돈으로 우리 직원들을 위해서 선물을 좀 살 수 있지 않을까 생각하고 있었어요. 괜찮을까요? 그렇게 하면 여기 많은 직원들에게 감명을 줄 것 같아요.

M: 동감이에요. 꼭 예산을 초과하지 않도록만 해주세요. 아, 초대 명단에 있는 이름을 꼭 확인해 주실래요? 이사들 누구도 빠뜨리지 않았다는 것을 확인하고 싶어요.

41. 남자는 무엇 때문에 놀라는가?
(A) 연장된 영업 시간
(B) 행사 장소
(C) 참석자 숫자
(D) 출장 요리 서비스의 가격 　　　　정답 (D)

42. 여자는 무엇을 하는 데 허락을 원하는가?
(A) 출장 요리 업체 고용
(B) 선물 구입
(C) 장소 변경
(D) 더 많은 사람 초대 　　　　　　　정답 (B)

43. 여자는 뒤이어 무엇을 해달라는 요청을 받는가?
(A) 가격 견적 받기
(B) 손님 명단 검토하기
(C) 초대장 보내기
(D) 이사와 얘기하기 　　　　　　　　정답 (B)

문제 44-46번은 다음 대화를 참조하시오. 미M 미W

M: **(44)Eastside Electronics. This is David speaking. What can I do for you?**

W: Hello. **(44)I am calling regarding the web cam I bought** at your store on Sunset Street. I do lots of videoconferencing with executives at my company's headquarters, (45)**but the audio keeps cutting in and out. To be honest, I'm pretty disappointed as I only purchased it two weeks ago.**

M: I'm terribly sorry, ma'am. How about if we walk you through a bit of troubleshooting now? First, have you tried unplugging the device and then plugging it back in?

W: Yes, but that didn't change anything.

M: Okay. How about the software? (46)**Did you get the most recent update?**

W: Hmm… Maybe not. (46)**Okay, let me take care of that, and then I'll call you back if there's still a problem.** Thanks.

M: 이스트사이드 전자제품 대리점입니다. 저는 데이비드입니다. 뭘 도와드릴까요?

W: 안녕하세요. 선셋 가 매장에서 제가 구매한 웹캠 때문에 전화드렸어요. 우리 회사 본사에서 임원들과 화상회의를 많이 하는데, 오디오가 계속해서 꺼졌다 켜졌다 해요. 솔직히 이것을 불과 2주 전에 구매했기 때문에 꽤 많이 실망했어요.

M: 정말 죄송합니다, 손님. 지금 문제 해결하는 것을 차근차근 알려 드리면서 도와드리면 어떨까요? 우선, 장치 플러그를 뺐다가 다시 꽂아 보셨어요?

W: 예, 그런데 그렇게 해도 아무런 변화도 없었어요.

M: 좋습니다. 소프트웨어는 어떤가요? 가장 최근 소프트웨어로 업데이트 하셨나요?

W: 음… 하지 않은 것 같아요. 그럼, 그렇게 해보고, 그 다음 계속 문제가 있으면 다시 전화드릴게요. 감사합니다.

44. 남자는 누구일 것 같은가?
(A) 영업 사원
(B) 인적자원부 직원
(C) 고객 서비스 담당 직원
(D) 제품 디자이너　　　　　　　　　　　정답 (C)

45. 여자가 "저는 이것을 불과 2주 전에 구매했어요"라고 말할 때 무엇을 함축하는가?
(A) 제품이 아직 작동해야 한다.
(B) 제품이 수송 중에 파손되었다.
(C) 주문품이 아직 배달되지 않았다.
(D) 그녀는 또 다른 오디오 장치를 구매하고 싶다.　정답 (A)

46. 여자는 이후에 무엇을 할 것 같은가?
(A) 소프트웨어 업데이트하기
(B) 제품에 대해 환불 받기
(C) 사용자 설명서 참조하기
(D) 장치의 플러그를 꽂기　　　　　　　　정답 (A)

문제 47-49번은 다음 대화를 참조하시오. 영M 미W

M: Lisa, (47)**do you have a moment to discuss your schedule here at the bakery?** (48)**Would you like to put in some more hours?**

W: That would be wonderful.

M: That's good. We could use another baker to work the morning shift on Saturday and Sunday. Lots of cakes and cookies are selling out by noon, so we need to make more. You'd begin your shift each day at 6 A.M. and finish at noon.

W: That's kind of early. (49)**How is the pay? Is the hourly rate**

the same as it is for my afternoon shifts on the weekday?

M: No. You'll get paid seven dollars more for each hour.

W: Whoa. That's impressive. I'll work both shifts then.

M: 리사, 여기 제과점에서의 당신 일정에 대해 잠시 얘기할 시간이 있어요? 몇 시간 더 근무를 하고 싶어요?

W: 그러면 좋죠.

M: 잘됐네요. 토요일과 일요일에 오전 근무로 일할 제빵사가 한 명 더 필요해요. 많은 케이크와 쿠키가 정오까지 다 매진되어서, 더 많이 만들 필요가 있어요. 매일 교대 근무를 아침 6시에 시작하여 정오에 마치게 돼요.

W: 그건 좀 이르네요. 급여는 어떤가요? 시간 당 급여가 주중에 오후 근무할 때와 똑같은가요?

M: 아뇨. 매 시간마다 7달러를 더 받게 될 거예요.

W: 와, 아주 인상적이네요. 그러면 교대 근무 둘 다 할게요.

47. 대화는 어디서 이루어지는가?
(A) 슈퍼마켓
(B) 제과점
(C) 식당
(D) 요리 학교　　　　　　　　　　　　　정답 (B)

48. 남자는 여자에게 어떤 기회를 제의하는가?
(A) 여자의 계약 갱신하기
(B) 다른 지점으로 전근 가기
(C) 제과점 관리하기
(D) 시간 외 근무 하기　　　　　　　　　정답 (D)

49. 여자는 어떤 정보에 대해 물어보는가?
(A) 근무 시간
(B) 회사 복리후생
(C) 시간당 급여
(D) 지불 방법　　　　　　　　　　　　　정답 (C)

문제 50-52번은 다음 3자 대화를 참조하시오. 호W 미M 미W

W1: Hello, Mr. Darvish. Thanks for agreeing to this meeting on short notice.

M: No problem. (50)**I'm eager to get started on the design of the new warehouse.**

W1: This is Alice Hastings, the warehouse manager. I've asked her to attend this meeting to discuss what needs to be done.

M: It's a pleasure to meet you, Alice. (51)**Did you look over my proposal?**

W2: (51)**Yes, each of us reviewed it this morning.** But I noticed there's a mistake in the specifications for the loading dock.

M: What mistake?

W2: (52)**We requested that there be enough room for ten trucks to load or unload simultaneously. But the specifications only noted that we'll be getting eight spots.** We're expanding, so we need those extra two slots.

W1: 안녕하세요, 다비시 씨. 급하게 연락드렸는데도 불구하고 이번 회의에 동의해 주셔서 감사합니다.

M: 괜찮습니다. 새 창고의 설계를 시작하고 싶어요.

W1: 이분은 앨리스 헤이스팅스로 창고 책임자입니다. 무엇을 해야 하는지 논의하기 위해서 그녀에게 이번 회의에 참석해 달라고 부탁했습니다.

M: 만나서 반갑습니다, 앨리스. 제 제안서는 검토하셨나요?

W2: 예, 우리 각자 오늘 오전에 그것을 검토했어요. 그런데 하역장의 세부 내용에 오류가 있는 것을 알게 되었어요.

M: 어떤 오류요?

W2: 우리는 10대의 트럭이 동시에 짐을 적재하거나 하역하기에 충분한 공간이 있어야 한다고 요청했어요. 그런데 세부내용에 8개가 생긴다고 되어 있더군요. 우리 회사는 확장 중이라서 추가로 그 2개가 필요해요.

50. 대화 주제는 무엇인가?
(A) 이전
(B) 인기 있는 제품
(C) 고용 기회
(D) 새 시설 　　　　　　　　　　　　　　정답 (D)

51. 여자들은 오늘 무엇을 했는가?
(A) 그들은 새 설계 작업을 했다.
(B) 그들은 창고를 직접 방문했다.
(C) 그들은 프로젝트 제안서를 검토했다.
(D) 그들은 입사 지원자들을 면접했다. 　　　정답 (C)

52. 앨리스에 따르면, 어떤 정보가 정확하지 않은가?
(A) 일부 품목의 비용
(B) 건물의 주소
(C) 창고의 크기
(D) 하역 장소의 개수 　　　　　　　　　정답 (D)

문제 53–55번은 다음 대화를 참조하시오. 호W 미M

W: Mr. Lewis, even though I just started here at the factory last month, I have an idea I'd like to discuss with you. (53)It's regarding how we can make the production process of our kitchen tiles more efficient and cost effective.

M: Okay. What's your idea on how to improve the process?

W: I noticed that we are manufacturing more tiles than we sell, and that's leaving us with plenty of leftover tiles. (54)But we don't have enough of those tiles to put in a single kitchen, so we can't sell them. Why don't we not make any tiles until we get an order?

M: You know, we tried doing that before. (55)But our customers weren't pleased with how much longer it took them to receive their orders than promised.

W: 루이스 씨, 저는 비록 지난달에 여기 공장에서 근무를 시작했지만, 의논하고 싶은 아이디어가 있어요. 그건 우리가 주방 타일 제조 과정을 얼마나 좀더 효율적이고 비용 효율적으로 만들 수 있는지에 관한 거예요.

M: 좋아요. 제조 과정을 향상시킬 방법에 대한 당신의 아이디어가 어떤 거예요?

W: 제가 알게 된 것은 우리가 판매하는 것보다 더 많은 타일을 제조하고 있어서, 우리에게 여분의 타일이 많이 남는다는 점이에요. 그런데 그 남은 타일들이 주방 하나에 깔 만큼 충분하게 있지는 않아서, 그것들을 판매할 수도 없어요. 다음 주문 들어올 때까지 더 이상 타일을 만들지 않는 게 어떨까요?

M: 있잖아요, 우리도 그것을 전에 시도해 봤어요. 그런데 고객들은 약속된 것보다 자신들의 주문을 받는 데 시간이 더 오래 걸리는 것을 좋아하지 않았어요.

53. 여자는 무엇을 논의하고 싶어하는가?
(A) 안전 규정 개선하기
(B) 다른 납품업체 고용하기

(C) 생산 과정 바꾸기
(D) 경쟁력 있는 가격 제시하기 　　　　　정답 (C)

54. 여자는 여분의 타일에 대해 어떤 문제점을 언급하는가?
(A) 그것들은 다 팔릴 수가 없다.
(B) 그것들을 보관할 공간이 없다.
(C) 그 중에 일부는 생산 중에 파손되었다.
(D) 그것들은 사이즈가 맞지 않다. 　　　정답 (A)

55. 남자가 고객들이 만족스러워하지 않았다고 말하는 이유는?
(A) 가격이 최근이 올랐다.
(B) 웹사이트에 문제가 있었다.
(C) 주문품을 제 시간에 받지 못했다.
(D) 작업의 품질이 형편 없었다. 　　　　정답 (C)

문제 56–58번은 다음 대화를 참조하시오. 미W 영M

W: Jason, do you know where we keep the paper cups in the employee lounge? (56)Since we relocated to this new office last week, I can't seem to find anything.

M: Look in the cupboard behind you. You know, it's good that we've moved a lot closer to our major clients, but this has been quite a change.

W: You can say that again. (57)The old office was so close to my apartment that I used to walk to work. But now I have to take the bus. It's not a big problem, but walking helped me stay in shape.

M: (58)Are you aware that the company is offering free gym memberships to all employees? You can talk to Fred if you're interested.

W: 제이슨, 직원 휴게실 어디에 우리가 종이컵을 보관하는지 알아요? 지난 주 이 새 사무실로 이전했기 때문에, 하나도 찾지 못하겠어요.

M: 당신 바로 뒤에 있는 찬장에서 찾아보세요. 있잖아요, 우리 주요 고객과 훨씬 더 가깝게 이사 온 것은 좋은데, 이건 너무도 큰 변화였어요.

W: 그 말이 백 번 옳아요. 예전 사무실은 제 아파트와 아주 가까워서 저는 회사에 걸어서 출근했어요. 그런데 이제는 버스를 타야 해요. 큰 문제는 아니지만, 걷는 게 몸매를 유지하는 데 도움되었거든요.

M: 우리 회사가 전 직원에게 헬스 회원권을 주는 거 알고 있어요? 관심 있으면 프레드와 얘기해 보세요.

56. 회사는 최근에 무엇을 했는가?
(A) 사무용품들을 다시 정리했다.
(B) 외국으로 확장했다.
(C) 직원들에게 더 많은 혜택을 제공했다.
(D) 다른 장소로 이전했다. 　　　　　　정답 (D)

57. 여자는 예전에 무엇을 한 적이 있었다고 말하는가?
(A) 매일 운동하기
(B) 걸어서 출근하기
(C) 회사에 점심 갖고 오기
(D) 늦게까지 일하기 　　　　　　　　　정답 (B)

58. 남자는 여자에게 무엇을 할 것을 제안하는가?
(A) 다른 장소로 이사하기
(B) 다른 부서로 전근 가기
(C) 헬스 클럽의 회원 되기
(D) 운전해서 출근하기 　　　　　　　　정답 (C)

문제 59-61번은 다음 대화를 참조하시오. 영M 호W

M: Jasmine, (59)we need to talk about the van design for the Rubicon model. I think there's a flaw in the design. The engine isn't powerful enough, and the van is too heavy for it to go very fast. (60)I'm worried because we're already running behind schedule.

W: (60)We have until August to finish the project. Have you considered making the engine more powerful?

M: Of course, but doing that would cost more than we've budgeted.

W: Okay, (61)let's have a meeting with Kevin to figure out what we can do. He's gone today and tomorrow, but he'll be back in the office on Thursday.

M: 재스민, 루비콘 모델에 대한 밴 설계에 대해 논의 좀 해야 해요. 설계에 결점이 있는 것 같아요. 엔진이 충분히 힘이 좋지 않고, 밴이 너무 무거워서 아주 빨리 달리지 못해요. 이미 일정보다 늦어지고 있어서 걱정돼요.

W: 프로젝트를 끝내는 데 8월까지는 시간이 있어요. 엔진을 좀 더 힘이 좋게 만드는 것은 생각해 봤어요?

M: 물론이죠. 그런데 그렇게 하려면 우리가 예산으로 잡아 놓은 것보다 비용이 더 들어갈 거예요.

W: 좋아요, 케빈과 회의를 해서 우리가 뭘 할 수 있는지 알아봅시다. 그는 오늘과 내일 부재중인데, 목요일에는 사무실에 돌아와 있을 거예요.

59. 대화의 주제는 무엇인가?
(A) 제품의 설계
(B) 광고의 변경
(C) 제품 시범 설명
(D) 신차의 출시일
정답 (A)

60. 여자가 "프로젝트를 끝내는 데 8월까지는 시간이 있어요"라고 말할 때 무엇을 암시하는가?
(A) 그들은 시간이 충분히 없다.
(B) 그들은 추가 직원을 고용할 필요가 있다.
(C) 그들은 더 신속하게 일해야 한다.
(D) 그들은 여전히 마감시한을 맞출 수 있다.
정답 (D)

61. 여자는 무엇을 할 것을 제안하는가?
(A) 자문위원 고용
(B) 동료와 대화
(C) 예산 증액
(D) 몇 가지 계산 검토
정답 (B)

문제 62-64번은 다음 대화와 설문지를 참조하시오. 미W 영M

W: (62)Craig, have you done any work on the survey we're doing for our newest video game? You know, the action one?

M: I've written something up. Could you look at it, please?

W: Sure. Let me look… I'd say you covered everything. (63) How did you decide which questions to put in the survey?

M: (63)I took a look at the reviews of other video games on the Internet. (62)These questions were mentioned the most by game players in the online reviews.

W: That was a good idea. Now, let me make one comment. (64) I've noticed that most people don't respond to surveys if they have to write any kind of explanation.

M: Ah, you're right. (64)I'll remove that item from the survey.

W: 크레이그, 우리 최신 비디오 게임을 위해 우리가 하려고 하는 설문조사 작업을 좀 했어요? 있잖아요, 액션 비디오 게임이요?

M: 좀 작성했어요. 한 번 봐 주실래요?

W: 좋아요. 어디 봐요… 모든 내용을 다 다루긴 했네요. 설문지에 어떤 질문을 넣을지는 어떻게 결정했어요?

M: 인터넷에서 다른 비디오 게임에 대한 후기들을 봤어요. 이 질문들이 온라인 후기에서 게임하는 사람들이 가장 많이 언급한 질문들이에요.

W: 잘 생각했군요. 자, 저도 의견 하나 낼게요. 제가 알게 된 것은, 대부분의 사람들이 어떤 종류의 설명이든 써야 한다면 설문에 답변을 하지 않더군요.

M: 아, 맞아요. 그 항목은 설문지에서 제외할게요.

설문조사		
	만족	불만족
1. 성능	☐	☐
2. 줄거리	☐	☐
3. 그래픽	☐	☐
(64)4. 뭔가 불만족스럽다면, 이유가 무엇인가요?		

62. 설문조사는 누구를 대상으로 하는 것인가?
(A) 디자이너
(B) 작가
(C) 게임하는 사람
(D) 컴퓨터 프로그래머
정답 (C)

63. 남자는 설문지에 열거된 항목들을 어떻게 선택했는가?
(A) 그는 온라인 후기를 참조했다.
(B) 그는 온라인 잡지에 있는 기사를 읽었다.
(C) 그는 동료들과 회의를 했다.
(D) 그는 제품 사용설명서를 봤다.
정답 (A)

64. 그래픽을 보시오. 어떤 항목이 설문지에서 제외되겠는가?
(A) 항목 1
(B) 항목 2
(C) 항목 3
(D) 항목 4
정답 (D)

문제 65-67번은 다음 대화와 그래프를 참조하시오. 미M 미W

M: Lisa, look at the numbers for the sales we made at the farmers' market last month. We sold a lot of strawberries.

W: (65)I think the new organic fertilizers we purchased last year helped us harvest high quality strawberries, so customers love them. But check out the graph. (66)We only managed to sell 15 kilograms of this.

M: (66)We'd better lower the price the next time we sell them at the farmer's market.

W: Good thinking. (67)Oh, did you see that segment on the news last night? It was all about the farmers' market. (67)It should help attract more people this weekend.

M: 리사, 농산물 시장에서 지난달에 우리가 이룬 매출 수치 좀 보세요. 딸기를 아주 많이 팔았어요.

W: 작년에 우리가 구입한 유기농 비료가 고품질의 딸기를 수확하는 데 도움이 된 것 같아요. 그래서 고객들이 딸기를 너무 좋아해요. 그런데 이 그래프 좀 보세요. 이거는 간신히 15kg만 팔았어요.

M: 다음에 농산물 시장에서 그것을 팔 때는 가격을 좀 낮추는 게 낫겠어요.

W: 좋은 생각이에요. 아, 어젯밤에 뉴스에 나온 그 부분 봤어요? 그게 온통 농산물 시장에 관한 것이었어요. 그게 이번 주말에 더 많은 사람들을 끌어모으는 데 도움이 될 거예요.

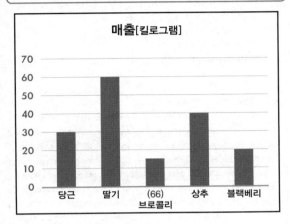

65. 화자들은 작년에 무엇을 했는가?
(A) 그들은 비료를 구매했다.
(B) 그들은 새로운 농업용 차량을 구매했다.
(C) 그들은 더 많은 농지를 얻었다.
(D) 그들은 더 많은 농장 노동자를 고용했다. 정답 (A)

66. 그래픽을 보시오. 이번 주말에 어떤 품목이 더 낮은 가격에 판매될 것인가?
(A) 딸기
(B) 브로콜리
(C) 상추
(D) 블랙베리 정답 (B)

67. 여자가 더 많은 고객이 시장에 갈 것이라고 생각하는 이유는?
(A) 뉴스 프로그램에 보도가 방송되었다.
(B) 신문에서 기사를 실었다.
(C) 더 많은 판매업체가 나중에 그곳에 갈 것이다.
(D) 모든 가격이 할인될 것이다. 정답 (A)

문제 68-70번은 다음 대화와 지도를 참조하시오. 미W 영M

W: Hello, Steve. It's Carla. (68)**I'm calling because Anderson Electric, one of our clients, wants to talk about the advertising campaign we're developing for them.**

M: Right. We're supposed to make some changes to the print advertisement that's going to run in the paper soon, right?

W: Correct. The team at Anderson wants to meet this Friday, so I said we'd be there at nine in the morning. (69)**The office is on the third floor of the building across from City Hall.**

M: Okay. I know where it is. Oh, no… I just remembered I'm meeting Mr. Gruber from HHW at ten on Friday. I can't cancel on him.

W: Don't worry. (70)**I'll reschedule the meeting for some time after lunch. Then, you can attend it.**

W: 안녕하세요, 스티브. 칼라예요. 우리 고객 중 하나인 앤더슨 전자회사에서 우리가 그 회사를 위해 개발하고 있는 광고 캠페인에 관해 논의하고 싶어서 전화했어요.

M: 그래요. 곧 신문에 낼 예정인 인쇄물 광고에 대해 우리가 변경 좀 하기로 되어 있죠, 그렇죠?

W: 맞아요. 앤더슨 사의 팀이 이번 주 금요일에 만나고 싶어 해서, 아침 9시에 거기로 가겠다고 말했어요. 사무실이 시청 맞은 편에 있는 건물 3층에 있어요.

M: 알았어요. 거기가 어디 있는지 알아요. 아, 이런… 제가 금요일 10시에 HHW 사의 그루버 씨를 만나기로 되어 있는 게 막 생각났어요. 그 사람과 만나는 것은 취소할 수가 없어요.

W: 걱정하지 마세요. 회의 일정을 점심 시간 후로 다시 잡을게요. 그러면, 당신이 참석할 수 있잖아요.

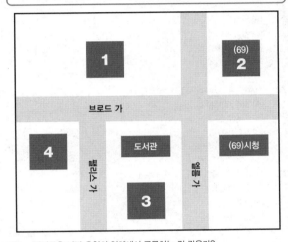

68. 화자들은 어떤 유형의 업체에서 근무하는 것 같은가?
(A) 광고 회사
(B) 회계 회사
(C) 전자제품 제조업체
(D) 전기 회사 정답 (A)

69. 그래픽을 보시오. 화자들은 금요일에 어느 건물을 방문하는가?
(A) 건물 1
(B) 건물 2
(C) 건물 3
(D) 건물 4 정답 (B)

70. 여자는 무엇을 하겠다고 제의하는가?
(A) 자신의 상사와 대화
(B) 회의 시간 변경
(C) 발표 자료 재작성
(D) 회의 장소 변경 정답 (B)

Part 4

문제 71-73번은 다음 광고를 참조하시오. 미M

M: Attention, anyone who loves cooking. Do you cook dishes that require exact amounts of certain ingredients? (71)**Then the Devers 1500 is the kitchen scale you need for all your cooking needs.** It's the most reliable product on the market. (72)**You'll get precise measurements to the nearest gram** each and every time you weigh something. (73)**The Devers 1500 is** so durable that we're ready and willing to immediately give you a special offer—a three-year extended warranty at no extra fee. That means, if it breaks, you can return it and get a new one for free.

요리를 사랑하는 사람은 누구든지 주목해 주세요. 특정 재료가 정확한 양으로 들어가야 하는 요리를 하시나요? 그렇다면 덴버 1500은 여러분의 모든 요리 요구에 필요한 주방용 저울입니다. 현재 시중에 나와 있는 것 중 가장 믿을 만한 제품입니다. 무게를 매번 잴 때마다 가장 근접한 그램까지 정확한 측정을 할 수 있습니다. 덴버 1500은 내구성이 매우 우수하여 우리는 즉시 특별 제공을 해 드릴 수 있는데, 바로 추가 비용 없이 3년 품질 보증 연장을 해드리는 것입니다. 그 말은, 고장 나면 그것을 반품하고 무료로 새것을 받으실 수 있다는 의미입니다.

71. 어떤 제품이 홍보되고 있는가?
(A) 믹서기
(B) 커피 메이커
(C) 토스터기
(D) 저울   정답 (D)

72. 화자는 제품에 대해 무엇을 칭찬하는가?
(A) 환경친화적이다.
(B) 비싸지 않다.
(C) 휴대용이다.
(D) 정확하다.   정답 (D)

73. 화자는 어떤 특별 거래를 제공하는가?
(A) 요리책에 대한 할인
(B) 무료 설치
(C) 품질 보증 연장
(D) 무료 배송   정답 (C)

문제 74-76번은 다음 전화 메시지를 참조하시오. 미W

W: Hello, Rick. This is Amy. Remember how Mr. Burgess asked us to come up with some ideas to save money? (74) (75)He said we needed to present our cost-reduction proposal next Friday. (75)But he just told me he wants the proposal to be done this Thursday. Apparently, he's meeting the CEO the following day, so he's counting completely on us to come up with some good ideas for saving money. I can start working on the slides, (76)but to get the presentation done, we'll need additional financial data. You do know Peter from Finance, don't you? Let me know what you get from him. I'll be in my office all day long. Thanks.

안녕하세요. 릭. 저는 에이미입니다. 버제스 씨가 우리에게 비용을 절감할 아이디어를 내라고 요청했던 거 기억하세요? 그는 다음 주 금요일에 우리가 비용 절감 제안서를 발표해야 한다고 말했잖아요. 그런데 그가 막 제게 제안서를 이번 주 목요일에 원한다고 했어요. 보아하니, 바로 그 다음 날 최고 경영자를 만날 예정이어서, 그는 비용을 아낄 수 있는 좋은 아이디어를 내놓는 데 우리에게 전적으로 의지하고 있는 것 같아요. 제가 슬라이드 작업을 시작할 수 있지만, 발표 자료를 끝내려면 추가적으로 재무 데이터가 필요할 거예요. 재무팀의 피터를 아시죠, 그렇죠? 그에게서 받는 것을 저에게 알려 주세요. 저는 하루 종일 사무실에 있을 거예요. 고마워요.

74. 화자는 무엇에 대한 프레젠테이션을 할 것인가?
(A) 더 많은 직원 보유하기
(B) 비용 절감 아이디어 제공하기

(C) 사무실 효율성 향상시키기
(D) 더 많은 견적서 받기   정답 (B)

75. 화자에 따르면, 무엇이 변경되었는가?
(A) 제안서 마감일
(B) 최고 경영자가 도착하는 날짜
(C) 고객의 방문
(D) 회의 장소   정답 (A)

76. 화자가 "재무팀의 피터를 아시죠, 그렇죠?"라고 말하는 이유는?
(A) 비용에 대한 우려를 표명하기 위해
(B) 회의 날짜를 확인하기 위해
(C) 직원 변경을 제안하기 위해
(D) 청자에게 동료에게 연락할 것을 요청하기 위해   정답 (D)

문제 77-79번은 다음 소개를 참조하시오. 영M

M: Hello. (77)I'm very pleased to announce that the winner of the employee of the year award is Susan Darcey, the head of the R&D Department. She not only manages a department with 120 people, (78)but she also successfully developed a more fuel-efficient engine that's being used in most of our vehicles now. Susan's contribution greatly helped our company, but she is also well known for her kindness. (79)Susan is always willing to mentor employees. She helps them improve themselves whenever she can. So, Susan, here's your award. Congratulations.

안녕하세요. 올해의 직원 상 수상자는 연구개발부의 부서장 수잔 다시라는 것을 발표하게 되어 매우 기쁩니다. 그녀는 120명이 있는 한 부서를 관리할 뿐만 아니라, 또한 좀 더 연비가 좋은 엔진을 성공적으로 개발했는데, 그 엔진은 현재 우리 대부분의 차량에 사용되고 있습니다. 수잔의 공헌은 우리 회사에 크게 도움이 되었고, 그녀는 또한 친절한 것으로도 잘 알려져 있습니다. 수잔은 항상 기꺼이 직원들에게 멘토가 되어 주려고 합니다. 그녀는 할 수 있는 한 언제든지 직원들이 스스로 실력을 기를 수 있도록 도와줍니다. 자, 수잔, 여기 당신에게 드리는 상이에요. 축하합니다.

77. 누가 소개되고 있는가?
(A) 최고 경영자
(B) 고객
(C) 중역
(D) 정부 관료   정답 (C)

78. 엔진에 대해 무엇이 언급되는가?
(A) 현재 사용 중이다.
(B) 가끔 고장이 난다.
(C) 개선될 필요가 있다.
(D) 현재 개발되는 과정에 있다.   정답 (A)

79. 수잔 다시에 대해 무엇이 시사되어 있는가?
(A) 그녀는 막 승진했다.
(B) 그녀는 종종 해외 여행을 다닌다.
(C) 그녀는 곧 은퇴할 예정이다.
(D) 그녀는 다른 사람을 도와주는 것을 좋아한다.   정답 (D)

요 – 플래시가 터지는 사진 촬영은 예술작품에 손상을 줄 수 있으므로 특별 허가가 없는 갤러리 안에서 금지됩니다. 대단히 감사합니다.

문제 80-82번은 다음 전화 메시지를 참조하시오. 호W

W: Hello. This message is for Mr. Griggs. (80)I'm calling from Orlando Restorations about the sofa that you dropped off here. The fabric on the seating part of the sofa needs replacing. I've checked with the furniture manufacturer to see if I could get some of the original fabric, (81)but unfortunately they don't have any in stock. The fabric for your sofa was a limited release design, so they didn't mass-produce it. However, I've found some other fabric that looks similar to it. I want to show it to you. (82)How about dropping by the store when you have a chance?

안녕하세요. 이 메시지는 그릭스 씨에게 보내는 메시지입니다. 고객님이 여기 맡긴 소파 건으로 올란도 복원 회사에서 전화드렸습니다. 소파의 앉는 부분의 천이 교체가 필요합니다. 원래 천을 좀 구할 수 있는지 알아보려고 그 가구 제조업체에 확인해 봤는데, 유감스럽게도 거기는 하나도 재고가 없더군요. 고객님의 소파에 들어간 천은 한정 출시 디자인이었고, 그래서 거기서 대량 생산하지 않았어요. 그런데 그것과 비슷하게 보이는 다른 천을 찾았습니다. 그것을 보여 드리고 싶어요. 기회 되실 때 가게에 들러 보시겠어요?

80. 화자는 무엇 때문에 전화하고 있는가?
(A) 가구에 대한 광고
(B) 소파 배달
(C) 그녀의 특별 주문에 대한 상황
(D) 가구 수리   정답 (D)

81. 화자는 어떤 문제를 언급하는가?
(A) 어떤 직물을 구할 수가 없다.
(B) 한 품목이 수리될 수 없다.
(C) 가격이 견적보다 더 높다.
(D) 마감시한이 지켜지지 않았다.   정답 (A)

82. 청자는 무엇을 해달라는 요청을 받는가?
(A) 다른 공급업체 물색
(B) 출시 날짜 변경
(C) 업체 방문
(D) 장비 찾아가기   정답 (C)

문제 83-85번은 다음 관람 정보를 참조하시오. 영M

M: Welcome to the Mandela Art Gallery. We'll start today's tour at the Impressionist Art Collection. (83)This is among our most popular exhibits because it features paintings by a different famous artist every other month. People enjoy seeing new artwork whenever they visit here. (84)After the tour, please feel free to ask any questions. But you should know that I'm an intern here. (85)Oh, one final reminder – flash photography is prohibited inside the gallery without special permission as it might damage artwork. Thank you very much.

만델라 아트 갤러리에 오신 것을 환영합니다. 오늘 관람은 인상주의 미술 컬렉션으로 시작하겠습니다. 이것은 우리의 가장 인기 있는 전시 중 하나인데, 왜냐하면 두 달에 한 번 각기 다른 유명 화가의 그림을 전시하기 때문입니다. 사람들은 여기에 방문할 때마다 새로운 예술작품 관람을 즐깁니다. 관람이 끝나면, 어떤 질문이든 편하게 해주세요. 그런데 저는 이곳의 인턴이란 것도 알아 두세요. 아, 그리고 마지막으로 한 가지 주의 사항이 있는데

83. 화자에 따르면, 인상주의 아트 컬렉션은 왜 인기 있는가?
(A) 입장료가 무료이다.
(B) TV 다큐멘터리에 나왔다.
(C) 미술관 최대의 컬렉션이다.
(D) 자주 업데이트된다.   정답 (D)

84. 화자가 "저는 이곳의 인턴이에요"라고 말할 때 무엇을 함축하는가?
(A) 그는 관람을 진행한 것에 대해 돈을 지급받지 않고 있다.
(B) 그는 동료의 도움이 필요하다.
(C) 그는 몇몇 질문에 답을 못할지도 모른다.
(D) 그는 방문객들에게 깊은 인상을 남기고 싶어한다.   정답 (C)

85. 화자는 청자들에게 무엇에 대해 잊지 말라고 주의를 주는가?
(A) 갤러리 방침
(B) 표 가격
(C) 문 닫는 시간
(D) 새로운 전시회   정답 (A)

문제 86-88번은 다음 방송을 참조하시오. 미W

W: WKEK is bringing you the news you need to know at 7 P.M. (86)First, let's cover the main story. All the votes have been counted, and Peter Shaw is the new mayor. Mr. Shaw is a leading member of the business community here in town. (87)Before running for mayor, he was the CEO of Shaw Construction for twenty years. He promised local residents to use his knowledge of the business world to improve the city's economy. (88)We'd love to know what our listeners think about the election. How about calling in to the station during our 8 P.M. talk show to discuss your opinions?

WKEK는 저녁 7시에 여러분들이 아셔야 하는 뉴스를 전해 드립니다. 우선, 주요 소식부터 다루겠습니다. 모든 투표가 집계되었고, 피터 쇼가 이제 새 시장입니다. 쇼 씨는 여기 이 도시의 재계의 선두주자입니다. 시장으로 출마하기 전에, 쇼 씨는 20년 동안 쇼 건설 회사의 최고 경영자였습니다. 쇼 씨는 지역 주민들에게 이 도시의 경제를 개선하는 데 재계에 대한 자신의 지식을 활용하겠다고 약속했습니다. 우리는 이 선거에 대해 우리 청취자들이 어떤 생각을 갖고 있는지 알고 싶습니다. 저녁 8시 우리 토크 쇼 시간에 방송국으로 전화주셔서 여러분의 의견에 대해 얘기하시는 게 어떨까요?

86. 방송은 주로 무엇에 대한 것인가?
(A) 경제 상황
(B) 회사 인수
(C) 선거 결과
(D) 완공된 공사 프로젝트   정답 (C)

87. 화자에 따르면, 피터 쇼는 어떤 분야에 경력이 있는가?
(A) 교육
(B) 상업
(C) 연예 오락
(D) 여행   정답 (B)

88. 청자들은 무엇을 하라는 초대를 받는가?
(A) 음악 신청
(B) 회원권 등록

(C) 생각 공유

(D) 경품 추첨 참여 　　　　　　　　정답 (C)

M: Hello. This is the voice mailbox of Ronald Martinson at Robinson Consulting. **(89)At Robinson Consulting, we provide our clients with the investment advice they need to make their money grow. (90)I'm going to be out of the office this week at an investment management training program.** I'll be back in the office on next Monday with knowledge to better serve you. **(91)If you need some urgent financial advice, please get in touch with Rodney Chapman, assistant supervisor.** He can be reached at extension 9548.

안녕하세요. 로빈슨 컨설팅, 로날드 마틴슨의 음성 사서함입니다. 로빈슨 컨설팅의 저희는 우리 고객들이 자금을 증식시키는 데 필요한 투자 조언을 제공해 드립니다. 이번 주는 투자 관리 연수 프로그램에 참석하느라 저는 사무실에 없을 겁니다. 여러분에게 더 잘 도움을 드릴 수 있는 지식을 가지고 다음 주 월요일에 사무실로 돌아올 것입니다. 긴급한 재정 조언이 필요하시다면, 부 책임자인 로드니 채프먼에게 연락하세요. 내선번호 9548로 그에게 연락하시면 됩니다.

89. 회사는 어떤 서비스를 제공하는가?

(A) 금융 컨설팅

(B) 웹 보안

(C) 온라인 마케팅

(D) 재산 관리 　　　　　　　　정답 (A)

90. 화자가 이번 주에 자리에 없는 이유는?

(A) 국외에 나가 있다.

(B) 총회에 참석 중이다.

(C) 직원 회의에 참석 중이다.

(D) 연수 과정에 참가 중이다. 　　　　정답 (D)

91. 청자들이 급한 조언이 필요하면 어떻게 해야 하는가?

(A) 이메일을 보낸다.

(B) 사무실을 방문한다.

(C) 다른 직원에게 전화한다.

(D) 관리자에게 휴대폰으로 전화한다. 　　정답 (C)

W: **(92)And our monthly meeting here at the Davidson Health Clinic is now over.** Oh, I need to mention one more thing. A local hospital is offering a two-day healthcare workshop. Leslie Smith will be leading the program. She's well-known in the medical industry as a leading health expert. You don't want to miss out on this program. We'd love for everyone to attend it. **(93)You can register tomorrow. Please keep in mind that lots of people know about Leslie. (94)When we meet next month, be sure to have next year's budget requests with you.**

자, 여기 데이비드슨 건강 클리닉의 월례 회의가 지금 끝났습니다. 아, 한 가지 더 말씀드려야겠습니다. 한 지역 병원이 2일간 보건 워크숍을 제공합니다. 레슬리 스미스가 그 프로그램을 진행하게 될 것입니다. 그녀는 유력

한 의료 전문가로 의료 업계에 잘 알려져 있습니다. 이 프로그램을 놓치지 마세요. 여러분 모두 이 프로그램에 참석하시면 좋겠습니다. 내일부터 등록할 수 있습니다. 수많은 사람들이 레슬리에 대해 알고 있다는 것을 명심하세요. 다음 달에 만날 때는, 내년 예산 요청서를 꼭 갖고 오십시오.

92. 청자들은 어디에서 근무하는가?

(A) 대학교

(B) 의료장비 회사

(C) 의료 시설

(D) 제약 회사 　　　　　　　　정답 (C)

93. 화자가 "수많은 사람들이 레슬리에 대해 알고 있다"고 말할 때 무엇을 함축하는가?

(A) 그녀는 더 많은 사무용품을 주문할 계획이다.

(B) 청자들은 빨리 등록할 필요가 있다.

(C) 회의 장소가 너무 작다.

(D) 그녀는 레슬리에게 당장 연락할 필요가 있다. 　정답 (B)

94. 화자는 청자들에게 무엇을 할 것을 상기시키는가?

(A) 제안서 작성

(B) 고객에게 연락

(C) 효율성 향상

(D) 서류 준비 　　　　　　　　정답 (D)

W: It's time for the local weather report. **(95)I'm pleased to say that the rain will end before the fall festival begins.** We'll have some cloudy weather, but no rain. In fact, it should be perfect fall weather. **(96)I'm looking forward to the festival because the Dingoes will be performing live.** I love that band, so I'll definitely be at the performance. **(97)And please remember that our radio station, KMSD, is giving away backstage passes.** Winners will also get the opportunity to meet the band after the concert ends. **(97)So visit our web page and enter.** You could be one of ten lucky winners.

지역 일기예보 시간입니다. 가을 축제가 시작되기 전에 비가 그친다는 것을 전하게 되어 기쁩니다. 날씨는 흐리겠지만, 비는 오지 않습니다. 사실, 완벽한 가을 날씨가 될 것입니다. 딩고스가 라이브로 공연할 것이기 때문에 저는 축제가 너무 기다려집니다. 저는 그 밴드를 너무 좋아해서 꼭 공연에 갈 것입니다. 그리고 우리 라디오 방송국 KMSD에서는 백스테이지 방문증을 드릴 것이니 잊지 마세요. 당첨자들은 또한 콘서트가 끝나고 나서 밴드를 만날 기회를 얻게 될 것입니다. 그러니 저희 웹 페이지를 방문해서 참가 신청을 하세요. 여러분도 운 좋은 10명의 당첨자들 중 한 명이 될 수도 있습니다.

일기 예보

월요일	화요일	(95)수요일	목요일	금요일
☔	☔	☁	☀	☔
비	비	(95)흐림	맑음	비

95. 그래픽을 보시오. 가을 축제는 언제 열리는가?

(A) 월요일

(B) 화요일

(C) 수요일

(D) 목요일 　　　　　　　　정답 (C)

96. 화자는 무엇 때문에 너무 신이 난다고 말하는가?
(A) 미술 전시회
(B) 음악 공연
(C) 스포츠 경기
(D) 음악에 대한 강연　　　　　　　　정답 (B)

97. 화자는 청자들에게 무엇을 할 것을 권하는가?
(A) 친구 데리고 오기
(B) 사전에 표 구매하기
(C) 방송국에 전화하기
(D) 경합에 참가 신청하기　　　　　　정답 (D)

문제 98-100번은 다음 회의 발췌 내용과 의제를 참조하시오. 영M

M: Hello, everyone. (98)Let me congratulate you on starting your first day of work here at Stephenson's. I'm Stuart Preston, and I'm the head of the HR Department. (99)Today, we'll let you know about what happens here at our camping equipment company. We would like everybody to understand how the different departments and teams work together to manufacture high-quality equipment including tents and sleeping bags we sell around the world. We were supposed to start with Jude Crow in R&D, but he's in a meeting. (100)So let's listen to the head of Sales instead.

안녕하세요, 여러분. 여기 스티븐스 회사에서의 여러분의 첫날 근무 시작을 축하드립니다. 저는 스튜어트 프레스턴이고, 인적자원부 부장입니다. 오늘 우리는 여기 캠핑장비 회사에서 어떻게 돌아가는지 알려 드리겠습니다. 우리는 여러분 모두 각기 다른 부서와 팀이 어떻게 함께 일하여 전세계 각지에서 우리가 판매하는 텐트와 침낭을 비롯한 고품질 장비들을 제조하는지 이해하시면 좋겠습니다. 연구개발부의 주드 크로우부터 시작하게 되어 있었으나, 그는 지금 회의 중에 있습니다. 그래서 대신에 영업부장 얘기부터 먼저 들어봅시다.

회의 의제	
13:45	소개
14:00	주드 크로우 – 연구개발 부장
14:15	엘리자베스 딘 – 인적자원부 총괄
14:30	(100)앤디 톰슨 – 영업 부장
14:45	윌마 패터슨 – 최고 경영자

98. 청자들은 누구일 것 같은가?
(A) 잠재 투자자
(B) 해외 고객
(C) 관리자
(D) 신입 사원　　　　　　　　　　정답 (D)

99. 회사는 어떤 종류의 제품을 만드는가?
(A) 캠핑 장비
(B) 차량
(C) 제약
(D) 스포츠 용품　　　　　　　　　정답 (A)

100. 그래픽을 보시오. 뒤이어 누가 연설을 하겠는가?
(A) 주드 크로우
(B) 엘리자베스 딘
(C) 앤디 톰슨
(D) 윌마 패터슨　　　　　　　　　정답 (C)

101. 국내 인기 있는 가수 중 한 명인 제임스 왓슨은 코코 보석회사가 다가오는 광고 캠페인에서 그의 이름을 사용하는 것을 허용하는 데 동의했다.　정답 (B)

102. 벨라 커뮤니케이션 회사는 지역 주민들에게 인터넷과 휴대 전화 서비스 둘 다 제공한다.　정답 (C)

103. 그 회사는 수년간 사람들이 광고 캠페인을 더 효율적으로 설계하도록 교육하는 데 있어 선도적인 기업이었다.　정답 (D)

104. 인사과에 있는 사무용 책상 중 일부는 브라이언과 해리 둘이서만 운반하기에는 너무 무겁다.　정답 (D)

105. 우리 회사는 원안대로 중국에 있는 두 은행의 합병을 추진하기로 결정했다.　정답 (B)

106. 신형 데스크톱 컴퓨터에는 최신 워드프로세서 소프트웨어와 고해상도 스크린이 탑재되어 있다.　정답 (C)

107. 2주간의 뮤지컬 추가 공연으로 인해, 이제 뮤지컬 〈로맨스 위드 캣츠〉는 우리 극장에서 11월 14일까지 공연될 것이다.　정답 (A)

108. 많은 회사들이 유럽 국가에서의 시장 점유율을 높이려는 희망으로 유럽 국가들과의 새로운 자유 무역 협정을 간절히 기다려왔다.　정답 (D)

109. 젠킨스 씨는 수출된 냉동 식품이 20개국의 식품 안전법을 준수하고 있다고 어제 말했다.　정답 (A)

110. 자료에 따르면, 지난 10년 간 화산 활동으로 인해 초래된 지진의 횟수가 상당히 증가해왔다.　정답 (B)

111. 깨끗하고 시각적으로 매력적인 근무 환경이 직원의 성과와 기분에 지대한 영향을 미칠 수 있다.　정답 (A)

112. 그 비행기의 일부 승객들은 국제 공항에 도착하자마자 아파서 즉시 병원에 입원했다.　정답 (C)

113. 우리 데이터는 분석과 피드백을 위해 중앙 데이터 저장소로 안전하게 전송되어야 한다는 점을 주지하시기 바랍니다.　정답 (A)

114. 귀하가 예약된 진료 예약을 지키지 못하신다면, 최소 이틀 전에 저희에게 알려 주십시오.　정답 (C)

115. 귀하의 사무용 건물이 화재 훈련과 안전 검사 의무로부터 면제되는지 확인하기 위해 서식을 작성해 주십시오.　정답 (B)

116. 저희 회사의 고객 서비스 담당자 중 한 명에게 전화를 걸어 문의할 때는, 사전에 질문 목록을 준비해 두는 것이 더 좋을 것입니다.　정답 (B)

117. 원 인터내셔널의 투자는 국내 금융 산업에 대한 단일 최대 규모 해외 직접 투자이다.　정답 (D)

118. 검증이 가능한 사실 및 증거와 함께, 발표는 논리적이고 분석적인 방식으로 실시되었다.　정답 (B)

119. 맥도날드 씨는 고작 두 달 전에 채용되었지만, 그럼에도 불구하고 회사를 위한 몇몇 효과적인 영업 전략들을 고안했다.　정답 (C)

120. 우리 회사 방침에 따르면, 마지막에 퇴근하는 사람이 누구든 사무실 내 모든 등을 소등하고 문을 잠가야 하는 책임이 있다. 　　　정답 (D)

121. 많은 직장인들이 업무와 일상에서 지치거나 스트레스를 받을 때마다 에너지 음료를 남용하는 것으로 보인다. 　　　정답 (B)

122. 그 잡지는 어느 누구든 예상했던 것보다 훨씬 더 많은 호를 판매하며 놀라운 성공을 거두었으나, 몇 년 사이에 그들의 판매 부수는 급격하게 하락했다. 　　　정답 (B)

123. 아시아의 상업용 웹사이트에 발주된 주문들은 대개 베트남에 있는 그들의 창고에 있는 상품으로 처리된다. 　　　정답 (A)

124. 만약 회사의 순이익이 이사회의 예상을 초과한다면, 우리 직원은 올해 말에 상당한 상여금을 받게 될 것이다. 　　　정답 (A)

125. 스타파크 스포츠 회사는 모두가 신고 싶어 하는 다양한 운동화를 디자인하고 생산하는 데 전념하고 있다. 　　　정답 (A)

126. 우리 브랜드가 현재처럼 인기가 좋은 상태를 유지하기 위해서는, 고품질의 콘텐츠가 인터넷에서 편리한 형태로 제공될 필요가 있다. 　　　정답 (D)

127. 높은 파도와 악천후에도 불구하고, 비행기에 탑승한 모든 승객들은 성공적으로 구조되었다. 　　　정답 (A)

128. 작은 텃밭을 만드는 것이 그리 어렵지 않은데도 불구하고, 도시 사람들은 자신들의 텃밭을 가꾸는 것에 대해 거의 생각하지 않는다. 　　　정답 (D)

129. 간혹, 우리 직원 대부분은 국경일 전에 평소보다 이른 퇴근이 허용된다. 　　　정답 (C)

130. 최근 몇 년간 전자제품의 소비가 너무 많이 증가하여 오늘날 이것은 환경적으로 가장 문제가 많은 제품군 중 하나를 대표한다. 　　　정답 (B)

Part 6

문제 131-134번은 다음 정보를 참조하시오.

> **벨라 항공사에 자주 묻는 질문**
>
> 만약 나의 벨라 항공편에 대한 이메일 확인서를 받지 못했다면요?
>
> <u>귀하의 항공편 정보는 고객님이 제공하신 이메일 주소로 발송될 것입니다.</u> 벨라 항공사는 예약 후 승객에게 이메일 확인서를 보내 드리는 데 통상 최대 3시간이 걸립니다. 예약 후에도 이메일 확인서를 받지 못한 경우, 고객님의 결제가 제대로 되었는지 확인하세요. 결제가 신용 카드 내역에 나타나지 않는 경우, 고객님의 항공권 예약이 제대로 처리되지 않았을 수 있습니다.
>
> 이런 경우, 저희가 그 문제를 조사할 수 있도록 692-9815로 전화 주십시오. 이 번호로 하는 전화는 벨라 항공사에서 비용이 지불되므로, 저희 고객님은 무료로 저희에게 연락하실 수 있습니다.

131. (A) 휴대 전화는 비행 중에는 어느 때라도 사용이 불가합니다.
(B) 거래 내역이 잘못 게시되었다면 저희가 귀하의 계정을 정정해 드리겠습니다.
(C) 귀하의 항공편 정보는 고객님이 제공하신 이메일 주소로 발송될 것입니다.
(D) 구입 주문서와 확인 번호를 출력된 자료로 보관해 주세요. 　　　정답 (C)

132. 　　　정답 (B)

133. 　　　정답 (B)

134. 　　　정답 (D)

문제 135-138번은 다음 광고를 참조하시오.

> **럭키 7 마트**
> "오직 신선함만을!"
> 선데일 애비뉴 5801번지
> 베이커스필드, 캘리포니아 93307
>
> 럭키 7 마트는 사계절 내내 구할 수 있는 가장 신선한 과일과 채소로 가득합니다!
>
> 캘리포니아 주, 애리조나 주, 플로리다 주 그리고 그 외 다른 지역에서 오는 우리 농산물은 굉장히 신선합니다! 입수 가능할 때 럭키 7 마트는 인근 지역 농부들이 재배하는 신선한 지역 농산물을 여러분의 가족에게 제공합니다.
>
> 럭키 7 마트는 여러분이 좋아하실 가격의 상품들을 보유하고 있습니다! 아주 다양한 점심 식사용 육류와 주문에 따라 바로 얇은 조각으로 갓 자른 치즈들을 판매하고 있습니다! 저희는 오직 최고 품질의 쇠고기와 A등급의 닭고기, A등급의 신선한 돼지고기, 수제 훈제 햄, 그리고 다진 고기만을 취급합니다. 여러분은 매일 제공되는 저렴한 가격, 세일 품목, 그리고 신상품들 <u>이 마음에 드실 것입니다.</u>
>
> 만약 쇼핑 중에 도움이 필요하시다면, 매장 직원에게 요청하세요. 그들이 해당 제품이 있는 곳으로 여러분을 기꺼이 안내해 드릴 것입니다.

135. 　　　정답 (C)

136. 　　　정답 (A)

137. 　　　정답 (A)

138. (A) 다가오는 특별 판촉 행사에 대해 알아보세요.
(B) 고객 후기들은 꾸준하게 긍정적이었습니다.
(C) 특히 빠르게 성장하는 시장에서 하는 회사들의 경쟁은 매우 치열할 수 있습니다.
(D) 여러분은 매일 제공되는 저렴한 가격, 세일 품목, 그리고 신상품들이 마음에 드실 것입니다. 　　　정답 (D)

문제 139-142번은 다음 이메일을 참조하시오.

> 수신: 샬롯 파커 〈cp@hdmail.com〉
> 발신: 리사 프레스턴 〈lpreston@nybc.com〉
> 제목: 귀하의 지원
> 날짜: 2월 14일
>
> 파커 씨에게,
>
> 행정 보조직 직에 지원해 주셔서 감사합니다. 저희 회사에 입사하려는 귀하의 관심에 대단히 감사드립니다. <u>귀하가 지원한 자리는 더 이상 공석이 아닙니다.</u> 그러나 저희 인사팀은 귀하의 이력서를 매우 관심 있게 읽었습니다. 귀하의 전문 경력과 학력이 매우 인상적이며, 따라서 귀하는 저희 회사에 우수한 충원 대상이 될 것입니다.
>
> 이의가 없으시다면, 저희는 귀하의 이력서를 파일로 보관해 두었다가 적당한 자리가 나는 대로 귀하에게 연락드리겠습니다.

그 동안 귀하의 구직 활동이 잘 되기를 바랍니다.

리사 프레스턴 드림
인사부장
뉴욕 비즈니스 컨설팅

139. 정답 (C)

140. (A) 저희는 귀하의 취업 면접 결과를 우려하고 있습니다.
(B) 귀하가 지원한 자리는 더 이상 공석이 아닙니다.
(C) 귀하는 행정 보조원이 되기에 자격이 충분합니다.
(D) 저희 채용 담당자들은 충원을 하기 위해 많은 지원서를 검토해야 합니다.
정답 (B)

141. 정답 (D)

142. 정답 (B)

문제 143-146번은 다음 편지를 참조하시오.

미라맥스 홈 임프루브먼트
피치트리 가 265번지
애틀랜타, 조지아 주 30303

6월 20일
클래식 세이드 주식회사
스콧 가 401번지
애틀랜타, 조지아 주 30303

관계자 분께:

우리는 어제 1갤런짜리 플로랄 화이트 가정용 페인트 40통을 수령했습니다만, 이는 저희가 귀사에 주문한 제품이 아닙니다. 따라서 저희는 메릴랜드에 있는 귀사의 록스빌 공장으로 그것들을 반품합니다.

귀하의 제품 카탈로그 번호 SF-909인 1파인트짜리 스노우플레이크 가정용 페인트 50통을 요청한 6월 12일자 구매 주문서 BK365020을 참조하십시오. 가능한 한 빨리 1-800-521-6313번의 팩스로 이 서신의 접수 및 요청의 이행을 확인해 주시기 바랍니다.

아울러, 저희가 고객의 요구를 신속하게 충족할 수 있도록 이 주문을 서둘러 처리해 주십시오.

오로라 레인 드림
조달 부장
미라맥스 홈 임프루브먼트

143. (A) 저희는 귀가 요청한 견적을 기꺼이 제공해 드리고자 합니다.
(B) 안타깝게도, 고객은 마감일이 지켜지지 못한 점에 대해 실망감을 표현했습니다.
(C) 따라서 저희는 메릴랜드에 있는 귀사의 록스빌 공장으로 그것들을 반품합니다.
(D) 귀사의 페인트 제품은 대상을 보호하거나 질감을 제공하는 데 가장 널리 사용됩니다.
정답 (C)

144. 정답 (B)

145. 정답 (B)

146. 정답 (D)

Part 7

문제 147-148번은 다음 양식을 참조하시오.

이스트 빌리지 주식회사
109 피츠 가, 도버, 델라웨어 주, 19028

주문일: 6월 5일

주문 번호:	0194570
(147)고객 이름:	**안젤라 로즈**
배송지:	42 채리티 드라이브, 하이랜드 에이커스 델라웨어 주, 19010
배송 날짜 및 시간:	6월 9일, 오후 12시
(148D)반납 날짜 및 시간:	6월 10일, 오전 10시

물품	수량	가격
(147)컬러 연회 식기 세트(대여)	2	24달러
꽃 장식 – 흰색과 노란색(대여)	5	20달러
접이식 연회 테이블 및 의자 세트(대여)	2	40달러
파티용 텐트(대여)	2	50달러
(148C)배송 및 세팅		50달러
합계		184달러

- (148B)기업 고객들에게는 10% 할인을 해드립니다.
- 픽업 비용은 배송 및 세팅 비용에 포함되어 있습니다.
- (148D)모든 물건들은 위에 명시된 반납 시간까지 픽업 준비가 되어 있어야 합니다.

147. 로즈 씨에 대해 시사되어 있는 것은 무엇인가?
(A) 피츠 가에 거주한다.
(B) 기업 고객이다.
(C) 한 행사를 준비하고 있다.
(D) 배송된 물건들을 오전에 사용할 것이다. 정답 (C)

148. 이스트 빌리지 주식회사에 대하여 나타나 있지 않은 것은 무엇인가?
(A) 늦은 반납에 대해 서비스 요금의 10%를 더 부과한다.
(B) 특정 고객들에게 할인을 제공한다.
(C) 고객들에게 배송비를 부과한다.
(D) 6월 10일에 대여된 물품들을 픽업할 것이다. 정답 (A)

문제 149-150번은 다음 문자 메시지를 참조하시오.

데이비드 로버츠 [오전 9시 11분]
칼라, (149)제 임무 마감일이 이틀 뒤인데, 아직 많이 남았어요.

칼라 존스 [오전 9시 12분]
도움이 좀 필요하세요?

데이비드 로버츠 [오전 9시 13분]
그러면 아주 좋을 것 같아요. (150)오늘 오전에 만날 수 있어요?

칼라 존스 [오전 9시 14분]
(150)점심 후가 어때요?

데이비드 로버츠 [오전 9시 15분]
좋아요. 1시 30분에 당신 사무실로 갈게요. 제가 완료한 작업을 갖고 갈게요. 어떻게 진행해야 할지 아이디어를 주시면 고맙겠어요.

칼라 존스 [오전 9시 16분]
혹시 도움이 더 필요하시면 오늘 밤 늦게까지 있어도 괜찮아요. 제 고객이 방금 저녁 모임을 취소했어요.

149. 로버츠 씨의 문제는 무엇인가?

(A) 그는 새로운 프로젝트를 위한 더 많은 아이디어가 필요하다.

(B) 그는 오늘 저녁까지 프로젝트를 완료해야 한다.

(C) 그의 고객이 방금 회의를 취소했다.

(D) 그는 아직 작업을 끝내지 못했다.   정답 (D)

150. 오전 9시 14분에, 존스 씨가 "점심 후가 어때요?"라고 쓰는 이유는?

(A) 예약을 변경하기 위해

(B) 제안을 거절하기 위해

(C) 사과하기 위해

(D) 위치를 제안하기 위해   정답 (B)

문제 151-153번은 다음 공고를 참조하시오.

제 2회 브라운 디자인 대회

선도적인 가정 용품 제조업체인 브라운 주식회사는 제 2회 브라운 디자인 대회를 열게 되어 기쁩니다. 올해의 디자인 출품작은 우리 회사 역사상 처음으로 개발하려고 하는 음식물 저장 용기가 될 것입니다.

여러 가지 미술 재료들을 사용한 초안이나 스케치들을 포함한 다양한 형태의 출품작을 환영합니다. www.browninc.com에서 브라운 주식회사의 이전 제품 디자인들을 참조하십시오. (151)**월터 조에 의해 디자인된 휴대용 찻주전자는 훌륭한 예시가 되는데, 이것이 브라운 주식회사의 이전 모든 판매 기록을 깬 작년 브라운 디자인 대회의 우승 디자인이기 때문입니다.**

올해 우승 출품작은 내년에 브라운 주식회사의 공식적인 제품으로 선정되어 시장에 출시될 것입니다. 또한, (152D)**1등 우승자는 정규직 고용 제의를 받을 것입니다.** (152B)**모든 수상자들은 도버의 본사에서 8월 20일에 예정이 된 시상식에 초대될 것입니다.** 상은 브라운 주식회사의 디자인 이사들에 의하여 수여될 것입니다.

또한, 수상자들은 총 6,000달러의 상금을 받게 될 것입니다.

(152A)**1등 상: 3,000달러**

2등 상: 2,000달러

3등 상: 1,000달러

만약 참가에 관심이 있으시면 저희 웹사이트 www.browninc.com/application을 방문해 제출을 위한 상세 지침을 내려받고 이메일로 출품작을 보내세요. 접수는 7월 1일에 시작되며, (153)**제출 마감일은 7월 31일입니다.**

---

151. 브라운 주식회사에 대해 시사되어 있는 것은 무엇인가?

(A) 식품 용기만 판매한다.

(B) 2년 동안 사업을 해 왔다.

(C) 휴대용 찻주전자가 고객들에게 인기 있었다.

(D) 이 대회의 시상식이 내년에 열릴 것이다.   정답 (C)

152. 1등 수상자에게 제공되지 않을 것은 무엇인가?

(A) 현금 3,000달러

(B) 공식 행사로의 초대

(C) 도버 행 항공권

(D) 브라운 주식회사에서의 정규직   정답 (C)

153. 신청자에 대해 나타나 있는 것은 무엇인가?

(A) 참가비를 요구한다.

(B) 7월 31일까지이다.

(C) 이사진에 의해 평가될 것이다.

(D) 우편으로 제출되어야 한다.   정답 (B)

문제 154-156번은 다음 이메일을 참조하시오.

수신: 존 베이커 〈jbaker@easymail.com〉

발신: 앰버 리 〈alee@hotelconcord.com〉

날짜: 9월 20일

제목: (155)**답장: 지난번 저의 방문에 관하여**

베이커 씨께,

먼저 콩코드 호텔 뉴올리언스를 최근 방문해 주신 것에 대해 감사드리고 싶습니다. 귀하께 서비스를 제공한 것은 저희에게 진심으로 영광이었습니다.

(155)**저희는 귀하의 문의를 받았습니다.** (154)**콩코드 호텔를 대표하여, 부디 지난주 불쾌한 저희 호텔 숙박에 대하여 저의 진심어린 사과를 받아 주시기 바랍니다. 예약 시스템에서 알 수 없는 오류가 발생하였고, 본래 예약하셨던 방을 제공해 드리지 못한 것에 대하여 사과드립니다.**

(154)**이번 불편에 대해 보상해 드리기 위하여,** (156)**미국 내의 어느 콩코드 호텔의 지점에서든 사용하실 수 있는 200달러 상품권을 제공하고자 합니다.** 저희의 공식 웹사이트인 www.hotelconcord.com에서 상품권을 내려받으실 수 있습니다.

감사드리며, 귀하를 다시 뵐 수 있기를 바랍니다.

앰버 리 드림

매니저, 콩코드 호텔 뉴올리언스

---

154. 이메일의 주요 목적은 무엇인가?

(A) 호텔 방문에 대하여 고객에게 감사하기 위한 것

(B) 예약 초과에 대해 변명하기 위한 것

(C) 예약을 확인하기 위한 것

(D) 최근의 실수를 보상하기 위한 것   정답 (D)

155. 베이커 씨에 대해 함축되어 있는 것은 무엇인가?

(A) 가족과 함께 콩코드 호텔을 방문했다.

(B) 최근에 콩코드 호텔에 이메일을 썼다.

(C) 뉴올리언스에 산다.

(D) 방에 대해 200달러를 지불했다.   정답 (B)

156. 이메일에 따르면, 콩코드 호텔에 대해 나타나 있는 것은 무엇인가?

(A) 웹사이트를 개설할 것이다.

(B) 방이 현재 모두 예약되었다.

(C) 두 개 이상의 지점이 있다.

(D) 처음 방문한 모든 고객들에게 쿠폰을 준다.   정답 (C)

문제 157-158번은 다음 쿠폰을 참조하시오.

샘의 피자

(157)**샘의 피자의 5주년을 기념**하여, 고객들에게 7월 내내 주중에 특별 할인 혜택을 제공합니다. 아래 쿠폰을 갖고 오셔서 특별한 가격에 맛있는 피자를 즐기세요.

쿠폰

3달러 할인 모든 스페셜 피자	〈무료〉 페퍼로니 롤 2개 또는 선택하시는 토핑 2종류 *라지 피자 구매시 이용 가능*
(158)**수요일 & 목요일** 대박 혜택 라지 치즈 피자 7.99달러 두 판 15달러	한 판을 사고 한 판을 무료로 받으세요 모든 라지 피자

– (158)모든 쿠폰들은 "포장" 전용입니다.

– 각 주문당, 한 개의 쿠폰만 사용 가능합니다.

157. 샘의 피자에 대해 추론될 수 있는 것은 무엇인가?

(A) 5년 동안 사업을 해 왔다.

(B) 주말에는 문을 닫는다.

(C) 고객들은 토핑 선택권이 없다.

(D) 배달 서비스를 제공하지 않는다. 정답 (A)

158. 고객이 라지 치즈 피자 두 판을 15달러에 사기 위해서 무엇을 해야 하는가?

(A) 현금으로 지불하기

(B) 7월의 목요일에 레스토랑에서 식사하기

(C) 특정한 날짜에 쿠폰 사용하기

(D) 정가 피자 한 판 더 구매하기 정답 (C)

문제 159–161번은 다음 광고를 참조하시오.

트리 하우스 솔루션

(159)흰개미와 빈대 같은 가정 해충으로 시달리고 계신가요? 트리 하우스 솔루션이 귀하의 집을 위한 맞춤형 3단계의 박멸 솔루션으로 곤충 문제를 해결해 드릴 수 있습니다.

1. 탐지
(161A)연간 10시간의 교육을 받아 잘 훈련된 검사관들이 (161B)귀하와 상담 후에 귀하의 집을 주의 깊게 검사하기 시작할 것입니다. 그 다음, 우리는 최대 보호를 위해 귀하의 고유 상황에 기반한 최적의 처리법을 처방할 것입니다.

2. 처리
탐지 이후, 해충 방제 처리제를 3회 사용함으로써 효율적이고 신속히 해충을 박멸합니다. (161D)무독성이며 환경적으로 안전한 액체와 거품으로 된 두 종류의 약제를 사용합니다. 액체 약제는 집의 토대에 사용되고, 거품 약제는 외부 벽과 파이프 같은 표면에 사용됩니다.

3. 관리
(160)저희 관리 서비스는 진행 중인 보호 효과를 확실하게 합니다. 2년 동안 분기별로 집을 방문하고 필요하다면 추가적인 약제를 사용합니다.

159. 무엇이 광고되고 있는 것 같은가?

(A) 집 청소 서비스

(B) 벌레 박멸 서비스

(C) 친환경 인테리어 디자인

(D) 정원 관리 서비스 정답 (B)

160. 트리 하우스 솔루션의 직원이 관리를 위하여 얼마나 자주 방문하는가?

(A) 1년에 한 번

(B) 1년에 두 번

(C) 1년에 세 번

(D) 1년에 네 번 정답 (D)

161. 트리 하우스 솔루션의 직원들에 대해 나타나 있지 않은 것은 무엇인가?

(A) 연례 교육을 받아야 한다.

(B) 원인 발견 전에 고객들과 증상에 대하여 의논한다.

(C) 계약을 갱신하는 고객들에게 약제 키트를 준다.

(D) 환경에 거의 해가 되지 않는 약제를 사용한다. 정답 (C)

문제 162–164번은 다음 이메일을 참조하시오.

수신: 제시카 시스네로스 (jcisneros@sevelia.com)
발신: 마크 데몬트 (mdemont@sku.edu)
날짜: 4월 15일
제목: 어제 저녁

시스네로스 씨께,

(163)세벨리아의 개업일 저녁에 처음 방문한 후로 저는 열혈 팬이 되었습니다. 저는 작은 지역 레스토랑이 훌륭한 서비스와 함께 이렇게 맛있는 태국 음식을 제공할 수 있다는 것을 믿을 수 없었습니다. 그 이후로, 저는 자주 세벨리아에 방문했고, (164)어제 저녁 전까지는 매번 즐거운 시간을 보냈습니다.

(162)저희는 두 개의 주요리를 주문했지만, 한 개만 제공받았습니다. 비록 우리는 이 실수에 대해 매우 화가 났지만, 기다릴 시간이 없어서 그 요리를 나눠 먹고 나서기로 결정했습니다. 식사를 마친 후, 신용 카드로 지불했는데, 청구서나 영수증을 확인하지는 않았습니다. 하지만, 나중에 영수증을 확인해 보니, 제게 한 개가 아닌 두 개의 주요리에 대해 청구했다는 것을 알게 되었습니다.

(163)귀 식당에서 식사했던 지난 2년 동안 제가 받았던 것 중 가장 실망스러운 서비스였습니다. 이번 경험 때문에, 앞으로 다시 귀 식당에 갈지 말지 여부를 고려해야겠습니다. 저는 이 문제에 대한 귀하의 즉각적인 조치를 요구합니다.

감사합니다.

마크 데몬트

162. 이메일의 목적은 무엇인가?

(A) 지역 레스토랑을 추천하기 위한 것

(B) 금전적 보상을 요구하기 위한 것

(C) 인상된 식사 가격에 대해 불평하기 위한 것

(D) 좋지 않은 서비스에 대해 알리기 위한 것 정답 (D)

163. 세벨리아에 대해 나타나 있는 것은 무엇인가?

(A) 큰 체인점이다.

(B) 많은 고객들을 보유하고 있지 않다.

(C) 약 2년 동안 영업을 해왔다.

(D) 최근에 새 직원을 고용했다. 정답 (C)

164. [1], [2], [3] 그리고 [4]로 표시된 곳 중에, 아래 문장이 들어가기에 가장 적절한 곳은?

"어제 저녁, 제 아내와 저는 저녁을 먹으러 귀 레스토랑에 갔습니다."

(A) [1]

(B) [2]

(C) [3]

(D) [4] 정답 (B)

문제 165–167번은 다음 기사를 참조하시오.

먼지 쌓인 구 시청이 다시 태어나다

6월 17일

바이 가에 위치한 오래된 시청은 지난 8개월간 많은 궁금증과 기대의 대상이 되어 왔다. 마침내, 그 건물은 인디애나폴리스 시립 미술관이라는 새로운 이름 아래에 7월 1일 밤에 대중에게 선보이게 될 것이다.

이 도시의 상징인 스파이럴 타워를 창조해낸 건축가 이안 켄싱턴이 이 미술관을 디자인하는 책임을 맡았다. 그는 그 공간을 친환경적으로 만들기 위해 도시 전력 시스템의 기술자인 도리안 웹스터와 긴밀하게 협력했다. 미술관을 조각 정원과 이어주는 두 개의 부속 건물이 추가되었다. 조각상의 모습을 한 풍차와 태양 전지판들이 미술관 전체를 돌아가게 할 만큼 충분한 전기를 생산할 것이다.

(165)개조 프로젝트는 사실 건축가 본인에 의해 시작되었다. 시 의회에 제안서를 제출한 후, 그는 또한 프로젝트에 상당한 액수의 자금을 기부했다. "제가 켄싱턴 씨가 이 프로젝트를 가능하게 했다고 말할 때, 그것은 과장이 아닙니다"라고 (166)인니애나폴리스의 시장, 케이틀린 트리스탄은 말했다. "그는 자선 모금 만찬을 주최하면서 필요한 개조 비용의 대부분의 금액을 모았습니다. 제가 한 것은 고작 그의 제안을 수락한 것이었습니다."

미술관은 유명한 사진작가, 에이미 니진스키의 전시회와 함께 개관할 것이다. (167)그녀는 그날 저녁 시 의회를 대신해서 켄싱턴 씨에게 감사 연설을 할 것이다.

미술관은 월요일부터 금요일 오전 9시부터 오후 7시까지 문을 열 것이다. 시 미술관에 대한 더 많은 정보를 위해서는 웹사이트 www.icma.org를 방문하면 된다.

165. 켄싱턴 씨는 미술관에 어떻게 기여했는가?
(A) 그의 사유지가 공사 현장으로 사용되는 것을 허용함으로써
(B) 예산이 어떻게 사용되어야 하는지 계획함으로써
(C) 시청 건물을 개조하자는 아이디어를 냄으로써
(D) 개관식을 준비함으로써　　　　　　　　정답 (C)

166. 트리스탄 씨는 누구일 것 같은가?
(A) 유명한 사진작가
(B) 박물관 큐레이터
(C) 시 공무원
(D) 전문 엔지니어　　　　　　　　　　　정답 (C)

167. 개관식에 대해 진술된 것은 무엇인가?
(A) 자선 모금 만찬이 이어질 것이다.
(B) 월요일에 열릴 것이다.
(C) 초대받은 사람만 올 수 있는 행사이다.
(D) 공식 연설을 포함할 것이다.　　　　　정답 (D)

문제 168-171번은 다음 온라인 채팅 토론을 참조하시오.

테레사 하퍼　　　　　　　　　　　[오전 10시 48분]
(168)오늘로 예정된 브레인스토밍 시간을 잊지 마세요. 장소가 453호로 바뀌었지만, 3시에 그대로 열릴 거예요.

케이트 마틴　　　　　　　　　　　[오전 10시 50분]
저는 거기에 제시간에 가지 못할 거예요. (169)던칸 주식회사에서의 제 회의가 2시 30분이나 끝나기로 되어 있어요. (171)제가 모두를 위한 다과를 갖고 갈까요?

테레사 하퍼　　　　　　　　　　　[오전 10시 51분]
(171)왜 안 되겠어요? 아, 여러분, 제가 오늘 아침에 이메일로 보낸 정보를 프린트해서 갖고 오시는 것을 잊지 마세요.

대릴 월트립　　　　　　　　　　　[오전 10시 52분]
받은 편지함을 보고 있는데, 당신에게서 온 게 아무것도 없어요.

에릭 리드　　　　　　　　　　　　[오전 10시 53분]
저도 그래요.

테레사 하퍼　　　　　　　　　　　[오전 10시 55분]
정말요? 제가 깜빡하고 그것을 안 보냈나 봐요. 지금 바로 모두에게 이메일로 보낼게요.

에릭 리드　　　　　　　　　　　　[오전 10시 56분]
알았어요. 고마워요.

대릴 월트립　　　　　　　　　　　[오전 10시 57분]
(170)회의에 대한 만반의 준비가 되도록 점심 시간에 읽을게요.

테레사 하퍼　　　　　　　　　　　[오전 10시 59분]
감사합니다. 여러분. 우리는 정말 이번 계약을 꼭 따내야 하는데, (168)우리 제안서에 대해 창의적인 아이디어를 내셨으면 합니다. 이번 주말로 예정되어 있어요.

168. 하퍼 씨가 작성자들을 회의에 초대하는 이유는?
(A) 설문조사 결과를 검토하기 위해
(B) 최근 제안을 고려하기 위해
(C) 계약 조건을 검토하기 위해
(D) 새로운 아이디어를 생각해내기 위해　　정답 (D)

169. 마틴 씨가 회의에 늦게 오는 이유는?
(A) 그녀는 아직 회의를 준비하지 않았다.
(B) 그녀는 작업 제안서를 완성해야 한다.
(C) 그녀는 비즈니스 회의에 참석해야 한다.
(D) 그녀는 그녀의 상사와 만날 것이다.　　정답 (C)

170. 월트립 씨는 무엇을 하겠다고 내비치는가?
(A) 정보 읽기
(B) 모두를 위해 문서 인쇄하기
(C) 회의실 준비하기
(D) 그의 동료들에게 회의에 대해 알리기　정답 (A)

171. 오전 10시 51분에, 하퍼 씨가 "왜 안 되겠어요?"라고 쓰는 이유는?
(A) 마틴 씨의 제안에 의문을 제기하기 위해
(B) 누구든 회의에 늦게 참석하는 것을 허용하지 않기 위해
(C) 회의에서 음식과 음료수를 먹는 것에 동의하기 위해
(D) 회의 시간 변경 요청을 승인하기 위해　　정답 (C)

문제 172-175번은 다음 기사를 참조하시오.

도쿄 데일리

(172)"저는 이것이 정말로 저에게 일어나고 있다고 여전히 믿지 못하겠습니다"라고 사쿠타로 기모토가 말했다. 겨우 16세밖에 되지 않았을 때, 기모토 씨는 그의 부모님과 함께 일본 도쿄에서 미국으로 이주했다. "제가 처음 뉴욕에 왔을 때, 저는 매우 외로웠습니다. 모든 것이 새로웠고 혼란스러웠기 때문에, 저는 학교가 끝난 후 대부분의 시간을 혼자 보냈습니다. 저의 지루함을 덜 수 있었던 단 하나의 방법은 집에서 요리를 하며 시간을 보내는 것이었습니다."

20세가 되었을 때, 기모토 씨는 대학에 진학하는 대신, 보스턴에 본사를 둔 이탈리아 식당인 찰리스에서 주방 직원으로 일하기 시작했다. 뛰어난 능력과 노력을 인정받아, 그는 고작 2년 만에 수석 주방장으로 승진했다. 거기서 그는 주방 직원을 관리하는 것과 다양한 이탈리아 음식을 요리하는 것을 배웠다. 주방장으로서 명성을 얻으면서, 기모토 씨는 자신의 식당을 여는 것을 고려하기 시작했다. 그곳에서 (173)수석 주방장으로서 3년 더 일한 후, 그는 찰리스를 떠나 고향으로 돌아갔고 일본과 이탈리아 퓨전 요리를 전문으로 하는 이랏샤이 이탈리아라는 이름의 작은 식당을 개업했다. (172)이 식당은 곧 그 지역의 상당한 관심을 얻었고 개업한 지 고작 1년만에 그 지역에서 가장 인기 있는 식당 중 하나가 되었다.

(175)식당은 이미 보수를 하고 두 번 확장했지만, 여전히 고객들의 수요를 충족하기 위하여 더 많은 공간이 필요하다. (174)사실, 이랏샤이 이탈리아의 두 번째 지점이 다음 주말에 일본 요코하마에서 개점할 것이다. "또 다른 식당을 개업하게 되어 몹시 흥분됩니다. 저에게 주어진 기회에 매우 감사하며, 지역 주민들에게 고급의 일본-이탈리아 음식을 제공하는 데 모든 노력을 기울일 것입니다"라고 기모토 씨는 말했다.

172. 기사에서 주로 논의하고 있는 것은 무엇인가?

    (A) 한 인물의 업적

    (B) 지역 사업체의 성공에 대한 요구 조건

    (C) 한 지역에서의 식사 경향

    (D) 식당을 개업할 때의 성공적인 방법　　　　정답 (A)

173. 자신의 식당을 열기 바로 전에 기모토 씨의 직업은 무엇이었는가?

    (A) 식당의 주방 직원

    (B) 찰리스의 주인

    (C) 대학교 학생

    (D) 지역 사업체의 관리자　　　　정답 (A)

174. 기사에 따르면, 기모토 씨는 곧 무엇을 할 것인가?

    (A) 더 많은 직원 채용하기

    (B) 기존 식당 이전하기

    (C) 또 다른 식당 시작하기

    (D) 다른 분야의 사업에 투자하기　　　　정답 (C)

175. [1], [2], [3] 그리고 [4]로 표시된 곳 중에, 아래 문장이 들어가기에 가장 적절한 곳은?

"기모토 씨의 식당은 규모가 커지고 있다."

    (A) [1]

    (B) [2]

    (C) [3]

    (D) [4]　　　　정답 (C)

문제 176-180번은 다음 영수증과 설문조사를 참조하시오.

---

(176)매지컬 인텔리전스

(176)우리가 고칠 수 없는 건 없습니다, 그러니 저희를 믿으세요!

(177)지점 위치:

■ 맨체스터　　　□ 런던　　　□ 브래드포드

(178)방문 및 픽업 날짜: 7월 6일

(179)작업 완료 날짜: 7월 22일　　　　서비스 번호: CR7902

고객 정보	서비스 정보
이름: 스티브 잭슨	품목: 세탁기
주소: 134 리지 애비뉴, 맨체스터	상표: 셜랏
연락처: 161-555-2267	모델: S3

서비스 내역	요금
• (176)세탁기 누수: 문 마개와 펌프 교체	65파운드
• 방문 및 픽업 서비스	15파운드
• 배송 및 설치비	12파운드
소계	92파운드
세금	9.20파운드
합계	101.20파운드

지불 받은 날짜	7월 22일
지불 방식	현금

(179)저희는 특히 서비스의 속도를 매우 중요시하며, 따라서 수리가 완료되고 댁으로 다시 갖다드리는 데 원래 예정되었던 시간보다 더 오래 걸리면 모든 서비스 금액의 30%를 환불해 드리겠습니다. 저희 기사가 제품을 픽업할 때 드렸던 설문조사지에 과정이 걸린 총 시간을 표시해 주십시오.

매지컬 인텔리전스

매지컬 인텔리전스를 선택해 주셔서 감사합니다! 부디 시간을 조금 내셔서 서비스를 개선하고 다음에 더 잘 모실 수 있도록 아래 설문조사를 작성해주십시오.

고객 이름	(178)스티브 잭슨
수령 날짜	(179)7월 22일
서비스 번호	CR7902
수리 기사	(178)윌리엄 루크

다음의 항목에 대한 만족도를 표시해 주십시오.

	매우 훌륭	좋음	양호	나쁨
속도				V
질	V			
비용		V		

수리 기사는 어땠습니까?

	매우 훌륭	좋음	양호	나쁨
프로다움	V			
정중함	V			
설명을 잘 해줌	V			

하실 말씀이 있다면 적어 주십시오:

저는 이번에 받은 서비스에 꽤 실망했습니다. (180)서비스의 품질은 언제나 그렇듯 괜찮고 만족스러웠으나, 시간이 얼마나 걸렸는지 정말 답답했습니다. 제가 매지컬 인텔리전스에 7월 2일 전화했을 때, (179)수리가 7월 10일까지 완료될 것이라고 통지받았습니다. 하지만 저는 2주 이상 지역 세탁소에 가야야 했고, 제 세탁기는 어제서야 도착했습니다. 앞으로 귀사 서비스를 다시 이용할지 한 번 생각해 봐야겠습니다.

176. 매지컬 인텔리전스는 어떤 사업체일 것 같은가?

    (A) 동네 세탁소

    (B) 운송 회사

    (C) 수리 서비스 제공업체

    (D) 전자제품 매장　　　　정답 (C)

177. 매지컬 인텔리전스에 대해 함축되어 있는 것은 무엇인가?

    (A) 고객들이 자신의 제품을 찾아가는 것을 요구한다.

    (B) 모든 고객에게 할인을 제공한다.

    (C) 하나 이상의 지점이 있다.

    (D) 무료 발송 제경비를 제공한다.　　　　정답 (C)

178. 루크 씨에 대해 사실인 것은?

    (A) 설문조사를 작성했다.

    (B) 셜랏에서 제조된 세탁기를 소유하고 있다.

    (C) 7월 6일 잭슨 씨를 방문했다.

    (D) 매지컬 인텔리전스의 새 직원이다.　　　　정답 (C)

179. 앞으로 어떤 일이 일어날 것 같은가?

    (A) 잭슨 씨가 일정 금액의 돈을 돌려받을 것이다.

    (B) 수리된 세탁기가 도착할 것이다.

    (C) 매지컬 인텔리전스가 잭슨 씨에게 수리 기사를 다시 보낼 것이다.

    (D) 할인 쿠폰이 만료될 것이다.　　　　정답 (A)

180. 설문조사에 나타나 있는 것은 무엇인가?

    (A) 잭슨 씨는 새 세탁기의 품질에 당황스럽다.

    (B) 매지컬 인텔리전스의 비용은 지역에서 제일 저렴하다.

    (C) 잭슨 씨는 전에 매지컬 인텔리전스를 이용한 적이 있다.

(D) 매지컬 인텔리전스는 출판물에 실린 적이 있다. 정답 (C)

문제 181-185번은 다음 이메일들을 참조하시오.

수신: (181)**니콜라스 카딘스키** ⟨nkadinsky@relectronics.com⟩
발신: (181)**에린 잭슨** ⟨ejackson@relectronics.com⟩
날짜: 10월 10일
제목: 10월 23일과 24일에 대한 스케줄

카딘스키 씨께,

10월 23일부터 24일까지 (181)**다가오는 도쿄 출장에 대해 잘 알고 계실 거라고 생각합니다만, 다시 상기시켜 드리고자 합니다.**

당신의 비행기는 10월 23일 오전 7시 15분에 로스앤젤레스 공항을 떠나 (183)**오후 12시 50분(현지 시각)에 도쿄 공항에 도착**할 예정입니다. (183)**우리 도쿄 지사의 직원 타쿠야 아키라가 당신을 픽업하기 위해서 공항에서 당신을 맞이할 것입니다.** 그 다음, 사쿠라 호텔에 도착하여 (도쿄) 지점장인 츠바사 혼다와 점심 식사를 하게 되실 것입니다.

(184)**당신이 기조 연설을 하실 퓨처스 컨퍼런스**는 사쿠라 호텔의 그랜드 컨퍼런스 홀에서 오후 4시에 시작할 것입니다. 그 다음, (184)**컨퍼런스에 참석하는 기업의 모든 최고 경영자들과 회장들이 초대되는 만찬에 참석하도록 예정되어 있습니다.**

다음 날, (182)**당신은 오전에 도쿄 지사의 회의실에서 다음 회계 연도의 회사의 방향에 대해 논의하는 이사회 회의에 참석하실 것입니다.** 귀국 항공편은 오후 4시 25분에 이륙하며, 도착하시면 제가 공항에서 픽업해 드리겠습니다.

에린 잭슨 드림
비서실장
라미 전자

수신: 츠바사 혼다 ⟨thonda@relectronics.com⟩
발신: 에린 잭슨 ⟨ejackson@relectronics.com⟩
날짜: 10월 23일
제목: 점심 약속 취소

혼다 씨께,

유감스럽게도 카딘스키 씨의 항공편이 기계적 문제로 인해 지연되었다는 사실을 알려 드리며, 따라서 오늘 귀하와 점심 식사를 하지 못하실 것이라는 것을 알려 드립니다. (183)**본래 예정보다 두 시간 늦게 출발하는 대체 항공편을 예약해 두었습니다.** 그에 따라 스케줄을 조정해 카딘스키 씨가 공항에서 지체 없이 픽업될 수 있도록 해주십시오.

카딘스키 씨는 귀하를 개인적으로 만날 수 없게 된 것에 대해 사과하며 다음에 또 한 번 기회가 있기를 바라십니다. 지연에도 불구하고, 컨퍼런스에서 기조 연설은 하실 수 있으며, (185)**나머지 스케줄은 변동이 없을 것입니다.**

에린 잭슨 드림
비서실장
라미 전자

181. 잭슨 씨가 카딘스키 씨에게 이메일을 보낸 이유는?
(A) 행사에 대한 세부 사항을 전달하기 위해
(B) 컨퍼런스의 안건에 대해 물어보기 위해
(C) 여행 계획의 개요를 알려 주기 위해
(D) 부서 회의에 대해 상기시켜 주기 위해 정답 (C)

182. 카딘스키 씨는 누구일 것 같은가?
(A) 회사 중역

(B) 지점장
(C) 분점 대표
(D) 비서실장 정답 (A)

183. 10월 23일에 아키라 씨가 무엇을 할 것 같은가?
(A) 오후 4시에 기조 연설을 할 것이다.
(B) 혼다 씨와 점심 식사를 할 것이다.
(C) 카딘스키 씨를 사쿠라 호텔에서 픽업할 것이다.
(D) 공항에 오후 2시 50분까지 갈 것이다. 정답 (D)

184. 퓨처스 컨퍼런스에 대해 시사되어 있는 것은 무엇인가?
(A) 라미 전자의 직원들만을 위한 것이다.
(B) 정식 만찬이 이어질 것이다.
(C) 로스앤젤레스에서 열릴 것이다.
(D) 잭슨 씨가 주최한다. 정답 (B)

185. 두 번째 이메일에서, 두 번째 단락의 3행에 있는 "rest"와 의미상 가장 가까운 것은?
(A) 휴식
(B) 세부 사항
(C) 나머지
(D) 추가 정답 (C)

문제 186-190번은 다음 안내문과 웹사이트 그리고 이메일을 참조하시오.

〈직접 만들기〉 잡지

닐슨 출판사는 당사의 다양한 잡지에 추가하여 또 하나의 추가 출판물을 발표하게 되어 기쁩니다. (187)**지난 10년 동안, 우리는 여성 관심 분야에서 다른 분야로 초점을 확장해 왔습니다.** 올해의 추가 출판물은 5월에 출간될 예정입니다.

〈직접 만들기〉는 이러한 종류의 잡지 중 최초의 잡지입니다. 〈직접 만들기〉로, (186) (189)**자신이 관심 있는 주제를 선정하여 개인 맞춤의 월간 잡지로 엮을 수 있습니다.** 닐슨 출판사는 사용자가 선택할 수 있는 12가지 다른 범주를 제공합니다. 원하는 범주의 수에 따라 구독 요금이 달라집니다.

회원 자격	주제 수	구독 요금
플래티넘	6	연 200달러
골드	4	연 170달러
실버	2	연 145달러

(190)**플래티넘 회원들은 무료 베스트셀러 소설 한 권뿐만 아니라 추가로 3개월치 잡지를 받게 될 것입니다.** 〈직접 만들기〉 구독 시, 원하는 소설의 책 코드를 입력하세요. 책과 코드 목록은 닐슨 출판사의 웹사이트에서 확인할 수 있습니다. 골드 회원은 잡지를 1개월 더 받게 됩니다.

닐슨 출판사의 잡지를 이미 구독하고 계신 분들을 위한 저희 독점 홍보 행사를 확인해 보세요. 그들은 〈직접 만들기〉 구독 첫 해 동안 50% 할인을 받게 됩니다. 이 할인 행사는 5월부터 8월까지 계속될 것입니다.

(188)**오늘 〈직접 만들기〉를 구독하셔서 30일 이내에 배송 받으세요!**

---

www.nielsenpublishing.com/subscribe/payment/confirmation

닐슨 출판사
체임버스 가 120번지, 뉴욕, 뉴욕 주 10007

홈	구독	기부	연락처

구독이 확인되었습니다.
〈직접 만들기〉를 구독해 주셔서 감사합니다!

날짜	(188)6월 19일
이름	켈시 페리
전화	917-659-7834
주소	마운틴 로드 98번지, 콘월-온-허드슨, 뉴욕 주 12520

결제액: $200

구독 세부 정보:

비즈니스 & 경제	V	과학 & 자연		스포츠 & 레크리에이션		패션 & 스타일	V
육아		(189)건강 & 신체 단련	V	문학		음악	V
V	라이프스타일	V	의학		뉴스 & 정치		아동

무료 도서 코드: _____

• 북 코드 칸을 비워 두는 플래티넘 단계의 회원에게는 도서가 무작위로 선정될 것입니다.

수신: ⟨customerservice@nielsonpublishing.com⟩
발신: ⟨kperry@personalmail.com⟩
날짜: 6월 20일
제목: 나의 구독

관계자 분께,

구독 신청과 함께 보내기로 되어 있던 특별 코드를 빠뜨린 것을 이제야 알았습니다. (190)제가 원하는 코드는 5954-93A입니다. 제 구독 기록에 꼭 추가되도록 해주세요. 정말 감사합니다.

곧 제 잡지의 첫 번째 호를 받기를 고대하고 있습니다.

켈시 페리 드림

186. ⟨직접 만들기⟩에 대해 언급된 것은 무엇인가?
(A) 그것은 독자들에게 인기가 있다.
(B) 그것은 월간으로 발행될 것이다.
(C) 그것은 5월에 서점에서 구입할 수 있을 것이다.
(D) 그것은 출판된 지 10년이 되었다. 　　　정답 (B)

187. 닐슨 출판사에 대해 나타나 있는 것은 무엇인가?
(A) 그것은 여성 전용 잡지를 전문으로 한다.
(B) 그것은 여러 나라에서 잡지를 발행한다.
(C) 그것의 본사는 체임버스 가에 위치해 있다.
(D) 그것은 많은 베스트셀러 소설을 출판했다. 　　　정답 (C)

188. 페리 씨는 언제 자신의 ⟨직접 만들기⟩ 첫 호를 받게 될 것인가?
(A) 5월
(B) 6월
(C) 7월
(D) 8월 　　　정답 (C)

189. 페리 씨가 관심 없는 주제는 어느 것인가?
(A) 문학
(B) 의학
(C) 패션 & 스타일
(D) 건강 & 신체 단련 　　　정답 (D)

190. 페리 씨가 이메일을 보낸 이유는?
(A) 무료 소설을 선택하기 위해
(B) 그녀가 원하는 보너스 잡지의 이름을 짓기 위해
(C) 잡지의 질을 칭송하기 위해

(D) 구독 연장을 요청하기 위해 　　　정답 (A)

문제 191-195번은 다음 기사와 이메일 그리고 보도 자료를 참조하시오.

국제 팰리버그 상 수여

프랭크 제임슨 작성

노스 알링턴(9월 19일) – (191)지난 80년 동안 늘 그래왔듯이, 문학에서 뛰어난 업적을 남긴 작가에게 수여되는 국제 팰리버그 상(IPA) 시상식이 9월 28일 팰리버그 센터에서 열린다. (195)수상자는 현금으로 8,000달러와 메달을 받게 된다. 올해는, 4명의 후보가 선정되었다: 로사 페리, 저스틴 오터, 제네비브 스위프트, 그리고 브루스 무어.

페리 씨와 무어 씨는 둘 다 수상 경력이 있는 작가들이다. 페리 씨의 후보작 ⟨불꽃놀이⟩는 그녀의 다른 많은 소설들과 마찬가지로 전기 장르이다. 무어 씨의 ⟨길⟩은 루크 웨스트라는 이름의 어린 소년의 비극적인 사랑 이야기이다.

후보에 저스틴 오터의 ⟨절대 안 된다고 말하지 말라⟩가 있다. 지난달 파리 도서 축제에서 우리와 인터뷰를 하면서, 오터 씨는 모험을 주제로 한 그의 작품이 고향 멜버른에서 어린 학생이었을 때의 자신의 경험에 어느 정도 기반을 둔 것이라고 말했다.

(192) (195)선정된 책 중 하나인 ⟨속성⟩에서 가장 눈에 띄는 점은 이것이 제네비브 스위프트의 첫 소설이라는 점이다. "작년에 저는 집필에 집중하려고 교직을 그만두었습니다. (193)서점에서 제 소설을 보았을 때, 저는 마침내 제 꿈을 실현했다고 생각했습니다"라고 스위프트 씨는 말했다.

자세한 정보와 과거 수상자 목록을 보려면, IPA의 웹사이트 www.ipalibergaward.org를 방문하라.

(194)수신: 저스틴 오터 ⟨jotter@ccpmail.com⟩
발신: 셀레나 젯슨 ⟨sjetson@kearnyhs.edu⟩
날짜: 9월 30일
제목: 축하해!

안녕, 저스틴.

(194)국제 팰리버그 상을 수상한 것을 축하한다. 후보 명단에 있는 네 소설을 보았을 때, 나는 네가 당선될 것이라는 것을 의심하지 않았어.

나는 그 책 속의 사과 농장이 내 아버지가 소유했던 곳이라는 것을 알아차렸어. 우리가 여름 방학 때 아버지를 도와드리곤 했던 것이 기억이 나. 네가 몇 년 전에 뉴욕으로 이사 간 후, 우리는 계속 연락하기가 꽤 어려웠지. 네 책을 읽으면서 우리가 고향에서 함께 보냈던 시간이 생각이 났어.

다시 한 번 축하해! 곧 답장 받길 고대할게.

셀레나

즉시 보도 용

프림로즈 출판사는 제네비브 스위프트와 독점 집필 계약을 맺었습니다. 스위프트 씨는 향후 6년 안에 5권의 책을 집필할 것입니다. (195)가칭 ⟨백조의 호수⟩라는 제목의 첫 번째 책은 스위프트 씨가 몇 개월 전에 출판한 ⟨속성⟩의 속편입니다. 이 새로운 계약에 대한 좀 더 자세한 내용은 www.primrosepublishing.com에서 확인할 수 있습니다.

191. 국제 팰리버그 상에 대해 시사되어 있는 것은 무엇인가?
(A) 그것은 약 80년 전에 제정되었다.
(B) 그것은 단 두 명의 소설 작가에게만 주어졌다.
(C) 그것은 지역 사업체의 후원을 받는다.
(D) 그것은 작가들로부터 개인적인 제출을 받는다. 　　　정답 (A)

192. 누가 전직 교육자인가?
(A) 프랭크 제임슨
(B) 로사 페리
(C) 제네비브 스위프트
(D) 루크 웨스트 정답 (C)

193. 기사에서 네 번째 단락 3행에 있는 단어 "realized"와 의미상 가장 가까운 것은?
(A) 사로잡았다
(B) 달성했다
(C) 인정했다
(D) 이해했다 정답 (B)

194. 오터 씨에 대해 사실인 것은 무엇인가?
(A) 그는 팰리버그 센터에 고용되었다.
(B) 그는 상금을 받았다.
(C) 그는 과거에 그의 작품으로 다른 상을 수상했다.
(D) 그는 문학을 전공했다. 정답 (B)

195. 스위프트 씨에 대해 시사되어 있는 것은 무엇인가?
(A) 그녀의 두 번째 소설의 제목은 〈백조의 호수〉가 될 것이다.
(B) 그녀가 시상식에 참석하는 것이 가능하지 않았다.
(C) 그녀는 새로운 작품을 오터 씨와 공동으로 작업할 것이다.
(D) 그녀는 낮에는 일하고 밤에는 글을 쓴다. 정답 (A)

문제 196-200번은 다음 회람과 이메일 그리고 의견서를 참조하시오.

수신: 전 직원
발신: 에린 린제이, 인사부 국장
제목: 직원 교육
날짜: 9월 21일

우리는 이번 주말에 새로운 기계를 설치할 예정입니다. 우리는 신스 주식회사로부터 컴퓨터, 컴퓨베스트에서 프린터, (197) (198)**파우더하우스에서 복사기**, 틴데일에서 스캐너를 구입합니다. 워낙 많은 장비를 교체하기 때문에, 모든 직원은 가능한 한 빨리 모든 것을 올바르게 사용하는 방법에 대해 교육을 반드시 받아야 합니다. (196)**아래는 9월 28일 월요일과 9월 29일 화요일에 진행되는 교육 과정에 대한 일정표입니다:**

날짜/시간	부서
9월 28일 오전 9시 – 오후 12:00	영업부
9월 28일 오후 1시 – 오후 4시	회계부, 인사부
9월 29일 오전 10시 – 오후 1시	연구개발부
(200)9월 29일 오후 2시 – 오후 5시	마케팅부

동료들과 함께 하는 적절한 교육에 꼭 참석해 주시기 바랍니다. 배정된 시간에 참석하실 수 없으면 내선 번호 89번으로 제게 연락 주십시오. 다른 시간에 배정할 수 있도록 최선을 다하겠습니다.

수신: 해롤드 마틴 〈harold_martin@powderhouse.com〉
발신: 에린 린제이 〈elindsey@watsontech.com〉
날짜: 9월 23일
제목: 감사합니다

마틴 씨,

(197) (198)**파우더하우스가 장기 고객에게 제공하고 있는 최근 세일에 대해 알려 주셔서 감사합니다.** 그 정보에 비추어 볼 때, 저는 XJ45를 5대 말고 6대를 구매하고 싶습니다. 저는 귀사에서 이 요청을 수용할 수 있기를 바랍니다. 그래도 오는 주말에 모든 기계가 회사에 배송되어 설치되었으면 합니

다. 저의 요청에 문제가 있다면 알려 주십시오.

에린 린제이 드림
왓슨 테크, 인사부 국장

직원 교육 의견서

(199)**교육 날짜/시간: 9월 29일 오후 2시**
직원 이름: 레지나 스튜어트

의견:
저는 이번 교육이 전반적으로 상당히 유익하다고 생각했습니다. 교육자들은 우리에게 사용법을 가르쳐 주는 장비에 대해 잘 알고 있었습니다. 그들은 또한 우리의 모든 질문에 기꺼이 대답해 주었습니다. (200)**하지만, 틴데일의 직원이 우리에게 유인물을 제공해 주었더라면 좋았을 것입니다. 대신 저는 그녀가 우리에게 말한 모든 것을 적어야 했고, 유감스럽게도 필요한 모든 정보를 기록할 수 없었습니다.**

---

196. 회람의 한 가지 목적은 무엇인가?
(A) 직원에게 작업 일정표를 요청하기 위한 것
(B) 다가오는 사무실 이전을 확인하기 위한 것
(C) 근로자들에게 교육 시간을 지정하기 위한 것
(D) 자원봉사자들에게 주말 근무를 요청하기 위한 것 정답 (C)

197. 왓슨 테크에 대해 시사되어 있는 것은 무엇인가?
(A) 주말에 사무실을 새로운 장소로 옮긴다.
(B) 다가오는 세션을 위해 자체 교육가를 제공할 것이다.
(C) 과거에 파우더하우스로부터 장비를 구매한 적이 있다.
(D) 최근에 직원을 더 고용했기 때문에 새로운 장비가 필요하다. 정답 (C)

198. 린제이 씨는 어떤 장비를 할인해서 구입할 수 있었는가?
(A) 컴퓨터
(B) 프린터
(C) 복사기
(D) 스캐너 정답 (C)

199. 스튜어트 씨가 어느 부서에서 근무하는 것 같은가?
(A) 영업부
(B) 회계부
(C) 연구개발부
(D) 마케팅부 정답 (D)

200. 스튜어트 씨는 어떤 문제를 언급하는가?
(A) 그녀가 물어본 질문들에 대해 대답이 없었다.
(B) 그녀의 교육 시간이 제시간에 시작되지 않았다.
(C) 그녀는 서면 사용 설명서를 받지 못했다.
(D) 그녀가 연습한 일부 장비가 제대로 작동하지 않았다. 정답 (C)

Part 1

1. [미M]
(A) A woman is reaching for a test tube on the shelf.
(B) A woman is wearing a lab coat.
(C) A woman is stocking some cabinets.
(D) A woman is pulling on some gloves.

(A) 여자가 선반에 있는 시험관을 잡으려고 손을 뻗고 있다.
(B) 여자가 실험실 가운을 입고 있다.
(C) 여자가 수납함에 물건을 채우고 있다.
(D) 여자가 장갑을 당겨서 착용하고 있다. 정답 (B)

2. [미W]
(A) The woman is lifting up some documents.
(B) The woman is leaning toward a display case.
(C) The woman is resting her arm on a cabinet.
(D) The woman is gazing out the window.

(A) 여자가 서류를 들어올리고 있다.
(B) 여자가 진열대 쪽으로 몸을 기대고 있다.
(C) 여자가 팔을 캐비닛에 올려놓고 있다.
(D) 여자가 창 밖을 물끄러미 보고 있다. 정답 (C)

3. [호W]
(A) Both of the men are putting on their masks.
(B) One of the men is pulling his suitcase on the runway.
(C) Some people are stepping out of a vehicle.
(D) They are gathered around the tour group.

(A) 남자 둘 다 마스크를 착용하고 있다.
(B) 남자 중 한 명이 활주로에서 여행가방을 끌고 있다.
(C) 몇 사람이 차에서 내리고 있다.
(D) 그들은 관광 단체 주변에 모여 있다. 정답 (B)

4. [미M]
(A) A piano is being worked on.
(B) A woman is singing to the piano.
(C) A man is seated at a piano.
(D) A piano is located near an entrance.

(A) 피아노가 수리되고 있다.
(B) 여자가 피아노 반주에 맞춰 노래를 부르고 있다.
(C) 남자가 피아노 앞에 앉아 있다.
(D) 피아노가 입구 근처에 놓여 있다. 정답 (C)

5. [호W]
(A) A man has stopped at a desk.
(B) A man is typing on a keyboard.
(C) A woman is drinking from her cup.
(D) A woman is arranging some office supplies.

(A) 남자가 책상 앞에서 멈춰 섰다.
(B) 남자가 키보드를 두드리고 있다.
(C) 여자가 컵에 있는 것을 마시고 있다.
(D) 여자가 사무용품을 정리하고 있다. 정답 (A)

6. [영M]
(A) A carpet is being installed in the conference room.
(B) A presentation slide is being projected on a screen.
(C) Refreshments are being served to the attendees.
(D) Some chairs have been arranged for a meeting.

(A) 카펫이 회의실에 놓이고 있다.
(B) 발표용 슬라이드가 화면에 비춰지고 있다.
(C) 다과가 참석자들에게 제공되고 있다.
(D) 의자들이 회의를 위해 정리정돈되어 있다. 정답 (D)

Part 2

7. [미M] [호W]
Do you know where the X-ray room is located?
(A) This morning, I think.
(B) Yes, she's a medical doctor.
(C) On the 3rd floor.

엑스레이실이 어디에 있는지 아세요?
(A) 오늘 아침인 것 같아요.
(B) 예, 그녀는 의사예요.
(C) 3층에요. 정답 (C)

8. [미W] [영M]
Will you be in the office this afternoon?
(A) Sure, here you are.
(B) The new copier in the office.
(C) No, I am supposed to meet a client.

오늘 오후에 사무실에 계실 건가요?
(A) 물론이죠, 여기 있어요.
(B) 사무실에 있는 새 복사기요.
(C) 아뇨, 저는 고객을 만나기로 되어 있어요. 정답 (C)

9. [호W] [미M]
When will the new landscaping crew arrive?
(A) I like your new garden.
(B) Right after noon.
(C) I didn't do it until this morning.

새 조경 직원들이 언제 도착하나요?
(A) 당신의 새 정원이 마음에 들어요.
(B) 정오 바로 지나서요.
(C) 저는 오늘 아침이 되어서야 그것을 했어요. 정답 (B)

10. [미W] [영M]
How long have you worked for Mr. Sanchez?
(A) Work extra hours.
(B) 3 kilometers away from here.
(C) For about one and a half years.

산체스 씨를 위해 얼마 동안 일했어요?
(A) 시간 외 근무를 하세요.
(B) 여기서 3킬로미터 떨어진 곳이요.
(C) 대략 1년 반이요. 정답 (C)

11. [미M] [미W]
How do you get to the laboratory from here?
(A) Aren't they included in the invoice?
(B) Just go upstairs and you'll see it on the right.
(C) I ordered more test tubes.

여기서 실험실에 어떻게 가죠?
(A) 그것들이 송장에 포함되지 않나요?
(B) 그냥 위층으로 가시면 오른쪽에 보일 거예요.

(C) 저는 더 많은 시험관을 주문했어요.   정답 (B)

12. 호W 영M

Who will take over now that Harry retires?
(A) In-Sook in Human resources.
(B) Yes, I'll send a technician over right away.
(C) I'm tired of working overtime.

해리가 은퇴하는데 누가 인계받을까요?
(A) 인적자원부의 인숙 씨요.
(B) 예, 지금 당장 기술자를 보낼게요.
(C) 저는 시간 외 근무하는 게 지겨워요.   정답 (A)

13. 미W 미M

The contract has to be sent out soon, doesn't it?
(A) Yes. I'll go ahead and mail it right away.
(B) You have the wrong contact information.
(C) You can get some at the post office downtown.

그 계약서는 곧 발송되어야 하죠, 그렇죠?
(A) 예, 제가 지금 바로 우편으로 발송할게요.
(B) 연락처를 잘못 알고 계시네요.
(C) 시내에 있는 우체국에서 좀 구매할 수 있어요.   정답 (A)

14. 영M 미W

The chef's special soup doesn't have any meat in it, does it?
(A) I'd like a steak, too.
(B) Actually, it does.
(C) It looks like the restaurant is open.

주방장의 특별 스프는 그 안에 고기가 안 들어가죠, 그렇죠?
(A) 저도 스테이크로 주세요.
(B) 사실, 들어가요.
(C) 식당이 문을 연 것 같아요.   정답 (B)

15. 미M 영M

What time does the out-of-town client want to meet?
(A) No, they aren't in town.
(B) Anytime in the afternoon is fine.
(C) Probably from a local supplier.

타지에서 온 고객은 몇 시에 만나고 싶어하나요?
(A) 아뇨, 그들은 시내에 있지 않아요.
(B) 오후 아무 때나 괜찮아요.
(C) 아마 현지 납품업체로부터요.   정답 (B)

16. 미W 호W

Make sure to reschedule your appointment for next week.
(A) I'm not sure if he did.
(B) I'll do it right away.
(C) An hour-long regular check-up.

예약을 꼭 다음 주로 일정을 변경해 주세요.
(A) 그가 했는지 확실치 않아요.
(B) 지금 당장 할게요.
(C) 한 시간 걸리는 정기 검진이에요.   정답 (B)

17. 미M 호W

Why is Joseph carrying a suitcase?
(A) Take it to the dry cleaners.
(B) His flight leaves at 7.
(C) We don't carry that suitcase brand.

조셉은 왜 여행가방을 들고 있는 거죠?
(A) 그것을 세탁소로 가져가세요.
(B) 그의 비행기가 7시에 출발하거든요.
(C) 우리는 그 여행가방 브랜드를 취급하지 않아요.   정답 (B)

18. 미W 영M

Have you heard about the new movie directed by Tom Cameron?
(A) The movie theater is newly built.
(B) I heard it got great reviews.
(C) Aren't they moving today?

톰 캐머론이 감독한 새 영화에 대해 들어봤어요?
(A) 그 영화관은 새로 지어졌어요.
(B) 그게 평이 아주 좋다고 들었어요.
(C) 그들은 오늘 이사 가지 않나요?   정답 (B)

19. 호W 미M

When can we see the safety training schedule?
(A) It was a great training session.
(B) Didn't you get the e-mail?
(C) We're expecting more than 100 people.

우리는 안전 교육 일정을 언제 볼 수 있어요?
(A) 그건 아주 괜찮은 교육이었어요.
(B) 이메일을 안 받았어요?
(C) 우리는 100명 이상을 예상하고 있어요.   정답 (B)

20. 영M 미W

Are you leading the workshop for new employees this afternoon or am I?
(A) He is unemployed at the moment.
(B) I work out every morning.
(C) Susan is going to take my place.

오늘 오후에 신입 사원을 위한 워크숍을 진행하실 건가요, 아니면 제가 할까요?
(A) 그는 지금은 실업자예요.
(B) 저는 매일 아침 운동해요.
(C) 수잔이 제 대신 할 거예요.   정답 (C)

21. 미M 영M

Could you let Elaine know that a package has been delivered for her?
(A) She's at a doctor's appointment.
(B) I'd like to send this to her by express mail.
(C) We are out of packing materials.

소포가 배달되었다고 일레인에게 알려 주실래요?
(A) 그녀는 진료 예약으로 병원에 있어요.
(B) 저는 이것을 그녀에게 속달로 보내고 싶어요.
(C) 우리는 포장재가 다 떨어졌어요.   정답 (A)

22. 미W 영M

Is Loraine here at the factory today?
(A) I saw her car in the parking area.
(B) Be sure to put on a safety helmet.
(C) Yours is down the hall.

로레인이 오늘 여기 공장에 왔어요?
(A) 주차장에서 그녀의 차를 봤어요.
(B) 꼭 안전모를 착용하세요.

(C) 당신 것은 복도 아래쪽에 있어요.
정답 (A)

23. 미M 호W

What location do you think would be good for a second store?
(A) There aren't any properties available nearby.
(B) You can buy it at a convenience store.
(C) Hang it on the wall above the table.

두 번째 매장을 위해 어느 위치가 좋을 것 같아요?
(A) 근처에는 구할 수 있는 부동산이 없어요.
(B) 편의점에서 그것을 사실 수 있어요.
(C) 그것을 테이블 위쪽 벽에 거세요.
정답 (A)

24. 미W 미M

You watched the video about the workplace safety, didn't you?
(A) It was a requirement for all the factory workers.
(B) My watch needs to be fixed.
(C) A cabinet for safety goggles.

직장 내 안전에 관한 비디오를 보셨죠, 그렇죠?
(A) 그건 모든 공장 근로자들에게는 필수 요건이었어요.
(B) 제 손목시계는 수리 받아야 해요.
(C) 보호 안경을 둘 비품함이요.
정답 (A)

25. 미M 호W

Where do you think these summer blouses should be displayed?
(A) Yes, around five degrees Celsius below zero.
(B) Don't we have to move some items?
(C) I prefer winter sports.

이 여름 블라우스는 어디에 진열되어야 할 것 같아요?
(A) 예, 약 영하 5도요.
(B) 일부 품목들을 옮겨야 하지 않나요?
(C) 저는 겨울 스포츠가 더 좋아요.
정답 (B)

26. 미W 영M

Why hasn't production on the commercial been finished?
(A) That sounds like a good idea.
(B) The deadline's been changed.
(C) Thirty seconds long.

그 상업 광고 제작은 왜 끝나지 않았어요?
(A) 그거 좋은 생각이네요.
(B) 마감일이 변경되었어요.
(C) 30초 길이예요.
정답 (B)

27. 미M 호W

Would you like me to show you where the human resources office is?
(A) Yes, I really enjoyed the talk show.
(B) All the positions have been filled.
(C) Nick gave me directions.

인적자원부가 어디에 있는지 안내해 드릴까요?
(A) 예, 저는 그 토크쇼가 정말 좋았어요.
(B) 모든 자리는 충원되었어요.
(C) 닉이 제게 길을 알려 주었어요.
정답 (C)

28. 영M 미W

You want to buy a pair of glasses, don't you?
(A) Somebody broke the window.

(B) I'm having trouble with my car.
(C) I purchased some reasonable contact lenses.

안경을 사고 싶으신 거죠, 그렇죠?
(A) 누군가가 창문을 깼어요.
(B) 제 차에 문제가 있어요.
(C) 가격이 적당한 콘택트 렌즈를 구매했어요.
정답 (C)

29. 미W 미M

Who's the sales representative for Janson Medical Supplies?
(A) I think I have their business card.
(B) She got a promotion.
(C) A 20% discount on oxygen tanks.

잰슨 의료 장비회사의 영업 사원이 누구예요?
(A) 저에게 그 회사 명함이 있는 것 같아요.
(B) 그녀는 승진했어요.
(C) 산소 탱크에 대해서 20% 할인이요.
정답 (A)

30. 미W 영M

Does Mr. Nelson have any experience in information technology?
(A) Yes, I am an experienced repairman.
(B) We need someone with a background in online marketing.
(C) It's a state-of-the-art technology.

넬슨 씨는 정보 기술 쪽에 경력이 있나요?
(A) 예, 저는 숙련된 수리공이에요.
(B) 우리는 온라인 마케팅에 경력 있는 사람이 필요해요.
(C) 그건 최첨단 기술이에요.
정답 (B)

31. 영M 호W

I'd like to promote Dan to marketing director.
(A) Do you have a promotional code for this item?
(B) No, it's already been on the market.
(C) He hasn't worked here long enough.

저는 댄을 마케팅 이사로 승진시키고 싶어요.
(A) 이 품목에 대한 할인 코드가 있으신가요?
(B) 아뇨, 그건 이미 시판되고 있어요.
(C) 그는 여기서 충분히 오래 근무하지 않았어요.
정답 (C)

Part 3

문제 32-34번은 다음 대화를 참조하시오. 호W 미M

W: Greg, (32)could I take a look at the budget for the yoga class I'm going to teach here at the community center this coming semester?
M: Of course. I'll be able to pull it up on my computer in no time. Why do you want to see it?
W: (33)I purchased some new yoga mats for some students yesterday, but they cost a lot. I wonder if there's any money in the budget to get some other equipment I could use.
M: It doesn't look like there's much left. (34)However, we could plan a community fundraiser for new supplies.
W: That's a great idea. How about meeting tomorrow morning to discuss what to do?

W: 그레그, 다가오는 이번 학기에 여기 커뮤니티 센터에서 제가 가르칠 요가 수업에 대한 예산을 좀 볼 수 있어요?

M: 물론이죠. 즉시 내 컴퓨터에 예산을 띄울 수 있을 거예요. 예산은 왜 보고 싶은 거예요?

W: 어제 일부 학생들을 위해서 새 요가 매트를 몇 개 구매했는데, 너무 돈이 많이 들었어요. 제가 사용할 다른 장비들을 구할 돈이 예산에 좀 있나 해서요.

M: 많이 남아 있는 것 같지 않아요. 하지만 새 물품을 살 수 있게 지역사회 기금 모금 행사를 계획해볼 수 있어요.

W: 그거 좋은 생각이네요. 내일 아침 만나서 할 일을 의논해 보는 게 어때요?

32. 여자는 누구일 것 같은가?
  (A) 요가 코치
  (B) 요리 선생님
  (C) 실험실 기술자
  (D) 컴퓨터 프로그래머 　　　　　　　　　정답 (A)

33. 여자는 최근에 무엇을 했다고 말하는가?
  (A) 피트니스 센터에 가입했다.
  (B) 부서를 변경했다.
  (C) 비품을 구입했다.
  (D) 예산을 검토했다. 　　　　　　　　　정답 (C)

34. 남자는 무엇을 제안하는가?
  (A) 물품 재사용
  (B) 장비 추가 구매
  (C) 상사와의 회의
  (D) 기금 모금 행사 개최 　　　　　　　　정답 (D)

문제 35-37번은 다음 대화를 참조하시오. 영M 미W

M: Good morning, Lucy. (35)**You are all prepared for the online marketing training session, aren't you?** I think I have all of the materials ready.

W: Yes, and the conference room is just about ready. (36)**The projector and the desks have been set up, but we need facility services to return. I requested 25 laptops.**

M: (36)**Oh, yeah? Okay, I'll give them a call.** In that case, why don't you go to the cafeteria? (37)**We are going to pick up the meal vouchers for the attendees before they arrive.**

M: 안녕하세요, 루시. 온라인 마케팅 교육 시간이 다 준비된 거죠, 그렇죠? 저는 모든 자료가 다 준비된 것 같아요.

W: 예, 그리고 회의실도 지금 거의 다 준비되었어요. 프로젝터와 책상은 설치되었는데, 시설팀이 다시 와야 해요. 제가 노트북을 25대 요청했어요.

M: 아, 그래요? 좋아요, 제가 시설팀에 전화할게요. 그러면 당신은 구내식당으로 가보시겠어요? 우리는 참석자들이 도착하기 전에 그들에게 줄 식권을 찾아오기로 했어요.

35. 화자들은 어떤 행사에 대해 논의하고 있는가?
  (A) 교육 프로그램
  (B) 오리엔테이션 시간
  (C) 자선 오찬
  (D) 제품 시연회 　　　　　　　　　　　정답 (A)

36. 여자가 "제가 노트북을 25대 요청했어요"라고 말할 때 무엇을 함축하는가?
  (A) 그녀는 온라인 회의를 실시할 계획이다.
  (B) 요청이 제대로 이행되지 않았다.
  (C) 모든 사람이 다 행사에 참석할 것은 아니다.

　　(D) 기계 몇 대가 작동하지 않고 있다. 　　정답 (B)

37. 남자는 여자에게 무엇을 할 것을 요청하는가?
  (A) 돈 지불
  (B) 식권 찾아오기
  (C) 행사 장소 예약
  (D) 방 청소 　　　　　　　　　　　　　정답 (B)

문제 38-40번은 다음 대화를 참조하시오. 호W 미M

W: Mr. Jacobs, I determined the nature of the problem. (38)**The leak is coming from your second-floor bathroom sink.**

M: Is that so?

W: Yes. I turned off the water there, so no more water is coming out. You're in luck because there doesn't appear to be any major water damage to the floor.

M: That's great. Thanks. (39)**Can you fix it now? I need to get this problem taken care of so that I can return to work.**

W: I don't know. (40)**Let me run out to my truck to see if I have the necessary parts.** I'll be back in a moment.

W: 제이콥스 씨, 문제의 본질을 파악했어요. 누수는 2층 욕실 세면대에서 되고 있어요.

M: 그래요?

W: 예. 거기 물을 잠궈서 더 이상 물은 나오지 않아요. 바닥에 큰 누수 피해가 없는 거 같아서 다행이에요.

M: 잘되었네요. 감사해요. 지금 고치실 수 있나요? 이 문제가 처리되어야 제가 회사로 복귀할 수 있거든요.

W: 잘 모르겠어요. 제 트럭에 빨리 가서 필요한 부품이 있는지 볼게요. 바로 돌아올게요.

38. 여자는 어떤 문제를 언급하는가?
  (A) 트럭의 엔진이 시동이 걸리지 않는다.
  (B) 오븐이 고장 났다.
  (C) 욕실 창문이 움직이지 않고 껴 있다.
  (D) 세면대가 새고 있다. 　　　　　　　정답 (D)

39. 남자는 무엇에 대해 물어보는가?
  (A) 연장이 있는 곳
  (B) 자신이 지불해야 하는 금액
  (C) 수리가 끝나는 때
  (D) 양식 작성 방법 　　　　　　　　　정답 (C)

40. 여자는 이후에 무엇을 할 것이라고 하는가?
  (A) 연장함 확인
  (B) 주택의 나머지 부분 점검
  (C) 부품 찾기
  (D) 상사에게 전화 　　　　　　　　　　정답 (C)

문제 41-43번은 다음 대화를 참조하시오. 미M 미W

M: Mr. Reynolds is sending me to Paris next week. (41)**He wants me to make a presentation on our latest findings at a seminar there.**

W: That sounds fun. Have you visited Paris before?

M: No, I've never been there.

W: I went there on vacation once. Aside from the popular

places, (42)be sure to visit La Salle. It serves the best food in the city.

M: Oh, yeah? Well, I do have one free evening. I wonder if I need to make a reservation. (43)I'll do an online search during my next break. Thanks.

M: 레이놀즈 씨가 다음 주에 저를 파리에 보낼 계획이에요. 그는 제가 거기 세미나에서 우리의 가장 최근 조사결과에 대해 발표하기를 원해요.
W: 재미있겠네요. 전에 파리에 가본 적이 있어요?
M: 아뇨, 한 번도 가본 적이 없어요.
W: 저는 휴가 차 거기에 한 번 갔었어요. 인기 있는 장소들뿐만 아니라, 라살도 꼭 방문해 보세요. 거기는 그 도시에서 최고의 음식을 제공해요.
M: 아, 그래요? 하루 저녁 한가하긴 해요. 예약할 필요가 있는지 모르겠네요. 다음 휴식 시간 중에 온라인 검색을 해봐야겠네요. 고마워요.

41. 남자의 출장 목적은 무엇인가?
(A) 어떤 결과를 발표하기 위한 것
(B) 신규 공급업체와 만나기 위한 것
(C) 계약에 서명하기 위한 것
(D) 제품을 시연하기 위한 것 　　　　　　　정답 (A)

42. 여자는 남자에게 어디를 방문하라고 제안하는가?
(A) 박물관
(B) 극장가
(C) 식당
(D) 기념비 　　　　　　　　　　　　　정답 (C)

43. 남자는 휴식 중에 무엇을 하겠다고 말하는가?
(A) 조사 실시하기
(B) 비행기표 예약하기
(C) 티켓 찾아보기
(D) 고객에게 연락하기 　　　　　　　　정답 (A)

문제 44-46번은 다음 대화를 참조하시오. 미W 영M

W: (44)On this morning's show, we've got Eric Stark, the CEO of Wilson Media. He's here to discuss his company's amazing rise to fame in the Internet news industry.
M: Thanks a lot for having me on.
W: Thank you for finding the time from your busy schedule to come to our show. (45)I also know that you made a presentation at the New Haven Online News Convention last week.
M: That's right. The convention was a lot of fun.
W: (46)What do you think the key to your success is?
M: (46)Well, my employees are incredibly dedicated and reliable.
W: I think that's a good point.

W: 오늘 아침 프로에는 윌슨 미디어의 최고 경영자 에릭 스타크 씨를 모셨습니다. 그가 이 자리에 온 이유는 그의 회사가 놀라울 정도로 성장해서 인터넷 뉴스 업계에서 명성을 얻게 된 것에 대해 얘기를 하기 위해서입니다.
M: 저를 초대해 주셔서 정말 감사합니다.
W: 바쁜 일정 중에 시간을 내서서 저희 프로에 나와 주셔서 감사합니다. 지난주에는 뉴 헤이번 온라인 뉴스 컨벤션에서 프레젠테이션을 하신 것도 알고 있습니다.
M: 맞습니다. 컨벤션이 아주 재미있었어요.
W: 당신의 성공의 열쇠는 무엇이라고 생각하시나요?

M: 음, 우리 직원들이 아주 헌신적이고 믿을 수 있습니다.
W: 좋은 지적 같네요.

44. 여자는 누구일 것 같은가?
(A) 신문 기자
(B) 회사 소유자
(C) 토크 쇼 진행자
(D) 광고 담당 중역 　　　　　　　　　정답 (C)

45. 여자에 따르면, 남자가 최근에 바빴던 이유는?
(A) 그는 컨벤션에 참석했다.
(B) 그는 신입 직원들을 교육하고 있었다.
(C) 그는 새로운 뉴스 보도를 작성했다.
(D) 그는 인터뷰를 몇 건 진행했다. 　　　정답 (A)

46. 남자가 "제 직원들이 아주 헌신적이고 믿을 수 있습니다"라고 말하는 이유는?
(A) 자기 직원들을 새 업무에 추천하기 위해
(B) 고객과 새로운 계약을 따내는 것을 돕기 위해
(C) 고객의 불만을 처리하기 위해
(D) 다른 사람들의 기여를 인정하기 위해 　정답 (D)

문제 47-49번은 다음 대화를 참조하시오. 호W 영M

W: Hello, Stan. How about an update on the things you are currently working on?
M: No problem. (47)I'm focusing on reading the results from customer satisfaction surveys about our travel magazine. Lots of readers have been complaining that we don't have many articles on foreign destinations.
W: (48)Well, the cost of traveling overseas has significantly increased. I'm afraid we can't afford to dispatch more writers abroad, which cost us a lot.
M: (49)Why don't we reach out to writers and travel guides living in foreign countries? I'm sure they would know about a lot of interesting stuff to do in their regions and (49)willingly work for us on a part-time basis.

W: 안녕하세요, 스탠. 현재 작업하고 있는 것들에 대한 최근 소식을 주시는 게 어때요?
M: 그럼요. 우리 여행 잡지에 대한 고객 만족도 설문조사 결과를 검토하는 데 집중하고 있어요. 많은 독자들이 우리가 해외 여행지에 대한 기사가 많지 않다고 불평하고 있어요.
W: 음, 해외 여행 비용이 크게 증가했어요. 안타깝지만 더 많은 작가들을 해외로 파견 보낼 여유가 없는데, 그게 비용이 많이 들어서요.
M: 외국에 사는 작가나 여행 가이드에게 연락을 해보는 것은 어떨까요? 분명히 자신들의 지역에서 할 수 있는 재미있는 것들을 많이 알고 있을 것이고, 기꺼이 파트 타임으로 우리 회사를 위해 일을 할 거라고 확신해요.

47. 남자는 무엇을 해왔는가?
(A) 입사 지원자 면접 보기
(B) 해외 여행에 대한 기사 쓰기
(C) 설문조사 결과 검토하기
(D) 일부 규칙 업데이트하기 　　　　　　정답 (C)

48. 여자는 어떤 문제를 언급하는가?
(A) 비용이 올랐다.
(B) 한 회사의 지사들이 폐쇄되고 있다.

(C) 일부 장비가 고장이다.
(D) 작가들이 해외로 가기를 꺼린다.   정답 (A)

49. 남자는 무엇을 할 것을 제안하는가?
(A) 직원 몇 명을 새 지사로 발령내기
(B) 전자 지불 허용하기
(C) 온라인 판의 잡지 제작하기
(D) 더 많은 직원 고용하기   정답 (D)

문제 50-52번은 다음 대화를 참조하시오. 호W 미M

W: (50)Jason, I just reviewed the budget proposal. I like it. I think we can make a presentation to the board of directors this Friday.
M: Oh, I was about to call you. (51)I was given some updated numbers from the Accounting Department. We have to revise the budget. There won't be major changes, but we need to start working on it now.
W: (52)Well, I have a meeting with a client in ten minutes. I don't have time to do it today.
M: I'll take care of it then. We can go over everything tomorrow morning.
W: Sounds great. Thanks.

- -

W: 제이슨, 방금 예산 제안서를 검토했어요. 맘에 들어요. 이번 주 금요일에 이사회에 발표하면 될 것 같아요.
M: 아, 제가 막 전화하려던 참이었는데요. 제가 회계과에서 갱신된 수치를 받았어요. 우리는 예산안을 수정해야 해요. 큰 변경은 없겠지만, 지금 작업을 시작해야 해요.
W: 음, 10분 후에 저는 고객과 미팅이 있어요. 저는 오늘 그걸 할 시간이 없어요.
M: 그러면 제가 처리할게요. 내일 아침에 모든 것을 우리 같이 검토하면 돼요.
W: 좋아요. 고마워요.

50. 화자들은 주로 무엇에 대해 논의하는가?
(A) 공석으로 나온 자리
(B) 예산 안
(C) 광고 캠페인
(D) 출장   정답 (B)

51. 남자는 무엇을 받았다고 말했는가?
(A) 일자리 제안
(B) 식권
(C) 새로운 정보
(D) 판매 수치   정답 (C)

52. 여자는 이후에 무엇을 할 것 같은가?
(A) 고객과 만나기
(B) 발표하기
(C) 회의 일정 변경하기
(D) 오찬 참석하기   정답 (A)

문제 53-55번은 다음 3자 대화를 참조하시오. 호W 미M 영M

W: (53)Pardon me, but could either of you recommend a marble cutter? I have to cut and install a lot of marble soon,

(54)but the cutting machine I have is heavy and bulky. I need something that's easy to use and carry to worksites by myself.
M1: Of course. The 840T is the best item on the market. It's tough but lightweight and even on wheels.
M2: In addition, you can fold up its legs, so you can fit it in your van easily.
W: That sounds fantastic, but I'm not really interested in spending $1,300.
M1: It's not cheap, but it's a great investment if you stay in the business. I'm sure it is worth the price. (55)Todd can demonstrate how to use it.
M2: (55)Sure. Let me show you how simple it is to use.

- -

W: 실례합니다만, 두 분 중 아무나 대리석 절단기를 추천해 주실 수 있나요? 곧 많은 대리석을 절단하고 설치해야 하는데, 제가 갖고 있는 대리석 절단기는 무겁고 부피가 커요. 사용하기 쉽고 저 혼자서 작업 현장으로 들고 가기 쉬운 것이 필요해요.
M1: 물론이죠. 840T는 시판되는 것 중에서 최상의 제품이에요. 강하지만 가볍고 바퀴까지 달렸어요.
M2: 게다가, 다리를 접을 수 있어서, 밴에 쉽게 넣을 수 있어요.
W: 아주 좋은 것 같긴 한데, 1300달러를 지불할 마음은 그다지 없네요.
M1: 저렴하지 않지만, 이 업종에 계속 계신다면, 아주 괜찮은 투자가 될 거예요. 그 금액의 가치가 있다고 확신해요. 토드가 제품 사용법을 설명해 드릴 수 있어요.
M2: 그럼요. 사용하기에 얼마나 간단한지 보여 드릴게요.

53. 대화는 어디에서 이루어지고 있는 것 같은가?
(A) 건설 현장
(B) 면세점
(C) 철물점
(D) 렌터카 대리점   정답 (C)

54. 여자는 제품에서 무엇을 찾고 있다고 말하는가?
(A) 품질 보증 연장
(B) 내구성 있는 재질
(C) 운반의 용이함
(D) 방수가 되는 것   정답 (C)

55. 토드는 이후에 무엇을 하겠는가?
(A) 사용자 설명서 보여 주기
(B) 배송 준비하기
(C) 제품 시연하기
(D) 할인 제공하기   정답 (C)

문제 56-58번은 다음 대화를 참조하시오. 미W 미M

W: (56)Thanks for coming to the Westside Hotel. What can I do for you?
M: Hello. (57)I'm the electrician you asked for. I heard there are some problems with the lighting in some of your guestrooms.
W: Oh, thanks for coming. Please follow me to the second floor. (58)We just underwent a few renovations on that floor last week, and everything seems to be working fine, but the lights in some of the rooms have been flickering since we were done with the work. I am wondering if there might be a problem with the circuit.

W: 웨스트사이드 호텔에 와주셔서 감사합니다. 뭘 도와드릴까요?

M: 안녕하세요. 저는 요청하셨던 전기 기사입니다. 객실 몇 개에 조명이 문제가 있다고 들었어요.

W: 아, 와주셔서 감사합니다. 2층으로 저를 따라와 주세요. 우리는 지난주에 2층에 몇 가지 개보수 작업을 했고, 모든 게 다 잘 되고 있는 것 같은데, 객실 몇 개의 조명이 작업을 끝낸 이후로 계속 깜빡거리고 있어요. 전기 회로에 문제가 있는 게 아닌지 모르겠어요.

56. 대화는 어디에서 이루어지는가?
(A) 공항
(B) 사무실 건물
(C) 호텔
(D) 슈퍼마켓   정답 (C)

57. 남자가 이 업체를 방문한 이유는?
(A) 조명기구를 설치하기 위해
(B) 전등을 수리하기 위해
(C) 방을 다시 장식하기 위해
(D) 벽을 페인트 칠하기 위해   정답 (B)

58. 여자는 지난주에 무슨 일이 있었다고 말하는가?
(A) 장비가 구입되었다.
(B) 새 세입자가 도착했다.
(C) 보수공사 작업이 이루어졌다.
(D) 영업 시간이 연장되었다.   정답 (C)

문제 59-61번은 다음 3자 대화를 참조하시오. 미M 미W 호W

M: Good morning. Thank you for visiting Star Bank.

W1: Hello. I'm Sarah Doyle. (59)I have a car dealership here, and I'd love to take out a small business loan to fund some advertisements.

M: That sounds great. (60)But I'm not in charge of discussing business loans. Let me talk to one of our loan officers. Excuse me, Justine. This is Ms. Doyle. She'd like to apply for a business loan.

W2: Wonderful. It's great to meet you, Ms. Doyle. Do you have an account with us?

W1: Yes, I have one.

W2: (61)Good because that's a requirement for customers requesting loans. Only current account holders qualify for loans.

M: 안녕하세요. 스타 은행에 방문해 주셔서 감사합니다.

W1: 안녕하세요. 저는 사라 도일입니다. 저는 이곳에 자동차 대리점을 소유하고 있는데, 광고에 자금을 대기 위해 중소기업 대출을 하고 싶습니다.

M: 좋습니다. 그런데 저는 기업 대출 상담은 담당하고 있지 않아요. 저희 대출 담당자 중 한 분에게 얘기해 보겠습니다. 실례해요, 저스틴. 이 분은 도일 씨인데요. 기업 대출을 신청하고 싶어 하십니다.

W2: 좋아요. 만나서 반갑습니다, 도일 씨. 저희 은행에 계좌를 갖고 계시나요?

W1: 예, 계좌 하나 있어요.

W2: 좋아요. 왜냐하면 그게 대출을 요청하는 고객들에게 필수 요건이라서요. 오직 현재 계좌 소유자만이 대출을 받을 자격이 있어요.

59. 사라 도일이 대출을 원하는 이유는?
(A) 장비를 구입하기 위해

(B) 월 임대료를 내기 위해
(C) 광고를 내기 위해
(D) 직원을 추가로 고용하기 위해   정답 (C)

60. 남자가 도움을 요청하는 이유는?
(A) 그는 특정 업무를 하지를 않는다.
(B) 그는 다른 고객을 돕고 있다.
(C) 그는 현재 휴식 중이다.
(D) 그는 질문을 이해하지 못한다.   정답 (A)

61. 대출에 대해 어떤 필수 요건이 언급되는가?
(A) 추천서
(B) 재산에 대한 법적 서류
(C) 금융 기록
(D) 은행 계좌   정답 (D)

문제 62-64번은 다음 대화와 식당 평가를 참조하시오. 영M 미W

M: Hello, Emily. (62) (63)I reviewed the presentation you'll be giving at tomorrow's meeting. It was really good, but I e-mailed some suggestions on how to improve it.

W: Thanks, Ken. (63)I'm a bit worried since this client has the potential to be big.

M: I'm sure you'll do fine.

W: Oh, (64)do you happen to know any good restaurants around here? The client wants to have dinner after the meeting ends.

M: (64)I know a really good one. It got four stars in a newspaper review last week, and it's right around the corner from the bank. I'll e-mail you a link to the website.

M: 안녕하세요, 에밀리. 내일 회의에서 당신이 발표할 프레젠테이션 내용을 검토해 봤어요. 아주 괜찮았는데, 그걸 어떻게 개선하면 좋은지 몇가지 제안을 이메일로 보냈어요.

W: 고마워요, 켄. 좀 걱정인데, 왜냐하면 이 고객은 아주 큰 고객이 될 가능성이 있거든요.

M: 분명히 잘할 거예요.

W: 오, 혹시 이 근처에 괜찮은 식당 아는 곳 있어요? 고객이 회의가 끝난 후에 저녁식사를 하고 싶어하네요.

M: 정말 좋은 곳 한 군데를 알아요. 지난주 신문 평가에서 별 4개를 받았고, 은행에서 모퉁이만 끼고 돌면 있어요. 거기 웹사이트 링크를 이메일로 보내 줄게요.

식당 평가	
수잔스 코너	★★☆☆☆
웨스트사이드 카페	★★★☆☆
(64)스테이크 45	★★★★☆
톰슨 플레이스	★★★★★

62. 남자는 여자를 위해서 무엇을 검토했는가?
(A) 제품 평가
(B) 회의 일정
(C) 발표 내용
(D) 회사 카탈로그   정답 (C)

63. 여자는 무엇에 대해 걱정하는가?
(A) 다가오는 교육 과정
(B) 세미나에서의 자신의 프레젠테이션
(C) 자신의 업무 평가
(D) 고객과의 미팅 　　　　　　　　정답 (D)

64. 그래픽을 보시오. 남자는 어떤 식당을 추천하는가?
(A) 수잔스 코너
(B) 웨스트사이드 카페
(C) 스테이크 45
(D) 톰슨 플레이스 　　　　　　　　정답 (C)

문제 65-67번은 다음 대화와 배송 조건을 참조하시오. 미M 호W

M: Hello. **(65)I'm Steve from Harrison Manufacturing. We've gotten some new clients in Europe**, so we need a shipping provider that can deliver our products there.
W: We provide shipping by both ground and air for flat rates if you use the boxes we provide. How many packages do you intend to ship?
M: **(66)We'll likely ship around 70 boxes each week.**
W: Air is the faster method, but you can save money by using ground shipping. It's slower, though.
M: **(66)We guarantee speedy delivery, so we need to use airmail.**
W: Okay. **(67)Why don't you let me know your address**, and I can send you enough boxes for the first week?

- -

M: 안녕하세요. 저는 해리슨 제조회사의 스티브입니다. 우리 회사는 유럽에 신규 고객이 생겨서, 거기로 우리 제품을 배송할 수 있는 운송업체가 필요합니다.
W: 저희가 제공하는 상자를 사용하시면 고정 요금으로 육상과 항공으로 모두 배송을 해드립니다. 소포를 몇 개 배송하시려고 하나요?
M: 매주 약 70개의 상자를 배송할 것 같아요.
W: 항공편이 더 빠른 방법이긴 한데, 육상 운송을 이용하시면 비용을 절감하실 수 있어요. 조금 더 느리긴 합니다.
M: 우리는 신속 배달을 보장해요, 그래서 항공편을 이용해야 해요.
W: 좋습니다. 주소를 알려 주세요. 그러면 첫 주에 쓸 만큼 충분한 상자를 보내 드릴 수 있어요.

	육상 (소포 당 가격)	**(66)항공** (소포 당 가격)
소포 1–20개	$3.00	$6.00
소포 21–50개	$2.50	$5.00
(66)소포 51–100개	$2.00	(66)$4.00

65. 해리슨 제조회사에 무슨 일이 생겼는가?
(A) 더 많은 직원을 고용했다.
(B) 신규 고객들을 확보했다.
(C) 유럽에 공장을 열었다.
(D) 납품업체와 계약을 맺었다. 　　　정답 (B)

66. 그래픽을 보시오. 소포 하나 보내는 데 비용이 얼마나 들 것 같은가?
(A) 2달러
(B) 2.50달러
(C) 4달러
(D) 5달러 　　　　　　　　　　　정답 (C)

67. 남자는 이후에 무엇을 할 것 같은가?
(A) 포장용 상자 보내기
(B) 자신의 연락처 제공하기
(C) 계약서에 서명하기
(D) 소포 몇 개 배송하기 　　　　　정답 (B)

문제 68-70번은 다음 대화와 회의 의제를 참조하시오. 미W 영M

W: **(68)Today, we need to discuss how to restore the Renaissance paintings in the B-wing.** I already handed out copies of the meeting agenda, **(69)but I'd like to skip ahead a bit and talk about who should lead the project.**
M: I'm in favor of letting Marcus do it. He'd be a great project leader since he has more than 10 years of experience in restoring paintings for many art galleries.
W: Hmm… He has never led a team before, has he? There is a huge difference between restoring individual paintings and taking care of multiple restorations while leading a massive team.
M: Well, I've worked on a few projects with him, and he's always been highly organized and efficient.
W: **(70)Sounds good to me. I'll give him a call and find out if he wants the assignment today.**

- -

W: 오늘, 우리는 B관에 있는 르네상스 회화들을 복원할 방법에 대해 논의를 해야 합니다. 제가 이미 회의 의제 사본을 나눠 드렸는데, 좀 건너뛰어 누가 프로젝트를 이끌어야 할지에 대해 얘기하고 싶습니다.
M: 저는 마커스가 그 일을 맡게 하는 데 찬성합니다. 많은 미술관의 그림을 복원하는 데 있어 10년 이상의 경력이 있기 때문에, 그는 훌륭한 프로젝트 리더가 될 것입니다.
W: 음… 마커스는 전에 팀을 이끌어 본 적이 없잖아요, 그렇죠? 그냥 개별 그림을 복원하는 것과 대규모 팀을 이끌면서 다수의 복원을 책임지는 것에는 엄청난 차이가 있습니다.
M: 음, 마커스와 몇 개의 프로젝트를 같이 작업한 적 있는데, 그는 항상 매우 체계적이고 유능했습니다.
W: 듣고 보니 괜찮을 것 같군요. 제가 오늘 마커스에게 전화해서 이 임무를 원하는지 알아보겠습니다.

프로젝트 관련 안건

1. 일정 시각표
(69)2. 프로젝트 관리
3. 예산
4. 물품 납품업체

---

68. 화자들은 어디에서 근무하는 것 같은가?
(A) 도서관
(B) 미술관
(C) 미술 화방
(D) 건축사 사무소 　　　　　　　　정답 (B)

69. 그래픽을 보시오. 화자들은 어떤 안건에 대해 논의하고 있는가?
(A) 항목 1
(B) 항목 2
(C) 항목 3
(D) 항목 4 　　　　　　　　　　　정답 (B)

70. 여자는 나중에 무엇을 하겠다고 말하는가?
(A) 동료에게 연락
(B) 제안서 검토
(C) 광고 게시
(D) 회의 소집 　　　　　　　　　정답 (A)

Part 4

문제 71-73번은 다음 전화 메시지를 참조하시오. ⊡M

M: Hello, Ms. Denton. This is David Stern from *Travel Magazine*. **(71)We received your application to work here as a writer.** **(72)Thanks for sending some of the articles you wrote in the past. I was quite impressed with them.** I would love for you to come in for an interview next week. **(73)Please call me back so that we can set up a day and time for you to come in.** My phone number is 596-2033. Thank you.

안녕하세요, 덴튼 씨. 저는 〈트래블 매거진〉의 데이비드 스턴입니다. 여기에서 작가로 일하시겠다는 지원서를 받았습니다. 과거에 쓰신 기사 몇 개를 보내 주셔서 감사합니다. 그 기사들이 무척 인상 깊었습니다. 다음 주에 면접 보러 와 주시면 좋겠습니다. 제게 다시 전화 주셔서 오실 수 있는 날짜와 시간을 정하면 좋겠네요. 제 전화 번호는 596-2033입니다. 감사합니다.

71. 청자는 누구일 것 같은가?
(A) 편집장
(B) 작가
(C) 사진사
(D) 교사 　　　　　　　　　정답 (B)

72. 화자에 따르면, 그는 무엇에 깊은 인상을 받았는가?
(A) 예산 제안서
(B) 직무 기술서
(C) 사진
(D) 작업 견본 　　　　　　　정답 (D)

73. 화자는 무엇을 하고 싶다고 말하는가?
(A) 이메일 주소 확인하기
(B) 인터뷰 일정 잡기
(C) 가격 견적 제공하기
(D) 출시일 일정 잡기 　　　　정답 (B)

문제 74-76번은 다음 광고를 참조하시오. ⊡W

W: The Jospin Institute can teach you everything you need to know about computers. **(74) (75)This Sunday from noon to three P.M., visit our building to learn more about us and computer courses we provide.** You can meet our instructors and sit in on some model classes. **(75)When you study at Jospin, you'll be taught by the best and get a computer programming certificate in as little as nine months. (76)Text 1234 on your cell phone in order to subscribe to our online version of the weekly newsletter.**

조스핀 연구소는 컴퓨터에 대해 여러분이 알아야 하는 모든 것들을 가르쳐 드립니다. 이번 주 일요일 정오부터 오후 3시까지, 저희 건물을 방문하셔서 우리 연구소와 우리가 제공하는 컴퓨터 강좌에 대해 더 알아보십시오. 저희 강사들도 만나고, 모델 수업을 청강하실 수 있습니다. 조스핀에서 공부하시

게 되면, 최고의 강사들에게 교육을 받게 되고, 고작 9개월만에 컴퓨터 프로그래밍 자격증도 받게 됩니다. 저희 주간 소식지 온라인 판을 구독하시려면 휴대폰으로 1234를 문자 주세요.

74. 일요일 무슨 일이 있겠는가?
(A) 제품 시연회
(B) 설명회
(C) 영업 총회
(D) 일자리 면접 　　　　　　정답 (B)

75. 조스핀 연구소는 무엇을 제공하는가?
(A) 기업 회계감사
(B) 컴퓨터 강좌
(C) 온라인 시장 조사
(D) 보안 상담 　　　　　　　정답 (B)

76. 청자들이 어떤 번호를 문자로 보내야 하는 이유는?
(A) 설문조사에 답하기 위해
(B) 소식지를 받기 위해
(C) 지원서를 요청하기 위해
(D) 의견을 제공하기 위해 　　정답 (B)

문제 77-79번은 다음 회의 발췌 내용을 참조하시오. 영M

M: **(77)The new phone system was installed in the conference room about a month ago.** This system is much better than the old one, but you may have noticed a problem regarding how it interacts with the two-way video. I've spoken with our IT expert, and he thinks the problem has been solved. **(78)But he wants us to let him know at once if any further problems arise.** Thanks to the new system, the conference room has become the most popular place for meetings, so we have to start reserving the room to avoid any conflicts. **(79)Call me whenever you want to use it since I'm handling the bookings now.**

새로운 전화 시스템이 한 달 전에 회의실에 설치되었습니다. 이 시스템은 이전 것보다 훨씬 더 좋습니다만, 이 시스템이 양방향 비디오로 소통하는 방식에서는 문제가 있음을 여러분도 알아차리셨을 겁니다. 우리 IT 전문가와 얘기를 나눴는데, 그는 그 문제가 해결되었다고 생각하고 있습니다. 그렇지만 IT 전문가는 추가 문제가 발생하면 즉시 그에게 알려 주기를 원합니다. 새로운 시스템 덕분에, 이 회의실이 회의를 위한 가장 인기 있는 장소가 되었고, 그래서 시간이 서로 겹치는 것을 막기 위해서 회의실 예약을 시작해야 합니다. 이제 제가 예약을 담당하고 있으므로 회의실을 사용하고 싶으면 언제든지 제게 전화 주세요.

77. 화자는 주로 무엇에 대해 얘기하고 있는가?
(A) 부서 예산
(B) 총회에서의 연설
(C) 새로운 전화 시스템
(D) 새 회의실 　　　　　　　정답 (C)

78. 화자에 따르면, 청자들은 추후 문제가 생기면 무엇을 해야 하는가?
(A) 전문가에게 알리기
(B) 온라인 후기 쓰기
(C) 다른 장비 사용하기
(D) 컴퓨터 다시 시작하기 　　정답 (A)

79. 화자가 청자들에게 전화하라고 요청하는 이유는?
(A) 회의실을 예약하기 위해
(B) 새로운 기계를 요청하기 위해
(C) 전근을 요청하기 위해
(D) 비품을 주문하기 위해　　　　　　　정답 (A)

문제 80-82번은 다음 발표 내용을 참조하시오. 호W

W: All of you are new members of the wait staff, so I want to speak with you before we get too busy at the dinner rush. (80) **First, you should know about this restaurant. I opened it twenty years ago**, and almost all the recipes I had were inherited from my mother and grandmother, and I wanted to share the delicious food recipes with people in the area. (81) **Even though many local restaurants have closed since then, our kitchen is always busy.** I'm pleased to welcome you here and I hope your first day goes well. (82)**In addition, please be sure to wear your name tags at all times.** That will enable both our diners and the other staff members to remember your names.

여러분 모두 서빙 직원으로 온 신입 사원들이므로, 저녁 식사 시간에 너무 바빠지기 전에 여러분과 얘기를 나누고 싶습니다. 우선, 이 식당에 대해 아셔야 하는데요. 제가 20년 전에 문을 열었는데, 제가 가진 거의 모든 조리법이 어머니와 할머니로부터 물려받은 것이고, 맛있는 음식 조리법을 이 지역 사람들과 같이 나누고 싶었습니다. 많은 지역 식당들이 그 때 이후 문을 닫았지만, 우리 주방은 항상 분주합니다. 여러분이 이 곳에 오신 것을 환영하고, 여러분의 첫날이 순조롭게 잘 지나가기를 바랍니다. 또한, 항상 이름표를 착용하도록 하십시오. 그렇게 해야 식사하시는 분들이나 다른 직원들이 여러분의 이름을 기억할 수 있을 겁니다.

80. 화자는 누구일 것 같은가?
(A) 식당 주인
(B) 정부 조사관
(C) 주방 직원
(D) 금융 자문관　　　　　　　정답 (A)

81. 화자가 "우리 주방은 항상 분주합니다"라고 말하는 이유는?
(A) 청자들에게 대기 시간이 더 길어질 수 있다고 말하기 위해
(B) 변경에 대한 이유를 설명하기 위해
(C) 업체가 성공적이라는 것을 보여 주기 위해
(D) 일이 어려울 것이라는 것을 입증하기 위해　　　정답 (C)

82. 화자는 청자들에게 무엇을 할 것을 요청하는가?
(A) 그들의 근무 일정 확인하기
(B) 시간 외 근무 하기
(C) 항상 안전모 착용하기
(D) 이름표 착용하기　　　　　　　정답 (D)

문제 83-85번은 다음 회의 발췌 내용을 참조하시오. 미W

W: Good afternoon, everybody. (83)**The R&D team just told me that work on our latest sneaker is almost complete.** They just need to implement a couple of changes suggested by the focus groups. The launch date has been moved up by two months. (84)**We therefore need to work on our marketing materials as quickly as possible.** We need both print and

---

radio advertisements, and we'll be active on social media, too. This is our main priority. (85)**This week, I'll meet individually with each of you to talk about the specific role I want you to have on the project.**

안녕하세요, 여러분. 연구개발팀에서 우리의 최신상 운동화에 대한 작업이 거의 끝났다고 저에게 막 전했습니다. 연구개발팀은 소비자 제품 평가단이 제안한 두 가지 정도의 변경을 할 필요가 있습니다. 출시일이 2개월 앞당겨졌습니다. 그래서 우리는 가능한 한 빨리 마케팅 자료 작업을 해야 합니다. 우리는 인쇄물 및 라디오 광고 둘 다 필요하고, 소셜 미디어에서도 적극적으로 활동을 하게 될 것입니다. 이 일이 우리의 최우선 순위입니다. 이번 주에 저는 여러분을 개별적으로 만나서 이 프로젝트에 대해 여러분이 맡아 주셨으면 하는 구체적인 역할에 대해 얘기를 하겠습니다.

83. 화자는 어떤 제품에 대해 논의하고 있는가?
(A) 운동 기구
(B) 소프트웨어 프로그램
(C) 피부 관리 품목
(D) 운동화　　　　　　　정답 (D)

84. 청자들은 무엇에 대한 작업을 시작하겠는가?
(A) 소비자 제품 평가단과 작업하기
(B) 마케팅 자료 만들기
(C) TV 광고 만들기
(D) 신입 직원 교육하기　　　　　정답 (B)

85. 화자는 이번 주에 무엇을 할 것이라고 말하는가?
(A) 각 직원 만나기
(B) 직원들과 전화 회의 준비하기
(C) 해외 출장 가기
(D) 회사의 공장 방문하기　　　　　정답 (A)

문제 86-88번은 다음 뉴스 보도를 참조하시오. 영M

M: And now for our next story, (86)**let's talk about an announcement by Martin Motors, which today said that every car model the company makes in the future** will have both a gasoline engine and an electric battery engine. Apparently, (87)**this action toward manufacturing hybrid vehicles, which utilize both fuel sources, has been taken in an effort to make the firm more ecofriendly.** During the press conference, Martin Motors' president also showed some pictures of the new vehicles, (88)**proving that caring for the environment can be paired with nice-looking cars.** In case you haven't seen them yet, let me say that I've already ordered a new one.

자, 다음 소식으로는, 마틴 모터스의 발표에 대해 얘기해 봅시다. 이 회사는 앞으로 마틴 모터스가 만드는 모든 자동차 모델은 휘발유 및 전기 배터리 엔진 둘 다 있을 거라고 오늘 밝혔습니다. 분명히, 두 연료원을 모두 사용하는 하이브리드 차량 제조를 향한 이런 조치는 회사를 좀 더 환경친화적으로 만들기 위한 노력의 일환으로 취해진 것 같습니다. 기자 회견 동안, 마틴 모터스의 사장은 또한 환경에 신경 쓰는 것이 멋진 외관의 차량과 짝을 이룰 수 있다는 것을 증명하면서 새 차량의 사진 몇 장을 보여 주었습니다. 여러분은 아직 이 차량들을 보지 못하셨다면, 저는 이미 새것을 주문했다는 것을 말씀 드리겠습니다.

86. 뉴스 보도는 주로 어떤 업종에 대한 것인가?
(A) 항공기 제조업체
(B) 렌터카 업체
(C) 자동차 제조업체
(D) 사진 스튜디오   정답 (C)

87. 화자에 따르면, 회사 조치의 목적은 무엇인가?
(A) 해외 시장으로 확장하기 위한 것
(B) 환경 보호를 돕기 위한 것
(C) 생산비를 줄이기 위한 것
(D) 원자재를 더 적게 사용하기 위한 것   정답 (B)

88. 화자가 "저는 이미 새것을 주문했습니다"라고 말할 때 무엇을 함축하는가?
(A) 그는 그 차량들이 수요가 높다고 생각한다.
(B) 일부 모델은 곧 구매할 수 없게 될 것이다.
(C) 차량의 가격이 그렇게 비싸지 않다.
(D) 그는 새 모델의 외관이 마음에 든다.   정답 (D)

문제 89-91번은 다음 회의 발췌 내용을 참조하시오. 호W

W: Good morning. (89)**This meeting was called due to the many recent complaints we've received about our items breaking while being shipped.** This is a major issue. After conducting an investigation, we determined that the damage to these items is caused by defective packaging. (90)**In an effort to fix that, our design team came up with three packaging options to protect the items better.** Since you're the employees who prepare the items to be shipped, we'd like your comments regarding which packaging works best. (91)**We've prepared samples of each package option.** Please come up here, take a good look, and let us know your thoughts on each type.

안녕하세요. 이 회의는 우리가 받은 최근의 많은 불만사항, 즉 우리 제품이 배송 중에 깨진다고 하는 것 때문에 소집되었습니다. 이것은 아주 큰 문제입니다. 조사를 한 끝에, 우리는 이들 제품에 대한 파손이 결함이 있는 포장으로 인한 것임을 확인했습니다. 그것을 해결하기 위한 노력의 일환으로, 우리 디자인팀은 제품들을 좀 더 잘 보호하기 위해서 세 가지 포장 방법을 아이디어로 내놨습니다. 여러분은 제품이 배송되도록 준비하는 직원들이기 때문에, 어떤 포장이 가장 괜찮은지에 대해 여러분의 의견을 주시면 좋겠습니다. 우리는 각각의 포장 방법에 대한 견본을 준비했습니다. 여기로 와서 잘 보시고, 각 유형에 대한 여러분의 생각을 알려 주세요.

89. 화자는 어떤 문제를 언급하는가?
(A) 배송업체가 제품을 늦게 발송하고 있다.
(B) 건물에 보수공사가 필요하다.
(C) 일부 제품이 파손되고 있다.
(D) 제품이 잘못 발송되었다.   정답 (C)

90. 회사는 무엇을 할 예정인가?
(A) 포장 옵션 변경
(B) 다른 배송업체 고용
(C) 더 많은 직원 혜택 제공
(D) 새로운 정책 지침 소개   정답 (A)

91. 직원들을 위해서 무엇이 준비되었는가?
(A) 음식과 음료

(B) 포장에 대한 교본
(C) 직원 안내책자
(D) 포장 견본   정답 (D)

문제 92-94번은 다음 담화를 참조하시오. 미M

M: Thanks for coming to today's volunteer orientation session. I'm glad so many local residents are willing to help out with the art program for children again this summer. (92)**As you know, the community center offers a five-week program every summer** for children to participate in art classes and learn about all kinds of art forms. (93)**This year, we'll be adding activities like woodcarving and sculpture.** Unfortunately, we're running a bit short of money because of the cost of all the art supplies we need. (94)**So any financial help that we can get from local residents would be great. We hope you feel the same way.** I'll be placing a collection box at the registration desk. Any amount will be appreciated.

오늘 자원봉사자 오리엔테이션에 와주셔서 감사합니다. 올 여름에도 다시 많은 지역 주민들이 기꺼이 어린이를 위한 미술 프로그램을 도와주시겠다고 해서 기쁩니다. 아시다시피, 지역사회 센터는 어린이들이 미술 수업에 참가해서 온갖 종류의 미술 양식을 배울 수 있도록 매년 여름에 5주 프로그램을 제공합니다. 올해는 목각과 조각과 같은 활동도 추가할 것입니다. 유감스럽게도, 우리가 필요로 하는 모든 미술용품의 비용 때문에 자금이 약간 부족합니다. 그래서 지역 주민들로부터 받을 수 있는 어떤 재정적 도움이든 있으면 정말 좋겠습니다. 여러분도 같은 생각이길 바랍니다. 등록대에 모금함을 놓아 두겠습니다. 금액이 얼마든 감사히 받겠습니다.

92. 화자는 어디서 근무하는가?
(A) 관공서
(B) 초등학교
(C) 미술용품점
(D) 지역사회 센터   정답 (D)

93. 화자에 따르면, 이번 여름의 프로그램은 무엇이 다른가?
(A) 추가적인 활동들이 포함될 것이다.
(B) 다른 장소에서 있게 될 것이다.
(C) 참가하는 데 돈이 들 것이다.
(D) 여름 늦게 시작할 것이다.   정답 (A)

94. 화자가 "우리는 여러분도 같은 생각이길 바랍니다"라고 말하는 이유는?
(A) 날짜를 변경한 데 대해 청자들에게 사과하기 위해
(B) 청자들에게 기부를 하라고 권장하기 위해
(C) 청자들에게 자원봉사를 해 준 데 대해 감사하기 위해
(D) 청자들로부터의 의견을 요청하기 위해   정답 (B)

문제 95-97번은 다음 전화 메시지와 카탈로그를 참조하시오. 미W

W: Hello, Ms. Watson. This is Erin Harper calling. Last week, I visited your home decorating store, and you gave me a catalog of the items you sell. I'd love to buy some wallpaper to redo my living room walls. (95)**It's product R4854.** I remember that it was being discounted by 25% last week, (96)**but I wonder if the sale price still applies.** Would you mind calling me back at 954-3827 to let me know? (97)**I'm out of the house all day, so you need to contact me after 8:00 P.M.** Thanks.

W: 안녕하세요, 왓슨 씨. 저는 에린 하퍼입니다. 지난주에 거기 홈 데코 매장을 방문했는데, 판매하시는 품목의 카탈로그를 저에게 주셨어요. 우리집 거실 벽을 다시 바꾸기 위해 벽지를 좀 사고 싶어요. 그게 제품 R4854예요. 제가 기억하기로 그 제품은 지난주에 25% 할인하고 있었는데, 그 할인가가 아직 적용되고 있는지 궁금하네요. 954-3827로 제게 다시 전화 주셔서 알려주시겠어요? 저는 오늘 하루 종일 집에 없을 거라서, 밤 8시 이후에 연락 주셔야 합니다. 감사합니다.

카탈로그

아이보리색 #R4852	하늘색 #R4853
(95)초록색 #R4854	크림색 #R4855

95. 그래픽을 보시오. 화자는 어느 색깔에 관심이 있는가?
(A) 아이보리색
(B) 하늘색
(C) 초록색
(D) 크림색   정답 (C)

96. 화자는 무엇을 알고 싶어하는가?
(A) 환불이 허용되는지
(B) 특별가 이용 가능한지
(C) 물건이 품절되었는지
(D) 배송을 무료로 받을 수 있는지   정답 (B)

97. 화자는 언제 연락되기를 원하는가?
(A) 오전에
(B) 점심 때
(C) 밤에
(D) 주말에   정답 (C)

문제 98-100번은 다음 담화와 지도를 참조하시오. M M

M: Welcome to Green Forest State Park. I'm Ranger Smith, and I'd like to give you some information before you set off. Take a look at this map. If you're an expert hiker, the south trail is the most challenging. It can get pretty steep as it goes up Mount Placid. (98)**However, the trail that goes around the pond is flat and is the easiest one.** Now, please remember that (99) **during this time of year, sudden rain showers can happen, so make sure you have a raincoat.** Okay, one last thing. (100) **I need you to look at these pictures of dangerous animals in the park.** Please familiarize yourself with them so that you can avoid them if necessary.

그린 포리스트 주립 공원에 오신 것을 환영합니다. 저는 공원 관리원 스미스이고, 출발하기 전에 몇 가지 정보를 드리고자 합니다. 이 지도를 보세요. 여러분이 전문 산악인이라면, 남 등산로가 가장 어려운 코스입니다. 이 등산로는 플래시드 산 위로 올라가기 때문에 아주 경사가 가파를 수 있습니다. 그렇지만, 연못 주위를 도는 이 등산로는 평평해서 가장 쉬운 코스입니다. 자, 이제 해마다 이맘 때쯤에는 갑작스런 소나기가 내릴 수 있다는 것을 잊지 마시고, 꼭 우비를 챙기도록 하십시오. 좋습니다. 마지막 한 가지 알려드립니다. 공원에 있는 이 위험한 동물들 사진을 보셔야 합니다. 필요할 때 이 동물들을 피할 수 있도록 그들 모습을 익혀 두시기 바랍니다.

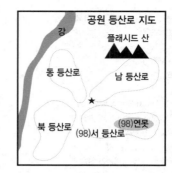

공원 등산로 지도

플래시드 산

동 등산로   남 등산로

★

북 등산로   (98)서 등산로   (98)연못

강

98. 그래픽을 보시오. 화자는 어느 등산로가 가장 쉽다고 말하는가?
(A) 북 등산로
(B) 남 등산로
(C) 동 등산로
(D) 서 등산로   정답 (D)

99. 화자에 따르면, 청자들은 무엇을 가지고 가야 하는가?
(A) 선크림 로션
(B) 우비
(C) 충분한 물
(D) 텐트   정답 (B)

100. 청자들은 뒤이어 무엇을 하라는 요청을 받는가?
(A) 등산객에 대한 설문 작성하기
(B) 단편 비디오 시청하기
(C) 사진 보기
(D) 등산 허가증 받기   정답 (C)

Part 5

101. 커피 하우스의 단골 고객들은 지난주 갑자기 시행된 급격한 가격 인상에 대해 놀랐다.   정답 (C)

102. 기상 위성 프로젝트는 10년 전에 시작되었지만, 그간 수차례의 지연으로 어려움을 겪었다.   정답 (D)

103. 최고 경영자의 연설은 젠킨스 씨와 인도에서의 그의 성공에 초점을 맞추었다.   정답 (B)

104. 경제적 불확실성은 이 도시에서 사업을 하는 동안 우리가 직면하는 최대 도전 중 하나인데, 이를 바로 잡기 위한 노력은 상대적으로 거의 없다.   정답 (B)

105. 우리 마을은 다양한 국적, 문화적 배경, 그리고 종교 집단들로 구성된 하나의 다양한 공동체이다.   정답 (C)

106. 스피드 화물 서비스의 사장은 2년 후에 토론토에 또 하나의 창고 건설을 고려하고 있다.   정답 (B)

107. 대부분의 직원들은 1년 간 근무한 후에 휴가와 휴가 수당을 받을 자격이 된다.   정답 (A)

108. 변제받기 원하는 고객은 구입 후 3일 이내에 결함 제품을 반납하고, 영수증 원본도 가지고 와야 한다.   정답 (B)

109. 우리가 받은 엄청난 양의 지원서로 인해, 다음 주에 자격 요건을 갖춘 지원자들에게만 연락이 갈 것이다.   정답 (A)

110. 벨라 모터스가 고작 6년 만에 하이브리드 자동차업계에서 선두가 되었다는 점은 상당히 놀랍다.　　정답 (B)

111. BK 제약회사 실험실의 모든 연구원들은 구내에서 필히 안전 장비를 착용해야 한다.　　정답 (B)

112. 정부는 최근 국내에서 사업을 하는 외국 기업들에게 관대한 세금 감면 혜택을 줄 것이라고 발표했다.　　정답 (C)

113. 환경 프로젝트는 해양의 심각한 쓰레기 문제에 대한 인식을 높이기 위해 고안되었다.　　정답 (C)

114. 컴퓨터 데이터 서버들의 운영 시스템의 개선 작업을 하기 위해 때로 서버들의 전원을 꺼야 할 필요가 있다.　　정답 (B)

115. 보통 야근을 하는 직원들은 생기를 되찾는 가장 좋은 방법이 에너지 드링크를 마시는 것이라고 생각하기 쉽다.　　정답 (A)

116. 자동차를 최상의 상태로 최대한 오래 가도록 하기 위해서는 필요한 수리나 정기 보수를 하는 것을 미루지 마십시오.　　정답 (A)

117. BK 케이블 텔레비전 회원으로 가입하여 수백 개의 채널뿐만 아니라 선택하신 3개의 스포츠 채널을 완전 무료로 보세요.　　정답 (B)

118. 우리 인사 기록에 따르면, 존스 씨가 치즈 브레드 팩토리에서 근무하는 전 직원을 통틀어 가장 열심히 일한다.　　정답 (C)

119. 의료 제도는 기본적으로 서비스 기반 산업이며, 기껏해야 다른 서비스 지향 부문들과 다를 바 없다.　　정답 (A)

120. 비록 현재 원유 가격이 급격히 상승하고 있어도, 대부분의 사람들은 자동차 공유에 대해 거의 생각하지 않고 있다.　　정답 (C)

121. 파커 씨는 작년에 관리직을 제안받았지만, 고임금 일자리를 찾고 있었기 때문에 거절하였다.　　정답 (C)

122. 투어리즘 인터내셔널은 어느 여행사든 이사진으로부터 가장 많은 표를 득표하는 여행사에 '올해의 여행사' 상을 수여할 것이다.　　정답 (B)

123. 인사과는 해외 시장에서 영업 직원들의 경쟁력을 높일 수 있도록 동기 부여를 할 여러 가지 방안을 내놓을 것이다.　　정답 (D)

124. 회사 구내식당은 주중에 오전 8시에서 오후 8시까지 운영되므로, 여러분은 그에 맞춰 점심 및 저녁 식사 시간을 계획하실 수 있습니다.　　정답 (D)

125. 브라운 씨가 언급한 대로, 실제 수익과 손실은 다음 회계 보고서에 정확히 반영되어야 한다.　　정답 (D)

126. 우리 방침에 따라, "휴대 전화 사용 금지" 규정을 어긴 사람은 극장에서 나가도록 요청받을 수 있다.　　정답 (D)

127. 우리 회사의 자산과 재무에 변화를 가져오는 모든 상업적 거래를 추적하는 책임이 있는 사람은 바로 수석 회계사인 브라이언 워커 씨이다.　　정답 (A)

128. 대부분의 고객들은 이 신제품이 사용하기 수월하다고 여기지만, 이에 덜 익숙한 사람들은 사용에 앞서 사용자 안내서를 참조해야 한다.　　정답 (A)

129. 로드리게스 씨는 그녀의 새로운 직책을 위한 연수 과정에 참여할 것이고, 그 직책에서 통계 분석을 담당하게 될 것이다.　　정답 (B)

130. 문제가 감지된 이후 새로운 모바일 기기의 출시가 최소 일주일 연기되었다.　　정답 (C)

Part 6

문제 131-134번은 다음 편지를 참조하시오.

쉬클러 씨에게;

전자 산업에 관한 저희 연례 심포지엄과 관련하여, 저희에게 강연을 해주실 업계의 전문가를 초빙합니다. 올해는 저희 주안점을 전자 산업의 미래에 두고 있기 때문에, 만약 귀하의 사업 경험을 바탕으로 강연을 해주신다면, 저희에겐 영광이겠습니다.

미래의 전자 산업 심포지엄은 10월 1일 로스앤젤레스 메트로폴리탄 호텔에서 오전 10시부터 오후 3시까지 개최될 것입니다. 저희는 오후 1시부터 2시까지 귀하의 연설 일정을 잡았으며, 질의 응답 시간을 포함하여 한 시간 동안 강연을 해주셨으면 합니다.

저희는 귀하의 여행 경비를 지불하고 소정의 사례비를 제공할 수 있게 되어 기쁩니다.

시오반 켈리 드림
부사장
안드로메다 전자

131.　　정답 (A)

132.　　정답 (C)

133.　　정답 (B)

134. (A) 10월 1일의 저희 프레젠테이션에 참석해 주셔서 대단히 감사합니다.
(B) 동의하신 대로, 우리 거래에 대한 귀하의 지불은 캐나다 달러로 이루어질 것입니다.
(C) 국제 사회와 관련된 여러 세미나와 프레젠테이션을 개최하게 되어 기쁩니다.
(D) 저희는 귀하의 여행 경비를 지불하고 소정의 사례비를 제공할 수 있게 되어 기쁩니다.　　정답 (D)

문제 135-138번은 다음 이메일을 참조하시오.

전 직원에게,

최근에 출장비 환급 정책을 개정했음을 여러분에게 알려 드리고자 이메일을 작성합니다. 이 정책은 회사를 대신하여 출장을 수행하는 직원과 회사가 출장 관련 비용을 환급하는 부분에 있어 적용되는 조건, 규정 및 절차를 정의합니다.

지금부터는, 출장 승인을 받은 후 항공권 및 호텔은 인사부를 통해 예약되어야 합니다. 이는 과거에 우리가 겪었던 혼란을 없애는 데 도움이 될 것입니다. 만약 여러분이 출장을 예약해야 하는 이유가 있다면, 출장 경비 보고서에 이유를 기록하고 모든 영수증을 인사부에 제출해야 합니다. 또한 직원들은 음식 및 지상 교통수단을 포함한 부수적인 비용을 지불하는 데 하루 최대 100달러까지 허용됩니다.

출장을 예약할 때 이 새로운 정책을 따르지 않으면 환급이 이루어지지 않음에 유의하시기 바랍니다.

질문이나 우려 사항이 있으시면 언제든 제게 연락하십시오.

제니퍼 그랜트
회계부장

135. 정답 (D)

136. (A) 여러분은 이곳의 저희 서비스 품질에 만족하실 것입니다.
(B) 우리는 다음 주에 부수적인 비용으로 허용되는 액수에 대해 논의해야 합니다.
(C) 이는 과거에 우리가 겪었던 혼란을 없애는 데 도움이 될 것입니다.
(D) 이번 기회를 이용하시려면, 5월 15일까지 답변을 주셔야 합니다.
정답 (C)

137. 정답 (A)

138. 정답 (D)

문제 139-142번은 다음 공지를 참조하시오.

업타운 가구

행사 안내

저희 소파 세트를 구매해 주셔서 대단히 고맙습니다. 고객님의 모든 가족이 편안하게 앉으실 수 있는 소파가 될 것입니다. 구매해 주셔서 대단히 감사드리며, 새로운 가구로 많은 즐거움을 누리고 계시리라 믿습니다.

저희는 항상 고객 관리를 개선하기 위해 노력합니다. 그러므로 잠시 시간을 내주셔서 동봉된 고객 만족도 설문조사를 작성해 주시면 감사하겠습니다. 고객님의 답변은 저희가 향후 고객들의 요구를 항상 충족시켜 드릴 수 있도록 하는 데 도움이 될 것입니다.

더욱이, 완료된 설문조사는 특별 경품 추첨에 들어갈 것입니다. 당첨되신 고객님께서는 매장에서 쓰실 수 있는 500달러 상품권을 받게 되실 것입니다. 추첨에 포함되려면, 7월 15일까지 설문지를 반송해 주십시오. 당첨자는 8월 1일에 발표될 것입니다.

---

139. 정답 (C)

140. (A) 이 직책은 이전 경력이 선호됩니다.
(B) 저희는 항상 고객 관리를 개선하기 위해 노력합니다.
(C) 여러분의 모든 불만사항은 각각 동등하게 처리될 것입니다.
(D) 그것은 종종 서랍장 및 식탁과 같은 무거운 물건에 자주 사용됩니다.
정답 (B)

141. 정답 (A)

142. 정답 (D)

문제 143-146번은 다음 기사를 참조하시오.

시라큐스 크로니클
문화 코너

새로운 사진 전시회가 이 마을에 오다
브랜든 리

11월 1일) 다음 주 수요일부터 국립 미술관에서 사진작가 세실 비튼 씨의 작품 전시회를 개최할 것이다. 비튼 씨의 사진은 국제적으로 많은 상들을 수상했다. 이 떠오르는 예술가는 사회적으로 억압받는 사람들을 보여 주는 흑백 사진으로 명성이 높다. 그녀는 원주민들의 삶을 포착하는 데 초점을 둔

저명한 사진작가 고 피터 잭슨의 유일한 제자였다. 비튼 씨는 잭슨 씨에게 배운 것을 토대로, 노숙자, 거지, 아동 노동자 그리고 사회적으로 무시당한 다른 시민들의 사진을 계속해서 찍었다. "전 세계적으로 완전히 인정받지 못하고 있는 원주민들처럼, 바로 우리 도시 안에도 무시당하고 있는 사람들이 있습니다"라고 비튼 씨는 말했다. "저는 사진을 통해 그들의 삶을 포착하여 제 관람객들이 그들의 잊혀진 이웃을 보고 그들과 다시 연결될 수 있도록 하고 싶었습니다." 이 사진작가는 자신의 작품을 통해 사회에 공헌할 수 있길 희망한다. 그녀는 전시회의 수익금 전액을 자선 단체에 기부할 계획이다. 전시회는 4개월 간 지속될 것이다.

143. 정답 (C)

144. 정답 (C)

145. 정답 (C)

146. (A) 전시회는 잭슨 씨의 원주민 사진들을 바탕으로 할 것이다.
(B) 몇몇 잡지사들이 그녀의 사진을 사용하기 위해서 조만간 그녀에게 연락할 것이다.
(C) 그녀는 전시회의 수익금 전액을 자선 단체에 기부할 계획이다.
(D) 그 사진작가는 노숙자들의 향후 사진 촬영 계획에 대해 언급했다.
정답 (C)

Part 7

문제 147-148번은 다음 이메일을 참조하시오.

수신: 브리트니 새들러 〈bsadler@runmail.com〉
발신: 〈customerservice@mccarleyonline.org〉
날짜: 6월 3일
제목: 재활성화 필요

(147)새들러 씨께,

(147)저희는 귀하의 온라인 계정을 정지시켰습니다. 귀하가 틀린 비밀번호로 세 번 로그인 시도를 했기 때문입니다. 계정을 재활성화시키려면, www.mccarleyonline.com/reactivation에서 비밀번호를 재설정하셔야 합니다.

보안상의 이유로, 귀하는 귀하의 사회 보장 번호와 집 주소를 포함한 몇 가지 정보를 제공하실 필요가 있습니다. **(148)계정을 재활성화시키고 나면, 저희의 온/오프라인 자료 모두의 대출을 제한 없이 이용할 수 있게 됩니다. 저희가 새롭게 시작한 전자책 자료실 이용에 관심을 가져 주시길 바랍니다.** 추가 정보를 원하시면 안내 데스크를 방문하세요.

고객 서비스
(148)맥칼리

---

147. 이메일이 새들러 씨에게 발송된 이유로 알맞은 것은?
(A) 그녀는 책 한 권을 온라인으로 구매할 수 없었다.
(B) 그녀는 맥칼리와의 거래를 취소했다.
(C) 그녀는 자신의 계정을 갱신해야 한다.
(D) 그녀는 비밀번호를 잊어버렸다.
정답 (D)

148. 맥칼리는 무엇일 것 같은가?
(A) 은행
(B) 온라인 서점
(C) 도서관
(D) 보안 기관
정답 (C)

문제 149-150번은 다음 전단을 참조하시오.

제 5회 연례 핫 포테이토 마켓
(149)로큰롤의 밤
이랏샤이 (지역 일식점) 제공

(149)오셔서 에너지가 가득한 밤을 즐기세요!
(149)초청 공연자: 그린 토마토 밴드

9월 4일, 금요일
오후 5시 40분 – (150C)오후 11시

벤슨 예술 극장
958 카일 가, 버틀랜드, 네브래스카 주 68927
2층

입장권 – 20달러(8월 30일에 판매 시작)
(150B)모든 수익금은 잭슨빌 음악 학교를 돕는 데 사용됩니다.
(150A)더 많은 정보와 표 예약은 www.hotpotatomarket.org를
방문해 주세요.
서두르시는 게 좋습니다! 표가 조기 매진될 것으로 예상됩니다.

• 이랏샤이 10% 할인 쿠폰이 모든 참석자에게 제공됩니다.

---

149. 어떤 종류의 행사가 광고되고 있는가?
(A) 레스토랑의 창립 기념일 파티
(B) 극장 개장
(C) 음악 공연
(D) 지역 음식 축제 　　　　　　　　　정답 (C)

150. 광고되고 있는 행사에 대해서 언급되지 않은 것은 무엇인가?
(A) 표는 온라인에서 구할 수 있다.
(B) 한 교육 기관을 도와줄 것이다.
(C) 오후 11시에 종료될 것이다.
(D) 표를 9월 4일에 살 수 있다. 　　　　정답 (D)

문제 151-152번은 다음 문자 메시지를 참조하시오.

조지 맥도날드　　　　　　　　　　　[오전 11시 19분]
새로운 마케팅 매니저가 임명됐다고 들었어요.

애덤 다니엘스　　　　　　　　　　　[오전 11시 20분]
맞아요, 나도 들었어요. 한 씨가 결국 은퇴하시네요. 그분이 보고 싶을 거예요.

조지 맥도날드　　　　　　　　　　　[오전 11시 22분]
(151)한 씨가 패스트 테크에서 거의 20년이나 일했다는 것이 믿겨져요? (152)그는 훌륭한 리더였어요.

(152)애덤 다니엘스　　　　　　　　　[오전 11시 25분]
저도 전적으로 동의해요.

조지 맥도날드　　　　　　　　　　　[오전 11시 26분]
(151)우리 회사의 몇 명 남지 않은 창업 구성원 중 또 한 분이 떠나는 걸 보니 마음이 좋지 않아요.

애덤 다니엘스　　　　　　　　　　　[오전 11시 27분]
당신 말이 맞아요, 그렇지만 힐리 씨도 한 씨 만큼이나 잘하실 거예요.

---

151. 패스트 테크에 대해 나타나 있는 것은 무엇인가?
(A) 사업 기간이 20년이 채 되지 않았다.
(B) 최근 신입 사원을 채용했다.
(C) 곧 구인 광고를 올릴 것이다.
(D) 회사의 마케팅부를 확장하고 있다. 　　정답 (A)

---

152. 오전 11시 25분에, 다니엘스 씨가 "저도 전적으로 동의해요"라고 쓸 때 무엇을 의미하는가?
(A) 맥도날드 씨가 잘못된 정보를 주고 있음을 지적하고 있다.
(B) 그 또한 한 씨를 훌륭하다고 생각한다.
(C) 그는 이제 가까운 동료가 하나도 없다.
(D) 그는 힐리 씨와 일하기를 거부한다. 　　정답 (B)

문제 153-154번은 다음 양식을 참조하시오.

퀄리티 프레임즈

1086 칼리지 애비뉴
데이턴, 오하이오 주 45434

고객 정보	
(154)이름:	빅터 클라크
전화번호:	(513) 555-2903

특별 메모:
저는 그림을 액자에 넣고 싶습니다. 이 그림은 저희 할아버지께서 그리신 것이고, 정서상 매우 큰 가치가 있습니다. (153)보시다시피, 그림이 낡았으므로 특별히 잘 다뤄 주십시오.

액자 종류:　　　미켈란젤로
색깔:　　　　　클래식 골드와 실버
(154)수령 날짜: 7월 10일

비용 요약:
– 공임:　　　　　　　　　　　　　　　　35달러
– 재료비: 미켈란젤로 액자(2 5/8 인치):　95달러
– 회원 할인 (10%):　　　　　　　　　　– 9.5달러
– 선불 보증금:　　　　　　　　　　　　– 30달러
(154)수령 시 지불 잔액:　　　　　　90.5달러

---

153. 그림에 대해 추론될 수 있는 것은 무엇인가?
(A) 유명한 예술가가 그렸다.
(B) 원래 액자가 부서졌다.
(C) 손상되기 쉽다.
(D) 비싸다. 　　　　　　　　　　　정답 (C)

---

154. 클라크 씨는 7월 10일에 얼마를 지불해야 하는가?
(A) 30달러
(B) 35달러
(C) 90.5달러
(D) 95달러 　　　　　　　　　　　정답 (C)

문제 155-157번은 다음 광고를 참조하시오.

재지 넘버스

(156B)재지 넘버스는 피아노, 색소폰, 클라리넷, 더블 베이스 그리고 드럼을 연주하는 구성원이 있는 3년 된 재즈 기악 밴드입니다. 저희는 원년 구성원 중 한 명인 아론 밀스를 포함한 많은 유명한 음악가들을 배출해 왔습니다. (156C) (156D)그는 최근에 수석 클라리넷 연주자로 명망 높은 에르셀 오케스트라에 합류했습니다.

당신은 재즈 음악에 대한 열정이 있습니까?
(155)그렇다면 주저하지 말고 멤버로 지원하세요! (157)프리랜서로 활동하는 재즈 밴드로서, 저희는 파티, 결혼식 그리고 기타 의식과 같은 다양한 행사를 위해 언제, 어디서든 연주합니다. (155)현재 우리는 새로운 구성원을

찾고 있습니다. 저희가 필요한 모든 것은 11월 3일까지 자신의 연주 녹음과 간단한 자기 소개서입니다. 저희가 일단 귀하의 제출물을 평가하고 나면, 오디션을 위한 전화를 드리겠습니다. 오디션 파일 제출이나 문의사항에 관해서는 제프리 헨더슨에게 jhenderson@boostmail.com으로 이메일을 보내 주세요.

155. 광고의 목적은 무엇인가?
(A) 은퇴를 알리기 위한 것
(B) 추가로 연주자들을 모집하기 위한 것
(C) 곧 있을 공연을 홍보하기 위한 것
(D) 기부를 요청하기 위한 것 　　　　　　　　　정답 (B)

156. 아론 밀스에 대해서 사실이 아닌 것은?
(A) 오디션을 심사할 것이다.
(B) 약 3년 전에 재지 넘버스에서 연주했다.
(C) 잘 알려진 클라리넷 연주자이다.
(D) 현재 에르셀 오케스트라의 구성원이다. 　　　정답 (A)

157. 재지 넘버스의 연주자들에 대해서 시사되어 있는 것은 무엇인가?
(A) 전자 파일 형태로 자신들의 공연을 녹음한다.
(B) 아마추어들이다.
(C) 여러 장소로 이동해 다닌다.
(D) 헨더슨 씨를 위해서 일을 한다. 　　　　　　정답 (C)

문제 158-160번은 다음 정보를 참조하시오.

바니즈 힐
바니즈 시그니처 시리얼 바

(159)바니즈 힐 시리얼 바는 캐나다 농부 바니 피에르가 개발한 전통적으로 집에서 만드는 가정 조리법으로 만들어졌습니다. 50년간, 피에르 씨가 사업을 운영해 왔지만, 지금은 그의 아들인 로메오 피에르 씨가 사업을 넘겨 받았습니다. (158)인공 감미료를 사용하지 않는 각각의 바는 구운 귀리, 캐슈 그리고 아몬드로 채워져 있고 진짜 메이플 시럽에 담그어져, 어디든지 가지고 갈 수 있는 달콤하고, 맛 좋고, 건강에 좋은 간식으로 만들어집니다. 저희의 시리얼 바는 클래식한 아삭함과 통곡물의 영양분으로 가득 채워져 있어서, 죄책감 없는 즐거움으로 포만감을 유지해 줄 영양가 있는 간식입니다.

– 높은 섬유질과 낮은 당분
– 트랜스지방 제로, 글루텐 무첨가
– 간편하고 쉽게 먹을 수 있음
– 에너지 보충
– (158)유기농 농장 협회(OFA) 인증

(160)저희 웹사이트 www.barneyshill.com/naturebars에 방문해서 인쇄할 수 있는 쿠폰을 내려받으세요. 12개의 바가 들어 있는 바니즈 힐 시리얼 바 한 상자를 구매하실 때, 계산원에게 쿠폰을 제시하고 또 한 상자를 무료로 받으세요!

---

158. 정보의 목적은 무엇인가?
(A) 한 사업체의 역사를 설명하기 위한 것
(B) 전통 음식을 소개하기 위한 것
(C) 천연 재료로 만든 제품을 광고하기 위한 것
(D) 집에서 만든 음식의 요리법을 보여 주기 위한 것 　정답 (C)

159. 바니즈 힐에 대해서 나타나 있는 것은 무엇인가?
(A) 피에르 씨의 서명을 제품에 인쇄한다.
(B) 제품이 농장에서 생산된다.
(C) 가족 소유의 사업체이다.

(D) OFA와 합병할 것이다. 　　　　　　　　　정답 (C)

160. 웹사이트에서 이용 가능한 것은 무엇인가?
(A) 시리얼 바 한 상자를 주문하는 것
(B) 신청서를 내려받는 것
(C) 무료 제품 샘플을 요청하는 것
(D) 1 + 1 교환권을 받는 것 　　　　　　　　　정답 (D)

문제 161-163번은 다음 이메일을 참조하시오.

수신: 소피아 엘리엇 〈selliot@neymail.com〉
발신: 오스카 비렌 〈oviren@valverdeshoes.com〉
날짜: 8월 13일, 월요일
제목: 답장: 요청

엘리엇 씨에게,

(162)고객님께서 8월 4일에 보내신 온라인 메시지에 대한 답변을 아직 받지 못하신 것을 알리기 위해 8월 9일에 저희에게 연락을 주신 것에 감사드립니다. 고객님이 8월 2일에 잘못된 사이즈의 신발을 받았다고 하신 고객님의 메시지는 저희 온라인 서버의 기술적 문제로 인해 지연이 되어 오늘 처리되었습니다.

(161)이미 알고 계시겠지만 발베르데 슈즈에 의해 초래된 문제로 인한 반품 요청은 무료로 처리됩니다. 또한, 저희가 고객님께 끼쳐 드린 불편에 대해 사과드리기 위해 20달러 할인 쿠폰을 제공해 드릴 것입니다. 저희 웹사이트에 접속하여 받아 주십시오.

고객님의 신발을 반품하시려면, 저희 웹사이트에서 반품 요청서를 내려받아 인쇄하여 작성해 주십시오. (163)원래의 상자에서, 선불 처리된 배송 라벨을 찾으실 수 있습니다. 반품 배송 상자에 신발, 영수증 원본, 그리고 작성하신 반품 요청서를 넣어 주셔야 합니다.

저희에게 반품 소포가 꼭 8월 20일까지 배송되도록 해주십시오.

오스카 비렌 드림
고객 서비스, 발베르데 슈즈

---

161. 발베르데 슈즈에 대해 함축되어 있는 것은 무엇인가?
(A) 반품 요청에 통상 비용을 청구한다.
(B) 배송품에 할인 쿠폰을 포함할 것이다.
(C) 현재 기술적 문제들을 겪고 있다.
(D) 재구매 고객들에게 할인 쿠폰을 제공한다. 　　정답 (A)

162. 엘리엇 씨는 발베르데 슈즈에 언제 처음으로 자신의 주문에 대한 문제점을 보고했는가?
(A) 8월 2일
(B) 8월 4일
(C) 8월 9일
(D) 8월 13일 　　　　　　　　　　　　　　정답 (B)

163. [1], [2], [3] 그리고 [4]로 표시된 곳 중에, 아래 문장이 들어가기에 가장 적절한 곳은?
"저희 사무실 주소가 표면에 인쇄되어 있으므로, 부치실 때 그것이 귀하의 배송품 위에 부착되어 있어야 합니다."
(A) [1]
(B) [2]
(C) [3]
(D) [4] 　　　　　　　　　　　　　　　　　정답 (C)

문제 164-167번은 다음 온라인 채팅 토론을 참조하시오.

아만다 미스터 [오후 7시 37분]
(165)나 방금 록킹 삭스의 콘서트 티켓을 샀어요! 나 말고 또 가는 사람 있어요?

리암 모리스 [오후 7시 41분]
난 오랫동안 그들 콘서트에 가고 싶었어요. **(165)그들의 새 앨범은 정말 놀라워요.**

페드로 루더 [오후 7시 42분]
맞아요, 그렇죠? **(165)몇몇 오프라인 매장에서 앨범을 구입하려고 했는데, 진짜 빨리 다 매진되어 버렸어요.**

리암 모리스 [오후 7시 43분]
티켓은 얼마였어요?

(164) (166) (167)아만다 미스터 [오후 7시 44분]
난 일반 입장권을 90달러에 구입했어요.

(164)페드로 루더 [오후 7시 44분]
우와. 난 120달러에 샀어요. 어느 웹사이트에서 샀어요?

(164) (166)아만다 미스터 [오후 7시 47분]
난 티켓 레전드의 회원이라서 할인 받을 수 있었어요.

(166) (167)리암 모리스 [오후 7시 48분]
말도 안 돼요! 보통 토지아 홀에서 하는 콘서트는 100달러를 거뜬히 넘거든요. 내가 회원 가입을 하면 할인 받을 수 있을까요?

아만다 미스터 [오후 7시 49분]
물론이죠. 그 회사가 최초 사용자에게는 추가 할인도 해줘요. 그것을 꼭 확인해 봐요.

페드로 루더 [오후 7시 50분]
나는 이제부터 그 웹사이트에서 모든 콘서트 티켓을 사야겠어요.

리암 모리스 [오후 7시 53분]
정보 고마워요, 아만다!

아만다 미스터 [오후 7시 54분]
뭘요. 그럼 콘서트에서 봐요!

---

164. 루더 씨의 티켓이 미스터 씨의 티켓보다 비싼 이유는?
(A) 그의 티켓은 팬 클럽 회원 전용이다.
(B) 그는 그의 티켓을 할인된 가격에 구입하지 않았다.
(C) 그는 앞줄 좌석표를 구매했다.
(D) 실수로 내야 할 금액보다 더 지불했다. 　　　　정답 (B)

165. 록킹 삭스에 대해 나타나 있는 것은 무엇인가?
(A) 곧 있을 그들의 콘서트 티켓이 매진되었다.
(B) 최근에 데뷔했다.
(C) 현재 순회 공연 중이다.
(D) 그들의 새 앨범이 큰 히트를 쳤다. 　　　　정답 (D)

166. 오후 7시 48분에, 모리스 씨가 "말도 안 돼요"라고 쓸 때 무엇을 의미하는가?
(A) 그는 그 웹사이트가 좋은 거래를 제공한다고 생각한다.
(B) 그는 미스터 씨에게 콘서트 당일에 집을 일찍 나설 것을 제안하고 있다.
(C) 그는 미스터 씨가 그를 위해 티켓을 사면 그녀에게서 그것을 받을 것이다.
(D) 온라인으로 티켓을 구매하는 것이 얼마나 쉬운지를 알게 되어 놀랐다. 　　　　정답 (A)

167. 온라인 채팅 토론에서 추론될 수 있는 것은 무엇인가?
(A) 모리스 씨는 그의 티켓을 환불 받을 것이다.

(B) 록킹 삭스 콘서트의 대기 줄이 길 것이다.
(C) 미스터 씨는 모리스 씨와 루더 씨의 콘서트에 갈 것이다.
(D) 곧 있을 록킹 삭스 콘서트는 토지아 홀에서 열릴 것이다.
　　　　정답 (D)

문제 168-171번은 다음 편지를 참조하시오.

12월 18일

(170)릴리 마르티네즈
부편집장
다이아트 출판사
551 이글스 로드
샌디에이고, 캘리포니아 주 92155

마르티네즈 씨에게,

(170)저는 커파우스 대학교의 언론학과 교수입니다. (169)저는 귀사의 웹사이트에 게재된 온라인 컬럼에서 귀하께서 설명하신 인터넷 출판물들을 제작하고 이용하는 것에 대한 혁신적인 아이디어에 매우 깊은 인상을 받았습니다. 편집과 출판 분야에서의 귀하의 지식과 전문성은 정말 존경스럽습니다.

(168) (170)전문 글쓰기 분야의 최신 정보를 제 학생에게 제공해 주고자, 저는 특별 초청 연사와 함께 하는 프로그램을 준비하고 있습니다. 제 수업에 오셔서 귀하의 온라인 컬럼과 같은 주제로 제 학생들을 만나 강연을 하시는 데 관심 있으실까요? (170)지난 학기에 귀 부서의 책임자 필립스 씨가 학생들에게 강의를 했고, 학생들은 그 강의로 많은 도움을 받았습니다.

(171)관심이 있으시다면, 브렌다 스미스에게 bsmith@cupouse.edu로 귀하의 방문 날짜와 시간을 논의할 수 있게 연락 주세요. 귀하를 만나뵙길 고대합니다.

조셉 클리블랜드 드림
커파우스 대학교, 언론학과 교수

---

168. 편지의 목적은 무엇인가?
(A) 곧 다가오는 행사에 대해 안내하기 위한 것
(B) 학생을 칭찬하기 위한 것
(C) 웹 디자인을 요청하기 위한 것
(D) 강연자를 초빙하기 위한 것 　　　　정답 (D)

169. 클리블랜드 씨는 마르티네즈 씨의 아이디어에 대해 어떻게 알게 되었는가?
(A) 그는 그녀가 쓴 온라인 기사를 읽었다.
(B) 그는 그녀가 진행한 세미나에 참석했다.
(C) 그는 그녀의 회사에서 강연했다.
(D) 그는 보도를 위해 그녀를 인터뷰했다. 　　　　정답 (A)

170. 편지에 따르면, 이전에 누가 커파우스 대학교를 방문했는가?
(A) 웹 디자이너들
(B) 한 출판사 직원
(C) 한 회사의 대표
(D) 한 세미나 시리즈의 조직자 　　　　정답 (B)

171. 마르티네즈 씨가 스미스 씨에게 연락해야 하는 이유는?
(A) 세미나의 자리를 예약하기 위해
(B) 몇 가지 서류들을 제출하기 위해
(C) 보상금에 대해 의논하기 위해
(D) 약속을 잡기 위해 　　　　정답 (D)

문제 172 – 175번은 다음 기사를 참조하시오.

8월 9일 – (172)문 서커스단은 자연의 놀라운 이야기를 바탕으로 한 공연 (174)〈조라〉를 선보이기 위해 뉴욕에서 첫 공연을 한다. (173D)이 최신의 화려한 공연은 2년의 동안의 제작 끝에 드디어 무대에 오를 준비가 되었다.

(173D) (173A)지난주 필라델피아에서 열린 기자 회견에서 〈조라〉의 감독인 그레고리 카민스키 씨는 공연이 어떻게 만들어졌는지 자세히 설명했다. 이 공연은 줄리아 심스의 인기 소설 작품 〈정글 이야기〉에 나오는 정글과 정글 서식 생물들의 장엄하고 야생적인 특징에서 영감을 얻었다.

카민스키 씨는 〈정글 이야기〉가 언어로 표현하는 자연의 색상을 무대 위에서 묘사하는 것에 중점을 두었다. 그는 최대한 사실적으로 보이도록 하기 위해 무대 디자인, 의상, 소품의 세심한 부분에 심혈을 기울였다. (173C) (175)그는 〈시애틀 지평선〉의 춤 동작을 짠 안무가 아리아 페르난데즈와 공동 작업으로 관객들이 실제 정글에 있다고 느끼게 만들 안무를 만들었다. (175)이러한 노력이 상상 이상의 서커스 대작을 만들어내는 데 크게 기여했다.

(174)로렌즈 극장에서의 〈조라〉의 첫 공연은 9월 3일에 선보여질 예정이다. 〈조라〉 전국 순회 공연은 후에 보스턴과 라스베이거스에도 갈 예정이다. 문 서커스단이 선보이는 역대 가장 멋진 공연인 〈조라〉를 감상할 기회를 놓치지 말자.

172. 기사의 주요 목적은 무엇인가?
(A) 소설을 원작으로 하는 영화를 광고하기 위한 것
(B) 데뷔하는 감독을 소개하기 위한 것
(C) 공연에 대한 정보를 공유하기 위한 것
(D) 정글의 동물이 등장하는 행사를 설명하기 위한 것　　　　정답 (C)

173. 카민스키 씨에 대해 나타나 있지 않은 것은 무엇인가?
(A) 그는 지난주에 기자단과 대화했다.
(B) 그는 공연을 준비하기 위해 정글을 찾아갔다.
(C) 그는 아리아 페르난데즈와 함께 작업했다.
(D) 그는 2년 동안 〈조라〉를 작업했다.　　　　정답 (B)

174. 로렌즈 극장은 어디에 있는가?
(A) 뉴욕
(B) 필라델피아
(C) 라스베이거스
(D) 보스턴　　　　정답 (A)

175. [1], [2], [3] 그리고 [4]로 표시된 곳 중에, 아래 문장이 들어가기에 가장 적절한 곳은?
"감독은 〈조라〉 극본을 만드는 데 수상 극작가 루이스 벨과도 긴밀하게 작업했다."
(A) [1]
(B) [2]
(C) [3]
(D) [4]　　　　정답 (C)

문제 176–180번은 다음 일정표와 이메일을 참조하시오.

(176) (179)밸리 피트니스 센터
~ 1주년을 기념하며 ~

(176)"지역 최고의 개인 트레이닝 제공업체가 되기까지
고작 1년 필요했습니다."

(178)12월 12~16일, 개인 트레이닝 201호실 수업

	(178)월요일	화요일	수요일	목요일	금요일
(178)오전 9시 – 오후 12시	(178)다니엘 앤드루스	로버트 스톤	로버트 스톤	알렉산더 닐슨	앨런 그레이슨
오후 1시 – 오후 4시	실비아 페레이라	앨런 그레이슨	로버트 스톤	알렉산더 닐슨	실비아 페레이라
오후 4시 – 오후 6시	다니엘 앤드루스	앨런 그레이슨	다니엘 앤드루스	빅토리아 버크	빅토리아 버크

이번 주는 로버트 스톤 씨가 가벼운 부상에서 회복 중인 애슐리 스나이더 씨를 대신해 그녀의 고객들에게 개인 트레이닝을 제공할 예정입니다. 매주 토요일은, 고객들이 놓친 수업을 보강하도록 모든 트레이닝실이 예약되어 있습니다.

수신: 린다 크로닌 〈lcronin@cuzmail.com〉
발신: 칼 존슨 〈cjohnson@valleyfitness.com〉
날짜: (178) (179)12월 10일
제목: 귀하의 개인 트레이닝

크로닌 씨에게,

(177)이번주 월요일과 화요일은 새크라멘토가 겪은 예상치 못한 폭설 때문에 밸리 피트니스 센터가 휴관할 것임을 알려 드리게 되어 죄송합니다. (178)따라서, 원래 201호에서 하기로 되어 있었던 고객님의 월요일 아침 개인 트레이닝은 취소되었습니다. 시간이 되실 때 가능한 한 빨리 저희 센터에 연락하셔서 고객님이 트레이닝 받기 편하신 날짜를 의논하십시오.

(179)저희 기록에 의하면 고객님의 연간 회원 자격이 12월 20일에 만료된다고 합니다. 12월 15일 이전에 회원 자격을 갱신해서 15%의 회원권 할인과 특별 선물을 받으십시오. (180)저희 웹사이트에 접속하셔서 손님께서 받으실 수 있는 20개 이상의 선물을 확인하십시오.

칼 존슨
밸리 피트니스 센터

176. 밸리 피트니스 센터에 대해 나타나 있는 것은 무엇인가?
(A) 빠르게 성장하는 사업체이다.
(B) 토요일마다 메이크업 전문가를 초대한다.
(C) 최근 스톤 씨를 고용했다.
(D) 다른 지점을 열 계획이다.　　　　정답 (A)

177. 이메일의 목적은 무엇인가?
(A) 거친 날씨에 대해 경고하기 위한 것
(B) 요청에 응답하기 위한 것
(C) 한 사업체의 폐업을 확인하기 위한 것
(D) 일정의 변동을 알리기 위한 것　　　　정답 (D)

178. 크로닌 씨는 누구로부터 개인 트레이닝을 받으려 했는가?
(A) 알렉산더 닐슨
(B) 앨런 그레이슨
(C) 다니엘 앤드루스
(D) 실비아 페레이라　　　　정답 (C)

179. 크로닌 씨에 대해 나타나 있는 것은 무엇인가?
(A) 새크라멘토에 산다.
(B) 토요일에 회원 자격을 갱신할 예정이다.
(C) 약 1년간 밸리 피트니스 센터의 회원이었다.
(D) 밸리 피트니스 센터의 개인 트레이너이다.　　　　정답 (C)

180. 크로닌 씨가 웹사이트를 방문해야 하는 이유는?

    (A) 약속을 잡기 위해

    (B) 목록을 확인하기 위해

    (C) 회원 자격을 갱신하기 위해

    (D) 할인을 받기 위해   정답 (B)

문제 181–185번은 다음 광고와 이메일을 참조하시오.

오카라

(181)오카라는 포츠빌에 위치한 컨벤션 센터로 포츠빌과 크링턴의 업체와 주민 모두에게 장소를 제공합니다. 저희 행사장 전문가들은 여러분이 완전히 만족할 때까지 멈추지 않을 것입니다.

주요 행사장

(183)바바라 홀	카탈리나 정원
버튼 빌딩의 이 메인 홀은 업체 그리고 개인 행사 모두에 완벽한 장소입니다. 스낵 바 포함입니다. 최대 200명까지 수용할 수 있습니다.	결혼식과 연회 같은 야외 행사를 위한 아름다운 정원입니다. 날씨 상태에 따라 이용 가능한 장소입니다. 추가 요금으로 음식 공급 서비스를 이용할 수 있습니다.
(184)디스키토 홀	프로페셔널즈 룸
이 회의장은 프로젝터, 6인용 원형 테이블, 그리고 안락한 의자가 갖춰져 있습니다. 40명 정도의 인원이 참석하는 발표와 세미나에 적합합니다.	세미나와 발표 그리고 강연에 이상적인 교실 유형의 방입니다. 화이트보드, 마이크, 레이저 포인터, 프로젝터, 그리고 기타 필요한 물건들이 있습니다. 약 50명의 인원을 수용합니다.

(182)이 페이지에 나와 있는 모든 장소에는 무료 무선 인터넷이 설치되어 있습니다. 세부사항과 각 장소의 가격, 그리고 오카라에 대한 더 많은 정보를 알아보시려면, 저희 웹사이트 www.auckara.com을 방문하십시오. 예약하시려면, 저희 행사장 매니저인, 캐서린 워싱턴에게 k.washington@ auckara.com으로 이메일을 보내십시오.

수신: 캐서린 워싱턴 〈k.washington@auckara.com〉
발신: 로즈 구아린 〈rguarin@voepublishing.com〉
날짜: 6월 10일
제목: 행사장

워싱턴 씨에게,

저는 7월에 홍보에 관한 세미나를 열 계획입니다. (183)행사기획부에서 근무하는 저의 동료 마이클 그린미어 씨가 4월에 바바라 홀에서 연회를 열어본 후 저에게 오카라를 소개해 주었습니다. 장소가 매우 잘 갖춰져 있고 가격도 적당하다고 그가 말해 주었습니다. (184)저는 약 35명을 위한 장소를 찾고 있습니다. 세미나에 토론 시간이 포함될 것이기 때문에, 참가자들을 조별로 나눌 수 있을 만한 곳이 필요합니다.

제 요구사항에 적합한 장소가 있다면, 추천하시는 장소와 함께 저에게 이 이메일에 답장 주세요. 추가적인 세부 사항들과 가격에 대해 의논하기 위해 전화상으로 얘기하고 싶습니다. (185)덧붙여, 저희 부서가 반년마다 세미나를 열기 때문에, 제가 할인을 받을 수 있는지도 알고 싶습니다. 귀하의 도움에 미리 감사드립니다.

로즈 구아린 드림

---

181. 오카라에 대해 언급된 것은 무엇인가?

    (A) 장소를 예약할 때 보증금이 필요하다.

    (B) 날씨 상태에 따라 영업을 하지 않을 수도 있다.

    (C) 업무 회의를 위한 장비들을 판매한다.

    (D) 다양한 행사를 위한 장소가 마련되어 있다.   정답 (D)

182. 광고에 따르면, 모든 주요 공간에서 이용할 수 있는 것은 무엇인가?

    (A) 다과

    (B) 프로젝터

    (C) 테이블과 의자

    (D) 인터넷 접속   정답 (D)

183. 그린미어 씨에 대해 언급된 것은 무엇인가?

    (A) 오카라에서 일한다.

    (B) 구아린 씨에게 이메일을 보낼 것이다.

    (C) 4월에 버튼 빌딩을 방문했다.

    (D) 그는 홍보에 관해 잘 안다.   정답 (C)

184. 워싱턴 씨는 구아린 씨에게 어느 장소를 추천할 것 같은가?

    (A) 바바라 홀

    (B) 디스키토 홀

    (C) 카탈리나 정원

    (D) 프로페셔널즈 룸   정답 (B)

185. 이메일에서 구아린 씨는 무엇을 물어보는가?

    (A) 할인을 받을 자격

    (B) 음식 공급 서비스 가격

    (C) 세미나 시리즈 날짜

    (D) 행사장의 크기   정답 (A)

문제 186–190번은 다음 공고와 웹 페이지들을 참조하시오.

제 3회 홈메이드 요리 경연대회

(190)〈푸드 엠파이어 잡지〉는 제 3회 홈메이드 요리 경연대회에 아마추어 요리사들을 초대합니다. 저희는 다음 4개 카테고리에서 요리를 찾고 있습니다:

카테고리	심사위원
중국 요리	레드 드래곤 식당의 주인이자 (186)〈최상의 재료, 최상의 요리〉의 저자 도날드 리우
프랑스 요리	그랜드 팰리스 호텔의 수석 요리사이자 (186)〈인생에서의 가장 중요한 요소: 음식〉의 저자 코린 데실레츠
(188) 이탈리아 요리	TV 프로그램 〈고메이 스폿〉의 음식 평론가이자 (186) (188)〈비밀의 요리법〉의 저자 마리오 파니쿠치
멕시코 요리	수상 경력이 있는 푸드 스타일리스트이자 (186)〈최고의 요리 스냅사진 찍는 법〉의 저자 알리시아 로드리게즈

(187)첫 번째 라운드는 참가자가 제출한 사진과 요리법을 기본으로 선발합니다. 7월 5일까지 저희 웹사이트에 출품작을 제출해 주세요. 7월 20일에 각 카테고리별 15명의 후보자가 발표됩니다. 선발되신 분들은 7월 30일에 푸드 엠파이어의 컨벤션 센터에 초대되어 심사위원들 앞에서 요리 실력과 요리들을 선보이게 됩니다. 8월 10일에 각 카테고리별로 두 명의 우승자가 발표됩니다. (189)모든 수상자들은 저희의 전문 사진작가가 찍은 그들의 주방 및 요리 사진과 함께 저희 9월호에 특집으로 실리게 됩니다. (190)1등상 수상자들은 상금으로 2,500달러를 받게 되고, 2등상 수상자들은 저희 잡지의 1년 무료 구독을 받습니다.

http://www.foodempire.com/contest_submission

홈메이드 요리 경연대회
온라인 제출 양식

이름: (188) (189)헬렌 맥다니엘스
이메일 주소: hmcdaniels@riomail.com
전화 번호: 843-555-5265
주소: 35 칼레 가, 로즈웰, 사우스 캐롤라이나 주 29455

요리에 대한 간단한 설명:

(188)버섯과 베이컨을 넣은 전형적인 크림 파스타와 집에서 구운 치즈 피자. 또한 디저트로 바닐라 아이스크림을 넣은 아포가토 포함.

 ✓ (189)경연대회의 우승자로 선정될 시, 〈푸드 엠파이어 잡지〉가 제 요리와 주방의 사진을 게재하는 것에 동의합니다.

요리의 사진과 요리법을 첨부해 주세요:

| 📄 파스타_맥다니엘스.jpg | 📄 아포가토_맥다니엘스.jpg |
| 📄 피자_맥다니엘스.jpg | 📄 레시피_맥다니엘스.doc |

---

http://www.foodempire.com/contest_winners

홈메이드 요리 경연대회
수상자 발표

드디어 저희가 제 3회 홈메이드 요리 경연대회의 수상자들을 발표할 시간이 됐습니다!

중국 요리	1등: 저스틴 하노이스	2등: 로버트 윌슨
이탈리아 요리	1등: 킴벌리 스미스	2등: 헬렌 맥다니엘스
프랑스 요리	1등: 브라이언 로페즈	2등: 타이스 설리반
멕시코 요리	(190)1등: 미쉘 메이슨	2등: 조셉 탕

수상하신 분들 축하합니다! 수상자들의 요리 사진과 요리법을 보시려면, 여기를 누르세요.

186. 심사위원들의 공통점은 무엇인가?
(A) 그들 모두 요리로 수상한 적이 있다.
(B) 그들은 같은 요리 학교에 다녔다.
(C) 그들 각자 이 경연대회를 세 번 심사했다.
(D) 그들 각자 음식에 관한 책을 썼다.   정답 (D)

187. 첫 번째 라운드 선발을 위한 제출 마감일은 언제인가?
(A) 7월 5일
(B) 7월 20일
(C) 7월 30일
(D) 8월 10일   정답 (A)

188. 누가 맥다니엘스 씨의 출품작을 평가했을 것 같은가?
(A) 리우 씨
(B) 데실레츠 씨
(C) 파니쿠치 씨
(D) 로드리게즈 씨   정답 (C)

189. 맥다니엘스 씨는 무엇을 하기로 동의하는가?
(A) TV 쇼에 출연하기
(B) 푸드 엠파이어가 그녀가 아마추어 요리사인지 확인하는 것을 허락하기
(C) 대회 수상자들의 주방 사진 찍기
(D) 푸드 엠파이어의 직원들이 그녀의 주방을 방문하게 해주기   정답 (D)

190. 메이슨 씨에 대해 나타나 있는 것은 무엇인가?
(A) 무료 잡지 구독권을 받게 된다.
(B) 상금을 받게 된다.
(C) 〈푸드 엠파이어 잡지〉에서 일한다.
(D) 멕시코 음식 전문 요리사이다.   정답 (B)

문제 191-195번은 다음 이메일들을 참조하시오.

수신: (191B) (193)조셉 킴, 앤드류 스미스, 안나 글리슨
발신: 로버트 루나
날짜: 5월 8일
제목: 환영합니다

안녕하세요, 여러분.

(191C)어린이들과 어른 모두를 위한 최고의 품질과 안전성을 갖춘 미니카, 인형, 그리고 퍼즐을 제공하기 위해 노력하는 던컨 주식회사에 입사하신 것을 환영합니다. (191B) (193)저희 던컨 주식회사는 여러분이 영업부에서 우리와 함께 일하게 되신 것을 기쁘게 생각합니다. 입사 첫날에, 인사부에 오셔서 사원증을 (192)교부 받으셔야 합니다. 또한, 인사부 부국장 미셸 윌리엄스와 사옥 내부를 돌아보시게 될 겁니다.

(191A) (194)5월 17일에 있을 신입 사원 교육에 참석하는 것은 의무입니다. (193)여러분 부서의 관리자가 교육 장소와 시간에 관해 연락할 것입니다. 다시 한 번, 던컨 주식회사에 오시는 것을 환영합니다!

로버트 루나 드림

수신: (193)조셉 킴, 앤드류 스미스, 안나 글리슨
발신: 크리스토퍼 페이지
날짜: 5월 14일
제목: 교육

안녕하세요,

여러분이 던컨 주식회사에서 일하는 것에 익숙해지고 있기를 바랍니다. (193)이 이메일은 곧 있을 여러분을 위한 교육에 관한 것입니다. 오후 1시 30분에 3층에 있는 회의실에서 교육을 실시합니다. (194)교육 다음 날에는, 신입 사원 모두를 위한 간단한 환영 연회도 열릴 예정입니다. 오후 6시까지 포스티오 식당으로 와 주세요.

(193)크리스토퍼 페이지 드림

수신: 크리스토퍼 페이지
발신: 로라 모건
날짜: 5월 21일
제목: 귀사의 거래 제의 건

페이지 씨에게.

(194)귀사의 신입 사원을 위한 최근 연회 장소로 포스티오 식당을 선택해 주셔서 감사합니다. 제 가게에서 모두 즐거운 시간을 보내셨기를 바랍니다. (194)파티에서 논의한 것처럼, 저희 포스티오는 6월에 귀사의 회의실에서 열릴 연례 기념행사에 기꺼이 음식을 제공하겠습니다. (195)계약 조건에 대

해 논의할 수 있도록 다시 한 번 방문해 주십시오.

감사합니다,

로라 모건

191. 던컨 주식회사에 대해 시사되어 있지 않은 것은 무엇인가?
(A) 회사 직원들을 위해 교육 과정을 제공한다.
(B) 최근 몇 명의 직원들을 채용했다.
(C) 어린이들을 위한 장난감을 판매한다.
(D) 직원의 여행 비용을 대준다.　　　　　정답 (D)

192. 첫 번째 메일의 첫 번째 단락 4행에 있는 단어 "issued"와 의미상 가장 가까운 것은?
(A) 인쇄되는
(B) 청구되는
(C) 주어지는
(D) 출판되는　　　　　정답 (C)

193. 페이지 씨는 누구일 것 같은가?
(A) 영업부 관리자
(B) 교육 강사
(C) 사업체 소유주
(D) 인사부 이사　　　　　정답 (A)

194. 모건 씨와 페이지 씨는 언제 만났을 것 같은가?
(A) 5월 14일
(B) 5월 17일
(C) 5월 18일
(D) 5월 21일　　　　　정답 (C)

195. 모건 씨는 페이지 씨에게 무엇을 할 것을 요청하는가?
(A) 음식 공급 서비스 제공
(B) 이메일 발송
(C) 최근 행사의 비용 지불
(D) 자신의 업체 방문　　　　　정답 (D)

문제 196-200번은 다음 광고와 주문서 그리고 이메일을 참조하시오.

(196)Booktree.com은 당신이 가장 합리적인 가격에 새 도서와 중고 도서를 모두 찾을 수 있는 인터넷 서점입니다. 20년 넘게 운영되면서, Booktree.com은 독서 애호가들에게 점점 더 인기를 끌고 있고, 작년에 〈트렌드 투데이 잡지〉의 '올해의 서점'으로 선정됐습니다.

(197)여름 특별 판촉 행사로, 현재 저희는 고객님이 도서를 구매하실 때 내신 금액의 20%를 북트리 포인트로 돌려 드리고 있습니다. 이것은 고객님이 평상시 받는 5%보다 15%나 더 많은 것입니다. 북트리 포인트는 앞으로 도서를 더 구매할 때 사용하실 수 있는 보상 포인트입니다. (197)이 혜택은 첫 구매에만 적용 가능하며 8월 30일까지 유효합니다.

단 3달러에 특급 배송을 신청하시고, 주문 2일 내로 배송을 받으세요. 이 서비스는 국내 고객에게만 가능합니다.

Booktree.com
언제나 최고의 책을 최상의 가격에

주문 번호:	FS094810	주문일:	8월 28일
북트리 계정	jbrown09	(198)발송일:	9월 2일
(197)고객 성명:	조셉 브라운		

주소:	425 캠브리지 드라이브 피닉스, 애리조나 주 85040

주문 명세

도서명	저자	상품 번호	가격
〈소프트웨어 디자인의 예술〉	레오나르도 카스트로	D148501	27.50달러
〈컴퓨터 프로그래밍 패턴〉	(200)프랭크 모슬리	R720958	(200)16.75달러
〈기초 프로그래밍〉	하워드 잭슨	R012290	31.10달러
〈생산적인 컴퓨터 사용〉	루시 로드리게즈	C890271	28.80달러
		소계:	104.15달러
		발송 제경비:	–
		세금 (8%):	8.33달러
		합계:	112.48달러

(197)이 거래에 제공된 북트리 포인트:
22.50포인트 (판촉 행사 혜택 - 20%)

• 반품 또는 환불 요청은 구매 10일 안에 하셔야 합니다. 온라인 요청서를 제출하시거나 returnrequest@booktree.com으로 이메일을 보내 주세요. 반품 및 환불에 관한 자세한 방침은 저희 웹사이트를 참조하세요.

수신: 조셉 브라운 〈jbrown@bkmail.com〉
발신: 고객 서비스 〈customerservice@booktree.com〉
날짜: 9월 5일
제목: 답장: 최근 주문

브라운 씨에게,

(200)주문하신 도서를 모슬리 박사가 집필한 〈컴퓨터 프로그래밍의 요소〉로 잘못 받으신 것을 오늘 오전에 들었는데 사과드립니다. 저희가 고객님의 배송품을 포장하면서 그 도서의 저자와 가격이 고객님이 실제로 주문하신 책과 같아서 실수가 있었던 것 같습니다. 저희가 고객님의 주소지로 주문하신 책을 신속히 보내 드리겠습니다. 가급적 빨리 55 일포드 애비뉴, 휴스턴, 텍사스 주 73550으로 받으셨던 도서를 보내 주십시오. 또한, 저희의 실수에 대해 사과드리고자, 10달러 할인 쿠폰을 제공해 드렸습니다; 저희 웹사이트에 고객님의 계정으로 접속하여 (199)받아 주십시오.

Booktree.com 고객 서비스 드림

196. Booktree.com에 대해 시사된 것은 무엇인가?
(A) 온라인으로 중고 서적을 판매한다.
(B) 여러 개의 상을 받았다.
(C) 도서를 국내 고객에게만 배송한다.
(D) 작년에 잡지를 출간했다.　　　　　정답 (A)

197. 브라운 씨에 대한 사실로 알맞은 것은?
(A) 그는 컴퓨터를 제조한다.
(B) 그는 〈트렌드 투데이 잡지〉를 구독한다.
(C) 그는 특급 배송을 요청했다.
(D) 그는 Booktree.com에서 처음으로 주문을 했다.　　　　　정답 (D)

198. 주문은 브라운 씨에게 언제 발송되었는가?
(A) 8월 28일
(B) 8월 30일
(C) 9월 2일
(D) 9월 5일　　　　　정답 (C)

199. 이메일의 첫 번째 단락 7행에 있는 단어 "claim"과 의미상 가장 가까운 것은?
(A) 주장하다
(B) 불평하다
(C) (돈을) 쓰다
(D) 가져가다 정답 (D)

200. 〈컴퓨터 프로그래밍의 요소〉는 얼마인가?
(A) 16.75달러
(B) 27.50달러
(C) 28.80달러
(D) 31.10달러 정답 (A)

1. 미M
(A) They are sitting across from each other.
(B) A man is pushing a chair under a table.
(C) A woman is writing on a pad of paper.
(D) They are removing a table from the room.

(A) 그들은 서로 마주 보고 앉아 있다.
(B) 남자가 의자를 테이블 아래로 밀어 넣고 있다.
(C) 여자가 종이 위에 글을 쓰고 있다.
(D) 그들이 방에서 테이블을 치우고 있다. 정답 (C)

2. 영M
(A) The woman is applying some makeup.
(B) The woman is removing an item from her purse.
(C) The woman is packing her suitcase.
(D) The woman is hanging a bag on her shoulder.

(A) 여자가 화장을 하고 있다.
(B) 여자가 핸드백에서 물건 하나를 꺼내고 있다.
(C) 여자가 여행가방을 싸고 있다.
(D) 여자가 어깨에 가방을 메고 있다. 정답 (B)

3. 미M
(A) He is washing a cutting board in a sink.
(B) He is stirring something in a bowl.
(C) He is placing some containers in a cabinet.
(D) He is preparing some food at a counter.

(A) 그는 개수대에서 도마를 씻고 있다.
(B) 그는 사발에 있는 것을 휘저어 섞고 있다.
(C) 그는 보관함에 용기를 넣고 있다.
(D) 그는 조리대에서 음식을 준비하고 있다. 정답 (D)

4. 미W
(A) The woman is turning off a water faucet.
(B) The woman is leaning against a windowsill.
(C) Some potted plants have been arranged in a row.
(D) Some tables are being moved into a room.

(A) 여자가 수도꼭지를 잠그고 있다.
(B) 여자가 창턱에 기대고 있다.
(C) 화분 몇 개가 한 줄로 줄지어 놓여 있다.
(D) 테이블 몇 개가 방 안으로 옮겨지고 있다. 정답 (C)

5. 호W
(A) One of the women is rowing a boat.
(B) Some people are boarding a boat.
(C) Some people are standing on a dock.
(D) One of the men is swimming across the river.

(A) 여자 중 한 명이 보트를 젓고 있다.
(B) 몇 사람이 배에 승선하고 있다.
(C) 몇 사람이 부두에 서 있다.
(D) 남자 중 한 명이 강을 가로질러 수영하고 있다. 정답 (C)

6. 미W
(A) Some trees are being planted near a river.
(B) A cabin overlooks a fishing pier.
(C) A bridge extends over a lake.

(D) Some trees border a river.

(A) 나무들이 강 가까이에 식수되고 있다.
(B) 오두막집이 낚시 잔교를 내려다보고 있다.
(C) 다리가 호수 위로 뻗어 있다.
(D) 나무 몇 그루가 강과 경계를 이루고 있다. 　　　정답 (D)

Part 2

7. 미W 영M
What are they constructing near the city park?
(A) On the 20th floor.
(B) A multi-complex shopping mall.
(C) The parking space is limited.

그들은 시립 공원 근처에 뭐를 짓고 있는 거예요?
(A) 20층에요.
(B) 복합 쇼핑몰이요.
(C) 주차 공간이 제한적이에요. 　　　정답 (B)

8. 미M 호W
We should consider Donald for the graphic designer position, shouldn't we?
(A) Yes, we're reviewing his application now.
(B) The repair should be done by 3.
(C) Can I come in for an interview?

그래픽 디자이너 자리에 도널드를 고려해 봐야죠, 그렇죠?
(A) 예, 우리는 지금 그의 지원서를 검토하고 있어요.
(B) 수리는 3시까지 완료되어야 합니다.
(C) 면접 보러 가도 될까요? 　　　정답 (A)

9. 미W 영M
When will the next marketing report become available?
(A) Not for another 2 weeks.
(B) Yes, it was last month.
(C) We are out of paper.

다음 마케팅 보고서는 언제 나오게 되나요?
(A) 앞으로 2주 동안은 아니에요.
(B) 예, 그건 지난달이었어요.
(C) 우리는 종이가 떨어졌어요. 　　　정답 (A)

10. 영M 호W
Who's in charge of the expansion budget?
(A) Neither did she.
(B) Forty thousand dollars.
(C) The project manager.

확장 예산을 누가 담당하고 있죠?
(A) 그녀도 안 했어요.
(B) 4만 달러요.
(C) 프로젝트 매니저요. 　　　정답 (C)

11. 미W 미M
Doesn't this supermarket have a section for bread?
(A) The catering service.
(B) There's a new bakery across from the entrance.
(C) Are you applying for the position right now?

이 슈퍼마켓에 빵 코너가 있지 않나요?
(A) 출장 요리 업체요.

(B) 입구 맞은 편에 새 제과점이 있어요.
(C) 지금 그 자리에 지원하시려고요? 　　　정답 (B)

12. 영M 호W
Will the prototype for the 3D printer be ready in time for the trade fair?
(A) The decision is not fair.
(B) Yes, it'll be finished in 2 days or so.
(C) The flight was behind time.

3D 프린터 제품 원형은 무역 박람회에 맞춰 늦지 않게 준비될까요?
(A) 결정이 공정하지 않아요.
(B) 예, 이틀 정도면 끝날 거예요.
(C) 비행기가 예정보다 늦었어요. 　　　정답 (B)

13. 미M 미W
Why didn't the shipment of computer keyboards arrive today?
(A) The truck broke down on the way.
(B) I like the computer game.
(C) The shipping department did yesterday.

컴퓨터 키보드 배송이 왜 오늘 도착하지 않았어요?
(A) 트럭이 오다가 고장 났어요.
(B) 저는 컴퓨터 게임을 좋아해요.
(C) 어제 배송부가 했어요. 　　　정답 (A)

14. 미W 영M
Our factory complex is locked on national holidays, isn't it?
(A) Go straight on Washington Boulevard.
(B) Just bring your company ID badge.
(C) To access the restricted area.

우리 공장 단지는 국경일에 문이 잠기죠, 그렇죠?
(A) 워싱턴 대로에서 곧장 가세요.
(B) 그냥 사원증만 가지고 오시면 됩니다.
(C) 제한 구역에 들어가기 위해서요. 　　　정답 (B)

15. 호W 미M
Do you want to purchase an inkjet printer or laser printer?
(A) I have the model number here.
(B) Yes, print it out, please.
(C) We are out of stock at the moment.

잉크젯 프린터를 사고 싶어요, 아니면 레이저 프린터를 사고 싶어요?
(A) 여기 모델 번호가 있어요.
(B) 예, 그거 출력해 주세요.
(C) 지금 품절이에요. 　　　정답 (A)

16. 영M 미W
Where can I sign up for the time management seminar?
(A) A new manager will be here soon.
(B) You can sign at the bottom.
(C) You can register on our website.

시간 관리 세미나를 어디서 신청할 수 있어요?
(A) 새 매니저가 곧 올 거예요.
(B) 아래 쪽에 서명하시면 됩니다.
(C) 우리 웹사이트에서 등록하시면 됩니다. 　　　정답 (C)

17. 영M 호W
You know the supervisor at this assembly line, don't you?
(A) Yes, I've met her several times.

(B) It comes preassembled.

(C) No, several units in the line are not working.

이 조립 라인에 있는 감독관 아시죠, 그렇죠?

(A) 예, 그녀를 여러 번 만났어요.

(B) 그건 사전 조립되어 나옵니다.

(C) 아뇨, 라인에 있는 장치 여러 개가 작동하지 않고 있어요.　　　　정답 (A)

18. 미W 호W

Can I help you rearrange your office furniture?

(A) I bought a filing cabinet last Monday.

(B) The furniture store on Oak Street.

(C) I think I can manage on my own.

사무 가구를 재배치하시는 것을 도와드릴까요?

(A) 저는 지난주 월요일에 서류함을 샀어요.

(B) 오크 가에 있는 가구점이요.

(C) 저 혼자서 할 수 있을 것 같아요. .　　　　정답 (C)

19. 미M 호W

Can you tell me how to open a corporate account?

(A) A new accountant.

(B) There are additional office supplies in the cabinet.

(C) Here is the form you need to fill out.

법인 계좌를 어떻게 개설하는지 알려 주실래요?

(A) 새로운 회계사요.

(B) 사물함에 추가 사무용품이 있어요.

(C) 여기 작성하셔야 할 양식이 있습니다.　　　　정답 (C)

20. 미W 영M

Which client are we supposed to meet with this afternoon?

(A) We could possibly discuss the upcoming merger.

(B) From a local catering service.

(C) The Cattel Company representative.

우리는 오늘 오후에 어떤 고객을 만나기로 되어 있나요?

(A) 우리는 다가오는 합병에 대해 논의할 가능성이 있어요.

(B) 현지의 출장 요리 업체로부터요.

(C) 캐텔 회사 직원이요.　　　　정답 (C)

21. 호W 미M

How do you like this seafood restaurant?

(A) I'd like to do it.

(B) No, I haven't met the chef.

(C) I'd say it's my favorite place to eat.

이 해산물 식당은 마음에 드세요?

(A) 그렇게 하고 싶어요.

(B) 아뇨, 아직 요리사를 만나지 못했어요.

(C) 식사하기에 제가 가장 좋아하는 곳이라고 말하겠어요.　　　　정답 (C)

22. 영M 미W

Is there anybody who knows how to start a video conference?

(A) Tracy can do it.

(B) The registration fee for the conference.

(C) Yes, the video will be available.

영상 회의를 어떻게 시작하는지 아는 사람 있어요?

(A) 트레이시가 할 수 있어요.

(B) 총회 등록비요.

(C) 예, 비디오를 사용할 수 있어요.　　　　정답 (A)

23. 미M 호W

I don't think today is the best day for an outdoor baseball game, right?

(A) Yes, he is one of the baseball players.

(B) I agree. It is rather hot and humid.

(C) Mondays from 8 to 5.

오늘은 야외 야구 경기를 하기에 최적의 날은 아닌 것 같아요, 그렇죠?

(A) 예, 그는 야구 선수 중 한 명이에요.

(B) 동감이에요. 다소 덥고 습하네요.

(C) 월요일 8시부터 5시까지요.　　　　정답 (B)

24. 미W 영M

It's raining so hard outside.

(A) With an umbrella and a raincoat.

(B) I can give you a ride to the store.

(C) Yes, that was really hard.

밖에 비가 너무 세게 쏟아지고 있네요.

(A) 우산하고 우비도 같이요.

(B) 제가 가게까지 태워다 드릴 수 있어요.

(C) 예, 그건 정말 어려웠어요.　　　　정답 (B)

25. 영M 호W

Which museum do you think I should take Mr. Ricardo to?

(A) I'm new to this town, actually.

(B) I'll take that one on the left.

(C) Thanks, but I've already submitted the report.

제가 리카르도 씨를 어느 박물관으로 모시고 가야 할 것 같아요?

(A) 사실, 저는 이 동네가 처음이에요.

(B) 왼쪽에 있는 저것으로 할게요.

(C) 고마워요, 그런데 저는 보고서를 이미 제출했어요.　　　　정답 (A)

26. 미W 미M

Greg, will you be available to call our foreign clients back?

(A) Aron left them a message.

(B) Yes, he'll be back shortly.

(C) Haven't we met before?

그레그, 우리 해외 고객에게 답신 전화를 하실 시간이 있어요?

(A) 아론이 그들에게 메시지를 남겼어요.

(B) 예, 그는 곧 돌아올 겁니다.

(C) 우리 전에 만나지 않았나요?　　　　정답 (A)

27. 미M 미W

Are the new clients from overseas flying in today or tomorrow?

(A) Salma already picked them up from the airport.

(B) Two roundtrip tickets, please.

(C) I'll give them the contract.

해외에서 비행기 타고 오는 새 고객은 오늘 오나요, 아니면 내일 오나요?

(A) 살마가 이미 그들을 공항에서 픽업했어요.

(B) 왕복 표 2장 주세요.

(C) 제가 그들에게 계약서를 줄게요.　　　　정답 (A)

28. 영M 미M

When do you think you'll be able to work on this designing project?

(A) I can't agree with you more.

(B) Yes, they brought in a new designer.

(C) I haven't been trained yet.

당신은 언제쯤 이 디자인 프로젝트 작업을 할 수 있을 것 같아요?
(A) 당신 말에 정말 동의해요.
(B) 예, 그들은 새 디자이너를 영입했어요.
(C) 저는 아직 교육을 받지 못했습니다.   정답 (C)

29. 미W 영M
This bill seems too high for the lunch we ordered, doesn't it?
(A) Okay, I'll add that dessert to the menu.
(B) No, that looks about right to me.
(C) I'll be right back with your bill.

우리가 주문한 점심에 대한 이 계산서는 금액이 너무 높아 보여요, 그렇지 않나요?
(A) 좋아요, 그 디저트를 메뉴에 추가할게요.
(B) 아뇨, 저는 맞아 보이는데요.
(C) 손님 계산서를 갖고 바로 다시 올게요.   정답 (B)

30. 호W 영M
Why will the warehouse be closed for the next week?
(A) We don't have any in stock, either.
(B) No, that's a new factory.
(C) Didn't you receive the memo?

다음 주에 창고가 왜 문을 닫죠?
(A) 우리 역시 재고가 하나도 없어요.
(B) 아뇨, 그곳은 새 공장이에요.
(C) 메모 받지 못했어요?   정답 (C)

31. 미W 영M
The all-weather tires here in this section are really costly.
(A) A 10-minute taxi ride.
(B) They last a very long time.
(C) Stay tuned for the weather update.

여기 이 코너에 있는 전천후 타이어는 정말 비싸요.
(A) 택시 타고 10분 거리요.
(B) 그 타이어들은 아주 오래 가요.
(C) 계속해서 일기예보를 시청해 주세요.   정답 (B)

Part 3

문제 32-34번은 다음 대화를 참조하시오. 영M 미W

M: (32)I'm pleasantly surprised by how well our clothing store is doing. Our customers seem satisfied with the blouses and sweaters we carry.
W: That's right. (33)And as soon as we install the new cash registers this weekend, customers will have shorter waits at checkout.
M: For sure. Oh, one more thing. (34)Since the holidays are approaching, several employees have asked about when you will have the overtime work schedule ready.
W: (34)I've been working on the schedule since this morning. I think I should be done with it by tomorrow.

M: 우리 옷 가게가 잘 되고 있어서 정말 깜짝 놀랐어요. 우리가 취급하는 블라우스와 스웨터들에 우리 고객들이 만족해하는 것 같아요.
W: 맞아요. 그리고 이번 주말에 새로운 계산대를 설치하는 즉시, 고객들은 계산대에서 덜 기다리게 될 거예요.
M: 확실히 그럴 거예요. 아, 한 가지 더 말씀드리면, 연휴가 다가오고 있기

때문에, 여러 직원들이 당신이 시간 외 근무 일정표를 언제 준비하실 건지에 대해 물어봤어요.
W: 오늘 아침부터 그 일정표 작업을 하고 있어요. 제 생각에 내일이면 다 끝마칠 수 있을 거예요.

32. 화자들은 어디에서 근무하는가?
(A) 소매점
(B) 섬유 제조업체
(C) 약국
(D) 슈퍼마켓   정답 (A)

33. 이번 주말에 무슨 일이 있겠는가?
(A) 세일이 있을 것이다.
(B) 직원들이 시간 외 근무를 할 것이다.
(C) 새 장비가 설치될 것이다.
(D) 교육 프로그램이 있을 것이다.   정답 (C)

34. 여자는 무엇을 준비하고 있다고 말하는가?
(A) 근무 일정표
(B) 매장 안내도
(C) 재고 목록
(D) 광고   정답 (A)

문제 35-37번은 다음 대화를 참조하시오. 미M 호W

M: Hello. (35)This is Jason in customer service at Harding International. How can I help you?
W: Oh, it's about time. I've been on hold for more than 40 minutes. (36)I'm so frustrated because I've never had to wait so long to talk to someone about a computer issue before.
M: I'm very sorry about the wait, ma'am. We're experiencing much higher call volume than normal today, and we're trying to answer them as quickly as we can. Now, before we continue speaking, (37)would you please let me know the eight-digit product code that's located on the back of your laptop?

M: 안녕하세요. 저는 하딩 인터내셔널의 고객 서비스과 제이슨입니다. 무엇을 도와드릴까요?
W: 아, 이제야 연결되네요. 40분 이상 대기 상태였어요. 전에 컴퓨터 문제 때문에 누군가와 상담하려고 이렇게 오래 기다려 본 적이 없어서 정말 불만스러워요.
M: 기다리시게 해서 너무 죄송합니다, 고객님. 오늘따라 평소보다 통화량이 훨씬 더 많은데, 가능하면 빨리 전화를 받으려고 애쓰고 있습니다. 자, 계속 얘기하기 전에, 우선 노트북 뒤에 있는 8자리 제품 코드를 알려 주시겠어요?

35. 남자는 누구일 것 같은가?
(A) 고객 서비스 직원
(B) 전기 기사
(C) 판매 상담원
(D) 마케팅 전문가   정답 (A)

36. 여자가 불만스러워 하는 이유는?
(A) 그녀는 영수증을 가지고 있지 않다.
(B) 그녀는 컴퓨터를 수리받지 못했다.
(C) 그녀는 환불을 받을 수가 없다.
(D) 그녀는 오래 기다려야 했다.   정답 (D)

37. 여자는 무엇을 제공해 달라고 요청받는가?
(A) 계좌 번호
(B) 제품 번호
(C) 쿠폰 코드
(D) 도로 주소　　　　　　　　　　　정답 (B)

문제 38-40번은 다음 3자 대화를 참조하시오. 미M 미W 영M

M1: Hello. (38)I'd like to confirm that the bus bound for Lexington is leaving in thirty minutes. I can't see a listing for it anywhere on the board.
W: (38) (39)I regret to inform you that the bus has been delayed by two hours. It's leaving at 10:30 now.
M1: Oh, no. That means we're going to miss our meeting with a customer in Lexington.
M2: (40)We'd better give her a call and let her know. Steve, would you mind doing that now?
M1: (40)Not at all. I'll see if she minds if we meet later in the evening.

M1: 안녕하세요. 렉싱턴 행 버스가 30분 후에 떠나는지 확인하고 싶습니다. 그 버스에 대한 시간 안내가 게시판 어디에도 안 보이네요.
W: 그 버스는 2시간 지연되었다는 사실을 알려 드리게 되어 유감입니다. 이제는 그 버스는 10시 30분에 떠나요.
M1: 아, 이런. 그 말은 우리가 렉싱턴에서 고객과 만나는 회의를 놓치게 될 거라는 말이잖아요.
M2: 그분에게 전화해서 알려 드리는 게 낫겠어요. 스티브, 지금 그렇게 해 주실래요?
M1: 물론이죠. 저녁에 좀 늦게 만나는 게 괜찮은지 알아볼게요.

38. 여자는 누구일 것 같은가?
(A) 버스 운전사
(B) 철도 엔지니어
(C) 렌터카 회사 직원
(D) 버스 정거장 직원　　　　　　　　정답 (D)

39. 여자는 어떤 문제를 언급하는가?
(A) 전화번호가 틀렸다.
(B) 회의가 취소되었다.
(C) 버스가 지연되었다.
(D) 인터넷 연결이 되지 않고 있다.　　정답 (C)

40. 스티브는 이후에 무엇을 하겠는가?
(A) 고객에게 연락
(B) 회의 취소
(C) 표 값 지불
(D) 표에 대한 환불 요청　　　　　　　정답 (A)

문제 41-43번은 다음 대화를 참조하시오. 호W 미M

W: Hi, John. (41)Is there a bicycle rack somewhere on the office building property here?
M: I'm not sure. Why do you ask?
W: (42)I just had to take my car to the garage. The mechanic said he can't work on it for a week, so I'm planning to ride my bike here until he's done.
M: Hmm… There might be a bicycle rack somewhere around

here. (43)But if there isn't, why don't you talk to Michelle? She lives in your neighborhood, so perhaps you could carpool to work together.
W: I had no idea about that. I'll call her after lunch.

W: 안녕하세요, 존. 여기 사무실 건물 부지 어딘가에 자전거 보관대가 있나요?
M: 잘 모르겠어요. 왜 물어요?
W: 방금 제 차를 정비소에 가져가야 했는데요. 정비사가 일주일 동안은 제 차 작업을 할 수 없다고 해서, 그가 수리를 끝낼 때까지는 자전거 타고 출근할 계획이에요.
M: 음… 이 근처 어딘가에 자전거 보관대가 있을 수 있어요. 만약에 없다면, 미셸과 얘기해 보시지 그래요? 그녀가 당신 동네에 사니까, 아마 카풀하여 같이 출근할 수 있을 거예요.
W: 그건 전혀 몰랐어요. 점심 후에 그녀에게 연락해 봐야겠네요.

41. 여자는 남자에게 무엇에 대해 물어보는가?
(A) 자동차 정비소
(B) 다가오는 세미나
(C) 자전거 주차
(D) 렌터카 예약　　　　　　　　　　정답 (C)

42. 여자에게 어떤 문제가 있는가?
(A) 그녀는 자동차 열쇠를 잃어버렸다.
(B) 그녀의 차가 정비소에 있다.
(C) 그녀의 컴퓨터가 작동하지 않는다.
(D) 그녀는 회사에 또 지각했다.　　　정답 (B)

43. 남자는 여자에게 무엇을 할 것을 제안하는가?
(A) 휴가 시간 가지기
(B) 회사 가까운 곳으로 이사하기
(C) 동료와 얘기해 보기
(D) 파일 출력하기　　　　　　　　　정답 (C)

문제 44-46번은 다음 대화를 참조하시오. 미W 영M

W: (44)Congratulations on being transferred to the new office in London, David. Here's a card that everyone in the office signed. We hope you enjoy working abroad.
M: Thanks. I'm going to miss working with everyone, (45)but I'm looking forward to the chance to manage my own office.
W: I know you'll do an outstanding job. We all wonder if you have some free time for dinner tonight. (46)We'd like to take you out to celebrate before you leave for London.
M: (46)I heard about a new Indian restaurant downtown.
W: Sounds great. Let's go there.

W: 런던의 새 사무소로 발령받은 것을 축하드립니다, 데이비드. 여기 사무실의 모든 직원이 서명한 카드가 있어요. 해외에서의 근무가 즐거우시길 바랍니다.
M: 감사해요. 여러분 모두와 같이 근무했던 것이 그리울 거예요. 그런데 제 사무소를 관리할 기회도 너무 기다려져요.
W: 정말 잘 하실 거라는 걸 알아요. 오늘 밤 저녁 식사 같이 할 시간이 있으신지 우리 모두 궁금해요. 런던으로 떠나시기 전에 모시고 나가서 축하드리고 싶어서요.
M: 시내에 있는 새 인도 식당에 관해 들었어요.
W: 좋아요. 거기에 갑시다.

44. 여자는 무엇에 관해 남자를 축하해 주는가?
(A) 승진
(B) 전근
(C) 상여금 수령
(D) 수상 　　　　　　　　　　　　　　　　정답 (B)

45. 남자는 무엇을 하는 것을 고대하고 있는가?
(A) 고향으로 이사 가는 것
(B) 새 계약서에 서명하는 것
(C) 관리자로 근무하는 것
(D) 해외에서 온 직원들을 맞이하는 것 　　정답 (C)

46. 남자가 "시내에 있는 새 인도 식당에 관해 들었어요"라고 말하는 이유는?
(A) 초대를 수락하기 위해
(B) 시내에 교통 체증이 심하다는 것을 나타내기 위해
(C) 메뉴 변경을 요청하기 위해
(D) 비용에 대한 우려를 표명하기 위해 　정답 (A)

문제 47-49번은 다음 3자 대화를 참조하시오. 미W 영M 호W

W1: Hello, Mr. Ames. I'm Deanna Morris. I'm the head of HR here at Peterson Software. This is Alice Boyle, my coworker. **(47) We'll both be interviewing you now.**
M: It's a pleasure to meet both of you.
W2: Likewise. Thanks for coming in for an interview today. **(48) I see from your application that you want to work here as a software developer.** So why are you interested in applying to our company?
M: Well, I've done a lot of research on your company. It's not only a great place to work, **(49)but you also provide your employees with great opportunities for career development and growth.** I think Peterson Software has a good reputation for investing a lot in training and educating its workers.
W1: Yes, we do encourage our employees to get as much training as they can.

W1: 안녕하세요, 에임스 씨. 저는 디애나 모리스입니다. 여기 피터슨 소프트웨어의 인적자원부 부장입니다. 여기는 앨리스 보일, 제 동료입니다. 우리 둘 다 에임스 씨를 지금 면접을 할 겁니다.
M: 두 분 다 뵙게 되어 반갑습니다
W2: 저희도 그렇습니다. 오늘 면접 보러 와 주셔서 감사합니다. 입사지원서에 보니, 소프트웨어 개발자로 이곳에 근무하고 싶어하시는군요. 그래서 우리 회사 지원에 왜 관심이 있으신 건가요?
M: 음, 이 회사에 대해 많은 조사를 했어요. 이 회사가 근무하기에 좋은 곳일 뿐만 아니라, 직원들에게 경력 발전 및 성장을 위한 좋은 기회도 제공하시더군요. 제 생각에는 피터슨 소프트웨어가 직원들을 훈련하고 교육시키는 데 투자를 많이 하는 것으로 평판이 좋은 것 같아요.
W1: 맞아요, 우리는 직원들에게 가능한 한 많은 교육을 받으라고 독려합니다.

47. 화자들이 만나는 이유는?
(A) 일자리 면접을 하기 위해
(B) 제품 시연회를 보기 위해
(C) 실험을 실시하기 위해
(D) 새 소프트웨어 프로그램에 대해 논의하기 위해 　정답 (A)

48. 남자의 직업은 무엇이겠는가?
(A) 화학 엔지니어

(B) 소프트웨어 개발자
(C) 자동차 디자이너
(D) 영업 담당자 　　　　　　　　　　　　정답 (B)

49. 남자는 회사에 대해 어떤 점이 마음에 든다고 하는가?
(A) 직원들에게 급여를 많이 준다.
(B) 개인의 성장을 위한 기회를 제공한다.
(C) 많은 외국에 지사가 있다.
(D) 직원들에게 헬스 회원권을 준다. 　　정답 (B)

문제 50-52번은 다음 대화를 참조하시오. 미W 미M

W: (50)**Jackson Health Clinic.** This is Melissa. How can I help you?
M: Hello. I need to make an appointment to see a doctor. My name is Stanley Peters.
W: Are you a current patient here?
M: That's right. I want to get a flu shot.
W: (51)**Just so you know, it's no longer necessary to make an appointment with a doctor to get a flu shot.** You can visit us anytime during hours of operation. One of our nurses can administer the shot.
M: Wonderful. I'd like to visit tomorrow during my lunch break. Are you busy then?
W: Lots of people come then. If you don't want to wait, you'd be better off coming in early in the morning.
M: Okay. (52)**I'll be there first thing tomorrow morning.**

W: 잭슨 헬스 클리닉입니다. 저는 멜리사입니다. 무엇을 도와드릴까요?
M: 안녕하세요. 예약을 해서 의사 선생님 진찰을 받아야 하는데요. 제 이름은 스탠리 피터스입니다.
W: 현재 이 병원의 환자세요?
M: 맞아요. 독감 주사를 맞고 싶습니다.
W: 참고로 말씀을 드리는데, 독감 주사 맞는 데 더 이상 의사 선생님과 예약을 하실 필요는 없습니다. 병원 운영 시간 언제든지 찾아오시면 됩니다. 간호사 중 한 명이 주사를 놓아 드릴 겁니다.
M: 잘됐군요. 내일 점심 시간에 방문하고 싶어요. 그 때는 바쁜 시간인가요?
W: 그때 많은 분들이 오세요. 기다리고 싶지 않으시다면, 오전 일찍 오시는 것이 나을 겁니다.
M: 좋습니다. 내일 아침 거기 먼저 갈게요.

50. 여자는 어디서 근무하는 것 같은가?
(A) 대학교
(B) 병원
(C) 쇼핑 센터
(D) 약국 　　　　　　　　　　　　　　　정답 (B)

51. 여자는 남자에게 어떤 새 정책에 대해 말하는가?
(A) 그는 소개를 받아야 한다.
(B) 그는 취소 비용을 내야 한다.
(C) 그는 미리 등록해야 한다.
(D) 그는 예약이 필요하지 않다. 　　　　정답 (D)

52. 남자는 무엇을 하겠다고 말하는가?
(A) 병원 서식 작성하기
(B) 예약을 내일로 변경하기
(C) 퇴근 후에 도착하기
(D) 아침에 방문하기 　　　　　　　　　정답 (D)

M: Hello, Sabrina.

W: Hello, Jason. What can I do for you?

M: (53)Some sales representatives and I had a meeting about the office renovations starting next week. It looks like some of us have to move during that time of construction. (54)I wonder if there's any room for us in the Marketing Department.

W: Oh, (54)we just got four new interns.

M: I see… Well, I know you've got several tables set up in the area. Don't you think they take up a lot of room? I guess some desks could fit in that space.

W: That's a good point. (55)I'll give a call to Facilities and have its team come to take them away.

M: 안녕하세요, 사브리나.

W: 안녕하세요, 제이슨. 뭘 도와드려요?

M: 몇몇 영업 직원들과 제가 다음 주부터 시작하는 사무실 보수공사 건 때문에 회의를 했어요. 우리 중 일부가 그 공사 기간 동안에 옮겨야 할 것 같아요. 마케팅부에 우리가 들어갈 공간이 있을까 모르겠네요.

W: 아, 저희는 막 새 인턴 4명을 받았어요.

M: 그렇군요… 거기에 테이블 몇 개가 설치되어 있는 걸로 알고 있어요. 그게 자리를 많이 차지한다고 생각하지 않으세요? 그 공간에 책상 몇 개는 들어갈 것 같은데요.

W: 좋은 지적이네요. 시설과에 전화해서, 그쪽 팀이 와서 테이블들을 치우게 할게요.

53. 화자들은 주로 무엇에 관한 얘기를 하고 있는가?
   (A) 일정이 바뀐 행사
   (B) 확장 제안서
   (C) 공사 프로젝트의 영향
   (D) 취업 기회
   정답 (C)

54. 여자가 "우리는 막 새 인턴 4명을 받았어요"라고 말할 때 무엇을 의미하는가?
   (A) 공간이 충분하지 않다.
   (B) 그녀는 추가 사무 장비가 필요하다.
   (C) 그들은 오리엔테이션이 필요하다.
   (D) 그녀의 부서는 예산을 초과했다.
   정답 (A)

55. 여자는 무엇을 하겠다고 제의하는가?
   (A) 시설부에 전화하기
   (B) 예산 보고서 보기
   (C) 고객과 얘기하기
   (D) 고객의 불평 처리하기
   정답 (A)

M: Hello, Wendy. (56)I'm hoping to put together a training session for the employees in this department all day next Monday. How does that sound?

W: That's fine. Everyone seems to be having trouble with the new software we've been working with, so having an instructor to go over how to use it at a slower pace would be helpful. (57) Since it's going to be so long, why don't we provide lunch for everyone?

M: That's a good idea. That should make everybody happy.

W: I know we can get some money from the departmental budget to buy lunch, but I don't know how much is available.

M: (58)I'll review the budget and let you know.

M: 안녕하세요, 웬디. 다음 주 월요일 하루 종일 이 부서 직원들을 위한 교육을 준비하고 싶어요. 그렇게 하는 게 어떨까요?

W: 좋아요. 모든 사람이 우리가 계속 작업하고 있는 그 새 소프트웨어에 대해 어려움을 겪고 있는 것 같아요. 그래서 강사로 하여금 더 느린 속도로 그것을 어떻게 사용하는지에 대해 검토하게 하면 도움이 될 거예요. 교육이 길어질 것이므로, 모두에게 점심을 제공하는 게 어때요?

M: 좋은 생각이에요. 그러면 모든 사람이 만족스러워하겠죠.

W: 제가 알기로 점심을 사는 데 부서 예산에서 자금을 받을 수 있을 건데, 얼마나 가능한지는 모르겠어요.

M: 예산을 검토해 보고 알려 드릴게요.

56. 남자는 무엇을 하고 싶어 하는가?
   (A) 업데이트된 소프트웨어 버전 설치
   (B) 더 많은 직원 고용
   (C) 교육 준비
   (D) 부서 회의 일정 잡기
   정답 (C)

57. 여자는 무엇을 할 것을 제안하는가?
   (A) 온라인 후기 보기
   (B) 컴퓨터 업그레이드하기
   (C) 고객을 모시고 나가서 점심 먹기
   (D) 음식 제공하기
   정답 (D)

58. 남자는 이후에 무엇을 할 것 같은가?
   (A) 없어진 물품 찾기
   (B) 출장 요리 업체 고용하기
   (C) 예산 보기
   (D) 전화 걸기
   정답 (C)

W: Hello, Mark. (59)I just completed the installation of the XLS 500, our new electronic time recorder. As of now, information about all of the employees is entered, so the system is going to start tracking employee timesheets electronically.

M: Employees just need to swipe their ID badges to clock in and out of work, right?

W: That's correct. (60)And at the departmental meeting this afternoon, I can distribute their new badges.

M: Okay. Do you think we need to extend the meeting to teach the employees how to use the new system?

W: Not at all. (61)The XLS 500 is very straightforward and user-friendly. I can demonstrate it if you want, but it's a simple process.

W: 안녕하세요, 마크. 제가 방금 우리 새로운 전자 시간 기록계인 XLS 500의 설치를 끝마쳤어요. 지금 이 시간 부로, 모든 직원들의 정보가 입력되어 있고, 그래서 시스템은 직원 근무시간 기록표를 전자적으로 추적할 거예요.

M: 직원들은 출퇴근 시간을 기록하는 데 자신의 신분증을 긁기만 하면 되는 거죠, 그렇죠?

W: 맞아요. 그리고 오늘 오후 부서 회의에서 새 신분증을 나눠줄 수 있어요.

M: 알겠습니다. 직원들에게 새 시스템 사용 방법을 가르쳐 주기 위해 회의

를 연장할 필요가 있을까요?

W: 전혀 아닙니다. XLS 500은 매우 간단하고 사용자 편의적이에요. 원하시면 시연해 드릴 수 있는데, 아주 간단한 과정이에요.

59. 화자들은 주로 무엇에 대해 논의하고 있는가?
(A) 고용 절차
(B) 내구성 있는 장치
(C) 근무시간 기록 시스템
(D) 디지털 도어록　　　　　　　　　　　정답 (C)

60. 오늘 오후에 직원들에게 무엇이 제공될 것인가?
(A) 수정된 근무 일정표
(B) 새로운 보안 코드
(C) 전자 신분증
(D) 노트북 컴퓨터　　　　　　　　　　　정답 (C)

61. 여자는 XLS 500에 대해 무엇을 나타내는가?
(A) 직원들이 사용하기 쉽다.
(B) 전사적으로 설치되는 데 비용이 많이 든다.
(C) 그것은 2년 품질 보증서가 같이 온다.
(D) 그 설치 작업이 오래 걸린다.　　　　정답 (A)

문제 62-64번은 다음 대화와 표를 참조하시오. 호W 영M

W: Hello, Steve. **(62)I'm just confirming that we have the necessary safety gear for the work we'll be doing on the four-story parking structure.**
M: That's the garage next to the river, right?
W: Yes, that's it. The project manager wants the workers on the site to wear color-coded safety helmets to keep track of the individual teams. **(63)But we don't have enough blue hard hats for the team that needs them.**
M: Hmm… **(63)Those construction workers won't be needed on the job site until one week from now.** Why don't we arrange to have some more blue hats delivered before then?
W: Yeah, that should be fine. **(64)I'll go ahead and place an order for them right now.**

W: 안녕하세요. 스티브. 우리가 4층 주차 건물 공사를 할 건데, 작업에 필요한 안전 장비를 우리가 갖추고 있는지 확인하고 있어요.
M: 그게 강 옆에 있는 주차 건물이죠, 그렇죠?
W: 예, 맞아요. 프로젝트 관리자는 개별 팀들을 파악하기 위해 현장 작업자들이 색깔별로 안전모를 착용하기를 원해요. 그런데, 파란 안전모가 필요한 팀을 위한 파란 안전모가 충분히 없어요.
M: 음… 그 공사 작업자들은 지금부터 일주일 후에나 현장에 필요할 거예요. 그 전에 파란 안전모가 추가로 배달되도록 하시는 게 어때요?
W: 예, 그러면 되겠네요. 지체없이 바로 지금 파란색 안전모를 주문할게요.

팀 안전모 색깔	
용접공	노란색
(63)배관공	**파란색**
벽돌공	주황색
지붕이는 사람	하얀색

62. 화자들은 어떤 유형의 건물에 대해 얘기하고 있는가?
(A) 스포츠 경기장
(B) 공장
(C) 주차 건물
(D) 쇼핑 센터　　　　　　　　　　　　정답 (C)

63. 그래픽을 보시오. 어느 팀 작업자들이 일주일 후에 일을 시작하는가?
(A) 용접공
(B) 배관공
(C) 지붕을 이는 사람
(D) 벽돌공　　　　　　　　　　　　　　정답 (B)

64. 여자는 이후에 무엇을 할 것인가?
(A) 온라인으로 광고 내기
(B) 프로젝트 현장 방문하기
(C) 공사 일정 시각표 확인하기
(D) 주문 넣기　　　　　　　　　　　　정답 (D)

문제 65-67번은 다음 대화와 게시판을 참조하시오. 미M 미W

M: Hello. Thank you for coming to Jackson's Ice Cream Shop.
W: Hello. **(65)I'm a teacher at Ridgewood Elementary School**, and I'd like to purchase some ice cream for our school party today.
M: Oh, my son is a student at your school. Today's your lucky day since we are having a sale on strawberry ice cream. I've got the price list right here.
W: My class is big, **(66)so I guess I'd better purchase a gallon of strawberry ice cream.** Oh, sorry. **(67)I left my purse in my car. I'll be back in just a moment.**
M: No problem.

M: 안녕하세요. 잭슨즈 아이스크림 가게에 와주셔서 감사합니다.
W: 안녕하세요. 저는 리지우드 초등학교 선생님인데, 오늘 우리 학교 파티를 위한 아이스크림을 구매하고 싶어요.
M: 아, 우리 아들이 그 학교 학생이에요. 딸기 아이스크림을 세일하고 있어서 오늘 운이 좋으시네요. 바로 여기 가격표가 있어요.
W: 우리 반은 규모가 커서, 딸기 아이스크림을 1갤런 구입해야 할 것 같아요. 아, 죄송해요. 제 지갑을 차에 두고 왔네요. 바로 돌아올게요.
M: 문제없어요.

잭슨즈 아이스크림 가게
오늘의 특별가

스쿱	$2.00
파인트	$3.50
쿼트	$5.00
(66)갤런	**$9.00**

65. 여자는 누구인가?
(A) 식당 주인

    (B) 배달하는 사람

    (C) 학교 선생님

    (D) 회사 관리자   정답 (C)

66. 그래픽을 보시오. 여자는 자신의 주문에 대해 얼마를 지불할 것인가?

    (A) 2달러

    (B) 3.50달러

    (C) 5달러

    (D) 9달러   정답 (D)

67. 여자는 이후에 무엇을 하겠는가?

    (A) 아이스크림 계산서 지불하기

    (B) 딸기 아이스크림 시식하기

    (C) 차에서 지갑 찾아오기

    (D) 자신의 차를 정비공에게 갖고 가기   정답 (C)

문제 68–70번은 다음 대화와 신용 카드 명세서를 참조하시오. 영M 호W

M: Thank you for contacting Lexington Bank. What can I do for you?

W: Hello. I just received this month's credit card statement, **(69) and I see an incorrect charge on it dated February 11.**

M: **(68)Could you tell me the name as it appears on your credit card, please?**

W: Sure. My name is Molly Carpenter.

M: Okay, Ms. Carpenter. It looks like you used your card at Jerry's Grill on February 11.

W: That's right. But the amount listed on the statement is different from the one on my receipt. I have the receipt I got from Jerry's Grill.

M: Okay. **(70)You'll need to fill out a form to dispute the charge.** I'll e-mail it to you at once.

M: 렉싱턴 은행에 연락 주셔서 감사합니다. 무엇을 도와드릴까요?

W: 안녕하세요. 방금 이번 달 신용 카드 명세서를 받았는데, 명세서에 2월 11일자 청구 금액이 잘못되었어요.

M: 고객님 신용 카드에 보이는 그대로 이름을 알려 주시겠습니까?

W: 예. 제 이름은 몰리 카펜터예요.

M: 알겠습니다. 카펜터 씨. 2월 11일 제리스 그릴에서 신용 카드를 사용하신 것 같네요.

W: 맞아요. 그런데 명세서에 적혀 있는 금액과 제 영수증에 있는 금액이 달라요. 제리스 그릴에서 받은 영수증을 가지고 있어요.

M: 좋습니다. 그 청구 금액에 대해 반박하는 양식을 작성해 주셔야겠습니다. 바로 이메일로 양식을 보내 드릴게요.

신용 카드 명세서

날짜	내역	금액
2월 5일	실반 의류	$73.45
2월 9일	버스 터미널	$15.00
(69)2월 11일	**제리스 그릴**	**$42.00**
2월 12일	웨스트사이드 식료품	$89.98

68. 여자는 어떤 정보를 제공하라는 요청을 받는가?

    (A) 그녀의 이름

    (B) 그녀의 이메일 주소

    (C) 그녀의 전화 번호

    (D) 그녀의 집 주소   정답 (A)

69. 그래픽을 보시오. 여자는 어떤 금액이 틀리다고 말하는가?

    (A) 73.45달러

    (B) 15달러

    (C) 42달러

    (D) 89.98달러   정답 (C)

70. 남자는 여자에게 무엇을 하라고 말하는가?

    (A) 직접 사무실 방문하기

    (B) 그녀의 계좌번호 제공하기

    (C) 서류양식 작성하기

    (D) 그의 매니저와 얘기하기   정답 (C)

Part 4

문제 71–73번은 다음 안내를 참조하시오. 미W

W: **(71)I'm so happy to be here with everyone today for the opening of the Meridian Library's new multi-media center.** Thanks to the generous donations everyone provided, **(72) we were able to buy a subscription to a movie streaming service**. This service will allow us to get fast and easy access to a wide selection of films available online. Best of all, all library members can enjoy the service for free. **(73)There's further information about the streaming service on the library's web page.** Now, why don't we celebrate with some snacks and beverages?

오늘 메리디언 도서관의 새 멀티미디어 센터 개막 행사에 여러분 모두와 이 자리를 같이하게 되어 참으로 기쁩니다. 여러분 모두가 해주신 후한 기부 덕분에, 우리는 영화 스트리밍 서비스를 구독할 수 있게 되었습니다. 이 서비스 덕분에 우리는 온라인에서 이용 가능한 아주 다양한 종류의 영화들을 빠르고 편하게 이용할 수 있게 되었습니다. 무엇보다도, 모든 도서관 회원들이 이 서비스를 무료로 즐기실 수 있습니다. 스트리밍 서비스에 대한 더 많은 정보는 도서관 웹 페이지에 있습니다. 자, 스낵과 음료를 같이 하면서 축하해 볼까요?

71. 안내는 어디에서 이루어지는가?

    (A) 영화관

    (B) 박물관

    (C) 텔레비전 방송국

    (D) 도서관   정답 (D)

72. 화자는 어떤 새로운 서비스가 제공된다고 말하는가?

    (A) 온라인 고객 지원

    (B) 무료 온라인 교본

    (C) 전자책 내려받기 서비스

    (D) 영화 스트리밍   정답 (D)

73. 청자들은 어떻게 더 많은 정보를 얻을 수 있는가?

    (A) 안내책자를 읽음으로써

    (B) 소식지를 구독함으로써

    (C) 사서와 상담함으로써

    (D) 웹 페이지를 방문함으로써   정답 (D)

문제 74-76번은 다음 워크숍의 발췌 내용을 참조하시오. 미M

M: My name is Tim Chambers, and I'm your instructor at today's workshop. I know most of you here today are business owners, and you know plenty about your professions. **(74)However, knowing how to market your products properly can be the difference between succeeding and failing.** In the past, you'd have to hire a marketing agency to help with promoting your products, and that could cost thousands of dollars. But today, **(75) I'm going to teach you some things you can do that will be much cheaper.** Now, before we get started, **(76)let's go around the room and introduce ourselves.** I want each of you to state your name and the business you run.

제 이름은 팀 챔버스이고, 제가 오늘 워크숍의 강사입니다. 오늘 이 자리에 오신 여러분 대다수가 사업주인 것을 알고 있고, 여러분은 여러분의 직업에 대해서는 많은 것들을 알고 계십니다. 그렇지만, 여러분의 제품을 적절하게 판매하는 방법을 아는 것이 성공하는 것과 실패하는 것을 가르는 차이점이 될 수 있습니다. 과거에 여러분은 마케팅 회사를 고용해서 여러분의 제품을 홍보하는 데 도움을 받으셔야 했을 것이고, 이는 수천 달러 비용이 들어갔을 것입니다. 그런데 오늘, 저는 여러분들에게 여러분이 할 수 있는 훨씬 더 저렴한 몇 가지를 가르쳐 드릴 것입니다. 자, 시작하기 전에, 방에서 돌면서 자기 소개를 합시다. 여러분 각자 이름을 말하고 자신이 운영하는 사업체도 말씀해 주세요.

74. 워크숍의 주제는 무엇인가?
(A) 신입 사원 채용하기
(B) 이력서 쓰기
(C) 상품 마케팅하기
(D) 직원 관리하기 　　　　　　　정답 (C)

75. 워크숍은 청자들에게 어떻게 도움을 줄 것인가?
(A) 고객을 더 유치하게 될 것이다.
(B) 고객을 계속 유지하게 해줄 것이다.
(C) 비용을 절감하게 해줄 것이다.
(D) 실적을 개선시켜 줄 것이다. 　　정답 (C)

76. 화자는 청자들에게 무엇을 할 것을 요청하는가?
(A) 양식에 서명하기
(B) 정보 비디오 시청하기
(C) 슬라이드 프로젝터 설치하기
(D) 자기 소개하기 　　　　　　　정답 (D)

문제 77-79번은 다음 회의의 발췌 내용을 참조하시오. 호W

W: I'm pleased all of you could make it for a morning team meeting. **(77)We're going to open the restaurant soon, so I want to keep this meeting short.** As you're well aware, summer is rapidly approaching, **(78)so that means the tourists are flocking to this area.** If any of you are interested in working additional hours, talk to me. I'd also like to remind everyone about our rules regarding changing schedules. **(79) If you trade shifts with anyone, don't forget to update the online calendar so that I know who will be working that day.**

아침 팀 회의에 여러분 모두 와주셔서 기쁘네요. 곧 식당 문을 열 것이니, 이 회의는 짧게 하고 싶습니다. 여러분 전부 다 잘 아시다시피, 여름이 빨리 다가오고 있는데, 이는 관광객이 이 지역으로 몰려온다는 의미죠. 여러분 중 누구든 시간 외 근무를 하고 싶으시면, 저에게 말씀해 주세요. 또한 일정을

변경하는 것과 관련하여 우리 규정에 대해 여러분에게 다시 한 번 상기시켜 드리고 싶어요. 다른 사람과 근무 시간을 바꾼다면, 제가 그 날 누가 근무하는지 알 수 있도록 여러분은 꼭 온라인 달력에 최신 정보로 수정하는 것을 잊지 마세요.

77. 청자들은 어디에서 근무하는가?
(A) 호텔
(B) 슈퍼마켓
(C) 식당
(D) 백화점 　　　　　　　　　　정답 (C)

78. 화자가 "관광객들이 이 지역으로 몰려온다"라고 말할 때 무엇을 함축하는가?
(A) 추가 직원들이 고용될 것이다.
(B) 주차할 곳을 찾기가 어려워질 것이다.
(C) 기한을 맞출 가능성이 없을 것이다.
(D) 업체가 더 분주해질 것이다. 　　정답 (D)

79. 화자는 청자들에게 무엇을 할 것을 상기시켜 주는가?
(A) 그들의 새 유니폼 찾아가기
(B) 직장에 제 시간에 오기
(C) 달력을 최신 정보로 수정하기
(D) 이름표 착용하기 　　　　　　정답 (C)

문제 80-82번은 다음 전화 메시지를 참조하시오. 영M

M: Hello, Craig. **(80)I'm calling to get an update on the mobile phone application for the travel guide we just published.** Ms. Chapman informed me that she wants to include a few more cities on the app, and one of those is Hartford. **(81)I know you grew up there, so I'm sure you know the best places to see and where to shop and eat in the city, so you would be a great fit for this updated app project.** I'd like to add your suggestions to the guide. **(82)We need to schedule a meeting to discuss this new project**, so please give me a call back as soon as possible to let me know when you have time. Thank you.

안녕하세요, 크레이그. 우리가 막 공개한 여행 가이드 휴대 전화 앱에 대한 업데이트 상황을 알고 싶어 전화드렸어요. 채프먼 씨가 앱에 도시 몇 개를 더 포함하고 싶은데, 그 중 하나가 하트포드라고 저에게 알렸어요. 제가 알기로 당신은 거기서 성장해서, 그 도시에서 볼 만한 가장 좋은 곳들, 어디서 쇼핑하고 식사할지를 잘 알고 있으리라 확신해요. 그래서 당신이 이 업데이트된 앱 프로젝트에 매우 적합할 거예요. 당신의 제안을 가이드에 추가하고 싶어요. 이 새 프로젝트를 논의하기 위해서 회의 일정을 잡아야 하니, 가능한 한 빨리 저에게 전화 주셔서 언제 시간이 되시는지 알려 주세요. 감사합니다.

80. 화자는 무엇 때문에 전화하고 있는가?
(A) 장비 주문
(B) 모바일 애플리케이션
(C) 빈 일자리
(D) 새 휴대 전화 출시 　　　　　정답 (B)

81. 청자가 새 프로젝트에 적합한 이유는?
(A) 그는 어떤 도시를 잘 안다.
(B) 그는 리더십 능력이 좋다.
(C) 그는 컴퓨터 프로그래머이다.
(D) 그는 아주 체계적이다. 　　　　정답 (A)

82. 화자는 무엇을 하고 싶어 하는가?

(A) 광고 게재

(B) 취업 기회에 관한 대화

(C) 전문가와 상담

(D) 회의 준비 정답 (D)

문제 83-85번은 다음 연설을 참조하시오. 미W

W: (83)**My newest book, *Starting Your Career*, is for those looking for a job or wanting a career change.** Job seekers spend long hours writing their résumés and completing job applications, but they seldom get a job interview call. (84)**My book explains some common mistakes people make in the job seeking process and also shows how to get the jobs and promotions you want.** I've worked as a recruiting manager at a few large companies for more than two decades. Following my presentation, I'll answer any questions you have and sign copies of my book. (85)**And be sure to visit my website, where you can sign up to get a free half-hour-long consultation from me regarding your career.**

저의 최신 저서, 〈경력 쌓기〉는 일자리를 찾거나 직업을 바꾸고자 하는 사람들을 위한 것입니다. 구직자들은 오랜 시간을 들여 이력서를 쓰고 입사 지원서를 작성합니다만, 면접 보러 오라는 전화를 좀처럼 받지 못합니다. 제 책은 직업을 구하는 과정에서 사람들이 흔하게 하는 실수에 대해 설명하고, 또한 어떻게 원하는 곳에 취업을 하고 승진하는지를 보여 줍니다. 저는 채용 담당 매니저로 몇몇 대기업에서 20년 이상 근무했습니다. 제 프레젠테이션 후에, 저는 어떤 질문이든 답해 드릴 것이고, 제 책에 서명도 해드릴 것입니다. 그리고 꼭 제 웹사이트를 방문해 보세요. 거기서 여러분의 경력에 관하여 제가 해드리는 30분짜리 무료 상담을 신청하실 수 있습니다.

83. 화자는 최근에 무엇을 했는가?

(A) 회사를 창업했다.

(B) 취업 면접을 요청했다.

(C) 책을 썼다.

(D) 발표를 했다. 정답 (C)

84. 화자가 "저는 채용 담당 매니저로 몇몇 대기업에서 20년 이상 근무했습니다"라고 말할 때 무엇을 함축하는가?

(A) 사람들은 그녀의 조언을 신뢰할 수 있다.

(B) 그녀는 훌륭한 직업을 가지고 있다.

(C) 그녀는 자신의 이력서를 철회했다.

(D) 그녀는 중소기업과 일하지 않는다. 정답 (A)

85. 청자들은 웹사이트를 확인함으로써 무엇을 받을 수 있는가?

(A) 강좌 자료에 대한 할인

(B) 소프트웨어 시험판

(C) 서명한 책

(D) 무료 상담 정답 (D)

문제 86-88번은 다음 방송을 참조하시오. 호W

W: Welcome back, everyone. I'm Meredith Warner, (86)**and we're halfway done with my show on Radio 103.4 here in Jacksonville.** You know, I often get asked how I chose this career, so I thought I'd share the answer with you. I've wanted to be a radio host since I was a kid. (87)**When I was nine, I**

was listening to the radio and heard an interview with a famous singer. I realized that it would be wonderful to have conversations with famous people. (88)**Now, I'm going to play some music by that musician.** Try to guess who it is.

돌아오신 것을 환영합니다, 여러분. 저는 메리디스 워너이고, 여기 잭슨빌 라디오 103.4의 제 프로그램이 반 정도 진행된 상태입니다. 있잖아요, 저는 이 직업을 어떻게 택하게 되었는지 종종 질문을 받는데, 그래서 그 답변을 여러분과 공유할까 생각했습니다. 저는 어릴 때부터 라디오 진행자가 되고 싶었어요. 9살 때 저는 라디오를 듣고 있었는데, 유명한 가수와의 인터뷰를 들었어요. 저는 유명한 사람들과 대화를 하는 것이 멋질 거라는 것을 깨달았죠. 이제, 그 뮤지션의 음악을 틀어 드릴게요. 누구인지 맞춰 보세요.

86. 화자는 누구인가?

(A) 가수

(B) 여배우

(C) 라디오 진행자

(D) 스포츠 리포터 정답 (C)

87. 화자는 자신의 직업을 고르는 데 무엇이 영감을 주었다고 말하는가?

(A) 유명한 가수와 얘기한 것

(B) 상을 수상한 것

(C) 인터뷰를 들은 것

(D) 전국을 여행한 것 정답 (C)

88. 화자는 뒤이어 무엇을 하겠는가?

(A) 소식 알리기

(B) 유명한 사람과 인터뷰하기

(C) 질문에 답하기

(D) 노래 틀기 정답 (D)

문제 89-91번은 다음 회의 발췌 내용을 참조하시오. 영M

M: Thank you for coming to this meeting here at the community center. (89)**As you're all aware, our annual fundraiser will be held this Friday night.** We hope to raise enough money to pay for the renovations the center badly needs. Now, we've gotten plenty of volunteers from the community who are willing to help out, which I am really grateful for. (90)**The volunteers will be putting up decorations around the auditorium and arranging tables for the fundraiser.** Unfortunately, however, the caterer for the event just had to cancel our order since there was some water damage to the business last night. (91)**Does anyone know a caterer that can provide food for 250 people on short notice?**

여기 지역사회 센터에서 하는 이 회의에 와 주셔서 감사합니다. 여러분 모두 아시다시피, 우리 연례 기금 모금 행사가 이번 주 금요일 밤에 열립니다. 우리는 센터가 절실히 필요한 보수공사의 비용을 댈 만큼 충분한 자금을 모금하기를 바랍니다. 지역사회에서 기꺼이 도움을 주려는 자원봉사를 하려는 분들이 많이 나왔는데, 이에 대해 정말 감사드립니다. 자원봉사자들은 기금 모금 행사를 위해 대강당에 장식을 하고, 테이블 배치도 하게 될 것입니다. 그런데 유감스럽게도, 이 행사의 출장 요리 업체가 어젯밤 사업장에 수해 피해가 생겨 우리 주문을 취소해야 했습니다. 촉박하게 알려 주는 상태에서 250인분 음식을 제공할 수 있는 출장 요리 업체를 아시는 분 있나요?

89. 어떤 행사가 계획되고 있는가?
(A) 자선 경매
(B) 스포츠 행사
(C) 기금 모금 행사
(D) 음악 콘서트
정답 (C)

90. 화자에 따르면, 행사를 위해 자원봉사자들은 무엇을 하게 될 것인가?
(A) 손님에게 음식 서빙하기
(B) 각 테이블에 꽃꽂이 놓기
(C) 입구에서 손님 맞이하기
(D) 방 준비하기
정답 (D)

91. 화자는 청자들에게 무엇을 요청하는가?
(A) 서명을 한 계약서
(B) 밴드에 대한 제안
(C) 신용 카드 번호
(D) 출장 요리 업체에 대한 추천
정답 (D)

문제 92–94번은 다음 담화를 참조하시오. 호W

W: (92)**Thank you for attending the annual marketing conference and for coming to my presentation.** As a marketing consultant, I have one final tip Before releasing new products, most businesses rely on outside product testers. (93)**In exchange for comments or any ideas to improve products, companies send products to these testers for free, which is costly. Your employees could turn out to be effective product testers.** It's because after all, they want their company to be successful. All you have to do is collect feedback from those who haven't worked on developing that particular product. That way, you get a new point of view. (94) **Here is a brochure that should be helpful.** It has my contact information on it, so feel free to get in touch with me.

연차 마케팅 총회에 참석해 주시고 제 프레젠테이션에 와 주셔서 감사합니다. 마케팅 컨설턴트로서 마지막 조언 하나를 드리겠습니다. 신제품을 출시하기 전에, 대부분의 업체들은 외부의 제품 시험자들에게 의존하게 됩니다. 의견이나 제품 개선을 위한 어떤 아이디어를 얻는 대가로, 회사들은 무료로 이 시험자들에게 제품을 보내 주게 되는데, 이것은 비용이 많이 듭니다. 여러분의 직원들이 효율적인 제품 시험자로 드러날 수도 있습니다. 그건 왜냐하면 결국 그들도 자신의 회사가 성공하기를 원하기 때문이죠. 여러분은 단지 그 특정 제품 개발 작업을 하지 않은 사람들에게서 의견을 받기만 하면 됩니다. 그렇게 하면 여러분은 새로운 관점을 얻게 됩니다. 여기 도움이 될 만한 안내책자가 있습니다. 거기에는 제 연락처가 있으니, 언제든 제게 편하게 연락 주십시오.

92. 연설은 어디에서 이루어지는가?
(A) 총회
(B) 교육
(C) 오리엔테이션 행사
(D) 취업 박람회
정답 (A)

93. 화자가 "여러분의 직원들이 효율적인 제품 시험자로 드러날 수도 있습니다"라고 말하는 이유는?
(A) 더 많은 제품 판매를 권하기 위해
(B) 다른 접근법을 제안하기 위해
(C) 일부 직원들을 칭찬하기 위해
(D) 더 많은 직원을 고용할 것을 권하기 위해
정답 (B)

94. 화자는 청자들에게 무엇을 주는가?
(A) 명함
(B) 웹사이트 주소
(C) 안내책자
(D) 사진
정답 (C)

문제 95–97번은 다음 회의 발췌 내용과 차트를 참조하시오. 미W

W: (95)**Thanks for attending this afternoon's design team meeting.** We need to discuss the design for the limited-edition necktie we sell every year in celebration of the company's anniversary. Remember that this item will only be available for purchase for two months. (96)**Now, I need everyone to divide into small groups and come up with at least a couple of ideas for the style for the item.** In case it helps to know what the primary color will be, this chart shows last quarter's sales broken down by colors of the ties we sold. (97)**The decision has already been made to use the top-selling color for the new product.**

오늘 오후 디자인 팀 회의에 참석해 주셔서 감사합니다. 우리는 회사 창립 기념일을 축하하여 해마다 판매하는 한정판 넥타이의 디자인에 대해 논의해야 합니다. 이 제품은 두 달 동안만 구매가 가능할 것이라는 점을 기억하십시오. 이제, 여러분 모두 소그룹으로 나누어서 이 제품 스타일에 대해 적어도 아이디어 두 개 정도는 의견을 내주셔야 합니다. 주 색상이 어떤 게 될지를 아는 것이 도움이 되신다면, 이 차트는 우리가 판매한 넥타이의 색깔별로 세분화된 지난 분기 매출을 보여 주고 있습니다. 새 상품에 대해서 가장 많이 팔린 색상을 사용하기로 이미 결정이 내려졌습니다.

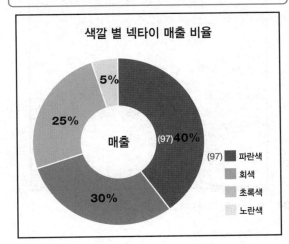

색깔 별 넥타이 매출 비율

매출
5%
25%
(97)40%
30%
(97) 파란색
회색
초록색
노란색

95. 청자들은 누구일 것 같은가?
(A) 마케터
(B) 디자이너
(C) 영업 사원
(D) 프로그래머
정답 (B)

96. 팀은 소그룹으로 신제품의 어떤 측면에 대해 논의할 것인가?
(A) 신제품의 사이즈
(B) 신제품의 색상
(C) 신제품의 스타일
(D) 신제품의 가격
정답 (C)

97. 그래픽을 보시오. 신제품의 색상은 무엇이 될 것인가?

    (A) 회색

    (B) 초록색

    (C) 노란색

    (D) 파란색   정답 (D)

문제 98~100번은 다음 담화와 지도를 참조하시오. 미M

M: **(98)All right, this is one of the most important days of the year at our furniture store.** It's our annual clearance sale. This is a huge event, so we're going to be full of customers all day long. **(99)Make sure that every customer who enters the store knows we're giving away free drinks and snacks in the customer lounge.** There is one more thing: I'll need a few people to put up a few more signs promoting our new membership program. We've already got some in front of the furniture display areas and by the cash registers, but **(100)we need some more in front of the customer service desk.**

- -

좋습니다. 오늘은 우리 가구점에서 연중 가장 중요한 날 중 하루입니다. 우리 연례 재고정리 세일을 하는 날입니다. 이것은 대단히 큰 행사여서, 하루종일 고객들로 가득 찰 것입니다. 매장에 들어오는 모든 고객에게 우리가 고객 라운지에서 무료 음료와 간식을 제공한다는 것을 꼭 알려 주세요. 한 가지 더 있습니다: 우리의 새 회원 프로그램을 홍보하는 표지판을 몇 개 더 붙일 몇 사람이 필요합니다. 이미 가구 전시 공간 앞과 계산대 옆에 몇 개 붙였는데, 고객 서비스 데스크 앞에도 몇 개 더 필요합니다.

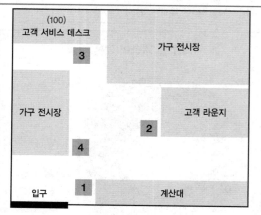

98. 화자는 주로 무엇에 대해 얘기하는가?

    (A) 교육 시간

    (B) 연례 재고정리 세일

    (C) 영업 총회

    (D) 고객 감사의 날   정답 (B)

99. 청자들은 사람들이 도착하면 무엇을 하라는 권고를 받는가?

    (A) 그들에게 쇼핑 카트 주기

    (B) 그들이 물건 찾는 것 도와주기

    (C) 홍보 전단지 나눠주기

    (D) 그들에게 다과에 대해 알려 주기   정답 (D)

100. 그래픽을 보시오. 추가 표지판은 어디에 위치하게 될 것인가?

    (A) 장소 1

    (B) 장소 2

    (C) 장소 3

    (D) 장소 4   정답 (C)

Part 5

101. 그 출장 요리 서비스 업체는 기념일 축하와 기업 연회와 같은 특별한 행사를 위해 다양한 이탈리아 요리와 후식을 제공한다.   정답 (A)

102. 소비자들은 해외 직구를 통해 구매하는 제품이 하자로 인해 회수된 상태인지 여부를 확인할 필요가 있다.   정답 (A)

103. 만약 특정한 책을 찾는 데 어려움이 있다면, 저희 도서 대출대로 오셔서 사서에게 도움을 요청하세요.   정답 (C)

104. 우리 레스토랑은 손님이 다른 손님들의 즐거운 식사를 방해한다면 서비스 제공을 거부할 권리를 갖고 있다.   정답 (C)

105. 인사부장은 내게 이사회가 새로운 제조 공장을 담당할 사람을 물색 중이라고 말했다.   정답 (B)

106. 신제품의 연구 및 개발 부족으로 인해, 코코 스포츠는 스포츠 용품 시장에서 선두 기업 자리를 유지할 수 없었다.   정답 (C)

107. 기사의 오류는 편집부로 신속히 보고되어 신문이 출간되기 전에 수정될 수 있도록 해야 한다.   정답 (B)

108. 몇몇 지역 기업인들이 소비자 보호를 위한 공정한 경쟁을 촉진하는 법이 통과되도록 하는 데 중요한 역할을 했다.   정답 (D)

109. 시는 5월 14일부터 19일까지 개최되는 영화제에 참여하는 사람에게 다양한 무료 음료를 제공할 것이다.   정답 (A)

110. 매장 관리자 자리를 위한 최종 면접에 합격한 지원자들은 다음 주 후반에 인사부장의 연락을 받게 될 것이다.   정답 (D)

111. BK 전자는 어제 앨라배마에 있는 자사 반도체 제조 시설을 확충하겠다는 새로운 계획을 발표했다.   정답 (C)

112. 고객 만족도를 높이고 회사 경쟁력을 더 강하게 유지하기 위해 더욱 노력하는 것이 필수적이다.   정답 (A)

113. 경제 성장이 둔화된 시기에 몇몇 투자 회사들은 수익률 가능성을 보고 신흥 시장에 맞춘 금융 상품을 출시했다.   정답 (B)

114. 이 선적에 대한 대금은 이 송장 수령 후 21일 내에 지급되어야 한다는 것을 유의해 주세요.   정답 (C)

115. 공항에 도착하자마자, 모든 승객은 세관을 통과해야 하며, 이는 25분 정도 소요될 것이다.   정답 (B)

116. 곧 있을 포럼의 모든 참가자들은 벨라 호텔이나 그랜드 호텔 중 자신이 쾌적하고 편리하다고 보는 어느 곳이든 숙박할 수 있다.   정답 (C)

117. 발생한 비용을 입증하기 위해서, 비용 청구 시에 영수증 원본이나 청구서가 제출되어야 한다.   정답 (B)

118. 원자재 가격 상승의 타격으로, 식품 가공, 철강, 그리고 섬유 산업에 대한 상당히 암울한 경제 전망이 지적되고 있다.   정답 (C)

119. 스탠포드 씨는 2년 전 최고 경영자 직책에서 물러남으로써 그의 아버지 회사의 경영권을 포기했다.   정답 (D)

120. 가격은 귀하의 여행 일자, 여행객 숫자, 출발 도시, 그리고 항공편, 호텔 등 기타 선택 항목에 따라 변경될 수 있다. 정답 (B)

121. 몇몇 주요 강들을 변화시키기 위해 행해지는 어떤 것도 결국 환경과 생태계를 회복할 수 없을 정도로 파괴하기만 할 것이다. 정답 (C)

122. 평가 보고서는 우리 유통 체계의 개선 덕분에 지난 2년간 수백만 달러 이상을 절약하는 결과에 이르렀다고 분명히 명시하고 있다. 정답 (A)

123. 이 가전제품 업계에서의 성공은 적시에 신제품을 시장에 출시할 수 있는 기술적인 능력에 달려 있다. 정답 (C)

124. 현재 경제 상황을 고려할 때, 대부분의 고객들은 우리의 값비싼 신제품을 구매할 여유가 없다. 정답 (B)

125. 에이스 메디컬은 여러 개의 저가 영상 기기들을 개발했으며, 그 중 두 개는 올해 브랜든 기술상 수상작으로 고려되고 있다. 정답 (D)

126. 만약 젯 레드 항공사에서 예약 업무를 해외에 외주로 맡기기 시작한다면, 올해 캘리포니아 지역에 약 천 개의 새 일자리가 창출될 것이다. 정답 (D)

127. 우리 각자 우리 자신과 가족뿐만 아니라 이웃과 사회를 위한 개인적 책임을 져야 한다. 정답 (B)

128. 회사의 인사부장은 일단 행정직이 충원되면 지원서 접수를 중단할 것이다. 정답 (B)

129. 신임 주지사는 증가하는 화물 수송량을 수용하고 교통 정체를 감소시키고자 4개의 주요 고속도로를 확장할 것을 제안했다. 정답 (D)

130. 만약 발표에 대한 도움이나 추가 지원이 필요하다면, 주저하지 말고 저희에게 연락하십시오. 정답 (C)

Part 6

문제 131-134번은 다음 기사를 참조하시오.

샌프란시스코 데일리

에이스 슈퍼마켓, 남미로 확장

피터 스미스

샌프란시스코 – 3월 3일) 미국에 본사를 둔 세계 최대 슈퍼마켓 체인인 에이스 슈퍼마켓이 남미 시장에 발판을 마련할 계획이다. 에이스 슈퍼마켓 본사는 어제 칠레와 브라질에 5개 지점이 들어갈 것이며, 첫 2개 슈퍼마켓은 3월 30일에 칠레에서 문을 열 예정이라고 발표했다. 나머지 3개 지점은 다음 달 말까지 브라질에서 문을 열 것이다. 기본적으로, 에이스 슈퍼마켓은 소규모 슈퍼마켓을 열어 자체 브랜드 제품과 지역 농산물을 저렴한 가격으로 제공하는 독특한 경영 전략을 펼친다. 에이스 슈퍼마켓의 대변인 벤자민 윌슨 씨는 "저희는 남미 지역에 저희 슈퍼마켓을 열어 고객들에게 저렴한 비용에 고품질 제품을 소개하기를 간절히 바라고 있습니다"라고 말했다.

131. 정답 (B)

132. (A) 나머지 3개 지점은 다음 달 말까지 브라질에서 문을 열 것이다.
(B) 올해 우리 슈퍼마켓의 약 5분의 1이 에너지 효율이 좋은 조명을 갖추게 될 것이다.
(C) 그들은 남미 전역에 걸쳐서 전통적인 식료품 체인들과 경쟁했다.
(D) 많은 상점이 토지가 부족한 인구 과밀 도시에 건설될 것이다. 정답 (A)

133. 정답 (B)

134. 정답 (D)

문제 135-138번은 다음 편지를 참조하시오.

에딘버러 미술 디자인 대학
로리스턴 플레이스 74번지
에딘버러, EH3 9DF
eca@ed.ac.uk
+44 (0)131 651 5800

5월 30일
루이스 버튼 씨
치담 힐 로드 184
맨체스터, 영국
M4 1PW

버튼 씨에게,

에딘버러 미술 디자인 대학의 저녁 강좌에 관한 귀하의 문의에 대해 감사드립니다. 귀하께서 요청하신 대로, 저희 강좌의 세부 내용, 특히 매주 화요일 또는 목요일에 운영하는 수업 때문에 연락드립니다.

우선, 기초 유화 강좌가 있는데, 기본 기법에 대해 교육을 하고 색채의 중요성을 강조합니다. 둘째로, 기술 도안 강좌가 있는데, 엔지니어링과 건축에 관심이 있는 분들을 위해 고안된 것입니다.

유감스럽게도, 현재 저희가 저녁 시간에 운영하는 주중 수업은 이것들뿐입니다. 하지만 저희는 또한 특히 일정이 바쁜 분들을 위해 다양한 온라인 강좌를 제공합니다. 이 강좌들에 등록하는 분들은 미리 구입해야 하는 필수 준비물 목록을 제공받습니다. 위에 나열된 모든 선택사항들에 관한 더 상세한 정보는 저희 웹사이트에서 찾아보실 수 있습니다.

애나벨 테일러 드림
학생 서비스 부장
에딘버러 미술 디자인 대학

135. 정답 (D)

136. 정답 (A)

137. 정답 (B)

136. (A) 저희 기관의 고용 기회에 관한 귀하의 관심에 감사드립니다.
(B) 위에 나열된 모든 선택사항들에 관한 더 상세한 정보는 저희 웹사이트에서 찾아보실 수 있습니다.
(C) 귀하의 강좌 등록 신청서가 현재 처리 중에 있습니다.
(D) 이 강좌들 중 어느 것이든 철회하고 싶으시면 제게 연락하십시오. 정답 (B)

문제 139-142번은 다음 이메일을 참조하시오.

수신: 스칼렛 웰시 〈sw@cocomail.com〉
발신: 엘리너 플레처 〈ef@sjfc.com〉
제목: 레코드 매장 공연
날짜: 4월 21일

웰시 씨에게,

스탠리 조던의 기획사에서 소중한 팬클럽 회원들을 위해 준비하고 있는 이번 공연에 관해 알려 드리게 되어 대단히 기쁩니다.

조던 씨는 사운드 팩토리 홀에서 25회의 공연을 열 것이며, 이 공연들은 팬들이 친근한 소형 무대에서 스탠리 조던의 공연을 즐겁게 경험할 수 있는 놀라운 기회를 제공하게 될 것입니다. 그 후에, 팬들은 사인회 동안 그들이 가장 좋아하는 팝 가수를 만날 수 있는데, 사인회 행사는 공연 직후에 이어질 것입니다. 스탠리 조던의 새로운 앨범이 구매 가능할 것이며, 팬들은 또한 사인회 동안 이 앨범에 사인을 받을 수 있습니다.

표는 적정한 가격으로 책정될 것이며, 온라인으로 구매 가능할 것입니다. 레코드 매장 콘서트는 5월 10일과 15일 사이에 열릴 것이며, 정확한 투어 일정은 앞으로 며칠 안에 www.sjfc.com에 게시될 것입니다. 사랑하는 아티스트를 가까이서 볼 수 있는 이번 기회를 놓치지 마세요.

엘리너 플레처 드림
스탠리 조던 팬클럽 관리자

139. 정답 (D)

140. 정답 (D)

141. 정답 (B)

142. (A) 스탠리 조던 씨에 대한 귀하의 최근 문의에 감사드립니다.
(B) 귀하는 7일 이내에 무료 입장권을 받으시게 될 것입니다.
(C) 사랑하는 아티스트를 가까이서 볼 수 있는 이번 기회를 놓치지 마세요.
(D) 첫 번째 공연은 이달 말에 개최될 예정입니다. 정답 (C)

문제 143–146번은 다음 정보를 참조하시오.

코르크는 본질적으로 코르크참나무로 알려진 떡갈나무 껍질 조각이다. 코르크참나무는 지중해 서부와 접한 지역에서 자연적으로 자란다. 세계의 다른 지역에서 이 종을 재배하기 위한 여러 노력이 있었다. 그러나 지금까지 그 결과는 고무적이지 않았다. 코르크가 약 2,000년 전에 마개로 사용되었음을 시사하는 역사적 증거가 있지만, 17세기에 유리병이 도입되면서 코르크가 더 널리 사용되었다. 최근 몇 년 동안, 플라스틱 마개와 같은 다른 대안이 포도주의 병마개로 도입되었다. 그러나 코르크는 여전히 고급 포도주의 주요 마개로 남아 있다.

143. 정답 (C)

144. (A) 세계의 다른 지역에서 이 종을 재배하기 위한 여러 노력이 있었다.
(B) 이는 지중해 기후에 적응한 나무들이 있음을 의미한다.
(C) 코르코 제작 기계는 제조업체의 지침에 따라 청소되고 유지 관리되어야 한다.
(D) 이 지역은 세계에서 가장 주목할 만한 포도와 포도주를 생산하고 있다. 정답 (A)

145. 정답 (C)

146. 정답 (D)

Part 7

문제 147–148번은 다음 정보를 참조하시오.

이스트 시애틀 론드리
이 지역에서 가장 좋고, 가장 깨끗한 빨래방!
24시간 영업

(147)1. 세탁물을 세탁기에 넣으십시오.
2. 세탁기에 세탁 세제를 넣으십시오. 세제는 정문 옆의 자판기에서 구입 가능합니다.
3. 세탁기 메뉴를 설정하십시오. 보통, 뜨거운 물은 하얀색 옷에 적절하고, 차가운 물은 색깔이 있는 옷에 적절합니다.
4. 동전 투입구에 각각의 세탁기에 요구되는 정확한 양의 동전을 삽입하십시오. 세탁 과정이 끝날 때까지 세탁기를 열지 마십시오.

(148)문제가 있으면 (206) 408–3180으로 전화 주세요.

147. 정보의 목적은 무엇인가?
(A) 세탁기 구매 방법을 알리기 위한 것
(B) 한 시설을 이용하는 절차를 설명하기 위한 것
(C) 장비 수리 서비스를 요청하는 방법을 알려 주기 위한 것
(D) 세탁 서비스를 광고하기 위한 것 정답 (B)

148. 만약 뜨거운 물이 나오지 않는다면, 고객은 무엇을 해야 하는가?
(A) 프런트에 가기
(B) 세탁기에 세탁물을 더 넣기
(C) 전화로 직원에게 알리기
(D) 추가로 동전을 더 넣기 정답 (C)

문제 149–150번은 다음 문자 메시지를 참조하시오.

해럴드 말론 [오전 10시 25분]
아이다. 디콘 호텔의 스톨링스 씨한테서 다시 연락 왔어요? (149)우리가 요청한 예약이 되었어요?

아이다 스튜어트 [오전 10시 27분]
그분이 막 5분 전쯤에 저에게 전화했어요. (149) (150)오렌지 룸은 9일에 예약이 됐지만, 우리가 원한다면 레드 룸으로 할 수 있다고 했어요.

해럴드 말론 [오전 10시 28분]
몇 명이 들어갈 수 있어요?

아이다 스튜어트 [오전 10시 29분]
최대 250명까지 충분한 공간이 있어요. (150)오렌지 룸보다 비용이 더 들어갈 거예요.

해럴드 말론 [오전 10시 31분]
(150)우리는 필요하다면 언제든지 추가 자금을 요청할 수 있어요.

아이다 스튜어트 [오전 10시 32분]
알겠습니다. 바로 그분에게 다시 전화할게요.

149. 문자 메시지 대화는 주로 무엇에 관한 것인가?
(A) 다가오는 행사를 위한 준비
(B) 방을 빌리는 가격
(C) 호텔 방 예약의 필요성
(D) 행사 날짜의 변경 정답 (A)

150. 오전 10시 31분에, 말론 씨가 "우리는 필요하다면 언제든지 추가 자금을 요청할 수 있어요"라고 쓸 때 무엇을 의미하는 것 같은가?
(A) 그는 예산 보고서를 제출해야 한다.
(B) 그는 곧 자신의 상사와 이야기해야 한다.

(C) 그는 방금 예산에 대해 더 많은 돈을 요청했다.

(D) 그는 기꺼이 레드 룸을 예약하려고 한다.　　　　　정답 (D)

문제 151-153번은 다음 광고를 참조하시오.

씨어트리컬 피자

영업 시간: 오전 10시 – 오후 11시

(153A)주 7일 영업

소	중	대	특대
12.95달러	14.95달러	18.95달러	20.95달러

모든 가격들은 공지 없이 바뀔 수 있습니다.

(153B)20달러 이상 주문 시 무료 배송됩니다.

(151)이달의 피자 (한 판 구매하시고 한 판 더 받으세요!)	
채식주의자	**(151)토마토**, 버섯, 빨간 양파, 초록색 피망, 고수, 올리브
슈프림	페퍼로니, **(151)토마토**, 버섯, 빨간 양파, 빨간색 및 초록색 피망, 올리브
BBQ 치킨	특별 BBQ 소스, 치킨, **(151)토마토**, 버섯, 양파, 피망

메뉴 전체를 보시려면

(153C)저희 웹사이트 www.theatricalpizza.com에 방문하세요.

(152)추가 토핑

소	중	대	특대
1.65달러	2.25달러	2.85달러	3.55달러

버섯, 토마토, 피망, 체다 치즈, 새우, 햄, 페퍼로니, 치킨, 구운 마늘, 양파, 올리브와 더 많은 것들이 있습니다!

모든 행사에 출장 요리 서비스를 제공합니다.
555-329-0504로 연락하셔서 가격을 알아보세요.

---

151. 이달의 피자에 모두 포함되어 있는 재료는 무엇인가?

(A) 고수

(B) 토마토

(C) 치킨

(D) 올리브　　　　　정답 (B)

152. 광고에 제공되어 있는 정보는 무엇인가?

(A) 음료의 가격

(B) 출장 요리 서비스의 가격

(C) 토핑 선택

(D) 가게 주소　　　　　정답 (C)

153. 씨어트리컬 피자에 대하여 나타나 있지 않은 것은 무엇인가?

(A) 일요일에 영업한다.

(B) 일부 고객들을 위해 주문을 무료로 배달해 준다.

(C) 웹사이트를 가지고 있다.

(D) 최근에 새 지점을 열었다.　　　　　정답 (D)

문제 154-156번은 다음 정보를 참조하시오.

나다니엘 쿠퍼 침대

(154)이 도시 최고급 가구 제공업체 나다니엘 가구 유한 책임회사에서 나다니엘 쿠퍼 침대를 구매해 주셔서 감사드립니다. (155)내구성으로 상을 받은 이 침대가 편안함으로 당신을 완벽하게 만족시킬 것이라고 믿습니다. 침대 조립을 시작하기 전에 아래의 설명을 주의 깊게 읽어 주십시오.

조립 설명

1단계. 머리맡 나무판을 희망하는 곳에 설치하십시오.

2단계. (156)안전 가드 하나의 빨간색 점을 머리맡 나무판의 점과 맞추어 안전 가드를 머리맡 나무판에 부착하십시오.

3단계. 안전 가드에 발밑 나무판을 부착하십시오.

4단계. 머리맡 나무판과 발밑 나무판에 볼트를 단단히 고정시키십시오.

5단계. 갈빗대를 (틀에) 넣고 드라이버로 나사를 조이십시오.

6단계. 매트리스를 틀에 놓으십시오.

이 단계들을 묘사하는 사진들을 보시려면 저희 웹사이트를 방문하세요. 제품에 관련된 질문이 있으시면, 1-555-932-3333으로 전화 주시거나 staff@nathanielbed.com으로 이메일을 보내 주세요.

---

154. 이 정보는 누구를 대상으로 하는 것인가?

(A) 가구 배송 회사의 직원

(B) 고객 서비스 직원

(C) 가구 제조업자

(D) 고객　　　　　정답 (D)

155. 제품에 대하여 나타나 있는 것은 무엇인가?

(A) 침대 레일들은 손잡이로 사용될 수 있다.

(B) 추가적인 구성품들이 침대를 조립하는 데에 사용될 수 있다.

(C) 어린이들을 위해 설계되었다.

(D) 침대가 튼튼한 구조에 대해 인정받았다.　　　　　정답 (D)

156. [1], [2], [3] 그리고 [4]로 표시된 곳 중에, 아래 문장이 들어가기에 가장 적절한 곳은?

"나머지 안전 가드에도 위의 과정을 반복하십시오."

(A) [1]

(B) [2]

(C) [3]

(D) [4]　　　　　정답 (B)

문제 157-158번은 다음 영수증을 참조하시오.

---

(157)케어링 핸즈

24 프랭클린 드라이브

시사이드, 오리건 주 97160

(503) 762-0847

4월 10일, 오전 9:35

품목	수량	가격	계
(157)포켓북, 〈응급 처치의 모든 것〉	1	$2.80	$2.80
(157)붕대 (2개입)	1	$2.00	$2.00
(157)살균 연고 (25mg)	1	$4.70	$4.70
(157)진통제 (10알)	1	$4.00	$4.00
총 품목(들)	4		
소계			$13.50
(158)단골 할인			– $2.00
지불할 금액			$11.50
신용 카드			$11.50
*********5621			
잔액			$0.00

감사합니다!

---

157. 케어링 핸즈는 어떤 종류의 사업체인 것 같은가?

(A) 병원

(B) 약국

(C) 서점

(D) 미용실

정답 (B)

158. 고객에 대해 나타나 있는 것은 무엇인가?

(A) 병원에서 일한다.

(B) 물건들을 오후에 구입했다.

(C) 현금으로 지불했다.

(D) 케어링 핸즈에서 자주 쇼핑을 한다.

정답 (D)

문제 159~161번은 다음 이메일을 참조하시오.

수신: 제이크 헤럴드 〈jherald@chelsea.com〉

발신: 릴리안 멀비 〈lmulvey@chelsea.com〉

날짜: 1월 23일

제목: 문의

(160)헤럴드 씨께,

1월 2일에 마케팅부의 복사기가 고장 났습니다. (159) (161)그래서 저는 새 복사기 요청서를 1월 8일에 (160)구매부에 제출했습니다. (159)당신은 그것이 일주일 이내에 처리될 것이라고 말해 주었지만, 신청서를 제출한 이래로 2주가 되었는데도 아무 조치도 취해지지 않았습니다.

저희 부서는 현재 인사부에 있는 복사기를 사용하고 있습니다. 이것은 저희가 1월 30일에 개최할 컨퍼런스 준비에 심각한 지연을 초래하고 있습니다.

이 문제가 곧 해결될 수 있기를 바랍니다. 만약 제가 할 수 있는 어떤 일이든 있다면 말씀해 주십시오.

감사합니다.

릴리안 멀비

159. 무엇이 문제인가?

(A) 물품이 교체되지 않았다.

(B) 회의가 지연되었다.

(C) 자금이 제공되지 않았다.

(D) 후임자가 채용되지 않았다.

정답 (A)

160. 헤럴드 씨는 어디에서 일하는가?

(A) 마케팅부

(B) 인사부

(C) 구매부

(D) 유지보수부

정답 (C)

161. 새 복사기에 대한 신청서는 언제 제출되었는가?

(A) 1월 2일

(B) 1월 8일

(C) 1월 23일

(D) 1월 30일

정답 (B)

문제 162~164번은 다음 이메일을 참조하시오.

수신: 〈jhbuskers@chmail.com〉

발신: 〈tmyers@ggmail.com〉

날짜: 12월 15일

제목: 축하합니다!

버스커스 멤버들께,

최근 크루즈 아레나에서 열린 콘서트의 성공에 대해 축하드리고 싶습니다. (164)〈세인트 크루즈 시티 해럴드〉를 읽고 데뷔한 지 겨우 3년 만에 그곳에서 콘서트를 연 첫 번째 뮤지션이란 것이란 것을 알게 되었습니다. 수익금의 일부를 소아 병원에 기부했다는 것에 대해 알게 되었을 때 특히 감명받았습니다.

(162) (163)바의 사장이자 여러분의 열렬한 팬으로서, 저는 여러분이 제 바에서 공연하시도록 초청하고 싶습니다. 저희 손님 대부분은 대학생들로 20대 중반이기 때문에, 여러분이 손님들에게 잘 맞을 것이라고 생각합니다. 저의 바인 세일보트는 세인트 크루즈 시티의 46 레인디어 드라이브에 있으며, 매일 오후 8시부터 오전 4시까지 영업합니다. 공연 시간과 비용은 협상이 가능합니다. 관심 있으시면 답장해 주십시오.

감사드리며.

(163)테사 마이어스

162. 이메일의 주요 목적은 무엇인가?

(A) 한 밴드의 업적을 다루기 위한 것

(B) 한 바에서의 일을 제의하기 위한 것

(C) 콘서트의 세부 사항에 대하여 알리기 위한 것

(D) 공연 스케줄을 확인하기 위한 것

정답 (B)

163. 테사 마이어스는 누구인가?

(A) 한 바의 손님

(B) 밴드 멤버

(C) 환자

(D) 음악 팬

정답 (D)

164. 버스커스에 대해 나타나 있는 것은 무엇인가?

(A) 4년 전에 구성되었다.

(B) 최근에 신입 멤버를 뽑았다.

(C) 지역 간행물에서 다루어졌다.

(D) 한 병원에서 콘서트를 열었다.

정답 (C)

문제 165~167번은 다음 기사를 참조하시오.

AMC 앞으로 나아가다

사만다 프로부스트 작성, 전속 기자

8월 7일 – 브뤼셀 소재 자동차 제조업체 아쿠아 자동차 회사(AMC)는 (167)이번 주 베이징에 있는 제조 공장의 공사가 마침내 완료됨에 따라 중국에서의 자동차 생산을 시작할 것이다.

"이것은 자동차 업계를 지배하고 중국에서 다른 경쟁업체들보다 (165)우위를 유지하기 위한 AMC 전략의 첫 번째 발걸음입니다"라고 AMC의 최고경영자인 진 버그만은 설명했다. "중국 시장에서 자동차 판매를 안정적으로 유지하고 향후 모델들을 홍보하기 위해 이 새 시설을 건설하기로 결정했던 것입니다."

AMC는 비평가들의 찬사를 받은 경차 모델인 조스가 지난해 시장에 출시된 이후로 중국에서 인기를 얻고 있다. "AMC의 차량들, 특히 (166C)조스 시리즈에 대한 수요가 급격히 증가했습니다. 현지 고객들이 (166A)저렴하고, (166B)연비가 좋고, 창의적으로 디자인되었기 때문에 조스 모델에 관심이 있는 것이라고 생각합니다"라고 상하이의 현지 자동차 딜러, 조 왕은 언급했다.

회사는 10월에 조스의 업그레이드된 버전 조스-2를 출시할 예정이다. 조스의 이 새 라인은 내장 네비게이션 시스템과 향상된 안전 기술 그리고 더욱 뛰어난 연료 효율성을 특징으로 삼을 것이다. (167)새로 지어진 공장은 충칭과 톈진 같은 중국의 주요 도시들에서의 수요를 충족시키기 위해, 주로 이 모델의 생산에 중점을 둘 것이다. AMC는 현재 유명한 벨기에 연예인인 필립 길리엄스 씨가 출연하는 TV 광고를 통해 중국 내에서 이 모델을 공격적으로 홍보할 준비를 하고 있다. 광고들은 조스–2가 출시되면 방송될 것이다.

165. 두 번째 단락 1행에 있는 단어 "edge"와 의미상 가장 가까운 것은?
(A) 칼날
(B) 수익
(C) 유리한 점
(D) 경향
정답 (C)

166. 왕 씨에 따르면, 조스 모델에 대해 시사되어 있지 않은 것은 무엇인가?
(A) 적절하게 가격이 매겨졌다.
(B) 비교적 적은 에너지를 소모한다.
(C) 판매가 중국에서 꽤 활발하다.
(D) 현재 중국에서 생산되고 있다.
정답 (D)

167. 조스–2는 주로 어디서 생산될 것인가?
(A) 브뤼셀
(B) 상하이
(C) 텐진
(D) 베이징
정답 (D)

문제 168–171번은 다음 온라인 채팅 토론을 참조하시오.

로즈마리 워터스 [오후 2시 42분]
안녕하세요, 실비아. 당신의 교육 프로그램은 어떻게 진행되고 있어요?

실비아 스미스 [오후 2시 43분]
(168)정말 교육적이에요. 여기서 많은 것을 배우고 있는데, 그 정보가 다음 주에 저의 공식 업무가 시작되면 큰 도움이 될 거예요.

로즈마리 워터스 [오후 2시 44분]
그 말을 들으니 기쁘군요. 당신은 여기서 정말 잘 맞을 거라고 확신해요.

실비아 스미스 [오후 2시 45분]
저를 믿어 주셔서 기뻐요.

트렌트 서터 [오후 2시 47분]
실비아, (169)다음 주 월요일에 이곳에 오면, 아침 10시에 제 사무실에 들러 주세요. 당신이 할 과제가 있어요.

실비아 스미스 [오후 2시 48분]
(169)그러고 싶지만, 9시부터 정오까지 인사과의 팻시 로스를 만나기로 되어 있어요. 점심 후에 만나도 될까요?

트렌트 서터 [오후 2시 49분]
저는 정오부터 회사 밖으로 나갈 예정이고, 금요일까지는 돌아오지 않을 거예요. (171)제가 이메일로 과제를 보내 주면 어때요?

실비아 스미스 [오후 2시 51분]
(171)저는 괜찮아요. (170)하지만 저는 아직 업무용 이메일 계정이 없어요.

로즈마리 워터스 [오후 2시 53분]
(170)제가 IT 쪽 사람을 시켜 지금 바로 당신을 위해 그것을 설정하게 할게요. 한 시간 안에 사용자명과 비밀번호를 문자로 보내 드릴게요.

실비아 스미스 [오후 2시 54분]
정말 감사합니다. 저의 새 이메일 주소를 받는 대로 알려 드릴게요, 트렌트. 그러면 우리가 일을 할 수 있어요.

---

168. 스미스 씨가 누구일 것 같은가?
(A) 관리자
(B) 수습 직원
(C) 손님
(D) 중역
정답 (B)

169. 스미스 씨에게 어떤 문제가 있는가?
(A) 그녀는 제안받은 시간에 만날 수 없다.
(B) 그녀는 충분한 경력이 없다.
(C) 그녀는 출장을 갈 수 없다.
(D) 그녀는 몇 가지 양식을 작성하지 않았다.
정답 (A)

170. 워터스 씨가 스미스 씨를 위해 해주겠다고 제의하는 것은 무엇인가?
(A) 새 컴퓨터 준비하기
(B) 그녀에게 새 책상 주문해 주기
(C) 온라인 계정 설정하기
(D) 그녀의 프로젝트 돕기
정답 (C)

171. 오후 2시 51분에, 스미스 씨가 "저는 괜찮아요"라고 쓰는 이유는?
(A) 새 과제에 대해 불평하기 위해
(B) 시간 외 근무를 하겠다고 제안하기 위해
(C) 그녀가 얼마나 바쁜지 나타내기 위해
(D) 서터 씨의 생각에 동의하기 위해
정답 (D)

문제 172–175번은 다음 기사를 참조하시오.

이곳에서 아프리카의 혼을 느끼세요!

브루클린, 4월 22일 – (172)아프리카의 소리가 이전 여러 해 동안 많은 음악 축제가 개최된 브루클린으로 온다. 놀라운 실외 아프리카 음악 축제인 아프리카 소울 축제는 (174)5월 30일과 31일에 브루클린 광장에서 열릴 것이다. 이 지역의 주민들뿐만 아니라 수백 명의 아프리카 음악 팬들도 올 것으로 예상된다.

브루클린의 레크리에이션부가 주최하는 아프리카 소울 축제에는 주목할 만한 특징들이 있다. 하나는 음악의 다양성이다. 동부, 중앙 그리고 남부 아프리카의 곡을 포함한 다양한 종류의 아프리카 음악이 연주될 것이다.

많은 유명 아프리카 뮤지션들이 아프리카 소울 축제에서 공연하기 위하여 비행기를 타고 브루클린으로 올 것이다. (175)제 4회 아프리카 뮤지션 대회의 우승자인 파파 켈레는 첫날에 공연할 것이다. 알란 가물라, 대디 솔로몬, 그리고 심바 오몽가 같은, 그들의 나라에서는 인기 있지만 아직 세계적으로 유명하지는 않은 아티스트들 또한 축제에서 공연할 것이다.

(174)행사 첫째 날, 시식용 아프리카 전통 음식과 음료가 무료로 입구 근처에서 저녁에 제공될 것이다.

티켓은 축제가 열리는 날에 브루클린 광장 입구 근처의 박스 오피스에서 구매 가능하다. (173)티켓은 또한 5월 20일까지 www.brooklinetickets.com에서 할인된 가격으로 구매할 수 있다.

---

172. 기사의 주제는 무엇인가?
(A) 주민들을 위한 무료 공연
(B) 아프리카로의 여행
(C) 아프리카 음악의 역사
(D) 실외 행사
정답 (D)

173. 티켓에 관해 언급된 것은 무엇인가?
(A) 제한된 시간 동안 할인될 것이다.
(B) 현장에서 구매할 수 없다.
(C) 지역 주민에게는 무료로 주어질 것이다.
(D) 레크리에이션부에 전화함으로써 예약될 수 있다.
정답 (A)

174. 언제 무료 음식이 제공될 것인가?

    (A) 4월 22일
    (B) 5월 20일
    (C) 5월 30일
    (D) 5월 31일   정답 (C)

175. [1], [2], [3] 그리고 [4]로 표시된 곳 중에, 아래 문장이 들어가기에 가장 적절한 곳은?

"둘째 날에는 TV 출연 후 지금은 유명한 스카 음악 밴드인 물랭 누아르가 참여할 것이다."

    (A) [1]
    (B) [2]
    (C) [3]
    (D) [4]   정답 (C)

문제 176–180번은 다음 전단과 웹사이트를 참조하시오.

콜 더 큐
시모어 공원, 런던
10월 1일 – 5일

(176) (179A)**국제 연극 협회(ITS)가 다섯 번째 콜 더 큐와 함께 또 돌아옵니다!** (180)**클레이모어 공연 예술 대학(CCPA)**을 포함한 대형 제작사와 독립 제작사 모두의 생동감 넘치는 공연들로 가득 찬 일주일 동안 이어지는 연례 축제에 함께 하세요!

(176)**주 무대 공연들은 다음과 같습니다:**

첫째 날: 제임스 가자와 록산느 스완슨이 공연하는 〈호랑이와 함께 있는 사람〉

둘째 날: 앤–소피 윈터가 공연하는 일련의 독백; 로얄 시어터 사가 공연하는 〈상인의 도시〉

셋째 날: 커튼 콜 사가 공연하는 〈색의 분수〉; 일레인 에디나의 원맨쇼

넷째 날: 러셀 찬의 〈노랑 우산〉을 비롯하여 (179D)**올해의 ITS의 단편 연극 대회에서 상을 받은 대본들**

다섯째 날: JMS 제작 및 로도스 배우 협회가 공연하는 〈드라고니아〉; (177) **로드릭 도허티가 공연하는 〈고독한 나무〉**

이 외에도 아주 많이 있습니다! 각 날짜 공연의 상세한 목록을 보려면, 저희 웹사이트 www.its.org/callthecue를 방문해 주세요.

(180)**CCPA에 재학 중인 이들에게는 특별 할인 혜택**이 (178)**제공됩니다.** 결제 시 할인 코드 CCASTD를 입력해 주세요. 입장 시 재학 증명서가 요구될 것입니다.

(179B)**국제 연극 협회**
1 패티슨 가 · 런던
0844 555 0787

---

www.ticketbook.com/theatre/its-call-the-cue/payment

입장권

환영합니다, (180)**크리스 파이프!** | 내 계정

메인 페이지	콘서트	(176)연극	전시	스포츠

빠른 검색	표 종류	일일 입장권
▬▬▬▬	날짜 선택	10월 3일
	배송 방법	현장 수령
오늘의 특가	할인 코드	(180)CCASTD
이번 주		표: 30달러
이번 달		배송: 0달러
		(180)요금 할인: −5달러
내 페이지		합계: 25달러
예약		
책갈피	결제 방법	신용 카드
내 포인트		xxxx–xxxx–xxxx–0333

176. 콜 더 큐는 어떤 종류의 행사일 것 같은가?

    (A) 미술 전시회
    (B) 동물 쇼의 시퀀스
    (C) 일련의 연극들
    (D) 학교 축제   정답 (C)

177. 누가 〈고독한 나무〉를 공연할 것인가?

    (A) 스완슨 씨
    (B) 가자 씨
    (C) 윈터 씨
    (D) 도허티 씨   정답 (D)

178. 전단지에서, 네 번째 단락 1행에 있는 단어 "extended"와 의미상 가장 가까운 것은?

    (A) 연기된
    (B) 창조된
    (C) 제공된
    (D) 확대된   정답 (C)

179. 국제 연극 협회에 대해 나타나 있지 않은 것은 무엇인가?

    (A) 전에 축제를 개최한 적이 있다.
    (B) 런던에 기반을 두고 있다.
    (C) 약 5년 전에 설립되었다.
    (D) 단편 연극 대회를 주최한다.   정답 (C)

180. 파이프 씨에 대해 시사되어 있는 것은 무엇인가?

    (A) 다른 누군가를 위해 표를 구매했다.
    (B) ITS의 회원이다.
    (C) 한 예술 학교의 학생이다.
    (D) 짧은 연극을 공연할 것이다.   정답 (C)

문제 181–185번은 다음 광고와 이메일을 참조하시오.

발포아 동굴 투어

자연이 창조해낸 놀라운 걸작인 발포아 동굴에 오시는 것을 환영합니다. 필리핀의 라구나 지방에 있는 국립 공원에 위치한 이 수천 년 된 동굴은 이 나라 최대 관광지 중 하나입니다. 다음 투어 중 하나를 고르고 숨을 멎게 할 자연의 위대함을 목격해 보세요! 각 투어에서 (185)**전국 관광 협회(NTA)에서 자격증을 받은 저희 가이드들의 도움을 받아 지역의 역사, 지리 그리고 문화에 대해 배우실 수 있습니다.**

일반 투어

SUV로 동굴까지 가는 편안한 차량 이동을 포함합니다. 성인 한 명당 450 페소, 어린이(4세~11세) 한 명당 300페소, 그리고 4세 미만의 어린이는 무료입니다.

황금 시간대 투어

하루 중 가장 많은 양의 햇빛이 동굴 안으로 들어올 때 출발합니다. 성인 한 명당 550페소, 어린이(4세~11세) 한 명당 380페소, 그리고 4세 미만의 어린이는 무료입니다.

사진 투어

당신만의 아름다운 발포아 동굴 사진을 찍으세요. 아마추어와 전문 사진 작가 모두를 위한 것입니다. 그곳에서 전문가들이 카메라 세팅과 각도에 대해 도움을 줄 것입니다. **(184)삼각대를 가지고 오셔도 됩니다. (184)성인 한 명당 650페소**, 어린이(4세~11세) 한 명당 470페소, 그리고 4세 미만의 어린이는 무료입니다.

(181)연중 365일 운영합니다. (182)예약과 더 자세한 사항들을 원하시면 www.valpoacave.com을 방문하세요. 질문이 있으시면, customerservice@valpoa.com에 이메일을 보내거나 632-555-9270에 전화하세요.

수신: 발포아 동굴 투어 〈customerservice@valpoa.com〉
발신: 커트 토카 〈ktoka@polemail.com〉
날짜: 7월 5일
제목: 제 지난번 투어에 대해서

관계자 분께,

(184)지난달에 저는 제 아내와 함께 발포아 동굴을 방문했습니다. 우리는 동굴의 아름다움을 매우 즐겼습니다. 하지만 그 장소는 너무 붐볐고, **(184) 제 삼각대를 설치할 공간이 충분하지 않았기 때문에** 동굴 사진을 찍는 데 어려움을 겪었습니다. 저는 이 불편함을 **(185)우리 투어 가이드인 데이비드 니슨**에게 말했고 그는 문제를 인정했습니다. 그는 부분적 환불과 **(183)보상으로 발포아 동굴 엽서 한 세트를 일주일 이내에 제 집으로 배송해 준다고 약속했습니다.** 저는 결제액의 일부였던 200페소를 받았고, 제가 동굴을 즐기긴 했기 때문에 이는 적당합니다. **(183)하지만 2주일이 넘었고 저는 아직 엽서를 받지 못했습니다.**

엽서를 아직 보내지 않았다면, 소포 안에 안내 책자를 함께 넣어 주실 수 있을까요? 귀하의 광고에서 할인 쿠폰이 있다는 것을 알게 되었고 저는 근시일 내에 발포아 동굴을 다시 방문하고 싶습니다.

감사합니다.

커트 토카

---

181. 발포아 동굴에서의 투어들에 대해 나타나 있는 것은 무엇인가?

(A) 방문객들에게 자신의 SUV를 직접 운전하여 올 것을 요구한다.

(B) 매 시간마다 출발한다.

(C) 1년 내내 이용 가능하다.

(D) 나이에 상관없이 동일한 요금을 부과한다. 　　　　정답 (C)

182. 고객은 어떻게 투어를 예약할 수 있는가?

(A) 가이드에게 이야기함으로써

(B) 이메일을 보냄으로써

(C) 웹사이트를 방문함으로써

(D) 전화를 함으로써 　　　　정답 (C)

183. 이메일의 목적은 무엇인가?

(A) 투어 가이드에 대해 불평하기 위한 것

(B) 배송되지 않은 물품에 대해 알리기 위한 것

(C) 전체 투어 일정을 요청하기 위한 것

(D) 동굴의 위치에 대해 물어보기 위한 것 　　　　정답 (B)

184. 토카 씨는 6월에 방문했을 때 원래 얼마를 지불했는가?

(A) 200페소

(B) 450페소

(C) 470페소

(D) 650페소 　　　　정답 (D)

185. 니슨 씨에 대해 시사되어 있는 것은 무엇인가?

(A) 토카 씨를 위한 다른 투어를 안내할 것이다.

(B) 토카 씨에게 엽서를 보낼 것이다.

(C) 한 기관에서 허가를 받았다.

(D) 자신의 삼각대를 발포아 동굴에 가져갔다. 　　　　정답 (C)

문제 186-190번은 다음 일정표와 이메일들을 참조하시오.

루돌프 토이즈

(186)루돌프 토이즈는 연례 직원 교육 과정이 다음 주에 실시될 것임을 알려 드리게 되어 기쁩니다. 이것은 직원의 능력 및 지식 향상을 위해 개최됩니다. 다음은 과정의 일정입니다:

프로젝트 계획

세츠코 아사다, 마케팅부 국장		
6월 10일 화요일	오전 9:00 - 오전 10:30	501호

엔지니어링 　　**(187)엔지니어링부의 모든 직원은 참석해야 합니다.**

올란도 이브라히모비치, 수석 엔지니어링 부장		
6월 10일 화요일	오후 1:00 - 오후 3:00	502호

의사소통 기술

안나 드보르킨, 회계부 과장		
6월 12일 목요일	오후 1:00 - 오후 2:30	401호

(188)안전 규정 및 장비 사용

(190)킴벌리 제이드, 공장장		
(188) (190) 6월 12일 목요일	(188) (190) 오후 3:00 - 오후 6:00	603호

(188)6월 12일 후반 시간에 이어, 참석자들에게 식사가 제공될 것입니다. 각 세션 시작 5분 전에 도착하여 자리에 앉으십시오. 음식이나 음료수는 반입이 안 됩니다. **(189)의견, 제안, 질문은 인사부로 제출되어야 합니다.**

수신: 레미 이브 〈ryves@rudolftoys.com〉
발신: 세츠코 아사다 〈sasada@rudolftoys.com〉
날짜: 6월 3일
제목: 교육 과정

(189)이브 씨에게,

(189)곧 있을 교육 과정과 관련하여 이메일을 씁니다. 제가 한 세션을 진행하기로 했는데, 제가 가야 하는 급한 출장으로 인해 그렇게 하지 못할 것 같습니다. 다행히도, 제 부서의 차장인 린다 소머스가 제 세션 당일에 시간이 있습니다. 그녀가 저를 대신하여 그 교육 과정을 담당할 것입니다.

혼선이 없도록 가급적 빨리 그 일정으로 게시물을 정정하여 주십시오. 불편을 끼쳐 드려 죄송합니다. 출장 중에는 제게 이메일이나 전화 (135)-555-6432로 연락하시면 됩니다.

세츠코 아사다 드림
국장, 마케팅부

수신: 레미 이브 〈ryves@rudolftoys.com〉
발신: 안나 드보르킨 〈annad@rudolftoys.com〉
날짜: 6월 13일
제목: 감사합니다

(189)이브 씨,

(189) (190)킴벌리와 과정 시간을 바꿀 수 있게 해 주신 데 대해 정말 감사드립니다. 고작 하루 전에 알려 드려 유감스럽게 생각하며, 변경을 해 주실 수 있었던 데 대해 진심으로 감사합니다.

게다가, 저는 이곳에서 교육 과정을 진행한 것이 처음이었습니다. 저는 그 과정이 대단히 즐거웠고, 앞으로 다시 할 기회가 있기를 바랍니다. 나중에 저의 도움이 더 필요하시면, 언제든지 요청하세요.

감사합니다.

안나 드보르킨

---

186. 일정표에 루돌프 토이즈에 대해 나타나 있는 것은 무엇인가?
(A) 교육 과정 참석자들에게 미리 신청할 것을 요구한다.
(B) 현재 신입 사원을 모집하고 있다.
(C) 곧 정기 행사를 열 계획이다.
(D) 매년 직원들의 성과를 평가한다.　　　　　정답 (C)

187. 이브라히모비치 씨가 진행하는 교육 과정에 대해 언급된 것은 무엇인가?
(A) 그것은 특정한 사람들이 참가할 것을 요구한다.
(B) 그것은 3시간 동안 계속될 것이다.
(C) 참석자들을 위한 다과가 제공될 것이다.
(D) 그것은 새로운 직원들을 대상으로 하는 것이다.　　　　　정답 (A)

188. 어느 세션 후에 무료 식사가 제공되는가?
(A) 프로젝트 계획
(B) 엔지니어링
(C) 의사소통 기술
(D) 안전 규정 및 장비 사용　　　　　정답 (C)

189. 이브 씨에 대해 추론될 수 있는 것은 무엇인가?
(A) 그는 교육 시간을 진행할 것이다.
(B) 그는 출장을 갈 계획이다.
(C) 그는 곧 아사다 씨에게 연락할 것이다.
(D) 그는 인사부에서 근무한다.　　　　　정답 (D)

190. 드보르킨 씨가 교육 과정을 진행한 때는 언제인가?
(A) 화요일 오전 9시
(B) 화요일 오후 1시
(C) 목요일 오후 1시
(D) 목요일 오후 3시　　　　　정답 (D)

문제 191~195번은 다음 광고와 웹 페이지 그리고 이메일을 참조하시오.

스칼라티움
특별한 날을 특별하게 만드세요

특별한 행사를 연다면 이 도시의 가장 선호하는 장소 스칼라티움을 선택하세요. 우리는 지난 5년 연속 행사 관리 분야에서 워싱턴 D.C. 최고의 서비스 제공업체로 선정되었습니다.

• 연회장
이 옵션에는 샹들리에가 비추는 대연회장이 포함되어 있어 우아한 모습을 창출합니다. 10인용 테이블에 200명의 손님이 편안하게 앉을 수 있으며 연설을 위한 무대가 있습니다.

• 로즈 가든
(191)귀하의 행사를 우아한 정자에서 태양 아래에서 개최하세요. 식사를 하지 않는 벤치 배치는 300명의 손님을 수용하고, 연회 배치는 150명의 손님을 수용합니다. 날씨 상황에 따라 비어 있는 대연회장으로 행사가 옮겨질 수 있으니 참고하시기 바랍니다.

• 예배당
(192)높은 아치와 대형 스테인드글라스 창문은 귀하의 하루를 위한 신성한 공간을 제공합니다. 이 방은 음식이 제공되지 않기 때문에 의식에만 사용 가능합니다. 요청 시 손님들은 다른 홀에서 식사를 제공받을 수 있습니다.

• 촬영
(194)지역 사진 스튜디오인 해밀턴즈가 그 날의 특별한 순간들을 담아 드릴 것입니다. 이 서비스는 성수기인 3~5월을 제외하고 무료로 제공됩니다.

---

www.scarlatium.com/testimonials

스칼라티움　특별한 날을 특별하게 만드세요!

홈	상담	예약	후기

완벽

– 나탈리 화이트 작성, 6월 13일 게시

(193)스칼라티움에서 결혼식을 올린 것은 후회되지 않는 결정이었다. 그날은 흠잡을 데 없었고, 내 행사 코디네이터인 에블린 조지에게 감사를 전한다. 에블린은 행사의 모든 세부 사항을 준비하는 데 있어 평가할 수 없을 정도였다. 아침에 내가 예약한 방의 오디오 시스템이 제대로 작동하지 않고 있다는 연락을 받아서 나는 스트레스를 많이 받았다. 다른 모든 대연회장은 예약이 다 되어 있다는 말을 듣고 한층 더 초조해졌다. 그 다음에, 에블린이 정원에서 행사가 열리도록 해주었다. (194) (195)그녀는 또한 사과의 표시로 내가 사진에 대해 지불한 돈을 환불해 주었다. 스칼라티움이 제공하는 음식도 기대 이상이었다. 더 이상은 요구할 수 있는 것이 없을 정도였다.

수신: 제이콥 토마스 〈jthomas@hamiltons.com〉
발신: 에블린 조지 〈egeorge@scarlatium.com〉
날짜: 6월 14일
제목: 답장: 결제

토마스 씨,

방금 당신이 보낸 이메일을 읽었습니다. (195)당신은 화이트 씨의 결혼식에서 당신이 제공한 서비스에 대해 결제를 받을 것이니 걱정하지 마세요. 우리가 그녀의 돈을 환불해 주었더라도, 우리는 여전히 당신에게 지불할 생각입니다. 우리가 당신으로부터 송장을 받으면, 대금은 영업일 기준으로 3일 이내에 당신의 계좌로 입금될 것입니다. 다른 우려 사항이 있으면 알려 주세요.

에블린 조지 드림
스칼라티움

---

191. 광고에서, 첫 번째 단락 1행에 있는 단어 "occasions"와 의미상 가장 가까운 것은?
(A) 사례
(B) 행사
(C) 휴식
(D) 날짜　　　　　정답 (B)

192. 스칼라티움에 대해 언급된 것은 무엇인가?
(A) 그것은 5년 전에 설립되었다.
(B) 그것은 결혼식만 수용한다.
(C) 그것은 화려하게 장식된 창문이 있는 공간이 있다.

(D) 그것은 한 번에 최대 300명의 손님을 수용할 수 있다.　정답 (C)

193. 화이트 씨가 웹 페이지에 글을 올린 이유는?
(A) 환불을 요청하기 위해
(B) 제안하기 위해
(C) 항의를 제기하기 위해
(D) 서비스를 칭찬하기 위해　정답 (D)

194. 화이트 씨에 대해 추론될 수 있는 것은 무엇인가?
(A) 그녀는 스칼라티움에 환불을 요청했다.
(B) 그녀는 처음에 자신의 행사를 밖에서 열 계획이었다.
(C) 그녀는 스칼라티움의 성수기 동안 자신의 행사를 열었다.
(D) 그녀는 외부 음식 공급 서비스를 이용했다.　정답 (C)

195. 토마스 씨는 누구일 것 같은가?
(A) 사진작가
(B) 스칼라티움 직원
(C) 결혼식 하객
(D) 스칼라티움 고객　정답 (A)

문제 196-200번은 다음 광고와 이메일들을 참조하시오.

오리엔탈 스타 호텔

(196)방콕의 중심부에 위치한 오리엔탈 스타 호텔은 지난 60년 동안 손님들을 모셔왔습니다. 호텔은 최근에 개조되었습니다. 이제 호텔 전체에서 무료 무선 인터넷을 이용할 수 있습니다. 새로 단장된 객실들의 특징은 다음과 같습니다:

표준	트윈 침대, 헤어 드라이어, 에어컨
(196)디럭스	트윈 침대 2개, 헤어 드라이어, (196)냉장고, 에어컨
스위트	트윈 침대 2개, 거실, 욕조가 딸린 욕실 2개, 헤어 드라이어, 냉장고, 최첨단 오디오 시스템, 고화질 텔레비전, 에어컨
(199) 이그제큐티브 스위트	2개의 침실, 거실, 욕조가 딸린 욕실 2개, 헤어 드라이어, 냉장고 2개, 오디오 시스템, 고화질 텔레비전 2대, 에어컨 및 (199)무료 조식

오리엔탈 스타 호텔의 레스토랑 블루 플레이츠는 (198D)세계적으로 명성 있는 (198B)상의 수상 경력이 있는 마스터 셰프 이스라 타가 준비한 음식을 제공합니다. (198C)타 씨는 태국, 한국, 일본, 이탈리아의 전통 음식을 요리한 15년의 경력이 있습니다.

오리엔탈 스타 호텔에 대한 자세한 내용을 보시려면 www.orientalstarhotel.com을 방문하십시오. (200)성수기 중에는 방문객이 많은 것을 감안하여, 2개월 전에 방을 예약하실 것을 추천드립니다.

수신: 고객 서비스 〈customerservice@orientalstarhotel.com〉
발신: 아누락 호르베이쿨 〈ahorvejkul@pmtextiles.com〉
날짜: 11월 20일
제목: 멋진 경험

관계자 분께,

귀 시설에서의 멋진 경험에 대해 감사드리고자 이 글을 씁니다. 지난주에 제 고객인 타한 산티사쿨이 업무 차 방콕을 방문했을 때 저는 그분이 귀 호텔에 묵을 수 있도록 주선했습니다. 산티사쿨 씨는 귀 호텔이 제공한 전반적인 서비스에 만족한다고 말했습니다. (199)그분은 매일 아침 즐겁게 식사했던 무료 조식을 높게 평가했습니다.

게다가, 산티사쿨 씨와 저 둘 다 블루 플레이츠에서 음식을 맛있게 먹었습

니다. 11월 16일에 우리 둘 다 연어 구이를 주문했습니다. 주방장님이 직접 우리에게 서빙해 주셨습니다. 전에 TV에서 본 적 있는 사람과 이야기를 나눈 것은 즐거운 경험이었습니다. 앞으로도 귀 호텔과 다시 거래를 할 수 있기를 기대합니다.

아누락 호르베이쿨 드림
회계 부장
PM 섬유 주식회사

수신: 〈reservations@orientalstarhotel.com〉
발신: 〈tahans@promenadecarpets.com〉
날짜: 12월 1일
제목: 예약

귀하에게,

제 이름은 타한 산티사쿨이고, 저는 귀 호텔에 예약을 하고자 합니다. 저는 지난달에 그곳에 머물렀고 숙박이 아주 좋았습니다. 저는 12월 6일부터 12일까지 방콕에 있을 것입니다. 지난번에 묵었던 방과 같은 종류의 방으로 하고 싶습니다.

(200)2개월 전에 이 예약을 했어야 하는 건 알고 있지만, 그래도 제 요청을 들어주실 수 있기를 바랍니다. 이용 가능한 방이 있으면 알려 주십시오.

타한 산티사쿨 드림

---

196. 광고에서 오리엔탈 스타 호텔에 대해 나타나 있는 것은 무엇인가?
(A) 그것은 일정 기간 동안 폐쇄되었다.
(B) 그것은 방콕에서 가장 큰 호텔이다.
(C) 그것은 여러 관광 명소 근처에 위치해 있다.
(D) 그것은 수십 년 동안 영업을 해왔다.　정답 (D)

197. 디럭스 룸에서 이용할 수 있는 것은 무엇인가?
(A) 고화질 TV
(B) 냉장고
(C) 거실
(D) 욕조　정답 (B)

198. 타 씨에 대해 시사되어 있지 않은 것은 무엇인가?
(A) 그녀는 오리엔탈 스타 호텔에서 15년 동안 근무했다.
(B) 그녀는 요리로 상을 받은 적이 있다.
(C) 그녀는 다양한 스타일의 요리를 한다.
(D) 그녀는 다른 나라 사람들에게 알려져 있다.　정답 (A)

199. 산티사쿨 씨에 대해 추론할 수 있는 것은 무엇인가?
(A) 그는 호르베이쿨 씨의 동료이다.
(B) 그는 방콕을 여러 번 방문했다.
(C) 그는 이그제큐티브 스위트에 묵었다.
(D) 그는 최근에 요리법에 관한 잡지를 읽었다.　정답 (C)

200. 산티사쿨 씨에 대해 나타나 있는 것은 무엇인가?
(A) 그는 12월 한 달 내내 방콕에 머무를 것이다.
(B) 그는 매일 호르베이쿨 씨를 만날 것이다.
(C) 그는 다음 여행에서는 다른 방으로 묵고 싶어 한다.
(D) 그는 성수기에 방콕을 방문할 계획이다.　정답 (D)

1. 미M
(A) A man is stacking some boxes on a shelf.
(B) A man is lifting a box.
(C) A man is carrying crates on a cart.
(D) A man is packing supplies into a box.

(A) 한 남자가 선반 위에 상자를 쌓고 있다.
(B) 한 남자가 상자를 들어올리고 있다.
(C) 한 남자가 상자를 카트로 운반하고 있다.
(D) 한 남자가 상자 안에 물품을 포장하고 있다.　　　정답 (C)

2. 호W
(A) Some pillows are piled up on a sofa.
(B) Some cartons are stacked on the floor.
(C) A ladder is leaning against the fence.
(D) Some plants are placed along the hallway.

(A) 베개 몇 개가 소파 위에 쌓여 있다.
(B) 종이 상자 몇 개가 바닥에 쌓여 있다.
(C) 사다리가 울타리에 기대어져 있다.
(D) 화분 몇 개가 복도를 따라 놓여 있다.　　　정답 (B)

3. 미M
(A) They are constructing a brick walkway.
(B) They are placing safety cones on a street.
(C) They are kneeling to inspect a machine.
(D) They are unloading bricks from a truck.

(A) 그들은 벽돌 보도를 만들고 있다.
(B) 그들은 도로에 안전용 삼각봉을 놓고 있다.
(C) 그들은 기계를 점검하기 위해 무릎을 꿇고 있다.
(D) 그들은 트럭에서 벽돌을 내리고 있다.　　　정답 (A)

4. 미W
(A) Plastic bags are being distributed to people.
(B) A broom has been propped up against a tree.
(C) They are putting waste in the recycling bins.
(D) They are cleaning up some debris.

(A) 비닐 봉지가 사람들에게 배포되고 있다.
(B) 빗자루가 받침대로 나무에 기대어 세워져 있다.
(C) 그들은 쓰레기를 재활용 수거함에 넣고 있다.
(D) 그들은 쓰레기를 깨끗이 치우고 있다.　　　정답 (D)

5. 영M
(A) The man is holding a cutting board.
(B) The woman is putting some pans on the counter.
(C) The man is placing some food onto a plate.
(D) The woman is turning off a stove.

(A) 남자가 도마를 들고 있다.
(B) 여자가 팬 몇 개를 조리대 위에 놓고 있다.
(C) 남자가 접시에 음식을 놓고 있다.
(D) 여자가 레인지를 끄고 있다.　　　정답 (C)

6. 미W
(A) There is a deck overlooking a river.
(B) Some people are disembarking from a boat.
(C) A motorboat is passing under an arched bridge.

(D) One of the people is diving off a pier.

(A) 강을 내려다보는 갑판이 있다.
(B) 몇 사람이 배에서 하선하고 있다.
(C) 모터보트가 아치형 다리 밑을 지나고 있다.
(D) 사람들 중 한 사람이 잔교에서 다이빙하고 있다.　　　정답 (A)

Part 2

7. 영M 미W
What kind of ice cream did you purchase?
(A) Yes, at the ice cream stand.
(B) I got the strawberry flavor.
(C) They seem to be reasonably priced.

어떤 종류의 아이스크림을 구매했어요?
(A) 예, 아이스크림 매대에서요.
(B) 저는 딸기 맛으로 샀어요.
(C) 그것들은 가격이 적당한 것 같아요.　　　정답 (B)

8. 호W 영M
When will the marketing expert arrive?
(A) The train will be here any minute.
(B) Right after noon.
(C) Sure, I will.

마케팅 전문가는 언제 도착하죠?
(A) 기차가 여기 곧 도착할 거예요.
(B) 정오 직후예요.
(C) 좋아요, 할게요.　　　정답 (B)

9. 미W 미M
Who is supposed to authorize this approval form?
(A) Yes, he is our new intern.
(B) The marketing director.
(C) By the end of the month.

누가 이 승인서를 승인하게 되어 있어요?
(A) 예, 그는 우리 새 인턴이에요.
(B) 마케팅 이사님이요.
(C) 이달 말까지요.　　　정답 (B)

10. 영M 미W
Please come here 15 minutes before your scheduled appointment.
(A) But I left work early yesterday.
(B) She is 10 minutes late.
(C) Okay. Is there parking for visitors nearby?

예정된 약속 시간보다 15분 일찍 여기로 오세요.
(A) 그런데 저는 어제 일찍 퇴근했어요.
(B) 그녀는 10분 늦어요.
(C) 알겠습니다. 근처에 방문객을 위한 주차장이 있나요?　　　정답 (C)

11. 영M 미M
When will remodeling at the cafeteria be finished?
(A) This Friday at the latest, I think.
(B) Reserve a table for three.
(C) Try the first door on the left.

구내식당 리모델링 공사는 언제 끝나요?
(A) 늦어도 이번 주 금요일일 것 같아요.

(B) 세 명 앉을 테이블을 예약해 주세요.
(C) 왼편에 있는 첫 번째 문을 열어 보세요.
정답 (A)

12. 미W 미M
How did your presentation for the board go?
(A) Actually it was a present from my mother.
(B) Is it okay if I join you?
(C) It really went well.

이사회에 한 발표는 어떻게 되었어요?
(A) 사실, 그건 제 어머니가 준 선물이었어요.
(B) 제가 함께해도 괜찮아요?
(C) 정말 잘 되었어요.
정답 (C)

13. 호W 미M
How much of the budget is allocated to our computer lab?
(A) It was too expensive to buy.
(B) The software tracks your budget.
(C) Less than 5 percent.

예산 중 얼마나 우리 컴퓨터실에 배정되어 있어요?
(A) 그건 사기에는 너무 비싸요.
(B) 그 소프트웨어는 당신 예산을 추적해요.
(C) 5퍼센트가 안 돼요.
정답 (C)

14. 미W 영M
Do you want to talk about the report after your conference call?
(A) The regional manager from Chicago.
(B) Yes, I report directly to Mr. Park.
(C) Actually, my call was postponed.

전화회의 후에 그 보고서에 대해 얘기하고 싶어요?
(A) 시카고에서 온 지역 담당 매니저요.
(B) 예, 저는 미스터 박에게 직접 보고합니다.
(C) 사실 제 전화는 연기되었어요.
정답 (C)

15. 영M 호W
Isn't the technician for routine maintenance coming later?
(A) Yes, after 3 in the afternoon.
(B) The renovation met our expectations.
(C) Downstairs and to the right.

정기 점검을 위한 기술자는 이따 오지 않나요?
(A) 예, 오후 3시 이후에요.
(B) 보수공사는 우리 기대를 충족시켰어요.
(C) 아래층으로 가서 오른쪽이요.
정답 (A)

16. 미W 미M
Who's responsible for taking meeting minutes today?
(A) You should take the train.
(B) There's an extra table upstairs.
(C) I'll take care of it.

오늘 회의록 기록하는 것은 누가 맡나요?
(A) 그 기차를 타셔야 해요.
(B) 위층에 여분의 테이블이 있어요.
(C) 제가 맡을 거예요.
정답 (C)

17. 영M 미W
Do you know why Sarah is out of the office this afternoon?
(A) The office space is rented out.
(B) She's picking up a client from the airport.

(C) You can take the stairs.

오늘 오후에 사라가 왜 사무실에 없는지 아세요?
(A) 그 사무 공간은 임대되었어요.
(B) 그녀는 공항에서 고객을 픽업하러 갔어요.
(C) 계단을 이용하시면 됩니다.
정답 (B)

18. 호W 영M
Could you lend me your webcam for a video conference tomorrow?
(A) Arrange a conference call.
(B) Post it on the website.
(C) Sure, but I need it tomorrow afternoon at 5.

내일 화상 회의를 위해 당신 웹캠을 빌려 주실래요?
(A) 전화 회의를 준비해 주세요.
(B) 그것을 웹사이트에 올리세요.
(C) 물론이죠, 그런데 내일 오후 5시에는 제가 웹캠이 필요해요.
정답 (C)

19. 미W 미M
What forms should I fill out on my first day of work?
(A) The ones in the welcome packet.
(B) Do it first thing in the morning.
(C) Sure, I'll fill it up.

근무 첫날에 제가 어떤 양식을 작성해야 하나요?
(A) 환영 패키지에 있는 것들이요.
(B) 아침에 맨 먼저 그것을 하세요.
(C) 좋아요, 가득 채워 드릴게요.
정답 (A)

20. 영M 호W
Didn't the attendees have time to fill out their paperwork?
(A) No, I didn't attend, either.
(B) A 30 minute taxi-ride.
(C) Not yet, but that's next.

참석자들이 서류를 작성할 시간이 없었어요?
(A) 아뇨, 저도 참석하지 않았어요.
(B) 택시 타고 30분 거리예요.
(C) 아직요, 그렇지만 그게 바로 다음이에요.
정답 (C)

21. 미W 미M
I think this water faucet has a leak.
(A) Water the plants for me.
(B) Carl has a list of things to repair.
(C) The old microwave has been replaced.

이 수도꼭지가 새는 것 같은데요.
(A) 저 대신 화분에 물 좀 주세요.
(B) 칼이 수리해야 할 것들의 목록을 가지고 있어요.
(C) 오래된 전자레인지는 교체되었어요.
정답 (B)

22. 영M 미W
We haven't already processed Ms. Wagner's order, have we?
(A) Place an order for more.
(B) I've gone over this book before.
(C) Yes, it was shipped out this morning.

우리는 이미 와그너 씨의 주문을 처리하지 않았나요, 그렇죠?
(A) 좀 더 주문하세요.
(B) 제가 전에 이 책을 검토해 본 적이 있어요.
(C) 예, 그건 오늘 아침에 발송되었어요.
정답 (C)

23. 호W 미M

Why don't we purchase the conference tables that Mr. Kwon recommended?
(A) A weeklong training session.
(B) We can't afford to get them.
(C) No, it's not in the conference room.

미스터 권이 추천한 회의 테이블을 구매하는 게 어때요?
(A) 일주일 동안 하는 교육이요.
(B) 우리는 그것들을 살 여유가 없어요.
(C) 아뇨, 그건 회의실에 없어요.   정답 (B)

24. 미W 영M

Are you driving yourself or taking a taxi to the art museum?
(A) Do the buses run on weekends, right?
(B) Just across the street.
(C) I get to work on foot.

미술관까지 직접 운전하고 갈 거예요, 아니면 택시를 탈 거예요?
(A) 주말에 버스가 운행되죠, 그렇죠?
(B) 바로 길 건너요.
(C) 저는 걸어서 출근합니다.   정답 (A)

25. 호W 미M

What street is the local community center on?
(A) They offer art classes at the center.
(B) Miranda's been there before.
(C) About a road repaving project.

지역사회 센터는 어느 도로에 있나요?
(A) 그들은 센터에서 미술 수업을 제공해요.
(B) 미란다가 전에 거기에 가본 적이 있어요.
(C) 도로 재포장 프로젝트에 대해서요.   정답 (B)

26. 영M 미W

Was the 10 o'clock ferry to the island canceled?
(A) She went there by plane, too.
(B) That's what I heard.
(C) Yes, at the restaurant downstairs.

섬까지 가는 10시 페리호는 취소되었어요?
(A) 그녀도 거기에 비행기로 갔어요.
(B) 저도 그렇게 들었어요.
(C) 예, 아래층 식당에서요.   정답 (B)

27. 미M 호W

Would you like me to give you a tour of the new motor parts factory today?
(A) Inspect assembly lines.
(B) I was there last Friday.
(C) A new automobile is launching today.

오늘 새 자동차 부품 공장을 견학시켜 드릴까요?
(A) 조립 라인을 점검하세요.
(B) 지난주 금요일에 거기에 갔어요.
(C) 새 자동차가 오늘 출시됩니다.   정답 (B)

28. 영M 호W

What's the fastest way to get to the modern art museum?
(A) Din might know.
(B) Just two more paintings.
(C) An hourly rate.

현대 미술관으로 가는 가장 빠른 방법이 뭐죠?
(A) 딘이 알지 몰라요.
(B) 그냥 그림 두 점 더요.
(C) 시간 당 요금이요.   정답 (A)

29. 미W 미M

Will the training for the new summer intern start on Monday or Tuesday?
(A) Can I come in for an interview?
(B) It wasn't a safety training session.
(C) The schedule hasn't been finalized.

신입 여름 인턴을 위한 교육이 월요일 시작하나요, 아니면 화요일 시작하나요?
(A) 면접 보러 가도 되나요?
(B) 그것은 안전 교육 시간이 아니었어요.
(C) 일정이 최종 결정되지 않았어요.   정답 (C)

30. 영M 미W

The copy machine in Marketing is out of order, isn't it?
(A) Yes, the manager's out of the office today.
(B) I used it 30 minutes ago.
(C) It's on the market now.

마케팅부에 있는 복사기는 고장 났죠, 그렇죠?
(A) 예, 부장님은 오늘 부재 중이에요.
(B) 제가 30분 전에 그걸 썼는데요.
(C) 그건 지금 시판되고 있어요.   정답 (B)

31. 호W 영M

Dr. Yoon has an appointment available this Friday after 3.
(A) Yes, I'm free at the moment.
(B) Chapter 7 starts on page 55.
(C) What about next Monday?

윤 박사님은 금주 금요일 3시 이후에 진료 예약이 가능해요.
(A) 예, 저는 지금은 한가해요.
(B) 7장은 55쪽에서 시작해요.
(C) 다음 주 월요일은 어떤가요?   정답 (C)

Part 3

문제 32-34번은 다음 대화를 참조하시오. 미M 미W

M: Carla, (32)**how did the trade show go yesterday?**
W: Very well. (32) (33)**I talked about the new sensor-laden smart watches we're producing, and people seemed really interested in it. We had an audience of more than 70 people, and everyone agreed that that's the future of our industry—designing high-tech devices that provide people with more immediate access to any information.**
M: Did you mention that (34)**we'll be conducting a product testing for our latest smart watches next Monday?**
W: I did. And several potential investors in the audience indicated that they'd be attending it.

M: 칼라, 어제 무역 전시회는 어떻게 되었어요?
W: 아주 잘됐어요. 우리가 생산하는 센서가 장착된 새 스마트 워치에 대해 얘기했는데, 사람들이 정말 관심이 많은 것 같았어요. 청중이 70명 정도 있었는데, 모두 그게 우리 산업의 미래라는 데 의견을 같이했어요 – 즉, 어떤

정보든 사람들이 좀 더 즉각적으로 이용할 수 있게 해주는 최첨단 장치를 디자인하는 거예요.

M: 다음 주 월요일 우리 최신형 스마트 워치에 대해 제품 테스트를 한다는 것도 언급했어요?

W: 했어요. 그리고 청중 중에 여러 잠재적인 투자자들이 거기에 참석하겠다고 언질을 주었어요.

32. 여자는 어제 무엇을 했는가?
(A) 인터뷰를 실시했다.
(B) 프레젠테이션을 했다.
(C) 신입 사원을 모집했다.
(D) 웹사이트를 업데이트했다.   정답 (B)

33. 화자들은 어느 산업에서 일하는가?
(A) 의류
(B) 전자제품
(C) 엔지니어링
(D) 출장 요리 서비스   정답 (B)

34. 회사는 다음 주 월요일에 무엇을 할 것인가?
(A) 고객과 회의
(B) 장치 교체
(C) 인수 협상
(D) 신제품 테스트   정답 (D)

문제 35-37번은 다음 대화를 참조하시오. 영M 호W

M: Elizabeth, (36)**I'm planning the event** that will be held in March. You know almost all the speakers. (35)**Would you mind introducing them to the audience before they talk?**

W: (35)**Not at all.** I would love to. Do you need any assistance with the planning? (36)**I know we're hoping to raise enough funds to finance some new projects, so it's vital for everything to go well.**

M: That's all right. I'm nearly finished. (37)**All I have to do is work on the invitations.** Thanks for offering, though.

- -

M: 엘리자베스, 3월에 열리는 행사에 대해 계획을 짜고 있는데, 거의 모든 연사들을 아시잖아요. 그러니 그들이 연설하기 전에 청중에게 그들을 소개해 주실래요?

W: 당연히요. 제가 소개하고 싶어요. 행사 계획하는 데 도움 필요하세요? 제가 알기로 우리는 새 프로젝트에 자금을 댈 정도로 충분한 기금을 모금하고 싶어하잖아요. 그래서 모든 게 순조롭게 돌아가는 게 아주 중요해요.

M: 괜찮습니다. 거의 끝냈어요. 초대장 작업만 하면 되거든요. 그래도 도와주겠다고 제안해 주셔서 감사해요.

35. 남자는 여자에게 행사장에서 무엇을 해줄 것을 요청하는가?
(A) 연사 소개
(B) 참석자 명단 만들기
(C) 장소 준비
(D) 표 판매   정답 (A)

36. 어떤 종류의 행사가 계획되고 있는가?
(A) 자선 경매
(B) 교육
(C) 기금모금 행사
(D) 제품 시연회   정답 (C)

37. 남자는 무엇을 할 필요가 있다고 말하는가?
(A) 초대장 만들기
(B) 초청 연사들에게 연락하기
(C) 출장 요리 업체 고용하기
(D) 계약금 지불하기   정답 (A)

문제 38-40번은 다음 대화를 참조하시오. 영M 미W

M: Hello, Lucy. (38)**You're leading the tours at the museum next week, right?**

W: That's right. I'll be here every day since Chester will be gone.

M: Okay. (39)**Then you should know we'll be getting a tour group from the local elementary school on Tuesday.** The kids are scheduled to take a special tour of the observatory.

W: Great. Do I need to do anything before they arrive?

M: Here's a list with the students' names on it. (40)**Make sure each of them has a visitor's badge when the group gets here.** They're scheduled to arrive at 10:00 A.M.

- -

M: 안녕하세요, 루시. 다음 주에 박물관에서 관람 안내를 하시죠, 맞죠?

W: 맞습니다. 체스터가 부재 중이기 때문에 제가 매일 이곳으로 오게 될 것입니다.

M: 좋아요. 그렇다면 화요일에 우리는 이 지역 초등학교 관람 단체를 받게 된다는 것을 알아 두세요. 아이들은 전망대 특별 관람을 할 예정입니다.

W: 좋습니다. 애들이 도착하기 전에 뭐든 제가 해야 할 일이 있나요?

M: 여기 학생 명단이 적힌 목록이 있어요. 그 단체가 여기 도착하게 되면, 그들 각각 방문증을 받도록 해주세요. 그들은 오전 10시에 도착할 예정이에요.

38. 화자들은 어디에서 근무하는가?
(A) 놀이 공원
(B) 은행
(C) 동물원
(D) 박물관   정답 (D)

39. 남자에 따르면, 화요일에 무슨 일이 있겠는가?
(A) 한 사람이 근무를 시작할 것이다.
(B) 한 단체가 건물을 방문할 것이다.
(C) 새 프로그램이 시작될 것이다.
(D) 전시회가 시작될 것이다.   정답 (B)

40. 남자는 여자가 무엇을 해야 한다고 말하는가?
(A) 배지 제공
(B) 표 수거하기
(C) 안내책자를 추가로 채워 넣기
(D) 관람 일정 출력하기   정답 (A)

문제 41-43번은 다음 대화를 참조하시오. 호W 미M

W: Eric, (41)**do you remember I said I'd research manufacturers for our new skateboard design?** Well, I think I found a good one.

M: Wonderful. Does the company have the ability to work with the lightweight materials we plan to use for the skateboards?

W: Yes, but the problem is that the company is in St. Louis.

M: Oh... You know that we have to make frequent site inspections to ensure quality. (42)**It would be pretty expensive** to fly to St. Louis every two weeks.

W: That's true. (43)But why don't we outsource by hiring a quality control inspector who lives in St. Louis? That would be much cheaper than having to travel there twice a month.

W: 에릭, 우리 새 스케이트보드 디자인을 위한 제조업체를 찾아보겠다고 제가 말한 거 기억나세요? 음, 괜찮은 곳을 찾은 것 같아요.

M: 잘되었네요. 그 회사는 우리가 스케이트보드 만드는 데 사용할 계획인 경량 재료로 작업할 능력이 있어요?

W: 예, 그런데 문제는 그 회사가 세인트루이스에 있다는 거예요.

M: 아… 품질을 보장하려면 현장 점검을 자주 해야 한다는 것을 아시잖아요. 2주마다 비행기 타고 세인트루이스로 가려면 비용이 꽤나 많이 들 거예요.

W: 그 말이 맞아요. 그렇긴 하지만 외부에 위탁해서 세인트루이스에 사는 품질 관리 검사원을 고용하는 것은 어떤가요? 그렇게 하는 게 한 달에 두 번씩 그곳으로 출장을 가는 것보다 비용이 훨씬 더 적게 들 거예요.

41. 화자들은 어떤 제품에 대해 얘기하고 있는가?
(A) 운동화
(B) 스포츠 음료
(C) 스케이트보드
(D) 자전거　　　　　　　　　　　　　　　　　　정답 (C)

42. 남자가 우려하는 이유는?
(A) 비행기가 결항되었다.
(B) 공장이 너무 멀리 위치해 있다.
(C) 업무량이 너무 많다.
(D) 프로젝트가 일정대로 되지 않고 있다.　　　　정답 (B)

43. 여자는 무엇을 할 것을 제안하는가?
(A) 연비가 좋은 차량 구매
(B) 공장 이전
(C) 생산 일정 시각표 변경
(D) 현지 검사원 물색　　　　　　　　　　　　　정답 (D)

문제 44-46번은 다음 대화를 참조하시오. 영M 미W

M: Hello, Tina. Welcome to Dylan Manufacturing. I'm Paul Bernstein, (44)and I'll be your trainer. I understand you have quite a bit of career experience in our field.

W: That's right. I worked for an automobile manufacturer in Dayton for seven years. (45)I took this job so that I can live closer to my parents.

M: That's wonderful. I'm sure this training should go smoothly then. But before we begin, you have to learn about the safety procedures we follow.

W: Sure. I understand.

M: (46)Here's the safety manual. Why don't you read it through now? I'll return to go over everything with you in about twenty minutes.

M: 안녕하세요, 티나. 딜란 제조회사에 오신 것을 환영합니다. 저는 폴 번스타인이고 당신의 담당 교육자예요. 당신은 이 분야에 직업 경력이 많은 걸로 알고 있어요.

W: 맞습니다. 7년 동안 데이턴에 있는 자동차 제조업체에서 일했어요. 부모님과 좀 더 가깝게 살 수 있도록 하려고 이 일을 맡았습니다.

M: 좋습니다. 그렇다면 이번 교육은 순조롭게 진행될 거라고 확신해요. 그런데 시작하기 전에, 우리가 준수하고 있는 안전 절차에 대해 알아야 해요.

W: 좋아요. 잘 알겠습니다.

M: 여기 안전 설명서가 있어요. 지금 그 설명서를 쭉 읽어 보시겠어요? 대략 20분 후에 다시 돌아와서 전부 같이 훑어 드릴게요.

44. 남자는 누구인가?
(A) 신입 사원 모집 담당자
(B) 교육 담당자
(C) 면접관
(D) 자동차 판매자　　　　　　　　　　　　　　정답 (B)

45. 여자가 새 일자리를 구한 이유는?
(A) 가족과 더 가까이에 있기 위해
(B) 더 많은 월급을 받기 위해
(C) 지역 대학교에서 강좌를 수강하기 위해
(D) 새로운 기술을 얻기 위해　　　　　　　　　정답 (A)

46. 여자는 이후에 무엇을 하겠는가?
(A) 직접적인 경험 하기
(B) 설명서 검토하기
(C) 서류 작성하기
(D) 제품 시연회 하기　　　　　　　　　　　　정답 (B)

문제 47-49번은 다음 3자 대화를 참조하시오. 미M 호W 미W

M: Hello. I'm Kevin Lester. I reserved a room here for tonight.

W1: Good afternoon, Mr. Lester. Welcome to the Omni. This is your room keycard. (47)Unfortunately, the elevator is out of service since it is being fixed right now. But you can take the stairs over there. Emily can show you to your room.

W2: Follow me, sir. (48)Do you have any luggage?

M: (48)Yes, I left them outside in my car. There are also a few boxes of books. Is that all right?

W2: (48)It's no problem at all.

M: Great. (49)I'm hoping to sell all those books at the international book fair tomorrow.

M: 안녕하세요. 저는 케빈 레스터인데요, 오늘 밤 여기 방을 예약했어요.

W1: 안녕하세요, 레스터 씨. 옴니에 오신 것을 환영합니다. 여기 객실 키카드가 있습니다. 유감스럽게도, 엘리베이터가 지금 수리 중이라서 운행을 하고 있지 않습니다. 저쪽에 있는 엘리베이터를 이용하시면 됩니다. 에밀리가 손님을 객실까지 안내해 드릴 것입니다.

W2: 손님, 저를 따라오세요. 짐은 있으세요?

M: 예, 밖에 제 차에 두었습니다. 그리고 책 몇 상자도 있어요. 그것도 괜찮나요?

W2: 전혀 문제가 되지 않습니다.

M: 잘됐네요. 내일 국제 도서 박람회에서 저 책들을 전부 다 팔고 싶거든요.

47. 엘리베이터는 무엇이 문제인가?
(A) 유지관리 때문에 운행이 중단되어 있다.
(B) 청소를 하고 있는 중이다.
(C) 충분히 크지 않다.
(D) 수리 중이다.　　　　　　　　　　　　　　정답 (D)

48. 에밀리는 무엇을 해주겠다고 제안하는가?
(A) 짐 옮기기
(B) 차 주차하기
(C) 남자를 공항까지 차로 데려다 주기
(D) 남자에게 할인 제공하기　　　　　　　　　정답 (A)

49. 남자는 내일 무엇을 하겠다고 말하는가?
(A) 차량 렌트
(B) 책 판매
(C) 서점에서 쇼핑
(D) 도서 박람회를 위한 부스 예약 　　　정답 (B)

문제 50~52번은 다음 대화를 참조하시오. 미M 미W

M: Hello, Tina. (50)**I need to speak with you for a moment before you begin your next tour of the park.**
W: No problem. I won't start my next one until three o'clock.
M: Great. (51)**I've got some surveys of the park tour for our guests. Please distribute them to everyone.**
W: Sure. What's the survey asking about?
M: We're thinking of making some changes to the tours. But we want to find out what aspects of it people like and dislike so that we can retain the popular parts.
W: Sounds good. I wonder if we'd get more responses by e-mail. (52)**I have lots of e-mail addresses of people who went on tours before. I can e-mail them the survey.**

M: 안녕하세요, 티나. 다음 공원 투어 시작하기 전에 잠시 얘기 좀 해요.
W: 좋아요. 3시나 되어야 다음 투어가 시작되니까요.
M: 잘되었네요. 손님들에게 줄 공원 투어에 대한 설문지가 있는데요. 모두에게 이 설문지를 나눠주세요.
W: 알았어요. 설문지는 무엇에 대해 묻는 건가요?
M: 우리는 투어에 약간 변경을 할까 생각 중인데요. 그런데 투어의 어떤 면을 사람들이 좋아하고 싫어하는지 알고 싶어요. 그래야 인기 있는 부문은 그냥 유지할 수 있으니까요.
W: 괜찮네요. 이메일로 더 많은 응답을 받을 수 있지 않을까요? 전에 투어를 했던 사람들의 이메일 주소를 많이 갖고 있어요. 그 사람들에게 설문지를 이메일로 보낼 수 있어요.

50. 여자는 누구이겠는가?
(A) 정부 조사관
(B) 버스 운전자
(C) 관광 가이드
(D) 여행사 직원 　　　정답 (C)

51. 남자는 여자가 무엇을 하기를 원하는가?
(A) 서류 검토하기
(B) 공원 투어 하기
(C) 설문지 나눠주기
(D) 자신에게 이메일 보내기 　　　정답 (C)

52. 여자는 자신이 무엇을 갖고 있다고 말하는가?
(A) 공원 지도
(B) 이름표
(C) 방문증
(D) 이메일 목록 　　　정답 (D)

문제 53~55번은 다음 대화를 참조하시오. 미W 영M

W: Sylvester Office Tower maintenance office. What can I do for you?
M: Hello. I'm calling from the Dustin Printing office on the fourth floor. (53)**The lights here in the office aren't working well.**

W: Maybe the light bulbs need to be replaced.
M: I did that, (53) (54)**but the lights go out a few seconds after I turn them on.**
W: Okay. (54)**Well, the maintenance team is working on some pipes this morning.**
M: (55)**Oh, unfortunately, I have to leave the office after twelve to inspect our warehouse.**
W: If you give us permission, we can access your office while you are gone.

W: 실베스터 오피스 타워 유지보수과입니다. 뭘 도와드릴까요?
M: 안녕하세요. 4층에 있는 더스틴 인쇄소에서 전화드리는데요. 여기 사무실의 등이 제대로 작동하지 않아요.
W: 어쩌면 전구를 교체해야 할 것 같은데요.
M: 교체했지만, 켜고 나서 전등이 몇 초 있다가 꺼지거든요.
W: 알겠습니다. 그런데 유지보수팀이 오늘 오전에 파이프 작업을 하고 있어요.
M: 아, 유감스럽게도 저는 12시 이후에 물류창고를 점검하러 사무실에서 나가야 해요.
W: 허락해 주신다면, 안 계시는 동안에 저희들이 사무실로 들어갈게요.

53. 대화는 주로 무엇에 관한 것인가?
(A) 누수되고 있는 파이프
(B) 고장 난 자물쇠
(C) 없어진 물건
(D) 전기 문제 　　　정답 (D)

54. 여자가 "유지보수팀이 오늘 오전에 파이프 작업을 하고 있어요"라고 말할 때 무엇을 의미하는가?
(A) 남자는 누군가 다른 사람에게 전화를 해야 한다.
(B) 수리 작업이 비용이 많이 들 것이다.
(C) 어떤 작업을 즉시 할 수 없다.
(D) 팀원들이 하루 종일 바쁘다. 　　　정답 (C)

55. 남자는 오후에 무엇을 하겠다고 말하는가?
(A) 물류창고 방문하기
(B) 고객 만나기
(C) 회사 야유회 참석하기
(D) 서류 준비하기 　　　정답 (A)

문제 56~58번은 다음 대화를 참조하시오. 호W 영M

W: Hello, Steve. I remember that you asked for some suggestions on how we can encourage our employees to be healthy. (56)**I know some companies acquire gym memberships for their employees. How does that sound?**
M: I think it would be a wonderful way to get people healthy. But (57)**we have lots of employees here.**
W: (57)**I figured you would say that. So I did some research** and learned that some local gyms offer corporate discounts.
M: Really? That's fascinating. Would you please forward me the information you found regarding that? (58)**I'll put it on the agenda for tomorrow's staff meeting.**

W: 안녕하세요, 스티브. 제가 기억하기로는, 우리 직원들에게 어떻게 건강 관리를 장려할지 제안 좀 해달라고 제게 요청했었잖아요. 일부 회사는 직원들을 위해 헬스 회원권을 얻는 것으로 알고 있어요. 그건 어떤가요?

M: 직원들의 건강 유지에는 아주 좋은 방법이겠네요. 그런데 우리는 여기에 직원이 많아요.

W: 그렇게 말하실 줄 알았어요. 그래서 제가 조사를 좀 해봤는데, 이 지역 내 일부 헬스 클럽들이 기업 할인을 해주는 것을 알게 되었어요.

M: 정말이에요? 아주 멋지군요. 그것과 관련해서 찾은 정보를 저에게 보내줄래요? 내일 직원 회의에 의제로 올릴게요.

56. 여자는 회사가 무엇을 할 것을 제안하는가?
(A) 운영 시간 변경
(B) 헬스 회원권 제공
(C) 더 나은 복리후생 제공
(D) 사내 헬스 센터 개설　　　　　　　　정답 (B)

57. 남자가 "우리는 여기에 직원이 많아요"라고 할 때 무엇을 함축하는가?
(A) 회사는 곧 더 많은 사무실을 추가할 것이다.
(B) 제안은 돈이 많이 들 것이다.
(C) 직원 몇 명이 전근 갈 것이다.
(D) 많은 직원들이 재택 근무를 해야 한다.　　정답 (B)

58. 남자는 무엇을 하겠다고 말하는가?
(A) 직원 회의 연기
(B) 예산 보고서 검토
(C) 혼자서 조사 실시
(D) 의제에 주제 추가　　　　　　　　　정답 (D)

문제 59-61번은 다음 3자 대화를 참조하시오. 미M 호W 영M

M1: Thanks for coming to Jackson's. My name is Peter. What can I do for you?

W: Hello. I work for a law firm downtown, and we relocated to a larger office last week. (59)I'd like to purchase some photo frames for our lobby.

M1: If you would like a unique look, we suggest that your picture frames be engraved. Our custom engraving services are highly rated. (60)We even won a Customer Satisfaction Award for our high-quality work this year.

W: Sounds good.

M1: Our engraver is here behind us. Jason, this woman wants to have some photo frames engraved.

M2: I can definitely do that. Would you be interested in a few samples of my work so that you can choose from?

W: That sounds great. Oh, what kind of price should I expect for having the work done?

M2: (61)As a first-time customer, you'll get 10% off the regular price and delivery is at no extra cost.

- -

M1: 잭슨즈에 오신 것을 환영합니다. 제 이름은 피터입니다. 뭘 도와드릴까요?

W: 안녕하세요. 저는 시내 법률 회사에 다니는데, 지난주에 더 큰 사무실로 이전했어요. 우리 로비에 놓을 사진 액자를 좀 사고 싶어요.

M1: 독특한 모습을 원하시면, 사진 액자 안에 모양을 새겨 넣는 것을 제안드려요. 우리의 고객 맞춤형 새김 서비스는 아주 평가가 좋습니다. 올해 고품질 작업으로 고객 만족상을 수상하기도 했어요.

W: 좋네요.

M1: 새김을 하는 작업자가 여기 우리 뒤에 있어요. 제이슨, 이 여자분께서 사진 액자에 모양을 새겨넣고 싶어 하시네요.

M2: 확실히 해드릴 수 있어요. 고르실 수 있게 제 작품 견본을 보여 드릴까요?

W: 좋아요. 아, 작업을 하는 데 비용은 얼마 정도 예상해야 하나요?

M2: 처음 오신 고객이므로, 정가에서 10% 할인 받으시고, 배송은 추가 비용 없습니다.

59. 여자는 무엇을 구매하고 싶어하는가?
(A) 그림엽서
(B) 사진 액자
(C) 매다는 화초
(D) 열쇠고리　　　　　　　　　　　　정답 (B)

60. 피터는 새김 서비스에 대해 무엇을 말하는가?
(A) 추가 시간이 요구될 것이다.
(B) 현재 재고가 없다.
(C) 올해 한 잡지에 특집으로 나왔다.
(D) 수상 경력이 있는 서비스이다.　　　정답 (D)

61. 제이슨은 무엇이 무료로 이용 가능하다고 말하는가?
(A) 새김 서비스
(B) 배송
(C) 유지보수
(D) 연장된 보증　　　　　　　　　　　정답 (B)

문제 62-64번은 다음 대화와 일정표를 참조하시오. 미W 미M

W: Hi, Jeff. (62)I'm going over a few details for the biomedical conference I'm organizing. I wonder if you can assist me with something.

M: Sure. What do you need?

W: Do you have some time available on Thursday? Kevin was supposed to be manning the information booth from 1:00 to 2:00, but he has to be away on business on that day. (63)I need someone to substitute for him for that hour.

M: Wait a second, let me check my calendar. Oh, sure. I can do it. (64)I have something scheduled for 1:00 on that day, but I can call Mr. Duncan and reschedule our meeting.

- -

W: 안녕하세요, 제프. 내가 준비하고 있는 생체의학 총회에 대한 몇 가지 세부사항을 검토하고 있는데요. 저를 좀 도와줄 수 있는지 모르겠네요.

M: 괜찮아요. 뭐가 필요하신가요?

W: 목요일에 여유 시간 있나요? 케빈이 1시에서 2시 사이에 안내 부스에서 일하게 되어 있었는데, 그날 출장을 가야 해요. 그 시간에 케빈을 대신할 사람이 필요해요.

M: 잠깐만요, 일정을 확인해 볼게요. 아, 돼요. 제가 할 수 있습니다. 그날 1시에 일정이 잡혀 있는 게 있긴 한데, 던컨 씨에게 전화해서 우리 회의 일정을 다시 조정하면 돼요.

제프의 일정
11월 5일, 목요일

오전 9:00 - 오전 10:00	튜더 제약과 전화 회의
오전 10:30 - 오후 12:00	에드워드 라이트와 제품 시연
(64)오후 1:00 - 오후 2:30	**스튜어트 던컨과 계약 협상**
오후 5:00 - 오후 6:00	하퍼 컨벤션 센터에서 프레젠테이션

62. 여자는 무엇을 준비하고 있는가?
(A) 제품 시연회
(B) 총회

(C) 자선 경매
(D) 오리엔테이션 행사 　　　　　　　정답 (B)

63. 여자는 남자에게 무엇을 해달라고 부탁하는가?
(A) 동료 대신 근무하기
(B) 리셉션 준비하기
(C) 출장 가기
(D) 고객과 만나기 　　　　　　　정답 (A)

64. 그래픽을 보시오. 남자는 어떤 활동의 일정을 변경할 것인가?
(A) 전화 회의
(B) 제품 시연회
(C) 계약 협상
(D) 프레젠테이션 　　　　　　　정답 (C)

문제 65–67번은 다음 대화와 원 그래프를 참조하시오. 영M 호W

M: Here is the sales report of my team for the store for last week.
W: Thank you. **(65)Oh, by the way, you know that the store manager is resigning next month, right?**
M: Yes, I heard about that.
W: I need someone who can take over her job. **(66)Your team has been pretty effective at selling refrigerators and air conditioners.** Would you be interested in the position?
M: Yes, I would. I think you ought to know that **(67)I actually had the third highest sales numbers last week**, but I was also out of town for three days. I still believe I'm the best person for the job.

M: 이거 지난주 제 팀의 매장 매출 보고서입니다.
W: 고마워요. 아, 그런데 다음 달에 매장 관리자가 사임하는 것을 알고 계시죠, 그렇죠?
M: 예, 그에 대해 들었어요.
W: 그녀가 하던 일을 맡아줄 수 있는 사람이 필요해요. 당신 팀이 냉장고와 에어컨을 파는 데 아주 유능하게 잘했죠. 그 자리에 관심 있으세요?
M: 예, 관심 있어요. 사실 지난주에 제가 매출이 세 번째로 높긴 했지만, 3일 동안 외지에 나가 있었다는 것을 알아 주셔야 할 거 같아요. 그래도 제가 그 자리에 최적임자라고 생각합니다.

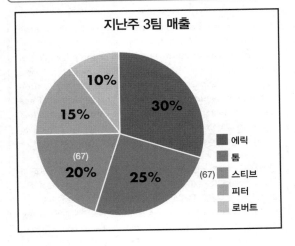

지난주 3팀 매출

- 10%
- 30%
- 15%
- (67)
- 20%
- 25%

■ 에릭
■ 톰
■ 스티브 (67)
■ 피터
■ 로버트

65. 여자에 따르면, 다음 주에 어떤 일이 있겠는가?
(A) 업무 일정이 바뀔 것이다.
(B) 새로운 직원이 전근 올 것이다.
(C) 영업 판촉행사가 있을 것이다.
(D) 한 직원이 일을 그만둘 것이다. 　　　　　정답 (D)

66. 화자들은 어디에서 근무하는 것 같은가?
(A) 가전제품 매장
(B) 옷 가게
(C) 야외 시장
(D) 연장 제조업체 　　　　　정답 (A)

67. 그래픽을 보시오. 남자의 이름은 무엇인가?
(A) 에릭
(B) 톰
(C) 스티브
(D) 피터 　　　　　정답 (C)

문제 68–70번은 다음 대화와 컴퓨터 화면을 참조하시오. 호W 미M

W: Hi, Walter. **(68)How do you like working at our marketing firm?**
M: I'm having a great time. In fact, I'm almost finished with my training program for new hires. However, I'm having some problems with the final assignment. I created a marketing plan, and I tried to e-mail it to my boss, Mr. Cameron. But I can't get it to go through. He's out of town on business and asked me to e-mail it to him.
W: The file is probably too big. You can't send files bigger than 30MBs.
M: **(69)Ah, the plan is around 40MBs.**
W: **(70)I think Mr. Cameron will return to the office tomorrow morning. Just wait until then and show the assignment to him.**

W: 안녕하세요, 월터. 우리 마케팅 회사 근무가 어떤 것 같습니까?
M: 아주 좋아요. 사실 신입 사원을 위한 교육 프로그램을 거의 끝냈습니다. 그런데 최종 임무는 좀 문제가 있네요. 마케팅 계획을 만들었고, 그것을 제 상사 캐머런 씨에게 이메일로 보내려고 했어요. 그런데 보내지지가 않더군요. 캐머런 씨는 출장차 외지에 나가 있는데 저에게 그것을 이메일로 보내 달라고 했어요.
W: 어쩌면 파일이 너무 커서인지도 모르겠네요. 30MB보다 크면 파일을 보낼 수가 없어요.
M: 아, 그 계획은 약 40MB예요.
W: 캐머런 씨가 내일 아침 사무실로 복귀할 것 같아요. 그 때까지 기다렸다가 그 과제를 그에게 보여 주세요.

파일명	용량
Kingswood.mov	15MB
Bernstein.mov	30MB
(69)Perez.mov	**40MB**
Littlebrook.mov	25MB

68. 화자들은 어떤 업종에서 일하는가?
(A) 마케팅
(B) 광고
(C) 제조
(D) 소프트웨어 　　　　　　　　　　정답 (A)

69. 그래픽을 보시오. 남자는 어느 파일을 이메일로 보내려고 했는가?
(A) Kingswood.mov
(B) Bernstein.mov
(C) Perez.mov
(D) Littlebrook.mov 　　　　　　　　정답 (C)

70. 여자는 남자에게 무엇을 할 것을 제안하는가?
(A) 파일을 다시 이메일로 보내 보기
(B) 관리자가 돌아오기를 기다리기
(C) IT 전문가와 얘기하기
(D) 컴퓨터 수리 받기 　　　　　　　　정답 (B)

Part 4

문제 71-73번은 다음 전화 메시지를 참조하시오. 미M

M: Hello, Ms. Hamilton. (71)**This is Kyle, your new tenant.** I have a quick question about the policy here at the apartment regarding the recycling of paper, plastic bottles, and metal items. (72)**When should I take out my recycling bin? Does the city do pickups on Mondays or Friday mornings?** (73) **I hope you can call me back with the correct information when you have the opportunity.** Thanks.

안녕하세요, 해밀턴 씨. 저는 새로 들어온 세입자 카일입니다. 종이, 플라스틱 병, 금속 제품 재활용에 관한 여기 아파트 정책에 대해 급한 질문이 있는데요. 재활용 통은 언제 밖으로 내놓아야 하나요? 시에서 월요일이나 금요일 아침에 수거를 하나요? 기회가 되시면 저에게 다시 전화 주셔서 맞는 정보를 알려 주시면 좋겠네요. 감사합니다.

71. 청자는 누구일 것 같은가?
(A) 정부 관료
(B) 가게 주인
(C) 아파트 관리인
(D) 배달하는 사람 　　　　　　　　정답 (C)

72. 화자는 어떤 정보에 대해 문의하는가?
(A) 아파트 주소
(B) 재활용품을 위한 장소
(C) 수거하는 날
(D) 수수료 금액 　　　　　　　　　정답 (C)

73. 화자는 청자에게 무엇을 할 것을 요청하는가?
(A) 정보를 이메일로 보내기
(B) 전화를 다시 하기
(C) 세입자에 대한 정책 확인하기
(D) 유지관리과에 전화하기 　　　　　정답 (B)

문제 74-76번은 다음 회의 발췌 내용을 참조하시오. 미W

W: (74)**The final thing we need to discuss is office supplies.** At the last meeting, I gave everyone some request forms for office supplies. (74)**If you need any paper, pens, staplers, or other similar items, write down what you need.** (75)**Just be sure you provide the correct information on the form**, or the order won't be processed. Some forms were rejected last month because they had been filled out improperly or incomplete. (76)**Sharon, the office manager, has the catalog in her office** if you need to consult it when completing the form.

우리가 논의해야 할 마지막 사항은 사무용품입니다. 지난번 회의에서 저는 모든 분에게 사무용품에 대한 요청서를 드렸습니다. 여러분이 종이, 펜, 스테이플러, 그 밖의 비슷한 물품들이 필요하다면, 필요한 것들을 적으십시오. 양식에 꼭 제대로 된 정보를 제시하세요, 그렇지 않으면 주문이 처리되지 않을 것입니다. 일부 양식이 지난달에 거부되었는데, 제대로 작성이 안 되었거나 덜 작성했기 때문입니다. 양식을 작성할 때 카탈로그를 참고하셔야 한다면, 사무실 책임자인 샤론이 자신의 사무실에 카탈로그를 갖고 있습니다.

74. 화자는 무엇에 대해 논의하는가?
(A) 규칙 변경
(B) 물품 주문
(C) 사무실 청소
(D) 다른 납품업체 물색 　　　　　정답 (B)

75. 화자는 청자에게 무엇을 할 것을 요청하는가?
(A) 근무시간 기록표 제출하기
(B) 오늘 저녁 회사에 늦게까지 남아 있기
(C) 정확하게 양식 작성하기
(D) 작업 효율을 위한 아이디어 공유하기 　정답 (C)

76. 화자는 샤론의 사무실에 무엇이 있다고 말하는가?
(A) 직원 연락명부
(B) 제품 카탈로그
(C) 사용자 설명서
(D) 방문증 　　　　　　　　　　정답 (B)

문제 77-79번은 다음 담화를 참조하시오. 호W

W: Hello, everybody. Before we close for the day, I have something to say. (77)**First, we haven't had any problems with the quality of our frozen pizzas or the packaging of them.** That's all thanks to your hard work. Next, I got some news from Justin Groceries, which is a big buyer. (78)**Due to the high demand for our pizzas, the supermarket has decided to increase its monthly order by fifty percent.** That means you'll be working a lot of overtime. (79)**Now, before we agree to the increase, I need to hear your thoughts.**

안녕하세요, 여러분. 오늘 마감하기 전에, 드릴 말씀이 있어요. 우선, 냉동 피자의 품질이나 포장에는 아무런 문제가 없었습니다. 그건 전부 여러분의 노고 덕분입니다. 다음은, 우리의 대형 구매업체인 저스틴 식품으로부터 소식을 들었는데요. 우리 피자에 대한 높은 수요 덕분에, 그 슈퍼마켓이 월별 주문량을 50% 늘이기로 결정했습니다. 그 말의 의미는 여러분이 시간 외 근무를 많이 하게 될 것이라는 것입니다. 이제, 이 주문 증가에 대해 동의하기 전에, 여러분의 생각을 좀 들어봐야겠습니다.

77. 어떤 제품이 논의되고 있는가?
(A) 피자
(B) 빵
(C) 커피
(D) 케이크   정답 (A)

78. 저스틴 식료품은 최근에 무엇을 했는가?
(A) 주문을 취소했다.
(B) 영업 시간을 변경했다.
(C) 피자 신제품을 출시했다.
(D) 주문을 늘렸다.   정답 (D)

79. 화자가 "여러분의 생각을 좀 들어봐야겠습니다"라고 할 때 무엇을 의미하는가?
(A) 수요를 맞추려면 더 많은 자금 지원이 필요할 것이다.
(B) 회의는 2주에 한 번 열릴 것이다.
(C) 일부 생산 라인이 제대로 작동되지 않고 있다.
(D) 결정을 하려면 정보가 좀 필요하다.   정답 (D)

문제 80-82번은 다음 안내 방송을 참조하시오. 미M

M: (80)Attention, passengers on Grant Air Flight 29 bound for London. We are still unable to find the problem with our electronic booking system, which means both passenger lists and boarding passes won't be available at the gate. (81) However, please be aware that this kind of issue has happened before and we have a good team working on it now. (82)We'll keep you posted on our progress. We'll make another announcement in just a few minutes. In the meantime, please be patient.

런던 행 그랜트 에어 29편 승객 여러분께 알려 드립니다. 우리는 아직도 우리 전자 예약 시스템에 생긴 문제를 찾지 못하고 있는데, 이는 탑승구에서 승객 명단과 탑승권을 확인할 수가 없다는 의미입니다. 그렇지만, 전에도 이런 문제가 발생했었고 지금 현재 훌륭한 팀이 이 문제를 해결하려고 작업 중이라는 것을 알고 계십시오. 우리의 처리 상황에 대해 계속해서 여러분에게 알려 드릴 것입니다. 조금 있다가 또 다시 안내 방송을 해드리겠습니다. 그 동안에 인내심을 갖고 기다려 주십시오.

80. 화자는 어디에서 근무하는가?
(A) 식당
(B) 병원
(C) 공항
(D) 극장   정답 (C)

81. 화자가 "지금 현재 훌륭한 팀이 그것을 작업 중입니다"라고 할 때 무엇을 함축하는가?
(A) 교체 부품이 곧 도착할 것이다.
(B) 문제가 곧 해결될 것이다.
(C) 모든 직원들이 너무 바쁘다.
(D) 추가 교육은 필요하지 않다.   정답 (B)

82. 화자는 이후에 무엇을 할 것이라고 말하는가?
(A) 모든 사람에게 환불해 주기
(B) 탑승구 번호 변경하기
(C) 누구의 질문에든 답변하기
(D) 곧 업데이트 내용 알려 주기   정답 (D)

문제 83-85번은 다음 회의 발췌 내용을 참조하시오. 호W

W: Hello. We are meeting because I was just informed by the vice president that (83)our most recent ad campaign for our running shoes has not been successful. Basically, we tried to attract too many people. Our market research shows that our shoes appeal mostly to 20 to 40-year-old age group. They like the style and are also physically active. (84)Our next campaign needs to specifically target this group. (85)We'll think about the details when we go over our new strategy at Friday's meeting.

안녕하세요. 우리가 회의를 하는 이유는 우리 운동화에 대한 가장 최근 광고 캠페인이 성공하지 못했다고 부사장님으로부터 방금 들었기 때문입니다. 기본적으로 우리는 너무 많은 사람을 끌어들이려고 했어요. 우리 시장 조사에 따르면 우리 신발은 주로 20-40세의 그룹에 어필합니다. 그들은 이 스타일을 좋아하고 육체적으로 활동을 많이 해요. 우리 다음 광고 캠페인은 특히 이 그룹을 목표로 해야 할 필요가 있습니다. 금요일 회의에서 우리의 새로운 전략을 검토할 때 세부사항에 관해 생각해 볼 것입니다.

83. 청자들은 무엇의 전문가이겠는가?
(A) 디자인
(B) 관광
(C) 마케팅
(D) 컴퓨터   정답 (C)

84. 화자는 무엇을 할 것을 제안하는가?
(A) 특정 개인들에 집중
(B) 신제품 운동화 출시
(C) 한 품목의 품질 개선
(D) 마케팅 컨설턴트의 추가 고용   정답 (A)

85. 금요일에 무슨 일이 있겠는가?
(A) 광고가 녹화될 것이다.
(B) 특정 그룹 대상으로 설문조사를 할 것이다.
(C) 취업 박람회가 열릴 것이다.
(D) 전략이 논의될 것이다.   정답 (D)

문제 86-88번은 다음 방송을 참조하시오. 미W

W: I hope you enjoyed listening to those songs on FM Radio 89.9. Right now, let's hear an important message from our sponsor. (86)Couper Kitchen Supplies is looking for people to act as product testers. (87)You'll receive some of its new products in the mail such as hand blenders, toasters and even small cooking utensils. What you have to do is use those products and simply report on how you liked using them. (88)If you would like to be picked, post your recipe that you think is best on our website. If you're selected, one of our customer service representatives will contact you.

FM 라디오 89.9에서 나오는 그 노래들을 잘 들으셨기를 바랍니다. 지금은 우리 후원업체가 전하는 중요한 메시지를 들어 봅시다. 쿠퍼 키친 서플라이즈는 제품 테스터 역할을 할 사람들을 찾고 있습니다. 여러분은 우편으로 손 믹서기, 토스터기 그리고 심지어는 작은 주방용품 같은 그 회사의 신제품들을 받게 될 것입니다. 여러분이 할 것은 그냥 그 제품들을 사용하고 사용할 때 그것들이 어땠는지 알려 주시기만 하면 됩니다. 여기에 뽑히고 싶다면, 여러분이 최고라고 생각하는 요리법을 우리 웹사이트에 올리세요. 여러분이

선정된다면, 저희 고객 서비스 담당 직원이 연락을 드릴 것입니다.

86. 방송에 따르면, 후원업체가 찾고 있는 것은 무엇인가?
(A) 요리 경연자
(B) 스타 요리사
(C) 제품 테스트 할 사람
(D) TV 아나운서
정답 (C)

87. 후원업체는 어떤 종류의 제품을 제조하는가?
(A) 컴퓨터 게임
(B) 주방 가전
(C) 원예 용품
(D) 스포츠 용품
정답 (B)

88. 참가에 관심이 있는 청자는 무엇을 해야 하는가?
(A) 매장 방문하기
(B) 우편으로 설문지 보내기
(C) 요리법 보내기
(D) 전화 걸기
정답 (C)

문제 89-91번은 다음 워크숍 발췌 내용을 참조하시오. 영M

M: Good morning. Welcome to our management seminar. (89)**During the next two days, you'll learn about how to run and grow a small business.** We're going to start with a presentation by my colleague and our speaker, Eric Hooper today. (90)**He's going to talk about his own past experiences with starting a small bookstore. Today, he owns a chain of stores all across the country.** So I strongly encourage you to listen carefully to what he advises. He is also the co-author of an award-winning book on management. (91)**Everybody will get a complimentary autographed copy when we are all done with this presentation today.**

안녕하세요. 우리 경영 세미나에 오신 것을 환영합니다. 앞으로 이틀 동안, 여러분은 작은 사업체를 어떻게 운영하고 키우는지 배우게 되실 겁니다. 오늘 우리는 제 동료이자 연사인 에릭 후퍼의 프레젠테이션으로 시작하겠습니다. 그는 작은 서점을 창업한 자신의 과거 경험에 대해 이야기할 것입니다. 오늘날, 그는 전국에 걸쳐서 서점 체인을 소유하고 있습니다. 그러니 그가 조언하는 것들을 주의깊게 경청하시라고 강력히 권해 드립니다. 그는 또한 수상 경력이 있는 경영에 관한 책의 공동 저자이기도 합니다. 오늘 이 프레젠테이션이 모두 끝나면 모든 분들은 서명이 들어간 책을 무료로 받으실 것입니다.

89. 청자들은 누구이겠는가?
(A) 대학생
(B) 작가
(C) 출판업자
(D) 사업체 소유주
정답 (D)

90. 화자가 "그는 전국에 걸쳐서 서점 체인을 소유하고 있습니다"라고 말하는 이유는?
(A) 연사의 자격을 강조하기 위해
(B) 동료에게 그의 공헌에 대해 감사하기 위해
(C) 청자들에게 최선을 다하라고 격려하기 위해
(D) 의제로 한 가지 주제를 제안하기 위해
정답 (A)

91. 이 날 마지막에 청자들은 무엇을 받게 될 것인가?
(A) 쿠폰집
(B) 서명을 한 포스터
(C) 서명을 한 책
(D) 무료 구독권
정답 (C)

문제 92-94번은 다음 회의 발췌 내용을 참조하시오. 미M

M: (92)**You should be aware that our winter clothing sale begins next week.** I need to tell you about a couple of things before the sale event. First, we're expecting plenty of customers since we advertised in many places. Our parking lot probably won't have enough room for all of the cars. (93)**I would therefore like you to park in the pay lot two blocks away.** You'll be reimbursed for the price of parking. Next, here's the list of the clothes on sale. (94)**Make sure to look it over by the end of the week so that you can answer any questions correctly that customers ask.**

다음 주에 우리 겨울 의류 세일이 시작된다는 것을 알아 두셔야 합니다. 세일 행사 전에 여러분에 몇 가지 드릴 말씀이 있습니다. 우선, 우리는 아주 많은 곳에 광고를 했기 때문에 많은 손님들이 올 것으로 예상하고 있습니다. 우리 주차장이 아마도 그 모든 차량을 수용하기에는 공간이 충분치 않을 겁니다. 그래서 여러분은 두 블록 떨어진 유료 주차장에 주차하시는 게 좋겠습니다. 주차 비용에 대해서는 환급받게 될 것입니다. 다음으로는, 여기 세일하는 의류 목록이 있습니다. 손님이 묻는 어떤 질문에든 정확하게 대답할 수 있도록 이번 주 말까지 이 목록을 꼭 훑어보세요.

92. 다음 주에 무슨 일이 있겠는가?
(A) 개장
(B) 송별 파티
(C) 세일
(D) 도로 폐쇄
정답 (C)

93. 화자는 청자들이 무엇을 하기를 원하는가?
(A) 제시간에 직장에 도착하기
(B) 유료 주차장에 주차하기
(C) 대중 교통 이용하기
(D) 매장 안내도 확인하기
정답 (B)

94. 화자는 청자들에게 이번 주 말까지 무엇을 하라고 말하는가?
(A) 세일 포스터 게시하기
(B) 교육 과정 이수하기
(C) 근무 시간 확인하기
(D) 문서 읽기
정답 (D)

문제 95-97번은 다음 전화 메시지와 일기예보를 참조하시오. 미W

W: Hi, Tim. This is Katherine, the symphony conductor. (95)**I'm calling about the concert we're supposed to perform tomorrow.** (96)**It looks like we'll be getting rain tomorrow. We need to reschedule it for the following day. It will be sunny then,** so there's no chance of rain. However, what do we do about the people who bought tickets but can't attend? I think we should refund their money. (97)**Please e-mail every ticket holder an announcement about the new date and also mention how to apply for a refund.** Thanks.

안녕하세요, 팀. 저는 심포니 지휘자 캐서린입니다. 내일 우리가 공연하게 되어 있는 콘서트 때문에 전화드렸는데요. 내일 비가 올 것 같네요. 그 다음 날로 공연 일정을 바꿔야 할 것 같아요. 그 때는 햇빛이 나서, 비 올 확률도 없고요. 그런데 티켓을 구매했지만 올 수 없는 사람은 어떻게 하면 좋을까요? 제 생각에는 환불을 해줘야 할 것 같아요. 모든 티켓 소지자에게 이메일로 안내문을 보내서 새로 바뀐 날짜에 대해 알려 주고 어떻게 환불 신청하면 되는지도 언급해 주세요. 감사합니다.

일기예보

일요일	월요일	화요일	(96)수요일	목요일
비	흐림	(96)비	(96)맑음	맑음

95. 화자는 어떤 행사 때문에 전화를 하고 있는가?
(A) 콘서트
(B) 스포츠 행사
(C) 인터뷰
(D) 총회 　　　　　　　　　　　　　　정답 (A)

96. 그래픽을 보시오. 행사는 언제 열릴 것인가?
(A) 월요일
(B) 화요일
(C) 수요일
(D) 목요일 　　　　　　　　　　　　　　정답 (C)

97. 청자는 무엇을 하라는 요청을 받는가?
(A) 안내문 발송
(B) 광고 게시
(C) 표 판매
(D) 콘서트 장소 변경 　　　　　　　　　정답 (A)

문제 98~100번은 다음 회의 발췌 내용과 지도를 참조하시오. 영M

M: (98)Right now, let's talk about some possible locations for our new restaurant. We need a place large enough to accommodate indoor and outdoor dining. Check out this map. You can clearly see the large building available beside the theater. (99)But I prefer the location across the street from the subway station. It's more accessible by public transportation. (100)Now, let's check out some photographs of the interior of that building. I want to know what you think after viewing them.

이제, 우리 새 식당을 위한 가능한 장소에 대해 얘기 좀 해봅시다. 우리는 실내 및 실외 식사를 수용할 정도로 큰 장소가 필요해요. 이 지도 좀 보세요. 극장 옆에 가능한 큰 건물이 분명히 보이죠. 그런데 저는 지하철역에서 길 건너편에 있는 장소가 더 마음에 들어요. 거기가 대중교통으로 더 접근이 쉬우니까요. 이제 그 건물 실내 사진 좀 확인해 봅시다. 사진들을 보고 난 다음 어떻게 생각하시는지 알고 싶네요.

98. 화자는 어떤 업종에 대해 논의하고 있는가?
(A) 소매점
(B) 식당
(C) 철물점
(D) 극장 　　　　　　　　　　　　　　정답 (B)

99. 그래픽을 보시오. 화자는 어떤 장소를 추천하는가?
(A) 장소 A
(B) 장소 B
(C) 장소 C
(D) 장소 D 　　　　　　　　　　　　　　정답 (D)

100. 화자는 이어서 무엇을 할 것이라고 말하는가?
(A) 사진 보여 주기
(B) 안내 책자 나눠주기
(C) 재정에 대해 얘기하기
(D) 질문에 답변하기 　　　　　　　　　정답 (A)

Part 5

101. 사회학자들은 사회적 문제가 해결되는 것을 막는 장애에 대해 우리가 인식하도록 도움을 준다. 　　　　　　　정답 (B)

102. 뮤지컬 공연 중에, 시각 효과를 극대화하기 위한 기본 조명뿐 아니라 레이저 빔 프로젝터나 안개 기계도 있다. 　　　정답 (D)

103. 해리슨 씨는 사업체를 소유하는 꿈을 추구했고, 기업 보험에서부터 기업 회계에 이르는 모든 것들을 배웠다. 　　　정답 (B)

104. 부티크 코코는 유럽에서 인기가 많은 의류 브랜드 중 하나로 여성 패션업계의 최신 트렌드를 창출한다. 　　　정답 (B)

105. 시 의회는 최근 모든 다국적 기업들이 사업 허가증을 매년 갱신할 것을 요구하는 법안을 마련했다. 　　　　　정답 (B)

106. 초기 단계에서 유해 바이러스의 확산을 막기 위해 모든 국가에서 이 도시로 입도하는 것이 엄격하게 통제되고 있다. 　　　정답 (C)

107. 몇몇 신문들은 새로 부임하는 우리 최고 경영자가 그의 경영 방식과 사업 방침을 좀처럼 바꾸지 않는 지도자라고 보도했다. 　　　정답 (B)

108. 잠재적인 관객들에게 입소문을 내어 표 판매를 늘리기 위해 다양한 방법들이 사용되었다. 　　　　　　　정답 (C)

109. 참석자들이 계획에 필요한 생각을 할 시간을 주기 위해 회의 안건을 훨씬 전에 나누어 주는 것이 중요하다. 　　　정답 (A)

110. 델타 증권회사는 시드니 투자회사와 자사의 은행 계열사와 합병함으로써 큰 시너지 효과를 추구하는 경영 개선 계획의 개요를 작성했다. **정답 (C)**

111. 콜린스 씨의 폭넓은 실무 경험으로 인해, 인사부장은 그가 영업팀에 환영받는 추가 인력이라고 생각한다. **정답 (D)**

112. 상업 지구의 사무 공간 임대 비용 상승으로 인해, 점점 더 많은 수의 회사들이 도시 근교 지역으로 옮기길 원한다. **정답 (B)**

113. 데본셔 가에 새로운 교통 신호등을 설치한 것은 교통 체증을 감소시키는 데 적당한 성공을 거뒀을 뿐이다. **정답 (D)**

114. 꼼꼼한 계획과 지속적인 TV 광고 덕분에, 벨라 앤 앤드류 회사는 마침내 전 세계 장난감 시장의 선두업체가 되었다. **정답 (C)**

115. 소셜 미디어는 참여, 개방성, 유대감 등을 특징으로 하는 새로운 유형의 온라인 미디어로 묘사될 수 있다. **정답 (D)**

116. 영업 분야에서 제한적인 경험을 소유한 지원자들은 일단 채용되면 연수 참가가 요구될 것이다. **정답 (A)**

117. 기내 탑승객들이 입국하기 전에 거쳐야 할 몇 가지 엄격한 세관 절차들이 있다. **정답 (D)**

118. 최근 항만 이용에 대한 조사에서, 많은 여행객들은 세관에서 오랜 대기 시간이 기진맥진하게 한다고 진술했다. **정답 (A)**

119. 고객들은 그들의 사무용 가구가 어떻게 제작되는지 직접 볼 수 있도록 원체스터 가구 제조 공장 견학에 초청 받았다. **정답 (D)**

120. 우리의 직원 실적 평가는 각 직원의 역량과 상대적인 장점 그리고 회사를 위한 가치를 이해하기 위해 필수이다. **정답 (C)**

121. 몇몇 광고주들은 펜, 수건, 열쇠고리와 같은 다른 홍보물보다는 냉장고 자석 배포를 더 선호한다. **정답 (A)**

122. 최근 눈 폭풍에도 불구하고, 우리 지역은 현재 더 따뜻하고 건조한 겨울을 겪고 있다. **정답 (B)**

123. 최근 유가 인상으로 인해, 그 회사는 새로운 중장비 한 대를 구매하려는 그들의 계약을 11월 말이나 심지어 12월 중순까지로 연기할 것이다. **정답 (D)**

124. 우리 회원은 전국에 있는 어느 가맹점에서든 구매할 때마다 보너스 포인트를 적립할 수 있다. **정답 (D)**

125. 의학 전문가에 따르면, 외출하는 사람은 누구든 바이러스 감염으로부터 보호하기 위해 마스크를 착용해야 한다. **정답 (A)**

126. 대중 교통이 무료이면 더 이상 승차권을 인쇄하지 않아도 되기 때문에 비용과 나무가 절약될 것이다. **정답 (B)**

127. 많은 공공 축제와 행사들이 1년 내내 개최되지만, 대부분은 보통 여름과 가을에 열린다. **정답 (A)**

128. 맥거완 씨가 우리의 새로운 휴대 전화에 관한 발표를 할 것이며, 그 후 10분간의 질의 응답 시간이 있을 것이다. **정답 (C)**

129. 우리 회사의 방침에 따라, 누구든 마지막으로 퇴근하는 사람은 책임지고 보안 경보 시스템의 전원을 켜야 한다. **정답 (C)**

130. 최근 몇 년간 전자제품의 소비가 너무 많이 증가해서 이것은 오늘날 가장 환경적으로 문제가 많은 제품군 중 하나를 대표한다. **정답 (B)**

Part 6

문제 131-134번은 다음 보도 자료를 참조하시오.

585번 고속도로에 대한 새로운 통행료

7월 17일 – 오클랜드) 켄우드 시장은 도시 외곽에 건설 중인 585번 고속도로의 공사 완료 즉시, 이에 부과하는 새로운 통행료를 승인했다.

시장의 새 통행료는 새 고속도로가 완공된 후 즉시 시행될 것이며, 요금소는 고속도로 1마일 표시 지점에 건설될 것이다. 전자 통행료 징수 시스템이 설치될 것이고, 운전자가 차를 세우고 통행료를 지불하지 않아도 된다.

시장은 새로운 고속도로 및 적용될 통행료에 관한 우려를 표명했다. 시장은 통행료가 환영받지 못할 것임을 알지만, 궁극적으로는 세금을 올릴 필요 없이 시에서 새로운 지방 도로의 비용을 지불할 능력이 생기는 동시에 교통량 감소에 도움이 될 것이라고 말했다.

131. **정답 (B)**

132. **정답 (A)**

133. **정답 (B)**

134. (A) 8월부터 11월까지는 도로 통행료를 현금으로 지불할 수 있다.
(B) 그는 관광 명소를 홍보하고 관광객 방문 의향을 불러일으키기 위해 관광부에 합류했다.
(C) 시장은 새로운 고속도로 및 적용될 통행료에 관한 우려를 표명했다.
(D) 고도로 발달된 고속도로 체계는 휴양을 목적으로 하는 관광객을 우리 도시로 유치하게 될 것이다. **정답 (C)**

문제 135-138번은 다음 정보를 참조하시오.

고객님이 방금 구매하신 에너지 배터리는 4년 이상 혹은 4만 마일 정도 사용할 수 있도록 설계되었습니다. 그럼에도 불구하고, 고객님의 배터리의 수명이 다하면 그것을 적절하게 폐기하셔야 합니다. 그것을 그냥 쓰레기통에 버리지 마십시오. 대부분의 자치단체는 현재 사용자들이 수명이 다된 배터리를 단순히 쓰레기와 함께 버리지 말 것을 권고합니다.

대부분 전문가들은 폐기된 배터리들이 금속 제품들이 있는 상자나 가방에 허술하게 보관되는 경우 화재와 폭발을 일으킬 수 있다고 말합니다. 그래서 저희 회사는 고객 분들에게 빠르고 간편한 폐기 방법을 제공해 드립니다. 고객님은 고객님의 지역에 있는 저희 재활용 센터 한 곳에 방전된 배터리를 반납하시기만 하면 됩니다. 그것들을 저희에게 넘기시면, 저희 재활용 전문가들이 추가 비용 없이 적절한 방식으로 그것들을 처리해 드립니다.

135. **정답 (B)**

136. **정답 (B)**

137. **정답 (B)**

138. (A) 오래된 배터리와 새 배터리, 다른 종류의 배터리 또는 서로 다른 제조사의 배터리를 함께 사용하지 마십시오.

(B) 차고에 남아 있는 일부 배터리는 여러 안전 문제의 원인이 될 수 있습니다.

(C) 고객님은 고객님의 지역에 있는 저희 재활용 센터 한 곳에 방전된 배터리를 반납하시기만 하면 됩니다.

(D) 새로운 소형 배터리는 휴대 전화와 전동 공구에 사용됩니다.　정답 (C)

문제 139-142번은 다음 광고를 참조하시오.

스피드 쇼핑의 VIP 회원

귀하의 택배가 도착하는 걸 기다리는 데 지치셨나요? 약간의 쇼핑 요법을 간절히 원하시나요? 매번 빠른 배송 비용을 지불하는 것이 싫으신가요? 오늘 VIP 회원이 되셔서 그러한 문제점들을 피하세요. 저희 VIP 회원은 매년 무제한 배송 횟수로 무료 당일 배송을 누리고 있습니다. 게다가, 그들은 분기마다 1회 매장과 온라인에서 모두 사용 가능한 30달러짜리 전자 상품권을 받습니다. 저희는 또한 VIP 회원에게 구매 시 특별 할인을 제공합니다. 단 18달러의 연간 회비로 오늘 저희 VIP 회원이 되세요. 황금 같은 이번 기회를 이용하세요! 결코 후회하지 않으실 겁니다!

139.　정답 (C)

140.　정답 (A)

141.　정답 (B)

142. (A) 저희는 또한 VIP 회원에게 구매 시 특별 할인을 제공합니다.
(B) $100 초과 지출 시 무료 당일 배송 혜택을 받으실 수 있습니다.
(C) 올해 최고의 매출 기록을 세운 여러분의 노고와 헌신에 감사드립니다.
(D) 저희는 고객님이 배송을 받지 못하신 것에 대해 놀랐으며 배송 지연에 대해 사과드립니다.　정답 (A)

문제 143-146번은 다음 회람을 참조하시오.

모든 직원에게.

해리 맥베인 씨가 창업을 하기 위해 6월 30일에 우리 회사를 떠난다는 것을 공식적으로 알려 드리고자 합니다. 맥베인 씨는 5년 전에 입사한 이후로, 우리 회사의 경쟁력을 향상시키는 데 핵심적인 역할을 해왔습니다. 결과적으로, 우리는 매출을 극적으로 신장시켰으며, 수익성이 훨씬 더 좋은 회사가 되었습니다.

맥베인 씨의 리더십 아래, 우리는 기획 절차를 재편성했으며, 엄격한 품질 기준을 도입했고, 전사적인 경쟁 전략을 개발했습니다. 변화의 과정이 항상 쉽지는 않았지만, 우리 모두 긍정적인 결과에 감사할 수 있습니다. 예를 들어, 지난 분기에 우리는 사상 처음으로 수익 및 단위 판매 모두에서 모든 경쟁사들을 추월한 것으로 추정합니다. 맥베인 씨는 이러한 성과에 대해 많은 공로를 인정 받을 자격이 있습니다.

저와 함께 맥베인 씨에게 앞으로의 그의 노력에 행운과 지속적인 성공이 있기를 기원해 주십시오.

샐리 머피
인사부장

143.　정답 (B)

144. (A) 우리가 우리 고객에게 보여준 헌신은 우리가 확장하는 데 도움이 되었습니다.
(B) 그는 최고 경영자로서 자신의 역할을 계속하고 주요 결정에 참여할 것입니다.

(C) 우리 서비스와 상품에 대한 가격은 매우 다양하며, 이는 종종 혼란을 야기합니다.
(D) 결과적으로, 우리는 매출을 극적으로 신장시켰으며, 수익성이 훨씬 더 좋은 회사가 되었습니다.　정답 (D)

145.　정답 (C)

146.　정답 (B)

문제 147-148번은 다음 광고를 참조하시오.

〈휴스턴 데일리〉 제공

당신의 가족을 위한 새로운 레시피를 찾고 계십니까?
(147)이 지역에서 가장 선호하는 레스토랑인 델리 네코의 지원을 받아, 〈휴스턴 데일리〉는 다음 주부터 지역 주민들에게 요리 수업을 제공할 것입니다. 수업은 델리 네코에서 열릴 것이며, 레스토랑의 주인인 미노루 토바가 수업을 가르칠 것입니다.

제공되는 수업은 다음과 같습니다:
당신만의 초밥을 만드세요　　- 월요일 오후 2시
일본 국수　　　　　　　　　- 월요일 오후 3시

(148)www.thehoustondaily.com에서 온라인으로 등록하실 수 있습니다. 비용을 포함한 상세한 정보를 원하시면, 바네사 코넬리에게 917-803-7552로 연락하세요.

147. 무엇이 광고되고 있는가?
(A) 레스토랑
(B) 지역 출판물
(C) 요리 수업
(D) 주택 개량 서비스　정답 (C)

148. 관심 있는 사람은 무엇을 해야 하는가?
(A) 웹사이트 방문
(B) 식당 주인에게 전화
(C) 코넬리 씨 방문
(D) 잡지 구매　정답 (A)

문제 149-150번은 다음 문자 메시지를 참조하시오.

더스틴 피터슨	[오후 6시 35분]

(150)낸시, 아직 사무실에 있어요? 공항으로 가는 중인데, 엘더슨 파일 한 부를 안 가지고 온 걸 방금 알았어요.

낸시 휘태커	[오후 6시 36분]

(150)운이 좋으세요. 그게 어디에 있어요?

더스틴 피터슨	[오후 6시 37분]

(149)제 사무실 책상 맨 위 서랍에 있어요. 앤디 플라워즈로부터 열쇠를 받을 수 있어요.

낸시 휘태커	[오후 6시 45분]

(149)됐어요, 제가 파일을 가지고 있어요. 어떻게 해야 하죠?

더스틴 피터슨   [오후 6시 46분]
모든 페이지를 스캔해서 이메일로 제게 보내 주세요.

낸시 휘태커   [오후 6시 48분]
큰 파일이에요. 30분까지 걸릴 수 있어요.

149. 휘태커 씨에 대해 시사되어 있는 것은 무엇인가?
  (A) 그녀는 피터슨 씨와 사무실을 같이 쓴다.
  (B) 그녀는 피터슨 씨의 사무실 안으로 들어갔다.
  (C) 그녀는 보통 늦게까지 사무실에 있다.
  (D) 그녀는 플라워 씨를 찾을 수 없었다.   정답 (B)

150. 오후 6시 36분에, 휘태커 씨가 "당신은 운이 좋으세요"라고 쓸 때 무엇을
  의미하는 것 같은가?
  (A) 그녀는 앨더슨 파일 작업을 하고 있다.
  (B) 그녀는 피터슨 씨가 필요한 파일을 찾았다.
  (C) 그녀는 공항에 갈 시간이 있다.
  (D) 그녀는 아직 퇴근하지 않았다.   정답 (D)

문제 151-153번은 다음 회람을 참조하시오.

해피 전자

수신: 모든 직원
발신: 마리 데이비스
날짜: 4월 1일 월요일
제목: 새로운 서비스 정책

여러분 모두가 3월 27일에 발표된 ST 전자의 새로운 고객 서비스 정책
에 관한 기사를 읽었으리라 짐작합니다. 우리의 가장 큰 경쟁사 중 하나
인 ST 전자가, 현장 수리 서비스를 시행할 것이라고 발표했습니다.

(151)업계에서 앞서고자, 이제 모든 제품에 대한 (152C) (153)기존의 1년
보증을 2년 더 연장할 것입니다. 또한 센터를 방문하는 고객에게 요금
없이 소프트웨어 업그레이드 서비스를 제공할 것입니다.

또한, 서비스의 질을 높이고 고객 만족도를 개선시키기 위하여 2시간 교
육이 (152B)각 매장에서 열릴 것입니다. 모든 영업 사원들이 이 교육을
받는 것은 필수입니다. 각 매장의 상세한 교육 일정은 다음 (152A)월례
회의 끝에 발표될 것입니다. 회의는 회의실 302A호에서 4월 8일에 열릴
것입니다.

마리 데이비스
마케팅 매니저
---

151. 이메일의 목적은 무엇인가?
  (A) 한 회사의 연혁을 제공하기 위한 것
  (B) 고객들에게서 피드백을 구하기 위한 것
  (C) 회의 안건을 요청하기 위한 것
  (D) 직원들에게 일부 변경에 대해 알리기 위한 것   정답 (D)

152. 해피 전자에 대해 나타나 있는 것은 무엇인가?
  (A) 정기적으로 회의를 개최한다.
  (B) 두 곳 이상의 매장을 가지고 있다.
  (C) 곧 3년짜리 보증을 제공할 것이다.
  (D) 현장 수리 서비스를 제공하기 시작할 것이다.   정답 (D)

153. [1], [2], [3] 그리고 [4]로 표시된 곳 중에, 아래 문장이 들어가기에 가장 적
  절한 곳은?
  "새로운 정책은 4월 5일 화요일에 시행될 것입니다."
  (A) [1]
  (B) [2]

  (C) [3]
  (D) [4]   정답 (B)

문제 154-156번은 다음 전단을 참조하시오.

샬럿에 오셔서 공연을 즐기세요!

(154)샬럿 시의회에서 다음의 멋진 공연 시리즈를 제공합니다!
저희 시를 방문하시고 여러 관광 명소들을 즐겨 보세요.

• 비가 올 경우에, 공연은 취소될 수 있습니다. •

5월 4일 / 사이키 **샬럿 어드벤처 월드 / 오후 7시**	**5월 18일 / 쿠웨이트 공연단** **(156)샬럿 극장 홀 / 오후 7시**
노르웨이의 올해의 뮤지션인 사이키가 그의 2집 앨범의 곡들을 연주할 것입니다. 세계에서 가장 열정적인 가수 중 한 명으로 알려져 있는 그는 〈뮤즈〉 잡지에 의해 올해의 음악인으로 뽑혔습니다.	(156)쿠웨이트 공연단이 쿠웨이트 악기인 루바바와 탄바라를 사용하여 쿠웨이트 댄스를 공연할 것입니다.
5월 11일 / 제임스 맥클린 **샬럿 놀이 공원 / 오후 8시**	**(155)5월 25일 / 제브라스** **샬럿의 라이트 공장 / 오후 7시**
스코틀랜드 전통 악기인 백파이프를 이용해서 맥클린이 여러분에게 그가 직접 작곡한 놀라운 곡을 들려줄 것입니다.	브룬디의 밴드 제브라스가 특유의 악기와 리듬을 이용해서 아프리카 전통 음악을 공연할 것입니다.
---

154. 콘서트가 개최되는 이유는?
  (A) 여행 패키지를 광고하기 위해
  (B) 새롭게 건설된 놀이 공원을 기념하기 위해
  (C) 샬럿 관광을 홍보하기 위해
  (D) 시민들에게 여러 종류의 음악을 연주할 것을 권장하기 위해   정답 (C)

155. 전단에 따르면, 제브라스는 언제 공연을 할 것인가?
  (A) 5월 4일
  (B) 5월 11일
  (C) 5월 18일
  (D) 5월 25일   정답 (D)

156. 댄스 공연이 어디에서 열릴 것인가?
  (A) 샬럿 어드벤처 월드
  (B) 샬럿 놀이 공원
  (C) 샬럿 시의회
  (D) 샬럿 극장 홀   정답 (D)

문제 157-158번은 다음 양식을 참조하시오.

피터스 가드닝

고객님 께,
(157)저희의 서비스를 이용해 주셔서 감사드립니다. 귀하의 소중한 의견을
받아 저희 서비스를 향상시킬 수 있도록 아래 양식의 작성을 요청드립니다.

이름: (158)스콧 헌트
전화번호: 214-860-2209
주소: 80 베어포 드라이브, 어빙, 텍사스 주

(157)1. 피터스 가드닝에서 어떤 서비스를 받으셨습니까?
☐ 가지 치기   ☐ 잔디 깎기   ☐ 청소   ☑ 토탈 솔루션
---

2. 가격에 대하여 만족하셨습니까?

☐ 매우 만족   ☐ 만족   ☑ 불만족   ☐ 매우 불만족

3. 서비스에 걸린 시간에 대하여 만족하셨습니까?

☑ 매우 만족   ☐ 만족   ☐ 불만족   ☐ 매우 불만족

4. 결과에 대하여 만족하셨습니까?

☐ 매우 만족   ☑ 만족   ☐ 불만족   ☐ 매우 불만족

5. 추가 의견:

피터스 가드닝의 토탈 솔루션 덕분에 저의 정원이 성공적으로 바뀌었습니다. 빠른 개조 과정과 결과 또한 좋았습니다. 하지만, 서비스 비용은 경쟁사에 비하여 조금 비싼 것 같습니다. (158)저와 같은 단골 고객을 위한 할인 추가를 권합니다.

157. 헌트 씨에게 양식이 발송된 이유는?

(A) 직원들의 의견을 수집하기 위해
(B) 완료된 일에 대한 피드백을 받기 위해
(C) 곧 있을 서비스에 대하여 고객에게 질문하기 위해
(D) 고객의 서비스 주문을 확인하기 위해   정답 (B)

158. 양식에 따르면, 헌트 씨에 대해 나타나 있는 것은 무엇인가?

(A) 그의 동료들에게 피터스 가드닝을 추천했다.
(B) 서비스 가격이 합리적이라고 생각한다.
(C) 그의 서비스에 대해 할인을 받았다.
(D) 피터스 가드닝에서 전에 서비스를 받은 적이 있다.   정답 (D)

문제 159-161번은 다음 웹사이트 정보를 참조하시오.

www.wholenewworlds.com/register

홀 뉴 월즈에 오신 것을 환영합니다

(159)새로운 언어를 배우고 싶었지만, 시간이나 기회가 없으셨습니까? 그렇다면 홀 뉴 월즈가 바로 귀하를 위한 것입니다. 홀 뉴 월즈는 강력하고 존경받는 교육 제공자로서 다음의 서비스들을 제공합니다:

- 50개가 넘는 나라의 원어민과의 1대1 페어링
- 인증된 강사들에 의해 이루어지는 동영상 강의
- 어휘와 관용구 플래시 카드를 이용한 편리한 자율 학습 도구
- 3일간의 무료 체험 기간
- 배치 고사

(160)홀 뉴 월즈의 수천 명의 회원들 중 한 명이 되어 오늘부터 당신의 언어 능력을 향상시키세요!

우리에게 당신에 대해 말해 주세요!	
성명:	앨버트 스탈
이메일 주소:	astahl@quickmail.com
출신국:	독일
구사 언어:	독일어
배우고 싶은 언어:	중국어

(161)홀 뉴 월즈를 사용하는 것이 이번이 처음입니까?

☐ 네   (161)☑ 아니오

등록 종류	이용 가능한 서비스
☐ 3일 체험 (무료)	배치 고사, 자율 학습 도구와 동영상 강의에 대한 이용
☐ 1개월 (30달러) ☑ 3개월 (80달러) ☐ 6개월 (150달러)	홀 뉴 월즈가 제공하는 모든 서비스 포함: 배치 고사, 1대1 페어링, 자율 학습 도구, 동영상 강의, 능력 평가 테스트, 그 외 다수

159. 이 정보의 목적은 무엇인가?

(A) 새 언어 강사를 모집하기 위한 것
(B) 온라인 발행물에 대한 할인을 제공하기 위한 것
(C) 번역 서비스를 광고하기 위한 것
(D) 교육 프로그램을 광고하기 위한 것   정답 (D)

160. 홀 뉴 월즈에 대해서 언급된 것은 무엇인가?

(A) 모든 서비스를 무료로 제공한다.
(B) 최근 설립되었다.
(C) 많은 사용자들을 보유하고 있다.
(D) 독일에 기반을 두고 있다.   정답 (C)

161. 스탈 씨에 대해 시사되어 있는 것은 무엇인가?

(A) 3일간의 체험에 등록할 계획이다.
(B) 중국어를 한다.
(C) 이 웹사이트를 전에 방문한 적이 있다.
(D) 최근에 배치 고사를 봤다.   정답 (C)

문제 162-164번은 다음 회람을 참조하시오.

회람

수신: 미스틱 폴즈 호텔의 전 직원
발신: 데이먼 살바토르
날짜: 2월 2일
제목: (162)추천의 결과

모든 직원 분들께,

(162)엘레나 길버트가 이 달의 직원으로 뽑혔다는 것을 발표하게 되어 기쁩니다. 호텔 소유주 로버트 후드가 (163)해마다 두 차례 열리는 6월의 미스틱 폴즈 밤에서 그녀에게 (공로로) 인정하는 상패를 수여할 것입니다. 이에 더하여, 그녀는 2일 유급 휴가 및 300달러의 상금을 받을 것입니다.

3년 전 그녀가 객실 청소부로 미스틱 폴즈 호텔에서 일하기 시작한 이래로, 길버트 씨는 계속적인 노력과 헌신을 보여 준 우수한 직원이었습니다. 그녀의 뛰어난 서비스는 고객들로부터 여러 차례 인정받았습니다.

(162)저는 모든 직원들이 이 뛰어난 업적에 대해 그녀를 축하해 주시기를 바랍니다. (164)사업 파트너이자 오랜 친구인 노만 후드 씨와 케빈 코스트너 씨가 이 호텔을 처음 설립한 이래로, 우리는 헌신과 열정을 보여준 직원에게 보상하는 전통을 계속해 왔고, 누구든지 이 달의 우수 직원 다음 수상자가 될 수 있을 거라고 믿습니다.

감사드리며,

데이먼 살바토르
총 지배인
미스틱 폴즈 호텔

162. 이 회람의 주제는 무엇인가?

(A) 수상자
(B) 곧 있을 축제
(C) 고객 만족도 조사 결과
(D) 직원들의 실적에 대한 검토   정답 (A)

163. 6월에 무슨 일이 있을 것인가?

(A) 살바토르 씨가 상을 받을 것이다.
(B) 추천에 대한 의견 개진이 시작될 것이다.
(C) 한 호텔 직원이 승진할 것이다.
(D) 길버트 씨가 행사에 참여할 것이다.   정답 (D)

ACTUAL TEST •••• 06

164. 코스트너 씨는 누구인가?

(A) 호텔의 주인
(B) 길버트 씨의 친구
(C) 한 사업체의 공동 설립자
(D) 객실 청소 직원

정답 (C)

문제 165-167번은 다음 판매 계약서를 참조하시오.

차량 판매 계약서

(주) J&G 자동차

계약 번호: 121590

이 판매 계약은 (167D)**(주) J&G 자동차** (판매자)와 <u>마이클 벨</u> (구매자) 사이에 성립되었다.

A. (165)판매자는 다음 차량을 구매자에게 <u>2월 28일</u>에 양도한다.

(167A)<u>제조사</u>: **젠슨**　　<u>종류</u>: 픽업 트럭
<u>모델</u>: J3000i　　<u>색상</u>: 로열 블루
<u>주행</u>: 76,291

B. (165)구매자는 판매자로부터 이 차량을 19,500달러(세금 포함)의 가격에 구매하는 데에 동의한다.

C. (165)구매자는 오늘 일부 금액인 14,500달러를 지불할 것이며, 차량 수령시에 남은 금액을 지불할 것이다.

D. 판매자는 구매자에게 차량의 모든 점검 기록을 제시하였으며, (167B)구매자는 품질 보증 없이 이 차량을 구매하는 데에 동의한다.

(166)(주) J&G 자동차의 <u>존스빌 시 지점</u>에서 <u>2월 20일</u>에 서명되었다.

<u>(167D)존 케일스</u>	<u>2월 20일</u>
(167D)판매자(대리점 직원)	날짜
<u>마이클 벨</u>	<u>2월 20일</u>
구매자	날짜
<u>카일 윌슨</u>	<u>2월 20일</u>
증인	날짜

---

165. 벨 씨는 2월 28일에 무엇을 할 것 같은가?

(A) J&G 자동차에 차량 판매
(B) 잔금 5,000달러 지불
(C) 1년 한정 품질 보증서 구매
(D) 케일스 씨에게 점검 기록서의 복사본 보내기

정답 (B)

166. 계약서에 따르면, J&G 자동차에 대하여 추론될 수 있는 것은 무엇인가?

(A) 2개 이상의 지점을 가지고 있다.
(B) 존스빌에 본사가 있다.
(C) 많은 영업 직원들이 있다.
(D) 마이클 벨에게 로열 블루 세단을 팔았다.

정답 (A)

167. 계약서에 나타나 있지 않은 것은 무엇인가?

(A) 차는 젠슨에서 제조되었다.
(B) 벨 씨는 어떠한 품질 보증도 받지 않을 것이다.
(C) 카일 윌슨이 차량의 이전 소유주였다.
(D) 존 케일스는 J&G 자동차에서 일한다.

정답 (C)

문제 168-171번은 다음 온라인 채팅 토론을 참조하시오.

글렌 카터	[오후 2시 29분]

앰버 카페의 재닛 루돌프가 제게 이메일을 보냈어요. 그녀는 주간 단위 주문을 두 배로 늘리고 싶어 해요. 우리가 처리할 수 있나요?

마커스 스테슨	[오후 2시 30분]

안 될 이유가 없죠. 그렇게 큰 것은 아니니, 우리가 할 수 있어요. 어떻게 생각해요, 그레그?

그레그 왓킨스	[오후 2시 31분]

제가 예상할 수 있는 유일한 문제는 배달이에요. 그녀는 매주 월요일 6개의 상자를 받는데, 만약 우리가 그것을 두 배로 12개로 늘리면, (168)**그녀의 배달량이 너무 커서 다른 모든 것과 함께 제 트럭에 실을 수 없을지 몰라요.**

마커스 스테슨	[오후 2시 33분]

아. 그건 미처 생각하지 못했어요.

글렌 카터	[오후 2시 34분]

배달 일정을 재조정할 수 있을까요? 어쨌든, 그녀의 업소는 고작 몇 블록 거리예요. (169)그녀의 물건을 그날 좀 더 일찍 배달해 주는 건 어때요?

에이미 존스	[오후 2시 35분]

(169)제가 할게요. 저는 매일 아침 그녀의 업소를 운전해서 지나가기 때문에, 해롤드의 피시 앤 칩스에 갈 때 모든 걸 갖다 줄 수 있어요. 아침 8시 30분까지 갈 수 있어요.

글렌 카터	[오후 2시 37분]

좋아요. (170)제가 재닛에게 전화해서 알려 줄게요. 제가 알아야 할 문제가 있나요?

마커스 스테슨	[오후 2시 38분]

(171)이번 주말에는 일손이 부족할 거예요. 브래드 하워드가 퇴사했는데, 후임자를 아직 구하지 못했어요.

에이미 존스	[오후 2시 40분]

(171)저는 주말에 아무 계획이 없어요.

글렌 카터	[오후 2시 41분]

고마워요, 에이미. 그럼 토요일에 봬요.

---

168. 왓킨스 씨에 대해 시사되어 있는 것은 무엇인가?

(A) 그는 배달 트럭을 운전한다.
(B) 그는 카페에서 일한다.
(C) 그는 루돌프 씨를 직접 만난 적이 있다.
(D) 그는 밤 늦게까지 일한다.

정답 (A)

169. 존스 씨가 하겠다고 제의하는 것은 무엇인가?

(A) 루돌프 씨와 대화하기
(B) 신입 사원 후보 찾기
(C) 일부 품목을 상점에 배달하기
(D) 매일 더 일찍 일 시작하기

정답 (C)

170. 카터 씨는 이후에 무엇을 할 것 같은가?

(A) 전화 걸기
(B) 일정 다시 짜기
(C) 하워드 씨와 대화하기
(D) 고객 방문하기

정답 (A)

171. 오후 2시 40분에, 존스 씨는 "저는 주말에 아무 계획이 없어요"라고 쓸 때 무엇을 시사하는가?

(A) 그녀는 돈을 더 벌어야 한다.
(B) 그녀는 이번 주에 많은 시간을 일하지 않았다.

(C) 그녀는 시간 외 근무 수당을 받기를 기대한다.
(D) 그녀는 하워드 씨의 교대 근무를 기꺼이 하려고 한다. 　　　정답 (D)

문제 172 – 175번은 다음 기사를 참조하시오.

패서디나, 4월 19일 – 오늘, 로스앤젤레스에 기반을 둔 **(172)국제 유제품 유통 공급업체인 브릴리언스 유업**은 지난 10년간 최고 경영자였던 잭슨 호프스태터 씨가 4월 30일 자로 은퇴할 것이라고 발표했다. 회사의 현 부회장인 페넬로페 가르시아 씨가 그의 자리를 대신할 것이다.

그의 직장 생활 전체를 브릴리언스 유업에서 보내면서, 호프스태터 씨는 35년 전 설립 이래로 회사에 충성을 바쳐왔다. "제 열정의 전부를 쏟아부은 회사가 성장하여 업계에서 최고의 기업이 되는 것을 보는 것은 즐거웠습니다"라고 호프스태터 씨는 과거를 회고하며 말했다.

호프스태터 씨의 후임자 또한 회사에서 그만큼 긴 근무 이력을 가지고 있다. 25년 전 보스턴 대학교에서 경영학 학위를 따고 난 직후, 가르시아 씨는 뉴욕에 있는 회사 계열사인 CBS 우유에 입사했다. 그녀는 브릴리언스 유업으로 옮기기 전에 CBS 우유에서 11년간 마케팅 이사로 근무했다.

"가르시아 씨는 이사회로서는 당연한 선택이었습니다. 저는 가르시아 씨와 **(173)함께 CBS 우유에서 마케팅 부책임자로서 일했을** 때 그녀가 선택될 것을 알았습니다. 그녀는 제가 만나본 사람들 중 가장 능률적이고 헌신적인 리더입니다"라고 현재 CBS 우유의 상무이사 **(173)션 쿠퍼 씨가** 말했다.

(175)브릴리언스 유업은 전 최고 경영자에게 작별 인사를 하고, 새로운 최고 경영자를 환영하기 위한 행사를 본사에서 마련하였다. 이번 행사에서는 또한 호프스태터 씨의 저서, 〈누구나 바닥에서 시작한다〉의 출간을 축하할 것이다. "저는 업계의 많은 사람들에게 여러 면에서 빚을 지고 있습니다. **(174)이제 제 경험과 지식을 책을 통해 나누면서 다른 이들을 도와줄 때입니다**"라고 호프스태터 씨가 말했다.

172. 브릴리언스 유업에 대해 나타나 있는 것은 무엇인가?

(A) 해외로 제품을 수출한다.
(B) CBS 우유의 경쟁업체이다.
(C) 패서디나에 큰 낙농장이 있다.
(D) 현재 새 직원을 모집 중이다. 　　　정답 (A)

173. 쿠퍼 씨는 누구인가?

(A) 브릴리언스 유업의 새 최고 경영자
(B) CBS 우유의 전 마케팅 부책임자
(C) 브릴리언스 유업의 현 부회장
(D) 〈누구나 바닥에서 시작한다〉의 저자 　　　정답 (B)

174. 호프스태터 씨는 무엇을 할 계획인가?

(A) 새 사업 창업
(B) 경영학 공부
(C) 가르시아 씨 교육
(D) 글을 통해 그의 전문 지식 공유 　　　정답 (D)

175. [1], [2], [3] 그리고 [4]로 표시된 곳 중에, 아래 문장이 들어가기에 가장 적절한 곳은?

"그것은 4월 30일에 열릴 것이다."

(A) [1]
(B) [2]
(C) [3]
(D) [4] 　　　정답 (D)

문제 176–180번은 다음 이메일들을 참조하시오.

수신: 챈들러 델리온 〈cdeleon@stranton.com〉
발신: 에이버리 빌링스 〈abillings@stranton.com〉
날짜: 9월 15일
(176)제목: 시스템 접근 오류

델리온 씨께,

아시다시피, 저희 부서는 현재 우리 태국 지사와 현지 기업인 디엠 홈 & 리빙 방콕과의 합동 화상 회의를 준비 중입니다. 제시카 디엠은 두 회사 간의 앞으로 있을 수 있는 협력에 대해 논의하기 위해 회의에 참석할 것입니다. **(177)이 회의는 우리 회사의 아시아 시장으로의 확장에 있어 아주 중요한 디딤돌이 될 것입니다.**

(179)하지만 9월 19일에 열릴 이 회의를 준비하는 도중에, 우리는 한 가지 문제에 직면했습니다. (176) **(178)에블린 포스터 차장이 현재 회사 인트라넷에 접속할 수 없다고 보고했습니다.** 그녀는 일주일 전에는 시스템에 로그인했을 때 아무 문제가 없었다고 언급했습니다.

그녀는 이 잠재적 사업 관계에 있어 핵심 멤버이며, 따라서 **(176)포스터 씨는 온라인으로 모든 자료들에 접근할 수 있어야 합니다.** 이 문제를 가능한 한 빨리 해결해 주십시오. 도움에 대해 미리 감사드립니다.

에이버리 빌링스 드림
마케팅 부장, 스트랜턴 주방 가전

수신: 에이버리 빌링스 〈abillings@stranton.com〉
발신: 챈들러 델리온 〈cdeleon@stranton.com〉
날짜: 9월 16일
제목: 답장: 시스템 접근 오류

빌링스 씨께,

문의하신 사안에 대해서 조사하여 문제의 원인을 알아냈습니다. 우리 지사들은 각각 회사 서버에 독립적인 액세스 포인트를 가지고 있기 때문에, 접속 코드는 공통적이지 않습니다. 따라서, **(178)차장이 방콕 지사에서 전근 오기 전에 받은 코드는 그곳에서만 유효할** 것입니다. 이곳 본사에서 사용할 새로운 코드를 받아야 합니다.

(179)시간적 제약을 고려해서, 임시 접근 코드를 발급했고, 별도의 이메일을 통해 보내 드리겠습니다. 그 코드는 회의 다음 날 만료될 것이라는 점을 숙지하여 주십시오. **(180)영구적인 코드를 받으려면 그 사람이 온라인으로 신청서를 제출해야 합니다.** 사원 매뉴얼에 나와 있듯이, http://intranet.stranton.com/form/100254에 있는 양식을 작성하고 제시된 자료들을 업로드하십시오.

저는 9월 22일부터 출장을 가기에 연락이 닿지 않을 것입니다. 제가 없는 동안 다른 문제점이 있다면, 제 비서 댄 해들리에게 연락하십시오.

챈들러 델리온 드림
기술 지원 부장, 스트랜턴 주방 가전

---

176. 첫 번째 이메일의 주요 목적은 무엇인가?

(A) 회의 참석을 요청하기 위한 것
(B) 기술적 지원을 요청하기 위한 것
(C) 사업 계획에 대해 알려 주기 위한 것
(D) 한 직원의 노력을 칭찬하기 위한 것 　　　정답 (B)

177. 스트랜턴 주방 가전에 대해 나타나 있는 것은 무엇인가?

(A) 재정적 어려움을 겪고 있다.
(B) 최근 새 직원들을 모집했다.
(C) 사업 확장을 하려고 한다.
(D) 새 시스템을 곧 도입할 것이다. 　　　정답 (C)

178. 누가 빌링스 씨의 부서에 최근에 합류했는가?

    (A) 델리온 씨

    (B) 디엠 씨

    (C) 포스터 씨

    (D) 해들리 씨   정답 (C)

179. 임시 코드는 언제 만료될 것인가?

    (A) 9월 16일

    (B) 9월 19일

    (C) 9월 20일

    (D) 9월 22일   정답 (C)

180. 포스터 씨는 이후에 무엇을 할 것 같은가?

    (A) 자신의 관리자에게 보고서 제출하기

    (B) 안내 책자 읽기

    (C) 새 승인 코드 신청하기

    (D) 회의 일정 잡기   정답 (C)

문제 181-185번은 다음 공고와 논평을 참조하시오.

제 4회 모래와 음악 축제
7월 13-14일, (184A)솔즈베리 해변

제 4회 모래와 음악 축제와 함께 여름의 낮과 밤을 즐기기 위해 (181)**많은 세계적으로 유명한 음악가들의 고향인 솔즈베리로 오세요.** 솔즈베리 해변에서 주말 동안 열리는 이 축제는 모든 방문객들에게 훌륭한 음식, 흥분과 잊을 수 없는 추억을 제공할 것입니다! 아래는 여러분이 참여할 수 있는 활동들의 목록입니다.

모래 조각 전시회
솔즈베리 해변의 아름다운 해안에 전시된 인상적인 모래 조각들을 따라 걸어 보세요. 올해 전시회의 테마는 '바다 아래서'입니다.

비치 발리볼 대회 (7월 14일만)
(182)혼성 비치 발리볼 대회에 참가하세요. 7월 8일까지 온라인에서 빠르고 쉽게 등록할 수 있습니다.

여름 밤 콘서트
일몰 속에서 울려 퍼지는 음악 소리를 즐기세요. 솔즈베리 해변의 해안에 무대가 설치될 것입니다. (184D) (185)**만약 비가 온다면 콘서트는 근처 바에서 열릴 것입니다.**

불꽃놀이
매일 밤 9시에 놀랍도록 아름다운 불꽃놀이를 감상하세요.

• 제 4회 모래와 음악 축제에 대한 추가적인 문의 사항이 있으시면, 555-0095로 저희에게 전화 주세요.

• (183)기자들은 축제를 취재하기 위하여 공식 허가를 받아야만 합니다. 7월 10일까지 제이크 세이즈에게 jseiz@salisbury.com으로 사전 등록이 요구됩니다.

솔즈베리 타임스

(183)헬리나 맬리오사 작성

7월 15일, 솔즈베리 – 지난 주말, 1만 명 이상의 사람들이 신나는 활동을 즐기기 위해 솔즈베리 해변에서의 제 4회 모래와 음악 축제에 참석했다. (184B) (184C)아들들과 나는 개인적으로 올해의 모래 조각 전시회를 가장 즐겼다. 지난해 아들들과 함께 축제를 방문했을 때는, 모래 조각 전시회에 약 10개의 조각들밖에 없었다. 올해의 거대한 바다 동물들의 마을은 분명히 멋진 광경을 연출했다. 전국에서 온 10명의 세계적인 모래 조각가들이 30개의 예술 작품들을 만들었다.

첫째 날 재즈 콘서트는 대성황이었다. 해안에 설치된 대형 무대가 많은 관중들 속에서 오히려 작아 보였다. (184D)재즈 콘서트와 달리, 둘째 날의 팝 콘서트는 실망스러웠다. (185)팝 콘서트는 근처 펍에서 열렸는데, 펍의 규모 때문에, 많은 사람들이 들어갈 수조차 없었다. 또한, 펍의 음향 장비는 너무 구식이어서 관중들이 음악을 제대로 들을 수 없었다. 내년 축제의 기획자는 콘서트를 위한 또 다른 실내 장소를 생각해내야 할 것 같다.

의심할 바 없이, 축제의 하이라이트는 매일 행사를 마무리 짓는 불꽃놀이였다. 지역의 최고 불꽃놀이 회사가 올해의 불꽃놀이를 설계했고 모든 방문객들은 무료로 이 멋진 쇼에 초대되었다.

181. 공고에서, 솔즈베리에 대해 언급된 것은 무엇인가?

    (A) 매주하는 불꽃놀이로 유명하다.

    (B) 여름에만 대중에게 개장한다.

    (C) 방문객들로 너무 붐빈다.

    (D) 몇몇 유명한 음악가들을 배출했다.   정답 (D)

182. 비치 발리볼 대회 등록은 언제까지 완료되어야 하는가?

    (A) 7월 8일

    (B) 7월 10일

    (C) 7월 14일

    (D) 7월 15일   정답 (A)

183. 맬리오사 씨는 축제 전에 무엇을 했을 것 같은가?

    (A) 회원으로 등록하기

    (B) 세이즈 씨에게 연락하기

    (C) 입장료 지불하기

    (D) (행사) 운영자들에게 전화하기   정답 (B)

184. 올해 축제에 대하여 시사되지 않은 것은 무엇인가?

    (A) 물 근처에서 열렸다.

    (B) 처음으로 모래 조각 전시회를 열었다.

    (C) 아이들에게 개방되었다.

    (D) 둘째 날에 비가 왔다.   정답 (B)

185. 맬리오사 씨가 논평에서 축제에 대해 나타내는 것은 무엇인가?

    (A) 축제에 아이들을 위한 행사가 부족하다.

    (B) 불꽃놀이는 더 많은 안전 요원들이 필요하다.

    (C) 콘서트를 위한 대체 장소가 부적절하다.

    (D) 방문객들이 식사할 수 있는 장소가 충분하지 않았다.   정답 (C)

문제 186-190번은 다음 광고와 설문조사 그리고 회람을 참조하시오.

인크레더블 로지
앨리스 스프링스, 노던 준주, 호주
+61 230777199

(186)독특한 휴가지를 찾고 계신가요? 그렇다면 호주 대륙의 중심부에서의 놀라운 만남을 위해 인크레더블 로지로 오세요. 고대의 땅과 접촉하여 모래 속에 묻힌 이야기들을 파헤쳐 보세요.

• 호주 토착민 가운데 하나인 원주민 부족 출신의 가이드와 함께 울루루 관광

• (189)지역 부족인 아난구족의 축제 참가

• 호주 중부를 탐험하는 일출 낙타 관광

• 사막의 아름다운 촘촘한 별빛 하늘 아래에서 식사

저희는 (187C)이 지역에서 가장 큰 호텔로서, (187B)무료로 공항 셔틀, 세탁 서비스, 청소 등 고객님의 모든 필요를 충족시켜 드립니다. (187D)10주년을 기념하여 모든 투숙객은 무료 아침 뷔페를 즐길 수 있습니다.

자세한 내용을 보려면 www.incrediblelodge.com을 방문하십시오. (188)
1월 말 이전에 방문하셔서 저희 기념품 가게에서 10% 할인을 받으세요.

인크레더블 로지
고객 의견

저희가 손님들을 더 잘 모실 수 있도록 이 간단한 설문조사를 작성해 주십시오.

이름: 키에런 아치노   이메일: kachino@mail.com

(190)숙박 날짜: 1월 20–25일

만족도를 표시하십시오(1 = 최고 / 4 = 최저)

	1	2	3	4
직원의 예의	○	●	○	○
직원의 응대	●	○	○	○
시설물의 청결	○	●	○	○
객실 품질	○	●	○	○

가장 기억에 남는 경험: 울루루 관광. (189)울루루에 방문했을 때, 훌륭한 이야기꾼이었던 바카나의 안내를 받았다. 그녀는 자기 부족의 전통적인 꿈의 시대 이야기를 들려주며, 내 경험에 깊이를 더해 주었다. (189)그날 밤 그녀의 부족 축제에서 그녀를 다시 볼 수 있어서 좋았고, 그곳에서 그녀는 더 많은 이야기를 해주었다.

겪으신 문제: (190)내가 머무는 이틀째 되던 날, 에어컨이 작동을 멈췄다. 하지만 신고하고 30분 내에 문제가 해결됐다. 나는 서비스 수준에 감명받았다.

수신: 전 직원, 유지관리부
발신: 제이슨 휠록
제목: 방 문제
(190)날짜: 1월 30일

(190)3층 34호실의 에어컨이 지난주에 두 번째로 고장이 났습니다. 문제를 조사해 보니 10년도 더 전에 그것을 구매했다는 것을 알았습니다. 그래서 저는 새로 한 대를 주문했습니다. 그것은 이틀 후에 도착할 예정입니다. 그것이 도착하면, 즉시 설치해 주세요. 그 방은 새 장치가 제대로 작동할 때까지 비어 있게 됩니다.

186. 광고는 누구를 대상으로 하는 것인가?
(A) 역사학자
(B) 사업주
(C) 관광객
(D) 전통 예술가   정답 (C)

187. 인크레더블 로지에 대해 시사되어 있지 않은 것은 무엇인가?
(A) 온라인 예약만 받는다.
(B) 손님들의 빨래를 무료로 해준다.
(C) 근처의 다른 모든 호텔보다 더 많은 손님을 수용할 수 있다.
(D) 10년 전에 문을 열었다.   정답 (A)

188. 광고에 따르면, 한정된 기간 동안 제공되는 것은 무엇인가?
(A) 방 업그레이드
(B) 무료 낙타 대여
(C) 무료 저녁 식사
(D) 선물 가게 할인   정답 (D)

189. 바카나에 대해 나타나 있는 것은 무엇인가?
(A) 그녀는 유명한 작가이다.
(B) 그녀는 아난구족 출신이다.
(C) 그녀는 최근에 인크레더블 로지에 고용되었다.
(D) 그녀는 최근의 여행에 만족했다.   정답 (B)

190. 아치노 씨에 대해 시사되어 있는 것은 무엇인가?
(A) 그는 인크레더블 로지가 너무 비싸다고 느꼈다.
(B) 그는 그의 여행이 다소 불쾌했다.
(C) 그는 인크레더블 로지의 3층에 머물렀다.
(D) 그는 올해 말 울루루로 다시 갈 예정이다.   정답 (C)

문제 191–195번은 다음 편지들과 쿠폰을 참조하시오.

7월 25일

바베이도스 그릴
97A 플레이트 애비뉴
토론토 M4C 5B5

점장님께,

(191)이것은 지난번 귀 식당에 방문했을 때 청구 과정에 대해 문의드리는 것입니다. (192)7월 20일 오후 6시 30분, 저와 제 아내는 콘서트 참석에 앞서 저녁을 위해 귀 식당을 방문했습니다. 아내는 이탈리아 허브가 들어간 양갈비를 주문했고 저는 두툼한 삼겹살을 주문했습니다. 음식 한 개당 가격이 60달러였습니다. 그런데, (195)주방장 특선 요리를 제공받았는데 아티초크가 곁들여진 돼지갈비였습니다.

(193)제가 귀하에게 말했을 때 귀하는 제게 맞는 요리를 기다릴 것인지 아니면 갖다 준 음식을 먹을 것인지 물었습니다. 귀하는 또한 그것은 귀하의 실수이기 때문에, 제가 원래 주문한 것과 같은 가격으로 (195)그 90달러짜리 요리를 제공하겠다고 말했습니다. 시간이 촉박해서 저는 돼지갈비를 먹었습니다.

우리는 떠날 때 너무 급해서 계산서를 꼼꼼히 검토하지 않았습니다. 하지만 월간 신용 카드 명세서를 받았을 때, (191)저는 그 식사에 150달러가 청구되었다는 것을 알게 되었습니다. 이에 30달러의 환불을 요청합니다.

우리는 거의 2년 동안 귀 레스토랑의 손님이었는데, 이번 일은 실망스러웠습니다. 다시는 비슷한 일이 일어나지 않으면 좋겠습니다.

브루스 맥기 드림

7월 31일

브루스 맥기
555 빅토리아 가
토론토, M3M 5G9

맥기 씨에게,

실수에 대한 저의 진심 어린 사과를 받아 주십시오. (193)마크 해링턴과 귀하의 방문에 대해 얘기했는데, 뜻하지 않게 잘못된 식사를 귀하께서 제공받았고, 그가 그것을 할인된 가격으로 귀하께 제공했다고 그가 확인해 주었습니다. 따라서 30달러가 귀하의 신용 카드로 환불되었습니다.

(194)귀하와 귀하의 아내 같은 소중한 고객들에게 이 같은 일이 일어나 유감입니다. 다음 방문 시 사용하실 수 있는 이 쿠폰을 받아 주십시오, 제가 해드릴 다른 일이 더 있으면 알려 주십시오.

로레인 브라코
로레인 브라코 드림
사장, 바베이도스 그릴

191. 첫 번째 편지가 작성된 이유는?
(A) 즐거운 경험을 묘사하기 위해
(B) 결제 오류를 보고하기 위해
(C) 식사를 예약하기 위해
(D) 메뉴에 대해 문의하기 위해   정답 (B)

192. 맥기 씨에 대해 나타나 있는 것은 무엇인가?
(A) 그는 콘서트에 늦었다.
(B) 그는 7월 20일 그의 배우자와 식사를 했다.
(C) 그는 새로운 메뉴들을 먹어 보는 것을 좋아한다.
(D) 그는 그 레스토랑에 다시는 가지 않을 것이다.   정답 (B)

193. 해링턴 씨에 대해 시사되어 있는 것은 무엇인가?
(A) 그는 7월 31일에 바베이도스 그릴에서 일하고 있었다.
(B) 그의 신용 카드가 잘못 청구되었다.
(C) 그는 바베이도스 그릴의 관리자이다.
(D) 그는 보통 손님들에게 양갈비를 추천한다.   정답 (C)

194. 바베이도스 그릴에 대해 추론될 수 있는 것은 무엇인가?
(A) 그곳은 오후 7시 30분에 문을 닫는다.
(B) 그곳은 모든 고객에게 상품권을 제공한다.
(C) 그곳은 영업을 시작한 지 2년 정도 되었다.
(D) 그곳의 주인은 손님들을 아낀다.   정답 (D)

195. 쿠폰의 가치는 얼마인가?
(A) 30달러
(B) 60달러
(C) 90달러
(D) 150달러   정답 (C)

문제 196-200번은 다음 기사와 회람 그리고 이메일을 참조하시오.

빅토리아 (10월 10일) – 잘 자라는 나무 협회(FTO)는 10월 13일 금요일, 오전 8시 30분부터 오후 6시까지 길모어 공원에서 모금 행사인 하나의 지구 축제를 개최할 것입니다. **(196)FTO는 사람들에게 환경과 자연의 중요성을 상기시키는 데 중점을 두는 비영리 단체입니다.** 이 축제는 빅토리아 주민들에게 환경을 홍보하기 위한 것입니다.

(197) (199)축제에서 윌로 로렌스를 포함한 초청 연사들의 연설이 있을 것입니다. "드디어 제 고향에서 이번 행사가 열리게 되어 기쁩니다. **(196)그것은 훌륭한 대의이고, 확실히 이 지역의 환경 의식을 높이는 데 도움이 될 것입니다**"라고 로렌스 씨가 말했습니다.

"**(197)**저는 다른 도시에서 열린 이전 축제에서 그랬던 것처럼 빅토리아의 모든 사람들이 축제를 즐겼으면 합니다. 음식 판매상, 짧은 공연, 그리고 지역 주민들의 음악 콘서트가 있을 것입니다"라고 덱스터 부어히스 FTO 대변인이 말했습니다. "**(198)**올해 축제의 특별한 점은 처음으로 야외에서 열린다는 것입니다."

축제에 오는 모든 사람들을 환영합니다. 모든 기부에 감사드립니다. **(200)**3천 달러 이상을 기부하는 기업들에게는 이 단체의 웹사이트의 첫 페이지와

안내 책자에 광고 자리가 제공될 것입니다. 더 자세한 정보를 원하시면, 기획 책임자 데클란 잭맨에게 852-555-0958로 전화하시거나 djackman@ftomail.com으로 이메일을 보내 주십시오.

수신: 데클란 잭맨, 펠리샤 스튜어트, 로드니 웨스트
발신: 제이슨 그린, 최고 경영자
날짜: 10월 11일
제목: 약간의 변경 사항

빅토리아에서 열리는 축제와 관련하여 몇 가지를 변경해야만 했습니다. 다음 직원의 새로운 직무에 유의하십시오:

아론 햄프턴: 오락 코디네이터
패트리샤 어민: 음식 공급 코디네이터
(199)로드니 웨스트: 대중 연설 조력자
낸시 마시: 홍보 고문

질문이 있으면 제게 바로 연락하세요. 올해 축제를 역대 최고의 축제로 만듭시다.

수신: 데클란 잭맨 〈djackman@ftomail.com〉
발신: 아놀드 자비에 〈axavier@lesfeuilles.com〉
날짜: 10월 17일
제목: 감사합니다!

잭맨 씨에게,

(200)귀 웹사이트와 안내 책자에 저희 식당의 로고를 올려 주셔서 감사합니다. 축제가 잘 진행되어서 기쁩니다. 행사 전체가 순조롭게 진행된 것 같았습니다. 저희 식당은 광고 덕분에 최근에 손님이 늘고 매출도 늘었습니다.

행사에 참여하게 되어 기뻤고, 앞으로도 그렇게 되기를 희망합니다. 나중에 생길 수 있는 어떤 기회든 저에게 계속 알려 주십시오.

감사합니다.

아놀드 자비에
사장
레 페이유

196. 기사에서, 두 번째 단락 4행에 있는 단어 "cause"와 의미상 가장 가까운 것은?
(A) 승진
(B) 목표
(C) 기금
(D) 결과   정답 (B)

197. 로렌스 씨에 대해 나타나 있는 것은 무엇인가?
(A) 그녀는 자원봉사자 팀을 이끌 것이다.
(B) 그녀는 FTO를 설립했다.
(C) 그녀는 빅토리아 출신이다.
(D) 그녀는 세계적으로 유명하다.   정답 (C)

198. 부어히스 씨에 따르면, 하나의 지구 축제에 대해 사실인 것은 무엇인가?
(A) 그것은 역대 최다 참석자를 예상하고 있다.
(B) 그것은 빅토리아에서 여러 번 개최되었다.
(C) 그것은 빅토리아 주민들만 받을 것이다.
(D) 그것은 작년에 실내에서 열렸다.   정답 (D)

199. 누가 로렌스 씨와 함께 일했을 것 같은가?

    (A) 햄프턴 씨

    (B) 어민 씨

    (C) 웨스트 씨

    (D) 마시 씨   정답 (C)

200. 자비에 씨에 대해 추론될 수 있는 것은 무엇인가?

    (A) 그는 축제에 3천 달러 이상 기부했다.

    (B) 그는 축제에서 자신의 식당의 음식을 판매했다.

    (C) 그는 몇 년 전에 레 페이유를 설립했다.

    (D) 그의 식당의 로고는 최근에 다시 디자인되었다.   정답 (A)

Answer Sheet

Actual Test 01

LISTENING (Part I ~ IV)

NO.	ANSWER				NO.	ANSWER				NO.	ANSWER				NO.	ANSWER			
	A	B	C	D		A	B	C	D		A	B	C	D		A	B	C	D
1	a	b	c		21	a	b	c	d	41	a	b	c		81	a	b	c	d
2	a	b	c		22	a	b	c	d	42	a	b	c		82	a	b	c	d
3	a	b	c		23	a	b	c	d	43	a	b	c		83	a	b	c	d
4	a	b	c		24	a	b	c	d	44	a	b	c		84	a	b	c	d
5	a	b	c		25	a	b	c	d	45	a	b	c		85	a	b	c	d
6	a	b	c		26	a	b	c	d	46	a	b	c		86	a	b	c	d
7	a	b	c		27	a	b	c	d	47	a	b	c		87	a	b	c	d
8	a	b	c		28	a	b	c	d	48	a	b	c		88	a	b	c	d
9	a	b	c		29	a	b	c	d	49	a	b	c		89	a	b	c	d
10	a	b	c		30	a	b	c	d	50	a	b	c	d	90	a	b	c	d
11	a	b	c		31	a	b	c	d	51	a	b	c	d	91	a	b	c	d
12	a	b	c		32	a	b	c	d	52	a	b	c	d	92	a	b	c	d
13	a	b	c		33	a	b	c	d	53	a	b	c	d	93	a	b	c	d
14	a	b	c		34	a	b	c	d	54	a	b	c	d	94	a	b	c	d
15	a	b	c		35	a	b	c	d	55	a	b	c	d	95	a	b	c	d
16	a	b	c		36	a	b	c	d	56	a	b	c	d	96	a	b	c	d
17	a	b	c		37	a	b	c	d	57	a	b	c	d	97	a	b	c	d
18	a	b	c		38	a	b	c	d	58	a	b	c	d	98	a	b	c	d
19	a	b	c		39	a	b	c	d	59	a	b	c	d	99	a	b	c	d
20	a	b	c		40	a	b	c	d	60	a	b	c	d	100	a	b	c	d

READING (Part V ~ VII)

NO.	ANSWER				NO.	ANSWER				NO.	ANSWER				NO.	ANSWER			
	A	B	C	D		A	B	C	D		A	B	C	D		A	B	C	D
101	a	b	c	d	121	a	b	c	d	141	a	b	c	d	181	a	b	c	d
102	a	b	c	d	122	a	b	c	d	142	a	b	c	d	182	a	b	c	d
103	a	b	c	d	123	a	b	c	d	143	a	b	c	d	183	a	b	c	d
104	a	b	c	d	124	a	b	c	d	144	a	b	c	d	184	a	b	c	d
105	a	b	c	d	125	a	b	c	d	145	a	b	c	d	185	a	b	c	d
106	a	b	c	d	126	a	b	c	d	146	a	b	c	d	186	a	b	c	d
107	a	b	c	d	127	a	b	c	d	147	a	b	c	d	187	a	b	c	d
108	a	b	c	d	128	a	b	c	d	148	a	b	c	d	188	a	b	c	d
109	a	b	c	d	129	a	b	c	d	149	a	b	c	d	189	a	b	c	d
110	a	b	c	d	130	a	b	c	d	150	a	b	c	d	190	a	b	c	d
111	a	b	c	d	131	a	b	c	d	151	a	b	c	d	191	a	b	c	d
112	a	b	c	d	132	a	b	c	d	152	a	b	c	d	192	a	b	c	d
113	a	b	c	d	133	a	b	c	d	153	a	b	c	d	193	a	b	c	d
114	a	b	c	d	134	a	b	c	d	154	a	b	c	d	194	a	b	c	d
115	a	b	c	d	135	a	b	c	d	155	a	b	c	d	195	a	b	c	d
116	a	b	c	d	136	a	b	c	d	156	a	b	c	d	196	a	b	c	d
117	a	b	c	d	137	a	b	c	d	157	a	b	c	d	197	a	b	c	d
118	a	b	c	d	138	a	b	c	d	158	a	b	c	d	198	a	b	c	d
119	a	b	c	d	139	a	b	c	d	159	a	b	c	d	199	a	b	c	d
120	a	b	c	d	140	a	b	c	d	160	a	b	c	d	200	a	b	c	d

Actual Test 02

LISTENING (Part I ~ IV)

NO.	A	B	C	D	NO.	A	B	C	D	NO.	A	B	C	D	NO.	A	B	C	D
1	ⓐ	ⓑ	ⓒ	ⓓ	21	ⓐ	ⓑ	ⓒ	ⓓ	41	ⓐ	ⓑ	ⓒ	ⓓ	81	ⓐ	ⓑ	ⓒ	ⓓ
2	ⓐ	ⓑ	ⓒ	ⓓ	22	ⓐ	ⓑ	ⓒ	ⓓ	42	ⓐ	ⓑ	ⓒ	ⓓ	82	ⓐ	ⓑ	ⓒ	ⓓ
3	ⓐ	ⓑ	ⓒ	ⓓ	23	ⓐ	ⓑ	ⓒ	ⓓ	43	ⓐ	ⓑ	ⓒ	ⓓ	83	ⓐ	ⓑ	ⓒ	ⓓ
4	ⓐ	ⓑ	ⓒ	ⓓ	24	ⓐ	ⓑ	ⓒ	ⓓ	44	ⓐ	ⓑ	ⓒ	ⓓ	84	ⓐ	ⓑ	ⓒ	ⓓ
5	ⓐ	ⓑ	ⓒ	ⓓ	25	ⓐ	ⓑ	ⓒ	ⓓ	45	ⓐ	ⓑ	ⓒ	ⓓ	85	ⓐ	ⓑ	ⓒ	ⓓ
6	ⓐ	ⓑ	ⓒ	ⓓ	26	ⓐ	ⓑ	ⓒ	ⓓ	46	ⓐ	ⓑ	ⓒ	ⓓ	86	ⓐ	ⓑ	ⓒ	ⓓ
7	ⓐ	ⓑ	ⓒ		27	ⓐ	ⓑ	ⓒ	ⓓ	47	ⓐ	ⓑ	ⓒ	ⓓ	87	ⓐ	ⓑ	ⓒ	ⓓ
8	ⓐ	ⓑ	ⓒ		28	ⓐ	ⓑ	ⓒ	ⓓ	48	ⓐ	ⓑ	ⓒ	ⓓ	88	ⓐ	ⓑ	ⓒ	ⓓ
9	ⓐ	ⓑ	ⓒ		29	ⓐ	ⓑ	ⓒ	ⓓ	49	ⓐ	ⓑ	ⓒ	ⓓ	89	ⓐ	ⓑ	ⓒ	ⓓ
10	ⓐ	ⓑ	ⓒ		30	ⓐ	ⓑ	ⓒ	ⓓ	50	ⓐ	ⓑ	ⓒ	ⓓ	90	ⓐ	ⓑ	ⓒ	ⓓ
11	ⓐ	ⓑ	ⓒ		31	ⓐ	ⓑ	ⓒ	ⓓ	51	ⓐ	ⓑ	ⓒ	ⓓ	91	ⓐ	ⓑ	ⓒ	ⓓ
12	ⓐ	ⓑ	ⓒ		32	ⓐ	ⓑ	ⓒ	ⓓ	52	ⓐ	ⓑ	ⓒ	ⓓ	92	ⓐ	ⓑ	ⓒ	ⓓ
13	ⓐ	ⓑ	ⓒ		33	ⓐ	ⓑ	ⓒ	ⓓ	53	ⓐ	ⓑ	ⓒ	ⓓ	93	ⓐ	ⓑ	ⓒ	ⓓ
14	ⓐ	ⓑ	ⓒ		34	ⓐ	ⓑ	ⓒ	ⓓ	54	ⓐ	ⓑ	ⓒ	ⓓ	94	ⓐ	ⓑ	ⓒ	ⓓ
15	ⓐ	ⓑ	ⓒ		35	ⓐ	ⓑ	ⓒ	ⓓ	55	ⓐ	ⓑ	ⓒ	ⓓ	95	ⓐ	ⓑ	ⓒ	ⓓ
16	ⓐ	ⓑ	ⓒ		36	ⓐ	ⓑ	ⓒ	ⓓ	56	ⓐ	ⓑ	ⓒ	ⓓ	96	ⓐ	ⓑ	ⓒ	ⓓ
17	ⓐ	ⓑ	ⓒ		37	ⓐ	ⓑ	ⓒ	ⓓ	57	ⓐ	ⓑ	ⓒ	ⓓ	97	ⓐ	ⓑ	ⓒ	ⓓ
18	ⓐ	ⓑ	ⓒ		38	ⓐ	ⓑ	ⓒ	ⓓ	58	ⓐ	ⓑ	ⓒ	ⓓ	98	ⓐ	ⓑ	ⓒ	ⓓ
19	ⓐ	ⓑ	ⓒ		39	ⓐ	ⓑ	ⓒ	ⓓ	59	ⓐ	ⓑ	ⓒ	ⓓ	99	ⓐ	ⓑ	ⓒ	ⓓ
20	ⓐ	ⓑ	ⓒ		40	ⓐ	ⓑ	ⓒ	ⓓ	60	ⓐ	ⓑ	ⓒ	ⓓ	100	ⓐ	ⓑ	ⓒ	ⓓ

READING (Part V ~ VII)

NO.	A	B	C	D	NO.	A	B	C	D	NO.	A	B	C	D	NO.	A	B	C	D
101	ⓐ	ⓑ	ⓒ	ⓓ	121	ⓐ	ⓑ	ⓒ	ⓓ	141	ⓐ	ⓑ	ⓒ	ⓓ	181	ⓐ	ⓑ	ⓒ	ⓓ
102	ⓐ	ⓑ	ⓒ	ⓓ	122	ⓐ	ⓑ	ⓒ	ⓓ	142	ⓐ	ⓑ	ⓒ	ⓓ	182	ⓐ	ⓑ	ⓒ	ⓓ
103	ⓐ	ⓑ	ⓒ	ⓓ	123	ⓐ	ⓑ	ⓒ	ⓓ	143	ⓐ	ⓑ	ⓒ	ⓓ	183	ⓐ	ⓑ	ⓒ	ⓓ
104	ⓐ	ⓑ	ⓒ	ⓓ	124	ⓐ	ⓑ	ⓒ	ⓓ	144	ⓐ	ⓑ	ⓒ	ⓓ	184	ⓐ	ⓑ	ⓒ	ⓓ
105	ⓐ	ⓑ	ⓒ	ⓓ	125	ⓐ	ⓑ	ⓒ	ⓓ	145	ⓐ	ⓑ	ⓒ	ⓓ	185	ⓐ	ⓑ	ⓒ	ⓓ
106	ⓐ	ⓑ	ⓒ	ⓓ	126	ⓐ	ⓑ	ⓒ	ⓓ	146	ⓐ	ⓑ	ⓒ	ⓓ	186	ⓐ	ⓑ	ⓒ	ⓓ
107	ⓐ	ⓑ	ⓒ	ⓓ	127	ⓐ	ⓑ	ⓒ	ⓓ	147	ⓐ	ⓑ	ⓒ	ⓓ	187	ⓐ	ⓑ	ⓒ	ⓓ
108	ⓐ	ⓑ	ⓒ	ⓓ	128	ⓐ	ⓑ	ⓒ	ⓓ	148	ⓐ	ⓑ	ⓒ	ⓓ	188	ⓐ	ⓑ	ⓒ	ⓓ
109	ⓐ	ⓑ	ⓒ	ⓓ	129	ⓐ	ⓑ	ⓒ	ⓓ	149	ⓐ	ⓑ	ⓒ	ⓓ	189	ⓐ	ⓑ	ⓒ	ⓓ
110	ⓐ	ⓑ	ⓒ	ⓓ	130	ⓐ	ⓑ	ⓒ	ⓓ	150	ⓐ	ⓑ	ⓒ	ⓓ	190	ⓐ	ⓑ	ⓒ	ⓓ
111	ⓐ	ⓑ	ⓒ	ⓓ	131	ⓐ	ⓑ	ⓒ	ⓓ	151	ⓐ	ⓑ	ⓒ	ⓓ	191	ⓐ	ⓑ	ⓒ	ⓓ
112	ⓐ	ⓑ	ⓒ	ⓓ	132	ⓐ	ⓑ	ⓒ	ⓓ	152	ⓐ	ⓑ	ⓒ	ⓓ	192	ⓐ	ⓑ	ⓒ	ⓓ
113	ⓐ	ⓑ	ⓒ	ⓓ	133	ⓐ	ⓑ	ⓒ	ⓓ	153	ⓐ	ⓑ	ⓒ	ⓓ	193	ⓐ	ⓑ	ⓒ	ⓓ
114	ⓐ	ⓑ	ⓒ	ⓓ	134	ⓐ	ⓑ	ⓒ	ⓓ	154	ⓐ	ⓑ	ⓒ	ⓓ	194	ⓐ	ⓑ	ⓒ	ⓓ
115	ⓐ	ⓑ	ⓒ	ⓓ	135	ⓐ	ⓑ	ⓒ	ⓓ	155	ⓐ	ⓑ	ⓒ	ⓓ	195	ⓐ	ⓑ	ⓒ	ⓓ
116	ⓐ	ⓑ	ⓒ	ⓓ	136	ⓐ	ⓑ	ⓒ	ⓓ	156	ⓐ	ⓑ	ⓒ	ⓓ	196	ⓐ	ⓑ	ⓒ	ⓓ
117	ⓐ	ⓑ	ⓒ	ⓓ	137	ⓐ	ⓑ	ⓒ	ⓓ	157	ⓐ	ⓑ	ⓒ	ⓓ	197	ⓐ	ⓑ	ⓒ	ⓓ
118	ⓐ	ⓑ	ⓒ	ⓓ	138	ⓐ	ⓑ	ⓒ	ⓓ	158	ⓐ	ⓑ	ⓒ	ⓓ	198	ⓐ	ⓑ	ⓒ	ⓓ
119	ⓐ	ⓑ	ⓒ	ⓓ	139	ⓐ	ⓑ	ⓒ	ⓓ	159	ⓐ	ⓑ	ⓒ	ⓓ	199	ⓐ	ⓑ	ⓒ	ⓓ
120	ⓐ	ⓑ	ⓒ	ⓓ	140	ⓐ	ⓑ	ⓒ	ⓓ	160	ⓐ	ⓑ	ⓒ	ⓓ	200	ⓐ	ⓑ	ⓒ	ⓓ

Actual Test 03

LISTENING (Part I ~ IV)

NO.	ANSWER A B C D	NO.	ANSWER A B C D	NO.	ANSWER A B C D	NO.	ANSWER A B C D
1	a b c d	21	a b c d	41	a b c d	81	a b c d
2	a b c d	22	a b c d	42	a b c d	82	a b c d
3	a b c d	23	a b c d	43	a b c d	83	a b c d
4	a b c d	24	a b c d	44	a b c d	84	a b c d
5	a b c d	25	a b c d	45	a b c d	85	a b c d
6	a b c d	26	a b c d	46	a b c d	86	a b c d
7	a b c	27	a b c d	47	a b c d	87	a b c d
8	a b c	28	a b c d	48	a b c d	88	a b c d
9	a b c	29	a b c d	49	a b c d	89	a b c d
10	a b c	30	a b c d	50	a b c d	90	a b c d
11	a b c	31	a b c d	51	a b c d	91	a b c d
12	a b c	32	a b c d	52	a b c d	92	a b c d
13	a b c	33	a b c d	53	a b c d	93	a b c d
14	a b c	34	a b c d	54	a b c d	94	a b c d
15	a b c	35	a b c d	55	a b c d	95	a b c d
16	a b c	36	a b c d	56	a b c d	96	a b c d
17	a b c	37	a b c d	57	a b c d	97	a b c d
18	a b c	38	a b c d	58	a b c d	98	a b c d
19	a b c	39	a b c d	59	a b c d	99	a b c d
20	a b c	40	a b c d	60	a b c d	100	a b c d

READING (Part V ~ VII)

NO.	ANSWER A B C D	NO.	ANSWER A B C D	NO.	ANSWER A B C D	NO.	ANSWER A B C D
101	a b c d	121	a b c d	141	a b c d	181	a b c d
102	a b c d	122	a b c d	142	a b c d	182	a b c d
103	a b c d	123	a b c d	143	a b c d	183	a b c d
104	a b c d	124	a b c d	144	a b c d	184	a b c d
105	a b c d	125	a b c d	145	a b c d	185	a b c d
106	a b c d	126	a b c d	146	a b c d	186	a b c d
107	a b c d	127	a b c d	147	a b c d	187	a b c d
108	a b c d	128	a b c d	148	a b c d	188	a b c d
109	a b c d	129	a b c d	149	a b c d	189	a b c d
110	a b c d	130	a b c d	150	a b c d	190	a b c d
111	a b c d	131	a b c d	151	a b c d	191	a b c d
112	a b c d	132	a b c d	152	a b c d	192	a b c d
113	a b c d	133	a b c d	153	a b c d	193	a b c d
114	a b c d	134	a b c d	154	a b c d	194	a b c d
115	a b c d	135	a b c d	155	a b c d	195	a b c d
116	a b c d	136	a b c d	156	a b c d	196	a b c d
117	a b c d	137	a b c d	157	a b c d	197	a b c d
118	a b c d	138	a b c d	158	a b c d	198	a b c d
119	a b c d	139	a b c d	159	a b c d	199	a b c d
120	a b c d	140	a b c d	160	a b c d	200	a b c d

Actual Test 04

READING (Part V ~ VII)

LISTENING (Part I ~ IV)

Actual Test 05

LISTENING (Part I ~ IV)

NO.	ANSWER	NO.	ANSWER	NO.	ANSWER	NO.	ANSWER	NO.	ANSWER
	A B C D		A B C D		A B C D		A B C D		A B C D
1	ⓐ ⓑ ⓒ ⓓ	21	ⓐ ⓑ ⓒ ⓓ	41	ⓐ ⓑ ⓒ ⓓ	61	ⓐ ⓑ ⓒ ⓓ	81	ⓐ ⓑ ⓒ ⓓ
2	ⓐ ⓑ ⓒ ⓓ	22	ⓐ ⓑ ⓒ ⓓ	42	ⓐ ⓑ ⓒ ⓓ	62	ⓐ ⓑ ⓒ ⓓ	82	ⓐ ⓑ ⓒ ⓓ
3	ⓐ ⓑ ⓒ ⓓ	23	ⓐ ⓑ ⓒ ⓓ	43	ⓐ ⓑ ⓒ ⓓ	63	ⓐ ⓑ ⓒ ⓓ	83	ⓐ ⓑ ⓒ ⓓ
4	ⓐ ⓑ ⓒ ⓓ	24	ⓐ ⓑ ⓒ ⓓ	44	ⓐ ⓑ ⓒ ⓓ	64	ⓐ ⓑ ⓒ ⓓ	84	ⓐ ⓑ ⓒ ⓓ
5	ⓐ ⓑ ⓒ ⓓ	25	ⓐ ⓑ ⓒ ⓓ	45	ⓐ ⓑ ⓒ ⓓ	65	ⓐ ⓑ ⓒ ⓓ	85	ⓐ ⓑ ⓒ ⓓ
6	ⓐ ⓑ ⓒ ⓓ	26	ⓐ ⓑ ⓒ ⓓ	46	ⓐ ⓑ ⓒ ⓓ	66	ⓐ ⓑ ⓒ ⓓ	86	ⓐ ⓑ ⓒ ⓓ
7	ⓐ ⓑ ⓒ	27	ⓐ ⓑ ⓒ ⓓ	47	ⓐ ⓑ ⓒ ⓓ	67	ⓐ ⓑ ⓒ ⓓ	87	ⓐ ⓑ ⓒ ⓓ
8	ⓐ ⓑ ⓒ	28	ⓐ ⓑ ⓒ ⓓ	48	ⓐ ⓑ ⓒ ⓓ	68	ⓐ ⓑ ⓒ ⓓ	88	ⓐ ⓑ ⓒ ⓓ
9	ⓐ ⓑ ⓒ	29	ⓐ ⓑ ⓒ ⓓ	49	ⓐ ⓑ ⓒ ⓓ	69	ⓐ ⓑ ⓒ ⓓ	89	ⓐ ⓑ ⓒ ⓓ
10	ⓐ ⓑ ⓒ	30	ⓐ ⓑ ⓒ ⓓ	50	ⓐ ⓑ ⓒ ⓓ	70	ⓐ ⓑ ⓒ ⓓ	90	ⓐ ⓑ ⓒ ⓓ
11	ⓐ ⓑ ⓒ	31	ⓐ ⓑ ⓒ ⓓ	51	ⓐ ⓑ ⓒ ⓓ	71	ⓐ ⓑ ⓒ ⓓ	91	ⓐ ⓑ ⓒ ⓓ
12	ⓐ ⓑ ⓒ	32	ⓐ ⓑ ⓒ ⓓ	52	ⓐ ⓑ ⓒ ⓓ	72	ⓐ ⓑ ⓒ ⓓ	92	ⓐ ⓑ ⓒ ⓓ
13	ⓐ ⓑ ⓒ	33	ⓐ ⓑ ⓒ ⓓ	53	ⓐ ⓑ ⓒ ⓓ	73	ⓐ ⓑ ⓒ ⓓ	93	ⓐ ⓑ ⓒ ⓓ
14	ⓐ ⓑ ⓒ	34	ⓐ ⓑ ⓒ ⓓ	54	ⓐ ⓑ ⓒ ⓓ	74	ⓐ ⓑ ⓒ ⓓ	94	ⓐ ⓑ ⓒ ⓓ
15	ⓐ ⓑ ⓒ	35	ⓐ ⓑ ⓒ ⓓ	55	ⓐ ⓑ ⓒ ⓓ	75	ⓐ ⓑ ⓒ ⓓ	95	ⓐ ⓑ ⓒ ⓓ
16	ⓐ ⓑ ⓒ	36	ⓐ ⓑ ⓒ ⓓ	56	ⓐ ⓑ ⓒ ⓓ	76	ⓐ ⓑ ⓒ ⓓ	96	ⓐ ⓑ ⓒ ⓓ
17	ⓐ ⓑ ⓒ	37	ⓐ ⓑ ⓒ ⓓ	57	ⓐ ⓑ ⓒ ⓓ	77	ⓐ ⓑ ⓒ ⓓ	97	ⓐ ⓑ ⓒ ⓓ
18	ⓐ ⓑ ⓒ	38	ⓐ ⓑ ⓒ ⓓ	58	ⓐ ⓑ ⓒ ⓓ	78	ⓐ ⓑ ⓒ ⓓ	98	ⓐ ⓑ ⓒ ⓓ
19	ⓐ ⓑ ⓒ	39	ⓐ ⓑ ⓒ ⓓ	59	ⓐ ⓑ ⓒ ⓓ	79	ⓐ ⓑ ⓒ ⓓ	99	ⓐ ⓑ ⓒ ⓓ
20	ⓐ ⓑ ⓒ	40	ⓐ ⓑ ⓒ ⓓ	60	ⓐ ⓑ ⓒ ⓓ	80	ⓐ ⓑ ⓒ ⓓ	100	ⓐ ⓑ ⓒ ⓓ

READING (Part V ~ VII)

NO.	ANSWER	NO.	ANSWER	NO.	ANSWER	NO.	ANSWER	NO.	ANSWER
	A B C D		A B C D		A B C D		A B C D		A B C D
101	ⓐ ⓑ ⓒ ⓓ	121	ⓐ ⓑ ⓒ ⓓ	141	ⓐ ⓑ ⓒ ⓓ	161	ⓐ ⓑ ⓒ ⓓ	181	ⓐ ⓑ ⓒ ⓓ
102	ⓐ ⓑ ⓒ ⓓ	122	ⓐ ⓑ ⓒ ⓓ	142	ⓐ ⓑ ⓒ ⓓ	162	ⓐ ⓑ ⓒ ⓓ	182	ⓐ ⓑ ⓒ ⓓ
103	ⓐ ⓑ ⓒ ⓓ	123	ⓐ ⓑ ⓒ ⓓ	143	ⓐ ⓑ ⓒ ⓓ	163	ⓐ ⓑ ⓒ ⓓ	183	ⓐ ⓑ ⓒ ⓓ
104	ⓐ ⓑ ⓒ ⓓ	124	ⓐ ⓑ ⓒ ⓓ	144	ⓐ ⓑ ⓒ ⓓ	164	ⓐ ⓑ ⓒ ⓓ	184	ⓐ ⓑ ⓒ ⓓ
105	ⓐ ⓑ ⓒ ⓓ	125	ⓐ ⓑ ⓒ ⓓ	145	ⓐ ⓑ ⓒ ⓓ	165	ⓐ ⓑ ⓒ ⓓ	185	ⓐ ⓑ ⓒ ⓓ
106	ⓐ ⓑ ⓒ ⓓ	126	ⓐ ⓑ ⓒ ⓓ	146	ⓐ ⓑ ⓒ ⓓ	166	ⓐ ⓑ ⓒ ⓓ	186	ⓐ ⓑ ⓒ ⓓ
107	ⓐ ⓑ ⓒ ⓓ	127	ⓐ ⓑ ⓒ ⓓ	147	ⓐ ⓑ ⓒ ⓓ	167	ⓐ ⓑ ⓒ ⓓ	187	ⓐ ⓑ ⓒ ⓓ
108	ⓐ ⓑ ⓒ ⓓ	128	ⓐ ⓑ ⓒ ⓓ	148	ⓐ ⓑ ⓒ ⓓ	168	ⓐ ⓑ ⓒ ⓓ	188	ⓐ ⓑ ⓒ ⓓ
109	ⓐ ⓑ ⓒ ⓓ	129	ⓐ ⓑ ⓒ ⓓ	149	ⓐ ⓑ ⓒ ⓓ	169	ⓐ ⓑ ⓒ ⓓ	189	ⓐ ⓑ ⓒ ⓓ
110	ⓐ ⓑ ⓒ ⓓ	130	ⓐ ⓑ ⓒ ⓓ	150	ⓐ ⓑ ⓒ ⓓ	170	ⓐ ⓑ ⓒ ⓓ	190	ⓐ ⓑ ⓒ ⓓ
111	ⓐ ⓑ ⓒ ⓓ	131	ⓐ ⓑ ⓒ ⓓ	151	ⓐ ⓑ ⓒ ⓓ	171	ⓐ ⓑ ⓒ ⓓ	191	ⓐ ⓑ ⓒ ⓓ
112	ⓐ ⓑ ⓒ ⓓ	132	ⓐ ⓑ ⓒ ⓓ	152	ⓐ ⓑ ⓒ ⓓ	172	ⓐ ⓑ ⓒ ⓓ	192	ⓐ ⓑ ⓒ ⓓ
113	ⓐ ⓑ ⓒ ⓓ	133	ⓐ ⓑ ⓒ ⓓ	153	ⓐ ⓑ ⓒ ⓓ	173	ⓐ ⓑ ⓒ ⓓ	193	ⓐ ⓑ ⓒ ⓓ
114	ⓐ ⓑ ⓒ ⓓ	134	ⓐ ⓑ ⓒ ⓓ	154	ⓐ ⓑ ⓒ ⓓ	174	ⓐ ⓑ ⓒ ⓓ	194	ⓐ ⓑ ⓒ ⓓ
115	ⓐ ⓑ ⓒ ⓓ	135	ⓐ ⓑ ⓒ ⓓ	155	ⓐ ⓑ ⓒ ⓓ	175	ⓐ ⓑ ⓒ ⓓ	195	ⓐ ⓑ ⓒ ⓓ
116	ⓐ ⓑ ⓒ ⓓ	136	ⓐ ⓑ ⓒ ⓓ	156	ⓐ ⓑ ⓒ ⓓ	176	ⓐ ⓑ ⓒ ⓓ	196	ⓐ ⓑ ⓒ ⓓ
117	ⓐ ⓑ ⓒ ⓓ	137	ⓐ ⓑ ⓒ ⓓ	157	ⓐ ⓑ ⓒ ⓓ	177	ⓐ ⓑ ⓒ ⓓ	197	ⓐ ⓑ ⓒ ⓓ
118	ⓐ ⓑ ⓒ ⓓ	138	ⓐ ⓑ ⓒ ⓓ	158	ⓐ ⓑ ⓒ ⓓ	178	ⓐ ⓑ ⓒ ⓓ	198	ⓐ ⓑ ⓒ ⓓ
119	ⓐ ⓑ ⓒ ⓓ	139	ⓐ ⓑ ⓒ ⓓ	159	ⓐ ⓑ ⓒ ⓓ	179	ⓐ ⓑ ⓒ ⓓ	199	ⓐ ⓑ ⓒ ⓓ
120	ⓐ ⓑ ⓒ ⓓ	140	ⓐ ⓑ ⓒ ⓓ	160	ⓐ ⓑ ⓒ ⓓ	180	ⓐ ⓑ ⓒ ⓓ	200	ⓐ ⓑ ⓒ ⓓ

Answer Sheet

Actual Test 06

LISTENING (Part I ~ IV)

NO.	ANSWER				NO.	ANSWER				NO.	ANSWER				NO.	ANSWER			
	A	B	C	D		A	B	C	D		A	B	C	D		A	B	C	D
1	a	b	c	d	21	a	b	c	d	41	a	b	c	d	61	a	b	c	d
2	a	b	c	d	22	a	b	c	d	42	a	b	c	d	62	a	b	c	d
3	a	b	c	d	23	a	b	c	d	43	a	b	c	d	63	a	b	c	d
4	a	b	c	d	24	a	b	c	d	44	a	b	c	d	64	a	b	c	d
5	a	b	c		25	a	b	c		45	a	b	c	d	65	a	b	c	d
6	a	b	c	d	26	a	b	c		46	a	b	c	d	66	a	b	c	d
7	a	b	c		27	a	b	c		47	a	b	c	d	67	a	b	c	d
8	a	b	c		28	a	b	c		48	a	b	c	d	68	a	b	c	d
9	a	b	c		29	a	b	c		49	a	b	c	d	69	a	b	c	d
10	a	b	c		30	a	b	c		50	a	b	c	d	70	a	b	c	d
11	a	b	c		31	a	b	c		51	a	b	c	d	71	a	b	c	d
12	a	b	c		32	a	b	c		52	a	b	c	d	72	a	b	c	d
13	a	b	c		33	a	b	c		53	a	b	c	d	73	a	b	c	d
14	a	b	c		34	a	b	c		54	a	b	c	d	74	a	b	c	d
15	a	b	c		35	a	b	c		55	a	b	c	d	75	a	b	c	d
16	a	b	c		36	a	b	c		56	a	b	c	d	76	a	b	c	d
17	a	b	c		37	a	b	c		57	a	b	c	d	77	a	b	c	d
18	a	b	c		38	a	b	c		58	a	b	c	d	78	a	b	c	d
19	a	b	c		39	a	b	c		59	a	b	c	d	79	a	b	c	d
20	a	b	c		40	a	b	c		60	a	b	c	d	80	a	b	c	d

NO.	ANSWER			
	A	B	C	D
81	a	b	c	d
82	a	b	c	d
83	a	b	c	d
84	a	b	c	d
85	a	b	c	d
86	a	b	c	d
87	a	b	c	d
88	a	b	c	d
89	a	b	c	d
90	a	b	c	d
91	a	b	c	d
92	a	b	c	d
93	a	b	c	d
94	a	b	c	d
95	a	b	c	d
96	a	b	c	d
97	a	b	c	d
98	a	b	c	d
99	a	b	c	d
100	a	b	c	d

READING (Part V ~ VII)

NO.	ANSWER				NO.	ANSWER				NO.	ANSWER				NO.	ANSWER			
	A	B	C	D		A	B	C	D		A	B	C	D		A	B	C	D
101	a	b	c	d	121	a	b	c	d	141	a	b	c	d	161	a	b	c	d
102	a	b	c	d	122	a	b	c	d	142	a	b	c	d	162	a	b	c	d
103	a	b	c	d	123	a	b	c	d	143	a	b	c	d	163	a	b	c	d
104	a	b	c	d	124	a	b	c	d	144	a	b	c	d	164	a	b	c	d
105	a	b	c	d	125	a	b	c	d	145	a	b	c	d	165	a	b	c	d
106	a	b	c	d	126	a	b	c	d	146	a	b	c	d	166	a	b	c	d
107	a	b	c	d	127	a	b	c	d	147	a	b	c	d	167	a	b	c	d
108	a	b	c	d	128	a	b	c	d	148	a	b	c	d	168	a	b	c	d
109	a	b	c	d	129	a	b	c	d	149	a	b	c	d	169	a	b	c	d
110	a	b	c	d	130	a	b	c	d	150	a	b	c	d	170	a	b	c	d
111	a	b	c	d	131	a	b	c	d	151	a	b	c	d	171	a	b	c	d
112	a	b	c	d	132	a	b	c	d	152	a	b	c	d	172	a	b	c	d
113	a	b	c	d	133	a	b	c	d	153	a	b	c	d	173	a	b	c	d
114	a	b	c	d	134	a	b	c	d	154	a	b	c	d	174	a	b	c	d
115	a	b	c	d	135	a	b	c	d	155	a	b	c	d	175	a	b	c	d
116	a	b	c	d	136	a	b	c	d	156	a	b	c	d	176	a	b	c	d
117	a	b	c	d	137	a	b	c	d	157	a	b	c	d	177	a	b	c	d
118	a	b	c	d	138	a	b	c	d	158	a	b	c	d	178	a	b	c	d
119	a	b	c	d	139	a	b	c	d	159	a	b	c	d	179	a	b	c	d
120	a	b	c	d	140	a	b	c	d	160	a	b	c	d	180	a	b	c	d

NO.	ANSWER			
	A	B	C	D
181	a	b	c	d
182	a	b	c	d
183	a	b	c	d
184	a	b	c	d
185	a	b	c	d
186	a	b	c	d
187	a	b	c	d
188	a	b	c	d
189	a	b	c	d
190	a	b	c	d
191	a	b	c	d
192	a	b	c	d
193	a	b	c	d
194	a	b	c	d
195	a	b	c	d
196	a	b	c	d
197	a	b	c	d
198	a	b	c	d
199	a	b	c	d
200	a	b	c	d

점수
환산표

자신의 정답 개수를 기준으로 본인의 점수를 개략적으로 환산해 볼 수 있는 자료입니다.
정확한 계산법이 아닌 추정치임을 참고하시기 바랍니다.

Listening Comprehension		Reading Comprehension	
정답 개수	환산점수	정답 개수	환산점수
96-100	470-495	96-100	470-495
91-95	440-470	91-95	450-470
86-90	410-440	86-90	420-450
81-85	370-410	81-85	380-420
76-80	340-370	76-80	350-380
71-75	310-340	71-75	330-350
66-70	280-310	66-70	300-330
61-65	250-280	61-65	270-300
56-60	230-250	56-60	240-270
51-55	200-230	51-55	210-240
46-50	170-200	46-50	190-210
41-45	150-170	41-45	170-190
36-40	120-150	36-40	140-170
31-35	90-120	31-35	110-140
26-30	70-90	26-30	90-110
21-25	40-70	21-25	70-90
16-20	30-40	16-20	50-70
11-15	10-30	11-15	30-50
6-10	5-10	6-10	10-30
1-5	5	1-5	0
0	5	0	0

900점 이상
고득점을 위한 책!

- **최신 출제 경향을 담은 12세트, 2400문제 제공!**
  900점 이상의 고득점을 위한 문제만 선별했습니다.

- **단기에 200점을 올려주는 학습 훈련 제공!**
  LC 통암기 훈련 노트와 RC 핵심 어휘집을 제공합니다.

- **출제 포인트를 쉽게 이해시켜주는 해설집 무료 제공!**
  핵심을 알기 쉽게 알려주는 해설집을 온라인 다운로드로 제공합니다.

- **학습용 MP3 제공!**
  실전용, 복습용 MP3를 무료로 제공합니다.

950 실전 모의고사 Crack the exam – 12 Actual Tests for 950

이 책을 권장하는 점수대	400 ╫╫╫ 500 ╫╫╫ 600 ╫╫╫ 700 ╫╫╫ 800 ╫╫╫ 900
실제 시험과 비교	쉬움 ├┼┼┼┼┼┼┼┼┤ 비슷함 ├┼┼┼┼┼┤ 어려움

03740
ISBN 979-11-407-0042-4

가격 25,000원

시나공
토익 공

고득점 완벽 마무리!
실전 12세트, 2400제

950

실전
모의고사

고경희, 김병기, 박재형 지음

2권

Actual Test 07~12

www.gilbut.co.kr

길벗
이지:톡

시험에 나오는 것만 공부한다!

시나공 토익

950

실전
모의고사

고경희, 김병기, 박재형 지음

Actual Test 07~12

길벗
이지:톡

시나공 토익
950 실전 모의고사

초판 1쇄 발행 · 2022년 7월 4일
초판 3쇄 발행 · 2024년 2월 21일

지은이 · 고경희, 김병기, 박재형
발행인 · 이종원
발행처 · ㈜도서출판 길벗
브랜드 · 길벗이지톡
출판사 등록일 · 1990년 12월 24일
주소 · 서울시 마포구 월드컵로 10길 56(서교동)
대표전화 · 02) 332-0931 | **팩스** · 02) 322-6766
홈페이지 · www.gilbut.co.kr | **이메일** · eztok@gilbut.co.kr

기획 및 책임편집 · 고경환 (kkh@gilbut.co.kr) | **디자인** · 윤석남 | **제작** · 이준호, 손일순, 이진혁, 김우식
마케팅 · 이수미, 장봉석, 최소영 | **영업관리** · 김명자, 심선숙 | **독자지원** · 윤정아, 최희창

CTP 출력 및 인쇄 · 북솔루션 | **제본** · 북솔루션

ISBN 979-11-407-0042-4 03740
(이지톡 도서번호 301092)

정가 25,000원

독자의 1초까지 아껴주는 정성 길벗출판사

(주)도서출판 길벗 | IT실용, IT/일반 수험서, 길벗캠퍼스, 경제경영, 취미실용, 인문교양(더퀘스트) **www.gilbut.co.kr**
길벗스쿨 | 국어학습, 수학학습, 어린이교양, 주니어 어학학습, 교과서 **www.gilbutschool.co.kr**

목차

＊자세한 해설을 확인하고 싶으시면 홈페이지에서 해설집을 다운로드하세요. (www.gilbut.co.kr)

Actual Test 07

MP3

해설집

적정 풀이 시간 120분

120 min

시작 시간 ___시 ___분
종료 시간 ___시 ___분

중간에 멈추지 말고 처음부터 끝까지 풀어보세요.
문제를 풀 때에는 실전처럼 답안지에 마킹하세요.

목표 개수 _____ / 200   **실제 개수** _____ / 200

예상 점수는 번역 및 정답에 있는 점수 환산표를 참조하세요.

LISTENING TEST

In the Listening test, you will be asked to demonstrate how well you understand spoken English. The entire Listening test will last approximately 45 minutes. There are four parts, and directions are given for each part. You must mark your answers on the separate answer sheet. Do not write your answers in the test book.

PART 1

Directions: For each question in this part, you will hear four statements about a picture in your test book. When you hear the statements, you must select the one statement that best describes what you see in the picture. Then find the number of the question on your answer sheet and mark your answer. The statements will not be printed in your test book and will be spoken only one time.

Statement (B), "They are sitting at a table." is the best description of the picture. So you should select answer (B) and mark it on your answer sheet.

1.

2.

▶ ▶ ▶ GO ON TO THE NEXT PAGE

3.

4.

5.

6.

▶ ▶ ▶GO ON TO THE NEXT PAGE

PART 2

Directions: You will hear a question or statement and three responses spoken in English. They will not be printed in your test book and will be spoken only one time. Select the best response to the question or statement and mark the letter (A), (B), or (C) on your answer sheet.

7. Mark your answer on your answer sheet.

8. Mark your answer on your answer sheet.

9. Mark your answer on your answer sheet.

10. Mark your answer on your answer sheet.

11. Mark your answer on your answer sheet.

12. Mark your answer on your answer sheet.

13. Mark your answer on your answer sheet.

14. Mark your answer on your answer sheet.

15. Mark your answer on your answer sheet.

16. Mark your answer on your answer sheet.

17. Mark your answer on your answer sheet.

18. Mark your answer on your answer sheet.

19. Mark your answer on your answer sheet.

20. Mark your answer on your answer sheet.

21. Mark your answer on your answer sheet.

22. Mark your answer on your answer sheet.

23. Mark your answer on your answer sheet.

24. Mark your answer on your answer sheet.

25. Mark your answer on your answer sheet.

26. Mark your answer on your answer sheet.

27. Mark your answer on your answer sheet.

28. Mark your answer on your answer sheet.

29. Mark your answer on your answer sheet.

30. Mark your answer on your answer sheet.

31. Mark your answer on your answer sheet.

PART 3

Directions: You will hear some conversations between two or three people. You will be asked to answer three questions about what the speakers say in each conversation. Select the best response to each question and mark the letter (A), (B), (C), or (D) on your answer sheet. The conversations will not be printed in your test book and will be spoken only one time.

32. Who is the woman?

(A) An event planner
(B) A caterer
(C) A conference organizer
(D) A photographer

33. What does the woman suggest the man do?

(A) Change the date of the event
(B) Pay her in cash
(C) Hire one of her colleagues
(D) Provide some more information

34. What does the man ask the woman for?

(A) A receipt
(B) An event program
(C) A sample
(D) A refund

35. What topic does the man bring up?

(A) A health program
(B) An employee get-together
(C) An upcoming conference
(D) A staff meeting

36. What does the woman say about her work?

(A) She has joined a new project team.
(B) She hasn't been able to complete a program.
(C) She has been busy.
(D) Her research needs more funding.

37. What will the man do next?

(A) Provide a demonstration
(B) Visit a health club
(C) Write down a phone number
(D) Speak with his manager

38. Why is the woman at the store?

(A) To exchange a product
(B) To ask about some repairs
(C) To return a laptop
(D) To apply for a job in technical support

39. What information does Dave provide?

(A) A new branch store will open soon.
(B) All laptops come with an extended warranty.
(C) Some of the new products are not available.
(D) The store is discounting some items.

40. What does Dave suggest the woman do?

(A) Complete some paperwork
(B) Place an order for another item
(C) Return later in the day
(D) Visit another store

41. Who most likely is the woman?

(A) A performer
(B) A concert organizer
(C) A talk show host
(D) A theater owner

42. What does the man say about the Lookout Theater?

(A) It has a very good sound system.
(B) It is located near where he was born.
(C) It is his favorite theater to perform music at.
(D) It is where he played his first concert.

43. What is the man pleased to learn?

(A) A theater is not closing.
(B) A restaurant is still open.
(C) An old building will be improved.
(D) A performance is sold out.

▶ ▶ ▶ **GO ON TO THE NEXT PAGE**

44. What do the men suggest doing?

(A) Expanding land used for berry farming
(B) Putting advertisements in a newspaper
(C) Taking part in a local festival
(D) Lowering the prices of their items

45. What does the woman think their business should do?

(A) Reserve a bigger booth at the festival
(B) Hire some more workers
(C) Provide coupons for free produce
(D) Give discounts to regular customers

46. What will the woman do next?

(A) Post a sign
(B) Distribute promotional flyers
(C) Sign up for an event
(D) Visit one of the fields

47. Why are the speakers traveling?

(A) To audit a foreign business
(B) To sign a rental agreement
(C) To purchase some materials
(D) To attend a ceremony

48. According to the woman, what skill does the man have?

(A) He can speak several languages.
(B) He is skilled at negotiating.
(C) He has great communication techniques
(D) He can repair broken items.

49. What does the woman imply when she says, "The local governor is going to be in attendance"?

(A) The event will be on television.
(B) A contract with government will be signed soon.
(C) They have to give a demonstration.
(D) They need to wear formal attires.

50. What does the man ask the woman about?

(A) A budget decision
(B) The results of a survey
(C) A new contract
(D) Some packaging materials

51. What product are the speakers discussing?

(A) Flashlights
(B) Lighting fixtures
(C) Power tools
(D) Solar panels

52. What will the woman do after lunch?

(A) Visit a warehouse
(B) Give a presentation
(C) Fill out a reimbursement request
(D) Work on some slides

53. What is the conversation mostly about?

(A) A grand opening
(B) The need to redecorate an office
(C) Some upcoming renovations
(D) A relocation to a new office space

54. Why does the woman say she is concerned?

(A) A work project will be noisy.
(B) Parking spaces are too small.
(C) Some materials for renovations are costly.
(D) A delivery has not arrived yet.

55. What is the woman informed about?

(A) A renovation project will be filmed.
(B) A staff meeting will be held weekly.
(C) A special work schedule has been arranged.
(D) A final payment has been made.

56. What type of business do the speakers work at?

(A) An advertising agency
(B) A clothing company
(C) A vehicle manufacturer
(D) A shipping service

57. Why does the woman say, "Your ideas for advertising are always creative"?

(A) To ask for help with a project
(B) To express her happiness
(C) To agree with a new suggestion
(D) To congratulate a colleague

58. What does the man suggest the woman do?

(A) Write a proposal
(B) Give a demonstration
(C) Send suggestions by e-mail
(D) Schedule a meeting

59. What type of organization do the speakers most likely work for?

(A) A sports team
(B) A research institute
(C) An acting group
(D) A government agency

60. What are the speakers mainly discussing?

(A) A new policy for customer service
(B) An election for a new president
(C) Increased advertising costs
(D) A corporate sponsorship

61. What does the man say about a proposal?

(A) He is satisfied with the results.
(B) He cannot agree to it right now.
(C) He thinks it will be rejected.
(D) He believes it will be expensive.

Instruction Booklet
Table of Contents

62. Where does the conversation most likely take place?

(A) In a conference room
(B) In a printer shop
(C) In an auditorium
(D) In a computer lab

63. Look at the graphic. Which page does the man turn to?

(A) Page 2
(B) Page 5
(C) Page 10
(D) Page 15

64. What does the woman say she will do next?

(A) Call a colleague
(B) Check a website
(C) Get some tools
(D) Set up some tables

▶ ▶ ▶ GO ON TO THE NEXT PAGE

Category	Number of Questions
Changing color	5
Printing	4
Changing size	6
Adding text	2
Graduated ruler	3

65. What needs to be printed?

(A) Some invitations
(B) Some business cards
(C) Some posters
(D) Some maps

66. Why is the woman unable to pick up the order?

(A) Her car is in the auto repair shop.
(B) She has to make a conference call.
(C) Her business trip has been rescheduled.
(D) She has a meeting with clients.

67. Look at the graphic. Which of the street names needs to be updated in the application?

(A) Grant Street
(B) Western Avenue
(C) Field Drive
(D) Orange Road

68. What happened on Monday?

(A) The woman went on a business trip.
(B) A manager posted a notice.
(C) The man was promoted.
(D) The company relocated to a different location.

69. Look at the graphic. How many questions will the woman respond to?

(A) 4
(B) 6
(C) 2
(D) 3

70. Why will the man put up a notice?

(A) To invite colleagues to a seminar
(B) To tell users that a website will not be available
(C) To ask for help with relocation
(D) To advertise a job opening for web design

PART 4

Directions: You will hear some short talks given by a single speaker. You will be asked to answer three questions about what the speaker says in each short talk. Select the best response to each question and mark the letter (A), (B), (C), or (D) on your answer sheet. The talks will not be printed in your test book and will be spoken only one time.

71. What kind of products does the store sell?

(A) Games
(B) Clothing
(C) Bicycles
(D) Tires

72. Why does the speaker suggest visiting the store soon?

(A) Some products will sell out quickly.
(B) A sale is going to end soon.
(C) A store is going out of business.
(D) A new shipment is expected to arrive today.

73. What extra service does the store provide?

(A) Free delivery
(B) Payment in installments
(C) Repairs
(D) International shipping

74. Who most likely are the listeners?

(A) Shoppers
(B) Gallery visitors
(C) Art students
(D) Restaurant workers

75. Why does the speaker say, "This won't be a big event"?

(A) To negotiate a price
(B) To express his surprise
(C) To give a warning
(D) To reassure the listeners

76. What does the speaker ask the listeners to bring to the event?

(A) Art supplies
(B) Photo identification
(C) Tickets
(D) Refreshments

77. What type of job is the listener being offered?

(A) Tour guide
(B) Bus driver
(C) History teacher
(D) Receptionist

78. What job qualification does the speaker say she is especially impressed with?

(A) Foreign language ability
(B) Positive references
(C) A college degree
(D) Writing experience

79. According to the speaker, what is the listener required to do?

(A) Wear a uniform
(B) Complete an online questionnaire
(C) Watch a tutorial video
(D) Take a physical checkup

80. Who is this talk intended for?

(A) Writers
(B) Photographers
(C) Tour guides
(D) Airline crews

81. What did the company recently do?

(A) It upgraded its website.
(B) It hired some freelance employees.
(C) It signed a rental contract for new office space.
(D) It relocated to Europe.

82. Where does the speaker say a publication will soon be available?

(A) On international flights
(B) In foreign supermarkets
(C) At train stations
(D) At travel agencies

▶ ▶ ▶ GO ON TO THE NEXT PAGE

83. What type of work does the speaker most likely do?

(A) Office remodeling
(B) Advertising
(C) Sales
(D) Food manufacturing

84. What does the speaker mean when she says, "I'm meeting a new client in Toronto"?

(A) She is out of town now.
(B) She is excited about her trip to Toronto.
(C) She wants to change a date.
(D) She cannot meet in person.

85. What does the speaker suggest that the listener do?

(A) Visit her in her office
(B) E-mail a script
(C) Reschedule a meeting
(D) Use some software

86. What has happened recently?

(A) Some products have been discontinued.
(B) Stores have closed.
(C) Sales have declined.
(D) A new line of soda has been popular.

87. What does the speaker imply when he says, "Companies are releasing many new products"?

(A) A new ad campaign needs to be launched.
(B) The company will stop making certain items.
(C) Prices need to be lowered immediately.
(D) The company has some competitors.

88. What will be given to the listeners at the next meeting?

(A) A list of successful products
(B) Product catalogues
(C) Some samples
(D) Next year's calendars

89. What is the mobile phone application for?

(A) Transferring money
(B) Placing orders for food
(C) Getting driving directions
(D) Buying performance tickets

90. According to the speaker, what do customers like about the mobile phone application?

(A) It provides a variety of restaurant choices.
(B) It costs nothing to use.
(C) It saves them time.
(D) It lets them leave comments.

91. According to the speaker, what will be added to the mobile phone application next week?

(A) Links to other websites
(B) A free delivery service
(C) Parking fee information
(D) A reward points program

92. What did the city council approve funding for?

(A) Adding some park trails
(B) Building a new parking lot
(C) Putting lights along a trail
(D) Buying bikes for residents

93. According to the speaker, what did some citizens do last month?

(A) They held an annual fundraiser.
(B) They got people to sign a petition.
(C) They made a presentation at a meeting.
(D) They completed a customer satisfaction survey.

94. What will the city council do next month?

(A) Make a hiring decision
(B) Have an election
(C) Visit a park
(D) Announce a new member

Song List

Track 1   *Wish You Were Here*

Track 2   *What's That?*

Track 3   *Time's Up*

Track 4   *Another Day*

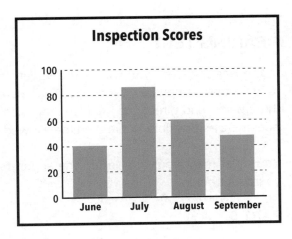

95. What did the speaker send by e-mail today?

(A) A contract form to sign
(B) A list of interview questions
(C) A price list of various sound equipment
(D) An album cover design

96. Look at the graphic. Which track number will Rick perform?

(A) Track 1
(B) Track 2
(C) Track 3
(D) Track 4

97. What does the woman say she will do this afternoon?

(A) Arrive the radio station early
(B) Buy some tickets
(C) Test some equipment
(D) Prepare some refreshments

98. Where do the listeners work?

(A) At a factory
(B) At a warehouse
(C) At a department store
(D) At a government agency

99. Look at the graphic. When was the last training session on workplace safety held?

(A) June
(B) July
(C) August
(D) September

100. According to the speaker, what will Peter do?

(A) Take notes from a meeting
(B) Demonstrate a safety procedure
(C) Lead a factory tour
(D) Hand out some copies

This is the end of the Listening test. Turn to Part 5 in your test book.

▶ ▶ ▶ **GO ON TO THE NEXT PAGE**

READING TEST

In the Reading test, you will read a variety of texts and answer several different types of reading comprehension questions. The entire Reading test will last 75 minutes. There are three parts, and directions are given for each part. You are encouraged to answer as many questions as possible within the time allowed.

You must mark your answer on the separate answer sheet. Do not write your answers in your test book.

PART 5

Directions: A word or phrase is missing in each of the sentences below. Four answer choices are given below each sentence. Select the best answer to complete the sentence. Then mark the letter (A), (B), (C), or (D) on your answer sheet.

101. The efficient and aggressive marketing strategies served a ------- role in supporting business success in several European countries.

(A) vitality
(B) vital
(C) vitalize
(D) vitally

102. The heavy snowfall led to a number of regional airline services being ------- until yesterday afternoon.

(A) delay
(B) delaying
(C) delayed
(D) delays

103. When we cannot attend an official event hosted by our partner, it is important to decline their invitations -------.

(A) respect
(B) respecting
(C) respectful
(D) respectfully

104. The city is doubling its efforts to lift some regulations to ------- corporate investment and create a very business-friendly environment.

(A) entitle
(B) qualify
(C) induce
(D) advise

105. All of our customers should be ------- that the store allow fourteen days for any refund or exchange to be processed.

(A) ready
(B) consistent
(C) aware
(D) responsible

106. The Long Beach Buffet accepts ------- personal checks nor credit cards, so customers must pay in cash.

(A) either
(B) neither
(C) both
(D) not only

107. ------- new business is adversely affected by the new regulations and the recent decline in the stock market.

(A) He
(B) Him
(C) His
(D) Himself

108. Every country has faced the global workforce crisis with an overall labor shortage, ------- this new artificial intelligence technology will help us to solve it.

(A) but
(B) or
(C) not only
(D) neither

109. For a ------- time only, customers can purchase our new powerful laptop computers with 0% financing and no money down.

(A) limit
(B) limits
(C) limiting
(D) limited

110. Mr. Singh ------- the features of the two products before choosing one to purchase.

(A) compared
(B) nominated
(C) designed
(D) simplified

111. Mr. Steven Chapman has been appointed as the new dean at our college ------- his impressive experience and his success at two previous universities.

(A) furthermore
(B) thanks to
(C) up to
(D) given that

112. The mayor ordered the replacement of several rows of street lights downtown, ------- find that the wiring is bad and the whole system needs to be replaced.

(A) only to
(B) even though
(C) in order that
(D) so as

113. Most of the local environmental groups are hoping ------- the construction projects that could devastate the region.

(A) stop
(B) to stop
(C) stopping
(D) stopped

114. The city government is devoted to ------- new methods for improving public health and welfare facilities.

(A) find
(B) finding
(C) found
(D) founded

115. Sociologists are concerned about many tensions and conflicts ------- arise from overcrowding in urban areas.

(A) that
(B) what
(C) how
(D) who

116. If you are interested in any of our new items, please contact us via e-mail, telephone, or fax so that we can send ------- information.

(A) further
(B) few
(C) little
(D) numerous

117. In an effort ------- prices, our company streamlined the production process and minimized package volume and weight.

(A) reduced
(B) reduces
(C) would reduce
(D) to reduce

118. HD Pharmaceuticals increased its third quarter net revenue due to the continued ------- of sales in North America.

(A) assets
(B) expansion
(C) decline
(D) compensation

▶ ▶ ▶ **GO ON TO THE NEXT PAGE**

119. In August, our city lost 5,500 jobs, a(n) ------- surprise for forecasters who had predicted employment growth.

(A) incremental
(B) anticipated
(C) pleasant
(D) unwelcome

120. There are some employees who prefer to work independently and others who do better when ------- with their colleagues.

(A) work
(B) to work
(C) working
(D) worked

121. The shutdown of our factory was very ------- as the mechanical problems were repaired more quickly than expected.

(A) prompt
(B) superior
(C) severe
(D) brief

122. The sales contract ------- indicates that some photo images can be used for commercial and non-commercial purposes.

(A) reassuringly
(B) courteously
(C) straightforwardly
(D) potentially

123. The airline company said its service was not disrupted ------- the cancelled flights to London and Berlin.

(A) except for
(B) including
(C) prior to
(D) between

124. The report said several countries in Asia will see steady growth this year on the ------- of an open international economy.

(A) analysis
(B) competition
(C) reliability
(D) strength

125. Of the two main factors interfering with the growth of new business models, one is outdated regulations, and ------- is the lack of new standards.

(A) some
(B) other
(C) others
(D) the other

126. Some industry experts predict that the worldwide market for cosmetics ------- by 20 percent in the next decade.

(A) are grown
(B) growing
(C) has grown
(D) will grow

127. ------- his flight arrived over an hour late, Dr. Hopkins could not be in attendance for the medical lecture.

(A) Nevertheless
(B) On account of
(C) Now that
(D) Providing that

128. ------- our order is delivered by next week, we will have to cancel it and search for another supplier.

(A) When
(B) Ever since
(C) Unless
(D) However

129. Mandoo Computers claims the new software is compatible with most computer operating systems, but some of its customers suggest -------.

(A) instead
(B) comparably
(C) otherwise
(D) on the other hand

130. Before Jia Technologies was named one of the best small businesses in the region, the company ------- expanding its operations nationwide.

(A) does not consider
(B) were considered
(C) will not consider
(D) had not considered

PART 6

Directions: Read the texts that follow. A word or phrase, or sentence is missing in parts of each text. Four answer choices for each question are given below the text. Select the best answer to complete the text. Then mark the letter (A), (B), (C), or (D) on your answer sheet.

Questions 131-134 refer to the following memo.

To: All employees
From: Lisa Hamilton, Head of Facilities Management
Date: January 21
Subject: Electricity Saving Tips and Fire Prevention

Please help us in reducing energy costs by cutting the use of electricity in our offices. Our

electricity bill has increased significantly this year, so we should make an effort to cut it in half.

Here are some simple energy saving tips. It is essential that you ------- any of your
                                                                    131.
personal electrical appliances such as under-desk heaters when not in use. At the end of

the working day, the last staff member to leave work should check each office to ensure

------- power is off with all the lights and electrical items. If you have a lot of things to plug
132.
in, use a power strip that can safely accommodate your needs. These can be a fire hazard

if left ------- overnight.
       133.

Please adjust your day-to-day behaviors and make small changes in habits. -------.
                                                                          134.

Thank you for your cooperation in advance.

131. (A) turning off
(B) turn off
(C) will turn off
(D) should be turned off

132. (A) while
(B) that
(C) which
(D) whether

133. (A) untouchable
(B) dissatisfied
(C) disabled
(D) unattended

134. (A) We're asking our customers to shift
energy use to off-peak hours.
(B) Fire prevention and energy savings
doesn't have to be high-tech.
(C) Before doing this, please consult the
company safety manual.
(D) Workplace safety will minimize the
risk of injuries on the job.

▶ ▶ ▶GO ON TO THE NEXT PAGE

July 5

Ms. Stacy Johnson
250 Hamilton Ave.
Palo Alto, CA 94301

The Red Rocks Amphitheater
3000 Tannery Way
Santa Clara, CA 95054

Dear Ms. Johnson,

The Five Metals Concert, which will take place on July 18 at the Red Rocks Amphitheater,

has been cancelled due to an unexpected car accident yesterday. Three of the band

members were badly injured in a collision. -------.
135.

Our record ------- that you purchased four tickets for Row C by cash last week. Therefore,
136.

we will give you a full refund of the price you paid. Just call at 1-800-575-4332 so that one

of our service representatives can assist you by ------- the refund.
137.

We sincerely apologize for any inconvenience and disappointment caused. Please accept

$20.00 gift certificate we have enclosed as a ------- of our apology.
138.

Thank you so much for your continuing support for our theater and arts in general.

Truly yours,

Brandon Hwang
General Manager
The Red Rocks Amphitheater

---

135. (A) Unfortunately, ride-sharing applications have declined sharply over recent weeks.
   (B) We would like to send our best wishes for their speedy and solid recovery.
   (C) The band has been known primarily for the stunning vocal talents of lead singer.
   (D) Remind all personnel that being careful can help to avoid accidents in the concert hall.

136. (A) illustrates
   (B) involves
   (C) indicates
   (D) concludes

137. (A) issue
   (B) issued
   (C) to issue
   (D) issuing

138. (A) gratitude
   (B) currency
   (C) reward
   (D) token

Century Real Estate
321 Union Landing Blvd.
Union City, NJ 94587
(510) 776-3232

Apartment For Lease
Walnut Creek Apt #310
1123 Harder Road

A clean, spacious two bedroom one bathroom apartment is ------- on Harder Road. The
139.
unit comes with basic kitchen appliances, a dishwasher, and in-unit laundry.

The apartment ------- conveniently at the heart of downtown. The nearest subway station
140.
is only a five-minute walk away and the nearest bus station is a ten-minute walk. There is

a convenient store within the apartment complex.

The rent is $1,250 a month inclusive of gas, electricity, and water. -------. Pets are strictly
141.
prohibited.

Please contact Mr. Andrew Kim at (510) 776-3232 for more information or to ------- an
142.
appointment for showing.

139. (A) applicable
(B) affordable
(C) comfortable
(D) available

140. (A) locating
(B) has located
(C) is locating
(D) is located

141. (A) There is also a supermarket that sells
kitchen supplies.
(B) Note that rent does not cover
Internet.
(C) Please visit our office to sign a lease
at your convenience.
(D) The rent increase is determined
based on taxes and maintenance
costs.

142. (A) arrange
(B) arranged
(C) arranging
(D) arrangement

To: Miranda Williams <mrw@beaglemedia.com>
From: Customer Service <cs@wwjc.com>
Date: October 26
Subject: About Your Registration

Dear Ms. Williams,

Welcome to the Worldwide Jobs Community, one of the leading online profession ------- **143.** in North America. Your personal information ------- your address and work experience will **144.** be securely kept only in our database if you allow us to do so.

The collected information will be used to analyze your job preferences, and we will provide it to employers who are ------- a job applicant just like you. Regular e-mail **143.** notifications about job openings in your area will be sent after you subscribe to our service.

-------. Therefore, we handle your personal information very carefully. If you want to join **145.** us, please visit our website at www.wwjc.com or call us at 1-800-857-6313.

Truly yours,

Worldwide Jobs Community
Customer Service

---

143. (A) responsibilities
(B) experiences
(C) developers
(D) matchmakers

144. (A) and
(B) now that
(C) such as
(D) as well as

145. (A) searching for
(B) relying upon
(C) laying off
(D) looking into

146. (A) Our job database is usually updated monthly.
(B) Your résumé has recently been reviewed by the board members.
(C) We know anyone can be a victim of identity theft.
(D) Customer satisfaction has always been our top priority.

PART 7

Directions: In this part you will read a selection of texts, such as magazine and newspaper articles, e-mails, and instant messages. Each text or set of texts is followed by several questions. Select the best answer for each question and mark the letter (A), (B), (C), or (D) on your answer sheet.

Questions 147-148 refer to the following letter.

Office Premium
4826 Mesa Drive
Manhattan, NY 10016

May 10
Stella Adams
4995 Yorkie Lane
Manhattan, NY 10016

Dear Ms. Adams,

This is to inform you that the rental fee of $150.00 for Office Premium's copying machine P039 is due on June 2. We are sending this letter as we were unsuccessful in reaching you at the e-mail address you provided in the rental contract. The contract states that you must pay for the machine in advance every two months. Please contact Office Premium at (912) 555-6218 at your earliest convenience.

Sincerely,

William Barnes
Store Manager, Office Premium

147. What is true about Office Premium?

(A) It wants Ms. Adams to sign a contract.
(B) It recommended a copying machine to Ms. Adams.
(C) It tried to contact Ms. Adams before.
(D) It wants Ms. Adams to respond by e-mail.

148. What is NOT mentioned in the letter?

(A) The initial date of the rental
(B) The serial number of the machine rented
(C) The location of Office Premium
(D) The frequency of payments

▶ ▶ ▶ GO ON TO THE NEXT PAGE

Pearson, Co.

32 Carters Rd.
Byron Bay, NSW 2481

Refund Reference Number:107C15

Refund Receipt Printed: June 21, 17:02:55

Approved By: Kenneth Dudley

Signature: *Kenneth Dudley*

Refunded To: Carlos Vestberg

Signature: *Carlos Vestberg*

The Amount Of: $58.20 (Cash)

Original Receipt Number:7138(June 15; 13:08:23)

Refund for...

Item	Quantity	Cost($)
Portable Stove	1	17.80
Folding Knife	1	11.35
Flashlight	1	3.20
6-Person Tent (Navy Blue)	1	25.85

---

149. What type of business most likely is Pearsons, Co.?

(A) An electronics shop
(B) A kitchenware manufacturer
(C) An outdoor equipment store
(D) A gardening gear retailer

150. What is indicated about Mr. Dudley?

(A) He approved the recall of some defective products.
(B) He was on duty on June 21.
(C) He received some money from Mr. Vestberg.
(D) He resides in the Byron Bay region.

Questions 151-152 refer to the following text message chain.

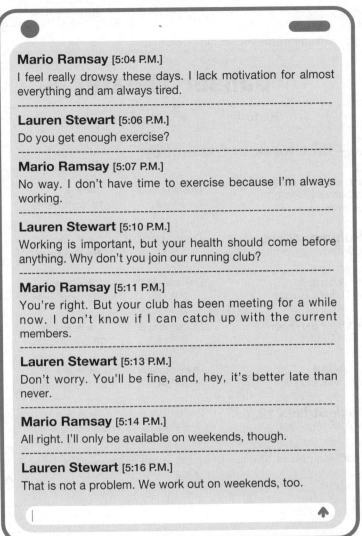

Mario Ramsay [5:04 P.M.]

I feel really drowsy these days. I lack motivation for almost everything and am always tired.

Lauren Stewart [5:06 P.M.]

Do you get enough exercise?

Mario Ramsay [5:07 P.M.]

No way. I don't have time to exercise because I'm always working.

Lauren Stewart [5:10 P.M.]

Working is important, but your health should come before anything. Why don't you join our running club?

Mario Ramsay [5:11 P.M.]

You're right. But your club has been meeting for a while now. I don't know if I can catch up with the current members.

Lauren Stewart [5:13 P.M.]

Don't worry. You'll be fine, and, hey, it's better late than never.

Mario Ramsay [5:14 P.M.]

All right. I'll only be available on weekends, though.

Lauren Stewart [5:16 P.M.]

That is not a problem. We work out on weekends, too.

---

151. At 5:13 P.M., what does Mr. Stewart mean when he writes, "it's better late than never"?

(A) He is concerned that Mr. Ramsay will not be able to run as fast as the others in the club.

(B) He is recommending that Mr. Ramsay get to work later than usual.

(C) He is encouraging Mr. Ramsay to start exercising.

(D) He is suggesting that Mr. Ramsay take weekends off from working.

152. What is indicated about Mr. Stewart?

(A) He will soon open a fitness club.

(B) He may run with Mr. Ramsay on weekends.

(C) He goes to work on weekends.

(D) He is a professional fitness trainer.

▶ ▶ ▶GO ON TO THE NEXT PAGE

Questions 153-154 refer to the following web page.

Danser Theater

Home	History	Show Times	Contact

Show time - first week of December

Return of the King Boston Broadway Company: Return Tour	December 1 7 P.M.	★★★☆☆ **16 comments**	**Buy tickets**
One Summer Night New York Broadway Company	December 2 3 P.M.	★★☆☆☆ **Be the first!**	**Buy tickets**
Anna Trinity Ballet Concert	December 3 2 P.M.	★★★★☆ **20 Comments**	**Canceled**
Over the Horizon Zen Circus	December 3 6 P.M.	★★★☆☆ **18 comments**	**Buy tickets**
Anna Trinity Ballet Concert	December 5 3 P.M.	★★★★☆ **20 Comments**	**Buy tickets**
The Clock Strikes 12 New York Musicals	December 5 8 P.M.	★★★★☆ **22 comments**	**Sold out**

* If payment is not made within 12 hours of seat reservation, the seat will be open to the public. Full refunds are available until 24 hours before the show.

153. According to the web page, what is true about *One Summer Night?*

(A) It is open to the public for free.
(B) It received harsh reviews.
(C) It is premiering at the Danser Theater.
(D) It does not have any comments yet.

154. For which show are tickets currently unavailable?

(A) *Return of the King*
(B) *Anna*
(C) *Over the Horizon*
(D) *The Clock Strikes 12*

Keep your house clean with Robocuum!

Are you too busy to clean your house? Then let Robocuum do the daily cleaning for you. Robocuum is an autonomous robot that removes dirt, dust, and hair from the floor. Robocuum's innovative technology ensures that the machine will avoid running into people or objects, so you never have to worry about your children or pets getting hurt.

With just 2 hours of charging, Robocuum runs for 7 hours, which is about 3 hours longer than similar models. In addition, the supplies used to run a Robocuum, such as dust bags and dust filters, are very reasonably priced so that they will be no burden for daily use.

To celebrate the coming of spring, we will provide a $30 discount on all orders made by March 31 in addition to providing free shipping, which usually costs $15. With the discount, a Robocuum is only $510! Customer will also be given a choice between a free 1-year warranty and a 2-year warranty that is currently available for $20, which is half the original price of $40.

155. What is NOT mentioned as an advantage of the Robocuum?

(A) It has a sensor that ensures safety.
(B) Supplies for it are inexpensive.
(C) It is energy efficient.
(D) It is the lightest model on the market.

156. What will happen in April?

(A) The price of the product will increase.
(B) Orders will not be accepted anymore.
(C) Free shipping on the product will be given.
(D) A celebratory event will take place.

157. How much does an extended warranty normally cost?

(A) $15
(B) $20
(C) $30
(D) $40

To:	Brian O'Dell <bodell@jettech.com>
From:	Janice Sullivan <jsullivan@kingdavidhotel.com>
Date:	October 5
Subject:	Reservation at King David
Attachment:	📎 Invoice

Dear Mr. O'Dell,

This is in regard to the reservation you made on September 29. Per your request submitted on October 3, your check-in date has now been changed from October 10 to November 10. The following is your new reservation summary:

Check In:	November 10 after 5:00 P.M.
Check Out:	November 16 before 11:00 A.M.
Number of Guest(s):	1
Loyalty Awards & Special Rates:	promotion code: MS292830 (10% discount)

Please find the attached invoice with detailed information about your reservation. The promotion code for Jet Tech, Inc. employees has been applied successfully. Payment can be made during check-in at the front desk. If you have any questions, feel free to e-mail me back or contact a customer service representative at (905) 555-2039. We have also reopened the fitness center after a comprehensive renovation, so don't forget to give it a try during your stay!

Janice Sullivan
Customer Service Representative

158. What is the purpose of the e-mail?

(A) To request an additional offer
(B) To book a hotel room
(C) To provide updated information
(D) To confirm the renewal of a membership

159. What is indicated about the King David Hotel?

(A) It has an exercise facility.
(B) It offers a discount to returning guests.
(C) It has partnerships with large companies.
(D) It has expanded to accommodate its growing clientele.

160. When did Mr. O'Dell originally plan to visit the hotel?

(A) On September 29
(B) On October 3
(C) On October 10
(D) On November 10

Questions 161-163 refer to the following online chat discussion.

Jonathan Stewart   3:10 P.M.
Have you seen the new episode of *Galaxy Combat*?

Haley Simmons   3:15 P.M.
Not yet. I'm planning on watching it next week.

Haley Simmons   3:16 P.M.
By the way, I heard that *Galaxy Combat* will be the last movie in the Galaxy series. Is that true?

Jonathan Stewart   3:17 P.M.
Not that I know of. The Winski brothers have been making every book of the series into a movie, and this is just the third episode.

Haley Simmons   3:20 P.M.
Wow! So there might actually be two more movies? That's so exciting.

Jonathan Stewart   3:21 P.M.
Well, that is what all we Galaxy fans are hoping for.

Haley Simmons   3:23 P.M.
I also heard that the character Marco is not played by Glen Duchson in *Galaxy Combat*. I really like him a lot as an actor.

Jonathan Stewart   3:25 P.M.
I do, too. His acting in the Galaxy series was truly amazing. He was great in the second episode of the series.

Jonathan Stewart   3:26 P.M.
However, the acting of the new actor, Jack Lemon, does not meet my expectations.

SEND

161. What is the main topic of the discussion?

    (A) A new TV show
    (B) A bestselling novel
    (C) An astronomical discovery
    (D) A movie series

162. At 3:17 P.M., what does Jonathan Stewart mean when he writes, "Not that I know of"?

    (A) He does not think *Galaxy Combat* will be the last of the series.
    (B) He is unsure if he wants to watch *Galaxy Combat*.
    (C) He does not know a lot about *Galaxy Combat*.
    (D) He has not met the Winski brothers yet.

163. What is indicated about Jonathan Stewart?

    (A) He is going to see *Galaxy Combat* next week.
    (B) He has seen the previous episode of the Galaxy series.
    (C) He has all five books in the Galaxy series.
    (D) He is a fan of Jack Lemon.

▶ ▶ ▶ GO ON TO THE NEXT PAGE

MEMO

To: All Employees of Frozen
From: Hayden de Witt
Date: May 8
Dear employees,

Congratulations for the excellent sales record we achieved last month! I thank you all for your dedication and hard work.

It seems that summer has come early this year as we are already receiving more customers. In order to meet the increased demand, the board has decided to open our stores for two more hours from May 17 to August 31. As this is a rather sudden decision, we have not been able to recruit additional employees yet. Therefore, I ask all employees to work longer shifts until recruitment takes place. Those who work overtime hours will be reimbursed with a bonus and additional paid day offs.

If you know a friend or a family member who can help us in the busy season, please let me know. I will arrange an interview for these temporary workers. Let's keep up the good work!

Regards,

Hayden de Witt
Human Resources Director

164. What is the purpose of the memo?

(A) To demand that employees work harder
(B) To introduce some new personnel
(C) To celebrate the company's anniversary
(D) To notify employees of future plans

165. The word "meet" in paragraph 2, line 2, is closest in meaning to

(A) face
(B) please
(C) greet
(D) fulfill

166. What is stated about Frozen?

(A) It is usually closed in the evening.
(B) It will extend its hours temporarily.
(C) It set a new sales record last month.
(D) It manufactures ice cream.

167. What are the recipients of the memo encouraged to do?

(A) Attend an interview
(B) Organize an event
(C) Design a job posting
(D) Refer a potential hire to Frozen

July 7 – The steamboat Suncoast is returning to the public on August 20. The Suncoast is a historical symbol of the Industrial Revolution in the U.S. as one of the first steam engine boats to travel along the Mississippi River. The Suncoast has traveled up and down the river while hauling agricultural exports for almost a decade. —[1]—.

After the invention of a high-pressure steam engine, the Suncoast was no longer needed. The Pollard Steamboat Company kept the Suncoast's original shape to maintain its historical value. To convey its historical significance to the community, it was donated to the New Orleans Engines Museum (NOEM) and was displayed at the South Shore Harbor beside the museum. —[2]—.

In order to show off the archaic beauty of the Suncoast to the world, NOEM has decided to use the steamboat itself to exhibit the history and evolution of waterway transportation on the Mississippi River during the Industrial Revolution. —[3]—. While preserving most of its inner structure, NOEM has built an indoor café, a restaurant, souvenir shops, and other facilities within the steamboat for visitors to enjoy. —[4]—.

An admission ticket for NOEM includes a free drink at the Suncoast Café. For ticket pricing and purchase, visit www.noem.com/suncoast.

168. What is the purpose of the article?

(A) To announce a change in a transportation schedule
(B) To advertise a new shopping mall
(C) To explain the history of steam engines
(D) To promote a new local attraction

169. What is mentioned as a change that was made to the Suncoast?

(A) It was sold to an institution.
(B) It was upgraded with a new steam engine.
(C) It was turned into a museum.
(D) It started to deliver agricultural goods.

170. What is NOT true about NOEM?

(A) It displays historical contents.
(B) It will reopen on August 20.
(C) It is located beside a body of water.
(D) It accepts admission fees.

171. In which of the positions marked [1], [2], [3], and [4] does the following sentence best fit?

"However, it was only for observing the exterior, and visitors were forbidden to enter."

(A) [1]
(B) [2]
(C) [3]
(D) [4]

http://www.leaderstoday.com/guides

Leaders Today

Home	Forum	Guides	FAQ

Cleaning a Laptop Computer

Clean your laptop computer efficiently and safely. Before anything else, make sure to unplug all the cords and remove the battery from your laptop. You will need a soft cloth, a can of compressed air, and a bottle of Leaders Cleaner.

Let's start with the surface. Put a drop or two of Leaders Cleaner on the cloth and wipe all the sides of your laptop. —[1]—. Using a mixture of water and regular soap is fine, but Leaders Cleaner is a better choice as it evaporates almost immediately, eliminating the danger of liquid getting into your laptop. —[2]—.

Next up is the keyboard. Removing the keys and putting them in a bowl filled with water to clean them is an option. —[3]—. However, simply using a can of compressed air to remove the debris underneath the keys will do the job just fine. Cleaning the monitor should be the last step, so you can prevent the screen from getting dirty with the dust you create while cleaning other parts. —[4]—.

Click here to order Leaders Cleaner. A brief video of our expert performing the laptop cleaning is available **here**. Talk with technical experts and other registered members of *Leaders Today* about tech-related issues **here**.

172. What is indicated as the first step in cleaning a laptop?

(A) Wiping the exterior of the laptop
(B) Studying all the laptop's components
(C) Turning off the laptop
(D) Brushing off the dust on the surface

173. According to the web page, what is mentioned as a strongly recommended item when cleaning a laptop?

(A) Some water
(B) A special solution
(C) Dishwashing detergent
(D) A bowl

174. What is indicated about *Leaders Today*?

(A) Its employees perform cleanings for customers.
(B) It sells laptop computers online.
(C) It encourages customers to clean their laptops on a regular basis.
(D) It provides an online space for discussions.

175. In which of the positions marked [1], [2], [3], and [4] does the following sentence best fit?

"Furthermore, it is more effective at removing oily residues."

(A) [1]
(B) [2]
(C) [3]
(D) [4]

Tucker Limitless-2 Nail Guns

Tucker is the world's favorite maker of hand tools and power tools for improvement jobs at homes. Our newly developed nail gun, the Limitless-2, will guarantee a safe and powerful performance for any kind of job. Check out the new features:

Handle: The Limitless-2's handle is very thin yet sturdy, which allows the user to hold and carry the nail gun easily. The innovative child-safety function on the handle is a feature of the new tool we are proud of.

Head LED: The LED at the tip of the nail gun will allow you to work on your task even in the dark, ensuring precision and safety.

Cordless: Unlike old models of nail guns, the Limitless-2 is a cordless unit that will free you from a compressor or messy fuel cells. Cordless does not mean less battery capacity as our lithium battery runs for as long as 6 hours straight with a single charge.

Operating Modes: With three different operating modes, now you can control the speed, power, and length of your duty with great precision. There is also a safety mode that disables the trigger when the tool is not in use.

---

  http://www.tucker.com/testimonials

TUCKER

HOME	PRODUCTS	TESTIMONIALS	ABOUT US

Tucker Limitless-2 Nail Gun

Submitted by Tony McCoy
Date: April 11

I have been using Tucker's Priority30 Drill since I purchased it three years ago. I was so satisfied with the drill that I did not hesitate to purchase a nail gun when I needed one to do some home improvement work at my new place. The nail gun is very convenient as it holds up to 120 nails at a time, which enables me to keep on working without having to stop every few moments. I also like the fact that the machine runs for almost an entire day. It is hard to believe how such a light and small battery can last for such a long time. If you purchase the Limitless-2, I can assure you that you will be as satisfied as me.

176. Where would the description most likely be found?

(A) In a military drill manual
(B) In a magazine for interior designers
(C) In a construction company's newsletter
(D) In a brochure for home-improvement items

177. What is indicated about Tucker?

(A) It is a fairly young business.
(B) It launched a nail gun for the second time.
(C) It considers the safety of its customers important.
(D) It has office locations worldwide.

178. What is suggested about Mr. McCoy?

(A) He works for a construction company.
(B) He will buy another drill for home-improvement purposes.
(C) He plans to move to a new location.
(D) He has done business with Tucker before.

179. What feature mentioned in the description is Mr. McCoy particularly satisfied with?

(A) The thin handle
(B) The lithium battery
(C) The nail capacity
(D) The year-long warranty

180. In the web page, the word "assure" in paragraph 1, line 7, is closest in meaning to?

(A) convince
(B) promise
(C) recommend
(D) enable

⊖ ▢ ⊗

To:	Customer Service <customerservice@howardelectronics.com>
From:	Jonathan Welsh <jwelsh@srmail.com>
Date:	August 9
Subject:	Recent Order
Attachment:	📎 Refrigerator

To whom it may concern,

I purchased a refrigerator (model number DO4018) and a microwave (AQ501) at Howard Electronics on August 3. I brought home the microwave the same day, and the refrigerator was delivered to my house the next day.

After your employees were done with the installation and were gone, I noticed that the door handle of the fridge was broken. I immediately visited Howard Electronics' website to file a claim (claim number IE46109). I was informed that another team of employees would visit my house on August 7 with another refrigerator to install. As of right now, however, I have neither received a response nor a visit. As I previously did, I am including a set of photos of the refrigerator and its broken part for reference. Please look into this matter as soon as possible.

Sincerely,

Jonathan Welsh

Resolved Claims Report

Howard Electronics Customer Service Department

Claims Resolved on: August 29
Representative: Susan Piercy
Submitted to: Eric Gardner

Claim Number	Description	Resolution
PQ23017	Delivery of a laptop computer (TE239) delayed by a week	A mouse worth $28 was sent along with the package.
CM31921	Malfunctioning printer (OJ3387) sold to a customer	A full refund of $49 was credited to the customer's credit card.
BA81274	Refrigerator (DL9387) malfunctioned because of improper installation	A check for $65 was issued for the contents of the refrigerator. A crew will visit again to fix the problem.
IE46109	Refrigerator (DO4018) damaged in transit and installation	Replacement with free shipping plus a $30 coupon will be provided.

• All claim forms and any supporting documents received from customers must be included with this report when submitting it to your manager.

181. What is indicated about Howard Electronics?

(A) It is conducting an online survey.
(B) It provides on-site installation service.
(C) It offers free shipping and handling.
(D) It will repair Mr. Welsh's refrigerator.

182. When was the refrigerator installed at Mr. Welsh's house?

(A) August 3
(B) August 4
(C) August 7
(D) August 9

183. According to the form, how much did Howard Electronics originally receive for the product OJ3387?

(A) $28
(B) $30
(C) $49
(D) $65

184. What was given to Mr. Welsh by Howard Electronics?

(A) A free home appliance
(B) A voucher
(C) A check
(D) A refund

185. What most likely was sent to Mr. Gardner along with the report?

(A) An original receipt
(B) A document on the store's return policy
(C) Credit card information
(D) Pictures of an appliance

7 August

Jasmine Castor
Creators, Inc.
2255 Fleming Way
Richville OH 5045

Dear Ms. Castor,

I am writing to apply for the position of construction coordinator at Creators, Inc., which was posted on Jobseekers.com on August 5. I graduated from the University of Appenn in Newport with a degree in architecture. After graduation, I worked at Palotas, a small construction company located in Cherry Hill, for two years and started working at my present place of employment, New Builders, as an assistant field engineer six years ago. Enclosed, please find my résumé, which will provide you with more information about my educational background and experience. I look forward to hearing from you soon.

Sincerely,

Mario Bevan
Enclosure

To:	Mario Bevan <jbevan@promail.com>
From:	Jasmine Castor <m.castor@creatorsinc.com>
Date:	August 11
Subject:	Interview
Attachment:	📎 Map

Dear Mr. Bevan,

Thank you for your interest in working with us at Creators, Inc. As we discussed on the phone, the position at our Burston office for which you applied has already been filled; you will instead be interviewed for a position at our branch located in the city where your university is. This unprecedented decision was based on your exceptional expertise, experience, and education.

The interview will take place at our headquarters in Richville. I have attached a map of the area for you to refer to. When you come outside from Exit 6 at Kearny Station, cross Eugene Road, pass by a tourist agency, and then take a left when you see a fairly big pharmacy on the corner of Lewin Street and Main Avenue. Then, walk for a couple of minutes until you find our corporate building next to a coffee shop. Good luck with your interview.

Regards,

Jasmine Castor

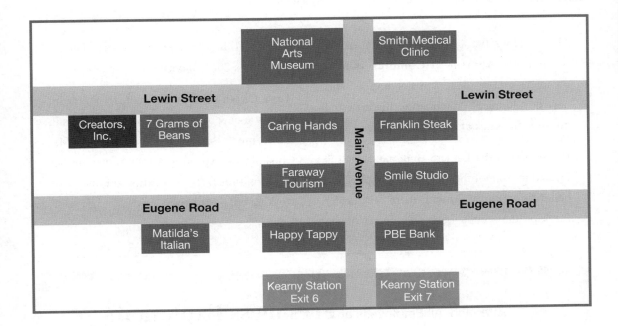

186. What is mentioned about Mr. Bevan?

(A) He used to own a business.
(B) He used to manage some websites.
(C) He currently works at New Builders.
(D) He has a master's degree in architecture.

187. What is the purpose of the e-mail?

(A) To follow up with a discussion
(B) To request information
(C) To give information about some roadwork
(D) To confirm an employment

188. Where will Mr. Bevan most likely work?

(A) In Richville
(B) In Newport
(C) In Cherry Hill
(D) In Burston

189. What is NOT suggested about Creators, Inc.?

(A) Its headquarters is located near a public transit center.
(B) It advertised a job opening online.
(C) It has more than one office location.
(D) It has been in operation for at least six years.

190. What kind of business most likely is Caring Hands?

(A) A coffee shop
(B) A tourist agency
(C) A daycare center
(D) A pharmacy

▶ ▶ ▶ GO ON TO THE NEXT PAGE

Murray (July 10) – The construction of the Rosemount Apartment Complex is now complete, and residents are flooding in. This new development is animating the area and boosting the sales of nearby businesses.

Businesses in the Lamere Building, which is located in front of the apartment complex, are benefiting greatly. Among them is Murphy Pizza on the second floor. The owner of the pizzeria, Hillary Dembowski, reports that she has "seen a 200% increase in revenue."

Rosa Chisholm is the owner of Dream Bakers, a new bakery that opened its doors in the Lamere Building just yesterday. Ms. Chisholm is expecting a high return on her new business. "Everything seems to be working out positively."

Attention, All Employees at **Freshness Explosion**

Thanks to the construction of the Rosemount Apartment Complex, we are seeing a sharp increase in the number of customers. To satisfy all customers and to deal with repeated requests from customers, we will spend the next week improving our facilities.

- A bathroom will be constructed inside the shop, thereby removing the need to share the bathroom with Murphy Pizza and Dream Bakers.
- The windows will be changed to thicker ones in order to improve energy efficiency.
- The parking lot will be repaved.
- The store will be widened and more cash registers installed, so customers will not have to wait in long lines anymore.

Thank you for your cooperation and dedication.

Posted August 11

Do you have something to say to Jack Rogers,

the owner of Freshness Explosion?

Write your opinions or suggestions below

and post this note on the board near the register.

I have been a customer of Freshness Explosion for about three years. Members of my fitness center especially love the onsite café's fresh tomato juice and carrot cake made out of ingredients that I receive from Freshness Explosion every day. I am writing this note in order to express my gratitude to one of your employees, Ms. Michelle Murdock. She delivers fruits and vegetables to the café at 7 o'clock in the morning every day. She has never been tardy, which shows her professionalism and ensures that the café operates without any problems. She truly deserves a reward for her hard work.

Herbert Warren

191. In the article, the word "animating" in paragraph 1, line 4, is closest in meaning to

(A) energizing
(B) filming
(C) welcoming
(D) extending

192. What is indicated about Freshness Explosion?

(A) It has a lot of staff members.
(B) It has decided to extend its business hours.
(C) Its owner also runs a pizzeria.
(D) It is located in the Lamere Building.

193. What has NOT been renovated at Freshness Explosion?

(A) The windows
(B) The waiting area
(C) The parking area
(D) The interior

194. Who most likely posted the notice?

(A) Mr. Rogers
(B) Mr. Warren
(C) Ms. Dembowski
(D) Ms. Murdock

195. What kind of business most likely is Freshness Explosion?

(A) A grocery store
(B) A café
(C) A fitness center
(D) A bakery

▶ ▶ ▶GO ON TO THE NEXT PAGE

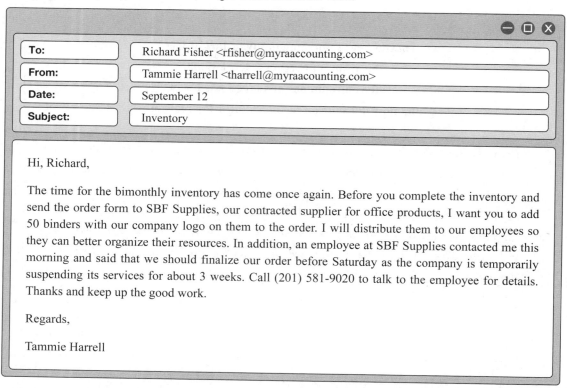

To: Richard Fisher <rfisher@myraaccounting.com>
From: Tammie Harrell <tharrell@myraaccounting.com>
Date: September 12
Subject: Inventory

Hi, Richard,

The time for the bimonthly inventory has come once again. Before you complete the inventory and send the order form to SBF Supplies, our contracted supplier for office products, I want you to add 50 binders with our company logo on them to the order. I will distribute them to our employees so they can better organize their resources. In addition, an employee at SBF Supplies contacted me this morning and said that we should finalize our order before Saturday as the company is temporarily suspending its services for about 3 weeks. Call (201) 581-9020 to talk to the employee for details. Thanks and keep up the good work.

Regards,

Tammie Harrell

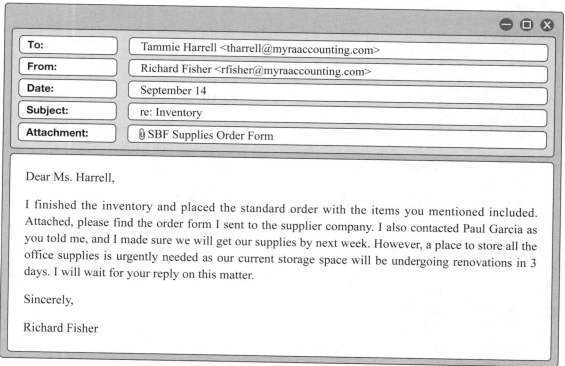

To: Tammie Harrell <tharrell@myraaccounting.com>
From: Richard Fisher <rfisher@myraaccounting.com>
Date: September 14
Subject: re: Inventory
Attachment: 📎 SBF Supplies Order Form

Dear Ms. Harrell,

I finished the inventory and placed the standard order with the items you mentioned included. Attached, please find the order form I sent to the supplier company. I also contacted Paul Garcia as you told me, and I made sure we will get our supplies by next week. However, a place to store all the office supplies is urgently needed as our current storage space will be undergoing renovations in 3 days. I will wait for your reply on this matter.

Sincerely,

Richard Fisher

SBF Supplies Order Form

Order Information:

Order Date:	September 14	Customer:	Myra Accounting
Contact:	Richard Fisher	Phone Number:	(201)555-6028

Order Description:

Lot Number	Item	Maker	Quantity
B9481	Computer Paper	Ratcliff	**70** boxes
P0349	Envelope (Company Name/Logo Imprinted)	Tate	**30** boxes
Y4251	Whiteboard Marker/Eraser Set	Twin Oaks	**15** sets
B2918	Binder (Company Name/Logo Imprinted)	Bungalow	**50** pieces
C5516	Paper Clip	Folio	**50** boxes

196. What is the purpose of the first e-mail?

(A) To confirm an order for supplies
(B) To provide instructions
(C) To offer a contract
(D) To call for a meeting

197. What is suggested about Myra Accounting?

(A) It receives discounts from SBF Supplies.
(B) It will be temporarily closed for a few weeks.
(C) It does business with SBF Supplies regularly.
(D) It hired another company to design its logo.

198. Who most likely is Paul Garcia?

(A) Ms. Harrell's colleague
(B) A representative at SBF Supplies
(C) A deliveryman
(D) A warehouse employee at Myra Accounting

199. What is indicated about SBF Supplies?

(A) It sells products made by other companies.
(B) It plans to renovate a facility.
(C) It shipped some items on September 14.
(D) Its sales are decreasing sharply.

200. Which product was newly added to the order form?

(A) B2918
(B) B9481
(C) C5516
(D) P0349

STOP! This is the end of the test. If you finish before time is called, you may go back to Parts 5, 6, and 7 and check your work.

Actual Test 08

MP3

해설집

적정 풀이 시간 120분

120 min

시작 시간 ___시 ___분
종료 시간 ___시 ___분

중간에 멈추지 말고 처음부터 끝까지 풀어보세요.
문제를 풀 때에는 실전처럼 답안지에 마킹하세요.

목표 개수 _____ / 200   **실제 개수** _____ / 200

예상 점수는 번역 및 정답에 있는 점수 환산표를 참조하세요.

LISTENING TEST

In the Listening test, you will be asked to demonstrate how well you understand spoken English. The entire Listening test will last approximately 45 minutes. There are four parts, and directions are given for each part. You must mark your answers on the separate answer sheet. Do not write your answers in the test book.

PART 1

Directions: For each question in this part, you will hear four statements about a picture in your test book. When you hear the statements, you must select the one statement that best describes what you see in the picture. Then find the number of the question on your answer sheet and mark your answer. The statements will not be printed in your test book and will be spoken only one time.

Statement (B), "They are sitting at a table." is the best description of the picture. So you should select answer (B) and mark it on your answer sheet.

1.

2.

3.

4.

5.

6.

▶ ▶ ▶**GO ON TO THE NEXT PAGE**

PART 2

Directions: You will hear a question or statement and three responses spoken in English. They will not be printed in your test book and will be spoken only one time. Select the best response to the question or statement and mark the letter (A), (B), or (C) on your answer sheet.

7. Mark your answer on your answer sheet.

8. Mark your answer on your answer sheet.

9. Mark your answer on your answer sheet.

10. Mark your answer on your answer sheet.

11. Mark your answer on your answer sheet.

12. Mark your answer on your answer sheet.

13. Mark your answer on your answer sheet.

14. Mark your answer on your answer sheet.

15. Mark your answer on your answer sheet.

16. Mark your answer on your answer sheet.

17. Mark your answer on your answer sheet.

18. Mark your answer on your answer sheet.

19. Mark your answer on your answer sheet.

20. Mark your answer on your answer sheet.

21. Mark your answer on your answer sheet.

22. Mark your answer on your answer sheet.

23. Mark your answer on your answer sheet.

24. Mark your answer on your answer sheet.

25. Mark your answer on your answer sheet.

26. Mark your answer on your answer sheet.

27. Mark your answer on your answer sheet.

28. Mark your answer on your answer sheet.

29. Mark your answer on your answer sheet.

30. Mark your answer on your answer sheet.

31. Mark your answer on your answer sheet.

PART 3

Directions: You will hear some conversations between two or three people. You will be asked to answer three questions about what the speakers say in each conversation. Select the best response to each question and mark the letter (A), (B), (C), or (D) on your answer sheet. The conversations will not be printed in your test book and will be spoken only one time.

32. What is the man preparing for?

(A) An anniversary event
(B) A grand opening
(C) A holiday raffle
(D) A charity fundraiser

33. What does the woman say she can do?

(A) Offer a discount
(B) Provide free shipping
(C) Rush an order
(D) Cater an event

34. What does the man ask about?

(A) The store's hours
(B) Color options
(C) Payment options
(D) Exchange policies

35. What will happen next week?

(A) A coworker will retire.
(B) A contract will be signed.
(C) A colleague will go on a business trip.
(D) A product will be released.

36. What is the man concerned about?

(A) A rental fee for a venue
(B) The number of attendees
(C) The deadline for a project
(D) The size of a venue

37. What will the man do next?

(A) Contact a caterer
(B) Reserve a picnic area
(C) Send some invitations
(D) Review a travel itinerary

38. Where most likely are the speakers?

(A) At a construction site
(B) At a car dealership
(C) At a car rental service
(D) At a restaurant

39. Which feature does the man say is important?

(A) Price
(B) Size
(C) Fuel efficiency
(D) Durability

40. What does the woman ask the man to provide?

(A) A travel itinerary
(B) A credit card information
(C) A ticket stump
(D) A driver's license

41. What most likely is the man's profession?

(A) Composer
(B) Event planner
(C) Musician
(D) Actor

42. Why is the woman calling?

(A) To schedule an interview
(B) To ask the man to sign a contract
(C) To offer the man a job
(D) To make a reservation

43. What does the man say might cause a problem?

(A) His place of residence
(B) A mechanical malfunction
(C) A schedule conflict
(D) His lack of experience

▶ ▶ ▶ GO ON TO THE NEXT PAGE

44. Who most likely is the man?

(A) A librarian
(B) A bank teller
(C) A student
(D) A book keeper

45. What does the man offer to do?

(A) Fix a problem
(B) Submit a request
(C) Secure funding for more books
(D) Waive a fee

46. Why is the woman worried?

(A) She does not have enough money.
(B) An item might not arrive in time.
(C) A late fee might be too expensive.
(D) Operating hours will not be extended.

---

47. What type of event did the man attend?

(A) An orientation session
(B) A professional conference
(C) A theatrical performance
(D) A board meeting

48. What does the man mean when he says, "That will not be easy"?

(A) He does not have any suggestions for budget cut.
(B) He wants to ask his manager for help.
(C) He agrees with a colleague's spending plan.
(D) He doesn't think he'll be able to meet a deadline.

49. What does the man say he will do next?

(A) Talk to an employee
(B) Cancel doctor's appointment
(C) Call in a meeting
(D) Complete some forms

50. According to the man, what is indicated about a company from the results of the survey?

(A) It needs to provide its employees with more benefits.
(B) It has some employees who are highly satisfied.
(C) Its employees are concerned about the environment.
(D) Its products are made of recycled materials.

51. What does the woman say she did last week?

(A) She saw a news report.
(B) She read an article in a magazine.
(C) She spoke with a colleague.
(D) She met her sales quota.

52. What does the man suggest that they do?

(A) Add a special promotion
(B) Modify a production process
(C) Hire an expert
(D) Promote some workers

---

53. Why does the woman say, "I eat there two or three times a week"?

(A) To agree with a comment
(B) To make an invitation
(C) To reject a suggestion
(D) To offer an alternative

54. Where do the speakers work?

(A) At a manufacturing plant
(B) At a warehouse
(C) At an engineering firm
(D) At a hardware store

55. Why does the man like his new job more than his previous job?

(A) The salary is much higher.
(B) He enjoys a greater variety of work.
(C) He has a flexible schedule.
(D) Much of the work is automated.

56. Who most likely is the man?

(A) A chef
(B) An engineer
(C) An interior designer
(D) A restaurant manager

57. Why will the man visit the woman's business this evening?

(A) To make a presentation
(B) To conduct an inspection
(C) To choose a product
(D) To have an interview

58. What does the woman recommend that the man bring?

(A) Some dimensions
(B) An architectural plan
(C) Some photographs
(D) A manual

59. Who most likely are the participants in the program?

(A) College interns
(B) Government workers
(C) Management trainees
(D) Potential employees

60. What does the woman ask about?

(A) A length of time
(B) A salary
(C) A location for a program
(D) A list of participants

61. How can the participants communicate a request?

(A) By speaking with a manager
(B) By sending an e-mail
(C) By making a telephone call
(D) By completing a form

Leasing Options

Rental Term	Monthly Rent
3 months	$1,000
6 months	$950
9 months	$900
12 months	$850

62. What reason does the man give for relocating?

(A) He recently got married.
(B) He wants a smaller apartment.
(C) He needs more rooms in his place.
(D) He has a new job.

63. Look at the graphic. How much will the man most likely pay for rent?

(A) $1,000
(B) $950
(C) $900
(D) $850

64. What will the speakers do next?

(A) Renew a lease
(B) Discuss some options
(C) Review a rental contract
(D) Take a tour

▶ ▶ ▶GO ON TO THE NEXT PAGE

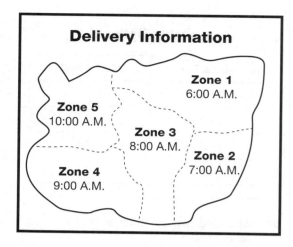

Delivery Information

Zone 1
6:00 A.M.

Zone 5
10:00 A.M.

Zone 3
8:00 A.M.

Zone 2
7:00 A.M.

Zone 4
9:00 A.M.

Doctor	Work Hours (Monday – Friday)
Dr. West	8:00 A.M. – 4:00 P.M.
Dr. Conners	9:00 A.M. – 5:00 P.M.
Dr. Mayweather	12:00 P.M. – 8:00 P.M.
Dr. Bell	10:00 A.M. – 6:00 P.M.

65. What type of business is the man calling?

(A) A delivery service
(B) A laundry service
(C) A caterer
(D) A repair shop

66. What does the woman say her business is well-known for?

(A) Having well-trained employees
(B) Having low prices
(C) Providing quality items
(D) Doing work on time

67. Look at the graphic. What time will the delivery be made?

(A) 7:00 A.M.
(B) 8:00 A.M.
(C) 9:00 A.M.
(D) 10:00 A.M.

68. Why does the woman want to change her appointment?

(A) She is going to be on vacation.
(B) She needs to be away on business.
(C) She is not feeling well.
(D) She has to leave for a family event.

69. Look at the graphic. Who will the woman see on Wednesday?

(A) Dr. West
(B) Dr. Conners
(C) Dr. Mayweather
(D) Dr. Bell

70. What will the woman most likely do next?

(A) Answer some questions
(B) Visit the office
(C) Provide new contact information
(D) Make an online payment

PART 4

Directions: You will hear some short talks given by a single speaker. You will be asked to answer three questions about what the speaker says in each short talk. Select the best response to each question and mark the letter (A), (B), (C), or (D) on your answer sheet. The talks will not be printed in your test book and will be spoken only one time.

71. Where is the announcement most likely being made?

(A) At a bus terminal
(B) At a business social event
(C) At a supermarket
(D) At a restaurant

72. According to the speaker, what should customers be told about the current situation?

(A) A price of an item has increased.
(B) A schedule has changed.
(C) An item is not available.
(D) A private room is closed for repairs.

73. What are the listeners encouraged to do?

(A) Work together as a team
(B) Greet customers at the entrance
(C) Work extra shifts this afternoon
(D) Serve meals to customers right away

74. What is the topic of the workshop?

(A) Gardening
(B) Programming
(C) Dairy farming
(D) Online vending

75. What does the speaker recommend?

(A) Register for a course
(B) Trying different activities
(C) Working with a partner
(D) Doing some research

76. What are the listeners doing next week?

(A) Taking a trip
(B) Paying a tuition fee
(C) Choosing a venue
(D) Buying some gardening supplies

77. What is the topic of the magazine in the advertisement?

(A) International business
(B) Information technology
(C) Personal finances
(D) Online marketing

78. What does the speaker say about the writers on the staff?

(A) They respond quickly to questions from readers.
(B) They are famous for their books.
(C) They have a lot of experience.
(D) They come from around the world.

79. What is indicated about the online version of the magazine?

(A) It comes with access to its archives.
(B) Its content is updated weekly.
(C) It is on sale for half the regular price.
(D) It is cheaper than the print version.

80. Who is this talk intended for?

(A) The board of directors
(B) Small business owners
(C) Potential investors
(D) Professional athletes

81. What type of products does the company sell?

(A) Footwear
(B) Neckties
(C) Business suits
(D) Swimwear

82. What does the speaker's business hope to buy?

(A) A warehouse
(B) A manufacturing plant
(C) Construction materials
(D) An athletic facility

▶ ▶ ▶GO ON TO THE NEXT PAGE

83. According to the speaker, what event will take place this evening?

(A) An awards ceremony
(B) A product launch
(C) A retirement party
(D) A stockholders' meeting

84. Why does the speaker say, "I'm driving to Jacksonville today"?

(A) To reject a suggestion
(B) To mention that she is not available
(C) To extend an offer
(D) To ask for driving directions

85. According to the speaker, what does she need to pick up?

(A) Some beverages for attendees
(B) Some floor plans for the event
(C) Some event programs
(D) Some promotional materials

86. Where most likely is the announcement being made?

(A) At an airport
(B) At a restaurant
(C) On a ferry
(D) On an airplane

87. Why does the speaker apologize?

(A) A stopover has been canceled.
(B) The departure was delayed.
(C) There was a mechanical problem.
(D) No more tickets are available.

88. What does the speaker mean when she says, "We take both cash and credit cards"?

(A) Some duty-free items are available.
(B) The new payment method is more convenient.
(C) The listeners will be charged for food.
(D) The listeners must present their photo identification.

89. Which department does the speaker most likely work for?

(A) Human Resources
(B) Research and Development
(C) Information Technology
(D) Product Development

90. According to the speaker, what has recently happened to the business?

(A) Some computers were affected by a virus.
(B) New security equipment were installed.
(C) Identification badges were handed out.
(D) No seats were available in the computer class.

91. What are the listeners asked to do?

(A) Look at the user's manuals
(B) Sign for a computer course
(C) Check security guidelines for any change
(D) Open a computer program

92. Who is the speaker?

(A) A museum curator
(B) The host of a radio program
(C) A historian
(D) A member of the city council

93. Why does the speaker say, "Moore House is going to open as the city's newest museum"?

(A) To give some directions to the museum
(B) To stress an accomplishment
(C) To recruit some volunteers for the event
(D) To correct a misunderstanding

94. What can be found on a website?

(A) The building directory
(B) An event schedule
(C) A video about the museum
(D) Some pictures

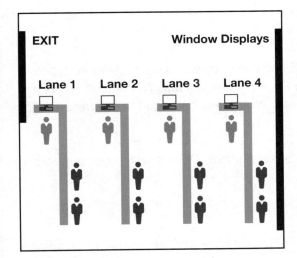

EXIT   Window Displays

Lane 1   Lane 2   Lane 3   Lane 4

August

Mon	Tues	Wed	Thurs	Fri
10 Painting Lesson	11 Arts & Crafts Class	12	13 Swimming Class	14
17	18 Music Class	19 Speech Class	20	21 Acting Class

95. Where most likely is the announcement being made?

(A) At a hardware store
(B) At a grocery store
(C) At a furniture store
(D) At a clothing store

96. Look at the graphic. Which lane is the express lane?

(A) Lane 1
(B) Lane 2
(C) Lane 3
(D) Lane 4

97. According to the speaker, what can listeners receive help with?

(A) Locating some merchandise
(B) Returning defective goods
(C) Moving big items
(D) Ordering items not in stock

98. Who most likely is the speaker?

(A) A music teacher
(B) An art instructor
(C) A swimming teacher
(D) An art dealer

99. What does the speaker ask the listeners to do?

(A) Help clean up the room
(B) Put their phones to silent mode
(C) Write a review of the class
(D) Check personal belongings

100. Look at the graphic. On which date will there be a special guest?

(A) August 10
(B) August 11
(C) August 18
(D) August 21

This is the end of the Listening test. Turn to Part 5 in your test book.

READING TEST

In the Reading test, you will read a variety of texts and answer several different types of reading comprehension questions. The entire Reading test will last 75 minutes. There are three parts, and directions are given for each part. You are encouraged to answer as many questions as possible within the time allowed.

You must mark your answer on the separate answer sheet. Do not write your answers in your test book.

PART 5

Directions: A word or phrase is missing in each of the sentences below. Four answer choices are given below each sentence. Select the best answer to complete the sentence. Then mark the letter (A), (B), (C), or (D) on your answer sheet.

101. To avoid any delays to your -------, please follow the guidelines below for citation and submission of your doctor's thesis.

(A) publish
(B) publisher
(C) published
(D) publication

102. In the factory workers' strike, neither management ------- labor appeared willing to give an inch.

(A) and
(B) but
(C) yet
(D) nor

103. An important aspect in the software development process is the ------- between various parts of the software system being designed.

(A) consist
(B) consisting
(C) consistent
(D) consistency

104. If you take the right steps, you can ------- remove the sticker from your car without causing damage to your car's paint.

(A) care
(B) careful
(C) carefully
(D) caring

105. Our company provides entrepreneurs with cost-effective and professional security services for ------- business facilities.

(A) they
(B) their
(C) them
(D) themselves

106. Instead of one huge goal at the beginning of the year, people should set numerous small and specific goals ------- the year.

(A) across
(B) within
(C) throughout
(D) between

107. Manufacturing companies must hire at least 10 workers to be ------- for the tax break, while tourism firms must hire five or more.

(A) eligible
(B) known
(C) eager
(D) responsible

108. Our goal is to provide every customer with full service and complete satisfaction, and we look forward to ------- you for many years to come.

(A) serve
(B) server
(C) serving
(D) served

109. If left ------- for more than one minute, the mobile phone screen usually will go into sleep mode automatically.

(A) inactive
(B) about
(C) narrow
(D) inside

110. The college offers on-campus ------- accommodation for over 2,000 students in both halls of residence and three bedroom self-catering apartments.

(A) suit
(B) suitable
(C) suiting
(D) suitably

111. Please visit our official website for side by side ------- of popular vehicles by pricing, interior and exterior features, and safety information.

(A) compare
(B) comparing
(C) comparable
(D) comparisons

112. Despite its short history, our company has ------- grown as a major player in the civil aircraft industry.

(A) succeed
(B) success
(C) successful
(D) successfully

113. A variety of changes will be made to our manufacturing process to ------- some of the issues arising from our new products.

(A) agree
(B) address
(C) proceed
(D) consume

114. Not only ------- genetic engineers change the structure of DNA, but they can put genes from one organ into another.

(A) does
(B) can
(C) had
(D) were

115. The employment contract states clearly that all of our employees must be in ------- with the company's confidentiality clause.

(A) comply
(B) complies
(C) compliant
(D) compliance

116. ------- about specific hygiene standards for restaurants, please contact our Public Health Center responsible for enforcing food hygiene regulations.

(A) Inquire
(B) To inquire
(C) Inquiry
(D) Inquired

117. A budget and time schedule for ------- of the new highways between two states are expected to be released next month.

(A) complete
(B) completed
(C) completion
(D) completing

118. Bella Apparel has made large donations to the local hospital for children ------- its commitment to community initiatives.

(A) as part of
(B) in place of
(C) regardless of
(D) in spite of

▶ ▶ ▶GO ON TO THE NEXT PAGE

119. According to the article, many of the complicated regulations will be ------- in efforts to help rejuvenate the auto insurance industry.

(A) eliminate
(B) eliminating
(C) eliminated
(C) elimination

120. ------- the two banking units, Ace Financial has an investment firm and three nonbank financial subsidiaries.

(A) Therefore
(B) Whichever
(C) Whereas
(D) In addition to

121. Some scientists worked on ------- the framework of the new physics theory and applied it to semiconductor manufacturing processes.

(A) imposing
(B) assisting
(C) refining
(D) revealing

122. A job application is the first impression ------- you will give your potential employer, so you should make a statement to catch the hiring manager's attention.

(A) then
(B) what
(C) when
(D) that

123. The Central Bank's decision on another interest rate cut implies its ------- to boost the economy by encouraging corporate investment.

(A) claim
(B) intent
(C) approval
(D) acquisition

124. The governmental agency provides assistance to families ------- houses are destroyed by natural disasters such as flooding and earthquake.

(A) their
(B) whenever
(C) whose
(D) which

125. If ------- by the board of directors, the relocation of Luna Steel Group to Pittsburgh will probably occur in September.

(A) approve
(B) approval
(C) approved
(D) approving

126. ------- the probationary period is completed, some of the interns will be employed full time, and the company will provide them with competitive salaries and extra benefits.

(A) While
(B) Once
(C) So that
(D) As though

127. As required by company insurance regulations, the new employees ------- physical checkups by the end of next month.

(A) had received
(B) received
(C) has received
(D) will have received

128. The local college offers German as a third foreign language, ------- is very rare in the country.

(A) it
(B) what
(C) that
(D) which

129. Because a wireless device usually relies on a small battery, ------- efficiently a microchip uses power becomes more important.

(A) how
(B) who
(C) whether
(D) when

130. ------- domestic companies rely on imported parts for the manufacture of high-tech products, they need to invest in research and development.

(A) Given that
(B) Therefore
(C) While
(D) Since

PART 6

Directions: Read the texts that follow. A word or phrase, or sentence is missing in parts of each text. Four answer choices for each question are given below the text. Select the best answer to complete the text. Then mark the letter (A), (B), (C), or (D) on your answer sheet.

Questions 131-134 refer to the following e-mail.

Dear Mr. Hopkins,

Our records show that your subscription to *World Economy Monthly* ------- on November
                                                                    131.
23. Please use the enclosed form to renew your subscription and continue to receive

------- of one of the country's most popular economic magazine.
 132.

To ensure that your service continues without interruption in the future, we also ------- you
                                                                                 133.
to register for our automatic billing program. This service is available at no extra charge to

help you make sure your bill is paid on time. -------.
                                              134.

Customers enroll in the program will be offered a 15 percent discount off the regular

subscription rate.

Act now and start saving today!

Customer Service
World Economy Monthly

131. (A) expire
     (B) will expire
     (C) has expired
     (D) will be expired

132. (A) awards
     (B) issues
     (C) benefits
     (D) aspects

133. (A) allow
     (B) reply
     (C) encourage
     (D) demonstrate

134. (A) You can change your payment and
        billing options at any time you want.
     (B) You can sign up by simply checking
        the "automatic billing" box on the
        form.
     (C) Many parents are ill-equipped to
        instruct their children in economics.
     (D) The recent customer reviews of our
        magazine have been consistently
        positive.

▶ ▶ ▶ GO ON TO THE NEXT PAGE

Oakland Telegraph
[Science & Environment Section]

Break Free From Plastic Waste - Plastic Recycling
By Jessica Holland

April 1 - People use nearly 14 billion kilograms of plastic every year, and they recycle only about 20% of it. In reality, recycled plastic can be made ------- a variety of goods, ranging
    135.
from food containers to modern furniture.

As most plastics are made from petroleum, recycling them conserve this valuable resources. In many cities and countrysides, plastic containers and beverage bottles can be returned to stores, some of ------- also accept plastic bags for reuse.
                       136.

-------. Particular types of plastic may not be accepted in certain areas. The most
 137.
commonly recycled plastics are ------- used in soft drink bottles, milk and water jugs, and
                    138.
cooking oil bottles.

135. (A) for
(B) into
(C) except
(D) throughout

136. (A) that
(B) them
(C) whom
(D) which

137. (A) You can find the closest landfill and recycling centers through the Internet.
(B) Local programs for reuse and recycling vary by region where you live.
(C) We should reduce street pollution through proper waste management.
(D) A money-back scheme for returning plastic bottles and cans has been proposed.

138. (A) we
(B) none
(C) those
(D) anyone

Blackthorn Ski Resort

Where the North Pole begins!

1 Whitehorn Rd.

Lake Louise, AB T0L 1E0, Canada

1 (877) 956-8473

Blackthorn Ski Resort is a place where anyone, no matter ------- their ability, can progress
139.

to a higher level in the sport of skiing. Enroll in one of our programs this winter and learn

from the professionals in the best snowboards and ski camp facility anywhere!

Located on Blackthorn Glacier on Mt. Hodong, we are the biggest winter ski resort in

Canada. Blackthorn Ski Resort has a staff of 60 men and women to give you the -------
140.

ski camp experience!

Many of our coaches are the same well-known skiers that you have seen ------- in
141.

magazines and televised competitions. -------. Everyone at Blackthorn Ski Resort, from
142.

the professionals to the service staff, is focused on making your ski camp experience

superb.

---

139. (A) when
(B) where
(C) how
(D) what

140. (A) selective
(B) proud
(C) ultimate
(D) necessary

141. (A) feature
(B) featured
(C) featuring
(D) being featured

142. (A) We offer great package deals,
affordable ticket prices, uncrowded
skiing and beautiful view.
(B) It is very important that you always
purchase or rent ski gear that you feel
comfortable in.
(C) Nowhere else in the world can you
find a more qualified group of expert
instructors.
(D) Find fun winter sports activities for
the slopes, trails, and ice rinks for
children of all ages.

▶ ▶ ▶GO ON TO THE NEXT PAGE

To: Kate Kiesling <katek@wonderib.com>
From: Christopher Winters <cwinters@andromeda.com>
Subject: Investment opportunity
Attachment: pamphlet.pdf

Dear Ms. Kiesling,

I obtained your name from Ms. Margaret Johnson, one of your board members.

We ------- in manufacturing liquid displays utilized for car navigations, computers, and
   143.
various control panels for home appliances.

Because of the superior quality of our semiconductors, and because of the increasing

popularity for our products in the industry, we want to seize the opportunity -------
   144.
immediately; however, in order to do so, we are asking for the help of outside investors.

I believe this is a great opportunity for a profitable investment. ------- are our pamphlets
   145.
explaining our services and the expansion plans.

-------. Please let me know when I should call to make an appointment.
146.

Very truly yours,

Christopher Winters
Chief Financial Officer, Andromeda Electronics

143. (A) commence
(B) trade
(C) develop
(D) specialize

144. (A) expand
(B) expanding
(C) expanded
(D) to expand

145. (A) Attach
(B) Attached
(C) Attaching
(D) Attachment

146. (A) You may want to meet as many
business prospects as you could.
(B) We have failed to provide
sufficient funds for developing key
technologies.
(C) I would like to discuss this exciting
offer with you early next week.
(D) Our investment will increase job
opportunities and improve living
standards.

PART 7

Directions: In this part you will read a selection of texts, such as magazine and newspaper articles, e-mails, and instant messages. Each text or set of texts is followed by several questions. Select the best answer for each question and mark the letter (A), (B), (C), or (D) on your answer sheet.

Questions 147-148 refer to the following e-mail.

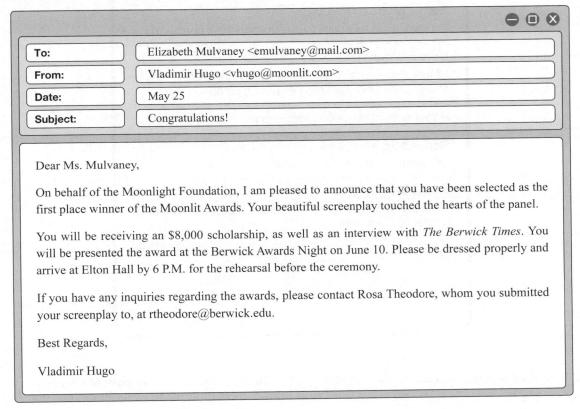

To:	Elizabeth Mulvaney <emulvaney@mail.com>
From:	Vladimir Hugo <vhugo@moonlit.com>
Date:	May 25
Subject:	Congratulations!

Dear Ms. Mulvaney,

On behalf of the Moonlight Foundation, I am pleased to announce that you have been selected as the first place winner of the Moonlit Awards. Your beautiful screenplay touched the hearts of the panel.

You will be receiving an $8,000 scholarship, as well as an interview with *The Berwick Times*. You will be presented the award at the Berwick Awards Night on June 10. Please be dressed properly and arrive at Elton Hall by 6 P.M. for the rehearsal before the ceremony.

If you have any inquiries regarding the awards, please contact Rosa Theodore, whom you submitted your screenplay to, at rtheodore@berwick.edu.

Best Regards,

Vladimir Hugo

147. Why was the e-mail sent to Ms. Mulvaney?

(A) To confirm the submission of her screenplay
(B) To announce the requirements for a competition
(C) To notify that she is an award winner
(D) To give details about the event that she will organize

148. What is NOT suggested about Ms. Mulvaney?

(A) She submitted her work to Ms. Theodore.
(B) She will be hired by the Moonlight Foundation.
(C) She will probably attend an event on June 10.
(D) She may answer some questions from a reporter.

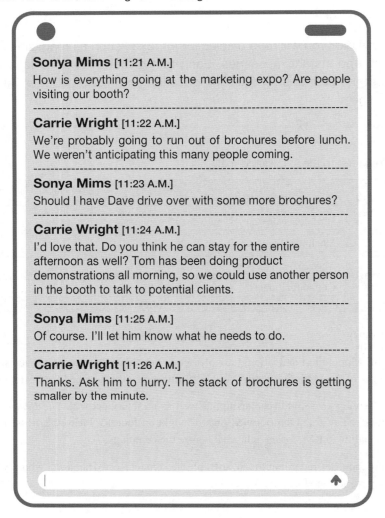

Sonya Mims [11:21 A.M.]

How is everything going at the marketing expo? Are people visiting our booth?

Carrie Wright [11:22 A.M.]

We're probably going to run out of brochures before lunch. We weren't anticipating this many people coming.

Sonya Mims [11:23 A.M.]

Should I have Dave drive over with some more brochures?

Carrie Wright [11:24 A.M.]

I'd love that. Do you think he can stay for the entire afternoon as well? Tom has been doing product demonstrations all morning, so we could use another person in the booth to talk to potential clients.

Sonya Mims [11:25 A.M.]

Of course. I'll let him know what he needs to do.

Carrie Wright [11:26 A.M.]

Thanks. Ask him to hurry. The stack of brochures is getting smaller by the minute.

149. What is suggested about the marketing expo?

(A) It is being held for the first time.
(B) It is located at the conference center.
(C) It is scheduled to end at lunchtime.
(D) It is within driving distance of Ms. Mims.

150. At 11:25 A.M., what does Ms. Mims most likely mean when she writes, "Of course"?

(A) She can drive to the expo in a few minutes.
(B) She will order more brochures to be printed.
(C) Dave can remain at the marketing expo.
(D) She approves of Tom doing demonstrations.

To: Richard Davis <rdavis@daniels.com>

From: Rachel Takashima <rtakashima@daniels.com>

Date: April 7

Subject: Congratulations

Dear Mr. Davis,

Congratulations on your promotion! I have heard about your integrity and excellent job performance when you were in the marketing department. I am very pleased to have you as a member of my team, and I look forward to working with you.

Before you officially start your duty next Wednesday, I would like you to become familiar with our tasks here in the human resources department. Our job is very different from those of other departments, so I want you to attend our weekly meeting on next Monday at 9:30 A.M. in H219.

As you already know, our company is preparing for next month's open recruitment. Therefore, your first task will be to create a formal document outlining creative ways to attract competent employees to our department. Call William Murphy (ext. 1244), who transferred to our department three weeks ahead of you, to work together on this project. Please submit the proposal no later than April 27.

Again, welcome to our team and I will see you next Monday!

Regards,

Rachel Takashima
Director, Human Resources Department

151. Why did Ms. Takashima write the e-mail?

(A) To offer a position at a company
(B) To give positive comments about an employee
(C) To give a set of instructions to an employee
(D) To announce a change in a meeting schedule

152. What can be implied about Ms. Takashima?

(A) She was recently promoted.
(B) She is newly hired.
(C) She is Mr. Davis's supervisor.
(D) She will submit a document.

153. According to the e-mail, what will Mr. Davis do soon?

(A) Confirm a schedule
(B) Recruit new employees
(C) Contact Mr. Murphy
(D) Organize an event

Open Position at Cosmo

Established in 1985, the leading publication in the industry, Cosmo, is currently recruiting a full-time editor-in-chief to contribute to its growing success in 20 different countries.

Job Description:

The editor-in-chief is in charge of the whole publication process. He or she hires assistant editors and creates an outline for each magazine edition. The editor-in-chief is also responsible for reviewing all the articles and pictures in the magazine before it is published. Another duty is to supervise budget plans for the magazine and attend meetings with publishers regularly.

Qualifications:

Candidates must have a minimum of seven years of work experience in the publication industry. A bachelor's degree is required — majors in communications/mass media are highly preferred. Communication skills are extremely important; candidates must have outstanding verbal and written communication skills. Proven leadership and managerial abilities are also necessary.

Candidates must submit an application form which is posted on our website at www.cosmo.com along with a résumé, a cover letter, two letters of reference and a portfolio of your previous publication works. Application must be submitted by mail. Send your documents to the personnel manager at the headquarters located in Edinburgh. Please contact Ms. Sandra Liang at sliang@cosmo.com for further inquiries.

154. What is mentioned about Cosmo?

(A) It is published in 20 different languages.
(B) Its main office is located in Edinburgh.
(C) It is currently looking for some editors.
(D) It is issued every month.

155. What is NOT a requirement of a candidate?

(A) An undergraduate degree of communications
(B) At least seven years of experience in the industry
(C) Good interpersonal skills
(D) Exceptional writing skills

156. What is NOT a necessary document for the application?

(A) Letters of recommendation
(B) A résumé
(C) A letter of self-introduction
(D) A list of references

To: Factory workers
From: Marcus Jacobs, CEO of HotDisplay
Date: March 12
Subject: Congratulations!

Dear all employees of HotDisplay,

As smartphones become increasingly vital in modern life, the smartphone market has been constantly expanding. Accordingly, last month, HotDisplay, a display manufacturer for cell phones, reached its highest sales volume since the establishment of the company. I would like to celebrate our monumental achievement and thank you for your contributions.

To meet the increased demand towards our displays, we will have to recruit about 100 more people. The recruitment process will commence next month. Until then, please be aware that extra work hours accompanied by extra pay will be unavoidable. If there is anyone who cannot afford to work overtime, report to your supervisor at your earliest convenience.

As the CEO, I will continuously try my best to provide an excellent working environment. I hope all of us can keep up the good work.

Thanks,

Marcus Jacobs
CEO, HotDisplay

157. What is the purpose of the memo?

(A) To recognize the recent performance of sales representatives
(B) To report on the latest economic trends
(C) To schedule an interview
(D) To announce a change in work hours

158. According to the memo, what change is being made to the factory?

(A) Its facility will be expanded.
(B) It will hire new employees.
(C) It will no longer manufacture smartphone displays.
(D) Its management will be changed.

Questions 159-161 refer to the following e-mail.

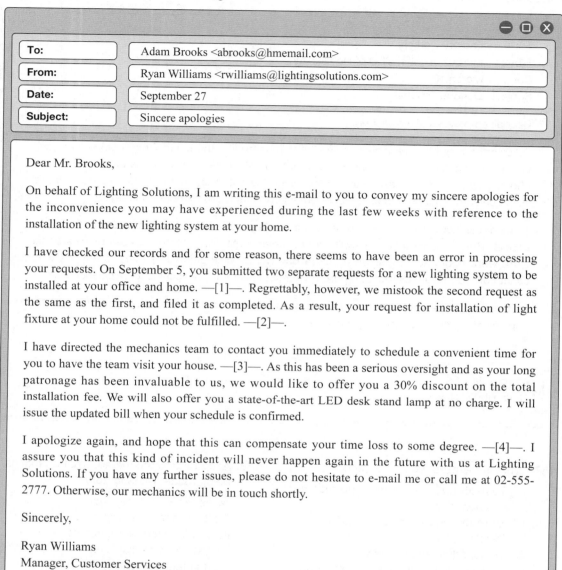

To: Adam Brooks <abrooks@hmemail.com>

From: Ryan Williams <rwilliams@lightingsolutions.com>

Date: September 27

Subject: Sincere apologies

Dear Mr. Brooks,

On behalf of Lighting Solutions, I am writing this e-mail to you to convey my sincere apologies for the inconvenience you may have experienced during the last few weeks with reference to the installation of the new lighting system at your home.

I have checked our records and for some reason, there seems to have been an error in processing your requests. On September 5, you submitted two separate requests for a new lighting system to be installed at your office and home. —[1]—. Regrettably, however, we mistook the second request as the same as the first, and filed it as completed. As a result, your request for installation of light fixture at your home could not be fulfilled. —[2]—.

I have directed the mechanics team to contact you immediately to schedule a convenient time for you to have the team visit your house. —[3]—. As this has been a serious oversight and as your long patronage has been invaluable to us, we would like to offer you a 30% discount on the total installation fee. We will also offer you a state-of-the-art LED desk stand lamp at no charge. I will issue the updated bill when your schedule is confirmed.

I apologize again, and hope that this can compensate your time loss to some degree. —[4]—. I assure you that this kind of incident will never happen again in the future with us at Lighting Solutions. If you have any further issues, please do not hesitate to e-mail me or call me at 02-555-2777. Otherwise, our mechanics will be in touch shortly.

Sincerely,

Ryan Williams
Manager, Customer Services

159. Why was the e-mail sent to Mr. Brooks?

(A) To apologize for a mechanical failure
(B) To recommend a new product
(C) To express regret for a delay in service
(D) To give an explanation for a policy change

160. What will Mr. Brooks receive as compensation?

(A) The free replacement of an ordered item
(B) A full refund
(C) A discount on his next purchase
(D) A gift

161. In which of the positions marked [1], [2], [3], and [4] does the following sentence best fit?

"We completed the delivery and installation at your workplace on September 13."

(A) [1]
(B) [2]
(C) [3]
(D) [4]

▶ ▶ ▶ GO ON TO THE NEXT PAGE

United States Wine Association
155 North Quarandell Dr.
Kearny, NJ 07030
USA

June 26

Jean Vernes
Millesima,113 Rue Albert Barraud
33000 Bordeaux, France

Dear Mr. Vernes,

On behalf of the United States Wine Association, I would like to invite you to the 4th Annual World Wine Forum. We hope you could share your insights and experiences with young winelovers in the US. Details about the event are outlined as below.

Title	The 4th World Wine Forum
Date	October 4 (Friday)
Venue	Elton Hall, the University of California
Host	The United States Wine Association
Participants	Expected around 1,000 (mostly professionals and students)

We provide all speakers round-trip airfares, a stay at a 5-star hotel, a set of wine accessories, and a $300 worth gift certificate for use at Restaurant Fearrington House, which is one of our sponsors.

If you would like to participate in the event, please contact us either by letter or e-mail at clopez@uc.edu by July 20. Thank you for your consideration in advance.

Best Regards,

Christine Lopez

162. What is the purpose of the letter?

(A) To inform about the wine culture in France
(B) To ask a lecturer to deliver a talk
(C) To give details about a registration process
(D) To advertise various types of wine

163. What will NOT be provided to the speaker at the wine forum?

(A) Complimentary air transportation
(B) Accommodation
(C) 300 dollars in cash
(D) Wine accessories

164. What is Mr. Vernes asked to do by July 20?

(A) Give a lecture
(B) Visit Restaurant Fearrington House
(C) Reply to the letter
(D) Give a written consent to be a sponsor

http://www.okanonpubliclibrary.or.us

OKANON PUBLIC LIBRARY
Frequently Asked Questions

| Library History | Library Card | Rental Policy | Donations |

What can I do with a library card?

With a library card, you can borrow books, CDs, DVDs, etc. You can also use it to access e-books, online newspapers, databases, and more. In addition, you can make a reservation for a computer in the library to create documents or surf the Internet.

How do I get a library card?

To receive a library card, an application must be completed. Also, the applicant should bring his or her personal identification card along with a photograph. The application form can be found at the customer service center where you submit the form. The library card can only be issued offline during our business hours from 9:00 A.M. to 6:00 P.M. Monday through Saturday.

How much does it cost to get a library card?

A library card is free to anyone who lives in Okanon. If you are a non-resident, the library card can be issued at a cost of $5. Also, monthly expense of $2 is charged to non-residents.

What should I do if I lose my library card?

If you lose your library card, it is very important that you report it to any staff at customer service center as soon as possible. Note that a cost of $4 will be charged to replace a lost card.

165. What is the purpose of the information?

(A) To introduce a new resident card
(B) To inform library users of how to use computers
(C) To explain about a membership
(D) To describe some changes to Okanon Public Library

166. What is NOT indicated in the information?

(A) A library card is needed to borrow a book.
(B) The library closes on Sundays.
(C) A non-resident is prohibited from using computers in the library.
(D) The library holds materials other than books.

167. What should cardholders do when they lose their library card?

(A) Pay $4 for card replacement
(B) Borrow a library card from another library member
(C) Ask for help on the library's website in order to find the lost card
(D) Complete an application form

Questions 168-171 refer to the following online chat discussion.

Cindy Murphy 11:17 A.M.

Okay, everyone. I'm glad we finally got the presentation out of the way. Overall, we did a good job.

Harold Stallings 11:18 A.M.

Have you heard anything from the people at DigiTech?

Cindy Murphy 11:20 A.M.

I spoke with Mr. Collins on his way out. He requested a meeting at his company this Friday.

Kim Thompson 11:21 A.M.

That's a good sign.

Cindy Murphy 11:22 A.M.

It sure is. Kim, I want you to accompany me because as an accountant, you know the financial details. Mr. Collins hinted that he wanted to negotiate the terms of an agreement.

Kim Thompson 11:23 A.M.

No problem. I was planning to attend the technology conference at the convention center on that day, but DigiTech is much more important.

Orlando Tenace 11:25 A.M.

I can go in your place, Kim. Is that all right, Cindy?

Harold Stallings 11:26 A.M.

I'm attending as well. We can ride together in my car if you want, Orlando.

Cindy Murphy 11:30 A.M.

Be my guest. That's fine with me.

Orlando Tenace 11:31 A.M.

Thanks, Cindy and Harold.

Cindy Murphy 11:32 A.M.

Oh, Harold, I need your notes from the presentation. I need to go over them to make sure I understand everything about the project. Can you bring them to my office before lunch, please?

SEND

168. Who most likely is Mr. Collins?

(A) An accountant
(B) A speaker at a conference
(C) A colleague of the writers
(D) An employee at DigiTech

169. What will Ms. Thompson do on Friday?

(A) Demonstrate how a product works
(B) Go to a technology conference
(C) Attend a meeting at DigiTech
(D) Prepare for a new presentation

170. What will Mr. Stallings probably do next?

(A) Make a visit to the convention center
(B) Provide Ms. Murphy with some documents
(C) Have lunch with Mr. Murphy
(D) Print some documents for a presentation

171. At 11:21 A.M., what does Ms. Thompson most likely suggest when she writes, "That's a good sign"?

(A) She believes the presentation went well.
(B) She likes the terms of the contract.
(C) She approves of a new advertisement.
(D) She is willing to work overtime tonight.

READ BEFORE USING:
Café Viva I-20

Thank you for purchasing the Café Viva I-20. This wonderful coffee maker, which won the Simmons' Best Product Design Award last month, is the best way to have excellent coffee at home. —[1]—. This new model, which hardly takes any counter space, will satisfy your senses.

Instructions

1. Turn on the Café Viva I-20 and wait for the green light on the left to blink.
2. Pull out the capsule tray and drop in one of your favorite flavors. —[2]—.
3. Lock the capsule in and place your cup underneath.
4. Press the BREW button.
   • Hot, pressurized water will be forced through the capsule and begin filling your cup. —[3]—.
5. Enjoy your cup of coffee ready with a rich layer of cream.
   • Please take out the used capsule after it cools down completely. —[4]—.

Flavors

Café Viva provides 10 different flavors of coffee capsules. Visit our website at www.cafeviva.com to explore a variety of coffee and milk capsules.

172. For whom is the information most likely intended?

(A) Café owners
(B) Customers
(C) Technicians
(D) Coffee bean suppliers

173. How can a customer purchase different kinds of coffee capsules?

(A) By signing up for delivery
(B) By calling a customer service center
(C) By going to a local dealership
(D) By visiting a website

174. What can be inferred from the information?

(A) Coffee capsules can be hot right after brewing.
(B) Another model of the coffee maker will soon be released.
(C) Coffee cups are included in the package.
(D) Steam is a sign that the machine is malfunctioning.

175. In which of the positions marked [1], [2], [3], and [4] does the following sentence best fit?

"Please be aware that this may create steam."

(A) [1]
(B) [2]
(C) [3]
(D) [4]

To: Courses Online <customersupport@coursesonline.com>

From: Barbara Sand <bsand@imail.com>

Date: April 19

Subject: Mobile App Payment Issue

To whom it may concern,

On April 16, I visited the website of Courses Online and discovered that you are now offering educational courses that I can view on my mobile phone. The advertisement also stated that users who are using the mobile course application for the first time will get a 50% off discount coupon. So I tried to purchase Food and Nutrition course (NF4017) with the discount coupon, but the code was repeatedly rejected on the payment page. Is this some kind of an error? I hope to use the discount coupon on this course since it is $80, which is a bit more expensive than other courses.

Instead, I bought Extreme Home Workout course (XW2551) for $60. However, I cannot watch the videos on my mobile phone and they did not appear on the list of purchased courses on the My Classrooms page of the application. My credit card bill clearly states that I have paid for the course. Please correct these errors as soon as possible.

Thank you,

Barbara Sand

To: Barbara Sand <bsand@imail.com>

From: Leonard Wich <lwich@coursesonline.com>

Date: April 20

Subject: re: Mobile App Payment Issue

Dear Ms. Sand,

This is in response to your inquiry dated April 19. The discount coupon you have attained is for first-time users on the entire Courses Online service, not just the mobile course application. Therefore, you would not have been able to use it on course number NF4017. We apologize for the confusion caused by the lack of clarity.

You also indicated that you are unable to access the course you purchased. Our app has been recently updated to solve the network traffic issues, and it seems that unexpected errors occurred in the process. All bugs in the system have now been adjusted, and you should now be able to access it. To apologize for the inconvenience we may have caused you, we have added $10 in reward points into your Courses Online account. You can check the points in My Wallet tab, located on the top right-hand corner of the website. This can be used towards purchasing any online lectures or e-books in the future.

If you experience any other issues, please report to us. Your feedback is very valuable to us.

Yours sincerely,

Leonard Wich
Manager, Courses Online

176. Why did Ms. Sand write the first e-mail?

(A) To report a problem
(B) To request cancellation of an order
(C) To explain the causes of a problem
(D) To apply for a new online course

177. How much did Ms. Sand pay for XW2551?

(A) $30
(B) $40
(C) $60
(D) $80

178. What is suggested about Courses Online?

(A) It recently developed a new type of service.
(B) It is currently experiencing a technical difficulty.
(C) It regularly updates its application.
(D) It limits the number of courses a customer can watch at a time.

179. What is NOT indicated about Ms. Sand?

(A) She paid with her credit card for her mobile educational course.
(B) She is probably concerned about health.
(C) She is dissatisfied with the contents of an online course.
(D) She has used services at Courses Online in the past.

180. What has been given to Ms. Sand?

(A) A reimbursement
(B) A free software
(C) Credit
(D) E-books

Bennington Herald

Bennington, Vermont

Wednesday, April 13

JOB OPENINGS: ALLIGATOR E&C

Alligator E&C is seeking additional site workers for the upcoming construction of a community center in Bennington, VT. Below are the descriptions of positions we are recruiting:

- **Electricians**

  An electrician's key role is to install and maintain wiring, fuses, and other electrical components. This position requires a valid electrical certification and minimum of one-year experience. Salary varies from $700 to $800 per week.

- **Plumbers**

  A plumber mainly installs and repairs water supply lines and waste disposal systems. This position requires a valid plumbing certification and minimum of two-year experience. Salary varies from $900 to $1,000 per week.

- **Concrete Mixer Truck Drivers**

  A concrete mixer's job includes delivering concrete mix to work sites, assembling the cement chute and cleaning the truck. This position requires a valid commercial driver's license and minimum of one-year experience. Note that drivers may be called to work on weekends. Salary varies from $650 to $750 per week.

- **Benefits**

  We have a flexible sick leave and paid holiday policy. A comprehensive medical coverage will be given to all of our office/on-site workers.

Contact Mr. Daniel Craig via e-mail at dcraig@aenc.com or call 207-360-9913 by April 30.

Bennington Daily

Around the Town

Bennington (June 1) – Alligator E&C, a local construction company, started building a new community center in Bennington last week. "Since I relocated the business from New York to Bennington ten years ago, its profit has been increasing rapidly. Last year, we even recorded the highest annual profits in the last decade. To express my deepest appreciation, I decided to contribute to the community by building a new facility and recruiting employees mainly from the region," said John Webber, the CEO of the company, about his intentions.

Alison Diamond, the mayor of Bennington, promptly welcomed the project. "I would like to thank Alligator E&C, especially for the recruitment decision. This will largely alleviate the chronic unemployment problem in the city," said Ms. Diamond.

Workers at the construction site are also pleased. "It was very lucky for me to have read about Alligator E&C's job posting in *Bennington Herald* two months ago. Although I am sometimes required to work on weekends, I am happy that I can contribute to my hometown," expressed Jake Clifferland, a newly employed worker of Alligator E&C.

The new community center will provide various facilities and programs. It will have a fitness center, a number of seminar rooms and multipurpose halls for people to use freely at a nominal charge. The construction is expected to take a year. For more information about the community center or Alligator E&C, visit www.aenc.com.

by Veena Khan

181. What is a qualification that all three positions in the advertisement require?

(A) Outstanding leadership skills
(B) A driver's license for commercial use
(C) An academic degree
(D) Previous involvement in the related field

182. What is NOT suggested about Alligator E&C?

(A) It recently recruited temporary workers for a project in New York.
(B) It provides full health insurance to its employees.
(C) It first started the business somewhere else than Bennington.
(D) It witnessed the highest profits in the last 10 years.

183. What is indicated about Mr. Clifferland?

(A) He repairs water supply lines.
(B) He moved to Bennington because of his new job.
(C) He works only on weekends.
(D) He transports concrete mix.

184. What can be inferred about Bennington?

(A) Its new mayor was recently elected.
(B) It is suffering a low employment rate.
(C) It has only one community center.
(D) It provides various benefits to new businesses.

185. What is NOT true about the community center?

(A) It will be open to the public for free.
(B) It will have a facility for exercise.
(C) It is expected to open to the public in about a year.
(D) It is being constructed by Alligator E&C to show its appreciation to the community.

To: Monica Vey, Lucy Hall
From: Roger Freeman
Date: December 19
Subject: Interview

We will be conducting the second round of interviews for those employees who applied to transfer to the open position in our department. Here are the names of the finalists along with their interview times. All interviews will take place on December 22.

Eric Marston – 10:00 A.M.
Maria Simon – 11:00 A.M.
Thaddeus Bean – 1:00 P.M.

All three of us will be interviewing the candidates a second time. Please be sure that your schedules are open at these times.

Tenn Design, Inc.

To: All employees, Design Department
From: Roger Freeman
Date: Thursday, January 8
Subject: A new face

Everyone,

I'm pleased to let you know that Maria Simon, an employee currently in the Accounting Department, will be transferring to our department next Monday.

Ms. Simon started working as an accountant at our company after she received her bachelor's degree in accounting at Bashkir University in Ufa. However, she has always been interested in design, so working part time, she attended graduate school at her old university. After earning her master's degree in graphic design, Ms. Simon applied to transfer to our department, and her application was just approved.

I'm sure many of you have seen Ms. Simon in the building, but I still encourage all of you to welcome her to the team. We'll be holding a welcome lunch for her following our weekly meeting, so please make sure that you all can attend. We'll be going out to eat at Morrison's on that day.

To:	Maria Simon <msimon@tenndesign.com>
From:	Roger Freeman <rfreeman@tenndesign.com>
Date:	January 9, Friday
Subject:	Welcome!

Dear Ms. Simon,

I'm happy to hear you'll be joining us here in the Design Department. I am sure you will like the work environment here.

You should know that we hold a departmental meeting each Wednesday at 11:00. You'll be expected to attend it. You will also need to attend a short training session that I'll be leading next Friday at 10:00 A.M.

I assume you won't need a tour of the building since you've been here for a couple of years. But if you need any help getting settled in to the department, let me know.

Sincerely,

Roger Freeman

186. What most likely is true about Ms. Vey and Ms. Hall?

(A) They will go on a business trip on December 22.
(B) They are good friends with Mr. Freeman.
(C) They are part-time employees.
(D) They work in the same department.

187. What is the purpose of the second memo?

(A) To acknowledge an employee's sales performance
(B) To announce a job opening at a company
(C) To profile a new employee
(D) To provide information about a design project

188. What is mentioned about Ms. Simon?

(A) She went to school and worked at the same time.
(B) She studied design as an undergraduate student.
(C) She is currently attending graduate school.
(D) She applied for a management position at her company.

189. When will Ms. Simon have lunch with her coworkers?

(A) On Monday
(B) On Tuesday
(C) On Wednesday
(D) On Friday

190. What does Mr. Freeman request that Ms. Simon do?

(A) Introduce herself to her new colleagues
(B) Take part in an educational course
(C) Show him some of her design work
(D) Familiarize herself with a building

▶ ▶ ▶ GO ON TO THE NEXT PAGE

The fifteenth annual

PORTLAND TRADE FAIR

will be held at the Duncan Convention Center
from 9:00 A.M. to 8:00 P.M. on March 10 and 11

More than 350 domestic and foreign companies involved in
the following industries will be attending:

medicine
manufacturing
logistics
software
shipbuilding

Attendance is free, but you must register in advance at
www.portlandtradefair.org/registration

For more information, visit our web page at
www.portlandtradefair.org

To:	Emily Rose <emily_r@watsontech.com>
From:	Hank Gathers <hankgathers@smm.com>
Date:	March 13
Subject:	Hello

Dear Ms. Rose,

Hello. This is Hank Gathers. I met you on the second day of the Portland Trade Fair earlier this week. It was a real pleasure speaking with you and learning about the products your company makes. I truly appreciate the fact that you took the time to speak to me individually even though you were quite busy.

I wonder if you are available to meet on March 21. I'm going to be in Seattle then, so I could visit your office anytime on that day. I'd like more information about the new appliances you spoke with me about. Are you able to negotiate on behalf of your firm? If not, could you make sure who will be in attendance at our meeting? Finally, does your firm offer discounts for bulk purchases?

I look forward to hearing from you.

Regards,

Hank Gathers
SMM, Inc.

To:	Hank Gathers <hankgathers@smm.com>
From:	Emily Rose <emily_r@watsontech.com>
Date:	March 14
Subject:	Re: Hello

Dear Mr. Gathers,

Thank you for your e-mail. It was also a pleasure to meet you at the trade fair. You asked insightful questions, and I learned a lot about your company.

I will be available in the morning on March 21, so how about meeting in my office at 9:00 A.M.? I have to head to the airport to go on a business trip at noon, so the earlier we meet, the better. I'll demonstrate all of the new appliances we have so that you can see exactly how they run. My boss, Howard Carter, will be in attendance as well. He can talk about the terms of any deals that you wish to make with us.

See you next week.

Regards,

Emily Rose

---

191. In the announcement, what is indicated about the Portland Trade Fair?

(A) It will take place over the course of two days.
(B) It only features companies from the Portland area.
(C) It is being held for the first time.
(D) It is expecting more visitors than ever before.

192. Why did Mr. Gathers write the e-mail?

(A) To request some brochures
(B) To apply for an open position
(C) To inquire about meeting in person
(D) To reconfirm the date of a meeting

193. When did Mr. Gathers meet Ms. Rose?

(A) On March 10
(B) On March 11
(C) On March 12
(D) On March 13

194. What will Ms. Rose do on March 21?

(A) Make a speech
(B) Attend a trade fair
(C) Take an airplane
(D) Interview a job candidate

195. Which concern of Mr. Gathers does Ms. Rose NOT address?

(A) Whether he can get reduced prices
(B) Who can negotiate terms of a deal
(C) When he can meet with her
(D) What kind of information he can get

Attention, residents of Beachside Apartments. Due to the flooding caused by the recent storm, Gravel Road and the sidewalk on the road's northern side suffered extensive damage. A work crew from Hampton Construction will be repairing the road and the sidewalk starting tomorrow, April 10. The roadwork is expected to be completed on April 17. The stretch of Gravel Road by the front entrance to the apartment complex will be closed during this entire time. Residents and visitors should therefore use the rear entrance on Pleasant Street. We apologize in advance for any excessive noise caused by the repair work.

To: Jeff Deacon, Beachside Apartments Manager
From: Carol Cross, Beachside Apartments Receptionist
Date: April 9
Time: 4:55 P.M.

Roberta Hall at the mayor's office just called. She mentioned that the repairs to the road and the sidewalk will begin tomorrow. The work is going to be done by Bowman Construction. She said that construction is going to begin at 7:00 A.M. each day and will continue until 7:00 P.M. She remarked that the mayor hopes the long workday will enable the crew to complete its work faster, which will be more convenient for the residents. She said she hopes you will let the residents know this information.

Gravel Road Opens Again

by staff reporter David Carlyle

Haven (April 20) – Three weeks after heavy thunderstorms caused flashfloods throughout Haven, the city is still undergoing repairs to fix the damage caused. Several roads in the city remain in poor condition.

However, Gravel Road, which runs adjacent to the coast, isn't one of them. A road repair crew worked tirelessly for more than a week to fix the street, and they just completed their work yesterday. "Gravel Road is crucial to transportation in Haven, so I'm pleased that vehicles can drive on it again," Mayor Glenn Goodway said. "Now, we just need to get those other roads fixed, and then life can get back to normal."

The mayor stressed that the city has a sufficient amount of money to pay for the repairs. Mr. Goodway noted that Haven has emergency funds it can draw on in case of natural disasters like the one the city endured.

196. What is the purpose of the notice?

(A) To advise tenants of construction work
(B) To respond to repeated requests
(C) To explain why the entrances are closed
(D) To ask residents to make donations

197. What information in the notice is different in the telephone message?

(A) The date work will start
(B) The company doing the work
(C) The time work will begin
(D) The cost of the work

198. Why did Ms. Hall leave a message?

(A) To explain a problem
(B) To respond to Mr. Deacon's request
(C) To ask for some advice
(D) To provide updated information

199. What does Mr. Goodway state about the roads in Haven?

(A) They are currently being widened.
(B) All of them have been paved.
(C) There are some still underwater.
(D) Some of them are not repaired.

200. What is indicated about the repair work done on Gravel Road?

(A) It was completed behind schedule.
(B) It cost too much money.
(C) It was done by two construction companies.
(D) It was paid for from private funds.

STOP! This is the end of the test. If you finish before time is called, you may go back to Parts 5, 6, and 7 and check your work.

Actual Test 09

MP3   해설집

적정 풀이 시간 120분

120 min

시작 시간 ___시 ___분

종료 시간 ___시 ___분

중간에 멈추지 말고 처음부터 끝까지 풀어보세요.
문제를 풀 때에는 실전처럼 답안지에 마킹하세요.

목표 개수 _____ / 200   실제 개수 _____ / 200

예상 점수는 번역 및 정답에 있는 점수 환산표를 참조하세요.

LISTENING TEST

In the Listening test, you will be asked to demonstrate how well you understand spoken English. The entire Listening test will last approximately 45 minutes. There are four parts, and directions are given for each part. You must mark your answers on the separate answer sheet. Do not write your answers in the test book.

PART 1

Directions: For each question in this part, you will hear four statements about a picture in your test book. When you hear the statements, you must select the one statement that best describes what you see in the picture. Then find the number of the question on your answer sheet and mark your answer. The statements will not be printed in your test book and will be spoken only one time.

Statement (B), "They are sitting at a table." is the best description of the picture. So you should select answer (B) and mark it on your answer sheet.

1.

2.

▶ ▶ ▶ GO ON TO THE NEXT PAGE

3.

4.

5.

6.

▶ ▶ ▶GO ON TO THE NEXT PAGE

PART 2

Directions: You will hear a question or statement and three responses spoken in English. They will not be printed in your test book and will be spoken only one time. Select the best response to the question or statement and mark the letter (A), (B), or (C) on your answer sheet.

7. Mark your answer on your answer sheet.

8. Mark your answer on your answer sheet.

9. Mark your answer on your answer sheet.

10. Mark your answer on your answer sheet.

11. Mark your answer on your answer sheet.

12. Mark your answer on your answer sheet.

13. Mark your answer on your answer sheet.

14. Mark your answer on your answer sheet.

15. Mark your answer on your answer sheet.

16. Mark your answer on your answer sheet.

17. Mark your answer on your answer sheet.

18. Mark your answer on your answer sheet.

19. Mark your answer on your answer sheet.

20. Mark your answer on your answer sheet.

21. Mark your answer on your answer sheet.

22. Mark your answer on your answer sheet.

23. Mark your answer on your answer sheet.

24. Mark your answer on your answer sheet.

25. Mark your answer on your answer sheet.

26. Mark your answer on your answer sheet.

27. Mark your answer on your answer sheet.

28. Mark your answer on your answer sheet.

29. Mark your answer on your answer sheet.

30. Mark your answer on your answer sheet.

31. Mark your answer on your answer sheet.

PART 3

Directions: You will hear some conversations between two or three people. You will be asked to answer three questions about what the speakers say in each conversation. Select the best response to each question and mark the letter (A), (B), (C), or (D) on your answer sheet. The conversations will not be printed in your test book and will be spoken only one time.

32. Where does the woman work?

(A) At a community center
(B) At a sporting goods store
(C) At an athletic facility
(D) At a supermarket

33. What does the man ask about?

(A) Prices
(B) Operating hours
(C) Employment opportunities
(D) Parking fees

34. What should the man do to receive a bonus gift?

(A) Show a coupon
(B) Purchase a subscription
(C) Post a review online
(D) Register before a deadline

35. Who most likely is the man?

(A) A store owner
(B) A travel agent
(C) An airline agent
(D) A hotel clerk

36. What service does the airport now offer?

(A) Foreign currency exchange
(B) Passenger lounges
(C) A shuttle service
(D) Local tours

37. What does the man ask the woman about?

(A) Why she is visiting the city
(B) How long she will be at the airport
(C) What she wants to see
(D) Which hotel she is staying at

38. Where do the speakers most likely work?

(A) At a shopping center
(B) At an interior design firm
(C) At a theater
(D) At a furniture store

39. What problem are the speakers discussing?

(A) A light is not working.
(B) A carpet keeps moving.
(C) It costs a lot to build a stage set.
(D) Some stairs are too steep.

40. What will the woman do next?

(A) Clean up a stage
(B) Replace some materials
(C) Call a repairperson
(D) Check a storage area

41. Why does the man say, "There were about two hundred people in attendance"?

(A) To mention that many tickets were sold
(B) To express his disappointment
(C) To indicate that they needed a larger conference room
(D) To indicate that an event was a success

42. What does the man say he is considering?

(A) Building some more robots
(B) Doing some more research for an article
(C) Designing a new type of robot
(D) Writing an article for publication

43. What does the woman offer to do?

(A) Proofread the man's article
(B) Contact an acquaintance
(C) Collaborate with the man
(D) Confirm a date for a meeting

▶ ▶ ▶ GO ON TO THE NEXT PAGE

44. What event are the speakers discussing?

(A) An employee running competition
(B) A company's health day
(C) An outdoor picnic
(D) An orientation session

45. According to the woman, what does the woman want to do differently from last year?

(A) Shorten an event schedule
(B) Provide food and drinks for attendees
(C) Have more fitness centers participate in the event
(D) Have more classes

46. What kind of gift does the woman plan to give away?

(A) Posters
(B) Notebooks
(C) Ballcaps
(D) T-shirts

47. What department does the man work in?

(A) Personnel
(B) Security office
(C) Maintenance
(D) Technical Support

48. Why does the woman say, "Are you sure you've come to the right place?"

(A) She is not expecting a delivery.
(B) She does not have any time now.
(C) She did not request assistance.
(D) She wants to get more specific directions.

49. What will the man probably do next?

(A) Return to his office
(B) Take a look at some equipment
(C) Call the Tech Department
(D) Repair a desktop computer

50. What kind of company do the speakers most likely work at?

(A) A food manufacturer
(B) A biochemical company
(C) A textile manufacturer
(D) A recycling company

51. What is the man's concern?

(A) An advertisement is not appealing.
(B) An item might become more costly.
(C) An item will become less popular.
(D) Some eco-friendly material is unavailable.

52. What do the speakers agree to do?

(A) Seek feedback from customers
(B) Create a new advertisement
(C) Speak with their supervisor
(D) Show customers around the factory

53. What are the speakers discussing?

(A) Wiring money overseas
(B) Withdrawing money from a cash machine
(C) Buying a train ticket
(D) Opening a corporate bank account

54. What are the speakers looking at?

(A) A boarding pass
(B) A smartphone
(C) A laptop
(D) A banking brochure

55. What information will the woman request?

(A) An e-mail address
(B) A street address
(C) A bank account number
(D) A telephone number

56. What position is the woman applying for?

(A) Computer programmer
(B) Sales associate
(C) Department supervisor
(D) Interior designer

57. What skill does the woman think is the most important?

(A) Departmental teamwork
(B) Work efficiency
(C) Budget management
(D) Communication

58. According to the man, what is the woman required to do?

(A) Train new employees
(B) Travel abroad frequently
(C) Use software programs
(D) Appraise staff members

59. What are the speakers mainly talking about?

(A) Removing a heater from the office
(B) Moving to a different location
(C) Adjusting the temperature in the office
(D) Fixing some broken machinery

60. What is the man concerned about?

(A) The office doors may be locked.
(B) The cost of electricity would be up.
(C) Heaters might be out of stock.
(D) Some pipes could get damaged.

61. What does the man say he will do?

(A) Contact the Maintenance Department
(B) Complete the repair request
(C) Prepare an energy-saving manual
(D) Work during the holiday

Annual Restaurant Festival

Restaurant	Cuisine	Location
Golden Dragon	Chinese	Tent 1
La Hasienda	Mexican	Tent 2
Firenze	Italian	Tent 3
Rio Delights	Brazilian	Tent 4

62. According to the woman, what are the speakers planning to do if it rains?

(A) Postpone the event until later
(B) Move ticket sales inside
(C) Provide visitors with umbrellas
(D) Have the event take place indoors

63. Look at the graphic. Which tent will be removed?

(A) Tent 1
(B) Tent 2
(C) Tent 3
(D) Tent 4

64. What will the woman ask a TV station to do?

(A) Announce a food contest
(B) Replay a commercial
(C) Make a donation
(D) Announce participating businesses

▶ ▶ ▶ GO ON TO THE NEXT PAGE

Today's Appointments

11:00 A.M.	Lucy Baldwin
12:00 P.M.	Irene West
1:00 P.M.	
2:00 P.M.	David Chun
3:00 P.M.	
4:00 P.M.	Jackie Reynolds
5:00 P.M.	
6:00 P.M.	Russ Powers

Time Sheet

Date	Code	Hours
November 11	None ▼	7
November 12	Sickness – 1	7
November 13	Personal Day – 2	7
November 14	Bad Weather – 3	7
	Holiday – 4	7

65. Where does the man work?

(A) At a newspaper
(B) At a doctor's office
(C) At a hair salon
(D) At a dental clinic

66. What problem has happened to the woman?

(A) Her car has a flat tire.
(B) She has to attend a meeting.
(C) Her car is not running.
(D) Her computer is broken.

67. Look at the graphic. What time will the woman's new appointment most likely be?

(A) 11:00 A.M.
(B) 1:00 P.M.
(C) 3:00 P.M.
(D) 5:00 P.M.

68. Where do the speakers work?

(A) At a catering service
(B) At a university
(C) At a library
(D) At a law firm

69. What most likely is the woman's job?

(A) Researcher
(B) Attorney
(C) Librarian
(D) Instructor

70. Look at the graphic. Which code should the woman select?

(A) Code 1
(B) Code 2
(C) Code 3
(D) Code 4

PART 4

Directions: You will hear some short talks given by a single speaker. You will be asked to answer three questions about what the speaker says in each short talk. Select the best response to each question and mark the letter (A), (B), (C), or (D) on your answer sheet. The talks will not be printed in your test book and will be spoken only one time.

71. What kind of event is being promoted?

(A) A career fair
(B) A marketing seminar
(C) A hotel anniversary
(D) A sales conference

72. What does the speaker say will be available this year?

(A) Online registration
(B) An information booth
(C) A catered lunch
(D) A complimentary shuttle

73. What are the listeners likely to do on a website?

(A) Read some feedback
(B) Enter a contest
(C) Register for an event
(D) Make a payment

74. What have the listeners decided to volunteer to do?

(A) Make tour brochures
(B) Clean artifacts of the museum
(C) Do research
(D) Guide tours

75. According to the speaker, what are the listeners supposed to do?

(A) Speak in a polite manner
(B) Arrive earlier than the scheduled time
(C) Distribute some promotional flyers
(D) Wear specific uniforms

76. What does the speaker say is available to the listeners?

(A) Free refreshments
(B) A discount at the souvenir shop
(C) A locker for personal use
(D) A free ticket to another museum

77. Who is this talk directed at?

(A) Restaurant workers
(B) Government inspectors
(C) Food critics
(D) Festival attendees

78. What is being discussed in the talk?

(A) Shipping schedules
(B) Packaging for beverages
(C) Recycling regulations
(D) Safety inspection

79. What does the speaker mean when she says, "I'm here every day"?

(A) She is aware of a scheduling conflict.
(B) She is the owner of the establishment.
(C) She agrees with the listeners' options.
(D) She can help the listeners.

80. What type of business is Kelvin Incorporated?

(A) An automobile maker
(B) A computer manufacturer
(C) A book publisher
(D) A pharmaceutical company

81. What has Kelvin Incorporated recently done?

(A) It has installed some new machines in the factory.
(B) It has introduced a new line of products.
(C) It has moved to a new plant.
(D) It has run some advertisements in the paper.

82. How has Kelvin Incorporated helped the community?

(A) By helping fund a local museum
(B) By donating money to renovate a school library
(C) By sponsoring a local sports team
(D) By donating equipment to schools

▶ ▶ ▶ GO ON TO THE NEXT PAGE

83. What is the speaker mainly discussing?

(A) A business competitor
(B) A new line of smartphone
(C) A job opening for sales staff
(D) A new budget for Information
     Technology

84. What type of company does the speaker most likely work for?

(A) An advertising agency
(B) A telephone service provider
(C) A computer repair firm
(D) A supplier for electronics

85. What will Pierre do now?

(A) Answer some questions
(B) Pass out some documents
(C) Show some slides
(D) Give a presentation

---

86. What topic is being discussed at today's show?

(A) Finding a furnished apartment
(B) Renovating a kitchen
(C) Choosing home furniture
(D) Tips for house relocation

87. What does the speaker recommend doing?

(A) Checking a furniture catalog
(B) Looking for low prices at stores
(C) Using multifunctional items
(D) Hiring a qualified designer

88. What does the speaker imply when she says, "There are plenty of companies out there you could choose from"?

(A) Affordable options are available.
(B) She can recommend the best
     companies.
(C) Some information is not accurate
     enough.
(D) A decision will be hard to make.

89. Who most likely are the listeners?

(A) Home owners
(B) Realtors
(C) Potential investors
(D) Landscaping crews

90. What will Mr. Howell talk about?

(A) Finding new customers
(B) Creating sales objectives
(C) Developing attractive advertisements
(D) Negotiating a business deal

91. What will the speaker do next?

(A) Distribute presentation materials
(B) Divide attendees into groups
(C) Show some photos
(D) Pass out some forms

---

92. What has been rescheduled?

(A) A software upgrade
(B) A training course
(C) A factory tour for clients
(D) A governmental safety inspection

93. What does the speaker imply when she says, "He's sending me a new version this weekend"?

(A) Some mistakes have been confirmed.
(B) A notice about some changes should
     be posted.
(C) She has asked for enough copies for
     everyone
(D) She had expected a faster reply.

94. What does the speaker say about Lucinda Lighting?

(A) It installed new production lines.
(B) It is relocating to another city.
(C) It requested some new
     advertisements.
(D) It has placed an order for a prototype.

OFFICE SUPPLY WAREHOUSE	
Wimberly Chair: $220 Rating: ★★★★	**Overton Chair:** $180 Rating: ★★★
Kline Chair: $160 Rating: ★★★★	**Lincoln Chair:** $120 Rating: ★

Monthly Pricing Plans

Bronze	$60
Silver	$90
Gold	$110
Platinum	$150

95. What problem does the speaker mention?

(A) A staff meeting has been canceled.
(B) A budget has been reduced lately.
(C) A shipment of office chairs are expected today.
(D) An order was submitted on time.

96. Look at the graphic. Which chair model does the speaker suggest buying?

(A) Wimberly Chair
(B) Overton Chair
(C) Kline Chair
(D) Lincoln Chair

97. What is the listener asked to do?

(A) Fill an order for 5 conference tables
(B) Get feedback from some colleagues
(C) Speak with the board of directors
(D) Find a way to raise more money

98. Who is the intended audience for the advertisement?

(A) Website designers
(B) The owners of small businesses
(C) Venture capitalists
(D) Computer programmers

99. What popular feature is being mentioned?

(A) Payment processing
(B) Automatic updates for software
(C) Inventory tracking
(D) Payment in installments

100. Look at the graphic. For which plan can listeners get one month free?

(A) Bronze
(B) Silver
(C) Gold
(D) Platinum

This is the end of the Listening test. Turn to Part 5 in your test book.

▶ ▶ ▶GO ON TO THE NEXT PAGE

READING TEST

In the Reading test, you will read a variety of texts and answer several different types of reading comprehension questions. The entire Reading test will last 75 minutes. There are three parts, and directions are given for each part. You are encouraged to answer as many questions as possible within the time allowed.

You must mark your answer on the separate answer sheet. Do not write your answers in your test book.

PART 5

Directions: A word or phrase is missing in each of the sentences below. Four answer choices are given below each sentence. Select the best answer to complete the sentence. Then mark the letter (A), (B), (C), or (D) on your answer sheet.

101. Ms. Baker established ------- as one of the most competent physicians in the country as she published three papers in *Medical World* last year alone.

(A) she
(B) her
(C) hers
(D) herself

102. If we hire two more house lawyers on staff, our office will reach its -------.

(A) routine
(B) capacity
(C) expansion
(D) abundance

103. The guest house has been renovated to a high standard in order to ------- modern day living while retaining its traditional features and charm.

(A) accommodate
(B) accommodates
(C) accommodation
(D) accommodating

104. Our company would like to upgrade your shipping option to next-day delivery at no extra ------- to you.

(A) cash
(B) charge
(C) interest
(D) price

105. To reduce the rate of financial fraud crimes, the government should reorganize all judicial procedures as ------- as possible.

(A) complete
(B) completed
(C) completion
(D) completely

106. Under the revised law, every customer should pay a special sales tax ------- all alcoholic beverages and tobacco products.

(A) on
(B) with
(C) by
(D) at

107. The Jia Gallery is ------- to hold exhibitions presenting four innovative local painters who currently produce modern art.

(A) upcoming
(B) recognized
(C) memorable
(D) honored

108. According to ------- reports, BK TV will buy out the AT Cable Company for a record price, making it the largest buyout in media history.

(A) confirmed
(B) confirming
(C) confirms
(D) confirmation

109. Please ------- that when the office renovations begin next Tuesday, we will not have access to the second floor for at least a week.

(A) advisable
(B) advised
(C) be advised
(D) have advised

110. Some major petroleum companies have been trying to gain access to the rights ------- crude oil in the oil fields in South America.

(A) produce
(B) production
(C) being produced
(D) to produce

111. ------- our recently launched accounting software, we offered one hundred copies of the complete versions to local accounting firms in the area.

(A) To promote
(B) Promotion
(C) After promoting
(D) For the promotion

112. Almost all local business owners responding to our survey are showing an interest in joint ventures with ------- companies.

(A) each other
(B) the others
(C) other
(D) another

113. Mimi Sports is committed to producing different types of fashionable sneakers and business casual shoes that ------- wants to wear.

(A) whoever
(B) everyone
(C) anywhere
(D) one another

114. *The Hayward Chronicle* has been awarded its highest ------- in the survey measuring the customer satisfaction levels.

(A) reliance
(B) altitude
(C) priority
(D) rating

115. Our company recently announced ------- Mr. Caine will be taking over as the chief financial officer at the end of the year.

(A) what
(B) because
(C) that
(D) while

116. ------- nervous did she get when she entered the conference room that she could hardly talk.

(A) So
(B) Very
(C) Too
(D) Quite

117. wawajamietravel.com is one of the leading online travel agencies that provides great travel packages at the most ------- prices.

(A) steep
(B) rising
(C) stringent
(D) affordable

118. Due to numerous requests, the ------- deadline for the submission of the revised annual marketing report is December 10.

(A) extend
(B) extension
(C) extensive
(D) extended

119. Coco Films has a vacancy for a(n) ------- accountant to manage the full accounting functions of the best movie production company in the country.

(A) optimal
(B) absolute
(C) experienced
(D) comparable

120. Century 48 Auto Insurance takes steps to ensure that all of the transaction records provided by our agents are kept ------- at all times.

(A) secure
(B) security
(C) securely
(D) secured

121. All information regarding health insurance and safety regulations will be posted ------- the Human Resources entrance.

(A) off
(B) for
(C) within
(D) beside

122. The economic situation of the region was so ------- that most multinational businesses started to shut down their branch offices.

(A) discourage
(B) discouraging
(C) discouraged
(D) discouragement

123. The government has so far not tried to raise the retirement age ------- questions regarding the long-term adequacy of the national pension plan.

(A) nevertheless
(B) however
(C) although
(D) in spite of

124. According to the National Forest Service, ------- who does not follow the rules will be fined or barred from visiting the mountain again.

(A) they
(B) those
(C) anyone
(D) people

125. ------- the company respects the principle of job security, the union will support the company's new wage system.

(A) As long as
(B) Afterward
(C) Though
(D) In order that

126. This type of heating unit is a good choice for the quick heating of enclosed spaces, but it should not be left -------.

(A) unused
(B) unorganized
(C) unattended
(D) unexpected

127. Due to the poor economy, most of the employees will put off taking a summer vacation until the domestic economy -------.

(A) improve
(B) had improved
(C) will improve
(D) has improved

128. Replacement car keys for your car may be ordered directly from our office ------- you can show evidence of your car title and car ownership.

(A) unless
(B) though
(C) since
(D) assuming that

129. Some of the product developers have given ------- attention to originality as to space efficiency in the new design.

(A) as many
(B) as much
(C) more
(D) the most

130. Our small jazz band, formed in Seoul, ------- a wide variety of audiences in many cities for the last twenty years.

(A) entertains
(B) entertaining
(C) is entertaining
(D) has entertained

PART 6

Directions: Read the texts that follow. A word or phrase, or sentence is missing in parts of each text. Four answer choices for each question are given below the text. Select the best answer to complete the text. Then mark the letter (A), (B), (C), or (D) on your answer sheet.

Questions 131-134 refer to the following advertisement.

Start Your Online Business

If you want to sell anything online, you need an web commerce platform. Web commerce is the most efficient way to ------- your business. -------.
                                    131.   **132.**

Learn about e-commerce from top-rated business instructors. You can take our free online business courses and learn digital strategy and marketing tactics to grow your company. First, we'll show you how to purchase a domain name and construct your own e-commerce site. -------, we'll show how to use sophisticated web tools for online
                              133.
shoppers.

You don't need any previous experience setting up websites at all! This online business course is designed for -------. Sign up today at https://bkecommerce.com/
                                134.
onlinebusinesscourse.

131. (A) grow
(B) grown
(C) growing
(D) growth

132. (A) Every big business in each industry sector started as a small one like yours.
(B) Find a thrift store in your area that fits your style, personality and budget.
(C) There have been numerous rise and fall of social media marketing sites in recent decades.
(D) Selling online can help your business reach new markets and increase your sales and revenues.

133. (A) Yet
(B) Next
(C) Instead
(D) Again

134. (A) technicians
(B) beginners
(C) patrons
(D) marketers

▶▶▶GO ON TO THE NEXT PAGE

To: James White <jw@goldsune.com>
From: Julia Baker <jbaker@mediatech.com>
Date: June 13
Subject: Official notification of price changes

Dear Mr. White:

Please accept this e-mail as notification of a slight rate adjustment, ------- July 1. The
                                                                    135.
adjustment is a result of increased transportation costs ------- the last twelve months.
                                                       136.

A summary of rate changes is located at the bottom of this e-mail. We anticipate no

additional rate adjustments for the next full year.

Should you have any further questions regarding our services, please contact our

company at 510-7767. -------.
                    137.

Thank you for understanding that this price increase means that we can continue to -------
                                                                              138.
the superior quality standards of our products and services for the coming year.

Very truly yours,

Julia Baker
Chief Executive Officer
Media Tech, Inc.

135. (A) acute
(B) good
(C) effective
(D) entitled

136. (A) with
(B) until
(C) over
(D) following

137. (A) Better service for all customers
should be a priority for us.
(B) Our customer service representatives
will be happy to assist you.
(C) We have great difficulty
communicating with overseas clients.
(D) Marketing is concerned with
customer needs and customer
satisfaction.

138. (A) maintain
(B) accomplish
(C) examine
(D) organize

Buckingham Plants

-------. Stick to these easy-to-follow guidelines to ------- your plants and help them to
   139.   **140.**
flourish.

First, your plants require water, light, and warmth in order to survive. Place your plants in

suitable pots or troughs filled with nutrient-rich soil. Then, ------- position them
                                             141.

somewhere where they can receive ample sunlight.

Make sure that you water your plants on a regular basis. -------, they will begin to wither
                                             142.

and will eventually die. By following these simple instructions, you can keep your plants

healthy for a long time.

139. (A) Thank you for purchasing plants from our store.
    (B) We are planning to open a new gardening store this week.
    (C) Our company is pleased to announce a new agricultural technology.
    (D) The evidence is very clear that plants promote health.

140. (A) select
    (B) order
    (C) review
    (D) preserve

141. (A) simple
    (B) simplify
    (C) simply
    (D) simplicity

142. (A) Thus
    (B) Altogether
    (C) Besides
    (D) Otherwise

Questions 143-146 refer to the following notice.

Tips for Staying Healthy at Work

Here at Coco Fashion, we genuinely care about and place the highest ------- on each and
143.
every single one of our employees. Working employees spend on average around 8.5

hours sitting a day with their computers. That is why we recommend taking a regular

break to our employees from their computers. -------, for every 90 minutes you work in a
144.
seated position, it is essential to get up and walk around for 15 minutes.

Encouraging employees to step away from their desk for a short break will give them the

opportunity to recharge, relax and prevent work burnout. Our attention spans and

concentration levels dwindle over time if there is no break, therefore a short break will

refresh attention spans and sustain concentration levels. It is also important to arrange

your computer workstation to be as ------- as possible. It is the first step to care for your
145.
overall health. Consider positioning your keyboard, computer, monitor, and other devices

so you do not have to strain yourself. -------.
146.

143. (A) style
(B) income
(C) commentary
(D) value

144. (A) As a result
(B) Meanwhile
(C) Despite that
(D) Specifically

145. (A) comfort
(B) comfortable
(C) comfortably
(D) comforted

146. (A) Location plays a huge role in attracting and retaining the best employees.
(B) Sometimes even a small adjustment can make a big difference.
(C) We always reward our staff for outstanding performance with special awards.
(D) Employers are often confronted with employee relations issues in the workplace.

PART 7

Directions: In this part you will read a selection of texts, such as magazine and newspaper articles, e-mails, and instant messages. Each text or set of texts is followed by several questions. Select the best answer for each question and mark the letter (A), (B), (C), or (D) on your answer sheet.

Questions 147-148 refer to the following advertisement.

We Make It Happen
Let your special days be extraordinary!

Everyone has special days to celebrate. All you need to do is enjoy. Red Antz will prepare everything for you.

We Manage:
Parties / Corporate Receptions / Proposals
From planning to catering! We handle personal requests!

• July's Special Offer
We provide a 15% discount to all customers who pay the deposit in July.
Please contact us now because our consulting schedule tends to fill up very quickly!

(212) 770-2431
www.redantz.com

147. Who would most likely be interested in the advertisement?

(A) A family who wants to go camping
(B) A person who plans to hold a banquet
(C) A corporation which has a meeting in the near future
(D) An organization which needs a place for a seminar

148. What is expected to happen on August 1?

(A) Red Antz will start offering a special discount.
(B) An unusual number of customers will request a quote.
(C) People will wait in line to receive a consultation.
(D) A special offer will no longer be available.

▶ ▶ ▶ GO ON TO THE NEXT PAGE

Questions 149-150 refer to the following text message chain.

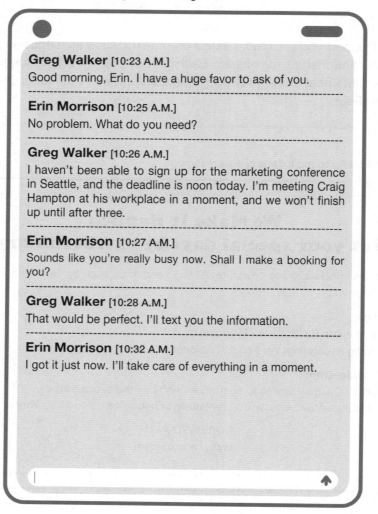

Greg Walker [10:23 A.M.]
Good morning, Erin. I have a huge favor to ask of you.

Erin Morrison [10:25 A.M.]
No problem. What do you need?

Greg Walker [10:26 A.M.]
I haven't been able to sign up for the marketing conference in Seattle, and the deadline is noon today. I'm meeting Craig Hampton at his workplace in a moment, and we won't finish up until after three.

Erin Morrison [10:27 A.M.]
Sounds like you're really busy now. Shall I make a booking for you?

Greg Walker [10:28 A.M.]
That would be perfect. I'll text you the information.

Erin Morrison [10:32 A.M.]
I got it just now. I'll take care of everything in a moment.

149. What is suggested about Mr. Walker?

(A) He is in his office now.
(B) He cannot meet a deadline.
(C) He lives in Seattle.
(D) He attended a conference recently.

150. At 10:32 A.M., what does Ms. Morrison mean when she writes, "I'll take care of everything in a moment"?

(A) She will give Mr. Hampton a telephone call.
(B) She will contact the organizers of the conference.
(C) She will send some information to Mr. Walker.
(D) She will register Mr. Walker for an event.

Welchs Daily
Expense Report

Name: Joanna Davalos   **Date:** June 16
Department: International Affairs   **Pay Period:** June 10 – June 12

Date	Description	Airfare	Lodging	Meals	Other	Total
June 10	Buenos Aires	$900.00	$95.00	$80.30		$1,075.30
June 11	International Children's Book		$95.00	$64.00		$159.00
June 12	Exhibition	$850.50		$70.50	$99.00	$1,020.00
					Total	**$2,254.30**
					Corporate Card Use	**$2,155.30**

Descriptions for "Other"

Date	Description	Amount
June 12	Camera films	$ 60.00
June 12	Voice recorder battery	$ 39.00

Purpose of the expenses:

I used up all my films and batteries in the middle of an interview, so I had to buy some on-site.

Approved By *Jeffrey McNeil*   **Date** *June 16*

• Reimbursement Policy

1. The expense report must be signed by the applicant's department manager before being handed in.
2. Any unofficial expenses will not be reimbursed.
3. Expenses not paid with a corporate card have to be specified in detail.
4. Turn in the completed document to Alex Aiken in the finance department.

ACTUAL TEST 09

151. Who most likely is Ms. Davalos?

(A) A member of an international institute
(B) A manufacturer of camera films
(C) An owner of a bookstore
(D) A reporter from a newspaper

152. What is NOT indicated in the form?

(A) Mr. McNeil leads the department of international affairs.
(B) Ms. Davalos paid for two nights of stay in Buenos Aires.
(C) Ms. Davalos used a corporate card for items irrelevant to the business.
(D) Ms. Aiken will process the transactions.

153. How much money will probably be reimbursed to Ms. Davalos?

(A) $99.00
(B) $159.00
(C) $2,155.30
(D) $2,254.30

▶ ▶ ▶**GO ON TO THE NEXT PAGE**

The Hometown of Angelica

by Leona Denver

Viceroy, a popular vacation spot that is a 30-minute-sail from Napoli, is the hometown of Angelica, the main character in the world-renowned cartoon series *Finding Angelica*. When you land at Prosch Port, you will soon find the view that you saw in the comic book. The beach where Angelica runs around with her friends is on your right, and you can see white houses with roofs in various colors lined up along the street as you walk into town. —[1]—.

"Angelica represents my happy, precious childhood memories in Viceroy," said Ms. Joanne Russo, the author of *Finding Angelica*. —[2]—. "I never knew Angelica would be this popular when I first created her. I feel blessed that she is loved by so many children."

Children can view the original sketches and animated pictures of Angelica at the museum in the center of town. A huge statue of Angelica standing in the center of Bruno Plaza is also a popular attraction.

The festival called "Happy Birthday, Angelica" will be held in Viceroy in the third week of July to celebrate Angelica's 10th anniversary this year. —[3]—. It is anticipated that more people than ever from all over the world will visit the town to attend this event. Since there are numerous hotels and guesthouses, especially for groups of 3 to 6 people, visitors do not have to worry about their stay in Viceroy. —[4]—.

154. Which group of people would most likely be interested in the article?

(A) Executives of a hotel chain
(B) Publishers of travel guides
(C) Festival volunteers
(D) Families planning trips

155. Who most likely is Ms. Russo?

(A) A visitor to Viceroy
(B) A tour guide
(C) A current resident of Viceroy
(D) A cartoonist

156. In which of the positions marked [1], [2], [3], and [4] does the following sentence best fit?

"It even has the ice cream store which often appears in the cartoon."

(A) [1]
(B) [2]
(C) [3]
(D) [4]

Notification for Passengers of
Casper Local Transit

Thanks to all residents of Casper for your continuous usage of Casper Local Transit.
We strive to provide safe and comfortable transportation.

However, fuel costs and wages are rapidly increasing. It is therefore inevitable for us to raise fares to cover these inflationary costs and to improve service levels. The following fare changes will go into effect in May.

Fares Effective from May:

Category	Adult	Students	Elderly	Monthly Pass
Local Bus	$1.50	$1.25	$1.00	$65.00
Commuter Bus	$2.50	$2.00	$1.50	$77.00

157. What is the purpose of the notice?

(A) To thank some customers
(B) To announce a change in policy
(C) To advertise new travel packages
(D) To discuss economic trends

158. What is suggested in the notice?

(A) Another notification will be posted soon.
(B) The number of passengers will decrease soon.
(C) Discounted fares are available for senior citizens.
(D) More bus routes will be added.

Questions 159-161 refer to the following schedule.

The 2nd Annual
Elk City Restaurants Association Seminar:
April 11

Time	Topic
09:00 – 09:10	**Opening Remarks** Stevie Chinitz (President of the Elk City Restaurants Association)
09:10 – 09:30	**Keynote Speech** **The Outlook for Organic Cuisine:** Introduction of the current culinary trends in organic cuisine • Jason Hunt (Senior researcher and chef at BobITso Restaurant)
09:30 – 10:30	**It's All About Local Ingredients:** Superiority of local ingredients and cheaper routes to procure them • Puerto Gonzales (Head of the Local Farmers Alliance)
10:30 – 11:30	**A Piece of Cookware Makes a Huge Difference:** State-of-the-art cookware to transform your kitchen into an up-to-date cooking environment • Heidi Howland (Sales manager of Lopal Electronics)
11:40 – 13:00	**Organic Recipe and Cooking Show** Presentation of the newest organic recipes — tasting session and luncheon held afterwards • Ralph Green (Executive Chef at Taste the Freshness)
13:00 – 14:00	**How to Successfully Run a Local Restaurant:** Success stories of local restaurants and tips on restaurant management • Daniel Milleren (Professor at the Elk City College)
14:00 – 15:30	**Discussion** All participants of the seminar will have a discussion with the speakers about prospects of organic cuisine and the local restaurant business.

159. Who will most likely be interested in the seminar?

(A) An interior designer
(B) A proprietor of a local restaurant
(C) A farmer of organic crops
(D) An executive of a food ingredients supplier

160. Who will present a live performance?

(A) Jason Hunt
(B) Puerto Gonzales
(C) Heidi Howland
(D) Ralph Green

161. When will a meal be provided?

(A) Before Jason Hunt's keynote speech
(B) During the Heidi Howland's session
(C) After the Ralph Green's presentation
(D) After the discussion

February 28

Steve Karowicz
Shine Kitchen Warehouse
196 Knox Street
Denver, CO 80111

Dear Mr. Karowicz,

We have recently received an application for employment from James Marley, who is seeking a job at our firm in the capacity of sales manager. We understand that this applicant is currently employed at Shine Kitchen Warehouse. We would appreciate a reference on the individual from you, especially because he has been under your supervision as vice sales manager for the last 2 years of his employment.

We were particularly impressed by the rapid promotion that Mr. Marley was granted, reaching the rank of vice sales manager from junior sales representative within only 5 years. We would like to find more about Mr. Marley's notable performance.

In your reference, please provide the following information:
• Confirmation of his dates of employment with you
• Responsibilities he held at your firm
• Performance evaluation (form enclosed)

Should you find it necessary to include any additional information, please feel free to do so.

Please understand that our sales manager position has been vacant for a very long time and we are in urgent need of a competent person to fill it. We would appreciate it if your answer could be received by no later than March 20. Thank you for your anticipated cooperation.

Sincerely,

Elizabeth Clarke
Director, Human Resources Department
Jackson Home Depo

Enclosure

162. Why was this letter sent?

(A) To acknowledge the receipt of personal information
(B) To request a letter of recommendation
(C) To recommend an employee for a position
(D) To provide instructions for application

163. The word "capacity" in paragraph 1, line 2, is closest in meaning to

(A) ability
(B) availability
(C) position
(D) size

164. What is true about Mr. Marley?

(A) He has worked for Shine Kitchen Warehouse for 2 years in total.
(B) His current position is vice sales manager.
(C) He has met Ms. Clarke in person.
(D) He is requested to send in some documents to Ms. Clarke.

▶ ▶ ▶ GO ON TO THE NEXT PAGE

April 25

Ms. Katie Callager
39 East Caroline Street
Seattle, WA 98105

Dear Ms. Katie Callager,

Thank you for continuously using our services at East Seattle Laundry.

Last Thursday, you requested dry cleaning service for your blouse to be returned to you on Monday. However, it went missing and was not returned to you as scheduled. We have discovered that it was mistakenly switched with another customer's shirt. We have found out where your blouse currently is and we will send it to your address as soon as we retrieve it.

We would like to make a sincere apology about your recent experience. Enclosed is a $50 gift certificate which you can use at East Seattle Laundry anytime for any service. Please feel free to give me a call at 206-408-3180 if you have further requests or concerns.

Best regards,

John Santos
Manager at East Seattle Laundry

Enclosure

165. What is the purpose of the letter?

   (A) To thank a customer for continued business
   (B) To respond to a customer's refund request
   (C) To apologize to a customer
   (D) To advertise a laundry service

166. What is sent with the letter?

   (A) A voucher
   (B) A $50 note
   (C) A blouse
   (D) A T-shirt

167. What is the customer asked to do if she has requests?

   (A) Call Mr. Santos
   (B) Visit the store
   (C) Complete a form
   (D) Contact another customer

▶ ▶ ▶ GO ON TO THE NEXT PAGE

Sheila West　　　　4:39 P.M.

Good afternoon, everyone. I need a status report on the Chamberlain project.

Derrek Steele　　　　4:41 P.M.

Work on stage 3 is nearly complete. The electricians and the plumbers are both expected to finish by the end of the week.

Sheila West　　　　4:43 P.M.

How about stage 4?

Rose Murphy　　　　4:44 P.M.

Everyone is set to go on Monday. But there's a slight problem with one of our contractors. He's requesting a higher payment.

Sheila West　　　　4:46 P.M.

Our budget is already pretty tight.

Rose Murphy　　　　4:47 P.M.

That's what I told him. If he insists on getting paid more, I'll find a replacement.

Peter Trimble　　　　4:48 P.M.

Are you talking about Eric Cotton, Rose?

Rose Murphy　　　　4:50 P.M.

Yes. Do you know him?

Peter Trimble　　　　4:51 P.M.

I worked with him a few years ago. Let me give him a call and explain things to him.

Sheila West　　　　4:52 P.M.

Thanks, Peter.

Sheila West　　　　4:54 P.M.

Okay, it sounds like things are going as well as we can expect. We really need this project to finish on time, especially after the problems we experienced with Grandview Plaza.

SEND

168. What is most likely true about stage 4?

(A) There is not enough funding for it.
(B) It is scheduled to begin next week.
(C) Plumbers will be working during it.
(D) It is the final stage of the construction process.

169. What will Mr. Trimble probably do next?

(A) Visit Grandview Plaza
(B) Contact a former colleague
(C) Speak with an electrician
(D) Submit some forms

170. What is suggested about Grandview Plaza?

(A) It took too long to complete.
(B) It has several construction flaws.
(C) It was finished over budget.
(D) Some people were hurt working on it.

171. At 4:46 P.M., why does Ms. West write, "Our budget is already pretty tight"?

(A) To approve a request for additional funding
(B) To express her unwillingness to negotiate
(C) To indicate she will speak with an accountant
(D) To stress the need to finish the work soon

January 11 - A chain of David's Pizzeria can be seen on almost every block across the country now. However, it took a long time and an enormous effort of its founder, David Keen, for the pizzeria to become this successful.

When he first came to the Philippines, Mr. Keen was only a student studying Physics at the University of Manila and his mother ran a small Thai food restaurant on the campus. —[1]—. One day, he was having pizza at the restaurant with some Thai side dishes. He thought then and there that he could make great things happen with these two very distinctive foods.

Mr. Keen then persuaded his mother to renovate the restaurant into a pizzeria. —[2]—. His mother agreed to do so and finally the famous David's Pizzeria opened. The pizzeria provides its own characteristic pizza, combinations of regular pizza and Thai food.

"It is true that we struggled at first, but my mother and I did not give up," Mr. Keen said. It took him 2 years to perfect his recipe, but once he did, the rest is history. —[3]—. "Our restaurant uses only naturally grown vegetables, organic cheese and organic grass-fed meat. I think this is the reason people love our pizza so much," Mr. Keen noted confidently.

As passionate as David's Pizzeria is about serving only healthy food to its customers, it is also dedicated to serving the communities where its stores are located. It spends funds and efforts to help those who are less fortunate. —[4]—. While enjoying a slice of pizza, a customer can also help the community we all live in.

For detailed information about David's Pizzeria, visit its website at www.davids.com. You can participate in David's Pizzeria's biannual charity events by registering online.

172. What is the topic of the article?

(A) A success of an international food chain
(B) A recipe for healthy pizza
(C) A management change of a restaurant
(D) A brief history of a business

173. The word "ran" in paragraph 2, line 3, is closest in meaning to

(A) moved fast
(B) left
(C) managed
(D) took over

174. What did Mr. Keen do before he founded David's Pizzeria?

(A) He delivered pizza.
(B) He owned a Thai restaurant.
(C) He attended a school.
(D) He wrote restaurant reviews.

175. In which of the positions marked [1], [2], [3], and [4] does the following sentence best fit?

"Although it is a fast-food restaurant, David's Pizzeria provides only healthy food to its customers."

(A) [1]
(B) [2]
(C) [3]
(D) [4]

http://www.slc.ca.gov/news

State Library Of California

| About Us | Search | Policies | News |

The State Library of California is one of the leading libraries in the United States that has world-class collections of books, videos, and many other resources. As a regional center for learning, we continuously provide quality educational programs to the public in affiliation with other public libraries in the region.

The State Library of California is operated mainly through city grants and has not received many individual contributions up to this point. However, we now have decided to accept personal donations to offer even better programs and services to our invaluable visitors. The first program open for donations is an educational program for children, which will begin in May at the library. Through this program, the participating children will learn proper reading skills. Please become donor members and help us make a difference in our communities.

Benefits of SLC Donor Members

Benefits	Friend ($50)	Sponsor ($75)	Patron ($100)	Benefactor ($150)
Free parking at the library	O	O	O	O
A discount at the library bookstore	N/A	O	O	O
Free entrance to partner museums and galleries in Southern California	N/A	N/A	O	O
A discount on our annual events & free admission to our seminars	N/A	N/A	N/A	O

For more information about our donation process, click **here** or call us at 555-1109.

Posted on March 1

To:	Mark Tanaka <mtanaka@domail.com>
From:	Lucy Diamond <ldiamond@slc.gov>
Date:	June 10
Subject:	Report

Dear Mr. Tanaka,

Thank you for your gracious support of the State Library of California as a Patron member. Today, we would like to inform you about our educational program for children which has been implemented with the assistance of generous donors like you.

Twice per week, 60 children visit the library to learn proper reading methods. We are currently receiving positive feedback from many of the children and their parents about the program. In appreciation of their generous support, our students wrote postcards to our donors last week, and I believe you may have already received one from Emily Johnson from South River Elementary School.

We are currently planning two additional projects including purchasing computers for computer classes and broadening our book collections. To discuss these projects, we would like to invite you to a meeting, which will be held on June 21 at the library. Please give us a call if you are interested.

Best Regards,

Lucy Diamond

176. On the website, what is mentioned as the major source of finance for operations of the State Library of California?

(A) Government budget
(B) Money donated by individuals
(C) Funding from other libraries
(D) Proceeds from selling books at the library

177. What is NOT a feature available at the State Library of California?

(A) Video materials
(B) A bookstore
(C) An art gallery
(D) A parking facility

178. What is the purpose of the e-mail?

(A) To ask for additional funding
(B) To request feedback about recent educational program
(C) To confirm the receipt of a membership fee
(D) To encourage participation in a meeting

179. What is a stated benefit Mr. Tanaka is being offered?

(A) A discount on entrance fees to other local facilities
(B) A discount on books sold at the library
(C) Free admission to seminars hosted by the library
(D) Invitation to the library's annual events

180. What is inferred about Emily Johnson?

(A) She can enter local museums free of charge.
(B) She has participated in an educational program since May.
(C) She will be given a new computer.
(D) She is an instructor of an educational program for children.

▶ ▶ ▶ GO ON TO THE NEXT PAGE

SCUBY REAL ESTATE

Serving Greater Sydney area for over 20 years

November 18

Veronica Michelin
35B Knights Road
Sydney, NSW 2111

Dear Ms. Michelin,

I am writing to you to follow up on our conversation on the phone last week. Some commercial properties that will be a perfect fit for your new business plan have recently been put on the market.

The first property is a single-story building located on Neich Street. Its construction was completed just last month, which means you will be the first owner of the property. It is situated in a business district, surrounded by numerous office suites. Thus, you will receive a lot of office workers during lunch hours.

Also, the store on the third floor of a building on Crimson Avenue is up for sale. The owner has offered to include several kitchen appliances in the deal, so you will not need to purchase new ones. Also, he is willing to leave the tables and chairs in the hall as well. The interior of the store is quite new and requires little refurnishing.

If you would like take a tour to the properties, please call me during our work hours, Monday to Friday between 9:00 A.M. and 5:00 P.M., or send me an e-mail. Regarding some financial concerns you expressed, we can discuss installment options when we meet.

We hope to serve you best today, tomorrow and always.

Best regards,

Mackenzie Robertson
Real Estate Consultant
Scuby Real Estate

To:	Mackenzie Robertson <mrobertson@scubyre.com>
From:	Veronica Michelin <vmichelin@plomail.com>
Date:	November 24
Subject:	Thank you

Dear Mr. Robertson,

Thank you for showing me around the properties this afternoon. With the terms you offered me, I have decided to purchase the brand-new property. The second option you recommended seems very appealing, but I plan to receive fresh ingredients from the suppliers every morning. Therefore, I need a place that would be more convenient for carrying produce into the building.

I would like to sign the contract as soon as possible. Please let me know when you would be available to meet with me with all the documents ready. Thank you for your assistance.

Regards,

Veronica Michelin

---

181. What is indicated about Scuby Real Estate?

(A) It specializes in only commercial estates.
(B) It currently does not have any fully furnished properties.
(C) It is located in a business district.
(D) Its client base is mainly in Sydney.

182. What type of business is Ms. Michelin probably planning to open?

(A) A kitchen appliance store
(B) A furniture store
(C) A dining establishment
(D) A real estate agency

183. In the letter, the word "installment" in paragraph 4, line 3, is closest in meaning to

(A) furniture assembly
(B) relocation service
(C) complimentary consultation
(D) partial payment

184. What is true about Mr. Robertson?

(A) He has about 20 years of experience in the real estate field.
(B) He works every day of the week.
(C) He recently met Ms. Michelin in person.
(D) He owns Scuby Real Estate.

185. What does Ms. Michelin plan to do in the future?

(A) Apply for loans from Scuby Real Estate
(B) Design the interior of her store
(C) Purchase the property on Neich Street
(D) Ship foods every morning to a local department store

▶ ▶ ▶ GO ON TO THE NEXT PAGE

Come to the Aberdeen Food Festival

This year's festival will take place from May 10-14. Enjoy food from some of the best restaurants in the city as well as food from more than 20 countries. There will be all kinds of exciting events, too. There will be cooking classes led by noted chefs such as Wayne Dupree, Lucinda de Miles, Carol Conner, and Jason Fifer. Visitors can watch how various foods are prepared. And, of course, there will be numerous types of fresh, dried, and canned foods available for people to buy. Admission for the entire five days is $3, but children 5 or younger and adults 65 or older get in for free. Call 495-9332 for more information.

To: Peter Griffin
From: Emily Dare
Subject: FYI
Date: May 8

It looks like everything is going well for the upcoming festival. All of the restaurants that said they would be there have reconfirmed their attendance. We've also sold more than 6,000 tickets, which is twice the number we sold last year. I'd say we're heading for our biggest turnout ever.

There's one thing you should know. Jason Fifer has fallen ill, so he won't be attending. However, I spoke with Irene Potter, whom you know, and she has agreed to replace Jason.

I'll let you know if anything else comes up.

Food Festival a Major Success

by staff reporter Kevin Drummond

Aberdeen (May 15) – The Aberdeen Food Festival came to an end yesterday, and it was widely acclaimed as the best in the event's twenty-seven-year history. Organizers said that more than 11,000 people attended at least one of the five days of the festival while others attended multiple days.

"I had a great time as I always do," said local resident Jackson Burgess. "I especially liked that I didn't have to pay to get in. That was a positive change from prior events." Mr. Burgess added that he especially enjoyed the food from Asia and South America which he sampled.

Festival organizer Peter Griffin said he was happy with how the event went. "Overall, I can't complain one bit. It was a great time for everyone."

186. According to the advertisement, what is true about the festival?

(A) People can purchase food products there.
(B) All attendees must pay to gain entry.
(C) It will be shown live on television.
(D) It will take place on a weekend.

187. What is the purpose of the memo?

(A) To ask for some assistance
(B) To give an update
(C) To praise an action
(D) To file a complaint

188. What did Ms. Potter do at the festival?

(A) She helped sell tickets.
(B) She provided cooking instruction.
(C) She sold canned and dried foods.
(D) She helped set up various booths.

189. In the article, what is indicated about the Aberdeen Food Festival?

(A) It lasted for one week.
(B) 11,000 people attended it every day.
(C) It featured food from different continents.
(D) It was being held for the first time.

190. What is suggested about Mr. Burgess?

(A) He comes from South America.
(B) He attended the festival every day.
(C) He helped organize the festival.
(D) He is at least sixty-five years old.

To: All Managers
From: Edward Silvan
Date: August 21
Subject: Survey Results

I was just provided the results of the survey from Arnold Consulting, the group which conducted the employee survey for us at MTT, Inc. It looks like we've got some problems we really need to take care of. Here are some of the results:

More than half of all employees feel they are underpaid.
45% of all employees think they work too much overtime.
35% of all employees feel they are not trained well enough.
75% of all employees would consider leaving this company if offered the same position, salary, and benefits at a competing firm.

We're having a brainstorming session in the conference room tomorrow at 9:00 A.M. It's going to be an all-day affair. Cancel all meetings scheduled and be sure to come with creative ideas.

To:	Edward Silvan <edsilvan@mtt.com>
From:	Lucy Jackson <lj@mtt.com>
Date:	August 23
Subject:	Yesterday

Ed,

That was a productive meeting yesterday. I thought a few people, especially Jeff Sacks and Helen Cross, had good ideas. I'm going to try to implement a few of them myself.

Are we planning on having another meeting? I think that would be the smart thing to do so that we can make sure everyone is using these new ideas. We could also provide updates on how the changes we're implementing are working out. What works for one person might be successful for others, too. We can also figure out which ideas are impractical or that employees don't care for.

Regards,

Lucy

To:	Edward Silvan <edsilvan@mtt.com>
From:	Helen Cross <helen@mtt.com>
Date:	September 4
Subject:	Update

Ed,

You should be aware that employees in the Shipping Department are still displeased with their overall work conditions. Many complained about having to work last weekend. In fact, this morning, two workers submitted their resignations. They said they've already accepted positions at Boscombe Tech. They pointed out that they'll get raises of more than $9,000 a year at their new jobs.

We've got to do something soon because I'm understaffed here. And fall is our busiest season of the year. If I can't get more employees soon, we're going to have plenty of unhappy customers.

Best,

Helen

191. What is the memo mainly about?

(A) How to improve working conditions
(B) Where to meet some other workers
(C) When a special event will happen
(D) Why employees are unhappy

192. What is indicated about Ms. Jackson?

(A) She is a manager at MTT, Inc.
(B) She is Mr. Silvan's supervisor.
(C) She works in the HR Department.
(D) She did not attend a recent meeting.

193. What does Ms. Jackson suggest doing?

(A) Advertising more on the Internet
(B) Conducting another survey
(C) Meeting again in the future
(D) Hiring more qualified employees

194. Which of the problems cited by workers does Ms. Cross NOT address in her e-mail?

(A) A desire to work elsewhere
(B) Underpaid employees
(C) A lack of training
(D) Working too much overtime

195. What problem does Ms. Cross mention in the second e-mail?

(A) She does not have enough workers.
(B) Her budget is too small.
(C) There are not enough delivery vehicles.
(D) The price of shipping items is increasing.

▶ ▶ ▶ GO ON TO THE NEXT PAGE

Hopewell Realty

Serving the Hillsdale community for more than fifty years

Check out these new places we have for sale. Thinking of starting a new business? Then you definitely want to take a look:

88 Hammer Street: 45-square-meter property on the first floor of the Marston Building; lots of foot traffic; great for a café or small restaurant; $45,000

12 Oak Street: entire top floor of the Greenville Building; the perfect location for an office; private elevator; basement parking garage; all-new facilities; $350,000

21 Dagger Road: 100 square meters on the second floor of Rosewood Tower; currently being used as a retail space; renovations may be required; $105,000

93 Kenmore Drive: small office space on the tenth floor of the Piedmont Building; ideal for a one-person private office; $20,000

E-mail us at inquries@hopewellrealty.com to see one of these properties or any of the others we have available.

To:	Tom Woodward <tomw@commercemail.com>
From:	Grace Dell <grace@hopewellrealty.com>
Date:	April 11
Subject:	Hello

Dear Mr. Woodward,

Thank you for your e-mail expressing interest in some of our properties. It would be a pleasure to show you around a few of them. I understand that you are working with a limited budget, so I am taking that into consideration when I think of which places to show you.

Let's start by meeting at 21 Dagger Road tomorrow at 9:00 A.M. After that, I can show you a few other places, including ones on Magnolia Drive and Pecan Street.

Please feel free to call me anytime. My number is 205-954-9022.

See you tomorrow.

Grace Dell
Hopewell Realty

Woodward and Smythe Used Bookstore
owned by Tom Woodward and Jack Smythe

will be holding its grand opening on
July 10

Come to see us at our new location at
95 Pecan Street

We have all kinds of books, but we specialize in
science-fiction, literature, and poetry

All sales on our opening day will be discounted at 20% off

---

196. According to the first advertisement, which place would a person who plans to sell food be interested in?

(A) 88 Hammer Street
(B) 12 Oak Street
(C) 21 Dagger Road
(D) 93 Kenmore Drive

197. In the e-mail, what is suggested about Mr. Woodward?

(A) He has met Ms. Dell in person before.
(B) He can only spend a certain amount of money.
(C) He will be visiting Hillsdale from another city.
(D) He will tour some properties on April 13.

198. What is the price of the place Ms. Dell wants to show Mr. Woodward first?

(A) $20,000
(B) $45,000
(C) $105,000
(D) $350,000

199. What is most likely true about Mr. Woodward?

(A) He has published some books in the past.
(B) He first saw the site of his bookstore on April 12.
(C) He is a noted author of science-fiction books.
(D) He has recently moved to Hillsdale.

200. What is indicated about Woodward and Smythe Used Bookstore?

(A) It will open during the month of June.
(B) It sells books that were recently released.
(C) It focuses on certain genres of books.
(D) It is offering a discount for an entire month.

STOP! This is the end of the test. If you finish before time is called, you may go back to Parts 5, 6, and 7 and check your work.

Actual Test 10

MP3

해설집

적정 풀이 시간 120분

120 min

시작 시간 ___시 ___분

종료 시간 ___시 ___분

중간에 멈추지 말고 처음부터 끝까지 풀어보세요.
문제를 풀 때에는 실전처럼 답안지에 마킹하세요.

목표 개수 _____ / 200   실제 개수 _____ / 200

예상 점수는 번역 및 정답에 있는 점수 환산표를 참조하세요.

LISTENING TEST

In the Listening test, you will be asked to demonstrate how well you understand spoken English. The entire Listening test will last approximately 45 minutes. There are four parts, and directions are given for each part. You must mark your answers on the separate answer sheet. Do not write your answers in the test book.

PART 1

Directions: For each question in this part, you will hear four statements about a picture in your test book. When you hear the statements, you must select the one statement that best describes what you see in the picture. Then find the number of the question on your answer sheet and mark your answer. The statements will not be printed in your test book and will be spoken only one time.

Statement (B), "They are sitting at a table." is the best description of the picture. So you should select answer (B) and mark it on your answer sheet.

1.

2.

▶ ▶ ▶ GO ON TO THE NEXT PAGE

3.

4.

5.

6.

▶ ▶ ▶ GO ON TO THE NEXT PAGE

PART 2

Directions: You will hear a question or statement and three responses spoken in English. They will not be printed in your test book and will be spoken only one time. Select the best response to the question or statement and mark the letter (A), (B), or (C) on your answer sheet.

7. Mark your answer on your answer sheet.

8. Mark your answer on your answer sheet.

9. Mark your answer on your answer sheet.

10. Mark your answer on your answer sheet.

11. Mark your answer on your answer sheet.

12. Mark your answer on your answer sheet.

13. Mark your answer on your answer sheet.

14. Mark your answer on your answer sheet.

15. Mark your answer on your answer sheet.

16. Mark your answer on your answer sheet.

17. Mark your answer on your answer sheet.

18. Mark your answer on your answer sheet.

19. Mark your answer on your answer sheet.

20. Mark your answer on your answer sheet.

21. Mark your answer on your answer sheet.

22. Mark your answer on your answer sheet.

23. Mark your answer on your answer sheet.

24. Mark your answer on your answer sheet.

25. Mark your answer on your answer sheet.

26. Mark your answer on your answer sheet.

27. Mark your answer on your answer sheet.

28. Mark your answer on your answer sheet.

29. Mark your answer on your answer sheet.

30. Mark your answer on your answer sheet.

31. Mark your answer on your answer sheet.

Directions: You will hear some conversations between two or three people. You will be asked to answer three questions about what the speakers say in each conversation. Select the best response to each question and mark the letter (A), (B), (C), or (D) on your answer sheet. The conversations will not be printed in your test book and will be spoken only one time.

32. Who is the man?

(A) A journalist
(B) A photographer
(C) A historian
(D) An artist

33. Why is the man calling?

(A) To cancel an appointment
(B) To confirm a reservation
(C) To ask about an art exhibit
(D) To offer the woman a job

34. What is the woman concerned about?

(A) A schedule
(B) A heavy workload
(C) An upcoming trip
(D) References

35. Where does the man most likely work?

(A) At a theater
(B) At a clothing store
(C) At a restaurant
(D) At a drugstore

36. What problem does the man mention?

(A) A shipment of sweaters has not arrived.
(B) The street is not accessible.
(C) An item is no longer available.
(D) Some equipment is not functioning.

37. What does the man offer to do?

(A) Keep some merchandise
(B) Provide a discount
(C) Get some items from the store room
(D) Issue a refund on the blouse

38. What does the woman inquire about?

(A) Ordering some food
(B) Paying by credit card
(C) Connecting to the Internet
(D) Changing seats

39. Where does the conversation take place?

(A) In a bookstore
(B) In a café
(C) On an express train
(D) On an airplane

40. What will the woman do next?

(A) Eat a meal
(B) Order a beverage
(C) Read a newspaper
(D) Turn on an electronic device

41. What is the conversation about?

(A) A TV advertisement
(B) A mobile application
(C) A new marketing strategy
(D) A mobile service provider

42. What does the woman say her team needs to do?

(A) Receive some feedback on a product
(B) Arrange video conferencing
(C) Hire an outside consultant
(D) Post information online

43. What will happen next week?

(A) A product will be launched.
(B) Team members will be divided into groups.
(C) A report will be submitted.
(D) An online catalog will be available.

▶ ▶ ▶GO ON TO THE NEXT PAGE

44. What good news does the man announce to the woman?

(A) A meeting with investors went well.
(B) A contract was signed.
(C) A company's product won an award.
(D) A merger was completed.

45. Why does the man need to go to the airport?

(A) To drop off an item
(B) To get his luggage
(C) To catch a flight
(D) To pick up a client

46. What does the woman offer to do for the man?

(A) Take his place at a meeting
(B) Put in extra hours
(C) Check a bus schedule online
(D) Give him a ride

47. What does the woman want to speak with the man about?

(A) Employee orientation
(B) Sales data
(C) A project deadline
(D) Job interviews

48. According to the woman, what is causing a problem?

(A) Some items are no longer in stock.
(B) Shipments are being delayed.
(C) The prices of raw materials have increased.
(D) A competing business has opened a shop.

49. What does the man say he will do?

(A) Speak with some customers
(B) Hire advertising experts
(C) Check an advertising budget
(D) Get an estimate from another supplier

50. Where does the conversation take place?

(A) At a furniture shop
(B) At a restaurant
(C) At a kitchen supply store
(D) At an appliance store

51. What does the man imply when he says, "I see some dishes on that table by the window"?

(A) Somebody has left items behind.
(B) Some missing items have been found.
(C) He wants to know an item's price.
(D) A task is not complete.

52. Why will the woman go to the breakroom before she goes home?

(A) To post her work schedule on the board
(B) To make sure a door is locked
(C) To sign a contract of employment
(D) To get her schedule

53. Who are the speakers?

(A) Architects
(B) Construction workers
(C) Hotel clerks
(D) Glassmakers

54. Why does Terry recommend using a specific material?

(A) It is easy to find.
(B) It is not costly
(C) It is popular.
(D) It is not heavy.

55. What problem does the woman point out?

(A) A project will go over budget.
(B) A deadline must be extended.
(C) A material is too heavy.
(D) Insulation will be needed.

56. What did Mayor Watson just do?

(A) He gave an interview on TV.
(B) He returned from another country.
(C) He hired a new assistant.
(D) He visited a factory in the city.

57. What is the man preparing?

(A) A press release
(B) A speech
(C) A budget report
(D) An article for a government newsletter

58. Why does the man say, "The conclusion needs to be redone"?

(A) To complain about a colleague
(B) To ask for assistance
(C) To turn down a request
(D) To agree with an opinion

59. What is the man's job?

(A) Factory foreman
(B) Company executive
(C) Safety inspector
(D) Security guard

60. What does Cindy say she will do?

(A) Change some vents
(B) Visit a factory floor
(C) Order more packaging materials
(D) Purchase a new item

61. According to the man, what will happen in one month?

(A) Some equipment will be cleaned.
(B) A factory will close down.
(C) Some software will be upgraded.
(D) A permit will expire.

Lunch Package

Standard	Sandwich, chips, and beverage	$10.00
Standard Plus	Includes dessert	$14.00
Deluxe	Includes dessert and salad	$17.00
Supreme	Includes salad, cookies and dessert bar	$20.00

62. What is the man organizing?

(A) A training session
(B) An awards ceremony
(C) A company picnic
(D) An outdoor job fair

63. Look at the graphic. Which package will the man choose?

(A) Standard
(B) Standard Plus
(C) Deluxe
(D) Supreme

64. What is being offered only in the summer?

(A) Tent rentals
(B) Free delivery
(C) Band performances
(D) Flower arrangements

Delta Pharmacy	
Aisle 1	Detergent
Aisle 2	Soap and Shampoo
Aisle 3	Health Supplements
Aisle 4	Medical items

65. What does the woman remind the man to update?

(A) His résumé
(B) His insurance information
(C) His timesheet
(D) His checklist for closing duties

66. Look at the graphic. Which aisle does the woman ask the man to go to?

(A) Aisle 1
(B) Aisle 2
(C) Aisle 3
(D) Aisle 4

67. What problem does the woman mention?

(A) Some shipments have not arrived.
(B) Some price tags are missing.
(C) Some items are damaged.
(D) Some coupons are not valid.

REST LOUNGE

Row A	A1	A2	A3	A4
Row B	B1	B2	B3	B4
Row C	C1	C2	C3	C4

INFORMATION BOOTH

68. Where are the speakers?

(A) At a company workshop
(B) At a job fair
(C) At a sales conference
(D) At a craft trade show

69. Look at the graphic. Where does the man plan to go first?

(A) Row A
(B) Row B
(C) Row C
(D) Rest lounge

70. According to the woman, what was included in the registration fee?

(A) Costs for hotels
(B) A test-drive
(C) Parking fees
(D) Sandwiches for lunch

PART 4

Directions: You will hear some short talks given by a single speaker. You will be asked to answer three questions about what the speaker says in each short talk. Select the best response to each question and mark the letter (A), (B), (C), or (D) on your answer sheet. The talks will not be printed in your test book and will be spoken only one time.

71. What event will take place next Saturday?

    (A) A book reading
    (B) A music concert
    (C) A play
    (D) A ballet performance

72. Where will the event be held?

    (A) At a library
    (B) At a school
    (C) At an auditorium
    (D) At a community center

73. What does the speaker say will happen at the end of the event?

    (A) Recordings will be available in the lobby.
    (B) Refreshments will be provided.
    (C) Children's art contest will take place.
    (D) A book signing will be held.

74. What is the speaker discussing?

    (A) A business takeover
    (B) A customer boycott
    (C) A government regulation
    (D) A departmental procedure

75. What has a printing company complained about?

    (A) Some instructions are confusing.
    (B) Payments are made late.
    (C) The printing company is understaffed.
    (D) Deadlines are too soon.

76. Who is Mr. Hammer?

    (A) A shop owner
    (B) An administrative assistant
    (C) A printer
    (D) A maintenance crew

77. What does the speaker thank the listener for?

    (A) Sending a brochure
    (B) Ordering carpets
    (C) Providing some samples
    (D) Paying for delivery

78. What does the speaker find impressive about the listener's business?

    (A) It has the lowest prices in the area.
    (B) It sends items quickly.
    (C) It imports high-quality items.
    (D) It has a wide variety of products.

79. Why does the speaker say, "I'm away on business next week"?

    (A) To reject an offer
    (B) To ask for a recommendation
    (C) To express her annoyance
    (D) To explain a method

80. What will be added to the office?

    (A) Framed pictures
    (B) Plants
    (C) An employee breakroom
    (D) More natural lighting

81. Why is a change being made?

    (A) To attract more tenants
    (B) To comply with regulations
    (C) To improve productivity
    (D) To address customer complaints

82. What are the listeners likely to do online?

    (A) View pictures
    (B) Fill out job application forms
    (C) Make requests
    (D) Write reviews on a product

▶ ▶ ▶ GO ON TO THE NEXT PAGE

83. What does Margorie Carter's company produce?

(A) Hairbrushes
(B) Toothbrushes
(C) Health supplements
(D) Toothpastes

84. What did Dr. Carter win an award for?

(A) Founding a company
(B) Donating money to charities
(C) Making a new product
(D) Contributing to the community

85. What will Margorie Carter talk about later?

(A) The reason for her invention
(B) Options for funding
(C) Online marketing strategies
(D) Hiring procedures

86. Who most likely are the listeners?

(A) Shop owners
(B) Game makers
(C) Reporters
(D) Sales representatives

87. What does the speaker imply when he says, "We've never done anything like this before"?

(A) A product development project failed.
(B) Some right information was not given.
(C) A date for product launching must be postponed.
(D) A product needs some extra work.

88. What does the speaker thank Jessica for?

(A) Setting up an updated version of software
(B) Organizing a focus group
(C) Providing feedback
(D) Arranging some equipment

89. Who is the speaker?

(A) A train conductor
(B) A mayor
(C) A government official
(D) A filmmaker

90. What change will take place at the train station?

(A) The ticket booths will be moved.
(B) Part of the station will be expanded.
(C) More railroad tracks will be added.
(D) A waiting area will be removed.

91. Why should the listeners sign up?

(A) To come in for a job interview
(B) To be eligible for a free ticket
(C) To get on a mailing list
(D) To be interviewed for a film

92. Where does the talk take place?

(A) At a construction site
(B) At an art gallery
(C) At an archaeological dig site
(D) At an astronomical observatory

93. What does the speaker imply when she says, "We get tons of visitors here during June and July"?

(A) Regular operating hours will be extended.
(B) Tourists should expect long waiting time.
(C) It's better to avoid visiting in the summer.
(D) A full staff will be needed in the summer.

94. What will each of the listeners be given?

(A) A guidebook
(B) A site map
(C) A list of visitors
(D) A T-shirt

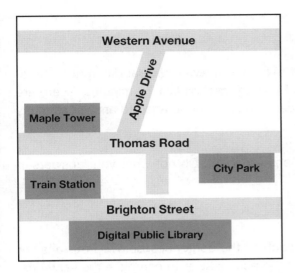

Management Workshop Series

Week	Location	Instructor
1	Room 110	Julie Crow
2	Room 111	Stella Thompson
3	Room 112	Erin May
4	Room 113	Suzie Powell

95. What type of company does the speaker work for?

(A) A manufacturing plant
(B) A publishing firm
(C) A library
(D) A bookstore

96. Look at the graphic. Which street does the speaker suggest parking on?

(A) Western Avenue
(B) Brighton Street
(C) Thomas Road
(D) Apple Drive

97. What does the speaker inquire about?

(A) Taking a tour of the company
(B) Going to lunch
(C) Raising a price
(D) Finishing a project on time

98. Look at the graphic. Who is the speaker?

(A) Julie Crow
(B) Stella Thompson
(C) Erin May
(D) Suzie Powell

99. What will the listeners learn about during the workshop?

(A) Improving work environment
(B) Communicating as a team effectively
(C) Reviewing employee performance
(D) Boosting employee morale

100. What are the listeners asked to do first?

(A) Sign up for a workshop
(B) Work with a partner
(C) Submit an assignment
(D) Introduce themselves

This is the end of the Listening test. Turn to Part 5 in your test book.

READING TEST

In the Reading test, you will read a variety of texts and answer several different types of reading comprehension questions. The entire Reading test will last 75 minutes. There are three parts, and directions are given for each part. You are encouraged to answer as many questions as possible within the time allowed.

You must mark your answer on the separate answer sheet. Do not write your answers in your test book.

PART 5

Directions: A word or phrase is missing in each of the sentences below. Four answer choices are given below each sentence. Select the best answer to complete the sentence. Then mark the letter (A), (B), (C), or (D) on your answer sheet.

101. More than twenty years have passed, ------- it is still one of the best-selling ice creams in the country.

(A) or
(B) but
(C) for
(D) too

102. If we fail to deliver your order ------- tomorrow, we will take 20 percent off the original price of $188.

(A) in
(B) by
(C) at
(D) to

103. Ms. Clinton opened her own law firm after ------- had passed the bar exam in New York.

(A) she
(B) her
(C) hers
(D) herself

104. The date on which the photograph has been taken should be clearly ------- on the photograph, otherwise it will be rejected.

(A) print
(B) printed
(C) printing
(D) printers

105. The new photocopying machine is also lower in cost and has a ------- production efficiency.

(A) high
(B) highly
(C) higher
(D) highest

106. Please allow ------- three to five days for any refund or exchange to be processed by our customer service representatives.

(A) heavily
(B) ironically
(C) approximately
(D) accurately

107. The board must decide to either cut salaries or lay off workers in order to ------- the company from going bankrupt.

(A) keep
(B) support
(C) demand
(D) lead

108. Several newspapers claimed that the new law is little different from the ------- law established ten years ago.

(A) strict
(B) original
(C) common
(D) fundamental

109. If you hear an emergency alarm, please make your way to the lighted exit signs in a calm and ------- fashion.

(A) stylish
(B) orderly
(C) apparent
(D) seasonal

110. Detailed instructions for proper operation and maintenance of the copy machine can be found in the ------- operation manual.

(A) enclosed
(B) trained
(C) discarded
(D) engaged

111. When manufacturing electronic components for automobiles or mobile devices, the cleanliness of a factory is ------- utmost importance.

(A) in
(B) of
(C) for
(D) by

112. Ms. McGowan went to Los Angeles to pursue studies in Film and Media Production, and then started ------- media firm.

(A) she
(B) hers
(C) her own
(D) herself

113. The company ------- signed a contract with the government to provide 60,000 units of the latest tablet computers.

(A) shortly
(B) favorably
(C) recently
(D) accordingly

114. Tourism is an important source of revenue for Switzerland, and it is the ------- largest business, right behind the watch manufacturing and the banking service industry.

(A) three
(B) triple
(C) third
(D) thirdly

115. National Commercial Bank updated its website to increase the amount of information available to customers ------- in investment options.

(A) interest
(B) interests
(C) interested
(D) interesting

116. Our new financial reporting software makes it ------- than before for companies to create their financial statements.

(A) easy
(B) easier
(C) ease
(D) more easily

117. We should review our new business proposal carefully ------- we have received it from our partner company.

(A) while
(B) since
(C) as soon as
(D) upon

118. The Head of Customer Service immediately told the board members about the complaints from customers abroad so that they could be ------- in the next day's board meeting.

(A) completed
(B) addressed
(C) described
(D) unclaimed

119. The changes now being felt ------- the IT industry reflect specific customer needs for simplicity and convenience.

(A) after
(B) throughout
(C) as
(D) yet

▶ ▶ ▶ GO ON TO THE NEXT PAGE

120. ------- posting an article to our online board, please review the group's frequently asked questions, also known as an FAQ.

(A) Alongside
(B) Prior to
(C) According to
(D) Nearby

121. Any items purchased at Mary's Superstore throughout February and March will be delivered ------- three business days.

(A) since
(B) between
(C) within
(D) above

122. ------- interested in purchasing property overseas should be aware that their actions have the potential to hurt the domestic economy.

(A) Which
(B) We
(C) Those
(D) Themselves

123. Unexpected technical complications which occurred during the final test caused the company ------- the launch of the new database system.

(A) delay
(B) delayed
(C) delaying
(D) to delay

124. Many researchers suggested that the company ------- on strengthening its R&D environment to attract investors.

(A) focus
(B) focuses
(C) will focus
(D) has been focused

125. ------- takes the chief executive officer job, the business situation facing our company is too difficult to expect a quick and sharp improvement.

(A) Whichever
(B) Whoever
(C) Since
(D) Even though

126. Our hotel suites feel like your own private paradise since the hotel is located on the island of Borneo and it is only ------- by boat.

(A) transported
(B) accessible
(C) operated
(D) adjacent

127. Due to the unexpected malfunction of the video conferencing equipment, our sales presentation ------- until further notice.

(A) will postpone
(B) has been postponed
(C) to postpone
(D) have postponed

128. The government will fail to sustain the national economy ------- it makes extra efforts to create more employment opportunities.

(A) who
(B) that
(C) unless
(D) therefore

129. The plant manager could not receive the replacement parts for some broken conveyor belts, because all of the components suppliers have ------- in stock.

(A) none
(B) every
(C) them
(D) little

130. Most of the meat processing companies will need more farmlands to raise more cows, ------- the beef consumption increases.

(A) if so
(B) provided that
(C) although
(D) in order that

PART 6

Directions: Read the texts that follow. A word or phrase, or sentence is missing in parts of each text. Four answer choices for each question are given below the text. Select the best answer to complete the text. Then mark the letter (A), (B), (C), or (D) on your answer sheet.

Questions 131-134 refer to the following letter.

Dear Mr. Watson,

Thank your for your interest in our vacant computer graphic designer position here at Hexagon Games, Inc. ------- on our evaluation of your skills and experience, you seem like
                                                    131.
an ideal candidate for the position.

We would like very much to talk with you in person ------- the computer graphic designer
                                                              132.
job. If it is a suitable time for you, We would like you to visit our headquarters at 2 P.M. on Wednesday, May 22.

At the job interview, you ------- to go into further detail about your strengths, and to
                                133.
describe your contributions to projects you have worked on in the past. If we feel that you would fit well into our computer graphic design team at Hexagon Games, Inc., we will then place you on a shortlist for the final round of interviews.

Please call me at (408) 535-3500 to let me know if the aforementioned meeting date and time are agreeable to you. -------.
                                134.

Scarlett Hwang

---

131. (A) Base
(B) Based
(C) Basing
(D) Basement

132. (A) toward
(B) among
(C) throughout
(D) concerning

133. (A) were asked
(B) will be asked
(C) had asked
(D) would have asked

134. (A) I look forward to receiving your call.
(B) I'd like to put you on our waiting list for future positions.
(C) I'm so sorry that the meeting will be delayed.
(D) Our company will be completely reorganized.

▶ ▶ ▶ GO ON TO THE NEXT PAGE

Cream Pharmaceutical Names New Director

London - August 10) Cream Pharmaceutical, one of the largest pharmaceutical supplies companies in England, announced yesterday that Dr. James Jackson has been hired as Director of Research and Development. With this -------, Cream Pharmaceutical hopes to
135.
raise its business profile and build a powerful influence in the industry.

Dr. Jackson ------- for over twenty five years in Phanza, Inc., including fifteen years
136.
in research and development of vaccines and medicines for the communicable and noncommunicable diseases. The CEO of Cream Pharmaceutical, Ms. Kelly Jenkins, stated "Dr. Jackson's medical expertise will be an invaluable tool for enhancing our quality of the medical products we produce. -------."
137.

Cream Pharmaceutical is a London-based company, with a medical research workforce of ------- 2,000 employees throughout England.
138.

135. (A) launch
(B) addition
(C) merger
(D) campaign

136. (A) working
(B) works
(C) has worked
(D) will work

137. (A) I am honored to have been offered this position.
(B) A new policy is committed to serving our customers better.
(C) I am thrilled to have the opportunity to work with him.
(D) We partner closely with experts to develop next generation product.

138. (A) approximate
(B) approximates
(C) approximating
(D) approximately

Golden Bear Real Estate

603 21st Street

Oakland, CA 94607

(510) 212-9267

www.gbre.com

Are you a dancer who is searching for a proper studio? We are currently renting out a

great dance studio, located at 1123 South River Road, which has plenty of space, high

ceilings, and a mix of natural and artificial lighting. It is a perfect place for ------- your
139.

dance rehearsal and performance.

The dance studio is ------- with maple flooring, full-length mirrors, retractable curtains,
140.

barres, and a state-of-the-art sound system. We now offer the ------- rental rate for it set
141.

at 15% below the average market rent. -------.
142.

If you want to inquire about this studio, or to book a visit, please contact Ms. Linda

Hopkins at (510) 913-9815 or lh@gbre.com.

139. (A) hold
(B) holder
(C) holding
(D) held

140. (A) talented
(B) developed
(C) equipped
(D) satisfied

141. (A) cooperative
(B) encouraging
(C) affordable
(D) thoughtful

142. (A) Moreover, your new pair of dance
shoes should be both comfortable
and functional.
(B) As a result, the new TV studios will be
built on an industrial park on South
River Road.
(C) In addition, if you are a college
student who majors in dancing, a
further discount will be given.
(D) In fact, the international festival was
launched ten years ago and has been
held annually ever since.

To: All private banking customers
From: Ronald Huxley <ronaldh@americanabank.com>
Subject: Personal information protection
Date: August 6

Dear our private banking customers,

At Americana Bank, we take our private online banking customers' security extremely seriously. That's why we will never request that you confirm your Internet banking log-in information or ------- security information by e-mail or telephone. -------.
       143.   **144.**

We recommend that customers take the extra ------- outlined below to protect their
       145.
personal information. Always choose a password that nobody would be able to guess and ensure that you change your password often. Never reply to e-mails that ask for your personal information, account numbers, etc. These e-mails will not be from us.

Finally, if you ------- suspect that an e-mail is fraudulent, contact our fraud prevention
       146.
department at 1-800-365-2020.

Thank you in advance for your support in protecting the confidentiality of your information.

Ronald Huxley

---

143. (A) each
    (B) most
    (C) any other
    (D) one another

144. (A) We will enhance regulations and penalties concerning identity theft.
    (B) We always treat your personal information with complete confidentiality.
    (C) We combine experienced professional bankers with the convenience of technology.
    (D) We are offering higher interest rates on savings accounts to acquire retail customers.

145. (A) savings
    (B) measures
    (C) ventures
    (D) speculations

146. (A) once
    (B) hardly
    (C) only
    (D) ever

PART 7

Directions: In this part you will read a selection of texts, such as magazine and newspaper articles, e-mails, and instant messages. Each text or set of texts is followed by several questions. Select the best answer for each question and mark the letter (A), (B), (C), or (D) on your answer sheet.

Questions 147-148 refer to the following invitation.

You are cordially invited to a banquet

Presenting

The new CD title
Chopin - Piano Concertos

(The Mozart Records Co.)

by

Claude Pawlowski

Professor, Guelf University of Classical Music

Friday, March 14
7:00 P.M. – 9:00 P.M.
The Walton Convention Center
Haven Hall

Sponsored by

Felts Classic Instruments

147. Why is the event taking place?

(A) To promote a concert
(B) To celebrate the establishment of a music school
(C) To honor a retiring professor
(D) To introduce a new album

148. Who will most likely pay for the event?

(A) Guelf University of Classical Music
(B) The Mozart Records Co.
(C) The Walton Convention Center
(D) Felts Classic Instruments

▶ ▶ ▶GO ON TO THE NEXT PAGE

Questions 149-150 refer to the following text message chain.

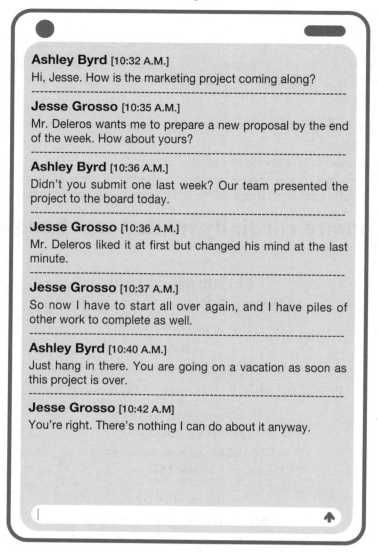

Ashley Byrd [10:32 A.M.]
Hi, Jesse. How is the marketing project coming along?

Jesse Grosso [10:35 A.M.]
Mr. Deleros wants me to prepare a new proposal by the end of the week. How about yours?

Ashley Byrd [10:36 A.M.]
Didn't you submit one last week? Our team presented the project to the board today.

Jesse Grosso [10:36 A.M.]
Mr. Deleros liked it at first but changed his mind at the last minute.

Jesse Grosso [10:37 A.M.]
So now I have to start all over again, and I have piles of other work to complete as well.

Ashley Byrd [10:40 A.M.]
Just hang in there. You are going on a vacation as soon as this project is over.

Jesse Grosso [10:42 A.M]
You're right. There's nothing I can do about it anyway.

---

149. What is indicated about Mr. Deleros?

(A) He is one of the board members.
(B) He has a meeting on the weekend.
(C) He rejected Mr. Grosso's previous proposal.
(D) He plans to take time off from work.

150. At 10:40 A.M., what does Ms. Byrd mean when she writes, "Just hang in there"?

(A) She expects Mr. Grosso will continue working for her.
(B) She hopes to go on a vacation with Mr. Grosso.
(C) She wants Mr. Grosso to keep working despite the stress.
(D) She would like Mr. Grosso to stay where he is now.

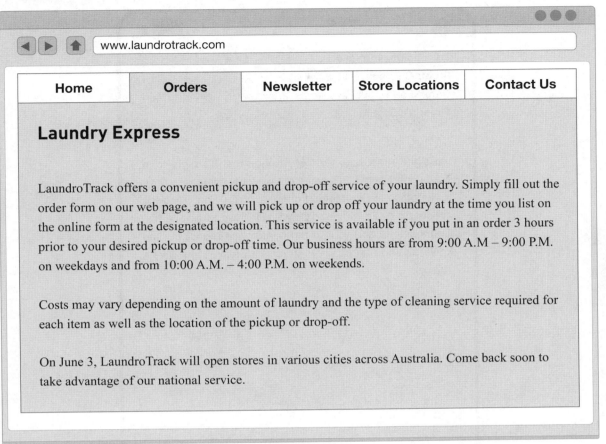

151. What is being advertised?

(A) A discount offer
(B) Updated business hours
(C) An improved service
(D) A new laundry store location

152. What is indicated about Laundry Express?

(A) Its prices may vary depending on the service hours.
(B) It is available nationally.
(C) It is cheaper for returning customers.
(D) It requires advance order placement.

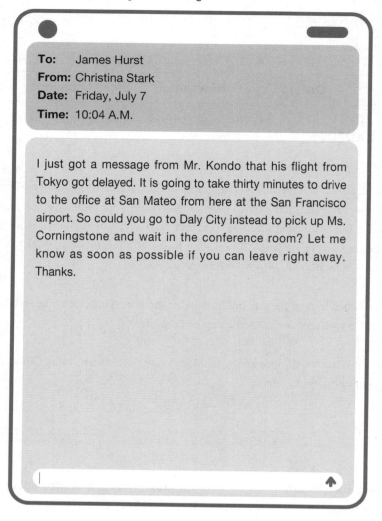

153. Where most likely is Ms. Stark now?

(A) In Tokyo
(B) In San Mateo
(C) In San Francisco
(D) In Daly City

154. What does Ms. Stark ask Mr. Hurst to do quickly?

(A) Book a conference room
(B) Wait for her to confirm a time
(C) Send a reply
(D) Call Ms. Corningstone

Yellowknife (August 28) – Tonight, it is expected that the Northern Lights will be visible at around 10:35 P.M. for about 10 minutes. Tonight should be one of the best nights to see aurora activity since there will be a very clear sky with no precipitation. There will be strong light activity in Cameron Valley, making it an ideal place to see the most colorful and brightest aurorae. The photography club will travel to Cameron Valley to see this remarkable sight. People can sign up for this exciting trip in Room #402 in the Wolfe Building on campus no later than 12:00 P.M. Interested students can contact club representative Jason Mayer at jmayer@fastmail.com or visit the club and ask one of the club members for more information. There is only room for 10 more students, so hurry and save a seat on the tour bus. At 8:00 P.M., they will depart for Cameron Valley, and they will return to campus at 12:00 A.M. Do not miss out on this chance to see a breathtaking display of the Northern Lights!

155. Where can the article most likely be found?

(A) In an art gallery
(B) In an astronomical observatory
(C) In a tourist catalogue
(D) In a college newspaper

156. According to the article, what are the people on the trip expected to see?

(A) Ancient local artifacts
(B) An event in the night sky
(C) A photography exhibition of aurorae
(D) A famous weather forecaster

157. At what time are the students leaving the campus?

(A) 4:00 P.M.
(B) 8:00 P.M.
(C) 10:35 P.M.
(D) 12:00 P.M.

Questions 158-160 refer to the following e-mail.

To:	Louis Smith <lsmith@boostmail.com>
CC:	<randerson@stylepoint.com>, <jmarsh@stylepoint.com>, <brivera@stylepoint.com>
From:	Sasha Martin <smartin@stylepoint.com>
Date:	January 11
Subject:	Style Point summer collection

Dear Mr. Smith,

We recently launched a new collection of Style Point summer sunglasses. You did such a wonderful job last season, and thanks to you, we experienced a 2% increase of sale in last season's handbag collection. Therefore, we would like you to work on our web page for the new products again. We loved the vibrant colors you worked with and your distinctive style of design.

We would like to meet with you to explain this season's concept and the specifics you need to include on the web page. Please let us know if you'll be available later this week. I have business meetings with some clients this week, so I may not be able to contact you directly at all times. Therefore, I have copied my marketing team on this e-mail so you can contact them with any inquiries or if you need assistance. If you are interested in working with us again, please let us know, and Ms. Anderson will send you some samples.

Sasha Martin.
Marketing manager, Style Point

158. What was Mr. Smith asked to do last year?

(A) Photograph some new products
(B) Distribute online catalogues to registered customers
(C) Design a web page
(D) Sell products online

159. According to Ms. Martin, what will Mr. Smith receive if he accepts the offer?

(A) Brand-new handbags
(B) A few pairs of glasses
(C) A contract
(D) A meeting schedule

160. Why did Ms. Martin make the e-mail available for others to see?

(A) To assign the job to a different person
(B) To let Mr. Smith be assisted when she is occupied
(C) To solicit design suggestions from them
(D) To ask them questions about an upcoming project

To:	Troy Miles <tmiles@boltmail.com>
From:	Gary Tennent <gtennent@boltmail.com>
Date:	March 2
Subject:	To-do list

Hi, Troy.

As you already know, I'm going on a family trip tomorrow and won't be back until next Monday. —[1]—. I need you to look after the store, and there are some things you need to do while I'm away. —[2]—. I already ordered 3 days' worth of products, so all you have to do is receive the deliveries and sign the forms that Mr. Torri, the deliveryman from Freshness First, hands you. Please organize the products on the shelves like you normally do during the day. Don't forget to throw out the expired products. Before you leave, make sure to turn off all the power except for the coolers. Lock the cash box and the doors. Place the keys inside the mailbox as always. If you have any questions, feel free to call me. —[3]—. Thanks for your hard work. I will double your pay for the time I'm gone.
—[4]—.

Gary

161. What type of business does Mr. Tennent most likely own?

(A) A travel equipment store
(B) A grocery store
(C) A delivery store
(D) A hotel restaurant

162. What is Mr. Miles' daily job at the store?

(A) Placing orders
(B) Signing forms
(C) Restocking the shelves
(D) Opening the doors

163. In which of the positions marked [1], [2], [3], and [4] does the following sentence best fit?

"I will have my phone on me at all times."

(A) [1]
(B) [2]
(C) [3]
(D) [4]

Summer Sun-Blast Tour

Welcome to New Zealand, the Land of Long White Cloud and Kiwis. Enjoy beautiful nature and summer events full of fun in New Zealand with Waitangi Tours. The following is a list of events you can take part in during the summer. Detailed information about the events is available on our website.

World Buskers Festival (January 14-25)
Join hundreds of the world's famous buskers and street performers on the streets of Christchurch. Feel the rhythm and sounds of diverse genres. The best part? It's completely free to participate for all!

Great Lake Cycling Trail (February 1-25)
Ride along the shores of Lake Taupo with the cool wind blowing through your hair. Options to ride on the full trail over two days or shorter sections are available.

Traditional Dance Nights (February 5-18)
Local dancers compete to win the Polyneori Prize. Join the dancers to make an unforgettable memory! The winner will be named on closing night.

Artifact and Jewelry Market (February 1-28)
Grab a souvenir to show your family and friends back home! Local craftsmen are ready to create special artifacts and jewelry upon request.

New Zealand's Treat Streets (February 10-20)
Martin Coleman, a professor at a local university, and his students will set up booths on the streets of Auckland to welcome all visitors and residents with traditional cuisine and dishes that they made in class.

164. For whom is the notice most likely intended?

(A) Local residents
(B) Event planners
(C) Tourists
(D) Volunteers

165. What is NOT listed among the events?

(A) Musical entertainment
(B) Watersports on a lake
(C) Sales of products
(D) A display of food

166. When will a winner of a contest be announced?

(A) On January 25
(B) On February 5
(C) On February 18
(D) On February 25

167. What is indicated about Mr. Coleman?

(A) He works for Waitangi Tours.
(B) He is knowledgeable about architecture.
(C) He goes on tours to New Zealand every summer.
(D) He teaches culinary arts.

Nathan Chen   6:03 P.M.

Kacey Co.'s brand-launching show in England will take place next month! This London launching show is highly anticipated by the board due to the huge success of our brand launching in Norway last year. How are things going?

Douglas Stanfield   6:06 P.M.

We received the fragrance collection from our factory in India and it is ready for display. Now, we are waiting for the new Kacey's skincare line to arrive from Germany.

Sajan Calen   6:10 P.M.

There will be a slight delay in the shipments.

Sajan Calen   6:12 P.M.

A severe rainstorm here has been going on for a few days, and no overseas transportation is operational. The good news is that all the products are safely packed and ready to go.

Douglas Stanfield   6:15 P.M.

Will this affect our brand-launching party schedule?

Sajan Calen   6:16 P.M

It most likely won't because there is still a month left until the grand opening, and the storm will pass in a couple of days.

Nathan Chen   6:18 P.M.

That is nice to hear.

Douglas Stanfield   6:20 P.M.

Mr. Calen, please keep me updated on all the shipping information.

Sajan Calen   6:23 P.M

Of course. I will let you know as soon as possible.

SEND

168. What kind of company is Kacey Co.?

(A) A shipping company
(B) A fashion boutique
(C) A cosmetics maker
(D) A travel agency

169. What has delayed the shipping of some display items?

(A) A schedule change of the launching party
(B) A manufacturing problem at a factory
(C) An accident during transportation
(D) Inclement weather conditions

170. Where does Mr. Calen work?

(A) In England
(B) In India
(C) In Norway
(D) In Germany

171. At 6:18 P.M., what does Mr. Chen mean when he writes, "That is nice to hear"?

(A) He is glad that the show can proceed as scheduled.
(B) He enjoys the rain.
(C) He thinks Kacey Co. will attract many customers.
(D) He appreciates Mr. Calen's hard work.

Community Report

Are you planning on advertising your business to attract more customers? Let *Community Report* take care of the difficult job of making your business known in the community for you!

Community Report is delivered to apartments, subway stations, businesses, and schools in Philadelphia. Using our service is the most effective and inexpensive way to advertise your establishment. For $20, your posting can be printed in an issue of *Community Report*. —[1]—. You can choose when your posting will be printed: the first week of the month or the third. We will also charge you only $35 for your posting to be printed in both issues of *Community Report* in a month.

When submitting your request on our website at www.communityreport.com/ads, please include a brief description of your business and your phone number and/or e-mail address. Relevant pictures should be sent as well to maximize the effectiveness of your posting. —[2]—.

Our experts can make, write, and edit a compelling advertisement for you. —[3]—. Contact us at (215) 555-8332 for details and more information. In addition, we heavily rely on donations from readers to continue our mission of providing trustworthy information about the community, careers, and local events to the people of Philadelphia. —[4]—. Go on our website to find out more about becoming a *Community Report* sponsor.

172. Who is the intended audience of the advertisement?

(A) Local tenants
(B) Job seekers
(C) Advertising company employees
(D) Business owners

173. What is indicated about *Community Report*?

(A) It charges $35 for a month subscription.
(B) It is attracting more subscribers than before.
(C) It donates its profits to local schools.
(D) It is delivered to residents twice a month.

174. What is NOT mentioned as information that should be submitted with a request for a posting?

(A) A description of a business
(B) A website address
(C) Images
(D) Contact information

175. In which of the positions marked [1], [2], [3], and [4] does the following sentence best fit?

"An extra fee will be charged for this service."

(A) [1]
(B) [2]
(C) [3]
(D) [4]

http://www.electrogitalmart.com/search

Electrogital Mart

HOME	PRODUCTS	SEARCH	CUSTOMER REVIEW

Click on the product names for detailed information. Orders placed in January will automatically be entered into a drawing for a chance to win an e-voucher. The voucher can be redeemed for a free set of Librio Headphones at Electrogital Mart's Louisville location.

Search results for: `Tablet PC`

Instinct Tablet PC Ace10 High-quality built-in microphone and speaker	$79.00 (**5** reviews)
Asuronic Tablet PC T100 Detachable keyboard dock included	$105.20 (**4** reviews)
Jemits Tablet PC Y80 7-inch screen with a stylus pen	$60.10 (**0** reviews)
Digimind Tablet PC XDL-2 High-definition wide screen and cameras on front and rear	$89.70 (**14** reviews)

  http://www.electrogitalmart.com/customerreview

Electrogital Mart

HOME	PRODUCTS	SEARCH	CUSTOMER REVIEW

Share your experience with us!

Trust your instincts! ★ ★ ★ ★ ☆
Posted February 17 by Isaac Martinez

I own and use the Digimind Tablet PC XDL-2 that I purchased from Electrogital Mart last year. It is indeed a good choice for anyone who likes to watch movies on the PC. The built-in cameras actually take good quality photographs, too.

Last month, I received free headphones from Electrogital Mart for buying another tablet PC. For my son's graduation, I purchased a tablet PC made by Asuronic, but its relatively heavy weight seemed to be a problem. So I returned it and ended up ordering an Instinct Tablet PC Ace10 online as his present. I thought about buying a Jemits Tablet PC Y80, but its small screen is probably not suitable for my son to use to do his college work.

176. Why would shoppers most likely buy an Asuronic Tablet PC T100?

(A) Because they like to listen to music while working on it.
(B) Because they have a limited budget.
(C) Because they plan on watching movies on it.
(D) Because they need to type in it.

177. What item has NOT been evaluated on the website by customers?

(A) Digimind Tablet PC XDL-2
(B) Asuronic Tablet PC T100
(C) Jemits Tablet PC Y80
(D) Instinct Tablet PC Ace10

178. In the first web page, the word "redeemed" in paragraph 1, line 2, is closest in meaning to

(A) reimbursed
(B) issued
(C) purchased
(D) exchanged

179. How much did the graduation gift cost?

(A) $60.10
(B) $79.00
(C) $89.70
(D) $105.20

180. What is indicated about Mr. Martinez?

(A) He visited an Electrogital Mart offline store.
(B) He works at a local college.
(C) He will buy another tablet PC.
(D) He received a discount on his recent purchase.

Better Tomorrow Citizens Association (BTCA)
Virginia Miller Schedule (April 10 – 14)

MONDAY	TUESDAY	WEDNESDAY	THURSDAY	FRIDAY
9:30 A.M. Meeting with Maria Manns	**9:10 A.M.** Training session for new volunteers	**9:00 A.M.** Returning to London by train	**9:00 A.M.** Meeting with Brian Clark (IT Team)	**8:50 A.M.** Meeting with a project planner from Southampton
2:30 P.M. Monthly board meeting	**1:20 P.M.** Lecture at a local high school	**12:00 P.M.** Lunch meeting with the advertising team	**1:00 P.M.** Volunteer campaign planning with Veronica Mabry	**10:00 A.M.** Interview (*London Today*)
5:00 P.M. Train trip to Manchester office	**4:30 P.M.** Meeting with student volunteers	**2:00 P.M.** Conference call with Paris office	**4:00 P.M.** Preparing for volunteer project in Cambodia	**1:00 P.M.** Meeting with a local sponsor
				5:00 P.M. Berlin office conference call

To:	Virginia Miller <vmiller@btca.org>
From:	Gregory Browning <gbrowning@btca.org>
Date:	April 10
Subject:	Update
Attachment:	📎 Copy of e-mail

Dear Ms. Miller,

This is to remind you of the updates to your schedule for this week. The IT team manager can no longer attend the meeting on Thursday due to an urgent business trip. The appointment has now been moved to next Monday at 8:30 A.M. I have arranged a meeting with Stephen Pulliam on that Thursday morning. He is the professor at the University of Fort Barns whom you want to meet to discuss his upcoming lecture at the Better Tomorrow Citizens Association.

Secondly, I have attached a copy of the e-mail from Alavis Car Rental that confirms the reservation of a vehicle for you to use during your business trip to Manchester. I believe you already have the train tickets and the hotel confirmation I previously sent you.

Lastly, David McLean of the local newspaper sent a list of questions he will ask you for his article on Friday. I will give you the list when you come back from you trip.

Sincerely,

Gregory Browning

181. What is indicated about the Better Tomorrow Citizens Association?

(A) It has offices in multiple cities.
(B) It has launched a new advertisement.
(C) It is currently recruiting new volunteers.
(D) It hired Ms. Miller recently.

182. According to the e-mail, what did Mr.Browning most likely do?

(A) He contacted a lecturer.
(B) He changed a website design.
(C) He solicited a donation.
(D) He delivered a speech at a university.

183. Whose meeting schedule has been changed?

(A) Maria Manns
(B) Brian Clark
(C) Veronica Mabry
(D) Gregory Browning

184. When will Ms. Miller meet with Mr. McLean on Friday?

(A) At 8:50 A.M.
(B) At 10:00 A.M.
(C) At 1:00 P.M.
(D) At 5:00 P.M.

185. What was sent with the e-mail?

(A) A train ticket
(B) A list of questions
(C) Accommodation details
(D) A car rental confirmation

MEMO

To: Managers of PE Ceramics
From: Nguyen Dinh
Date: June 2
Subject: Business World

This is in regard to the Professional Development Association's upcoming series of seminars, Business World, to be held from June 20 to 22. Attending the seminars is obligatory for all new managers. For all managers, the price of admission will be covered by the company, but hotel room reservations should be covered individually. If you choose the Golden Castle Hotel, you will pay $75 per night instead of $130 thanks to the seminar-attendee discount. For reimbursement, please contact the manager of the Accounting Department. Refer to the notice posted on the bulletin board at the employee lounge.

Sincerely,

Nguyen Dinh
President

Business World – Essential Management Skills

June 20 – June 22
Bloomberg Convention Center
455 Long Street, New York, NY 10055

Join our popular seminars that are led by well-known authors, educators, senior executives, consultants, and even current chief executive officers of large corporations! Seminars begin at 9:00 A.M. and end at 5:00 P.M. each day. Lunch will be provided. Through our seminars, you can learn to set mutual goals, maximize team performance, value differences and ideas, and communicate effectively. Please wear business casual attire in layers to the seminars as the room temperatures may vary.

To:	William Gonzalez <w.gonzalez@peceramics.com>
From:	Marlene Karp <m.karp@peceramics.com>
Date:	July 6
Subject:	Reimbursement

Dear Mr. Gonzalez,

I attended the Business World seminars for all three days. I will stop by your office to drop off the receipts and expense report for the reimbursement process.

By the way, I should mention that it was a bit difficult to reach the Bloomberg Convention Center, where the seminars took place, from the Golden Castle Hotel. The public transit in the neighborhood is neither very convenient nor on time. I would appreciate it if PE Ceramics could arrange a contract with a hotel that is closer to the seminar location or that provides shuttle service next time.

Sincerely,

Marlene Karp
Advertising Department

186. What is the purpose of the memo?

(A) To confirm a reservation at a hotel
(B) To offer a discounted registration fee for a seminar
(C) To recommend joining an organization
(D) To encourage employees to attend an event

187. In the memo, the word "covered" in paragraph 1, line 3, is closest in meaning to

(A) included
(B) paid for
(C) exempted
(D) applied

188. What are the participants asked to do?

(A) Follow a dress code
(B) Arrive early at the venue
(C) Bring food to the seminars
(D) Ask questions to the presenters

189. Who most likely is Mr. Gonzalez?

(A) A supervisor at PE Ceramics
(B) A seminar instructor
(C) A new accountant
(D) A manager of Golden Castle Hotel

190. What is NOT implied about Ms. Karp?

(A) She is in a managerial position.
(B) She will be reimbursed for her flight.
(C) She received a discount at the Golden Castle Hotel.
(D) She was in New York on June 21.

A disturbance in *The Unity*

Fans of Warren Diaz's pop phenomenon sci-fi series, *The Space Empire*, will have to wait five additional months to see the fourth and final film of the movie series, *The Unity*. Thinkers Production announced today that the release of *The Unity* has been postponed to December 15 from July 21 in North America. The production company pushed back the release date in the hope that the Christmas season will bring more people to the theaters.

The success of the movie series was actually rather unexpected in the film industry as its first film, *The March to Mars*, was watched by a relatively low number of people. The second and third films of the series made in total of $3.2 billion, breaking records with impressive figures and shocking the whole industry.

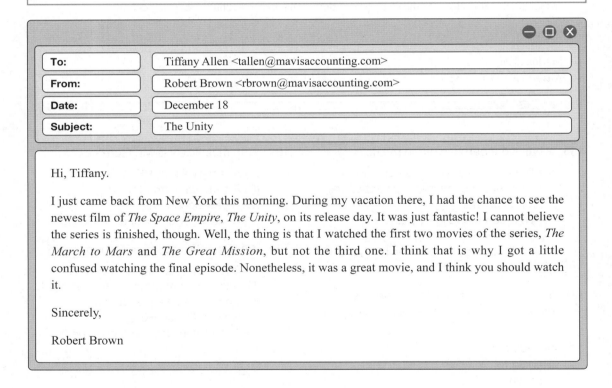

To:	Tiffany Allen <tallen@mavisaccounting.com>
From:	Robert Brown <rbrown@mavisaccounting.com>
Date:	December 18
Subject:	The Unity

Hi, Tiffany.

I just came back from New York this morning. During my vacation there, I had the chance to see the newest film of *The Space Empire*, *The Unity*, on its release day. It was just fantastic! I cannot believe the series is finished, though. Well, the thing is that I watched the first two movies of the series, *The March to Mars* and *The Great Mission*, but not the third one. I think that is why I got a little confused watching the final episode. Nonetheless, it was a great movie, and I think you should watch it.

Sincerely,

Robert Brown

To:	Robert Brown <rbrown@mavisaccounting.com>
From:	Tiffany Allen <tallen@mavisaccounting.com>
Date:	December 19
Subject:	re: The Unity

Hi, Robert.

I am sorry for the late reply. As you may know, I was busy all day long yesterday preparing for the company seminar. I am glad you enjoyed your recent vacation. I actually watched *The Unity* with my family on December 17. It is indeed a very well-made movie. The final action scene took my breath away.

I can't believe you haven't seen *The Collapse of the Throne* yet! How could you possibly have missed it? I have a DVD of every episode of the series, so maybe we can watch the one you missed together sometime. Let me know when you are available.

Regards,

Tiffany Allen

191. According to the article, why was the release of the film postponed?

(A) Because the director is going to change the script.
(B) Because the graphic work was not complete.
(C) Because the advertisements for the film have yet to be prepared.
(D) Because Thinkers Production wanted more people to see the film.

192. In the article, the word "figures" in paragraph 2, line 3, is closest in meaning to

(A) people
(B) numbers
(C) reviews
(D) graphics

193. When did Mr. Brown most likely watch *The Unity*?

(A) On November 21
(B) On December 15
(C) On December 17
(D) On December 18

194. What is the third film of *The Space Empire*?

(A) *The Collapse of the Throne*
(B) *The Great Mission*
(C) *The March to Mars*
(D) *The Unity*

195. What is implied about Ms. Allen?

(A) She will attend a seminar next week.
(B) She is surprised that Mr. Brown likes *The Unity*.
(C) She will buy another DVD for Mr. Brown.
(D) She is a fan of *The Space Empire*.

▶ ▶ ▶ GO ON TO THE NEXT PAGE

Thank you for being a loyal sponsor of the Philadelphia Art Museum (PAM). To mark Susan McCabe's upcoming exhibition at our museum, we would like to invite all our sponsors to join us in welcoming her. Ms. McCabe is a young cartoonist who is emerging as a rising star in today's cartoon world.

We invite all sponsors to the preopening of the exhibition, which will be held on April 4. Special gifts will be given to those who attend according to their sponsorship level.

The gifts available to sponsors are as follow:

Sponsorship Level	*Gift(s)
Friend	A postcard
Associate	A postcard and a mug
Partner	A postcard, a mug, and Ms. McCabe's latest cartoon book, *The Zeppelin*
Benefactor	All of the above and a plaque with the sponsor's name engraved on it

*All gift items are designed by Ms. McCabe.

The grand opening will take place on April 8, and it is open to the public as well as sponsors. All visitors will be able to enjoy a tour around the exhibition and some refreshments.

We look forward to seeing you at the exhibition!

To:	Annie Rivera <arivera@pam.org>
From:	Clyde Harper <charper@onemail.com>
Date:	April 12
Subject:	Sponsor gift

Dear Ms. Rivera,

Thank you for inviting me to such a great exhibition by a local artist who is becoming a true star in both the cartoon and art scene. It was a wonderful and well-organized exhibition that fully demonstrated Ms. McCabe's great skills and unique style. The reason I am writing is to report that I did not receive my gift items at the exhibition. I was told that you will send me the gifts by mail within a few days. However, I have yet to receive them. As I am really looking forward to reading *The Zeppelin*, I want a prompt response from you.

Sincerely,

Clyde Harper

To: Clyde Harper <charper@onemail.com>
From: Annie Rivera <arivera@pam.org>
Date: April 13
Subject: re: Sponsor gift

Dear Mr. Harper,

I am very sorry to hear that you have not received your gifts yet. We will send the gift items to your address by express mail, so they will be delivered by April 16. However, we should make clear that you will only receive a mug and a postcard, not the cartoon book, just like the other sponsors in the same sponsorship level as you did. Thank you for your commitment to our museum and the community.

Truly yours,

Annie Rivera

196. In the notice, the word "mark" in paragraph 1, line 1, is closest in meaning to

(A) distinguish
(B) indicate
(C) brighten
(D) celebrate

197. What is indicated about Ms. McCabe?

(A) She lives in Philadelphia.
(B) She donated money to the PAM.
(C) She will serve light snacks to visitors.
(D) She recently graduated from her university.

198. When did Mr. Harper visit the PAM?

(A) On April 4
(B) On April 8
(C) On April 12
(D) On April 13

199. What is a purpose of the second e-mail?

(A) To report an error in an order
(B) To apologize for the poor quality of a gift
(C) To ask for a donation
(D) To clarify some information

200. What sponsorship level does Mr. Harper have?

(A) Friend
(B) Associate
(C) Partner
(D) Benefactor

STOP! This is the end of the test. If you finish before time is called, you may go back to Parts 5, 6, and 7 and check your work.

Actual Test 11

MP3

해설집

적정 풀이 시간 120분

120
min

시작 시간 ___시 ___분

종료 시간 ___시 ___분

중간에 멈추지 말고 처음부터 끝까지 풀어보세요.
문제를 풀 때에는 실전처럼 답안지에 마킹하세요.

목표 개수 _____ / 200   **실제 개수** _____ / 200

예상 점수는 번역 및 정답에 있는 점수 환산표를 참조하세요.

LISTENING TEST

In the Listening test, you will be asked to demonstrate how well you understand spoken English. The entire Listening test will last approximately 45 minutes. There are four parts, and directions are given for each part. You must mark your answers on the separate answer sheet. Do not write your answers in the test book.

PART 1

Directions: For each question in this part, you will hear four statements about a picture in your test book. When you hear the statements, you must select the one statement that best describes what you see in the picture. Then find the number of the question on your answer sheet and mark your answer. The statements will not be printed in your test book and will be spoken only one time.

Statement (B), "They are sitting at a table." is the best description of the picture. So you should select answer (B) and mark it on your answer sheet.

1.

2.

▶ ▶ ▶ GO ON TO THE NEXT PAGE

3.

4.

5.

6.

▶ ▶ ▶GO ON TO THE NEXT PAGE

Directions: You will hear a question or statement and three responses spoken in English. They will not be printed in your test book and will be spoken only one time. Select the best response to the question or statement and mark the letter (A), (B), or (C) on your answer sheet.

7. Mark your answer on your answer sheet.

8. Mark your answer on your answer sheet.

9. Mark your answer on your answer sheet.

10. Mark your answer on your answer sheet.

11. Mark your answer on your answer sheet.

12. Mark your answer on your answer sheet.

13. Mark your answer on your answer sheet.

14. Mark your answer on your answer sheet.

15. Mark your answer on your answer sheet.

16. Mark your answer on your answer sheet.

17. Mark your answer on your answer sheet.

18. Mark your answer on your answer sheet.

19. Mark your answer on your answer sheet.

20. Mark your answer on your answer sheet.

21. Mark your answer on your answer sheet.

22. Mark your answer on your answer sheet.

23. Mark your answer on your answer sheet.

24. Mark your answer on your answer sheet.

25. Mark your answer on your answer sheet.

26. Mark your answer on your answer sheet.

27. Mark your answer on your answer sheet.

28. Mark your answer on your answer sheet.

29. Mark your answer on your answer sheet.

30. Mark your answer on your answer sheet.

31. Mark your answer on your answer sheet.

PART 3

Directions: You will hear some conversations between two or three people. You will be asked to answer three questions about what the speakers say in each conversation. Select the best response to each question and mark the letter (A), (B), (C), or (D) on your answer sheet. The conversations will not be printed in your test book and will be spoken only one time.

32. Who most likely is the woman?

(A) A delivery person
(B) A web designer
(C) A photographer
(D) A security guard

33. What is the woman concerned about?

(A) Getting enough lighting
(B) Carrying some equipment
(C) Getting a parking ticket validated
(D) Finishing a project on time

34. What does the man provide the woman?

(A) A parking pass
(B) A nametag
(C) An employee ID card
(D) A key to the conference room

35. What will be constructed at a stadium?

(A) A fueling station
(B) A storage warehouse
(C) A parking area
(D) An athletic facility

36. What is the biggest concern the residents have?

(A) Noise from the construction
(B) Safety for children
(C) Decreasing population
(D) An increase in traffic

37. Why has a new meeting venue been chosen?

(A) It is closer to the stadium.
(B) It costs less to use.
(C) It is not far from public transportation.
(D) It provides more room.

38. Who most likely is the man?

(A) A departmental manager
(B) A computer programmer
(C) A financial consultant
(D) A vendor for office supplies

39. What did the woman request for the man?

(A) A laptop computer
(B) New office supplies
(C) Some office furniture
(D) A corporate credit card

40. What does the woman suggest the man do?

(A) Get an estimate from another supplier
(B) Call a new client immediately
(C) Make sure to keep his receipts
(D) Spend less money for travel expenses

41. What will the woman do next week?

(A) Meet with clients from Sydney
(B) Complete a project
(C) Visit her relatives
(D) Go on a business trip

42. What does the woman want the man to recommend?

(A) Guided tours
(B) Restaurants
(C) Affordable hotels
(D) A city's tourist attractions

43. What does the woman say she will do next?

(A) Send an e-mail at once
(B) Make a payment for traveling
(C) Check her air ticket
(D) Find an address

▶ ▶ ▶ GO ON TO THE NEXT PAGE

44. What does the man want to talk about?

(A) A job opportunity
(B) The results of a survey
(C) Supplier selections
(D) Responses to customer complaints

45. Why does the woman say, "The report is just two pages long"?

(A) To express her annoyance
(B) To confirm she is available
(C) To request more work
(D) To turn down an offer

46. What does the man remind the woman about?

(A) Ordering food from a caterer
(B) Filling in for a colleague
(C) Calling her supervisor
(D) Making a reservation

47. What department does the woman work in?

(A) Buildings and Grounds
(B) Public Works
(C) Parks and Recreation
(D) Information Technology

48. Why is the man calling?

(A) To ask about a new program
(B) To inquire about the registration fee
(C) To report a fallen tree in the street
(D) To find out when is the tree planting

49. What does the woman tell the man to do?

(A) Submit a form in person
(B) Pay for trees in advance
(C) Call her back later
(D) Fill in an online form

50. What did the man recently review?

(A) A policy for safety
(B) A product review
(C) A sales report
(D) Guidelines for assembly lines

51. What does the man ask the woman about?

(A) Extending a deadline
(B) Hiring new workers
(C) Approving overtime work
(D) Checking inventory of the warehouse

52. What information will the man be provided after lunch?

(A) An inventory status
(B) Rescheduled shifts
(C) A new date for shipping
(D) Sales data for the new computer

53. What project are the speakers working on?

(A) A press release
(B) An advertising campaign
(C) A reconstruction project
(D) An orientation session

54. What is the problem that the woman has mentioned?

(A) She cannot finish a project on time.
(B) There are not enough funds in a budget.
(C) She has a scheduling conflict.
(D) A coworker has been absent repeatedly.

55. What will the woman do next?

(A) Call a colleague
(B) Go home for the day
(C) Go to see a doctor
(D) Share some pictures

56. Where does the conversation most likely take place?

(A) At a grocery store
(B) At an automobile manufacturer
(C) At a computer chip maker
(D) At a clothing factory

57. What did the woman have trouble with this morning?

(A) Her parking pass
(B) Her timesheet
(C) Her office computer
(D) Her identification badge

58. What will the speakers most likely do next?

(A) Practice a skill
(B) Watch an instructional video
(C) Complete a form
(D) Take a tour of the facility

59. What industry do the speakers most likely work in?

(A) Manufacturing
(B) Entertainment
(C) Medicine
(D) Food service

60. What does the man mean when he says, "I've given presentations there in the past"?

(A) He has no time to meet now.
(B) He does not enjoy giving presentations.
(C) He understands the woman's situation.
(D) He can give the woman some help.

61. What do the speakers decide to do?

(A) Work on presentation slides together
(B) Work overtime in the evening
(C) Postpone finding a new employee
(D) Take a short break for lunch

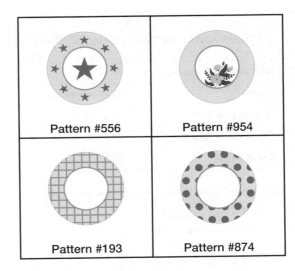

Pattern #556   Pattern #954

Pattern #193   Pattern #874

62. Look at the graphic. Which plate pattern is the woman interested in?

(A) #954
(B) #193
(C) #874
(D) #556

63. What does the woman say will happen in October?

(A) A new product line will be released.
(B) A store will check inventory of the plates.
(C) A new business will open.
(D) A branch office will be relocated.

64. What problem does the man mention?

(A) Several items were damaged in transit.
(B) A catalog contains incorrect information.
(C) Some items will be unavailable.
(D) A shipping fee will be applied to all orders.

▶ ▶ ▶ GO ON TO THE NEXT PAGE

Ticket Confirmation Code: 8590AW	
Number of Passengers	4
Date	September 21
Departure Time	10 A.M.
Price per Ticket	$15
Total Price	$60

Electronic Trackers

Company	Battery Life
Sully	6 months
Best Electronics	1 year
Waverly	2 years
TRM, Inc.	9 months

65. What type of business is the man calling?

(A) A bus company
(B) A ferry service
(C) An airline
(D) A train company

66. Look at the graphic. Which number will be updated?

(A) 4
(B) 21
(C) 10
(D) 15

67. What will the woman most likely do next?

(A) Send an e-mail
(B) Ask for account information
(C) Confirm a phone number
(D) Check a seat assignment

68. What does the woman ask the man for?

(A) Some plastic bags
(B) A list of potential clients
(C) Some zip ties
(D) Some computer cables

69. What is the woman going to do tomorrow?

(A) Order more electrical cables
(B) Go on a business trip
(C) Meet her supervisor
(D) Keep track of inventory

70. Look at the graphic. Which company did the woman make a purchase from?

(A) Sully
(B) Best Electronics
(C) Waverly
(D) TRM, Inc.

PART 4

Directions: You will hear some short talks given by a single speaker. You will be asked to answer three questions about what the speaker says in each short talk. Select the best response to each question and mark the letter (A), (B), (C), or (D) on your answer sheet. The talks will not be printed in your test book and will be spoken only one time.

71. What is most likely being advertised?

(A) A restaurant
(B) A hotel
(C) A convention center
(D) A logistics company

72. What is the business well-known for?

(A) Its prices
(B) Its staff
(C) Its location
(D) Its attention to detail

73. According to the speaker, what can be found on a web page?

(A) Driving directions to the center
(B) Some catering options
(C) Contact numbers
(D) Hours of operation

74. Who most likely are the listeners?

(A) Product developers
(B) Attorneys
(C) Potential investors
(D) Book publishers

75. According to the speaker, what is favorable to the listeners about a contract?

(A) A product will be advertised heavily.
(B) An interest rate is getting low.
(C) An immediate payment will be made.
(D) An extended warranty is offered.

76. What does the speaker imply when he says, "I'll e-mail the document this afternoon"?

(A) He wants the listeners to fill out the forms.
(B) He wants to hear the listeners' opinions
(C) He won't be able to meet the deadline.
(D) He suggests that the listeners meet the lawyer.

77. Where is the tour taking place?

(A) At a warehouse
(B) At a motor parts factory
(C) At a construction site
(D) At a solar panel factory

78. What are the listeners reminded to do?

(A) Mind personal belongings
(B) Wear some protective gear
(C) Stay with the group
(D) Follow posted signs

79. What will the listeners view first on the tour?

(A) Some product models
(B) A floor plan of the factory
(C) Some pictures of the assembly lines
(D) Some safety goggles

80. What is the focus of the episode?

(A) Changing careers
(B) Negotiating contracts
(C) Improving communication skills
(D) Serving customers better

81. What does the speaker say is important in career transition?

(A) Highlighting transferable skills
(B) Becoming more educated
(C) Attending meetings on online marketing
(D) Complying with industry regulations

82. Who is Jeremy Nelson?

(A) A radio host
(B) A business management instructor
(C) A company executive
(D) A government official

▶ ▶ ▶GO ON TO THE NEXT PAGE

83. What is the telephone message mainly about?

(A) Checking a seat assignment
(B) Finding performers
(C) Designing a set
(D) Revising a script

84. Why does the speaker say, "My team is large"?

(A) To explain a problem
(B) To make an apology
(C) To turn down an offer
(D) To provide reassurance

85. Why is the speaker unable to meet this evening?

(A) She has to interview some performers.
(B) She is traveling out of town on business.
(C) She has to see some family members.
(D) She has a doctor's appointment.

86. Who is this talk most likely intended for?

(A) Managers
(B) Trainers
(C) Interns
(D) Financial analysts

87. What did the listeners receive?

(A) A cost estimate for a project
(B) An information packet
(C) A customer survey
(D) A parking pass for employees

88. What does the speaker say the listeners will do in an hour?

(A) Take a short tour of the office
(B) Submit timesheets
(C) Receive security badges
(D) Have their pictures taken

89. What did the speaker do last week?

(A) He took part in a conference.
(B) He made a demonstration at a seminar.
(C) He trained some employees.
(D) He traveled abroad on business.

90. What do some customers have trouble finding?

(A) Account archives
(B) Contact information
(C) Membership requirements
(D) Complaint forms

91. What will the speaker do next?

(A) Turn on the slide projector
(B) Introduce the next speaker
(C) Give a presentation
(D) Pass out some pamphlets

92. Who is the speaker?

(A) A city official
(B) A tour guide
(C) A history instructor
(D) A film director

93. What happened in the town last year?

(A) An international tour convention was held.
(B) A historic event took place.
(C) Some roads were damaged.
(D) A documentary was filmed there.

94. Why does the speaker say, "Those old roads weren't constructed for traffic"?

(A) To express a complaint
(B) To explain a new project
(C) To express concern
(D) To extend a gratitude

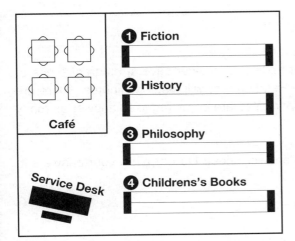

Safety Course

Please sign up for one of these courses:

| March 11, 3 P.M. – 6 P.M. |
| March 15, 10 A.M. – 1 P.M. |
| March 22, 2 P.M. – 5 P.M. |
| March 28, 11 A.M. – 2 P.M. |

95. According to the speaker, what will happen this Saturday?

(A) A bookstore will close.
(B) An author will visit.
(C) A shipment of new books will be delivered.
(D) A season sale will begin.

96. Look at the graphic. Which aisle are the listeners directed to?

(A) Aisle 1
(B) Aisle 2
(C) Aisle 3
(D) Aisle 4

97. What can the listeners win?

(A) A free book
(B) A gift card
(C) A homemade baked goods
(D) A discount coupon

98. Where does the speaker most likely work?

(A) At a job training school
(B) At a machine repair shop
(C) At a warehouse
(D) At a harbor dock

99. What is the speaker's department supposed to do at the end of the month?

(A) Hold monthly meetings
(B) Work extra hours
(C) Prepare a large order
(D) Repair some equipment

100. Look at the graphic. Which session does the speaker want to sign up for?

(A) March 11
(B) March 15
(C) March 22
(D) March 28

This is the end of the Listening test. Turn to Part 5 in your test book.

READING TEST

In the Reading test, you will read a variety of texts and answer several different types of reading comprehension questions. The entire Reading test will last 75 minutes. There are three parts, and directions are given for each part. You are encouraged to answer as many questions as possible within the time allowed.

You must mark your answer on the separate answer sheet. Do not write your answers in your test book.

PART 5

Directions: A word or phrase is missing in each of the sentences below. Four answer choices are given below each sentence. Select the best answer to complete the sentence. Then mark the letter (A), (B), (C), or (D) on your answer sheet.

101. As of next Friday, retail stores can admit customers in their establishments ------- 10 P.M. on weekdays.

(A) at
(B) for
(C) until
(D) within

102. The house near the mountain was built in the middle of the 18th century, but still stands in excellent -------.

(A) style
(B) condition
(C) example
(D) architecture

103. According to our recent survey, labor shortages were the number one obstacle to ------- increased demand.

(A) creating
(B) meeting
(C) hinting
(D) commanding

104. One possible ------- is that the new system will streamline the manufacturing process and increase productivity.

(A) conclusive
(B) conclude
(C) conclusion
(D) concluding

105. In order to help ------- wasted energy at the office, it is important that each employee checks that their computers are turned off at the end of each day.

(A) reduce
(B) reducing
(C) reduced
(D) reduction

106. Public health experts are ------- to finding new methods for preventing diseases and improving health care facilities in the city.

(A) devote
(B) devoting
(C) devotion
(D) devoted

107. Internet users must ------- their identity to access sites, but companies are urged to delete all personal information once the identification process is complete.

(A) hide
(B) release
(C) undergo
(D) verify

108. If your flight is delayed or cancelled ------- inclement weather, we may change your flight without any charge only once.

(A) through
(B) due to
(C) notwithstanding
(D) in place of

109. Since the negative reviews of the new restaurant hit the newspaper, the number of reservations has ------- declined over the last few weeks.

(A) notice
(B) noticing
(C) noticeable
(D) noticeably

110. The stronger and more eloquent your voice is, the greater the likelihood of you making a good first ------- with your clients.

(A) support
(B) intelligence
(C) impression
(D) statement

111. Leisure and sports gear manufacturers are rushing to sell clothes and shoes ------- for walking and trekking instead of heavy hiking clothes.

(A) popular
(B) honored
(C) suitable
(D) eligible

112. The city is home to many companies within the maritime industry, ------- of which are among the world's largest shipping companies and maritime insurance brokers.

(A) another
(B) some
(C) nothing
(D) those

▶ ▶ ▶ GO ON TO THE NEXT PAGE

113. Please be aware that orders for office supplies we need should be placed ------- through the personnel manager.

(A) seldom
(B) quite
(C) only
(D) significantly

114. Given the rapidly aging population, the labor market is unlikely to rise soon, and ------- is youth unemployment.

(A) so
(B) but for
(C) never
(D) neither

115. Health experts suggest that people wash their hands ------- and not share towels or tissues to avoid being infected with a virus.

(A) frequently
(B) absolutely
(C) immediately
(D) additionally

116. Here is a quick and easy guide to show you ------- easy it is to install our new software program on your computer.

(A) and
(B) when
(C) how
(D) otherwise

117. According to the recent survey, the number of women employees in the information industry is ------- higher than that of men.

(A) even
(B) quite
(C) very
(D) so

118. Last month's accounting seminar was the most successful one so far with more than 150 certified public accountants in -------.

(A) attend
(B) attendants
(C) attendees
(D) attendance

119. The price of crude oil has risen ------- on the back of a recovery in global demand as the world economy recovers from the recession.

(A) highly
(B) mutually
(C) sharply
(D) economically

120. A specific date is ------- to be revealed, but some industry experts predicted the both companies may undertake a merger within the first half of next year.

(A) only
(B) once
(C) still
(D) yet

121. ------- Mr. Ryan was not available to attend the staff meeting, he asked one of his colleagues to send the minutes to come up with the staff meeting.

(A) Once
(B) So that
(C) Although
(D) Whenever

122. Even though Mr. Keller's novels were praised by readers, some critics were totally unsatisfied with his works since they were the ------- reviewers.

(A) harsh
(B) harsher
(C) harshest
(D) harshly

123. These days, many of the people are used ------- the latest news and various forms of entertainment online.

(A) share
(B) to share
(C) sharing
(D) to sharing

124. The city government will create a safer environment for international tourists ------- they can enjoy shopping more pleasantly and visit the city's must-see attractions more safely.

(A) and
(B) in order that
(C) where
(D) unless

125. At a time when investment is shrinking and the unemployment rate is rising, it is essential that big businesses ------- investments.

(A) make
(B) will make
(C) are making
(D) have been made

126. The major issue we face is the fact ------- the government has suffered a revenue loss and its spending will exceed its annual budget within the next six months.

(A) which
(B) that
(C) what
(D) whether

127. Drivers over 60 should not be allowed to renew their licenses through the mail, ------- is the standard practice in many cities.

(A) who
(B) whose
(C) which
(D) what

128. This agreement is ------- from the date of signature by both parties and will continue until such time as it is cancelled or terminated.

(A) agreeable
(B) ambiguous
(C) instructive
(D) effective

129. Thanks to the success of the advertising campaign, the number of our mobile phone subscribers ------- at a steady pace for the last six months.

(A) to grow
(B) is growing
(C) will grow
(D) has been growing

130. ------- wants to continue this medical research needs to report to the headquarters and get an approval from the board of directors.

(A) Some
(B) Whoever
(C) Those
(D) Whatever

PART 6

Directions: Read the texts that follow. A word or phrase, or sentence is missing in parts of each text. Four answer choices for each question are given below the text. Select the best answer to complete the text. Then mark the letter (A), (B), (C), or (D) on your answer sheet.

Questions 131-134 refer to the following notice.

Sunrise Apartments
3411 Lake Tahoe Blvd.
South Lake Tahoe, CA 96150

NOTICE NUMBER: 3124
DATE: APRIL 10

NOTICE TO ALL RESIDENTS

The renovation of our tennis courts ------- on April 7, one week ahead of schedule.
                                     131.

The tennis courts can be reserved by calling the Apartment Recreation Division at 445-

9815. When making a reservation, please provide the ------- when it is needed and the
                                                       132.

number of people expected to use it.

Reservations are accepted in the order in which they are received. So please make your

reservation several days in advance. ------- there is no charge for using the tennis courts,
                                     133.

a deposit of $50 is required to hold the reservation. -------.
                                                      134.

131. (A) complete
     (B) is completing
     (C) was completed
     (D) will be completed

132. (A) expenses
     (B) methods
     (C) dates
     (D) transportations

133. (A) Although
     (B) Since
     (C) During
     (D) Despite

134. (A) Tennis is a good sport for maintaining health, fitness, strength and agility.
     (B) If any damage to the tennis courts occurs while you are playing, the deposit will not be refunded.
     (C) Repair costs can be minimized through an aggressive facility management program.
     (D) If you are unsure if a facility is open, please call ahead to the Apartment Recreation Division.

▶▶▶GO ON TO THE NEXT PAGE

Prime Publications

To: All employees
From: Hellen Hunt, Head of Personnel
Subject: Environmental Sustainability Policy – Ink Cartridges
Date: January 10

As an environmentally aware business, we are committed to making sure that all of our

office consumables are recycled wherever possible. As such, it is mandatory that all used

ink cartridges be recycled ------- thrown away.
                          135.

We make this easy for staff to achieve. Around the office, there are a number of recycling

canisters ------- "Used Ink Cartridges." -------. We then return the cartridges to the
              136.   **137.**

manufacturers for recycling.

It is very important that we recycle our cartridges as this is a key part of our environmental

policy. For further information on the company-wide policy, please see the ------- section
                                                                        138.

on the intranet.

135. (A) in addition to
(B) pursuant to
(C) further to
(D) rather than

136. (A) label
(B) labels
(C) labeling
(D) labeled

137. (A) All you need to do is drop any used cartridges into these containers.
(B) Refilling cartridges can save you a lot as opposed to buying a new cartridge.
(C) Recycled paper uses less energy, water, and produces low carbon emissions.
(D) Plastic containers that are safe in the microwave are sturdy, resistant to high temperature.

138. (A) major
(B) certain
(C) relevant
(D) controversial

Dear Ms. Jenkins,

Many thanks for choosing Smith Protective Services as your security system provider for

your home. We can assure you that you have made a wise decision in relying on us to

------- your house.
139.

For the last 20 years, we have been the country's number one choice for home security.

-------. We are always improving our systems and services ------- that you benefit from
140.   **141.**

the highest possible levels of safety.

If you have any questions about anything related to your security system or our services,

please do get in touch with us. We take pride in making sure that all our customers are

------- pleased with our performance and products.
142.

Yours sincerely,

Brian Smith
Chief Executive Officer
Smith Protective Services

139. (A) purchase
(B) modernize
(C) improve
(D) safeguard

140. (A) We also provide security for some of
the biggest companies nationwide.
(B) The theft of office supplies accounts
for a significant portion of the loss.
(C) You can contact us for experienced
high quality security guard services.
(D) Hackers will be able to gather
personal data, such as e-mails and
bank details.

141. (A) ensure
(B) to ensure
(C) have ensured
(D) will have ensured

142. (A) officially
(B) completely
(C) appropriately
(D) fundamentally

The State Tribune

Local News / Economics / Society / **Health** / Science

Mental health: What role does sleep play?
By Juliet Farrish

Advocates of a good night's sleep often claim that it can improve our lives by increasing concentration and raising energy levels. A group of researchers has sought to demonstrate this scientifically ------- a series of experiments.
143.

The researchers selected 200 people of varying ages, and asked half of them to go to bed at 10 P.M. every evening. -------- 100 people were told to stay up late and get up early.
144.

After two weeks, the researchers measured the participants' performance in a number of tests aimed at ------- their mental acuity.
145.

The tests conclusively showed that those who had slept a lot had benefited considerably in terms of alertness and energy. -------.
146.

143. (A) for
(B) through
(C) over
(D) along

144. (A) Other
(B) Others
(C) The other
(D) Each other

145. (A) boosting
(B) predicting
(C) gauging
(D) programming

146. (A) Getting too much sleep can be a sign of underlying health problems.
(B) We should increase our daytime working hours to attain a goal of production.
(C) The danger far outweighs the benefits of using energy drinks.
(D) It seems advisable to get to bed early the night before a test or an important meeting.

PART 7

Directions: In this part you will read a selection of texts, such as magazine and newspaper articles, e-mails, and instant messages. Each text or set of texts is followed by several questions. Select the best answer for each question and mark the letter (A), (B), (C), or (D) on your answer sheet.

Questions 147-148 refer to the following invitation.

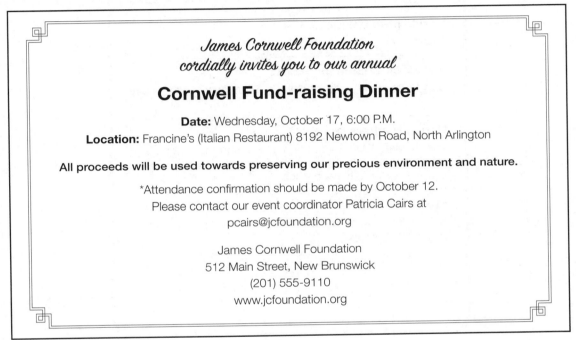

James Cornwell Foundation
cordially invites you to our annual

Cornwell Fund-raising Dinner

Date: Wednesday, October 17, 6:00 P.M.
Location: Francine's (Italian Restaurant) 8192 Newtown Road, North Arlington

All proceeds will be used towards preserving our precious environment and nature.

*Attendance confirmation should be made by October 12.
Please contact our event coordinator Patricia Cairs at
pcairs@jcfoundation.org

James Cornwell Foundation
512 Main Street, New Brunswick
(201) 555-9110
www.jcfoundation.org

147. Why is the event being held?

(A) To promote tourism in a city
(B) To provide complimentary food to local residents
(C) To help preserve the environment
(D) To celebrate a grand opening of a restaurant

148. What is NOT mentioned about James Cornwell Foundation?

(A) It holds an event on a regular basis.
(B) It is located on Newtown Road.
(C) It can be contacted by phone.
(D) It has a website.

ACTUAL TEST ・・・ 11

Questions 149-150 refer to the following text message chain.

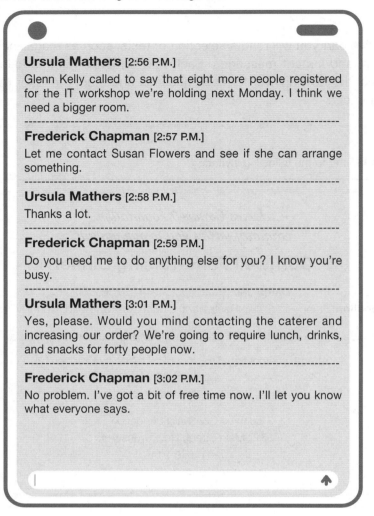

Ursula Mathers [2:56 P.M.]

Glenn Kelly called to say that eight more people registered for the IT workshop we're holding next Monday. I think we need a bigger room.

Frederick Chapman [2:57 P.M.]

Let me contact Susan Flowers and see if she can arrange something.

Ursula Mathers [2:58 P.M.]

Thanks a lot.

Frederick Chapman [2:59 P.M.]

Do you need me to do anything else for you? I know you're busy.

Ursula Mathers [3:01 P.M.]

Yes, please. Would you mind contacting the caterer and increasing our order? We're going to require lunch, drinks, and snacks for forty people now.

Frederick Chapman [3:02 P.M.]

No problem. I've got a bit of free time now. I'll let you know what everyone says.

149. What does Ms. Mathers want to do?

(A) Cease advertising for the workshop
(B) Change the location of an event
(C) Find a second instructor by next week
(D) Speak with Ms. Flowers today

150. At 3:02 P.M., what does Mr. Chapman suggest when he writes, "I've got a bit of free time now"?

(A) He will attend the workshop.
(B) He needs more work assignments.
(C) He can provide some documents now.
(D) He will call the caterer soon.

To:	Tessa Soto, Marcus Ortiz, Victoria Patel
From:	Miranda O'Neil
Date:	Friday, May 3
Subject:	News

—[1]—. Thank you all for greatly contributing to the Abandoned Pet Care Association. This is to remind everyone of some important issues within our association, discussed today in our weekly meeting.

First, there will be a change of personnel in the board of directors. One of our directors, Tessa Soto is retiring next Friday. We are having a farewell reception for her on the day. —[2]—. Mr. Peter Davidson will replace her seat from the following Monday. Please give a warm welcome to Mr. Davidson.

—[3]—. Also, Mr. Marcus Ortiz will deliver a series of presentations at a local elementary school about the preciousness of life. The presentations will take place every Thursday for 4 weeks starting next week.

If you have any concerns, feel free to contact me anytime. —[4]—.

Thanks,

Miranda

151. For whom is the e-mail most likely intended?

(A) Volunteers for an event
(B) Board members of an organization
(C) Employees of an animal hospital
(D) Donors of an animal protection association

152. What is expected to happen on May 9?

(A) The Abandoned Pet Care Association will post a job opening.
(B) All board members will submit an event proposal by then.
(C) Mr. Ortiz will give a presentation for young students.
(D) Mr. Davidson will start working.

153. In which of the positions marked [1], [2], [3], and [4] does the following sentence best fit?

"I expect all of you to be present."

(A) [1]
(B) [2]
(C) [3]
(D) [4]

JWF
Jolly Wood Furniture
220 Washington Street
Palo Alto, CA 94300

October 11

Andy Stark
85 Travis Boulevard
Palo Alto, CA 94307

Dear Mr. Stark,

After talking to you in person on October 8, I am happy to offer you the position of Sales Director. As I have already informed you at the interview, your responsibilities will include managing the employees of our sales department, writing a monthly report and holding weekly department meetings. Since you have a record of working as sales director at your current employment, Duckpit Interior, I am sure that you are familiar with the tasks entailed in the position and that you will do very well.

I have enclosed some documents outlining the specific responsibilities, terms and conditions and salary rate with this letter. Please read them carefully, sign them if you find the conditions acceptable and submit the documents to the human resources team of JWF no later than October 20.

Please feel free to call me at 649-555-1010 if you have any problem or questions. I am looking forward to seeing you soon.

Sincerely,

Philippa Natividad
Assistant Director, Human Resources Department
Jolly Wood Furniture

Enclosure

154. What can be inferred about Mr. Stark?

(A) He worked at Duckpit Interior for a long time.
(B) He applied for a job on October 8.
(C) He met Ms. Natividad recently.
(D) He will move to another city.

155. What is mentioned as a duty Mr. Stark is expected to fulfill at JWF?

(A) Reviewing his employees' reports
(B) Leading a regular meeting
(C) Writing e-mails to Ms. Natividad
(D) Going on business trips

156. What is sent along with the letter?

(A) A list of employees
(B) Presentation materials
(C) A contract
(D) A record of past jobs

Phoenix Zoo

Become a member of Phoenix Zoo
and receive a FREE GIFT!

Exclusive Benefits

- Unlimited entry throughout the year
- Free admission for children under 7 when accompanied by an adult with membership
- A 10% discount at all souvenir shops and restaurants
- Invitations to special performances

Membership Types and Pricing

	1 Year	2 Year
Kids (Age 7 – 13)	$45	$70
Student (with valid student ID)	$50	$80
Adult	$70	$120
Seniors	$45	$70

Special Offer in August

FREE stuffed animals will be given to those who sign up for the membership.

157. How can a customer receive a free gift?

(A) By bringing a pre-school child
(B) By purchasing a family membership
(C) By registering within a certain period of time
(D) By buying an animal toy from the souvenir shop

158. How much does a one-year membership cost for a 7-year-old child?

(A) $0.00
(B) $45.00
(C) $50.00
(D) $70.00

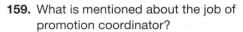

JOB OPENING FOR EVENT PROMOTION COORDINATOR

Red Antz Ltd., Singapore's best event management company, is now recruiting a promotion coordinator. The promotion coordinator is in charge of the promotions department and works closely with the sales department to advertise our company to the public. This position involves participating in important decision making processes with the event director as a part of the organizing committee, planning the company's advertising policies, arranging interviews with newspapers, magazines and TV programs, and regularly preparing promotional events.

A successful candidate must have:
• Outstanding communication skills both in verbal and written language
• At least five years of experience in the event planning or promotion field
• A bachelor's degree in Marketing or Management
In addition, candidates with fluency in a language other than English will be given preference.

Candidates who would like to apply for the position should fill out an application form which is available on our website at www.redantz.com. Please mail the completed application to Barbara Galliano, our human resources director, along with a résumé and a cover letter. Completed documents should arrive no later than September 15 and interviews will take place on September 20 for the final five candidates. Inquiries will not be accepted.

Posted on August 16

---

159. What is mentioned about the job of promotion coordinator?

(A) It is closely linked to recruiting employees.
(B) It involves cooperation with the event director.
(C) It includes interviewing celebrities for TV commercials.
(D) It requires editing newspapers.

160. What is a stated qualification of the position?

(A) A doctor's degree in management
(B) Bilingualism
(C) At least five years of experience in a related field
(D) Experience at broadcasting stations

161. What is true about the application process?

(A) An application can be submitted by e-mail.
(B) An applicant must use the company's own application form.
(C) Inquiries can be directed to Ms. Galliano.
(D) Further details about the interview will be given through the website.

The 2nd Annual Seminar in Marketing

The 2nd Annual Marketing Seminar will be held from May 1 to May 3 in the Laura L. Taylor auditorium at Carnegie University. This year's special features include:

Determining the Right Target for Your Business
By Tim Williams, Emeritus Professor at Carnegie University
Determining the right target for your business is the key to your success. Detailed steps from proper market segmentation to positioning will be outlined.

Rational Decision Making in Business
By Randall Yaksitch, CEO of Lily Healthcare
When you own a business, there are right moments to enter or exit the market. The CEO of Lily Healthcare, one of the nation's largest pharmaceutical companies, will recount real stories of success and failure.

The Effects of Humor in Advertising
By Erica J. Lee, Professor at Roche University
Successful advertisements always contain a sense of humor. Appropriate usage of humor to draw the audiences' attention as well as to increase the effectiveness of the advertisement and the familiarity of the product will be lectured on.

Panel Discussion: Business Ethics and Marketing
Moderated by Paige Button
A panel of experts will discuss business ethics and how it affects marketing.

For those who want to participate in the seminar, please contact Ms. Lisa Mellon at lmellon@carnegie.edu with contact information. Detailed information about the seminar is available at www.carnegie.edu/asim.

162. Who will NOT give a lecture in the seminar?

(A) Tim Williams
(B) Randall Yaksitch
(C) Erica J. Lee
(D) Paige Button

163. The word "draw" in paragraph 4, line 4, is closest in meaning to

(A) paint
(B) attract
(C) persuade
(D) elect

164. What are those who want to participate asked to do?

(A) Register at the Laura L. Taylor auditorium
(B) Complete a registration form
(C) Visit a website
(D) Submit contact information to Lisa Mellon

▶ ▶ ▶GO ON TO THE NEXT PAGE

Smith's Legacy

by Christopher Robin, Local Reporter

Melbourne (July 10) — Adam Smith, the secretary general of the world-renowned NGO, the Spring Bud Foundation, will be stepping down in August. "I will never forget my beautiful memories at Spring Bud," said Mr. Smith.

When asked about how his 26-year-long devotion to Spring Bud began, Mr. Smith commented that he had always known what his passions were. "I had been working as an office clerk in Sydney for three years when I saw their advertisement for an assistant field manager at their Brazil office. I had always been eager to work hands-on in the field, helping others. So I submitted my résumé without hesitation."

As an assistant field manager at Spring Bud's Piracicaba office, he devoted his full efforts to educating pre-school children in the province. His hard work promoted him to a field manager in just three years.

"I found being a field staff rough and I kept wondering about the true meaning of this hard job. However, Mr. Smith's enthusiasm and love towards children touched my heart deep down. He has been the most influential figure in my 13-year career," said Caitlin Montclair, the current field manager in Brazil.

After spending ten years as a field manager, Mr. Smith was transferred to Toronto, Canada in 2000, where the headquarters of Spring Bud is located. In Toronto, he attained his advanced degree in Social Welfare Studies, and he was promoted to the general manager of the education department. He became the secretary general of Spring Bud there, and served in the position for the rest of his career.

His retirement reception will be held in Toronto next month. He plans to continuously help the organization as a senior advisor.

165. What is the topic of the article?

(A) A vacant position in an organization
(B) History of an organization
(C) Introduction of international NGOs
(D) Achievements of an individual

166. For how long has Mr. Smith been working at Spring Bud?

(A) 3 years
(B) 10 years
(C) 13 years
(D) 26 years

167. What city is the Spring Bud Foundation based in?

(A) Melbourne
(B) Piracicaba
(C) Toronto
(D) Sydney

Questions 168-171 refer to the following online chat discussion.

Miranda Carter 11:40 A.M.
How is the work on the brochure proceeding?

Tony Neagle 11:41 A.M.
The text has been written and sent to the proofreaders. I was assured that it would be returned to me by this afternoon.

Linda Barksdale 11:43 A.M.
We've run into a problem with the pictures. Some are fine, but three or four are blurry. I think we'd better get more photos.

Miranda Carter 11:44 A.M.
The printer is expecting the completed brochure by tomorrow. If we want copies before the sales convention begins next week, we can't miss the deadline.

Linda Barksdale 11:45 A.M.
I'll talk to Allan Porter. I'll get him to retake some photos today.

Miranda Carter 11:46 A.M.
Thanks. Tony, are you sure you're going to receive everything by today?

Tony Neagle 11:47 A.M.
I will speak with Deanna Moore to confirm.

Miranda Carter 11:49 A.M.
We simply have to finish the brochure before we go home tonight.

Linda Barksdale 11:50 A.M.
We'd better plan on eating dinner here in that case.

Tony Neagle 11:52 A.M.
That's fine with me. I know a great new Italian place that delivers. I'll handle that if you don't mind.

SEND

168. What is the main topic of the discussion?

  (A) A sales convention
  (B) Plans for the afternoon
  (C) Progress on a work project
  (D) A completed brochure

169. Why do the writers need copies of the brochure?

  (A) To use for an upcoming professional event
  (B) To mail to the company's customers
  (C) To hand out to job applicants
  (D) To send to interested individuals abroad

170. What is suggested by Ms. Barksdale?

  (A) The writers will work overtime this evening.
  (B) She has to cancel an appointment this afternoon.
  (C) There is not enough time to complete some work.
  (D) She is willing to pick up food at a restaurant.

171. At 11:47, what does Mr. Neagle most likely suggest when he writes, "I will speak with Deanna Moore to confirm"?

  (A) Ms. Moore is not working hard enough.
  (B) He is unhappy with some work.
  (C) Ms. Moore works as a proofreader.
  (D) He has not received any updates.

Questions 172-175 refer to the following review.

 http://www.napoli.com/review

NAPOLI Espresso

HOME	ONLINE SHOP	REVIEW	CONTACT	CUSTOMER SUPPORT

"Good Value"

Submitted by:	Amanda Robertson
Submitted on:	July 24
Product Name:	Napoli Capsule Espresso Machine
Product Number:	M23
Customer Rating:	★★★★☆

I recently purchased Napoli's Espresso Machine M23 through this website at a very reasonable price. The machine was delivered two days ago, and I opened the box with excitement. —[1]—. Contrary to other customers, whose reviews indicated that they were unsatisfied with the color of the machine, I found the overall design suited my tastes.

As demonstrated in the product manual that came with the package, the machine has four detachable parts, which makes it easy to wash after use. —[2]—. The machine also hardly makes any noise while it runs, which was my favorite aspect. —[3]—. The reason I replaced my old espresso machine was that it was too loud when operating.

Given the fact that Napoli is relatively new to the espresso machine industry, its single-serve capsules are difficult to locate in regular stores and supermarkets. —[4]—. The capsules are currently only available online and at certain stores, so I recommend making sure that nearby stores carry Napoli espresso capsules or ordering a few along with the machine.

172. What is NOT indicated in the review?

(A) The machine can be taken apart for cleaning.
(B) The package was delivered 2 days earlier than expected.
(C) It has not been long since Napoli started making espresso machines.
(D) Some people do not like the appearance of the machine.

173. What can be inferred about Ms. Robertson?

(A) She purchased the machine at a nearby store.
(B) She tried making coffee by using Napoli's espresso machine.
(C) She bought another machine from Napoli before.
(D) She requested help with locating single-serve capsules.

174. What feature of the M23 does Ms. Robertson like the most?

(A) Its quiet performance
(B) Its overall design
(C) Its affordable price
(D) Its customer support

175. In which of the positions marked [1], [2], [3], and [4] does the following sentence best fit?

"This is somewhat inconvenient."

(A) [1]
(B) [2]
(C) [3]
(D) [4]

Questions 176-180 refer to the following letters.

19 June

Casting Department
Global Media Inc.
Cinema City, CA 91006

To whom it may it concern,

I am writing to submit my application for an audition. My agency, Star Academy, has informed me of *The Adventurers* and I believe I would contribute positively to the new movie.

I have a total of 14 years of acting experience in both film and theater and in many genres. I was the main character's best friend in the award-winning film *The Botanic*, directed by Jane Cameron. Also, I played a role as one of the extraterrestrial soldiers in Jessica Abram's sci-fi themed movie, *The Summer Kingdom*.

As for the theater industry, I had a minor role in *Start Again*, which was the first stage production of Walter Dane, the director of *The Search for a Ring*. I was also involved in a number of major productions written by the world-renowned playwright, Samuel Freeman. These include *Clay Potter* and *Outerspace*. Please refer to the enclosed résumé for the complete list of productions I have participated in.

As you can see, I am highly passionate and enthusiastic for acting. I would greatly appreciate an opportunity to act for your new production. I look forward to hearing from you soon.

Sincerely,

Anita Hathaway

29 June

Anita Hathaway
91B Northumberland Avenue
Los Angeles, CA 90124

Dear Ms. Hathaway,

Thank you for applying for an audition in our new film. I have heard about your diligence and passion in acting from the many directors you have worked with.

We appreciate your filmography in a wide range of genres. I believe your experience with the film *The Summer Kingdom* in particular will be very useful for our new film since the two films are of the same genre. Therefore, we would like to invite you to the audition on July 10. It will be held not at our head office, but at the Media Center on 10 Casterleigh Street. You will not need to bring any supplementary materials except for any props you wish to utilize.

Should you be unavailable on this date or have any questions regarding the audition, please feel free to call me at 210-555-1235. I hope to see you soon.

Best Wishes,

Trent Burton
Casting Director, Global Media Inc.

---

176. Why did Ms. Hathaway send the first letter?

(A) To accept an application
(B) To apply for a director position
(C) To obtain a role in a movie
(D) To offer a role in a new production

177. What is a production that Ms. Hathaway did NOT take part in?

(A) *The Search for a Ring*
(B) *Start Again*
(C) *The Botanic*
(D) *Outerspace*

178. What is indicated about Ms. Hathaway?

(A) She won a prize for her acting prowess.
(B) She was the main character in Ms. Cameron's film.
(C) She started acting right after her graduation from college.
(D) She sent some additional information along with the letter.

179. What is implied about *The Adventurers*?

(A) It will be directed by Mr. Burton.
(B) It is a sci-fi movie.
(C) It will be premiered on July 10.
(D) It is sponsored by Star Academy.

180. What will Ms. Hathaway most likely do in the future?

(A) She will visit the head office in July.
(B) She will ask Mr. Burton to prepare some props for her.
(C) She will meet the casting director in person.
(D) She will provide more information about her filmography.

CHATEAU CATERING

PO BOX 605248, Las Vegas, NV 81930
Contact: 709-222-7199
Account Number: 517698124

Estimate Sent: Oct. 7
Order Number: 39476
Customer: Amelia Cyrus
E-mail: acyrus@kmail.com
Mobile: 090-555-7230

Event Date/ Start Time: Oct. 23 at 7:00 P.M.
Duration: 4 hours
Location: Cello Hall, Hillside Hotel
Guests: 90

Description	Cost	Quantity	Total
Food:			
Standard Canapé Package	$27	95	$2,565.00
Vegetarian Package	$23	10	$230.00
Beverages:			
Standard Drink Package	$10	105	$1,050.00
Cocktails	$8	105	$840.00
Staff:			
Caterer	$100	4	$400.00
Subtotal:			**$5,085.00**
Corporate Customer Discount (10%):			**-$508.50**
Tax:			**$366.12**
Total:			**$4,942.62**

*Cutlery hire provided at no charge

TERMS AND CONDITIONS: Please check the details thoroughly and confirm your booking with the office. Any changes must be requested five working days prior to the event. Otherwise, a penalty fee may be charged. Payment must be made two working days in advance of the event date.

To:	Justin Lake <jlake@ccatering.com>
From:	Amelia Cyrus <acyrus@kmail.com>
Date:	October 20
Subject:	URGENT – About October 23 at Hillside

Dear Mr. Lake,

I have to make some alterations to my colleague's retirement party. Unfortunately, some of the guests are now unable to attend. That will reduce the final number by ten and I will now be requiring 85 Standard Canapé Packages and 95 of each beverage package. Since there are fewer people now, I have decided to move to a smaller banquet hall. Please deliver the food to Viola Gallery in the premises, instead of the original location.

I understand that this will make some changes to the total price. Please send me a revised estimate and I will make the payment before the deadline.

Regards,

Amelia Cyrus

181. According to the bill, by when does the payment for catering have to be made?

(A) October 7
(B) October 20
(C) October 21
(D) October 23

182. What is indicated about Chateau Catering?

(A) It requires customers to provide their specific dietary needs.
(B) It is based at Hillside Hotel.
(C) It extends a special offer to a certain type of customers.
(D) It hired Ms. Cyrus to prepare for an event.

183. What is the purpose of the e-mail?

(A) To request additional items
(B) To update scheduled plans
(C) To cancel a reservation
(D) To announce a resignation

184. What is expected to happen in the near future?

(A) A retirement party will be rescheduled.
(B) Ms. Cyrus will be retiring soon.
(C) Ms. Cyrus will be charged an additional fee.
(D) Mr. Lake will attend a retirement party as a guest.

185. What is suggested about Hillside Hotel?

(A) It has more than one banquet room.
(B) It has a number of caterers in its staff.
(C) It has ample parking spaces.
(D) It will change the price of its services.

Enjoy a special offer from
Sewell Windows
during the entire month of June

Purchase four or more windows from us
and we will go to your home or office and install them absolutely free.

If you aren't satisfied for any reason,
we'll give you 50% off the price you paid for the windows.

We carry windows made by companies such as
Glass Pro, Maddox, Westside, and KTR.

Visit our store at 37 Forest Lane to see what we have in stock.

We are open every day of the week from 9:30 A.M. to 8:00 P.M.

To: All Employees, Sewell Windows
From: Mitch Murray, Owner
Subject: Work Schedule
Date: June 20

A few of our window installers are on vacation this week, so here's the revised schedule. Everyone, please take note of it. If you sell somebody windows, make sure that the person working on the day the customer wants the windows installed has time.

Monday, June 20:   Peter Croft
Tuesday, June 21:   Larry Medford
Wednesday, June 22:   Orlando Smith
Thursday, June 23:   Eric Hopkins
Friday, June 24:   Peter Croft, Orlando Smith

The schedule for the weekend is yet to be determined. I'll update it as soon as I can.

June 27

Dear Mr. Murray,

My name is Jeremy Toole, and I'm a long-time customer at your store. I've been purchasing windows from you for more than eight years. I was delighted to see your special offer for this month, so I went to the store and bought ten windows for my home.

Imagine my surprise when nobody showed up to install them on June 22. I called your store, and the person I spoke with told me that my windows were supposed to be installed at 10:00 in the morning, but nobody came. It was particularly upsetting because I had to wait at home all day, which resulted in my missing a day of work.

When the windows were installed the next day, the person who did the job actually cracked one but didn't even apologize.

I hope that you take the required steps to fix these problems.

Regards,

Jeremy Toole

186. According to the advertisement, what is true about Sewell Windows?

(A) It has a website customers can visit.
(B) It manufactures its own windows.
(C) It sells items from different companies.
(D) It is open five days a week.

187. In the memo, what does Mr. Murray indicate about the schedule?

(A) It will be updated later in the day.
(B) It is incomplete for part of the week.
(C) It can be changed by the employees.
(D) It requires some people to work overtime.

188. Why did Mr. Toole write the letter?

(A) To complain about a service
(B) To request a rebate
(C) To demand an apology
(D) To respond to a letter

189. Who was originally scheduled to install Mr. Toole's windows?

(A) Peter Croft
(B) Larry Medford
(C) Orlando Smith
(D) Eric Hopkins

190. What will Mr. Murray most likely do for Mr. Toole?

(A) Visit his home to apologize in person
(B) Give him half off the price he paid
(C) Have the windows installed at once
(D) Send him a coupon to use later

▶ ▶ ▶GO ON TO THE NEXT PAGE

October 23

Molly Rhodes
58 Seaside Lane
Portland, Oregon

Dear Molly,

Hello. This is Samantha Bree. We worked together at Gladstone Consulting a couple of years ago. I heard from one of our old colleagues, Brian Hastings, that you're currently looking for a job.

You might be interested in knowing that my current firm, Westside, Inc., will be hiring soon. We're located in Lexington, Kentucky. This is a great place to work, and I think you'd love it here. We're in need of people with computer programming skills, and you're one of the best.

If you want, I can put in a good word for you with my boss. Let me know if you're interested in any of the positions. Good luck.

Regards,

Samantha

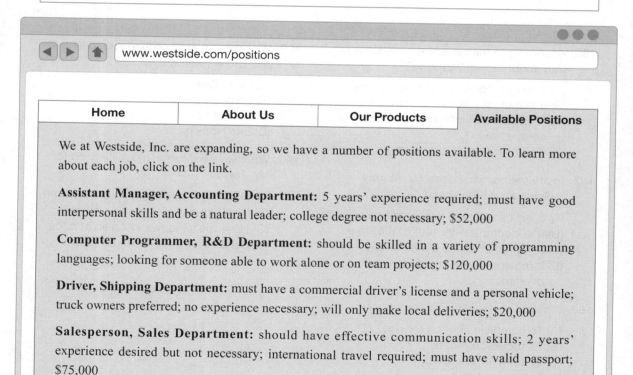

www.westside.com/positions

| Home | About Us | Our Products | Available Positions |

We at Westside, Inc. are expanding, so we have a number of positions available. To learn more about each job, click on the link.

Assistant Manager, Accounting Department: 5 years' experience required; must have good interpersonal skills and be a natural leader; college degree not necessary; $52,000

Computer Programmer, R&D Department: should be skilled in a variety of programming languages; looking for someone able to work alone or on team projects; $120,000

Driver, Shipping Department: must have a commercial driver's license and a personal vehicle; truck owners preferred; no experience necessary; will only make local deliveries; $20,000

Salesperson, Sales Department: should have effective communication skills; 2 years' experience desired but not necessary; international travel required; must have valid passport; $75,000

To:	All Employees
From:	Carla Hunt
Date:	December 2
Subject:	New Week

Please be advised that we'll be having two new employees start working with us as of Monday, December 7. Their names are Ronald Burgher and Molly Rhodes. Ronald is transferring to us from our Knoxville office while Molly is moving across the country from Portland. But don't worry about her too much. She's returning to her hometown. Please make sure that you welcome both of them and help them get used to their jobs as quickly as possible.

We'll be having a welcome event for them next week. The date and the time have yet to be decided. I'll send out a company-wide e-mail as soon as those are settled.

191. Why did Ms. Bree send the letter?

(A) To request some personal information
(B) To schedule a time for an interview
(C) To inform a person about an open position
(D) To offer a person a new job

192. Which position requires a person to visit other countries?

(A) Assistant manager
(B) Computer programmer
(C) Driver
(D) Salesperson

193. Which department will Ms. Rhodes most likely apply to work in?

(A) The Accounting Department
(B) The R&D Department
(C) The Shipping Department
(D) The Sales Department

194. What is most likely true about Ms. Rhodes?

(A) She will be working with Mr. Burgher.
(B) She interviewed personally with Ms. Hunt.
(C) She has a large amount of work experience.
(D) She grew up in Lexington, Kentucky.

195. What does Ms. Hunt indicate about the welcome event?

(A) It will take place at a restaurant.
(B) It will be held in the morning.
(C) Its time will be determined later.
(D) It will occur next Monday.

Payless Stationery

585 Robinson Road

(304) 223-8563

Item	Item Number	Quantity	Price
Copy Paper, 5,000 Pages	588-KLW	3	$99.00
Pen, Black Ink (20/Box)	933-JRD	4	$40.00
Stapler	484-VFM	1	$12.00
Printer Ink	495-AKE	2	$80.00
		Subtotal	$231.00
		Tax	$11.55
		Total	$242.55

Thank you for shopping at Payless Stationery, where you pay less than you do at other shops.

To:	Alicia Watson <aw@brandon.com>
From:	Glenn Morris <g_morris@payless.com>
Date:	July 16
Subject:	Re: My Purchase

Dear Ms. Watson,

Thank you for bringing this issue to my attention. I checked the purchase you recently made, and I realized you were not sent item 484-VFM. As such, you will be refunded the proper amount to your credit card. That should be reflected on your bill within the next three business days.

In addition, I'd like to inform you about a special offer we are promoting. If you recommend a new customer who starts a business account with us during the next three months, you will receive 15% of all purchases you make until the end of the year.

Have a wonderful day.

Glenn Morris
Manager, Payless Stationery Store

To: Alicia Watson <aw@brandon.com>

From: Romeo Boothe <romeob@grovertech.com>

Date: August 29

Subject: Thank You

Dear Ms. Watson,

It was a pleasure to meet you at the Orlando Trade Fair last week. I'm positive that our two firms will be able to do business with each other. Since our offices are so close, it should be easy to meet in person. I'm going to be in Europe on business for the next two weeks, but I'll get in touch with you when I return in the middle of September.

I'd also like to thank you for letting me know about Payless Stationery. I checked it out and decided to open a corporate account there. Of course, I let the owner know that you were the one who told me all about it.

Thanks again.

Regards,

Romeo Boothe
Grover Tech

196. According to the receipt, which of the following statements is true?

(A) Pens are sold individually.
(B) The customer spent less than $200.
(C) Tax was not applied to the purchase.
(D) The store sells items at cheap prices.

197. What is one purpose of the first e-mail?

(A) To advertise a store's newest products
(B) To let a customer know about a promotion
(C) To apologize for sending an item late
(D) To offer a discount on a recent purchase

198. How much money will Ms. Watson be refunded?

(A) $12
(B) $40
(C) $80
(D) $99

199. What is one reason Mr. Boothe sent the second e-mail to Ms. Watson?

(A) To request more information from her
(B) To confirm the terms of an agreement
(C) To let her know about his schedule
(D) To ask her about meeting this week

200. What is indicated about Ms. Watson's company?

(A) It has an office that is located in Orlando.
(B) It will receive a discount on future purchases at Payless Stationery.
(C) It makes frequent purchases from Payless Stationery.
(D) It is planning to expand to Europe in the next few months.

STOP! This is the end of the test. If you finish before time is called, you may go back to Parts 5, 6, and 7 and check your work.

Actual Test 12

 MP3

 해설집

적정 풀이 시간 120분

120 min

시작 시간 ___시 ___분

종료 시간 ___시 ___분

중간에 멈추지 말고 처음부터 끝까지 풀어보세요.
문제를 풀 때에는 실전처럼 답안지에 마킹하세요.

목표 개수 _____ / 200   실제 개수 _____ / 200

예상 점수는 번역 및 정답에 있는 점수 환산표를 참조하세요.

LISTENING TEST

In the Listening test, you will be asked to demonstrate how well you understand spoken English. The entire Listening test will last approximately 45 minutes. There are four parts, and directions are given for each part. You must mark your answers on the separate answer sheet. Do not write your answers in the test book.

PART 1

Directions: For each question in this part, you will hear four statements about a picture in your test book. When you hear the statements, you must select the one statement that best describes what you see in the picture. Then find the number of the question on your answer sheet and mark your answer. The statements will not be printed in your test book and will be spoken only one time.

Statement (B), "They are sitting at a table." is the best description of the picture. So you should select answer (B) and mark it on your answer sheet.

1.

2.

▶ ▶ ▶GO ON TO THE NEXT PAGE

3.

4.

5.

6.

PART 2

Directions: You will hear a question or statement and three responses spoken in English. They will not be printed in your test book and will be spoken only one time. Select the best response to the question or statement and mark the letter (A), (B), or (C) on your answer sheet.

7. Mark your answer on your answer sheet.

8. Mark your answer on your answer sheet.

9. Mark your answer on your answer sheet.

10. Mark your answer on your answer sheet.

11. Mark your answer on your answer sheet.

12. Mark your answer on your answer sheet.

13. Mark your answer on your answer sheet.

14. Mark your answer on your answer sheet.

15. Mark your answer on your answer sheet.

16. Mark your answer on your answer sheet.

17. Mark your answer on your answer sheet.

18. Mark your answer on your answer sheet.

19. Mark your answer on your answer sheet.

20. Mark your answer on your answer sheet.

21. Mark your answer on your answer sheet.

22. Mark your answer on your answer sheet.

23. Mark your answer on your answer sheet.

24. Mark your answer on your answer sheet.

25. Mark your answer on your answer sheet.

26. Mark your answer on your answer sheet.

27. Mark your answer on your answer sheet.

28. Mark your answer on your answer sheet.

29. Mark your answer on your answer sheet.

30. Mark your answer on your answer sheet.

31. Mark your answer on your answer sheet.

PART 3

Directions: You will hear some conversations between two or three people. You will be asked to answer three questions about what the speakers say in each conversation. Select the best response to each question and mark the letter (A), (B), (C), or (D) on your answer sheet. The conversations will not be printed in your test book and will be spoken only one time.

32. Where does the conversation most likely take place?

    (A) At a bank
    (B) At a government office
    (C) At a doctor's office
    (D) At an eyeglasses shop

33. What did the man do in advance?

    (A) He completed some paperwork.
    (B) He made a deposit for a service online.
    (C) He called the person on duty after hours.
    (D) He asked about a parking lot.

34. What does the man say he will do?

    (A) Sit in the waiting area
    (B) Pay for parking
    (C) Retrieve a missing item
    (D) Log on to the Internet

35. What department does Jacob work in?

    (A) Sales
    (B) Personnel
    (C) Marketing
    (D) Accounting

36. What does the man say he will do?

    (A) Make a booking
    (B) Speak with a manager
    (C) Contact a supplier
    (D) Look over a marketing report

37. According to the woman, why should the man visit the manager's office?

    A) To donate some money
    (B) To receive a report
    (C) To sign a card
    (D) To turn in a receipt

38. What type of business do the men work for?

    (A) At a building material business
    (B) At an interior design company
    (C) At a warehouse
    (D) At a construction company

39. What is the woman's job?

    (A) Sales representative
    (B) Building inspector
    (C) Construction worker
    (D) Architect

40. What does Jeff plan to do in ten minutes?

    (A) Contact a client
    (B) Depart the conference event
    (C) See a demonstration
    (D) Finalize a construction contract

41. What project are the speakers discussing?

    (A) Recording an upcoming event
    (B) Editing an advertisement
    (C) Negotiating a contract
    (D) Developing a new product

42. Why does the woman apologize?

    (A) She made a technical mistake.
    (B) She forgot to review the commercial script.
    (C) She was late for an advertising team meeting.
    (D) She does not like the man's idea.

43. What does the man say he likes?

    (A) The color pattern of a printed ad
    (B) The length of a commercial
    (C) The way an actress speaks
    (D) The packaging design

▶ ▶ ▶ GO ON TO THE NEXT PAGE

44. What problem do the speakers discuss?

(A) Cleaning work was done poorly.
(B) A project was not completed.
(C) A price has risen.
(D) A schedule has been altered.

45. Why does the man say, "The firm upstairs has a cleaning crew of its own"?

(A) To make a suggestion
(B) To offer to help with cleaning
(C) To approve of an idea
(D) To apologize for poor work performance

46. What does the woman ask the man to do?

(A) Book some plane tickets
(B) Print some documents
(C) Make a dinner reservation
(D) Purchase some refreshments

---

47. Why was the woman late for work?

(A) She had to visit a car repair shop.
(B) She missed the subway.
(C) She was stuck in traffic.
(D) She had a dental appointment.

48. What is scheduled to arrive today?

(A) Laptop computers
(B) Art supplies
(C) Fabric
(D) Store catalogs

49. What business will the woman contact?

(A) An electronics store
(B) A recycling center
(C) A stationery store
(D) A department store

50. What did the woman do recently?

(A) She conducted a market research.
(B) She started working this week.
(C) She won a contract.
(D) She traveled abroad on business.

51. What does the man encourage the woman to consider?

(A) Reviewing a job description
(B) Applying for a position
(C) Accepting a new project
(D) Requesting a transfer

52. What does the man say he will do next?

(A) Have a meal
(B) Visit a supplier
(C) Sign a contract
(D) Attend a meeting

---

53. Who is the woman?

(A) A store manager
(B) A real estate broker
(C) A financial advisor
(D) A paint supplier

54. What does the man say happened last month?

(A) He got a raise.
(B) He bought a building.
(C) He moved to the city.
(D) He started a new job.

55. What does the woman recommend doing?

(A) Making some promotional flyers
(B) Using mobile marketing strategies
(C) Making a bulk purchasing
(D) Using a mobile application

56. Who most likely is the woman?

(A) A delivery driver
(B) A repair person
(C) A factory manager
(D) An assembly-line worker

57. What do the men express concern about?

(A) A potential expense
(B) A shortage of supplies
(C) A broken machine
(D) A heavy workload

58. According to the woman, why can she determine the problem quickly?

(A) She knows about the equipment.
(B) She does not have any other tasks.
(C) Some product specifications are straightforward.
(D) A manufacturing plant is not very large.

59. Where do the speakers most likely work?

(A) At a magazine publisher
(B) At a bookstore
(C) At a graphic design company
(D) At a library

60. What does the woman mean when she says, "There are tons of images"?

(A) She is impressed with the man's creativity.
(B) The man should use more images.
(C) A design should be made simpler.
(D) A written description is necessary.

61. What will the company celebrate in August?

(A) A retirement
(B) A successful acquisition
(C) A new contract
(D) An anniversary

Item	Item Number	Price
Men's T-shirt	3490544	$25
Men's Running Shoes	3095343	$99
Men's Sweater	8574400	$50
Men's Shorts	6834233	$65

62. What problem does the man have?

(A) What he wants is out of stock.
(B) His credit card is missing.
(C) His address was input incorrectly.
(D) A payment has not been accepted.

63. What does the woman say will happen tomorrow?

(A) A discount will be applied.
(B) A clearance sale will end.
(C) A new store will open.
(D) An order will go out.

64. Look at the graphic. What is the price of the item the man wants to purchase?

(A) $25
(B) $50
(C) $65
(D) $99

Employee Orientation Schedule

Building Tour	10:00 A.M.
Workshop	11:00 A.M.
Lunch	12:30 P.M.
Welcome Speech	2:00 P.M.

65. What industry do the speakers work in?

(A) Finance
(B) Manufacturing
(C) Information Technology
(D) Advertising

66. Look at the graphic. When will a Human Resources employee join the speakers?

(A) At 10:00 A.M.
(B) At 11:00 A.M.
(C) At 12:30 P.M.
(D) At 2:00 P.M.

67. Where will the speakers most likely go next?

(A) To the auditorium
(B) To the cafeteria
(C) To the man's office
(D) To the conference room

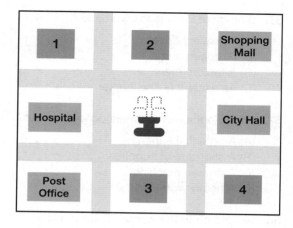

68. What field do the speakers most likely work in?

(A) Real estate
(B) Medicine
(C) Education
(D) Publishing

69. Look at the graphic. Which building does the woman say she likes?

(A) Building 1
(B) Building 2
(C) Building 3
(D) Building 4

70. What does the man ask the woman to do?

(A) Speak with a colleague
(B) Copy some documents
(C) Call a real estate agent
(D) Read over a contract

PART 4

Directions: You will hear some short talks given by a single speaker. You will be asked to answer three questions about what the speaker says in each short talk. Select the best response to each question and mark the letter (A), (B), (C), or (D) on your answer sheet. The talks will not be printed in your test book and will be spoken only one time.

71. Why is the speaker calling?

    (A) To request approval for some spending
    (B) To ask if she could come in for an interview
    (C) To cancel a previously scheduled meeting
    (D) To confirm her attendance at a luncheon

72. What does the speaker say about a job applicant?

    (A) His qualifications are impressive.
    (B) He does not live locally.
    (C) He requires additional on-the-job training.
    (D) He has worked in a foreign country.

73. What did the speaker say she sent in an e-mail?

    (A) Presentation notes
    (B) A meeting agenda
    (C) A travel itinerary
    (D) A price estimate

74. What product has the speaker's company developed?

    (A) A bicycle helmet
    (B) A new line of microphone
    (C) An inflatable massage ball
    (D) An adjustable stick

75. What does the speaker say is important to him?

    (A) Affordability
    (B) Durability
    (C) Lightweight
    (D) Compatibility

76. What will the speaker do next?

    (A) Collect some forms
    (B) Go over a brochure
    (C) Hand out some samples
    (D) Show a video

77. Where do the listeners most likely work?

    (A) At a restaurant
    (B) On a farm
    (C) At a farmers' market
    (D) At a grocery store

78. What event are the listeners preparing for?

    (A) A weekend sale
    (B) A grand opening
    (C) A cooking competition
    (D) A special cooking class

79. Who is David Atwell?

    (A) An award-winning chef
    (B) A photographer
    (C) A newspaper journalist
    (D) A health trainer

▶ ▶ ▶ GO ON TO THE NEXT PAGE

80. What will the listeners learn during the workshop?

(A) How to register for a course
(B) How to complete a tax form
(C) How to be an efficient accountant
(D) How to use a software program

81. What kind of work do the listeners most likely do?

(A) Manufacturing
(B) Engineering
(C) Accounting
(D) Programming

82. What does the speaker ask the listeners to do?

(A) Pair with a partner
(B) Bring in a computer
(C) Pick up registration packets
(D) Fill out a form

83. According to the speaker, what is a top priority?

(A) Keeping quality workers
(B) Improving employee morale
(C) Increasing company profits
(D) Reducing manufacturing costs

84. Who is Allison Hyatt?

(A) A spokesperson for a company
(B) A human resources consultant
(C) A market researcher
(D) A company executive

85. Why does the speaker say, "This is something that affects everybody"?

(A) To give a warning on errors
(B) To pass on some bad news
(C) To encourage participation
(D) To apologize for shortage of workers

86. Where is the tour taking place?

(A) At an electronics store
(B) At a tire factory
(C) At a museum
(D) At a clothing manufacturer

87. Why does the speaker say, "We also ship our products to countries around the world"?

(A) To emphasize how popular some items are
(B) To explain why a place is so large
(C) To apologize for some recent delays
(D) To confirm that a special service is available

88. What does the speaker say is available to the listeners?

(A) Entry in a prize raffle
(B) A free event calendar
(C) A discount on a purchase
(D) An audio tour

89. What did Wrangler Travel announce yesterday?

(A) It made a profit during the last quarter.
(B) It was approved for a business license.
(C) It received an award for innovation.
(D) It acquired a competing business.

90. What will Wrangler Travel offer to new drivers?

(A) Designated free parking
(B) Flexible working hours
(C) Rental vehicles
(D) Competitive salaries

91. What will take place in Salem next month?

(A) A marketing expo
(B) An arts and crafts festival
(C) An automobile trade fair
(D) A sporting event

92. What is the speaker organizing?

(A) A job fair
(B) A charity auction
(C) A company get-together
(D) A factory inspection

93. What does the speaker imply when he says, "I had to ask him to repeat himself"?

(A) He had a bad connection on the phone.
(B) An explanation was not clear.
(C) He is not qualified for the assigned task.
(D) A decision surprised him.

94. What is the listener asked to do?

(A) Contact a sponsor
(B) Update a list
(C) Make a donation
(D) Reply by e-mail

Ticket Booth	Booth 1	Booth 2
Main Street		
	Freight Elevator	
Refreshment Area	Booth 3	Booth 4

95. What does the speaker's business produce?

(A) Office equipment
(B) Office furniture
(C) Baked goods
(D) Construction materials

96. What are the listeners asked to do?

(A) Work on a weekend
(B) Take inventory of food
(C) Promote some products
(D) Take the stairs only

97. Look at the graphic. Which booth will the company use?

(A) Booth 1
(B) Booth 2
(C) Booth 3
(D) Booth 4

Lecture Series

Name	Date
Barry Arnold	September 13
Wilson Roth	October 29
Frederick Harper	November 15
Darren Matisse	December 3

98. Who is this talk intended for?

(A) Architects
(B) Teachers
(C) Librarians
(D) Interior designers

99. Look at the graphic. Which lecturer is the speaker excited to hear?

(A) Barry Arnold
(B) Wilson Roth
(C) Frederick Harper
(D) Darren Matisse

100. What will the listeners most likely do next?

(A) Discuss a new work project
(B) Complete some forms
(C) Consider some potential workers
(D) Go over this year's budget

This is the end of the Listening test. Turn to Part 5 in your test book.

▶ ▶ ▶ GO ON TO THE NEXT PAGE

READING TEST

In the Reading test, you will read a variety of texts and answer several different types of reading comprehension questions. The entire Reading test will last 75 minutes. There are three parts, and directions are given for each part. You are encouraged to answer as many questions as possible within the time allowed.

You must mark your answer on the separate answer sheet. Do not write your answers in your test book.

PART 5

Directions: A word or phrase is missing in each of the sentences below. Four answer choices are given below each sentence. Select the best answer to complete the sentence. Then mark the letter (A), (B), (C), or (D) on your answer sheet.

101. A number of new laws and legal studies will be introducing some ------- to crime and corruption control.

(A) damages
(B) approaches
(C) investigations
(D) implementations

102. Starpark Bridge was recently chosen as the ------- construction structure in North America by architectural professionals.

(A) fine
(B) finer
(C) finest
(D) fineness

103. While piano tuning is normally done by ------- technicians, guitars are usually tuned by the guitarist themselves.

(A) train
(B) training
(C) trainer
(D) trained

104. A number of ------- airlines have stirred up air travel within Europe by radically cutting fares in exchange for eliminating some traditional passenger services.

(A) major
(B) lucrative
(C) budget
(D) official

105. The company ------- chose to relocate to Hayward, and they quote themselves by saying they were drawn to Hayward's innovation.

(A) properly
(B) consistently
(C) cooperatively
(D) deliberately

106. The economic crisis of a nation usually develops ------- a global thing which must be solved by international efforts.

(A) for
(B) into
(C) from
(D) along with

107. Among several assignments that Ms. Ryan has been given ------- an important project with the task force committee.

(A) to be
(B) is
(C) are
(D) have been

108. Surfing Services offers a wide ------- of surfboards, as well as wet suits and T-shirts for short or long term rentals.

(A) region
(B) margin
(C) distribution
(D) selection

109. ------- we receive your payment before midnight, we will still be able to ship your package tomorrow morning.

(A) While
(B) Unless
(C) Despite
(D) As long as

110. Mr. Andrew Kim, Head of Financial, will be held ------- if the financial situation of the company worsens in the pandemic flu.

(A) responsible
(B) responsive
(C) responsibly
(C) responsibility

111. The country has achieved ------- economic growth and poverty reduction in the past decade, thanks mainly to economic reforms in the past few years.

(A) affordable
(B) impressive
(C) beneficial
(D) collaborative

112. Scientists are almost finished ------- a major genetic project that will open up new opportunities in biotechnology.

(A) for
(B) by
(C) with
(D) upon

ACTUAL TEST ••• **12**

▶ ▶ ▶ GO ON TO THE NEXT PAGE

113. When one of our long-term employees decided to stay home after her maternity leave, the company hired her temporary -------.

(A) shelter
(B) production
(C) workplace
(D) replacement

114. The market analysis report contains some errors that Mr. Porter ------- before the board meeting scheduled to take place tomorrow.

(A) correct
(B) to correct
(C) has been corrected
(D) will correct

115. For ------- to the National Gallery of Contemporary Art's fundraiser, donors were sent a thank-you card signed by twelve famous painters.

(A) contributors
(B) contributing
(C) contribution
(D) contributed

116. Our Research & Development Team is currently developing a new type of mobile phone battery which will last at least 48 hours on a single -------.

(A) usage
(B) function
(C) practice
(D) charge

117. Our fast-food franchises are expanding quickly through Europe and they are handling a high ------- of customers every day.

(A) size
(B) section
(C) volume
(D) total

118. To produce hydroelectric power and provide irrigation, the Grand Valley Dam was built, ------- has been in operation since 1973.

(A) who
(B) that
(C) which
(D) there

119. The recommendation of the board was that more emphasis should be put ------- research and development in the coming year.

(A) for
(B) on
(C) against
(D) through

120. Doctor Choi has had numerous medical breakthroughs over the past four decades, so she is treated with ------- by her colleagues.

(A) consent
(B) influence
(C) reverence
(D) accomplishment

121. Please ------- that January 10 is a hard deadline for submission of applications and no extensions will be given.

(A) notify
(B) assure
(C) advise
(D) note

122. The theater should turn on dim floor lights to show people where to go ------- they need to leave.

(A) where
(B) in case
(C) by the time
(D) now that

123. The Bella Hospitable Solutions received the Star Diamond Award, one of the most prestigious awards in the tourism and hospitality industry, in recognition of its ------- services to tourists.

(A) talented
(B) respective
(C) exceptional
(D) complimentary

124. The borrowers from our bank make payments ------- the agreed-upon schedule until they pay back in full.

(A) on account of
(B) in efforts to
(C) according to
(D) with regard to

125. ------- you have already paid for a yearly membership, you may come in and out of the exhibition as many times as you want.

(A) In the event of
(B) Except
(C) As long as
(D) Nevertheless

126. ------- hundreds of certified public tax accountants at the Tax Accounting Convention in Berlin last week.

(A) Several
(B) Having had
(C) There were
(D) Many of the

127. ------- our company is growing in terms of revenues, we are not strong enough yet to compete with other foreign companies.

(A) When
(B) Even though
(C) In case
(D) Nonetheless

128. Different jobs require different skilled employees, and should ------- have various mandatory retirement ages.

(A) however
(B) furthermore
(C) therefore
(D) often

129. The city government is still uncertain about ------- it will hold the festival in November as originally planned or wait until the peak tourist season in spring.

(A) whether
(B) although
(C) where
(D) however

130. The new green car is more efficient and economical than common vehicles, ------- it is powered by electricity or solar energy.

(A) while
(B) thanks to
(C) in order that
(D) considering that

PART 6

Directions: Read the texts that follow. A word or phrase, or sentence is missing in parts of each text. Four answer choices for each question are given below the text. Select the best answer to complete the text. Then mark the letter (A), (B), (C), or (D) on your answer sheet.

Questions 131-134 refer to the following memo.

Dear all tax accountants,

I am writing to ------- you that all of our tax accountants will need to put in extra hours
      131.
through the end of tax season.

This year, we have a ------- number of clients who demand more hard work from
      132.
everyone. However, your efforts will be rewarded once the tax season is finished. Any

requests for leave during this tax season must be approved ------- by me. Your supervisor
      133.
or team leader cannot approve requests at this critical time.

-------. Additionally, we will give all of you extra time off in appreciation of your hard work.
  134.

Thank you, in advance, for your cooperation.

Daniel McGowan
President, One Tax Accounting

131. (A) note
(B) notify
(C) notice
(D) notification

132. (A) pleasant
(B) favorable
(C) remarkable
(D) definite

133. (A) promptly
(B) presumably
(C) cooperatively
(D) directly

134. (A) Your contract includes a clause that requires employees to work extra hours.
(B) We will host a fabulous office party for you after the busy period.
(C) Good reward management can improve employee motivation and engagement.
(D) Our headquarters are too small for the current number of employees or for future growth.

▶▶▶GO ON TO THE NEXT PAGE

Dear Ms. Brown,

-------. These sessions help companies to reduce stress-related absenteeism and maintain
135.

a high level of productivity in the workplace. Workshop participants learn to ------- the
136.

most effective stress reduction and relaxation methods known in the field. Our sessions

------- the staff members of your organization practical and simple methods to minimize
137.

and stop the stress response before it has a chance to build up.

Our relaxation workshops are run at our downtown location, but we can also arrange

for them to be conducted at your place of business, if you prefer. I have enclosed

some information about available workshops and dates ------- you to review at your
138.

convenience.

For more details, please contact directly the Department of Public Events at (907)

247-1971.

Yours respectfully,

The Department of Public Events
The National Research Institute of Mental Health

---

135. (A) We will offer our employees free
medical help for their injuries at work.
(B) The research organization has
provided people with a lot of valuable
information.
(C) We appreciate your interest in our
new series of relaxation workshops.
(D) Mental health services reduce the risk
of chronic diseases related to stress.

136. (A) apply
(B) validate
(C) explain
(D) formulate

137. (A) be taught
(B) will teach
(C) has taught
(D) is teaching

138. (A) from
(B) across
(C) for
(D) past

Mimi Bags

Thank you for purchasing the Mimi luggage bags. Mimi luggage bags with two wheels are designed to ------- moisture and dirt as well as the wear and tear of everyday travel.
139.

Mimi luggage bags are made with a great deal of care and attention, and defects are ------, but we provide our customers with a 24-month free guarantee from the date of
140.

purchase. -------. If you detect a fault within this period, the bag will be repaired or, if
141.

necessary, replaced at no extra cost. An original proof of purchase will be required.

Outside of this period, repairs will ------- an additional cost.
142.

If you visit our official website at www.mimibags.com, you can find an authorized repair center in your area. Contact the local repair center and discuss the work that needs to be done to your bag. You can also send your bag to our headquarters in Seoul for exchanges, returns and repairs.

139. (A) reserve
(B) vacation
(C) arrange
(D) withstand

140. (A) rare
(B) sturdy
(C) detrimental
(D) complicated

141. (A) Our products are usually sold in duty-free shops in airports.
(B) Please use this guide to narrow down your needs to make the best selection.
(C) Our customers do not need to take additional action to be covered.
(D) We can repair items such as zips and locks, as well as offer a cleaning service.

142. (A) obtain
(B) discount
(C) provide
(D) carry

▶ ▶ ▶ GO ON TO THE NEXT PAGE

Questions 143-146 refer to the following announcement.

AWARDS NOMINATION ANNOUNCEMENT

The Macro IT Solutions has recently announced the candidates for its annual Telstra Award, a grant ------- to a particularly promising entrepreneur who runs a company in a
143.
technology-related field.

Among this year's candidates are Mr. Steve Kensington and Ms. Martha McDonald, two ex-employees of electronics firm, BK Technologies. ------- you wish to find out more
144.
about each candidate, you can read their biographies online. ------- can be found at www.
145.
macroitsolutions.com/telstraaward/list.

-------. A prize of $240,000 will be awarded to the winner in order to assist them in
146.
developing new technologies for the benefit of humanity.

---

143. (A) give
(B) gives
(C) giving
(D) given

144. (A) If
(B) Since
(C) Instead
(D) Despite that

145. (A) It
(B) They
(C) Them
(D) Which

146. (A) We are glad to inform you that you
have been selected as a winner.
(B) Starting your own business can be
thrilling and exciting.
(C) The winner will be announced on
December 23 on our website.
(D) A completed application should arrive
by no later than next Friday.

Directions: In this part you will read a selection of texts, such as magazine and newspaper articles, e-mails, and instant messages. Each text or set of texts is followed by several questions. Select the best answer for each question and mark the letter (A), (B), (C), or (D) on your answer sheet.

Questions 147-148 refer to the following advertisement.

Maximum Real Estate

For Lease: cozy and antique beauty salon space

Bernard Watford

bwatford@joinmail.com

(520) 555-2938

- Two storage areas and one staff lounge
- Ample street parking nearby
- Salon chairs and mirrors in good shape—available for use
- Located in high-traffic area across from King's University campus
- $3,000/month—two-year contract
- Immediate move-in available

147. What is indicated about the advertised space?

(A) It is on sale for $3,000.
(B) It is located near a highway.
(C) It has an enclosed parking space.
(D) It may attract student customers.

148. What option is mentioned in the advertisement?

(A) The option to renovate the space
(B) The option to pay a rent yearly
(C) The option to use some furniture
(D) The option to use an additional storage area

ACTUAL TEST ··· 12

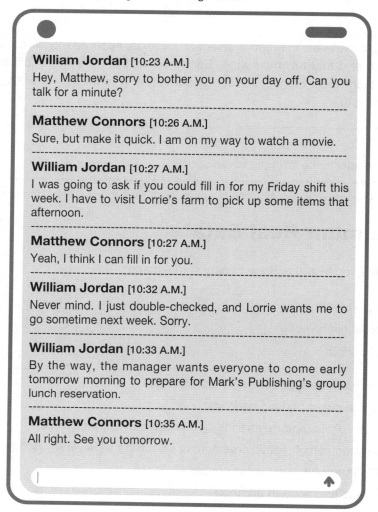

149. Where do Mr. Jordan and Mr. Connors probably work?

A) At a food establishment
(B) At a publishing company
(C) At a farm
(D) At a movie theater

150. At 10:32 A.M., what does Mr. Jordan mean when he writes, "Never mind"?

(A) He realized that he has another task to finish.
(B) He is making an apology for giving short notice.
(C) He is indicating it is too late to reschedule.
(D) He wants to withdraw his earlier request.

While You Were Out

For:	Gabriella Hayes		
Date:	October 14	Time:	3:25 P.M.

Caller	Daniel Newell
Of	Newell Electricity
Phone Number:	(555) 510-9010
Details:	Mr. Newell called to tell you that he will be visiting with his team on October 16 to fix the light in the lobby and to install more lighting in the garden. Signs need to be put up to notify the hotel guests about the disturbance. Contact Mr. Michael Mayson in the Maintenance Department for details about which part of the garden will be affected.
Message Taken By:	Adriano Gentile

151. Who will visit the hotel on October 16?

(A) Gabriella Hayes
(B) Daniel Newell
(C) Adriano Gentile
(D) Michael Mayson

152. Why does Ms. Hayes have to contact Mr. Mayson?

(A) To confirm the time of visit
(B) To find out where to put up posts
(C) To notify him of an interruption
(D) To return his call

Questions 153-154 refer to the following e-mail.

To:	Lisa Keller <lkeller@gomail.com>
From:	Mario Henderson <mhenderson@arlingtonpubliclibrary.org>
Date:	November 14
Subject:	Important notice

Dear Ms. Keller,

Your Arlington Public Library card will expire in December. To renew your card, visit the information desk with a photo ID and a legal document that confirms your current address. Note that any late fees remaining on your current card must be paid before the renewal. Please talk to a librarian on duty for assistance with late fee payments. You can view the remaining balance on your account at the library's website at www.arlingtonpubliclibrary.org.

Please be advised that you cannot check out any library materials without a valid library card. If you miss the deadline for renewal, you will have to make a new card at a cost of $10. For further questions, contact the library at (571) 555-2930.

Mario Henderson
Library Assistant

153. Why did Mr. Henderson write to Ms. Keller?

(A) To notify her of a late payment
(B) To apply for a library card
(C) To inform her about a change in the policy
(D) To issue a reminder

154. What can Ms. Keller do online?

(A) Check for any overdue fees
(B) Submit questions about library use
(C) Request help from a library employee
(D) Donate to the library

Solar Barbershop for Men

120 Main Street, Chicago

open from noon to 8:00 P.M.

- **Regular Haircut** $30.00

Includes shampoo and rinse service before and after the haircut. Hairstyling can be done for an extra $2.00.

- **Hair Dyeing** $65.00

Various colors available. The price may vary depending on the length of your hair. Hair treatment service afterward available for $5.00.

- **Scalp Massage** $18.00

A 30-minute massage by an expert. Add just $4.00 to receive a Solar Special Shampoo, good for hair growth.

- **Waxing** $12.00

Have a clean back, chest, arms, or legs with our waxing service. Special chemicals to minimize skin irritation are used. Hair & beard trimming can be added with just $3.00 more.

- **Shampoo** $3.00

A quick shampoo and hair-drying service.

Bring a friend who is new to Solar Barbershop
and receive $5 off both your bills.
This offer is valid until August 31.

155. What is indicated about Solar Barbershop?

(A) It was recently established.
(B) It has only men on its staff.
(C) It is well-known in Chicago.
(D) It is closed in the morning.

156. To which service can a hair-care item be provided for an additional cost?

(A) A regular haircut
(B) A shampoo
(C) A scalp massage
(D) Waxing

157. How can a customer receive a discount on a haircut?

(A) By recommending Solar Barbershop to an acquaintance
(B) By spending more than a certain amount of money
(C) By ordering a hairstyling service within August
(D) By talking to the manager of Solar Barbershop

Questions 158-160 refer to the following web page.

www.onlibtree.com/announcements

OnLibTree.com
The world's biggest online bookshelf

| Home | Search | Announcements | Order | Contact Us |

Author of the Month

Robert Whitlow
Author of *Hear Me*
Published by Rocking Chair

Robert Whitlow majored in Sociolinguistics and Speech Sciences as an undergraduate at McGill University in Ottawa. During his master's program at the same school, he published his first book, *Science in Communication*, which deals with the importance of communication in daily life and ways to improve it. After receiving his master's degree in Linguistics and Sociology, Mr. Whitlow moved to Boston to work at Bright Finance Corp. As a business communication mentor, he taught employees persuasive communication in business operations. Now, he is a linguistics professor at the University of Chicago. Currently on a tour to promote his first novel, *Hear Me*, Mr. Whitlow is visiting several cities in England. As of June 10, he is in London, and he will soon visit Manchester, Bristol, and Cardiff.

158. What kind of business is OnLibTree?

(A) A research company
(B) An online furniture store
(C) A bookstore
(D) A publisher

159. Where did Mr. Whitlow begin his writing career?

(A) In Ottawa
(B) In Chicago
(C) In Boston
(D) In London

160. What is mentioned about Mr. Whitlow?

(A) He designed a chair.
(B) He works for a financial institution.
(C) He used to teach at McGill University.
(D) He is staying in England temporarily.

To:	Customer Service <customerservice@toptracks101.com>
From:	Doris Hogue <dhogue@walkmail.com>
Date:	October 10
Subject:	Order #10009283

To whom it may concern,

I tried calling the Toptracks 101 customer service directly but could not reach any of the workers. I purchased some albums on your website not long ago. —[1]—. After I paid for the selected items, I realized that I had accidently ordered the Rock Station's Delux album, which I did not mean to purchase as I had already done so last month. For some reason, it still remained in my shopping cart and got checked out along with my new list of items, so I accidently paid for it. —[2]—.

On the website, the notice says that I should contact customer service and that a refund will be available within 24 hours of purchase. —[3]—. If by any chance, the refund of a single item is not available, could you just cancel my whole order? The Rock Station's Delux album is not cheap and I certainly don't need two of them. —[4]—. Please get back to me with the available options.

Thank you.

Doris Hogue

161. Why does Ms. Hogue send the e-mail?

(A) To file a complaint about a recent purchase
(B) To add an additional item to her order
(C) To inquire about missing items
(D) To ask for a refund

162. What is stated about Ms. Hogue?

(A) She has shopped at Toptracks 101 before.
(B) She is not a fan of the Rock Station.
(C) She downloads music frequently.
(D) She already has two copies of the same album.

163. In which of the positions marked [1], [2], [3], and [4] does the following sentence best fit?

"It has only been about 20 minutes since my purchase, so I believe the opportunity to get a refund is still valid."

(A) [1]
(B) [2]
(C) [3]
(D) [4]

Questions 164-167 refer to the following online chat discussion.

Shannon Grant   6:39 P.M.

Hey, guys, we need to sort out who's going to bring what to our annual birdwatching club outing to Crimson Falls next week.

Thomas Gagne   6:41 P.M.

I'll bring the kitchen utensils. I think we should all bring our own cutlery instead of using plastic ones to minimize the amount of garbage.

Larry Olson   6:43 P.M.

That's a good idea.

Shannon Grant   6:46 P.M.

I can bring a tent and some other outdoor equipment. My dad goes rock climbing a lot, so he has loads of outdoor equipment in the garage. I'll pick up some things from his pile.

Jamie Smith   6:50 P.M.

Sam and I will be in charge of food. We are going grocery shopping tomorrow. Any special requests?

Larry Olson   6:52 P.M.

I'll bring some extra blankets in case it rains or it gets too cold inside the tent at night.

Shannon Grant   6:53 P.M.

That's a great idea. Thanks, Larry.

Thomas Gagne   6:53 P.M.

Jamie, don't forget the marshmallows!

Jamie Smith   6:54 P.M.

You know that will never happen. Even if I did, Sam would definitely be there to remind me.

Sam Lorenzo   6:55 P.M.

Certainly, they are the first on my shopping list.

Shannon Grant   6:56 P.M.

Okay. I will check up with you guys again in two days to go over the final preparations and our activity schedule.

SEND

164. What type of event is being prepared for?

(A) Rock climbing
(B) An animal experiment
(C) A camping trip
(D) An environmental seminar

165. What is Mr. Lorrenzo supposed to do?

(A) Gather outdoor equipment from his father's garage
(B) Plan activities for the group
(C) Bring warm blankets to share with the others
(D) Buy some groceries

166. What will probably happen a couple of days later?

(A) Ms. Grant will contact the club members.
(B) The club members will decide on the final location of their outing.
(C) Mr. Smith will prepare some kitchen utensils.
(D) The club members will leave for Crimson Falls.

167. At 6:54 P.M., what does Mr. Smith mean when he writes, "You know that will never happen"?

(A) He does not want to waste money on snacks.
(B) He would not leave out a specific item.
(C) He does not want to follow the activity schedule.
(D) He will remind Mr. Lorenzo to revise his shopping list.

Wallington (March 17) – Cosette's, the most popular independent jewelry shop in Wallington's Polio district, is closing its doors on March 21 after 10 years of service at its current location. Owner Richard Cooper will open a new jewelry shop just 2 blocks away under the name of Joyeria, Inc.

The Polio district was able to draw an increasing number of visitors over the years thanks to a few successful shops, including Cosette's. The success, however, actually ended up being the main reason Cosette's was forced out of business. The building's landlord increased the rent on the property to a level Mr. Cooper could no longer manage.

When Cosette's was about to fade away into history, Joyeria, Inc. reached out with a helping hand. "I have been a big fan of Cosette's since its establishment. Mr. Cooper is such a gifted jewelry craftsman," says Ms. Prasad, the chief executive officer of Joyeria. "That is why I did not miss the chance to recruit him as our senior designer."

Mr. Cooper will now operate a Joyeria shop and design jewelry for the company. "Although I was not able to keep my old shop," said Mr. Cooper. "I am just grateful that I can continue working in my hometown."

168. What is indicated about the Polio district?

(A) It was established 10 years ago.
(B) It is where Joyeria, Inc. is based.
(C) It is the busiest district in Wallington.
(D) It has become more popular.

169. The word "just" in paragraph 1, line 6, is closest in meaning to

(A) fairly
(B) approximately
(C) only
(D) accurately

170. Who most likely is Ms. Prasad?

(A) An old customer of Cosette's
(B) A resident of Wallington
(C) The landlord of a property
(D) The founder of Joyeria, Inc.

171. According to the article, why is Mr. Cooper happy?

(A) Because he does not have to leave Wallington.
(B) Because he was able to hire Ms. Prasad.
(C) Because he is gaining a large sum of money.
(D) Because he will return to his birthplace.

CE Corporation - Organic Chemistry Lab Safety Rules

1. Before lab activity

Wear safety goggles and an apron to protect yourself from hazardous chemicals during experiments and research. Avoid wearing clothing that could easily catch fire. Otherwise, make sure to wear a lab coat over your clothing. —[1]—.

2. Restricted items

With the exception of authorized heat sources, no items that can cause fires or explosions are allowed in the lab. Our lab activities are confidential, so filming devices are highly restricted in the lab. —[2]—.

3. Organization

It is evident that lab stations are clean and organized at all times to prevent accidents and chemical residues from causing reactions. Before and after lab activities, all chemicals should be put away with lids closed tightly. —[3]—.

4. Emergencies

Accidents can happen anytime during the lab, and thus you must be aware of the use and location of safety equipment. In case of a fire or chemical contamination, a siren will go off, and everyone must leave the lab immediately. —[4]—.

172. For whom is the information most likely intended?

(A) Safety inspectors
(B) Lab researchers
(C) Science students
(D) Maintenance staff

173. What is NOT mentioned as an item the readers should avoid bringing into the lab?

(A) A camera
(B) A lighter
(C) Food
(D) Cotton fabric clothing

174. According to the information, under what circumstance is evacuation necessary?

(A) When a text message arrives
(B) When the alarm rings
(C) When there is an announcement from the speakers
(D) When a warning signal light is turned on

175. In which of the positions marked [1], [2], [3], and [4] does the following sentence best fit?

"Lab materials should be cleaned thoroughly and be placed where they belong."

(A) [1]
(B) [2]
(C) [3]
(D) [4]

To: Henry Cohen <hcohen@deliciousdream.com>

From: Audrey Miller <amiller@deliciousdream.com>

Date: March 10

Subject: Delicious Dream Seminar

Hi, Henry.

This is in regard to the upcoming Delicious Dream Seminar scheduled to take place on March 20. I have a few things to let you know before you finalize the schedule for the seminar.

This morning, Ms. Barbara Kennedy called to tell me that she can no longer lead a session at the scheduled time on the day of the seminar as she will be leaving for Buffalo, New York, in the afternoon. Mr. Emmanuel Colon graciously agreed to switch presentation times with Ms. Kennedy. Please reflect this in the schedule in order to avoid any confusion.

As you already know, Mr. Anthony Hartley is such a famous and influential figure that we expect his session to attract a lot more people than the other sessions. I would like you to reserve a room that will be able to hold all the attendees without any problem for his presentation.

Thank you for your assistance. See you in the office tomorrow.

Audrey

5th Annual Delicious Dream Seminar
Franco Conference Center
350 Walnut Avenue, New Orleans
March 20, Wednesday

Time	Seminar Title / Presenter
10:00 A.M. – 11:00 A.M.	*You Are What You Eat* in Room 201 by Tracee Smith, author of *Eat Well, Live Well*
11:00 A.M. – 12:00 P.M.	*Happy Family Meals* in Room 201 by Barbara Kennedy, renowned culinary artist
12:00 P.M. – 1:30 P.M.	Lunch Break (Meals will be provided by Shari Catering.)
1:30 P.M. – 2:30 P.M.	*Successfully Creating New Dishes* in Room 302 by Mary Agnes, head chef at the Grand Paris Hotel
2:30 P.M. – 3:30 P.M.	*Selecting the Right Ingredients* in Room 205 by Emmanuel Colon, founder and owner of Colon's Mexican Cuisine
3:30 P.M. – 4:30 P.M.	*How to Get into the Food Business* in Room 306 by Anthony Hartley, producer of the TV show *Dining Paradise*

*Updated on March 11

176. What is a purpose of the e-mail?

(A) To arrange an appointment
(B) To provide an update on a change in plans
(C) To invite a guest speaker
(D) To inquire about a seminar venue

177. What is true about Ms. Miller?

(A) She works for Mr. Cohen.
(B) She will be going on a business trip soon.
(C) She recently talked to Ms. Kennedy.
(D) She is very well-known nationally.

178. Which seminar was originally planned to commence at 11:00 A.M.?

(A) *Selecting the Right Ingredients*
(B) *How to Get into the Food Business*
(C) *Successfully Creating New Dishes*
(D) *You Are What You Eat*

179. What is true about the Delicious Dream Seminar?

(A) It will be broadcast on TV.
(B) Its subject is related to food.
(C) It requires an admission fee.
(D) It received donations from local businesses.

180. What is probably different about Room 306 compared to other rooms in the Franco Conference Center?

(A) It is larger in terms of its capacity.
(B) It is less expensive.
(C) It has better audio equipment.
(D) It is a boardroom-style venue.

▶ ▶ ▶ GO ON TO THE NEXT PAGE

To:	Robert Miller <Rmiller@dmail.com>
From:	Brenda Pierce <Brenda@thefirstcarrental.com>
Date:	October 10
Subject:	Car rental

Dear Mr. Miller,

Thank you for your interest in renting a vehicle from First Class Rental. First Class Rental provides cars that are in the best condition at the best prices, a proven fact as we won the Best Vehicle Rental Dealer Award last year. Below is a list of several vehicles with their specifications that may suit your needs.

Make	Model	Capacity	Features	Price (per day)
Autobahn	S019	6	Air conditioning, built-in GPS, four-wheel drive, sunroof	$179
Autobahn	E998	4	Air conditioning, built-in GPS, front-wheel drive	$137
Clever	3-50	4	Air conditioning, high-performance tires, sunroof	$140
FNR	Tracker 6	5	Air conditioning, four-wheel drive, sunroof	$165

Please come by our shop to test-drive the vehicles yourself. The First Class Rental branch I work at is located at 455 Willow Oaks Lane, Lafayette. You can ask for me or my assistant, Mr. Stanley Ciula, when you visit the shop.

Thank you,

Brenda Pierce

To:	Brenda Pierce <Brenda@thefirstcarrental.com>
From:	Robert Miller <Rmiller@dmail.com>
Date:	October 27
Subject:	Feedback

Dear Ms. Pierce,

I was able to greatly enjoy my recent trip to the Grand Canyon thanks to your assistance. I guess it would have been even better if I had gone along with your recommendation of the car with the built-in GPS and a sunroof, but the Tracker 6 was not bad after all.

I also completed the survey on your website, and I received a discount coupon for another rental at your shop. I would like to know how long it is good for as that information is not specified on the coupon.

Sincerely,

Robert Miller

181. What is suggested about First Class Rental?

(A) It has more than one location.
(B) It is an internationally well-known business.
(C) It provides free repair service to its customers.
(D) It provides award-winning vehicles.

182. What does Ms. Pierce ask Mr. Miller to do?

(A) Drop off some documents
(B) Visit a website
(C) Pay her a call
(D) Send an e-mail to her assistant

183. In the second e-mail, the word "guess" in paragraph 1, line 1, is closest in meaning to

(A) wonder
(B) question
(C) gather
(D) provide

184. Which vehicle did Ms. Pierce most likely recommend to Mr. Miller?

(A) 3-50
(B) E998
(C) S019
(D) Tracker 6

185. What can be inferred about Mr. Miller?

(A) He conducted a survey on a website.
(B) He intends to use First Class Rental again.
(C) He used a coupon when he rented a vehicle.
(D) He will visit the Grand Canyon soon.

▶ ▶ ▶GO ON TO THE NEXT PAGE

Questions 186-190 refer to the following advertisement, e-mail, and ticket.

Boston Concert Hall

An internationally well-known theater production, *Broken Promises*, will be shown at the Boston Concert Hall from December 5 to 7. Periso Dramatists Award-winning playwright and director Lisa Adams has been on tour with her crew around the world since last month, visiting South Africa and Canada so far. Do not miss out on this once-in-a-lifetime chance to see the thought-provoking and enthralling play. Tickets are $90 each for the general public and $75 for members of the Boston Concert Hall. Tickets are available at the door or at www.bostonconcerthall.com. A membership discount can be applied to up to 2 tickets per member. A complete list of the crew members, photos of the play from the past, and a brief background history of the playwright can also be viewed on the website.

To:	Samuel Ferris <s.ferris@donaldaccounting.com>
From:	Melinda Nafure <m.nafure@donaldaccounting.com>
Date:	November 26
Subject:	*Broken Promises*

Hi, Samuel.

Did you know that the play *Broken Promises* is coming to Boston in December? Since I personally know the director, as she used to live next door to me when I went to college in Sydney, I am eager to see her production and to talk to her. Would you like to watch the play with me? I will pay for the tickets if you say yes.

Sincerely,

Melinda

Boston Concert Hall
Online Ticket

Broken Promises

December 6, 7:15 P.M.

Customer Name: Melinda Nafure
E-mail Address: m.nafure@donaldaccounting.com

Admission for 2 ($75 each)
Seats: B25, B26

FOR YOUR INFORMATION:
- Please print out this ticket and present it at the door for admission.
- Go on www.bostonconcerthall.com for cancelation or change of tickets.
- Please show up at the concert hall 15 minutes before the stated time to be seated.
- There will be a brief picture-taking session after the play.

Thank you.

---

186. What is suggested about *Broken Promises*?

(A) It has received an award.
(B) It has been performed in more than one country.
(C) Its last performance will take place in Boston.
(D) It stars Lisa Adams in the role of a playwright.

187. What is available on the Boston Concert Hall's website?

(A) Reviews written by critics
(B) Advance purchase discount offers
(C) Biographical information of the main cast
(D) A list of performers

188. Who is Ms. Nafure?

(A) A current resident of Sydney
(B) A former neighbor of Ms. Adams
(C) An actress
(D) A director

189. What is indicated about Ms. Nafure?

(A) She has seen *Broken Promises* in the past.
(B) She will change the details of her ticket.
(C) She went to college with Mr. Ferris.
(D) She is a member of the Boston Concert Hall.

190. What are ticketholders requested to do?

(A) Purchase their tickets at the door
(B) Avoid taking pictures
(C) Arrive early at the venue
(D) Remain seated when the play ends

The Irvine Community Foundation (ICF) awards local nonprofit organizations need-based grants to help improve our community through the Better Irvine Funds Program. The grants range in size from $2,000 to $10,000.

Applications for grants must be submitted on the ICF's website to be considered. On the application form, a detailed plan for community improvement, at least 35 signatures from organization members who have committed to their participation in the project, and other information about the potential project must be included. For more information and to apply, go to the ICF's website at www.irvinecf.org/betterirvine.

Irvine Community Foundation

150 Valley Avenue, Irvine, CA 92602
(949) 555-1023

July 1

Adriana Grill
Ersel Parents Association
77 Vineyard Drive
Irvine, CA 92603

Dear Ms. Grill,

We at the Irvine Community Foundation are happy to announce that the Ersel Parents Association will be given a grant of $6,000 for the initiative you proposed for a playground in the city. We believe the addition will improve our city and community greatly. As the president of your organization, you are encouraged to come to our office this week to discuss more about the plan. Please call (949) 510-9057 to arrange a date.

Thank you,

Richard Kwan

Irvine (November 21) – The construction of Irvine Paradise for the Young, a new playground for the children of Irvine, was completed yesterday. The playground is a collaborative work by the Ersel Parents Association (EPA) and the Irvine Community Foundation (ICF). Children will be able to embark on adventures at Irvine Paradise starting on November 25. The president of the EPA will be present at the opening ceremony to deliver a speech regarding the importance of providing safe places for children to have fun and to exercise.

191. What is mentioned about the Irvine Community Foundation?

(A) It is currently hiring volunteers.
(B) It receives grant requests online.
(C) It is made up of Irvine residents only.
(D) It posts grant recipients' names on its website.

192. In the information, the word "committed" in paragraph 2, line 3, is closest in meaning to

(A) sacrificed
(B) promised
(C) contributed
(D) decided

193. What is a purpose of the letter?

(A) To invite Ms. Grill to a meeting
(B) To solicit a donation
(C) To persuade Ms. Grill to construct a playground
(D) To announce grant application procedures

194. What is NOT suggested about the Ersel Parents Association?

(A) It is based in Irvine.
(B) It has merged with the Irvine Community Foundation.
(C) It has at least 35 members.
(D) It is a nonprofit organization.

195. When will Ms. Grill most likely show up at Irvine Paradise for the Young?

(A) On July 1
(B) On November 20
(C) On November 21
(D) On November 25

http://www.sunbursthotel.com/aboutus

Sunburst Hotel

HOME	ABOUT US	RESERVATION	TESTIMONIAL

Welcome to the Sunburst Hotel

155 Rissik Street, Sun City 0355, South Africa

The Sunburst Hotel is a 4-star hotel that was rated number one among 8 hotels in the area. With our 50-year-long history, we have been successfully welcoming both local and foreign tourists to Sun City.

Our main goal is to provide all visitors with a perfectly relaxing stay, and we believe the top-quality food provided by world-famous cook Marilyn Yi contributes to achieving it. Press the button for the second floor in the elevator, and it will take you to a place where you can taste magic.

We are currently offering tickets to a local museum to all returning visitors. Find out more about the promotional event **HERE**. Offer valid from June 1 to July 31.

http://www.sunbursthotel.com/testimonial

Sunburst Hotel

HOME	ABOUT US	RESERVATION	TESTIMONIAL

Fabulous Stay! ★★★★★ (5 stars out of 5)

Reviewed by **Stephanie Vallejo** on **June 16**

I visited South Africa on vacation for 7 days from June 4 to June 11. I stayed at three different hotels during my trip and went to the Sunburst Hotel on June 9 and stayed there for my last 3 days in South Africa. I am confident in saying that the Sunburst is simply the best hotel in the area. Its parking lot is unbelievably huge, and there are staff members everywhere to assist visitors with the utmost level of service and attentiveness. I also loved swimming at the beach, which was just a 3-minute walk away from the hotel. Great food, great location, great staff, and great price. What more can you ask for?

Sunburst Hotel

HOME	ABOUT US	RESERVATION	TESTIMONIAL

No more "bursting Sun" ★☆☆☆☆ (1 star out of 5)

Reviewed by **Renato Segatto** on **August 9**

I visited the Sunburst Hotel on July 20 and stayed there for 5 nights. I appreciated the free ticket to a museum I received from the hotel very much, but I must express how I really felt about the hotel itself. The Sunburst Hotel used to be the best hotel in the region, but I personally think it has lost its old glory. The building is undeniably old, all the doors squeak every time I open them, and the wireless Internet is just way too slow. Worst of all, the street the hotel is located on has become very developed, so there are bright lights shining through the windows and many people making loud noises at night. I do not recommend the Sunburst Hotel if you are looking to have a quiet, relaxing vacation.

196. What is indicated about the Sunburst Hotel?

(A) It is managed by Marilyn Yi.
(B) It is the oldest establishment in Sun City.
(C) It receives the highest number of visitors in June.
(D) Its building consists of more than one floor.

197. When did Ms. Vallejo leave the Sunburst Hotel?

(A) On June 4
(B) On June 9
(C) On June 11
(D) On June 16

198. What is NOT mentioned as a feature available at the Sunburst Hotel?

(A) A restaurant
(B) A swimming pool
(C) Internet access
(D) A parking lot

199. What is suggested about Mr. Segatto?

(A) He is complaining about the Sunburst Hotel's poor customer service.
(B) He has visited the Sunburst Hotel more than once.
(C) He drove a vehicle to the Sunburst Hotel.
(D) He personally knows the staff members at the Sunburst Hotel.

200. What can be inferred about Rissik Street?

(A) It is noisy at night.
(B) There are eight hotels on it.
(C) It will be widened soon.
(D) It needs to be renovated.

STOP! This is the end of the test. If you finish before time is called, you may go back to Parts 5, 6, and 7 and check your work.

Actual Test 정답표

Listening Comprehension **Reading Comprehension**

07

1. (B)	2. (B)	3. (C)	4. (D)	5. (C)
6. (C)	7. (B)	8. (A)	9. (C)	10. (C)
11. (C)	12. (B)	13. (A)	14. (C)	15. (B)
16. (B)	17. (A)	18. (A)	19. (A)	20. (B)
21. (B)	22. (C)	23. (C)	24. (B)	25. (C)
26. (B)	27. (A)	28. (C)	29. (C)	30. (C)
31. (A)	32. (D)	33. (C)	34. (D)	35. (A)
36. (C)	37. (A)	38. (B)	39. (D)	40. (C)
41. (C)	42. (D)	43. (B)	44. (C)	45. (C)
46. (A)	47. (D)	48. (A)	49. (D)	50. (B)
51. (A)	52. (D)	53. (C)	54. (A)	55. (C)
56. (B)	57. (A)	58. (D)	59. (A)	60. (D)
61. (B)	62. (A)	63. (B)	64. (C)	65. (B)
66. (D)	67. (C)	68. (C)	69. (A)	70. (B)
71. (C)	72. (A)	73. (C)	74. (C)	75. (D)
76. (D)	77. (A)	78. (D)	79. (D)	80. (A)
81. (B)	82. (A)	83. (B)	84. (D)	85. (D)
86. (C)	87. (D)	88. (D)	89. (B)	90. (C)
91. (D)	92. (C)	93. (C)	94. (A)	95. (B)
96. (D)	97. (C)	98. (A)	99. (B)	100. (D)

101. (B)	102. (C)	103. (D)	104. (C)	105. (C)
106. (B)	107. (C)	108. (A)	109. (D)	110. (A)
111. (B)	112. (A)	113. (B)	114. (B)	115. (A)
116. (A)	117. (D)	118. (B)	119. (D)	120. (C)
121. (D)	122. (C)	123. (A)	124. (D)	125. (D)
126. (D)	127. (C)	128. (C)	129. (D)	130. (D)
131. (B)	132. (B)	133. (D)	134. (B)	135. (B)
136. (C)	137. (D)	138. (D)	139. (D)	140. (D)
141. (B)	142. (A)	143. (D)	144. (C)	145. (A)
146. (C)	147. (C)	148. (A)	149. (C)	150. (B)
151. (C)	152. (B)	153. (D)	154. (D)	155. (D)
156. (A)	157. (D)	158. (C)	159. (A)	160. (C)
161. (D)	162. (A)	163. (B)	164. (D)	165. (D)
166. (B)	167. (D)	168. (D)	169. (C)	170. (B)
171. (B)	172. (C)	173. (B)	174. (D)	175. (B)
176. (B)	177. (C)	178. (B)	179. (B)	180. (B)
181. (B)	182. (B)	183. (C)	184. (B)	185. (D)
186. (C)	187. (A)	188. (B)	189. (D)	190. (D)
191. (A)	192. (D)	193. (B)	194. (A)	195. (A)
196. (B)	197. (C)	198. (B)	199. (A)	200. (A)

08

1. (B)	2. (B)	3. (D)	4. (D)	5. (B)
6. (A)	7. (C)	8. (A)	9. (A)	10. (B)
11. (A)	12. (C)	13. (C)	14. (C)	15. (A)
16. (A)	17. (C)	18. (B)	19. (A)	20. (A)
21. (C)	22. (A)	23. (B)	24. (B)	25. (B)
26. (A)	27. (A)	28. (B)	29. (C)	30. (B)
31. (B)	32. (A)	33. (C)	34. (B)	35. (A)
36. (A)	37. (C)	38. (B)	39. (B)	40. (D)
41. (C)	42. (C)	43. (C)	44. (A)	45. (B)
46. (B)	47. (B)	48. (D)	49. (A)	50. (C)
51. (A)	52. (C)	53. (A)	54. (B)	55. (D)
56. (C)	57. (C)	58. (A)	59. (C)	60. (A)
61. (D)	62. (D)	63. (D)	64. (D)	65. (B)
66. (D)	67. (B)	68. (B)	69. (C)	70. (A)
71. (D)	72. (C)	73. (A)	74. (A)	75. (D)
76. (A)	77. (C)	78. (C)	79. (D)	80. (C)
81. (A)	82. (B)	83. (B)	84. (C)	85. (D)
86. (D)	87. (B)	88. (C)	89. (C)	90. (A)
91. (D)	92. (B)	93. (B)	94. (D)	95. (A)
96. (A)	97. (C)	98. (B)	99. (A)	100. (C)

101. (D)	102. (D)	103. (D)	104. (C)	105. (B)
106. (C)	107. (A)	108. (C)	109. (A)	110. (B)
111. (D)	112. (D)	113. (B)	114. (B)	115. (D)
116. (B)	117. (C)	118. (A)	119. (C)	120. (D)
121. (C)	122. (D)	123. (B)	124. (C)	125. (C)
126. (B)	127. (D)	128. (D)	129. (A)	130. (A)
131. (B)	132. (B)	133. (C)	134. (B)	135. (B)
136. (D)	137. (B)	138. (C)	139. (D)	140. (C)
141. (B)	142. (C)	143. (D)	144. (D)	145. (B)
146. (C)	147. (C)	148. (B)	149. (D)	150. (C)
151. (C)	152. (C)	153. (C)	154. (B)	155. (A)
156. (D)	157. (D)	158. (B)	159. (C)	160. (D)
161. (A)	162. (B)	163. (C)	164. (C)	165. (C)
166. (C)	167. (A)	168. (D)	169. (C)	170. (B)
171. (A)	172. (B)	173. (D)	174. (A)	175. (C)
176. (A)	177. (C)	178. (A)	179. (C)	180. (C)
181. (D)	182. (B)	183. (D)	184. (B)	185. (A)
186. (D)	187. (C)	188. (A)	189. (C)	190. (B)
191. (A)	192. (C)	193. (B)	194. (C)	195. (A)
196. (A)	197. (B)	198. (D)	199. (D)	200. (A)

Actual Test 정답표

Listening Comprehension　　　　　　　　**Reading Comprehension**

09

1. (A)	**2.** (B)	**3.** (A)	**4.** (D)	**5.** (B)	**101.** (D)	**102.** (B)	**103.** (A)	**104.** (B)	**105.** (D)
6. (B)	**7.** (C)	**8.** (B)	**9.** (B)	**10.** (B)	**106.** (A)	**107.** (D)	**108.** (A)	**109.** (C)	**110.** (D)
11. (B)	**12.** (B)	**13.** (B)	**14.** (A)	**15.** (C)	**111.** (A)	**112.** (C)	**113.** (B)	**114.** (D)	**115.** (C)
16. (C)	**17.** (A)	**18.** (A)	**19.** (C)	**20.** (C)	**116.** (A)	**117.** (D)	**118.** (D)	**119.** (C)	**120.** (A)
21. (B)	**22.** (C)	**23.** (A)	**24.** (B)	**25.** (C)	**121.** (D)	**122.** (B)	**123.** (D)	**124.** (C)	**125.** (A)
26. (A)	**27.** (A)	**28.** (C)	**29.** (A)	**30.** (C)	**126.** (C)	**127.** (D)	**128.** (D)	**129.** (B)	**130.** (D)
31. (C)	**32.** (C)	**33.** (A)	**34.** (D)	**35.** (B)	**131.** (A)	**132.** (D)	**133.** (B)	**134.** (B)	**135.** (C)
36. (D)	**37.** (B)	**38.** (C)	**39.** (B)	**40.** (D)	**136.** (C)	**137.** (B)	**138.** (A)	**139.** (A)	**140.** (D)
41. (D)	**42.** (D)	**43.** (B)	**44.** (B)	**45.** (D)	**141.** (C)	**142.** (D)	**143.** (D)	**144.** (D)	**145.** (B)
46. (B)	**47.** (D)	**48.** (C)	**49.** (B)	**50.** (A)	**146.** (B)	**147.** (B)	**148.** (D)	**149.** (B)	**150.** (D)
51. (B)	**52.** (A)	**53.** (A)	**54.** (B)	**55.** (C)	**151.** (D)	**152.** (C)	**153.** (A)	**154.** (D)	**155.** (D)
56. (C)	**57.** (D)	**58.** (C)	**59.** (C)	**60.** (D)	**156.** (A)	**157.** (B)	**158.** (C)	**159.** (B)	**160.** (D)
61. (A)	**62.** (B)	**63.** (B)	**64.** (B)	**65.** (B)	**161.** (C)	**162.** (B)	**163.** (C)	**164.** (B)	**165.** (D)
66. (C)	**67.** (D)	**68.** (D)	**69.** (A)	**70.** (D)	**166.** (A)	**167.** (A)	**168.** (B)	**169.** (B)	**170.** (A)
71. (A)	**72.** (D)	**73.** (A)	**74.** (D)	**75.** (B)	**171.** (B)	**172.** (D)	**173.** (C)	**174.** (C)	**175.** (C)
76. (C)	**77.** (A)	**78.** (C)	**79.** (D)	**80.** (B)	**176.** (A)	**177.** (A)	**178.** (D)	**179.** (B)	**180.** (B)
81. (C)	**82.** (B)	**83.** (A)	**84.** (B)	**85.** (D)	**181.** (D)	**182.** (B)	**183.** (D)	**184.** (C)	**185.** (C)
86. (C)	**87.** (C)	**88.** (A)	**89.** (B)	**90.** (B)	**186.** (A)	**187.** (B)	**188.** (B)	**189.** (C)	**190.** (D)
91. (C)	**92.** (B)	**93.** (A)	**94.** (D)	**95.** (B)	**191.** (D)	**192.** (A)	**193.** (C)	**194.** (C)	**195.** (A)
96. (C)	**97.** (B)	**98.** (B)	**99.** (A)	**100.** (B)	**196.** (A)	**197.** (B)	**198.** (C)	**199.** (B)	**200.** (C)

10

1. (A)	**2.** (D)	**3.** (B)	**4.** (C)	**5.** (D)	**101.** (B)	**102.** (B)	**103.** (A)	**104.** (B)	**105.** (C)
6. (D)	**7.** (C)	**8.** (B)	**9.** (C)	**10.** (B)	**106.** (C)	**107.** (A)	**108.** (B)	**109.** (B)	**110.** (A)
11. (A)	**12.** (A)	**13.** (C)	**14.** (C)	**15.** (C)	**111.** (B)	**112.** (C)	**113.** (C)	**114.** (C)	**115.** (C)
16. (A)	**17.** (A)	**18.** (C)	**19.** (C)	**20.** (B)	**116.** (B)	**117.** (C)	**118.** (B)	**119.** (B)	**120.** (B)
21. (A)	**22.** (C)	**23.** (B)	**24.** (A)	**25.** (A)	**121.** (C)	**122.** (C)	**123.** (D)	**124.** (A)	**125.** (B)
26. (C)	**27.** (C)	**28.** (A)	**29.** (C)	**30.** (C)	**126.** (B)	**127.** (B)	**128.** (C)	**129.** (A)	**130.** (B)
31. (B)	**32.** (A)	**33.** (D)	**34.** (A)	**35.** (B)	**131.** (B)	**132.** (D)	**133.** (B)	**134.** (A)	**135.** (B)
36. (D)	**37.** (A)	**38.** (C)	**39.** (D)	**40.** (C)	**136.** (C)	**137.** (C)	**138.** (B)	**139.** (C)	**140.** (C)
41. (B)	**42.** (A)	**43.** (C)	**44.** (B)	**45.** (B)	**141.** (C)	**142.** (C)	**143.** (C)	**144.** (B)	**145.** (B)
46. (D)	**47.** (B)	**48.** (D)	**49.** (C)	**50.** (B)	**146.** (D)	**147.** (D)	**148.** (D)	**149.** (C)	**150.** (C)
51. (D)	**52.** (D)	**53.** (A)	**54.** (B)	**55.** (D)	**151.** (C)	**152.** (D)	**153.** (C)	**154.** (C)	**155.** (D)
56. (B)	**57.** (B)	**58.** (C)	**59.** (C)	**60.** (A)	**156.** (B)	**157.** (B)	**158.** (C)	**159.** (B)	**160.** (D)
61. (D)	**62.** (C)	**63.** (D)	**64.** (A)	**65.** (C)	**161.** (D)	**162.** (C)	**163.** (C)	**164.** (C)	**165.** (B)
66. (A)	**67.** (C)	**68.** (B)	**69.** (A)	**70.** (C)	**166.** (C)	**167.** (D)	**168.** (C)	**169.** (D)	**170.** (D)
71. (C)	**72.** (A)	**73.** (B)	**74.** (D)	**75.** (A)	**171.** (A)	**172.** (D)	**173.** (D)	**174.** (B)	**175.** (C)
76. (B)	**77.** (A)	**78.** (D)	**79.** (A)	**80.** (B)	**176.** (D)	**177.** (C)	**178.** (D)	**179.** (B)	**180.** (A)
81. (C)	**82.** (C)	**83.** (B)	**84.** (D)	**85.** (B)	**181.** (A)	**182.** (A)	**183.** (B)	**184.** (B)	**185.** (D)
86. (B)	**87.** (D)	**88.** (D)	**89.** (C)	**90.** (B)	**186.** (D)	**187.** (B)	**188.** (A)	**189.** (A)	**190.** (B)
91. (D)	**92.** (C)	**93.** (D)	**94.** (D)	**95.** (B)	**191.** (D)	**192.** (B)	**193.** (B)	**194.** (A)	**195.** (D)
96. (B)	**97.** (B)	**98.** (C)	**99.** (C)	**100.** (B)	**196.** (D)	**197.** (A)	**198.** (A)	**199.** (D)	**200.** (B)

Actual Test 정답표

Listening Comprehension　　　　　　　　**Reading Comprehension**

11

1. (B)	2. (A)	3. (A)	4. (B)	5. (D)	101. (C)	102. (B)	103. (B)	104. (C)	105. (A)
6. (D)	7. (B)	8. (C)	9. (C)	10. (C)	106. (D)	107. (D)	108. (B)	109. (D)	110. (C)
11. (C)	12. (C)	13. (A)	14. (B)	15. (C)	111. (C)	112. (B)	113. (C)	114. (D)	115. (A)
16. (B)	17. (B)	18. (A)	19. (B)	20. (B)	116. (C)	117. (A)	118. (D)	119. (C)	120. (D)
21. (B)	22. (A)	23. (A)	24. (C)	25. (C)	121. (C)	122. (C)	123. (D)	124. (B)	125. (A)
26. (B)	27. (B)	28. (B)	29. (C)	30. (A)	126. (B)	127. (C)	128. (D)	129. (D)	130. (B)
31. (A)	32. (C)	33. (B)	34. (A)	35. (C)	131. (C)	132. (C)	133. (A)	134. (B)	135. (D)
36. (D)	37. (D)	38. (A)	39. (D)	40. (C)	136. (D)	137. (A)	138. (C)	139. (D)	140. (A)
41. (D)	42. (B)	43. (D)	44. (B)	45. (D)	141. (B)	142. (B)	143. (B)	144. (C)	145. (C)
46. (D)	47. (A)	48. (A)	49. (D)	50. (C)	146. (D)	147. (C)	148. (B)	149. (B)	150. (D)
51. (B)	52. (A)	53. (B)	54. (C)	55. (D)	151. (B)	152. (C)	153. (B)	154. (C)	155. (B)
56. (D)	57. (D)	58. (A)	59. (C)	60. (C)	156. (C)	157. (D)	158. (B)	159. (B)	160. (C)
61. (C)	62. (B)	63. (C)	64. (C)	65. (B)	161. (B)	162. (D)	163. (B)	164. (D)	165. (D)
66. (C)	67. (A)	68. (C)	69. (B)	70. (C)	166. (D)	167. (C)	168. (C)	169. (A)	170. (A)
71. (A)	72. (B)	73. (B)	74. (A)	75. (C)	171. (C)	172. (B)	173. (B)	174. (A)	175. (D)
76. (B)	77. (D)	78. (B)	79. (A)	80. (A)	176. (C)	177. (A)	178. (D)	179. (B)	180. (D)
81. (A)	82. (C)	83. (C)	84. (D)	85. (C)	181. (A)	182. (C)	183. (B)	184. (C)	185. (A)
86. (C)	87. (B)	88. (C)	89. (A)	90. (B)	186. (C)	187. (B)	188. (A)	189. (C)	190. (B)
91. (C)	92. (A)	93. (D)	94. (C)	95. (B)	191. (C)	192. (D)	193. (B)	194. (D)	195. (C)
96. (A)	97. (B)	98. (C)	99. (C)	100. (B)	196. (D)	197. (B)	198. (A)	199. (C)	200. (B)

12

1. (C)	2. (B)	3. (A)	4. (D)	5. (B)	101. (B)	102. (C)	103. (D)	104. (C)	105. (D)
6. (C)	7. (C)	8. (C)	9. (A)	10. (B)	106. (B)	107. (B)	108. (D)	109. (D)	110. (A)
11. (B)	12. (B)	13. (B)	14. (B)	15. (A)	111. (B)	112. (C)	113. (D)	114. (D)	115. (B)
16. (B)	17. (A)	18. (C)	19. (B)	20. (A)	116. (D)	117. (C)	118. (C)	119. (B)	120. (C)
21. (C)	22. (C)	23. (A)	24. (C)	25. (C)	121. (D)	122. (B)	123. (C)	124. (C)	125. (C)
26. (A)	27. (B)	28. (A)	29. (B)	30. (A)	126. (C)	127. (B)	128. (C)	129. (A)	130. (D)
31. (C)	32. (C)	33. (A)	34. (C)	35. (C)	131. (B)	132. (C)	133. (D)	134. (B)	135. (C)
36. (A)	37. (C)	38. (D)	39. (A)	40. (C)	136. (A)	137. (B)	138. (C)	139. (D)	140. (A)
41. (B)	42. (A)	43. (C)	44. (C)	45. (A)	141. (C)	142. (D)	143. (D)	144. (A)	145. (B)
46. (D)	47. (C)	48. (A)	49. (A)	50. (C)	146. (C)	147. (D)	148. (C)	149. (A)	150. (D)
51. (B)	52. (A)	53. (A)	54. (B)	55. (D)	151. (B)	152. (B)	153. (D)	154. (A)	155. (D)
56. (B)	57. (A)	58. (A)	59. (A)	60. (C)	156. (C)	157. (A)	158. (C)	159. (A)	160. (D)
61. (D)	62. (D)	63. (D)	64. (A)	65. (A)	161. (D)	162. (A)	163. (D)	164. (C)	165. (D)
66. (B)	67. (B)	68. (B)	69. (D)	70. (A)	166. (A)	167. (B)	168. (D)	169. (C)	170. (A)
71. (A)	72. (B)	73. (D)	74. (A)	75. (A)	171. (A)	172. (B)	173. (C)	174. (B)	175. (C)
76. (D)	77. (A)	78. (B)	79. (C)	80. (D)	176. (B)	177. (C)	178. (A)	179. (B)	180. (A)
81. (C)	82. (D)	83. (A)	84. (B)	85. (C)	181. (A)	182. (C)	183. (C)	184. (C)	185. (B)
86. (B)	87. (A)	88. (C)	89. (B)	90. (C)	186. (B)	187. (D)	188. (B)	189. (D)	190. (C)
91. (D)	92. (B)	93. (D)	94. (B)	95. (C)	191. (B)	192. (B)	193. (A)	194. (B)	195. (D)
96. (A)	97. (D)	98. (A)	99. (C)	100. (C)	196. (D)	197. (C)	198. (B)	199. (B)	200. (A)

Actual Test

07
08
09
10
11
12

번역 및 정답

Part 1

1. 미W
(A) She is working with a keyboard.
(B) She is using the touchscreen.
(C) She is sipping a cup of coffee.
(D) She is looking into her bag.

(A) 그녀는 키보드로 작업하고 있다.
(B) 그녀는 터치스크린 화면을 사용하고 있다.
(C) 그녀는 커피 한 잔을 마시고 있다.
(D) 그녀는 가방 안을 들여다보고 있다.　　　　정답 (B)

2. 영M
(A) All of them are facing the same direction.
(B) The men are shaking hands.
(C) They are drinking from cups.
(D) They are sitting back to back.

(A) 그들 모두 같은 방향을 향하고 있다.
(B) 남자들이 악수하고 있다.
(C) 그들은 컵에 있는 것을 마시고 있다.
(D) 그들은 등을 맞대고 앉아 있다.　　　　정답 (B)

3. 호W
(A) Some people are fishing at the water's edge.
(B) One of the men is securing a boat to the dock.
(C) Some of the boats are floating next to the dock.
(D) One of the boats is filled with passengers.

(A) 몇 사람이 물가에서 낚시하고 있다.
(B) 남자 중 한 명이 선착장에 배를 안전하게 묶고 있다.
(C) 배들 중 몇 척이 선착장 옆에 떠 있다.
(D) 배들 중 한 척이 승객들로 가득 차 있다.　　　　정답 (C)

4. 미M
(A) They are removing a computer from the desk.
(B) They are putting on their helmets.
(C) One of the men is distributing flyers.
(D) One of the men is pointing at a computer screen.

(A) 그들은 책상에서 컴퓨터를 치우고 있다.
(B) 그들은 헬멧을 쓰고 있는 중이다.
(C) 남자 중 한 명이 전단지를 돌리고 있다.
(D) 남자 중 한 명이 컴퓨터 화면을 가리키고 있다.　　　　정답 (D)

5. 영M
(A) The back of the door of a truck is being opened.
(B) Both of the men are standing inside the truck.
(C) Some boxes have been stacked near a truck.
(D) A moving truck has been parked in a garage.

(A) 트럭 문 뒤쪽이 열리고 있다.
(B) 남자 둘 다 트럭 안쪽에 서 있다.
(C) 상자 몇 개가 트럭 근처에 쌓여 있다.
(D) 이삿짐 트럭이 차고에 세워져 있다.　　　　정답 (C)

6. 미W
(A) Some instruments are being polished.
(B) Some guitars are being loaded onto carts.
(C) Some guitars haven't been hung on a wall.

(D) A woman is playing a musical instrument.

(A) 악기 몇 대가 윤이 나게 닦이고 있다.
(B) 기타 몇 대가 카트 위에 실리고 있다.
(C) 기타 몇 대가 벽에 걸려 있다.
(D) 여자가 악기를 연주하고 있다.　　　　정답 (C)

Part 2

7. 미M 미W
Doesn't the bus stop at Sunset Street?
(A) A round-trip ticket.
(B) Let me show you the schedule.
(C) No, I don't have a car.

그 버스는 선셋 가에 서지 않나요?
(A) 왕복 티켓이요.
(B) 일정표를 보여 드릴게요.
(C) 아뇨, 저는 차가 없어요.　　　　정답 (B)

8. 호W 미M
Why haven't the trees in front of the building been trimmed yet?
(A) Because it rained this morning.
(B) Across from the white building.
(C) The gardening tool is on sale.

건물 앞에 있는 나무들은 왜 아직 가지치기가 안 되어 있죠?
(A) 오늘 아침에 비가 왔기 때문이에요.
(B) 하얀색 건물 건너편이요.
(C) 그 원예도구는 세일 중이에요.　　　　정답 (A)

9. 영M 미W
What does your factory manufacture?
(A) No, just a year ago.
(B) Routine maintenance.
(C) Motor parts.

당신 공장에서는 무엇을 만드나요?
(A) 아뇨, 딱 1년 전에요.
(B) 정기 유지보수요.
(C) 자동차 부품이요.　　　　정답 (C)

10. 미M 호W
Do you know what time Ms. Roberts is picking up her laptop?
(A) They can fix the computer.
(B) Yes, he knows the brand name.
(C) Two hours or so later.

로버츠 씨가 몇 시에 노트북을 찾아갈지 아세요?
(A) 그들이 컴퓨터를 수리할 수 있어요.
(B) 예, 그는 그 브랜드 명을 알아요.
(C) 두 시간 정도 후에요.　　　　정답 (C)

11. 영M 미W
Who will you work on the business proposal assignment with?
(A) I proposed to Nancy.
(B) Sign here on the contract, please.
(C) I'll be working with Jackson.

사업 제안서 작성 과제는 누구와 같이 작업하실 건가요?
(A) 저는 낸시에게 청혼했어요.
(B) 여기 계약서에 서명하세요.

(C) 잭슨과 같이 작업할 거예요.   정답 (C)

12. 미M 호W
Where do the plastic bags belong?
(A) Sure, I'll unfold the tablecloth.
(B) In the bottom shelf of the cabinet.
(C) Personal belongings.

비닐 봉지는 어디에 들어가죠?
(A) 알았어요, 제가 식탁보를 펼게요.
(B) 캐비닛의 아래 선반에요.
(C) 개인 소지품이요.   정답 (B)

13. 미W 영M
Isn't the marathon for charity next week?
(A) No, it's this Saturday.
(B) Sure, I'll have some more.
(C) Teams of nine.

자선 마라톤 대회는 다음 주가 아닌가요?
(A) 네, 이번 주 토요일이에요.
(B) 좋아요, 저는 좀 더 먹을게요.
(C) 9명으로 구성된 팀들이요.   정답 (A)

14. 미M 미W
I thought I'd left my toolbox here in the conference room.
(A) Did you reserve a venue for the conference?
(B) I got a great deal.
(C) I put it back in the supply closet.

제가 연장함을 여기 회의실에 두고 간 거 같아요.
(A) 회의 장소를 예약하셨어요?
(B) 저는 아주 싸게 샀어요.
(C) 제가 비품실에 다시 갖다 놨어요.   정답 (C)

15. 호W 영M
Mr. Park delivered an excellent keynote speech.
(A) Communication techniques.
(B) I'm very glad to hear that.
(C) No, the meeting time has changed.

박 씨는 훌륭한 기조 연설을 했어요.
(A) 의사소통 기술이요.
(B) 그런 얘기를 듣게 되어 기쁘군요.
(C) 아뇨, 회의 시간이 변경되었어요.   정답 (B)

16. 호W 미M
Do you know where Mr. Yoon's office is?
(A) Yes, he does.
(B) I'm going that way now.
(C) I've already signed up for the course.

윤 씨의 사무실이 어디인지 아세요?
(A) 예, 그는 그렇습니다.
(B) 제가 지금 그쪽으로 가는 길이에요.
(C) 저는 이미 그 강좌를 신청했어요.   정답 (B)

17. 미W 영M
Have you ever managed a research and development team?
(A) Yes, I have lots of leadership experience.
(B) He got promoted to manager.
(C) A new model has been developed.

연구개발팀을 관리해 보신 적이 있으세요?
(A) 예, 저는 리더십 경력이 많습니다.
(B) 그는 관리자로 승진했어요.
(C) 새로운 모델이 개발되었어요.   정답 (A)

18. 미M 호W
Where can I find information about our company's history?
(A) Try our website.
(B) Did you get a refund on your device?
(C) Put it over here.

우리 회사 연혁에 대한 정보는 어디에서 찾을 수 있나요?
(A) 우리 웹사이트에 가보세요.
(B) 당신 장치에 대한 환불을 받았어요?
(C) 그것을 이쪽에 놓으세요.   정답 (A)

19. 미W 영M
Didn't you go to the dental clinic last Friday?
(A) I had my appointment rescheduled.
(B) Go ahead and do it.
(C) No, the lost and found section has it.

지난주 금요일에 치과에 가지 않았어요?
(A) 제 진료 예약 일정을 바꿨어요.
(B) 어서 가서 하세요.
(C) 아뇨, 유실물 센터에 그게 있어요.   정답 (A)

20. 호W 영M
How do I turn on this paper shredding machine?
(A) Try the hardware section in aisle five.
(B) Press the button on the top righthand side.
(C) We are out of paper.

이 종이 분쇄기는 어떻게 전원을 켜나요?
(A) 5번 통로에 있는 철물 코너에 가보세요.
(B) 맨 위 오른쪽에 있는 버튼을 누르세요.
(C) 우리는 종이가 떨어졌어요.   정답 (B)

21. 미M 호W
Who's going to train the bank tellers we hired yesterday?
(A) We take cash only.
(B) I'll make the schedule today.
(C) You have to wait at platform B.

어제 우리가 채용한 은행 창구 직원들을 누가 교육시킬 건가요?
(A) 우리는 현금만 받아요.
(B) 제가 오늘 일정표를 만들게요.
(C) B 승강장에서 기다리셔야 해요.   정답 (B)

22. 미W 영M
Would you prefer to use a laptop or a desktop computer?
(A) Yes, I was in the computer lab.
(B) It is not plugged in.
(C) Well, I travel a lot for work.

노트북 사용이 더 좋으세요, 아니면 데스크톱 컴퓨터 사용이 더 좋으세요?
(A) 예, 저는 컴퓨터실에 있었어요.
(B) 그건 플러그 연결이 안 되어 있어요.
(C) 그게, 저는 업무 때문에 출장을 많이 다녀요.   정답 (C)

23. 호W 미M

What should I do about the copy machine that is stuck again?
(A) Ten double sided copies should be enough.
(B) It will be here anytime soon.
(C) Call maintenance.

또 다시 종이가 낀 복사기는 어떻게 하면 좋아요?
(A) 양면 복사로 10장이면 충분해요.
(B) 그건 곧 여기에 도착할 거예요.
(C) 유지보수과에 전화해 보세요.   정답 (C)

24. 미M 미W

Make sure to read the laboratory security policy.
(A) It is not open yet.
(B) OK, can you tell me where I can find it?
(C) Don't forget to bring your photo ID.

실험실 보안 정책을 꼭 읽어 두세요.
(A) 거기는 아직 안 열었어요.
(B) 알겠죠, 그것을 어디서 찾을 수 있는지 알려 주실래요?
(C) 사진이 부착된 신분증을 갖고 오는 것을 잊지 마세요.   정답 (B)

25. 미W 영M

Would you like me to go over the notes for your presentation?
(A) He is present, too.
(B) The fee is $150.
(C) Yes, that would be great. Thanks.

당신 발표 초고를 제가 검토해 드릴까요?
(A) 그 사람도 참석했어요.
(B) 수수료는 150달러예요.
(C) 예, 그렇게 해주시면 좋죠. 감사합니다.   정답 (C)

26. 미W 미M

The paper shredding machine is not working, is it?
(A) Call another paper vendor.
(B) They're taking a look at it now.
(C) He left work early today.

종이 분쇄기는 고장 난 거 아니죠, 그렇죠?
(A) 다른 종이 납품업체에 전화해 보세요.
(B) 그들이 그것을 지금 보고 있어요.
(C) 그는 오늘 조퇴했어요.   정답 (B)

27. 미W 영M

Why is that pharmaceutical company revising their logo?
(A) You haven't seen their current logo, have you?
(B) He advised me to do it right away.
(C) Take 3 pills after each meal.

그 제약 회사는 자사 로고를 왜 수정하고 있나요?
(A) 거기 현재 로고를 본 적 없죠, 그렇죠?
(B) 그는 제게 당장 그것을 하라고 권했어요.
(C) 매 식사 후에 세 알씩 복용하세요.   정답 (A)

28. 미M 호W

Do you want tickets for the jazz concert on Saturday or Sunday?
(A) It was a great performance.
(B) We are expecting a large audience.
(C) Whichever is cheaper.

재즈 콘서트 티켓을 토요일로 원하세요, 아니면 일요일로 원하세요?
(A) 아주 좋은 공연이었어요.
(B) 많은 청중을 기대하고 있어요.
(C) 어느 것이든 더 싼 것으로요.   정답 (C)

29. 미W 영M

When's the next customer service staff meeting?
(A) An hour-long workshop.
(B) Sure, I'll e-mail you a reminder.
(C) It's only for new hires.

다음 고객 서비스과 직원 회의는 언제예요?
(A) 한 시간짜리 워크숍이에요.
(B) 물론이에요, 이메일로 상기시켜 드릴게요.
(C) 그건 신입 직원들만 위한 거예요.   정답 (C)

30. 호W 미M

Why is Nancy working the evening shift at the hospital?
(A) Seven doctors and ten nurses.
(B) Yes, in the intensive care unit.
(C) Didn't you get the memo about the schedule change?

낸시가 왜 병원 저녁 근무를 하고 있어요?
(A) 의사 7명과 간호사 10명이요.
(B) 예, 중환자실에서요.
(C) 일정 변경에 대한 메모를 받지 못하셨어요?   정답 (C)

31. 미W 영M

I need to get my dress shirt cleaned before our sales conference.
(A) A shop is across the street that can do it quickly.
(B) Cleaners haven't arrived yet.
(C) How long did the workshop last?

영업 총회 전에 제 와이셔츠를 클리닝 맡겨야 해요.
(A) 빨리 할 수 있는 업소가 길 건너편에 있어요.
(B) 청소업체 직원들이 아직 도착하지 않았어요.
(C) 워크숍은 얼마 동안 했어요?   정답 (A)

Part 3

문제 32-34번은 다음 대화를 참조하시오. 미W 영M

W: Hello. This is Tina Stewart. (32)**You hired me as a photographer for your office event this Thursday.**
M: Hello, Tina.
W: I'm really sorry, but I don't think I'll be able to make it there.
M: I'm sorry to hear that. Are you all right?
W: Yes, I am. I just have a family matter which I need to attend to. However, (33)**I have a colleague who is highly professional and can take my place.** Would you like to have her contact information?
M: Yes, I'd love that. (34)**Could you reimburse me the deposit I paid you?**
W: Sure. I'll give you your money back later today.

W: 안녕하세요. 저는 티나 스튜어트예요. 이번 주 목요일 귀사의 행사에 저를 사진사로 고용하셨어요.
M: 안녕하세요, 티나.
W: 정말 죄송하지만 거기 갈 수 없을 것 같아요.

M: 그 얘기를 들으니 유감이네요. 괜찮으신 건가요?

W: 예, 괜찮아요. 지금 제가 처리해야 할 가족 문제가 생겨서요. 그런데, 아주 프로페셔널한 동료가 있는데, 저 대신 할 수 있어요. 그녀의 연락처를 드릴까요?

M: 예, 주세요. 제가 지급한 계약금은 반환해 주시겠어요?

W: 물론이죠. 오늘 이따 환급해 드릴게요.

32. 여자는 누구인가?
(A) 행사 기획자
(B) 출장 요리 업자
(C) 총회 준비 위원
(D) 사진사 　　　　　　　　　　정답 (D)

33. 여자는 남자에게 무엇을 할 것을 제안하는가?
(A) 행사 날짜 변경
(B) 그녀에게 현금 지불
(C) 동료 중 한 명 고용
(D) 추가 정보 제공 　　　　　　정답 (C)

34. 남자는 여자에게 무엇을 달라고 요청하는가?
(A) 영수증
(B) 행사 프로그램
(C) 샘플
(D) 환불 　　　　　　　　　　　정답 (D)

문제 35-37번은 다음 대화를 참조하시오. [미M] [호W]

M: Hello, Wilma. (35)**Do you intend to register for the company's new wellness program?**

W: (36)**I've been so busy with work lately that I haven't had time to do anything else, let alone check the memo about it.** Can you tell me the details?

M: All participants need to spend a few hours a week doing various activities that will improve their lives. For instance, they can do exercise.

W: How are we supposed to keep track of what we do?

M: That's easy. You download a spreadsheet and then enter whatever you do.

W: How long does it take to enter the information?

M: Not very long. (37)**Here, uh, I can show you what to do.**

- -

M: 안녕하세요, 윌마. 회사의 새 건강 프로그램에 등록할 생각인가요?

W: 그것에 대한 회람을 확인하는 거는 고사하고, 최근에는 일 때문에 너무 바빠서 다른 것을 할 시간이 없었어요. 자세한 내용 좀 알려 주실래요?

M: 참석자들은 전부 일주일에 몇 시간은 자신들의 삶을 향상시켜 줄 여러 다양한 활동을 하면서 시간을 보낼 필요가 있어요. 예를 들어, 운동을 할 수 있어요.

W: 우리가 하는 것을 어떻게 파악하게 되어 있어요?

M: 그건 쉬워요. 스프레드시트를 내려받아서 당신이 무엇을 하든 거기에 입력만 하면 됩니다.

W: 정보를 입력하는 데 얼마나 오래 걸려요?

M: 오래 걸리지 않아요. 여기요, 어, 내가 어떻게 하는지 보여 드릴게요.

35. 남자는 어떤 주제를 꺼내는가?
(A) 건강 프로그램
(B) 직원 모임
(C) 다가오는 총회
(D) 직원 회의 　　　　　　　　정답 (A)

36. 여자는 자신의 일에 대해 무엇을 말하는가?
(A) 그녀는 새 프로젝트 팀에 합류했다.
(B) 그녀는 프로그램을 이수할 수 없었다.
(C) 그녀는 바빴다.
(D) 그녀의 연구는 자금이 더 필요하다. 　정답 (C)

37. 남자는 뒤이어 무엇을 할 것인가?
(A) 제품 시연하기
(B) 헬스 클럽 방문하기
(C) 전화번호 적기
(D) 자신의 매니저와 얘기하기 　　정답 (A)

문제 38-40번은 다음 3자 대화를 참조하시오. [미M] [미W] [영M]

M1: Thank you for coming to Kelvin Electronics.

W: Hi. (38)**I need some help from someone in technical support. There's something wrong with my laptop.**

M1: Sure. Dave, our top technician, is available right now.

M2: Hi. I'm Dave. What seems to be the problem?

W: My laptop's battery keeps running down very quickly. I can only use it when there is a wall outlet available.

M2: Hmm… It sounds like you need a new battery. (39)**You'll be happy to know that we're having a sale on laptop batteries.**

W: Wonderful. Can you take care of this problem now?

M2: I've got a couple of other things to do first. (40)**How about coming by again at 4:00?**

- -

M1: 켈빈 전자를 방문해 주셔서 감사합니다.

W: 안녕하세요. 기술지원부 사람의 도움이 필요해요. 제 노트북에 문제가 생겼어요.

M1: 알았습니다. 우리 최고 기술자인 데이브가 지금 바로 시간이 돼요.

M2: 안녕하세요. 데이브입니다. 뭐가 문제인 것 같으세요?

W: 제 노트북 배터리가 계속 너무 빨리 닳아버리네요. 벽 콘센트가 있을 때에만 노트북을 사용할 수 있어요.

M2: 흠… 듣고 보니 새 배터리가 필요한 것 같아요. 우리가 현재 노트북 배터리를 세일하고 있다는 것을 아시면 좋을 겁니다.

W: 잘되었네요. 지금 이 문제를 처리해 주실 수 있나요?

M2: 먼저 두어 가지 해야 할 다른 일이 있어요. 4시에 다시 들르시는 게 어떠세요?

38. 여자가 가게에 와 있는 이유는?
(A) 제품을 교환하기 위해
(B) 수리에 대해 물어보기 위해
(C) 노트북 컴퓨터를 반품하기 위해
(D) 기술지원부 자리에 지원하기 위해 　정답 (B)

39. 데이브는 어떤 정보를 제공하는가?
(A) 새 지점이 곧 문을 열 것이다.
(B) 모든 노트북이 연장된 품질 보증서가 같이 나온다.
(C) 신제품 일부는 구할 수 없다.
(D) 가게가 일부 품목을 할인하고 있다. 　정답 (D)

40. 데이브는 여자에게 무엇을 할 것을 제안하는가?
(A) 서류 작성하기
(B) 다른 물건 주문하기
(C) 그날 나중에 다시 오기
(D) 다른 가게 방문하기 　　　　　정답 (C)

문제 41-43번은 다음 대화를 참조하시오. [호W] [미M]

W: (41)On today's show, I'll be speaking with Calvin Harper. He's here in town to perform in concert at the Lookout Theater. Mr. Harper, thanks so much for dropping by this morning.

M: It's a pleasure to be here. (42)You know, my first show ever was at the Lookout Theater.

W: Is that so? I knew you had performed there before, but I didn't realize that you had debuted there.

M: I remember it really well. (43)I also recall that there was an amazing seafood restaurant right across the street from it.

W: You must be referring to Catch of the Day. (43)It's still open, but it moved to Amber Drive.

M: (43)That's great to hear. I'll be sure to stop by there later today.

W: 오늘 프로에서는 캘빈 하퍼와 얘기를 나누겠습니다. 그는 룩아웃 극장에서 콘서트 공연을 하기 위해서 여기 이 도시에 와 있습니다. 하퍼 씨, 오늘 아침에 들러 주셔서 정말 감사합니다.

M: 이 자리에 오게 되어 기쁩니다. 있잖아요, 저의 첫 공연이 룩아웃 극장에서였어요.

W: 그래요? 전에 거기서 공연하셨다는 것을 알긴 했지만, 거기서 데뷔를 하신 것은 몰랐네요.

M: 그 때 기억이 정말 잘 나요. 또한 그 극장 길 바로 건너편에 멋진 해산물 식당이 있었다는 것도 기억이 나요.

W: 캐치오브더데이를 언급하고 계신 것 같네요. 아직도 식당이 영업을 하고 있는데, 앰버 드라이브로 옮겼어요.

M: 듣던 중 반가운 소리네요. 오늘 나중에 거기에 한 번 꼭 들러 봐야겠네요.

41. 여자는 누구일 것 같은가?
(A) 공연자
(B) 콘서트 준비 위원
(C) 토크 쇼 진행자
(D) 극장 소유주   정답 (C)

42. 남자는 룩아웃 극장에 대해 무엇을 말하는가?
(A) 그곳의 음향 시스템이 아주 좋다.
(B) 자신이 태어난 곳과 가까운 곳에 있다.
(C) 음악 공연을 하기에 자신이 가장 좋아하는 극장이다.
(D) 자신이 첫 콘서트를 했던 곳이다.   정답 (D)

43. 남자는 무엇을 알게 되어 기뻐하는가?
(A) 극장이 문을 닫지 않았다.
(B) 식당이 아직도 영업 중이다.
(C) 낡은 건물이 개량될 것이다.
(D) 공연이 매진되었다.   정답 (B)

문제 44-46번은 다음 3자 대화를 참조하시오. [영M] [미M] [호W]

M1: Hello, Susan. (44)The city's summer festival will be held soon. Todd and I think we should sell some of our berry pies there.

M2: We're known mostly for our vegetables, but our berry fields have started producing well. Selling pies could help promote our products.

W: That's right. Lots of other farmers will be selling pies, too, so the competition will be fierce. (45)We should provide a coupon for some free fruit with each purchase.

M1: Great idea. That will encourage people to visit the farm.

W: Right. (46)I'll put up a big sign by the entrance to the farm. That will help customers driving by know when they have arrived here.

M1: 안녕하세요, 수잔. 시에서 주최하는 여름 축제가 곧 열려요. 토드와 제가 생각해 봤는데, 거기서 우리 베리 파이를 좀 파는 게 좋을 것 같아요.

M2: 우리는 주로 채소로 알려져 있지만, 우리 베리 농장이 수확이 아주 좋아지기 시작했어요. 파이를 파는 게 우리 제품을 홍보하는 데 도움이 될 수 있어요.

W: 맞아요. 다른 많은 농부들도 파이를 팔 거니까, 경쟁이 치열할 거예요. 우리는 매번 구매를 할 때마다 무료 과일 쿠폰을 제공하는 게 어떨까요.

M1: 좋은 생각이네요. 그게 사람들이 농장을 방문하도록 촉진할 거예요.

W: 맞아요. 저는 농장으로 들어오는 입구 옆에 큰 표지판을 세워 놓을게요. 그러면, 차를 몰고 지나가던 손님들이 이곳에 도착했을 때 알아보는 데 도움이 될 거예요.

44. 남자들은 무엇을 할 것을 제안하는가?
(A) 베리 경작을 위해 사용되는 농지 확장
(B) 신문에 광고 게재
(C) 지역 축제 참가
(D) 자신들의 제품 가격 인하   정답 (C)

45. 여자는 자신들의 업체가 무엇을 해야 한다고 생각하는가?
(A) 축제에서 더 큰 부스 예약하기
(B) 더 많은 직원 고용하기
(C) 무료 농산물 쿠폰 제공하기
(D) 단골 고객에게 할인해 주기   정답 (C)

46. 여자는 뒤이어 무엇을 할 것인가?
(A) 표지판 세우기
(B) 홍보 전단지 나눠주기
(C) 행사에 등록하기
(D) 농장 중 한 곳 방문하기   정답 (A)

문제 47-49번은 다음 대화를 참조하시오. [미W] [미M]

W: Is everyone ready for next week's trip?

M: I am. (47)I can't wait to attend the groundbreaking ceremony for the new textile factory in Indonesia.

W: (48)I'm really glad you're fluent in several languages. That talent should come in handy when we visit some other countries nearby.

M: Oh, (49)what kind of clothes should we wear to the ceremony?

W: (49)The local governor is going to be in attendance.

W: 모두 다 다음 주 출장 준비는 되었어요?

M: 예. 되었어요. 인도네시아의 새 섬유 공장 기공식에 참석하는 게 너무 기다려져요.

W: 당신이 여러 개 언어에 유창해서 정말 다행이에요. 그 재능은 우리가 근처 다른 몇 나라를 방문할 때 정말 도움이 될 거예요.

M: 오, 식에 어떤 종류의 옷을 입고 가야 하는 거죠?

W: 현지 주지사가 참석할 예정이에요.

47. 화자들이 출장을 가는 이유는?
(A) 해외 업체에 대한 회계감사를 하기 위해
(B) 임대 계약서에 서명하기 위해

(C) 자재를 구매하기 위해
(D) 식에 참석하기 위해　　　　　　　　　　정답 (D)

48. 여자에 따르면, 남자는 어떤 능력을 가지고 있는가?
(A) 몇 개 언어를 할 수 있다.
(B) 협상에 능력이 있다.
(C) 우수한 의사소통 기술이 있다.
(D) 고장 난 물건을 고칠 수 있다.　　　　정답 (A)

49. 여자가 "현지 주지사가 참석할 예정이에요"라고 말할 때 무엇을 함축하는가?
(A) 행사가 TV에 방영될 것이다.
(B) 정부와의 계약이 곧 서명될 것이다.
(C) 그들은 제품 시연을 해야 한다.
(D) 그들은 정장 차림을 해야 할 필요가 있다.　　　　정답 (D)

문제 50-52번은 다음 대화를 참조하시오. 영M 미W

M: (50)Deborah, have the results of the survey arrived yet? (51)We need to see the data before we determine whether we can make a profit by designing and making solar-powered flashlights.
W: More than half of the respondents indicated that they'd love to use solar power rather than put batteries in their flashlights. They also mentioned that they believe our other products are well made and high quality, so they will strongly consider buying new items from us.
M: Wonderful. Thanks for letting me know. I am wondering if you could put together a presentation for the board of directors this Friday.
W: Of course. (53)I think I'll be able to start creating the slides right after lunch.

M: 데보라, 설문조사 결과가 도착했어요? 태양열로 작동하는 손전등을 설계하고 제조해서 수익을 낼 수 있는지 결정하기 전에 그 데이터를 봐야 해요.
W: 응답자 중 절반 이상이 손전등에 배터리를 넣는 것보다 태양열을 이용하는 게 더 좋겠다고 표시했어요. 그들은 또한 우리 다른 제품들도 잘 만들어졌고 품질이 좋다고 생각하고, 그래서 그들은 우리 회사 신제품 구매를 강력히 고려해볼 거라고 언급했어요.
M: 잘되었네요. 알려 줘서 감사해요. 이번 주 금요일 이사회에 발표할 프레젠테이션 내용을 준비해줄 수 있는지 모르겠네요.
W: 물론이죠. 점심 먹자마자 슬라이드를 만들기 시작할 수 있을 것 같아요.

50. 남자는 여자에게 무엇에 대해 물어보는가?
(A) 예산 결정
(B) 설문조사 결과
(C) 새 계약
(D) 포장 재료　　　　　　　　　　정답 (B)

51. 화자들은 어떤 제품에 대해 논의하는가?
(A) 손전등
(B) 조명 기구
(C) 전동 도구
(D) 태양 전지판　　　　　　　　　　정답 (A)

52. 여자는 점심 이후에 무엇을 할 것인가?
(A) 창고 방문
(B) 발표하기
(C) 환급 요청서 작성
(D) 슬라이드 작업　　　　　　　　　　정답 (D)

문제 53-55번은 다음 대화를 참조하시오. 미M 미W

M: Hello, Kate. (53)Sylvester Interior sent me the plans for the renovations we're doing in the eating area of the employee lounge.
W: Wonderful. I'd like to take a look at them. I know all of the employees are looking forward to the improvements we'll be making.
M: Yeah. This project will be expensive, but the employees will have a much better place to relax and to enjoy their meals.
W: (54)The only thing that I'm a bit worried about is the noise the construction work will cause. Some of us have offices near the lounge.
M: I had the same concern, so I spoke to Mr. Jackson at Sylvester Interior. (55)He said his team would only work on weekends. That should solve the problem.

M: 안녕하세요, 케이트. 실베스터 인테리어에서 저에게 직원 휴게실의 식사 공간에 대해 우리가 하려고 하는 보수공사 설계도를 보냈어요.
W: 잘되었네요. 그 설계도를 보고 싶어요. 전 직원이 우리가 하고 있는 개선작업을 고대하고 있다는 것을 알아요.
M: 예. 이 프로젝트는 비용이 많이 들겠지만, 직원들은 편히 쉬고 식사도 즐길 훨씬 더 좋은 장소가 생길 거예요.
W: 한 가지 좀 걱정스러운 것은 공사로 인해 생길 소음이에요. 우리 중 일부는 직원 휴게실 가까이에 사무실이 있잖아요.
M: 저도 우려사항이 같아서 실베스터 인테리어의 잭슨 씨와 얘기해 봤어요. 잭슨 씨는 자신의 팀이 주말에만 작업하겠다고 얘기하더군요. 그렇게 되면 문제가 해결될 거예요.

53. 대화는 주로 무엇에 대한 것인가?
(A) 개업
(B) 사무실을 다시 꾸밀 필요성
(C) 다가오는 보수 공사
(D) 새 사무 공간으로 이전　　　　　　정답 (C)

54. 여자가 우려하고 있다고 말하는 이유는?
(A) 공사 프로젝트가 시끄러울 것이다.
(B) 주차 공간이 너무 비좁다.
(C) 보수 공사 자재가 너무 비싸다.
(D) 배달물건이 아직 도착하지 않았다.　　정답 (A)

55. 여자가 알게 되는 것은 무엇인가?
(A) 보수 공사가 촬영될 것이다.
(B) 직원 회의가 일주일마다 열릴 것이다.
(C) 특별 작업 일정이 마련되었다.
(D) 최종 지급이 이루어졌다.　　　　　정답 (C)

문제 56-58번은 다음 대화를 참조하시오. 호W 미M

W: Nick, are you busy?

M: (56)I'm just reviewing the marketing budget for our new line of women's business attire. I'll have some time in about an hour. Is that all right?

W: Sure. (57)I'm just working on a marketing project for our winter coats, and your ideas for advertising are always creative.

M: (58)Why don't you set up a time to meet me so we can talk about your ideas? I'll be happy to make a few suggestions for you.

W: Perfect. I'll schedule our meeting at once.

W: 닉, 바빠요?

M: 지금 여성 정장 신제품에 대한 마케팅 예산을 검토 중이에요. 한 시간 정도 있으면 시간이 날 거예요. 괜찮아요?

W: 물론이에요. 저는 우리 겨울 코트의 마케팅 프로젝트 건을 작업 중인데, 광고에 대한 당신의 아이디어는 항상 창의적이잖아요.

M: 당신의 아이디어에 대해 얘기 나눌 수 있게 저와 회의할 시간을 정하는 게 어떤가요? 기꺼이 몇 가지 제안해 드릴 수 있어요.

W: 아주 잘됐네요. 당장 우리 회의 일정을 잡을게요.

56. 화자들은 어떤 업종에서 근무하는가?
(A) 광고 회사
(B) 의류 회사
(C) 차량 제조업체
(D) 배송업체   정답 (B)

57. 여자가 "당신의 광고 아이디어는 항상 창의적이잖아요"라고 말하는 이유는?
(A) 프로젝트에 대한 도움을 요청하기 위해
(B) 자신의 행복을 표현하기 위해
(C) 새 제안에 동의하기 위해
(D) 동료를 축하하기 위해   정답 (A)

58. 남자는 여자에게 무엇을 할 것을 제안하는가?
(A) 제안서 작성하기
(B) 제품 시연하기
(C) 이메일로 제안 보내기
(D) 회의 일정 잡기   정답 (D)

문제 59-61번은 다음 대화를 참조하시오. 영M 미W

M: Cindy, (59)the executives of our baseball team are meeting tomorrow. (60)I have to give them an update on our sponsorship agreement with Verhoeven Manufacturing. Is the new deal for three years?

W: Yes, that's what we agreed to. Having Verhoeven sponsor us will tremendously help our finances. Oh, the company wants some of our players to appear in TV advertisements.

M: I was expecting that request. The players have a provision in their contracts regarding that. (61)However, I need more information on the ads before I agree to them.

M: 신디, 우리 야구팀 임원들이 내일 회의를 하는데요. 임원들에게 베호벤 제조회사와 우리 협찬 계약에 대해 최신 정보를 알려 드려야 해요. 새 스폰서 계약이 3년인가요?

W: 예, 그렇게 하기로 합의했어요. 베호벤이 우리를 협찬하게 하는 것은 우리 재정에 엄청나게 도움이 될 거예요. 오, 그 회사는 우리 일부 선수들이 TV 광고에 출연하기를 원해요.

M: 그런 요청은 예상하고 있었어요. 선수들은 그와 관련된 계약 조항이 있어요. 그런데 내가 그 광고들에 대해 동의하기 전에 광고에 대한 더 많은 정보가 필요해요.

59. 화자들은 어떤 종류의 기관에서 근무하는 것 같은가?
(A) 스포츠 팀
(B) 연구 기관
(C) 연기 단체
(D) 정부 기관   정답 (A)

60. 화자들은 주로 무엇에 대해 논의하고 있는가?
(A) 고객 서비스를 위한 새 정책
(B) 새 회장에 대한 선거
(C) 늘어난 광고 비용
(D) 회사의 협찬   정답 (D)

61. 남자는 제안에 대해 무엇을 말하는가?
(A) 그는 결과에 만족하고 있다.
(B) 그는 그것에 당장은 동의할 수 없다.
(C) 그는 그것이 거부될 것이라고 생각한다.
(D) 그는 그것이 비용이 많이 들 것이라고 생각한다.   정답 (B)

문제 62-64번은 다음 대화와 소책자를 참조하시오. 호W 미M

W: (62)Thanks for offering to assist me with installing the speakers for the computer in the conference room.

M: You're welcome. We need to make sure the sound system is perfect for the demonstration we're giving.

W: Yeah. I tried to do it by myself, but I just got confused.

M: Isn't there an instruction booklet?

W: Yes, I have it right here.

M: Hmm… (63)Here's the section on installation. (64)It looks like we might need a couple of screwdrivers. We'd better get them now before we start the work.

W: Okay. (64)I'll go to Mr. Fields's office and ask him to borrow a couple.

W: 회의실에 있는 컴퓨터용 스피커를 설치하는 데 도와주겠다고 해서 감사해요.

M: 괜찮아요. 우리가 하게 될 설명회를 위해서 음향 시스템을 꼭 완벽하게 해둘 필요가 있어요.

W: 예, 혼자서 하려고 해봤는데, 헷갈리기만 했어요.

M: 사용 설명서가 없나요?

W: 있어요, 바로 여기 갖고 있어요.

M: 음… 여기 설치에 관한 부분이 있네요. 드라이버 몇 개가 필요할 것 같네요. 작업을 시작하기 전에 드라이버를 가져오는 게 낫겠어요.

W: 알았어요. 필즈 씨의 사무실로 가서 드라이버 두어 개 정도 빌려 달라고 해볼게요.

<table>
<tr><td colspan="2">사용 설명서
목차</td></tr>
</table>

시작하기	2페이지
(63)설치	**5페이지**
소프트웨어 다운로드하기	10페이지
프린터와 연결하기	15페이지

62. 대화가 어디에서 이루어지는 것 같은가?
(A) 회의실
(B) 인쇄소
(C) 대강당
(D) 컴퓨터실 　　　　　　　　　정답 (A)

63. 그래픽을 보시오. 남자는 어느 페이지로 넘기는가?
(A) 2페이지
(B) 5페이지
(C) 10페이지
(D) 15페이지 　　　　　　　　　정답 (B)

64. 여자는 이후에 무엇을 하겠다고 말하는가?
(A) 동료에게 전화하기
(B) 웹사이트 확인하기
(C) 공구 가져오기
(D) 테이블 설치하기 　　　　　　　정답 (C)

문제 65-67번은 다음 대화와 주행 안내를 참조하시오. 미W 미M

W: **(65)Tim, has the printer called regarding the business cards we're getting printed for our new landscaping firm?**
M: I e-mailed the design to the printer yesterday, and Mr. Wakefield said the cards will be done by noon.
W: Perfect. **(66)Do you mind picking them up? I need to meet with clients from the department store** to discuss what kind of trees and flowers to plant.
M: Sure. I can do that.
W: Do you know where the shop is?
M: No, but I found the directions on this navigation app on my cell phone. Here it is.
W: Hmm… **(67)There's a mistake because the app hasn't been updated. One of the street names has changed. The last road that you need to turn left on has been changed to Bailey Drive.**

W: 팀, 우리 새 조경 회사를 위해서 우리가 인쇄하려는 명함 건으로 인쇄소에서 전화왔어요?
M: 어제 디자인을 이메일로 인쇄소에 보냈는데, 웨이크필드 씨가 명함이 정오까지 될 거라고 했어요.
W: 아주 잘되었네요. 그것 좀 찾아와 주실래요? 백화점에서 온 고객들을 만나서 어떤 종류의 나무와 꽃을 심어야 할지 의논해야 하거든요.
M: 좋아요. 할게요.
W: 그 인쇄소가 어디 있는지 알아요?
M: 아뇨, 그런데 제 휴대폰의 이 내비게이션 앱으로 거기 가는 길을 찾았어요. 여기 있어요.
W: 흠… 앱이 업데이트가 안 되어 있어서 오류가 있네요. 도로 이름 중 하나가 바뀌었어요. 좌회전해야 하는 마지막 도로가 베일리 드라이브로 바뀌었어요.

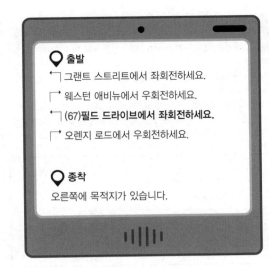

출발
그랜트 스트리트에서 좌회전하세요.
웨스턴 애비뉴에서 우회전하세요.
(67)필드 드라이브에서 좌회전하세요.
오렌지 로드에서 우회전하세요.

종착
오른쪽에 목적지가 있습니다.

65. 인쇄되어야 하는 것은 무엇인가?
(A) 초대장
(B) 명함
(C) 포스터
(D) 지도 　　　　　　　　　　정답 (B)

66. 여자가 주문한 물건을 찾으러 갈 수 없는 이유는?
(A) 그녀의 자동차가 정비소에 있다.
(B) 그녀는 전화 회의를 해야 한다.
(C) 그녀의 출장 일정이 변경되었다.
(D) 그녀는 고객들과 회의가 있다. 　　정답 (D)

67. 그래픽을 보시오. 도로 이름 중 앱에서 갱신되어야 하는 것은 어느 것인가?
(A) 그랜트 스트리트
(B) 웨스턴 애비뉴
(C) 필드 드라이브
(D) 오렌지 로드 　　　　　　　　정답 (C)

문제 68-70번은 다음 대화와 표를 참조하시오. 호W 미M

W: Hello, Brent. **(68)Congratulations on getting a promotion on Monday.**
M: Thanks. It's great to be appreciated.
W: You're doing a wonderful job here. Oh, I noticed that the question-and-answer chat group for our new version of 3D software has been launched. Well done.
M: It's been up for two days, and we've already gotten several questions. They're divided into a few categories. I may need some assistance responding to a few of them.
W: Hmm… **(69)I know a lot about the printing, so I'd be happy to answer those questions.**
M: Sounds perfect. Thanks. **(70)Oh, after you finish answering the questions, I'm going to take the chat group offline for a bit. I need to fix some technical problems. I'll put up a notice letting users know what's going to happen.**

W: 안녕하세요, 브렌트. 월요일 승진하신 것을 축하드려요.
M: 고마워요. 인정받게 되어서 좋네요.
W: 여기서 정말 일을 잘하고 계세요. 오, 우리 3D소프트웨어 새 버전에 대

한 질의 응답 단체 채팅방이 시작되었더군요. 정말 잘했어요.

M: 한 지 2일 되었고, 벌써 질문이 여러 개 들어왔어요. 질문들은 몇 개 카테고리로 나뉘어져 있어요. 질문 몇 개에 답변하는 데 제가 도움이 필요할지 몰라요.

W: 음… 출력에 대해서는 제가 좀 많이 알고 있으니, 기꺼이 그 질문들에 답변해 드릴게요.

M: 잘됐네요. 고마워요. 아, 질문에 답변을 다 끝내고 난 후, 저는 그 단체 채팅방을 잠시 오프라인 상태로 둘 거예요. 기술적인 문제 몇 가지를 고쳐야 해서요. 이용자들에게 무슨 일이 있을지 알리는 공지를 올릴게요.

카테고리	질문 숫자
색깔 변경	5
(69)출력	4
사이즈 변경	6
텍스트 추가	2
눈금 자	3

68. 월요일 무슨 일이 있었는가?
(A) 여자가 출장을 갔다.
(B) 관리자가 공지를 올렸다.
(C) 남자가 승진되었다.
(D) 회사가 다른 장소로 이전했다. 　　　정답 (C)

69. 그래픽을 보시오. 여자가 답할 질문의 개수는?
(A) 4
(B) 6
(C) 2
(D) 3 　　　정답 (A)

70. 남자가 공지를 올리려는 이유는?
(A) 동료들을 세미나에 초대하기 위해
(B) 이용자들에게 웹사이트 이용이 안 된다는 것을 알리기 위해
(C) 이전에 대한 도움을 요청하기 위해
(D) 웹 디자인 공석을 광고하기 위해 　　　정답 (B)

Part 4

문제 71-73번은 다음 광고를 참조하시오. 호W

W: (71)Look at all of these bicycles we have that are both great quality and affordable. We also just received a large shipment of Trendy Max's latest styles. With five different models we offer, you'll be sure to find a bike that suits your needs from Trendy Max. (72)Be sure to hurry to our store soon, though. These bikes are already selling quickly. Everyone loves our low prices. And don't forget that we don't just sell bikes. (73)We fix them, too. If yours needs repairing, bring it in, and let us take care of it.

우리가 보유하고 있는 품질도 아주 좋고 가격도 비싸지 않은 이 자전거들을 전부 보세요. 또한 지금 막 트랜디 맥스의 최신 스타일 자전거를 대량으로 배송 받았습니다. 각기 다른 모델 5개가 준비되어 있어서, 여러분의 필요에 딱 맞는 트렌디 맥스 자전거를 꼭 찾게 될 것입니다. 그렇지만 서둘러서 곧 가게를 방문해 주세요. 이 자전거들은 벌써 빠르게 판매되고 있습니다. 모두가 다 낮은 가격을 무척 좋아하네요. 그리고 우리가 자전거만 파는 것이 아니라는 것을 잊지 마세요. 수리도 합니다. 여러분의 자전거가 수리가 필요하다면, 가지고 오세요. 그러면 저희들이 책임지고 해드리겠습니다.

71. 가게는 어떤 종류의 제품을 파는가?
(A) 게임
(B) 의류
(C) 자전거
(D) 타이어 　　　정답 (C)

72. 화자가 가게를 빨리 방문할 것을 제안하는 이유는?
(A) 일부 제품이 빨리 품절될 것이다.
(B) 세일이 곧 끝날 것이다.
(C) 가게가 폐업할 것이다.
(D) 새 배송물건이 오늘 도착할 예정이다. 　　　정답 (A)

73. 가게는 어떤 추가 서비스를 제공하는가?
(A) 무료 배달
(B) 할부 결제
(C) 수리
(D) 국제 배송 　　　정답 (C)

문제 74-76번은 다음 발표를 참조하시오. 영M

M: Let me make a quick announcement while all of you are putting your supplies away. (74)It's been a pleasure having you in my intermediate learners' painting class this month. Next week, we're going to put on a small show to display the works you've created so far. (75)I know some of you are shy about showing off your work. But this won't be a big event. Just invite some family members and close friends. The exhibition will be on Saturday, August 12, and will run from 1:00 to 4:00 P.M. (76)We need some refreshments, so let me know if you can bring some snacks or drinks. I'll put a signup sheet out tomorrow.

여러분 전부 물품을 치우는 동안에, 간단한 안내 하나 해드리겠습니다. 이번 달에 중급자 회화반에서 여러분과 같이 하게 되어 즐거웠습니다. 다음 주에, 우리는 지금까지 여러분이 만든 작품들을 보여 주는 조그만 전시회를 하게 될 것입니다. 여러분 중 일부는 자신의 작품을 자랑하는 것에 대해 부끄러워 한다는 것을 압니다. 그런데 이것은 큰 행사가 아닙니다. 그냥 가족과 가까운 친구들을 초대하세요. 전시회는 8월 12일 토요일, 오후 1시에서 4시까지 하게 될 것입니다. 우리는 다과가 좀 필요한데, 간식이나 음료를 갖고 오실 수 있으면 저에게 알려 주세요. 내일 신청서를 꺼내 놓겠습니다.

74. 청자들은 누구일 것 같은가?
(A) 쇼핑객
(B) 미술관 방문객
(C) 미술반 학생
(D) 식당 직원 　　　정답 (C)

75. 화자가 "이것은 큰 행사가 아닙니다"라고 말하는 이유는?
(A) 가격을 협상하기 위해
(B) 놀라움을 표현하기 위해
(C) 경고를 하기 위해
(D) 청자들을 안심시키기 위해 　　　정답 (D)

76. 화자는 청자들에게 행사장에 무엇을 가지고 오라고 요청하는가?
(A) 미술용품
(B) 사진이 부착된 신분증
(C) 티켓
(D) 다과류 　　　정답 (D)

문제 77-79번은 다음 전화 메시지를 참조하시오. 미W

> W: Hello. This is Emily Green from Sandy Tours calling about your job application. Congratulations. **(77)You've been chosen to lead historical tours of our city.** We love your work history. **(78)The fact that you have written articles about local landmarks for several magazines should help you considerably.** Since the job you'll be in charge of is physically demanding, **(79)you need to take a physical examination before you begin.** My assistant will call you later to make a reservation with a doctor.
>
> ---
>
> 안녕하세요. 저는 샌디 투어의 에밀리 그린인데, 당신의 인사 지원 때문에 전화드렸습니다. 축하드립니다. 우리 도시의 역사 투어를 진행하시도록 뽑히셨습니다. 우리는 당신의 업무 이력이 마음에 듭니다. 여러 잡지사를 위해서 지역 랜드마크에 대한 기사를 썼다는 사실이 당신에게 상당히 도움이 될 것입니다. 당신이 맡게 될 일은 육체적으로 힘든 일이기 때문에, 시작하시기 전에 건강 검진을 받을 필요가 있습니다. 제 직원이 나중에 전화드려 의사와의 진료 예약을 잡아 드릴 것입니다.

77. 청자에게 어떤 종류의 일이 제의되고 있는가?
- (A) 관광 안내원
- (B) 버스 운전사
- (C) 역사 선생님
- (D) 접수 담당자   정답 (A)

78. 화자는 어떤 업무 자격 요건에 특히 깊은 인상을 받았다고 말하는가?
- (A) 외국어 능력
- (B) 긍정적인 추천서
- (C) 대학 학위
- (D) 집필 경력   정답 (D)

79. 화자에 따르면, 청자는 무엇을 해야 하는가?
- (A) 유니폼 착용
- (B) 온라인 설문지 작성
- (C) 사용 지침 비디오 시청
- (D) 신체 검사 받기   정답 (D)

문제 80-82번은 다음 회의 발췌 내용을 참조하시오. 영M

> M: **(80)We're having this meeting of our magazine writers** so that I can give you a quick update on some news. **(81)I just hired six new freelance writers, all of whom live in different countries around the world.** They're going to be on our travel writing team and should be able to contribute to our diverse collection of articles each month. We're also going to sign a contract to create a partnership with Atlantic Airlines. **(82)As a result, all of its flights bound for Asia and Europe will feature copies of our travel magazine for passengers to read.** That means more people will be reading your work soon.
>
> ---
>
> 우리는 몇몇 소식들을 여러분들에게 신속하게 업데이트해 드리기 위해 이번 우리 잡지사 작가 회의를 하게 되었습니다. 저는 막 신규 프리랜서 작가 6명을 고용했는데, 이들 전부 전세계 각지의 다른 나라에 살고 있습니다. 이들은 우리 여행 작가 팀에 속하게 될 것이고, 매달 우리의 다양한 기사 모음에 기여하게 될 것입니다. 우리는 또한 애틀랜틱 항공사와 파트너십을 맺는 계약을 체결할 것입니다. 그래서 아시아 및 유럽으로 향하는 모든 비행편에 승객들이 읽을 수 있도록 우리 여행 잡지가 비치될 것입니다. 이는 곧 더 많은

> 사람들이 여러분의 글을 읽게 된다는 뜻이기도 합니다.

80. 이 담화는 누구를 대상으로 하는 것인가?
- (A) 작가
- (B) 사진사
- (C) 여행 가이드
- (D) 항공사 직원   정답 (A)

81. 화사는 최근에 무엇을 했는가?
- (A) 웹사이트를 업그레이드했다.
- (B) 프리랜서 직원을 몇 명 고용했다.
- (C) 새 사무 공간을 위한 임대 계약에 서명했다.
- (D) 유럽으로 이전했다.   정답 (B)

82. 화자는 간행물을 곧 어디에서 볼 수 있다고 말하는가?
- (A) 국제 비행편
- (B) 외국의 슈퍼마켓
- (C) 기차 역
- (D) 여행사   정답 (A)

문제 83-85번은 다음 전화 메시지를 참조하시오. 미W

> W: Hello, Eric. This is Jill. **(83)I'm glad to hear that we'll be collaborating on the script for the new fast-food restaurant commercial.** I've seen some of your previous ad campaigns you've worked on, and I think we'll do well together. Anyway, I'm calling about your request to meet this Friday. Thank you for booking the conference room for us, **(84)but I'm meeting a new client in Toronto.** I was informed that the video conferencing software we have is effective. **(85)Why don't we try it out before we have a meeting?** I'm looking forward to sharing ideas with you.
>
> ---
>
> 안녕하세요 에릭. 저는 질이에요. 우리가 패스트푸드 식당 새 광고에 대한 대본 작업을 공동으로 할 거라는 소식을 듣고 기뻤어요. 당신이 이전에 작업했던 광고 캠페인 일부를 봤는데, 우리 둘이 같이 잘하게 될 것 같아요. 어쨌든, 저는 이번 주 금요일 만나자는 당신의 요청 때문에 전화드렸는데요. 우리를 위해서 회의실을 예약해 주신 건 감사한데, 저는 토론토에서 신규 고객을 만날 거예요. 우리가 가지고 있는 화상 회의 소프트웨어가 효율적이라고 들었어요. 우리 회의하기 전에 그 소프트웨어를 사용해 보는 것은 어떤가요? 당신과 같이 의견을 나누게 되는 게 너무 기다려져요.

83. 화자는 어떤 종류의 일을 하는 것 같은가?
- (A) 사무실 개조
- (B) 광고
- (C) 영업
- (D) 식품 제조   정답 (B)

84. 화자가 "저는 토론토에서 신규 고객을 만날 거예요"라고 말할 때 무엇을 의미하는가?
- (A) 그녀는 지금 다른 지역에 가 있다.
- (B) 그녀는 토론토 여행에 대해 신이 나 있다.
- (C) 그녀는 날짜를 변경하고 싶어한다.
- (D) 그녀는 직접 만날 수 없다.   정답 (D)

85. 화자는 청자에게 무엇을 할 것을 제안하는가?
- (A) 자신의 사무실로 찾아오기
- (B) 대본을 이메일로 보내기

(C) 회의 일정 변경하기

(D) 소프트웨어 사용해 보기　　　　　　　　　　정답 (D)

문제 86-88번은 다음 회의 발췌 내용을 참조하시오. 영M

M: It's time to discuss our future plans. We've been selling soda for more than thirty years, and we've been very successful. (86) (87)But sales have been decreasing lately. Nowadays, (87) companies are releasing many new products. We need to develop some other unique products with new flavors to get back the customers we've lost. Our R&D Department is working hard on it right now. (88)At the next meeting, we'll get to do a taste test of some of the new flavors they've created and they want us to give some comments.

우리의 미래 계획에 대해 논의할 때입니다. 우리는 청량 음료를 30년 이상 판매해 왔고 매우 성공적이었습니다. 그런데 최근 들어 매출이 하락했습니다. 요새는 여러 회사들이 많은 신제품을 출시하고 있습니다. 우리가 잃어버린 고객들이 다시 되돌아오게 하기 위해서 우리는 새로운 맛의 다른 독특한 제품을 개발할 필요가 있습니다. 현재 우리 연구개발부에서는 그에 대해 열심히 작업 중입니다. 다음 회의에서는 연구개발부가 만든 새로운 맛에 대해 시음 테스트를 하게 될 것인데, 그들은 우리가 의견을 내주기를 원합니다.

86. 최근에 무슨 일이 있었는가?

(A) 일부 제품이 단종되었다.

(B) 가게들이 문을 닫았다.

(C) 매출이 하락했다.

(D) 청량 음료 신제품이 인기를 얻었다.　　　　정답 (C)

87. 화자가 "여러 회사들이 많은 신제품을 출시하고 있습니다"라고 말할 때 무엇을 함축하는가?

(A) 새로운 광고 캠페인이 시작될 필요가 있다.

(B) 회사는 특정한 제품 생산을 중단할 것이다.

(C) 당장 가격이 인하될 필요가 있다.

(D) 회사가 경쟁업체들이 생겼다.　　　　　　정답 (D)

88. 청자들은 다음 회의에서 무엇을 받게 될 것인가?

(A) 성공한 제품 목록

(B) 제품 카탈로그

(C) 샘플

(D) 내년 달력　　　　　　　　　　　　　　정답 (C)

문제 89-91번은 다음 광고를 참조하시오. 미M

M: Do you enjoy purchasing lunch from one of the city's numerous food trucks? If so, you're in luck. (89)There's a new mobile application that can help you get the food you want. Download the Lunch on Wheels app, and you'll be able to see where every food truck is at all times. You can place an order through the app, and it will be ready for you to pick up when you arrive at the truck. (90)Customers love this app because they can save time. They don't have to wait in lines anymore. (91)Starting next week, customers will also earn points from their purchases at food trucks which can be redeemed for free meals. Download Lunch on Wheels today.

도시의 수많은 푸드 트럭에서 점심을 구입하는 것을 좋아하세요? 그렇다

면, 여러분은 운이 좋으십니다. 여러분이 원하는 음식을 살 수 있게 도와주는 새로운 모바일 앱이 있습니다. 런치 온 휠즈 앱을 내려받으세요. 그러면, 여러분은 모든 푸드 트럭이 항상 어디에 있는지 보실 수 있습니다. 이 앱을 통해서 주문을 하시면, 트럭에 도착할 때쯤에는 여러분이 찾아갈 수 있도록 음식이 준비되어 있을 것입니다. 고객들은 시간을 절감할 수 있어서 이 앱을 아주 좋아합니다. 더 이상 줄 서서 기다릴 필요가 없습니다. 다음 주부터, 고객들은 또한 푸드 트럭에서 구매할 때 포인트를 받을 수 있는데, 이 포인트는 무료 식사로 교환할 수 있습니다. 오늘 런치 온 휠즈를 내려받으세요.

89. 휴대폰 앱은 무엇을 위한 것인가?

(A) 돈 이체하기

(B) 음식 주문하기

(C) 운전 길 안내 받기

(D) 공연 티켓 구매하기　　　　　　　　　　정답 (B)

90. 화자에 따르면, 고객들이 휴대폰 앱에 대해 좋아하는 것은 무엇인가?

(A) 다양한 식당 선택을 제공한다.

(B) 사용하는 데 비용이 들어가지 않는다.

(C) 시간을 절감시켜 준다.

(D) 의견을 남기게 해준다.　　　　　　　　　정답 (C)

91. 화자에 따르면, 다음 주에 휴대폰 앱에 무엇이 추가될 것인가?

(A) 다른 웹사이트 링크

(B) 무료 배달 서비스

(C) 주차비 정보

(D) 보상 포인트 프로그램　　　　　　　　　정답 (D)

문제 92-94번은 다음 방송을 참조하시오. 미W

W: Good morning. This is Trisha Mayweather with a news update. Last night, (92)the city council appropriated funds to install lampposts on the Centennial Park Trail. The trail which is popular with walkers and bikers currently is not open to the public after sunset. The decision was definitely influenced by a group of concerned citizens. (93)Last month, they attended the city council's meeting and made a presentation regarding the need for lighting installation. Now, the city council needs to select a contractor to do the work. (94) The city council is sorting out bids for the project and the winning one will be announced at next month's meeting.

안녕하세요. 저는 최신 소식의 트리샤 메이웨더입니다. 어젯밤 시 의회는 센테니얼 공원 산책로에 가로등을 설치하는 데 자금을 책정했습니다. 산책하는 사람들과 자전거 타는 사람들에게 인기 있는 이 산책로는 현재는 일몰 이후에는 일반 대중에게 개방되지 않습니다. 이번 결정은 분명히 관심이 있는 시민 단체로부터 영향을 받은 것 같습니다. 지난달에, 이들은 시 의회 회의에 참석했는데, 조명 설치의 필요성에 대해 프레젠테이션을 했습니다. 이제, 시 의회는 이 일을 할 계약업체를 선정해야 합니다. 시 의회에서는 이 프로젝트에 대한 입찰을 선별 분류 중이고, 뽑힌 입찰이 다음 달 회의에서 발표될 것입니다.

92. 시 의회는 무엇을 위한 자금을 승인했는가?

(A) 공원 산책로 추가

(B) 새 주차장 건설

(C) 산책로를 따라 조명 설치

(D) 주민들을 위한 자전거 구입　　　　　　　정답 (C)

93. 화자에 따르면, 일부 시민은 지난달에 무엇을 했는가?
(A) 연례 기금모금 행사를 열었다.
(B) 사람들에게 진정서에 서명하게 했다.
(C) 회의에서 발표를 했다.
(D) 고객 만족도 설문을 작성했다. 정답 (C)

94. 다음 달 시 의회에서 무엇을 할 것인가?
(A) 고용 결정 내리기
(B) 선거 하기
(C) 공원 방문하기
(D) 새 위원 발표하기 정답 (A)

문제 95-97번은 다음 전화 메시지와 곡 목록을 참조하시오. Ⓜ️Ⓦ

M: Hello, Rick. This is Julia Montana from the radio station. I can't wait to interview you about your new concert tour this evening. **(95)I just e-mailed you some questions I intend to ask on the show.** In addition, I have the results of a survey of our listeners that we conducted. We asked which song they want you to perform in the studio. **(96)Sixty percent really want to hear *Another Day*.** I hope you don't mind performing it live. Just so you know, we have some new sound equipment. **(97)I'll check it out personally to make sure it's operating fine this afternoon.**

안녕하세요, 릭. 저는 라디오 방송국의 줄리아 몬태나예요. 오늘 저녁 새 콘서트 투어에 대해 당신과 인터뷰하는 것이 너무 기다려집니다. 지금 막 이메일로 방송 프로에서 묻고자 하는 질문 몇 가지를 보냈습니다. 그 외에, 저는 우리가 청취자 대상으로 실시했던 설문조사 결과를 가지고 있는데요. 그들은 스튜디오에서 당신이 어떤 노래를 라이브로 공연해 주기를 원하는지를 물어봤습니다. 60퍼센트가 정말로 〈또 하루〉를 듣고 싶어했어요. 그 곡을 라이브로 연주해 주셨으면 합니다. 그리고 참고로 드리는 말씀인데, 우리는 새로운 음향 장비를 들여놨습니다. 오늘 오후에 그게 제대로 작동하도록 하기 위해서 그 음향 장비를 직접 점검해 보겠습니다.

곡 목록	
트랙 1	네가 여기에 있었으면 좋겠어
트랙 2	그게 뭐지?
트랙 3	시간이 다됐어
(96)트랙 4	**또 하루**

95. 화자는 오늘 이메일로 무엇을 보냈는가?
(A) 서명할 계약 서식
(B) 인터뷰 질문 목록
(C) 다양한 음향 장비의 가격 목록
(D) 앨범 커버 디자인 정답 (B)

96. 그래픽을 보시오. 릭이 연주할 트랙 번호는 어느 것인가?
(A) 트랙 1
(B) 트랙 2
(C) 트랙 3
(D) 트랙 4 정답 (D)

97. 여자는 오늘 오후에 무엇을 할 것이라고 말하는가?
(A) 라디오 방송국에 일찍 도착
(B) 티켓 구매

(C) 장비 테스트
(D) 다과 준비 정답 (C)

문제 98-100번은 다음 회의 발췌 내용과 그래프를 참조하시오. 영️Ⓜ️

W: It's time to start our managers' meeting. **(98)First, let me talk about the safety inspections we conduct here at the factory each month.** Check out this graph. **(99)Notice the month in which we got our highest score. I think that happened probably because we held a training session on workplace safety at the start of that month before the inspection was conducted. But our scores have declined since then,** and that indicates me the staff needs a reminder on how to prevent accidents in the workplace on a regular basis. So this month, have everyone on your team review the safety manual prior to the inspection. **(100)Peter has copies for you. Pick them up from him for your team members when the meeting ends.**

우리 관리자 회의를 시작할 시간입니다. 우선, 매달 우리가 여기 공장에서 실시하는 안전 점검에 대해서 얘기하겠습니다. 이 그래프를 확인해 보세요. 가장 점수가 높았던 달을 주목해서 보세요. 이런 일이 생긴 이유는 아마 안전 점검이 실시되기 전에 그 달 초에 우리가 근무지 안전에 대한 교육을 했기 때문인 것 같습니다. 그렇지만 우리 점수는 그 때 이후로 하락했고, 그게 시사하는 바는 정기적으로 근무지 내에서 어떻게 사고를 방지할지에 대해 직원들에게 다시 한 번 알려 줘야 한다는 것입니다. 그래서 이번 달에는, 점검 전에 여러분 팀원들 전부가 안전 지침서를 검토하게 하십시오. 피터가 여러분이 가져갈 수 있도록 지침서 사본을 준비했습니다. 회의가 끝나면 여러분 팀원들을 위해 그에게서 사본을 받아 가십시오.

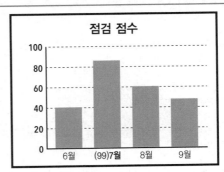

점검 점수

| 6월 | (99)7월 | 8월 | 9월 |

98. 청자들은 어디에서 근무하는가?
(A) 공장
(B) 창고
(C) 백화점
(D) 정부 기관 정답 (A)

99. 그래픽을 보시오. 근무지 안전에 관한 마지막 교육은 언제 있었는가?
(A) 6월
(B) 7월
(C) 8월
(D) 9월 정답 (B)

100. 화자에 따르면, 피터는 무엇을 할 것인가?
(A) 회의 내용 받아 적기
(B) 안전 절차 시연하기
(C) 공장 견학 진행하기
(D) 사본 나누어 주기 정답 (D)

101. 효율적이고 적극적인 마케팅 전략들은 여러 유럽 국가에서의 사업 성공을 뒷받침하는 데 필수적인 역할을 담당했다. 　정답 (B)

102. 폭설로 인해 어제 오후까지 많은 지역의 항공편 운항이 지연되었다. 　정답 (C)

103. 우리 제휴사가 주최하는 공식 행사에 참석하지 못할 때, 그들의 초청을 정중하게 거절하는 것이 중요하다. 　정답 (D)

104. 시에서는 기업 투자를 유도하고 매우 기업 친화적인 환경을 조성하고자 몇 가지 규제를 철폐하기 위한 노력을 배가하고 있다. 　정답 (C)

105. 모든 고객 분들은 이 매장에서 환불 혹은 교환이 처리되는 데 14일을 허용한다는 사실을 알고 계셔야 합니다. 　정답 (C)

106. 롱 비치 뷔페에서는 개인 수표도 신용 카드도 받지 않기 때문에, 고객들은 현금으로 지불해야 한다. 　정답 (B)

107. 그의 새로운 사업은 새로운 규제와 주식 시장의 최근 주가 하락에 의해 부정적인 영향을 받고 있다. 　정답 (C)

108. 모든 나라가 전반적인 노동력 부족과 함께 세계의 노동력 위기에 직면했지만, 이 새로운 인공 지능 기술이 우리가 그것을 해결하는 데 도움이 될 것이다. 　정답 (A)

109. 한정된 시간 동안 고객들은 우리의 강력한 새 노트북 컴퓨터를 계약금 없이 0% 대출을 통해 구입할 수 있다. 　정답 (D)

110. 싱 씨는 구매할 제품 한 개를 선택하기 전에 두 제품의 특성을 비교했다. 　정답 (A)

111. 스티븐 채프먼 씨는 그의 인상적인 경력과 이전 두 대학에서의 성공 덕분에 우리 대학의 신임 학장으로 임명되었다. 　정답 (B)

112. 시장은 시내에 있는 몇 줄의 가로등 교체를 지시했으나, 배선이 불량해 전체 시스템이 교체되어야 한다는 점을 알게 되었다. 　정답 (A)

113. 지역 환경 단체 대부분은 그 지역을 파괴할 수 있는 건설 프로젝트를 중단하기를 바라고 있다. 　정답 (B)

114. 시 정부에서는 공중 보건 및 복지 시설을 개선할 새로운 방법을 찾는 데 전념하고 있다. 　정답 (B)

115. 사회학자들은 도시 지역의 인구 과밀로 인해 발생하는 많은 긴장과 갈등에 관해 우려하고 있다. 　정답 (A)

116. 만약 당사의 신상품에 관심이 있으시면, 이메일, 전화, 혹은 팩스를 통해 저희에게 연락하시면 추가 정보를 보내 드리도록 하겠습니다. 　정답 (A)

117. 가격을 낮추기 위해, 우리 회사는 생산 공정을 간소화하고 포장의 부피와 무게를 최소화했다. 　정답 (D)

118. HD 제약 회사는 북미 지역에서의 지속적인 매출의 확대로 인해 3분기의 순수익이 증가했다. 　정답 (B)

119. 8월에 우리 시는 5,500개의 일자리를 잃었는데, 고용 증가를 예상했던 예측가들에게는 반갑지 않은 놀라운 일이었다. 　정답 (D)

120. 독립적으로 일하는 것을 선호하는 직원들도 있고, 동료들과 일할 때 일을 더 잘하는 직원들도 있다. 　정답 (C)

121. 기계적인 문제들이 예상보다 더 빠르게 수리되어서 우리 공장의 폐쇄는 매우 짧았다. 　정답 (D)

122. 판매 계약서는 일부 사진 이미지들이 상업적, 비상업적인 목적으로 사용될 수 있음을 직접적으로 명시하고 있다. 　정답 (C)

123. 그 항공사는 결항된 런던 및 베를린 행 항공편들을 제외하고는 서비스가 중단되지 않았다고 밝혔다. 　정답 (A)

124. 보고서는 아시아의 여러 국가들이 개방된 국제 경제에 힘입어 올해 꾸준한 성장을 보게 될 것이라고 했다. 　정답 (D)

125. 새로운 사업 모델의 성장을 방해하는 두 개의 주된 요인 중, 하나는 고루한 규제이며, 다른 하나는 새로운 기준의 부재이다. 　정답 (D)

126. 업계 일부 전문가들은 전 세계 화장품 시장이 향후 10년간 20퍼센트 성장할 것이라고 예측한다. 　정답 (D)

127. 그의 비행기가 한 시간 이상 늦게 도착했기 때문에, 홉킨스 박사는 의학 강연에 참석할 수 없었다. 　정답 (C)

128. 우리 주문이 다음 주까지 배송되지 않는다면, 우리는 그것을 취소하고 다른 공급업체를 물색해야 할 것이다. 　정답 (C)

129. 만두 컴퓨터 회사는 새로운 소프트웨어가 대부분의 컴퓨터 운영 체제들과 호환된다고 주장하지만, 일부 고객들은 그렇지 않다고 말한다. 　정답 (C)

130. 지아 테크놀로지 회사는 그 지역 최고의 중소기업 가운데 하나로 선정되기 전에는, 전국적으로 사업을 확장하는 것을 고려하지 않았었다. 　정답 (D)

Part 6

문제 131-134번은 다음 회람을 참조하시오.

> 수신: 전 직원
> 발신: 리사 해밀턴, 시설 관리 부장
> 날짜: 1월 21일
> 제목: 전기 절약 정보 및 화재 예방
>
> 사무실에서 전기 사용을 줄여 에너지 비용을 줄이는 데 도와주세요. 올해 전기 요금이 크게 증가해서, 우리는 이를 반으로 줄이도록 노력해야 합니다.
>
> 다음은 몇 가지 간단한 에너지 절약 정보입니다. 책상 아래에 두는 난방기와 같은 개인 전기 제품을 사용하지 않을 때는 전원을 반드시 꺼야 합니다. 일이 끝나면 마지막으로 퇴근하는 직원이 사무실마다 모든 전등과 전기 제품의 전원이 꺼져 있는지 필히 확인해야 합니다. 플러그를 꽂을 물건이 많다면 여러분의 필요를 안전하게 수용할 수 있는 멀티탭을 사용하십시오. 이것들은 밤새 방치되어 있으면 화재 위험이 될 수 있습니다.
>
> 일상의 행동을 조정하고 습관에 작은 변화를 가져오세요. 화재 예방 및 에너지 절약이 첨단 기술일 필요는 없습니다.
>
> 여러분의 협조에 미리 감사의 말씀을 드립니다.

131. 　정답 (B)

132. 　정답 (B)

133. 정답 (D)

134. (A) 우리는 고객에게 에너지 사용을 전력 소비량이 많지 않은 시간으로 전
환해줄 것을 요청하고 있습니다.
(B) 화재 예방 및 에너지 절약이 첨단 기술일 필요는 없습니다.
(C) 이를 수행하기 전에, 회사 안전 매뉴얼을 참조하십시오.
(D) 작업장 안전은 업무 중 부상 위험을 최소화할 것입니다. 정답 (B)

문제 135-138번은 다음 편지를 참조하시오.

> 레드 록스 원형극장
> 태너리 로 3000번지
> 산타클라라, 캘리포니아 주 95054
>
> 7월 5일
>
> 스테이시 존슨 씨
> 해밀턴 애비뉴 250번지
> 팔로 알토, 캘리포니아 주 94301
>
> 존슨 씨에게,
>
> 7월 18일 레드 록스 원형극장에서 개최 예정인 파이브 메탈스의 콘서트가
> 어제 발생한 예상치 못한 교통사고로 취소되었습니다. 밴드 멤버 세 명이
> 충돌로 중상을 입었습니다. 저희는 그들의 빠르고 확실한 쾌유를 기원합니
> 다.
>
> 저희 기록에는 고객님께서 지난주에 현금으로 C열 표를 4장 구매하신 것으
> 로 나와 있습니다. 그러므로 고객님이 지불하신 가격의 전액을 환불해 드리
> 겠습니다. 1-800-575-4332로 전화 주시면 서비스 담당자가 환불 처리를
> 도와드릴 것입니다.
>
> 야기된 불편과 실망을 드린 점에 대해 진심으로 사과드립니다. 부디 저희가
> 사과의 표시로 동봉한 20달러의 상품권을 받아 주십시오.
>
> 저희 공연장과 예술 전반에 대한 지속적인 지지에 대단히 감사드립니다.
>
> 브랜든 황 드림
> 단장
> 레드 록스 원형극장

135. (A) 불행히도, 최근 몇 주간 차량 공유 신청이 급격하게 감소했습니다.
(B) 저희는 그들의 빠르고 확실한 쾌유를 기원합니다.
(C) 그 밴드는 주로 리드 싱어의 놀라운 가창력으로 알려져 왔습니다.
(D) 주의를 기울이는 것이 공연장에서 사고를 방지하는 데 도움이 될 수 있
음을 모든 직원에게 상기시키십시오. 정답 (B)

136. 정답 (C)

137. 정답 (D)

138. 정답 (D)

문제 139-142번은 다음 광고를 참조하시오.

> **센트리 부동산**
> 유니언 랜딩 대로 321번지
> 유니언 시티, 뉴저지 주 94587
> (510) 776-3232
>
> **아파트 임대**
> 월넛 크릭 아파트 310호
> 하더 로드 1123번지

하더 로드에 위치한 깨끗하고, 넓은 두 개의 침실과 한 개의 욕실이 있는 아
파트가 임대 가능합니다. 이 아파트는 기본적인 주방 시설, 식기 세척기, 그
리고 주인이 제공하는 세탁기가 구비되어 있습니다.

이 아파트는 시내 중심부에 편리하게 위치해 있습니다. 가장 가까운 지하철
역은 도보로 고작 5분 거리에, 그리고 가장 가까운 버스 정류장은 도보로
10분 거리에 있습니다. 아파트 단지 안에 편의점이 있습니다.

임대료는 가스, 전기, 그리고 수도를 포함하여 월 1,250달러입니다. 임대료
에 인터넷은 포함되지 않는다는 점에 유의하십시오. 반려동물은 엄격히 금
지되어 있습니다.

더 많은 정보를 원하시거나 아파트 구경을 위한 예약을 하시려면 앤드류 김
씨에게 (510) 776-3232로 연락 주십시오.

139. 정답 (D)

140. 정답 (D)

141. (A) 주방용품을 판매하는 슈퍼마켓도 있습니다.
(B) 임대료에 인터넷이 포함되지 않는다는 점에 유의하십시오.
(C) 임대 계약서에 서명하기 위해 편하신 시간에 저희 사무실을 방문해 주
십시오.
(D) 임대료 인상은 세금과 유지비에 기초하여 결정됩니다. 정답 (B)

142. 정답 (A)

문제 143-146번은 다음 이메일을 참조하시오.

> 수신: 미란다 윌리엄스 〈mrw@beaglemedia.com〉
> 발신: 고객 서비스 〈cs@wwjc.com〉
> 날짜: 10월 26일
> 제목: 귀하의 등록에 관해
>
> 윌리엄스 씨에게,
>
> 북미의 선도적인 온라인 직업 소개소 중 하나인 월드와이드 잡스 커뮤니티
> 에 오신 것을 환영합니다. 귀하의 주소와 직업 경력과 같은 개인 정보는 귀
> 하께서 허용하신다면 저희 데이터베이스에 안전하게 보관될 것입니다.
>
> 수집된 정보는 귀하의 직업 선호도를 분석하는 데 사용될 것이며, 귀하와
> 같은 취업 지원자들을 찾고 있는 고용주들에게 제공할 것입니다. 귀하가 저
> 희 서비스에 가입한 후에 귀하 지역의 일자리에 대한 정기적인 이메일 통지
> 가 발송될 것입니다.
>
> 저희는 누구나 신원 도용의 피해자가 될 수 있다는 점을 알고 있습니다. 그
> 러므로 저희는 귀하의 개인 정보를 매우 신중하게 다루고 있습니다. 만약
> 저희 서비스에 가입하고자 하신다면, 저희 웹사이트 www.wwjc.com을
> 방문하시거나 1-800-857-6313으로 전화 주십시오.
>
> 월드와이드 잡스 커뮤니티
> 고객 서비스

143. 정답 (D)

144. 정답 (C)

145. 정답 (A)

146. (A) 저희의 직업 데이터베이스는 통상 매달 갱신됩니다.
(B) 귀하의 이력서는 최근 이사진에 의해 검토되었습니다.
(C) 저희는 누구나 신원 도용의 피해자가 될 수 있다는 점을 알고 있습니다.
(D) 고객 만족이 항상 저희의 최우선 순위에 있습니다. 정답 (C)

문제 147-148번은 다음 편지를 참조하시오.

오피스 프리미엄
(148C)4826 메사 드라이브
맨해튼, 뉴욕 주 10016

5월 10일

스텔라 아담스
4995 요키 레인
맨해튼, 뉴욕 주 10016

애덤스 씨께,

오피스 프리미엄의 **(148B)P039 복사기 대여** 요금 150달러가 6월 2일까지 납입되어야 함을 알려 드립니다. **(147)귀하께서 대여 계약서에 제공하신 이 메일 주소로 연락이 닿지 않아, 이 편지를 보냅니다. (148D)계약서에는 귀하께서 두 달마다 선불로 복사기 대여 비용을 지불해야 한다**고 명시되어 있습니다. 가급적 빨리 (912) 555-6218로 오피스 프리미엄에 연락 주십시오.

윌리엄 반스 드림
매장 매니저, 오피스 프리미엄

---

147. 오피스 프리미엄에 관하여 사실인 것은?
　(A) 애덤스 씨가 계약서에 서명하기를 원한다.
　(B) 애덤스 씨에게 복사기를 추천했다.
　(C) 전에 애덤스 씨에게 연락하려고 했다.
　(D) 애덤스 씨가 이메일로 답장하기를 원한다.　　정답 (C)

148. 편지에 언급되지 않은 것은 무엇인가?
　(A) 대여 시작 날짜
　(B) 대여한 기계의 일련번호
　(C) 오피스 프리미엄의 위치
　(D) 지불 빈도　　정답 (A)

문제 149-150번은 다음 영수증을 참조하시오.

피어슨 회사
32 카터스 로드
바이런 베이, 뉴사우스웨일스 주 2481

환불 조회 번호:　　　107C15
(150)환불 영수증 인쇄 일자: 6월 21일, 17시 2분 55초
(150)승인자:　　　　케네스 더들리
서명:　　　　　　*케네스 더들리*

환불받는 사람:　　카를로스 베스트버그
서명:　　　　　　*카를로스 베스트버그*
총 (환불) 금액:　　$58.20 (현금)

최초 발행 영수증 번호: 7138 (6월 15일; 13시 8분 23초)
다음의 물품(들)에 대해 환불함

물품	수량	가격(달러)
(149)휴대용 난로	1	17.80
(149)접이식 칼	1	11.35
(149)손전등	1	3.20
(149)6인용 텐트 (네이비 블루색)	1	25.85

---

149. 피어슨 회사는 어떤 종류의 사업체일 것 같은가?
　(A) 전자제품 가게
　(B) 부엌용품 제조업체
　(C) 야외 장비 상점
　(D) 원예 장비 소매업체　　정답 (C)

150. 더들리 씨에 대해서 나타나 있는 것은 무엇인가?
　(A) 그가 몇몇 결함 있는 제품의 리콜을 승인했다.
　(B) 6월 21일에 근무했다.
　(C) 베스트버그 씨로부터 돈을 받았다.
　(D) 바이런 베이 지역에 살고 있다.　　정답 (B)

문제 151-152번은 다음 문자 메시지를 참조하시오.

마리오 램지　　　　　　　　　[오후 5시 4분]
나 요즘 너무 축 처지는 느낌이에요. 거의 모든 것에 의욕도 없고 항상 피곤해요.

로런 스튜어트　　　　　　　　[오후 5시 6분]
운동은 충분히 하고 있어요?

마리오 램지　　　　　　　　　[오후 5시 7분]
전혀요. 맨날 일하고 있어서 운동할 시간이 없어요.

로런 스튜어트　　　　　　　　[오후 5시 10분]
일하는 것도 중요하지만, 건강이 무엇보다도 먼저예요. **(151)우리 달리기 동호회에 들어오지 않을래요?**

마리오 램지　　　　　　　　　[오후 5시 11분]
당신 말이 맞아요. 그렇지만 당신 동호회는 이미 모임을 오랫동안 해 왔잖아요. 내가 지금 회원들을 잘 따라갈 수 있을지 모르겠어요.

로런 스튜어트　　　　　　　　[오후 5시 13분]
(151)걱정하지 마요. 당신은 잘할 거예요. 그리고 늦어도 안 하느니보다 나아요.

마리오 램지　　　　　　　　　[오후 5시 14분]
좋아요. 그런데 **(152)주말에만 시간이 될 거예요.**

로런 스튜어트　　　　　　　　[오후 5시 16분]
(152)그건 괜찮아요. 우리도 주말에 운동하니까요.

---

151. 오후 5시 13분에, 스튜어트 씨가 "늦어도 안 하느니보다 나아요"라고 쓸 때 무엇을 의미하는가?
　(A) 그는 램지 씨가 동호회의 다른 사람들만큼 빨리 달리지 못할 것을 우려한다.
　(B) 그는 램지 씨에게 평소보다 좀 늦게 출근하라고 권고하고 있다.
　(C) 그는 램지 씨에게 운동을 시작하도록 권장하고 있다.
　(D) 그는 램지 씨에게 주말에 일을 쉬라고 제안하고 있다.　　정답 (C)

152. 스튜어트 씨에 대해 나타나 있는 것은 무엇인가?
　(A) 그는 곧 헬스장을 열 것이다.
　(B) 그는 주말마다 램지 씨와 달리기를 할 것이다.
　(C) 그는 주말마다 일하러 나간다.
　(D) 그는 전문 헬스 트레이너이다.　　정답 (B)

문제 153-154번은 다음 웹 페이지를 참조하시오.

http://www.dansertheater.com/showtimes

단서 극장

홈	역사	공연 시간	연락처

공연 시간 - 12월 첫째 주

〈왕의 귀환〉 보스턴 브로드웨이 사: 앵콜 투어	12월 1일 오후 7시	★★★☆☆ 16개 관람 평	입장권 구매
(153)〈어느 여름밤〉 뉴욕 브로드웨이	12월 2일 오후 3시	★★☆☆☆ (153) 최초로 (평을) 써주세요!	입장권 구매
〈안나〉 트리니티 발레 콘서트	12월 3일 오후 2시	★★★★☆ 20개 관람 평	취소
〈지평선 너머〉 젠 서커스	12월 3일 오후 6시	★★★☆☆ 18개 관람 평	입장권 구매
〈안나〉 트리니티 발레 콘서트	12월 5일 오후 3시	★★★★☆ 20개 관람 평	입장권 구매
(154)〈시계가 12시를 알리면〉 뉴욕 뮤지컬스	12월 5일 오후 8시	★★★★☆ 22개 관람 평	(154)매진

• 만약 결제가 좌석 예약 후 12시간 내에 이뤄지지 않으면, (예약된) 좌석은 다른 이용자들에게 열릴 것입니다. 전액 환불은 공연 24시간 전까지만 가능합니다.

153. 웹 페이지에 따르면, 〈어느 여름밤〉에 대해 사실인 것은?
(A) 일반인들에게 무료로 개방된다.
(B) 혹평을 받았다.
(C) 단서 극장에서 초연한다.
(D) 아직 관람 평이 없다. 　　　　　정답 (D)

154. 현재 어떤 공연의 입장권을 구할 수 없는가?
(A) 왕의 귀환
(B) 안나
(C) 지평선 너머
(D) 시계가 12시를 알리면 　　　　　정답 (D)

문제 155-157번은 다음 브로셔를 참조하시오.

로보큠으로 당신의 집을 깨끗하게 유지하세요!

집을 청소하시기에 너무 바쁘신가요? 그렇다면, 로보큠이 당신을 위해서 매일 청소하게 해보세요. 로보큠은 자동으로 움직이는 로봇으로 바닥의 흙, 먼지 그리고 머리카락을 제거합니다. (155A)로보큠의 혁신적인 기술은 기계가 사람이나 물건과의 충돌을 피해 가는 것을 보장하므로, 자녀나 애완동물이 다칠까 절대 걱정하실 필요가 없습니다.

(155C)단 2시간의 충전만으로, 로보큠은 7시간 동안 작동합니다, 이것은 비슷한 모델들보다 3시간 정도 더 깁니다. (155B)게다가, 먼지 봉투나 먼지 필터 같은 로보큠을 작동하는 데 사용되는 소모품들도 매일 사용하는 데 부담이 되지 않도록 매우 합리적인 가격으로 제공합니다.

(156)봄을 맞이하여, 저희는 보통 15달러인 배송을 무료로 제공할 뿐만 아니라 3월 31일까지의 모든 주문 건에 대해서 30달러의 할인도 제공합니다. 할인을 받으면, 로보큠은 고작 510달러입니다! (157)구매 고객은 또한 1년 무상 품질 보증과 정상가 40달러의 절반인 20달러에 현재 이용 가능한 2년 품질 보증 중에서 선택하실 수 있습니다.

---

155. 로보큠의 장점으로 언급되지 않은 것은 무엇인가?
(A) 안전을 보장하는 센서가 있다.
(B) 소모품들의 값이 비싸지 않다.
(C) 에너지 효율적이다.
(D) 시중에서 가장 가벼운 모델이다. 　　　　　정답 (D)

156. 4월에 무슨 일이 있을 것인가?
(A) 제품의 가격이 오를 것이다.
(B) 주문이 더 이상 받아들여지지 않을 것이다.
(C) 제품에 대한 무료 배송이 주어질 것이다.
(D) 축하 행사가 열릴 것이다. 　　　　　정답 (A)

157. 연장된 품질 보증은 평상시 가격이 얼마인가?
(A) 15달러
(B) 20달러
(C) 30달러
(D) 40달러 　　　　　정답 (D)

문제 158-160번은 다음 이메일을 참조하시오.

수신: 브라이언 오델 〈bodell@jettech.com〉
발신: 제니스 설리반 〈jsullivan@kingdavidhotel.com〉
날짜: 10월 5일
제목: 킹 데이비드 호텔 예약
첨부: 송장

오델 씨게,

이 이메일은 9월 29일에 귀하께서 하신 예약에 관한 것입니다. (158)10월 3일에 제출된 귀하의 요청에 따라, (160)체크인 날짜가 이제 10월 10일에서 11월 10일로 변경됐습니다. 다음은 귀하의 새로운 예약 정보 개요입니다:

체크인:	11월 10일 오후 5시 이후
체크아웃:	11월 16일 오전 11시 이전
숙박객 수:	1
고객 보상 및 특별 요금:	프로모션 코드: MS292830 (10% 할인)

귀하의 예약에 관한 세부적인 정보가 있는 첨부된 송장을 확인해 주세요. 젯테크 주식회사의 직원용 프로모션 코드가 성공적으로 적용되었습니다. 결제는 프런트에서 체크인하실 때 하시면 됩니다. 질문이 있으시면, 편하게 저에게 이메일 답장을 주시거나, (905) 555-2039로 고객 서비스 담당자에게 연락 주십시오. (159)저희는 또한 대대적인 보수공사 끝에 피트니스 센터를 다시 열었습니다. 그러니 머무르시는 동안 잊지 말고 꼭 한 번 이용해 보세요!

제니스 설리반
고객 서비스 담당자

158. 이메일의 목적은 무엇인가?
(A) 추가적인 혜택을 요청하기 위한 것
(B) 호텔 방을 예약하기 위한 것
(C) 업데이트된 정보를 제공하기 위한 것
(D) 회원권의 갱신을 확인하기 위한 것 　　　　　정답 (C)

159. 킹 데이비드 호텔에 대해 나타나 있는 것은 무엇인가?
(A) 운동 시설이 있다.
(B) 재방문 고객에게 할인해 준다.
(C) 대기업들과 제휴를 맺고 있다.
(D) 증가하는 고객을 수용하려고 확장했다. 　　　　　정답 (A)

160. 오델 씨는 원래 언제 호텔을 방문할 계획이었는가?

    (A) 9월 29일
    (B) 10월 3일
    (C) 10월 10일
    (D) 11월 10일   정답 (C)

문제 161-163번은 다음 온라인 채팅 토론을 참조하시오.

조나단 스튜어트   [오후 3시 10분]
〈갤럭시 컴뱃〉의 새 에피소드를 봤어요?

할리 시몬스   [오후 3시 15분]
아뇨, 아직. 다음 주에 볼 계획이에요.

할리 시몬스   [오후 3시 16분]
그런데, (161) (162)〈갤럭시 컴뱃〉이 갤럭시 시리즈의 마지막 영화가 될 거라고 들었어요. 그게 사실이에요?

조나단 스튜어트   [오후 3시 17분]
(162)내가 아는 한 아니에요. 윈스키 형제가 그 시리즈의 모든 책을 영화로 만들어 왔고, 이것은 단지 세 번째 에피소드예요.

할리 시몬스   [오후 3시 20분]
(163)와! 그럼 실제로 두 편의 영화가 더 나올지도 모른다고요? 정말 신나요.

조나단 스튜어트   [오후 3시 21분]
음, 그게 모든 우리 갤럭시 팬들이 바라고 있는 거죠.

할리 시몬스   [오후 3시 23분]
〈갤럭시 컴뱃〉에서는 글렌 더치슨이 마르코 역을 맡지 않는다는 것도 들었어요. 난 그를 배우로서 정말 좋아해요.

조나단 스튜어트   [오후 3시 25분]
나도 그래요. (163)갤럭시 시리즈에서 그의 연기는 정말 대단했어요. 시리즈의 두 번째 에피소드에서 그는 연기를 너무 잘했어요.

조나단 스튜어트   [오후 3시 26분]
그런데, 새로운 배우 잭 레먼의 연기는 내 기대에 못 미쳤어요.

---

161. 대화의 주요 주제는 무엇인가?

    (A) 새로운 TV 프로그램
    (B) 베스트셀러 소설
    (C) 천문학적 발견
    (D) 영화 시리즈   정답 (D)

162. 오후 3시 17분에, 조나단 스튜어트가 "내가 아는 한 아니에요"라고 쓸 때 무엇을 의미하는가?

    (A) 〈갤럭시 컴뱃〉이 시리즈의 마지막 편일 것으로 생각하지 않는다.
    (B) 자신이 〈갤럭시 컴뱃〉을 보기를 원하는지 잘 모른다.
    (C) 〈갤럭시 컴뱃〉에 대해서 잘 모른다.
    (D) 윈스키 형제를 아직 만난 적이 없다.   정답 (A)

163. 조나단 스튜어트에 대해 나타나 있는 것은 무엇인가?

    (A) 다음 주에 〈갤럭시 컴뱃〉을 보러 갈 것이다.
    (B) 갤럭시 시리즈의 이전 에피소드를 보았다.
    (C) 갤럭시 시리즈의 책 다섯 권을 모두 가지고 있다.
    (D) 잭 레먼의 팬이다.   정답 (B)

문제 164-167번은 다음 회람을 참조하시오.

회람

수신: 프로즌의 전 직원
발신: 헤이든 드 위트
날짜: 5월 8일

직원 여러분께,

지난달 우리가 달성한 우수한 매출 실적을 축하합니다! 모두의 헌신과 노고에 감사드립니다.

벌써 손님들이 더 많아지는 것을 보니 올해는 여름이 빨리 온 듯하네요. (164)증가하는 수요에 (165)맞추기 위해서, (166)이사회가 5월 17일부터 8월 31일까지 매장을 2시간 더 열기로 결정했습니다. 이것은 꽤 급작스러운 결정이라서, 저희는 추가 인원을 아직 모집하지 못했습니다. 따라서, 모집이 이루어질 때까지, 모든 직원이 연장 교대 근무를 해줄 것을 요청합니다. 초과 근무를 하는 직원들은 상여금과 추가적인 유급 휴가로 보상받을 것입니다.

(167)성수기 동안 우리를 도와줄 수 있는 친구나 가족이 있다면, 저에게 알려 주세요. 그 임시 직원들에 대한 면접을 잡겠습니다. 앞으로도 열심히 합시다!

헤이든 드 위트 드림
인사과 국장

---

164. 회람의 목적은 무엇인가?

    (A) 직원들에게 더 열심히 일할 것을 요구하기 위한 것
    (B) 몇 명의 새로운 직원을 소개하기 위한 것
    (C) 회사의 기념일을 축하하기 위한 것
    (D) 직원들에게 향후 계획을 알리기 위한 것   정답 (D)

165. 두 번째 단락 2행에 있는 단어 "meet"와 의미상 가장 가까운 것은?

    (A) 직면하다
    (B) 기쁘게 하다
    (C) 환대하다
    (D) 충족시키다   정답 (D)

166. 프로즌에 대해 진술된 것은 무엇인가?

    (A) 평소 저녁에 문을 닫는다.
    (B) 임시로 운영 시간을 연장할 것이다.
    (C) 지난달 새로운 판매 기록을 세웠다.
    (D) 아이스크림을 제조한다.   정답 (B)

167. 회람의 수신자들은 무엇을 하도록 권장받는가?

    (A) 면접 참석
    (B) 행사 준비
    (C) 채용 공고 디자인
    (D) 프로즌에 채용 희망자 소개   정답 (D)

문제 168-171번은 다음 기사를 참조하시오.

7월 7일 – (168)증기선 선코스트가 8월 20일 대중에게 돌아온다. 선코스트는 미시시피 강을 따라 항해하던 첫 증기 기관선 중 하나로 미국 산업 혁명의 역사적 상징물이다. 선코스트는 거의 10년 동안 농업 수출품을 수송하면서 미시시피 강을 따라 오르내리며 항해했다.

고압 증기 엔진의 발명 이후로, 선코스트는 더는 필요가 없어졌다. 폴라드 스팀보트 회사는 선코스트의 역사적 가치를 보존하기 위해 원형을 보존했다. 이 역사적 중요성을 지역사회에 알리기 위해, (170C)이것은 뉴올리언스 엔진 박물관(NOEM)에 기증되어 박물관 옆의 사우스 쇼어 하버

에 전시되었다.

(168) (169) (170A) (171) **선코스트의 고풍스러운 아름다움을 전 세계에 보여 주기 위해**, NOEM은 증기선 그 자체를 산업 혁명 동안 미시시피 강에서 수상 운송의 역사와 발전 과정을 전시하는 용도로 사용하기로 결정했다. (171)이 배의 내부 구조를 대부분 보존하며, NOEM은 관람객들이 이용할 수 있도록 선내에 실내 카페, 식당, 기념품 가게 및 기타 시설들을 만들었다.

NOEM의 입장권에는 선코스트 카페의 무료 음료가 포함되어 있다. (168) (170D)**입장권의 가격을 알고 싶거나 구매를 원하면**, www.noem.com/suncoast를 방문하라.

168. 기사의 목적은 무엇인가?
(A) 운반 일정의 변경을 알리기 위한 것
(B) 새로운 쇼핑몰을 광고하기 위한 것
(C) 증기 엔진의 역사를 설명하기 위한 것
(D) 새로운 지역 명소를 홍보하기 위한 것　　　정답 (D)

169. 선코스트에 생긴 변화로 언급된 것은 무엇인가?
(A) 한 기관에 매각되었다.
(B) 새로운 증기 엔진으로 개선되었다.
(C) 박물관으로 바뀌었다.
(D) 농산물들을 운반하기 시작했다.　　　정답 (C)

170. NOEM에 대해 사실이 아닌 것은?
(A) 역사적 내용물을 전시한다.
(B) 8월 20일에 다시 개장될 것이다.
(C) 물가에 위치해 있다.
(D) 입장료를 받는다.　　　정답 (B)

171. [1], [2], [3] 그리고 [4]로 표시된 곳 중에, 아래 문장이 들어가기에 가장 적절한 곳은?
"그러나, 그것은 단지 외관만을 보기 위해서였고, 관광객들이 입장하는 것은 금지되었다."
(A) [1]
(B) [2]
(C) [3]
(D) [4]　　　정답 (B)

문제 172-175번은 다음 웹 페이지를 참조하시오.

http://www.leaderstoday.com/guides

리더스 투데이

메인 페이지	포럼	가이드	자주 묻는 질문

노트북 청소하기

(172)**당신의 노트북 컴퓨터를 효율적이고 안전하게 청소하세요.** 무엇보다 먼저, 모든 코드를 뽑고 노트북에서 배터리를 분리하는 것을 잊지 마세요. 부드러운 천, 압축 공기 한 캔, 그리고 리더스 클리너 한 병이 필요합니다.

표면부터 시작합시다. 리더스 클리너 한두 방울을 천에 떨어뜨리고 노트북의 모든 면을 닦습니다. (173) (175)물과 일반 비누의 혼합액을 사용하시는 것도 좋지만, (175)리더스 클리너는 거의 즉시 증발해 버려서 노트북 내부로 액체가 들어갈 위험성을 없애기 때문에 더 좋은 선택이 됩니다.

다음은 키보드입니다. 자판을 모두 떼어내어 물이 채워진 그릇에 넣고 씻는 것은 하나의 선택사항입니다. 그러나, 간단히 압축 공기 캔을 사용하여 자판 아래의 오염 물질들을 제거하는 것이 그만큼 효과가 있을 것입니다. 모니터를 닦는 것이 마지막 순서가 되어야 다른 부분을 청소하다 생기는 먼지

가 화면을 더럽히는 것을 막을 수 있습니다.

여기를 눌러 리더스 클리너를 주문하세요. 저희 전문가가 노트북 청소를 시연하는 짧은 동영상을 여기에서 보실 수 있습니다. (174)여기에서 기술 전문가 및 〈리더스 투데이〉에 등록된 다른 회원들과 기술 관련 문제들에 관해 얘기를 나눠 보세요.

172. 노트북을 청소하는 첫 번째 단계로 나타나 있는 것은 무엇인가?
(A) 노트북 컴퓨터의 외부 닦기
(B) 노트북 컴퓨터의 모든 부품에 대해 알아보기
(C) 노트북 컴퓨터의 전원 끄기
(D) 표면의 먼지 털어내기　　　정답 (C)

173. 웹 페이지에 따르면, 노트북을 청소할 때 강력히 추천되는 물품으로 언급되는 것은 무엇인가?
(A) 약간의 물
(B) 특별한 용액
(C) 설거지용 세제
(D) 그릇　　　정답 (B)

174. 〈리더스 투데이〉에 대해 나타나 있는 것은 무엇인가?
(A) 직원들이 고객을 위해 청소를 해준다.
(B) 온라인으로 노트북 컴퓨터를 판매한다.
(C) 고객들에게 주기적으로 노트북을 청소하도록 권장한다.
(D) 온라인 대화 공간을 제공한다.　　　정답 (D)

175. [1], [2], [3] 그리고 [4]로 표시된 곳 중에, 아래 문장이 들어가기에 가장 적절한 곳은?
"그뿐 아니라, 기름기 있는 잔여물을 제거하는 데 더 효과적입니다."
(A) [1]
(B) [2]
(C) [3]
(D) [4]　　　정답 (B)

문제 176-180번은 다음 설명서와 웹 페이지를 참조하시오.

터커 리미틀리스-2 못 박는 기계

(176)**터커는 세계에서 가장 선호하는 집 개보수 작업용 수공구와 전동 공구 제조사입니다.** 새로 개발된 저희의 못 박는 기계, 리미틀리스-2는 어떤 작업에도 안전하고 강력한 성능을 보장합니다. 새로운 특징을 확인해 보세요:

핸들: 리미틀리스-2의 핸들은 매우 얇지만 견고해서, 사용자가 못 박는 기계를 쉽게 들고 옮길 수 있습니다. (177)핸들의 혁신적인 어린이 안전 보호 기능은 저희가 자랑하는 이 새로운 공구의 특징입니다.

헤드 LED: 못 박는 기계의 끝부분에 달린 LED 등은 (177)어두운 곳에서도 정확하고 안전성 있게 작업하는 것을 가능하게 합니다.

무선: 이전 모델의 못 박는 기계들과 다르게, 리미틀리스-2는 무선 제품으로 컴프레서나 너저분한 연료 전지들로부터 당신을 자유롭게 할 것입니다. 무선이라고 해서 배터리 용량이 적다는 의미는 아닙니다. (179)저희 리튬 배터리는 한 번의 충전으로 최대 6시간 연속 사용이 가능하기 때문입니다.

작동 모드: 세 가지의 다른 작동 모드로, 이제는 아주 정확하게 작업의 속도, 강도, 그리고 시간을 조절할 수 있습니다. 그리고 (177)공구를 이용하지 않을 때 방아쇠가 작동하지 않도록 하는 안전 모드도 있습니다.

터커

메인 페이지	제품	고객 평가	회사 소개

터커 리미틀리스-2 못 박는 기계

(178)토니 맥코이 제출
날짜: 4월 11일

(178)저는 터커 사의 프라이어리티30 드릴을 3년 전에 구매했을 때부터 쭉 사용하고 있어요. 저는 이 드릴에 정말 만족하기 때문에 새로 이사 온 집의 개조 작업을 하며 못 박는 기계가 하나 필요했을 때 구매하는 것을 망설이지 않았습니다. 이 못 박는 기계는 한 번에 120개까지 못을 넣을 수가 있어서 제가 수시로 멈출 필요 없이 계속 작업할 수 있어 매우 편리합니다. (179)그리고 이 기계가 거의 온종일 작동한다는 사실이 마음에 듭니다. 이렇게 가볍고 작은 배터리가 그렇게 긴 시간 지속된다는 것이 믿기 어려울 정도입니다. 만약 리미틀리스-2를 구매하신다면, 저만큼이나 만족할 것이라고 (180)장담합니다.

176. 설명서는 어디에서 볼 수 있을 것 같은가?
  (A) 군사 훈련 안내서
  (B) 인테리어 디자이너를 위한 잡지
  (C) 건설 회사의 사보
  (D) 주택 개조 제품의 소개 책자   정답 (D)

177. 터커 사에 대해 나타나 있는 것은 무엇인가?
  (A) 꽤 신생 업체이다.
  (B) 못 박는 기계를 두 번째로 출시했다.
  (C) 고객의 안전을 중요하게 여긴다.
  (D) 전 세계적으로 지점을 갖고 있다.   정답 (C)

178. 맥코이 씨에 대해 시사된 것은 무엇인가?
  (A) 건설 회사에서 일한다.
  (B) 주택 개조 목적으로 드릴을 하나 더 살 것이다.
  (C) 새로운 곳으로 이사할 계획이다.
  (D) 전에 터커 사와 거래를 한 적이 있다.   정답 (D)

179. 설명서에 언급된 특징 중 맥코이 씨가 특히 만족하는 것은 무엇인가?
  (A) 얇은 손잡이
  (B) 리튬 배터리
  (C) 못 저장량
  (D) 일 년 품질 보증서   정답 (B)

180. 웹 페이지의 첫 번째 단락 7행에 있는 단어 "assure"와 의미상 가장 가까운 것은?
  (A) 납득시키다
  (B) 약속하다
  (C) 추천하다
  (D) 가능하게 하다   정답 (B)

문제 181-185번은 다음 이메일과 양식을 참조하시오.

수신: 고객 서비스 〈customerservice@howardelectronics.com〉
발신: 조나단 웰시 〈jwelsh@srmail.com〉
날짜: 8월 9일
제목: 최근의 주문
첨부: 냉장고

담당자 분께,

(182) (184)저는 8월 3일에 하워드 전자에서 냉장고(모델 번호 DO4018)와 전자레인지(AQ501)를 구매했습니다. 전자레인지는 당일 제가 집에 가져왔고, 냉장고는 다음 날 집에 배송됐습니다.

(181) (182)귀사 직원이 설치 작업을 마치고 돌아간 후에, 냉장고의 문 손잡이가 망가져 있는 것을 알아챘습니다. (184)즉시 하워드 전자의 웹사이트를 방문해서 클레임을 제기했습니다(클레임 번호 IE46109). 다른 팀 직원이 8월 7일에 다른 냉장고를 가져와서 설치할 것이라고 안내 받았습니다. 하지만 지금까지 어떠한 응답도 방문도 받지 못했습니다. (185)이전에 그랬듯이, 냉장고와 부러진 부분의 사진들을 참조하실 수 있게 첨부해 보냅니다. 가능한 한 빨리 이 문제에 대해 알아봐 주세요.

조나단 웰시 드림

해결된 클레임 보고서
하워드 전자 고객 서비스부

클레임 해결일: 8월 29일
담당자: 수잔 피어시
(185)수신자: 에릭 가드너

클레임 번호	설명	해결책
PQ23017	노트북 컴퓨터(TE239)의 배송이 일주일간 지연됨	28달러짜리 마우스가 제품과 함께 발송됨.
CM31921	(183)결함 있는 프린터(OJ3387)가 고객에게 판매됨	고객의 신용 카드로 49달러가 전액 환불 처리됨.
BA81274	냉장고(DL9387)를 잘못 설치해서 제대로 작동하지 않음	냉장고의 내용물에 대해 65달러의 수표가 발행됨. 직원이 문제 해결을 위해 다시 방문할 예정.
(184)IE46109	냉장고(DO4018)가 운반과 설치 도중 파손됨	무료 배송품으로 교체되고 30달러 쿠폰이 제공될 것임.

(185) • 고객으로부터 받은 모든 클레임 양식과 증빙 서류들은 담당 관리자에게 제출할 때 꼭 이 보고서와 함께 제출해야 한다.

181. 하워드 전자에 대해 나타나 있는 것은 무엇인가?
  (A) 온라인 설문조사를 시행한다.
  (B) 현장 설치 서비스를 제공한다.
  (C) 무료로 운반 배송을 한다.
  (D) 웰시 씨의 냉장고를 수리할 것이다.   정답 (B)

182. 웰시 씨의 집에 냉장고가 설치된 때는 언제인가?
  (A) 8월 3일
  (B) 8월 4일
  (C) 8월 7일
  (D) 8월 9일   정답 (B)

183. 양식에 따르면, 하워드 전자는 OJ3387 제품에 대해 원래 얼마를 받았는가?
  (A) 28달러
  (B) 30달러
  (C) 49달러
  (D) 65달러   정답 (C)

184. 하워드 전자로부터 웰시 씨가 받은 것은 무엇인가?
  (A) 무료 가전제품
  (B) 상품권
  (C) 수표

(D) 환불　　　　　　　　　　　　정답 (B)

185. 가드너 씨에게 보고서와 함께 무엇이 발송되었을 것 같은가?
(A) 영수증 원본
(B) 매장의 반품 규칙에 대한 문서
(C) 신용 카드 정보
(D) 전자 제품의 사진　　　　　　정답 (D)

문제 186-190번은 다음 편지와 이메일 그리고 지도를 참조하시오.

8월 7일

재스민 캐스터
크리에이터스 주식회사
2255 플레밍 웨이
리치빌, 오하이오 주 5045

캐스터 씨에게,

(189B)8월 5일 Jobseekers.com에 게시된 크리에이터스 주식회사의 건설 코디네이터 자리에 지원하고자 편지를 보냅니다. (188)저는 뉴포트에 있는 에펜 대학에서 건축학 학위를 받고 졸업했습니다. 졸업 후에는, 2년 동안 체리 힐에 있는 작은 건설 회사, 팔로타스에서 일했고, (186)6년 전부터 저의 현 직장인 뉴 빌더스에서 부 현장 엔지니어로 일하기 시작했습니다. 제 학력과 경력사항에 대해 더 자세한 정보가 적힌 이력서를 첨부하였으니 읽어 주십시오. 곧 연락 받기를 기다리겠습니다.

마리오 베번 드림

동봉물 재중

수신: 마리오 베번 〈jbevan@promail.com〉
발신: 재스민 캐스터 〈m.castor@creatorsinc.com〉
날짜: 8월 11일
제목: 면접
첨부: 지도

베번 씨에게,

저희 크리에이터스 주식회사에서의 근무에 관심을 가져 주셔서 감사드립니다. (187) (189C)전화로 얘기한 대로, 귀하가 지원하신 버스턴 사무소의 자리는 이미 충원되었습니다. (188)대신, 귀하가 졸업한 대학이 소재한 도시에 있는 저희 지점의 자리에 대해 면접을 보시게 될 것입니다. 이 전례 없는 결정은 귀하의 뛰어난 전문 지식과 경력 그리고 학력에 따른 것입니다.

(189A) (189C)면접은 리치빌에 있는 저희 본사에서 진행될 예정입니다. 참고하실 수 있도록 그 지역의 지도를 첨부했습니다. (189A) (190)커니 역의 6번 출구로 나와서, 유진 로드를 건너고, 여행사를 지나쳐서 르윈 거리와 메인 애비뉴의 모퉁이에 있는 대형 약국이 보이면 좌회전하세요. 그 다음, 커피숍 옆에 있는 우리 회사 건물이 보일 때까지 몇 분 정도 걸으세요. 면접에 행운이 따르기를 바랍니다.

재스민 캐스터 드림

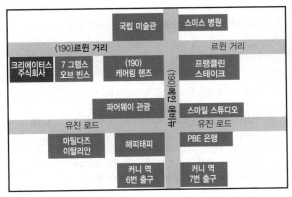

186. 베번 씨에 대해 언급된 것은 무엇인가?
(A) 사업체를 소유했던 적이 있었다.
(B) 몇몇 웹사이트를 운영했었다.
(C) 현재 뉴 빌더스에서 일한다.
(D) 건축학 석사 학위를 갖고 있다.　　정답 (C)

187. 이메일의 목적은 무엇인가?
(A) 한 대화에 대한 후속 조치를 취하기 위한 것
(B) 정보를 요청하기 위한 것
(C) 도로공사에 대한 정보를 주기 위한 것
(D) 고용을 확정하기 위한 것　　　　정답 (A)

188. 베번 씨는 어디서 일할 것 같은가?
(A) 리치빌
(B) 뉴포트
(C) 체리 힐
(D) 버스턴　　　　　　　　　　정답 (B)

189. 크리에이터스 주식회사에 대해 시사되지 않은 것은 무엇인가?
(A) 본사가 대중교통 센터 근처에 있다.
(B) 인터넷에 구인광고를 올렸다.
(C) 지점이 한 군데 이상 있다.
(D) 적어도 6년 동안 운영되고 있다.　정답 (D)

190. 케어링 핸즈는 어떤 종류의 사업체일 것 같은가?
(A) 커피숍
(B) 여행사
(C) 어린이 집
(D) 약국　　　　　　　　　　　정답 (D)

문제 191-195번은 다음 기사와 공지 그리고 쪽지를 참조하시오.

머레이 (7월 10일) – 로즈마운트 아파트 단지의 건축이 이제 완료되어, 주민이 물밀듯이 입주하고 있다. 이 새로운 개발은 지역에 (191)생기를 불어넣고 주변 상가의 매출도 신장시키고 있다.

(192)아파트 단지 앞에 있는 라미어 빌딩의 가게들은 매우 큰 이득을 보고 있다. 그중 하나가 2층의 머피 피자이다. 피자 가게의 주인, 힐러리 뎀보브스키는 "수익이 200% 증가했다"고 말한다.

로사 치스홀름은 바로 어제 라미어 빌딩에 문을 연 새 제과점, 드림 베이커스의 주인이다. 치스홀름 씨는 새 가게에서 높은 수익을 기대하고 있다. "모든 것이 잘 풀리고 있는 듯합니다"라고 말했다.

(192) (194)프레시니스 익스플로전의 직원 여러분에게 알려 드립니다

(192)로즈마운트 아파트 단지의 건설 덕에, 고객의 수가 급격히 늘고 있습니다. 모든 고객을 만족시키고, 고객의 재차 반복되는 요청을 처리하기 위해, 우리는 다음 주 중에 시설을 개선하겠습니다.

- (192)상점 안에 화장실이 설치될 것인데, 이로써 머피 피자 및 드림 베이커스와 화장실을 공유해야 할 필요가 없어질 것입니다.
- (193A)창문은 에너지 효율을 높이기 위해, 더 두꺼운 것으로 교체될 것입니다.
- (193C)주차장 바닥이 새로 포장될 것입니다.
- (193D)가게가 확장될 것이고 더 많은 계산대가 설치되어, 고객들이 더는 오랫동안 줄을 서서 기다릴 필요가 없을 것입니다.

여러분의 협조와 헌신에 감사드립니다.

8월 11일 게시

(194)프레시니스 익스플로전의 점주, 잭 로저스에게 하실 말씀이 있으신가요? 아래에 고객님의 의견이나 제안사항을 써서 계산대 가까이에 있는 게시판에 이 쪽지를 붙여 주세요.

저는 대략 3년 동안 프레시니스 익스플로전을 이용하고 있습니다. (195)제 헬스장의 회원님들은 프레시니스 익스플로전에서 매일 받는 재료로 만든 헬스장 내 카페의 신선한 토마토 주스와 당근 케이크를 특히 좋아합니다. 저는 귀사의 직원, 미셸 머독 씨에게 감사를 표하기 위해 이 쪽지를 씁니다. 그녀는 매일 아침 7시에 과일과 야채를 카페에 배달합니다. 그녀는 한 번도 늦은 적이 없는데, 그것은 그녀의 직업 정신을 보여 주는 것이고, 카페가 아무 문제 없이 운영되도록 보장해 줍니다. 정말 그녀의 근면함은 보상 받을 만합니다.

허버트 워렌

191. 기사에서 첫 번째 단락 4행에 있는 단어 "animating"과 의미상 가장 가까운 것은?
(A) 활기를 북돋우는
(B) 촬영하는
(C) 환대하는
(D) 확장하는
정답 (A)

192. 프레시니스 익스플로전에 대해 나타나 있는 것은 무엇인가?
(A) 직원이 많다.
(B) 영업 시간을 연장하기로 결정했다.
(C) 주인이 피자 가게도 운영한다.
(D) 라미어 빌딩에 있다.
정답 (D)

193. 프레시니스 익스플로전에서 수리되지 않은 것은 무엇인가?
(A) 창문
(B) 대기실
(C) 주차장
(D) 실내
정답 (B)

194. 누가 공지를 올린 것 같은가?
(A) 로저스 씨
(B) 워렌 씨
(C) 뎀보브스키 씨
(D) 머독 씨
정답 (A)

195. 프레시니스 익스플로전은 어떤 종류의 업소일 것 같은가?
(A) 식료품점

(B) 카페
(C) 헬스장
(D) 제과점
정답 (A)

문제 196-200번은 다음 이메일들과 주문서를 참조하시오.

수신: 리처드 피셔 〈rfisher@myraaccounting.com〉
발신: 태미 해럴 〈tharrell@myraacounting.com〉
날짜: 9월 12일
제목: 재고 목록

안녕하세요, 리처드,

(197)두 달에 한 번씩 있는 재고 조사 시간이 다시 왔네요. (196) (200)당신이 재고 목록을 작성해서 (197) (199)우리의 계약된 사무용품 공급업체인 SBF 공급회사에 주문을 보내기 전에, (200)우리 회사 로고가 새겨진 바인더 50개를 주문에 추가해 줄 바라요. 제가 직원들에게 자료들을 더 잘 정리할 수 있도록 바인더들을 나누어 줄 예정이에요. 그리고, (198)SBF 공급회사의 한 직원이 오늘 오전에 제게 연락했는데, 그 회사가 3주 정도 일시적으로 서비스를 중단하기 때문에 우리가 토요일 이전에 주문을 마무리 지어야 한다고 했어요. (198)(201) 581-9020으로 전화해서 그 직원과 자세한 내용에 대해 얘기하세요. 감사하고요, 앞으로도 수고해 주세요.

태미 해럴 드림

수신: 태미 해럴 〈tharrell@myraaccounting.com〉
발신: 리처드 피셔 〈rfisher@myraaccounting.com〉
날짜: 9월 14일
제목: 답장: 재고 목록
첨부: SBF 공급회사 주문서

해럴 씨에게,

저는 재고 파악을 끝내고 당신이 언급한 물건들이 포함된 기본 주문을 넣었어요. 제가 첨부한 공급 회사에 보낸 주문서를 확인해 주세요. (198)그리고 당신이 말한 대로 폴 가르시아 씨에게 연락해서 다음 주까지 확실히 우리 물품을 받을 수 있도록 했어요. 하지만 3일 후에 지금 사용 중인 창고가 수리에 들어가기 때문에, 모든 사무용품들을 보관할 장소가 시급히 필요합니다. 이 건에 대해 당신의 답변을 기다릴게요.

리처드 피셔 드림

SBF 공급회사 주문서

주문 정보:

주문일:	9월 14일	고객명:	미라 회계
연락 담당자:	리처드 피셔	전화번호:	(201) 555-6028

주문 내역:

제품 번호	품목	(199)제조사	수량
B9481	인쇄용 종이	랫클리프	70상자
P0349	봉투 (회사명/로고 인쇄)	테이트	30상자
Y4251	화이트보드 펜/지우개 세트	트윈 옥스	15세트
(200) B2918	바인더 (회사명/로고 인쇄)	벙갈로	50개
C5516	종이 클립	폴리오	50상자

196. 첫 번째 이메일의 목적은 무엇인가?
(A) 물품 주문을 확인하기 위한 것
(B) 지시를 내리기 위한 것
(C) 계약을 제안하기 위한 것
(D) 회의를 요청하기 위한 것　　　　　　　　정답 (B)

197. 미라 회계에 대해 시사된 것은 무엇인가?
(A) SBF 공급회사에서 할인을 받는다.
(B) 몇 주 동안 일시적으로 문을 닫는다.
(C) 정기적으로 SBF 공급회사와 거래를 한다.
(D) 로고를 디자인하기 위해 다른 회사를 고용했다.　　정답 (C)

198. 폴 가르시아 씨는 누구일 것 같은가?
(A) 해럴 씨의 동료
(B) SBF 공급회사의 직원
(C) 배달원
(D) 미라 회계의 창고 직원　　　　　　　　정답 (B)

199. SBF 공급회사에 대해 나타나 있는 것은 무엇인가?
(A) 다른 회사에서 만든 제품들을 판매한다.
(B) 시설을 수리할 계획이다.
(C) 9월 14일에 물품들을 배송했다.
(D) 매출이 급격히 줄어들고 있다.　　　　　정답 (A)

200. 주문서에 새롭게 추가된 제품은 어느 것인가?
(A) B2918
(B) B9481
(C) C5516
(D) P0349　　　　　　　　　　　　정답 (A)

Actual Test 08
Part 1

1. 미M
(A) A woman is drying her hair with a towel.
(B) A woman is drinking from a bottle.
(C) A woman is folding a yoga mat.
(D) A woman is mopping the floor.

(A) 여자가 타월로 머리를 말리고 있다.
(B) 여자가 병에 있는 것을 마시고 있다.
(C) 여자가 요가 매트를 접고 있다.
(D) 여자가 바닥을 대걸레로 닦고 있다.　　정답 (B)

2. 영M
(A) He is installing a board on the wall.
(B) He is pointing at notices.
(C) He is giving a presentation.
(D) He is writing on the notice board.

(A) 그는 벽에 게시판을 설치하고 있다.
(B) 그는 게시물들을 손으로 가리키고 있다.
(C) 그는 발표를 하고 있다.
(D) 그는 게시판에 뭔가 적고 있다.　　정답 (B)

3. 미W
(A) The woman is putting a picture into a frame.
(B) Some tools are resting on a shelf.
(C) All of the pictures have been hung on a wall.
(D) The woman is hammering a nail into a wall.

(A) 여자가 사진을 액자 속에 넣고 있다.
(B) 연장 몇 개가 선반에 놓여 있다.
(C) 모든 사진이 벽에 걸려 있다.
(D) 여자가 벽에 망치로 못을 치고 있다.　　정답 (D)

4. 미M
(A) He is trimming branches off a tree.
(B) He is directing traffic at the intersection.
(C) He is parking a truck on the street.
(D) He is spraying a sidewalk with water.

(A) 그는 나뭇가지를 자르고 있다.
(B) 그는 교차로에서 교통 정리를 하고 있다.
(C) 그는 거리에 트럭을 주차하고 있다.
(D) 그는 인도에 물을 뿌리고 있다.　　정답 (D)

5. 호W
(A) He is carrying a tool box into the warehouse.
(B) He is kneeling down to look at an item.
(C) A power tool is being assembled in a shop.
(D) Some items are stacked in the aisle.

(A) 그는 연장함을 창고로 옮기고 있다.
(B) 그는 무릎을 꿇고 물건을 보고 있다.
(C) 전동 공구가 가게에서 조립되고 있다.
(D) 몇 개의 물건이 통로에 쌓여 있다.　　정답 (B)

6. 미M
(A) Some appliances are placed on a counter.
(B) Some cabinets are being installed in a kitchen.
(C) Some utensils are being used.

(D) Some plates are piled up in a sink.

(A) 가전제품 몇 개가 카운터 위에 놓여 있다.
(B) 수납장 몇 개가 부엌에 설치되고 있다.
(C) 주방기구들이 사용되고 있다.
(D) 접시 몇 개가 개수대에 쌓여 있다. 정답 (A)

Part 2

7. 미M 호W

Why was tonight's welcome reception postponed?
(A) Yes. It'll be ready shortly.
(B) I'll be right back with your bill.
(C) Because our client's train arrived late.

오늘 저녁의 환영회가 왜 연기되었어요?
(A) 예. 그것은 곧 준비될 것입니다.
(B) 계산서 가지고 바로 돌아오겠습니다.
(C) 우리 고객의 기차가 늦게 도착했기 때문이에요. 정답 (C)

8. 영M 미W

Were you able to reserve the booth for the fair we used last year?
(A) No, the ones in the center were all booked.
(B) They are expecting more than 100 people.
(C) Thanks for supporting the event.

작년에 우리가 사용했던 박람회 부스를 예약할 수 있었어요?
(A) 아뇨, 중앙에 있는 부스들은 다 예약이 차 있었어요.
(B) 그들은 100명 이상을 예상하고 있어요.
(C) 행사를 지원해 주셔서 감사합니다. 정답 (A)

9. 미M 호W

When does the customer service staff usually arrive?
(A) At 8:30.
(B) Whichever is faster.
(C) The service is reasonably priced.

고객 서비스 담당 직원은 보통 몇 시에 도착해요?
(A) 8시 30분에요.
(B) 어느 것이든 더 빠른 것으로요.
(C) 그 서비스는 적정 가격이에요. 정답 (A)

10. 미W 미M

How did you learn about that high-end household appliance?
(A) I didn't think so, either.
(B) From a television commercial.
(C) I went there on foot.

그 최고급 가전제품에 대해서 어떻게 알게 되었어요?
(A) 저 역시 그렇게 생각하지 않았어요.
(B) 텔레비전 광고에서요.
(C) 저는 거기에 걸어서 갔습니다. 정답 (B)

11. 미W 영M

Our new sales representatives have been doing a great job.
(A) I can't agree with you more.
(B) Sales are up this month.
(C) Thanks. It was not that difficult.

새로 온 우리 영업 직원들이 정말 일을 잘하고 있어요.
(A) 정말 동감이에요.

(B) 이번 달에 매출이 올랐어요.
(C) 고마워요. 그건 그렇게 어렵지 않았어요. 정답 (A)

12. 미M 호W

Why didn't you like the presentation led by Peter?
(A) I read the article, too.
(B) Yes, in the conference room.
(C) It lasted too long.

피터가 진행한 프레젠테이션이 왜 마음에 들지 않으셨어요?
(A) 저도 그 기사를 읽었어요.
(B) 예, 회의실에서요.
(C) 너무 오래 갔어요. 정답 (C)

13. 영M 미W

Could you turn in the receipts from your business trip?
(A) Yes, turn right at the second block.
(B) A direct flight, if it's available.
(C) Absolutely, I'll send them to you this afternoon.

당신의 출장 영수증들을 제출해 주시겠어요?
(A) 예, 두 번째 블록에서 우회전하세요.
(B) 가능하다면 직항편으로요.
(C) 물론이죠, 오늘 오후에 보내 드릴게요. 정답 (C)

14. 미M 호W

Where do we keep reimbursement forms?
(A) Some of the receipts are missing.
(B) Purchase some conference tables, too.
(C) I have an extra printout.

우리 환급 요청서를 어디에 보관해요?
(A) 영수증 몇 장이 없어요.
(B) 회의 테이블도 좀 구매하세요.
(C) 저한테 여분으로 출력해둔 게 있어요. 정답 (C)

15. 미W 영M

When was that accounting firm established?
(A) I started working there yesterday.
(B) I opened a corporate account.
(C) On the corner of Pine Street.

그 회계 회사는 언제 설립되었어요?
(A) 저는 거기에 어제 근무하기 시작했어요.
(B) 저는 법인 계좌를 개설했어요.
(C) 파인 가 모퉁이에요. 정답 (A)

16. 호W 미M

Which dishes are highly recommended at this restaurant?
(A) The chef changed the menu recently.
(B) On Jefferson Boulevard.
(C) How about a lunch break now?

이 식당에서는 어떤 요리를 제일 많이 추천하나요?
(A) 주방장이 최근에 메뉴를 바꿨어요.
(B) 제퍼슨 대로에요.
(C) 지금 점심 시간을 가지는 게 어때요? 정답 (A)

17. 미W 영M

Why can't I access the research study folder anymore?
(A) The road is not accessible.
(B) It's hotter than usual inside.

(C) We were sent an e-mail about that.

저는 왜 더 이상 연구 폴더에 접근이 안 되는 거죠?
(A) 그 도로는 통행이 안 됩니다.
(B) 평소보다 안이 더 덥네요.
(C) 그 건에 대해 우리는 이메일을 받았잖아요. **정답 (C)**

18. [호W] [미M]
Should the company dinner be on a Thursday or a Friday?
(A) I'm not sure what role he played.
(B) Fridays are always best.
(C) We hired two different caterers.

회식을 목요일에 할까요, 아니면 금요일에 할까요?
(A) 그가 어떤 역할을 맡았는지 저는 잘 몰라요.
(B) 금요일이 항상 제일 좋죠.
(C) 우리는 각기 다른 두 개의 출장 요리 업체를 고용했어요. **정답 (B)**

19. [미W] [영M]
We should move the copier closer to the entrance, shouldn't we?
(A) Yes, that sounds like a good idea.
(B) One of the energy efficient machines.
(C) There aren't any in the drawer.

우리는 복사기를 입구 가까이로 옮겨야 해요, 그렇지 않아요?
(A) 예, 그거 좋은 생각 같아요.
(B) 에너지 효율이 좋은 기계 중 하나예요.
(C) 서랍에 하나도 없어요. **정답 (A)**

20. [미M] [영M]
Have you applied for the position in the IT company yet?
(A) The deadline isn't until next Monday.
(B) Yes, find it in the employee orientation packet.
(C) Yes, it is a state-of-the-art technology.

IT 회사의 자리에 지원했어요?
(A) 마감시한이 다음 주 월요일까지예요.
(B) 예, 직원 오리엔테이션 서류 속에서 찾아보세요.
(C) 예, 그건 최첨단 기술이에요. **정답 (A)**

21. [미W] [영M]
What's the cover story for next month's newsletter issue?
(A) No. Jane is having an issue with her laptop.
(B) They'll cover the cost this month.
(C) The editors are having a meeting this afternoon to decide.

다음 달 소식지의 커버 스토리는 뭐예요?
(A) 아뇨, 제인은 노트북에 문제가 있어요.
(B) 그들이 이번 달 비용을 부담해줄 거예요.
(C) 편집자들이 오늘 오후에 회의를 열어 결정할 거예요. **정답 (C)**

22. [미M] [미W]
Will you tell me what the complimentary breakfast at the hotel was like?
(A) I had an early morning meeting with some clients.
(B) I'd like to stay at a nearby hotel.
(C) Your meal will be served in a minute.

호텔의 무료 조식은 어땠는지 얘기해 주실래요?
(A) 저는 고객들과 이른 아침 회의가 있었어요.
(B) 저는 근처 호텔에 묵고 싶어요.
(C) 손님 식사는 잠시 후에 나올 거예요. **정답 (A)**

23. [미W] [영M]
You are going to attend tomorrow's safety workshop, aren't you?
(A) On an attendance sheet here.
(B) Do you think that's mandatory?
(C) It doesn't depart until 11.

내일 안전 워크숍에 참석하실 거죠, 그렇지 않아요?
(A) 여기 출석부예요.
(B) 그게 의무적인 것 같으세요?
(C) 그것은 11시가 되어야 출발해요. **정답 (B)**

24. [호W] [미M]
Where can I sign up for the company baseball team?
(A) I picked the tickets up for you.
(B) On the sheet in the staff breakroom.
(C) He left for the stadium.

회사 야구팀은 어디서 가입할 수 있나요?
(A) 당신을 위해서 제가 티켓을 샀어요.
(B) 직원 휴게실에 있는 종이에요.
(C) 그는 경기장으로 떠났어요. **정답 (B)**

25. [미W] [영M]
Who's leading today's focus group discussion?
(A) Janice grouped the blouses by price.
(B) I just saw Mario with them.
(C) About an hour ago.

오늘 소비자 제품평가단 토론회는 누가 진행해요?
(A) 제니스가 블라우스를 가격별로 분류했어요.
(B) 방금 마리오가 그들과 있는 것을 봤어요.
(C) 약 한 시간 전에요. **정답 (B)**

26. [미M] [호W]
Excuse me, do you have these sandals in a larger size in stock?
(A) Sorry, we're sold out.
(B) I have the receipt with me.
(C) Yes, we are open for business tomorrow.

실례지만, 이 샌들이 좀 더 큰 사이즈로 재고가 있나요?
(A) 죄송하지만, 다 팔렸어요.
(B) 영수증을 지금 가지고 있어요.
(C) 예, 내일 저희는 영업합니다. **정답 (A)**

27. [미W] [영M]
Isn't tomorrow's workshop about multi-tasking skills?
(A) No, that one is rescheduled for this Friday.
(B) Sure, I'll be available to do that.
(C) He came in for an interview.

내일 워크숍은 다중 작업 처리 능력에 관한 게 아닌가요?
(A) 네, 그건 이번 주 금요일로 일정이 변경되었어요.
(B) 물론이죠, 제가 그거 할 시간은 있을 거예요.
(C) 그는 면접 보러 왔어요. **정답 (A)**

28. [미M] [호W]
Can you show me how to operate the rotary saw?
(A) The technician didn't come.
(B) The user's guide is in the box.
(C) The first show starts at 10.

회전 톱을 어떻게 작동하는지 좀 가르쳐 주실래요?
(A) 기술자가 오지 않았어요.
(B) 사용자 설명서가 상자 안에 있어요.
(C) 첫 상영이 10시에 시작해요.　　　　　정답 (B)

29. 미W 영M

How can we find new interns for the marketing department?
(A) The marketing expert reviewed it.
(B) I'll check the supply room for more pens.
(C) Why don't we post some announcements on campus?

마케팅부에서 일할 새 인턴을 어떻게 찾을 수 있을까요?
(A) 마케팅 전문가가 그것을 검토했어요.
(B) 펜이 더 있는지 비품실을 확인해 볼게요.
(C) 캠퍼스에 공지를 하는 게 어때요?　　　　　정답 (C)

30. 미W 미M

Would you like your connecting flight to go through Philadelphia or New York?
(A) I am going through the manual now.
(B) I'd like the shortest possible layover.
(C) None of the seats are available.

연결편은 필라델피아를 통해서 가고 싶으세요, 아니면 뉴욕을 통해서 가고 싶으세요?
(A) 지금 사용 설명서를 검토하고 있어요.
(B) 가능하면 가장 짧은 경유지로 하고 싶어요.
(C) 좌석이 하나도 남아 있지 않아요.　　　　　정답 (B)

31. 미W 영M

I can't find any folders in the storage room.
(A) Fold the newspaper in half.
(B) Check with Simon.
(C) Try another store.

보관실에는 폴더가 하나도 없네요.
(A) 신문을 반으로 접으세요.
(B) 사이먼에게 확인해 보세요.
(C) 다른 가게에 가보세요.　　　　　정답 (B)

Part 3

문제 32-34번은 다음 대화를 참조하시오. 호W 미M

W: Hello. This is Jasmine Clothing. How may I help you?
M: Hi. I want to order 300 T-shirts with my store's logo. (32) **We're having a special event for our fifth anniversary next week.** I need the shirts by next Thursday.
W: Oh, that's very fast. (33)**If I make this an express order, we can meet the deadline.** But that will cost more, and you'll need to e-mail the logo to us.
M: That's fine with me. (34)**What color shirts do you have available? I want a variety of options so that customers can make a choice.**

W: 안녕하세요. 여기는 재스민 의류인데요. 무엇을 도와드릴까요?
M: 안녕하세요. 저희 가게 로고가 박힌 티셔츠 300벌을 주문하고 싶어요. 다음 주에 창립 5주년을 위해서 특별 행사를 열 거예요. 다음 주 목요일까지 셔츠가 필요해요.
W: 오, 그건 너무 빠른데요. 이걸 급행 주문으로 하면, 마감시간을 맞출 수

있긴 해요. 그런데 그게 비용이 좀 더 들 거예요. 그리고 로고를 이메일로 저희에게 보내 주셔야 해요.
M: 좋아요. 티셔츠 색깔은 어떤 게 가능한가요? 고객들이 선택할 수 있도록 다양한 옵션을 원해요.

32. 남자는 무엇을 준비하고 있는가?
(A) 기념일 행사
(B) 개업
(C) 휴일 경품추첨
(D) 자선 기금 모금 행사　　　　　정답 (A)

33. 여자는 무엇을 할 수 있다고 말하는가?
(A) 할인 제공
(B) 무료 배송 제공
(C) 서둘러 주문 처리
(D) 행사에 음식 조달　　　　　정답 (C)

34. 남자는 무엇에 대해 물어보는가?
(A) 가게의 영업 시간
(B) 색깔 옵션
(C) 결제 옵션
(D) 교환 정책　　　　　정답 (B)

문제 35-37번은 다음 대화를 참조하시오. 영M 미W

M: Sylvia, do you have a moment?
W: Sure. What's going on?
M: (35)**You know that Becky is retiring next week, right?** She's been here for more than three decades. I think we should do something special for her. You've worked with her a lot. Do you have any idea what she would like?
W: Well, how about having a picnic at Lakeside Park?
M: That sounds good. (36)**But we'll need to rent the picnic area there. Our funds are a bit limited.**
W: Actually, there's no charge, and you don't even need a reservation. There's lots of room for people there.
M: Wonderful. (37)**I'll send out the invitations then.**

M: 실비아, 잠시 시간 돼요?
W: 물론이죠. 무슨 일이 있어요?
M: 다음 주에 베키가 은퇴하는 거 아시죠, 그렇죠? 30년 이상 여기서 근무하셨잖아요. 그녀를 위해서 우리가 특별한 뭔가를 해야 할 것 같아요. 베키와 많이 같이 일하셨잖아요. 그녀가 뭘 좋아할지 아세요?
W: 음, 레이크사이드 공원에서 피크닉을 하는 것은 어때요?
M: 그거 괜찮네요. 그런데 거기 피크닉 공간을 임대해야 할 거예요. 우리 기금이 약간 제한적이에요.
W: 사실, 비용이 안 들고, 심지어 예약할 필요도 없어요. 그곳에는 사람들을 위한 공간이 아주 많아요.
M: 잘됐네요. 그렇다면 내가 초대장을 보낼게요.

35. 다음 주에 무슨 일이 있겠는가?
(A) 동료가 은퇴할 것이다.
(B) 계약서에 서명할 것이다.
(C) 동료가 출장을 갈 것이다.
(D) 제품이 출시될 것이다.　　　　　정답 (A)

36. 남자는 무엇에 대해 우려하는가?
(A) 장소에 대한 임대 사용료

(B) 참석자 수
(C) 프로젝트에 대한 마감시한
(D) 장소의 크기   정답 (A)

37. 남자는 이후에 무엇을 할 것인가?
(A) 출장 요리 업체에 연락
(B) 피크닉 공간 예약
(C) 초대장 발송
(D) 여행 일정표 검토   정답 (C)

문제 38-40번은 다음 3자 대화를 참조하시오. 미W 미M 호W

W1: (38)Welcome to Dan's Automotive. How may I help you today?
M: (38)I'd like to get a pickup truck for my catering business.
W1: Sure. We have a customer representative who specializes in trucks. Lisa, this customer would like a pickup truck for his company.
W2: Sounds good. (39)What particular features are you looking for?
M: (39)I need a vehicle big enough to carry lots of items. I transport large crates and big coolers at times.
W2: Okay, I can show you a few models that would be perfect for you. (40)Do you have your driver's license with you? I can let you test-drive them if you have it with you.

W1: 댄스 오토모티브에 오신 것을 환영합니다. 오늘 무엇을 도와드릴까요?
M: 제 출장 요리 사업 때문에 픽업 트럭을 사고 싶어요.
W1: 알겠습니다. 트럭을 전문으로 담당하는 고객 담당 직원이 있어요. 리사, 이 손님이 자신의 회사를 위해서 픽업 트럭을 원하세요.
W2: 좋습니다. 특히 어떤 기능이 있는 것을 찾으세요?
M: 많은 물건들을 싣고 다닐 만큼 충분히 큰 차량이 필요해요. 때로는 대형 상자와 큰 아이스박스를 수송해요.
W2: 알겠습니다. 손님에게 안성맞춤인 모델 몇 개를 보여 드릴게요. 운전 면허증을 지금 갖고 계세요? 운전 면허증이 있다면 트럭들을 시운전하게 해드릴 수 있거든요.

38. 화자들은 어디에 있는 것 같은가?
(A) 공사 현장
(B) 자동차 대리점
(C) 렌터카 회사
(D) 식당   정답 (B)

39. 남자는 어떤 특징이 중요하다고 말하는가?
(A) 가격
(B) 크기
(C) 연료 효율성
(D) 내구성   정답 (B)

40. 여자는 남자에게 무엇을 제시할 것을 요청하는가?
(A) 여행 일정표
(B) 신용 카드 정보
(C) 티켓 조각
(D) 운전 면허증   정답 (D)

문제 41-43번은 다음 대화를 참조하시오. 미W 미M

W: Hello. Is this Steve?
M: Yes, this is Steve.
W: Hello. (41)It's Rose Desmond from the city orchestra.
M: Thank you for calling, Ms. Desmond. I've been waiting to hear from you.
W: (41)The hiring committee and I listened to the recordings you sent us. We really liked the performance you gave at Jamestown.
M: I'm happy to hear that.
W: You also did well at the interview. (42)So we'd like to offer you a position with us.
M: Thank you very much. However, I should let you know one thing. (43)I noticed that rehearsals for this coming season start in mid-May, but I'm going to be out of town until June 1. Is that a problem?

W: 안녕하세요, 스티브인가요?
M: 예, 스티브입니다.
W: 안녕하세요. 시립 오케스트라의 로즈 데스몬드입니다.
M: 전화 주셔서 감사해요, 데스몬드 씨. 연락 오기를 기다리고 있었어요.
W: 고용 위원회와 저는 당신이 저희에게 보내준 녹음을 들어봤어요. 제임스타운에서 당신이 한 공연은 정말 마음에 들었어요.
M: 그 말을 들으니 좋네요.
W: 면접에서도 잘 하셨어요. 그래서 우리 오케스트라의 자리를 제안하고 싶어요.
M: 대단히 감사합니다. 그런데, 알려 드려야 할 게 한 가지가 있는데요. 보니까 이번 돌아오는 시즌에 대한 리허설이 5월 중순에 시작하는데, 저는 6월 1일까지는 외지에 나가 있어서 여기 없습니다. 그게 문제가 될까요?

41. 남자의 직업은 무엇일 것 같은가?
(A) 작곡가
(B) 행사 기획자
(C) 음악가
(D) 배우   정답 (C)

42. 여자가 전화를 거는 이유는?
(A) 면접 일정을 잡기 위해
(B) 남자에게 계약서에 서명할 것을 요청하기 위해
(C) 남자에게 일자리를 제안하기 위해
(D) 예약을 하기 위해   정답 (C)

43. 남자는 무엇 때문에 문제가 생길 수 있다고 말하는가?
(A) 자신의 주거지
(B) 기계적인 결함
(C) 일정 충돌
(D) 자신의 경험 부족   정답 (C)

문제 44-46번은 다음 대화를 참조하시오. 영M 미W

M: Good afternoon. Can I assist you with something?
W: Yes, please. (44)I need a book for some research I'm conducting. The title is *The Origins of Banking in the Middle Ages*. I couldn't find the book on the online catalog. Is it not available here?
M: I'm sorry, but (44)we don't have that book in the library. (45)I could, however, put in a request for it through

interlibrary loan. If it's at another library, we can have the book sent here.

W: Okay. But how long will that take? (46)My report is due in two weeks, so I'm concerned that I won't get it in time.

M: 안녕하세요. 뭐 도와드릴까요?

W: 예, 도와주세요. 제가 하고 있는 연구를 위한 책이 필요해요. 제목이 〈중세 시대 금융의 기원〉입니다. 온라인 카탈로그에서 그 책을 찾을 수 없었어요. 그 책이 여기에는 없는 건가요?

M: 죄송하지만, 우리 도서관에서는 그 책을 구비하고 있지 않네요. 그런데 도서관 간 대여 시스템을 통해서 그 책을 요청 넣을 수 있어요. 그 책이 다른 도서관에 있으면, 이쪽으로 보내 달라고 할 수 있어요.

W: 좋습니다. 그런데 그게 얼마나 걸릴까요? 제 보고서가 2주 후 마감이라서, 시간 내에 그 책을 받을 수 없을까 걱정이네요.

44. 남자는 누구일 것 같은가?
(A) 도서관 사서
(B) 은행의 창구직원
(C) 학생
(D) 회계장부 담당자 정답 (A)

45. 남자는 무엇을 해주겠다고 제의하는가?
(A) 문제 해결
(B) 요청서 제출
(C) 더 많은 책을 위한 기금 확보
(D) 수수료 면제 정답 (B)

46. 여자가 걱정하는 이유는?
(A) 돈이 충분하게 없다.
(B) 물건이 제 시간에 도착하지 않을지 모른다.
(C) 연체료가 너무 비쌀지 모른다.
(D) 운영 시간이 연장되지 않을 것이다. 정답 (B)

문제 47–49번은 다음 대화를 참조하시오. 호W 미M

W: (47)Stuart, how did you enjoy the conference on interior design in Cleveland?

M: I had a good time there. The sessions on color coordination were quite good. I definitely learned a lot from them.

W: Good. Oh, have you seen the most recent expense report for our office spending?

M: No, I haven't. Why?

W: We've already spent our entire quarterly budget. We need to reduce spending now. I want everyone to come up with some ideas on how to cut our department's spending. (48)I'm wondering if you could write up some ideas by 3:00 P.M. today.

M: (48)That will not be easy.

W: I know you just got back to the office, but this is really important.

M: Okay. (49)I'll speak to my assistant and have him clear my schedule for the rest of this afternoon and get to work right away.

W: 스튜어트, 클리블랜드에서 열렸던 인테리어 디자인 총회는 어땠어요?

M: 거기서 좋은 시간 보냈어요. 색채 조정에 대한 시간이 아주 좋았어요. 거기에서 정말 많은 것을 배웠어요.

W: 잘됐네요. 아, 우리 사무실 지출에 대한 가장 최근의 비용 보고서

봤어요?

M: 아뇨, 안 봤어요. 왜요?

W: 우리는 이미 전체 분기별 예산을 다 썼어요. 우리는 지금 지출을 줄일 필요가 있어요. 모두가 우리 부서의 지출을 삭감할 방안에 대해 아이디어를 내주면 좋겠어요. 오늘 오후 3시까지 당신이 아이디어 좀 써줄 수 있을지 모르겠네요.

M: 그건 쉽지 않겠는데요.

W 당신이 이제 막 사무실로 돌아온 것을 알지만 이게 정말 중요해요.

M: 알았어요. 내 비서에게 얘기해서 오늘 오후 내 나머지 일정을 비우게 하고 당장 작업할게요.

47. 남자는 어떤 종류의 행사에 참석했는가?
(A) 오리엔테이션
(B) 전문직업인 총회
(C) 극장 공연
(D) 이사회 회의 정답 (B)

48. 남자가 "그건 쉽지 않겠는데요"라고 말할 때 무엇을 의미하는가?
(A) 예산 삭감에 대해 제안할 게 없다.
(B) 자신의 매니저에게 도움을 요청하고 싶어한다.
(C) 동료의 지출 계획에 동의한다.
(D) 마감시한을 맞출 수 있을 것이라고 생각하지 않는다. 정답 (D)

49. 남자는 이후에 무엇을 할 것이라고 말하는가?
(A) 직원과 대화
(B) 진료 예약 취소
(C) 회의 소집
(D) 양식 작성 정답 (A)

문제 50–52번은 다음 대화를 참조하시오. 미W 미M

W: Russ, do you have the result of last week's employee satisfaction survey?

M: Yes, I do. (50)On the basis of their comments, most of our workers think the company isn't environmentally friendly enough. Apparently, they want us to do more to encourage everyone to recycle.

W: Hmm... (51)You know, last week, I saw a news report that mentioned that ecofriendly companies usually have employees who are highly satisfied.

M: (52)Well, I think we should hire an outside consultant then. Let's find someone who can advise us on what we can do to promote sustainability.

W: 러스, 지난주의 직원 만족도 조사 결과를 가지고 있어요?

M: 예, 가지고 있어요. 그들의 의견을 바탕으로 보면, 직원들 대부분이 회사가 충분히 환경 친화적이지 않다고 생각하고 있어요. 보아하니, 직원들은 우리가 좀 더 노력해서 모두에게 재활용할 것을 독려하기를 원해요.

W: 음... 있잖아요. 지난주에 제가 뉴스 보도를 봤는데, 거기서 환경 친화적인 회사들은 보통 직원들이 아주 만족해 한다고 언급하더군요.

M: 음. 그렇다면 우리는 외부 컨설턴트를 고용해야 할 것 같아요. 지속가능성을 촉진시키는 데 우리가 할 수 있는 일이 무엇인지 조언해줄 수 있는 사람을 찾아봅시다.

50. 남자에 따르면, 설문 결과에서 회사에 대하여 나타나 있는 것은 무엇인가?
(A) 직원들에게 더 많은 복리후생을 제공할 필요가 있다.
(B) 매우 만족스러워 하는 직원들이 있다.
(C) 직원들이 환경에 대해 염려한다.

(D) 이 회사의 제품은 재활용 물질로 만들어진다.　　　정답 (C)

51. 여자는 지난주에 무엇을 했다고 말하는가?
(A) 뉴스 보도를 봤다.
(B) 잡지에서 기사를 읽었다.
(C) 동료와 얘기를 나눴다.
(D) 매출 할당량을 충족시켰다.　　　정답 (A)

52. 남자는 무엇을 할 것을 제안하는가?
(A) 특별 판촉행사 추가하기
(B) 생산 과정 수정하기
(C) 전문가 고용하기
(D) 일부 직원 승진시키기　　　정답 (C)

문제 53~55번은 다음 대화를 참조하시오. 호W 영M

W: Hi, Chris. Have you had lunch yet?
M: Yes, I have. (53)**I dropped by Bernardino's. I had some delicious lasagna.**
W: (53)**That's nice. I eat there two or three times a week.** So how do you like your work? (54)**Are you getting acclimated to warehouse you are in?**
M: Everything here is fine. Filling shipping orders is much easier here than at my previous job. The robots really help out.
W: They do, don't they?
M: Yeah. (55)**At my previous place of employment, we did almost everything including picking and packing manually. But all of the automation here makes the job a lot easier.**

W: 안녕하세요, 크리스. 점심은 먹었어요?
M: 예, 먹었어요. 버나디노즈에 들렀어요. 라자냐를 맛있게 먹었어요.
W: 잘되었네요. 나는 일주일에 두세 번 거기서 식사해요. 그런데 일하는 거는 어때요? 지금 있는 물류창고에 잘 적응되고 있어요?
M: 여기 모든 게 다 좋아요. 여기서 배송 주문을 처리하는 게 제 이전 직장보다 훨씬 수월하네요. 로봇들이 정말 도움이 돼요.
W: 그렇죠, 도움되죠?
M: 예. 제 이전 직장에서는 물건을 들어올리고 포장하는 것을 포함하여 거의 모든 것을 수작업으로 했거든요. 그런데 여기는 자동화된 모든 것이 일을 훨씬 수월하게 만들어 주네요.

53. 여자가 "나는 일주일에 두세 번 거기서 식사해요"라고 말하는 이유는?
(A) 의견에 공감하기 위해
(B) 초대를 하기 위해
(C) 제안을 거절하기 위해
(D) 대안을 제시하기 위해　　　정답 (A)

54. 화자들은 어디에서 근무하는가?
(A) 제조 공장
(B) 물류창고
(C) 엔지니어링 회사
(D) 철물점　　　정답 (B)

55. 남자가 이전 직장보다 새 직장을 더 좋아하는 이유는?
(A) 급여가 훨씬 더 높다.
(B) 더욱 다양한 업무를 즐긴다.
(C) 근무 일정이 유연하다.
(D) 업무의 많은 부분이 자동화되어 있다.　　　정답 (D)

문제 56~58번은 다음 대화를 참조하시오. 미M 미W

M: Hello. (56)**I'm calling you because I'm renovating a client's restaurant kitchen, and I need a stone kitchen countertop.**
W: (57)**We have both granite and marble here at our store. Why don't you visit us and see which you prefer?**
M: Wonderful. I'll drop by in the evening. Oh, how long will it take for the countertop to get installed?
W: If it's rectangular in shape, we require three days to cut it and polish it. Then, we can install it the next day. (58)**If you let me know the precise length and width, we can get to work on it once you make your choice.**
M: Okay. (58)**I'll bring the measurements with me.**

M: 안녕하세요. 제가 고객의 식당 주방을 개조하고 있어서 전화드렸는데, 돌 재질의 주방 카운터 상판이 필요해요.
W: 여기 우리 매장에 화강석과 대리석 둘 다 있어요. 저희 매장에 오셔서 어느 게 더 마음에 드는지 보실래요?
M: 좋아요. 저녁에 들를게요. 아, 카운터 상판 설치하는 데는 얼마나 걸리나요?
W: 모양이 직사각형이면, 그걸 자르고 광 내고 하는 데 3일이 요구됩니다. 그리고 나면 그 다음 날 그것을 설치할 수 있어요. 저희에게 정확한 길이와 넓이를 알려 주시면, 그리고 일단 돌을 선택하시면 바로 작업에 들어갈 수 있습니다.
M: 알았어요. 치수도 같이 가져갈게요.

56. 남자는 누구일 것 같은가?
(A) 요리사
(B) 엔지니어
(C) 인테리어 디자이너
(D) 식당 매니저　　　정답 (C)

57. 남자가 오늘 저녁에 여자의 사업체에 방문하는 이유는?
(A) 발표를 하기 위해
(B) 점검을 하기 위해
(C) 제품을 고르기 위해
(D) 인터뷰를 하기 위해　　　정답 (C)

58. 여자는 남자에게 무엇을 가지고 오라고 권하는가?
(A) 치수
(B) 설계 도면
(C) 사진
(D) 사용 설명서　　　정답 (A)

문제 59~61번은 다음 3자 대화를 참조하시오. 미M 영M 미W

M1: Congratulations. You are some of the best employees here at KL Bradley. (59)**You have all been selected for our future managers program.** You'll rotate through several different jobs in different departments so that you can learn everything you need to know about working here. Now, let's listen to Mr. Marsh, my colleague, speak.
M2: Thanks, Josh. This program is crucial to your becoming a successful manager here. Oh, do you have a question back there?
W: Yes, Mr. Marsh. (60)**How long will we work in each division?**

M2: You'll work in one place for three months and then move to another one. (61)**Regarding preferences for assignments, they will be taken into consideration. I mean you can indicate your preference for your first assignment on the form in front of you.**

M1: 축하합니다. 여러분은 여기 KL 브래들리에서 최우수 직원 가운데 몇 분입니다. 여러분은 전부 다 우리 미래 관리자 프로그램에 선정되셨습니다. 여러분은 여기서 근무하면서 알아야 할 모든 것을 배울 수 있도록, 각기 다른 부서에서 다양한 일을 돌아가면서 해보게 될 것입니다. 이제, 제 동료 마시 씨가 말하는 것을 들어봅시다.
M2: 고마워요, 조시. 이 프로그램은 여기에서 성공한 관리자가 되는 데 아주 중요합니다. 오, 거기 뒤에 질문 있으세요?
W: 예, 마시 씨. 각 부서에서 우리는 얼마나 근무하게 되나요?
M2: 한 곳에서 3개월 근무하고, 그 다음 다른 곳으로 이동합니다. 맡을 업무에 대한 선도도는 고려될 것입니다. 제 말은, 여러분의 첫 배정 업무에 대한 선호도는 여러분 앞에 있는 양식에 표시하면 된다는 말입니다.

59. 프로그램의 참석자들은 누구일 것 같은가?
(A) 대학 인턴
(B) 공무원
(C) 관리직 교육생
(D) 채용 가능성 있는 직원　　　　　　　　정답 (C)

60. 여자는 무엇에 대해 물어보는가?
(A) 기간
(B) 급여
(C) 프로그램 장소
(D) 참석자 명단　　　　　　　　　　　　　정답 (A)

61. 참석자들이 요청사항을 전달할 수 있는 방법은?
(A) 한 관리자와 얘기함으로써
(B) 이메일을 보냄으로써
(C) 전화를 함으로써
(D) 양식을 작성함으로써　　　　　　　　　정답 (D)

문제 62-64번은 다음 대화와 표를 참조하시오. 호W 영M

W: Welcome to Dinsmore Apartments. What can I do for you?
M: (62)**I'm moving here to start a new job next month**, and I need a place to live close to work. Do you have any two-bedroom apartments available?
W: Let me check… Yes, we will have a couple of units available. Here are our leasing options for two-bedroom units. Notice that the price per month declines the longer you stay. (63)**How long are you planning to rent for here?**
M: (63)**At least a year.**
W: All right. So here is the rent on a 12-month lease. (64)**I can show you around a unit to see if you like it right now.**
M: Perfect. Let's do it.

W: 딘스모어 아파트에 오신 것을 환영합니다. 뭘 도와드릴까요?
M: 다음 달 새 일을 시작하느라 이곳으로 이사오는데, 회사 가까운 곳에 살 곳이 필요해요. 방 두 개짜리 아파트 나와 있는 거 있나요?
W: 확인해 볼게요… 예, 현재 두 개 정도 나올 게 있어요. 여기 방 두 개짜리 아파트에 대한 임대 옵션들이 있어요. 주목하실 것은 월 가격이 오래 체류할수록 줄어든다는 거예요. 여기서 얼마 동안 임차하실 건가요?
M: 적어도 1년이요.

W: 좋아요. 여기 12개월 임대에 대한 임대료가 있어요. 지금 원하신다면, 볼 수 있는 아파트를 구경시켜 드릴 수 있어요.
M: 아주 잘됐네요. 그렇게 해요.

임대 옵션

임대 기간	월 임대료
3개월	1,000달러
6개월	950달러
9개월	900달러
(63)12개월	850달러

62. 남자는 이사에 대해 어떤 이유를 말하는가?
(A) 최근에 결혼했다.
(B) 더 작은 아파트를 원한다.
(C) 자신의 집에 더 많은 방이 필요하다.
(D) 새 직장을 얻었다.　　　　　　　　　　정답 (D)

63. 그래픽을 보시오. 남자는 임대료로 얼마를 낼 것 같은가?
(A) 1000달러
(B) 950달러
(C) 900달러
(D) 850달러　　　　　　　　　　　　　　정답 (D)

64. 화자들은 이후에 무엇을 할 것인가?
(A) 임대 계약서 갱신
(B) 일부 옵션에 대한 논의
(C) 임대 계약서 검토
(D) 구경　　　　　　　　　　　　　　　　정답 (D)

문제 65-67번은 다음 대화와 지도를 참조하시오. 미W 미M

W: Hello. (65)**This is Martin Laundry.**
M: Hi. This is Jim Jackson, and I'm calling from the Waterside Hotel. We need an outside vendor to wash our bedding and towels daily, and you come highly recommended.
W: Thanks for saying that. (66)**Our customers all say that we provide reliable service in a timely manner.**
M: So what time could you deliver our items to us each day?
W: That depends on your location. (67)**According to the online delivery map that you should have, you're located in Zone 3.**
M: Ah, okay. That's fine. Our housekeepers don't start on rooms until nine in the morning, so that will give us enough time.

W: 안녕하세요. 마틴 세탁소입니다.
M: 안녕하세요. 저는 짐 잭슨이고, 워터사이트 호텔에서 전화드립니다. 저희는 우리 침구류 및 타올을 매일 세탁해줄 외부 업체가 필요한데, 그 업체 추천을 아주 많이 하더군요.
W: 그렇게 말씀해 주셔서 감사합니다. 우리 고객 모두 저희 업체가 제 시간에 맞춰 서비스를 제공한다고 말씀하세요.
M: 그러면 매일 우리가 맡긴 것들을 어느 시간에 배달해 주실 수 있나요?
W: 그곳 위치에 달려 있어요. 손님께서 가지고 계신 온라인 배달 지도에 따르면, 그곳은 3번 구역에 위치하고 있네요.
M: 아, 알았어요. 좋습니다. 우리 호텔 객실 청소원들이 아침 9시에야 객실 정리 업무를 시작하니까, 시간이 충분할 것 같네요.

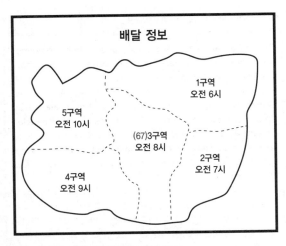

배달 정보

5구역
오전 10시

1구역
오전 6시

(67)3구역
오전 8시

2구역
오전 7시

4구역
오전 9시

65. 남자는 어떤 업종에 전화를 걸고 있는가?
(A) 택배업체
(B) 세탁업체
(C) 출장 요리 업체
(D) 수리점 　　　　　　　　　　　　　정답 (B)

66. 여자는 자신의 회사가 무엇으로 잘 알려져 있다고 말하는가?
(A) 잘 교육 받은 직원 보유
(B) 저가의 가격
(C) 품질이 좋은 물건 제공
(D) 제 시간에 맞춰 일하는 것 　　　　　정답 (D)

67. 그래픽을 보시오. 배달은 몇 시에 이루어질 것인가?
(A) 오전 7시
(B) 오전 8시
(C) 오전 9시
(D) 오전 10시 　　　　　　　　　　　정답 (B)

문제 68-70번은 다음 대화와 일정표를 참조하시오. 영M 호W

M: Hello. This is the Westside Dental Clinic.
W: Hello. I have an appointment with Dr. Conners on Thursday at 3:00 P.M., (68)but I need to reschedule it. I have to go out of town to meet a client on that day.
M: No problem. When can you come here then?
W: I finish work at 6:00 every day, so any time after that would be perfect.
M: Well, Dr. Conners doesn't have anything after 5:00 every day. (69)However, I can fit you in at 6:30 on Wednesday with another doctor.
W: (69)That's fine with me.
M: Okay. (70)Now, I need to ask you a few questions to make sure your personal information is still the same.

M: 안녕하세요. 웨스트사이드 덴탈 클리닉입니다.
W: 안녕하세요. 목요일 오후 3시에 코너스 의사 선생님과 진료 예약이 되어 있는데, 일정을 조정해야 해요. 그 날 고객을 만나러 타지로 가야 하거든요.
M: 괜찮습니다. 그러면 여기에 언제 오실 수 있으세요?
W: 저는 매일 6시에 퇴근해서 그 시간 이후 언제든 괜찮습니다.
M: 저, 코너스 의사 선생님은 매일 5시 이후에는 어떤 예약도 받지 않습니다. 그런데, 수요일 6시 30분에 다른 의사 선생님하고 예약을 넣어 드릴 수 있어요.

W: 그거 괜찮네요.
M: 알겠습니다. 이제, 개인 정보가 여전히 동일한지 확인하기 위해 몇 가지 질문을 드려야 합니다.

의사	근무 시간 (월요일 – 금요일)
웨스트 의사 선생님	오전 8:00 – 오후 4:00
코너스 의사 선생님	오전 9:00 – 오후 5:00
(69)메이웨더 의사 선생님	오후 12:00 – 오후 8:00
벨 의사 선생님	오전 10:00 – 오후 6:00

68. 여자가 자신의 진료 약속을 변경하고 싶어 하는 이유는?
(A) 휴가를 갈 것이다.
(B) 출장 차 외지로 나가야 한다.
(C) 몸이 좋지 않다.
(D) 가족 행사를 위해 가야 한다. 　　　　정답 (B)

69. 그래픽을 보시오. 여자는 수요일에 누구에게 진료를 받을 것인가?
(A) 웨스트 의사 선생님
(B) 코너스 의사 선생님
(C) 메이웨더 의사 선생님
(D) 벨 의사 선생님 　　　　　　　　　정답 (C)

70. 여자는 이후에 무엇을 할 것 같은가?
(A) 몇 가지 질문에 답변
(B) 사무실 방문
(C) 새 연락처 제공
(D) 온라인으로 지불 　　　　　　　　정답 (A)

Part 4

문제 71-73번은 다음 공지를 참조하시오. 미M

M: (71)Before today's lunch shift begins, I need to tell you all a few things. (72)First, the baked salmon was so popular yesterday that we wound up selling out our entire stock of it. Please let your customers know it's unavailable today. We'll also be dividing up the service areas this afternoon. Half of you will be in the main dining room while the rest of you will be in the room for special events such as a private party. There's a company retirement party going on in there. We're going to have a busy afternoon. (73)So please cooperate with each other to provide the best possible service for every customer.

오늘 점심 근무 시작하기 전에, 여러분 모두에게 몇 가지 드릴 말씀이 있습니다. 우선, 어제 연어 구이가 너무 인기 있어서 전체 연어 재고가 품절되고 말았습니다. 고객들에게 오늘 연어 구이가 품절되었다는 것을 알려 주세요. 또한 우리는 오늘 오후에 서비스 구역을 나누게 될 것입니다. 여러분 중에 반은 메인 식사 공간에서 근무하게 될 것이고, 반면 나머지는 사적인 파티 같은 특별 행사를 위한 방에서 근무하게 될 것입니다. 거기에서 한 회사의 은퇴 파티가 열리게 됩니다. 오늘 오후는 바쁜 시간을 보내게 될 것입니다. 그러니 서로 협력해서 모든 고객들에게 가능한 최선의 서비스를 제공하시기 바랍니다.

71. 안내 공지는 어디서 이루어지고 있는 것 같은가?
(A) 버스 터미널

(B) 사업 상 사교 행사
(C) 슈퍼마켓
(D) 식당　　　　　　　　　　　　　　　　　정답 (D)

72. 화자에 따르면, 고객들은 현 상황에 대해 어떤 말을 듣게 될 것인가?
(A) 어떤 품목의 가격이 올랐다.
(B) 일정이 변경되었다.
(C) 어떤 품목이 품절되었다.
(D) 개별 방이 수리 때문에 폐쇄된다.　　　　정답 (C)

73. 청자들은 무엇을 하도록 권유받는가?
(A) 팀으로 함께 일하기
(B) 입구에서 고객 맞이하기
(C) 오늘 오후에 추가 근무 하기
(D) 바로 고객들에게 식사 제공하기　　　　정답 (A)

문제 74-76번은 다음 워크숍 발췌 내용을 참조하시오. ⓜⓦ

W: **(74)Welcome to our annual spring gardeners workshop here at the Wentworth Community Center.** We're going to discuss how to grow vegetables in your backyard garden. Today, I'm going to give you a general overview. **(75)What I recommend you do is learn as much as you can about the various types of vegetables that you're interested in growing before you plant them.** Different vegetables require different types of soil to grow. **(76)Next week, we'll visit a local farm, where you'll learn about how to fertilize your garden.**

여기 웬트워스 지역사회 센터에서 하는 우리 연례 봄 원예가 워크숍에 오신 것을 환영합니다. 우리는 여러분의 뒷마당에 채소를 어떻게 키울 것인가에 대해 얘기하게 될 것입니다. 저는 오늘 일반적인 개관을 설명해 드릴 것입니다. 여러분에게 추천드리는 것은 여러분이 재배에 관심 있는 다양한 종류의 채소에 대해 그것들을 심기 전에 가능한 한 많이 배워 두라는 것입니다. 다양한 채소들은 키우는 데 다양한 종류의 토양이 요구됩니다. 다음 주에 우리는 지역 농장 한 군데를 방문하는데, 거기서 여러분의 정원에 비료를 어떻게 줄 것인지에 대해 배우게 될 것입니다.

74. 워크숍의 주제는 무엇인가?
(A) 원예
(B) 프로그래밍
(C) 낙농업
(D) 온라인 판매　　　　　　　　　　　　　정답 (A)

75. 화자는 무엇을 추천하고 있는가?
(A) 강좌 등록하기
(B) 다양한 활동 시도하기
(C) 파트너와 일하기
(D) 조사하기　　　　　　　　　　　　　　정답 (D)

76. 다음 주에 청자들은 무엇을 할 것인가?
(A) 견학 가기
(B) 수강료 내기
(C) 장소 고르기
(D) 원예용품 구매하기　　　　　　　　　정답 (A)

문제 77-79번은 다음 광고를 참조하시오. 영ⓜ

M: **(77)Do you want to save money to retire, to buy property, or to start your own business? Then you should subscribe to** *Finance Magazine*. It features articles authored by some of the leading personal financial advisors in the country. **(78)The writers working for us have more years of experience than you could find on the writing staff of any other financial magazine. (79)You can have 12 issues delivered to your home for just $50 a year. Or subscribe to the online version, and you only need to pay $35.** Get your subscription today, and learn how to grow your savings.

은퇴를 대비해서, 집을 사기 위해, 또는 창업하기 위해서 돈을 모으고 싶으세요? 그렇다면 〈파이낸스 매거진〉을 구독하셔야 합니다. 이 잡지는 전국 일류의 개인 금융 자문관 몇 분이 글을 쓴 기사를 특징으로 합니다. 우리 회사를 위해서 글을 쓰는 작가들은 여러분이 찾을 수 있는 다른 어떤 금융 잡지의 필진들보다 더 많은 경력을 갖고 있습니다. 1년에 50달러만 내시면 12호를 집으로 배달 받을 수 있습니다. 또는 온라인 판을 구독하시면 35달러만 지불하면 됩니다. 오늘 구독하시고, 어떻게 저축을 늘릴지 배워 보세요.

77. 광고에 나온 잡지의 주제는 무엇인가?
(A) 국제 비즈니스
(B) 정보 기술
(C) 개인 금융
(D) 온라인 마케팅　　　　　　　　　　　정답 (C)

78. 화자는 필진에 대해 무엇을 말하는가?
(A) 독자들의 질문에 신속하게 답한다.
(B) 그들의 책으로 유명하다.
(C) 경력이 많다.
(D) 전세계 각지에서 온 사람이다.　　　　정답 (C)

79. 잡지의 온라인 판에 대해 나타나 있는 것은 무엇인가?
(A) 그것의 아카이브에 대한 이용권이 같이 딸려 나온다.
(B) 그 내용이 일주일에 한 번 갱신된다.
(C) 정가의 반 가격에 세일하고 있다.
(D) 인쇄물 버전보다 더 저렴하다.　　　　정답 (D)

문제 80-82번은 다음 회의 발췌 내용을 참조하시오. ⓜⓜ

M: Good afternoon. **(80)I'm pleased to have this chance to speak with you about investing in our company.** After you hear my presentation, I'm sure you'll all agree that our newest product is something you should invest in. **(81)Weston Footwear has been selling athletic shoes for more than four decades.** Recently, our researchers designed a new pair of sneakers that provides a more comfortable fit and doesn't hurt your feet when running or jogging. These sneakers have become quite popular in the past few months. **(82)If you invest with us, we'll be able to purchase a second facility that will permit us to more than double our production.**

안녕하세요. 우리 회사에 투자하시는 것에 대해 여러분과 얘기할 이번 기회를 가지게 되어 기쁩니다. 제 프레젠테이션을 듣고 난 후, 확신컨대 여러분 모두 우리 최신 제품이 투자할 만한 것이라는 데 완전히 동의하실 것입니다. 웨스턴 풋웨어는 40년 이상 운동화를 팔았습니다. 최근에, 우리 연구원들이 새로운 운동화를 디자인했는데, 이 운동화는 더욱 편안한 딱 맞는 착용감을

주고 달리거나 조깅할 때 발에 통증을 주지 않습니다. 이 운동화는 지난 몇 개월 동안 아주 많은 인기가 있었습니다. 우리에게 투자를 해주시면, 우리는 생산량을 두 배 이상 늘려줄 두 번째 시설을 매입할 수 있을 것입니다.

80. 이 담화는 누구를 대상으로 한 것인가?
(A) 이사회
(B) 중소업체 소유주
(C) 잠재적인 투자자
(D) 프로 운동선수 　　　　　　　　　　　　정답 (C)

81. 회사는 어떤 종류의 제품을 판매하는가?
(A) 신발류
(B) 넥타이
(C) 양복
(D) 수영복 　　　　　　　　　　　　　　　정답 (A)

82. 화자의 업체는 무엇을 사기를 바라는가?
(A) 물류창고
(B) 제조 공장
(C) 건축 자재
(D) 운동 시설 　　　　　　　　　　　　　정답 (B)

문제 83–85번은 다음 전화 메시지를 참조하시오. 미W

W: Hello, Jason. (83)**I'm calling about this evening.** I know you're going to be at the product release in Jacksonville where we are going to unveil our newest laptop. You said that you're taking the orange subway line to that launch event. (84) **Well, I just learned that the subway line will be taken out of service temporarily for urgent repairs.** (84)**I thought you might like to know that I'm driving to Jacksonville today.** (85) **I need to stop at the print shop on the way to pick up some promotional flyers that we're going to be handing out to the attendees tonight.** But there's still plenty of time to stop there and to make it to Jacksonville by 6:00 P.M.

안녕하세요, 제이슨. 오늘 저녁 일 때문에 전화드렸는데요. 우리 최신 노트북을 공개할 예정인 잭슨빌의 제품 공개 행사장에 당신이 가는 것을 알고 있어요. 당신은 그 공개 행사에 주황색 지하철 노선을 타고 갈 거라고 하셨잖아요. 그런데 지금 막 알게 된 건데, 그 지하철 노선이 급한 수리 때문에 임시로 운행을 하지 않으려고 해요. 제 생각에 오늘 제가 잭슨빌로 운전해서 간다는 것을 아시면 좋아하실 것 같아요. 가는 길에 인쇄소에 들러서, 오늘 밤 참석자들에게 배포할 홍보 전단지를 찾아서 가야 해요. 그런데 거기 들르고도 오후 6시까지 잭슨빌에 갈 시간이 충분합니다.

83. 화자에 따르면, 오늘 저녁 어떤 행사가 열릴 것인가?
(A) 시상식
(B) 제품 공개
(C) 은퇴 파티
(D) 주주 총회 　　　　　　　　　　　　　정답 (B)

84. 화자가 "오늘 제가 잭슨빌로 운전해서 가요"라고 말하는 이유는?
(A) 제안을 거절하기 위해
(B) 자신이 시간이 안 된다는 것을 언급하기 위해
(C) 제안을 하기 위해
(D) 운전 길 안내를 요청하기 위해 　　　　정답 (C)

85. 화자에 따르면, 그녀는 무엇을 찾아야 하는가?
(A) 참석자들을 위한 음료
(B) 행사장의 평면도
(C) 행사 프로그램
(D) 홍보 자료 　　　　　　　　　　　　　정답 (D)

문제 86–88번은 다음 안내 방송을 참조하시오. 호W

W: Good morning, everyone. (86)**You can remove your seatbelts and move around the cabin now since we've reached our cruising altitude.** (87)**We're sorry about the slight delay.** We had a minor issue with the baggage handling system. Our new arrival time in Berlin is 1:05 P.M. That's about twenty minutes later than normally scheduled. (88)**In just a moment, our flight attendants will start serving breakfast.** If you want to order anything, we take both cash and credit cards.

여러분, 안녕하세요. 이제 우리가 순항 고도에 들어섰기 때문에 안전벨트를 풀고 객실을 돌아다니셔도 됩니다. 약간 지연된 것에 대해서는 죄송합니다. 수하물 처리 시스템에 사소한 문제가 있었습니다. 새로운 베를린 도착 시간은 오후 1시 5분이 되겠습니다. 정상적인 일정보다 20분 정도 늦어지게 됩니다. 잠시 후에 저희 승무원이 아침식사를 제공할 것입니다. 무엇이든 주문하시고자 한다면, 현금과 신용 카드 둘 다 받습니다.

86. 안내 방송은 어디에서 진행되고 있는가?
(A) 공항
(B) 식당
(C) 페리
(D) 기내 　　　　　　　　　　　　　　　정답 (D)

87. 화자가 사과를 하는 이유는?
(A) 경유지 단기 체류가 취소되었다.
(B) 출발이 지연되었다.
(C) 기계 결함이 있다.
(D) 표가 더 이상 남아 있지 않다. 　　　　정답 (B)

88. 화자가 "우리는 현금과 신용 카드 둘 다 받습니다"라고 말할 때 무엇을 의미하는가?
(A) 일부 면세 품목이 구입 가능하다.
(B) 새로운 지불 방법이 좀 더 편리하다.
(C) 청자들은 음식값을 청구 받을 것이다.
(D) 청자들은 사진이 부착된 신분증을 제시해야 한다. 　정답 (C)

문제 89–91번은 다음 소개를 참조하시오. 영M

M: (89)**Welcome to the IT Department's workshop on computer security.** Please feel free to ask questions anytime you have them during this interactive workshop. We're holding this event because (90)**quite a few employees' computers have recently been infected with a virus,** apparently caused by downloading files from suspicious sites. We simply can't allow that to happen anymore. Now, we all need to learn how to update the antivirus security software. (91)**Please open the program on your computers by clicking on the icon at the top of the screen on the left-hand side.**

컴퓨터 보안에 관한 IT부 워크숍에 오신 것을 환영합니다. 이 대화 방식의 워크숍을 하는 동안 질문을 있을 경우에는 언제든지 편하게 질문해 주십시오. 이 행사를 갖게 된 이유는 꽤 많은 직원들의 컴퓨터가 최근에 바이러스에 감염되었기 때문인데, 보아하니 의심스러운 사이트에서 파일들을 내려받은 것이 원인인 것 같습니다. 우리는 이런 상황이 더 이상 발생하는 것을 허용할 수 없습니다. 이제 우리는 모두 바이러스 퇴치 보안 소프트웨어를 어떻게 업데이트하는지 배울 필요가 있습니다. 화면 왼쪽 위에 있는 아이콘을 클릭하여 여러분의 컴퓨터에 있는 프로그램을 열어 주십시오.

89. 화자는 어느 부서에서 근무하는 것 같은가?
(A) 인적 자원부
(B) 연구 개발부
(C) 정보 기술부
(D) 제품 개발부 정답 (C)

90. 화자에 따르면, 이 업체에 최근에 무슨 일이 있었는가?
(A) 일부 컴퓨터가 바이러스의 영향을 받았다.
(B) 새 보안 장비가 설치되었다.
(C) 신분증이 배포되었다.
(D) 컴퓨터 수업에 자리가 없었다. 정답 (A)

91. 청자들은 무엇을 하라는 요청을 받는가?
(A) 사용 설명서 보기
(B) 컴퓨터 강좌 등록하기
(C) 변경 내용이 있는지 보안 지침 확인하기
(D) 컴퓨터 프로그램 열기 정답 (D)

문제 92-94번은 다음 방송을 참조하시오. 미W

W: Hello, everyone. (92)I'm Julie Hamilton, the host of *Our Town* here on Radio FM 103.2. Today's guest is Robert Landon. He's a local historian who's interested in preserving some of the city's oldest landmarks. Recently, he has secured funds with the help of the city council and worked on the childhood home of Darren Moore, the founder of our city. This weekend, Moore House is going to open as the city's newest museum. (93)I already toured it and was simply amazed by it. I strongly urge everyone listening to go there sometime because you're going to be impressed. (94)If you look on our website, you can see some photographs of the house before it was renovated as well as the house right now.

안녕하세요, 여러분. 저는 여기 라디오 FM 103.2, 〈우리 마을〉의 진행자 줄리 해밀턴입니다. 오늘의 초대 손님은 로버트 랜던입니다. 랜던 씨는 지역 역사학자인데, 이 도시의 가장 오래된 랜드마크들을 보존하는 데 관심이 있습니다. 최근에 랜던 씨는 시 의회의 도움으로 자금을 확보해서, 우리 도시의 창시자 다렌 무어의 어린시절 저택에 대한 작업을 했습니다. 이번 주말에 무어 하우스가 이 도시의 최신 박물관으로 개관을 할 예정입니다. 저는 이미 그 박물관을 둘러보았는데 그저 놀라울 따름이었습니다. 청취하고 계신 여러분 모두가 언제 한 번 거기에 꼭 가보실 것을 강력히 권해 드립니다. 왜냐하면 여러분도 깊은 인상을 받게 될 것이기 때문입니다. 우리 웹사이트를 보시면, 무어 하우스의 현재 모습뿐만 아니라 보수공사 하기 전의 저택 사진들을 볼 수 있습니다.

92. 화자는 누구인가?
(A) 박물관 큐레이터
(B) 라디오 프로그램 진행자
(C) 역사학자

(D) 시 의회 의원 정답 (B)

93. 화자가 "무어 하우스는 이 도시의 최신 박물관으로 개관할 예정입니다"라고 말하는 이유는?
(A) 박물관으로 가는 길 안내를 해주기 위해
(B) 업적을 강조하기 위해
(C) 행사를 위한 자원봉사자를 모집하기 위해
(D) 오해를 정정하기 위해 정답 (B)

94. 웹사이트에서 무엇을 찾을 수 있는가?
(A) 건물 안내도
(B) 행사 일정표
(C) 박물관에 대한 비디오
(D) 사진 정답 (D)

문제 95-97번은 다음 안내 방송과 상점 지도를 참조하시오. 영M

M: Attention, shoppers. Thank you for visiting Arnold's for our summer sale. (95)As you know, we have the lowest prices in the city for all your hardware needs. Today, we've got plenty of shoppers here to take advantage of our special deals, so the checkout lines are getting long. To speed up the checkout process, (96)please proceed to the express lane located right by the exit if you're purchasing six items or fewer. In addition, (97)if you are buying a large item and need assistance carrying it, just talk to any of our employees. Somebody will then help you transport the item to your car.

안내 말씀드립니다, 쇼핑객 여러분. 우리 여름 세일에 아놀즈를 방문해 주셔서 감사합니다. 아시다시피, 우리는 여러분이 필요로 하는 모든 철물에 대해서 이 도시에서 최저가로 제공하고 있습니다. 오늘 여기에 특별 할인 혜택을 보고자 아주 많은 쇼핑객들이 오셔서, 계산대 줄이 길어지고 있습니다. 계산하고 나가는 과정을 신속하게 하시려면, 6개 이하의 물품을 구매하신 경우 출구 바로 옆에 있는 빠른 계산대로 가십시오. 그 밖에, 대형 물건을 사서 그걸 운반하는 데 도움이 필요하시다면, 우리 직원 누구에게든 말씀만 하십시오. 그러면 누군가 고객님의 차량까지 그 물건을 운반하는 것을 도와드릴 것입니다.

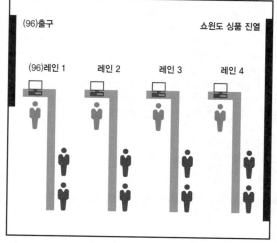

95. 안내 방송은 어디에서 이루어지고 있는 것 같은가?
(A) 철물점
(B) 식료품점
(C) 가구점

  (D) 의류점   **정답 (A)**

96. 그래픽을 보시오. 어느 레인이 빠른 레인인가?
 (A) 레인 1
 (B) 레인 2
 (C) 레인 3
 (D) 레인 4   **정답 (A)**

97. 화자에 따르면, 청자들은 무엇을 하는 데 도움을 받을 수 있는가?
 (A) 상품의 위치 찾기
 (B) 불량품 반품하기
 (C) 큰 물건 옮기기
 (D) 품절된 물건 주문하기   **정답 (C)**

문제 98-100번은 다음 담화와 달력을 참조하시오. 미M

M: **(98)Thanks for attending our drawing class here at the Croft Community Center.** I hope you all had fun and learned a lot tonight. **(99)Now, if you wouldn't mind collecting your pens, pencils, and sketchbooks and putting them on the table in the back, I'd really appreciate it.** That will make my cleanup much easier. In addition, before you leave, why don't you take some time and check out some of the other activities you can do here? You can get a copy of this month's schedule right by the door. **(100)I highly recommend you attend the music class because there will be a special guest instructor, Gina Wilson, who's a noted soprano.**

여기 크로프트 지역사회 센터에서 하는 드로잉 수업에 참여해 주셔서 감사합니다. 오늘 밤 여러분 모두 다 즐거운 시간을 보내고 많은 것들을 배웠기를 바랍니다. 이제, 펜, 연필, 스케치북들을 수거해서 뒤에 있는 테이블 위로 갖다 놔주시면 정말로 감사하겠습니다. 그렇게 해주시면 제 청소가 훨씬 더 수월해질 것입니다. 그 외에, 여기서 나가기기 전에 시간 좀 내서 여기서 여러분이 하실 수 있는 다른 활동들도 좀 확인해 보시겠습니까? 바로 문 옆에 있는 이번 달 일정표를 한 부씩 가져가셔도 됩니다. 음악 수업에 참석하실 것을 강력히 추천드립니다. 왜냐하면 특별 초대 강사 지나 윌슨이 오는데, 이 분은 유명한 소프라노입니다.

8월

월	화	수	목	금
10 회화 강습	**11** 미술 및 공예 수업	**12**	**13** 수영 수업	**14**
17	**18** (100) **음악 수업**	**19** 연설 수업	**20**	**21** 연기 수업

98. 화자는 누구일 것 같은가?
 (A) 음악 교사
 (B) 미술 강사
 (C) 수영 강사
 (D) 미술작품 거래상   **정답 (B)**

99. 화자는 청자들에게 무엇을 할 것을 요청하는가?
 (A) 방 청소 도와주기
 (B) 전화기를 무음으로 해 놓기
 (C) 수업에 대한 후기 쓰기
 (D) 개인 소지품 확인하기   **정답 (A)**

100. 그래픽을 보시오. 어느 날짜에 특별 게스트가 올 것인가?
 (A) 8월 10일
 (B) 8월 11일
 (C) 8월 18일
 (D) 8월 21일   **정답 (C)**

Part 5

101. 출판이 지연되는 일을 피하려면, 박사 논문 인용 및 제출에 대한 아래 지침을 따라 주십시오.   **정답 (D)**

102. 공장 노동자들의 파업에서, 경영진도 노조도 한치의 양보도 하려는 것 같아 보이지 않았다.   **정답 (D)**

103. 소프트웨어 개발 과정에서 중요한 측면은 설계되고 있는 소프트웨어 시스템의 다양한 부분 간의 일관성이다.   **정답 (D)**

104. 올바른 단계를 취하면, 자동차 페인트에 손상을 입히지 않고 자동차에서 스티커를 조심스럽게 제거할 수 있다.   **정답 (C)**

105. 우리 회사는 기업인들에게 그들의 사업 시설에 대해 비용 효율적이면서 전문적인 보안 서비스를 제공한다.   **정답 (B)**

106. 연초의 한 가지 거대한 목표 대신에, 사람들은 한 해 동안 이룰 작고 구체적인 목표들을 많이 정해야 한다.   **정답 (C)**

107. 제조업체는 최소 10명의 근로자를 고용해야 세금 우대 혜택을 받을 수 있지만, 관광 회사는 5명 이상을 고용해야 한다.   **정답 (A)**

108. 우리의 목표는 모든 고객에게 완전한 서비스 및 최대의 만족을 제공하는 것이며, 앞으로도 오랫동안 귀하에게 서비스할 수 있길 기대합니다.
             정답 (C)

109. 휴대 전화의 화면이 1분 이상 비활성 상태로 있으면, 대개 자동적으로 절전 상태가 될 것이다.   **정답 (A)**

110. 그 대학은 기숙사동과 방이 3개인 직접 취사가 가능한 아파트에서 2천 명이 넘는 학생들을 위한 캠퍼스 내 적절한 숙소를 제공한다.   **정답 (B)**

111. 가격, 내부 및 외부 기능, 안전 정보로 인기 차량을 나란히 비교하려면 저희 공식 웹사이트를 방문해 주세요.   **정답 (D)**

112. 짧은 역사에도 불구하고, 우리 회사는 민간 항공기 산업 분야에서의 주요 업체로 성공적으로 성장하였다.   **정답 (D)**

113. 우리 신제품에서 발생하는 일부 문제점들을 처리하기 위해서 우리 제조 공정에 다양한 변화가 이뤄질 것이다. 　　　　　　　정답 (B)

114. 유전 공학자들은 DNA 구조를 변경시킬 수 있을 뿐만 아니라, 하나의 신체 기관에서 다른 기관으로 유전자를 이식할 수도 있다. 　　　정답 (B)

115. 고용 계약서에는 우리 직원 모두가 회사의 비밀 유지 조항을 준수해야 한다고 명확하게 언급되어 있다. 　　　　　　　정답 (D)

116. 식당의 구체적인 위생 기준에 대해 문의하려면, 식품 위생 규정의 시행을 담당하고 있는 우리 보건소에 연락하십시오. 　　　정답 (B)

117. 두 개 주 사이의 새로운 고속도로 건설의 완공에 필요한 예산과 시간 계획표는 다음 달에 발표될 것으로 예상된다. 　　　정답 (C)

118. 벨라 어패럴은 지역사회 계획에 대한 헌신의 일환으로 지역 아동 병원에 큰 기부를 해왔다. 　　　　　　　정답 (A)

119. 기사에 따르면, 자동차 보험 산업의 활성화를 돕기 위한 노력으로 다수의 복잡한 규제들이 폐지될 것이라고 한다. 　　　정답 (C)

120. 에이스 금융 회사는 두 개의 은행 계열사 외에도 투자사 한 개와 세 개의 비은행 금융 계열사를 보유하고 있다. 　　　정답 (D)

121. 일부 과학자들이 새로운 물리학 이론의 틀을 다듬고 이를 반도체 제조 공정에 적용시켰다. 　　　　　　　정답 (C)

122. 입사 지원서는 잠재적 고용주에게 주는 첫 인상이므로, 채용 담당자의 주의를 끌 수 있는 진술을 해야 한다. 　　　정답 (D)

123. 중앙 은행의 추가 금리 인하에 관한 결정은 기업 투자를 장려함으로써 경기를 부양하겠다는 의도를 내포한다. 　　　정답 (B)

124. 정부 기관에서 홍수나 지진과 같은 자연재해로 가옥이 파괴된 가족들에게 도움을 제공한다. 　　　　　　　정답 (C)

125. 만약 이사회에 의해 승인된다면, 루나 철강 그룹의 피츠버그 이전은 아마도 9월에 있게 될 것이다. 　　　정답 (C)

126. 일단 수습 기간이 끝나면, 인턴 중 일부는 정규직으로 채용될 것이고, 회사는 그들에게 경쟁력 있는 급여와 추가 혜택을 제공할 것이다. 　정답 (B)

127. 회사 보험 규정에서 요구하는 바에 따라, 신입 직원들은 다음 달 말까지 건강 검진을 받게 될 것이다. 　　　정답 (D)

128. 그 지방 대학은 제3외국어로 독일어를 제공하는데, 이는 이 나라에서 매우 보기 드문 일이다. 　　　정답 (D)

129. 무선 기기는 대개 소형 배터리에 의존하기 때문에, 마이크로칩이 전력을 얼마나 효율적으로 사용하는지가 더 중요해진다 　　　정답 (A)

130. 국내 회사들이 최첨단 제품 제조를 위해 수입 부품들에 의존한다는 점을 고려하면, 그들은 연구 및 개발에 투자할 필요가 있다. 　정답 (A)

Part 6

문제 131-134번은 다음 이메일을 참조하시오.

> 홉킨스 씨에게.
>
> 당사 기록에 따르면 귀하의 〈월간 월드 이코노미〉 구독이 11월 23일에 만료됩니다. 동봉된 양식을 사용하여 구독을 갱신하고 국내에서 가장 인기 있는 경제 잡지 중 하나의 발행물을 계속해서 받아 보세요.
>
> 앞으로 서비스가 중단되지 않고 계속될 수 있도록, 저희 자동 청구 프로그램에 등록하실 것을 권장해 드립니다. 이 서비스는 고객님의 청구서가 제때에 납부되도록 하는 데 추가 비용 없이 이용하실 수 있습니다. 양식의 "자동 결제" 란에 체크 표시만 함으로써 가입하실 수 있습니다.
>
> 이 프로그램에 등록하는 고객에게는 일반 구독 요금에서 15% 할인이 제공됩니다.
>
> 지금 실행하시고 오늘 구독료를 절약하세요!
>
> 고객 서비스부
> 〈월간 월드 이코노미〉

131. 　　　　　　　정답 (B)

132. 　　　　　　　정답 (B)

133. 　　　　　　　정답 (C)

134. (A) 귀하는 언제든지 결제 및 청구 선택 사항을 변경할 수 있습니다.
　　(B) 양식의 "자동 결제" 란에 체크 표시만 함으로써 가입하실 수 있습니다.
　　(C) 많은 부모들이 자녀에게 경제학을 가르칠 준비가 되어 있지 않습니다.
　　(D) 우리 잡지의 최근 고객 평들은 한결같이 긍정적이었습니다.
　　　　　　　정답 (B)

문제 135-138번은 다음 기사를 참조하시오.

> **오클랜드 텔레그래프**
> [과학 및 환경란]
>
> **플라스틱 폐기물에서 벗어나야 한다 – 플라스틱 재활용**
> 제시카 홀랜드 작성
>
> 4월 1일 – 사람들은 매년 거의 140억 킬로그램의 플라스틱을 사용하고, 그 중 약 20%만 재활용한다. 실제로 재활용된 플라스틱은 식품 용기에서 현대 가구에 이르기까지 다양한 제품으로 제작될 수 있다.
>
> 대부분의 플라스틱은 석유로 만들어지므로, 재활용하면 이 귀중한 자원을 절약할 수 있다. 많은 도시와 시골에서 플라스틱 용기와 음료수 병이 상점에 반환될 수 있으며, 그 중 일부는 재사용을 위해 비닐봉지도 받는다.
>
> 지역의 재사용 및 재활용 프로그램은 살고 있는 지역에 따라 다르다. 특정 유형의 플라스틱이 어떤 지역에서는 받아들여지지 않을 수도 있다. 가장 흔히 재활용되는 플라스틱은 청량 음료 병, 우유 및 물통, 식용유 병에 사용되는 플라스틱이다.

135. 　　　　　　　정답 (B)

136. 　　　　　　　정답 (D)

137. (A) 여러분은 인터넷을 통해 가장 가까운 매립지와 재활용 센터를 찾을 수 있다.
　　(B) 지역의 재사용 및 재활용 프로그램은 살고 있는 지역에 따라 다르다.
　　(C) 우리는 적절한 폐기물 관리를 통해 거리의 오염을 감소시켜야 한다.

(D) 플라스틱 병과 캔들을 반환하는 환불 제도가 제안되었다.　　　정답 (B)

138.　　　정답 (C)

ACTUAL
TEST
08

문제 139–142번은 다음 광고를 참조하시오.

블랙손 스키 리조트
북극이 시작되는 곳!
화이트혼 로드 1번지
레이크 루이스, 앨버타 주 T0L 1E0, 캐나다
1 (877) 956–8473

블랙손 스키 리조트는 실력에 상관없이 누구나 스키 스포츠에서 더 높은 수준으로 나아갈 수 있는 곳입니다. 올 겨울에 저희 프로그램 중 하나에 등록하고, 최고의 스노보드와 스키 캠프 시설에서 전문가들로부터 배우세요!

호동 산의 블랙손 빙하에 위치하고 있는 저희는 캐나다 최대의 겨울 스키 리조트입니다. 블랙손 스키 리조트는 최고의 스키 캠프 경험을 선사하기 위해 60명의 남녀 직원이 있습니다!

많은 코치들이 잡지와 TV로 중계된 대회에 나온 것을 보셨던 바로 그 유명한 스키 선수들입니다. 세계 어디에서도 더 훌륭한 자격을 갖춘 전문 강사 그룹을 찾을 수 없습니다. 전문가부터 서비스 담당 직원에 이르기까지 블랙손 스키 리조트의 모든 사람들은 스키 캠프 경험을 최고로 만들어드리는 데 집중하고 있습니다.

139.　　　정답 (D)

140.　　　정답 (C)

141.　　　정답 (B)

142. (A) 저희는 훌륭한 패키지 상품, 저렴한 표 가격, 사람이 붐비지 않는 환경에서 즐기는 스키와 아름다운 풍경을 제공합니다.
(B) 여러분이 항상 편안하게 느끼는 스키 장비를 구입하거나 임대하는 것이 매우 중요합니다.
(C) 세계 어디에서도 더 훌륭한 자격을 갖춘 전문 강사 그룹을 찾을 수 없습니다.
(D) 슬로프, 산책로 및 아이스 링크에서 모든 연령대의 어린이를 위한 재미있는 겨울 스포츠 활동을 찾으세요.　　　정답 (C)

문제 143–146번은 다음 이메일을 참조하시오.

수신: 케이트 키슬링 〈katek@wonderib.com〉
발신: 크리스토퍼 윈터스 〈cwinters@andromeda.com〉
제목: 투자 기회
첨부: pamphlet.pdf

키슬링 씨에게,

저는 귀사의 이사진 중 한 분인 마가렛 존슨 씨에게 귀하의 이름을 받았습니다.

저희는 자동차 항법 장치, 컴퓨터, 그리고 가전제품 용 각종 제어판에 활용되는 액정 화면 생산을 전문으로 하고 있습니다.

저희 반도체의 우수한 품질과 저희 제품에 대한 업계에서의 인기 상승 덕분에, 저희는 바로 확장할 수 있는 기회를 잡기를 원하는데, 그렇게 하기 위해서 외부 투자가들의 도움을 요청하고 있습니다.

저는 이것이 수익성이 좋은 투자를 위한 좋은 기회라고 믿습니다. 첨부된 것은 저희의 서비스와 사업 확장 계획을 설명하는 소책자입니다.

저는 다음 주 초에 귀하와 이 흥미로운 제안에 대해 의논하고 싶습니다. 약속을 정하기 위해 제가 언제 전화드려야 할지 알려 주십시오.

크리스토퍼 윈터스 드림
최고 재무 책임자, 안드로메다 전자

143.　　　정답 (D)

144.　　　정답 (D)

145.　　　정답 (B)

146. (A) 귀하는 가능한 한 많은 비즈니스 잠재 고객을 만나는 것이 좋습니다.
(B) 저희는 핵심 기술 개발에 필요한 충분한 자금을 제공하는 데 실패했습니다.
(C) 저는 다음 주 초에 귀하와 이 흥미로운 제안에 대해 의논하고 싶습니다.
(D) 저희 투자는 일자리 기회를 증가시키고 생활 수준을 향상시킬 것입니다.　　　정답 (C)

Part 7

문제 147–148번은 다음 이메일을 참조하시오.

수신: 엘리자베스 멀베이니 〈emulvaney@mail.com〉
발신: 블라디미르 휴고 〈vhugo@moonlit.com〉
날짜: 5월 25일
제목: 축하드립니다!

멀베이니 씨께,

(147)문라이트 재단을 대표해, 저는 귀하가 문릿 어워즈의 1등 수상자로 선정되신 것을 알리게 되어 기쁩니다. 귀하의 아름다운 대본은 패널들의 마음을 감동시켰습니다.

(148D)귀하는 〈버윅 타임즈〉와의 인터뷰뿐만 아니라, 8,000달러의 장학금을 받으실 것입니다. (148C)귀하는 6월 10일에 버윅 어워즈의 밤에서 상을 수여받을 것입니다. 격식에 맞게 옷을 입으시고 식전 리허설을 위하여 오후 6시까지 엘튼 홀로 와 주시기 바랍니다.

이 상에 대하여 문의 사항이 있으시면, (148A)대본을 제출하셨던 로사 시어도어에게 rtheodore@berwick.edu로 연락하십시오.

블라디미르 휴고 드림

---

147. 멀베이니 씨에게 이메일이 발송된 이유는?
(A) 그녀의 대본 제출을 확인해 주기 위해
(B) 대회의 자격 조건을 알리기 위해
(C) 그녀가 수상자임을 통지하기 위해
(D) 그녀가 준비할 행사에 대한 자세한 정보를 주기 위해　　　정답 (C)

148. 멀베이니 씨에 대해 시사되지 않은 것은 무엇인가?
(A) 그녀는 시어도어 씨에게 그녀의 작품을 제출했다.
(B) 그녀는 문라이트 재단에 의해 고용될 것이다.
(C) 그녀는 아마도 6월 10일 행사에 참석할 것이다.
(D) 그녀는 기자로부터 몇 가지 질문에 답할 수 있다.　　　정답 (B)

문제 149-150번은 다음 문자 메시지를 참조하시오.

소냐 밈스 　　　　　　　　　　　[오전 11시 21분]

마케팅 박람회는 어떻게 진행되고 있나요? 우리 부스에 사람들이 오고 있나요?

캐리 라이트 　　　　　　　　　　[오전 11시 22분]

점심시간 전에 안내책자가 다 떨어질 것 같아요. 이렇게 많은 사람들이 올 줄 예상하지 못했어요.

소냐 밈스 　　　　　　　　　　　[오전 11시 23분]

(149)데이브한테 운전해서 안내책자를 더 가지고 가게 할까요?

캐리 라이트 　　　　　　　　　　[오전 11시 24분]

그러면 좋겠어요. (150)그도 오후 내내 머무를 수 있을까요? 톰이 오전 내내 제품 시연회를 하고 있어서, 부스에서 또 한 사람이 잠재 고객들과 얘기할 수 있으면 돼요.

소냐 밈스 　　　　　　　　　　　[오전 11시 25분]

(150)물론이에요. 내가 그에게 무엇을 해야 하는지 알려 줄게요.

캐리 라이트 　　　　　　　　　　[오전 11시 26분]

감사합니다. 그에게 서둘러 달라고 해주세요. 안내책자 더미가 시시각각으로 줄어들고 있어요.

---

149. 마케팅 박람회에 대해 시사되어 있는 것은 무엇인가?

(A) 처음으로 열리고 있다.

(B) 회의 센터에 위치해 있다.

(C) 점심시간에 끝날 예정이다.

(D) 밈스 씨로부터 운전할 수 있는 거리 내에 있다.　　　정답 (D)

150. 오전 11시 25분에, 밈스 씨가 "물론이에요"라고 쓸 때 무엇을 의미하는 것 같은가?

(A) 그녀는 몇 분 안에 박람회까지 운전해서 갈 수 있다.

(B) 그녀는 더 많은 안내책자가 인쇄되도록 주문할 것이다.

(C) 데이브는 마케팅 박람회에 남아도 된다.

(D) 그녀는 톰이 시범 설명을 보이는 것을 승인한다.　　　정답 (C)

문제 151-153번은 다음 이메일을 참조하시오.

수신: 리차드 데이비스 〈rdavis@daniels.com〉

(152)발신: 레이첼 타카시마 〈rtakashima@daniels.com〉

날짜: 4월 7일

제목: 축하드립니다

데이비스 씨께,

승진을 축하드립니다! 마케팅부에 계셨을 때 당신의 성실함과 훌륭한 업무 성과에 대하여 들었습니다. (152)당신이 제 팀의 구성원이 되어 매우 기쁘고, 당신과 함께 일하는 것을 고대하고 있습니다.

(151)다음 주 수요일에 공식적으로 당신의 업무를 시작하기 전에, 이곳 인사부에서의 업무에 당신이 친숙해지기를 바랍니다. 우리의 업무는 다른 부서들의 것과는 많이 다르므로, 당신이 다음 주 월요일 오전 9시 30분 H2219에 있을 우리 주간 회의에 참석하기를 바랍니다.

당신도 알다시피, 회사는 다음 달 공개 모집을 준비 중입니다. 그러므로 (151)당신의 첫 번째 임무는, 우리 부서로 능력 있는 직원들을 끌어올 창의적인 방안의 개요를 서술할 공식 문서를 만드는 것입니다. (153)이 프로젝트를 함께 하기 위해, 당신보다 3주 먼저 우리 부서로 전근 온 윌리엄 머피 씨에게 전화하세요(내선번호 1244). 제안서를 늦어도 4월 27일까지 제출해 주세요.

다시 한 번, 우리 팀에 오신 것을 환영하며 다음 주 월요일에 뵙겠습니다!

레이첼 타카시마 드림

부장, 인사부

---

151. 타카시마 씨가 이메일을 작성한 이유는?

(A) 회사의 자리를 제안하기 위해

(B) 한 직원에 대한 긍정적인 평가를 하기 위해

(C) 한 직원에게 일련의 지시 사항을 주기 위해

(D) 회의 일정의 변경을 알리기 위해　　　정답 (C)

152. 타카시마 씨에 대해 함축되어 있는 것은 무엇인가?

(A) 최근에 승진되었다.

(B) 신규 고용되었다.

(C) 데이비스 씨의 상사이다.

(D) 서류를 제출할 것이다.　　　정답 (C)

153. 이메일에 따르면, 데이비스 씨는 곧 무엇을 할 것인가?

(A) 스케줄 확정

(B) 신규 사원 모집

(C) 머피 씨에게 연락

(D) 행사 조직　　　정답 (C)

문제 154-156번은 다음 광고를 참조하시오.

코스모의 일자리

1985년에 설립된 출판계의 선두 기업인 코스모는 20개 국에서의 지속적인 성공에 기여할 전임 편집장을 현재 모집 중입니다.

직무 기술:

편집장은 모든 출판 과정을 담당하게 됩니다. 편집장은 편집 조수들을 채용하고 그들과 함께 잡지 각 호의 개요를 만듭니다. 편집장은 또한 출판 전에 잡지의 기사들과 사진 검토에 대한 책임을 맡습니다. 편집장의 또 다른 업무는 잡지의 예산 계획을 감독하고 정기적으로 출판인들과의 회의에 참석하는 것입니다.

자격 요건:

(155B)지원자는 출판계에서 적어도 7년간의 업무 경력이 있어야 합니다. 학사 학위가 요구됩니다. 커뮤니케이션/매스미디어 전공이 매우 선호됩니다. 커뮤니케이션 능력이 매우 중요합니다. (155D)지원자는 뛰어난 구두 및 서면 커뮤니케이션 기술을 가지고 있어야 합니다. (155C)증명된 리더십과 관리 능력 또한 필수적입니다.

지원자는 코스모의 웹사이트 www.cosmo.com에 게시된 지원서를 (156B)이력서, (156C)자기소개서, (156A)2개의 추천서, 그리고 이전 출판 작업의 포트폴리오와 함께 제출해야 합니다. 지원서는 우편으로 제출되어야 합니다. 서류들을 (154)에든버러에 있는 본사의 인사 부장에게 보내십시오. 추가적인 문의 사항이 있다면 산드라 리앙 씨에게 sliang@cosmo.com으로 연락하시기 바랍니다.

---

154. 코스모에 대하여 언급된 것은 무엇인가?

(A) 20개의 다른 언어로 출판된다.

(B) 본사가 에든버러에 있다.

(C) 현재 여러 명의 편집자들을 찾고 있다.

(D) 매달 발행된다.　　　정답 (B)

155. 지원자의 자격 요건이 아닌 것은 무엇인가?

(A) 커뮤니케이션의 학사 학위

(B) 최소 7년의 업계 경력

(C) 좋은 대인 관계 기술

(D) 훌륭한 글 솜씨　　　정답 (A)

156. 지원에 필요한 서류가 아닌 것은 무엇인가?

(A) 추천서

(B) 이력서

(C) 자기소개서

(D) 추천인의 목록 　　　　　　　　　　정답 (D)

문제 157-158번은 다음 회람을 참조하시오.

수신: 공장 직원들

발신: 마커스 제이콥스, 핫디스플레이의 최고 경영자

날짜: 3월 12일

제목: 축하드립니다!

핫디스플레이의 모든 직원 분들께,

현대 생활에 스마트폰이 점점 필수품이 되면서, 스마트폰 시장이 끊임없이 확장하고 있습니다. 이에 따라, 휴대폰 디스플레이 제조업체인 핫디스플레이는 지난달 회사 설립 이래로 최고 판매량을 달성했습니다. 저는 우리의 역사적인 성과를 축하하고 여러분의 기여에 감사드리고 싶습니다.

디스플레이 수요 증가를 충족하기 위하여, (158)대략 100명의 직원을 더 모집해야 할 것입니다. 모집 절차는 다음 달에 시작될 것입니다. (157)그때까지는, 추가적인 급료가 수반된 추가 업무가 불가피하다는 것을 알고 계시기 바랍니다. 만약 초과 근무를 할 수 없는 사람이 있다면, 가급적 빨리 상사에게 보고하십시오.

최고 경영자로서, 훌륭한 근무 환경을 제공하기 위하여 계속적으로 최선을 다할 것입니다. 모든 직원들이 앞으로도 열심히 일하기를 기대합니다.

감사합니다.

마커스 제이콥스

최고 경영자, 핫디스플레이

---

157. 회람의 목적은 무엇인가?

(A) 영업 사원들의 최근 성과를 인정하기 위한 것

(B) 최근 경제 동향을 보고하기 위한 것

(C) 면접 일정을 잡기 위한 것

(D) 근무 시간 변경을 알리기 위한 것 　　　정답 (D)

158. 회람에 따르면, 공장에 어떤 변화가 있을 것인가?

(A) 시설이 확장될 것이다.

(B) 새로운 직원들을 채용할 것이다.

(C) 스마트폰 디스플레이를 더 이상 제조하지 않을 것이다.

(D) 경영진이 바뀔 것이다. 　　　　　　　정답 (B)

문제 159-161번은 다음 이메일을 참조하시오.

수신: 아담 브룩스 〈brooks@hmemail.com〉

발신: 라이언 윌리엄스 〈rwilliams@lightingsolutions.com〉

날짜: 9월 27일

제목: 진심어린 사과

브룩스 씨께,

라이팅 솔루션즈를 대표하여, (159)지난 몇 주간 새 조명 시스템을 귀하의 댁에 설치하는 것과 관련하여 겪으셨을 불편에 대해 진심으로 사과를 전해 드리기 위해 이 이메일을 씁니다.

기록을 살펴보니, 어떤 까닭인지 귀하의 주문을 처리하는 데 실수가 있었던 것으로 보입니다. (161)9월 5일에 귀하의 사무실과 댁에 새로운 조명 시스템이 설치되도록 두 건의 요청을 내셨습니다. 하지만, 유감스럽게도, 저희는 두 번째 요청을 첫 번째 것과 같은 것으로 착각했고 그것을 완료했다고

처리했습니다. (159)그 결과, 댁의 새 조명 기구의 설치 요청은 이행되지 못했습니다.

저희의 정비 팀에게 귀하께 즉시 연락하여 귀하의 댁을 방문하기에 편리한 시간을 잡도록 지시했습니다. 이번 일은 심각한 실수였고, 귀하는 오랜 고객으로 저희에게 매우 소중하기에, 총 설치비에 대해 30% 할인을 제공해 드리고자 합니다. 또한, (160)최신 LED 책상 스탠드를 무료로 드리도록 하겠습니다. 일정이 확정되면 갱신된 청구서를 발행해 드리겠습니다.

다시 한 번 사과드리며, 이것이 귀하의 시간 손실에 대해 조금이라도 보상이 될 수 있기를 바랍니다. 이러한 일이 앞으로는 우리 라이팅 솔루션즈에서 절대로 다시 일어나지 않을 것이라고 약속드립니다. 어떤 다른 문제점이 있으시다면, 망설이지 말고 이메일을 보내시거나 02-555-2777로 저에게 전화하세요. 그렇지 않다면, 저희 정비공들이 곧 연락을 드릴 것입니다.

라이언 윌리엄스 드림

매니저, 고객 상담부

---

159. 이메일이 브룩스 씨에게 발송된 이유는?

(A) 기계 오작동에 대해 사과하기 위해

(B) 신제품을 추천하기 위해

(C) 서비스의 지연에 대해 사과하기 위해

(D) 정책 변경에 대해 설명하기 위해 　　　정답 (C)

160. 브룩스 씨는 보상으로 무엇을 받을 것인가?

(A) 주문한 상품의 무료 교체

(B) 전액 환불

(C) 다음 구매에 대한 할인

(D) 선물 　　　　　　　　　　　　　　정답 (D)

161. [1], [2], [3] 및 [4]로 표시된 위치 중 아래 문장이 들어가기에 가장 적절한 곳은?

"우리는 9월 13일에 귀하의 직장에 배송과 설치를 완료했습니다."

(A) [1]

(B) [2]

(C) [3]

(D) [4] 　　　　　　　　　　　　　　정답 (A)

문제 162-164번은 다음 편지를 참조하시오.

미국 와인 협회

155 노스 코랜델 드라이브

커니, 뉴저지 주 07030

미국

6월 26일

진 번스 씨

밀레지마, 113 뤼 알베르 바흐

33000 보르도, 프랑스

진 번스 씨께,

미국 와인 협회를 대표하여, 귀하를 제 4회 연차 세계 와인 포럼에 초대하고 싶습니다. (162)귀하의 통찰력과 경험을 미국의 젊은 와인 애호가들과 공유해 주시기 바랍니다. 행사의 세부 사항은 아래에 요약되어 있습니다.

행사명	제 4회 세계 와인 포럼
날짜	10월 4일 (금요일)
장소	엘튼 홀, 캘리포니아 대학교
주최	미국 와인 협회
참가자	약 1,000명 예상 (대부분 전문가 및 학생)

---

(162)모든 연사들에게 (163A)왕복 항공권, (163B)5성급 호텔 숙박, (163D) 와인 액세서리 세트 그리고 우리의 후원사 가운데 하나인 (163C)레스토랑 피어링턴 하우스에서 사용할 수 있는 300달러 상당의 상품권을 제공할 것입니다.

(164)만약 행사에 참여하고 싶으시다면, 7월 20일까지 편지 혹은 clopez@uc.edu에 이메일로 저희에게 연락하십시오. 귀하의 고려에 미리 감사드립니다.

크리스틴 로페즈 드림

162. 편지의 목적은 무엇인가?
(A) 프랑스의 와인 문화에 대하여 알리기 위한 것
(B) 강사에게 강연을 해달라고 요청하기 위한 것
(C) 등록 절차에 대한 세부 사항을 알리기 위한 것
(D) 다양한 종류의 와인을 광고하기 위한 것　　정답 (B)

163. 와인 포럼 강연자들에게 제공되지 않을 것은 무엇인가?
(A) 무료 항공 이동
(B) 숙소
(C) 현금 300달러
(D) 와인 액세서리　　정답 (C)

164. 번스 씨는 7월 20일까지 무엇을 할 것을 요청받는가?
(A) 강연하기
(B) 레스토랑 피어링턴 하우스 방문하기
(C) 편지에 답장하기
(D) 후원자가 되겠다는 서면 동의를 하기　　정답 (C)

문제 165-167번은 다음 안내문을 참조하시오.

http://www.okanonpubliclibrary.or.us

오카논 공립 도서관

자주 묻는 질문

도서관 역사	도서관 카드	대여 정책	기부

(165)도서관 카드로 무엇을 할 수 있습니까?
(166A) (166D)도서관 카드로 책과 CD, DVD 등을 대여할 수 있습니다. 또한 전자책, 온라인 신문, 데이터베이스 등에 접근할 때에도 사용할 수 있습니다. 그 외에도, (166C)도서관 내 컴퓨터에서 문서를 작성하거나 인터넷 서핑을 하기 위한 예약을 할 수 있습니다.

(165)도서관 카드를 어떻게 받을 수 있습니까?
도서관 카드를 받기 위해서는 신청서가 작성되어야 합니다. 또한, 신청자는 사진과 함께 자신의 신분증을 가지고 와야 합니다. 신청서는 양식을 제출하는 고객 서비스 센터에서 찾을 수 있습니다. 도서관 카드는 (166B)운영 시간 동안인 월요일부터 토요일, 오전 9시부터 오후 6시 사이에 오프라인에서만 발급될 수 있습니다.

(165)도서관 카드를 받는 데 얼마의 비용이 듭니까?
도서관 카드는 오카논에 거주하고 있는 분은 누구에게나 무료입니다. 만약 (166C)주민이 아니라면, 도서관 카드는 5달러의 비용으로 발급될 수 있습니다. 또한, 주민이 아닌 분들에게는 2달러의 월별 요금이 부과됩니다.

(165) (167)만약 도서관 카드를 분실하면 어떻게 해야 하나요?
만약 도서관 카드를 분실하면, 고객 서비스 센터의 직원 누구에게든 가능한 빨리 보고하는 것이 매우 중요합니다. (167)분실한 카드를 교체하기 위하여 4달러의 비용이 부과될 것이라는 점을 알아 두세요.

165. 안내문의 목적은 무엇인가?
(A) 새로운 주민 카드를 소개하기 위한 것
(B) 도서관 사용자들에게 컴퓨터 사용 방법에 대하여 알리기 위한 것
(C) 회원 자격에 대하여 설명하기 위한 것
(D) 오카논 공립 도서관에 대한 몇 가지 변동 사항을 설명하기 위한 것　　정답 (C)

166. 안내문에서 나타나 있지 않은 것은 무엇인가?
(A) 책을 대여하기 위하여 도서관 카드가 필요하다.
(B) 도서관은 일요일에 문을 닫는다.
(C) 비거주자들은 도서관에서 컴퓨터를 사용하는 것이 금지되어 있다.
(D) 도서관에는 책 외에도 자료들을 소장하고 있다.　　정답 (C)

167. 카드 소지자들은 도서관 카드를 잃어버렸을 때 무엇을 해야 하는가?
(A) 카드 교체를 위하여 4달러 지불
(B) 다른 도서관 회원으로부터 도서관 카드 빌리기
(C) 분실한 카드를 찾기 위해 도서관의 웹사이트에 도움 요청
(D) 신청서 작성　　정답 (A)

문제 168-171번은 다음 온라인 채팅 토론을 참조하시오.

신디 머피	[오전 11시 17분]

네, 여러분. (171)드디어 발표가 끝나서 다행이에요. 전체적으로 잘했어요.

해럴드 스톨링스	[오전 11시 18분]

(168)디지테크 사람들한테서 들은 거 있어요?

신디 머피	[오전 11시 20분]

(168)나가는 길에 콜린스 씨와 얘기했어요. (169) (171)그분이 이번 주 금요일에 그의 회사에서 회의를 요청했어요.

킴 톰슨	[오전 11시 21분]

(171)그거 좋은 징조군요.

신디 머피	[오전 11시 22분]

그렇고 말고요. 킴, (169)회계사로서 재정적인 세부사항을 잘 아시기 때문에 저와 동행해 주셨으면 해요. 콜린스 씨가 계약 조건을 협상하고 싶다는 뜻을 내비쳤어요.

킴 톰슨	[오전 11시 23분]

(169)문제없어요. 그날 컨벤션 센터에서 열리는 기술 총회에 참석할 계획이었지만, 디지테크가 훨씬 더 중요해요.

올랜도 테니스	[오전 11시 25분]

제가 대신 갈 수 있어요, 킴. 그래도 괜찮아요, 신디?

해럴드 스톨링스	[오전 11시 26분]

저도 참석할 거예요. 원하신다면 제 차에 같이 타고 가도 돼요, 올랜도.

신디 머피	[오전 11시 30분]

그렇게 하세요. 저는 좋습니다.

올랜도 테니스	[오전 11시 31분]

고마워요, 신디와 해럴드.

신디 머피	[오전 11시 32분]

아, (170)해럴드, 발표에 대한 당신 메모가 필요해요. 그 프로젝트에 대한 모든 것을 제가 확실히 이해하도록 하기 위해 그것들을 검토해야 해요. 점심 전에 제 사무실로 갖다 주실 수 있어요?

168. 콜린스 씨는 누구이겠는가?
(A) 회계사
(B) 총회의 강연자
(C) 작성자들의 동료
(D) 디지테크의 직원　　정답 (D)

169. 톰슨 씨는 금요일에 무엇을 할 것인가?
(A) 제품 작동 방식 시연하기
(B) 기술 총회에 가기
(C) 디지테크에서 회의에 참석하기
(D) 새 발표 준비하기 　　　　　　　　정답 (C)

170. 스톨링스 씨는 이후에 무엇을 하겠는가?
(A) 컨벤션 센터 방문
(B) 머피 씨에게 문서 제공
(C) 머피 씨와 점심 식사
(D) 발표를 위한 문서 인쇄 　　　　　　정답 (B)

171. 오전 11시 21분에, 톰슨 씨가 "그건 좋은 징조군요"라고 쓸 때 무엇을 시사하는 것 같은가?
(A) 그녀는 발표가 잘 되었다고 생각한다.
(B) 그녀는 계약 조건이 마음에 든다.
(C) 그녀는 새로운 광고를 승인한다.
(D) 그녀는 오늘 밤 시간 외 근무를 기꺼이 할 것이다. 　정답 (A)

문제 172 - 175번은 다음 안내문을 참조하시오.

---
(172)사용하기 전에 읽으세요:
카페 비바 I-20

카페 비바 I-20을 구매해 주셔서 감사합니다. 지난달에 시몬스 최고의 제품 디자인 상을 수상한 이 훌륭한 커피 메이커는 집에서 훌륭한 커피를 마실 수 있는 가장 좋은 방법입니다. 카운터 공간을 거의 차지하지 않는 이 새 모델은 당신의 감각을 만족시킬 것입니다.

사용 설명
1. 카페 비바 I-20을 켜고 왼쪽에 초록색 불빛이 깜박일 때까지 기다리세요.
2. 캡슐 트레이를 꺼내어 가장 좋아하는 맛 중 하나를 넣으세요.
3. 캡슐을 안으로 넣어 잠그고 컵을 아래에 놓으세요.
4. 가열 버튼을 누르세요.
　• (175)뜨겁고, 압축된 물이 캡슐을 통과해서 나와 컵을 채우기 시작할 것입니다.
5. 풍부한 크림 층과 함께 준비된 커피 한 잔을 즐기세요.
　• (174)사용된 캡슐은 완전히 식은 후에 꺼내시기 바랍니다.

맛
(173)카페 비바는 10개의 다양한 맛의 커피 캡슐들을 제공합니다. 저희 웹사이트 www.cafeviva.com을 방문해 다양한 커피와 밀크 캡슐을 알아보세요.

---

172. 안내문은 누구를 대상으로 하는 것 같은가?
(A) 카페 주인
(B) 고객
(C) 기술자
(D) 커피 콩 공급업자 　　　　　　　　정답 (B)

173. 고객이 다양한 종류의 커피 캡슐을 구매할 수 있는 방법은?
(A) 배송을 신청함으로써
(B) 고객 서비스 센터에 전화함으로써
(C) 지역 대리점에 찾아감으로써
(D) 웹사이트에 방문함으로써 　　　　　정답 (D)

174. 안내문에서 추론될 수 있는 것은 무엇인가?
(A) 끓인 직후의 커피 캡슐은 뜨거울 수 있다.
(B) 다른 모델의 커피 메이커가 곧 출시될 것이다.
(C) 커피 컵이 패키지에 포함되어 있다.

(D) 증기는 기계가 오작동하고 있다는 표시이다. 　정답 (A)

175. [1], [2], [3] 그리고 [4]로 표시된 곳 중에, 아래 문장이 들어가기에 가장 적절한 곳은?
"이것은 증기를 발생시킬 수 있다는 것을 알아 두세요."
(A) [1]
(B) [2]
(C) [3]
(D) [4] 　　　　　　　　　　　　　　정답 (C)

문제 176-180번은 다음 이메일들을 참조하시오.

수신: 코스 온라인 〈customersupport@coursesonline.com〉
(176)발신: 바바라 샌드 〈bsand@imail.com〉
날짜: 4월 19일
제목: 모바일 앱 결제 문제

관계자 분께,

(178)4월 16일에 저는 코스 온라인의 웹사이트를 방문했고, 이제 휴대 전화로 볼 수 있는 교육 과정들을 제공하고 있다는 사실을 알게 되었습니다. 그 광고는 또한 모바일 강좌 애플리케이션을 처음 이용하는 사용자들은 50% 할인 쿠폰을 받을 것이라고 했습니다. (176)그래서 저는 (179B)음식과 영양 강좌(NF4017)를 할인 쿠폰으로 구매하려고 했으나, (179D)결제 페이지에서 코드가 계속해서 거부되었습니다. 이것은 일종의 오류입니까? 이 강좌는 다른 강좌들보다 조금 더 비싼 80달러이기 때문에, 저는 이 강좌에 할인 쿠폰을 사용하고 싶습니다.

대신, (177)60달러에 (179B)익스트림 홈 운동 강좌(XW2551)를 구매했습니다. (176)하지만, 그 영상들을 제 휴대 전화에서 시청할 수 없고 애플리케이션의 내 강의실 페이지에 있는 구매 강좌 목록에도 나타나지 않았습니다. (179A)제 신용 카드 청구서는 분명히 그 강좌를 결제한 것으로 보여 줍니다. 이 오류를 최대한 빨리 정정해 주십시오.

감사합니다.

바바라 샌드

수신: 바바라 샌드 〈bsand@imail.com〉
발신: 레너드 위치 〈lwich@coursesonline.com〉
날짜: 4월 20일
제목: 답장: 모바일 앱 결제 문제

샌드 씨께,

이것은 귀하의 4월 19일자 문의에 대한 답변입니다. 받으신 할인 쿠폰은 단지 모바일 강좌 애플리케이션이 아닌, (179D)코스 온라인 서비스 전체에 대한 신규 이용자들을 위한 것입니다. 따라서, 귀하는 그 쿠폰을 강좌 번호 NF40170에 사용하실 수 없었을 겁니다. 명확하지 않은 설명으로 혼란을 끼친 것에 대해 사과드립니다.

또한 귀하께서 구매하신 강좌를 이용하실 수 없다고 하셨습니다. 저희 앱은 네트워크 통신량 문제를 해결하기 위해 최근 업데이트 되었으며, 그 과정에서 예상치 못한 오류들이 발생한 것으로 보입니다. 시스템 상의 모든 버그들이 이제 수정되었으며, 그 강좌에 이제 접근하실 수 있을 겁니다. 저희가 끼쳤을 수 있는 불편에 사과를 드리고자, (180)귀하의 코스 온라인 계정에 10달러의 보상 포인트를 적립해 드렸습니다. 이 포인트는 웹사이트 우측 상단 끝에 있는 내 지갑에서 확인하실 수 있습니다. 그것은 향후에 온라인 강좌나 전자책을 구매하실 때 사용하실 수 있습니다.

다른 문제점을 겪게 되시면, 저희에게 보고해 주십시오. 귀하의 피드백은 저희에게 매우 소중합니다.

레너드 위치 드림
매니저, 코스 온라인

176. 샌드 씨가 첫 번째 이메일을 작성한 이유는?
(A) 문제를 보고하기 위해
(B) 주문 취소를 요청하기 위해
(C) 문제의 원인을 설명하기 위해
(D) 새 온라인 강좌 신청하기 위해 　　　　정답 (A)

177. 샌드 씨가 XW2551에 대해 지불한 금액은 얼마인가?
(A) 30달러
(B) 40달러
(C) 60달러
(D) 80달러 　　　　정답 (C)

178. 코스 온라인에 대해 시사되어 있는 것은 무엇인가?
(A) 최근 새로운 종류의 서비스를 개발했다.
(B) 현재 기술적 어려움을 겪고 있다.
(C) 정기적으로 애플리케이션을 업데이트한다.
(D) 고객이 한 번에 시청할 수 있는 강좌의 수를 제한한다. 　　　　정답 (A)

179. 샌드 씨에 대해 나타나 있지 않은 것은 무엇인가?
(A) 모바일 교육 강좌를 신용 카드로 결제했다.
(B) 아마도 건강에 관심이 많을 것이다.
(C) 한 온라인 강좌의 내용에 대해 불만족스러워한다.
(D) 과거에 코스 온라인의 서비스를 이용한 적이 있다. 　　　　정답 (C)

180. 샌드 씨에게 무엇이 주어졌는가?
(A) 환불
(B) 무료 소프트웨어
(C) 포인트
(D) 전자책 　　　　정답 (C)

문제 181-185번은 다음 광고와 기사를 참조하시오.

베닝턴 헤럴드
베닝턴, 버몬트 주
　　　　　　　　　　　　　　　4월 13일 수요일
구인: 앨리게이터 E&C

앨리게이터 E&C는 버몬트 주의 베닝턴에 곧 있을 지역사회 센터의 건설을 위한 건설 현장 근로자들을 추가로 구하고 있습니다. 아래에는 저희가 모집 중인 자리에 대한 설명입니다:

• **전기 기사**
전기 기사의 주된 업무는 전선, 퓨즈, 그리고 다른 전기 부품들을 설치하고 유지하는 것입니다. 이 자리는 유효한 전기 기사 자격증과 (181)**최소 1년의 경력을 요구합니다.** 급여는 주당 700달러에서 800달러 사이입니다.

• **배관공**
배관공은 주로 상수도관과 오수 처리 시스템(하수도)을 설치하고 수리합니다. 이 자리는 유효한 배관 자격증과 (181)**최소 2년의 경력이 요구됩니다.** 급여는 주당 900달러에서 1,000달러 사이입니다.

• **레미콘 트럭 운전자**
(183)레미콘 트럭 운전자는 작업 현장으로 콘크리트 믹스를 운반하고 시멘트 활송 장치를 조립하는 것과 트럭 청소를 포함합니다. 이 자리는 유효한 상용 운전 면허증과 (181)**최소 1년의 경력을 요구합니다.** (183)운전자는 주말 근무를 위해 호출될 수도 있다는 점을 알아 두세요. 급여는 주당 650달러에서 750달러 사이입니다.

• **혜택**
융통성 있는 병가와 유급 휴가 정책을 가지고 있습니다. (182B)**종합 의료 혜택이 모든 사무/현장 직원들에게 제공됩니다.**
4월 30일까지 다니엘 크레이그 씨에게 dcraig@aenc.com으로 이메일을 보내시거나 207-360-9913으로 전화 주세요.

　　　　　　　　　　　　　　　　　　　　베닝턴 데일리
마을 동정

베닝턴 (6월 1일) - (185D)지역 건설 회사인 앨리게이터 E&C가 지난주 베닝턴에 새로운 지역사회 센터를 짓기 시작했다. "(182C)10년 전 사업체를 뉴욕에서 베닝턴으로 이전한 이래로, 회사의 수익이 급격히 증가하고 있습니다. (182D)심지어 작년, 저희는 10년만에 가장 큰 연간 수익을 기록했습니다. (185D)진심어린 감사를 표하기 위해, 저는 새 시설을 짓고 주로 이 지역에서 직원들을 모집함으로써 이 지역사회에 기여하기로 결정했습니다"라고 회사의 CEO인 존 웨버가 그의 의도에 대해 말했다.

베닝턴의 시장 앨리슨 다이아몬드는 즉각적으로 이 프로젝트를 환영했다. "저는 특히 모집 결정에 대해 앨리게이터 E&C에 감사하고 싶습니다. 이는 (184)이 도시의 만성적인 실업 문제를 크게 완화해 줄 것입니다"라고 다이아몬드 씨가 말했다.

공사 현장의 현장 근로자들 또한 기뻐하고 있다. (183)"두 달 전 〈베닝턴 헤럴드〉에서 앨리게이터 E&C의 구인 공고를 본 것이 저에게 큰 행운이었습니다. 가끔씩 주말에도 일해야 하지만, 저의 고향에 기여할 수 있다는 것에 기쁩니다"라고 새롭게 채용된 앨리게이터 E&C 직원인 (183)제이크 클리퍼랜드가 말했다.

새로운 지역사회 센터는 다양한 시설들과 프로그램들을 제공할 것이다. 사람들이 (185A)적은 요금으로 자유롭게 사용할 수 있는 (185B)피트니스 센터, 많은 세미나 룸, 그리고 다목적 홀이 들어설 것이다. (185C)공사는 일년이 걸릴 것으로 예상된다. 지역사회 센터나 앨리게이터 E&C에 대한 더 많은 정보를 위해서는 www.aenc.com을 방문하면 된다.

　　　　　　　　　　　　　　　　　　　　비나 칸 작성
---

181. 광고의 3개 자리 모두가 요구하는 자격 조건 하나는 무엇인가?
(A) 뛰어난 지도력
(B) 상용 운전 면허
(C) 학위
(D) 관련 분야에서의 이전 종사 여부 　　　　정답 (D)

182. 앨리게이터 E&C에 대해 시사되지 않은 것은 무엇인가?
(A) 뉴욕에서의 프로젝트를 위하여 최근에 임시 직원들을 모집했다.
(B) 회사의 직원들에게 종합 의료 보험을 제공한다.
(C) 처음에 베닝턴이 아닌 다른 곳에서 사업을 시작했다.
(D) 지난 10년 중 가장 높은 수익을 보게 되었다. 　　　　정답 (A)

183. 클리퍼랜드 씨에 대해 나타나 있는 것은 무엇인가?
(A) 상수도관을 수리한다.
(B) 그의 새로운 직업 때문에 베닝턴으로 이사했다.
(C) 주말에만 근무한다.
(D) 콘크리트 믹스를 운반한다. 　　　　정답 (D)

184. 베닝턴에 대해 추론될 수 있는 것은 무엇인가?
(A) 새로운 시장이 최근에 선출되었다.
(B) 낮은 취업률을 보이고 있다.
(C) 하나의 지역사회 센터만 가지고 있다.
(D) 새로운 사업체에 다양한 혜택을 제공한다. 　　　　정답 (B)

185. 지역사회 센터에 대해 사실이 아닌 것은?

(A) 무료로 대중들에게 개방될 것이다.

(B) 운동을 위한 시설을 갖게 될 것이다.

(C) 약 일 년 후에 대중에게 개방될 것으로 예상된다.

(D) 지역사회에 감사를 표하기 위해 앨리게이터 E&C에 의해 건설되고 있다. 　　　　　　　　　　　　　　　　　정답 (A)

문제 186-190번은 다음 회람들과 이메일을 참조하시오.

---

(186)수신: 모니카 베이, 루시 홀

발신: 로저 프리먼

날짜: 12월 19일

제목: 면접

(186)우리 부서의 공석으로 이동을 신청한 직원들을 대상으로 2차 면접을 실시할 예정입니다. 다음은 최종 후보들의 면접 시간과 명단입니다. 모든 면접은 12월 22일에 진행될 예정입니다.

에릭 마스턴　　– 오전 10시

마리아 사이먼　– 오전 11시

대디어스 빈　　– 오후 1시

우리 세 명이 후보들을 다시 한 번 면접 볼 것입니다. 여러분의 스케줄을 이 시간에 비워 두도록 해주십시오.

텐 디자인 주식회사

수신: 전 직원, 디자인부

발신: 로저 프리먼

날짜: 1월 8일 목요일

제목: (187)새로운 얼굴

여러분,

현재 경리부의 직원인 마리아 사이먼이 다음 주 월요일에 우리 부서로 온다는 것을 알려 드리게 되어 기쁩니다.

(187)사이먼 씨는 우파에 있는 바시키르 대학교에서 회계학 학사 학위를 받은 후 우리 회사에서 회계사로 일하기 시작했습니다. 하지만, (188)그녀는 항상 디자인에 관심이 있어서 시간제로 일하며 그녀가 다녔던 대학의 대학원에 다녔습니다. 사이먼 씨는 그래픽 디자인 석사 학위를 받은 후, 우리 부서로의 이동을 신청했고, 그녀의 신청이 방금 승인되었습니다.

여러분 중 많은 분들이 건물에서 사이먼 씨를 보셨겠지만, 저는 그래도 여러분 모두 그녀가 팀에 온 것을 환영해 주시기를 권합니다. (189)주간 회의에 이어 그녀를 위한 환영 점심식사를 할 예정이니, 모두 참석하실 수 있도록 하십시오. 우리는 그날 모리슨즈에서 식사를 하러 나갈 것입니다.

수신: 마리아 사이먼 〈msimon@tenndesign.com〉

발신: 로저 프리먼 〈rfreeman@tenndesign.com〉

날짜: 1월 9일, 금요일

제목: 환영합니다!

사이먼 씨에게,

여기 디자인부에서 우리와 함께 하시게 되어 기쁩니다. 귀하는 분명히 이곳의 근무 환경을 좋아하실 것입니다.

(189)매주 수요일 11시에 부서 회의를 개최한다는 것을 알아 두셔야 합니다. 귀하는 그 회의에 참석하셔야 할 것입니다. (190)제가 다음 주 금요일 오전 10시에 진행하는 짧은 교육 시간에도 참석하셔야 합니다.

귀하가 이곳에 근무한 지 몇 년 됐으니 건물 구경은 필요 없을 것으로 짐작합니다. 하지만 부서에 적응하는 데 도움이 필요하시면 알려 주세요.

로저 프리먼 드림

186. 베이 씨와 홀 씨에 대해 사실인 것은?

(A) 그들은 12월 22일에 출장을 갈 것이다.

(B) 그들은 프리먼 씨와 좋은 친구이다.

(C) 그들은 시간제 직원이다.

(D) 그들은 같은 부서에서 근무한다. 　　　　　　정답 (D)

187. 두 번째 회람의 목적은 무엇인가?

(A) 직원의 판매 실적을 인정하기 위한 것

(B) 회사에 채용 공고를 발표하기 위한 것

(C) 신규 직원의 프로필을 알려 주기 위한 것

(D) 디자인 프로젝트에 대한 정보를 제공하기 위한 것 　정답 (C)

188. 사이먼 씨에 대해 언급된 것은 무엇인가?

(A) 그녀는 학교에 다니면서 동시에 일했다.

(B) 그녀는 학부생으로 디자인을 공부했다.

(C) 그녀는 현재 대학원에 다니고 있다.

(D) 그녀는 자기 회사의 관리직에 지원했다. 　정답 (A)

189. 사이먼 씨는 언제 동료들과 점심을 먹겠는가?

(A) 월요일

(B) 화요일

(C) 수요일

(D) 금요일 　　　　　　　　　　　　　정답 (C)

190. 프리먼 씨가 사이먼 씨에게 무엇을 할 것을 요청하는가?

(A) 새로운 동료들에게 자기 소개하기

(B) 교육 과정에 참가하기

(C) 그녀의 디자인 작품을 그에게 보여 주기

(D) 건물에 익숙해지기 　　　　　　　　정답 (B)

문제 191-195번은 다음 공지와 이메일들을 참조하시오.

제 15회 연차

포틀랜드 무역 박람회

(191) (193)3월 10일과 11일 오전 9시부터 오후 8시까지 던컨 컨벤션 센터에서 개최됩니다.

다음 업계에 몸담고 있는 350개 이상의 국내외 기업이 참석할 예정입니다:

의료

제조업

물류

소프트웨어

조선업

참석은 무료이지만, 다음 웹사이트에서 사전 등록해야 합니다.

www.portlandtradefair.org/registration

좀 더 자세한 내용을 원하시면 저희 웹 페이지를 방문하십시오.

www.portlandtradefair.org

수신: 에밀리 로즈 〈emily_r@watsontech.com〉

발신: 행크 개더스 〈hankgathers@smm.com〉

날짜: 3월 13일

제목: 안녕하세요

로즈 씨에게,

안녕하세요, 행크 개더스입니다. **(193)이번 주 초 포틀랜드 무역 박람회 둘째 날 귀하를 만났습니다.** 귀하와 이야기를 나누고 귀사가 제조하는 제품에 대해 알게 되어 정말 즐거웠습니다. 상당히 바쁘신데도 불구하고 저와 개인적으로 얘기하는 데 시간을 내주신 사실에 대해 진심으로 감사드립니다.

(192) (195C)3월 21일에 만날 시간이 되시는지 궁금합니다. 제가 그때 시애틀에 있을 예정이기 때문에, 그날 언제든지 귀하의 사무실을 방문할 수 있습니다. **(195D)말씀하신 새로운 가전제품에 대해 좀 더 자세히 알고 싶습니다.** **(195B)귀사를 대표해서 협상하실 수 있습니까?** 그렇지 않다면, 우리 회의에 누가 참석할지 확인해 주실 수 있을까요? **(195A)마지막으로, 귀사는 대량 구매에 대한 할인을 제공하나요?**

답장 기다리겠습니다.

행크 개더스 드림
SMM 주식회사

수신: 행크 개더스 〈hankgathers@smm.com〉
발신: 에밀리 로즈 〈emily_r@watsontech.com〉
날짜: 3월 14일
제목: 답장: 안녕하세요

개더스 씨에게,

이메일을 보내 주셔서 감사합니다. 무역 박람회에서 귀하를 만나서 역시 반가웠습니다. 통찰력 있는 질문을 하셨고, 저는 귀사에 대해 많은 것을 알게 되었습니다.

(194) (195C)3월 21일 오전에 시간이 되시니까, 제 사무실에서 오전 9시에 만나는 게 어떨까요? 저는 정오에 출장을 가기 위해 공항으로 가야 해서 일찍 만날수록 더 좋습니다. **(195D)새로 나온 가전제품 전부를 시연해서 정확히 어떻게 작동하는지 아실 수 있게 하겠습니다.** **(195B)제 상사 하워드 카터도 참석할 예정입니다.** 그분이 귀하께서 우리와 거래하기를 원하는 조건에 대해 말할 수 있습니다.

다음 주에 뵙겠습니다.

에밀리 로즈 드림

191. 안내문에서 포틀랜드 무역 박람회에 대해 나타나 있는 것은 무엇인가?
(A) 그것은 2일에 걸쳐 열릴 것이다.
(B) 그것은 오직 포틀랜드 지역의 기업들만 대상으로 한다.
(C) 그것은 처음으로 개최되고 있다.
(D) 그 어느 때보다도 더 많은 방문객을 예상하고 있다.

정답 (A)

192. 개더스 씨가 이메일을 작성한 이유는?
(A) 안내책자를 요청하기 위해
(B) 공석에 지원하기 위해
(C) 직접 만나는 것에 대해 문의하기 위해
(D) 회의 날짜를 재확인하기 위해

정답 (C)

193. 개더스 씨가 로즈 씨를 만난 날짜는 언제였는가?
(A) 3월 10일
(B) 3월 11일
(C) 3월 12일
(D) 3월 13일

정답 (B)

194. 로즈 씨는 3월 21일에 무엇을 할 것인가?
(A) 연설
(B) 무역 박람회 참석
(C) 비행기 탑승
(D) 입사 지원자 면접

정답 (C)

195. 로즈 씨가 다루지 않는 개더스 씨의 관심사는 어느 것인가?
(A) 그가 할인된 가격을 받을 수 있는지 여부
(B) 거래 조건을 협상할 수 있는 사람
(C) 그가 그녀를 만날 수 있는 때
(D) 그가 얻을 수 있는 정보의 종류

정답 (A)

문제 196-200번은 다음 안내문과 전화 메시지 그리고 기사를 참조하시오.

비치사이드 아파트 주민 여러분께 알립니다. 최근의 폭풍으로 인한 침수 피해로, 그레이블 로드와 도로 북쪽 인도가 크게 파손되었습니다. **(196) (197)햄프턴 건설의 작업팀이 4월 10일 내일부터 도로와 인도를 수리할 예정입니다.** **(200)도로 보수 작업은 4월 17일에 완료될 것으로 예상됩니다.** 이 기간 내내 아파트 단지 정문 쪽 그레이블 로드 구간이 폐쇄될 것입니다. 따라서 주민과 방문객들은 플레전트 스트리트의 후문을 이용해야 합니다. 수리 작업으로 인한 과도한 소음에 대해 미리 사과드립니다.

수신: 제프 디콘, 비치사이드 아파트 관리인
발신: 캐롤 크로스, 비치사이드 아파트 안내원
날짜: 4월 9일
시간: 오후 4시 55분

시장실의 로베르타 홀에게서 방금 전화가 왔어요. 그녀는 내일부터 도로와 인도에 대한 수리가 시작된다고 말했어요. **(197)작업은 보우만 건설에서 할 예정입니다.** 그녀는 공사가 매일 오전 7시에 시작하여 오후 7시까지 계속될 것이라고 말했어요. 그녀는 시장이 긴 작업 시간으로 작업반원들이 작업을 더 빨리 끝낼 수 있게 되길 바라며, 그렇게 되면 주민들에게 더 편리해질 것이라고 말했어요. **(198)그녀는 당신이 이 정보를 주민들에게 알려 주길 바란다고 말했습니다.**

그레이블 로드가 다시 열리다

데이비드 칼라일 기자 작성

헤이븐 **(200)(4월 20일)** – 심한 뇌우 때문에 헤이븐 전역에 갑작스런 범람이 생긴 지 3주가 지났지만, **(199)도시는 여전히 그로 인해 생긴 파손을 손보기 위해 수리 중이다.** 도시의 몇몇 도로들은 상태가 좋지 않다.

하지만, 해안과 인접해 있는 그레이블 로드는 그런 도로에 속하지 않는다. 도로 보수반이 도로 수리를 위해 일주일 넘게 지칠 줄 모르고 작업했고, **(200)어제 막 작업을 마쳤다.** "그레이블 로드는 헤이븐의 교통에 매우 중요하기 때문에, 차량이 다시 그 위를 달릴 수 있어 기쁩니다"라고 글렌 굿웨이 시장은 말했다. "이제, **(199)우리는 나머지 도로들을 수리하기만 하면, 생활이 정상으로 돌아갈 수 있습니다.**"

시장은 수리비를 지불할 충분한 자금을 시가 보유하고 있다고 강조했다. 굿웨이 시장은 헤이븐이 시에서 견뎌낸 것과 같은 자연 재해가 생길 경우 의지할 수 있는 긴급 자금을 보유하고 있다고 언급했다.

196. 안내문의 목적은 무엇인가?
(A) 세입자에게 공사 작업에 대해 알리기 위한 것
(B) 반복된 요청에 응하기 위한 것
(C) 출입구가 폐쇄된 이유를 설명하기 위한 것
(D) 주민들에게 기부를 요청하기 위한 것

정답 (A)

197. 안내문의 어떤 정보가 전화 메시지와 다른가?
(A) 작업이 시작되는 날짜
(B) 작업을 하는 회사
(C) 작업이 시작될 시간
(D) 작업 비용

정답 (B)

198. 홀 씨가 메시지를 남긴 이유는?
(A) 문제를 설명하기 위해
(B) 디콘 씨의 요청에 응하기 위해
(C) 조언을 요청하기 위해
(D) 갱신된 정보를 제공하기 위해 　　　　　정답 (D)

199. 굿웨이 씨가 헤이븐의 도로에 대해 무엇을 말하는가?
(A) 그것들은 현재 확장되고 있다.
(B) 모두 포장되었다.
(C) 아직 물에 잠겨 있는 것들이 있다.
(D) 그 중 일부는 수리되지 않았다. 　　　　　정답 (D)

200. 그레이블 로드에서 실시된 수리 작업에 대해 나타나 있는 것은 무엇인가?
(A) 그것은 예정보다 늦게 완료되었다.
(B) 그것은 돈이 너무 많이 들었다.
(C) 그것은 2개 건설 회사에 의해 실시되었다.
(D) 그것은 개인 자금으로 지불되었다. 　　　　　정답 (A)

1. 미W
(A) Both of the women are wheeling their luggage.
(B) They are leaning against the railing.
(C) A woman is placing her suitcase on a cart.
(D) They are rolling a cart down the aisle.

(A) 여자 둘 다 바퀴 달린 가방을 끌고 가고 있다.
(B) 그들은 난간에 기대고 있다.
(C) 여자 한 명이 여행가방을 카트 위에 올려놓고 있다.
(D) 그들은 바퀴 달린 카트를 통로 아래로 밀고 가고 있다. 　　정답 (A)

2. 호W
(A) They are driving through the park.
(B) The man is pointing at something on a map.
(C) The man is folding a map in half.
(D) They have stopped for gas.

(A) 그들은 차를 몰고 공원을 통과하고 있다.
(B) 남자가 지도의 어떤 것을 손으로 가리키고 있다.
(C) 남자가 지도를 반으로 접고 있다.
(D) 그들은 가스를 넣기 위해 멈춰 섰다. 　　　　　정답 (B)

3. 영M
(A) A ramp is leading to the back of the truck.
(B) A man is pushing a box up on the ramp.
(C) A container has been left open.
(D) A vehicle is being worked on in a garage.

(A) 경사판이 트럭 뒷편에 이어져 있다.
(B) 한 남자가 상자를 경사판에서 위로 밀어 올리고 있다.
(C) 용기가 열린 채로 있다.
(D) 차량이 정비소에서 수리되고 있다. 　　　　　정답 (A)

4. 미W
(A) She is picking some flowers.
(B) She is carrying some dirt in a wheelbarrow.
(C) She is building a greenhouse.
(D) She is using a garden tool.

(A) 그녀는 꽃을 꺾고 있다.
(B) 그녀는 외바퀴 손수레에 흙을 실어 나르고 있다.
(C) 그녀는 온실하우스를 짓고 있다.
(D) 그녀는 정원용 도구를 사용 중이다. 　　　　　정답 (D)

5. 영M
(A) Some books are piled up on the floor.
(B) Many books have been shelved in rows.
(C) A man is reading a sign on the wall.
(D) A man is sorting through some books.

(A) 책 몇 권이 바닥에 쌓여 있다.
(B) 많은 책들이 줄 맞춰 선반에 놓여 있다.
(C) 남자가 벽에 있는 표지판을 읽고 있다.
(D) 남자가 책들을 종류별로 분류하고 있다. 　　　　　정답 (B)

6. 미M
(A) A server is setting a table for two people.
(B) They are facing the same direction.
(C) A photographer is taking a photo of a couple.

(D) Some customers are paying for a meal.

(A) 서빙하는 사람이 2인용 식탁을 차리고 있다.
(B) 그들은 같은 방향을 향하고 있다.
(C) 사진가가 커플의 사진을 찍어 주고 있다.
(D) 몇 명의 고객들이 식사값을 치르고 있다. **정답 (B)**

Part 2

7. [미M] [호W]
When does the new sci-fi movie come out?
(A) At a movie theater nearby.
(B) Movie director of the year.
(C) This Saturday.

새로운 공상과학 영화는 언제 나오나요?
(A) 근처 극장에서요.
(B) 올해의 영화감독이요.
(C) 이번 주 토요일이요. **정답 (C)**

8. [영M] [미W]
Where is the company library?
(A) The book is not printed anymore.
(B) At the end of the hallway.
(C) Put it back on the shelf.

회사 도서관이 어디에 있어요?
(A) 그 책은 더 이상 인쇄되지 않아요.
(B) 복도 끝이요.
(C) 그것을 선반에 다시 놓으세요. **정답 (B)**

9. [호W] [미M]
What airline is the vice-president flying to Madrid?
(A) An aisle seat, please.
(B) Top Airlines.
(C) That's a full flight.

부사장님은 어느 항공사 비행기를 타고 마드리드에 가시죠?
(A) 통로 쪽 자리로 주세요.
(B) 탑 항공사요.
(C) 그건 만석 항공편이에요. **정답 (B)**

10. [미W] [영M]
How long is the non-stop flight to Frankfurt?
(A) No, I went there by train.
(B) Only six hours.
(C) There is a long line at the terminal entrance.

프랑크푸르트 행 직항편은 얼마나 걸리나요?
(A) 아뇨, 저는 거기에 기차로 갔어요.
(B) 6시간밖에 안 걸려요.
(C) 터미널 입구에 줄이 길게 섰어요. **정답 (B)**

11. [미M] [호W]
Can I have the check, please?
(A) He checked out yesterday.
(B) Of course. Here it is.
(C) No, it wasn't inspected thoroughly.

계산서 갖다 주실래요?
(A) 그는 어제 퇴실했어요.
(B) 물론이죠. 여기 있어요.

(C) 아뇨. 그건 철저히 점검되지 않았어요. **정답 (B)**

12. [미W] [영M]
Who should be our target audience for this online advertisement?
(A) The TV commercial is on channel 9.
(B) Mainly young adults.
(C) Linda in marketing did.

이 온라인 광고의 대상층은 누가 되어야 할까요?
(A) 그 텔레비전 광고는 9번 채널에서 나와요.
(B) 주로 젊은이들이요.
(C) 마케팅 팀의 린다가 했어요. **정답 (B)**

13. [미M] [호W]
Excuse me. How much does this printer cost?
(A) I already printed it out.
(B) It's on sale for just 90 dollars.
(C) Go to aisle 5 next to the scanner section.

실례합니다. 이 프린터는 얼마인가요?
(A) 저는 이미 그것을 출력했어요.
(B) 고작 90달러에 세일 중이에요.
(C) 스캐너 코너 옆에 있는 5번 통로로 가세요. **정답 (B)**

14. [영M] [미W]
Would you like me to give you a copy of your medical records?
(A) No, I've already got one.
(B) Just iced water, please.
(C) The dental clinic on 5th Avenue.

당신의 의료 기록 한 부를 드릴까요?
(A) 아뇨, 이미 한 부 갖고 있어요.
(B) 그냥 얼음물만 주세요.
(C) 5번가에 있는 치과 의원이요. **정답 (A)**

15. [호W] [미M]
You met Miss. Schneider at the trade fair, didn't you?
(A) It is fairly expensive.
(B) Reserve a booth for the trade show.
(C) Yes, she gave me her card.

무역 박람회에서 슈나이더 씨를 만나셨죠, 그렇죠?
(A) 그것은 꽤 비싸요.
(B) 무역 전시회 부스를 예약하세요.
(C) 예. 그분이 제게 명함을 주었어요. **정답 (C)**

16. [미W] [영M]
Have you received the invitation for the annual event?
(A) The head of information technology.
(B) Sign for the package instead.
(C) I've been in meetings with clients all day.

연례 행사에 대한 초대장을 받으셨어요?
(A) 정보기술부 부장이요.
(B) 대신 그 소포를 서명하고 받아 주세요.
(C) 저는 하루 종일 고객들과 회의를 했어요. **정답 (C)**

17. [호W] [미M]
Which photograph should we use for the cover of our next issue magazine?
(A) The one with the award-winning building.

(B) We'll cover the transportation.
(C) Take our photographer there.

다음 호 잡지 표지로 어떤 사진을 써야 할까요?
(A) 수상 경력이 있는 건물이 있는 사진이요.
(B) 우리가 교통비를 대겠습니다.
(C) 우리 사진작가를 그곳에 데려가세요.　　　　　정답 (A)

18. 호W 영M
Do I have a patient at 2 P.M. on Wednesday, don't I?
(A) Mr. Lopez just called to reschedule.
(B) No, it's on the righthand side.
(C) I called in sick yesterday.

수요일 오후 2시에 나에게 환자가 있나요, 그렇지 않죠?
(A) 로페즈 씨가 지금 막 전화해서 일정을 바꿨어요.
(B) 아뇨, 그건 오른쪽에 있어요.
(C) 저는 어제 아파서 결근하겠다고 전화했어요.　　　정답 (A)

19. 미M 호W
Is it possible to connect my laptop to the television?
(A) Mostly talk shows.
(B) I left my laptop behind in the lobby.
(C) Yes. Let me just find the cord.

제 노트북을 텔레비전과 연결하는 게 가능한가요?
(A) 주로 토크쇼예요.
(B) 로비에 제 노트북을 두고 왔어요.
(C) 예. 코드를 찾아볼게요.　　　　　　　　　정답 (C)

20. 영M 미W
I would like to see the dessert menu.
(A) At a classical music concert.
(B) Have you seen the film?
(C) Our kitchen closed just now.

디저트 메뉴 좀 보고 싶은데요.
(A) 클래식 음악 콘서트에서요.
(B) 그 영화를 보셨어요?
(C) 우리 주방이 지금 막 닫았어요.　　　　　　정답 (C)

21. 미M 호W
Didn't Bryan fix that machine in the assembly line on Monday?
(A) It is preassembled.
(B) He did, but it stopped again.
(C) Would you like to have your lunch delivered?

월요일에 브라이언이 조립 라인의 그 기계를 수리하지 않았어요?
(A) 그것은 사전에 조립되어 있는 거예요.
(B) 그랬는데, 또 다시 기계가 멈췄어요.
(C) 점심을 배달시키실래요?　　　　　　　　정답 (B)

22. 영M 미W
How soon will the out-of-town clients arrive at the office?
(A) It didn't last long.
(B) It began half an hour ago.
(C) They had to cancel.

타지에서 오는 고객들이 얼마나 빨리 이 사무실에 도착할까요?
(A) 그건 오래 하지 않았어요.
(B) 그것은 30분 전에 시작했어요.
(C) 그들은 취소해야 했어요.　　　　　　　정답 (C)

23. 호W 미M
Are you going to present your research findings this Friday or next Monday?
(A) I'll be away on business next week.
(B) Let's move to the room on the third floor.
(C) It was a gift from my sister.

연구 결과를 이번 주 금요일이나 다음 주 월요일 발표하실 거예요?
(A) 다음 주는 제가 출장 갈 거예요.
(B) 3층에 있는 방으로 옮깁시다.
(C) 제 여동생이 준 선물이었어요.　　　　　정답 (A)

24. 영M 미W
Where are the new line of hats that needs to be displayed?
(A) Two machines at the assembly line.
(B) They're not here yet.
(C) He hasn't seen this play, either.

전시되어야 하는 신제품 모자들이 어디에 있어요?
(A) 조립 라인의 기계 두 대요.
(B) 그것들은 아직 여기에 도착하지 않았어요.
(C) 그 역시 이 연극을 보지 않았어요.　　　　정답 (B)

25. 호W 미M
I forgot to sign up to attend the biotechnology conference.
(A) The keynote speaker hasn't arrived yet.
(B) Twenty dollars is enough.
(C) Registration is closed.

생명공학 총회에 참석 신청하는 것을 깜빡 잊었어요.
(A) 기조 연설자가 아직 도착하지 않았어요.
(B) 20달러면 충분해요.
(C) 등록이 마감되었어요.　　　　　　　　정답 (C)

26. 호W 영M
Is there a discount for children or do they have to pay the full price?
(A) They're charged half-price.
(B) Yes, the price is reasonable.
(C) Yes. They are having a clearance sale.

어린이를 위한 할인이 있나요, 아니면 전액 지불해야 하나요?
(A) 어린이들은 반값 청구됩니다.
(B) 예, 가격이 합리적이네요.
(C) 예. 거기는 재고정리 세일을 하고 있어요.　　정답 (A)

27. 영M 미W
Why haven't you restocked the women's blouses yet?
(A) There have been a lot of unexpected customers today.
(B) We accept either cash or credit cards.
(C) They have been on sale this week.

여성용 블라우스는 왜 아직도 다시 채워 놓지 않았어요?
(A) 오늘 예상치 않게 고객들이 많았어요.
(B) 우리는 현금이나 신용 카드를 받아요.
(C) 그것들은 이번 주에 세일했어요.　　　　정답 (A)

28. 미M 호W
Didn't Maria install the new accounting software program?
(A) Count me in, please.
(B) It is a popular TV program.
(C) No. She's been busy.

마리아가 새로 나온 회계 소프트웨어 프로그램을 설치하지 않았나요?
(A) 저도 끼워 주세요.
(B) 그건 인기 있는 텔레비전 프로예요.
(C) 아뇨, 그녀는 바빴어요. 　　　　　　　　　　　　정답 (C)

29. [호W] [미M]

Isn't the annual banquet for staff going to be held outdoors?
(A) None of the others have been.
(B) Flower arrangements on each table.
(C) It was a great meal.

직원들을 위한 연례 연회는 야외에서 열리지 않을까요?
(A) 다른 연례 연회 그 어느 것도 그런 적이 없어요.
(B) 각 테이블에 있는 꽃꽂이요.
(C) 그건 정말 괜찮은 식사였어요. 　　　　　　　　정답 (A)

30. [호W] [영M]

The projector in the conference room isn't functioning.
(A) I don't agree. The screen is large enough.
(B) She won't miss the deadline.
(C) I could print out copies of your presentation.

회의실에 있는 프로젝터가 작동하지 않고 있어요.
(A) 저는 동의하지 않아요. 스크린은 충분히 커요.
(B) 그녀는 마감시한을 놓치지 않을 거예요.
(C) 제가 당신 발표 자료 사본을 출력해 드릴 수 있어요. 　정답 (C)

31. [미M] [호W]

Are you opening a corporate or a personal account?
(A) No, it doesn't open on Mondays.
(B) The accountant position has been filled.
(C) I'm considering both.

법인 계좌를 개설하시나요, 아니면 개인 계좌를 개설하시나요?
(A) 아뇨, 그곳은 월요일에는 문을 열지 않아요.
(B) 회계사 자리는 충원이 되었어요.
(C) 둘 다 생각하고 있어요. 　　　　　　　　　　　정답 (C)

Part 3

문제 32-34번은 다음 대화를 참조하시오. [미W] [미M]

W: **(32)Welcome to Shape Up Fitness.**
M: Hello. I'm thinking about becoming a member, **(33)but I'd like to know how much it costs.**
W: Sure. We have several options depending upon what kind of membership you're interested in. Here's a list with all of our rates on it. If you're thinking of using the gym on a regular basis, you should probably get a one-year membership.
M: Is that the best deal?
W: Yes, and as an additional incentive, **(34)if you sign up for a 12-month membership before September 1, you'll get two complimentary tickets to the Louisville Rock Festival.**
M: Great. You've convinced me.

W: 쉐이프업 피트니스에 오신 것을 환영합니다.
M: 안녕하세요. 회원이 될까 생각중인데, 가격이 얼마나 하는지 알고 싶어요.
W: 알겠습니다. 우리는 여러 옵션이 있는데, 관심 있으신 회원권 종류에 따라 다릅니다. 여기 회원권에 대한 우리의 모든 요금이 나와 있는 목록입니

다. 규칙적으로 헬스 클럽을 이용할 생각이시라면, 아마 1년 회원권을 하시는 게 괜찮을 겁니다.
M: 그게 가장 좋은 가격 조건인가요?
W: 예, 그리고 추가 인센티브로 9월 1일 전에 1년 회원권 등록을 하시게 되면, 루이빌 록 페스티벌에 갈 수 있는 무료 티켓 2장도 받게 됩니다.
M: 잘되었네요. 저를 설득하셨네요.

32. 여자는 어디에서 근무하는가?
(A) 지역사회 센터
(B) 스포츠 용품 매장
(C) 운동 시설
(D) 슈퍼마켓 　　　　　　　　　　　　　　　　　정답 (C)

33. 남자는 무엇에 대해 물어보는가?
(A) 가격
(B) 영업 시간
(C) 취업 기회
(D) 주차비 　　　　　　　　　　　　　　　　　　정답 (A)

34. 보너스 선물을 받으려면 남자는 무엇을 해야 하는가?
(A) 쿠폰 보여 주기
(B) 구독하기
(C) 온라인에 후기 올리기
(D) 마감 전에 등록하기 　　　　　　　　　　　　정답 (D)

문제 35-37번은 다음 대화를 참조하시오. [영M] [호W]

M: **(35)Hello. Sandy Beach Travel.** This is David speaking. How may I be of assistance?
W: Hello. I'm going on a trip next week and happen to have a layover several hours long in your city. Are there any places I can see which are close to the airport?
M: You're in luck. **(36)There's a new service at the airport called Quick Tours. It has tours that leave from the airport. I can sign you up for one.**
W: Wonderful. I'd love that.
M: **(37)First, how long is your layover?** If I know that, I can choose a good tour for you.

M: 안녕하세요. 샌디 비치 트래블입니다. 저는 데이비드입니다. 무엇을 도와드릴까요?
W: 안녕하세요. 다음 주에 여행을 가는데, 마침 그 도시에서 대여섯 시간 체류하게 되어서요. 공항과 가까운 곳으로 구경할 수 있는 장소가 있나요?
M: 운이 좋으시네요. 공항에 퀵 투어스라는 새로운 서비스가 생겼어요. 서비스에 공항에서 출발하는 투어들이 있어요. 하나 신청해 드릴 수 있어요.
W: 잘 되었네요. 그러고 싶어요.
M: 우선, 단기체류 시간은 얼마나 되나요? 그걸 안다면, 제가 괜찮은 투어를 골라 드릴 수 있어요.

35. 남자는 누구인 것 같은가?
(A) 가게 주인
(B) 여행사 직원
(C) 항공사 직원
(D) 호텔 직원 　　　　　　　　　　　　　　　　정답 (B)

36. 공항은 이제 어떤 서비스를 제공하는가?
(A) 외화 환전
(B) 승객용 라운지

(C) 셔틀 서비스
(D) 지역 투어 　　　　　　　　　　　정답 (D)

37. 남자는 여자에게 무엇에 대해 물어보는가?
(A) 그녀가 그 도시를 방문하는 이유
(B) 그녀가 공항에 있게 되는 시간
(C) 그녀가 보고 싶어 하는 것
(D) 그녀가 체류하는 호텔 　　　　　　　정답 (B)

문제 38-40번은 다음 3자 대화를 참조하시오. [미M] [호W] [영M]

M1: Hello. (38)**You're a stagehand, right? I'm Greg Stewart, the play's director. Can you look at something on the stage for me?**
W: Of course, Mr. Stewart. Is there a problem?
M1: Unfortunately, yes. This is Peter, one of the performers. Can you explain the problem, Peter?
M2: Sure. (39)**This carpet is a huge problem. We have to walk around on the stage a lot, but whenever we step on the carpet, it moves.** I almost slipped and fell twice.
W: Ah, I see. It needs to be secured to the floor. Let me put some carpet tape on it. (40)**I saw some in the storage room behind the stage a while ago. Let me go and get it.**

M1: 안녕하세요. 무대 담당자시죠, 그렇죠? 저는 그레그 스튜어트, 연극 연출가예요. 저 대신 무대에 있는 것을 좀 점검해 주실래요?
W: 물론이죠, 스튜어트 씨. 문제가 있나요?
M1: 유감스럽게도 그렇네요. 여기는 피터인데 연기자 중 한 명이에요. 문제 좀 설명해 줄래요, 피터?
M2: 알았어요. 이 카펫이 큰 문제예요. 우리는 무대 위를 많이 돌아다녀야 하는데, 우리가 카펫을 밟을 때마다 그게 움직여요. 두 번이나 미끄러져 거의 넘어질 뻔했어요.
W: 아, 알았어요. 카펫을 바닥에 고정할 필요가 있어요. 카펫에 테이프를 붙일게요. 조금 전에 무대 뒤 보관실에서 테이프를 봤어요. 가서 가져올게요.

38. 화자들은 어디에서 근무하는 것 같은가?
(A) 쇼핑 센터
(B) 인테리어 디자인 회사
(C) 극장
(D) 가구점 　　　　　　　　　　　정답 (C)

39. 화자들은 어떤 문제를 논의하고 있는가?
(A) 등이 작동하지 않고 있다.
(B) 카펫이 계속 움직인다.
(C) 무대 세트를 만드는 데 비용이 많이 든다.
(D) 일부 계단이 너무 가파르다. 　　　　정답 (B)

40. 여자는 이후에 무엇을 할 것인가?
(A) 무대 청소
(B) 일부 자재 교체
(C) 수리공에게 전화
(D) 보관실 확인 　　　　　　　　　정답 (D)

문제 41-43번은 다음 대화를 참조하시오. [미M] [미W]

W: Hello, Jim. How did your presentation at the robotics conference go last week?
M: Great. (41)**There were about two hundred people in attendance.**
W: (41)**That's impressive.** What did you talk about in your presentation?
M: I discussed the potential uses of robots in factories in the future. I researched that topic a lot. In fact, (42)**I'm going to write an article and submit it to a major robotics journal for publication.**
W: Good thinking. You know, (43)**I went to university with the editor-in-chief of *Robotics Today*.** I'd be happy to contact him when you're done with the article.

W: 안녕하세요, 짐. 지난주에 했던 로봇공학 총회에서 당신 발표는 어떻게 되었어요?
M: 잘되었어요. 200명 정도가 참석했어요.
W: 너무 인상적이네요. 당신은 발표에서 무슨 얘기를 했나요?
M: 저는 미래의 공장에서 가능한 로봇 사용에 대해 얘기했어요. 그 주제에 대해 조사를 많이 했어요. 사실, 주요 로봇공학 저널에 발표할 수 있도록 글을 하나 써서 제출하려고요.
W: 좋은 생각이에요. 있잖아요, 제가 〈로봇공학 투데이〉의 수석 편집장과 대학을 같이 다녔어요. 당신이 그 글을 다 쓰게 되면 제가 기꺼이 그 사람에게 연락해 볼게요.

41. 남자가 "200명 정도가 참석했어요"라고 말하는 이유는?
(A) 많은 티켓이 팔렸다는 것을 언급하기 위해
(B) 실망감을 표현하기 위해
(C) 더 큰 회의실이 필요했다는 것을 나타내기 위해
(D) 행사가 성공적이었다는 것을 나타내기 위해 　정답 (D)

42. 남자는 무엇을 고려 중이라고 말하는가?
(A) 더 많은 로봇을 만드는 것
(B) 글을 위해 더 많은 조사를 하는 것
(C) 새로운 유형의 로봇을 설계하는 것
(D) 출판을 위한 글을 쓰는 것 　　　　정답 (D)

43. 여자는 무엇을 하겠다고 제의하는가?
(A) 남자의 글 교정 보기
(B) 지인에게 연락하기
(C) 남자와 공동으로 작업하기
(D) 회의 날짜 확정하기 　　　　　　정답 (B)

문제 44-46번은 다음 대화를 참조하시오. [호W] [미M]

W: Mr. Murphy, (44)**I'm in charge of our company's physical fitness day, and I have a question regarding it.**
M: Sure. I heard you need to discuss the budget.
W: That's right. (45)**Last year, we had one exercise class. But it was really popular, so we'd like to offer five of them this time.** But it will cost us an additional 400 dollars to hire a trainer for the full day.
M: Is there any way you can reduce spending elsewhere?
W: I have one idea if the budget can't be raised. (46)**We were planning to hand out T-shirts and ballcaps to everybody, but we could just give T-shirts away instead.**

M: I recommend doing that. It would be best if you didn't go over the original budget. To stay within the existing budget is our priority at the moment.

W: 머피 씨, 제가 우리 회사의 체력 단련의 날을 담당하고 있는데, 그것에 대해 질문이 있어요.

M: 그래요. 예산에 대해 논의할 필요가 있다고 들었어요.

W: 맞습니다. 작년에 우리는 운동 수업이 하나 있었어요. 그런데 그게 정말 인기가 많아서 이번에는 그런 수업 5개를 제공하고 싶어요. 하지만 하루 종일 트레이너를 고용하려면 400달러가 추가로 들어가요.

M: 다른 부문에서 비용을 줄일 수 있는 방법이 있을까요?

W: 예산을 증액할 수 없다면, 좋은 생각 하나 있긴 해요. 우리는 모든 사람에게 티셔츠와 야구모자를 나눠 줄 계획이었는데, 그냥 티셔츠만 줄 수도 있어요.

M: 저도 그렇게 하는 것을 권할게요. 원래 예산을 넘지 않는 게 최선일 겁니다. 현재 예산 한도 내에서 버티는 것이 현재로서는 최우선 사항이에요.

44. 화자들은 무슨 행사에 대해 논의하고 있는가?
(A) 직원 달리기 대회
(B) 회사의 건강의 날
(C) 야유회
(D) 오리엔테이션   정답 (B)

45. 여자에 따르면, 여자는 작년과 무엇을 다르게 하고 싶어 하는가?
(A) 행사 일정을 줄이는 것
(B) 참석자들에게 음식과 음료를 제공하는 것
(C) 더 많은 헬스 클럽을 행사에 참석시키는 것
(D) 더 많은 수업을 여는 것   정답 (D)

46. 여자는 어떤 종류의 선물을 나눠 줄 계획인가?
(A) 포스터
(B) 공책
(C) 야구모자
(D) 티셔츠   정답 (D)

문제 47-49번은 다음 대화를 참조하시오. ⓜM ⓜW

M: Pardon me. (47)**I'm Silas Edwards, and I work in the Tech Department.** (48)**I heard you're having a problem with your desktop computer.**

W: Um… Hello. (48)**Are you sure you've come to the right place?**

M: Oh, sorry. I guess I must have been given the wrong information. I'm sorry that I bothered you.

W: No problem. (49)**Actually, while you're here, would you mind checking my laptop?** There's a problem with some software I just downloaded.

M: (49)**I've got a few minutes to spare, so sure, I can help you out.**

M: 실례합니다, 저는 실라스 에드워즈이고, 기술지원부에서 근무합니다. 데스크톱 컴퓨터에 문제가 있다고 들었어요.

W: 음… 사무실을 제대로 찾아오신 것이 맞나요?

M: 오, 죄송해요. 제 생각에 제가 잘못된 정보를 받았나봐요. 번거롭게 해드려서 죄송해요.

W: 괜찮아요. 사실, 여기 오신 김에, 제 노트북 컴퓨터 좀 봐 주실래요? 제가 막 내려받은 소프트웨어에 문제가 생겨서요.

M: 몇 분 여유가 있으니, 물론, 도와드릴게요.

47. 남자는 어느 부서에서 근무하는가?
(A) 인사부
(B) 보안부
(C) 유지보수부
(D) 기술지원부   정답 (D)

48. 여자가 "사무실을 제대로 찾아오신 것이 맞나요?"라고 말하는 이유는?
(A) 그녀는 배달을 기대하지 않고 있다.
(B) 그녀는 지금 어떤 시간도 낼 수 없다.
(C) 그녀는 지원을 요청하지 않았다.
(D) 그녀는 좀 더 구체적인 지시를 받고 싶어 한다.   정답 (C)

49. 남자는 이후에 무엇을 하겠는가?
(A) 자신의 사무실로 돌아가기
(B) 장비 점검하기
(C) 기술지원부에 전화하기
(D) 데스크톱 컴퓨터 수리하기   정답 (B)

문제 50-52번은 다음 3자 대화를 참조하시오. ⓜW ⓗW ⓜM

W1: (50)**Let's discuss some of the packaging options for our new candy bar.** I have an idea. Instead of wrapping it in regular plastic, why don't we use that new kind of biodegradable plastic which breaks down quicker?

W2: I like that idea. Customers these days are becoming more interested in the environment, so the move would appeal to them. How do you feel, Mark?

M: Hmm… (51)**That new plastic is more expensive, so it would add to the total cost of the candy bar.**

W1: Well, if the biodegradable packaging attracts more buyers, the extra expense will be worth it. (52)**Why don't we organize some focus groups and ask them what they think?**

W2: Yeah, the discussion is worth trying.

M: I agree.

W1: 새로 나오는 캔디 바의 포장 옵션에 대해 얘기해 봅시다. 내게 아이디어가 있는데요. 일반 비닐로 캔디 바를 포장하는 대신에, 좀 더 빨리 분해되는 새로운 종류의 생분해 비닐을 사용하는 것은 어떨까요?

W2: 그 생각은 좋은데요. 요즘 고객들은 환경에 좀 더 관심이 많아서, 그런 조치가 그들의 관심을 끌 거예요. 어떻게 생각해요, 마크?

M: 음… 그 새 비닐은 더 비싸서, 캔디 바의 전체 원가에 비용이 추가될 텐데요.

W1: 글쎄요, 생분해 비닐 포장이 좀 더 많은 구매자들을 끌어들인다면, 추가 비용은 그만한 가치가 있을 거예요. 소비자 제품 평가단을 구성해서 그들에게 어떻게 생각하는지 물어보는 것은 어떨까요?

W2: 예, 그 토론은 시도해 볼 만해요.

M: 동의해요.

50. 화자들은 어떤 종류의 회사에서 근무하는 것 같은가?
(A) 식품 제조업체
(B) 생화학 회사
(C) 섬유 제조업체
(D) 재활용 회사   정답 (A)

51. 남자의 우려 사항은 무엇인가?
(A) 광고가 사람들의 관심을 끌지 못하고 있다.
(B) 제품이 더 비싸질지 모른다.
(C) 제품이 인기가 더 떨어질 것이다.

(D) 친환경 재료를 구할 수 없다.　　　　　정답 (B)

52. 화자들은 무엇을 하기로 동의하는가?
(A) 고객들로부터 의견 구하기
(B) 새 광고 만들기
(C) 상사와 대화하기
(D) 고객들에게 공장 구경시켜 주기　　　정답 (A)

문제 53-55번은 다음 대화를 참조하시오. 호W 영M

> W: Cliff, (53)**do you know how to transfer money abroad?** I have to send some money to my brother in Venezuela. I think I can use my smartphone to do that, but I'm not sure.
>
> M: You're right. (54)**If you have an online banking app on your phone**, look for the button that reads "transfer" or something like that. Hmm… (54)**Okay, here it is. It's right next to the "balance" button on your screen.**
>
> W: Oh, thanks. My brother said that I could just use his e-mail address, (55)**but according to the app, I need to know his bank account number.** I need to call him to find out what it is.

> W: 클리프, 해외로 송금을 어떻게 하는지 아세요? 베네수엘라에 있는 남동생에게 송금을 해야 해서요. 송금하는 데 스마트폰을 사용할 수 있을 것 같은데 확실히 모르겠어요.
>
> M: 맞아요. 전화기에 온라인 뱅킹 앱이 있으면, "송금"이라고 적혀 있는 버튼이나 그런 비슷한 것을 찾아보세요. 흠… 됐어요, 여기 있네요. 화면에서 "잔고" 버튼 바로 옆에 있어요.
>
> W: 오, 고마워요. 제 남동생이 그냥 자신의 이메일 주소를 사용하면 된다고 했는데, 앱에 따르면, 동생의 은행 계좌 번호를 알아야 하네요. 동생에게 전화해서 계좌 번호가 뭔지 알아봐야겠어요.

53. 화자들은 무엇에 대해 논의하고 있는가?
(A) 해외로 송금하기
(B) 현금 인출기에서 돈 인출하기
(C) 기차 표 구매하기
(D) 법인 은행 계좌 개설하기　　　　　정답 (A)

54. 화자들은 무엇을 보고 있는가?
(A) 탑승권
(B) 스마트폰
(C) 노트북 컴퓨터
(D) 은행 안내책자　　　　　　　　　　정답 (B)

55. 여자는 어떤 정보를 요청할 것인가?
(A) 이메일 주소
(B) 거리 주소
(C) 은행 계좌 번호
(D) 전화 번호　　　　　　　　　　　　정답 (C)

문제 56-58번은 다음 대화를 참조하시오. 영M 미W

> M: (56)**Thanks for coming in for this interview for the supervisor of the Design Department position.** I see from your résumé that you have some supervisory experience in your past, first at a computer software firm and then at an engineering company.

> W: That's right. I really learned a lot at those jobs.
>
> M: (57)**Which skill that you learned is the most important?**
>
> W: (57)**Communication for sure.** If you don't communicate well with your staff, they won't be able to do exactly what you want them to do.
>
> M: That's right. (58)**Are you okay working with computers? This job will require you to use some advanced software.**
>
> W: Actually, I have led computer software training programs in the past, so I'm familiar with various types of software.

> M: 디자인부의 관리자 자리에 대한 이번 면접에 와 주셔서 감사합니다. 이력서를 보니까, 과거에 관리 경력이 있으신데, 처음은 컴퓨터 소프트웨어 회사에서, 그 다음은 엔지니어링 회사에서요.
>
> W: 맞아요. 그 자리들에서 정말 많은 것들을 배웠습니다.
>
> M: 배운 것 중에 어떤 능력이 제일 중요한가요?
>
> W: 확실히 의사소통 능력이죠. 직원들과 의사소통을 잘하지 않으면, 직원들은 당신이 그들에게 하기를 바라는 대로 정확히 일을 할 수 없을 거예요.
>
> M: 맞습니다. 컴퓨터로 작업하는 것은 괜찮으세요? 이 일은 고급 소프트웨어를 이용해야 하거든요.
>
> W: 사실, 과거에 컴퓨터 소프트웨어 교육 프로그램을 진행해 왔거든요. 그래서 여러 유형의 소프트웨어를 잘 압니다.

56. 여자는 어떤 자리에 지원하고 있는가?
(A) 컴퓨터 프로그래머
(B) 영업 직원
(C) 부서장
(D) 인테리어 디자이너　　　　　　　　정답 (C)

57. 여자는 어떤 능력이 가장 중요하다고 생각하는가?
(A) 부서의 팀워크
(B) 업무 효율성
(C) 예산 관리
(D) 의사소통　　　　　　　　　　　　정답 (D)

58. 남자에 따르면, 여자는 무엇을 할 것이 요구되는가?
(A) 신입 사원 교육
(B) 잦은 해외 출장
(C) 소프트웨어 프로그램 사용
(D) 직원 평가　　　　　　　　　　　　정답 (C)

문제 59-61번은 다음 대화를 참조하시오. 미W 영M

> W: Luke, (59)**I'm going to have someone from the Maintenance Department turn the heat in the office down during the long holiday.**
>
> M: Sure, Wendy. (60)**But don't forget that the water pipes froze and then burst last year. It's going to be even colder this year, so I'd hate for the same thing to happen again.**
>
> W: You're right. And I guess a few workers will be coming into the office during the holiday. So it shouldn't be turned down too low. We need to try to save energy while keeping the office temperature comfortable.
>
> M: Okay. (61)**Let me call the maintenance crew to turn the heat down a bit then.**

> W: 루크, 긴 연휴 동안 유지보수과 사람으로 하여금 사무실 난방기 온도를 좀 낮추게 해야겠어요.
>
> M: 알았습니다. 웬디. 그런데 작년에 배수관이 얼어서 터졌던 거 잊지 마세

요. 올해는 훨씬 더 추울 거라서, 같은 일이 또 일어나는 것은 싫어요.

W: 맞아요. 그리고 직원 몇 명이 휴일 동안 사무실에 올 것 같아요. 그래서 온도를 너무 낮게 하면 안 되죠. 사무실 온도를 쾌적하게 유지하면서 에너지를 절감하도록 노력할 필요가 있어요.

M: 알겠습니다. 그러면 유지보수과 직원에게 전화해서 난방기를 약간만 낮추라고 할게요.

59. 화자들은 주로 무엇에 대해 논의하고 있는가?
(A) 사무실에서 난방기 치우기
(B) 다른 장소로 이전하기
(C) 사무실의 온도 조정하기
(D) 고장 난 장비 고치기
정답 (C)

60. 남자는 무엇에 대해 우려하는가?
(A) 사무실 문이 잠길지 모른다.
(B) 전기료가 올라갈 것이다.
(C) 난방기가 품절될지 모른다.
(D) 파이프 일부가 손상될 수 있다.
정답 (D)

61. 남자는 무엇을 할 것이라고 말하는가?
(A) 유지보수과에 연락
(B) 수리 요청서 작성
(C) 에너지 절감 설명서 준비
(D) 휴일 동안 근무
정답 (A)

문제 62~64번은 다음 대화와 차트를 참조하시오. [미M] [미W]

M: All right, Susanna. We need to go over the details of the restaurant festival that's taking place this weekend. The weather forecast is calling for rain, so…

W: Yeah. The food areas will be covered with tents, but the ticket sellers will be out in the open. (62)**If it rains, we can move the ticket booths into the main office at the park.**

M: That's perfect. Okay, the Chinese and Brazilian restaurants confirmed they'll be coming, (63)**but the Mexican restaurant can't make it. So we need to remove that tent.**

W: No problem.

M: We're also running behind our goal for advance ticket sales. (64)**Please contact the local TV station and have our ad get run again.**

W: I'll get on it.

M: 좋아요, 수잔나. 이번 주말에 열리는 식당 페스티벌의 세부사항에 대해 검토할 필요가 있어요. 일기예보에 따르면 비가 오네요, 그러니…

W: 예, 음식이 있는 구역은 텐트로 가려지긴 하는데, 티켓 판매자들은 아무것도 없는 야외 공간에 있게 됩니다. 만약 비가 오면, 티켓 부스를 공원의 주 사무실로 옮길 수 있어요.

M: 완벽해요. 좋아요, 중국 식당과 브라질 식당은 참석할 거라고 확인해 주었는데, 멕시코 식당은 올 수 없대요. 그래서 그 텐트는 제거해야 해요.

W: 그러죠.

M: 또한 티켓 예매가 목표를 달성하지 못하고 있어요. 지역 TV 방송국에 연락해서 우리 광고가 다시 나가게 해주세요.

W: 바로 처리할게요.

연례 식당 페스티벌

식당	요리	위치
골든 드래곤	중국 음식	텐트 1
라 하시엔다	(63)멕시코 음식	텐트 2
피렌체	이탈리아 음식	텐트 3
리오 딜라이츠	브라질 음식	텐트 4

62. 여자에 따르면, 비가 오면 화자들은 무엇을 할 계획인가?
(A) 행사를 나중으로 연기하기
(B) 티켓 판매를 안으로 옮기기
(C) 방문객들에게 우산 제공하기
(D) 행사를 실내에서 개최하기
정답 (B)

63. 그래픽을 보시오. 어느 텐트가 치워질 것인가?
(A) 텐트 1
(B) 텐트 2
(C) 텐트 3
(D) 텐트 4
정답 (B)

64. 여자는 TV 방송국에 무엇을 해달라고 요청할 것인가?
(A) 음식 콘테스트 알리기
(B) 광고 재방송하기
(C) 기부하기
(D) 참가 업체 알리기
정답 (B)

문제 65~67번은 다음 대화와 일정표를 참조하시오. [미M] [호W]

M: (65)**Thanks for calling the Duncan Health Clinic.** How may I help you?

W: Hello. This is Lucy Baldwin. I'm scheduled to have a physical checkup this morning at eleven o'clock, (66)**but my car won't start. The engine has some kind of a problem.** Can I reschedule my appointment for the afternoon?

M: I'm really sorry to hear that, Ms. Baldwin. (67)**You can come at 3:00 P.M.**

W: (67)**That's too early for me. Is there another time later in the day?**

M: Let me see if there are any other openings.

M: 던컨 헬스 클리닉에 전화 주셔서 감사합니다. 무엇을 도와드릴까요?

W: 안녕하세요. 저는 루시 볼드윈인데요. 오늘 오전 11시에 건강 검진을 받게 되어 있었는데, 제 자동차가 시동이 걸리지 않아요. 엔진에 뭔가 문제가 있어요. 제 진료 예약을 오후로 조정할 수 있을까요?

M: 그렇게 되어 정말 유감이네요. 볼드윈 씨. 오후 3시에 오시면 되겠습니다.

W: 그 시간은 제게 너무 일러요. 오늘 더 늦게 다른 시간이 있나요?

M: 다른 비어 있는 시간이 있는지 볼게요.

오늘의 진료 예약

오전 11:00	루시 볼드윈
오후 12:00	아이린 웨스트
오후 1:00	
오후 2:00	데이비드 전
오후 3:00	
오후 4:00	재키 레이놀즈
(67)오후 5:00	
오후 6:00	러스 파워스

65. 남자는 어디에서 근무하는가?
(A) 신문사
(B) 병원
(C) 미용실
(D) 치과 　　　　　　　　　　　　　정답 (B)

66. 여자에게 어떤 문제가 생겼는가?
(A) 자동차 타이어에 펑크가 났다.
(B) 회의에 참석해야 한다.
(C) 자동차가 작동이 안 된다.
(D) 컴퓨터가 고장 났다. 　　　　　　정답 (C)

67. 그래픽을 보시오. 여자의 새 진료 예약은 몇 시가 될 것 같은가?
(A) 오전 11시
(B) 오후 1시
(C) 오후 3시
(D) 오후 5시 　　　　　　　　　　　정답 (D)

문제 68–70번은 다음 대화와 근무 시간 기록표를 참조하시오. 미M 호W

M: Hello, Cynthia. This is Larry from Payroll. I met you during the orientation session. (68)**How are you enjoying your first week of work here at Peterson Legal Services?**
W: (69)**I'm having a great time. I've been doing lots of research in the library for two of our attorneys, so everything is going pretty well.** Oh, I appreciate that the firm provides me with the laptop. That's very useful. Is there something I can do for you?
M: Yes. This is with regard to the timesheet you submitted yesterday.
W: Is there a problem?
M: It's a small thing. (70)**Since Tuesday was a holiday, you have to use the holiday code.** You can see it as an option on the drop-down menu.
W: Ah, thanks for telling me. I'll fix it right now.

M: 안녕하세요, 신시아. 저는 급여담당부의 래리입니다. 오리엔테이션 때 만났었죠. 여기 피터슨 법률 서비스에서 첫 주 근무는 어떻게 재미있으신가요?
W: 좋은 시간 보내고 있어요. 변호사 두 분을 위해 도서관에서 많은 조사를 하고 있고, 그래서 모든 게 다 잘 돌아가고 있어요. 오, 회사에서 저에게 노트북을 제공해 주신 것을 감사드려요. 아주 유용해요. 제가 뭐 해드릴 일이라도 있나요?

M: 예. 어제 당신이 제출한 근무 시간 기록표에 관한 것이에요.
W: 문제가 있나요?
M: 사소한 거예요. 화요일이 공휴일이었기 때문에, 휴일 코드를 사용해야 해요. 드롭다운 메뉴에서 옵션으로 그것을 볼 수 있어요.
W: 아, 말씀해 주셔서 감사해요. 당장 고칠게요.

근무 시간 기록

날짜	코드	근무시간
11월 11일	**없음** ▼	7
11월 12일	병가 – 1	7
11월 13일	개인 용무 – 2	7
11월 14일	악천후 – 3 / (70)**공휴일 – 4**	7

68. 화자들은 어디에서 근무하는가?
(A) 출장 요리 업체
(B) 대학교
(C) 도서관
(D) 법률 회사 　　　　　　　　　　정답 (D)

69. 여자의 직업은 무엇일 것 같은가?
(A) 조사원
(B) 변호사
(C) 도서관 사서
(D) 강사 　　　　　　　　　　　　　정답 (A)

70. 그래픽을 보시오. 여자는 어떤 코드를 선택해야 하는가?
(A) 코드 1
(B) 코드 2
(C) 코드 3
(D) 코드 4 　　　　　　　　　　　정답 (D)

Part 4

문제 71–73번은 다음 광고를 참조하시오. 호W

W: Looking for a job? Look no further. (71)**Just drop by the Richmond Job Fair at the Manfred Hotel this weekend.** More than 200 domestic firms will be there in the hope of finding and hiring new workers. (72)**This year, there will be a free shuttle bus from the train station to the hotel**, so you won't have any problems arriving there. If you're attending the fair for the first time, (73)**visit our website to read some reviews previous attendees have written.**

일자리를 찾으세요? 더 이상 찾아보지 마세요. 그냥 이번 주말에 맨프레드 호텔에서 하는 리치몬드 취업 박람회에 들르시기만 하면 됩니다. 200여 개의 국내 기업들이 새 직원들을 찾아 고용하고자 그 자리에 참석합니다. 올해는 기차역과 호텔 사이에 무료 셔틀 버스가 제공되므로, 그곳에 도착하는 데 아무 문제가 없을 겁니다. 이번에 취업 박람회에 처음 참석하신다면, 저희 웹사이트를 방문해서 이전 참석자들이 적어 놓은 후기들을 읽어 보십시오.

71. 어떤 종류의 행사가 홍보되고 있는가?
(A) 취업 박람회
(B) 마케팅 세미나
(C) 호텔 기념일
(D) 영업 총회 　　　　　　　　　　정답 (A)

72. 화자는 올해에 무엇이 이용 가능할 것이라고 말하는가?
  (A) 온라인 등록
  (B) 안내소
  (C) 출장 요리 업체가 제공하는 점심
  (D) 무료 셔틀 버스 　　　　　　　　　　정답 (D)

73. 청자들은 웹사이트에서 무엇을 할 가능성이 있는가?
  (A) 의견 읽기
  (B) 콘테스트 참가하기
  (C) 행사에 등록하기
  (D) 지불하기 　　　　　　　　　　　　정답 (A)

문제 74-76번은 다음 담화를 참조하시오. 영M

M: Hello, everybody. **(74)I'm so pleased to see how many people have volunteered to work at the museum.** We have tours running every fifteen minutes, **(74)but we also need some people to lead tours for special guests. (75)So we want each of you to show up a quarter of an hour before your scheduled tour begins.** When you are fully trained, you'll get your weekly volunteer assignment every Sunday. **(76)Please feel free to put your belongings in one of the employee lockers.** What you just need to remember is bring your own lock.

안녕하세요, 여러분. 얼마나 많은 사람들이 박물관에서 자원봉사 근무를 해 주시겠다고 했는지 정말 기쁩니다. 우리는 매 15분마다 투어를 운영하고 있습니다만, 우리는 또한 특별 손님들을 위한 투어를 안내할 사람들이 필요합니다. 그래서 우리는 여러분 모두 일정으로 잡힌 투어가 시작되기 15분 전에 나와 주셨으면 합니다. 여러분이 완전히 교육을 받게 되면, 여러분은 매주 일요일 주간 자원봉사 근무 배정을 받게 될 것입니다. 우리 직원 사물함 중 하나에 편하게 여러분의 소지품을 보관하세요. 단, 기억해 두셔야 할 것은 자신의 자물쇠를 가져와야 한다는 것입니다.

74. 청자들은 무엇을 자원해서 하기로 결정했는가?
  (A) 투어 안내책자를 만드는 것
  (B) 박물관의 공예품을 청소하는 것
  (C) 조사하는 것
  (D) 투어 안내를 하는 것 　　　　　　　정답 (D)

75. 화자에 따르면, 청자들은 무엇을 하기로 되어 있는가?
  (A) 공손하게 말하기
  (B) 예정된 시간보다 더 일찍 도착하기
  (C) 홍보용 전단지 나눠 주기
  (D) 특정 유니폼 입기 　　　　　　　　정답 (B)

76. 화자는 청자들에게 무엇을 이용 가능하다고 말하는가?
  (A) 무료 다과
  (B) 기념품점에서 할인
  (C) 개인용 사물함
  (D) 다른 박물관의 무료 티켓 　　　　　정답 (C)

문제 77-79번은 다음 안내를 참조하시오. 미W

W: Hello. **(77)Before you start your work shift,** I have a reminder to go over with you. We got a letter from the recycling office of the city today. **(77) (78)Apparently, our café isn't sorting garbage properly. (78)So let me cover a**

few guidelines. We have to separate food items from other packaging materials. We must also put glass, paper, and plastic products into the correct recycling bins. I know that things can be a bit confusing at times, **(79)but I'm here every day. Just let me know if you have a question.**

안녕하세요, 여러분의 교대시간 근무를 시작하기 전에, 여러분과 같이 검토할 주의사항이 있습니다. 오늘 시 재활용과로부터 편지를 하나 받았습니다. 보아하니, 우리 카페가 쓰레기를 적절하게 분류하지 않는 것 같습니다. 그래서 제가 몇 가지 지침사항들을 얘기하겠습니다. 우리는 다른 포장 재료에서 식품들을 별도로 분리해야 합니다. 또한 유리, 종이, 플라스틱 제품은 올바른 재활용 통에 넣어야 합니다. 몇 가지는 때때로 혼동스럽다는 것도 잘 압니다만, 제가 이 곳에 매일 상주합니다. 질문 있으시면 저에게 알려 주시기만 하면 됩니다.

77. 이 담화는 누구를 대상으로 한 것인가?
  (A) 식당 직원
  (B) 정부 검사관
  (C) 음식 비평가
  (D) 축제 참석자 　　　　　　　　　　정답 (A)

78. 담화에서 무엇이 논의되고 있는가?
  (A) 배송 일정
  (B) 음료에 대한 포장
  (C) 재활용 규정
  (D) 안전 점검 　　　　　　　　　　　정답 (C)

79. 화자가 "제가 이 곳에 매일 상주합니다"라고 말할 때 무엇을 의미하는가?
  (A) 그녀는 일정이 겹치는 것을 알고 있다.
  (B) 그녀는 그 사업체의 소유주이다.
  (C) 그녀는 청자들의 옵션에 동의한다.
  (D) 그녀는 청자들을 도와줄 수 있다. 　정답 (D)

문제 80-82번은 다음 방송을 참조하시오. 미M

M: I'm Doug Harper reporting for Channel 8, the leader in local news. **(80)Today, our main story is about computer maker Kelvin Incorporated.** It announced this morning that **(81)they have now completely relocated into their new factory which is finally operating at 100% capacity.** The company makes high-end desktop and laptop computers. **(82)It is also a major contributor to the welfare of the community. It has donated more than 500 machines to local schools in the past three months.** The donation will help students get a better education.

저는 더그 하퍼이고, 지역 뉴스의 리더, 채널 8을 위해 보도하고 있습니다. 오늘, 우리 주요 소식은 컴퓨터 제조업체 켈빈 주식회사에 관한 것입니다. 이 회사는 오늘 아침에, 이제 새 공장으로 완전히 이전했으며, 그 공장은 마침내 생산능력 100%로 가동되고 있다고 발표했습니다. 이 업체는 첨단 데스크톱과 노트북 컴퓨터를 제조합니다. 이 업체는 또한 이 지역사회의 복지에 대한 주요 기부업체이기도 합니다. 이 업체는 지난 3개월 동안 여러 지역 학교에 500대 이상의 컴퓨터를 기증했습니다. 이 기증은 학생들이 더 나은 교육을 받는 데 도움을 줄 것입니다.

80. 켈빈 주식회사는 어떤 종류의 업체인가?
  (A) 자동차 제조업체
  (B) 컴퓨터 제조업체
  (C) 출판업체

(D) 제약회사   정답 (B)

81. 켈빈 주식회사는 최근에 무엇을 했는가?
(A) 공장에 새 기계를 설치했다.
(B) 신제품을 출시했다.
(C) 새 공장으로 이전했다.
(D) 신문에 광고를 냈다.   정답 (C)

82. 켈빈 주식회사는 지역사회를 어떻게 도왔는가?
(A) 지역 박물관에 자금 지원하는 것을 도와줌으로써
(B) 학교 도서관을 보수공사할 수 있도록 돈을 기부함으로써
(C) 지역 스포츠 팀을 후원함으로써
(D) 학교에 장비를 기증함으로써   정답 (D)

문제 83~85번은 다음 회의 발췌 내용을 참조하시오. 호W

W: Thanks for coming to this afternoon's meeting. (83) (84) **You may not be aware that we have a new competitor in the local mobile service market.** The company is Blue Field, and it's offering cheap data packages to draw new customers. I'm worried that some of our customers may leave us and switch over to Blue Field. We can't afford to lose any business to a competitor. (85)**So now Pierre is going to take over the meeting. He has some ideas on how we can remain competitive in the market.**

오늘 오후 회의에 와 주셔서 감사합니다. 아실지 모르겠지만, 이 지역 휴대폰 서비스 시장에 새 경쟁업체가 생겼습니다. 이 회사는 블루 필드이고, 신규 고객을 끌어들이기 위해 저렴한 데이터 패키지 상품을 제공하고 있습니다. 걱정되는 것은 우리 고객 일부가 우리 업체를 떠나서 블루 필드로 갈아탈지도 모른다는 것입니다. 우리는 경쟁업체에 우리 고객을 빼앗길 수 없습니다. 그래서 이제 피에르가 이 회의를 주재할 것입니다. 우리가 시장에서 어떻게 경쟁력을 유지할 수 있을지에 대해 피에르에게 아이디어가 있습니다.

83. 화자는 주로 무엇에 대해 논의하고 있는가?
(A) 사업 경쟁업체
(B) 스마트폰 신제품
(C) 영업 사원에 대한 공석
(D) 정보기술부에 대한 새로운 예산   정답 (A)

84. 화자는 어떤 종류의 회사에서 근무하는 것 같은가?
(A) 광고 회사
(B) 전화 서비스 제공업체
(C) 컴퓨터 수리회사
(D) 전자제품 공급업체   정답 (B)

85. 피에르는 지금 무엇을 할 것인가?
(A) 질문에 답변하기
(B) 자료 나눠 주기
(C) 슬라이드 보여 주기
(D) 발표하기   정답 (D)

문제 86~88번은 다음 방송을 참조하시오. 미W

W: (86)On today's episode of *Designing Your Home with Melinda*, I'll be talking about furnishing one-bedroom

apartments. If you don't have much space, you need to maximize what you have. (87)**So I suggest getting multipurpose furniture.** You could have a sofa which pulls out into a full-sized bed and a folding counter that could be turned into a kitchen table. Having furniture that fulfills multiple roles can make your apartment feel bigger than it really is. (88)**I know some of you have limited budgets. But don't worry. There are plenty of companies out there you could choose from.**

〈멜린다와 함께하는 집 꾸미기〉오늘의 회차에서는 원룸 아파트에 가구를 채워 넣는 것에 대해 얘기해 보겠습니다. 공간이 많지 않다면, 가지고 있는 것으로 최대한 활용할 필요가 있습니다. 그래서 저는 다목적 가구를 구입할 것을 제안합니다. 잡아당기면 풀사이즈 침대로 바뀌는 소파와 부엌 식탁으로 변할 수 있는 접는 카운터를 둘 수 있습니다. 다목적 역할을 충실히 수행하는 가구를 두게 되면 여러분의 아파트가 실제보다 더 크게 느껴질 수 있습니다. 여러분 중 일부는 예산 제약이 있다는 것을 압니다. 그렇지만 걱정하지 마세요. 밖에 나가 보면 여러분이 고를 수 있는 회사들이 많습니다.

86. 오늘 프로에서는 어떤 주제가 논의되고 있는가?
(A) 가구가 딸린 아파트 찾기
(B) 주방 보수공사 하기
(C) 가정용 가구 고르기
(D) 집 이전에 관한 팁   정답 (C)

87. 화자는 무엇을 할 것을 추천하는가?
(A) 가구 카탈로그 확인하기
(B) 매장에서 저가 찾기
(C) 다기능 제품 사용하기
(D) 자격이 있는 디자이너 고용하기   정답 (C)

88. 화자는 "밖에 나가 보면 여러분들이 고를 수 있는 회사들이 많습니다"라고 말할 때 무엇을 함축하는가?
(A) 가격이 알맞은 옵션들이 이용 가능하다.
(B) 그녀는 최고의 회사들을 추천할 수 있다.
(C) 일부 정보는 충분히 정확하지 않다.
(D) 결정을 하기 어려울 것이다.   정답 (A)

문제 89~91번은 다음 소개를 참조하시오. 영M

M: (89)It's my great pleasure to introduce our keynote speaker for our annual conference. Martin Howell is one of the top real estate agents in the state of Texas. (90)Today, Mr. Howell will discuss the importance of developing sales goals with specific steps and then reaching them. He has a highly successful systematic sales method which documents every process from start to finish, including how a deal is negotiated and closed. He's managed to sell more homes than anyone else in Texas in the past five years. (91)Before Mr. Howell starts, however, let me show you some pictures of the home he sold just yesterday.

우리 연례 총회의 기조 연설자를 소개하게 되어 대단히 기쁩니다. 마틴 하월은 텍사스 주에서 최고의 부동산 중개사 중 한 명입니다. 오늘날, 하월 씨는 구체적인 단계가 있는 판매 목표 개발, 그 다음 그 목표 달성의 중요성에 대해 얘기하게 될 것입니다. 하월 씨에게는 아주 성공적인 체계적인 판매 방법이 있는데, 거래를 어떻게 협상하고 체결하는지를 포함하여, 처음부터 끝까지 모든 과정을 문서화하는 것입니다. 그는 지난 5년 동안 텍사

스에서 그 어느 누구보다도 더 많은 주택을 매매했습니다. 그런데 하월 씨가 시작하기 전에, 바로 어제 그가 판매한 주택 사진들을 보여 드리겠습니다.

89. 청자들은 누구일 것 같은가?
(A) 주택 소유자
(B) 부동산 중개사
(C) 잠재적인 투자자
(D) 조경회사 직원　　　　　　　　　　　　　　정답 (B)

90. 하월 씨는 무엇에 대해 얘기할 것인가?
(A) 새 고객을 찾는 것
(B) 판매 목표를 만드는 것
(C) 매력적인 광고를 개발하는 것
(D) 사업 거래를 협상하는 것　　　　　　　　　정답 (B)

91. 화자는 뒤이어 무엇을 할 것인가?
(A) 발표 자료 나눠 주기
(B) 참석자들을 그룹으로 나누기
(C) 사진 보여 주기
(D) 양식 나눠 주기　　　　　　　　　　　　　정답 (C)

문제 92–94번은 다음 회의 발췌 내용을 참조하시오. 〖M〗〖W〗

W: **(92)Let me update you on the safety training program. It was supposed to happen on Wednesday, but it has been postponed until next week.** Mr. Robinson in HR just updated the course material and sent me a new manual. When I previewed the documents though, I noticed a few problems, **(93)so I asked Mr. Robinson if there were any mistakes in the manual. He said he'd double-check for me. He's happy he did that**. He's sending me a new version this weekend. **(94)In the meantime, we should go ahead with our work for Lucinda Lighting. We need to manufacture a prototype of their newest product they asked us to do.**

- -

안전 교육 프로그램에 대해 최신 소식을 알려 드리겠습니다. 교육이 수요일에 열리기로 되어 있었는데, 다음 주로 연기되었습니다. 인적자원부의 로빈슨 씨가 지금 막 강좌 자료를 새로 업데이트해서 새로운 지침서를 저에게 보냈습니다. 그런데 제가 자료들을 미리 보고 몇 가지 문제를 발견하여, 로빈슨 씨에게 지침서에 실수가 있는 게 아닌지 물어봤습니다. 그는 저를 위해 다시 확인해 본다고 했습니다. 그렇게 다시 확인하게 되어서 다행이라고 하네요. 이번 주말에 그가 저에게 새로운 버전을 보낼 것입니다. 그 동안, 우리는 루신다 조명을 위해서 우리가 맡은 일을 추진해야 합니다. 그들이 만들어 달라고 요청한 대로 그들의 최신 제품 원형을 만들어야 합니다.

92. 무엇의 일정이 변경되었는가?
(A) 소프트웨어 업그레이드
(B) 교육 과정
(C) 고객을 위한 공장 견학
(D) 정부의 안전 점검　　　　　　　　　　　　정답 (B)

93. 화자가 "이번 주말에 그가 저에게 새 버전을 보낼 것입니다"라고 말할 때 무엇을 함축하는가?
(A) 몇 개의 실수가 확인되었다.
(B) 변경에 대한 공지가 게시되어야 한다.
(C) 그녀는 모든 사람에게 돌아갈 만큼 충분한 사본을 요청했다.
(D) 그녀는 더 빠른 답변을 기대했었다.　　　　정답 (A)

94. 루신다 조명에 대해 화자는 무엇을 말하는가?
(A) 새로운 생산 라인을 설치했다.
(B) 다른 도시로 이전한다.
(C) 새로운 광고를 요청했다.
(D) 제품 원형에 대한 주문을 했다.　　　　　　정답 (D)

문제 95–97번은 다음 전화 메시지와 웹사이트를 참조하시오. 〖M〗〖M〗

M: Hello, Richard. This is Allen. I'm calling about the order for office chairs you submitted to me yesterday when we had a staff meeting. I know you need some new chairs in your office, but I don't think we'll be able to purchase the ones you want. **(95)The budget has been lowered this quarter**, so buying chairs for $220 each isn't possible. **(96)I checked out the website you sent me and noticed a nice-looking chair for $160 which still has positive ratings. (97)How about asking your employees if they think it would be all right to buy that chair for them?**

- -

안녕하세요, 리처드. 앨런이에요. 어제 우리가 직원 회의를 할 때 당신이 내게 제출한 사무용 의자에 대한 주문서 때문에 전화했어요. 당신 부서에 새 의자가 필요하다는 것은 알겠는데, 당신이 원하는 의자로 구매할 수 있을 것 같지는 않아요. 이번 분기에 예산이 내려갔어요, 그래서 개당 220달러에 의자를 구매하는 것은 가능하지가 않아요. 당신이 내게 보내 준 웹사이트를 확인해 봤는데, 여전히 긍정적인 평점이면서도 좋아 보이는 의자가 160달러라는 것을 알게 되었어요. 당신 직원들이 그 의자를 사는 게 괜찮다고 생각하는지 직원들에게 물어보시는 게 어때요?

사무용품 웨어하우스

윔벌리 의자: 220달러 평점: ★★★★	오버톤 의자: 180달러 평점: ★★★
(96)클라인 의자: 160달러 평점: ★★★★	링컨 의자: 120달러 평점: ★

95. 남자는 무슨 문제를 언급하는가?
(A) 직원 회의가 취소되었다.
(B) 예산이 최근에 줄어들었다.
(C) 사무실 의자 배송이 오늘 올 예정이다.
(D) 주문서가 제 시간에 제출되었다.　　　　　정답 (B)

96. 그래픽을 보시오. 화자는 어느 의자 모델을 구매할 것을 제안하는가?
(A) 윔벌리 의자
(B) 오버톤 의자
(C) 클라인 의자
(D) 링컨 의자　　　　　　　　　　　　　　　정답 (C)

97. 청자는 무엇을 해달라는 요청을 받는가?
(A) 회의용 테이블 5개에 대한 주문 처리하기
(B) 동료들로부터 의견 받기
(C) 이사회와 대화하기
(D) 돈을 더 모금할 방법 찾기 　　　　　　　　정답 (B)

문제 98-100번은 다음 광고와 차트를 참조하시오. 호W

W: (98)Do you own a small business and want to sell your products online? If you answered yes, then E-Systems is the company you need to contact at once. E-Systems helps small retailers attract customers by providing everything that is needed such as setting them up with a website and selling items online for them. (99)One of our most popular services is our payment processing feature that lets customers pay for their orders just by clicking on a single button. (100)For a limited time, you can sign up for our most popular plan for free for one month. That's a $90 value. For more details about our service, check out our website.

소규모 사업체를 소유하고 있고 온라인으로 물건을 판매하고 싶으세요? 그렇다면, 이-시스템즈가 여러분이 바로 연락하셔야 할 회사입니다. 이-시스템즈는 작은 소매업체들에게 웹사이트를 설치해 주고 그들을 위해서 온라인에서 물건을 판매하는 것과 같은 필요한 모든 것들을 제공함으로써, 중소 소매업체들이 고객들을 끌어들이는 것을 도와드립니다. 우리의 가장 인기 있는 서비스 중 하나는 우리의 결제 처리 기능인데, 이것은 고객들이 그냥 버튼 하나만 클릭함으로써 그들이 주문한 것에 대해 돈을 지불할 수 있도록 해줍니다. 한정된 기간 동안, 무료로 1개월 간 가장 인기 있는 요금제를 신청할 수 있습니다. 그것은 90달러의 가치입니다. 우리 서비스에 대한 더 자세한 내용을 알고 싶다면, 우리 웹사이트를 확인해 보십시오.

월별 가격 요금제

브론즈	60달러
(100)실버	90달러
골드	110달러
플래티넘	150달러

98. 이 광고는 누구를 대상으로 하는 것인가?
(A) 웹사이트 디자이너
(B) 소규모 업체 소유주
(C) 벤처사업 투자자
(D) 컴퓨터 프로그래머 　　　　　　　　정답 (B)

99. 어떤 인기 있는 특징이 언급되고 있는가?
(A) 결제 처리
(B) 소프트웨어에 대한 자동 업데이트
(C) 재고 관리
(D) 할부 결제 　　　　　　　　정답 (A)

100. 그래픽을 보시오. 청자들은 어떤 요금제에 대해 1개월 간 무료로 받을 수 있는가?
(A) 브론즈
(B) 실버
(C) 골드
(D) 플래티넘 　　　　　　　　정답 (B)

101. 베이커 씨는 작년 한 해에만 〈의학 세계〉에 세 편의 논문을 공개하며 국내에서 가장 유능한 내과의사 중 한 명이라는 명성을 쌓았다. 　　정답 (D)

102. 만약 우리가 직원으로 두 명의 사내 변호사를 더 고용한다면, 우리 사무실은 정원에 도달할 것이다. 　　정답 (B)

103. 그 게스트하우스는 전통적인 특징과 매력을 유지하는 동시에 현대적인 생활을 할 수 있게 높은 수준으로 개조되었다. 　　정답 (A)

104. 당사는 귀하의 배송 옵션을 추가 비용 없이 익일 배송으로 업그레이드해 드리고자 합니다. 　　정답 (B)

105. 금융 사기 범죄율을 감소시키기 위해. 정부는 모든 사법 절차를 가능한 한 완전하게 재편해야 한다. 　　정답 (D)

106. 개정된 법에 따라, 모든 고객은 모든 주류와 담배 제품에 대해 특별 판매세를 지불해야 한다. 　　정답 (A)

107. 지아 미술관은 현재 현대 미술을 생산하는 네 명의 혁신적인 지역 화가를 선보이는 전시회를 개최하게 되어 영광이다. 　　정답 (D)

108. 확인된 보도에 의하면, BK TV는 AT 케이블 회사를 기록적인 가격에 인수할 것인데, 미디어 역사상 가장 큰 규모의 매수가 될 것이다. 　　정답 (A)

109. 다음 주 화요일에 사무실 보수공사가 시작되면 최소 일주일간 2층에 접근할 수 없다는 점을 알아 두시기 바랍니다. 　　정답 (C)

110. 일부 주요 석유 회사들은 남미의 유전에서 원유를 생산할 수 있는 권리를 얻고자 노력해 왔다. 　　정답 (D)

111. 최근에 출시된 회계 소프트웨어를 홍보하기 위해. 우리는 그 지역 내 현지 회계 회사들에 전체 버전 100개를 제공했다. 　　정답 (A)

112. 우리의 설문조사에 응답한 거의 모든 지역 자영업자들이 다른 회사들과의 합작 사업에 관심을 보이고 있다. 　　정답 (C)

113. 미미 스포츠는 누구나 착용하고 싶어 하는 다양한 종류의 유행에 맞는 스니커즈 운동화와 비즈니스 캐주얼화를 생산하는 데 전념하고 있다. 　　정답 (B)

114. 〈헤이워드 크로니클〉은 고객 만족도를 측정하는 설문조사에서 가장 높은 평가를 받았다. 　　정답 (D)

115. 우리 회사는 최근에 케인 씨가 올해 말 최고 재무 책임자를 맡게 될 것이라고 발표했다. 　　정답 (C)

116. 그녀는 회의실에 들어갔을 때 너무 긴장해서 거의 말을 할 수 없었다. 　　정답 (A)

117. wawajamietravel.com은 좋은 여행 상품을 가장 저렴한 가격에 제공하는 손꼽히는 온라인 여행사 중 한 곳이다. 　　정답 (D)

118. 많은 요청으로 인해. 개정된 연간 마케팅 보고서에 대한 연장된 제출 마감 시한은 12월 10일이다. 　　정답 (D)

119. 코코 영화사는 국내 최고 영화 제작사의 모든 회계 업무를 관리할 경력 회계사 자리가 비어 있다. 　　정답 (C)

120. 센트리 48 오토 보험회사는 당사 대리점에 의해 제공되는 모든 거래 기록이 늘 안전하게 유지되도록 관련 조치를 취한다.   정답 (A)

121. 건강 보험과 안전 규정에 관한 모든 정보는 인사부 입구 옆에 게시될 것이다.   정답 (D)

122. 그 지역의 경제 상황이 좌절감을 주고 있어 대부분의 다국적 기업들은 지사들을 폐쇄하기 시작했다.   정답 (B)

123. 국민연금 제도의 장기 적절성에 관한 의문에도 불구하고 정부는 지금까지도 은퇴 연령을 높이려 하지 않고 있다.   정답 (D)

124. 국립 산림청에 따르면, 규정을 준수하지 않는 자는 벌금이 부과되거나 다시 산을 방문하는 것이 금지될 것이다.   정답 (C)

125. 회사에서 고용 안정의 원칙을 존중하는 한, 노조는 회사의 새로운 임금 체제를 지지할 것이다.   정답 (A)

126. 이러한 종류의 난방 장치는 밀폐된 공간에서의 빠른 난방을 위한 좋은 선택이지만, 관리하는 사람 없이 방치되어서는 안 된다.   정답 (C)

127. 불경기로 인해, 대부분의 직원들은 국내 경기가 좋아질 때까지 여름 휴가 가는 것을 미룰 것이다.   정답 (D)

128. 만약 귀하가 차량 명의와 차량 소유권 증빙을 제시할 수 있다면 저희 사무실에서 차량의 대체 열쇠를 직접 주문하는 것이 가능합니다.   정답 (D)

129. 제품 개발자 중 일부는 새로운 디자인에 있어서 공간 효율성만큼이나 독창성에 주목하고 있다.   정답 (B)

130. 서울에서 결성된 우리 소규모 재즈 밴드는 지난 20년간 많은 도시에서 다양한 관객들에게 즐거움을 안겨 주었다.   정답 (D)

Part 6

문제 131-134번은 다음 광고를 참조하시오.

온라인 사업을 시작하세요

온라인으로 무엇이든 판매하고 싶다면, 웹 상거래 플랫폼이 필요합니다. 웹 상거래는 사업을 성장시키는 데 가장 효율적인 방법입니다. 온라인 판매는 귀하의 사업이 새로운 시장에 진출하고 매출 및 수익을 증대하는 데 도움이 될 수 있습니다.

최고의 비즈니스 강사로부터 전자 상거래에 대해 알아보십시오. 저희 무료 온라인 비즈니스 과정을 수강하고 디지털 전략 및 마케팅 전술을 학습하여 회사를 성장시킬 수 있습니다. 먼저, 도메인 이름을 구매하고 자신만의 전자 상거래 사이트를 구축하는 방법을 알려 드리겠습니다. 그 다음으로, 저희는 온라인 쇼핑객들을 위한 정교한 웹 도구의 사용법을 보여줄 것입니다.

웹사이트를 제작해본 이전 경험은 전혀 필요하지 않습니다! 이 온라인 비즈니스 과정은 초보자를 위해 설계되었습니다. 오늘 바로 https://bkecommerce.com/onlinebusinesscourse에서 등록하십시오.

131.   정답 (A)

132. (A) 각 산업 부문의 모든 대기업도 귀사와 같은 소기업으로 시작했습니다.
(B) 귀하의 지역에서 귀하의 스타일, 개성 및 예산에 맞는 중고품 할인 상점을 찾으십시오.

(C) 최근 수십 년 동안 소셜 미디어 마케팅 사이트의 무수한 흥망성쇠가 있었습니다.
(D) 온라인 판매는 귀하의 사업이 새로운 시장에 진출하고 매출 및 수익을 증대하는 데 도움이 될 수 있습니다.   정답 (D)

133.   정답 (B)

134.   정답 (B)

문제 135-138번은 다음 이메일을 참조하시오.

수신: 제임스 화이트 〈jw@goldsune.com〉
발신: 줄리아 베이커 〈jbaker@mediatech.com〉
날짜: 6월 13일
제목: 가격 변동에 대한 공식 통보

화이트 씨에게:

이 이메일을 7월 1일부로 시행되는 약간의 요금 조정에 대한 공지로 받아 주시기 바랍니다. 조정은 지난 12개월 간 운송비 증가에 따른 결과입니다.

요금 변동에 대한 요약은 이 이메일 하단에 있습니다. 내년 한 해 동안에는 추가적인 요금 조정이 없을 것으로 예상합니다.

저희 서비스에 관한 추가 질문이 있으시면, 510-7767로 저희 회사에 연락 주십시오. 저희 고객 서비스 담당자가 귀하를 기꺼이 도와 드릴 것입니다.

이번 가격 인상은 내년에도 우리가 저희 제품과 서비스의 우수한 품질 기준을 계속 유지할 수 있다는 의미임을 이해해 주셔서 감사드립니다.

줄리아 베이커 드림
최고 경영자
미디어 테크 (주)

135.   정답 (C)

136.   정답 (C)

137. (A) 모든 고객을 위한 더 나은 서비스가 우리에게 최우선 사항이 되어야 합니다.
(B) 저희 고객 서비스 담당자가 귀하를 기꺼이 도와 드릴 것입니다.
(C) 저희는 해외 고객들과 소통하는 것에 어려움이 있습니다.
(D) 마케팅은 고객의 필요와 고객의 만족에 관한 것입니다.   정답 (B)

138.   정답 (A)

문제 139-142번은 다음 설명서를 참조하시오.

버킹엄 플랜트

저희 매장에서 식물을 구입해 주셔서 감사합니다. 식물을 보존하고 잘 자랄 수 있도록 돕기 위해 따라하기 쉬운 이 지침을 따르세요.

첫째로, 식물들은 생존하기 위해서 물과 햇빛, 그리고 온기를 필요로 합니다. 식물을 영양분이 풍부한 흙으로 가득 찬 적절한 화분 또는 통에 놓으세요. 그런 후에, 식물을 충분한 햇빛을 받을 수 있는 곳에 놓기만 하면 됩니다.

반드시 주기적으로 식물에 물을 주도록 하세요. 그렇지 않으면, 식물이 시들기 시작해서 결국 죽게 될 것입니다. 간단한 이 지시사항을 따름으로써, 여러분은 오랫동안 식물을 건강하게 유지하실 수 있습니다.

139. (A) 저희 매장에서 식물을 구입해 주셔서 감사합니다.
(B) 저희는 이번 주에 새로운 원예 매장을 열 계획입니다.
(C) 우리 회사는 새로운 농업 기술을 발표하게 된 것을 기쁘게 생각합니다.
(D) 식물이 건강을 증진시킨다는 증거는 아주 분명합니다. 　　정답 (A)

140. 　　정답 (D)

141. 　　정답 (C)

142. 　　정답 (D)

문제 143-146번은 다음 공지를 참조하시오.

직장에서의 건강 유지에 대한 정보

이곳 코코 패션에서는 진심으로 우리 직원 한 명 한 명을 아끼고 그들에게 최고의 가치를 부여합니다. 일하는 직원은 하루 평균 약 8.5시간을 컴퓨터 앞에 앉아 보냅니다. 그것이 바로 직원들에게 주기적으로 컴퓨터에서 떨어져 휴식을 취할 것을 추천하는 이유입니다. 구체적으로 말하면, 앉은 자세로 일하는 90분마다 일어나서 15분 동안 걸어다니는 것이 필수적입니다.

잠깐의 휴식을 위해 직원들에게 책상에서 떨어져 있을 것을 권장하는 것은 직원들이 재충전하고 긴장을 풀고 업무 과로를 예방할 수 있는 기회를 줄 것입니다. 휴식 시간이 없다면 주의력의 지속 시간과 집중력 수준은 시간이 지남에 따라 감소하므로, 짧은 휴식 시간은 주의력의 지속 시간을 다시 늘리고 집중력 수준을 유지하도록 할 것입니다. 컴퓨터가 있는 업무 공간이 가능한 한 편해지도록 배치하는 것도 중요합니다. 이것이 직원들이 전반적인 건강을 돌보는 첫 번째 단계입니다. 키보드, 컴퓨터, 모니터 및 기타 기기를 몸에 무리가 가지 않도록 배치하는 것을 고려하십시오. 때로는 작은 조정으로도 큰 차이를 만들 수 있습니다.

143. 　　정답 (D)

144. 　　정답 (D)

145. 　　정답 (B)

146. (A) 회사의 위치는 최고의 직원을 끌어들이고 유지하는 데 큰 역할을 합니다.
(B) 때로는 작은 조정으로도 큰 차이를 만들 수 있습니다.
(C) 우리는 항상 특별 포상으로 뛰어난 성과를 거둔 직원에게 보상합니다.
(D) 고용주는 종종 직장에서 직원 관계 문제에 직면합니다. 　　정답 (B)

Part 7

문제 147-148번은 다음 광고를 참조하시오.

우리가 가능하게 해드립니다
당신의 특별한 날을 더욱 특별하게 만드세요!

누구든지 기념해야 할 특별한 날들이 있습니다. 여러분들은 그저 즐기기만 하시면 됩니다. 레드 앤츠가 모든 것을 준비해 드리겠습니다.

(147)우리가 취급하는 행사들은 다음과 같습니다:

(147)파티 / 기업 연회 / 청혼
계획부터 출장 요리까지! 개인적인 요청을 처리해 드립니다.

(148) • 7월의 특별 혜택
(148)7월에 계약금을 지불하는 모든 고객 분들께 15퍼센트의 할인을 제공

합니다.
– 상담 스케줄은 매우 빠르게 예약이 차기 때문에 지금 연락하세요!

(212) 770-2431
www.redantz.com

147. 광고에 누가 가장 관심을 가질 것 같은가?
(A) 캠핑을 가고 싶어 하는 가족
(B) 연회 개최를 계획하는 사람
(C) 가까운 장래에 회의를 여는 기업
(D) 세미나를 위한 장소가 필요한 기관 　　정답 (B)

148. 8월 1일에 무슨 일이 있을 것으로 예상되는가?
(A) 레드 앤츠가 특별 할인 제공을 시작할 것이다.
(B) 많은 고객들이 견적을 요청할 것이다.
(C) 사람들이 상담을 받기 위하여 줄을 설 것이다.
(D) 특별 할인이 더 이상 이용 불가능할 것이다. 　　정답 (D)

문제 149-150번은 다음 문자 메시지를 참조하시오.

그레그 워커	[오전 10시 23분]
좋은 아침이에요, 에린. 당신에게 큰 부탁이 하나 있어요.	
에린 모리슨	[오전 10시 25분]
문제없어요. 뭐가 필요하세요?	
그레그 워커	[오전 10시 26분]
(149) (150)시애틀에서 열리는 마케팅 총회에 등록하지 못했는데, 마감시한이 오늘 정오예요. 잠시 후에 크레이그 햄프턴의 직장에서 그를 만나기로 했는데, 3시 후에나 끝날 것 같아요.	
에린 모리슨	[오전 10시 27분]
지금 정말 바쁘신 것 같군요. (150)제가 예약해 드릴까요?	
그레그 워커	[오전 10시 28분]
그러면 아주 좋죠. 제가 문자로 정보를 보내 드릴게요.	
에린 모리슨	[오전 10시 32분]
방금 받았어요. (150)제가 금방 모든 것을 처리할게요.	

149. 워커 씨에 대해 시사되어 있는 것은 무엇인가?
(A) 그는 지금 자신의 사무실에 있다.
(B) 그는 마감시한을 맞출 수 없다.
(C) 그는 시애틀에 산다.
(D) 그는 최근에 총회에 참석했다. 　　정답 (B)

150. 오전 10시 32분에, 모리슨 씨가 "제가 금방 모든 것을 처리할게요"라고 쓸 때 무엇을 의미하는가?
(A) 그녀는 햄프턴 씨에게 전화할 것이다.
(B) 그녀는 총회 주최 측에 연락할 것이다.
(C) 그녀는 워커 씨에게 정보를 보낼 것이다.
(D) 그녀는 워커 씨를 행사에 등록할 것이다. 　　정답 (D)

문제 151-153번은 다음 양식을 참조하시오.

(151)웰치스 데일리
경비 보고서

(151)이름: 조안나 다발로스　날짜: 6월 16일
(151) (152A)부서: 국제부　지출 기간: 6월 10일-6월 12일

날짜	내역	항공료	(152B)숙박	식사	(153)기타	합계
6. 10	(152B)부에노스 아이레스 국제 아동 도서 전시회	900.00달러	95.00달러	80.30달러		1075.30달러
6. 11			95.00달러	64.00달러		159.00달러
6. 12		850.50달러		70.50달러	99.00달러	1,020.00달러
					합계	2,254.30달러
					법인 카드 사용액	2,155.30달러

(153)"기타" 내역

날짜	내역	금액
6. 12	카메라 필름	60.00달러
6. 12	녹음기 배터리	39.00달러

지출 목적:
(151) (153)인터뷰 도중 필름과 배터리를 모두 사용해, 현장에서 몇 개를 구매해야 했습니다.

(152A)승인: 제프리 맥닐　날짜: 6. 16
• 상환 정책
(152A)1. 경비 보고서는 제출 전 신청인의 부서장에 의해 서명되어야 합니다.
(153)2. 업무와 관계 없는 경비는 상환되지 않을 것입니다.
(153)3. 법인 카드로 결제되지 않은 경비는 상세하게 기술되어야 합니다.
(152D)4. 회계부의 알렉스 에이켄 씨에게 작성 완료된 문서를 제출하십시오.

151. 다발로스 씨는 누구일 것 같은가?
(A) 국제 기관의 회원
(B) 카메라 필름 제조업자
(C) 서점 주인
(D) 신문사 기자　　　　　정답 (D)

152. 양식에 나타나 있지 않은 것은 무엇인가?
(A) 맥닐 씨가 국제부를 이끌고 있다.
(B) 다발로스 씨는 부에노스 아이레스에서 2박의 숙박료를 냈다.
(C) 다발로스 씨는 업무와 상관없는 물품에 법인 카드를 사용했다.
(D) 에이켄 씨가 결제를 처리할 것이다.　　정답 (C)

153. 다발로스 씨에게 얼마가 상환될 것인가?
(A) 99.00달러
(B) 159.00달러
(C) 2,155.30달러
(D) 2,254.30달러　　　　　정답 (A)

문제 154-156번은 다음 기사를 참조하시오.

(154)주간 여행 가이드

안젤리카의 고향

리오나 덴버 작성

(154)나폴리에서 배로 30분 거리에 있는 인기 있는 휴가지 바이스로이는 (155)세계적으로 유명한 만화 시리즈 〈안젤리카 찾기〉의 주인공 안젤리카의 고향이다. (156)프로쉬 항구에 내리면, 곧 만화책에서 보았던 광경을 보게 될 것이다. 안젤리카가 친구들과 뛰어노는 해변이 오른편에 있고, 마을로 걸어들어가면서 거리를 따라 줄지어 있는 색색의 지붕들을 가진 하얀 집들을 볼 수 있다.

(155)"안젤리카는 바이스로이에서의 저의 행복하고 소중한 어린시절의 추억을 나타냅니다"라고 〈안젤리카 찾기〉의 작가인 조앤 루소 씨가 말했다. "처음 그녀를 만들었을 때 안젤리카가 이렇게 인기 있을 줄은 전혀 알지 못했습니다. 그녀가 많은 아이들에게 사랑 받고 있어 축복 받는 느낌입니다."

아이들은 마을의 중심부에 위치한 박물관에서 안젤리카의 원본 스케치와 애니메이션을 즐길 수 있다. 브루노 광장의 중심에 서 있는 안젤리카의 거대한 동상 또한 인기 있는 명소이다.

(154)올해, 안젤리카의 열 번째 기념일을 축하하기 위하여, "안젤리카, 생일 축하해"라는 축제가 7월의 셋째 주에 바이스로이에서 열릴 것이다. 전 세계에서 그 어느 때보다 더 많은 사람들이 이 행사에 참가하기 위해 마을을 방문할 것으로 예상된다. 특히 3명에서 6명의 방문객들을 위한 많은 수의 호텔과 게스트하우스들이 있기 때문에, 방문객들은 바이스로이에서의 숙박에 대하여 걱정하지 않아도 된다.

154. 어떤 부류의 사람들이 이 기사에 가장 관심 있을 것 같은가?
(A) 호텔 체인의 간부
(B) 여행 가이드의 출판업자
(C) 축제 자원봉사자
(D) 가족 여행객　　　　　정답 (D)

155. 루소 씨는 누구일 것 같은가?
(A) 바이스로이 방문객
(B) 여행 가이드
(C) 바이스로이의 현재 주민
(D) 만화가　　　　　정답 (D)

156. [1], [2], [3] 및 [4]로 표시된 위치 중 아래 문장이 들어가기에 가장 적절한 곳은?
"만화에 자주 등장하는 아이스크림 가게도 있다."
(A) [1]
(B) [2]
(C) [3]
(D) [4]　　　　　정답 (A)

문제 157-158번은 다음 공고를 참조하시오.

캐스퍼 지역 교통의 승객들을 위한 공고

캐스퍼 지역 교통의 지속적인 이용에 대하여 캐스퍼의 모든 주민 분들께 감사드립니다. 저희는 안전하고 편리한 교통을 제공하기 위하여 노력하고 있습니다.

(157)하지만, 연료비와 임금이 급격히 상승하고 있습니다. 따라서, 이러한 물가 상승에 의한 비용을 충당하고 서비스 수준을 개선하기 위하여 요금을 인상하는 것이 불가피합니다. 다음 요금 변경은 5월부터 적용될 것입니다.

5월부터 적용되는 요금:

카테고리	성인	학생	노인	월 정기권
지역 버스	(158)1.50달러	1.25달러	(158)1.00달러	65.00달러
통근 버스	(158)2.50달러	2.00달러	(158)1.50달러	77.00달러

157. 이 공고의 목적은 무엇인가?
(A) 고객에게 감사하기 위한 것
(B) 정책의 변경을 알리기 위한 것
(C) 새로운 여행 패키지를 광고하기 위한 것
(D) 경제 동향에 관해 논하기 위한 것 　　　　정답 (B)

158. 공고에 시사되어 있는 것은 무엇인가?
(A) 또 다른 공고가 곧 게시될 것이다.
(B) 승객들의 수가 곧 줄어들 것이다.
(C) 노인은 할인된 요금으로 이용할 수 있다.
(D) 더 많은 버스 노선이 추가될 것이다. 　　　　정답 (C)

문제 159-161번은 다음 일정표를 참조하시오.

(159)제 2회 연차 엘크 시 레스토랑 협회 세미나
4월 11일

시간	주제
09:00 – 09:10	**개회사** • 스티브 치니츠 (엘크 시 레스토랑 협회장)
09:10 – 09:30	**기조 연설** **유기농 요리의 전망:** 유기농 요리에서의 최근 요리 동향 소개 • 제이슨 헌트 (보빗소 레스토랑의 선임 연구원이자 요리사)
09:30 – 10:30	**모든 건 지역산 재료에 달려 있다:** 지역산 재료의 우수함과 그것들을 얻을 수 있는 보다 저렴한 방법 • 푸에르토 곤잘레스 (지역 농부 연합회 회장)
10:30 – 11:30	**조리 기구 하나가 큰 차이를 만든다:** 당신의 주방을 최신식 조리 환경으로 변화시킬 첨단 조리 기구 • 하이디 하울랜드 (로팔 전자회사의 영업 부장)
11:40 – 13:00	**(160)유기농 레시피와 요리 쇼:** 최신 유기농 레시피 시연 – (161)이후에 시식 시간과 오찬이 있음 • (160)랄프 그린 (신선함을 맛보세요의 주방장)
13:00 – 14:00	**지역 레스토랑을 성공적으로 운영하는 방법:** (159)지역 레스토랑의 성공 이야기들과 레스토랑 경영에 대한 팁 • 다니엘 밀러렌 (엘크 시립 대학 교수)
14:00 – 15:30	**토론** 세미나의 모든 참가자들은 강연자와 함께 유기농 요리의 전망과 지역 레스토랑 사업에 대한 토론을 할 것입니다.

159. 누가 세미나에 관심이 있을 것 같은가?
(A) 인테리어 디자이너
(B) 지역 레스토랑의 소유주
(C) 유기농 작물 농부
(D) 음식 재료 공급업체의 경영 간부 　　　　정답 (B)

160. 누가 현장 시연을 할 것인가?
(A) 제이슨 헌트
(B) 푸에르토 곤잘레스
(C) 하이디 하울랜드
(D) 랄프 그린 　　　　정답 (D)

161. 식사는 언제 제공될 것인가?
(A) 제이슨 헌트의 기조 연설 전
(B) 하이디 하울랜드의 세션 동안
(C) 랄프 그린의 프레젠테이션 이후
(D) 토론 이후 　　　　정답 (C)

문제 162-164번은 다음 편지를 참조하시오.

2월 28일

스티브 카로비츠
샤인 키친 웨어하우스
196 녹스 가
덴버, 콜로라도 주 80111

카로비츠 씨께,

저희는 최근 제임스 말리에게서 입사 지원서를 받는데, (163)영업 부장직으로 저희 회사의 일자리를 구하고 있습니다. 이 지원자가 현재 샤인 키친 웨어하우스에 고용되어 있다는 것을 알고 있습니다. 특히 그가 최근 2년의 고용 기간 중 귀하 밑에서 (164)영업 차장으로 지내왔기 때문에, (162)귀하께서 그에 대한 추천서를 주시면 감사하겠습니다.

저희는 하급 영업 사원에서 겨우 5년 만에 (164)영업 차장 직에 오른, 말리 씨의 고속 승진에 특히 깊은 인상을 받았습니다. 저희는 말리 씨의 주목할 만한 실적에 대해 더 알고 싶습니다.

추천서에, 다음의 정보를 제공해 주십시오:
• 그가 귀하와 일한 날짜 확인
• 그가 귀사에서 맡았던 책무
• 실적 평가 (양식 동봉)

만약 추가적인 정보를 제공해야 한다고 보시면, 거리낌 없이 그렇게 해주십시오.

저희 영업 부장 자리가 매우 오랫동안 비어 있었으며 저희는 그 자리를 채울 능력 있는 사람이 급히 필요하다는 점을 이해해 주십시오. 늦어도 3월 20일까지 답장 주시면 감사하겠습니다. 협조에 감사드립니다.

엘리자베스 클라크 드림
국장, 인사부
잭슨 홈 디포

동봉물

162. 이 편지가 발송된 이유는?
(A) 개인 정보 수령을 확인해 주기 위해
(B) 추천장을 요청하기 위해
(C) 직원을 어떤 자리에 추천하기 위해
(D) 지원에 대한 지침을 제공하기 위해 　　　　정답 (B)

163. 첫 번째 단락 2행에 있는 단어 "capacity"와 의미상 가장 가까운 것은?
(A) 능력
(B) 이용 가능성
(C) 직책
(D) 크기 　　　　정답 (C)

164. 말리 씨에 대해 사실인 것은?
- (A) 샤인 키친 웨어하우스에서 총 2년간 근무했다.
- (B) 현재 직위는 영업 차장이다.
- (C) 클라크 씨를 직접 만난 적이 있다.
- (D) 클라크 씨에게 서류를 보내달라는 요청을 받았다.   정답 (B)

문제 165-167번은 다음 편지를 참조하시오.

4월 25일

케이티 캘러거 씨
39 이스트 캐롤라인 가
시애틀, 워싱턴 주 98105

케이티 캘러거 씨께,

이스트 시애틀 세탁소의 저희 서비스를 지속적으로 이용해 주셔서 감사드립니다.

지난주 목요일, 귀하의 블라우스의 드라이 클리닝 서비스를 월요일까지 요청하셨습니다. 하지만 블라우스가 분실되어 예정되어 있던 날에 돌려받지 못하셨습니다. 실수로 블라우스가 다른 고객의 셔츠와 바뀌었기 때문인 것을 알게 되었습니다. 귀하의 블라우스가 현재 어디에 있는지 알아냈고 옷을 회수하는 대로 귀하의 주소로 보내 드리겠습니다.

(165)최근 겪으신 일에 대하여 진심어린 사과를 하고 싶습니다. (166)이스트 시애틀 세탁소에서 어떠한 서비스에든 언제든지 사용하실 수 있는 50달러 상품권이 동봉되었습니다. (167)추가 요청이나 우려가 있으시다면 206-408-3180으로 저에게 언제든 전화 주십시오.

존 산토스 드림
이스트 시애틀 세탁소 매니저

동봉물

165. 편지의 목적은 무엇인가?
- (A) 고객에게 지속적인 거래에 대해 감사하기 위한 것
- (B) 고객의 환불 요청에 응답하기 위한 것
- (C) 고객에게 사과하기 위한 것
- (D) 세탁 서비스를 광고하기 위한 것   정답 (C)

166. 무엇이 편지와 함께 발송되었는가?
- (A) 상품권
- (B) 50달러 지폐
- (C) 블라우스
- (D) 티셔츠   정답 (A)

167. 만약 고객이 요청 사항이 있다면 무엇을 할 것을 요청받는가?
- (A) 산토스 씨에게 전화하기
- (B) 가게 방문하기
- (C) 양식 작성하기
- (D) 다른 고객에게 연락하기   정답 (A)

문제 168-171번은 다음 온라인 채팅 토론을 참조하시오.

쉴라 웨스트	[오후 4시 39분]

좋은 오후입니다, 여러분. 체임벌린 프로젝트에 대한 현황 보고가 필요해요.

데릭 스틸	[오후 4시 41분]

3단계 작업이 거의 완료되었어요. 전기공과 배관공 둘 다 이번 주 말까지 끝낼 것으로 예상돼요.

쉴라 웨스트	[오후 4시 43분]

(168)4단계는 어때요?

로즈 머피	[오후 4시 44분]

(168)모든 사람들이 월요일에 갈 준비가 되어 있어요. 그런데 계약자 중 한 명에게 약간의 문제가 생겼어요. (171)그는 더 높은 임금을 요구하고 있어요.

쉴라 웨스트	[오후 4시 46분]

(171)우리의 예산은 이미 꽤 빠듯해요.

로즈 머피	[오후 4시 47분]

저도 그에게 그렇게 말했어요. 만약 그가 돈을 더 받겠다고 고집한다면, 제가 대신할 사람을 찾아볼게요.

피터 트림블	[오후 4시 48분]

에릭 코튼에 대해서 말하시는 건가요, 로즈?

로즈 머피	[오후 4시 50분]

네. 아는 분인가요?

피터 트림블	[오후 4시 51분]

(169)몇 년 전에 그와 함께 일했어요. 제가 그분에게 전화해서 설명해 드릴게요.

쉴라 웨스트	[오후 4시 52분]

고마워요, 피터.

쉴라 웨스트	[오후 4시 54분]

좋아요, 예상만큼 잘 진행되고 있는 것 같아요. (170)특히 그랜드뷰 플라자로 우리가 겪었던 문제 후라서, 우리는 정말 이 프로젝트를 제시간에 끝내야 해요.

168. 4단계에 대해 사실인 것은?
- (A) 그것을 위한 충분한 자금이 없다.
- (B) 그것은 다음 주에 시작될 예정이다.
- (C) 배관공들이 그 기간 동안 일을 할 것이다.
- (D) 그것은 공사 과정의 마지막 단계이다.   정답 (B)

169. 트림블 씨는 이후에 무엇을 하겠는가?
- (A) 그랜드뷰 플라자 방문
- (B) 이전 동료에게 연락
- (C) 전기기사와 대화
- (D) 양식 제출   정답 (B)

170. 그랜드뷰 플라자에 대해 시사되어 있는 것은 무엇인가?
- (A) 그것은 완료하는 데 너무 오래 걸렸다.
- (B) 그것은 몇 가지 시공상의 결함이 있다.
- (C) 그것은 예산 초과로 끝났다.
- (D) 몇 사람이 그곳 작업 중에 다쳤다.   정답 (A)

171. 오후 4시 46분에, 웨스트 씨가 "우리의 예산은 이미 꽤 빠듯해요"라고 쓰는 이유는?
- (A) 추가 자금 지원 신청을 승인하기 위해
- (B) 그녀가 협상하고 싶지 않다는 것을 나타내기 위해
- (C) 그녀가 회계사와 이야기할 것임을 나타내기 위해
- (D) 작업을 빨리 끝내야 하는 필요성을 강조하기 위해   정답 (B)

문제 172-175번은 다음 기사를 참조하시오.

1월 11일 - (172)데이비드의 피자리아의 체인점은 이제 전국의 거의 모든 블록마다 볼 수 있다. 하지만, 이 피자 가게가 이만큼 성공하기까지는 창업자인 데이비드 킨의 많은 시간과 엄청난 노력이 필요했다.

(174)필리핀으로 그가 처음 왔을 때, 킨 씨는 마닐라 대학교에서 물리학을 공부하는 학생일 뿐이었고 그의 어머니는 캠퍼스에서 작은 태국 음식점을 (173)운영했다. 어느 날, 그는 식당에서 몇몇 태국 곁들임 요리와 함께 피자를 먹고 있다. 그는 그때 그곳에서 그 두 개의 매우 독특한 요리들로 위대한 일들이 일어나게 할 수 있을 것이라고 생각했다.

그 다음, 킨 씨는 식당을 피자 전문점으로 개조하자고 어머니를 설득했다. 어머니는 그렇게 하기로 동의했고 마침내 그 유명한 데이비드의 피자리아가 개업했다. 이 피자 전문점은 보통의 피자와 태국 음식의 결합물인 이 가게 특유의 피자를 제공한다.

"처음에 힘들었던 것은 사실이지만 어머니와 저는 포기하지 않았습니다"라고 킨 씨가 말했다. 레시피를 완성하는 데 2년이 걸렸지만, 일단 완성하자, 그 나머지는 역사가 되었다. (175)"저희 식당은 자연산 채소, 유기농 치즈와 유기농 풀을 먹인 고기만을 사용합니다. 제 생각에는 이것이 사람들이 저희 피자를 많이 사랑하는 이유인 것 같습니다"라고 킨 씨가 자신 있게 말했다.

데이비드의 피자리아는 고객에게 건강에 좋은 음식만을 제공하는 데 열정적인 만큼, 체인점이 위치한 지역사회에 기여하는 데 또한 헌신적이다. 그 가게는 불우한 이들을 돕기 위해 돈과 노력을 쏟는다. 피자 한 조각을 즐기면서, 손님은 또한 우리 모두가 살고 있는 사회를 도울 수 있다.

데이비드의 피자리아에 대한 자세한 정보를 위해서는 웹사이트 www.davids.com을 방문하면 된다. 온라인에서 등록함으로써 연 2회 열리는 데이비드의 피자리아의 자선 행사에 참여할 수 있다.

172. 기사의 주제는 무엇인가?
(A) 국제적 식당 체인의 성공
(B) 건강에 좋은 피자의 레시피
(C) 한 레스토랑의 경영 변화
(D) 한 사업체의 간략한 역사 　　　　　　　정답 (D)

173. 기사에서, 두 번째 단락 3행에 있는 단어 "ran"과 의미상 가장 가까운 것은?
(A) 빠르게 움직였다
(B) 떠났다
(C) 운영했다
(D) 인수했다 　　　　　　　정답 (C)

174. 킨 씨는 데이비드의 피자리아를 설립하기 전에 무엇을 했는가?
(A) 피자를 배달했다.
(B) 태국 식당을 소유했다.
(C) 학교에 다녔다.
(D) 식당 후기를 썼다. 　　　　　　　정답 (C)

175. [1], [2], [3] 그리고 [4]로 표시된 곳 중에, 아래 문장이 들어가기에 가장 적절한 곳은?
"비록 그곳은 패스트푸드점이지만, 데이비드의 피자리아는 고객들에게 건강에 좋은 음식만을 제공한다."
(A) [1]
(B) [2]
(C) [3]
(D) [4] 　　　　　　　정답 (C)

문제 176-180번은 다음 웹사이트와 이메일을 참조하시오.

http://www.slc.ca.gov/news

소개	검색	정책	소식

세계적인 수준의 도서 컬렉션, (177A)비디오와 많은 기타 자료들을 보유하

고 있는 캘리포니아 주립 도서관은 미국 내 선두 도서관들 중 하나입니다. 지역의 학습 중심지로서, 저희는 지역의 다른 공공 도서관들과 협력하여 지속적으로 대중에게 양질의 교육 프로그램을 제공합니다.

(176)캘리포니아 주립 도서관은 주로 시 보조금으로 운영되며 지금까지는 개인 기부금을 많이 받아오지는 않았습니다. 하지만, 이제 소중한 방문객들께 훨씬 더 나은 프로그램 및 서비스를 제공해 드리기 위해 개인 기부금을 받기로 결정했습니다. (180)기부금으로 하는 첫 번째 프로그램은 도서관에서 5월에 시작할 아동을 위한 교육 프로그램입니다. 이 프로그램을 통하여, 참가하는 아동들은 올바른 읽기 기술을 배우게 될 것입니다. 기부 회원이 되어서 우리 지역사회에서 변화를 만들어 낼 수 있도록 저희를 도와주십시오.

SLC 기부자 회원 혜택

혜택	친구 (50달러)	후원자 (75달러)	(179) 고위 후원자 (100달러)	최고 후원자 (150달러)
(177D) 도서관 무료 주차	O	O	O	O
(177B) (179) 도서관 내 서점 할인	해당 없음	O	O	O
캘리포니아 남부에 있는 파트너 박물관과 미술관 무료 입장	해당 없음	해당 없음	O	O
연례 행사 할인 & 세미나 무료 입장	해당 없음	해당 없음	해당 없음	O

저희 기부 절차에 대한 추가적인 정보를 위해서는 **여기**를 클릭하시거나 555-1109로 전화 주시기 바랍니다.

3월 1일 게시

수신: 마크 다나카 〈mtanaka@gmail.com〉
발신: 루시 다이아몬드 〈ldiamond@slc.gov〉
날짜: 6월 10일
제목: 보고

다나카 씨께,

(179)캘리포니아 주립 도서관에 대한 고위 후원자로서의 귀하의 자애로운 지원에 대하여 감사드립니다. 오늘, 우리는 귀하와 같은 자애로운 후원자들의 도움으로 실시된 아이들을 위한 교육 프로그램에 대하여 귀하께 알려 드리고자 합니다.

(180)60명의 아이들이 일주일에 두 번 도서관을 방문하여 올바른 독서 방법을 배웁니다. 현재 많은 아이들과 그들의 부모님들로부터 이 프로그램에 대하여 긍정적인 피드백을 받고 있습니다. 자애로운 후원에 감사하는 의미로, 우리 학생들이 지난주에 후원자들에게 엽서를 썼고, 이미 사우스 리버 초등학교의 에밀리 존슨에게서 엽서를 받으셨을 겁니다.

우리는 컴퓨터 수업을 위한 컴퓨터 구매와 소장 도서를 확대하는 것을 포함하는 두 가지의 추가 프로젝트를 현재 계획 중에 있습니다. 이 프로젝트에 대해 논의하기 위해, (178)도서관에서 6월 21일에 열릴 회의에 귀하를 초대하고 싶습니다. 만약 관심이 있으시면 전화 주시기 바랍니다.

루시 다이아몬드 드림

176. 웹사이트에서, 캘리포니아 주립 도서관의 운영을 위한 주요 자금 원천으로 언급된 것은 무엇인가?
(A) 정부 예산
(B) 개인 후원금
(C) 다른 도서관으로부터의 기금
(D) 도서관의 서적 판매 수익금 　　　　　　　정답 (A)

177. 캘리포니아 주립 도서관에서 이용할 수 있는 것이 아닌 것은?

    (A) 비디오 자료

    (B) 서점

    (C) 미술관

    (D) 주차 시설   정답 (C)

178. 이메일의 목적은 무엇인가?

    (A) 추가적인 기금을 요청하기 위한 것

    (B) 최근의 교육 프로그램에 대한 의견을 요청하기 위한 것

    (C) 회비의 수령을 확인하기 위한 것

    (D) 회의 참여를 권장하기 위한 것   정답 (D)

179. 다나카 씨가 제공받고 있는 혜택으로 진술된 것은 무엇인가?

    (A) 이 지역의 다른 시설 입장료 할인

    (B) 도서관에서 판매되는 서적 할인

    (C) 도서관이 주최하는 세미나 무료 입장

    (D) 도서관의 연례 행사 초대   정답 (B)

180. 에밀리 존슨에 대해 추론될 수 있는 것은 무엇인가?

    (A) 지역 박물관에 무료로 입장할 수 있다.

    (B) 5월부터 교육 프로그램에 참여해 왔다.

    (C) 새 컴퓨터를 받을 것이다.

    (D) 아이들을 위한 교육 프로그램의 강사이다.   정답 (B)

문제 181–185번은 다음 편지와 이메일을 참조하시오.

스쿠비 부동산

(181)시드니와 그 주변 지역에서 20년 이상 서비스하고 있습니다

11월 18일

베로니카 미쉐린

35B 나이츠 로드

시드니, 뉴사우스웨일스 주 2111

미쉐린 씨께,

지난주에 했던 전화 통화에 이어서 편지를 씁니다. 귀하의 새 사업 계획에 딱 맞는 몇 개의 상가 부동산이 최근에 시장에 나왔습니다.

(185)첫 번째 건물은 니치 가에 있는 1층짜리 건물입니다. 바로 지난달 건축이 완료되었고, 이는 귀하가 그 건물의 첫 번째 소유주가 될 것이라는 걸 의미합니다. 이것은 많은 사무실들로 둘러싸인 상업 지구에 위치해 있습니다. 따라서 귀하는 점심 시간에 많은 직장인들을 받게 될 것입니다.

또한, 크림슨 거리에 있는 건물의 3층에 있는 가게도 매물로 나왔습니다. **(182)가게 주인이 몇몇 주방 기구들을 거래에 포함시키겠다고 제안해서, 당신은 새것들을 구매할 필요가 없을 것입니다.** 또한 그는 기꺼이 홀의 테이블과 의자들도 남겨둘 것입니다. 가게의 인테리어는 제법 새것이라 재단장할 필요가 거의 없습니다.

만약 이 부동산들을 둘러보고 싶으시면, **(184B)근무 시간인 월요일부터 금요일 오전 9시와 오후 5시 사이에 저에게 전화 주시거나**, 이메일을 보내 주십시오. 귀하가 표한 몇몇 금전적 우려들에 관해서는, 만났을 때 (183)할부금 옵션에 대해 논의할 수 있습니다.

저희는 오늘, 내일, 그리고 항상 귀하를 최고로 모실 수 있길 바랍니다.

맥킨지 로버트슨 드림

부동산 컨설턴트

스쿠비 부동산

수신: 맥킨지 로버트슨 〈mrobertson@scubyre.com〉

발신: 베로니카 미쉐린 〈vmichelin@plomail.com〉

날짜: 11월 24일

제목: 감사합니다

로버트슨 씨께,

(184)오늘 오후 저에게 부동산을 보여 주셔서 감사합니다. 귀하께서 저에게 제안한 조건으로 저는 (185)신축 부동산을 사기로 결정했습니다. 추천해 주신 두 번째 옵션도 굉장히 매력적이지만, **(182)저는 매일 아침 공급업체들로부터 신선한 재료들을 받을 계획입니다. 따라서 농산물을 빌딩 안으로 옮기기 더 편리한 장소가 필요합니다.**

계약서에 최대한 빨리 서명하기를 원합니다. 귀하께서 언제 서류를 모두 준비해 저와 만날 수 있는지 알려 주십시오. 도움에 감사드립니다.

베로니카 미쉐린 드림

---

181. 스쿠비 부동산에 대해 나타나 있는 것은 무엇인가?

    (A) 상업용 부동산만 전문적으로 다룬다.

    (B) 현재 가구가 완비된 부동산을 하나도 가지고 있지 않다.

    (C) 상업 지구에 위치해 있다.

    (D) 고객층은 주로 시드니에 기반을 두고 있다.   정답 (D)

182. 미쉐린 씨는 어떤 종류의 업체를 개업할 것 같은가?

    (A) 주방 기기 상점

    (B) 가구점

    (C) 식당

    (D) 부동산   정답 (C)

183. 편지에서, 네 번째 단락 3행에 있는 단어 "installment"와 의미상 가장 가까운 것은?

    (A) 가구 조립

    (B) 이사 서비스

    (C) 무료 컨설팅

    (D) 분할 지불   정답 (D)

184. 로버트슨 씨에 대해 사실인 것은?

    (A) 부동산 분야에서 약 20년의 경력이 있다.

    (B) 일주일 내내 매일 일한다.

    (C) 최근에 미쉐린 씨를 직접 만났다.

    (D) 스쿠비 부동산을 소유하고 있다.   정답 (C)

185. 미쉐린 씨는 앞으로 무엇을 할 계획인가?

    (A) 스쿠비 부동산에서 대출 신청

    (B) 자신의 가게 인테리어 디자인

    (C) 니치 가에 있는 건물 구입

    (D) 매일 아침 근처 백화점에 식품 배송   정답 (C)

문제 186-190번은 다음 광고와 메모 그리고 기사를 참조하시오.

애버딘 음식 축제에 오세요

올해의 축제는 5월 10일부터 14일까지 열릴 것입니다. 20개 이상의 국가에서 온 음식뿐만 아니라 이 도시에서 가장 좋은 레스토랑 몇 군데의 음식도 즐기세요. 온갖 종류의 신나는 행사들도 있을 것입니다. 웨인 듀프리, 루신다 드 마일스, 캐롤 코너, **(188)제이슨 피퍼와 같은 유명한 요리사들이 진행하는 요리 수업이 있을 것입니다.** 방문객들은 다양한 음식이 준비되는 과정을 볼 수 있습니다. 그리고 물론, **(186)사람들이 살 수 있는 수많은 종류의 신선 식품, 건조 식품, 통조림이 있을 것입니다.** 5일 전체에 대한 입장료는 3달러이

지만, (190)5세 이하의 어린이와 65세 이상의 성인은 무료로 입장할 수 있습니다. 더 자세한 정보는 495-9332로 전화하세요.

수신: 피터 그리핀
발신: 에밀리 데어
제목: 참고
날짜: 5월 8일

다가오는 축제는 모든 것이 잘 되어가고 있는 것 같습니다. (187)참석하겠다고 밝힌 식당들이 모두 참석을 재확인했습니다. 표도 6,000장 넘게 판매했는데, 이는 지난해 판매량의 두 배입니다. 사상 최대 규모의 참석률을 향해 가는 것 같습니다.

(187)한 가지 알아 두셔야 할 게 있습니다. (188)제이슨 피퍼가 아파서 참석하지 못할 것입니다. 하지만, 당신이 알고 있는 아이린 포터와 얘기했는데, 그녀가 제이슨을 대신하기로 동의했습니다.

다른 일이 생기면 알려 드리겠습니다.

음식 축제, 대 성공
케빈 드러먼드 기자 작성

애버딘 (5월 15일) - 애버딘 음식 축제가 어제 막을 내렸고, 이것은 행사의 27년 역사상 최고라는 찬사를 받았다. 주최 측은 축제 기간 5일 중 최소 1일 이상 11,000여 명이 참석한 반면, 다른 사람들은 여러 날 참석했다고 밝혔다.

"저는 항상 그렇듯이 즐거운 시간을 보냈습니다"라고 지역 주민 잭슨 버제스가 말했다. (190)저는 특히 입장하기 위해 돈을 낼 필요가 없어서 좋았어요. 그 점이 이전 행사와는 다른 긍정적인 변화였어요." (189)버제스 씨는 특히 자신이 시식한 아시아와 남아메리카의 음식을 즐겼다고 덧붙였다.

축제 주최자인 피터 그리핀은 행사가 진행된 방식에 만족한다고 말했다. "전반적으로, 저는 조금도 불평할 게 없습니다. 모두에게 즐거운 시간이었습니다."

186. 광고에 따르면, 축제에 대한 설명으로 사실인 것은?
(A) 사람들은 그곳에서 식품을 살 수 있다.
(B) 모든 참석자는 입장하기 위해 돈을 지불해야 한다.
(C) 그것은 텔레비전으로 생중계될 것이다.
(D) 그것은 주말에 열릴 것이다.   정답 (A)

187. 메모의 목적은 무엇인가?
(A) 도움을 요청하기 위한 것
(B) 최신 소식을 주기 위한 것
(C) 행동을 칭찬하기 위한 것
(D) 고소하기 위한 것   정답 (B)

188. 포터 씨는 축제에서 무엇을 했는가?
(A) 그녀는 티켓 판매를 도왔다.
(B) 그녀는 요리 지도를 했다.
(C) 그녀는 통조림과 건조 식품을 판매했다.
(D) 그녀는 여러 부스 설치를 도왔다.   정답 (B)

189. 기사에서, 애버딘 음식 축제에 대해 나타나 있는 것은 무엇인가?
(A) 그것은 일주일 동안 계속되었다.
(B) 축제에 매일 11,000명이 참석했다.
(C) 그것은 다양한 대륙의 음식을 특징으로 했다.
(D) 그것은 처음으로 개최되고 있었다.   정답 (C)

190. 버제스 씨에 대해 시사되어 있는 것은 무엇인가?
(A) 그는 남아메리카 출신이다.
(B) 그는 축제에 매일 참석했다.
(C) 그는 축제를 조직하는 것을 도왔다.
(D) 그는 최소 65세이다.   정답 (D)

문제 191-195번은 다음 회람과 이메일들을 참조하시오.

---

(192)수신: 전 관리자
발신 : 에드워드 실번
(192)날짜: 8월 21일
제목: 설문조사 결과

(192)저는 방금 MTT 주식회사를 위해 직원 설문조사를 실시한 그룹인 아놀드 컨설팅으로부터 설문조사 결과를 제공받았습니다. 우리가 정말 처리해야 할 문제가 좀 있을 것 같습니다. 다음은 몇 가지 결과입니다:

(191) (194B)전체 직원의 절반 이상이 저임금이라고 느낀다.
(191) (194D)전체 직원의 45%가 시간 외 근무를 너무 많이 한다고 생각한다.
(191) (194C)전체 직원의 35%가 충분한 교육을 받지 못한다고 느낀다.
(191) (194A)전체 직원의 75%가 경쟁 회사에서 동일한 직급, 급여, 혜택을 제공한다면 이 회사를 떠나는 것을 고려할 것이다.

(192)내일 오전 9시에 회의실에서 브레인스토밍을 할 예정입니다. 종일 업무가 될 것입니다. 예정된 회의는 모두 취소하고 창의적인 아이디어를 갖고 오도록 하세요.

수신: 에드워드 실번 〈edsilvan@mtt.com〉
발신: 루시 잭슨 〈lj@mtt.com〉
(192)날짜: 8월 23일
제목: 어제

에드,

(192)어제 그것은 생산적인 회의였어요. 나는 몇몇 사람들, 특히 제프 색스와 헬렌 크로스가 좋은 아이디어를 가지고 있다고 생각했어요. 그 중 몇 가지는 제가 직접 시행해 보려고 해요.

(193)우리 회의를 또 할 계획인가요? 모두가 이러한 새로운 아이디어를 이용하고 있는지 확인할 수 있도록 하는 것이 현명한 일이라고 생각해요. 또한 우리가 시행해 보고 있는 변화가 잘 진행되고 있는지에 대한 최신 정보도 제공할 수 있어요. 한 사람에게 효과가 있는 것이 다른 사람들에게 성공할 수도 있어요. 우리는 또한 어떤 아이디어가 비현실적이거나 직원들이 좋아하지 않는지도 파악할 수 있어요.

루시

수신: 에드워드 실번 〈edsilvan@mtt.com〉
발신: 헬렌 크로스 〈helen@mtt.com〉
날짜: 9월 4일
제목: 최신 정보

에드,

운송부의 직원들은 여전히 전반적인 작업 여건에 불만을 품고 있다는 것을 알고 계셔야 합니다. (194D)많은 사람들이 지난 주말에 일을 해야 하는 것에 대해 불평했어요. (194A)실제로 오늘 오전에는 2명의 근로자가 사표를 제출했어요. 그들은 이미 보스콤 테크의 자리를 수락했다고 말했어요. (194B)그들은 새 직장에서 연 9,000달러 이상 올려 받을 것이라고 했어요. (195)여기 일손이 부족해서 빨리 조치를 취해야 해요. 그리고 가을은 일년 중 가장 바쁜 계절입니다. 추가 직원을 빨리 받지 못하면, 불만스러워하는 고객들이 많아질 거예요.

헬렌

191. 회람은 주로 무엇에 관한 것인가?
  (A) 근로 환경 개선 방안
  (B) 다른 직원들을 만날 장소
  (C) 특별 행사가 있을 시기
  (D) 직원들이 불만족스러워 하는 이유   정답 (D)

192. 잭슨 씨에 대해 나타나 있는 것은 무엇인가?
  (A) 그녀는 MTT 주식회사의 관리자이다.
  (B) 그녀는 실번 씨의 상사이다.
  (C) 그녀는 인사부에서 근무한다.
  (D) 그녀는 최근 회의에 참석하지 않았다.   정답 (A)

193. 잭슨 씨는 무엇을 할 것을 제안하는가?
  (A) 인터넷에 더 많은 광고 내기
  (B) 또 한 번의 설문조사 실시하기
  (C) 앞으로 다시 회의하기
  (D) 자격 있는 직원 채용하기   정답 (C)

194. 직원들이 제기한 문제 가운데 크로스 씨가 자신의 이메일에서 다루지 않는 것은 무엇인가?
  (A) 다른 곳에서 일하고 싶은 욕구
  (B) 제대로 보수를 못 받는 직원
  (C) 교육 부족
  (D) 너무 많은 초과 근무   정답 (C)

195. 크로스 씨가 두 번째 이메일에서 언급하는 문제는 무엇인가?
  (A) 그녀는 직원이 충분히 있지 않다.
  (B) 그녀의 예산이 너무 적다.
  (C) 배송 차량이 충분하지 않다.
  (D) 물품 배송 가격이 상승하고 있다.   정답 (A)

문제 196-200번은 다음 광고들과 이메일을 참조하시오.

호프웰 부동산
힐사이드 지역사회에서 50년 이상 운영

저희가 매물로 내놓은 이 새로운 장소들을 확인해 보세요. 새로운 사업을 시작할 생각이신가요? 그럼 분명 한 번 보셔야 할 것입니다:

(196)**해머 스트리트 88: 마스턴 건물 1층에 있는 45평방미터 규모의 부동산; 유동 인구가 많음; 카페나 작은 레스토랑에 적격; 45,000달러**

오크 스트리트 12: 그린빌 건물의 꼭대기 층 전체; 사무실에 완벽한 위치; 전용 엘리베이터; 지하 주차장; 완전히 새로운 시설; 350,000달러

(198)**대거 로드 21: 로즈우드 타워 2층에 있는 100평방미터; 현재 소매점 공간으로 사용되고 있음; 수리가 필요할 수 있음; 105,000달러**

켄모어 드라이브 93: 피드먼트 건물 10층에 있는 작은 사무실 공간; 1인 개인 사무실에 알맞음; 20,000달러

이 부동산 중 하나 또는 저희가 매물로 갖고 있는 그외 다른 곳을 보시려면 inquiries@hopewellrealty.com으로 이메일을 보내 주십시오.

수신: 톰 우드워드 〈tomw@commercemail.com〉
발신: 그레이스 델 〈grace@hopewellrealty.com〉
(199)**날짜: 4월 11일**

제목: 안녕하세요

우드워드 씨에게,

저희 일부 부동산에 관심을 나타내 주신 이메일에 감사드립니다. 그 중 몇 군데 보여 드릴 수 있다면 기쁘겠습니다. (197)**한정된 예산으로 일하시는 거로 알고 있는데,** 어느 곳을 보여 드릴지 생각할 때 그 부분을 고려하고 있습니다.

(198) (199)**내일 오전 9시에 대거 로드 21번지에서 만나서 시작합시다.** 그 다음 매그놀리아 드라이브와 피칸 스트리트에 있는 매물을 포함한 몇 군데 다른 곳들을 보여 드릴 수 있습니다.

언제든지 제게 전화 주세요. 제 번호는 205-954-9022입니다.

내일 뵙겠습니다.

그레이스 델
호프웰 부동산

---

(199)**우드워드와 스미스 중고 서점**
톰 우드워드와 잭 스미스 소유

7월 10일에
개점합니다.

새로운 위치로 찾아오세요.
(199)**피칸 스트리트 95번지**

모든 종류의 책을 보유하고 있습니다.
그러나 (200)**저희는 공상과학 소설, 문학, 시를 전문으로 하고 있습니다.**

개점 당일의 모든 판매는 20% 할인됩니다.

---

196. 첫 번째 광고에 따르면, 음식을 판매하려는 사람이 관심을 가질 장소는 어디인가?
  (A) 해머 스트리트 88
  (B) 오크 스트리트 12
  (C) 대거 로드 21
  (D) 켄모어 드라이브 93   정답 (A)

197. 이메일에서, 우드워드 씨에 대해 시사되어 있는 것은 무엇인가?
  (A) 그는 이전에 델 씨를 직접 만난 적이 있다.
  (B) 그는 일정 금액의 돈만 쓸 수 있다.
  (C) 그는 다른 도시에서 힐즈데일을 방문할 것이다.
  (D) 그는 4월 13일에 몇 군데 부동산을 둘러볼 것이다.   정답 (B)

198. 델 씨가 우드워드 씨에게 먼저 보여 주고 싶은 곳의 가격은 얼마인가?
  (A) 2만 달러
  (B) 4만 5천 달러
  (C) 10만 5천 달러
  (D) 35만 달러   정답 (C)

199. 우드워드 씨에 관해 사실인 것은?
  (A) 그는 과거에 몇 권의 책을 출판한 적이 있다.
  (B) 그는 4월 12일에 처음 그의 서점 위치를 보았다.
  (C) 그는 유명한 공상과학 도서의 작가이다.
  (D) 그는 최근에 힐즈데일로 이사했다.   정답 (B)

200. 우드워드와 스미스 중고 서점에 대해 나타나 있는 것은 무엇인가?
  (A) 그곳은 6월 한 달 동안 문을 열 것이다.
  (B) 그곳은 최근에 출판된 책들을 판매한다.
  (C) 그곳은 특정한 장르의 책에 초점을 맞추고 있다.
  (D) 그곳은 한 달 내내 할인을 제공하고 있다.   정답 (C)

1. 미W
(A) She is turning a control knob.
(B) She is tying her apron.
(C) She is removing something from an oven.
(D) She is reaching into a microwave oven.

(A) 그녀는 조절 손잡이를 돌리고 있다.
(B) 그녀는 앞치마를 매고 있다.
(C) 그녀는 오븐에서 뭔가를 꺼내고 있다.
(D) 그녀는 전자레인지 안으로 손을 뻗고 있다.　　　정답 (A)

2. 영M
(A) She is installing a shelving unit.
(B) She is assembling a sofa.
(C) She is putting a plant on the windowsill.
(D) She is looking at items in a box.

(A) 그녀는 선반을 설치하고 있다.
(B) 그녀는 소파를 조립하고 있다.
(C) 그녀는 식물을 창턱에 놓고 있다.
(D) 그녀는 상자 안의 물건을 보고 있다.　　　정답 (D)

3. 호W
(A) The men are removing their hats.
(B) One of the men is unloading a chair from a vehicle.
(C) There is a truck parked in front of the store.
(D) A car is being inspected on the street.

(A) 남자들이 모자를 벗고 있다.
(B) 남자 중 한 명이 차량에서 의자를 내리고 있다.
(C) 가게 앞에 주차되어 있는 트럭 한 대가 있다.
(D) 차 한 대가 길거리에서 점검을 받고 있다.　　　정답 (B)

4. 미W
(A) The staircase is leading up to the roof.
(B) Some flags are being raised on the rooftop.
(C) They are doing construction work on a house.
(D) They are transporting the ladders.

(A) 계단이 지붕 위쪽으로 이어져 있다.
(B) 깃발들이 지붕 꼭대기에 게양되고 있다.
(C) 그들은 주택 공사 작업을 하고 있다.
(D) 그들은 사다리를 운반하고 있다.　　　정답 (C)

5. 미M
(A) A cart with books on it is being pulled down the hallway.
(B) One of the men is climbing a ladder.
(C) Some people are browsing in a library.
(D) Some shelving units line the walls of the room.

(A) 책들이 올려져 있는 카트를 복도 아래쪽으로 끌고 내려가고 있다.
(B) 남자 중 한 명이 사다리를 올라가고 있다.
(C) 몇 명의 사람들이 도서관을 둘러보고 있다.
(D) 몇 개의 선반들이 방의 벽을 따라 늘어서 있다.　　　정답 (D)

6. 영M
(A) Some pizzas are being sliced into pieces.
(B) A pizza is being taken out of an oven.
(C) A pizza box is being unfolded.
(D) Some boxes are stacked on a counter area.

(A) 피자가 조각으로 잘리고 있다.
(B) 피자를 오븐에서 꺼내고 있다.
(C) 피자 상자가 펼쳐지고 있다.
(D) 상자 몇 개가 카운터 위에 쌓여 있다.　　　정답 (D)

Part 2

7. 미M 미W
Why isn't the drugstore store open today?
(A) Here is your prescription.
(B) They don't serve breakfast.
(C) Since it's a national holiday.

약국이 왜 오늘 문을 열지 않죠?
(A) 여기 당신의 처방전이 있어요.
(B) 그들은 아침을 제공하지 않아요.
(C) 국경일이라서요.　　　정답 (C)

8. 호W 미M
You hired a new nutritionist, right?
(A) It's next to the cafeteria.
(B) Yes, he starts next Monday.
(C) Hang it a little higher.

영양사를 새로 채용하셨죠, 그렇죠?
(A) 그것은 구내식당 옆에 있어요.
(B) 예, 그는 다음 주 월요일에 시작해요.
(C) 그걸 좀 더 높이 거세요.　　　정답 (B)

9. 미W 영M
Why don't we take the express train this time?
(A) Yes, it's a safety training.
(B) I sent it by express mail.
(C) Sure, let's do that.

이번에 급행 열차를 타는 게 어때요?
(A) 예, 그건 안전 교육이에요.
(B) 저는 그것을 속달로 보냈어요.
(C) 좋아요, 그렇게 합시다.　　　정답 (C)

10. 미M 호W
When does the art museum close?
(A) It is close to the station.
(B) It stays open until 6 every day.
(C) No, I don't have a ticket.

미술관은 언제 닫아요?
(A) 그건 역과 가까워요.
(B) 거긴 매일 6시까지 문을 열어요.
(C) 아뇨, 저는 표가 없어요.　　　정답 (B)

11. 호W 미M
What do you think we should bring to the training?
(A) A pen and something to write on.
(B) Only interns will attend.
(C) Whenever you are late.

교육에 무엇을 가지고 가면 좋을까요?
(A) 펜과 적을 수 있는 종이요.
(B) 인턴만 참석할 거예요.

(C) 당신이 지각할 때마다요.　　　　　　　　　　　정답 (A)

12. 미W 영M

Whose large black suitcase is this?
(A) It belongs to Perry.
(B) No, it's not large enough.
(C) Which suitcase do you like?

이 대형 까만색 여행가방은 누구 건가요?
(A) 페리 것입니다.
(B) 아뇨, 그건 충분히 크지 않아요.
(C) 어떤 여행가방이 마음에 드시겠어요?　　　　정답 (A)

13. 미M 호W

Why won't we be able to submit the application forms online?
(A) Make sure the forms are straightforward.
(B) Here's your receipt.
(C) There's a problem with our website.

우리 온라인으로 신청서를 제출할 수 없을까요?
(A) 양식은 꼭 간단하게 만드세요.
(B) 여기 영수증 있습니다.
(C) 우리 웹사이트에 문제가 있어요.　　　　　　정답 (C)

14. 호W 미M

Do you need help taking the chairs to the conference room?
(A) He is the chairman.
(B) All the seats are already reserved.
(C) Sure, that would be great.

회의실로 의자를 가져가는 데 도움 필요하세요?
(A) 그는 의장입니다.
(B) 모든 좌석이 이미 예약되었어요.
(C) 좋아요, 그렇게 해주시면 좋죠.　　　　　　정답 (C)

15. 미W 영M

Can we talk about the issue in your office or should we go to the meeting room?
(A) A two-hour meeting.
(B) Yes, I went there yesterday.
(C) In my office is fine.

그 문제에 대해 당신 사무실에서 얘기할까요, 아니면 회의실로 갈까요?
(A) 두 시간짜리 회의요.
(B) 예, 저는 어제 거기에 갔어요.
(C) 제 사무실에서 하는 게 좋아요.　　　　　　정답 (C)

16. 미M 미W

It seems like the shipment is missing two boxes.
(A) OK. We should notify the vendor immediately.
(B) No, they're going by plane.
(C) It was shipped out yesterday.

배송품에서 상자 2개가 분실된 것 같아요.
(A) 알았어요. 당장 업체에 알려야겠네요.
(B) 아뇨, 그들은 비행기로 갑니다.
(C) 그건 어제 발송되었어요.　　　　　　　　정답 (A)

17. 미M 미W

How many attendees are you expecting?
(A) Chuck has the list.
(B) I didn't attend, either.

(C) Those plants belong in the entryway.

몇 명의 참석자를 예상하시나요?
(A) 척이 명단을 가지고 있어요.
(B) 저 역시 참석하지 않았어요.
(C) 저 화분들은 입구 통로에 있으면 돼요.　　　정답 (A)

18. 미W 영M

Who's working on the account for Jefferson Law Firm?
(A) A corrected invoice will be sent out.
(B) I discussed it with my lawyer.
(C) Laura's taking care of that.

제퍼슨 법률회사 계정은 누가 작업하고 있어요?
(A) 수정된 송장이 발송될 거예요.
(B) 저는 변호사와 그것에 대해 의논했어요.
(C) 로라가 그것을 담당하고 있어요.　　　　　정답 (C)

19. 영M 미W

Aren't you going to send the budget proposal in the e-mail to Mr. Yoon?
(A) Show him the photo ID.
(B) Oh, are they?
(C) Yes. Thank you for reminding me.

미스터 윤에게 이메일로 예산 제안서를 보내지 않을 거예요?
(A) 그에게 사진이 있는 신분증을 보여 주세요.
(B) 아, 그들이 그래요?
(C) 보낼 거예요. 잊지 않게 다시 알려 주셔서 감사해요.　　정답 (C)

20. 미M 호W

Have you finished drafting the proposal or do you need some more time?
(A) Management proposed the changes.
(B) I'm almost done.
(C) A new watch is needed.

제안서 초안 작성을 마치셨어요, 아니면 시간이 더 필요하세요?
(A) 경영진은 변경을 제안했어요.
(B) 거의 끝냈어요.
(C) 새 손목시계가 필요해요.　　　　　　　　정답 (B)

21. 미W 영M

When are the paintings for the hallway going to be finished?
(A) The artist is away on vacation.
(B) At an art supply store.
(C) How can you tell the difference?

복도에 설치할 그림들은 언제 끝나요?
(A) 화가가 휴가 차 다른 데 갔습니다.
(B) 화방에서요.
(C) 어떻게 차이를 구분하시죠?　　　　　　　정답 (A)

22. 호W 영M

Wasn't the photocopy machine supposed to be fixed after lunch?
(A) I've already eaten.
(B) Please put it up over here.
(C) That's been put off.

점심 후에 복사기가 수리 받게 되어 있지 않았나요?
(A) 저는 벌써 먹었어요.

(B) 그걸 이쪽에 올려 주세요.
(C) 그건 미루어졌어요. 　　　　　　　　정답 (C)

23. 호W 영M
We have an extra ticket for the rock concert tonight.
(A) No, it shouldn't be cheaper than the red one.
(B) You should ask Brenden to join you.
(C) The forms are not in the drawer.

우리는 오늘 밤 록 콘서트 티켓이 한 장 더 있어요.
(A) 아뇨, 그게 빨간 거보다 더 싸지는 않을 거예요.
(B) 브렌든에게 같이 가자고 해보세요.
(C) 그 서식은 서랍에 없어요. 　　　　　　정답 (B)

24. 미M 미W
How can I open the filing cabinet?
(A) Ibrahim has a key.
(B) Office supplies are in the cabinet upstairs.
(C) We don't open on Mondays.

서류함을 어떻게 열 수 있나요?
(A) 이브라힘이 열쇠를 가지고 있어요.
(B) 사무용품은 위층 캐비닛에 있어요.
(C) 우리는 월요일마다 문을 열지 않아요. 　　정답 (A)

25. 호W 영M
We should purchase more potted plants for the waiting area.
(A) We do have room in the budget.
(B) Sorry. We don't accept credit cards.
(C) I have plans this afternoon.

우리는 대기실에 놓을 화분을 더 구입해야 해요.
(A) 예산에 여유가 있어요.
(B) 죄송합니다. 저희는 신용 카드를 받지 않습니다.
(C) 저는 오늘 오후에 약속이 있어요. 　　　정답 (A)

26. 미M 호W
The deadline for your presentation is tomorrow, isn't it?
(A) There are five laptops in the room.
(B) About the upcoming acquisition.
(C) I just have to finish two more slides.

당신 발표자료 마감일이 내일이죠, 그렇죠?
(A) 방에 노트북 컴퓨터가 5대 있어요.
(B) 다가오는 인수에 대해서요.
(C) 슬라이드 2개 더 끝내기만 하면 돼요. 　정답 (C)

27. 미W 영M
Excuse me, where can I find the spring jackets your store carries?
(A) It doesn't have a price tag.
(B) I'm not sure where I left it.
(C) New inventory won't be available until next month.

실례지만, 여기 가게에서 취급하는 봄 재킷은 어디에서 찾을 수 있나요?
(A) 그것은 가격표가 없어요.
(B) 제가 그것을 어디에 두고 왔는지 모르겠어요.
(C) 새 재고는 다음 달이나 되어야 들어올 거예요. 　정답 (C)

28. 호W 미M
I'm leaving on an urgent business trip this afternoon.
(A) I'll reschedule our discussion.

(B) Leave it turned on.
(C) He got in by plane yesterday.

제가 오늘 오후에 급한 출장을 떠나요.
(A) 우리 토론 일정을 다시 조정할게요.
(B) 그것을 그냥 켠 채로 두세요.
(C) 그는 어제 비행기로 도착했어요. 　　　정답 (A)

29. 미W 영M
What's the status of the expansion project proposal?
(A) The numbers have increased as projected.
(B) For the research and development team.
(C) We need to get the manager's approval.

확장 프로젝트 제안서의 상황이 어떤가요?
(A) 예상한 대로 수치가 증가했어요.
(B) 연구개발팀을 위해서요.
(C) 우리는 부장님의 승인을 받아야 해요. 　정답 (C)

30. 미M 미W
How much funding did you get for our library renovations?
(A) By posting it online.
(B) It was a fundraising event.
(C) Enough for the whole project.

우리 도서관 보수공사를 위한 기금을 얼마나 모았어요?
(A) 그것을 온라인에 올려서요.
(B) 그것은 기금 모금 행사였어요.
(C) 전체 프로젝트에 충분할 만큼이요. 　　정답 (C)

31. 미W 영M
Where are you going on your next summer vacation?
(A) The menu is different in the summer.
(B) We are still deciding.
(C) Bring some of your friends to the party.

다음 여름 휴가를 어디로 가세요?
(A) 여름에는 메뉴가 달라요.
(B) 우리는 아직 결정하는 중이에요.
(C) 파티에 친구를 몇 명 데려오세요. 　　정답 (B)

Part 3

문제 32-34번은 다음 대화를 참조하시오. 영M 미W

M: Hello. May I speak with Lucy Watkins? (32)**This is Eric Thomas from the *Lancaster Daily*.**
W: Hello. This is Lucy.
M: Hi. (32)**I'm working on an article about the art exhibit from Korea at the museum.** I'm going to conduct some interviews, and (33)**I want to hire you as a Korean-English translator. I've heard good things about you.**
W: That sounds interesting. (34)**But you should know that I'm busy until May 10. Is that a problem?**
M: Not at all. The interviews will be conducted at the end of the month.

M: 여보세요. 루시 왓킨스와 통화 가능할까요? 저는 〈랭카스터 데일리〉의 에릭 토마스입니다.
W: 여보세요. 제가 루시입니다.
M: 안녕하세요. 저는 미술관에서 열리는 한국 미술 전시회에 대해 기사 작

업을 하고 있는데요. 인터뷰를 좀 할 계획인데, 한영 통역관으로 선생님을 고용하고 싶어서요. 선생님에 대해선 좋은 이야기 많이 들었습니다.

W: 흥미로운 일이군요. 그런데 아셔야 할 게 제가 5월 10일까지는 바쁘네요. 이게 문제 될까요?

M: 전혀요. 인터뷰가 이달 말에 진행되거든요.

32. 남자는 누구인가?
    (A) 기자
    (B) 사진사
    (C) 역사학자
    (D) 화가   정답 (A)

33. 남자가 전화를 건 이유는?
    (A) 약속을 취소하기 위해
    (B) 예약을 확인하기 위해
    (C) 미술 전시회에 대해 문의하기 위해
    (D) 여자에게 일을 제안하기 위해   정답 (D)

34. 여자는 무엇에 대해 우려하는가?
    (A) 일정
    (B) 많은 업무량
    (C) 다가오는 출장
    (D) 추천서   정답 (A)

문제 35-37번은 다음 대화를 참조하시오. [미M] [미W]

M: Okay, ma'am. **(35)The total cost of the sweater and the blouse is $65.**

W: Here's my credit card.

M: I'm very sorry, but we are only taking cash now. **(36)Our credit card terminal hasn't been working properly all afternoon because of an unknown device error.**

W: Oh, well, I only have a few dollars on me. I wish I'd known that.

M: There's an ATM right across the street in the convenience store. **(37)If you want to go there to get some cash, I can hold these items here at the checkout counter until you return.**

M: 좋습니다. 고객님. 스웨터와 블라우스 총 금액은 65달러입니다.

W: 여기 제 신용 카드예요.

M: 대단히 죄송합니다만, 지금은 현금만 받고 있어요. 우리 신용 카드 단말기가 알 수 없는 장치 오류로 오후 내내 제대로 작동을 하지 않네요.

W: 오, 음, 제 수중에는 몇 달러밖에 없어요. 진작에 알았더라면 좋았을 텐데요.

M: 바로 길 건너 편의점에 현금 인출기가 있어요. 거기 가서 돈을 뽑아오신다면, 돌아오실 때까지 여기 계산대에 이 물건들을 보관해 드릴 수 있어요.

35. 남자는 어디에서 근무하는 것 같은가?
    (A) 극장
    (B) 옷 가게
    (C) 식당
    (D) 약국   정답 (B)

36. 남자는 어떤 문제를 언급하는가?
    (A) 스웨터 배송품이 도착하지 않았다.
    (B) 도로가 접근이 불가능하다.
    (C) 한 품목이 더 이상 구입 가능하지 않다.
    (D) 어떤 장비가 작동되지 않고 있다.   정답 (D)

37. 남자는 무엇을 해주겠다고 제안하는가?
    (A) 상품 보관하기
    (B) 할인 제공하기
    (C) 보관실에서 물건 가져오기
    (D) 블라우스 환불 처리하기   정답 (A)

문제 38-40번은 다음 대화를 참조하시오. [미W] [영M]

W: Pardon me, but **(38) (39)I'm wondering if this flight is equipped with wireless Internet.**

M: Yes. **(39)As soon as we reach our cruising altitude, the captain will make an announcement. (38)Then you'll be able to connect your electronic device to the Internet.**

W: Wonderful. I hope I can start working online quickly using my laptop. About how long will I have to wait?

M: It should take around twenty minutes. **(40)While you wait, would you like something to read?** We have an assortment of both foreign and domestic newspapers you can choose from.

W: **(40)Sure. Any local paper would be great.**

W: 실례합니다만, 이 기내에 무선 인터넷 설비가 되어 있나 모르겠네요.

M: 예, 순항 고도에 이르자마자, 기장님이 안내 방송을 할 것입니다. 그러면 전자 장치를 인터넷에 연결하실 수 있습니다.

W: 좋아요. 노트북을 이용해서 빨리 온라인으로 작업을 시작할 수 있으면 좋겠네요. 얼마 정도 기다려야 할까요?

M: 20분 정도 걸릴 거예요. 기다리시는 동안, 뭐 읽을 거라도 드릴까요? 골라서 읽을 수 있는 온갖 종류의 국내외 신문들이 있습니다.

W: 좋습니다. 국내신문 어떤 것이든 괜찮겠네요.

38. 여자가 무엇에 대해 문의하는가?
    (A) 음식 주문하기
    (B) 신용 카드로 지불하기
    (C) 인터넷에 연결하기
    (D) 좌석 바꾸기   정답 (C)

39. 대화가 벌어지는 장소는 어디인가?
    (A) 서점
    (B) 카페
    (C) 급행 열차
    (D) 비행기   정답 (D)

40. 여자는 이후에 무엇을 할 것인가?
    (A) 식사
    (B) 음료 주문
    (C) 신문 읽기
    (D) 전자장치 전원 켜기   정답 (C)

문제 41-43번은 다음 대화를 참조하시오. [미M] [호W]

M: Hello, Louis. **(41)Your team has been working on the design of our new instant messaging application for mobile devices.** My supervisor wanted an update on the progress your team is making on it.

W: It's going well. We've come up with a new feature that will provide group audio or video calls.

M: Perfect. And everything remains on track for the planned launch in October, right?

W: (42)Well, we still need to get comments from a focus group. We are going to ask participants to fill out a questionnaire telling us what they particularly like or dislike about the new feature.

M: I want to know the results as soon as they come in. (43)Can I get a report summarizing the focus group's feedback by next week?

W: (43)Of course. I'll have that information ready for you by next Wednesday.

M: 안녕하세요, 루이스. 당신 팀이 휴대 기기를 위한 새 인스턴트 메신저 앱의 디자인 작업을 계속 하고 있잖아요. 제 상사가 당신 팀이 하고 있는 그 일의 진척 상황에 대해 업데이트해 주길 원하세요.

W: 잘 되어 가고 있어요. 우리는 새로운 기능을 내놨는데, 그룹으로 음성 통화나 영상 통화를 제공할 거예요.

M: 완벽하군요. 그리고 계획된 10월 출시를 위해 모든 게 제대로 진행되고 있죠, 그렇죠?

W: 음, 아직 소비자 제품 평가단으로부터 의견을 받아야 해요. 참가자들에게 설문지를 작성해 달라고 부탁할 건데, 새 기능에 대해 그들이 특히 뭐가 마음에 드는지 혹은 마음에 들지 않는지 알게 될 거예요.

M: 결과가 들어오는 대로 알고 싶네요. 다음 주까지 소비자 제품 평가단의 의견을 요약한 보고서를 내가 받아 볼 수 있어요?

W: 물론이죠. 다음 주 수요일까지 그 자료를 준비해 놓겠습니다.

---

41. 대화는 무엇에 관한 것인가?
(A) TV 광고
(B) 모바일 앱
(C) 새로운 마케팅 전략
(D) 모바일 서비스 제공업체　　　　정답 (B)

42. 여자는 자신의 팀이 무엇을 할 필요가 있다고 말하는가?
(A) 제품에 대한 의견 받기
(B) 화상 회의 준비하기
(C) 외부 컨설턴트 고용하기
(D) 온라인에 자료 올리기　　　　정답 (A)

43. 다음 주에 무슨 일이 일어날 것인가?
(A) 제품이 출시될 것이다.
(B) 팀원들이 그룹으로 나뉠 것이다.
(C) 보고서가 제출될 것이다.
(D) 온라인 카탈로그가 나올 것이다.　　　　정답 (C)

문제 44-46번은 다음 대화를 참조하시오. 미W 영M

W: Good afternoon, James. How did your trip to Vancouver go?

M: (44)It really went well. The CEO of Avery Groceries signed a contract with us, so we'll be supplying that chain of stores with all of our frozen food products.

W: Outstanding. Will you be attending the meeting in a few minutes?

M: Sorry, but I can't make it. The airline put my suitcase on the wrong flight in Vancouver, and I just got a call telling me that it arrived. (45)I'll be taking a bus to the airport to get my bag soon.

W: (46)If you are all right waiting, I can drive you there once the meeting ends.

M: Is that so? I'd appreciate that.

W: 안녕하세요, 제임스. 밴쿠버 출장은 어떻게 되었어요?

M: 아주 잘되었어요. 애브리 식료품 회사의 최고 경영자가 우리와의 계약에 서명했어요. 그래서 우리는 그 업체의 체인 매장에 우리의 모든 냉동 식품을 납품하게 될 겁니다.

W: 아주 잘되었네요. 조금 있다가 회의에 참석하실 거예요?

M: 죄송하지만, 참석 못해요. 항공사가 밴쿠버에서 내 여행가방을 다른 비행기에 잘못 실었는데, 지금 막 전화로 내 여행가방이 도착했다고 알려 주었어요. 곧 공항까지 버스 타고 가서 내 가방을 가져와야 해요.

W: 기다려도 괜찮다면, 회의 끝나는 대로 내 차로 거기까지 데려다 줄게요.

M: 그래요? 그렇게 해주면 감사하죠.

---

44. 남자는 여자에게 어떤 좋은 소식을 알려 주는가?
(A) 투자자들과의 회의가 잘 되었다.
(B) 계약이 체결되었다.
(C) 회사의 제품이 상을 받았다.
(D) 합병이 완료되었다.　　　　정답 (B)

45. 남자가 공항에 가야 하는 이유는?
(A) 물건을 갖다 주기 위해
(B) 자신의 짐을 찾기 위해
(C) 비행기를 타기 위해
(D) 고객을 모시러 가기 위해　　　　정답 (B)

46. 여자는 남자를 위해서 무엇을 해주겠다고 제의하는가?
(A) 회의에 그 남자 대신 참석하기
(B) 시간 외 근무 하기
(C) 온라인에서 버스 일정 확인하기
(D) 남자를 차에 태워 주기　　　　정답 (D)

문제 47-49번은 다음 대화를 참조하시오. 미W 영M

W: Hello, Gordon. (47)Can we talk about the sales numbers from last quarter for a moment, please?

M: Sure, Sabrina. Is there a problem?

W: Yes, I see from the report that our sales declined last quarter.

M: I noticed that, too. Do you have any theories on why they've been down for the last few months?

W: (48)We've been losing some customers to the new clothing store down the street. It opened 3 months ago. You know, we might need to advertise the store a bit more.

M: Yeah, I think you're right. (49)I'll see if we can budget some more money for advertising. That should help improve next quarter's numbers.

W: 안녕하세요, 고든. 지난 분기 판매 수치에 대해 잠시 얘기할 수 있어요?

M: 그럼요, 사브리나. 문제 있어요?

W: 예, 보고서를 보니 우리 매출이 지난 분기에 하락했네요.

M: 저도 봤어요. 지난 몇 달 동안 매출이 왜 하락했는지에 대해 뭐 생각하는 거 있어요?

W: 길 아래쪽에 생긴 새 옷가게에 고객을 뺏기고 있어요. 그곳이 3개월 전에 문을 열었잖아요. 저기, 우리 매장을 좀 더 광고해야 할지도 모르겠네요.

M: 예, 당신 말이 맞는 것 같아요. 광고를 위해 좀 더 예산을 세울 수 있는지 알아볼게요. 그렇게 하면 다음 분기 수치 향상에 도움이 될 거예요.

---

47. 여자는 남자와 무엇에 대해 얘기하고 싶어하는가?
(A) 직원 오리엔테이션
(B) 매출 데이터
(C) 프로젝트 마감일
(D) 취업 면접　　　　정답 (B)

48. 여자에 따르면, 무엇 때문에 문제가 생기고 있는가?

    (A) 일부 품목이 더 이상 재고가 없다.

    (B) 배송품이 지연되고 있다.

    (C) 원자재 가격이 올랐다.

    (D) 경쟁업체가 가게를 열었다.   정답 (D)

49. 남자는 무엇을 할 것이라고 말하는가?

    (A) 고객과 대화

    (B) 광고 전문가 고용

    (C) 광고 예산 확인

    (D) 다른 공급업체로부터 견적 받기   정답 (C)

문제 50-52번은 다음 대화를 참조하시오. 미M 호W

M: (50)Ramona, could you go into the kitchen and see if the chefs have everything ready to start making lunch tomorrow? You have also gone over your checklist for closing procedures, haven't you?

W: (51)I'm almost done. I cleared off all the tables, and now I need to restock the silverware, glasses and dishes.

M: (51)I see some dishes on that table by the window.

W: Oh, thanks for pointing them out.

M: No problem. (52)Your work shift schedule for next week is in the breakroom. Make sure to pick it up before you leave for the day.

M: 라모나, 주방으로 가서 내일 점심 조리를 시작하는 데 요리사들이 모든 걸 준비했는지 알아볼래요? 그리고 식당 마감 절차에 대한 체크리스트도 다 훑어본 거죠, 그렇죠?

W: 거의 다 했어요. 테이블을 전부 다 치웠고, 이제 포크 나이프, 글라스, 그리고 접시들을 다시 채워넣어야 해요.

M: 창가 옆 저 테이블에 접시 몇 개가 보이네요.

W: 오, 접시 있다는 것을 지적해 주셔서 감사해요.

M: 괜찮아요. 다음 주 당신 교대근무 일정표가 휴게실에 있어요. 퇴근하기 전에 그거 꼭 가지고 가세요.

50. 대화가 벌어지는 곳은 어디인가?

    (A) 가구점

    (B) 식당

    (C) 주방용품 가게

    (D) 가전제품 매장   정답 (B)

51. 남자가 "창가 옆 저 테이블에 접시가 몇 개 보이네요"라고 말할 때 무엇을 함축하는가?

    (A) 누군가가 물건을 두고 갔다.

    (B) 일부 누락된 물건이 발견되었다.

    (C) 그는 물건의 가격을 알고 싶어 한다.

    (D) 업무가 완료되지 않았다.   정답 (D)

52. 여자가 집에 가기 전에 휴게실에 가는 이유는?

    (A) 자신의 근무 일정표를 게시판에 붙이기 위해

    (B) 문이 잠겼는지 확인하기 위해

    (C) 고용 계약서에 서명하기 위해

    (D) 자신의 일정표를 가져가기 위해   정답 (D)

문제 53-55번은 다음 3자 대화를 참조하시오. 미M 영M 미W

M1: I talked to the real estate developers this morning. (53)They want to see the first draft of the blueprints for the Maddox Hotel. How is the work going, Terry and Alice?

M2: The design for the entire structure is done. Now, we're trying to figure out what kind of glass to use in the windows. I like the glass made by Timmons Incorporated. (54)It's inexpensive but of very high quality.

M1: Is that glass going to be able to keep heat from escaping? It can get cold in Albany during winter.

W: It lets some heat get out, but overall, it's better than most windows. (55)So we might need some more insulation if we use these windows.

M1: 오늘 아침 부동산 개발업자들과 얘기를 해봤어요. 매독스 호텔의 청사진 첫 초안을 보고 싶어해요. 테리, 앨리스, 작업이 어떻게 되어가고 있어요?

M2: 전체 구조물 설계는 끝났어요. 이제, 창문에 어떤 종류의 유리를 사용할 것인지 머리를 짜내고 있어요. 티몬스 주식회사에서 만든 유리가 마음에 들어요. 비싸지 않은데, 품질이 아주 좋아요.

M1: 그 유리는 열기가 빠져나가는 것을 막아줄 수 있나요? 겨울에 올버니는 추울 수 있어요.

W: 열기가 일부는 빠져나가는데, 전반적으로 대부분의 창들보다 나아요. 그러니 우리가 이 창들을 사용한다면, 단열재가 좀 더 필요할지 몰라요.

53. 화자들은 누구인가?

    (A) 건축가

    (B) 건설 근로자

    (C) 호텔 직원

    (D) 유리 제조업자   정답 (A)

54. 테리가 특정 자재 사용을 추천하는 이유는?

    (A) 구하기 쉽다.

    (B) 비싸지 않다.

    (C) 인기 있다.

    (D) 무겁지 않다.   정답 (B)

55. 여자는 어떤 문제점을 지적하는가?

    (A) 프로젝트가 예산을 초과할 것이다.

    (B) 마감시한이 연장될 것이다.

    (C) 자재가 너무 무겁다.

    (D) 단열재가 필요할 것이다.   정답 (D)

문제 56-58번은 다음 대화를 참조하시오. 호W 영M

W: Hello, Grant. This is Sally, Mayor Watson's assistant.

M: Hello, Sally. (56)Has the mayor returned from his trip abroad? I hope he had a good time.

W: (56)Yes, he came back this morning. He wants to look over the speech he's going to give at the grand opening of the civic center, which is why I'm calling. (57)I know you've been working on the speech. (58)Can you send me a copy of it for the mayor to review now?

M: (58)Actually, the conclusion needs to be redone. The tone wasn't right, so I need to refine some words and expressions a bit more.

W: Ah, I see. Okay. He's not giving the speech until Saturday, so we still have some time.

W: 안녕하세요, 그랜트, 저는 왓슨 시장님의 비서 샐리예요.

M: 안녕하세요, 샐리. 시장님은 해외 여행에서 돌아오셨나요? 좋은 시간 보 냈으면 좋겠네요.

W: 예, 오늘 아침 돌아오셨어요. 시장님께서 시민 회관의 개관 행사에서 하실 연설문을 검토하고 싶어 하시는데, 그래서 전화했습니다. 연설문 작업을 해오신 것을 알아요. 지금 시장님이 검토하실 수 있도록 사본 한 부를 저에게 보내 주실 수 있으세요?

M: 사실, 결론을 다시 써야 해요. 어조가 맞지 않아서, 단어와 표현들을 좀 더 다듬을 필요가 있어요.

W: 아, 알겠습니다. 좋아요. 시장님 연설은 토요일 되서야 하니, 아직 우리는 시간이 좀 있어요.

56. 왓슨 시장은 지금 막 무엇을 했는가?
(A) TV에서 인터뷰를 했다.
(B) 다른 나라에서 돌아왔다.
(C) 새 비서를 뽑았다.
(D) 도시에 있는 공장을 방문했다. 정답 (B)

57. 남자는 무엇을 준비하고 있는가?
(A) 보도 자료
(B) 연설문
(C) 예산 보고서
(D) 관보 기사 정답 (B)

58. 남자가 "결론을 다시 써야 해요"라고 말하는 이유는?
(A) 동료에 대해 불평하기 위해
(B) 도움을 요청하기 위해
(C) 요청을 거절하기 위해
(D) 의견에 동의하기 위해 정답 (C)

문제 59~61번은 다음 3자 대화를 참조하시오. [미W] [호W] [미M]

W1: Ms. Fortuna, pardon me. **(59)This is Mr. Daimler, the safety inspector.** He just took a tour of our factory. We have to make one change before our permit can be renewed.

W2: I see. Please sit down, Mr. Daimler.

M: Thank you. Almost everything in the factory is in compliance, but the ventilation system in the packaging area isn't operating properly. It should let fresh air in and out of the area at all times.

W2: I see. **(60)I think the exhaust vents need to be replaced.** Cindy, could you…

W1: **(60)I'll take care of that as soon as possible.**

M: Thanks. **(61)You still have one month before your permit expires.** Call me when everything is in compliance, and I'll come back to check it out.

W1: 포투나 씨, 실례합니다. 이 분은 안전 검사관, 다임러 씨입니다. 이 분이 지금 막 우리 공장을 둘러봤습니다. 우리 허가증이 갱신될 수 있기 전에 한 가지 변경을 해야 해요.

W2: 알겠습니다. 앉으세요. 다임러 씨.

M: 감사합니다. 공장의 거의 모든 것이 규정을 잘 준수하고 있지만, 포장 구역의 환기 시스템이 제대로 작동하지 않고 있어요. 신선한 공기가 그 구역 안팎으로 항상 순환이 되어야 합니다.

W2: 알겠습니다. 제 생각에는 배기관 통풍구가 교체될 필요가 있는 것 같아요. 신디, 해줄 수 있겠어요…

W1: 가능한 한 빨리 처리하겠습니다.

M: 감사합니다. 허가증이 만료되려면 아직 한 달이 남았습니다. 모든 것이 규정 준수가 되면 전화주세요. 그러면 다시 와서 점검할게요.

59. 남자의 직업은 무엇인가?
(A) 공장의 작업반장
(B) 회사 임원
(C) 안전 검사관
(D) 경비원 정답 (C)

60. 신디는 무엇을 할 것이라고 말하는가?
(A) 통풍구 교체
(B) 공장 현장 방문
(C) 추가 포장재료 주문
(D) 새로운 물건 구매 정답 (A)

61. 남자에 따르면, 한 달 후에 무슨 일이 있겠는가?
(A) 장비가 청소될 것이다.
(B) 공장이 폐쇄될 것이다.
(C) 소프트웨어가 업그레이드될 것이다.
(D) 허가증이 만료될 것이다. 정답 (D)

문제 62~64번은 다음 대화와 메뉴를 참조하시오. [미M] [미W]

M: Hello. **(62)I'm organizing an outdoor picnic for an orientation session my company is having on August 1.** I want to check if you would be able to cater it for us.

W: Let me see… Yes, we will be available. How many people are expected to attend?

M: There will be 120 people in attendance. I took a look at your online menu, but I'm not sure which one I should select.

W: The standard option is the most popular one. But if you want dessert, you'll need to choose another option. **(63)We can also provide a dessert bar if you want.**

M: **(63)Oh, the dessert bar sounds perfect.** We'll also need a tent. Do you know a company that can rent one to us?

W: **(64)Actually, we also provide tent rentals for outside events only in the summer.** Should I put that on your order?

M: 안녕하세요. 8월 1일 우리 회사에서 하는 오리엔테이션 시간에 야외 소풍을 준비하고 있는데요. 우리에게 식사를 제공하는 게 가능한지 확인하고 싶어요.

W: 어디 봅시다… 예, 그 때 가능하네요. 몇 명이나 참석할 예정인가요?

W: 120명이 참석할 거예요. 거기 온라인 메뉴를 봤는데, 어떤 것을 골라야 할지 잘 모르겠어요.

W: 스탠다드 옵션이 가장 인기 있어요. 그런데 디저트를 원하시면 다른 옵션을 고르셔야 할 거예요. 그리고 원하시면 디저트 바도 또한 제공할 수 있습니다.

M: 오, 디저트 바가 아주 괜찮겠네요. 우리는 텐트도 필요할 거예요. 텐트를 대여할 수 있는 회사를 아시나요?

W: 사실, 저희도 여름에만 야외 행사를 위한 텐트 대여를 해드립니다. 그것도 주문서에 넣을까요?

점심 패키지		
스탠다드	샌드위치, 칩, 그리고 음료	$10.00
스탠다드 플러스	디저트 포함	$14.00
디럭스	디저트와 샐러드 포함	$17.00
(63)슈프림	샐러드, 쿠키 그리고 (63)디저트 바 포함	$20.00

62. 남자는 무엇을 준비하고 있는가?
(A) 연수
(B) 시상식
(C) 회사 야유회
(D) 야외 취업 박람회   정답 (C)

63. 그래픽을 보시오. 남자는 어떤 패키지를 고를 것인가?
(A) 스탠다드
(B) 스탠다드 플러스
(C) 디럭스
(D) 슈프림   정답 (D)

64. 무엇이 여름에만 제공되고 있는가?
(A) 텐트 대여
(B) 무료 배달
(C) 밴드 공연
(D) 꽃꽂이   정답 (A)

문제 65-67번은 다음 대화와 표지판을 참조하시오. 호W 미M

W: Hi, Jeff. **(65)You just started working here, so I want to remind you to remember to update your timesheet.** Employees should do that at the end of each work shift.
M: Thanks. I won't forget.
W: Okay. **(66)Now, uh, first, you need to put this shipment of laundry detergent on the shelves.** Make sure the label is facing outward. That way, customers can see everything easily.
M: No problem. I'll do that at once.
W: Oh, one thing. **(67)Some of the bottles got scratched or damaged while being shipped.** Those shouldn't be on display. Just leave them in the original box and I'll have them returned to the manufacturer later.

W: 안녕하세요, 제프. 여기서 이제 막 일을 시작하셨으니, 근무 시간 기록표를 업데이트하는 것 잊지 말라고 상기시켜 드리고 싶어요. 직원들은 각 근무 교대가 끝날 때 그것을 해야 해요.
M: 감사합니다. 잊지 않을게요.
W: 좋아요. 이제, 어, 우선 배송된 이 세탁세제를 선반에 정리하셔야 해요. 라벨은 꼭 바깥쪽으로 향하게 해주세요. 그래야 고객들이 모든 것을 쉽게 볼 수 있으니까요.
M: 알겠습니다. 지금 당장 하겠습니다.
W: 오, 한 가지 더요. 세제 병 일부가 운송 중에 긁히거나 손상을 입었어요. 그것들은 진열되면 안 됩니다. 그냥 원래 상자에 두시면 제가 나중에 그것들을 제조업체에 반품할게요.

델타 약국	
(66)통로 1	세제
통로 2	비누와 샴푸
통로 3	건강 보조제
통로 4	의료 용품

65. 여자는 남자에게 무엇을 업데이트하라고 상기시켜 주는가?
(A) 이력서
(B) 보험 정보
(C) 근무 시간 기록표
(D) 업무 마감 체크 목록   정답 (C)

66. 그래픽을 보시오. 여자는 남자에게 어느 통로로 갈 것을 요청을 하는가?
(A) 통로 1
(B) 통로 2
(C) 통로 3
(D) 통로 4   정답 (A)

67. 여자가 어떤 문제를 언급하는가?
(A) 일부 배송물건이 도착하지 않았다.
(B) 일부 가격표가 없다.
(C) 일부 제품이 파손되었다.
(D) 일부 쿠폰이 유효하지 않다.   정답 (C)

문제 68-70번은 다음 대화와 지도를 참조하시오. 미W 영M

W: Thanks for signing up, Mr. Bradley. **(68)Here's your registration packet. You can find information about the participating businesses inside.** That can help you determine what type of employers you want to speak with.
M: Thanks a lot. I'm impressed by the number of exhibitors here.
W: What are you looking for?
M: I'm an engineer, so I'm planning to look for some companies involved in manufacturing.
W: **(69)Those are all in the same row. They're located in the row closest to the rest lounge.**
M: Ah, I see. Thanks a lot.
W: By the way, did you drive here? If you did, let me validate your parking ticket. **(70)The parking fee is included in the cost of attending this event.**

W: 등록해 주셔서 감사합니다, 브래들리 씨. 여기 등록 안내서 묶음이에요. 안에 보시면 참가업체들에 대한 정보를 찾아볼 수 있어요. 그게 어떤 종류의 회사와 상담하고 싶은지 결정하는 데 도움을 줄 거예요.
M: 감사합니다. 여기 전시관을 차린 업체들 수가 인상적이네요.
W: 뭘 찾고 계십니까?
M: 저는 엔지니어예요. 그래서 제조 관련 회사들을 찾을 계획입니다.
W: 그 회사들은 전부 같은 열에 있습니다. 휴게 라운지에서 가장 가까운 열에 위치해 있습니다.
M: 아, 알겠습니다. 대단히 감사합니다.
W: 그런데 여기까지 차 운전하고 오셨나요? 그러셨다면, 제가 주차권을 확인해 드릴게요. 주차비가 이 행사 참가 비용에 포함되어 있습니다.

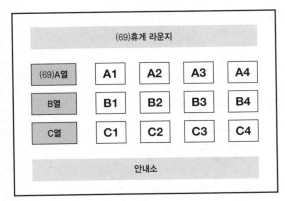

68. 화자들은 어디에 있는가?
(A) 회사 워크숍
(B) 취업 박람회
(C) 영업 총회
(D) 공예 박람회　　　　　　　　　　정답 (B)

69. 그래픽을 보시오. 남자는 어디를 먼저 갈 계획인가?
(A) A열
(B) B열
(C) C열
(D) 휴게 라운지　　　　　　　　　　정답 (A)

70. 여자에 따르면, 무엇이 등록비에 포함되었는가?
(A) 호텔비
(B) 시운전
(C) 주차비
(D) 점심 샌드위치　　　　　　　　　정답 (C)

Part 4

문제 71-73번은 다음 방송을 참조하시오. 미M

M: This is WGAM, the leader in local news. **(71)This Saturday at 1:00 P.M., students at the Jackson Academy of Performing Arts will put on a theatrical performance of** *Peter and the Wolf.* **(72)The play will be held at the Waterman Public Library.** This is a performance that both children and adults are sure to love, so go there and enjoy it with your entire family. **(73)There will be free snacks and beverages in the lobby following the performance.** Desmond Food is catering the event.

지역 뉴스의 선두주자, WGAM입니다. 이번 주 토요일 오후 1시에 잭슨 공연 예술 아카데미의 학생들이 〈피터와 늑대〉라는 연극 공연을 올릴 것입니다. 이 연극은 워터맨 공립 도서관에서 합니다. 이 연극은 어린이와 성인 모두 분명히 좋아할 공연이니, 여러분의 전 가족과 함께 가서 좋은 시간을 보내십시오. 공연에 이어 로비에 무료 스낵 및 음료가 제공될 것입니다. 데스몬드 푸드에서 이 행사에 음식을 제공합니다.

71. 다음 주 토요일에 무슨 행사가 있을 것인가?
(A) 책 낭송
(B) 음악 콘서트
(C) 연극
(D) 발레 공연　　　　　　　　　　정답 (C)

72. 행사는 어디에서 개최될 것인가?
(A) 도서관
(B) 학교
(C) 대강당
(D) 지역사회 센터　　　　　　　　　정답 (A)

73. 화자는 행사 끝에 무엇이 있을 것이라고 말하는가?
(A) 녹화된 것이 로비에서 구입 가능할 것이다.
(B) 다과류가 제공될 것이다.
(C) 어린이 미술 대회가 열릴 것이다.
(D) 저자 서명회가 열릴 것이다.　　　정답 (B)

문제 74-76번은 다음 회의 발췌 내용을 참조하시오. 영M

M: Before this meeting ends, **(74)I'd like to discuss the new procedure being implemented in the Sales Department.** Anytime we have large printing orders, **(75)we contact Davis Printing, but the manager there has been complaining that the instructions we provide aren't always clear.** As a result, he needs to contact us to clarify matters. So we're going to change how we submit orders. Starting next week, **(76)all printing orders will be made through Fred Hammer, our administrative assistant.** He'll make sure the instructions are clear. In addition, that way the print shop will have a single person to contact if they have questions about printing orders.

이 회의가 끝나기 전에, 영업부에서 실시되고 있는 새로운 절차에 대해 논의하고 싶네요. 대량 인쇄 주문이 있을 때마다 우리는 데이비스 프린팅에 연락하는데, 거기 관리자가 우리가 제시하는 지시사항이 항상 명료하지 않다고 불평을 하고 있어요. 결과적으로 그는 문제를 명확하게 하기 위해서 우리에게 연락을 해야 하고요. 그래서 우리는 주문을 제출하는 방식을 바꿀 예정이에요. 다음 주부터, 모든 인쇄 주문은 우리 행정 보조 직원인 프레드 해머를 통해서 하게 될 거예요. 프레드 해머가 지시사항이 명확하도록 확실히 할 거예요. 또한 그렇게 해야 인쇄소가 인쇄 주문에 관한 문의사항이 있을 때, 연락할 사람이 단 한 사람만 있게 되는 거고요.

74. 화자는 무엇에 대해 논의하고 있는가?
(A) 사업체 인수
(B) 고객의 불매운동
(C) 정부 규정
(D) 부서의 절차　　　　　　　　　　정답 (D)

75. 인쇄소에서 무엇에 대해 불평해 왔는가?
(A) 일부 지시사항이 혼란을 준다.
(B) 결제가 늦게 이루어진다.
(C) 인쇄소가 일손이 부족하다.
(D) 마감시한이 너무 빠르다.　　　　정답 (A)

76. 해머 씨는 누구인가?
(A) 가게 주인
(B) 행정 보조 직원
(C) 인쇄업자
(D) 유지보수 관리 직원　　　　　　정답 (B)

문제 77-79번은 다음 전화 메시지를 참조하시오. 미W

W: Hello, Ms. Burdett. This is Stephanie from the Maple Home Improvement Store. (77)**Thanks for sending me a brochure for your company.** (78)**I took a look at it and really like the great selection of carpets.** There are quite a lot of options. (79)**I noticed you added a note reading that you could give a presentation to our sales department at our store next Thursday or Friday.** Well, (79)**I'm away on business next week**, but I'll definitely contact you as soon as I return to the office.

안녕하세요. 버뎃 씨. 메이플 홈임프루먼트 스토어의 스테파니입니다. 저에게 귀사의 안내책자를 보내 주셔서 감사합니다. 그것을 봤는데, 카펫이 아주 다양해서 정말 좋습니다. 아주 많은 옵션이 있네요. 추가하신 쪽지도 봤는데, 다음 주 목요일이나 금요일 우리 매장에서 우리 영업팀에 프레젠테이션을 할 수 있다고 적혀 있더군요. 음, 제가 다음 주에 출장을 갑니다만, 사무실로 돌아오자마자 꼭 연락을 드리겠습니다.

77. 화자는 청자에게 무엇에 대해 감사하는가?
(A) 안내책자를 보내준 것
(B) 카펫을 주문한 것
(C) 견본을 제공한 것
(D) 배달한 물건에 대해 돈을 지불한 것   정답 (A)

78. 화자는 청자의 업체에 대해 무엇이 인상적이라고 생각하는가?
(A) 그 지역 내에서 최저가이다.
(B) 물건을 빨리 보내 준다.
(C) 고품질 물건들을 수입한다.
(D) 아주 다양한 제품을 갖추고 있다.   정답 (D)

79. 화자가 "제가 다음 주에 출장을 갑니다"라고 말하는 이유는?
(A) 제안을 거절하기 위해
(B) 추천을 요청하기 위해
(C) 성가시다는 것을 표현하기 위해
(D) 방법을 설명하기 위해   정답 (A)

문제 80-82번은 다음 회의 발췌 내용을 참조하시오. 영M

M: Thanks for coming to our staff meeting. (80)**First, I'd like you all to know that we'll be placing lots of plants throughout the office**, about one per every two square meters of floor space. Recent studies show that plants not only look good (81)**but can also reduce employee stress levels, which can lead to increasing employee productivity.** We'll be bringing in many plants, so if you have any preferences for what kind of green plants you want in your work area, let me know. (82)**You can fill out a form online, and I'll do my best to accommodate what you request.**

직원 회의에 와주셔서 감사합니다. 우선, 여러분 전부 다 아셨으면 하는 것은 사무실 이곳 저곳에, 대략 바닥 공간 2평방미터 당 하나씩, 많은 화분을 갖다 놓을 것이라는 것입니다. 최근의 연구에 따르면, 식물은 보기에도 좋을 뿐만 아니라 직원들의 스트레스 수준을 줄일 수 있으며, 이는 직원들의 생산성 증가로 이어질 수 있습니다. 우리는 많은 화분을 들여놓을 것이니, 여러분의 근무 공간에 어떤 종류의 녹색 식물을 원하는지 선호하는 게 있다면 저에게 알려 주세요. 온라인으로 양식을 작성하실 수 있으며, 제가 최선을 다해서 여러분이 요청하는 것을 수용할 것입니다.

80. 사무실에 무엇이 추가될 것인가?
(A) 사진 액자
(B) 화분
(C) 직원 휴게실
(D) 더 많은 자연 채광   정답 (B)

81. 변화가 이루어지고 있는 이유는?
(A) 더 많은 세입자를 끌어들이기 위해
(B) 규정을 준수하기 위해
(C) 생산성을 향상시키기 위해
(D) 고객의 불만을 처리하기 위해   정답 (C)

82. 청자들은 온라인에서 무엇을 할 것 같은가?
(A) 사진 보기
(B) 입사 지원서 작성하기
(C) 요청하기
(D) 제품에 대해 후기 작성하기   정답 (C)

문제 83-85번은 다음 방송을 참조하시오. 미W

W: Welcome to today's episode of *Good Health*. On our program, we're going to be interviewing Margorie Carter, the founder of the dental clinic, (83)**Best Smile Dental that produces a wide variety of toothbrushes.** (84)**Dr. Carter is the most recent winner of the Samuels Award, which is given annually to a local business owner who practices community service for donating her firm's products generously** to underprivileged sections of the community. Today, we'll talk to Dr. Carter about many topics including the story of how she came up with a patented toothbrush for children, which was designed to facilitate the proper brushing. (85)**A bit later in the program, Dr. Carter will tell us her interesting experience with some options for securing funding for her startup** from some venture capital groups to crowdfunding.

오늘의 〈굿 헬스〉 에피소드에 오신 것을 환영합니다. 우리 프로에서 마고리 카터와 인터뷰를 할 예정인데, 이 분은 아주 다양한 칫솔을 만드는 베스트 스마일 덴탈이라는 치과 클리닉의 창업주입니다. 닥터 카터는 가장 최근의 새뮤얼스 상 수상자로, 이 상은 매년 지역사회에 봉사를 하는 지역 사업 소유주에게 주는 상인데, 지역사회의 소외된 구역에 자신의 회사 제품을 아낌없이 기증을 한 덕분입니다. 오늘, 저희는 닥터 카터와 많은 주제에 대해 얘기를 나눌 것인데, 그 주제 중에는 그녀가 어떻게 해서 어린이들을 위한 특허 받은 칫솔을 내놓게 되었는지에 대한 이야기도 있으며, 그 칫솔은 올바른 칫솔질을 용이하게 하도록 설계되었습니다. 방송 프로 후반에, 닥터 카터는 자신의 창업 자금을 확보하는 데 벤처 캐피탈 그룹에서부터 크라우드 펀딩까지 여러 옵션이 있던 흥미로운 경험담을 얘기할 것입니다.

83. 마고리 카터의 회사는 무엇을 생산하는가?
(A) 헤어브러시
(B) 칫솔
(C) 건강 보조제
(D) 치약   정답 (B)

84. 닥터 카터는 무엇에 대한 상을 수상했는가?
(A) 회사 창업
(B) 자선기관에 돈 기부
(C) 신제품 제조

(D) 지역사회에 기여   정답 (D)

85. 마고리 카터는 나중에 무엇에 대해 얘기할 것인가?
(A) 그녀의 발명에 대한 이유
(B) 자금 모금의 옵션
(C) 온라인 마케팅 전략
(D) 고용 절차   정답 (B)

문제 86-88번은 다음 회의 발췌 내용을 참조하시오. 미M

M: (86)It's my great pleasure to let you know that we've completed developing the preliminary version of our video game, Gatekeeper. As you all know, (87)we're known for making board games and puzzles. We've never done anything like this before. As a result, we've got a group of gamers who will test Gatekeeper. Today, they'll play it and rate it on its storyline, playability, graphics, and other features. (88) I'd like to thank Jessica for setting up the computers and monitors in the conference room. We're all set for the testers to get to work this afternoon. I'll let you know the results of their feedback tomorrow at our team meeting.

우리 비디오 게임, 게이트키퍼의 초기 버전 개발을 완료했음을 알려 드리게 되어 아주 기쁩니다. 여러분 전부 아시다시피, 우리는 보드 게임과 퍼즐을 만드는 것으로 알려져 있습니다. 우리는 전에 이런 것을 해본 적이 없습니다. 그래서, 우리는 게이트키퍼를 테스트할 게이머 그룹을 모집했습니다. 오늘, 그들이 게이트키퍼로 게임을 해보고, 이 게임의 스토리라인, 플레이 능력, 그래픽 그리고 그 밖의 다른 특징들에 대해 평가할 것입니다. 회의실에 컴퓨터와 모니터들을 설치해 줘서 제시카에게 감사드리고 싶습니다. 오늘 오후에 테스터들이 게임을 할 준비가 다 되었습니다. 내일 우리 팀 회의에서 게이머들의 피드백 결과를 알려 드리겠습니다.

86. 청자들은 누구일 것 같은가?
(A) 가게 주인
(B) 게임 제작자
(C) 기자
(D) 영업부 직원   정답 (B)

87. 화자가 "우리는 전에 이런 것을 해본 적이 없습니다"라고 말할 때 무엇을 함축하는가?
(A) 제품 개발 프로젝트가 실패했다.
(B) 올바른 정보가 주어지지 않았다.
(C) 제품 출시 날짜가 연기 되어야 한다.
(D) 제품이 추가적인 작업이 필요하다.   정답 (D)

88. 화자는 무엇에 대해 제시카에게 감사하는가?
(A) 소프트웨어 업데이트 버전 설치
(B) 소비자 제품 평가단 조직
(C) 의견 제시
(D) 장비 준비   정답 (D)

문제 89-91번은 다음 발표를 참조하시오. 호W

W: (89)Welcome to this meeting of the Chandler City Department of Transportation. I'd like to thank all the members of the public here today for coming. As you're aware, next month, (90)we'll be doing some renovation work to accommodate more seats in the waiting area on the Chandler City Train Station. Consequently, we're going to demolish a couple of the buildings there. They were made a long time ago, for which reason there is some history in the area. So, we're planning to make a documentary about the station. (91)We'll be interviewing Chandler City residents about the station for the documentary. If you want to be interviewed, be sure to put your name and phone number on the signup sheet by the door.

이번 챈들러 시 교통부 회의에 오신 것을 환영합니다. 오늘 여기 와주신 모든 시민들에게 감사드리고 싶습니다. 아시다시피, 다음 달에, 우리는 챈들러 시 기차역 대합실에 더 많은 좌석을 수용하기 위해서 보수공사를 할 것입니다. 따라서, 거기 있는 건물 두 동을 철거할 예정입니다. 이 건물들은 오래 전에 지어진 것인데, 그런 이유로 그곳에 역사가 좀 있습니다. 그래서 우리는 역에 대한 다큐멘터리를 제작할 계획입니다. 다큐멘터리를 위해 역에 대해서 챈들러 시 주민을 인터뷰할 것입니다. 인터뷰 대상이 되고 싶으시면, 문 옆에 있는 신청서에 이름과 전화 번호를 꼭 적어 주십시오.

89. 화자는 누구인가?
(A) 기차 차장
(B) 시장
(C) 정부 관리
(D) 영화 제작자   정답 (C)

90. 기차 역에 어떤 변화가 생길 것인가?
(A) 매표소가 옮겨질 것이다.
(B) 기차역 일부가 확장될 것이다.
(C) 더 많은 기차 선로가 추가될 것이다.
(D) 대합실을 없앨 것이다.   정답 (B)

91. 청자들이 등록해야 하는 이유는?
(A) 취업 면접에 오기 위해
(B) 무료 티켓을 받을 자격이 되기 위해
(C) 우편물 목록에 오르기 위해
(D) 촬영을 위한 인터뷰를 받기 위해   정답 (D)

문제 92-94번은 다음 담화를 참조하시오. 미W

W: (92)This is the first day of the training session for summer guides for the Western Hills archaeological site. During the past few years, our archaeologists have uncovered several buildings and many artifacts more than a thousand years old. You'll mostly be responsible for leading tours of the dig site. (93)You might think that we don't need so many guides since the site isn't very large. But we get tons of visitors here during June and July. (94)Each of you will get a special T-shirt to wear that will help identify you as summer guides (92)here at the site. You can pick yours up at the back office.

오늘은 웨스턴 힐스 고고학 현장의 여름 가이드를 위한 교육 첫날입니다. 지난 몇 년 동안, 우리 고고학자들은 천년 이상 된 여러 채의 건물과 많은 유물들을 발굴해 냈습니다. 여러분은 주로 발굴 현장의 투어 안내를 책임지게 될 것입니다. 여러분은 발굴 현장이 그다지 크지 않으므로 그렇게 많은 가이드가 필요하지 않다고 생각할지 모릅니다. 그런데, 6월과 7월에는 여기에 엄청나게 많은 방문객들이 찾아옵니다. 여러분 각자 착용할 특별 티셔츠를 받게 되는데, 여기 현장에서 여러분을 여름 가이드로 구분하는 데 도움을 줄 것입니다. 뒤쪽 사무실에 가서 여러분의 티셔츠를 받아 가십시오.

92. 이 담화는 어디에서 이루어지는가?
(A) 건설 현장
(B) 미술관
(C) 고고학 발굴 현장
(D) 천문 관측대 　　　　　　　　　　　정답 (C)

93. 화자는 "6월과 7월에는 여기에 엄청나게 많은 방문객들이 찾아옵니다"라고 말할 때 무엇을 함축하는가?
(A) 정규 영업 시간이 연장될 것이다.
(B) 관광객들은 긴 대기 시간을 예상해야 한다.
(C) 여름에 방문하는 것을 피하는 게 낫다.
(D) 여름에는 아주 많은 직원이 필요할 것이다. 　정답 (D)

94. 청자들은 각각 무엇을 받게 되는가?
(A) 안내 책자
(B) 현장 지도
(C) 방문객 명단
(D) 티셔츠 　　　　　　　　　　　　　　정답 (D)

문제 95-97번은 다음 전화 메시지와 지도를 참조하시오. [미M]

M: Hi, Jacob. This is Robert from the Stillwater Agency. (95) I'm looking forward to meeting you tomorrow so that we can talk about some revisions to the book manuscript you submitted. My office is in Maple Tower. (96)If you're driving, free street parking is available right in front of the public library. In addition, after our morning meeting concludes, (97) how about having lunch with our graphic designer? She has a few ideas on what the front cover should look like.

안녕하세요, 제이콥. 저는 스틸워터 에이전시의 로버트입니다. 내일 만나 제출하신 책 원고에 대한 수정사항을 논의할 수 있게 되어 기대됩니다. 제 사무실은 메이플 타워에 있습니다. 운전하고 오신다면, 공립 도서관 바로 앞에 무료 거리 주차가 가능합니다. 그 밖에, 오전 회의가 끝나고 나서, 우리 그래픽 디자이너와 점심을 같이 하시는 게 어떨까요? 그녀에게 앞 표지가 어떤 모습이 되면 좋을지 몇 가지 아이디어가 있습니다.

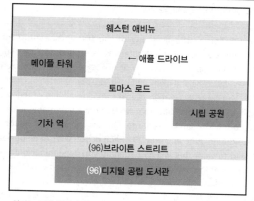

95. 화자는 어떤 종류의 회사에서 근무하는가?
(A) 제조 공장
(B) 출판사
(C) 도서관
(D) 서점 　　　　　　　　　　　　　　정답 (B)

96. 그래픽을 보시오. 화자는 어떤 거리에 주차할 것을 제안하는가?
(A) 웨스턴 애비뉴
(B) 브라이튼 스트리트
(C) 토마스 로드
(D) 애플 드라이브 　　　　　　　　　　정답 (B)

97. 화자는 무엇에 대해 물어보는가?
(A) 회사를 둘러보는 것
(B) 점심 먹으러 가는 것
(C) 가격을 올리는 것
(D) 제 시간에 프로젝트를 끝내는 것 　　정답 (B)

문제 98-100번은 다음 워크숍 발췌 내용과 일정표를 참조하시오. [호W]

W: Hello, everyone. (98)I'm glad you found room 112 with no problems. Thanks for attending this week's session. (99) In today's workshop, I'm going to talk about how to evaluate employees and what metrics to consider the most important when measuring employee performance. Now, let's get started by doing a quick brainstorming idea. (100) Pair up with the person sitting next to you. Together, come up with three ways that you can evaluate performance results. When you're finished, be prepared to discuss your thoughts with everyone else here.

안녕하세요, 여러분. 여러분이 아무 문제없이 112호실을 찾으셔서 기쁘네요. 이번 주 세션에 참석해 주셔서 감사합니다. 오늘 워크숍에서는 어떻게 직원들을 평가할 것인가 그리고 직무 능력을 측정할 때 어떤 고려 기준이 가장 중요한지에 대해 얘기할 예정입니다. 이제, 빨리 아이디어를 브레인스토밍하면서 시작합시다. 옆에 앉아 있는 사람과 짝을 지어 보세요. 함께 성과 결과를 평가할 수 있는 세 가지 방법을 생각해 보세요. 다 끝나면, 이곳의 다른 모든 사람들과 같이 여러분의 생각을 논의할 준비를 하세요.

경영 워크숍 시리즈

주	장소	강사
1	110호	줄리 크로우
2	111호	스텔라 톰슨
3	(98)112호	**에린 메이**
4	113호	수지 파월

98. 그래픽을 보시오. 누가 화자인가?
(A) 줄리 크로우
(B) 스텔라 톰슨
(C) 에린 메이
(D) 수지 파월 　　　　　　　　　　　정답 (C)

99. 청자들은 워크숍 동안에 무엇을 배우게 될 것인가?
(A) 근무 환경을 개선하는 것
(B) 팀으로서 효율적으로 의사소통하는 것
(C) 직무 능력을 평가하는 것
(D) 직원들의 사기를 진작시키는 것 　　정답 (C)

100. 청자들은 맨 먼저 무엇을 하라는 요청을 받는가?
(A) 워크숍 신청하기
(B) 파트너와 작업하기
(C) 과제물 제출하기
(D) 자기소개 하기　　　　　　　　　　　　정답 (B)

Part 5

101. 20년 이상이 흘렀지만, 그것은 여전히 국내에서 가장 잘 팔리는 아이스크림 중의 하나이다.　　　　　　　　　　　정답 (B)

102. 만약 저희가 고객님의 주문품을 내일까지 배송하지 못한다면, 원래 가격 188달러에서 20%를 할인해 드리겠습니다.　　정답 (B)

103. 클린턴 씨는 뉴욕에서 변호사 시험에 합격한 후 자신의 법률 사무소를 열었다.　　　　　　　　　　　　　　정답 (A)

104. 사진이 촬영된 날짜가 사진에 선명하게 인쇄되어 있어야 하며, 그렇지 않은 경우 사진은 거부될 것이다.　　　　정답 (B)

105. 새로운 복사기는 또한 비용이 더 저렴하고 생산 효율성은 더 높다.　정답 (C)

106. 저희 고객 서비스 담당자들에 의해 환불이나 교환이 처리되는 데 3일에서 5일가량이 소요된다는 점을 감안해 주시기 바랍니다.　정답 (C)

107. 이사회는 회사가 파산하는 것을 막기 위해 임금을 삭감하거나 직원들을 정리 해고하기로 결정해야 한다.　　　　정답 (A)

108. 몇몇 신문사들은 새로운 법이 십년 전에 제정된 원래의 법과 거의 다르지 않다고 주장했다.　　　　　　　　정답 (B)

109. 만약 비상 경보가 들리면, 불이 켜진 비상구 표지판 쪽으로 차분하고 질서 정연하게 가도록 하세요.　　　　　　정답 (B)

110. 복사기의 적절한 작동 및 관리를 위한 세부적인 지침은 동봉된 작동 설명서에서 찾아볼 수 있다.　　　　　　정답 (A)

111. 자동차나 모바일 기기용 전자 부품을 제조할 때는 공장의 청결이 가장 중요하다.　　　　　　　　　　　정답 (B)

112. 맥거완 씨는 영상 및 미디어 제작 공부를 하기 위해 로스앤젤레스로 갔고, 그 후 자신의 미디어 회사를 시작했다.　정답 (C)

113. 그 회사는 최근 정부와 6만 대의 최신 태블릿 컴퓨터를 공급하는 계약을 체결했다.　　　　　　　　　　정답 (C)

114. 관광은 스위스의 중요한 수입원이며, 이는 시계 제조업과 금융 서비스업에 뒤이은 세 번째로 큰 규모의 산업이다.　정답 (C)

115. 국립 상업 은행은 투자 옵션에 관심이 있는 고객들이 이용할 수 있는 정보의 양을 늘리고자 은행의 웹사이트를 업데이트했다.　정답 (C)

116. 우리의 새로운 재무 보고 소프트웨어는 기업들이 이전보다 더 쉽게 재무제표를 작성할 수 있도록 한다.　　　정답 (B)

117. 협력사로부터 새로운 사업 제안서를 수령하는 대로 우리는 이를 신중하게 검토해야 한다.　　　　　　　　정답 (C)

118. 고객 서비스 부장은 해외 고객들의 불만사항이 다음 날 이사회 회의에서 다뤄질 수 있도록 이를 바로 이사진에게 알렸다.　정답 (B)

119. 현재 IT 산업 전반에서 느껴지고 있는 변화들은 단순성과 편의성에 대한 고객들의 구체적인 요구를 반영한다.　정답 (B)

120. 저희 온라인 게시판에 글을 올리기에 앞서, FAQ로도 알려져 있는 그룹의 자주 묻는 질문을 검토하십시오.　정답 (B)

121. 2월과 3월 내내 우리 메리즈 슈퍼스토어에서 구매되는 모든 물품들은 영업일 기준 3일 이내에 배송될 것이다.　정답 (C)

122. 해외 부동산 매입에 관심 있는 사람들은 그들의 행동이 국내 경제를 해칠 가능성이 있음을 인식해야 한다.　　정답 (C)

123. 최종 테스트 중에 발생한 예상치 못한 기술적인 문제로 인해 회사는 새로운 데이터베이스 시스템의 출시를 연기하게 되었다.　정답 (D)

124. 많은 연구원들은 회사가 투자자를 유치하기 위해서는 연구개발 환경 강화에 초점을 맞춰야 한다고 제안했다.　정답 (A)

125. 누가 최고 경영자 직을 맡든, 우리 회사가 직면한 경영 상황이 너무 어려워서 빠르고 급격한 개선을 기대할 수 없다.　정답 (B)

126. 우리 호텔은 보르네오 섬에 위치하고 있으며 배로만 접근 가능하므로, 호텔 객실들이 자신만의 개인적인 천국처럼 느껴진다.　정답 (B)

127. 예상치 못한 화상 회의 장비의 오작동으로 인해, 우리의 영업 발표는 추후 공지가 있을 때까지 연기되었다.　정답 (B)

128. 정부가 더 많은 고용 기회를 창출하고자 추가의 노력을 기울이지 않는다면 국가 경제를 유지하는 데 실패할 것이다.　정답 (C)

129. 모든 부품 공급업체들의 재고가 동이 나서 공장장은 고장 난 컨베이어 벨트를 위한 교체 부품을 받지 못했다.　정답 (A)

130. 만약 쇠고기 소비가 증가한다면, 대부분의 육가공 업체들은 더 많은 소를 사육하기 위한 더 많은 농지가 필요할 것이다.　정답 (B)

Part 6

문제 131-134번은 다음 편지를 참조하시오.

왓슨 씨에게,

여기 헥사곤 게임즈 주식회사의 공석인 컴퓨터 그래픽 디자이너 자리에 관심을 가져 주셔서 감사합니다. 귀하의 기술과 경험에 대한 저희 평가에 따르면, 귀하는 그 자리에 이상적인 후보자로 보입니다.

저희는 귀하와 컴퓨터 그래픽 디자이너 업무에 대해 직접 만나서 많은 이야기를 나누고 싶습니다. 시간이 괜찮으시다면, 5월 22일 수요일 오후 2시에 저희 본사를 방문해 주시면 좋겠습니다.

취업 면접에서, 귀하의 장점에 대해 더 자세히 설명하고 과거에 작업한 프로젝트에 대한 귀하의 기여도를 설명하라는 요청을 받을 것입니다. 헥사곤 게임즈 주식회사의 컴퓨터 그래픽 디자인 팀에 귀하가 적합하다고 판단되면, 귀하를 최종 면접의 최종 후보자 명단에 올릴 것입니다.

(408) 535-3500으로 제게 전화하여 앞서 언급한 만남 날짜와 시간이 귀하에게 적합한지 알려주세요. 귀하의 전화를 기다리고 있겠습니다.

131. 정답 (B)

132. 정답 (D)

133. 정답 (B)

134. (A) 귀하의 전화를 기다리고 있겠습니다.
(B) 저는 귀하를 장래의 자리에 대한 대기자 명단에 올려 두고 싶습니다.
(C) 회의가 지연되어 정말 죄송합니다.
(D) 우리 회사는 완전히 재편될 것입니다. 정답 (A)

문제 135-138번은 다음 기사를 참조하시오.

크림 제약회사, 신임 이사 임명하다

런던 - 8월 10일) 영국에서 가장 큰 제약 공급업체 중 하나인 크림 제약회사는 어제 제임스 잭슨 박사가 연구 개발 이사로 고용되었다고 발표했다. 이번 인력 보강을 통해, 크림 제약회사는 업계에서 회사의 인지도를 높이고 강력한 영향력을 구축하길 희망하고 있다.

잭슨 박사는 전염병 및 비전염성 질환에 대한 백신과 의약품의 연구 및 개발 분야에서의 15년을 포함하여 판자 주식회사에서 25년 이상을 근무했다. 크림 제약회사의 최고 경영자 켈리 젠킨스 씨는 "잭슨 박사의 의학 전문지식은 우리가 생산하는 의료 제품의 품질을 향상시키는 데 귀중한 도구가 될 것입니다. 저는 그와 함께 일할 수 있는 기회를 가지게 되어 기쁩니다"라고 말했다.

크림 제약회사는 런던에 기반을 둔 회사로 영국 전역에 약 2,000명의 의료 연구 인력을 보유하고 있다.

135. 정답 (B)

136. 정답 (C)

137. (A) 저는 이 자리를 제안받게 되어 영광입니다.
(B) 새로운 방침은 고객에게 더 나은 서비스를 제공하는 부분에 집중하고 있습니다.
(C) 저는 그와 함께 일할 수 있는 기회를 가지게 되어 기쁩니다.
(D) 우리는 차세대 제품을 개발하고자 전문가들과 긴밀하게 협력합니다. 정답 (C)

138. 정답 (D)

문제 139-142번은 다음 광고를 참조하시오.

골든 베어 부동산
21번가 603번지
오클랜드, 캘리포니아 주 94607
(510) 212-9267
www.gbre.com

귀하는 적당한 스튜디오를 찾고 있는 무용가인가요? 저희는 현재 사우스 리버 로드, 1123번지에 위치한 훌륭한 댄스 스튜디오를 임대하고 있는데, 이곳은 충분한 공간과 높은 천장, 그리고 자연 조명과 인공 조명이 혼합되어 있습니다. 이 곳은 귀하의 무용 리허설 및 공연을 하기에 완벽한 장소입니다.

댄스 스튜디오는 단풍나무 바닥, 전신 거울, 개폐식 커튼, 무용 바 및 최첨

단 사운드 시스템을 갖추고 있습니다. 저희는 현재 시중의 평균 임대료보다 15% 낮게 책정된 저렴한 임대료를 제공합니다. 또한 무용을 전공하는 대학생이라면 추가 할인이 주어질 것입니다.

이 스튜디오에 대해 문의하거나 둘러보기를 예약하고자 하시면, (510) 913-9815 또는 lh@gbre.com으로 린다 홉킨스 씨에게 연락하십시오.

139. 정답 (C)

140. 정답 (C)

141. 정답 (C)

142. (A) 덧붙여, 귀하의 새로운 무용화는 편안하고 기능적이어야 합니다.
(B) 결과적으로 새로운 TV 스튜디오는 사우스 리버 로드의 산업 단지에 건설될 것입니다.
(C) 또한 무용을 전공하는 대학생이라면 추가 할인이 주어질 것입니다.
(D) 사실, 국제 페스티벌은 10년 전에 시작되었고, 그 이후로 매년 개최되고 있습니다. 정답 (C)

문제 143-146번은 다음 이메일을 참조하시오.

수신: 모든 프라이빗 뱅킹 고객
발신: 로날드 헉슬리 〈ronaldh@americanabank.com〉
제목: 개인 정보 보호
날짜: 8월 6일

저희 프라이빗 뱅킹 고객님들에게.

아메리카나 은행에서는 프라이빗 온라인 뱅킹 고객의 보안을 매우 중요하게 생각합니다. 그래서 저희는 결코 이메일이나 전화로 고객님의 인터넷 뱅킹 로그인 정보나 어떠한 다른 보안 정보도 확인해줄 것을 요청하지 않습니다. 저희는 항상 고객님의 개인 정보를 철저히 기밀로 취급합니다.

고객의 개인 정보 보호를 위해 아래에 설명된 추가 조치를 취할 것을 고객님들께 권장합니다. 항상 아무도 짐작하지 못할 비밀번호를 선택하시고, 반드시 비밀번호를 자주 변경하십시오. 개인 정보, 계좌번호 등을 요청하는 이메일에 절대 회신하지 마십시오. 이러한 이메일들은 저희가 발송한 것이 아닙니다.

마지막으로, 이메일이 사기로 의심된다면, 저희 사기방지부에 1-800-365-2020으로 연락 주십시오.

귀하의 정보 기밀을 보호하는 것에 대한 지원에 미리 감사드립니다.

로날드 헉슬리

143. 정답 (C)

144. (A) 저희는 신원 도용에 대한 규정 및 처벌을 강화하겠습니다.
(B) 저희는 항상 고객님의 개인 정보를 철저히 기밀로 취급합니다.
(C) 저희는 숙련된 전문 은행가와 기술의 편리함을 결합합니다.
(D) 저희는 소매 고객을 유치하기 위해 저축 계좌에 대해 더 높은 금리를 제공하고 있습니다. 정답 (B)

145. 정답 (B)

146. 정답 (D)

Part 7

문제 147-148번은 다음 초대장을 참조하시오.

귀하를 연회에 정중히 초대합니다

(147)새로운 CD 음반 소개

쇼팽 - 피아노 협주곡
(모차르트 레코드 회사)

연주자
클로드 파울로프스키
구엘프 클래식 음악 대학교, 교수

3월 14일, 금요일
오후 7시 – 오후 9시
월튼 컨벤션 센터
헤이븐 홀

(148)후원
펠츠 클래식 악기

---

147. 행사가 열리는 이유는?
(A) 콘서트를 홍보하기 위해
(B) 음악 학교의 설립을 축하하기 위해
(C) 은퇴하는 교수에게 경의를 표하기 위해
(D) 새로운 앨범을 소개하기 위해   정답 (D)

148. 누가 행사 비용을 지불할 것 같은가?
(A) 구엘프 클래식 음악 대학교
(B) 모차르트 레코드 회사
(C) 월튼 컨벤션 센터
(D) 펠츠 클래식 악기   정답 (D)

문제 149-150번은 다음 문자 메시지를 참조하시오.

애슐리 버드   [오전 10시 32분]
안녕하세요, 제시. 마케팅 프로젝트가 어떻게 되어가고 있어요?

제시 그로소   [오전 10시 35분]
(149)델레로스 씨는 이번 주 말까지 내가 새로운 제안서를 준비하길 원하고 있어요. 당신 것은 어때요?

애슐리 버드   [오전 10시 36분]
(149)지난주에 제안서를 제출하지 않았어요? 우리 팀은 오늘 이사회에 프로젝트를 제출했어요.

제시 그로소   [오전 10시 36분]
(149)델레로스 씨가 처음에는 좋아했는데, 마지막 순간에 마음을 바꾸셨어요.

제시 그로소   [오전 10시 37분]
(150)그래서 지금 처음부터 다시 시작해야 해요. 그리고 또한 끝내야 할 일들이 많아요.

애슐리 버드   [오전 10시 40분]
(150)조금만 버텨봐요. 이 프로젝트가 끝나자마자 휴가를 가져요.

제시 그로소   [오전 10시 42분]
맞아요. 어쨌든, 이것에 대해서 내가 할 수 있는 것이 아무것도 없어요.

---

149. 델레로스 씨에 대해서 나타나 있는 것은 무엇인가?
(A) 이사회 위원 중 한 명이다.
(B) 주말에 회의가 있다.

(C) 그로소 씨의 이전 제안서를 거부했다.
(D) 휴가를 낼 예정이다.   정답 (C)

150. 오전 10시 40분에, 버드 씨가 "조금만 버텨요"라고 쓸 때 무엇을 의미하는가?
(A) 그로소 씨가 그녀를 위해 계속 일할 것으로 기대한다.
(B) 그로소 씨와 같이 휴가 가기를 바란다.
(C) 그로소 씨가 스트레스에도 불구하고 계속 일을 하기를 원한다.
(D) 그로소 씨가 현재 있는 곳에 그대로 있기를 바란다.   정답 (C)

문제 151-152번은 다음 웹 페이지에 있는 안내문을 참조하시오.

---

www.laundrotrack.com

| 메인 페이지 | 주문 | 소식지 | 매장 위치 | 문의 |

런더리 익스프레스

(151)런드로트랙은 귀하의 세탁물의 편리한 수거 및 배달 서비스를 제공합니다. 저희 웹 페이지에서 주문서를 작성하시기만 하면 저희가 귀하께서 온라인 양식에 기재한 시간에 지정된 장소에서 세탁물을 수거하거나 돌려 드립니다. **(152)이 서비스는 원하는 수거 또는 배송 3시간 전에 주문하신 경우에 이용할 수 있습니다.** 저희 영업 시간은 주중에는 오전 9시부터 오후 9시까지이고 주말에는 오전 10시부터 오후 4시까지입니다.

비용은 수거나 배송 장소뿐만 아니라 세탁물의 양 및 각 세탁물에 요구되는 세탁 서비스의 종류에 따라 다를 수 있습니다.

6월 3일, 런드로트랙은 호주 전역의 여러 도시에서 매장을 열 것입니다. 곧 다시 오셔서 저희 전국 서비스를 이용해 주세요.

---

151. 무엇이 광고되고 있는가?
(A) 할인가 제공
(B) 변경된 영업 시간
(C) 향상된 서비스
(D) 새로운 세탁소 매장 위치   정답 (C)

152. 런더리 익스프레스에 대해 나타나 있는 것은 무엇인가?
(A) 서비스 시간에 따라서 가격이 다를 수 있다.
(B) 전국적으로 이용 가능하다.
(C) 재방문 고객들에게는 더 저렴하다.
(D) 사전 주문이 요구된다.   정답 (D)

문제 153-154번은 다음 문자 메시지를 참조하시오.

---

(154)수신: 제임스 허스트
(153)발신: 크리스티나 스타크
날짜: 7월 7일, 금요일
시간: 오전 10시 4분

방금 콘도 씨로부터 도쿄 발 자신의 비행기가 지연되었다는 메시지를 받았습니다. **(153)여기 샌프란시스코 공항으로부터 샌 마티오의 사무실까지 운전해서 가면 30분이 걸릴 거예요.** 그래서 말인데 데일리 시로 대신 가서 코닝스턴 씨를 픽업한 후 회의실에서 기다려 줄 수 있나요? **(154)지금 당장 떠날 수 있으면 가능한 한 빨리 알려 주세요.** 고마워요.

---

153. 스타크 씨는 지금 어디에 있을 것 같은가?
(A) 도쿄
(B) 샌 마티오
(C) 샌프란시스코

(D) 데일리 시   정답 (C)

154. 스타크 씨는 허스트 씨가 무엇을 빨리 해줄 것을 요청하는가?

    (A) 회의실 예약하기
    (B) 자신이 시간 확정하는 것을 기다려 주기
    (C) 답장 보내기
    (D) 코닝스톤 씨에게 전화하기   정답 (C)

문제 155-157번은 다음 기사를 참조하시오.

옐로우나이프 (8월 28일) – 오늘 밤, 북극광이 오후 10시 35분경에 약 10분 동안 보일 것으로 기대됩니다. 오늘 밤은 강수 확률 없이, 매우 깨끗한 하늘이 될 것이므로 오로라의 활동을 볼 수 있는 가장 좋은 밤 중 하나가 될 것입니다. (156)캐머론 계곡에서 강한 빛의 활동이 있을 것이고, 그 장소가 가장 다채로운 색상의 가장 밝은 오로라를 볼 수 있는 이상적인 곳이 될 것입니다. 사진 클럽이 캐머론 계곡으로 이동하여 이 경이로운 광경을 볼 것입니다. (155)오후 12시까지 캠퍼스의 울프 빌딩 402호로 이 신나는 여행을 신청할 수 있습니다. 관심이 있는 학생들은 클럽 대표인 제이슨 메이어에게 jmayer@fastmail.com으로 연락하거나 많은 정보를 클럽을 방문하여 클럽 회원에게 물어보시면 됩니다. 단 10명의 자리만 남아 있으니, 서둘러서 투어 버스의 자리를 맡으세요. (157)오후 8시에 캐머론 계곡으로 출발하여, 자정에 캠퍼스로 돌아올 것입니다. (156)북극광의 숨막히는 광경을 볼 이번 기회를 놓치지 마세요!

155. 기사는 어디에서 볼 것 같은가?

    (A) 미술관
    (B) 천문대
    (C) 관광 카탈로그
    (D) 대학 신문   정답 (D)

156. 기사에 따르면, 여행을 가는 사람들은 무엇을 볼 것으로 기대되는가?

    (A) 지역의 고대 유물
    (B) 밤하늘의 현상
    (C) 오로라 사진 전시회
    (D) 유명한 일기 예보 진행자   정답 (B)

157. 학생들은 몇 시에 캠퍼스를 떠나는가?

    (A) 오후 4시
    (B) 오후 8시
    (C) 오후 10시 35분
    (D) 오후 12시   정답 (B)

문제 158-160번은 다음 이메일을 참조하시오.

수신: 루이스 스미스 〈lsmith@boostmail.com〉
(160)참조: 〈randerson@stylepoint.com〉, 〈jmarsh@stylepoint.com〉, 〈brivera@stylepoint.com〉
발신: 샤샤 마틴〈smartin@stylepoint.com〉
(158)날짜: 1월 11일
제목: 스타일 포인트 여름 컬렉션

스미스 씨께,

(159)저희는 최근에 스타일 포인트 여름 선글라스의 새 상품군을 출시했습니다. (158)당신이 지난 시즌에 훌륭하게 일을 했고, 그 덕분에 저희는 지난 시즌 핸드백 상품군의 매출이 2% 증가했습니다. 그러므로, 저희는 한 번 더 당신이 저희의 신상품을 위한 웹 페이지 작업을 다시 해주셨으면 합니다. 저희는 당신이 사용하는 생기 넘치는 색깔과 독특한 디자인 스타일이

좋았습니다.

저희는 이번 시즌의 콘셉트와 웹 페이지에 포함해야 하는 세부사항을 설명하기 위해 당신을 만나고 싶습니다. 이번 주 후반에 시간이 되는지 알려 주십시오. (160)제가 이번 주에 몇 명의 고객과 사업 미팅이 있어서, 언제든지 바로 연락드릴 수 없을지도 모릅니다. 따라서, 제가 이 이메일에 저희 마케팅팀을 참조로 넣었고, 어떤 문의사항이나 도움이 필요하면 그들에게 연락하시면 됩니다. (159)저희와 다시 일하는 데 관심이 있으시면, 저희에게 알려 주십시오. 그러면 앤더슨 씨가 몇 가지 샘플을 보내 드릴 겁니다.

샤샤 마틴
마케팅 매니저, 스타일 포인트

158. 스미스 씨는 지난해에 무엇을 해달라고 요청 받았는가?

    (A) 몇몇 신상품 사진 촬영하기
    (B) 온라인 카탈로그를 등록된 고객들에게 나눠 주기
    (C) 웹 페이지 디자인하기
    (D) 온라인으로 제품 팔기   정답 (C)

159. 마틴 씨에 따르면, 스미스 씨가 제안을 받아들인다면 무엇을 받게 되는가?

    (A) 새 핸드백
    (B) 안경 몇 개
    (C) 계약서
    (D) 회의 스케줄   정답 (B)

160. 마틴 씨가 다른 사람들이 이메일을 볼 수 있게 한 이유는?

    (A) 다른 이에게 이 일을 할당하기 위해
    (B) 그녀가 바쁠 때 스미스 씨가 도움을 받게 하기 위해
    (C) 그들로부터 디자인 제안을 요청하기 위해
    (D) 그들에게 다가오는 프로젝트에 대해 질문을 하기 위해   정답 (B)

문제 161-163번은 다음 이메일을 참조하시오.

수신: 트로이 마일스 〈tmiles@boltmail.com〉
발신: 게리 테넌트 〈gtennent@boltmail.com〉
날짜: 3월 2일
제목: 해야 할 목록

안녕하세요, 트로이.

당신도 이미 알다시피, 내가 내일 가족 여행을 떠나서 다음 주 월요일에나 돌아올 거예요. 당신이 가게를 봐주었으면 하고, 내가 없는 동안에 당신이 해줘야 할 것들이 있어요. (161)내가 이미 사흘 치의 물건들을 주문했으니, 그냥 배달 오는 것을 받고 프레시니스 퍼스트의 배달원 토리 씨가 건네주는 양식에 서명하기만 하면 돼요. (161) (162)당신이 평소에 하던 대로 제품들을 선반에 잘 정리해 주세요. 유통기한이 지난 제품을 버리는 것을 잊지 마세요. 퇴근 전에는, 냉장고를 제외한 모든 전원을 꼭 끄도록 하세요. 금고와 문도 잠그세요. 언제나처럼 열쇠는 우편함 안에 넣으세요. (163)물어볼 게 있으면 편하게 전화하세요. 수고해 주셔서 고마워요. 내가 없는 동안의 당신 임금은 두 배로 줄게요.

게리

161. 테넌트 씨는 어떤 종류의 업체를 소유하고 있는 것 같은가?

    (A) 여행 장비 가게
    (B) 식료품점
    (C) 배달 업체
    (D) 호텔 식당   정답 (B)

162. 가게에서 마일스 씨가 매일 하는 업무는 무엇인가?

    (A) 주문하기

(B) 양식에 서명하기

(C) 선반에 물건 채워 넣기

(D) 가게 문 열기 　　　　　　　정답 (C)

163. [1], [2], [3] 그리고 [4]로 표시된 곳 중에, 아래 문장이 들어가기에 가장 적절한 곳은?

"전화기를 항상 갖고 있을 거예요."

(A) [1]

(B) [2]

(C) [3]

(D) [4] 　　　　　　　정답 (C)

문제 164-167번은 다음 공지문을 참조하시오.

---

(164)서머 선-블래스트 투어

길고 하얀 구름과 키위의 땅, 뉴질랜드에 오시는 것을 환영합니다. (164)뉴질랜드에서 아름다운 자연과 즐거움으로 가득 찬 여름 행사를 와이탕기 여행사와 함께 즐기세요. 다음은 이번 여름 동안 여러분이 참여할 수 있는 행사들의 목록입니다. 행사에 관한 자세한 정보는 저희 웹사이트에서 보실 수 있습니다.

(165A)세계 거리의 악사 페스티벌 (1월 14일~25일)

크라이스처치의 거리에서 세계적으로 유명한 수백 명의 거리 악사들과 거리 공연자들과 함께하세요. 다양한 장르의 리듬과 소리를 느껴 보세요. 가장 좋은 점은? 모두가 완전히 무료로 참여할 수 있다는 겁니다!

멋진 호수 자전거 코스 (2월 1일~25일)

머리카락 사이로 부는 시원한 바람과 함께 타우포 호숫가를 자전거로 달려 보세요. 이틀에 걸친 완주 코스와 좀 더 짧은 코스 중 선택하실 수 있습니다.

전통 춤의 밤 (166)(2월 5일~18일)

현지 댄서들이 폴리너리 상을 타기 위해 경연합니다. 잊지 못할 추억을 댄서들과 함께 만드세요! (166)우승자는 마지막 날 밤에 호명될 것입니다.

(165C)공예품과 장신구 시장 (2월 1일~28일)

고향에 있는 가족과 친구들에게 보여줄 기념품을 사세요! 이 지역의 장인들이 요청에 따라 특별한 공예품과 장신구를 만들 준비가 되어 있습니다.

(165D)뉴질랜드의 먹거리 거리 (2월 10일~20일)

(167)현지의 한 대학교 교수인 마틴 콜맨과 그의 학생들이 오클랜드의 거리에 부스를 설치하여 그들이 수업 시간에 만든 전통 요리들로 모든 방문객들과 주민들을 맞이할 것입니다.

---

164. 공지문은 누구를 대상으로 하는 것 같은가?

(A) 지역 주민

(B) 행사 기획자

(C) 관광객

(D) 자원 봉사자 　　　　　　　정답 (C)

165. 행사 가운데 열거되어 있지 않은 것은 무엇인가?

(A) 음악 공연

(B) 호수에서의 수상 스포츠

(C) 상품 판매

(D) 음식 전시 　　　　　　　정답 (B)

166. 대회의 우승자는 언제 발표될 것인가?

(A) 1월 25일

(B) 2월 5일

(C) 2월 18일

(D) 2월 25일 　　　　　　　정답 (C)

167. 콜맨 씨에 대해 나타나 있는 것은 무엇인가?

(A) 와이탕기 여행사에서 일한다.

(B) 건축에 대해 박식하다.

(C) 매년 여름 뉴질랜드로 여행을 간다.

(D) 요리법을 가르친다. 　　　　　　　정답 (D)

문제 168-171번은 다음 온라인 채팅 토론을 참조하시오.

네이선 첸　　　　　　　　　　　　　[오후 6시 3분]

(168)케이시 회사의 영국에서의 브랜드 런칭 쇼가 다음 주에 열립니다! 작년 노르웨이에서의 브랜드 런칭의 큰 성공으로 이사회가 이번 런던 런칭 쇼를 매우 기대하고 있어요. (168)어떻게 진행되고 있나요?

더글라스 스탠필드　　　　　　　　　[오후 6시 6분]

(168)인도의 우리 공장에서 향수 컬렉션을 받았고 진열할 준비가 되었습니다. (170)지금은, 독일에서 케이시의 새로운 피부관리 제품이 도착하기를 기다리고 있습니다.

(170)서전 캘런　　　　　　　　　　　[오후 6시 10분]

배송이 약간 지연될 거예요.

(170)서전 캘런　　　　　　　　　　　[오후 6시 12분]

(169) (170)이곳에서 며칠 동안 심한 폭풍우가 계속되고 있어서, 해외 배송이 진행되지 않고 있어요. 다행히 모든 제품이 안전하게 포장됐고 배송 준비는 끝났어요.

더글라스 스탠필드　　　　　　　　　[오후 6시 15분]

(171)이게 우리 브랜드 런칭 연회 일정에 지장을 줄까요?

서전 캘런　　　　　　　　　　　　　[오후 6시 16분]

(171)그렇지는 않을 것 같습니다. 오프닝까지 아직 한 달의 시간이 있고, 폭풍우도 며칠 후면 지나갈 거라서요.

(171)네이선 첸　　　　　　　　　　　[오후 6시 18분]

듣던 중 반가운 소식이네요.

더글라스 스탠필드　　　　　　　　　[오후 6시 20분]

캘런 씨, 저에게 모든 수송 건에 대한 최신 정보를 계속 알려 주세요.

서전 캘런　　　　　　　　　　　　　[오후 6시 23분]

물론이죠, 가능한 한 빠르게 알려 드릴게요.

---

168. 케이시 회사는 어떤 종류의 회사인가?

(A) 운송 회사

(B) 패션 부티크

(C) 화장품 제조회사

(D) 여행사 　　　　　　　정답 (C)

169. 무엇이 진열 제품들의 배송을 지연시켰는가?

(A) 론칭 연회의 일정 변경

(B) 공장의 제조 문제

(C) 운송 중의 사고

(D) 악천후 　　　　　　　정답 (D)

170. 캘런 씨는 어디에서 근무하는가?

(A) 영국

(B) 인도

(C) 노르웨이

(D) 독일 　　　　　　　정답 (D)

171. 오후 6시 18분에, 첸 씨가 "듣던 중 반가운 소식이네요"라고 쓸 때 무엇을 의미하는가?

(A) 예정대로 쇼가 진행될 수 있어서 기쁘다.

(B) 그는 비를 즐긴다.

(C) 그는 케이시 회사가 많은 손님을 끌어들일 것이라고 생각한다.

(D) 캘런 씨의 노고에 감사한다.   정답 (A)

문제 172-175번은 다음 광고를 참조하시오.

커뮤니티 리포트

(172)더 많은 고객을 유치하기 위해 귀 사업체를 광고할 계획이신가요? 지역 사회에 귀 사업체를 알리는 힘든 일을 〈커뮤니티 리포트〉에 맡겨 주십시오!

(173)〈커뮤니티 리포트〉는 필라델피아의 아파트, 지하철역, 사업장, 그리고 학교에 배송됩니다. 저희 서비스를 이용하는 것이 귀 사업체를 광고하는 가장 효과적이고 저렴한 방법입니다. 20달러에, 〈커뮤니티 리포트〉 1회분에 귀하의 게시물이 인쇄될 것입니다. (173)게시물이 인쇄될 시기를 선택할 수 있습니다: 매달 첫째 주 또는 셋째 주. 그리고 한 달 동안 발행되는 〈커뮤니티 리포트〉 2회분 모두에 게시물이 인쇄되면 단 35달러를 청구합니다.

저희의 웹사이트 www.communityreport.com/ads에 귀하의 요청서를 제출하실 때, (174A)업체에 대한 간략한 설명 그리고 (174D)전화번호와 이메일 주소 둘 다 혹은 그 중 하나를 포함해 주시길 바랍니다. 귀하의 게시물의 효과를 극대화할 수 있도록 (174C)관련 사진 또한 보내 주십시오.

(175)저희 전문가들이 귀하를 대신해 이목을 끄는 광고를 만들고, 작성하고, 편집해 드릴 수 있습니다. 자세한 사항들과 추가 정보에 대해서는 저희에게 (215) 555-8332로 연락하세요. 또한, 저희는 필라델피아의 주민들에게 지역사회, 직업, 그리고 지역 행사들에 대한 신뢰성 있는 정보들을 제공하는 저희의 임무를 지속적으로 수행하기 위해 독자의 기부금에 많이 의존하고 있습니다. 저희 웹사이트에 접속하셔서 〈커뮤니티 리포트〉의 후원자가 되는 것에 대해 더 알아보세요.

---

172. 광고의 대상은 누구인가?

(A) 지역 주민

(B) 구직자

(C) 광고 회사 직원

(D) 업체 소유주   정답 (D)

173. 〈커뮤니티 리포트〉에 대해 나타나 있는 것은 무엇인가?

(A) 한 달 구독료로 35달러를 받는다.

(B) 예전보다 더 많은 구독자들을 끌어모으고 있다.

(C) 수익금을 지역의 학교에 기부한다.

(D) 한 달에 두 번 주민들에게 배송된다.   정답 (D)

174. 게시 신청과 함께 제출되어야 하는 정보로서 언급되지 않은 것은 무엇인가?

(A) 업체에 관한 설명

(B) 웹사이트 주소

(C) 사진

(D) 연락처 정보   정답 (B)

175. [1], [2], [3] 그리고 [4]로 표시된 곳 중에, 아래 문장이 들어가기에 가장 적절한 곳은?

"이 서비스에는 추가 요금이 부과됩니다."

(A) [1]

(B) [2]

(C) [3]

(D) [4]   정답 (C)

문제 176-180번은 다음 웹 페이지들을 참조하시오.

---

http://www.electrogitalmart.com/search

일렉트로지털 마트

메인 페이지	제품	검색	고객 후기

세부적인 정보를 원하시면 제품명을 클릭하세요. (180)1월의 주문 건들은 자동으로 인터넷 교환권을 받으실 수 있는 추첨 대상이 됩니다. 해당 교환권은 일렉트로지털 마트 루이빌 지점에서 무료 리브리오 헤드폰 하나로 (178)교환될 수 있습니다.

검색 결과: 태블릿 PC

(177D) (179)인스틴트 태블릿 PC 에이스10 고급의 내장 마이크와 스피커	79.00달러	(5개 후기)
(176) (177B)아수로닉 태블릿 PC T100 분리 가능한 키보드 독 포함	105,20달러	(4개 후기)
(177C)제미츠 태블릿 PC Y80 7인치 화면과 스타일러스 펜	60,10달러	(177C)(0개 후기)
(177A)디지마인드 태블릿 PC XDL-2 고해상도의 넓은 화면과 전후방 카메라	89,70달러	(14개 후기)

---

http://www.electrogitalmart.com/customerreview

일렉트로지털 마트

메인 페이지	제품	검색	고객 후기

당신의 경험을 함께 공유해 주세요!

당신의 직감을 믿으세요! ★★★★☆

(180)아이작 마르티네즈, 2월 17일 게시

저는 작년에 일렉트로지털 마트에서 구매한 디지마인드 태블릿 PC XDL-2를 소유하여 사용하고 있습니다. 이건 분명 PC로 영화 보는 것을 즐기는 사람에게 좋은 선택입니다. 또한, 내장된 카메라로 정말 좋은 화질의 사진을 찍을 수 있어요.

지난달에, (180)저는 일렉트로지털 마트에서 태블릿 PC를 하나 더 구매해서 공짜 헤드폰을 받았어요. (179)제 아들의 졸업선물로 아수로닉 제조의 태블릿 PC를 구매했는데, 비교적 무거운 무게가 문제가 되는 것 같았어요. 그래서 저는 그걸 반품시키고 결국엔 온라인으로 인스틴트 태블릿 PC 에이스10을 아들의 선물로 주문했습니다. 저는 제미츠 태블릿 PC Y180을 구매하는 것도 고려해 보았지만, 화면이 작아서 제 아들이 대학교 학업을 하는 데 사용하기에는 적합하지 않은 것 같습니다.

---

176. 소비자들이 아수로닉 태블릿 PC T100을 구매하려고 할 것 같은 이유는?

(A) 이것으로 작업하는 동안 음악 듣는 것을 좋아하기 때문이다.

(B) 예산이 제한되어 있기 때문이다.

(C) 이것으로 영화를 볼 계획하기 때문이다.

(D) 타이핑을 해야 하기 때문이다.   정답 (D)

177. 웹사이트에 어떤 제품이 고객들에게 평가되지 않았는가?

(A) 디지마인드 태블릿 PC XDL-2

(B) 아수로닉 태블릿 PC T100

(C) 제미츠 태블릿 PC Y80

(D) 인스틴트 태블릿 PC 에이스10   정답 (C)

178. 첫 번째 웹 페이지의 첫 번째 단락 2행에 있는 단어 "redeemed"와 의미상 가장 가까운 것은?

(A) 변제된

(B) 발행된

(C) 구매된

(D) 교환된 정답 (D)

179. 졸업 선물은 얼마였는가?

(A) 60.10달러

(B) 79.00달러

(C) 89.70달러

(D) 105.20달러 정답 (B)

180. 마르티네즈 씨에 대해 나타나 있는 것은 무엇인가?

(A) 그는 일렉트로지털 마트의 오프라인 매장을 방문했다.

(B) 그는 한 지역 대학에서 일한다.

(C) 그는 다른 태블릿 PC를 구매할 것이다.

(D) 그는 그의 최근 구매에 대해 할인을 받았다. 정답 (A)

문제 181-185번은 다음 일정표와 이메일을 참조하시오.

베터 투모로우 시민 협회 (BTCA)

(183)버지니아 밀러의 일정표 (4월 10일~14일)

월요일	화요일	수요일	(183)목요일	(184)금요일
오전 9:30 마리아 만스와 회의	오전 9:10 새로운 자원봉사자들을 위한 교육 시간	오전 9:00 (181)기차로 런던에 돌아오기	(183)오전 9:00 브라이언 클라크 (IT 팀)와 회의	오전 8:50 사우샘프턴 의 프로젝트 기획자와 회의
오후 2:30 월례 이사회 회의	오전 1:20 지역 고등학교에서 강의	오후 12:00 광고팀과 점심 식사 모임	오후 1:00 베로니카 매브리와 자원봉사 운동 계획 짜기	(184) 오전 10:00 인터뷰 (런던 투데이)
오후 5:00 (181) 맨체스터 지사까지 기차 이동	오후 4:30 학생 자원봉사자들과 만남	오후 2:00 (181)파리 지사와 전화 회의	오후 4:00 캄보디아의 자원봉사 프로젝트 준비하기	오후 1:00 지역 후원자와 만남
				오후 5:00 (181)베를린 지사 전화 회의

---

(183)**수신: 버지니아 밀러 〈vmiller@btca.org〉**

발신: 그레고리 브라우닝 〈gbrowning@btca.org〉

(183)**날짜: 4월 10일**

제목: 업데이트

첨부: 이메일 사본

밀러 씨에게,

이것은 이번 주 일정의 최신 변경 사항을 상기시켜 드리기 위한 것입니다. (183)IT팀 부장님이 급한 출장 때문에 목요일에 회의에 더 이상 참석할 수 없다고 합니다. 약속은 다음 주 월요일 오전 8시 30분으로 옮겨졌습니다. (182)그 목요일 오전에 스티븐 풀리엄 씨와 회의를 잡아 놓았습니다. 그는 곧 다가올 베터 투모로우 시민 협회를 위한 그의 강의에 대해 당신이 만나서 의논하고 싶어 하시는 포트 반스 대학교의 교수입니다.

(185)두 번째로, 맨체스터 출장 중 이용하실 차량의 예약을 확인하는 알라비스 렌터카에서 보내온 이메일의 사본을 첨부하였습니다. 이미 전에 제가 보내 드린 기차표와 호텔 예약 확인서는 가지고 계실 것으로 생각합니다.

마지막으로, (184)지역 신문사의 데이비드 맥클린이 그의 기사를 위해 금요

일에 당신에게 물어볼 질문 목록을 보냈습니다. 출장에서 돌아오시면 목록을 드리도록 하겠습니다.

그레고리 브라우닝 드림

---

181. 베터 투모로우 시민 협회에 대해 나타나 있는 것은 무엇인가?

(A) 여러 도시에 사무실이 있다.

(B) 새로운 광고를 시작했다.

(C) 현재 새로운 자원봉사자를 모집하고 있다.

(D) 최근 밀러 씨를 채용했다. 정답 (A)

182. 이메일에 따르면, 브라우닝 씨는 무엇을 했을 것 같은가?

(A) 강연자에게 연락했다.

(B) 웹사이트 디자인을 변경했다.

(C) 기부를 요청했다.

(D) 대학에서 연설을 했다. 정답 (A)

183. 누구의 회의 일정이 변경되었는가?

(A) 마리아 만스

(B) 브라이언 클라크

(C) 베로니카 매브리

(D) 그레고리 브라우닝 정답 (B)

184. 밀러 씨는 맥클린 씨와 금요일 언제 만날 것인가?

(A) 오전 8:50

(B) 오전 10:00

(C) 오후 1:00

(D) 오후 5:00 정답 (B)

185. 이메일과 함께 무엇이 발송되었는가?

(A) 기차표

(B) 질문 목록

(C) 숙소 세부사항

(D) 자동차 대여 확인서 정답 (D)

문제 186-190번은 다음 회람과 공지문 그리고 이메일을 참조하시오.

회람

수신: PE 세라믹스 관리자

발신: 응구옌 딘

날짜: 6월 2일

제목: 비즈니스 월드

(190D)6월 20일부터 22일까지 개최되는 전문 개발 협회의 일련의 세미나, 비즈니스 월드에 관한 내용입니다. (186) (190A)세미나 참석은 모든 신임 관리자에게 의무적입니다. 모든 관리자를 위해 참가비는 회사가 (187)부담할 것이지만, 호텔 객실의 예약은 개인적으로 부담하셔야 합니다. (190C)만약에 골든 캐슬 호텔을 선택한다면, 세미나 참석자 할인으로 하루 숙박에 130달러 대신 75달러만 내시면 됩니다. (189)환불에 대해서는 회계부의 관리자에게 연락하십시오. 직원 휴게실의 게시판에 붙은 공고를 참조하세요.

응구옌 딘 드림

회장

비즈니스 월드 - 필수적인 관리 기술

6월 20일 – 6월 22일

블룸버그 컨벤션 센터

455 롱 스트리트, (190D)뉴욕, 뉴욕 주 10055

유명한 작가, 교육자, 고위 간부, 컨설턴트 그리고 심지어 현직 대기업 최고 경영자들이 진행하는 저희의 인기 있는 세미나에 참석하세요! 세미나는 매일 오전 9시에 시작해서 오후 5시에 끝납니다. 점심이 제공될 것입니다. 저희 세미나를 통해, 여러분은 공통의 목표를 정하고, 팀 성과를 극대화하고, 개인의 차이점과 아이디어를 존중하며, 효과적으로 의사소통하는 법을 배울 수 있습니다. (188)방의 온도가 때마다 다를 수 있으니, 일상 근무복 복장으로 여러 겹 겹쳐 입고 세미나에 와주세요.

---

(189)수신: 윌리엄 곤잘레스 〈w.gonzalez@peceramics.com〉
발신: 마를렌 카프 〈m.karp@peceramics.com〉
날짜: 7월 6일
제목: 환급

곤잘레스 씨에게.

(190D)저는 비즈니스 월드 세미나에 3일 모두 참석했습니다. (189) (190A)환급 처리를 위해 영수증들과 지출 보고서를 전달하러 당신의 사무실에 들르겠습니다.

그런데, (190C)골든 캐슬 호텔에서 세미나가 열렸던 블룸버그 컨벤션 센터까지 가기가 약간 힘들었다는 것을 얘기해야겠습니다. 그 근방의 대중 교통은 아주 편리하지도 시간에 맞춰 다니지도 않았습니다. 저는 PE 세라믹스에서 다음 번에는 세미나 위치와 좀 더 가까운 곳에 있거나 아니면 셔틀 서비스를 제공하는 호텔과 계약을 맺을 수 있으면 감사하겠습니다.

마를렌 카프 드림
홍보부

186. 회람의 목적은 무엇인가?
(A) 호텔 예약을 확인하기 위한 것
(B) 세미나 등록비 할인을 제공하기 위한 것
(C) 한 단체 가입을 추천하기 위한 것
(D) 직원들에게 행사 참석을 권장하기 위한 것 정답 (D)

187. 회람에서 첫 번째 단락 3행에 있는 단어 "covered"와 의미상 가장 가까운 것은?
(A) 포함된
(B) 지급된
(C) 면제된
(D) 적용된 정답 (B)

188. 참석자들은 무엇을 할 것을 요청 받는가?
(A) 복장 규정 따르기
(B) 장소에 일찍 도착하기
(C) 세미나에 음식 가져오기
(D) 발표자들에게 질문하기 정답 (A)

189. 곤잘레스 씨는 누구일 것 같은가?
(A) PE 세라믹스의 관리자
(B) 세미나 강연자
(C) 새로운 회계사
(D) 골든 캐슬 호텔의 관리자 정답 (A)

190. 카프 씨에 대해 암시되지 않은 것은 무엇인가?
(A) 그녀는 관리직에 있다.
(B) 그녀는 자신의 비행기 티켓 값을 환급 받을 것이다.
(C) 골든 캐슬 호텔에서 할인을 받았다.
(D) 그녀는 6월 21일에 뉴욕에 있었다. 정답 (B)

문제 191-195번은 다음 기사와 이메일들을 참조하시오.

〈통합〉의 소동

워렌 디아즈의 폭발적 인기를 끈 공상 과학 시리즈 (194)〈우주 제국〉의 팬들은 영화 시리즈의 네 번째이자 마지막 편인 〈통합〉을 보려면 5개월을 더 기다려야 할 것이다. (193)싱커스 프로덕션은 오늘 〈통합〉의 북미 지역 개봉이 7월 21일에서 12월 15일로 연기되었다고 발표했다. (191)제작사는 크리스마스 시즌으로 극장에 더 많은 관람객이 오기를 바라며 개봉일을 연기했다.

이 영화 시리즈의 성공은 사실 시리즈 첫 편 〈화성으로의 행진〉을 비교적 적은 수의 사람들이 관람했기 때문에 영화업계에서는 다소 예상치 못한 것이었다. 시리즈의 두 번째와 세 번째 영화가 총 32억 달러를 벌어들이며, 놀라운 (192)수치로 기록을 깨면서 영화업계 전체를 깜짝 놀라게 했다.

수신: 티파니 앨런 〈tallen@mavisaccounting.com〉
발신: 로버트 브라운 〈rbrown@mavisaccounting.com〉
날짜: 12월 18일
제목: 〈통합〉

안녕하세요, 티파니.

나 오늘 아침에 막 뉴욕에서 돌아왔어요. 거기서 휴가를 보내는 동안, (193)〈우주 제국〉 시리즈의 최신 편 〈통합〉을 개봉 당일에 볼 기회가 있었어요. 정말 환상적이었어요! 그런데 시리즈가 이제 다 끝났다는 걸 믿을 수가 없어요. (194)그런데 실은 이 시리즈의 첫 두 편인 〈화성으로의 행진〉과 〈위대한 사명〉은 보았는데 세 번째 편은 보지 못했어요. 그래서인지 내가 마지막 편을 보면서 약간 헷갈린 거 같아요. 그렇더라도 정말 좋은 영화이니 당신도 꼭 보는 게 좋을 것 같아요.

로버트 브라운

수신: 로버트 브라운 〈rbrown@mavisaccounting.com〉
발신: 티파니 앨런 〈tallen@mavisaccounting.com〉
날짜: 12월 19일
제목: 답장: 〈통합〉

안녕하세요, 로버트.

답장이 늦어서 미안해요. 알다시피, 어제 난 온종일 회사 세미나를 준비하느라 바빴어요. 당신은 이번 휴가를 즐기고 왔다니 기뻐요. 나 실은 12월 17일에 가족과 〈통합〉을 봤어요. 정말 아주 잘 만들어진 영화예요. 마지막 액션 장면은 정말 숨이 막혔어요.

(194)당신이 아직 〈왕좌의 몰락〉을 보지 않았다는 게 안 믿겨요! 어떻게 그걸 못 볼 수가 있었어요? (195)내가 시리즈 전체 에피소드 DVD를 소장하고 있으니까, 언제 당신이 못 본 에피소드를 함께 볼 수 있을 거예요. 시간 될 때 알려 주세요.

티파니 앨런

191. 기사에 따르면, 영화의 개봉일이 연기된 이유는?
(A) 감독이 대본을 변경할 것이기 때문이다.
(B) 그래픽 작업이 완성되지 않았기 때문이다.
(C) 아직 영화 광고가 준비되지 않았기 때문이다.
(D) 싱커스 프로덕션이 더 많은 사람이 영화를 관람하길 원했기 때문이다. 정답 (D)

192. 기사의 두 번째 단락 3행에 있는 단어 "figures"와 의미상 가장 가까운 것은?
(A) 사람
(B) 숫자

(C) 논평
(D) 그래픽   정답 (B)

193. 브라운 씨는 언제 〈통합〉을 봤을 것 같은가?
(A) 11월 21일
(B) 12월 15일
(C) 12월 17일
(D) 12월 18일   정답 (B)

194. 〈우주 제국〉의 세 번째 편은 무엇인가?
(A) 〈왕좌의 몰락〉
(B) 〈위대한 사명〉
(C) 〈화성으로의 행진〉
(D) 〈통합〉   정답 (A)

195. 앨런 씨에 대해 암시된 것은 무엇인가?
(A) 다음 주에 세미나에 참석할 것이다.
(B) 브라운 씨가 〈통합〉을 좋아한다는 것이 놀랍다.
(C) 브라운 씨에게 또 다른 DVD를 사 줄 것이다.
(D) 〈우주 제국〉의 팬이다.   정답 (D)

문제 196-200번은 다음 공지문과 이메일들을 참조하시오.

필라델피아 미술관 (PAM)의 충실한 후원자가 되어 주셔서 감사합니다. (197)곧 다가올 우리 미술관의 수잔 맥카베 전을 (196)기념하기 위하여, 저희는 모든 후원자 분들을 초대해 그녀를 환영해 주고자 합니다. 맥카베 씨는 요즘 만화계의 기대주로서 떠오르고 있는 젊은 만화가입니다.

(198)저희는 4월 4일에 열릴 전시회의 사전 개막식에 모든 후원자를 초대합니다. 참석하시는 모든 분께 후원 등급에 따라 특별 선물을 드릴 것입니다.

후원자들에게 준비된 선물들은 다음과 같습니다:

후원 등급	*선물(들)
친구	엽서
(200)동료	**엽서와 머그잔**
파트너	엽서, 머그잔, 그리고 맥카베 씨의 최신 만화책 〈더 제펠린〉
후원자	위의 모든 항목과 후원자의 이름이 새겨진 명판

• 모든 선물은 맥카베 씨가 디자인하셨습니다.

정식 개막식은 4월 8일에 열리며, 후원자들뿐만 아니라 일반인에게도 공개합니다. 모든 방문객은 전시회를 둘러보고 몇 가지 다과도 즐기실 수 있습니다.

전시회에서 뵙기를 기대합니다!

수신: 애니 리베라 〈arivera@197-3pam.org〉
발신: 클라이드 하퍼 〈charper@onemail.com〉
날짜: 4월 12일
제목: 후원자 선물

리베라 씨에게,

(197)만화와 예술계 양쪽에서 진짜 스타가 되어 가고 있는 지역 예술가의 정말 멋진 전시회에 저를 초대해 주셔서 감사합니다. (198)맥카베 씨의 뛰어난 실력과 독특한 스타일을 충분히 보여준 멋지고 잘 기획된 전시회였어요. 제가 이메일을 쓰는 이유는 전시회에서 선물들을 받지 못한 걸 알리기 위함입니다. 며칠 안으로 미술관에서 선물들을 우편으로 보낼 것이라고 들었거든요. 그런데 아직 받지 못했어요. 저는 정말 〈더 제펠린〉을 읽는 것을 고대하고 있어서, 빠른 회신을 원합니다.

클라이드 하퍼 드림

수신: 클라이드 하퍼 〈charper@onemail.com〉
발신: 애니 리베라 〈arivera@pam.org〉
날짜: 4월 13일
제목: 답장: 후원자 선물

하퍼 씨에게,

아직 선물을 못 받으셨다니 정말 죄송합니다. 저희가 선물이 4월 16일까지 배송되도록 후원자님 주소로 특급 우편으로 보내 드리겠습니다. (199)(200)하지만, 후원자님과 같은 등급의 다른 후원자 분들과 마찬가지로 만화책은 받지 못하시고 머그잔과 엽서만 받게 되신다는 점을 확실히 알려 드립니다. 우리 미술관과 지역사회에 대한 헌신에 감사드립니다.

애니 리베라 드림

196. 공고문의 첫 번째 단락 1행에 있는 단어 "mark"와 의미상 가장 가까운 것은?
(A) 구별하다
(B) 나타내다
(C) 밝히다
(D) 축하하다   정답 (D)

197. 맥카베 씨에 대해 나타나 있는 것은 무엇인가?
(A) 필라델피아에서 산다.
(B) PAM에 기부금을 냈다.
(C) 방문객들에게 가벼운 간식을 제공할 것이다.
(D) 최근에 대학을 졸업했다.   정답 (A)

198. 하퍼 씨는 언제 PAM을 방문했는가?
(A) 4월 4일
(B) 4월 8일
(C) 4월 12일
(D) 4월 13일   정답 (A)

199. 두 번째 이메일의 한 가지 목적은 무엇인가?
(A) 주문의 오류를 보고하기 위한 것
(B) 선물의 나쁜 품질에 대해 사과하기 위한 것
(C) 기부를 요청하기 위한 것
(D) 어떤 정보를 명확하게 하기 위한 것   정답 (D)

200. 하퍼 씨의 후원 등급은 무엇인가?
(A) 친구
(B) 동료
(C) 파트너
(D) 후원자   정답 (B)

Part 1

1. 미M

(A) People are using ladders to shelve books.
(B) People are visiting a library.
(C) Some books have been placed on a cart.
(D) A doorway is crowded with people standing in line.

(A) 사람들이 사다리를 이용해서 책들을 선반에 놓고 있다.
(B) 사람들이 도서관을 방문하고 있다.
(C) 책 몇 권이 카트 위에 놓여 있다.
(D) 출입구가 줄 서 있는 사람들로 붐비고 있다.　　　정답 (B)

2. 미W

(A) They are walking through the doorway.
(B) They are pulling their suitcases.
(C) They are arranging flower pots.
(D) They are ready to pay for their purchases.

(A) 그들은 출입구를 통해서 걸어가고 있다.
(B) 그들은 그들의 여행가방을 끌고 있다.
(C) 그들은 화분을 정리하고 있다.
(D) 그들은 자신들의 구매품에 대해 돈을 지불할 준비가 되어 있다.
　　　정답 (A)

3. 영M

(A) One of the people is pointing at some flowers.
(B) One of the women is emptying out a paper bag.
(C) They are selecting some fruits at a market stall.
(D) They are writing on the board in the store.

(A) 사람들 중 한 명이 꽃을 가리키고 있다.
(B) 여자 중 한 명이 종이 봉지를 비우고 있다.
(C) 그들은 시장 가판대에서 과일을 고르고 있다.
(D) 그들은 가게에 있는 게시판에 뭔가를 적고 있다.　　　정답 (A)

4. 호W

(A) The man is operating heavy machinery.
(B) The man is wiping some windows.
(C) The man is working on the roof.
(D) The man is inspecting a house.

(A) 남자가 중장비를 작동하고 있다.
(B) 남자가 창문을 닦고 있다.
(C) 남자가 지붕에서 일하고 있다.
(D) 남자가 집을 점검하고 있다.　　　정답 (B)

5. 미M

(A) Some curtains have been drawn over the windows.
(B) Some plants are being carried into a room.
(C) A framed picture is hanging above the mirror.
(D) A cushion has been set on an armchair.

(A) 창문 위로 커튼이 쳐져 있다.
(B) 화분 몇 개가 방 안으로 옮겨지고 있다.
(C) 액자 그림이 거울 위에 걸려 있다.
(D) 쿠션이 안락의자에 놓여 있다.　　　정답 (D)

6. 미W

(A) He is hanging up a phone.
(B) He is putting on a safety helmet.
(C) He is standing in the entranceway.
(D) He is holding a laptop under his arm.

(A) 그는 전화를 끊고 있다.
(B) 그는 안전모를 착용하고 있다.
(C) 그는 출입구에 서 있다.
(D) 그는 노트북을 겨드랑이에 끼고 있다.　　　정답 (D)

Part 2

7. 미W 영M

Do you prefer walking or cycling along the river?
(A) The bike race is in May.
(B) I like running.
(C) He is riding the bike.

강을 따라서 걷는 것을 더 좋아하세요, 아니면 자전거 타는 거를 더 좋아하세요?
(A) 자전거 경주는 5월에 있어요.
(B) 저는 달리는 것을 좋아해요.
(C) 그는 자전거를 타고 있어요.　　　정답 (B)

8. 호W 미M

Where is the parking garage for visitors?
(A) The local park is nearby.
(B) His commute to work is long enough.
(C) Next to the office building.

방문객을 위한 주차장이 어디에 있나요?
(A) 그 지역 공원은 근처에 있어요.
(B) 그의 통근 거리는 충분히 길어요.
(C) 사무실 건물 옆에요.　　　정답 (C)

9. 영M 미W

When will the product development team meet?
(A) No, I purchased five.
(B) In the bottom drawer.
(C) Sometime next week.

제품 개발 팀은 언제 만나나요?
(A) 아뇨, 저는 5개 구매했어요.
(B) 맨 아래 서랍에요.
(C) 다음 주쯤이요.　　　정답 (C)

10. 영M 미M

How long is the film we talked about?
(A) Sure, I can go to the movies.
(B) I like any kind of action movie.
(C) It lasts about two hours.

우리가 얘기했던 그 영화는 얼마나 오래해요?
(A) 좋아요, 저는 영화 보러 갈 수 있어요.
(B) 저는 액션 영화는 어떤 종류든 좋아요.
(C) 2시간 정도 해요.　　　정답 (C)

11. 미W 영M

How did you like the meal served at the banquet?
(A) I'd like to have it.
(B) It looks like a restaurant.
(C) It was excellent.

연회에서 제공된 식사는 어땠어요?

(A) 저는 그것을 먹고 싶어요.
(B) 그곳은 식당처럼 보이네요.
(C) 아주 좋았어요.　　　　　　　　　　　　정답 (C)

12. 호W 미M
Can I have a pitcher of iced water?
(A) We stay open until 10 P.M. on weekends.
(B) I'd like my coffee without cream and sugar.
(C) Sure. I'll be right back.

얼음물 한 주전자 주실래요?
(A) 우리는 주말에는 밤 10시까지 문을 열어요.
(B) 제 커피는 크림과 설탕 없이 주세요.
(C) 물론입니다. 금방 돌아올게요.　　　　정답 (C)

13. 미W 영M
Why did the R&D manager send you an e-mail?
(A) Because he wants me to work on a proposal.
(B) Yes, he is a new manager.
(C) Post it on the website now.

연구개발 부장님이 왜 당신에게 이메일을 보냈나요?
(A) 제가 제안서 작업을 해주길 원하셔서요.
(B) 예, 그는 새로 온 부장님입니다.
(C) 그것을 지금 웹사이트에 올리세요.　　정답 (A)

14. 미M 호W
Do you know who needed to reschedule their dental appointments?
(A) James has a doctor's appointment this afternoon.
(B) Let me check our patient list.
(C) We need another medication.

누가 치과 진료 예약 일정을 변경해야 했는지 아세요?
(A) 제임스는 오늘 오후에 진료 예약이 있어요.
(B) 우리 환자 명단을 확인해 볼게요.
(C) 우리는 다른 약이 필요해요.　　　　　정답 (B)

15. 영M 미W
Both of these food orders can be delivered during the same trip, right?
(A) It got damaged in transit.
(B) Actually, the trip was really nice.
(C) Sure, they go to the same part of the area.

이 음식 주문 둘 다 한 번 나갈 때 같이 배달될 수 있죠, 그렇죠?
(A) 그게 수송 중에 파손되었어요.
(B) 사실, 그 여행은 정말 좋았어요.
(C) 물론이죠, 그것들은 그 지역 같은 부분으로 가요.　　정답 (C)

16. 미M 미W
Should I work on the report now, or can it wait until later this week?
(A) The conference room is occupied.
(B) Any time this week's fine.
(C) Yes, the ticket's valid until this Sunday.

보고서 작업을 지금 해야 하나요, 아니면 이번 주 후반까지 기다릴 수 있나요?
(A) 회의실은 사용 중이에요.
(B) 이번 주 아무 때나 괜찮아요.
(C) 예, 표는 이번 주 일요일까지 유효해요.　　정답 (B)

17. 호W 영M
What do you think of the last month's company newsletter?
(A) About five pages long.
(B) It had some informative articles.
(C) Try an online version of the newsletter.

지난달 사보에 대해 어떻게 생각했어요?
(A) 대략 5페이지 길이요.
(B) 거기에 유익한 기사가 좀 있었어요.
(C) 온라인 버전의 소식지로 보세요.　　　정답 (B)

18. 미W 영M
Isn't Ms. Baker's office on the second floor?
(A) No, it moved to the third floor.
(B) I need to buy more conference tables.
(C) The door is usually left open.

베이커 씨의 사무실이 2층에 있지 않아요?
(A) 아뇨, 3층으로 옮겼어요.
(B) 저는 회의 테이블을 더 사야 해요.
(C) 그 문은 보통 연 채로 놔둡니다.　　　정답 (A)

19. 호W 미M
Why did Mrs. Craig resign from her position?
(A) About 5 days ago.
(B) She found a better job.
(C) The contract has just been signed.

크레이그 씨는 왜 자리에서 사임했나요?
(A) 약 5일 전이요.
(B) 더 좋은 일자리를 찾으셨어요.
(C) 계약이 지금 막 체결되었어요.　　　　정답 (B)

20. 미W 영M
I think I'm going to a rock festival in the city park on Sunday.
(A) Some tables and chairs on the patio.
(B) Isn't it supposed to rain?
(C) That song is my favorite.

일요일에 시립 공원에서 하는 록 페스티벌에 갈 것 같아요.
(A) 옥외 테라스에 있는 테이블과 의자 몇 개요.
(B) 비 온다고 하지 않나요?
(C) 그 노래는 제가 제일 좋아하는 노래예요.　　정답 (B)

21. 호W 미M
Weren't the light bulbs in the conference room replaced recently?
(A) Actually, this place isn't suitable.
(B) Yes, we changed all of them.
(C) Yes, put it up in the corner.

회의실에 있는 전구들이 최근에 교체되지 않았어요?
(A) 사실, 이 장소는 적당하지 않아요.
(B) 예, 우리는 그것들을 전부 바꿨어요.
(C) 예, 그것을 구석에 놓으세요.　　　　정답 (B)

22. 미W 영M
How about we go to that traditional dance performance this evening?
(A) I would like to.
(B) Go up on the stage.
(C) The performers were late.

오늘 저녁에 그 전통 춤 공연에 가는 게 어때요?
(A) 그러고 싶어요.
(B) 무대 위로 올라가세요.
(C) 공연자들이 늦었어요.　　　　　　　　　정답 (A)

23. 영M 호W
What should I do with the extra packing supplies?
(A) Leave them on the table.
(B) Yes, they should now.
(C) From a local supplier.

여분의 포장 용품을 어떻게 할까요?
(A) 테이블 위에 놔두세요.
(B) 예, 그들은 지금 해야 해요.
(C) 현지 납품업체로부터요.　　　　　　　　정답 (A)

24. 영M 미W
I haven't reserved our plane tickets yet.
(A) What time does the theater open?
(B) Just one carry-on luggage.
(C) Airfares will go up soon.

우리 비행기표를 아직 예약하지 못했어요.
(A) 극장이 몇 시에 열어요?
(B) 휴대용 짐 딱 하나요.
(C) 비행기 요금이 곧 오를 거예요.　　　　정답 (C)

25. 호W 미M
How many servers are we supposed to need waiting tables at the banquet?
(A) Yes, I reserved a table for 3 people.
(B) At a nearby restaurant.
(C) We have a party of 35 coming in.

연회에서 식사 시중을 드는 데, 서빙하는 사람이 몇 명 필요한가요?
(A) 예, 제가 3인용 테이블을 예약했어요.
(B) 근처 식당에서요.
(C) 35명의 일행이 와요.　　　　　　　　정답 (C)

26. 미W 영M
Are you interested in our membership program?
(A) Yes, I'll be on the TV program.
(B) I've been a member for more than 5 years.
(C) The train will arrive on platform B.

우리 회원 프로그램에 관심 있으세요?
(A) 예, 저는 그 텔레비전 프로에 나갈 거예요.
(B) 저는 회원이 된 지 5년 넘었어요.
(C) 기차가 B 승강장으로 도착할 거예요.　정답 (B)

27. 영M 호W
Our quarterly sales numbers were lower than we anticipated.
(A) It's a difficult hiking trail.
(B) We do have a new competitor.
(C) Yes, they are on sale today.

우리 분기별 판매 수치가 우리가 예상한 것보다 더 낮았어요.
(A) 그곳은 어려운 등산로예요.
(B) 우리는 새 경쟁업체가 생겼어요.
(C) 예, 그것들은 오늘 세일 중이에요.　　정답 (B)

28. 미W 미M
When's the next workplace efficiency workshop?
(A) It's on Main Street.
(B) I didn't sign up for that.
(C) Mark took the slide projector just now.

다음 번 직장내 효율성 워크숍은 언제 있나요?
(A) 그것은 메인 가에 있어요.
(B) 저는 그것을 신청하지 않았어요.
(C) 마크가 지금 막 슬라이드 프로젝터를 가져갔어요.　정답 (B)

29. 영M 미W
I'll be glad to take photos at the company retreat.
(A) With some refreshments.
(B) Yes, can I see a digital camera?
(C) They hired a photographer.

회사 연수회에서 제가 기꺼이 사진을 찍어드릴 거예요.
(A) 다과류도 함께요.
(B) 예, 디지털 카메라를 볼 수 있을까요?
(C) 그들은 사진사를 고용했어요.　　　　정답 (C)

30. 영M 호W
We should discuss how to increase our sales revenue for this quarter.
(A) Kate's going to hire a consultant.
(B) You will have to use carpooling.
(C) Sure, I'd like to join you for the sales conference.

이번 분기에 어떻게 하면 판매 수익을 올릴 수 있는지 논의해야 해요.
(A) 케이트가 자문위원을 고용할 거예요.
(B) 카풀을 이용하셔야 할 거예요.
(C) 좋아요, 영업 총회에 저도 같이 가고 싶어요.　정답 (A)

31. 미W 영M
Why aren't the attendees in the conference room now?
(A) Didn't they e-mail you a copy of the updated schedule?
(B) I didn't pay for the registration.
(C) Pay closer attention to the speaker.

참석자들이 왜 지금 회의실에 없는 거죠?
(A) 그들이 갱신된 일정을 한 부 당신에게 이메일로 보내지 않았어요?
(B) 저는 등록 비용을 지불하지 않았어요.
(C) 연설자의 말에 더욱 집중하세요.　　　정답 (A)

Part 3

문제 32-34번은 다음 대화를 참조하시오. 미M 미W

M: Hello. Welcome to Parker International.
W: Hello. (32)**I'm from Freeze Frame. I'm supposed to take photos of the staff for your website.**
M: Wonderful. I have a conference room reserved on the second floor for the staff photo shoot.
W: Sounds good. (33)**But, well, I have a lot of heavy lighting equipment that I need to use. It's in my truck, but for free parking I had to park several rows back from the entrance to the building.** Is there anything I can do to use...
M: Oh, sure. (34)**Here's a parking pass.** Put it on your car's windshield, and then you can park in one of the reserved places in the front row.

W: Excellent. I'll do that right now.

M: 안녕하세요. 파커 인터내셔널에 오신 것을 환영합니다.

W: 안녕하세요. 저는 프리즈 프레임에서 왔는데요. 귀사의 웹사이트에 들어갈 직원 사진을 찍기로 되어 있습니다.

M: 좋아요. 직원 사진 촬영을 할 수 있도록 2층에 회의실을 예약해 두었어요.

W: 좋아요. 그런데 사용해야 하는 무거운 조명 장비가 많아요. 그게 제 트럭에 있는데, 무료 주차를 위해 건물 입구에서 몇 줄 한참 뒤쪽에 주차해야 했어요. 제가 할 수 있는 뭐 이용 가능한…

M: 오, 물론이죠. 여기 주차권이 있어요. 자동차 앞유리창에 꽂아 두시면, 앞쪽 줄에 있는 지정 주차 공간에 주차할 수 있어요.

W: 아주 좋네요. 지금 그렇게 하겠습니다.

32. 여자는 누구일 것 같은가?
(A) 배달하는 사람
(B) 웹 디자이너
(C) 사진사
(D) 경비원   정답 (C)

33. 여자는 무엇에 대해 우려하고 있는가?
(A) 충분한 조명을 얻는 것
(B) 장비를 옮기는 것
(C) 주차권 확인을 받는 것
(D) 프로젝트를 제시간에 끝내는 것   정답 (B)

34. 남자는 여자에게 무엇을 제공하는가?
(A) 주차권
(B) 이름표
(C) 직원 신분증
(D) 회의실 열쇠   정답 (A)

문제 35-37번은 다음 3자 대화를 참조하시오. 호W 미M 영M

W: Hello, Craig and Ozzie. (35)**Since our design for the new parking lot at the stadium was selected,** we need to start pushing forward to the next step. Ozzie, do you have an update for me?

M1: Yes, I do. We have to think about the effects on local residents and the neighborhood by the stadium. A preliminary survey we conducted indicated that (36)**people are concerned about the possible increase in traffic.**

W: Craig, don't we have a meeting scheduled to take place for local residents to discuss their concerns?

M2: That's right. It's scheduled for March 10. (37)**However, we had to change the location because there wasn't enough space in the library conference room.** Instead, it will be at the local community center.

W: 안녕하세요. 크레이그, 오지. 경기장의 새 주차장에 대한 우리 설계가 선정되었기 때문에, 우리는 다음 단계로의 추진을 시작할 필요가 있어요. 오지, 나에게 전할 새로운 소식이 있나요?

M1: 예, 있어요. 지역 주민들과 경기장 옆에 있는 동네에 끼치는 영향에 대해 생각해 봐야 합니다. 우리가 실시한 예비 설문조사에 따르면, 사람들은 교통량 증가 가능성에 대해 우려하고 있어요.

W: 크레이그, 지역 주민들이 우려하는 것에 대해 논의할 수 있도록 회의 개최 일정이 잡혀 있는 거 아닌가요?

M2: 맞아요. 3월 10일에 일정이 잡혀 있어요. 그런데, 도서관 회의실의 공

간이 충분하지 않아서 장소를 변경해야 했어요. 대신에, 지역사회 센터에서 열릴 거예요.

35. 경기장에 무엇이 건설될 것인가?
(A) 주유소
(B) 보관 창고
(C) 주차장
(D) 운동 시설   정답 (C)

36. 주민들이 가지고 있는 가장 큰 우려는 무엇인가?
(A) 공사로부터 나오는 소음
(B) 어린이들을 위한 안전
(C) 감소하는 인구
(D) 교통량 증가   정답 (D)

37. 회의 장소가 새로 선정된 이유는?
(A) 경기장과 더 가깝다.
(B) 사용하는 데 비용이 덜 든다.
(C) 대중교통과 멀지 않다.
(D) 더 많은 공간을 제공한다.   정답 (D)

문제 38-40번은 다음 대화를 참조하시오. 미W 영M

W: Thanks for dropping by to see me, Glenn. How are you enjoying your new position with us?

M: I'm really happy. The management training that I got from the Personnel Department was of great help.

W: Good. (38)**Now that you are part of the management team here,** (39)**I put in a request for a company credit card for you. I just got it.** Here you are.

M: Thanks. I need to use this when I make small daily purchases in my department, right? I mean, like for office supplies.

W: Exactly. You can use it for bigger expenses, like when you're out of town on business, too. (40)**But save all your receipts because you'll be expected to fill out a reimbursement request form for your travel expenses when you come back.**

W: 저를 보러 잠깐 들러 줘서 고마워요, 글렌. 우리 회사에서 새 직책은 어때요, 좋아요?

M: 정말 만족스럽습니다. 인사과로부터 제가 받은 관리자 교육이 아주 도움이 되었어요.

W: 잘되었네요. 이제 여기 관리직 팀의 일원이니까, 제가 당신을 위해서 회사 신용 카드를 신청했어요. 지금 막 받았어요. 여기 있어요.

M: 감사합니다. 제 부서에서 소량의 일일 구매를 할 때 이 신용 카드를 써야 되는 거죠, 그렇죠? 제 말은 사무용품 같은 거요.

W: 정확해요. 좀 더 큰 비용에도 쓸 수 있는데, 예를 들어 타지로 출장갈 때 말이에요. 그런데 영수증은 전부 보관해야 해요. 왜냐하면 돌아왔을 때 출장비 환급 신청서를 작성하게 되어 있으니까요.

38. 남자는 누구일 것 같은가?
(A) 부서 관리자
(B) 컴퓨터 프로그래머
(C) 금융 컨설턴트
(D) 사무용품 판매자   정답 (A)

39. 여자는 남자를 위해서 무엇을 요청했는가?
(A) 노트북 컴퓨터

(B) 새 사무용품
(C) 사무용 가구
(D) 법인 카드　　　　　　　　　　　　　정답 (D)

40. 여자는 남자에게 무엇을 할 것을 제안하는가?
(A) 다른 납품업체로부터 견적 받기
(B) 당장 신규 고객에게 전화하기
(C) 영수증 반드시 보관하기
(D) 출장비로 돈 더 적게 쓰기　　　　　정답 (C)

문제 41-43번은 다음 대화를 참조하시오. 호W 미M

W: Hi, George. (41)**I'm attending a seminar in Sydney next week.**
M: That's my hometown.
W: I know. That's why I mentioned it. I don't think I'll have time to do any sightseeing, (42)**but I wonder if you can recommend any good restaurants for me.** I want to make sure I eat well while I'm there.
M: No problem. Which part of the city is your hotel in? If I know that, I can suggest some nearby places.
W: I'm not sure. (43)**I can get the hotel's address from the confirmation e-mail I just got. Let me log on to my e-mail and check.**

W: 안녕하세요, 조지. 다음 주에 시드니에서 하는 세미나에 참석해요.
M: 거기 제 고향인데요.
W: 알아요. 그래서 말한 거예요. 뭐 관광을 할 시간은 없을 것 같은데, 그래도 괜찮은 식당을 추천해 주실 수 있는지 모르겠네요. 거기 있는 동안, 맛있는 거라도 꼭 먹고 싶어서요.
M: 당연히 되죠. 당신 호텔이 시드니 어느 지역에 있어요? 그걸 알면, 근처 식당을 추천할 수 있어요.
W: 잘 모르겠어요. 제가 방금 받은 이메일 확인서에서 호텔 주소를 알 수 있어요. 제 이메일에 로그온해서 확인해 볼게요.

41. 여자는 다음 주에 무엇을 할 것인가?
(A) 시드니에서 온 고객 만나기
(B) 프로젝트 끝내기
(C) 친척 방문하기
(D) 출장 가기　　　　　　　　　　　　정답 (D)

42. 여자는 남자가 무엇을 추천해 주기를 원하는가?
(A) 가이드를 동반한 관광
(B) 식당
(C) 저렴한 호텔
(D) 도시의 관광지　　　　　　　　　　정답 (B)

43. 여자가 뒤이어 무엇을 할 것이라고 말하는가?
(A) 즉시 이메일 보내기
(B) 여행에 대한 비용 결제
(C) 자신의 항공권 확인
(D) 주소 찾기　　　　　　　　　　　　정답 (D)

문제 44-46번은 다음 대화를 참조하시오. 영M 미W

M: (44)**We have to talk about the results of the online customer questionnaires we e-mailed two weeks ago. I**

know you've had a lot to do lately, but have you had a chance to review the data yet?
W: Actually, I'm just finished with the report. I'm giving a presentation in the Sales Department this afternoon.
M: Already? Well done. (45)**Do you need me to review it before the meeting?**
W: (45)**The report is just two pages long.**
M: I see. Oh, one more thing. (46)**I'd like to remind you to book a table for us at your friend's restaurant.** The sales team would like to eat there after tomorrow's meeting ends.
W: Okay. I'll do that now.

M: 2주 전에 우리가 이메일로 보낸 온라인 고객 설문지 결과에 대해 논의해야 해요. 최근 할 일이 엄청 많은 것을 알긴 하지만, 그 데이터를 검토해 볼 기회는 있었어요?
W: 사실, 지금 막 보고서를 끝냈어요. 오늘 오후에 영업부에서 프레젠테이션을 할 겁니다.
M: 벌써요? 잘했어요. 회의 전에 내가 그것을 검토할 필요가 있을까요?
W: 보고서는 2페이지밖에 안 됩니다.
M: 알았어요. 아, 한 가지 더 있는데요. 당신 친구 식당에 우리를 위한 테이블을 예약하는 거 잊지 마셨으면 해요. 영업팀이 내일 회의 끝나고 거기서 식사하고 싶어 해요.
W: 알겠어요. 지금 할게요.

44. 남자는 여자가 무엇에 대해 논의하기를 바라는가?
(A) 취업 기회
(B) 설문조사 결과
(C) 납품업체 선정
(D) 고객 불만에 대한 대응　　　　　　정답 (B)

45. 여자가 "보고서는 2페이지밖에 안 됩니다"라고 말하는 이유는?
(A) 성가심을 표현하기 위해
(B) 자신이 시간이 된다는 것을 확인시켜 주기 위해
(C) 더 많은 일을 요청하기 위해
(D) 제안을 거절하기 위해　　　　　　　정답 (D)

46. 남자는 여자에게 무엇에 대해 잊지 말라고 하는가?
(A) 출장 요리 업체에 음식을 주문하는 것
(B) 동료 대신 근무하는 것
(C) 상사에게 전화하는 것
(D) 예약하는 것　　　　　　　　　　　정답 (D)

문제 47-49번은 다음 대화를 참조하시오. 호W 미M

W: (47)**Davis County Building and Grounds Department.** How may I be of assistance?
M: Hello. (48)**I heard you have a new tree-planting program and I'd like to know more about it.**
W: Sure. Residents have the chance to have a tree planted near their street in commemoration of someone special. It's a part of our effort for the county's new beautification project.
M: That sounds good. How do I make a request for it?
W: (49)**You can complete a form that you download from our website. Fill in all of the necessary information and submit the form online.** Then, you'll receive a confirmation e-mail from us.

W: 데이비스 카운티의 건물 및 토지부입니다. 무엇을 도와드릴까요?

M: 안녕하세요. 거기에서 새로운 식목 프로그램을 진행한다고 들었는데, 그것에 대해 좀 더 알고 싶습니다.

W: 물론이죠. 주민들은 누군가 특별한 사람을 기려서, 자신이 살고 있는 거리 근처에 나무를 심을 기회를 갖게 됩니다. 이것은 이 카운티의 새로운 미화 프로젝트를 위한 노력의 일환입니다.

M: 좋은 생각이네요. 그거 어떻게 신청하면 되나요?

W: 우리 웹사이트에서 내려받은 양식을 작성하시면 됩니다. 필요한 모든 정보를 기입하고 그 양식을 온라인으로 제출하세요. 그러면, 우리에게서 이메일 확인서를 받게 될 거예요.

47. 여자는 어떤 부서에서 근무하는가?
(A) 건물 및 토지부
(B) 공공사업부
(C) 공원 및 레크리에이션부
(D) 정보기술부   정답 (A)

48. 남자가 전화를 거는 이유는?
(A) 새로운 프로그램에 대해 물어보기 위해
(B) 등록비에 대해 문의하기 위해
(C) 거리에 쓰러진 나무가 있음을 신고하기 위해
(D) 나무 심는 날이 언제인지 알아보기 위해   정답 (A)

49. 여자는 남자에게 무엇을 하라고 말하는가?
(A) 양식을 직접 제출하기
(B) 나무 값을 미리 지불하기
(C) 나중에 그녀에게 다시 전화하기
(D) 온라인 양식 기입하기   정답 (D)

문제 50-52번은 다음 대화를 참조하시오. 미M 미W

M: Wendy, I have a question about the production of our new Destiny tablet computers. (50)**I saw the latest sales report.** Sales are even better than our most optimistic prediction.

W: Yeah, apparently, it looks like consumer demand is sharply increasing for the new device.

M: So... (51)**Do you think we should hire some temporary workers to run the assembly line?** The holidays are coming up, and I wonder if we'll be able to keep up with the demand.

W: Well, we've got many items in inventory at the warehouse, so we might not need to hire more line workers. (52)**I'll find out exactly how many Destiny tablet computers are available at the warehouse now and let you know after lunch.**

M: 웬디, 새로 나온 우리 데스티니 태블릿 컴퓨터 생산에 대해 질문이 있는데요. 가장 최근에 나온 영업 보고서를 봤어요. 매출이 우리가 가장 낙관적으로 예측했던 것보다도 훨씬 더 좋네요.

W: 맞아요. 보아하니, 그 새 장치에 대한 소비자 수요가 급격히 증가하고 있는 것 같아요.

M: 그래서... 조립 라인을 돌리는데, 임시 직원을 고용해야 할 것 같지 않아요? 연휴가 다가오고 있어서, 우리가 수요에 맞출 수 있을지 모르겠어요.

W: 음, 물류창고에 물건 재고가 많이 있어서, 조립 라인 직원을 더 고용할 필요는 없을지 몰라요. 물류창고에 정확히 데스티니 태블릿 컴퓨터가 몇 대 준비되어 있는지 알아보고 점심시간 후에 알려 드릴게요.

50. 남자는 최근에 무엇을 검토했는가?
(A) 안전 정책
(B) 제품 평가
(C) 영업 보고서
(D) 조립 라인에 대한 지침   정답 (C)

51. 남자는 여자에게 무엇에 대해 질문하는가?
(A) 마감시한을 연장하는 것
(B) 새로 직원을 채용하는 것
(C) 시간 외 근무를 승인하는 것
(D) 물류창고의 재고를 확인하는 것   정답 (B)

52. 남자는 점심 이후에 어떤 자료를 제공받게 되는가?
(A) 재고 상황
(B) 일정이 재조정된 교대근무
(C) 새로운 배송 날짜
(D) 새 컴퓨터에 대한 매출 데이터   정답 (A)

문제 53-55번은 다음 대화를 참조하시오. 호W 영M

W: Mr. Randolph, I'm so glad you haven't left the office for the day yet. About tomorrow's meeting...

M: Yes. It's scheduled for 1:00 P.M., right? (53)**We need to go over the designs for the advertising campaign for Green Thumb Groceries.**

W: I'm really sorry, but I think we should reschedule it. (54)**I forgot that I have a dental appointment at that time.**

M: Okay. Well, we're meeting the representative from Green Thumb the day after tomorrow, so we really have to meet tomorrow. Are you available at 9:00 A.M. instead?

W: That's perfect.

M: Good. Oh, (55)**why don't you post the images for the campaign in a shared folder in drive after we are done?** I want to check them out in advance.

W: (55)**Of course. I'll do that right away.**

W: 랜돌프 씨, 아직 퇴근 안 하셔서 너무 다행이에요. 내일 회의 건 때문에…

M: 예. 오후 1시에 일정이 잡혀 있죠, 맞죠? 그린 썸 그로서리를 위한 광고 캠페인 디자인을 검토해야 하고요.

W: 정말 죄송한데, 그 일정을 다시 조정해야 할 것 같아요. 그 때 제가 치과 진료 예약 있는 것을 깜빡했네요.

M: 알았어요. 그런데 모레 그린 썸 대표로 오는 사람을 만날 거잖아요, 그래서 내일은 정말 회의해야 해요. 대신에 아침 9시에는 시간이 가능해요?

W: 그러면 아주 괜찮죠.

M: 좋아요. 오, 우리 얘기 다 끝나면, 드라이브 공유 폴더에 그 캠페인에 대한 이미지들을 올려 주실래요? 미리 그 이미지들을 확인하고 싶어요.

W: 물론이죠. 지금 당장 할게요.

53. 화자들은 어떤 프로젝트를 작업하고 있는가?
(A) 보도 자료
(B) 광고 캠페인
(C) 재건 공사
(D) 오리엔테이션   정답 (B)

54. 여자가 언급한 문제는 무엇인가?
(A) 그녀는 제 시간에 프로젝트를 끝낼 수가 없다.
(B) 예산에 자금이 충분히 없다.
(C) 그녀는 일정이 겹치는 게 있다.
(D) 동료가 반복적으로 결근했다.   정답 (C)

55. 여자는 뒤이어 무엇을 할 것인가?
(A) 동료에게 전화
(B) 퇴근

(C) 의사에게 진료 보러 가기

(D) 사진 공유

정답 (D)

문제 56-58번은 다음 3자 대화를 참조하시오. 미M 미W 영M

M1: Hello, everybody, (56)**welcome to your third day of training to become industrial fabric workers.** All of you ran the sewing machines well yesterday. Now before we get started, are there any questions?

W: I need to mention something not connected to the training. (57)**This morning, my security badge didn't function properly.** I had to ask the guard to let me into the factory.

M1: Okay. Come and talk to me the first time we take a break. Anything else?

M2: (58)**Mr. Cross, yesterday, you showed us how to keep the thread from tangling. Can we practice doing that?**

M1: Sure, that's a very important thing you all need to know. Please turn on your sewing machines, and let's get started.

M1: 안녕하세요, 여러분. 공업용 직물을 만드는 근로자가 되기 위한 3일째 교육에 오신 것을 환영합니다. 어제는 여러분 전부 다 재봉틀을 잘 돌렸어요. 이제 시작하기 전에, 질문 있으신가요?

W: 교육과 관계없는 것을 언급해야겠는데요. 오늘 아침, 제 보안 신분증이 제대로 작동하지 않았어요. 경비원에게 공장 안으로 들여보내 달라고 부탁해야 했어요.

M1: 알겠습니다. 우리 첫 번째 휴식을 할 때 저에게 오셔서 말씀해 주세요. 그 밖에 다른 거는 없나요?

M2: 크로스 씨, 어제 실이 엉키지 않도록 하는 방법을 저희에게 보여 주셨잖아요. 그것을 연습해볼 수 있을까요?

M1: 좋아요, 그건 여러분 전부가 알아야 하는 아주 중요한 것입니다. 재봉틀 전원을 켜시고 시작해 봅시다.

---

56. 대화는 어디에서 이루어지는 것 같은가?

(A) 식료품점

(B) 자동차 제조업체

(C) 컴퓨터 칩 제조업체

(D) 의류 공장

정답 (D)

57. 오늘 아침 여자는 무엇 때문에 문제를 겪었는가?

(A) 그녀의 주차권

(B) 그녀의 근무 시간 기록표

(C) 그녀의 사무실 컴퓨터

(D) 그녀의 신분증

정답 (D)

58. 화자들은 뒤이어 무엇을 할 것 같은가?

(A) 기술 연습

(B) 교육용 비디오 시청

(C) 양식 작성

(D) 시설 견학

정답 (A)

문제 59-61번은 다음 대화를 참조하시오. 호W 영M

W: Hello, Harold. (59)**I know we made plans to review the applications for a medical assistant today. But, well, (60) I'm still working on my slides for the healthcare conference next week.**

M: Sure. (60)**I've given presentations there in the past.** You

---

have to be well prepared.

W: So should we look at the applications next week?

M: (61)**Why don't we just hold off on hiring someone until a month from now?**

W: That's fine with me. But are you sure we can wait that long?

M: It's all right. (61)**Denise said she's willing to stay here until we find her replacement.**

W: 안녕하세요, 해럴드. 오늘 의료 조무사를 위한 지원서를 검토하기로 계획한 것을 알고 있는데요. 그런데, 음, 제가 아직도 다음 주에 있을 의료보건 총회를 위한 슬라이드를 작업하고 있어요.

M: 알았어요. 과거에 저도 거기서 프레젠테이션을 한 적이 있어요. 준비를 잘 하셔야 할 거예요.

W: 그러니 다음 주에 지원서를 검토해도 될까요?

M: 그냥 지금부터 앞으로 한 달 후로 사람 뽑는 것을 미루는 게 어때요?

W: 저는 괜찮아요. 그런데 그렇게 오래 기다렸다 해도 되나요?

M: 괜찮아요. 우리가 자기 후임을 찾을 때까지 데니스가 기꺼이 여기 계속 남아 있겠다고 했거든요.

---

59. 화자들은 어떤 산업에서 일하는 것 같은가?

(A) 제조

(B) 오락 연예

(C) 의료

(D) 음식 서비스

정답 (C)

60. 남자가 "과거에 저도 거기서 프레젠테이션을 한 적이 있어요"라고 말할 때 무엇을 의미하는가?

(A) 그는 지금 만날 시간이 없다.

(B) 그는 프레젠테이션 하는 것을 즐기지 않는다.

(C) 그는 여자의 상황을 이해한다.

(D) 그는 여자에게 도움을 줄 수 있다.

정답 (C)

61. 화자들은 무엇을 하기로 결정했는가?

(A) 같이 프레젠테이션 슬라이드 작업하기

(B) 저녁에 시간 외 근무 하기

(C) 신입 직원 찾는 것을 연기하기

(D) 점심을 위해 잠깐 쉬기

정답 (C)

문제 62-64번은 다음 대화와 카탈로그를 참조하시오. 미M 미W

M: This is Delmont Ceramics. How may I help you?

W: I'd like to order some plates that are advertised in your catalog for my new café. (62)**They're the ones which have crisscrossed stripes on them.**

M: Yes, I know them. Are you aware that those are a limited edition?

W: Really? Are they still available? (63)**My café will be opening its doors in October.**

M: They're still in stock, but (64)**that pattern will be discontinued at the end of December. It will be hard to get replacements after that.**

W: Thanks for letting me know. I'll order some extra ones in that case.

M: 델몬트 세라믹입니다. 무엇을 도와드릴까요?

W: 귀사의 카탈로그에 광고된 접시를 저의 새 카페를 위해서 주문하고 싶습니다. 접시 위에 열십자 모양의 줄무늬가 있는 접시예요.

M: 예, 어떤 접시인지 압니다. 그 접시가 한정판이란 것을 아세요?

W: 정말이에요? 아직도 구입할 수 있어요? 제 카페가 10월에 문을 열거든요.
M: 그 접시는 아직 재고가 있긴 하지만, 그 패턴이 12월 말에 단종될 거예요. 그 이후로는 대체품을 구하기가 어려울 거예요.
W: 알려 줘서 감사해요. 그렇다면 여분으로 그 접시를 더 주문해야겠네요.

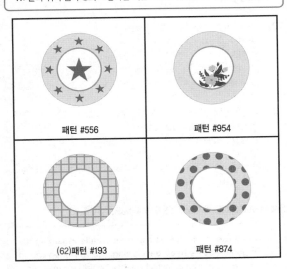

패턴 #556

패턴 #954

(62)패턴 #193

패턴 #874

62. 그래픽을 보시오. 어느 접시 패턴에 여자가 관심이 있는가?
(A) 954번
(B) 193번
(C) 874번
(D) 556번　　　　　　　　　　　　　　정답 (B)

63. 여자는 10월에 무슨 일이 있을 거라고 말하는가?
(A) 신제품이 출시될 것이다.
(B) 가게가 접시의 재고조사를 할 것이다.
(C) 새로운 업체가 문을 열 것이다.
(D) 지사가 이전할 것이다.　　　　　　정답 (C)

64. 남자는 어떤 문제를 언급하는가?
(A) 여러 품목이 수송 중에 파손되었다.
(B) 카탈로그에 잘못된 정보가 들어 있다.
(C) 어떤 물품은 구입할 수 없을 것이다.
(D) 모든 주문에 대해 배송비가 적용될 것이다.　정답 (C)

문제 65–67번은 다음 대화와 티켓 확인서를 참조하시오. 호W 미M

W: Good morning. (65)**This is Bayside Ferry.**
M: Hello. I have a question about my reservation for my trip to Andover. My confirmation code is 8590AW.
W: Okay. Hold on a minute… I'll look it up. Ah, you have four tickets.
M: Correct. (66)**But I wonder if you have a ferry leaving earlier in the day.**
W: Yes, (66)**we do have one that leaves two hours earlier in the day.** Tickets are available at the same price.
M: Great. Can you change my tickets, please?
W: Sure. (67)**Should I send the new information to the same e-mail address that we sent the original reservation to?**
M: (67)**Yes.** That would be perfect.

W: 안녕하세요, 베이사이드 페리입니다.
M: 안녕하세요. 앤도버행 여행에 대한 제 예약 건 때문에 질문이 있어요. 확인 코드가 8590AW입니다.
W: 알겠습니다. 잠깐 기다려 보세요… 찾아볼게요. 아, 티켓 4장이 예약되어 있네요.
M: 맞습니다. 그런데 그 날 좀 더 일찍 떠나는 페리가 있나 모르겠네요.
W: 예, 그 날 두 시간 일찍 떠나는 페리가 하나 있어요. 티켓은 같은 가격에 구입 가능합니다.
M: 잘됐네요. 제 티켓을 변경할 수 있나요?
W: 물론이죠. 원래 예약 정보를 보냈던 같은 이메일 주소로 새 정보를 보낼까요?
M: 예, 그렇게 해주시면 아주 좋죠.

티켓 확인 코드: 8590AW	
승객 숫자	4
날짜	9월 21일
(66)출발 시간	오전 10시
티켓당 가격	$15
총 가격	$60

65. 남자는 어떤 종류의 업체에 전화하는가?
(A) 버스 회사
(B) 페리 회사
(C) 항공사
(D) 기차 회사　　　　　　　　　　　정답 (B)

66. 그래픽을 보시오. 어떤 숫자가 갱신될 것인가?
(A) 4
(B) 21
(C) 10
(D) 15　　　　　　　　　　　　　　정답 (C)

67. 여자는 뒤이어 무엇을 할 것 같은가?
(A) 이메일 보내기
(B) 계정 정보 물어보기
(C) 전화번호 확인하기
(D) 좌석 배정 확인하기　　　　　　정답 (A)

문제 68–70번은 다음 대화와 비교 차트를 참조하시오. 미W 영M

W: Greg, (68)**where are the plastic zip ties? We used them a couple of days ago to tie some computer cables together.**
M: I still have them on my desk. What do you need them for?
W: I've got to attach some electronic trackers to my suitcase. (69)**I'm flying to Greece tomorrow to have a meeting with some potential clients.** I want to make sure I keep track of my luggage while I'm travelling.
M: I could use some of those. I'm always losing things. How did you decide which ones to buy?
W: The feature that I think is the most important is battery life. (70)**I just purchased the one that had the longest lasting battery.**

W: 그레그, 플라스틱 케이블 타이가 어디에 있어요? 이틀 전에 컴퓨터 케이블들을 같이 묶느라 그것들을 사용했는데요.

M: 아직도 내 책상에 있어요. 무엇 때문에 케이블 타이가 필요해요?

W: 내 여행가방에 전자 추적장치를 붙여야 해요. 내일 잠재 고객들과 회의를 하기 위해 비행기 타고 그리스로 가거든요. 여행하는 동안 내 짐들이 어디에 있는지 확실하게 계속해서 파악하고 싶어요.

M: 나도 그런 것을 사용해볼 수 있겠군요. 저도 항상 물건들을 잃어버리거든요. 어떤 것을 사야 할지 어떻게 결정했어요?

W: 내가 생각하는 가장 중요한 기능은 배터리 수명이에요. 저는 배터리 수명이 가장 오래 가는 것으로 막 구매했어요.

전자 추적장치

회사	배터리 수명
설리	6개월
베스트 일렉트로닉스	1년
(70)웨이벌리	2년
TRM 주식회사	9개월

68. 여자는 남자에게 무엇을 요청하는가?
(A) 비닐 봉지
(B) 잠재 고객 명단
(C) 케이블 타이
(D) 컴퓨터 케이블 　　　　　　　　정답 (C)

69. 여자는 내일 무엇을 할 것인가?
(A) 더 많은 전선 케이블 주문하기
(B) 출장 가기
(C) 상사 만나기
(D) 재고 파악하기 　　　　　　　　정답 (B)

70. 그래픽을 보시오. 여자는 어느 회사로부터 구매했는가?
(A) 설리
(B) 베스트 일렉트로닉스
(C) 웨이벌리
(D) TRM 주식회사 　　　　　　　　정답 (C)

Part 4

문제 71-73번은 다음 광고를 참조하시오. [미M]

M: Are you looking for a venue to hold your next business event? Then, look no further than Davidson's. (71)**We have great food and private dining rooms which combine to make Davidson's the best place for business gatherings.** But there are more reasons to choose Davidson's. (72)**We've got a friendly and experienced wait staff. Our chefs are also the best in the business.** Do you plan to host an event at your office? That's fine. We can bring the food to you. (73)**Check out our catering packages on our web page.**

다음 회사 행사를 치를 장소를 찾고 계시나요? 그렇다면 더 멀리 볼 것도 없이 데이비드슨즈가 있습니다. 우리는 맛있는 음식과 전용 다이닝룸도 갖추고 있는데요, 이 두 개가 결합하여 데이비드슨즈를 사업 모임을 위한 최적의 장소로 만들고 있습니다. 그런데 데이비드슨즈를 선택할 이유들이 더 있습니다. 우리는 친절하고 경력이 많은 서빙 직원들을 두고 있습니다. 우리 요리사는 또한 업계에서 최고입니다. 사무실에서 행사를 치를 계획이신가요? 그것도 좋습니다. 우리가 음식을 갖고 갈 수 있습니다. 우리 웹 페이지에서 출장 요리 패키지 상품을 확인해 보세요.

71. 무엇이 광고되고 있는 것 같은가?
(A) 식당
(B) 호텔
(C) 컨벤션 센터
(D) 물류 회사 　　　　　　　　정답 (A)

72. 이 사업체는 무엇으로 잘 알려져 있는가?
(A) 가격
(B) 직원
(C) 위치
(D) 세심한 정성 　　　　　　　　정답 (B)

73. 화자에 따르면, 웹 페이지에서 무엇을 찾을 수 있는가?
(A) 센터까지 운전해서 가는 길 안내
(B) 출장 요리 옵션
(C) 연락처
(D) 영업 시간 　　　　　　　　정답 (B)

문제 74-76번은 다음 회의 발췌 내용을 참조하시오. [영M]

M: (74)**I'd like to provide you with an update regarding the video game you've been developing.** We've just agreed to partner with a video game publishing firm that will help market our product. I have the initial contract they sent me. (75)**I'm happy to say that the terms being proposed are favorable to us. We'll get a payment as soon as we sign the contract.** (76)But our lawyers want to make sure that the programmers are satisfied with the terms of the contract so that they can negotiate a few other provisions in the contract. I'll e-mail the document this afternoon.

여러분이 개발하고 있는 비디오 게임에 관해서 최신 소식을 알려 드리고 싶습니다. 우리는 지금 비디오 게임 출판업체와 제휴하기로 했는데, 이 회사가 우리 제품을 내놓는 데 도움을 줄 것입니다. 그들이 저에게 보낸 초기 계약서를 가지고 있습니다. 제시되고 있는 조건들이 우리에게 유리하다고 말씀드리게 되어 기쁩니다. 계약에 서명을 하자마자 돈을 지불받을 것입니다. 그렇지만 우리 쪽 변호사들은 프로그래머들이 그 계약 조건에 만족하는지 확실히 해두고 싶어합니다. 그래야 계약서의 다른 조항을 몇 개 더 협상할 수 있으니까요. 오늘 오후에 그 서류를 이메일로 보내 드리겠습니다.

74. 청자들은 누구인가?
(A) 제품 개발업자
(B) 변호사
(C) 잠재적인 투자자
(D) 서적 출판업자 　　　　　　　　정답 (A)

75. 화자에 따르면, 계약에 대해 청자들에게 무엇이 유리한가?
(A) 제품이 아주 많이 광고될 것이다.
(B) 이자율이 낮아지고 있다.
(C) 즉각적인 지불이 이루어질 것이다.
(D) 연장된 품질보증서가 제공될 것이다. 　정답 (C)

76. 화자가 "오늘 오후에 그 서류를 이메일로 보내 드리겠습니다"라고 말할 때 무엇을 함축하는가?
(A) 그는 청자들이 양식을 작성하기를 원한다.
(B) 그는 청자들의 의견을 듣고 싶어한다.
(C) 그는 마감시간에 맞출 수 없을 것이다.
(D) 그는 청자들에게 변호사를 만날 것을 제안한다. 　정답 (B)

W: (77)Thanks for taking part in this tour of our solar-panel manufacturing plant. Here at Chandler Solar Power Limited, we believe it's important for people to get a firsthand look at the production of the solar panels that convert light energy into electricity, which we can then use to power our homes and businesses. (78)Before the tour begins, you need to be aware that safety always comes first here. You must wear your hardhats you were provided and keep them on at all times while in the factory. Now, (79)the first place we're going to visit will be the showroom. Let me show you the newest models of our solar panels so that you can fully understand how they work.

태양열판 제조 공장에 대한 이번 투어에 참가해 주셔서 감사합니다. 여기 챈들러 태양열 발전 주식회사에서는, 사람들이 태양열판 생산과정을 직접 보는 게 중요하다고 생각합니다. 태양열판은 빛 에너지를 전기로 바꿔 주고, 그러면 우리는 그 전기를 이용해서 가정과 사업체에 전기 동력을 제공합니다. 투어가 시작되기 전에, 여기서는 먼저 안전이 항상 최우선이라는 것을 아셔야 합니다. 여러분은 제공받은 안전모를 착용하고, 공장에 있는 동안 항상 계속 착용하고 있어야 합니다. 이제, 우리가 방문하게 될 첫 번째 곳은 제품 전시실입니다. 여러분이 태양열판이 어떻게 작동하는지 충분히 이해하실 수 있도록 우리 태양열판의 최신 모델을 보여 드리겠습니다.

77. 투어는 어디서 이루어지고 있는가?
(A) 물류창고
(B) 자동차 부품 공장
(C) 공사 현장
(D) 태양열판 공장 　　　　　　　　　정답 (D)

78. 청자들은 무엇을 잊지 말라는 주의를 받는가?
(A) 개인소지품에 신경 쓰기
(B) 보호장비 착용하기
(C) 일행과 같이 있기
(D) 게시된 표지 따라가기 　　　　　　정답 (B)

79. 청자들은 투어에서 맨 먼저 무엇을 보는가?
(A) 제품 모델
(B) 공장의 평면도
(C) 조립 라인의 사진
(D) 보호 안경 　　　　　　　　　　　정답 (A)

M: Thank you for listening to *Business Today*. (80)This evening, we're going to take a deep dive into the topic of making a transition to a new career. Transitioning to a new field is not always easy. In fact, it can be challenging. (81)You'll need to emphasize any transferable skills you have which can be useful at your new job. Basically, what specific skills and expertise do you currently own that could add value to your new role? And how can you promote yourself on professional social media platforms? To explore this together, (82)Jeremy Nelson, the CEO of Make it Yours, a popular job search app, is here with us in the studio today. Welcome, Mr. Nelson.

〈비즈니스 투데이〉를 청취해 주셔서 감사합니다. 오늘 저녁은, 새로운 직업

으로 전환하는 주제에 심층적으로 들어가 보겠습니다. 새로운 분야로 이동하는 것은 항상 쉽지만은 않습니다. 사실 어려울 수 있습니다. 여러분은 새 직장에서 도움이 될 수 있는, 이전 가능한 여러분의 능력을 강조할 필요가 있습니다. 기본적으로 여러분은 현재 새 역할에 부가적인 가치를 더해줄 수 있는 어떤 구체적인 능력과 전문지식을 가지고 있나요? 그리고 전문적인 소셜 미디어 플랫폼에서 여러분 자신을 어떻게 홍보할 수 있을까요? 이것을 함께 탐색하기 위해서, 인기 있는 구직 앱인 메이크 잇 유어스의 최고 경영자인 제레미 넬슨이 여기 스튜디오에 오늘 함께 하셨습니다. 환영합니다, 넬슨 씨.

80. 에피소드의 초점은 무엇인가?
(A) 직업을 바꾸는 것
(B) 계약을 협상하는 것
(C) 커뮤니케이션 능력을 개선하는 것
(D) 고객을 좀 더 잘 모시는 것 　　　정답 (A)

81. 화자는 직업 전환에 있어서 무엇이 중요하다고 말하는가?
(A) 다른 직종에서도 바꿔 쓸 수 있는 능력을 강조하는 것
(B) 더 많은 교육을 받는 것
(C) 온라인 마케팅에 관한 회의에 참여하는 것
(D) 업계 규정을 따르는 것 　　　　　정답 (A)

82. 제레미 넬슨은 누구인가?
(A) 라디오 진행자
(B) 경영학 강사
(C) 회사 임원
(D) 정부 관료 　　　　　　　　　　　정답 (C)

W: Hello. (83)This is Delilah Murray, the set designer for the Octagon Theater. I met you a couple of days ago. As you're directing the new play at the theater, I'd like to meet to discuss a few suggestions I have. I reviewed the script and have a few ideas for the background. (83) (84)You mentioned you're concerned about a lack of time to create a set. Just so you know, (84)my team is large, and we have numerous props we used for previous productions. (85)I'll be away to visit some relatives this evening. But if you are available to meet this weekend, I have a flexible schedule then.

안녕하세요. 저는 옥타곤 극장의 무대 디자이너, 딜라일라 머레이입니다. 이틀 전에 뵈었었죠. 당신이 극장에서 새 연극을 연출하시므로, 제가 갖고 있는 몇 가지 제안에 대해 만나서 논의하고 싶습니다. 대본을 검토했는데, 배경에 대한 몇 가지 아이디어가 떠올랐습니다. 무대를 만들 시간이 부족하기 때문에 걱정된다고 언급하셨잖아요. 참고로 드리는 말씀인데, 제 팀은 규모가 크고, 이전 작품들에 우리가 사용했던 수많은 연극 소품들이 있습니다. 오늘 저녁 저는 친척을 만나러 타지로 나갑니다. 그런데 이번 주말에 만날 시간이 있으시다면, 그때는 일정이 유연합니다.

83. 전화 메시지는 주로 무엇에 관한 것인가?
(A) 좌석 배치도 확인하기
(B) 연기자들 찾기
(C) 세트 디자인하기
(D) 대본 수정하기 　　　　　　　　　정답 (C)

84. 화자가 "제 팀은 규모가 커요"라고 말하는 이유는?
(A) 문제를 설명하기 위해

ACTUAL TEST 11

(B) 사과하기 위해
(C) 제안을 거절하기 위해
(D) 안심시켜 주기 위해　　　　　　　　정답 (D)

85. 화자가 오늘 저녁 만날 수 없는 이유는?
(A) 공연자들을 면접 봐야 한다.
(B) 시외로 출장 갈 것이다.
(C) 가족 구성원들을 만나야 한다.
(D) 진료 예약이 있다.　　　　　　　　정답 (C)

문제 86-88번은 다음 담화를 참조하시오. 미W

W: Welcome to Peterman Financial. (86)**I'm Sarah Brentwood, the coordinator of our internship program. I hope your summer internship here is entertaining and rewarding.** Before the training session starts, we need to handle some administrative matters. When you entered here, (87)**you were given a packet full of documents.** It contains information about how to log on to your e-mail and how to submit timesheets. Let me discuss those issues now. (88)**In an hour or so, you'll go to the security desk to get your identification badges.** Those are necessary to enter and exit the office.

피터맨 파이낸셜에 오신 것을 환영합니다. 저는 사라 브렌트우드이고 우리 인턴십 프로그램의 코디네이터입니다. 이곳에서의 여러분의 여름 인턴십이 즐거우면서도 보람되기를 바랍니다. 교육을 시작하기 전에, 몇 가지 행정적인 문제를 처리할 필요가 있습니다. 여러분이 여기로 들어오실 때, 여러분은 서류가 가득한 봉투를 받았습니다. 거기에는 여러분의 이메일에 로그인하는 방법과 근무 시간 기록표를 제출하는 방법에 관한 정보가 들어 있습니다. 지금 그 문제들에 대해 말씀드리겠습니다. 한 시간 정도 후에, 여러분은 보안과로 가서 여러분의 신분증을 받게 될 것입니다. 그 신분증은 사무실을 출입할 때 필요합니다.

86. 담화는 누구를 대상으로 하는 것 같은가?
(A) 매니저
(B) 트레이너
(C) 인턴
(D) 금융 분석가　　　　　　　　정답 (C)

87. 청자들은 무엇을 받았는가?
(A) 프로젝트에 대한 견적서
(B) 자료 봉투
(C) 고객 설문서
(D) 직원용 주차권　　　　　　　　정답 (B)

88. 화자는 청자들이 한 시간 후에 무엇을 하게 될 것이라고 말하는가?
(A) 사무실의 간단한 구경
(B) 근무 시간 기록표 제출
(C) 보안 신분증 수령
(D) 사진 촬영　　　　　　　　정답 (C)

문제 89-91번은 다음 회의 발췌 내용을 참조하시오. 영M

M: (89)**Last week, I attended a conference** where I had the opportunity to speak with other small business owners located throughout the region. We exchanged quite a few helpful ideas. For instance, a few of them talked about how hard it can be for

customers to navigate corporate web pages. (90)**This is a big problem when customers are looking for information like an e-mail address or a phone number** to contact someone to discuss a matter. I talked to Mitch in IT and asked him to redesign our website to make it more user friendly and more navigable. Look up here. (91)**I'll demonstrate the new design for our website that I think should be ready soon.**

지난주에 저는 어떤 총회에 참석했었는데, 거기서 이 지역 전역의 다른 소기업 소유주들과 얘기를 나눌 기회가 있었습니다. 우리는 꽤나 많은 유용한 아이디어를 교환했습니다. 예를 들어, 그들 중 몇 명은 고객들이 회사 웹 페이지에서 자료를 찾아 돌아다니는 것이 얼마나 힘들 수 있는지에 관해 얘기했습니다. 이것은 고객들이 문제를 논의하기 위해서 누군가에게 연락할 이메일 주소나 전화번호 같은 정보를 찾을 때는 아주 큰 문제입니다. 저는 정보기술부의 미치에게 우리 웹사이트가 좀 더 사용자 편의적이고 좀 더 돌아다니기 편하게 되도록 다시 디자인하라고 요청했습니다. 여기를 보세요. 제 생각에 곧 준비가 될 우리 웹사이트의 새로운 디자인에 대해 설명을 드리겠습니다.

89. 화자는 지난주에 무엇을 했는가?
(A) 총회에 참석했다.
(B) 세미나에서 시연회를 했다.
(C) 직원 몇 명을 교육시켰다.
(D) 출장으로 해외에 갔다.　　　　　　　　정답 (A)

90. 고객들은 무엇을 찾는 데 어려움을 겪고 있는가?
(A) 계정 아카이브
(B) 연락처
(C) 회원 자격 요건
(D) 불편신고 서식　　　　　　　　정답 (B)

91. 화자는 뒤이어 무엇을 할 것인가?
(A) 슬라이드 프로젝터 켜기
(B) 다음 연사 소개하기
(C) 프레젠테이션 하기
(D) 팸플릿 나눠 주기　　　　　　　　정답 (C)

문제 92-94번은 다음 연설을 참조하시오. 미W

W: Thanks for coming to today's city council meeting. (92) **I'm Mayor Sellers**, and we're going to talk about tourism first. We're all pleased that (93)**the documentary about our town's history, which was filmed here a year ago, is succeeding at the box office.** We've already gotten hundreds of inquiries from travel agents around the world asking about accommodations and tours. That will be great news for local businesses. However, some residents are concerned about the sudden influx of large numbers of tourists, which may cause damage to their streets. (94)**I think they have a point. We should come up with some suggestions to handle the expected issue.** Those old roads weren't constructed for traffic.

오늘 시의회 회의에 와주셔서 감사합니다. 저는 시장 셀러스이고, 우선 관광에 대해 얘기해 보겠습니다. 1년 전에 여기서 촬영을 한 우리 마을의 역사에 대한 다큐멘터리가 박스 오피스에서 성공을 거두고 있다고 해서 우리 모두 기뻐하고 있습니다. 우리는 이미 전세계의 여행사 직원들로부터 숙박 시설과 관광에 대해 물어보는 문의를 수백 건이나 받았습니다. 이것은 지역 사업체들에게는 좋은 소식일 것입니다. 그렇지만 일부 주민들은 엄청난

수의 관광객 유입으로 그들의 도로에 손상을 줄지도 모른다고 우려하고 있습니다. 그들의 말이 일리가 있다고 생각합니다. 예상되는 문제를 처리하기 위해서 제안들을 내야 합니다. 그 오래된 도로들은 차들이 왕래하게 건설된 것은 아니니까요.

92. 화자는 누구인가?
(A) 시 관료
(B) 관광 가이드
(C) 역사 강사
(D) 영화 감독 　　　　　　　　　　정답 (A)

93. 마을에 작년에 무슨 일이 있었는가?
(A) 국제 관광 컨벤션이 개최되었다.
(B) 역사적인 행사가 열렸다
(C) 일부 도로가 파손되었다.
(D) 다큐멘터리 영화가 그곳에서 촬영되었다. 　정답 (D)

94. 화자가 "그 오래된 도로들은 차들이 왕래하게 건설된 것은 아니었어요"라고 말하는 이유는?
(A) 불만을 표현하기 위해
(B) 새로운 프로젝트를 설명하기 위해
(C) 우려를 표하기 위해
(D) 감사를 표하기 위해 　　　　　　　정답 (C)

문제 95-97번은 다음 안내와 매장 배치도를 참조하시오. 영M

M: We at Diamond Books are pleased to announce that it's time for our annual meet-the-author series to begin. (95)This Saturday afternoon, famous author Reggie Goodman will visit us. He'll read an excerpt from his newest novel, which is set in Asia. He'll also sign copies and answer your questions. (96) Be sure to visit the fiction aisle to find copies of his work. And (97)don't forget to enter the drawing to win a $10 gift card that you can use at our café. We've got all kinds of coffees and homemade baked goods.

우리 다이아몬드 서점에서는 연례 저자와의 만남 시리즈가 시작될 시간임을 알리게 되어 기쁩니다. 이번 주 토요일 오후에 유명한 작가인 레지 굿맨이 저희 서점을 방문하십니다. 그는 아시아를 배경으로 한 자신의 최신 소설에서 발췌한 내용을 낭독할 것입니다. 그는 또한 책에 서명을 할 것이며 질문에 답할 것입니다. 꼭 소설 코너를 방문하셔서 그의 작품들을 찾아보십시오. 그리고 잊지 말고 저희 카페에서 사용 가능한 10달러 기프트 카드를 받을 수 있는 추첨에 참가하세요. 모든 종류의 커피와 홈메이드 제빵류를 다 갖추고 있습니다.

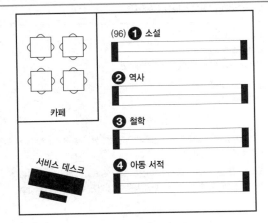

(96) ❶ 소설
❷ 역사
❸ 철학
❹ 아동 서적

카페
서비스 데스크

95. 화자에 따르면, 토요일에 무슨 일이 있을 것인가?
(A) 서점이 문을 닫을 것이다.
(B) 저자가 방문할 것이다.
(C) 새로운 도서 배송품이 배달될 것이다.
(D) 시즌 세일이 시작될 것이다. 　　　정답 (B)

96. 그래픽을 보시오. 청자들에게 어느 통로로 가라고 안내하는가?
(A) 통로 1
(B) 통로 2
(C) 통로 3
(D) 통로 4 　　　　　　　　　　　정답 (A)

97. 청자들은 무엇을 탈 수 있는가?
(A) 무료 도서
(B) 기프트 카드
(C) 홈메이드 빵
(D) 할인 쿠폰 　　　　　　　　　　정답 (B)

문제 98-100번은 다음 전화 메시지와 공고문을 참조하시오. 미W

W: Hello, Mr. Deacon. I'm Jessica Miller. (98)I operate a forklift in the Shipping Department. I'm calling regarding the safety course I'm supposed to take. I need to change the date I'm scheduled for. I'm registered for the session on March 28. However, (99)I was just informed that we need to fill a huge order at the end of the month, so I'm going to be busy all that week. (100)I would like to attend the session that starts at 10:00 A.M. Could you please sign me up for it? Thank you.

안녕하세요, 디콘 씨. 저는 제시카 밀러입니다. 배송부에서 지게차를 운전하고 있습니다. 제가 받기로 되어 있는 안전 과정 때문에 전화드렸어요. 제가 일정이 잡혀 있는 날짜를 변경해야 합니다. 3월 28일 세션에 등록되어 있어요. 그런데 이달 말에 대량 주문을 처리해야 한다는 소식을 방금 들어서, 그 주 내내 바쁠 거예요. 오전 10시에 시작하는 세션에 참석하고 싶은데요. 그 시간으로 저를 등록해 주시겠습니까? 감사합니다.

안전 과정
과정 중 하나를 신청해 주세요:
3월 11일, 오후 3시 – 오후 6시
(100)3월 15일, 오전 10시 – 오후 1시
3월 22일, 오후 2시 – 오후 5시
3월 28일, 오전 11시 – 오후 2시

98. 화자는 어디에서 근무하는 것 같은가?
(A) 직업 훈련 학교
(B) 기계 수리점
(C) 물류창고
(D) 항구 선착장 　　　　　　　　　　정답 (C)

99. 화자의 부서는 이달 말에 무엇을 하기로 되어 있는가?
(A) 월례 회의 개최
(B) 시간 외 근무
(C) 대량 주문 준비
(D) 장비 수리 　　　　　　　　　　　정답 (C)

100. 그래픽을 보시오. 화자는 어느 세션에 신청하고 싶어 하는가?
(A) 3월 11일
(B) 3월 15일
(C) 3월 22일
(D) 3월 28일
　　　　　　　　　　　　　　　　　정답 (B)

Part 5

101. 다음 주 금요일부터 소매점은 주중 오후 10시까지 매장에 고객을 들일 수 있다.
　　　　　　　　　　　　　　　　　정답 (C)

102. 산 근처에 있는 주택은 18세기 중반에 건축되었지만, 여전히 주택은 훌륭한 상태로 남아 있다.
　　　　　　　　　　　　　　　　　정답 (B)

103. 최근 우리의 설문 조사에 따르면, 노동력 부족이 증가하는 수요를 충족시키는 데 있어 가장 큰 걸림돌이었다.
　　　　　　　　　　　　　　　　　정답 (B)

104. 한 가지 가능한 결론은 새로운 시스템이 제조 공정을 능률화시켜 생산성을 증대시킬 것이라는 점이다.
　　　　　　　　　　　　　　　　　정답 (C)

105. 사무실에서 낭비되는 에너지를 줄이기 위해서는, 직원 개개인이 매일 퇴근 시에 컴퓨터가 꺼져 있는지 확인하는 것이 중요하다.
　　　　　　　　　　　　　　　　　정답 (A)

106. 공중 보건 전문가들은 시에서 질병을 예방하고 의료 시설의 개선을 위한 새로운 방안을 모색하는 데 전념하고 있다.
　　　　　　　　　　　　　　　　　정답 (D)

107. 인터넷 사용자는 사이트에 접속하기 위해서는 본인 확인을 해야 하며, 기업들은 본인 확인 절차가 완료되면 모든 개인 정보를 삭제해야 한다.
　　　　　　　　　　　　　　　　　정답 (D)

108. 악천후로 인해 항공편이 지연되거나 취소되는 경우, 1회에 한하여 무료로 항공편을 변경해 드릴 수 있습니다.
　　　　　　　　　　　　　　　　　정답 (B)

109. 새 레스토랑에 대한 부정적인 평이 신문에 실린 후, 지난 몇 주간 예약 건수가 확연히 감소했다.
　　　　　　　　　　　　　　　　　정답 (D)

110. 목소리가 강하고 말주변이 더 유창할수록, 고객에게 좋은 첫인상을 줄 가능성이 더 커진다.
　　　　　　　　　　　　　　　　　정답 (C)

111. 요즘 레저 스포츠용품 제조업체들은 무거운 등산복 대신 도보와 트레킹에 적합한 의류와 신발 판매를 서두르고 있다.
　　　　　　　　　　　　　　　　　정답 (C)

112. 이 도시는 해양산업 내의 많은 기업들이 위치한 곳으로, 그 중 일부는 세계 최대의 운송 회사들과 해상 보험 회사들이다.
　　　　　　　　　　　　　　　　　정답 (B)

113. 우리가 필요한 사무용품에 대한 주문은 인사부장을 통해서만 이뤄져야 함을 알아 두시길 바랍니다.
　　　　　　　　　　　　　　　　　정답 (C)

114. 급속한 인구 노령화를 고려할 때, 노동 시장이 곧 상승할 것 같지 않으며, 청년 실업 또한 그러하다.
　　　　　　　　　　　　　　　　　정답 (D)

115. 건강 전문가들은 사람들이 바이러스 감염을 피하기 위해서는 손을 자주 씻고 수건이나 휴지를 같이 쓰지 말 것을 제안한다.
　　　　　　　　　　　　　　　　　정답 (A)

116. 여기 우리의 새로운 소프트웨어 프로그램을 컴퓨터에 설치하는 것이 얼마나 쉬운지 보여 주는 빠르고 쉬운 안내서가 있다.
　　　　　　　　　　　　　　　　　정답 (C)

117. 최근 설문조사에 따르면, 정보업계의 여성 직원의 수가 남성의 수보다 훨씬 더 높다.
　　　　　　　　　　　　　　　　　정답 (A)

118. 지난달의 회계 세미나는 150명이 넘는 공인 회계사들이 참석하여 지금까지 가장 성공적인 것이었다.
　　　　　　　　　　　　　　　　　정답 (D)

119. 세계 경제가 불경기에서 회복되면서 세계 수요 회복에 힘입어 원유 가격이 급격히 올랐다.
　　　　　　　　　　　　　　　　　정답 (C)

120. 구체적인 날짜는 아직 밝혀지지 않았지만, 일부 업계 전문가들은 양사가 내년 상반기에 합병에 착수할 수도 있다고 예측했다.
　　　　　　　　　　　　　　　　　정답 (D)

121. 라이언 씨는 직원 회의에 참석할 수 없었지만, 그는 회의 내용을 파악하기 위해 동료에게 회의록을 보내 달라고 요청했다.
　　　　　　　　　　　　　　　　　정답 (C)

122. 비록 켈러 씨의 소설은 독자들로부터 격찬을 받았지만, 일부 비평가들은 가장 엄격한 비평가들이었기 때문에 그의 작품에 완전히 불만족스러워했다.
　　　　　　　　　　　　　　　　　정답 (C)

123. 요즘, 많은 사람들은 최신 소식과 다양한 오락거리를 온라인으로 공유하는 것에 익숙하다.
　　　　　　　　　　　　　　　　　정답 (D)

124. 시 정부는 국제 관광객들이 더욱 쾌적하게 쇼핑을 즐길 수 있고, 꼭 가봐야 할 시의 명소를 좀 더 안전하게 방문할 수 있도록 더욱 안전한 환경을 조성할 것이다.
　　　　　　　　　　　　　　　　　정답 (B)

125. 투자가 감소하고 실업률이 증가할 때는 대기업들이 투자하는 것이 극히 중요하다.
　　　　　　　　　　　　　　　　　정답 (A)

126. 우리가 직면한 가장 큰 문제는 바로 정부가 세수 감소로 어려움을 겪고 있으며, 정부의 지출은 향후 6개월 안에 연간 예산을 초과할 것이라는 사실이다.
　　　　　　　　　　　　　　　　　정답 (B)

127. 60세 이상의 운전자들은 우편으로 그들의 운전면허증을 갱신하는 것이 허용되어서는 안 되는데, 이것은 많은 도시의 표준 관행이다.
　　　　　　　　　　　　　　　　　정답 (C)

128. 이 계약은 양 당사자가 서명한 날짜부터 유효하며 계약이 취소 또는 종료될 때까지 그 효력이 지속될 것이다.
　　　　　　　　　　　　　　　　　정답 (D)

129. 광고 캠페인의 성공 덕분에, 최근 6개월 간 우리 휴대 전화 가입자 수가 꾸준하게 증가해왔다.
　　　　　　　　　　　　　　　　　정답 (D)

130. 이 의학 연구를 계속하고 싶은 자는 누구든 본사에 보고해야 하며, 이사회로부터 승인을 받아야 한다.
　　　　　　　　　　　　　　　　　정답 (B)

Part 6

문제 131-134번은 다음 안내문을 참조하시오.

선라이즈 아파트
레이크 타호 대로 3411번지
사우스 레이크 타호, 캘리포니아 주 96150

공지 번호: 3124
날짜: 4월 10일

주민 공고

우리 테니스 코트에 대한 보수 공사가 일정보다 한 주 빠른 4월 7일에 완료되었습니다.

테니스 코트는 아파트 레크리에이션부 445-9815로 전화하셔서 예약될 수 있습니다. 예약할 때, 필요한 날짜와 사용 예정 인원 수를 알려 주십시오.

예약은 받는 순서대로 접수됩니다. 따라서 미리 며칠 전에 예약해 주십시오. 테니스 코트를 사용하는 데는 비용이 없지만, 예약을 유지하기 위해 50달러의 보증금이 필요합니다. 테니스를 치시는 동안 테니스 코트에 파손이 발생하는 경우, 보증금은 환불되지 않습니다.

131. 정답 (C)

132. 정답 (C)

133. 정답 (A)

134. (A) 테니스는 건강, 체력, 근력 및 민첩성을 유지하는 데 좋은 스포츠입니다.
(B) 테니스를 치시는 동안 테니스 코트에 파손이 발생하는 경우, 보증금은 환불되지 않습니다.
(C) 적극적인 시설 관리 프로그램을 통해 수리 비용이 최소화될 수 있습니다.
(D) 시설이 열려 있는지 확실하지 않은 경우, 아파트 레크리에이션부로 미리 전화하십시오.
정답 (B)

문제 135-138번은 다음 회람을 참조하시오.

프라임 출판사

수신: 전 직원
발신: 헬렌 헌트, 인사부장
제목: 환경 지속 가능성 정책 – 잉크 카트리지
날짜: 1월 10일

환경을 생각하는 기업으로서, 우리는 될 수 있는 대로 사무실의 모든 소모품이 재활용되도록 하기 위해 최선을 다하고 있습니다. 따라서 사용한 모든 잉크 카트리지는 모두 버리지 말고 재활용되도록 해야 합니다.

저희는 직원들이 이를 쉽게 달성할 수 있도록 합니다. 사무실 주변에, "사용된 잉크 카트리지"라는 라벨이 붙은 재활용 용기가 많이 있습니다. 여러분은 사용한 카트리지를 이 용기에 버리기만 하면 됩니다. 그 다음 우리는 재활용을 위해 제조업체에 카트리지를 반환합니다.

카트리지를 재활용하는 것은 우리 환경 정책의 핵심 부분이므로 매우 중요합니다. 전사적 정책에 대한 좀 더 자세한 내용은 인트라넷에서 관련 부문을 참조하시오.

135. 정답 (D)

136. 정답 (D)

137. (A) 여러분은 사용한 카트리지를 이 용기에 버리기만 하면 됩니다.
(B) 카트리지를 리필하면 새 카트리지를 구입하는 것보다 훨씬 절약할 수 있습니다.
(C) 재활용 종이는 에너지와 물을 덜 사용하고 탄소 배출량이 적습니다.
(D) 전자레인지에 안전한 플라스틱 용기는 견고하고 고온에 강합니다.
정답 (A)

138. 정답 (C)

문제 139-142번은 다음 편지를 참조하시오.

젠킨스 씨께,

귀댁의 보안 시스템 업체로 스미스 보안 서비스를 선택해 주셔서 대단히 감사합니다. 귀하가 귀하의 집을 보호하기 위해 저희에게 의지하는 현명한 결정을 내리셨다는 것을 보장할 수 있습니다.

지난 20년간 저희는 주택 보안 분야에서 전국 최고의 선택이었습니다. 저희는 또한 전국에 있는 일부 대기업들에도 보안 서비스를 제공합니다. 저희는 가능한 최고 수준의 안전의 혜택을 받으시도록 보장하기 위해 항상 시스템과 서비스를 개선하고 있습니다.

귀하의 보안 시스템 또는 저희 서비스와 관련된 것에 대한 질문이 있으시면 저희에게 연락 주십시오. 저희는 모든 고객 분들이 저희 업무 및 제품에 완전히 만족하시도록 하는 데에 자부심을 느낍니다.

브라이언 스미스 드림
최고 경영자
스미스 보안 서비스

139. 정답 (D)

140. (A) 저희는 또한 전국에 있는 일부 대기업들에도 보안 서비스를 제공합니다.
(B) 사무용품 도난은 손실의 상당 부분을 차지합니다.
(C) 경험이 풍부한 고급 보안 요원 서비스에 대해서는 저희에게 연락하시면 됩니다.
(D) 해커는 이메일 및 은행 세부 정보와 같은 개인 데이터를 수집할 수 있을 것입니다.
정답 (A)

141. 정답 (B)

142. 정답 (B)

문제 143-146번은 다음 기사를 참조하시오.

더 스테이트 트리뷴

지역 뉴스 / 경제 / 사회 / **건강** / 과학

정신 건강: 수면은 어떤 역할을 할까?

줄리엣 패리시 작성

숙면 옹호자들은 숙면이 집중력을 늘리고 에너지 수준을 높여줌으로써 우리의 삶을 향상시킬 수 있다고 종종 주장한다. 한 연구자 집단이 일련의 실험을 통해 이를 과학적으로 입증하고자 노력해왔다.

연구자들은 다양한 연령대의 200명을 선정하였고, 그 중 절반에게 매일 밤 10시에 잠자리에 들 것을 요청했다. 나머지 100명에게는 늦게 자고 일찍 일어나라고 했다. 2주 후 연구자들은 정신적 예민함을 측정하기 위한 여러 가지 테스트에서 참가자들의 수행 정도를 측정했다.

테스트들은 결론적으로 많이 잔 사람들이 정신적 기민함과 에너지 면에서 상당히 이득을 본 것으로 나타났다. 시험이나 중요한 회의 전날 밤에는 일찍 잠자리에 드는 것이 바람직해 보인다.

143. 정답 (B)

144. 정답 (C)

145. 정답 (C)

146. (A) 너무 많은 수면을 취하는 것은 근본적인 건강 문제의 징후일 수 있다.
(B) 우리가 생산 목표를 달성하려면 주간 노동 시간을 늘려야 한다.
(C) 에너지 음료를 이용하는 이점보다 위험이 훨씬 더 크다.
(D) 시험이나 중요한 회의 전날 밤에는 일찍 잠자리에 드는 것이 바람직해 보인다.

정답 (D)

Part 7

문제 147–148번은 다음 초대장을 참조하시오.

> **제임스 콘웰 재단**
>
> (148A)연례 콘웰 기금 모금 만찬에
> 진심 어린 마음으로 귀하를 초대합니다.
>
> 날짜: 10월 17일 수요일, 오후 6시
> 장소: (148B)프란치네 (이탈리아 레스토랑)
> 8192 뉴타운 로드, 노스 알링턴
>
> (147)모든 수익금은 소중한 환경과 자연을 보존하는 데 사용될 것입니다.
> *10월 12일까지 참석이 확인되어야 합니다.
> 행사 진행자인 패트리샤 케어스에게
> pcairs@jcfoundation.org로 연락해 주십시오.
>
> 제임스 콘웰 재단
> 512 메인 스트리트, 뉴 브룬스윅
> (148C)(201) 555-9110
> (148D)www.jcfoundation.org

147. 행사가 개최되는 이유는?
(A) 도시의 관광을 촉진하기 위해
(B) 지역 주민들에게 무료 음식을 제공하기 위해
(C) 환경을 보존하는 것에 도움을 주기 위해
(D) 레스토랑의 개업을 축하하기 위해

정답 (C)

148. 제임스 콘웰 재단에 대해 나타나 있지 않은 것은 무엇인가?
(A) 정기적으로 행사를 개최한다.
(B) 뉴타운 로드에 위치해 있다.
(C) 전화로 연락 가능하다.
(D) 웹사이트를 갖고 있다.

정답 (B)

문제 149–150번은 다음 문자 메시지를 참조하시오.

> 우르술라 매더스 [오후 2시 56분]
> 글렌 켈리가 전화했는데 다음 주 월요일에 우리가 개최하는 IT 워크숍에 8명이 더 등록했다고 합니다. (149)좀 더 큰 방이 필요할 것 같아요.
>
> 프레더릭 채프먼 [오후 2시 57분]
> 수잔 플라워스에게 연락해서 뭔가를 준비할 수 있는지 알아볼게요.
>
> 우르술라 매더스 [오후 2시 58분]
> 정말 고마워요.
>
> 프레더릭 채프먼 [오후 2시 59분]
> 제가 해드릴 일이 더 있나요? 당신, 바쁘시잖아요.
>
> 우르술라 매더스 [오후 3시 1분]
> 네, 해주세요. (150)출장 요리 업체에 연락해서 주문을 늘려 주실 수 있나요? 지금은 40인분의 점심, 음료, 간식이 필요할 거예요.
>
> 프레더릭 채프먼 [오후 3시 2분]
> 문제없어요. (150)저는 지금 여유 시간이 좀 있어요. 다들 뭐라고 하시는지 알려 드릴게요.

149. 매더스 씨는 무엇을 하고 싶어 하는가?
(A) 워크숍에 대한 광고 중단
(B) 행사장 변경
(C) 다음 주까지 두 번째 강사 물색
(D) 오늘 플라워 씨와 통화

정답 (B)

150. 오후 3시 2분에, 채프먼 씨가 "저는 지금 여유 시간이 좀 있어요"라고 쓸 때 무엇을 시사하는가?
(A) 그는 워크숍에 참석할 것이다.
(B) 그는 더 많은 업무 과제가 필요하다.
(C) 그는 지금 몇 가지 서류를 제공할 수 있다.
(D) 그는 곧 출장 요리 업체에 전화할 것이다.

정답 (D)

문제 151–153번은 다음 이메일을 참조하시오.

> (151)수신: 테사 소토, 마커스 오티즈, 빅토리아 패텔
> 발신: 미란다 오닐
> (152)날짜: 5월 3일, 금요일
> 제목: 뉴스
>
> 유기 애완동물 보호 협회에 기부해 주신 여러분 모두에게 감사드립니다. 여러분 모두에게 오늘 주간 회의에서 논의된 협회 내 중요한 사안들에 대하여 알려 드리고자 합니다.
>
> (151)먼저, 이사회의 인원에 변화가 있을 것입니다. 이사 중 한 분인 테사 소토 씨가 다음 주 금요일에 은퇴합니다. (153)그 날 그녀를 위한 송별회를 열 것입니다. 피터 데이비드슨 씨가 그 다음 주 월요일부터 그녀의 자리를 대신할 것입니다. 데이비드슨 씨를 따뜻하게 환영해 주십시오.
>
> 또한, (152)마커스 오티즈 씨가 지역의 한 초등학교에서 생명의 소중함에 대한 일련의 프레젠테이션을 할 것입니다. 프레젠테이션은 다음 주부터 4주 동안 매주 목요일에 열릴 것입니다.
>
> 만약 우려 사항이 있으시다면, 저에게 언제라도 연락하십시오.
>
> 감사드리며,
>
> 미란다

151. 이메일은 누구를 대상으로 하는 것 같은가?
(A) 행사의 자원봉사자
(B) 기관의 이사회 위원
(C) 동물 병원의 직원
(D) 동물 보호 협회의 기부자

정답 (B)

152. 5월 9일에 무슨 일이 있을 것인가?
(A) 유기 애완동물 보호 협회가 일자리를 공고할 것이다.
(B) 모든 이사회 위원들이 그때까지 행사 제안서를 제출할 것이다.
(C) 오티즈 씨가 어린 학생들을 위한 프레젠테이션을 할 것이다.
(D) 데이비드슨 씨가 근무를 시작할 것이다.

정답 (C)

153. [1], [2], [3] 및 [4]로 표시된 위치 중 아래 문장이 들어가기에 가장 적절한 곳은?
"여러분 모두 참석해 주시기 바랍니다."
(A) [1]
(B) [2]
(C) [3]
(D) [4]

정답 (B)

문제 154-156번은 다음 편지를 참조하시오.

JWF

졸리 원목 가구

220 워싱턴 스트리트

팔로 알토, 캘리포니아 주 94300

10월 11일

앤디 스타크

85 트래비스 대로

팔로 알토, 캘리포니아 주 94307

(154)스타크 씨께,

(154)10월 8일 귀하와 직접 대화를 나눈 후, 귀하에게 영업 부장 직책을 제안하게 되어 기쁩니다. 면접에서 이미 귀하에게 알려 드렸듯이, 영업부 직원들 관리, 월간 보고서 작성, 그리고 **(155)주간 부서 회의 개최와 같은 업무를 하게 됩니다.** 귀하의 현재 직장인 덕핏 인테리어에서 영업 부장으로서 일한 경력이 있기 때문에, 이미 이 직책에 수반되는 일들에 익숙하고 매우 잘 하시리라 믿습니다.

(156)업무, 조건 및 연봉을 자세하게 설명한 문서들을 이 편지와 함께 동봉했습니다. 자세하게 읽은 후, 그 조건들을 수락하시면 그것에 서명해서 JWF의 인사부로 늦어도 10월 20일까지 제출하십시오.

만약 어떤 문제나 질문이 있으시다면 언제든지 저에게 649-555-1010으로 전화 주십시오. 곧 뵙기를 기대하고 있겠습니다.

(154)필리파 나티비다드 드림

차장, 인사부

졸리 원목 가구

동봉물

---

154. 스타크 씨에 대해 추론될 수 있는 것은 무엇인가?
(A) 덕핏 인테리어에서 오랫동안 근무했다.
(B) 10월 8일에 일자리에 지원했다.
(C) 최근에 나티비다드 씨를 만났다.
(D) 다른 도시로 이사할 것이다.　　　　정답 (C)

155. 스타크 씨가 JWF에서 해야 할 업무로 언급된 것은 무엇인가?
(A) 직원들의 보고서 검토하기
(B) 정기적인 회의 진행하기
(C) 나티비다드 씨에게 이메일 쓰기
(D) 출장 가기　　　　정답 (B)

156. 편지와 함께 발송된 것은 무엇인가?
(A) 직원 명단
(B) 발표 자료
(C) 계약서
(D) 경력 서술서　　　　정답 (C)

문제 157-158번은 다음 광고를 참조하시오.

피닉스 동물원

피닉스 동물원의 회원이 되시고
무료 선물을 받으세요!

독점 혜택

– 1년 내내 무제한 입장
– 회원 가입한 성인과 동반 시 7세 미만의 어린이 무료 입장
– 모든 기념품 가게와 레스토랑에서 10퍼센트 할인

– 특별 공연 초대권

회원권 종류와 가격

	(158)1년	2년
(158)어린이(7 – 13세)	(158)45달러	70달러
학생 (유효한 학생증이 있어야 함)	50달러	80달러
성인	70달러	120달러
노인	45달러	70달러

(157)8월의 특별 혜택

회원 가입하는 분들은 무료 동물 인형을 받으실 수 있습니다.

157. 고객이 무료 선물을 받을 수 있는 방법은?
(A) 유치원생을 데려감으로써
(B) 가족 회원권을 구매함으로써
(C) 특정 기간 안에 등록함으로써
(D) 기념품 가게에서 동물 장난감을 구입함으로써　　　　정답 (C)

158. 7세 어린이의 1년 회비는 얼마인가?
(A) 0달러
(B) 45달러
(C) 50달러
(D) 70달러　　　　정답 (B)

문제 159-161번은 다음 일자리 공고를 참조하시오.

행사 홍보 담당자 구인

싱가폴 최고의 행사 관리 회사인 레드 앤츠 주식회사가 지금 홍보 담당자를 모집합니다. 홍보 담당자는 홍보부를 책임지며, 우리 회사를 대중에 알리기 위하여 영업부와 긴밀히 협력합니다. **(159)이 직책에는 조직 위원회의 한 구성원으로서 행사 책임자와 함께 중요한 결정을 내리는 과정에 참여하고,** 회사의 광고 정책을 기획하며, 신문과 잡지 및 TV 프로그램과의 인터뷰를 주선하고, 정기적으로 홍보 행사를 준비하는 것이 포함됩니다.

합격자는 다음을 갖추어야 합니다:

• 구두와 서면에서의 뛰어난 소통 능력
• **(160)행사 기획이나 홍보 분야에서의 최소 5년 경력**
• 마케팅 또는 경영 학사 학위

추가적으로, 영어 외의 언어에 능숙한 지원자는 우대를 받을 것입니다.

(161)이 자리에 지원하고 싶은 지원자는 웹사이트 www.redantz.com에서 받을 수 있는 지원서를 작성해야 합니다. 이력서 및 자기소개서와 함께 인사부장 바바라 갈리아노에게 작성된 지원서를 우편으로 보내십시오. 완성된 서류들은 늦어도 9월 15일까지 도착해야 하며, 최종 5명의 후보자들을 위한 면접이 9월 20일에 있을 것입니다. 문의는 받지 않습니다.

8월 16일 게시

---

159. 홍보 담당자의 업무로 언급된 것은 무엇인가?
(A) 직원 모집에 밀접하게 관련되어 있다.
(B) 행사 책임자와의 협력이 포함된다.
(C) TV 광고를 위하여 연예인들과 인터뷰하는 것을 포함한다.
(D) 신문 편집이 요구된다.　　　　정답 (B)

160. 이 일자리의 자격 요건으로 명시된 것은 무엇인가?
(A) 경영학 박사 학위
(B) 2개 국어 사용
(C) 관련 분야의 최소 5년 경력

(D) 방송국 경력 정답 (C)

161. 지원 절차에 대하여 사실인 것은?
(A) 지원서는 이메일로 제출될 수 있다.
(B) 지원자는 회사의 자체적인 지원서를 사용해야 한다.
(C) 문의 사항들을 갈리아노 씨에게 보낼 수 있다.
(D) 면접에 대한 추가 사항들은 웹사이트를 통하여 제공될 것이다.

정답 (B)

문제 162–164번은 다음 공고를 참조하시오.

제 2회 연차 마케팅 세미나

제 2회 연차 마케팅 세미나가 카네기 대학교의 로라 엘 테일러 강당에서 5월 1일부터 3일까지 열릴 것입니다. 올해의 특별 강연들은 다음을 포함합니다:

올바른 사업 목표 결정하기
카네기 대학교 명예 교수 (162A)팀 윌리엄스
사업의 올바른 목표를 결정하는 것이 성공의 열쇠입니다. 적절한 시장 분할부터 포지셔닝까지의 상세한 단계들이 소개될 것입니다.

경영에서의 합리적인 결정
릴리 헬스케어의 최고 경영자 (162B)랜들 약시치
사업을 운영할 때, 시장에 뛰어들거나 나와야 할 딱 맞는 순간들이 있습니다. 국내 최대 제약 회사중 하나인 릴리 헬스케어의 최고 경영자가 성공과 실패의 실제 이야기를 들려드립니다.

광고의 유머 효과
로슈 대학교 교수 (162C)에리카 제이 리
성공적인 광고에는 언제나 유머가 있습니다. 고객의 이목을 (163)끌고 더불어 광고의 효과와 제품의 친숙함을 증가시킬 수 있는 유머의 적절한 사용에 관해 강연할 것입니다.

패널 토론: 비즈니스 윤리와 마케팅
(162D)사회자: 페이지 버튼
기업 윤리와 그것이 마케팅에 어떻게 영향을 주는지에 대하여 전문가 패널이 토론할 것입니다.

(164)세미나에 참석하고 싶으신 분들은, 연락처와 함께 리사 멜론 씨에게 lmellon@carnegie.edu로 연락하십시오. 세미나에 대한 상세한 정보는 웹사이트 www.carnegie.edu/asim에서 이용하실 수 있습니다.

---

162. 세미나에서 강연을 하지 않을 사람은 누구인가?
(A) 팀 윌리엄스
(B) 랜들 약시치
(C) 에리카 제이 리
(D) 페이지 버튼 정답 (D)

163. 네 번째 단락 4행에 있는 단어 "draw"와 의미상 가장 가까운 것은?
(A) 칠하다
(B) 끌다
(C) 설득하다
(D) 선출하다 정답 (B)

164. 참가하고 싶은 사람들은 무엇을 할 것을 요청받는가?
(A) 로라 엘 테일러 강당에서 등록하기
(B) 등록 양식 작성하기
(C) 웹사이트 방문하기
(D) 리사 멜론에게 연락처 제출하기 정답 (D)

문제 165–167번은 다음 기사를 참조하시오.

스미스의 유산

현지 기자, 크리스토퍼 로빈 작성

멜버른 (7월 10일) – (165)세계적으로 유명한 비정부 기구인 스프링 버드 재단의 사무총장 아담 스미스가 8월에 물러날 것이다. "저는 스프링 버드에서의 저의 아름다운 기억을 절대 잊지 못할 것입니다"라고 스미스 씨가 말했다.

(166)26년간의 스프링 버드에 대한 헌신이 어떻게 시작되었는지에 대해 질문받았을 때, 스미스 씨는 자신의 열정이 무엇이었는지 늘 알고 있었다고 말했다. (165)스프링 버드 브라질 지사에서 일할 부 현장 관리자에 대한 공고를 보았을 때, 저는 시드니에서 3년째 사무 직원으로 근무하고 있었습니다. 늘 현장에서 다른 사람들을 돕는 일을 직접 하고 싶었고, 그래서 망설임 없이 이력서를 제출했습니다."

(165)스프링 버드 피라시카바 지사의 부 현장 관리자로서, 그는 시골 유치원생을 교육하는 데에 모든 노력을 쏟아부었다. 열심히 일한 결과 그는 3년만에 현장 관리자로 승진하게 되었다.

"저는 직원으로서 일하는 것이 힘들다고 느꼈고, 이 힘든 업무의 참된 의미에 대해 계속 생각하고 있었습니다. 하지만, 스미스 씨의 아이들을 향한 열정과 사랑이 저의 가슴 속 깊은 곳을 감동시켰습니다. 그는 저의 13년 간의 경력 중에서 가장 영향력 있는 인물이었습니다"라고 브라질의 현재 현장 관리자인 케이틀린 몽클레어가 말했다.

(167)현장 관리자로서 10년을 보낸 후, 스미스 씨는 2000년에 스프링 버드의 본사가 있는 캐나다의 토론토로 오게 되었다. 토론토에서, 그는 사회복지학 분야에서 석사 학위를 받았고, 교육부의 총괄 관리자로 승진했다. 그곳 스프링 버드의 사무총장이 되었고 남은 경력 동안 그 직책에서 근무했다.

그의 은퇴 연회는 다음 달 토론토에서 열릴 것이다. 그는 선임 고문으로서 지속적으로 이 기구를 도울 계획이다.

---

165. 기사의 주제는 무엇인가?
(A) 한 단체의 빈 일자리
(B) 한 단체의 역사
(C) 국제 비정부 기구들의 소개
(D) 한 개인의 업적 정답 (D)

166. 스미스 씨는 스프링 버드에서 얼마나 오랫동안 일해 왔는가?
(A) 3년
(B) 10년
(C) 13년
(D) 26년 정답 (D)

167. 스프링 버드 재단은 어느 도시에 기반을 두고 있는가?
(A) 멜버른
(B) 피라시카바
(C) 토론토
(D) 시드니 정답 (C)

문제 168–171번은 다음 온라인 채팅 토론을 참조하시오.

미란다 카터 [오전 11시 40분]
(168)안내책자 작업이 어떻게 진행되고 있나요?

토니 니글 [오전 11시 41분]
(171)본문은 이미 작성되어 교정자들에게 보내졌어요. 저는 오늘 오후까지는 그것이 제게 다시 돌아올 것이라고 확신하고 있었어요.

린다 박스데일   [오전 11시 43분]
사진에 문제가 생겼어요. 일부는 괜찮은데, 서너 장은 흐릿해요. 사진 좀 더 받아야 할 것 같아요.

미란다 카터   [오전 11시 44분]
인쇄소에서 내일까지 완성된 안내책자를 기다리고 있어요. (169)다음 주에 **영업 컨벤션이 시작되기 전에 우리가 복제본을 원한다면, 우리는 마감일을 놓쳐서는 안 돼요.**

린다 박스데일   [오전 11시 45분]
앨런 포터에게 말해 볼게요. 오늘 사진 몇 장을 다시 찍으라고 할게요.

미란다 카터   [오전 11시 46분]
고마워요. 토니. (171)오늘까지 모든 것을 확실히 받으시나요?

토니 니글   [오전 11시 47분]
(171)디애나 무어에게 얘기해서 확인해 볼게요.

미란다 카터   [오전 11시 49분]
오늘 밤 집에 가기 전에 안내책자를 끝내기만 하면 돼요.

린다 박스데일   [오전 11시 50분]
(170)그렇다면 여기서 저녁 식사를 하는 게 좋겠어요.

토니 니글   [오전 11시 52분]
저는 좋아요. 배달하는 훌륭한 새 이탈리아 레스토랑을 제가 알고 있어요. 괜찮으시다면 제가 처리할게요.

168. 토론의 주제는 무엇인가?
(A) 영업 컨벤션
(B) 오후 계획
(C) 작업 프로젝트 진행률
(D) 완성된 안내책자   정답 (C)

169. 작성자들이 안내책자의 복제본이 필요한 이유는?
(A) 곧 있을 전문적인 행사에 사용하기 위해
(B) 회사의 고객들에게 우편으로 보내기 위해
(C) 구직들에게 나누어 주기 위해
(D) 해외의 이해 당사자에 보내기 위해   정답 (A)

170. 박스데일 씨에 의해 시사되어 있는 것은 무엇인가?
(A) 작성자들은 오늘 저녁에 시간 외 근무를 할 것이다.
(B) 그녀는 오늘 오후 약속을 취소해야 한다.
(C) 작업을 완료하기에 시간이 충분하지 않다.
(D) 그녀는 기꺼이 음식점에서 음식을 찾아올 것이다.   정답 (A)

171. 오전 11시 47분에 니글 씨가 "디애나 무어에게 얘기해서 확인해 볼게요"라고 쓸 때 무엇을 시사하는 것 같은가?
(A) 무어 씨는 충분히 열심히 일하지 않고 있다.
(B) 그는 작업에 불만이 있다.
(C) 무어 씨는 교정자로 일한다.
(D) 그는 어떠한 최근 정보도 받지 못했다.   정답 (C)

문제 172-175번은 다음 후기를 참조하시오.

http://www.napoli.com/review

나폴리 에스프레소

메인 페이지	온라인 매장	후기	연락처	고객 지원

"좋은 값어치"
제출자: 아만다 로버트슨
제출일: 7월 24일

제품명: 나폴리 캡슐 에스프레소 머신
제품번호: M23
고객 평가: ★★★★☆

저는 최근 나폴리의 에스프레소 머신 M23을 이 웹사이트를 통해 굉장히 합리적인 가격에 구매했습니다. 기계는 이틀 전에 배송되었고, 신이 나서 상자를 열었습니다. (172D)이 기계의 색상에 대해 불만족스러웠다는 다른 고객들의 후기와 달리, 저는 전체적인 디자인이 제 취향에 맞다는 것을 알았습니다.

패키지에 함께 딸려온 제품 설명서에 묘사된 대로, (172A)기계에는 사용 후 씻기 편하도록 분리가 되는 네 개의 부품이 있습니다. (173) (174)또한 기계가 작동하는 동안 거의 어떠한 소음도 내지 않는데, 이것이 제가 가장 좋아했던 점입니다. 이전 에스프레소 기계를 교체한 이유는 기계가 작동할 때 너무 시끄러웠기 때문이었습니다.

(172C)나폴리가 에스프레소 머신 업계에 진출한 지 얼마 안됐다는 사실을 고려할 때, (175)일회용 캡슐은 일반 가게나 슈퍼마켓에서 찾기가 어렵습니다. 캡슐은 현재 오직 온라인과 특정 가게에서만 구입할 수 있어서, 근처 가게들이 나폴리 에스프레소 캡슐을 취급하는지 확인해 보거나 혹은 기계와 함께 몇 개를 주문할 것을 추천합니다.

172. 후기에 나타나 있지 않은 것은 무엇인가?
(A) 기계가 청소를 위해 분리될 수 있다.
(B) 패키지가 예상보다 이틀 일찍 배송되었다.
(C) 나폴리가 에스프레소 기계를 만들기 시작한 지 얼마 되지 않았다.
(D) 몇몇 사람들은 기계의 외형을 좋아하지 않는다.   정답 (B)

173. 로버트슨 씨에 대해 추론될 수 있는 것은 무엇인가?
(A) 근처 가게에서 기계를 구매했다.
(B) 나폴리 에스프레소 머신을 사용해 커피를 만들어 보았다.
(C) 나폴리에서 전에 다른 기계를 구입했다.
(D) 일회용 캡슐을 찾는 것에 대한 도움을 요청했다.   정답 (B)

174. 로버트슨 씨는 M23의 특징 중 무엇을 가장 좋아하는가?
(A) 조용한 작동
(B) 전체적인 디자인
(C) 알맞은 가격
(D) 고객 지원   정답 (A)

175. [1], [2], [3] 그리고 [4]로 표시된 곳 중에, 아래 문장이 들어가기에 가장 적절한 곳은?
"이것은 다소 불편합니다."
(A) [1]
(B) [2]
(C) [3]
(D) [4]   정답 (D)

문제 176-180번은 다음 편지들을 참조하시오.

6월 19일

캐스팅부
글로벌 미디어 주식회사
시네마 시티, 캘리포니아 주 91006

관계자 분께,

(176)오디션 지원서를 제출하기 위해 편지를 씁니다. 제 소속사, 스타 아카데미가 〈모험가들〉에 대해 알려 주었고 저는 제가 그 새 영화에 분명히 기여할 것으로 믿습니다.

저는 수많은 장르의 영화와 연극, 두 분야에서 총 14년의 연기 경력이 있습니다. 저는 제인 카메론이 연출한 수상작 (177C)〈식물〉에서 주연의 절친한 친구였습니다. (179)제시카 아브람의 공상 과학 주제 영화, 〈여름 왕국〉에서 한 외계 병사의 역할을 연기했습니다.

연극계에서는 (177A)〈반지를 찾아서〉의 감독인 월터 데인의 첫 연극 작품이었던 (177B)〈다시 스타되기〉에서 조연을 맡았습니다. (177D)또한 세계적으로 유명한 극작가인 사무엘 프리먼의 여러 주요 작품들에 참여했습니다. 그것들에는 〈클레이 포터〉와 〈아우터스페이스〉가 있습니다. (178)제가 참가했던 작품들의 전체 목록을 보시려면 동봉된 이력서를 참조해 주십시오.

보시다시피, 저는 연기에 굉장히 열정적입니다. 귀사의 새 작품에서 연기할 수 있는 기회가 생긴다면 대단히 감사할 것입니다. 곧 답을 듣기를 기대하고 있겠습니다.

애니타 해서웨이 드림

6월 29일

애니타 해서웨이
91B 노섬버랜드 애비뉴
로스앤젤레스, 캘리포니아 주 90124

해서웨이 씨께,

저희의 새 영화를 위한 오디션에 지원해 주셔서 감사합니다. 당신이 함께 일한 많은 감독들에게서 당신의 성실함과 연기에 대한 열정에 대해 들었습니다.

저희는 다양한 장르에서의 당신의 필모그래피가 매우 가치 있다고 생각합니다. (179)두 영화가 같은 장르이기 때문에, 특히 〈여름 왕국〉 영화에서의 당신의 경험이 우리 새 영화에 굉장히 도움이 될 것이라고 생각합니다. (180)따라서 당신을 7월 10일 오디션에 초대하고 싶습니다. 오디션은 본사가 아니라, 캐스터레이 가 10번지에 있는 미디어 센터에서 열릴 것입니다. 사용하고자 하시는 소품 외에 다른 추가 준비물은 가져오실 필요가 없을 것입니다.

만약 이날 오실 수 없거나 오디션에 대해 질문이 있으시다면, 210–555–1235로 저에게 언제든지 연락하십시오. (180)곧 뵙기를 기대하고 있겠습니다.

트렌트 버튼 드림
(180)캐스팅 감독, 글로벌 미디어 주식회사

176. 해서웨이 씨가 첫 번째 편지를 보낸 이유는?
(A) 지원서를 수락하기 위해
(B) 감독 자리에 지원하기 위해
(C) 영화의 배역을 따내기 위해
(D) 새 작품에서의 역할을 제안하기 위해　　정답 (C)

177. 해서웨이 씨가 참여하지 않았던 작품은 무엇인가?
(A) 〈반지를 찾아서〉
(B) 〈다시 스타되기〉
(C) 〈식물〉
(D) 〈아우터스페이스〉　　정답 (A)

178. 해서웨이 씨에 대해 나타나 있는 것은 무엇인가?
(A) 연기 실력으로 상을 받았다.
(B) 캐머론 씨의 영화에서 주인공이었다.
(C) 대학 졸업 후 바로 연기를 시작했다.
(D) 편지와 함께 추가 정보를 보냈다.　　정답 (D)

179. 〈모험가들〉에 대해 암시된 것은 무엇인가?
(A) 버튼 씨에 의해 연출될 것이다.

(B) 공상 과학 영화이다.
(C) 7월 10일 개봉할 것이다.
(D) 스타 아카데미의 후원을 받는다.　　정답 (B)

180. 해서웨이 씨가 앞으로 무엇을 할 것 같은가?
(A) 7월에 본사에 찾아갈 것이다.
(B) 버튼 씨에게 자신을 위해 소품을 준비해 달라고 요청할 것이다.
(C) 캐스팅 감독을 직접 만날 것이다.
(D) 자신의 필모그래피에 대한 정보를 더 제공할 것이다.　　정답 (C)

문제 181–185번은 다음 청구서와 이메일을 참조하시오.

샤토 케이터링

우편 사서함 605248, 라스베이거스, 네바다 주 81930
연락처: 709–222–7199
계정 번호: 517698124

견적서 발송: 10월 7일
주문 번호: 39476
고객: 아멜리아 사이러스
이메일: acyrus@kmail.com
핸드폰: 090–555–7230
(181)행사 날짜/시작 시간: 10월 23일, 저녁 7시
행사 소요 시간: 4시간
(185)장소: 첼로 홀, 힐사이드 호텔
손님: 90명

내역	가격	수량	합계
음식:			
기본 카나페 패키지	27달러	95	2,565.00달러
채식주의자 패키지	23달러	10	230.00달러
음료:			
기본 음료 패키지	10달러	105	1,050.00달러
칵테일	8달러	105	840.00달러
직원:			
음식 제공 서비스 담당자	100달러	4	400.00달러
		소계	5,085.00달러
	(182)기업 고객 할인 (10%):		−508.50달러
		세금:	366.12달러
		합계	4,942.62달러

• 식사 도구 대여는 무료 제공

조건: 세부 사항을 자세히 검토하고 사무실에 예약을 확인해 주십시오. (184)변경 사항은 근무일 기준 행사 5일 전에 요청하셔야 합니다. 그렇지 않으면, 벌금이 부과될 수 있습니다. (181)결제는 근무일 기준 행사 날짜 2일 전까지 되어야 합니다.

수신: 저스틴 레이크 〈jlake@ccatering.com〉
발신: 아멜리아 사이러스 〈acyrus@kmail.com〉
(184)날짜: 10월 20일
제목: 긴급 – 10월 23일 힐사이드 행사에 대하여

레이크 씨께,

(183)동료의 은퇴 파티에 몇 가지 변경을 해야 합니다. 유감스럽게도, (184)손님 몇 분이 이제 참석하지 못하게 되었습니다. 그래서 최종 인원 수가 10

명이 줄어, 이제 기본 카나페 패키지 85개와 각 음료 패키지가 95개씩 필요할 것입니다. (185)이제 인원이 더 적으므로, 저는 더 작은 연회홀로 옮기기로 결정했습니다. 음식을 원래 장소가 아니라, 시설 내의 비올라 갤러리로 배달해 주십시오.

이로 인해 총 가격이 변경될 거라고 생각합니다. 수정된 견적서를 보내 주시면 기한 전에 결제하겠습니다.

아멜리아 사이러스 드림

181. 청구서에 따르면, 음식 공급 서비스에 대한 결제가 언제까지 되어야 하는가?
(A) 10월 7일
(B) 10월 20일
(C) 10월 21일
(D) 10월 23일
정답 (C)

182. 샤토 케이터링에 대해 나타나 있는 것은 무엇인가?
(A) 고객들에게 특정 식단 요구 사항에 대해 알려줄 것을 요구한다.
(B) 힐사이드 호텔에 기반을 두고 있다.
(C) 특정 유형의 고객들에게 특별 혜택을 제공한다.
(D) 행사를 준비하기 위해 사이러스 씨를 고용했다.
정답 (C)

183. 이메일의 목적은 무엇인가?
(A) 추가 물품을 요청하기 위한 것
(B) 계획된 일정을 갱신하기 위한 것
(C) 예약을 취소하기 위한 것
(D) 은퇴를 발표하기 위한 것
정답 (B)

184. 가까운 미래에 무슨 일이 일어날 것으로 예상되는가?
(A) 은퇴 파티의 일정이 변경될 것이다.
(B) 사이러스 씨가 곧 은퇴할 것이다.
(C) 사이러스 씨에게 추가 요금이 청구될 것이다.
(D) 레이크 씨가 손님으로 은퇴 파티에 참석할 것이다.
정답 (C)

185. 힐사이드 호텔에 대해 시사되어 있는 것은 무엇인가?
(A) 두 개 이상의 연회 홀을 가지고 있다.
(B) 직원 중에 음식 제공 서비스를 하는 사람들이 많다.
(C) 충분한 주차 공간을 보유하고 있다.
(D) 서비스 가격을 변경할 것이다.
정답 (A)

문제 186-190번은 다음 광고와 회람 그리고 편지를 참조하시오.

수엘 윈도우즈에서
6월 한 달 내내
특별 행사를 즐기세요.

4개 이상의 창문을 구입하세요.
그러면 저희가 여러분의 집이나 사무실로 가서 그것들을
완전히 무료로 설치해 드립니다.

(190)어떤 이유로든 만족하시지 못하면
창문에 지불한 가격의 50%를 할인해 드리겠습니다.

(186)우리는 다음과 같은 회사에서 만든 창문을 취급합니다.
글래스 프로, 매독스, 웨스트사이드 그리고 KTR

포레스트 레인 37에 있는 저희 매장에 방문하셔서 재고가 있는지
확인해 보세요.

저희는 일주일 내내 오전 9시 30분부터 오후 8시까지 영업합니다.

수신: 전 직원, 수엘 윈도우즈
발신: 미치 머레이, 사장
제목: 근무 일정
날짜: 6월 20일

이번 주에 창문 설치자 몇 명이 휴가입니다. 따라서 다음은 수정된 일정표입니다. 여러분, 주목해 주세요. 누군가에게 창문을 판매하면, 고객이 창문을 설치 받기를 원하는 날에 근무하는 사람이 시간이 있는지 확인하세요.

6월 20일 월요일: 피터 크로프트
6월 21일 화요일: 래리 메드포드
(189)6월 22일 수요일: **올랜도 스미스**
6월 23일 목요일: 에릭 홉킨스
6월 24일 금요일: 피터 크로프트, 올랜도 스미스

(187)주말 일정은 아직 정해지지 않았습니다. 최대한 빨리 갱신하겠습니다.

6월 27일

머레이 씨에게,

제 이름은 제레미 툴이고, 저는 귀 매장의 장기 고객입니다. 저는 8년 넘게 거기에서 창문을 구매해 왔습니다. 이 달 특별 행사를 보고 반가워서 매장에 가서 집을 위한 창문을 열 개 샀습니다.

(188) (189)6월 22일에 창문을 설치하러 아무도 오지 않았을 때 제가 놀란 것을 상상해 보십시오. 귀 매장에 전화했더니, 저와 통화한 사람이 아침 10시에 제 창문이 설치되기로 되어 있다고 했는데 아무도 안 왔습니다. 하루 종일 집에서 기다려야 했고, 이로 인해 하루 결근하는 일이 생겼기 때문에 특히 속상했습니다.

(188)다음 날 창문이 설치되었을 때, 그 일을 한 사람이 사실 창문 하나에 금이 가게 했는데 사과조차 하지 않았습니다.

(190)필요한 조치를 취하셔서 이 문제들을 해결해 주시기를 바랍니다.

제레미 툴 드림

186. 광고에 따르면, 수엘 윈도우즈에 대해 사실인 것은?
(A) 그곳은 고객들이 방문할 수 있는 웹사이트를 갖고 있다.
(B) 그곳은 창문을 자체 생산한다.
(C) 그곳은 다른 회사들의 물건들을 판매한다.
(D) 그곳은 주 5일 문을 연다.
정답 (C)

187. 회람에서 머레이 씨가 일정에 대해 언급하는 것은 무엇인가?
(A) 그날 늦게 최신 정보로 수정될 것이다.
(B) 일주일의 일부분이 미완성이다.
(C) 직원들에 의해 변경될 수 있다.
(D) 시간 외 근무를 할 몇 사람이 필요하다.
정답 (B)

188. 툴 씨가 편지를 작성한 이유는?
(A) 서비스에 대해 불평하기 위해
(B) 환불을 요청하기 위해
(C) 사과를 요구하기 위해
(D) 편지에 답장하기 위해
정답 (A)

189. 원래 누가 툴 씨의 창문을 설치하기로 예정되어 있었는가?
(A) 피터 크로프트
(B) 래리 메드포드
(C) 올랜도 스미스
(D) 에릭 홉킨스
정답 (C)

190. 머레이 씨가 툴 씨를 위해 무엇을 할 것 같은가?
    (A) 그의 집에 직접 가서 사과하기
    (B) 그가 지불한 가격의 반을 그에게 할인해 주기
    (C) 창문이 즉시 설치되도록 하기
    (D) 그에게 나중에 사용할 쿠폰 보내기   정답 (B)

문제 191-195번은 다음 편지와 웹사이트 그리고 회람을 참조하시오.

10월 23일

몰리 로즈
58 시사이드 레인
포틀랜드, 오리건 주

몰리 씨에게,

안녕하세요. 저는 사만다 브리입니다 우리는 몇 년 전에 글래드스톤 컨설팅에서 함께 일했습니다. (191)우리 옛 동료 중 한 명인 브라이언 헤이스팅스에게서 당신이 현재 일자리를 찾고 계신다고 들었습니다.

(191)현재 제가 다니고 있는 회사인 웨스트사이드 주식회사가 곧 채용할 예정이라는 사실에 관심이 있으실 것 같아서요. (194)우리는 켄터키 주 렉싱턴에 위치해 있습니다. 이곳은 일하기 좋은 곳이고, 당신이 이곳을 좋아할 것 같아요. (193)우리는 컴퓨터 프로그래밍 기술을 가진 사람들이 필요한데, 당신은 최고 적임자 중 한 명입니다.

원하신다면, 제 상사에게 당신을 추천해 드릴 수 있습니다. 관심 있는 자리가 있으면 알려 주세요. 행운을 빌겠습니다.

사만다 드림

---

www.westside.com/positions

홈	소개	제품	채용

웨스트사이드 주식회사는 사업을 확장하고 있어서 여러 자리가 비어 있습니다. 각 업무에 대해 자세히 알아보려면 링크를 클릭하십시오.

대리, 경리부: 5년 경력 필수; 대인관계 능력이 뛰어나고 타고난 리더여야 함; 학사 학위 필요 없음' $52,000

(193)컴퓨터 프로그래머, 연구개발부: 다양한 프로그래밍 언어에 능숙해야 함; 혼자 또는 팀 프로젝트에서 일할 수 있는 사람을 구함; $120,000

운전기사, 배송부: 상용 운전면허 및 개인 차량 소유하고 있어야 함; 트럭 소유자 우대; 경력 불필요; 지역 배송만 함; $20,000

(192)영업사원, 영업부: 효과적인 커뮤니케이션 기술 보유해야 함; 2년 경력 희망, 필수 사항은 아님; (192)해외 여행 필수; 유효한 여권 보유; $75,000

수신: 전 직원
발신: 칼라 헌트
날짜: 12월 2일
제목: 새로운 주간

우리는 12월 7일 월요일 부로 2명의 새로운 직원이 근무를 시작한다는 것을 알려 드립니다. 그들의 이름은 로널드 버거와 몰리 로즈입니다. 몰리는 포틀랜드에서 이 나라를 가로질러 오는 반면, 로널드는 우리 녹스빌 사무실에서 우리 쪽으로 옮겨오는 것입니다. 하지만 그녀에 대해 너무 많이 걱정하지 마세요. (194)그녀는 자신의 고향으로 돌아오는 것입니다. 두 분 모두 환영해 주시고, 그들이 아무쪼록 빨리 업무에 익숙해지도록 도와주세요.

(195)우리는 다음 주에 그들을 위한 환영 행사를 열 것입니다. 날짜와 시간은 아직 정해지지 않았습니다. 그들이 자리잡는 대로 제가 전사 차원의 이

메일을 보내겠습니다.

---

191. 브리 씨가 편지를 보낸 이유는?
    (A) 개인 정보를 요청하기 위해
    (B) 면접 시간을 잡기 위해
    (C) 어떤 사람에게 공석에 관해 알리기 위해
    (D) 어떤 사람에게 새로운 일을 제의하기 위해   정답 (C)

192. 다른 나라를 방문해야 하는 직책은 어느 것인가?
    (A) 대리
    (B) 컴퓨터 프로그래머
    (C) 운전사
    (D) 영업사원   정답 (D)

193. 로즈 씨는 어느 부서에 근무를 지원할 것 같은가?
    (A) 경리부
    (B) 연구개발부
    (C) 배송부
    (D) 영업부   정답 (B)

194. 로즈 씨에 대해 사실인 것은?
    (A) 그녀는 버거 씨와 함께 일할 것이다.
    (B) 그녀는 헌트 씨와 직접 면접을 봤다.
    (C) 그녀는 많은 업무 경력이 있다.
    (D) 그녀는 켄터키 주 렉싱턴에서 성장했다.   정답 (D)

195. 헌트 씨가 환영 행사에 대해 나타내는 것은 무엇인가?
    (A) 그것은 레스토랑에서 열릴 것이다.
    (B) 그것은 오전에 열릴 것이다.
    (C) 그것의 시간은 나중에 결정될 것이다.
    (D) 그것은 다음 주 월요일에 있을 것이다.   정답 (C)

문제 196-200번은 다음 영수증과 이메일들을 참조하시오.

페이리스 문구점
로빈슨 로드 585
(304) 223-8563

품목	품목 번호	수량	가격
복사지, 5,000페이지	588–KLW	3	$99.00
펜, 검은색 잉크 (20/박스)	933–JRD	4	$40.00
(198)스테이플러	484–VFM	1	$12.00
프린터 잉크	495–AKE	2	$80.00
		소계	$231.00
		세금	$11.55
		총계	$242.55

(196)다른 가게보다 돈을 적게 지불하는 페이리스 문구점에서 구매해 주셔서 감사합니다.

(C) 그녀에게 그의 일정을 알려 주기 위해
(D) 그녀에게 이번 주 회의에 대해 물어보기 위해 .... 정답 (C)

200. 왓슨 씨의 회사에 대해 나타나 있는 것은 무엇인가?
(A) 올랜도에 위치해 있는 사무실이 있다.
(B) 페이리스 문구점에서 향후 구매 시 할인을 받을 것이다.
(C) 페이리스 문구점에서 자주 구매한다.
(D) 다음 몇 달 안에 유럽으로 확장할 계획이다. .... 정답 (B)

수신: 앨리샤 왓슨 〈aw@brandon.com〉
발신: 글렌 모리스 〈g_morris@payless.com〉
날짜: 7월 16일
제목: 답장: 저의 구매

왓슨 씨에게,

이 문제를 저에게 알려 주셔서 감사합니다. 최근에 구매하신 것을 제가 확인해 보니, **(198)484-VFM 품목이 발송되지 않은 것을 확인했습니다.** 따라서, 귀하의 신용 카드 적정 금액을 환불받으실 것입니다. 그것은 앞으로 영업일 기준 3일 이내에 귀하의 청구서에 반영될 것입니다.

(197)추가로 저희가 홍보하고 있는 특가 행사에 대해 알려 드립니다. (200) 향후 3개월 동안 저희와 함께 거래 계정을 시작하는 신규 고객을 추천해 주시면 연말까지 전체 구매액의 15%를 받게 됩니다.

좋은 하루 보내십시오.

글렌 모리스
관리자, 페이리스 문구점

수신: 앨리샤 왓슨 〈aw@brandon.com〉
발신: 로메오 부스 〈romeob@grovertech.com〉
날짜: 8월 29일
제목: 감사합니다

왓슨 씨에게,

지난주 올랜도 무역 박람회에서 당신을 만나서 반가웠습니다. 저는 우리 두 회사가 서로 거래할 수 있을 것이라고 확신합니다. **(199)사무실이 가까우니까, 직접 만나기가 쉬울 것입니다. 앞으로 2주 동안 업무차 유럽에 있을 예정이지만, 9월 중순에 돌아오면 연락드리겠습니다.**

또한 페이리스 문구점을 알려 주신 데 대해 감사드리고 싶습니다. **(200)그곳을 확인해 보았고 거기에 법인 계정을 개설하기로 결정했습니다. 물론, 그에 대해 제게 모두 알려준 사람이 당신이라고 사장에게 말했습니다.**

다시 한 번 감사합니다.

로미오 부스 드림
그로버 테크

---

196. 영수증에 따르면, 다음 중 사실인 것은?
(A) 펜은 낱개로 판매된다.
(B) 고객이 200달러 미만으로 지출했다.
(C) 구매에 세금이 적용되지 않았다.
(D) 상점이 물건을 저렴한 가격에 판매한다. .... 정답 (D)

197. 첫 번째 이메일의 한 가지 목적은 무엇인가?
(A) 상점의 최신 제품을 광고하기 위한 것
(B) 고객에게 판촉 활동에 대해 알리기 위한 것
(C) 물건을 늦게 보낸 데 대해 사과하기 위한 것
(D) 최근 구매에 대해 할인을 제공하기 위한 것 .... 정답 (B)

198. 왓슨 씨가 환불 받을 금액은 얼마인가?
(A) 12달러
(B) 40달러
(C) 80달러
(D) 99달러 .... 정답 (A)

199. 부스 씨가 왓슨 씨에게 두 번째 이메일을 보낸 한 가지 이유는?
(A) 그녀에게 더 많은 정보를 요청하기 위해
(B) 계약 조건을 확인하기 위해

1. 미M
(A) One of the women is looking through the window.
(B) They are standing across from each other.
(C) They are adjusting the window shade.
(D) One of the women is reaching across the table.

(A) 여자 중 한 명이 창문을 통해 보고 있다.
(B) 그들은 서로 마주보고 서 있다.
(C) 그들은 창문 블라인드를 조정하고 있다.
(D) 여자 중 한 명이 책상을 가로질러 손을 뻗고 있다.   정답 (C)

2. 미W
(A) They are waiting in a checkout line.
(B) One of the women is trying on a pair of sunglasses.
(C) They are hanging merchandise on a wall.
(D) One of the women is putting a price tag on a product.

(A) 그들은 계산대 줄에서 기다리고 있다.
(B) 여자 중 한 명이 선글라스를 착용해 보고 있다.
(C) 그들은 벽에 상품을 걸고 있다.
(D) 여자 중 한 명이 가격표를 제품에 붙이고 있다.   정답 (B)

3. 영M
(A) A man is approaching a sign in a parking area.
(B) A man is getting a parking ticket from a machine.
(C) A pathway is leading to the city park.
(D) One of the cars is parked in a tow-away zone.

(A) 남자가 주차 구역에 있는 표지판 쪽으로 다가가고 있다.
(B) 남자가 기계에서 주차권을 뽑고 있다.
(C) 보도가 시립 공원으로 이어지고 있다.
(D) 차량 중 한 대가 견인 지역에 주차되어 있다.   정답 (A)

4. 호W
(A) There are documents spread out on a table.
(B) A woman is working on a vehicle.
(C) A woman is reaching for a laptop.
(D) There are some power cords lying on a table.

(A) 테이블 위에 펼쳐진 서류들이 있다.
(B) 여자가 차량을 작업하고 있다.
(C) 여자가 노트북 컴퓨터 쪽으로 손을 뻗고 있다.
(D) 테이블 위에 전원 코드들이 놓여 있다.   정답 (D)

5. 호W
(A) A dock is being built in a harbor.
(B) Some boats have been docked under a canopy.
(C) A boat is racing through the water.
(D) There are some people fishing from a pier.

(A) 항구에 선착장이 건설되고 있다.
(B) 몇 대의 배들이 캐노피 아래 정박되어 있다.
(C) 배 한 척이 물살을 가르고 질주하고 있다.
(D) 잔교에서 낚시하고 있는 사람들이 있다.   정답 (B)

6. 영M
(A) A man is waiting at a baggage claim area.
(B) Some suitcases are going through a security check.
(C) A woman is examining a document.
(D) A woman is entering some information into a laptop.

(A) 남자가 수화물 찾는 곳에서 기다리고 있다.
(B) 여행가방들이 보안 검사대를 통과하고 있다.
(C) 여자가 서류를 검사하고 있다.
(D) 여자가 노트북 컴퓨터에 정보를 입력하고 있다.   정답 (C)

Part 2

7. 미M 호W
Why was the launch of our new line rescheduled?
(A) I'm having pizza for lunch.
(B) Sample this new line of wine.
(C) We have yet to finish testing.

우리 신제품 출시는 왜 일정이 조정되었나요?
(A) 저는 점심으로 피자를 먹을 거예요.
(B) 이 신제품 와인을 시음해 보세요.
(C) 우리는 아직 테스트를 끝내지 못했어요.   정답 (C)

8. 미M 미W
I like having some flower plants in the lobby.
(A) At the flower shop.
(B) I have plans for this weekend.
(C) I do, too.

저는 로비에 화초가 있는 게 좋아요.
(A) 꽃집에서요.
(B) 저는 이번 주말에 약속이 있어요.
(C) 저도요.   정답 (C)

9. 호W 미M
How much food should I purchase for the company outing?
(A) Enough for two dozens people.
(B) It costs more than 100 dollars.
(C) In the park on Elm Avenue.

회사 야유회를 위한 음식을 얼마나 사야 하나요?
(A) 24명이 먹기에 충분할 만큼이요.
(B) 100달러 이상 들어가요.
(C) 엘름 애비뉴에 있는 공원에서요.   정답 (A)

10. 미M 미W
We have plenty of paper left in the copy room, don't we?
(A) He left it in the conference room.
(B) I think there's enough.
(C) Two cups of coffee, please.

복사실에 용지가 많이 남아 있는 거죠, 그렇죠?
(A) 그는 그것을 회의실에 두고 왔어요.
(B) 충분하게 있는 것 같아요.
(C) 커피 두 잔 주세요.   정답 (B)

11. 미M 호W
Who is supposed to update our security procedures?
(A) Yes, it's up to you.
(B) I think it might be Annie.
(C) Show it to the security desk.

우리 보안 절차를 누가 업데이트하기로 되어 있나요?
(A) 예, 그건 당신에게 달려 있어요.
(B) 애니일 것 같아요.

(C) 그것을 경비과에 보여 주세요.　　　　　　정답 (B)

12. 영M 호W
Do you want me to call your work phone or your mobile phone?
(A) From the previous month.
(B) I only use my mobile phone.
(C) Please call me to let me know.

직장 전화로 전화드릴까요, 아니면 당신 휴대폰으로 전화드릴까요?
(A) 지난달 거예요.
(B) 저는 제 휴대폰만 사용해요.
(C) 저에게 전화해서 알려 주세요.　　　　　정답 (B)

13. 영M 미W
The plane hasn't left yet, has it?
(A) I had some leftovers from yesterday's party.
(B) No, you've got more than five minutes.
(C) I got here by train.

비행기는 아직 출발하지 않았죠, 그렇죠?
(A) 저는 어제 파티에서 남은 음식을 먹었어요.
(B) 예, 5분 이상 남아 있어요.
(C) 저는 여기에 기차로 왔어요.　　　　　　정답 (B)

14. 미M 호W
Would you like to come over and see the soccer match tonight?
(A) Our team won the competition.
(B) Yeah, that sounds great.
(C) It's an exact match.

오늘 밤 축구 시합을 보러 올래요?
(A) 우리 팀이 시합에서 이겼어요.
(B) 예, 그거 좋은데요.
(C) 그게 정확히 일치해요.　　　　　　　　정답 (B)

15. 미W 미M
There is a pharmacy on Main Street, isn't there?
(A) Yes, it's near the post office.
(B) Here is your prescription.
(C) No, take two pills after each meal.

메인 가에 약국이 있죠, 그렇지 않나요?
(A) 예, 우체국 근처에 있어요.
(B) 여기 손님의 처방전입니다.
(C) 아뇨, 식후마다 두 알씩 복용하세요.　　정답 (A)

16. 호W 영M
Traffic is unusually heavy on the highway this morning.
(A) I get to work by bus.
(B) I hope I don't miss my plane.
(C) The package is very light.

오늘 아침 고속도로의 교통체증이 평소와 달리 심하네요.
(A) 저는 버스로 출근해요.
(B) 제 비행기를 놓치지 않길 바랍니다.
(C) 그 소포는 아주 가볍군요.　　　　　　정답 (B)

17. 미M 미W
Excuse me, where can I find the dairy products?
(A) At the end of aisle 5.
(B) I heard it's high in demand.
(C) Yes, all the items are on sale.

실례합니다. 유제품은 어디에 있나요?
(A) 5번 통로 끝에 있어요.
(B) 그게 수요가 높다고 들었어요.
(C) 예, 모든 품목이 세일 중이에요.　　　　정답 (A)

18. 영M 미W
Did Chuck send the registration packets by e-mail or regular mail?
(A) In the registration desk.
(B) Yes, put it in my mailbox.
(C) Probably by express delivery.

척이 등록 서류 묶음을 이메일로 보냈어요, 아니면 일반우편으로 보냈어요?
(A) 등록 창구에서요.
(B) 예, 그것을 제 우편함에 넣어 주세요.
(C) 아마 속달로요.　　　　　　　　　　정답 (C)

19. 호W 미M
Will the store stay open late for the sales event?
(A) No, it is close to the station.
(B) We usually get an e-mail about that.
(C) Turn left at the intersection.

그 상점은 세일 행사 때 늦게까지 문을 여나요?
(A) 아뇨, 거긴 역에 가까워요.
(B) 우리는 보통 그것에 대해 이메일을 받아요.
(C) 교차로에서 좌회전하세요.　　　　　　정답 (B)

20. 영M 미W
I've lost my company identification badge.
(A) You will be issued a new one today.
(B) The new office looks more spacious.
(C) Yes, I joined the company last month.

제가 회사 신분증을 잃어버렸어요.
(A) 오늘 새것을 발급 받으실 거예요.
(B) 새 사무실이 더 넓어 보이네요.
(C) 예, 저는 지난달에 입사했어요.　　　　정답 (A)

21. 미M 호W
Didn't you sign up for the webinar?
(A) Yes, I resigned two weeks ago.
(B) Proceed to the cash register.
(C) No, I'll be away at that time.

웹 세미나를 신청하지 않으셨어요?
(A) 예, 저는 2주 전에 사임했어요.
(B) 계산대로 가세요.
(C) 네, 그 때는 제가 여기에 없을 거예요.　정답 (C)

22. 영M 미W
When did we carry out a health and safety inspection last?
(A) Only for two hours at a time.
(B) Yes, the meal this morning was very healthy.
(C) The records are available online.

우리는 건강 및 안전 검사를 마지막으로 언제 실시했죠?
(A) 한 번에 두 시간 동안만요.
(B) 예, 오늘 아침 식사는 아주 건강식이었어요.
(C) 기록을 온라인으로 볼 수 있어요.　　　정답 (C)

ACTUAL TEST···**12**

23. 미M 호W

I'm wondering where I should mail the short story I wrote.
(A) I can suggest a few of the leading literary magazines.
(B) Yes, I'll be back shortly.
(C) Send it by express mail, please.

제가 쓴 단편 소설을 어디로 우편 발송해야 하는지 궁금해요.
(A) 일류 문학 잡지 몇 개를 추천해 드릴 수 있어요.
(B) 예, 곧 돌아올게요.
(C) 그것을 속달로 보내세요.   정답 (A)

24. 영M 미W

When did you call the technician to come over?
(A) The copier should be over there.
(B) No, it wasn't functioning properly.
(C) I called him just now.

기술자에게 와 달라고 언제 전화했어요?
(A) 복사기는 저쪽에 있을 거예요.
(B) 아뇨, 그게 제대로 작동하지 않고 있었어요.
(C) 지금 막 그에게 전화했어요.   정답 (C)

25. 미M 호W

How often am I supposed to replace these batteries in the machine?
(A) We are looking for a replacement.
(B) It is a great place to relax.
(C) They're rechargeable.

기계의 이 배터리들을 얼마나 자주 교체해야 하는 거죠?
(A) 우리는 대체할 것을 찾고 있어요.
(B) 그곳은 휴식을 취하기에 좋은 장소예요.
(C) 그것들은 재충전되는 거예요.   정답 (C)

26. 영M 호W

Who is going to order the cake for Michelle's retirement party?
(A) Ice cream will be served instead.
(B) No, I didn't order it.
(C) We replaced that tire with the new one.

미셸의 은퇴 파티를 위해서 누가 케이크를 주문할 건가요?
(A) 아이스크림이 대신 제공될 거예요.
(B) 아뇨, 저는 그것을 주문하지 않았어요.
(C) 우리는 그 타이어를 새 것으로 교체했어요.   정답 (A)

27. 미M 미W

Do you know where we can pick up the tickets to the performance?
(A) The band was fantastic.
(B) I don't think I can go.
(C) It starts at about 7 o'clock.

공연 표를 어디서 구매할 수 있는지 아세요?
(A) 그 밴드는 환상적이었어요.
(B) 저는 갈 수 없을 것 같아요.
(C) 그것은 7시쯤에 시작해요.   정답 (B)

28. 호W 미M

Before we present these certificates, we should put them in frames.
(A) An art supply store is nearby, I think.
(B) No, you should proceed to the podium.

(C) I'm afraid the microphone is not working again.

이 증서들을 수여하기 전에, 액자에 넣어야 해요.
(A) 화방이 근처에 있는 거 같아요.
(B) 아뇨, 연단으로 가셔야 합니다.
(C) 마이크가 다시 작동하지 않는 것 같아요.   정답 (A)

29. 미M 미W

Could you tell me where Mr. Schmitz's office is?
(A) Only on weekends.
(B) All directors are on the 3rd floor.
(C) Put it over there in the corner.

슈미츠 씨의 사무실이 어디에 있는지 알려 주실래요?
(A) 주말에만요.
(B) 모든 이사님들이 3층에 계세요.
(C) 그것을 저쪽 구석에 놓으세요.   정답 (B)

30. 영M 미W

Why don't we design new jackets for the winter collection?
(A) Our current collection is a little outdated, isn't it?
(B) Yes, the art museum design is amazing.
(C) Did you put the price tags?

윈터 컬렉션을 위해서 새 재킷을 디자인하는 게 어때요?
(A) 현재 우리 컬렉션은 약간 구식이죠, 그렇죠?
(B) 예, 미술관 디자인은 놀라워요.
(C) 가격표를 붙였어요?   정답 (A)

31. 호W 미M

Don't hesitate to contact me if you have any more technical difficulties with the machine.
(A) The contract was signed yesterday.
(B) Press the red button on the side.
(C) Thanks. I have your business card.

기계에 기술적인 문제가 더 있다면, 주저하지 말고 저에게 연락 주세요.
(A) 계약서는 어제 서명되었어요.
(B) 옆에 있는 빨간색 버튼을 누르세요.
(C) 고마워요. 저에게 당신 명함이 있어요.   정답 (C)

Part 3

문제 32~34번은 다음 대화를 참조하시오. 영M 미W

M: Hello. I'm Eric Strauss. (32)**I've got an appointment at 4:30.**
W: Let me see… (32)**Yes, you'll be seeing Dr. Hampton.** Since this is your first time at the office, you need to fill out some paperwork.
M: (33)**Oh, someone from the office e-mailed me about that, so I completed the forms online and already submitted them.**
W: That's great. In that case, why don't you take a seat over there? The doctor will be with you in a moment.
M: Wait a minute. (34)**I just realized that I left my wallet in my car. I need to go back out to the parking lot.**
W: Sure.

M: 안녕하세요. 저는 에릭 스트라우스인데요. 진료 예약이 4시 30분에 있습니다.
W: 좀 볼게요… 예, 닥터 햄프턴에게 진료 받으시네요. 이 병원에 이번이

처음 오신 거니까, 서식을 좀 작성하셔야 합니다.

M: 오, 병원의 누군가가 그 건에 대해 저에게 이메일을 보내 주어서 온라인으로 양식을 작성하고 이미 제출했습니다.

W: 잘되었네요. 그렇다면 저쪽에 앉아 계시겠어요? 의사 선생님이 금방 환자 분을 보실 거예요.

M: 잠깐만요. 제 지갑을 차에 두고 왔다는 것을 방금 깨달았어요. 밖에 주차장으로 다시 가봐야겠어요.

W: 좋습니다.

32. 대화는 어디에서 이루어지는 것 같은가?
(A) 은행
(B) 관공서
(C) 병원
(D) 안경점 ...... 정답 (C)

33. 남자는 미리 무엇을 했는가?
(A) 서류를 작성했다.
(B) 온라인으로 서비스에 대한 예약금을 지불했다.
(C) 근무 시간 이후에 당직자에게 전화했다.
(D) 주차장에 대해 물어봤다. ...... 정답 (A)

34. 남자는 자신은 무엇을 할 것이라고 말하는가?
(A) 대기 구역에 앉아 있기
(B) 주차비 내기
(C) 두고 온 물건 찾아오기
(D) 인터넷 접속하기 ...... 정답 (C)

문제 35-37번은 다음 대화를 참조하시오. 호W 미M

W: You're aware that Jacob is going to be relocated to work at the Denver branch starting in July, right?

M: Yes, I heard that. (35)**Everyone on the marketing team is going to miss him.** But I'm sure he'll be a big asset in the Denver office.

W: Why don't we take him out to dinner on his last day of work?

M: That sounds great. (36)**I can reserve a table at the Italian restaurant he loves.** Should we get him a gift?

W: His manager is buying something for him for everyone on the team. (37)**But don't forget to drop by her office to sign the farewell card for him.**

- -

W: 7월부터 제이콥이 덴버 지사로 옮겨서 근무할 거 알고 있죠, 그렇죠?

M: 예, 들었어요. 마케팅 팀의 모두가 그를 그리워할 거예요. 그렇지만, 그는 덴버 지사에 큰 자산이 될 것임을 확신해요.

W: 근무 마지막 날에 그를 데리고 나가서 저녁 먹는 게 어떨까요?

M: 좋은 생각이네요. 그가 무척 좋아하는 이탈리아 식당에 테이블 하나를 제가 예약할 수 있어요. 그에게 선물도 할까요?

W: 그의 매니저가 팀 전원을 대신해서 그를 위한 선물을 사는 것 같아요. 그런데 매니저 사무실에 들러서 제이콥을 위한 송별 카드에 사인하는 거 잊지 마세요.

35. 제이콥은 어느 부서에서 근무하는가?
(A) 영업과
(B) 인사과
(C) 마케팅과
(D) 회계과 ...... 정답 (C)

36. 남자는 무엇을 하겠다고 말하는가?
(A) 예약하기
(B) 매니저와 얘기하기
(C) 납품업체에 연락하기
(D) 마케팅 보고서 검토하기 ...... 정답 (A)

37. 여자에 따르면, 남자가 매니저 사무실에 들러야 하는 이유는?
(A) 돈을 기부하기 위해
(B) 보고서를 받기 위해
(C) 카드에 사인하기 위해
(D) 영수증을 제출하기 위해 ...... 정답 (C)

문제 38-40번은 다음 3자 대화를 참조하시오. 영M 미M 미W

M1: Jeff, this builders' conference is fascinating. I'm glad Mr. Arnold allowed us to attend it.

M2: I agree. (38)**Our construction firm should benefit from everything we're learning here.** Oh, check out this booth on textile concrete.

W: Hello. Do you have any questions? (39)**My name is Anna, and I'm on the sales team at Madison Construction Materials.**

M2: What kind of concrete is this? I've never seen anything like it.

W: It's more lightweight and less costly to manufacture, and a lot stronger than reinforced concrete while using less material. (40)**I'll be giving a product demonstration in ten minutes.**

M1: (40)**I've got to meet a client, but you should attend, Jeff.**

M2: (40)**I think I will.**

- -

M1: 제프, 이 건축업체 총회는 너무 괜찮네요. 아놀드 씨가 우리가 총회에 참석할 수 있도록 허락해 줘서 다행이에요.

M2: 동감이에요. 우리 건설 회사는 우리가 여기서 알게 되는 모든 것에서 도움을 받을 거예요. 오, 직물 콘크리트에 관한 이 부스 좀 보세요.

W: 안녕하세요? 질문 있으세요? 제 이름은 안나인데, 매디슨 건축 자재 회사의 영업 팀에 있어요.

M2: 이것은 어떤 종류의 콘크리트인가요? 이런 것은 본 적이 없어요.

W: 이것은 더 경량이며 제조할 때 비용이 덜 들어가고, 재료는 덜 쓰면서도 강화 콘크리트보다 훨씬 더 강해요. 10분 후에 제가 제품 시연회를 할 겁니다.

M1: 나는 고객을 만나야 하는데, 당신은 참석하는 게 좋겠어요, 제프.

M2: 그럴까 생각해요.

38. 남자들은 어떤 종류의 업체에서 근무하는가?
(A) 건축 자재 회사
(B) 실내 디자인 회사
(C) 물류창고
(D) 건설 회사 ...... 정답 (D)

39. 여자의 직업은 무엇인가?
(A) 영업 사원
(B) 빌딩 검사관
(C) 건설 근로자
(D) 건축가 ...... 정답 (A)

40. 제프는 10분 후에 무엇을 할 계획인가?
(A) 고객에게 연락하기

(B) 총회 행사장 떠나기
(C) 시연회 보기
(D) 건설 계약을 최종 결정하기   정답 (C)

문제 41-43번은 다음 대화를 참조하시오. 영M 미W

M: (41)Tina, I reviewed the chocolate candy commercial which you edited.

W: How did you like it?

M: I agree with what you said previously. The new camera angle works much better. (42)However, there's a problem with the audio which is out of sync with the video.

W: (42)Oh, sorry. I will use the new software we bought to fix it. It shouldn't take long.

M: Yeah, that software is amazing. The rest of the ad looks great. (43)I love the actress you hired. She does a wonderful job and says her lines really well.

M: 티나, 당신이 편집한 초콜릿 캔디 광고를 검토했어요.

W: 어땠어요?

M: 전에 당신이 얘기한 것에 공감해요. 새 카메라 앵글 작업이 훨씬 낫네요. 그런데 오디오에 문제가 좀 있는데, 비디오와 잘 맞지 않아요.

W: 오, 죄송해요. 우리가 산 새 소프트웨어를 이용해서 그걸 수정할게요. 오래 걸리지 않을 거예요.

M: 예, 그 소프트웨어는 놀라워요. 광고 나머지 부분은 괜찮아 보여요. 당신이 고용한 여배우가 정말 마음에 들어요. 정말 잘하고 대사를 정말 잘 말해요.

41. 화자들은 어떤 프로젝트에 대해 논의하는가?
(A) 다가오는 행사 녹화하기
(B) 광고 편집하기
(C) 계약 협상하기
(D) 신제품 개발하기   정답 (B)

42. 여자가 사과하는 이유는?
(A) 그녀는 기술적인 실수를 했다.
(B) 그녀는 광고 대본을 검토하는 것을 잊었다.
(C) 그녀는 광고 팀 회의에 늦었다.
(D) 그녀는 남자의 아이디어가 마음에 들지 않는다.   정답 (A)

43. 남자는 무엇이 마음에 든다고 말하는가?
(A) 인쇄물 광고의 색 패턴
(B) 광고의 길이
(C) 여배우가 말하는 투
(D) 포장 디자인   정답 (C)

문제 44-46번은 다음 대화를 참조하시오. 호W 미M

W: I just received this month's bill from the cleaning service we hire. We might have to do something.

M: What's wrong? (44)Did the price go up?

W: (44)Almost double. You know, the people it sends us do good work. They keep the office nice and tidy, but we wouldn't be able to sustain it if they continued to charge us at this rate.

M: Well, (45)the firm upstairs has a cleaning crew of its own.

W: (45)Really? I'll go up and talk to Ms. Archer now. In the meantime, (46)would you mind getting some pastries and

coffee for the eleven A.M. meeting?

M: Not at all. I'll head to the café across the street.

W: 우리가 고용하고 있는 청소업체로부터 방금 이번 달 청구서를 받았어요. 뭔가 조치를 취해야 할지 모르겠네요.

M: 뭐가 잘못되었어요? 가격이 올랐어요?

W: 거의 두 배로 올랐어요. 아시잖아요, 거기서 보내 주는 사람들이 일을 잘하긴 해요. 사무실을 계속해서 좋고 깔끔하게 유지해 주긴 하지만, 그 업체에서 이 요금으로 계속 청구한다면 우리는 버틸 수 없을 거예요.

M: 음, 위층에 있는 회사는 자체적으로 청소 직원을 두고 있어요.

W: 정말이에요? 지금 올라가서 아처 씨와 얘기해 볼게요. 그 동안 괜찮다면 오전 11시 회의에 필요한 페이스트리와 커피 좀 사다 주실래요?

M: 그럼요. 길 건너 카페로 가 볼게요.

44. 화자들은 어떤 문제에 대해 논의하는가?
(A) 청소 작업이 잘 안 되었다.
(B) 프로젝트가 완료되지 않았다.
(C) 가격이 올랐다.
(D) 일정이 변경되었다.   정답 (C)

45. 남자가 "위층에 있는 회사는 자체적으로 청소 직원을 두고 있어요"라고 말하는 이유는?
(A) 제안을 하기 위해
(B) 청소를 도와주겠다고 제의하기 위해
(C) 아이디어에 대해 찬성하기 위해
(D) 부진한 업무 성과에 대해 사과하기 위해   정답 (A)

46. 여자는 남자에게 무엇을 해달라고 요청하는가?
(A) 비행기 티켓 예약
(B) 서류 출력
(C) 저녁 예약
(D) 다과류 구입   정답 (D)

문제 47-49번은 다음 대화를 참조하시오. 미W 미M

W: Hello, Mr. Martin. (47)I'm sorry I'm late. The roads were full of cars today. Everyone's driving slowly because of the unexpected snow.

M: No problem, Erica. We haven't had many customers yet. I just hope the delivery truck isn't delayed by this weather.

W: Are we expecting something to be delivered?

M: (48)We're getting three new laptop computers for the office. They're supposed to get here today. I was planning to ask you to help format them.

W: No problem. Um… What are you doing with the old laptops? (49)I know of an electronics store that might buy them.

M: Wonderful. (49)Could you give a call to someone there?

W: Of course.

W: 안녕하세요, 마틴. 늦어서 죄송해요. 오늘 도로가 차로 가득했어요. 예상치 못한 눈 때문에 다들 서행 운전하고 있어요.

M: 괜찮아요, 에리카. 아직은 고객이 많지 않았어요. 저는 그냥 배달 트럭이 이런 날씨 때문에 늦어지지 않았으면 좋겠네요.

W: 뭐 배달될 것을 기다리고 있어요?

M: 사무실용 새 노트북 컴퓨터 세 대를 구매하거든요. 그 노트북 컴퓨터들이 오늘 여기 도착하게 되어 있어요. 그거 포맷하는 거 도와달라고 부탁하려고 했어요.

W: 문제없죠. 음… 낡은 노트북 컴퓨터는 어떻게 할 건가요? 전자제품 매

장 한 군데를 알고 있는데, 그 노트북들을 구입해 줄지 몰라요.
M: 잘되었네요. 거기 사람에게 전화해볼 수 있어요?
W: 물론이에요.

47. 여자가 직장에 지각한 이유는?
(A) 자동차 정비소에 들러야 했다.
(B) 지하철을 놓쳤다.
(C) 교통체증으로 길이 막혔다.
(D) 치과 진료 예약이 있었다. 　　　　　정답 (C)

48. 오늘 무엇이 도착할 예정인가?
(A) 노트북 컴퓨터
(B) 미술 용품
(C) 옷감
(D) 상점 카탈로그 　　　　　정답 (A)

49. 여자는 어떤 업체에 연락할 것인가?
(A) 전자제품 매장
(B) 재활용 센터
(C) 문구점
(D) 백화점 　　　　　정답 (A)

문제 50-52번은 다음 대화를 참조하시오. 영M 미W

M: I thought you'd like to know that management is impressed with your performance, Molly. (50)Your landing the biggest sales contract in the company's history last month is quite an achievement.
W: Thank you. Working here in the Sales Department has been a great experience so far.
M: You know, there's going to be a management position opening in the Sales Department next month. Even though you haven't been here for very long, (51)I think you should consider applying for it.
W: It sounds interesting, but I wonder if you could let me know what my duties entail.
M: Sure. (52)But I have to leave now to meet a client for lunch. How about stopping by my office around four this afternoon?

M: 몰리, 경영진이 당신의 성과에 대해 깊은 인상을 받았다는 것을 알고 싶을 텐데요. 지난달에 당신이 회사 역사상 최대의 판매 계약을 따낸 것은 엄청난 성과입니다.
W: 감사합니다. 여기 영업부에서 근무하는 것은 지금까지 정말 좋은 경험이었어요.
M: 있잖아요. 다음 달에 영업부에 관리자 자리가 하나 빌 거예요. 당신은 여기에서 그렇게 오래 근무하지는 않았지만, 내 생각에는 당신이 그 자리 지원을 고려해 보면 좋을 것 같아요.
W: 흥미롭게 들리긴 하는데, 내가 맡을 업무에 어떤 것이 수반되는지 알려 주실 수 있을까요?
M: 물론이죠. 그런데 고객을 만나 점심 먹으러 지금 나가야 해요. 오늘 오후 4시쯤에 내 사무실에 들르는 게 어때요?

50. 여자는 최근에 무엇을 했는가?
(A) 그녀는 시장조사를 했다.
(B) 그녀는 이번 주에 근무를 시작했다.
(C) 그녀는 계약을 따냈다.
(D) 그녀는 업무차 해외로 출장 갔다. 　　　　　정답 (C)

51. 남자는 여자에게 무엇을 고려할 것을 권하는가?
(A) 직무기술서 검토하기
(B) 자리에 지원하기
(C) 새 프로젝트 수락하기
(D) 전근 요청하기 　　　　　정답 (B)

52. 남자는 이후에 무엇을 할 것이라고 말하는가?
(A) 식사
(B) 납품업체 방문
(C) 계약 서명
(D) 회의 참석 　　　　　정답 (A)

문제 53-55번은 다음 대화를 참조하시오. 미W 미M

W: (53)Thank you for visiting Watson Paint. I'm the manager. What can I do for you?
M: Hello. (54)I acquired an office building nearby last month, and I'd like to have all of the interior walls repainted.
W: Of course. Have you decided on which color you'd like them to be?
M: I haven't decided yet. Could you show me some samples?
W: Yes. (55)You know, our store has a mobile application that many customers find handy.
M: Is that so?
W: (55)Sure. It lets you visualize what your office will look like with various colored walls. You take a picture, upload it to the app, and then apply different colors. Then, you can see what it will look like.

W: 왓슨 페인트를 방문해 주셔서 감사합니다. 저는 매니저인데, 뭘 도와드릴까요?
M: 안녕하세요. 지난달에 근처 사무실 빌딩을 매입했는데, 실내 모든 벽을 다시 페인트 칠하고 싶어요.
W: 물론 되죠. 벽이 어떤 색깔이면 좋을지 결정하셨어요?
M: 아직 결정 안했어요. 샘플 좀 보여 주시겠어요?
W: 예. 있잖아요, 우리 매장은 많은 고객들이 유용하다고 생각하는 모바일 앱이 있어요.
M: 그래요?
W: 그럼요. 그 앱은 다양한 색깔의 벽으로 사무실이 어떻게 보일지 시각화시켜 줘요. 사진을 찍어서 그것을 앱에 업로드한 다음, 다양한 색깔을 적용시켜 보세요. 그러면 사무실이 어떤 모습으로 보일지 볼 수 있을 거예요.

53. 여자는 누구인가?
(A) 매장 매니저
(B) 부동산 중개인
(C) 금융 자문관
(D) 페인트 납품업체 　　　　　정답 (A)

54. 남자는 지난달에 무슨 일이 있었다고 말하는가?
(A) 그는 봉급이 올랐다.
(B) 그는 건물을 매입했다.
(C) 그는 도시로 이사했다.
(D) 그는 새로운 일을 시작했다. 　　　　　정답 (B)

55. 여자는 무엇을 할 것을 권장하는가?
(A) 홍보용 전단지 제작
(B) 모바일 마케팅 전략 사용
(C) 대량 구매

(D) 모바일 앱 이용

정답 (D)

문제 56-58번은 다음 3자 대화를 참조하시오. 영M 호W 미M

M1: Hello, Kay. (56)Thanks for coming here to the factory to fix the problem on such short notice. This is Steve, the floor manager.

W: Pleased to meet you.

M2: The feeling is mutual. Yesterday, we noticed that one of our laser cutters was not functioning properly.

M1: (57)It's an expensive machine, so we hope it doesn't cost too much to fix.

M2: (57)Right. We're especially concerned about that.

W: Well, I can't tell you a quote of how much the repairs will be until I take a look at it. (58)But I'm familiar with this type of machine, so I'll be able to determine the problem quickly.

M1: 안녕하세요, 케이. 그렇게 급하게 연락 드렸음에도 불구하고 문제를 해결하기 위해 여기 공장에 와주셔서 감사합니다. 공장 현장 감독인 스티브입니다.

W: 만나 뵙게 되어 반갑습니다.

M2: 저도 같은 마음입니다. 어제, 레이저 커팅 기계 중 하나가 제대로 작동하지 않고 있다는 것을 알게 되었습니다.

M1: 그게 비싼 기계라서, 수리하는 데 비용이 너무 많이 들지 않으면 좋겠어요.

M2: 맞습니다. 우리는 특히 그것이 우려가 됩니다.

W: 글쎄, 제가 그 기계를 볼 때까지는 수리비가 얼마나 될지 견적을 알려드릴 수 없어요. 그렇지만 이런 종류의 기계는 제가 익숙해서 문제를 빨리 파악할 수 있을 거예요.

56. 여자는 누구일 것 같은가?
(A) 배달 운전사
(B) 수리하는 사람
(C) 공장장
(D) 조립라인 직원

정답 (B)

57. 남자들은 무엇에 대해 우려를 나타내는가?
(A) 잠재적인 비용
(B) 비품 부족
(C) 고장 난 기계
(D) 많은 업무량

정답 (A)

58. 여자에 따르면, 그녀가 문제를 빨리 파악할 수 있는 이유는?
(A) 그녀는 장비에 대해 알고 있다.
(B) 그녀는 다른 업무가 없다.
(C) 제품 일부 사양이 간단하다.
(D) 제조 공장이 그다지 넓지 않다.

정답 (A)

문제 59-61번은 다음 대화를 참조하시오. 미W 영M

W: Hello, Jeff. (59)How is the work on the cover of next month's magazine going?

M: I'm nearly finished. Since next month's theme is summer trends, I combined a few images from some local gardens.

W: Great idea. You know, the design of the cover looks nice, but (60)there are tons of images.

M: Hmm… (60)Maybe I should remove a few.

W: That would be perfect. Once you are done, let's talk about our next issue. It's going to be the fiftieth edition of the magazine, (61)so we need to create a special cover for it and reveal it at our anniversary celebration in August.

W: 안녕하세요, 제프. 다음 달 잡지 표지 작업이 어떻게 되어가고 있어요?

M: 거의 끝냈어요. 다음 달 주제는 여름철 유행이기 때문에, 이 지역 정원의 일부 이미지를 몇 개 합쳐서 만들었어요.

W: 좋은 생각이에요. 있잖아요. 표지 디자인이 멋있어 보이긴 하는데, 이미지가 너무 많아요.

M: 음… 이미지 몇 개를 빼야 할까 봐요.

W: 그렇게 하면 아주 좋죠. 일단 다 끝내면, 우리 다음 호에 대해서 논의합시다. 잡지 50주년 에디션이 될 거라서, 그를 위한 특별한 표지를 만들어서 8월 우리 기념일 축하 때 공개해야 해요.

59. 화자들은 어디에서 근무하는 것 같은가?
(A) 잡지 출판사
(B) 서점
(C) 그래픽 디자인 회사
(D) 도서관

정답 (A)

60. 여자가 "이미지가 너무 많아요"라고 말할 때 무엇을 의미하는가?
(A) 그녀는 남자의 창의성에 깊은 인상을 받았다.
(B) 남자는 더 많은 이미지를 사용해야 한다.
(C) 디자인이 더 단순하게 만들어져야 한다.
(D) 서면 설명이 필요하다.

정답 (C)

61. 회사는 8월에 무엇을 축하할 것인가?
(A) 은퇴
(B) 성공적인 인수
(C) 새 계약
(D) 기념일

정답 (D)

문제 62-64번은 다음 대화와 상품 명세서를 참조하시오. 호W 미M

W: Hello. This is Susan from customer service at Anderson Clothing.

M: Hello. I'm trying to make a purchase from your online shop. (62)However, when I attempt to check out, my credit card gets rejected.

W: I'm sorry about that. Why don't you make your order over the phone right now?

M: When would the items get mailed to me if I did that?

W: (63)They'd be shipped out first thing tomorrow.

M: Great. (64)I would like the men's long-sleeved T-shirt in a size large. It should be red.

W: No problem at all. Could you give me your credit card number, please?

W: 안녕하세요. 앤더슨 의류회사의 고객 서비스과 수잔입니다.

M: 안녕하세요. 거기 온라인 매장에서 구매를 하려고 하는데요. 그런데, 계산하려고 하는데, 제 신용 카드가 거부되네요.

W: 그거 죄송하게 되었네요. 지금 전화상으로 주문하시겠어요?

M: 그렇게 하면, 언제쯤 물건이 저에게 발송되나요?

W: 내일 아침 가장 먼저 발송될 거예요.

M: 좋아요. 그럼 라지 사이즈로 남성용 긴 소매 셔츠로 하고 싶어요, 빨간색이어야 하고요.

W: 전혀 문제 없어요. 신용 카드 번호를 알려 주시겠습니까?

품목	품목 번호	가격
(64)남성용 티셔츠	3490544	(64)$25
남성용 운동화	3095343	$99
남성용 스웨터	8574400	$50
남성용 반바지	6834233	$65

62. 남자는 어떤 문제를 가지고 있는가?
(A) 그가 원하는 것이 품절되었다.
(B) 그의 신용 카드가 분실되었다.
(C) 그의 주소가 잘못 입력되었다.
(D) 결제가 받아들여지지 않았다.　　　　정답 (D)

63. 여자는 내일 무슨 일이 있을 것이라고 말하는가?
(A) 할인이 적용될 것이다.
(B) 재고정리 세일이 끝날 것이다.
(C) 새 매장이 문을 열 것이다.
(D) 주문한 물건이 발송될 것이다.　　　　정답 (D)

64. 그래픽을 보시오. 남자가 구매하고 싶어하는 물건의 가격은 얼마인가?
(A) 25달러
(B) 50달러
(C) 65달러
(D) 99달러　　　　정답 (A)

문제 65-67번은 다음 대화와 일정표를 참조하시오. 영M 미W

M: It's a pleasure to meet you, Emily. Welcome to your first day of work. I'm John, your manager, and I'll help you get through orientation. You should have received an e-mail about the schedule of everything I'd like us to handle today.
W: Thanks. (65)I'm excited to be working at the city's top financial consulting company. I have a question. What will we be doing during the workshop?
M: We'll discuss how to work with clients and what to do when you encounter various problems and issues. (66)That session will be led by a representative from HR. Now, (67)let's go to the cafeteria to get some coffee before starting.

M: 만나서 반가워요, 에밀리. 근무 첫날을 환영합니다. 저는 당신의 관리자 존이고, 오리엔테이션 끝내는 것을 도와드릴게요. 오늘 우리가 다루었으면 하는 모든 것의 일정에 대해 이메일을 이미 받으셨을 거예요.
W: 감사합니다. 이 도시 최고의 재무 컨설팅 회사에서 일하게 되어 너무 좋습니다. 질문이 있는데요. 워크숍 동안에 무엇을 하게 되나요?
M: 고객과 어떻게 일을 진행할지, 여러 다양한 문제에 봉착했을 때 어떻게 해야할지에 대해 논의하게 될 거예요. 그 세션은 인적자원부 직원이 진행하게 될 거예요. 자, 시작하기 전에 구내식당에 가서 커피 좀 마십시다.

직원 오리엔테이션 일정

건물 구경	오전 10:00
(66)워크숍	오전 11:00
점심	오후 12:30
환영사	오후 2:00

65. 화자들은 어떤 산업에서 일하는가?
(A) 금융
(B) 제조
(C) 정보 기술
(D) 광고　　　　정답 (A)

66. 그래픽을 보시오. 인적자원부 직원은 언제 화자들과 합류할 것인가?
(A) 오전 10시
(B) 오전 11시
(C) 오후 12시 30분
(D) 오후 2시　　　　정답 (B)

67. 화자들은 뒤이어 어디에 갈 것 같은가?
(A) 대강당
(B) 구내식당
(C) 남자의 사무실
(D) 회의실　　　　정답 (B)

문제 68-70번은 다음 대화와 지도를 참조하시오. 호W 미M

W: Hello, Greg. I sent you a map featuring some office buildings. I also attached some pictures of the rooms along with their dimensions. (68)Which do you think would be best for our new dental clinic?
M: The one nearest the local hospital would be ideal.
W: Well, (69)I think the one across the street from City Hall would work better because it has a better layout and its rent is cheaper.
M: Okay. That's fine with me. (70)Why don't you talk to David and see when he is available? Then, we can all visit that place together.

W: 안녕하세요, 그레그. 사무실 건물들이 있는 지도를 보냈어요. 또한 크기와 더불어 방 사진도 첨부했어요. 어느 것이 우리 새 치과를 하기에 가장 좋을 것 같아요?
M: 지역 병원과 가장 가까운 곳이 이상적이긴 해요.
W: 음, 내 생각에는 시청 맞은 편에 있는 건물이 더 좋을 것 같아요. 왜냐하면 배치가 더 낫고 임대료도 더 저렴해요.
M: 알겠습니다. 저도 괜찮아요. 데이비드에게 얘기해서 그가 언제 시간이 되는지 알아봐 주실래요? 그러면 우리 모두 함께 그 장소를 방문할 수 있으니까요.

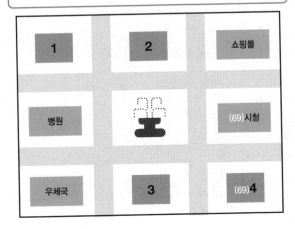

68. 화자들은 어떤 분야에서 일하는 것 같은가?
(A) 부동산
(B) 의료
(C) 교육
(D) 출판
정답 (B)

69. 그래픽을 보시오. 여자는 어느 건물이 좋다고 말하는가?
(A) 건물 1
(B) 건물 2
(C) 건물 3
(D) 건물 4
정답 (D)

70. 남자는 여자에게 무엇을 할 것을 요청하는가?
(A) 동료에게 얘기하기
(B) 서류 복사하기
(C) 부동산 중개인에게 전화하기
(D) 계약서 검토하기
정답 (A)

Part 4

문제 71-73번은 다음 전화 메시지를 참조하시오. 미W

W: Hello, Kevin. This is Samantha. I just spoke on the phone with one of the leading candidates for the head engineer position. (71)I'd like to have him visit for an interview, but I need to check about the cost with you. Can we cover his travel expenses? (72)He doesn't live around here. He'd be flying in from Seattle. I'd like to arrange everything by the end of the day if possible. (73)I just e-mailed you a cost estimate. Could you tell me what you think of it?

안녕하세요. 케빈. 사만다예요. 지금 막 수석 엔지니어 자리에 지원한 주요 지원자 중 한 명과 전화 통화를 했어요. 그 사람을 면접 보러 오게 하고 싶은데, 비용에 대해 당신에게 확인해야 해서요. 그의 여행 경비를 우리가 충당해줄 수 있나요? 그는 여기에 살지 않아요. 시애틀에서 비행기 타고 올 거예요. 가능하면 오늘 중으로 모든 것을 준비하고 싶어요. 지금 막 당신에게 이메일로 비용 견적서를 보냈어요. 이에 대해 어떻게 생각하는지 말씀해 주시겠어요?

71. 화자가 전화를 거는 이유는?
(A) 지출에 대해 승인을 요청하기 위해
(B) 자신이 면접 보러 갈 수 있는지 물어보기 위해
(C) 이전에 일정이 잡힌 회의를 취소하기 위해
(D) 오찬 참석을 확인하기 위해
정답 (A)

72. 화자는 입사 지원자에 대해 무엇을 말하는가?
(A) 그의 자격요건이 인상적이다.
(B) 그는 이 지역에 살지 않는다.
(C) 그는 추가적인 현장 교육이 더 필요하다.
(D) 그는 외국에서 근무했다.
정답 (B)

73. 화자는 이메일로 무엇을 보냈다고 말했는가?
(A) 발표 메모
(B) 회의 의제
(C) 여행 일정표
(D) 가격 견적서
정답 (D)

문제 74-76번은 다음 연설을 참조하시오. 영M

M: It's wonderful to be here at the International Sports Expo. (74)I'd like to let everyone know that my company will be releasing one of the most anticipated designs of the year, the smart bike helmet next week. The helmet uses state-of-the-art technology to provide built-in Bluetooth speakers and wind-resistant microphones for hands-free communication. (75)What's especially important to me is that the smart helmet is offered at a reasonable price. Despite its low price, this bike helmet shares many smart features as its more expensive counterparts. (76)Please pay attention to the screen behind me and I'll show you a video so that you can get a first-hand look at the smart helmet in action.

여기 국제 스포츠 엑스포에 오게 되어 너무 좋습니다. 여러분에게 알려 드리고 싶은 것은 우리 회사가 올해 가장 기대되는 디자인 중 하나인, 스마트 자전거 헬멧을 다음 주에 출시한다는 것입니다. 이 헬멧은 최첨단 기술을 이용해서 내장된 블루투스 스피커와 핸즈프리 통화를 위한 바람에 견딜 수 있는 마이크를 제공한다는 것입니다. 특히 저에게 중요한 점은 스마트 헬멧이 적정 가격에 제공된다는 것입니다. 낮은 가격에도 불구하고, 이 자전거 헬멧은 다른 더 비싼 헬멧들처럼 많은 스마트 기능을 공유하고 있습니다. 제 뒤에 있는 화면을 봐주시면, 스마트 헬멧이 작동하는 것을 직접 보실 수 있도록 비디오를 보여 드리겠습니다.

74. 화자의 회사는 무슨 제품을 개발했는가?
(A) 자전거 헬멧
(B) 마이크 신제품
(C) 공기 주입식 마사지 공
(D) 조절 가능한 지팡이
정답 (A)

75. 화자는 자신에게 무엇이 중요하다고 말하는가?
(A) 감당할 수 있는 가격
(B) 내구성
(C) 경량성
(D) 호환성
정답 (A)

76. 화자는 뒤이어 무엇을 할 것인가?
(A) 양식 수거하기
(B) 안내책자 검토하기
(C) 샘플 나눠 주기
(D) 비디오 보여 주기
정답 (D)

문제 77-79번은 다음 회의 발췌 내용을 참조하시오. 호W

W: (77)This meeting is for everybody—cooks, servers, hosts, and cleaners—because we all need to work together to succeed. Today is very important. (78)First, thanks for coming in early to get ready for our grand opening. Second, (79)you should know that a journalist from the local paper, David Atwell, has made a reservation for 7:30. Mr. Atwell will be writing a review about his experience here as well as the quality of the food we serve. So please take good care of him. A positive review will help us attract more customers.

이 회의는 - 요리사, 서빙하는 사람, 손님을 모시는 사람, 청소하는 사람 - 모두를 위한 회의입니다. 왜냐하면 우리는 모두 성공하기 위해서 협력해야 하기 때문입니다. 오늘은 아주 중요합니다. 우선, 우리의 개업을 준비하기 위

해서 일찍 와주셔서 감사합니다. 두 번째로, 지역 신문사 기자인 데이비드 애트웰 씨가 7시 30분에 예약이 되어 있다는 것을 알아 두셔야 합니다. 애트웰 씨는 우리가 제공하는 음식의 질뿐만 아니라 이곳에서의 자신의 경험에 대해서도 비평을 쓸 것입니다. 그러니, 그 분을 잘 모셔 주세요. 긍정적인 평은 우리가 더 많은 고객들을 끌어들이는 데 도움이 될 것입니다.

77. 청자들은 어디에 근무하는 것 같은가?
(A) 식당
(B) 농장
(C) 농산물 시장
(D) 식료품점 　　　　　　　　　　　　　　　정답 (A)

78. 청자들은 어떤 행사를 준비하고 있는가?
(A) 주말 세일
(B) 개업
(C) 요리 경연대회
(D) 특별 요리 수업 　　　　　　　　　　　　정답 (B)

79. 데이비드 애트웰은 누구인가?
(A) 수상 경력이 있는 요리사
(B) 사진사
(C) 신문사 기자
(D) 헬스 트레이너 　　　　　　　　　　　　정답 (C)

문제 80-82번은 다음 담화를 참조하시오. 영M

M: Hello. My name is David Cartwright, and I'll be your instructor for this workshop. (80) (81)Today, I'm going to show you how to use your company's newest accounting software. During this session, I'll demonstrate how to utilize all of the functions of this software in the most efficient way. I want you to learn as much as possible so that you can help your clients with their finances. Now, before we begin, I'd like to know which computer programs you're already familiar with. (82)Please complete the survey sheet that I just handed out. When you're done, I'll pick them up.

- -

안녕하세요. 제 이름은 데이비드 카트라이트이고 이 워크숍 강사입니다. 오늘, 저는 여러분 회사의 최신 회계 소프트웨어를 어떻게 사용하는지 보여 드릴 것입니다. 이 워크숍 세션 동안, 저는 이 소프트웨어의 모든 기능을 어떻게 하면 가장 효율적으로 활용할 수 있는지 예시를 들면서 가르쳐 드릴 것입니다. 여러분이 여러분 고객의 재무상황을 도와 드릴 수 있도록 가능한 한 많이 배우시기를 바랍니다. 이제 시작하기 전에, 여러분이 이미 익숙한 컴퓨터 프로그램이 어떤 것인지 알고 싶네요. 지금 막 나눠 드린 설문지를 작성해 주십시오. 작성이 다 끝나시면, 제가 수거하겠습니다.

80. 워크숍 중에 청자들은 무엇을 배우게 될 것인가?
(A) 코스를 등록하는 방법
(B) 세금 서식을 작성하는 방법
(C) 유능한 회계사가 되는 방법
(D) 소프트웨어 프로그램을 사용하는 방법 　　정답 (D)

81. 청자들은 어떤 종류의 일을 할 것 같은가?
(A) 제조
(B) 엔지니어링
(C) 회계
(D) 프로그래밍 　　　　　　　　　　　　　정답 (C)

82. 화자는 청자들에게 무엇을 할 것을 요청하는가?
(A) 파트너와 짝 이루기
(B) 컴퓨터 가져오기
(C) 등록 서류 묶음 가져가기
(D) 양식 작성하기 　　　　　　　　　　　　정답 (D)

문제 83-85번은 다음 회의 발췌 내용을 참조하시오. 미W

W: (83)Okay, the next item on the agenda is how to retain quality personnel. That's a top priority at our firm. We believe offering competitive salaries and comprehensive benefits packages should let us both recruit and keep talented employees. That's why we hired Allison Hyatt. (84)Allison is an HR consultant who's going to work here for a few months to help us restructure our compensation packages. Right now, (85)she needs feedback from the staff. To that end, she has put together a questionnaire that she's going to distribute to the staff when we are finished today. I know we're all busy, but (85)this is something that affects everybody.

- -

좋아요, 의제의 다음 항목은 어떻게 하면 우수한 인재들을 유지할 수 있는지에 대한 것입니다. 이것은 우리 회사의 최우선 사항입니다. 경쟁력 있는 급여와 포괄적인 복리후생 패키지를 제공하게 되면 우리는 유능한 직원들을 모집하고 계속 보유할 수 있게 될 것입니다. 그래서 우리는 앨리슨 하이엇을 고용했습니다. 앨리슨은 인적자원부 컨설턴트인데, 이 분은 몇 달 동안 여기에서 근무하면서 우리의 보상 패키지를 재편성하는 것을 도와줄 것입니다. 지금, 그녀는 직원들의 의견이 필요합니다. 그 목적을 위해서 그녀가 설문지를 만들었는데, 오늘 회의가 끝날 때 직원들에게 나눠줄 것입니다. 우리 전부 바쁜 것은 압니다만, 이것은 우리 모두에게 영향을 주는 중요한 것입니다.

83. 화자에 따르면, 최우선 사항은 무엇인가?
(A) 우수한 직원들을 보유하는 것
(B) 직원들의 사기를 높이는 것
(C) 회사의 이윤을 증진시키는 것
(D) 제조 비용을 줄이는 것 　　　　　　　　정답 (A)

84. 앨리슨 하이엇은 누구인가?
(A) 회사 대변인
(B) 인적자원부 컨설턴트
(C) 시장 조사원
(D) 회사 중역 　　　　　　　　　　　　　　정답 (B)

85. 화자가 "이것은 우리 모두에게 영향을 주는 중요한 것입니다"라고 말하는 이유는?
(A) 실수에 대한 경고를 하기 위해
(B) 안 좋은 소식을 전하기 위해
(C) 참여를 독려하기 위해
(D) 직원 부족에 대해 사과하기 위해 　　　　정답 (C)

문제 86-88번은 다음 투어 안내를 참조하시오. 호W

W: Thank you for taking this tour of Freeport Manufacturing. Our town has become famous for the tires produced here. (86) In fact, this tire factory is the major employer in town. (87) While everyone locally is familiar with our tires, we also ship our products to countries around the world. Today, you'll see the process of making tires from start to finish. After the tour ends, you can visit our gift shop, where you can find all sorts of things that will remind you of your visit. Please remember to keep your tour ticket. (88)Present it to the cashier, and you can get ten percent off everything you buy.

이번 프리포트 제조회사 투어에 참여해 주셔서 감사합니다. 우리 지역은 여기서 생산되는 타이어로 유명해졌습니다. 사실, 이 타이어 공장은 이 마을의 주요 고용업체입니다. 이 지역의 모든 사람이 우리 타이어를 잘 알지만, 우리는 또한 전세계 나라들로 우리 제품을 배송합니다. 오늘, 여러분은 처음부터 끝까지 타이어를 만드는 과정을 보게 될 것입니다. 투어가 끝나고 난 이후에는 선물 가게를 방문하실 수 있는데, 거기서 여러분은 여러분의 방문을 기억나게 할 온갖 종류의 물건들을 보실 수 있습니다. 여러분의 투어 티켓을 꼭 간직하고 계십시오. 그것을 계산원에게 제시하면, 여러분이 구매하시는 모든 물건에서 10% 할인을 받으실 수 있습니다.

86. 투어는 어디에서 이루어지고 있는가?
(A) 전자제품 매장
(B) 타이어 공장
(C) 박물관
(D) 의류 제조업체 　　　　　　　　정답 (B)

87. 화자가 "우리는 또한 전세계 나라들로 우리 제품을 배송합니다"라고 말하는 이유는?
(A) 제품이 얼마나 인기 있는지 강조하기 위해
(B) 장소가 왜 그렇게 넓은지 설명하기 위해
(C) 최근의 지연에 대해 사과하기 위해
(D) 특별 서비스가 이용 가능하다는 것을 확인하기 위해 　　정답 (A)

88. 화자는 청자들에게 무엇을 이용할 수 있다고 말하는가?
(A) 경품 추첨행사 참가
(B) 무료 행사 캘린더
(C) 구매물건에 대한 할인
(D) 오디오 투어 　　　　　　　　정답 (C)

문제 89-91번은 다음 방송을 참조하시오. 미|M

M: This is your local news update. (89)Yesterday, Wrangler Travel, a ride-sharing company, announced that it has received a permit to operate here in Salem. (90)To recruit new drivers, Wrangler will lease electric vehicles to individuals without their own cars and will charge very low rates. The city's spokesman, Jason Cates, stated that the permit was awarded due to the lack of transportation options in the city, especially for people in low-income groups. (91)Given that Salem will be hosting the Golden Games next month, many people are expected to flock to the town to watch the athletes in action and Wrangler is likely to be very busy soon.

최신 지역 뉴스입니다. 어제, 랭글러 트래블, 승차 공유 회사가 여기 살렘에서 사업을 운영할 수 있는 허가증을 받았다고 발표했습니다. 새로운 운전자를 모집하기 위해서, 랭글러는 본인 소유의 차가 없는 개인들에게 전기차를 임대하고 아주 낮은 요금을 부과하게 될 것입니다. 시의 대변인 제이슨 케이츠에 따르면, 도시 내에서의 교통 옵션의 부족 때문에, 특히 저소득층의 사람들을 위해서 허가가 내려진 것이라고 했습니다. 살렘이 다음 달 골든 게임즈를 개최하는 것을 감안하면, 많은 사람들이 선수들이 뛰는 것을 보기 위해서 이 도시로 몰려들 것으로 예상되므로, 랭글러는 곧 아주 바빠지게 될 것 같습니다.

89. 랭글러 트래블은 어제 무엇을 발표했는가?
(A) 지난 분기에 수익을 냈다.
(B) 사업자 등록증으로 승인되었다.
(C) 혁신 상을 수상했다.
(D) 경쟁업체를 인수했다. 　　　　　　정답 (B)

90. 랭글러 트래블은 새로운 운전자들에게 무엇을 제공할 것인가?
(A) 지정된 곳에 무료 주차
(B) 유연한 근무 시간
(C) 임대 차량
(D) 경쟁력 있는 급여 　　　　　　　정답 (C)

91. 다음 달에 살렘에 무슨 일이 있겠는가?
(A) 마케팅 엑스포
(B) 예술 공예품 축제
(C) 자동차 박람회
(D) 스포츠 행사 　　　　　　　　정답 (D)

문제 92-94번은 다음 전화 메시지를 참조하시오. 영M

M: Hello, Deborah. (92)I've got some good news about next month's charity auction that we're organizing. Remember how I asked Deacon Motors to make a donation? (93)Well, the CEO decided to donate two new cars that can be auctioned off. I just got off the phone with him. (93)I had to ask him to repeat himself. (94)Please be sure to add Deacon Motors to the list of sponsors of the event. Please do that as soon as you can.

안녕하세요, 데보라. 우리가 준비하고 있는 다음 달 자선 경매에 대해 좋은 소식이 있어요. 디콘 모터스에 기부를 해달라고 내가 어떻게 부탁했는지 기억나세요? 저, 거기 최고 경영자가 경매에 부쳐질 수 있는 새 자동차 두 대를 기부하기로 결정했어요. 지금 막 그 분과 통화를 끝냈어요. 그 분에게 다시 한 번 말해 달라고 해야 했어요. 행사 후원사 명단에 디콘 모터스를 꼭 추가하도록 하세요. 가능하면 빨리 그렇게 해주세요.

92. 화자는 무엇을 준비하고 있는가?
(A) 취업 박람회
(B) 자선 경매
(C) 회사 모임
(D) 공장 점검 　　　　　　　　정답 (B)

93. 화자가 "저는 그 분에게 다시 한 번 말해 달라고 해야 했어요"라고 말할 때 무엇을 함축하는가?
(A) 그는 전화 연결이 안 좋았다.
(B) 설명이 명료하지 않았다.
(C) 그는 할당된 업무에 자격이 맞지 않았다.
(D) 어떤 결정이 그를 놀라게 했다. 　　　　정답 (D)

94. 청자는 무엇을 해달라는 요청을 받는가?
(A) 후원업체에 연락하기
(B) 명단 갱신하기
(C) 기부하기
(D) 이메일로 답장하기 　　　　　　정답 (B)

문제 95-97번은 다음 담화와 지도를 참조하시오. 호W

W: Great news, everybody. Our application to take part in the Denver International Food Festival this weekend was just approved. (95)We'll be able to show off our entire line of pastries while we're there. Unfortunately, (96)it means that you'll all have to work this weekend. I would like you all to help me carry some boxes of food to our booth. They're a bit heavy, (97)but I requested the booth that's closest to the freight elevator. That means we won't have to carry anything too far.

여러분, 좋은 소식이에요. 이번 주말 덴버 국제 식품 축제 참가 신청이 지금 막 승인되었습니다. 우리는 거기에 참가하는 동안 우리의 전체 페이스트리 제품을 보여줄 수 있을 것입니다. 유감스럽게도, 이 말은 여러분 모두 이번 주말에 근무해야 한다는 것입니다. 여러분 모두 우리 부스로 식품 상자 옮기는 것을 도와주셨으면 합니다. 상자들은 약간 무겁긴 하지만, 화물 엘리베이터와 가장 가까운 부스로 신청했습니다. 그 말은 너무 멀리 물건을 옮길 필요는 없을 것이라는 것입니다.

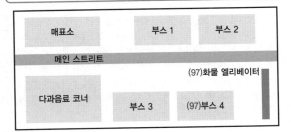

95. 화자의 업체는 무엇을 만드는가?
(A) 사무 장비
(B) 사무용 가구
(C) 제과제빵류
(D) 건축 자재
정답 (C)

96. 청자들은 무엇을 할 것을 요청받는가?
(A) 주말 근무
(B) 식품 재고조사
(C) 제품 홍보
(D) 계단만 이용
정답 (A)

97. 그래픽을 보시오. 회사는 어느 부스를 이용할 것인가?
(A) 부스 1
(B) 부스 2
(C) 부스 3
(D) 부스 4
정답 (D)

문제 98-100번은 다음 회의 발췌 내용과 일정표를 참조하시오. 영M

M: Thanks for coming to this month's meeting. (98)We have a few things to talk about regarding architecture. First is our lecture series, which will be starting next week. We've got several excellent speakers. (99)I can't wait to see November's speaker, who will be talking about some ecofriendly homes that he recently designed. Next, we have to hire a new employee. (100)Jason is going to pass around the résumés we've received. I want everyone to review them quickly.

이번 달 회의에 와주셔서 감사합니다. 건축에 대해 논의해야 할 몇 가지가 있습니다. 첫 번째는 우리 강연 시리즈인데, 다음 주부터 시작됩니다. 우리에게는 훌륭한 연사들이 여러 명 있습니다. 11월 연사가 너무 기다려지는데, 그는 최근에 자신이 설계한 친환경 주택들에 대해 얘기할 것입니다. 다음은, 신입 사원을 고용해야 하는데, 제이슨이 우리가 받은 이력서를 나눠 드릴 것입니다. 여러분 모두가 그 이력서를 빨리 검토해 주셨으면 합니다.

강연 시리즈

이름	날짜
배리 아놀드	9월 13일
윌슨 로스	10월 29일
(99)프레데릭 하퍼	11월 15일
대런 매티스	12월 3일

98. 이 담화는 누구를 대상으로 한 것인가?
(A) 건축설계사
(B) 교사
(C) 도서관 사서
(D) 인테리어 디자이너
정답 (A)

99. 그래픽을 보시오. 화자는 어느 강연자의 강연을 듣는 것에 들떠 있는가?
(A) 배리 아놀드
(B) 윌슨 로스
(C) 프레데릭 하퍼
(D) 대런 매티스
정답 (C)

100. 청자들은 뒤이어 무엇을 할 것 같은가?
(A) 새로운 업무 프로젝트에 대해 논의하기
(B) 일부 양식 작성하기
(C) 잠재적인 직원을 고려하기
(D) 올해의 예산 검토하기
정답 (C)

Part 5

101. 많은 새로운 법과 법률 연구는 범죄와 부패 통제에 대한 몇 가지 접근법을 도입할 것이다.
정답 (B)

102. 스타파크 대교는 최근 건축 전문가들에 의해 북미 지역에서 가장 훌륭한 건축물로 선정되었다.
정답 (C)

103. 피아노 튜닝은 일반적으로 숙련된 기술자가 수행하지만, 기타는 대개 기타 연주자가 직접 튜닝한다.
정답 (D)

104. 많은 저가 항공사들이 전통적인 승객 서비스를 없애는 대가로 요금을 대폭 인하하여 유럽 내 항공 여행을 촉진시켰다.
정답 (C)

105. 그 회사는 의도적으로 헤이워드로 이전하기로 선택했고, 그들은 헤이워드의 혁신에 이끌렸다고 그들 자신의 말을 인용했다.
정답 (D)

106. 한 국가의 경제 위기는 보통 국제적인 노력으로 해결되어야 하는 세계적인 문제로 발전한다.
정답 (B)

107. 라이언 씨에게 주어진 몇 가지 업무 중에는 특별 업무 위원회와 함께 하는 중요한 프로젝트가 있다.
정답 (B)

108. 서핑 서비스는 다양한 종류의 서핑 보드뿐 아니라, 단기 또는 장기 대여를 위한 잠수복과 티셔츠도 제공한다. 정답 (D)

109. 자정 전에 귀하의 대금을 받는다면, 저희는 귀하의 소포를 여전히 내일 아침 배송할 수 있을 것입니다. 정답 (D)

110. 재무 책임자인 앤드류 김 씨는 전 세계적으로 유행하는 독감으로 회사의 재무 상태가 악화될 경우 책임을 지게 될 것이다. 정답 (A)

111. 그 나라는 주로 지난 몇 년간의 경제 개혁 덕분에 지난 10년 동안 인상적인 경제 성장과 빈곤 감소를 달성했다. 정답 (B)

112. 과학자들은 생명공학의 새로운 기회를 열어줄 주요 유전 프로젝트를 거의 마무리지었다. 정답 (C)

113. 장기근속 직원 중 한 명이 출산 휴가 후에 집에 있기로 결정하자, 회사는 그녀를 임시로 대신할 사람을 고용했다. 정답 (D)

114. 시장 분석 보고서에는 내일 열리기로 예정된 이사회 회의 전에 포터 씨가 수정할 몇 가지 오류가 포함되어 있다. 정답 (D)

115. 국립 현대 미술관의 기금 모금에 기여해준 데 대해 기부자들에게 12명의 유명 화가들이 서명한 감사 카드가 발송되었다. 정답 (B)

116. 우리 연구개발팀은 현재 한 번의 충전으로 최소 48시간 지속되는 새로운 종류의 휴대 전화 배터리를 개발하고 있다. 정답 (D)

117. 우리 패스트푸드 프랜차이즈는 유럽 전역으로 빠르게 확장하고 있으며 그들은 매일 많은 수의 고객들을 대하고 있다. 정답 (C)

118. 수력 발전을 생산하고 관개시설을 제공하기 위해서, 그랜드 밸리 댐이 건설되었으며, 이것은 1973년 이후 가동되어 오고 있다. 정답 (C)

119. 이사회의 권고사항은 내년에 연구개발 분야에 더욱 역점을 두어야 한다는 것이었다. 정답 (B)

120. 최 박사는 지난 40년 동안 수많은 의학적 돌파구를 마련해 왔으며, 동료들로부터 존경을 받고 있다. 정답 (C)

121. 신청서 제출 마감일은 1월 10일이며 절대로 연장되지 않음에 유의하십시오. 정답 (D)

122. 극장은 사람들이 떠나야 할 경우 어디로 가야 할지 알려 주기 위해 희미한 바닥 조명을 켜야 한다. 정답 (B)

123. 벨라 호스피터블 솔루션은 관광객에 대한 탁월한 서비스를 인정받아 관광 및 접객업계에서 가장 권위 있는 상 중 하나인 스타 다이아몬드 상을 수상했다. 정답 (C)

124. 우리 은행의 대출자들은 전액 상환할 때까지 합의된 일정에 따라 납부한다. 정답 (C)

125. 연간 회원권 가격을 이미 지불했다면 원하는 만큼 전시회를 드나들 수 있다. 정답 (C)

126. 지난주에 베를린에서 열린 세무 회계 총회에 수백 명의 공인 세무사들이 있었다. 정답 (C)

127. 비록 우리 회사가 수익 면에서는 성장하고 있지만, 다른 외국 회사들과 경쟁하기에는 아직 역부족이다. 정답 (B)

128. 다양한 일자리들은 다양한 기술의 숙련된 직원들이 필요하며, 따라서 그에 맞는 다양한 정년 퇴직 연령이 있어야 한다. 정답 (C)

129. 시 당국은 당초 계획대로 11월에 축제를 개최할지, 아니면 봄철 관광 성수기까지 기다릴지 여전히 확신이 없다. 정답 (A)

130. 새로운 친환경 자동차가 전기나 태양 에너지로 움직인다는 점을 고려할 때, 일반 차량보다 더 효율적이고 경제적이다. 정답 (D)

Part 6

문제 131-134번은 다음 회람을 참조하시오.

> 모든 세무사들에게.
>
> 세금 신고 기간이 끝날 때까지 모든 세무사들은 추가 근무 시간을 투입해야 한다는 점을 알려 드리기 위해 회람을 작성합니다.
>
> 올해. 모두에게 더 많은 노력을 요구하는 놀라운 수의 고객들이 있습니다. 하지만 여러분들의 노고는 세금 신고 기간이 끝나면 보상받게 될 것입니다. 이번 세금 신고 기간 중의 휴가 신청은 저에게 직접 승인받아야 합니다. 이 중요한 시기에는 여러분의 상사나 팀장이 휴가 신청을 승인할 수 없습니다.
>
> <u>바쁜 시기가 지나면 회사에서 여러분을 위한 멋진 사무실 파티를 열 것입니다. 뿐만 아니라 여러분의 노고에 감사하는 뜻으로 여러분 모두에게 별도의 휴가를 드릴 것입니다.</u>
>
> 여러분의 협조에 미리 감사드립니다.
>
> 다니엘 맥거완
> 사장. 원택스 회계 회사

131. 정답 (B)

132. 정답 (C)

133. 정답 (D)

134. (A) 귀하의 계약에는 직원에게 추가 시간 근무를 요구하는 조항이 포함되어 있습니다.
(B) 바쁜 시기가 지나면 회사에서 여러분을 위한 멋진 사무실 파티를 열 것입니다.
(C) 좋은 보상 관리는 직원의 동기 부여 및 참여를 향상시킬 수 있습니다.
(D) 우리 본사는 현재 직원 수나 향후 성장에 비해 너무 작습니다. 정답 (B)

문제 135-138번은 다음 편지를 참조하시오.

> 브라운 씨에게.
>
> <u>새로운 저희 긴장 완화 워크숍 시리즈에 대한 귀하의 관심에 감사드립니다.</u> 이 세션들은 기업들이 스트레스와 관련된 결근을 줄이고 직장에서 높은 수준의 생산성을 유지하는 데 도움을 드립니다. 워크숍 참가자들은 이 분야에서 알려진 가장 효과적인 스트레스 감소 및 휴식 방법을 적용하는 법을 배웁니다. 저희 세션은 귀 단체의 직원들에게 스트레스 반응이 더 커지기 전에 그것을 최소화하고 멈출 수 있는 실질적이고 간단한 방법들을 가르쳐 드릴 것입니다.
>
> 저희 스트레스 이완 워크숍은 저희 시내 지점에서 운영되는데, 원하시는 경우. 귀하의 사업장에서 실시되도록 준비할 수도 있습니다. 귀하께서 편리한

시간에 검토하실 수 있도록 이용 가능한 워크숍과 날짜에 관한 정보를 동봉했습니다.

더 자세한 정보를 원하시면, (907) 247-1971로 공공 행사부에 직접 연락 주십시오.

공공 행사부
국립 정신 건강 연구소

135. (A) 저희는 직원들에게 업무 중 부상에 대한 무상 의료 지원을 제공할 것입니다.
(B) 그 연구 단체는 사람들에게 많은 귀중한 정보를 제공했습니다.
(C) 새로운 저희 긴장 완화 워크숍 시리즈에 대한 귀하의 관심에 감사드립니다.
(D) 정신 건강 서비스는 스트레스와 관련된 만성 질환의 위험을 감소시킵니다. 　　　　　　　　　　　　　　　　정답 (C)

136. 　　　　　　　　　　　　　　　　정답 (A)

137. 　　　　　　　　　　　　　　　　정답 (B)

138. 　　　　　　　　　　　　　　　　정답 (C)

문제 139-142번은 다음 광고를 참조하시오.

미미 가방

미미 여행 가방을 구매해 주셔서 감사합니다. 두 개의 바퀴가 달린 미미 여행 가방은 습기와 먼지는 물론 일상적인 여행의 마모를 견딜 수 있도록 설계되었습니다.

미미 여행 가방은 세심한 관리와 정성으로 제작되어 결함이 드물지만, 저희는 고객님께 구매일로부터 24개월 무상 보증을 제공합니다. <u>저희 고객님은 무상 보증을 위해 추가 조치를 취하실 필요가 없습니다.</u> 이 기간 내에 결함을 발견하시면, 가방을 수리 받거나 필요한 경우 추가 비용 없이 교체 받으실 것입니다. 구매 증빙 원본이 요구될 것입니다. 이 기간 외의 수리는 추가 비용이 수반됩니다.

고객님이 저희 공식 웹사이트 www.mimibags.com을 방문하시면, 자신의 지역에 있는 공인 수리 센터를 찾으실 수 있습니다. 지역 수리 센터에 연락하셔서 가방에 필요한 작업에 대해 의논하십시오. 또한 서울에 있는 저희 본사로 교환, 반품 및 수리를 위해 고객님의 가방을 보내셔도 됩니다.

139. 　　　　　　　　　　　　　　　　정답 (D)

140. 　　　　　　　　　　　　　　　　정답 (A)

141. (A) 저희 제품은 보통 공항의 면세점에서 판매됩니다.
(B) 이 지침을 사용하여 최상의 선택을 하기 위한 필요한 범위를 좁히십시오.
(C) 저희 고객님은 무상 보증을 위해 추가 조치를 취하실 필요가 없습니다.
(D) 저희는 지퍼 및 자물쇠와 같은 품목을 수리할 수 있을 뿐만 아니라 청소 서비스도 제공할 수 있습니다. 　　　　　　　　정답 (C)

142. 　　　　　　　　　　　　　　　　정답 (D)

문제 143-146번은 다음 발표를 참조하시오.

수상 후보 발표

매크로 IT 솔루션은 기술 관련 분야에서 회사를 경영하는 특히 유망한 기업가에게 지원금을 수여하는 연례 텔스트라 상에 대한 후보자들을 최근에 발표했습니다.

올해의 후보자들 중에 스티브 켄싱턴 씨와 마사 맥도날드 씨가 있는데, 이두 분은 전자 회사인 BK 테크놀로지의 전 직원이었습니다. 각 후보자에 관해 더 많은 것을 알아보고 싶다면, 온라인으로 약력을 읽어볼 수 있습니다. 약력은 www.macroitsolutions.com/telstraaward/list에서 찾아볼 수 있습니다.

<u>수상자는 우리 웹사이트에서 12월 23일에 발표될 것입니다.</u> 인류의 이익을 위한 새로운 기술을 개발하는 것을 돕기 위해 수상자에게 24만 달러의 상금이 수여될 것입니다.

143. 　　　　　　　　　　　　　　　　정답 (D)

144. 　　　　　　　　　　　　　　　　정답 (A)

145. 　　　　　　　　　　　　　　　　정답 (B)

146. (A) 우리는 귀하가 수상자로 선정되었음을 알려 드리게 되어 기쁩니다.
(B) 자신의 사업을 시작하는 것은 신나고 매우 흥미진진할 수 있습니다.
(C) 수상자는 우리 웹사이트에서 12월 23일에 발표될 것입니다.
(D) 작성 완료된 지원서는 늦어도 다음 주 금요일까지 도착해야 합니다. 　　　　　　　　정답 (C)

Part 7

문제 147-148번은 다음 광고를 참조하시오.

맥시멈 부동산

임대: 아늑하고 고풍스런 미용실 공간

버나드 왓포드
bwatford@joinmail.com
(520) 555-2938

– 2개 창고와 1개 직원 휴게실
– 근처에 충분한 거리 주차공간
– (148)상태가 좋은 미용실 의자와 거울 – 사용 가능함
– (147)킹 대학교 캠퍼스 건너편의 통행량이 많은 지역에 위치
– 3,000달러/월 – 2년 계약
– 즉시 이사 가능

147. 광고된 공간에 대해 나타나 있는 것은 무엇인가?
(A) 3,000달러에 판다.
(B) 고속도로 근처에 위치해 있다.
(C) 밀폐된 주차장이 있다.
(D) 학생 고객들을 끌 수도 있다. 　　　　정답 (D)

148. 광고에서 언급된 선택권은 무엇인가?
(A) 공간을 개조할 선택권
(B) 연 임대료를 지불하는 선택권
(C) 일부 가구를 사용할 선택권
(D) 추가 창고를 이용할 선택권 　　　　정답 (C)

문제 149-150번은 다음 문자 메시지를 참조하시오.

윌리엄 조던 [오전 10시 23분]
안녕하세요, 매튜. 쉬는 날 방해해서 미안해요. 잠시 이야기할 수 있을까요?

매튜 코너스 [오전 10시 26분]
물론이죠. 그런데 빨리 하세요. 나 영화 보러 가는 길이에요.

윌리엄 조던 [오전 10시 27분]
(150)이번 주 금요일 근무 좀 대신해 줄 수 있는지 물어보려고 했어요. (149)그날 오후에 로리의 농장으로 물건을 가지러 가야 해요.

매튜 코너스 [오전 10시 27분]
알았어요, 내가 대신해 줄게요.

윌리엄 조던 [오전 10시 32분]
(150)신경 쓰지 마세요. (150)방금 다시 확인해 봤는데, 로리가 다음 주중에 왔으면 하네요. 미안해요.

윌리엄 조던 [오전 10시 33분]
(149)그런데, 매니저가 내일 아침에 모두 일찍 와서, 마크 출판사의 단체 점심 예약을 준비하길 원하고 있어요.

매튜 코너스 [오전 10시 35분]
알겠어요. 내일 봐요.

149. 조던 씨와 코너스 씨는 어디서 일할 것 같은가?
(A) 식당
(B) 출판사
(C) 농장
(D) 극장
정답 (A)

150. 오전 10시 32분에, 조던 씨가 "신경 쓰지 마세요"라고 쓸 때 무엇을 의미하는가?
(A) 자신이 끝내야 하는 또 다른 일이 있다는 것을 깨달았다.
(B) 촉박하게 통보를 한 것을 사과하고 있다.
(C) 일정을 재조정하기에 너무 늦었음을 나타내고 있다.
(D) 앞서 한 부탁을 철회하고 싶어 한다.
정답 (D)

문제 151-152번은 다음 전화 메시지를 참조하시오.

부재중 메시지

수신자:	(152)가브리엘라 헤이스		
날짜:	10월 14일	시간:	오후 3시 25분

발신자	다니엘 뉴웰
소속	뉴웰 전자
전화 번호:	(555) 510-9010
내용:	(151)뉴웰 씨가 전화하여 10월 16일에 로비의 전등 수리와 (152)정원에 조명을 더 설치하기 위해서 그의 팀과 함께 방문하겠다고 말했습니다. 호텔의 손님들에게 이 불편에 대해서 알리기 위해서 안내판이 게시되어야 합니다. 정원의 어느 부분이 영향 받을지에 대한 세부사항은 관리부의 마이클 메이슨 씨에게 연락하십시오.

전화 받은 사람:	아드리아노 젠틸레

151. 10월 16일에 누가 호텔을 방문할 것인가?
(A) 가브리엘라 헤이스
(B) 다니엘 뉴웰
(C) 아드리아노 젠틸레
(D) 마이클 메이슨
정답 (B)

152. 헤이스 씨가 메이슨 씨에게 연락해야 하는 이유는?
(A) 방문 시간을 확인하기 위해
(B) 안내판을 게시할 곳을 알아보기 위해
(C) 그에게 중단에 대해 알리기 위해
(D) 그의 전화에 회신하기 위해
정답 (B)

문제 153-154번은 다음 이메일을 참조하시오.

수신: 리사 켈러 〈lkeller@gomail.com〉
발신: 마리오 헨더슨 〈mhenderson@arlingtonpubliclibrary.org〉
날짜: 11월 14일
제목: 중요한 알림

켈러 씨에게,

(153)귀하의 알링턴 공공 도서관 카드가 12월에 만료됩니다. 귀하의 카드를 갱신하시려면, 사진이 부착된 신분증과 현재 주소를 확인할 법적인 효력이 있는 서류를 소지하고 안내 데스크를 방문해 주세요. 현재 카드에 남아 있는 연체료는 갱신 전에 반드시 내셔야 합니다. 연체료 납부에 도움이 필요하시면 근무 중인 도서관 사서에게 얘기하세요. (154)귀하 계정의 잔여 금액은 도서관 웹사이트 www.arlingtonpubliclibrary.org에서 확인할 수 있습니다.

유효한 도서관 카드 없이는 어떤 도서관 자료도 빌릴 수 없다는 것을 알려 드립니다. 만약 갱신 마감일을 놓치면, 10달러의 비용으로 카드를 만드셔야 합니다. 더 궁금한 점이 있으시면 (571) 555-2930으로 도서관에 연락하세요.

마리오 헨더슨
도서관 사서 보조원

153. 헨더슨 씨가 켈러 씨에게 편지를 쓴 이유는?
(A) 그녀에게 연체를 통지하기 위해
(B) 도서관 카드를 신청하기 위해
(C) 정책 변경에 관해 그녀에게 알려 주기 위해
(D) 상기시켜 주는 메시지를 전하기 위해
정답 (D)

154. 켈러 씨는 온라인으로 무엇을 할 수 있는가?
(A) 연체료 확인
(B) 도서관 사용에 대한 질문 제출
(C) 도서관 직원의 도움 요청
(D) 도서관에 기부
정답 (A)

문제 155-157번은 다음 가격표를 참조하시오.

남성을 위한 솔라 이발소
120 메인 가, 시카고
(155)정오부터 오후 8시까지 영업

- **일반 이발**   30달러
이발 전후에 샴푸와 린스 서비스 포함. 2달러 추가 요금으로 헤어스타일링 제공.

- **머리 염색**   65달러
다양한 색상 가능. 가격은 머리 길이에 따라 다름. 염색 후 헤어 트리트먼트 서비스 5달러에 이용 가능.

- **(156)두피 마사지**   18달러
전문가에 의한 30분 마사지. (156)머리카락 성장에 좋은 솔라 특별 샴푸를 받으시려면 4달러만 더 추가하세요.

- **제모**   12달러
저희 제모 서비스로 깨끗한 등, 가슴, 팔, 혹은 다리를 가져 보세요. 피부 자극을 최소화하는 특수 화학제품이 사용됩니다. 털 또는 턱수염 다듬기는 단 3달러 추가 요금으로 추가 가능.

- **샴푸**   3달러
빠른 샴푸와 머리 말리기 서비스.

(157)솔라 이발소가 처음인 친구를 데려와
두 계산서에서 다 5달러 할인을 받으세요.
이 할인은 8월 31일까지 유효합니다.

155. 솔라 이발소에 대해 나타나 있는 것은 무엇인가?
(A) 최근에 개업했다.
(B) 오직 남자 직원만 있다.
(C) 시카고에서 유명하다.
(D) 오전에는 문을 닫는다.   정답 (D)

156. 추가 비용으로 헤어 관리 제품이 제공될 수 있는 서비스는 어느 것인가?
(A) 일반 이발
(B) 샴푸
(C) 두피 마사지
(D) 제모   정답 (C)

157. 손님이 이발에 대해 할인을 받을 수 있는 방법은?
(A) 지인에게 솔라 이발소를 추천함으로써
(B) 특정 금액 이상을 더 냄으로써
(C) 8월 안에 헤어스타일링 서비스를 주문함으로써
(D) 솔라 이발소의 매니저와 이야기함으로써   정답 (A)

문제 158-160번은 다음 웹 페이지를 참조하시오.

www.onlibtree.com/announcements

OnLibTree.com
(158)세계에서 가장 큰 온라인 책장

홈	검색	알림	주문	문의처

(158)이 달의 작가

로버트 휘틀로우
〈내 말을 들어줘〉의 저자
록킹 체어 출판

로버트 휘틀로우 씨는 (159)오타와의 맥길 대학교에서 학부생으로 사회 언어학과 언어 과학을 전공했다. 같은 학교에서 석사 과정 중에, 그는 일상생활에서의 의사소통의 중요성과 그것을 향상하는 방법들을 다루는 그의 첫 번째 저서 〈의사소통에서의 과학〉을 출판했다. 휘틀로우 씨는 언어학과 사회학에서 석사 학위를 받은 후에, 브라이트 금융 회사에서 일하기 위해 보스턴으로 옮겨갔다. 비즈니스 의사소통 멘토로서, 그는 직원들에게 비즈니스 활동에서 설득적 의사소통을 가르쳤다. 현재 그는 시카고 대학교의 언어

학 교수이다. (160)그의 첫 번째 소설 〈내 말을 들어줘〉를 홍보하기 위해서 순회 중인 휘틀로우 씨는 현재 영국의 여러 도시를 방문하고 있다. 6월 10일 현재, 그는 런던에 있다. 그리고 곧 맨체스터, 브리스틀 그리고 카디프를 방문할 것이다.

158. 온리브트리는 어떤 종류의 사업체인가?
(A) 연구 회사
(B) 온라인 가구 상점
(C) 서점
(D) 출판사   정답 (C)

159. 휘틀로우 씨는 어디에서 집필 경력을 시작했는가?
(A) 오타와
(B) 시카고
(C) 보스턴
(D) 런던   정답 (A)

160. 휘틀로우 씨에 대해서 언급된 것은 무엇인가?
(A) 의자를 디자인했다.
(B) 금융 기관에서 일한다.
(C) 맥길 대학교에서 가르쳤다.
(D) 현재 영국에 잠시 머물고 있다.   정답 (D)

문제 161-163번은 다음 이메일을 참조하시오.

수신: 고객 서비스 〈customerservice@toptracks101.com〉
발신: 도리스 호그 〈dhogue@walkmail.com〉
날짜: 10월 10일
제목: 주문 번호 10009283

담당자 분께,

제가 탑트랙 101 고객 서비스에 직접 전화하려고 시도했는데, 상담원 누구와도 연결되지 않았어요. 저는 근래 귀사의 웹사이트에서 앨범 몇 장을 구매했어요. 선택한 상품들을 결제한 후, 제가 실수로 〈록 스테이션 디럭스〉 앨범을 주문했다는 것을 알게 되었어요. (162)저는 지난달에 이미 그 앨범을 구입했기 때문에 그것을 구매할 의도가 없었어요. 어떤 이유 때문인지, 그 앨범이 제 장바구니에 여전히 남아 있었고, 새 상품 목록들과 함께 선택되어, 제가 뜻하지 않게 그 앨범도 결제했어요.

(163)웹사이트의 공지에 따르면, 제가 고객 서비스에 연락하면 구매 24시간 이내에 환불이 가능하다고 되어 있어요. (161)만약 혹시라도 한 개의 상품에 대한 환불이 되지 않는다면, 저의 전체 주문을 취소해 주시겠어요? 〈록 스테이션 디럭스〉 앨범은 싸지도 않을뿐더러 정말 두 개가 필요하지도 않거든요. 어떤 선택이 가능한지 저에게 연락 주시기 바랍니다.

감사합니다.

도리스 호그

161. 호그 씨가 이메일을 보내는 이유는?
(A) 최근의 구매에 대한 항의를 제기하기 위해
(B) 주문에 다른 품목을 추가하기 위해
(C) 빠진 물품들에 관하여 문의하기 위해
(D) 환불을 요청하기 위해   정답 (D)

162. 호그 씨에 대하여 진술된 것은 무엇인가?
(A) 전에 탑트랙 101에서 구매한 적이 있다.
(B) 록 스테이션의 팬이 아니다.
(C) 음악을 자주 내려받는다.
(D) 이미 같은 앨범 두 장을 가지고 있다.   정답 (A)

163. [1], [2], [3] 그리고 [4]로 표시된 곳 중에, 아래 문장이 들어가기에 가장 적절한 곳은?

"구매 후 고작 20분 정도 되었기 때문에, 제가 환불 받을 기회는 아직 유효하다고 봅니다."

(A) [1]
(B) [2]
(C) [3]
(D) [4]   정답 (C)

문제 164-167번은 다음 온라인 채팅 토론을 참조하시오.

섀넌 그랜트   [오후 6시 39분]
안녕, 얘들아, (164)다음 주에 크림슨 폭포로 가는 우리 조류 관찰 클럽 연차 야유회에 누가 무엇을 가져올지 정해야 해.

토마스 가네   [오후 6시 41분]
내가 조리 기구들을 가져갈게. 내 생각엔 쓰레기 양을 최소화할 수 있게 플라스틱 용기를 사용하는 대신에 모두가 개인 식사 도구를 가져와야 할 것 같아.

래리 올슨   [오후 6시 43분]
그거 좋은 생각이야.

섀넌 그랜트   [오후 6시 46분]
(164)내가 텐트와 다른 야외 활동 장비를 가지고 갈게. 우리 아빠가 암벽 등반을 많이 가셔서 차고에 야외 활동 장비가 엄청나게 많아. 내가 아빠의 장비 더미에서 몇 가지를 챙겨 갈게.

제이미 스미스   [오후 6시 50분]
(165)샘과 내가 음식을 담당할 거야. 우리 내일 식료품 장을 보러 갈 건데. 뭐 특별히 필요한 거 있니?

래리 올슨   [오후 6시 52분]
혹시라도 비가 온다거나 밤에 텐트 안이 너무 추울 경우를 대비해서 난 여분의 담요를 더 가져갈게.

섀넌 그랜트   [오후 6:시 53분]
좋은 생각이야. 고마워, 래리.

토마스 가네   [오후 6:시 53분]
(167)제이미, 마시멜로를 잊지 마!

(167)제이미 스미스   [오후 6시 54분]
그런 일은 절대 일어나지 않을 거라는 걸 알잖아. 설령 내가 그러더라도, 샘이 거기에 가니까 분명히 내가 잊지 않도록 말해 줄 거야.

(165)샘 로렌조   [오후 6시 55분]
물론이지, 그게 내 쇼핑 목록 1순위인 걸.

(166)섀넌 그랜트   [오후 6시 56분]
좋아. 최종 준비와 활동 일정을 점검해야 하니까, 이틀 후에 다시 너희와 확인할게.

---

164. 어떤 종류의 행사가 준비되고 있는가?

(A) 암벽 등반
(B) 동물 실험
(C) 캠핑 여행
(D) 환경 세미나   정답 (C)

165. 로렌조 씨는 무엇을 하기로 되어 있는가?

(A) 그의 아버지의 창고에서 야외 활동 장비 챙기기
(B) 단체 활동 계획하기
(C) 다른 사람들과 함께 쓸 따뜻한 담요 가져오기
(D) 식료품 구입하기   정답 (D)

166. 이틀 후에, 어떤 일이 있을 것 같은가?

(A) 그랜트 씨가 클럽 회원들에게 연락할 것이다.
(B) 클럽 회원들이 그들의 야유회 최종 장소를 결정할 것이다.
(C) 스미스 씨가 조리 기구들을 준비할 것이다.
(D) 클럽 회원들이 크림슨 폭포로 떠날 것이다.   정답 (A)

167. 오후 6시 54분에, 스미스 씨가 "그런 일은 절대 일어나지 않을 거라는 걸 알잖아"라고 쓸 때 무엇을 의미하는가?

(A) 그는 간식에 돈을 낭비하고 싶지 않다.
(B) 그는 특정 물건을 빠뜨리지 않을 것이다.
(C) 그는 활동 일정을 따르고 싶지 않다.
(D) 그는 로렌조 씨에게 쇼핑 목록을 수정하도록 상기시켜 줄 것이다.
                                                           정답 (B)

문제 168-171번은 다음 기사를 참조하시오.

월링턴 (3월 17일) – (171)월링턴의 폴리오 지구에서 가장 인기 있는 독립 보석 상점 코제트스가 현 위치에서 (170)10년 동안의 영업을 끝내고 3월 21일에 문을 닫는다. 점주인 리차드 쿠퍼 씨는 (169)단지 두 블록 떨어진 곳에 조예리아 주식회사라는 이름으로 보석 가게를 새로 시작한다.

(168)폴리오 지구는 코제트스를 포함한 몇몇 성공한 가게들 덕에 수년 동안 점점 많은 수의 방문객들을 끌어들일 수 있었다. 하지만, 그 성공은 사실 코제트스가 폐업할 수밖에 없었던 주된 이유가 되고 말았다. 건물주는 쿠퍼 씨가 더 이상 감당하지 못할 정도로 가게 임대료를 올렸다.

코제트스가 역사 속으로 사라지려 할 때, 조예리아가 도움의 손길을 뻗었다. (170)"저는 코제트스가 처음 문을 열었을 때부터 열성적인 팬이었습니다. 쿠퍼 씨는 정말 천재적인 보석공입니다"라고 조예리아의 최고 경영자인 프라사드 씨는 말한다. "그래서 저는 그를 우리의 선임 디자이너로 채용할 기회를 놓치지 않았던 것입니다."

쿠퍼 씨는 이제 조예리아 가게를 운영하며 회사를 위해 보석을 디자인할 예정이다. (171)"비록 제가 예전의 가게를 지킬 수는 없었지만, 계속해서 제 고향에서 일할 수 있다는 것에 감사할 따름입니다"라고 쿠퍼 씨는 말한다.

---

168. 폴리오 지구에 대해 나타나 있는 것은 무엇인가?

(A) 10년 전에 설립되었다.
(B) 조예리아 주식회사가 본사를 둔 곳이다.
(C) 월링턴에서 가장 붐비는 지역이다.
(D) 더 인기를 얻게 되었다.   정답 (D)

169. 첫 번째 단락 6행에 있는 단어 "just"와 의미상 가장 가까운 것은?

(A) 공정하게
(B) 대략적으로
(C) 단지
(D) 정확히   정답 (C)

170. 프라사드 씨는 누구일 것 같은가?

(A) 코제트스의 오랜 고객
(B) 월링턴의 주민
(C) 건물의 주인
(D) 조예리아 주식회사의 설립자   정답 (A)

171. 기사에 따르면, 쿠퍼 씨가 행복한 이유는?

(A) 월링턴을 떠나지 않아도 되기 때문이다.
(B) 프라사드 씨를 고용할 수 있었기 때문이다.
(C) 많은 돈을 벌고 있기 때문이다.
(D) 그의 고향으로 돌아갈 것이기 때문이다.   정답 (A)

문제 172-175번은 다음 안내문을 참조하시오.

---

(172)CE 기업 – 유기 화학 실험실 안전 규칙

1. 실험실 활동 전:
실험과 연구 중에 인체에 해로운 화학 물질로부터 자신을 보호하기 위한 보호 안경과 앞치마를 착용한다. 쉽게 불이 붙을 수 있는 옷의 착용은 피한다. 입었다면, 옷 위에 실험복을 꼭 입도록 한다.

2. (173)제한 물품:
허가받은 열원을 제외하고, 화재나 폭발을 일으킬 수 있는 물품들은 실험실에 들어올 수 없다. 우리의 실험 활동은 기밀이며, 따라서 촬영 장비는 실험실에서 엄격히 제한된다.

3. (175)정리정돈:
사고를 예방하고 화학 잔여물들이 반응을 일으키는 것을 막기 위해 실험대는 항상 깨끗하고 정돈되어 있어야 한다. 실험실 활동 전후로, 모든 화학 물질은 마개가 꼭 막힌 상태로 치워야 한다.

4. 비상사태:
실험 중 언제든 사고가 일어날 수 있으므로, 안전 장비의 사용법과 위치를 잘 알아야 한다. (174)화재나 화학물질 오염의 경우, 사이렌이 울릴 것이며, 모두 즉시 실험실을 떠나야 한다.

---

172. 안내문은 누구를 대상으로 하는 것 같은가?
(A) 안전 조사원
(B) 실험실 연구원
(C) 과학 전공 학생
(D) 유지관리 직원 　　　　　　　정답 (B)

173. 실험실 내부 반입을 피해야 하는 물품으로 언급되지 않은 것은 무엇인가?
(A) 카메라
(B) 라이터
(C) 음식
(D) 면 재질의 옷 　　　　　　　정답 (C)

174. 안내문에 따르면, 어떤 상황에서 대피가 필요한가?
(A) 문자 메시지가 도착했을 때
(B) 경보 음이 울릴 때
(C) 스피커에서 안내 방송이 나올 때
(D) 경고 신호등이 켜졌을 때 　　　　　　　정답 (B)

175. [1], [2], [3] 그리고 [4]로 표시된 곳 중에, 아래 문장이 들어가기에 가장 적절한 곳은?
"실험실 물품들은 철저하게 세척한 후, 제 위치에 놓여야 한다."
(A) [1]
(B) [2]
(C) [3]
(D) [4] 　　　　　　　정답 (C)

문제 176-180번은 다음 이메일과 일정표를 참조하시오.

수신: 헨리 코헨 〈hcohen@deliciousdream.com〉
발신: (177)오드리 밀러 〈amiller@deliciousdream.com〉
날짜: 3월 10일
제목: 맛있는 꿈 세미나

안녕하세요, 헨리,

(176)3월 20일에 개최 예정인 다가오는 맛있는 꿈 세미나에 관련된 내용이에요. 당신이 세미나 일정을 마무리하기 전 알려줄 몇 가지 사항들이 있어요.

---

(177) (178)오늘 아침, 바바라 케네디 씨가 전화해서, 세미나 당일 오후에 뉴욕 주 버팔로로 떠나야 해서 그날 예정된 시간에 세미나를 더 이상 진행할 수 없다고 하셨어요. 엠마누엘 콜론 씨가 고맙게도 케네디 씨와 프레젠테이션 시간을 바꾸는 데 동의하셨어요. 혼선이 없도록 이 사항을 일정에 반영해 주세요.

(180)당신도 이미 알다시피, 앤서니 하틀리 씨는 정말 유명하고 영향력 있는 인물이라서 우리도 그의 세미나가 다른 세미나보다 훨씬 더 많은 사람을 끌어모을 것으로 기대하고 있죠. 그의 프레젠테이션에 차질이 없도록 모든 참석자를 수용할 수 있는 방을 예약해 주길 바랍니다.

당신의 도움에 감사해요. 내일 사무실에서 봬요.

오드리

제 5회 연차 맛있는 꿈 세미나
프랑코 컨퍼런스 센터
350 월넛 애비뉴, 뉴올리언스
3월 20일, 수요일

시간	세미나 제목 / 발표자
오전 10:00 – 오전 11:00	(179)〈당신이 먹는 것이 곧 당신이다〉 201호 〈잘 먹어야 잘 산다〉의 저자 트레이시 스미스
(178) 오전 11:00 – 오후 12:00	(178) (179)〈행복한 가정 식단〉 201호 저명한 요리 연구가 바바라 케네디
오후 12:00 – 오후 1:30	점심 시간 (식사는 샤리 케이터링으로부터 제공될 것입니다.)
오후 1:30 – 오후 2:30	(179)〈성공적으로 새로운 요리 개발하기〉 302호 그랜드 파리 호텔의 수석 요리사 메리 아그네스
(178) 오후 2:30 – 오후 3:30	(178) (179)〈올바른 재료 고르기〉 205호 콜론의 멕시코 요리의 설립자이자 소유주 엠마누엘 콜론
오후 3:30 – 오후 4:30	(179) (180)〈요식업을 시작하는 법〉 306호 TV 프로 〈식사 천국〉의 프로듀서 앤서니 하틀리

* 3월 11일 수정

176. 이메일의 목적은 무엇인가?
(A) 약속을 잡기 위한 것
(B) 계획 변동에 대한 업데이트를 제공하기 위한 것
(C) 초빙 강사를 초대하기 위한 것
(D) 세미나 장소에 대해 문의하기 위한 것 　　　　　　　정답 (B)

177. 밀러 씨에 대해 사실인 것은?
(A) 코헨 씨를 위해 일한다.
(B) 곧 출장을 갈 것이다.
(C) 최근 케네디 씨와 얘기했다.
(D) 그녀는 전국적으로 매우 유명하다. 　　　　　　　정답 (C)

178. 원래 오전 11시에 시작하기로 계획되어 있던 세미나는 어느 것인가?
(A) 올바른 재료 고르기
(B) 요식업을 시작하는 법
(C) 성공적으로 새로운 요리 개발하기
(D) 당신이 먹는 것이 곧 당신이다 　　　　　　　정답 (A)

179. 맛있는 꿈 세미나에 대해 사실인 것은?

(A) TV에 방영될 예정이다.

(B) 주제는 음식과 관련된 것이다.

(C) 입장료가 요구된다.

(D) 지역 사업체들로부터 기부금을 받았다. 정답 (B)

180. 306호실은 프랑코 컨퍼런스 센터의 다른 방들과 비교하여 무엇이 다른 것 같은가?

(A) 수용력 면에서 더 크다.

(B) 덜 비싸다.

(C) 오디오 장비가 더 좋다.

(D) 회의실 스타일의 장소이다. 정답 (A)

문제 181-185번은 다음 이메일들을 참조하시오.

---

(182)**수신: 로버트 밀러 〈Rmiller@dmail.com〉**

(182)**발신: 브렌다 피어스 〈Brenda@thefirstcarrental.com〉**

날짜: 10월 10일

제목: 자동차 렌트

밀러 씨에게,

저희 퍼스트 클래스 렌탈에서 차량을 빌리는 데 관심을 가져 주셔서 감사합니다. 퍼스트 클래스 렌탈이 최적의 가격에 최상의 차량을 제공해 드리는 것은, 저희가 작년 최우수 차량 대여 사업자 상을 수상한 만큼 입증된 사실입니다. 아래는 고객님의 요구에 맞을 수 있는 사양의 몇몇 차량 목록입니다.

제조사	모델	수용 인원	특징	가격 (하루)
아우토반	(184)S019	6	(184)에어컨, 내장 GPS, 4륜 구동, 선루프	179달러
아우토반	E998	4	에어컨, 내장 GPS, 전륜 구동	137달러
클레버	3-50	4	에어컨, 고성능 타이어, 선루프	140달러
FNR	트래커 6	5	에어컨, 4륜 구동, 선루프	165달러

(182)저희 매장에 들러서 직접 차량을 시운전해 보세요. (181)제가 일하고 있는 퍼스트 클래스 렌탈 지점은 라파예트의 윌로우 오크 레인 455번지에 위치해 있습니다. 매장을 방문하시면, 저를 찾으시거나 저의 조수 스탠리 시울라 씨를 찾으시면 됩니다.

감사합니다.

브렌다 피어스

---

(184)**수신: 브렌다 피어스 〈Brenda@thefirstcarrental.com〉**

(184)**발신: 로버트 밀러 〈Rmiller@dmail.com〉**

날짜: 10월 27일

제목: 피드백

피어스 씨에게,

당신의 도움 덕분에 최근에 그랜드 캐넌으로 떠난 여행을 잘 다녀올 수 있었어요. (184)당신이 추천해준 내장 GPS와 선루프가 달린 차로 갔더라면 훨씬 더 좋았을 거라는 (183)생각이 들긴 하지만, 트래커 6도 전혀 나쁘

지 않았어요.

웹사이트의 설문 조사도 다 작성했고, (185)당신 매장에서 다른 차를 대여할 때 사용 가능한 할인 쿠폰도 받았습니다. 쿠폰에 정보가 명시되어 있지 않아 이 쿠폰의 유효 기간을 알고 싶습니다.

로버트 밀러 드림

---

181. 퍼스트 클래스 렌탈에 대해 시사되어 있는 것은 무엇인가?

(A) 2개 이상의 지점을 보유하고 있다.

(B) 국제적으로 유명한 사업체이다.

(C) 손님들에게 무상 수리 서비스를 제공한다.

(D) 수상 경력이 있는 차량들을 제공한다. 정답 (A)

182. 피어스 씨가 밀러 씨에게 무엇을 할 것을 요청하는가?

(A) 서류 갖다 주기

(B) 웹사이트 방문하기

(C) 그녀를 방문하기

(D) 그녀의 조수에게 이메일 보내기 정답 (C)

183. 두 번째 이메일에서, 첫 번째 단락 1행에 있는 단어 "guess"와 의미상 가장 가까운 것은?

(A) 궁금해하다

(B) 질문하다

(C) 추정하다

(D) 제공하다 정답 (C)

184. 피어스 씨가 밀러 씨에게 추천한 차량은 무엇인것 같은가?

(A) 3-50

(B) E998

(C) S019

(D) 트래커 6 정답 (C)

185. 밀러 씨에 대해 추론할 수 있는 것은 무엇인가?

(A) 웹사이트에서 설문조사를 시행했다.

(B) 퍼스트 클래스 렌탈을 다시 이용할 의향이 있다.

(C) 차량을 빌릴 때 쿠폰을 사용했다.

(D) 곧 그랜드 캐넌을 방문할 것이다. 정답 (B)

문제 186-190번은 다음 광고와 이메일 그리고 입장권을 참조하시오.

보스턴 콘서트 홀

(186)국제적으로 잘 알려진 연극 작품 〈깨진 약속〉이 12월 5일부터 7일까지 보스턴 콘서트 홀에서 공연됩니다. 페리소 극작가 상을 수상한 (188)극작가 겸 감독 리사 애덤스는 그녀의 단원들과 지난달부터 전 세계 순회 공연을 하고 있으며, 지금까지 남아프리카 캐나다를 방문했습니다. 시사하는 바가 많은 매혹적인 연극을 볼 수 있는 생애 단 한 번뿐인 이번 기회를 놓치지 마세요. 입장권은 일반인에게는 장당 90달러, (189)보스턴 콘서트 홀의 회원에게는 75달러입니다. 입장권은 극장 정문이나 www.bostonconcerthall.com에서 구매 가능합니다. 회원제 할인은 회원 당 표 2매까지 적용 가능합니다. (187)단원 전체 명단과 지난 연극 공연 사진들, 그리고 극작가의 간단한 이력도 웹사이트에서 볼 수 있습니다.

수신: 사무엘 페리스 〈s.ferris@donaldaccounting.com〉

(188)**발신: 멜린다 나푸레 〈m.nafure@donaldaccounting.com〉**

날짜: 11월 26일

제목: 〈깨진 약속〉

안녕하세요, 사무엘.

(188)12월에 연극 〈깨진 약속〉이 보스턴에 오는 거 알고 있어요? 내가 개인적으로 감독을 아는데, 시드니에서 대학을 다닐 때 내 옆집에 살았어요. 난 정말로 그녀의 작품도 보고 그녀와 얘기도 나누고 싶어요. 나랑 같이 연극을 볼래요? 당신이 그러겠다고 말하면, 내가 표를 살게요.

멜린다 드림

보스턴 콘서트 홀
온라인 입장권

〈깨진 약속〉
12월 6일, 오후 7:15

(189)고객명: 멜린다 나푸레
이메일 주소: m.nafure@donaldaccounting.com

(189)입장 인원: _2_ (장당 75달러)
좌석: B25, B26

안내사항:
• 이 입장권을 인쇄해서 입장 시 입구에서 제시하세요.
• 입장권의 취소나 변경은 www.bostonconcerthall.com에서 하세요.
• (190)착석하라고 안내되는 시간 15분 전에 콘서트 홀에 와주세요.
• 연극이 끝난 후 짧은 사진 촬영 시간이 있습니다.

감사합니다.

---

186. 〈깨진 약속〉에 관해 시사되어 있는 것은 무엇인가?
(A) 상을 받았다.
(B) 2개 이상의 국가에서 공연되었다.
(C) 마지막 공연이 보스턴에서 열릴 것이다.
(D) 극작가 역으로 리사 애덤스가 주연한다.　　　정답 (B)

187. 보스턴 콘서트 홀의 웹사이트에서 이용 가능한 것은?
(A) 비평가들이 쓴 논평
(B) 사전 구매 할인 혜택
(C) 주연의 약력 사항
(D) 공연자 명단　　　정답 (D)

188. 나푸레 씨는 누구인가?
(A) 현 시드니 주민
(B) 애덤스 씨의 예전 이웃
(C) 여배우
(D) 감독　　　정답 (B)

189. 나푸레 씨에 대해 나타나 있는 것은 무엇인가?
(A) 〈깨진 약속〉을 예전에 본 적이 있다.
(B) 그녀의 티켓 세부사항을 변경할 것이다.
(C) 페리스 씨와 함께 대학을 다녔다.
(D) 보스턴 콘서트 홀의 회원이다.　　　정답 (D)

190. 입장권 구매자들은 무엇을 할 것을 요청받는가?
(A) 입구에서 입장권 구매하기
(B) 사진 찍지 않기
(C) 장소에 일찍 도착하기
(D) 연극이 끝날 때까지 착석해 있기　　　정답 (C)

문제 191-195번은 다음 안내문과 편지 그리고 기사를 참조하시오.

어바인 지역사회 재단 (ICF)은 (194A) (194D)지역 비영리 단체에 우리 지역사회의 발전을 돕는 데 필요한 보조금을 베터 어바인 펀드 프로그램을 통해

지급합니다. 보조금은 2,000달러부터 10,000달러까지 액수가 다양합니다.

(191)보조금에 대한 신청서는 심의를 받기 위해 ICF의 웹사이트에서 제출되어야 합니다. 신청서에는, 지역사회의 발전을 위한 상세한 계획과, (194)해당 프로젝트에 참여하기로 (192) (193C)서약한 단체 회원에게 받은 최소 35개의 서명, 그리고 그 잠재 프로젝트에 대한 다른 정보들이 포함되어야 합니다. 추가적인 정보를 원하거나 신청하시려면, ICF의 웹사이트 www.irvinecf.org/betterirvine에 접속하세요.

어바인 지역사회 재단
150 밸리 애비뉴, 어바인, 캘리포니아 주 92602
(949) 555-1023

7월 1일

(195)아드리아나 그릴
어셀 부모 연합회
77 비녀드 드라이브
어바인, 캘리포니아 주 92603

그릴 씨에게,

(194)저희 어바인 지역사회 재단에서는 어셀 부모 연합회가 도시의 놀이터를 위해 제안하신 계획에 대해 6,000달러의 보조금을 받게 되는 것을 기쁜 마음으로 알려 드립니다. 우리는 그것이 우리 도시와 지역사회를 크게 발전시킬 것이라고 믿습니다. (193) (195)귀 단체의 회장으로서, 그 계획에 대해 더 논의할 수 있도록 이번 주에 저희 사무실을 방문해 주시기 바랍니다. 날짜를 잡을 수 있도록 (949) 510-9057로 전화 주세요.

감사합니다.

리차드 콴

어바인 (11월 21일) – 어바인의 어린이들을 위한 새로운 놀이터, 어바인 어린이 파라다이스의 공사가 어제 완료되었습니다. 놀이터는 어셀 부모 연합회(EPA)와 어바인 지역사회 재단(ICF)의 공동 작업입니다. (195)어린이들은 11월 25일부터 어바인 파라다이스에서의 모험을 시작할 수 있게 됩니다. EPA의 회장이 개장식에 참석하여 어린이들이 즐겁게 놀고 운동할 수 있는 안전한 장소를 제공하는 것의 중요성에 대해 연설할 예정입니다.

191. 어바인 지역사회 재단에 대해 언급된 것은 무엇인가?
(A) 현재 자원봉사자를 채용하고 있다.
(B) 온라인으로 보조금 신청을 받는다.
(C) 어바인 주민으로만 구성되어 있다.
(D) 웹사이트에 보조금 수령자의 이름을 게시한다.　　　정답 (B)

192. 안내문에서, 두 번째 단락 3행에 있는 단어 "committed"와 의미가 가장 가까운 것은?
(A) 희생한
(B) 약속한
(C) 기여한
(D) 결정한　　　정답 (B)

193. 편지의 한 가지 목적은 무엇인가?
(A) 그릴 씨를 회의에 초대하기 위한 것
(B) 기부를 요청하기 위한 것
(C) 놀이터를 짓도록 그릴 씨를 설득하기 위한 것
(D) 보조금 신청 절차를 발표하기 위한 것　　　정답 (A)

194. 어셀 부모 연합회에 대해 시사되지 않은 것은 무엇인가?
(A) 어바인에 기반을 두고 있다.
(B) 어바인 지역사회 재단과 합병했다.

(C) 적어도 35명의 회원이 있다.

(D) 비영리 단체이다. 정답 (B)

195. 그릴 씨는 언제 어바인 어린이 파라다이스에 나타날 것 같은가?

(A) 7월 1일

(B) 11월 20일

(C) 11월 21일

(D) 11월 25일 정답 (D)

문제 196–200번은 다음 웹 페이지들을 참조하시오.

```
http://www.sunbursthotel.com/aboutus
```

선버스트 호텔

메인 페이지	호텔 소개	예약	평가

선버스트 호텔에 오신 것을 환영합니다

(200)155 리식 스트리트, 선시티 0355, 남아프리카

선버스트 호텔은 이 지역의 8개 호텔 중 1위로 평가된 4급급 호텔입니다. 50년의 역사를 가지고 있는 저희는 선시티를 방문하시는 국내 그리고 외국 여행객 모두를 성공적으로 맞이하고 있습니다.

저희의 주된 목표는 모든 방문객에게 완벽하게 편안한 숙박을 제공하는 것이고, (198A)세계적으로 유명한 요리사 마릴린 이 씨가 제공하는 최상의 음식이 그러한 목표를 달성하는 데 이바지한다고 생각합니다. (196)엘리베이터에서 2층으로 가는 버튼을 누르시면, 마법의 맛을 볼 수 있는 곳으로 데려다줄 것입니다.

(199)저희는 현재 모든 재방문 고객에게 지역 박물관의 입장권을 제공하고 있습니다. 이 홍보 행사에 대해 여기에서 더 알아보세요. 행사는 6월 1일부터 7월 31일까지 유효합니다.

```
http://www.sunbursthotel.com/testimonial
```

선버스트 호텔

메인 페이지	호텔 소개	예약	평가

멋진 숙박! ★★★★★ (별 5개 중 5개)

6월 16일, (197)스테파니 발레이오 평가

저는 6월 4일부터 11일까지 7일 동안 휴가로 남아프리카를 방문했습니다. 여행 동안 세 개의 다른 호텔에서 묵었는데 (197)6월 9일에 선버스트 호텔로 가서 남아프리카에서의 마지막 3일을 그곳에서 보냈습니다. 저는 선버스트가 가히 그 지역의 최고 호텔이라고 자신 있게 말할 수 있습니다. (198D)주차장은 믿기지 않을 만큼 크고, 직원들이 곳곳에서 최고 수준의 서비스와 정중함으로 방문객들을 도와줍니다. 저는 또한 해변에서 수영하는 것도 무척 마음에 들었는데, 호텔에서 걸어서 단지 3분 거리에 있었습니다. 좋은 음식, 좋은 위치, 좋은 직원, 그리고 좋은 가격. 무엇을 더 요구할 수 있을까요?

```
http://www.sunbursthotel.com/testimonial
```

선버스트 호텔

메인 페이지	호텔 소개	예약	평가

더는 "이글거리지 않는 태양" ★☆☆☆☆ (별 5개 중 1개)

8월 9일, (199)레나토 세가토 평가

(199)저는 7월 20일에 선버스트 호텔을 방문하여 그곳에서 5일 동안 머물렀습니다. 호텔에서 받은 박물관 무료 입장권은 매우 감사하게 생각하지만,

저는 호텔 자체에 대해 제가 정말로 느꼈던 점을 말해야만 하겠어요. 선버스트 호텔은 이 지역 최고의 호텔이었지만, 개인적으로는 예전의 영광을 잃어버렸다고 생각해요. 건물은 부인할 수 없을 정도로 낡았고, 모든 문들은 제가 열 때마다 끽 소리가 나며, (198C)무선 인터넷은 그냥 너무 느려요. 최악인 점은, (200)호텔이 위치해 있는 거리가 개발이 아주 많이 되어서, 밤에 창문을 통해 밝은 불빛이 번쩍거리고 많은 사람이 시끄럽게 해요. 조용하고 편안한 휴가를 기대한다면 저는 선버스트 호텔을 추천하지 않습니다.

196. 선버스트 호텔에 대해 나타나 있는 것은 무엇인가?

(A) 마릴린 이에 의해 운영된다.

(B) 선시티의 가장 오래된 시설이다.

(C) 6월에 가장 많은 수의 방문객을 받는다.

(D) 건물이 2개 층 이상으로 되어 있다. 정답 (D)

197. 발레이오 씨는 언제 선버스트 호텔을 떠났는가?

(A) 6월 4일

(B) 6월 9일

(C) 6월 11일

(D) 6월 16일 정답 (C)

198. 선버스트 호텔에서 이용 가능한 특징으로 언급되지 않은 것은 무엇인가?

(A) 식당

(B) 수영장

(C) 인터넷 접속

(D) 주차장 정답 (B)

199. 세가토 씨에 대해 시사되어 있는 것은 무엇인가?

(A) 그는 선버스트 호텔의 형편없는 고객 서비스에 대해 불평하고 있다.

(B) 그는 두 번 이상 선버스트 호텔을 방문했다.

(C) 그는 선버스트 호텔까지 차량을 운전해서 갔다.

(D) 그는 선버스트 호텔의 직원들을 개인적으로 안다. 정답 (B)

200. 리식 스트리트에 대해 추론될 수 있는 것은 무엇인가?

(A) 밤에 시끄럽다.

(B) 이 거리에 8개의 호텔이 있다.

(C) 곧 확장될 예정이다.

(D) 수리가 필요하다. 정답 (A)

Actual Test 07

LISTENING (Part I ~ IV)

NO.	ANSWER	NO.	ANSWER	NO.	ANSWER	NO.	ANSWER	NO.	ANSWER
	A B C D		A B C D		A B C D		A B C D		A B C D
1	a b c	21	a b c d	41	a b c d	61	a b c d	81	a b c d
2	a b c	22	a b c d	42	a b c d	62	a b c d	82	a b c d
3	a b c	23	a b c d	43	a b c d	63	a b c d	83	a b c d
4	a b c	24	a b c d	44	a b c d	64	a b c d	84	a b c d
5	a b c	25	a b c d	45	a b c d	65	a b c d	85	a b c d
6	a b c	26	a b c d	46	a b c d	66	a b c d	86	a b c d
7	a b c	27	a b c d	47	a b c d	67	a b c d	87	a b c d
8	a b c	28	a b c d	48	a b c d	68	a b c d	88	a b c d
9	a b c	29	a b c d	49	a b c d	69	a b c d	89	a b c d
10	a b c	30	a b c d	50	a b c d	70	a b c d	90	a b c d
11	a b c	31	a b c d	51	a b c d	71	a b c d	91	a b c d
12	a b c	32	a b c d	52	a b c d	72	a b c d	92	a b c d
13	a b c	33	a b c d	53	a b c d	73	a b c d	93	a b c d
14	a b c	34	a b c d	54	a b c d	74	a b c d	94	a b c d
15	a b c	35	a b c d	55	a b c d	75	a b c d	95	a b c d
16	a b c	36	a b c d	56	a b c d	76	a b c d	96	a b c d
17	a b c	37	a b c d	57	a b c d	77	a b c d	97	a b c d
18	a b c	38	a b c d	58	a b c d	78	a b c d	98	a b c d
19	a b c	39	a b c d	59	a b c d	79	a b c d	99	a b c d
20	a b c	40	a b c d	60	a b c d	80	a b c d	100	a b c d

READING (Part V ~ VII)

NO.	ANSWER	NO.	ANSWER	NO.	ANSWER	NO.	ANSWER	NO.	ANSWER
	A B C D		A B C D		A B C D		A B C D		A B C D
101	a b c d	121	a b c d	141	a b c d	161	a b c d	181	a b c d
102	a b c d	122	a b c d	142	a b c d	162	a b c d	182	a b c d
103	a b c d	123	a b c d	143	a b c d	163	a b c d	183	a b c d
104	a b c d	124	a b c d	144	a b c d	164	a b c d	184	a b c d
105	a b c d	125	a b c d	145	a b c d	165	a b c d	185	a b c d
106	a b c d	126	a b c d	146	a b c d	166	a b c d	186	a b c d
107	a b c d	127	a b c d	147	a b c d	167	a b c d	187	a b c d
108	a b c d	128	a b c d	148	a b c d	168	a b c d	188	a b c d
109	a b c d	129	a b c d	149	a b c d	169	a b c d	189	a b c d
110	a b c d	130	a b c d	150	a b c d	170	a b c d	190	a b c d
111	a b c d	131	a b c d	151	a b c d	171	a b c d	191	a b c d
112	a b c d	132	a b c d	152	a b c d	172	a b c d	192	a b c d
113	a b c d	133	a b c d	153	a b c d	173	a b c d	193	a b c d
114	a b c d	134	a b c d	154	a b c d	174	a b c d	194	a b c d
115	a b c d	135	a b c d	155	a b c d	175	a b c d	195	a b c d
116	a b c d	136	a b c d	156	a b c d	176	a b c d	196	a b c d
117	a b c d	137	a b c d	157	a b c d	177	a b c d	197	a b c d
118	a b c d	138	a b c d	158	a b c d	178	a b c d	198	a b c d
119	a b c d	139	a b c d	159	a b c d	179	a b c d	199	a b c d
120	a b c d	140	a b c d	160	a b c d	180	a b c d	200	a b c d

Actual Test 08

LISTENING (Part I ~ IV)

NO.	ANSWER				NO.	ANSWER				NO.	ANSWER				NO.	ANSWER			
	A	B	C	D		A	B	C	D		A	B	C	D		A	B	C	D
1	ⓐ	ⓑ	ⓒ	ⓓ	21	ⓐ	ⓑ	ⓒ		41	ⓐ	ⓑ	ⓒ	ⓓ	61	ⓐ	ⓑ	ⓒ	ⓓ
2	ⓐ	ⓑ	ⓒ	ⓓ	22	ⓐ	ⓑ	ⓒ		42	ⓐ	ⓑ	ⓒ	ⓓ	62	ⓐ	ⓑ	ⓒ	ⓓ
3	ⓐ	ⓑ	ⓒ	ⓓ	23	ⓐ	ⓑ	ⓒ		43	ⓐ	ⓑ	ⓒ	ⓓ	63	ⓐ	ⓑ	ⓒ	ⓓ
4	ⓐ	ⓑ	ⓒ	ⓓ	24	ⓐ	ⓑ	ⓒ		44	ⓐ	ⓑ	ⓒ	ⓓ	64	ⓐ	ⓑ	ⓒ	ⓓ
5	ⓐ	ⓑ	ⓒ	ⓓ	25	ⓐ	ⓑ	ⓒ		45	ⓐ	ⓑ	ⓒ	ⓓ	65	ⓐ	ⓑ	ⓒ	ⓓ
6	ⓐ	ⓑ	ⓒ	ⓓ	26	ⓐ	ⓑ	ⓒ		46	ⓐ	ⓑ	ⓒ	ⓓ	66	ⓐ	ⓑ	ⓒ	ⓓ
7	ⓐ	ⓑ	ⓒ		27	ⓐ	ⓑ	ⓒ		47	ⓐ	ⓑ	ⓒ	ⓓ	67	ⓐ	ⓑ	ⓒ	ⓓ
8	ⓐ	ⓑ	ⓒ		28	ⓐ	ⓑ	ⓒ		48	ⓐ	ⓑ	ⓒ	ⓓ	68	ⓐ	ⓑ	ⓒ	ⓓ
9	ⓐ	ⓑ	ⓒ		29	ⓐ	ⓑ	ⓒ		49	ⓐ	ⓑ	ⓒ	ⓓ	69	ⓐ	ⓑ	ⓒ	ⓓ
10	ⓐ	ⓑ	ⓒ		30	ⓐ	ⓑ	ⓒ	ⓓ	50	ⓐ	ⓑ	ⓒ	ⓓ	70	ⓐ	ⓑ	ⓒ	ⓓ
11	ⓐ	ⓑ	ⓒ		31	ⓐ	ⓑ	ⓒ	ⓓ	51	ⓐ	ⓑ	ⓒ	ⓓ	71	ⓐ	ⓑ	ⓒ	ⓓ
12	ⓐ	ⓑ	ⓒ		32	ⓐ	ⓑ	ⓒ	ⓓ	52	ⓐ	ⓑ	ⓒ	ⓓ	72	ⓐ	ⓑ	ⓒ	ⓓ
13	ⓐ	ⓑ	ⓒ		33	ⓐ	ⓑ	ⓒ	ⓓ	53	ⓐ	ⓑ	ⓒ	ⓓ	73	ⓐ	ⓑ	ⓒ	ⓓ
14	ⓐ	ⓑ	ⓒ		34	ⓐ	ⓑ	ⓒ	ⓓ	54	ⓐ	ⓑ	ⓒ	ⓓ	74	ⓐ	ⓑ	ⓒ	ⓓ
15	ⓐ	ⓑ	ⓒ		35	ⓐ	ⓑ	ⓒ	ⓓ	55	ⓐ	ⓑ	ⓒ	ⓓ	75	ⓐ	ⓑ	ⓒ	ⓓ
16	ⓐ	ⓑ	ⓒ		36	ⓐ	ⓑ	ⓒ	ⓓ	56	ⓐ	ⓑ	ⓒ	ⓓ	76	ⓐ	ⓑ	ⓒ	ⓓ
17	ⓐ	ⓑ	ⓒ		37	ⓐ	ⓑ	ⓒ	ⓓ	57	ⓐ	ⓑ	ⓒ	ⓓ	77	ⓐ	ⓑ	ⓒ	ⓓ
18	ⓐ	ⓑ	ⓒ		38	ⓐ	ⓑ	ⓒ	ⓓ	58	ⓐ	ⓑ	ⓒ	ⓓ	78	ⓐ	ⓑ	ⓒ	ⓓ
19	ⓐ	ⓑ	ⓒ		39	ⓐ	ⓑ	ⓒ	ⓓ	59	ⓐ	ⓑ	ⓒ	ⓓ	79	ⓐ	ⓑ	ⓒ	ⓓ
20	ⓐ	ⓑ	ⓒ		40	ⓐ	ⓑ	ⓒ	ⓓ	60	ⓐ	ⓑ	ⓒ	ⓓ	80	ⓐ	ⓑ	ⓒ	ⓓ
															81	ⓐ	ⓑ	ⓒ	ⓓ
															82	ⓐ	ⓑ	ⓒ	ⓓ
															83	ⓐ	ⓑ	ⓒ	ⓓ
															84	ⓐ	ⓑ	ⓒ	ⓓ
															85	ⓐ	ⓑ	ⓒ	ⓓ
															86	ⓐ	ⓑ	ⓒ	ⓓ
															87	ⓐ	ⓑ	ⓒ	ⓓ
															88	ⓐ	ⓑ	ⓒ	ⓓ
															89	ⓐ	ⓑ	ⓒ	ⓓ
															90	ⓐ	ⓑ	ⓒ	ⓓ
															91	ⓐ	ⓑ	ⓒ	ⓓ
															92	ⓐ	ⓑ	ⓒ	ⓓ
															93	ⓐ	ⓑ	ⓒ	ⓓ
															94	ⓐ	ⓑ	ⓒ	ⓓ
															95	ⓐ	ⓑ	ⓒ	ⓓ
															96	ⓐ	ⓑ	ⓒ	ⓓ
															97	ⓐ	ⓑ	ⓒ	ⓓ
															98	ⓐ	ⓑ	ⓒ	ⓓ
															99	ⓐ	ⓑ	ⓒ	ⓓ
															100	ⓐ	ⓑ	ⓒ	ⓓ

READING (Part V ~ VII)

NO.	ANSWER				NO.	ANSWER				NO.	ANSWER				NO.	ANSWER			
	A	B	C	D		A	B	C	D		A	B	C	D		A	B	C	D
101	ⓐ	ⓑ	ⓒ	ⓓ	121	ⓐ	ⓑ	ⓒ	ⓓ	141	ⓐ	ⓑ	ⓒ	ⓓ	161	ⓐ	ⓑ	ⓒ	ⓓ
102	ⓐ	ⓑ	ⓒ	ⓓ	122	ⓐ	ⓑ	ⓒ	ⓓ	142	ⓐ	ⓑ	ⓒ	ⓓ	162	ⓐ	ⓑ	ⓒ	ⓓ
103	ⓐ	ⓑ	ⓒ	ⓓ	123	ⓐ	ⓑ	ⓒ	ⓓ	143	ⓐ	ⓑ	ⓒ	ⓓ	163	ⓐ	ⓑ	ⓒ	ⓓ
104	ⓐ	ⓑ	ⓒ	ⓓ	124	ⓐ	ⓑ	ⓒ	ⓓ	144	ⓐ	ⓑ	ⓒ	ⓓ	164	ⓐ	ⓑ	ⓒ	ⓓ
105	ⓐ	ⓑ	ⓒ	ⓓ	125	ⓐ	ⓑ	ⓒ	ⓓ	145	ⓐ	ⓑ	ⓒ	ⓓ	165	ⓐ	ⓑ	ⓒ	ⓓ
106	ⓐ	ⓑ	ⓒ	ⓓ	126	ⓐ	ⓑ	ⓒ	ⓓ	146	ⓐ	ⓑ	ⓒ	ⓓ	166	ⓐ	ⓑ	ⓒ	ⓓ
107	ⓐ	ⓑ	ⓒ	ⓓ	127	ⓐ	ⓑ	ⓒ	ⓓ	147	ⓐ	ⓑ	ⓒ	ⓓ	167	ⓐ	ⓑ	ⓒ	ⓓ
108	ⓐ	ⓑ	ⓒ	ⓓ	128	ⓐ	ⓑ	ⓒ	ⓓ	148	ⓐ	ⓑ	ⓒ	ⓓ	168	ⓐ	ⓑ	ⓒ	ⓓ
109	ⓐ	ⓑ	ⓒ	ⓓ	129	ⓐ	ⓑ	ⓒ	ⓓ	149	ⓐ	ⓑ	ⓒ	ⓓ	169	ⓐ	ⓑ	ⓒ	ⓓ
110	ⓐ	ⓑ	ⓒ	ⓓ	130	ⓐ	ⓑ	ⓒ	ⓓ	150	ⓐ	ⓑ	ⓒ	ⓓ	170	ⓐ	ⓑ	ⓒ	ⓓ
111	ⓐ	ⓑ	ⓒ	ⓓ	131	ⓐ	ⓑ	ⓒ	ⓓ	151	ⓐ	ⓑ	ⓒ	ⓓ	171	ⓐ	ⓑ	ⓒ	ⓓ
112	ⓐ	ⓑ	ⓒ	ⓓ	132	ⓐ	ⓑ	ⓒ	ⓓ	152	ⓐ	ⓑ	ⓒ	ⓓ	172	ⓐ	ⓑ	ⓒ	ⓓ
113	ⓐ	ⓑ	ⓒ	ⓓ	133	ⓐ	ⓑ	ⓒ	ⓓ	153	ⓐ	ⓑ	ⓒ	ⓓ	173	ⓐ	ⓑ	ⓒ	ⓓ
114	ⓐ	ⓑ	ⓒ	ⓓ	134	ⓐ	ⓑ	ⓒ	ⓓ	154	ⓐ	ⓑ	ⓒ	ⓓ	174	ⓐ	ⓑ	ⓒ	ⓓ
115	ⓐ	ⓑ	ⓒ	ⓓ	135	ⓐ	ⓑ	ⓒ	ⓓ	155	ⓐ	ⓑ	ⓒ	ⓓ	175	ⓐ	ⓑ	ⓒ	ⓓ
116	ⓐ	ⓑ	ⓒ	ⓓ	136	ⓐ	ⓑ	ⓒ	ⓓ	156	ⓐ	ⓑ	ⓒ	ⓓ	176	ⓐ	ⓑ	ⓒ	ⓓ
117	ⓐ	ⓑ	ⓒ	ⓓ	137	ⓐ	ⓑ	ⓒ	ⓓ	157	ⓐ	ⓑ	ⓒ	ⓓ	177	ⓐ	ⓑ	ⓒ	ⓓ
118	ⓐ	ⓑ	ⓒ	ⓓ	138	ⓐ	ⓑ	ⓒ	ⓓ	158	ⓐ	ⓑ	ⓒ	ⓓ	178	ⓐ	ⓑ	ⓒ	ⓓ
119	ⓐ	ⓑ	ⓒ	ⓓ	139	ⓐ	ⓑ	ⓒ	ⓓ	159	ⓐ	ⓑ	ⓒ	ⓓ	179	ⓐ	ⓑ	ⓒ	ⓓ
120	ⓐ	ⓑ	ⓒ	ⓓ	140	ⓐ	ⓑ	ⓒ	ⓓ	160	ⓐ	ⓑ	ⓒ	ⓓ	180	ⓐ	ⓑ	ⓒ	ⓓ
															181	ⓐ	ⓑ	ⓒ	ⓓ
															182	ⓐ	ⓑ	ⓒ	ⓓ
															183	ⓐ	ⓑ	ⓒ	ⓓ
															184	ⓐ	ⓑ	ⓒ	ⓓ
															185	ⓐ	ⓑ	ⓒ	ⓓ
															186	ⓐ	ⓑ	ⓒ	ⓓ
															187	ⓐ	ⓑ	ⓒ	ⓓ
															188	ⓐ	ⓑ	ⓒ	ⓓ
															189	ⓐ	ⓑ	ⓒ	ⓓ
															190	ⓐ	ⓑ	ⓒ	ⓓ
															191	ⓐ	ⓑ	ⓒ	ⓓ
															192	ⓐ	ⓑ	ⓒ	ⓓ
															193	ⓐ	ⓑ	ⓒ	ⓓ
															194	ⓐ	ⓑ	ⓒ	ⓓ
															195	ⓐ	ⓑ	ⓒ	ⓓ
															196	ⓐ	ⓑ	ⓒ	ⓓ
															197	ⓐ	ⓑ	ⓒ	ⓓ
															198	ⓐ	ⓑ	ⓒ	ⓓ
															199	ⓐ	ⓑ	ⓒ	ⓓ
															200	ⓐ	ⓑ	ⓒ	ⓓ

Actual Test 09

LISTENING (Part I ~ IV)

NO.	ANSWER				NO.	ANSWER				NO.	ANSWER				NO.	ANSWER			
	A	B	C	D		A	B	C	D		A	B	C	D		A	B	C	D
1	a	b	c		21	a	b	c	d	41	a	b	c	d	61	a	b	c	d
2	a	b	c		22	a	b	c	d	42	a	b	c	d	62	a	b	c	d
3	a	b	c		23	a	b	c	d	43	a	b	c	d	63	a	b	c	d
4	a	b	c		24	a	b	c	d	44	a	b	c	d	64	a	b	c	d
5	a	b	c		25	a	b	c	d	45	a	b	c	d	65	a	b	c	d
6	a	b	c		26	a	b	c	d	46	a	b	c	d	66	a	b	c	d
7	a	b	c		27	a	b	c	d	47	a	b	c	d	67	a	b	c	d
8	a	b	c		28	a	b	c	d	48	a	b	c	d	68	a	b	c	d
9	a	b	c		29	a	b	c	d	49	a	b	c	d	69	a	b	c	d
10	a	b	c		30	a	b	c	d	50	a	b	c	d	70	a	b	c	d
11	a	b	c		31	a	b	c	d	51	a	b	c	d	71	a	b	c	d
12	a	b	c		32	a	b	c	d	52	a	b	c	d	72	a	b	c	d
13	a	b	c		33	a	b	c	d	53	a	b	c	d	73	a	b	c	d
14	a	b	c		34	a	b	c	d	54	a	b	c	d	74	a	b	c	d
15	a	b	c		35	a	b	c	d	55	a	b	c	d	75	a	b	c	d
16	a	b	c		36	a	b	c	d	56	a	b	c	d	76	a	b	c	d
17	a	b	c		37	a	b	c	d	57	a	b	c	d	77	a	b	c	d
18	a	b	c		38	a	b	c	d	58	a	b	c	d	78	a	b	c	d
19	a	b	c		39	a	b	c	d	59	a	b	c	d	79	a	b	c	d
20	a	b	c		40	a	b	c	d	60	a	b	c	d	80	a	b	c	d
															81	a	b	c	d
															82	a	b	c	d
															83	a	b	c	d
															84	a	b	c	d
															85	a	b	c	d
															86	a	b	c	d
															87	a	b	c	d
															88	a	b	c	d
															89	a	b	c	d
															90	a	b	c	d
															91	a	b	c	d
															92	a	b	c	d
															93	a	b	c	d
															94	a	b	c	d
															95	a	b	c	d
															96	a	b	c	d
															97	a	b	c	d
															98	a	b	c	d
															99	a	b	c	d
															100	a	b	c	d

READING (Part V ~ VII)

NO.	ANSWER				NO.	ANSWER				NO.	ANSWER				NO.	ANSWER			
	A	B	C	D		A	B	C	D		A	B	C	D		A	B	C	D
101	a	b	c	d	121	a	b	c	d	141	a	b	c	d	161	a	b	c	d
102	a	b	c	d	122	a	b	c	d	142	a	b	c	d	162	a	b	c	d
103	a	b	c	d	123	a	b	c	d	143	a	b	c	d	163	a	b	c	d
104	a	b	c	d	124	a	b	c	d	144	a	b	c	d	164	a	b	c	d
105	a	b	c	d	125	a	b	c	d	145	a	b	c	d	165	a	b	c	d
106	a	b	c	d	126	a	b	c	d	146	a	b	c	d	166	a	b	c	d
107	a	b	c	d	127	a	b	c	d	147	a	b	c	d	167	a	b	c	d
108	a	b	c	d	128	a	b	c	d	148	a	b	c	d	168	a	b	c	d
109	a	b	c	d	129	a	b	c	d	149	a	b	c	d	169	a	b	c	d
110	a	b	c	d	130	a	b	c	d	150	a	b	c	d	170	a	b	c	d
111	a	b	c	d	131	a	b	c	d	151	a	b	c	d	171	a	b	c	d
112	a	b	c	d	132	a	b	c	d	152	a	b	c	d	172	a	b	c	d
113	a	b	c	d	133	a	b	c	d	153	a	b	c	d	173	a	b	c	d
114	a	b	c	d	134	a	b	c	d	154	a	b	c	d	174	a	b	c	d
115	a	b	c	d	135	a	b	c	d	155	a	b	c	d	175	a	b	c	d
116	a	b	c	d	136	a	b	c	d	156	a	b	c	d	176	a	b	c	d
117	a	b	c	d	137	a	b	c	d	157	a	b	c	d	177	a	b	c	d
118	a	b	c	d	138	a	b	c	d	158	a	b	c	d	178	a	b	c	d
119	a	b	c	d	139	a	b	c	d	159	a	b	c	d	179	a	b	c	d
120	a	b	c	d	140	a	b	c	d	160	a	b	c	d	180	a	b	c	d
															181	a	b	c	d
															182	a	b	c	d
															183	a	b	c	d
															184	a	b	c	d
															185	a	b	c	d
															186	a	b	c	d
															187	a	b	c	d
															188	a	b	c	d
															189	a	b	c	d
															190	a	b	c	d
															191	a	b	c	d
															192	a	b	c	d
															193	a	b	c	d
															194	a	b	c	d
															195	a	b	c	d
															196	a	b	c	d
															197	a	b	c	d
															198	a	b	c	d
															199	a	b	c	d
															200	a	b	c	d

Answer Sheet

Actual Test 10

LISTENING (Part I ~ IV)

NO.	ANSWER				NO.	ANSWER				NO.	ANSWER			
	A	B	C	D		A	B	C	D		A	B	C	D
1	ⓐ	ⓑ	ⓒ	ⓓ	21	ⓐ	ⓑ	ⓒ	ⓓ	41	ⓐ	ⓑ	ⓒ	ⓓ
2	ⓐ	ⓑ	ⓒ	ⓓ	22	ⓐ	ⓑ	ⓒ	ⓓ	42	ⓐ	ⓑ	ⓒ	ⓓ
3	ⓐ	ⓑ	ⓒ	ⓓ	23	ⓐ	ⓑ	ⓒ	ⓓ	43	ⓐ	ⓑ	ⓒ	ⓓ
4	ⓐ	ⓑ	ⓒ	ⓓ	24	ⓐ	ⓑ	ⓒ	ⓓ	44	ⓐ	ⓑ	ⓒ	ⓓ
5	ⓐ	ⓑ	ⓒ	ⓓ	25	ⓐ	ⓑ	ⓒ	ⓓ	45	ⓐ	ⓑ	ⓒ	ⓓ
6	ⓐ	ⓑ	ⓒ	ⓓ	26	ⓐ	ⓑ	ⓒ	ⓓ	46	ⓐ	ⓑ	ⓒ	ⓓ
7	ⓐ	ⓑ	ⓒ	ⓓ	27	ⓐ	ⓑ	ⓒ	ⓓ	47	ⓐ	ⓑ	ⓒ	ⓓ
8	ⓐ	ⓑ	ⓒ		28	ⓐ	ⓑ	ⓒ	ⓓ	48	ⓐ	ⓑ	ⓒ	ⓓ
9	ⓐ	ⓑ	ⓒ		29	ⓐ	ⓑ	ⓒ	ⓓ	49	ⓐ	ⓑ	ⓒ	ⓓ
10	ⓐ	ⓑ	ⓒ		30	ⓐ	ⓑ	ⓒ	ⓓ	50	ⓐ	ⓑ	ⓒ	ⓓ
11	ⓐ	ⓑ	ⓒ		31	ⓐ	ⓑ	ⓒ	ⓓ	51	ⓐ	ⓑ	ⓒ	ⓓ
12	ⓐ	ⓑ	ⓒ		32	ⓐ	ⓑ	ⓒ	ⓓ	52	ⓐ	ⓑ	ⓒ	ⓓ
13	ⓐ	ⓑ	ⓒ		33	ⓐ	ⓑ	ⓒ	ⓓ	53	ⓐ	ⓑ	ⓒ	ⓓ
14	ⓐ	ⓑ	ⓒ		34	ⓐ	ⓑ	ⓒ	ⓓ	54	ⓐ	ⓑ	ⓒ	ⓓ
15	ⓐ	ⓑ	ⓒ		35	ⓐ	ⓑ	ⓒ	ⓓ	55	ⓐ	ⓑ	ⓒ	ⓓ
16	ⓐ	ⓑ	ⓒ		36	ⓐ	ⓑ	ⓒ	ⓓ	56	ⓐ	ⓑ	ⓒ	ⓓ
17	ⓐ	ⓑ	ⓒ		37	ⓐ	ⓑ	ⓒ	ⓓ	57	ⓐ	ⓑ	ⓒ	ⓓ
18	ⓐ	ⓑ	ⓒ		38	ⓐ	ⓑ	ⓒ	ⓓ	58	ⓐ	ⓑ	ⓒ	ⓓ
19	ⓐ	ⓑ	ⓒ		39	ⓐ	ⓑ	ⓒ	ⓓ	59	ⓐ	ⓑ	ⓒ	ⓓ
20	ⓐ	ⓑ	ⓒ		40	ⓐ	ⓑ	ⓒ	ⓓ	60	ⓐ	ⓑ	ⓒ	ⓓ

NO.	ANSWER				NO.	ANSWER			
	A	B	C	D		A	B	C	D
61	ⓐ	ⓑ	ⓒ	ⓓ	81	ⓐ	ⓑ	ⓒ	ⓓ
62	ⓐ	ⓑ	ⓒ	ⓓ	82	ⓐ	ⓑ	ⓒ	ⓓ
63	ⓐ	ⓑ	ⓒ	ⓓ	83	ⓐ	ⓑ	ⓒ	ⓓ
64	ⓐ	ⓑ	ⓒ	ⓓ	84	ⓐ	ⓑ	ⓒ	ⓓ
65	ⓐ	ⓑ	ⓒ	ⓓ	85	ⓐ	ⓑ	ⓒ	ⓓ
66	ⓐ	ⓑ	ⓒ	ⓓ	86	ⓐ	ⓑ	ⓒ	ⓓ
67	ⓐ	ⓑ	ⓒ	ⓓ	87	ⓐ	ⓑ	ⓒ	ⓓ
68	ⓐ	ⓑ	ⓒ	ⓓ	88	ⓐ	ⓑ	ⓒ	ⓓ
69	ⓐ	ⓑ	ⓒ	ⓓ	89	ⓐ	ⓑ	ⓒ	ⓓ
70	ⓐ	ⓑ	ⓒ	ⓓ	90	ⓐ	ⓑ	ⓒ	ⓓ
71	ⓐ	ⓑ	ⓒ	ⓓ	91	ⓐ	ⓑ	ⓒ	ⓓ
72	ⓐ	ⓑ	ⓒ	ⓓ	92	ⓐ	ⓑ	ⓒ	ⓓ
73	ⓐ	ⓑ	ⓒ	ⓓ	93	ⓐ	ⓑ	ⓒ	ⓓ
74	ⓐ	ⓑ	ⓒ	ⓓ	94	ⓐ	ⓑ	ⓒ	ⓓ
75	ⓐ	ⓑ	ⓒ	ⓓ	95	ⓐ	ⓑ	ⓒ	ⓓ
76	ⓐ	ⓑ	ⓒ	ⓓ	96	ⓐ	ⓑ	ⓒ	ⓓ
77	ⓐ	ⓑ	ⓒ	ⓓ	97	ⓐ	ⓑ	ⓒ	ⓓ
78	ⓐ	ⓑ	ⓒ	ⓓ	98	ⓐ	ⓑ	ⓒ	ⓓ
79	ⓐ	ⓑ	ⓒ	ⓓ	99	ⓐ	ⓑ	ⓒ	ⓓ
80	ⓐ	ⓑ	ⓒ	ⓓ	100	ⓐ	ⓑ	ⓒ	ⓓ

READING (Part V ~ VII)

NO.	ANSWER				NO.	ANSWER				NO.	ANSWER			
	A	B	C	D		A	B	C	D		A	B	C	D
101	ⓐ	ⓑ	ⓒ	ⓓ	121	ⓐ	ⓑ	ⓒ	ⓓ	141	ⓐ	ⓑ	ⓒ	ⓓ
102	ⓐ	ⓑ	ⓒ	ⓓ	122	ⓐ	ⓑ	ⓒ	ⓓ	142	ⓐ	ⓑ	ⓒ	ⓓ
103	ⓐ	ⓑ	ⓒ	ⓓ	123	ⓐ	ⓑ	ⓒ	ⓓ	143	ⓐ	ⓑ	ⓒ	ⓓ
104	ⓐ	ⓑ	ⓒ	ⓓ	124	ⓐ	ⓑ	ⓒ	ⓓ	144	ⓐ	ⓑ	ⓒ	ⓓ
105	ⓐ	ⓑ	ⓒ	ⓓ	125	ⓐ	ⓑ	ⓒ	ⓓ	145	ⓐ	ⓑ	ⓒ	ⓓ
106	ⓐ	ⓑ	ⓒ	ⓓ	126	ⓐ	ⓑ	ⓒ	ⓓ	146	ⓐ	ⓑ	ⓒ	ⓓ
107	ⓐ	ⓑ	ⓒ	ⓓ	127	ⓐ	ⓑ	ⓒ	ⓓ	147	ⓐ	ⓑ	ⓒ	ⓓ
108	ⓐ	ⓑ	ⓒ	ⓓ	128	ⓐ	ⓑ	ⓒ	ⓓ	148	ⓐ	ⓑ	ⓒ	ⓓ
109	ⓐ	ⓑ	ⓒ	ⓓ	129	ⓐ	ⓑ	ⓒ	ⓓ	149	ⓐ	ⓑ	ⓒ	ⓓ
110	ⓐ	ⓑ	ⓒ	ⓓ	130	ⓐ	ⓑ	ⓒ	ⓓ	150	ⓐ	ⓑ	ⓒ	ⓓ
111	ⓐ	ⓑ	ⓒ	ⓓ	131	ⓐ	ⓑ	ⓒ	ⓓ	151	ⓐ	ⓑ	ⓒ	ⓓ
112	ⓐ	ⓑ	ⓒ	ⓓ	132	ⓐ	ⓑ	ⓒ	ⓓ	152	ⓐ	ⓑ	ⓒ	ⓓ
113	ⓐ	ⓑ	ⓒ	ⓓ	133	ⓐ	ⓑ	ⓒ	ⓓ	153	ⓐ	ⓑ	ⓒ	ⓓ
114	ⓐ	ⓑ	ⓒ	ⓓ	134	ⓐ	ⓑ	ⓒ	ⓓ	154	ⓐ	ⓑ	ⓒ	ⓓ
115	ⓐ	ⓑ	ⓒ	ⓓ	135	ⓐ	ⓑ	ⓒ	ⓓ	155	ⓐ	ⓑ	ⓒ	ⓓ
116	ⓐ	ⓑ	ⓒ	ⓓ	136	ⓐ	ⓑ	ⓒ	ⓓ	156	ⓐ	ⓑ	ⓒ	ⓓ
117	ⓐ	ⓑ	ⓒ	ⓓ	137	ⓐ	ⓑ	ⓒ	ⓓ	157	ⓐ	ⓑ	ⓒ	ⓓ
118	ⓐ	ⓑ	ⓒ	ⓓ	138	ⓐ	ⓑ	ⓒ	ⓓ	158	ⓐ	ⓑ	ⓒ	ⓓ
119	ⓐ	ⓑ	ⓒ	ⓓ	139	ⓐ	ⓑ	ⓒ	ⓓ	159	ⓐ	ⓑ	ⓒ	ⓓ
120	ⓐ	ⓑ	ⓒ	ⓓ	140	ⓐ	ⓑ	ⓒ	ⓓ	160	ⓐ	ⓑ	ⓒ	ⓓ

NO.	ANSWER				NO.	ANSWER			
	A	B	C	D		A	B	C	D
161	ⓐ	ⓑ	ⓒ	ⓓ	181	ⓐ	ⓑ	ⓒ	ⓓ
162	ⓐ	ⓑ	ⓒ	ⓓ	182	ⓐ	ⓑ	ⓒ	ⓓ
163	ⓐ	ⓑ	ⓒ	ⓓ	183	ⓐ	ⓑ	ⓒ	ⓓ
164	ⓐ	ⓑ	ⓒ	ⓓ	184	ⓐ	ⓑ	ⓒ	ⓓ
165	ⓐ	ⓑ	ⓒ	ⓓ	185	ⓐ	ⓑ	ⓒ	ⓓ
166	ⓐ	ⓑ	ⓒ	ⓓ	186	ⓐ	ⓑ	ⓒ	ⓓ
167	ⓐ	ⓑ	ⓒ	ⓓ	187	ⓐ	ⓑ	ⓒ	ⓓ
168	ⓐ	ⓑ	ⓒ	ⓓ	188	ⓐ	ⓑ	ⓒ	ⓓ
169	ⓐ	ⓑ	ⓒ	ⓓ	189	ⓐ	ⓑ	ⓒ	ⓓ
170	ⓐ	ⓑ	ⓒ	ⓓ	190	ⓐ	ⓑ	ⓒ	ⓓ
171	ⓐ	ⓑ	ⓒ	ⓓ	191	ⓐ	ⓑ	ⓒ	ⓓ
172	ⓐ	ⓑ	ⓒ	ⓓ	192	ⓐ	ⓑ	ⓒ	ⓓ
173	ⓐ	ⓑ	ⓒ	ⓓ	193	ⓐ	ⓑ	ⓒ	ⓓ
174	ⓐ	ⓑ	ⓒ	ⓓ	194	ⓐ	ⓑ	ⓒ	ⓓ
175	ⓐ	ⓑ	ⓒ	ⓓ	195	ⓐ	ⓑ	ⓒ	ⓓ
176	ⓐ	ⓑ	ⓒ	ⓓ	196	ⓐ	ⓑ	ⓒ	ⓓ
177	ⓐ	ⓑ	ⓒ	ⓓ	197	ⓐ	ⓑ	ⓒ	ⓓ
178	ⓐ	ⓑ	ⓒ	ⓓ	198	ⓐ	ⓑ	ⓒ	ⓓ
179	ⓐ	ⓑ	ⓒ	ⓓ	199	ⓐ	ⓑ	ⓒ	ⓓ
180	ⓐ	ⓑ	ⓒ	ⓓ	200	ⓐ	ⓑ	ⓒ	ⓓ

Actual Test 11

LISTENING (Part I ~ IV)

NO.	ANSWER	NO.	ANSWER	NO.	ANSWER	NO.	ANSWER	NO.	ANSWER
	A B C D		A B C D		A B C D		A B C D		A B C D
1	a b c d	21	a b c d	41	a b c d	61	a b c d	81	a b c d
2	a b c d	22	a b c d	42	a b c d	62	a b c d	82	a b c d
3	a b c d	23	a b c d	43	a b c d	63	a b c d	83	a b c d
4	a b c d	24	a b c d	44	a b c d	64	a b c d	84	a b c d
5	a b c d	25	a b c d	45	a b c d	65	a b c d	85	a b c d
6	a b c d	26	a b c d	46	a b c d	66	a b c d	86	a b c d
7	a b c d	27	a b c d	47	a b c d	67	a b c d	87	a b c d
8	a b c	28	a b c d	48	a b c d	68	a b c d	88	a b c d
9	a b c	29	a b c d	49	a b c d	69	a b c d	89	a b c d
10	a b c	30	a b c d	50	a b c d	70	a b c d	90	a b c d
11	a b c	31	a b c d	51	a b c d	71	a b c d	91	a b c d
12	a b c	32	a b c d	52	a b c d	72	a b c d	92	a b c d
13	a b c	33	a b c d	53	a b c d	73	a b c d	93	a b c d
14	a b c	34	a b c d	54	a b c d	74	a b c d	94	a b c d
15	a b c	35	a b c d	55	a b c d	75	a b c d	95	a b c d
16	a b c	36	a b c d	56	a b c d	76	a b c d	96	a b c d
17	a b c	37	a b c d	57	a b c d	77	a b c d	97	a b c d
18	a b c	38	a b c d	58	a b c d	78	a b c d	98	a b c d
19	a b c	39	a b c d	59	a b c d	79	a b c d	99	a b c d
20	a b c	40	a b c d	60	a b c d	80	a b c d	100	a b c d

READING (Part V ~ VII)

NO.	ANSWER	NO.	ANSWER	NO.	ANSWER	NO.	ANSWER	NO.	ANSWER
	A B C D		A B C D		A B C D		A B C D		A B C D
101	a b c d	121	a b c d	141	a b c d	161	a b c d	181	a b c d
102	a b c d	122	a b c d	142	a b c d	162	a b c d	182	a b c d
103	a b c d	123	a b c d	143	a b c d	163	a b c d	183	a b c d
104	a b c d	124	a b c d	144	a b c d	164	a b c d	184	a b c d
105	a b c d	125	a b c d	145	a b c d	165	a b c d	185	a b c d
106	a b c d	126	a b c d	146	a b c d	166	a b c d	186	a b c d
107	a b c d	127	a b c d	147	a b c d	167	a b c d	187	a b c d
108	a b c d	128	a b c d	148	a b c d	168	a b c d	188	a b c d
109	a b c d	129	a b c d	149	a b c d	169	a b c d	189	a b c d
110	a b c d	130	a b c d	150	a b c d	170	a b c d	190	a b c d
111	a b c d	131	a b c d	151	a b c d	171	a b c d	191	a b c d
112	a b c d	132	a b c d	152	a b c d	172	a b c d	192	a b c d
113	a b c d	133	a b c d	153	a b c d	173	a b c d	193	a b c d
114	a b c d	134	a b c d	154	a b c d	174	a b c d	194	a b c d
115	a b c d	135	a b c d	155	a b c d	175	a b c d	195	a b c d
116	a b c d	136	a b c d	156	a b c d	176	a b c d	196	a b c d
117	a b c d	137	a b c d	157	a b c d	177	a b c d	197	a b c d
118	a b c d	138	a b c d	158	a b c d	178	a b c d	198	a b c d
119	a b c d	139	a b c d	159	a b c d	179	a b c d	199	a b c d
120	a b c d	140	a b c d	160	a b c d	180	a b c d	200	a b c d

Answer Sheet

Actual Test 12

LISTENING (Part I ~ IV)

NO.	ANSWER	NO.	ANSWER	NO.	ANSWER	NO.	ANSWER	NO.	ANSWER
	A B C D		A B C D		A B C D		A B C D		A B C D
1	a b c d	21	a b c d	41	a b c d	61	a b c d	81	a b c d
2	a b c d	22	a b c d	42	a b c d	62	a b c d	82	a b c d
3	a b c d	23	a b c d	43	a b c d	63	a b c d	83	a b c d
4	a b c	24	a b c d	44	a b c d	64	a b c d	84	a b c d
5	a b c	25	a b c d	45	a b c d	65	a b c d	85	a b c d
6	a b c	26	a b c d	46	a b c d	66	a b c d	86	a b c d
7	a b c	27	a b c	47	a b c d	67	a b c d	87	a b c d
8	a b c	28	a b c	48	a b c d	68	a b c d	88	a b c d
9	a b c	29	a b c	49	a b c d	69	a b c d	89	a b c d
10	a b c	30	a b c	50	a b c d	70	a b c d	90	a b c d
11	a b c	31	a b c	51	a b c d	71	a b c d	91	a b c d
12	a b c	32	a b c	52	a b c d	72	a b c d	92	a b c d
13	a b c	33	a b c	53	a b c d	73	a b c d	93	a b c d
14	a b c	34	a b c	54	a b c d	74	a b c d	94	a b c d
15	a b c	35	a b c	55	a b c d	75	a b c d	95	a b c d
16	a b c	36	a b c	56	a b c d	76	a b c d	96	a b c d
17	a b c	37	a b c	57	a b c d	77	a b c d	97	a b c d
18	a b c	38	a b c	58	a b c d	78	a b c d	98	a b c d
19	a b c	39	a b c	59	a b c d	79	a b c d	99	a b c d
20	a b c	40	a b c	60	a b c d	80	a b c d	100	a b c d

READING (Part V ~ VII)

NO.	ANSWER	NO.	ANSWER	NO.	ANSWER	NO.	ANSWER
	A B C D		A B C D		A B C D		A B C D
101	a b c d	121	a b c d	141	a b c d	181	a b c d
102	a b c d	122	a b c d	142	a b c d	182	a b c d
103	a b c d	123	a b c d	143	a b c d	183	a b c d
104	a b c d	124	a b c d	144	a b c d	184	a b c d
105	a b c d	125	a b c d	145	a b c d	185	a b c d
106	a b c d	126	a b c d	146	a b c d	186	a b c d
107	a b c d	127	a b c d	147	a b c d	187	a b c d
108	a b c d	128	a b c d	148	a b c d	188	a b c d
109	a b c d	129	a b c d	149	a b c d	189	a b c d
110	a b c d	130	a b c d	150	a b c d	190	a b c d
111	a b c d	131	a b c d	151	a b c d	191	a b c d
112	a b c d	132	a b c d	152	a b c d	192	a b c d
113	a b c d	133	a b c d	153	a b c d	193	a b c d
114	a b c d	134	a b c d	154	a b c d	194	a b c d
115	a b c d	135	a b c d	155	a b c d	195	a b c d
116	a b c d	136	a b c d	156	a b c d	196	a b c d
117	a b c d	137	a b c d	157	a b c d	197	a b c d
118	a b c d	138	a b c d	158	a b c d	198	a b c d
119	a b c d	139	a b c d	159	a b c d	199	a b c d
120	a b c d	140	a b c d	160	a b c d	200	a b c d

Columns 161–180 (READING): a b c d for each from 161 through 180.

시험에 나오는 것만 공부한다!

시나공 토익

900점 이상
고득점을 위한 책!

- **최신 출제 경향을 담은 12세트, 2400문제 제공!**
  900점 이상의 고득점을 위한 문제만 선별했습니다.

- **단기에 200점을 올려주는 학습 훈련 제공!**
  LC 통암기 훈련 노트와 RC 핵심 어휘집을 제공합니다.

- **출제 포인트를 쉽게 이해시켜주는 해설집 무료 제공!**
  핵심을 알기 쉽게 알려주는 해설집을 온라인 다운로드로 제공합니다.

- **학습용 MP3 제공!**
  실전용, 복습용 MP3를 무료로 제공합니다.

950 실전 모의고사 Crack the exam – 12 Actual Tests for 950

이 책을 권장하는 점수대	400	500	600	700	800	900

실제 시험과 비교	쉬움	비슷함	어려움

03740

9 791140 700424
ISBN 979-11-407-0042-4

가격 25,000원